PUBLIC RECORD OFFICE HANDBOOKS

No. 26

Economic Planning 1943–1951

A Guide to Documents in the Public Record Office

B.W.E. Alford, Rodney Lowe and Neil Rollings

LONDON: HMSO

© Crown copyright 1992

Applications for reproduction should be made to HMSO

First published 1992

ISBN 0 11 440238 8

British Library Cataloguing in Publication Data

A CIP catalogue of this book

is available from the British Library

HMSO publications are available from:

HMSO Publications Centre
(Mail and telephone orders only)
PO Box 276, London, SW8 5DT
Telephone orders 071-873 9090
General enquiries 071-873 0011
(queuing system in operation for both numbers)

HMSO Bookshops
49 High Holborn, London WC1V 6HB 071-873 0011 (counter service only)
258 Broad Street, Birmingham, B1 2HE 021-643 3740
Southey House, 33 Wine Street, Bristol, BS1 2BQ 0272-264306
9-21 Princess Street, Manchester, M60 8AS 061-834 7201
80 Chichester Street, Belfast, BT1 4JY 0232-238451
71 Lothian Road, Edinburgh, EH3 9AZ 031-228 4181

HMSO's Accredited Agents
(see Yellow Pages)

and through good booksellers

Contents

Acknowledgements

The authors and the Public Record Office would like to acknowledge the generous financial assistance of the Economic and Social Research Council, without which this handbook could not have been compiled. They would also like to thank Mandy Banton, Jonathan Bradbury, Gwynn-fyl Lowe, Sue Lowe and Ann Morton for copy-editing; Anita Hathway and, above all, Rosemary Graham for the typing; and Enid Zaig for compiling the index.

BWEA, RL, NR

Preface

So large a handbook requires some explanation of its structure, the nature of its contents and the range of conventions used. This preface is designed to provide a brief, general explanation. More detailed information concerning the criteria for the selection and presentation of material can be found in each chapter.

Structure

The handbook starts with an introduction to the broad political and administrative context within which economic planning evolved between 1943 and 1951. The records of the Cabinet (chapter 2) and Cabinet committees (chapters 3–16) are then covered, followed by the papers of the Prime Minister (chapter 17), of the two departments most closely identified with economic planning (chapters 18 and 19) and finally of the other most relevant Whitehall departments. Within each section or chapter the material is broadly ordered by the P.R.O. class number, although on occasion it was felt to be more appropriate to group smaller classes together. Where such grouping occurs, the location of each class is clearly indicated in the list of contents. The presentation of the records in other ways, for example chronologically or by some definition of 'importance', was considered but deemed impractical given the manner in which they have been preserved and classified.

Selection criteria

It was recognized at an early stage that no precise criteria for the selection of material would wholly satisfy all potential users of the handbook – if only because the term 'economic planning' assumed different meanings at the time and (at its broadest) embraced many of the traditional, as well as the novel, economic activities of government. On the advice of the P.R.O., the criteria finally chosen were fairly broad and designed to satisfy not just the specialist interested in 'economic planning' *per se* but also the general user interested in how, for example, economic planning impinged on a particular region or industry. Accordingly the departmental and committee records selected are those most relevant to the new attempts by government to control, or plan, the economy; but in the more general classes, such as Cabinet minutes and memoranda, references are retained to closely related subjects such as nationalization and overseas trade. Housing has not been covered in any detail as it is included in the P.R.O. handbook *The Development of the Welfare State 1939–1951: A Guide to Documents in the Public Record Office.* Overseas finance, except where it imposed constraints on domestic policy, is also largely excluded and would provide an excellent subject for another handbook.

The same broad criteria were used to determine how fully the records of each class should be described. There are four levels of description. The files of classes central to planning (such as the Production Committee, chapter 15.35) have been listed in full, with the content of the most significant individually summarized. In other important classes, files have been listed selectively with the criteria for selection specified, where necessary, in the introduction to the relevant chapter or sub-section. This is true, for example, for Cabinet minutes and memoranda (chapter 2). At the third level, the contents of a whole class of records have been summarized (as in chapter 21, covering the Board of Trade) with only the individual piece numbers of particularly important files identified. Finally with more marginal classes (such as those recorded in chapter 15.37) the subject of each class has been described even more concisely.

In all these summaries the objective has been consistently to help the reader to follow through a particular decision or to locate related material amongst the vast range of government records, whether it be specifically recorded in this handbook or not. To this end, a comprehensive index has been compiled. Wherever possible, cross-references and suggestions for further reading have also been included, and the departments of officials identified since (especially in relation to Cabinet committee secretaries) this may indicate where related files can be located. In none of these three areas, however, is there any claim to comprehensiveness.

The period covered by the handbook also requires some explanation. January 1943 was regarded as an appropriate starting date because, as explained in the introduction, this was when reconstruction planning in Whitehall commenced seriously. October 1951 was regarded as an equally appropriate closing date since that was when the Labour government lost office. This choice of dates, however, raises two issues. First, the handbook is concerned only with peace-time planning. Wartime records, therefore, are included only where they specifically cover the planning of peace-time policy or the establishment of important precedents for it. Secondly, some files registered after 1951 have been included (especially in chapters 18 and 19), because they include material that was in use before October 1951 or retrospective assessments of the earlier period.

Conventions

The handbook employs certain conventions designed to provide the maximum of information in the minimum of space.

(i) To enable the reader to distinguish between ministers and officials, the latter alone have been given initials. The problem of two ministers having similar names is solved by placing initials after their surname. This convention does not apply to the introduction.

(ii) A similar distinction has been made between committee meetings and memoranda with (as in the first entry to chapter 15.37) the former being styled AM(49)1st–4th and the latter AM(49)1–20. At a glance, therefore, the reader is provided before ordering a document with the relevant file code, the date (in this case 1949) and the number of meetings and memoranda included within the file, which will provide some indication of its potential value.

(iii) To economize on space, some very long file titles have been abbreviated (as in chapter 17.2) and long runs of files covering the same topic have have been grouped together (as in chapters 18 and 19). A due warning is provided at the start of the relevant chapter.

(iv) In departmental records (chapters 20–22) where long lists of committee papers are recorded, the committees covered are identified in the final paragraph of the relevant entry and – to avoid endless repetition – the word 'committee' omitted from their titles.

(v) There is a list of abbreviations at the end of the handbook.

The records' limitations

Finally, two major limitations of the official records covered here – regardless of any failings of the editors – must be stressed. The first concerns their incompleteness. Many files for the period have been destroyed; and the existence of others, which have survived, has yet to be officially acknowledged. In the past whole classes of records (such as T 273 and T 278) have not been notified to the P.R.O. until after the appropriate release date under the thirty-year rule. Other such classes undoubtedly exist today. Similarly the existence has not been acknowledged of long-running series of files on specific topics, although it is only the later files that are restricted under the thirty-year rule. The subjects covered by such series can only be surmised. Moreover, even when the existence of records has been notified to the P.R.O. public access to them can be limited. Many files may be closed for over thirty years where issues of privacy, defence or sensitive commercial negotiations are concerned. Others have been retained in Whitehall departments. The handbook, consequently, cannot claim to be a complete guide to all relevant records. It covers only records notified to the P.R.O. up to December 1987, and access to known records was not always permitted. Where access was restricted, the reasons have been specified.

The second limitation is the very nature of official records, which should never be taken to provide a comprehensive or even a wholly reliable guide to policy-formulation on any given topic. The records relating to economic planning are no exception. Some important decisions, for instance, were deliberately left unrecorded (see, for example, P.M. Williams (ed), *The Diary of Hugh Gaitskell* (1983), p 130). Many others were taken outside the formal committee structure in informal meetings or during personal discussions between ministers or officials (see D.N. Chester in G.D.N. Worswick and P.H. Ady (eds), *The British Economy, 1945-1950* (1952), p 350). Such understandings, owing to the increasing use of the telephone, would frequently go unminuted. The committee system was also used at times to obstruct rather than to expedite decisions, and at others was simply inherently ineffective. 'At ministerial committees', wrote Gaitskell in 1947, 'there tends to be too much bickering, talking, woolliness, ignorance and personal feeling. At purely official committees there tends to be too little drive'. (*Diary*, p 38–39). Where effective decisions were regularly taken, in his opinion, was in relatively humble official committees such as the Materials Committee (15.26) chaired by junior ministers like himself. These are the kinds of committee to which historians might not immediately turn.

Factors such as these led one insider to conclude that 'historians will have difficulty in tracing changes of policy merely from a study of Cabinet or Cabinet committees... Indeed formal committee decisions were perhaps the least important of the devices of the central machine'. (D.N. Chester in *Lessons of the War Economy* (1951), p 21). Such a conclusion would seem to be unduly pessimistic, but it serves as a timely warning to those who are tempted to take official records too readily at face value and without due reference to other sources of written and oral testimony. It serves also to underline the fundamental purpose of this handbook which is not just to provide a guide to the policy-making process, but to make readily accessible, to as many users of the P.R.O. as possible, the wealth of information preserved in the official records of economic planning at so critical a period in Britain's history.

Chapter 1 Introduction

Economic Planning before 1945

Economic planning has a mixed pedigree. In the nineteenth century John Stuart Mill, the arch-priest of classical economics, claimed that there was much virtue in systems of communism or socialism 'which would be superior to the present state of society with all its suffering and injustices'.[1] But it was not until the advent of Soviet communism and, in particular, the Five-year Plans in the 1920s, that central economic planning became a reality. Planning did not, moreover, remain for long a prerogative of the left. During the 1920s and 1930s centralized economic direction became an essential element in the growing power of fascist regimes.

Great Britain was not unaffected by these later developments and a number of writers on political economy presented central planning as the panacea for the country's economic ills. There was, however, little agreement over what planning entailed, so that planning proposals amounted to an amalgam of utopian ideas and attempts to devise practical programmes for the cure of unemployment. On the left of British politics John Strachey, G.D.H. Cole, Stafford Cripps, Hugh Dalton, Evan Durbin, Oswald Mosley, the Independent Labour Party and various elements within the trade union movement, contributed to the debate. Mosley was a special case because whilst his memorandum of radical proposals for dealing with unemployment and industrial organization was prepared for a Labour cabinet, it clearly embodied a nascent corporatism which found its full expression in his later political extremism. The Liberal Party's flirtation with planning was heralded by Keynes's celebrated essay, *The End of Laissez-Faire* (1926), and the engagement was announced by the publication of the Party's programme, *Britain's Industrial Future* (1928). Outside party politics a number of organizations – of which Political and Economic Planning is the best known – developed and promoted what they considered to be politically neutral proposals for economic planning which would overcome shortcomings and failures within the existing system. Even elements within the Conservative Party were affected by planning ideas, the best examples being the Next Five Years Group and Harold Macmillan who published his ideas in his book *The Middle Way* in 1938.[2]

These ideas and schemes did not take practical root, however. Apart from the problem of justifying them in ways which were consistent with the British system of government, there was a significant public reaction against central planning as details of the excesses of the Soviet government gradually became known. Few could match the self-righteous certainty of Beatrice Webb and view Soviet communism as a new and desirable form of civilization. More in tune with existing values and institutions was the blueprint of Keynes's economics as set out in *The General Theory of Employment Interest and Money* published in 1936. Yet even Keynes's ideas failed to gain wide acceptance in the 1930s in Britain, partly because of political and institutional inertia but also because of the growing belief that economic recovery was occurring satisfactorily under existing policies.

Britain's entry into war with Germany in 1939 changed everything. War on such a scale involved not just mobilization of the armed services but the maximum commitment of manpower and material resources to the war effort. The full extent of this commitment was not at first recognized by the government since it was assumed that the combined might of Britain, France and their allies would soon bring the German aggressors to heel. Once the reality was understood, the establishment of a command economy was rapidly achieved. A form of economic planning and economic planners had arrived *force majeure*.

For the longer term, practical demonstration of the central government's competence to control the economy was matched by changing public attitudes which could only mean that – unlike in 1919 – the return to peace would be accompanied by popular demands for greater state intervention. The whole country had combined not just to defeat fascism but to ensure a return to a better material world for the majority than had existed in the 1930s. The new world would offer high levels of employment and wide measures of social welfare; and the state would play the central role in its creation and regulation. What was far from clear, however, was just how central government would combine the will and the means to match the ends.

Economic planning in wartime was a unique creature. Whilst not an easy task, planning was simpler than in peace-time because the objectives were clear and predetermined. Planning was further facilitated by the wartime innovation of manpower budgeting and the techniques of national income accounting. Moreover, the degree of popular acceptance of state direction was, despite expectations of post-war economic and social change, greater than could be sustained in peace-time. Nowhere was this more evident than in relation to trade unions and the operation of the labour market, as will be shown later.

From late 1940 onwards, members of the wartime coalition government were aware of the economic problems which would arise with the transition from war to peace and of the formidable task of reconstruction. By 1945 the economy was near exhaustion and since 1941 it had been kept alive by aid from the U.S.A. in the form of Lend-Lease, and generous assistance from Canada. The dominant fear was that a brief inflationary post-war boom would be followed by deflation and deep depression. Thus it was felt that the only way of avoiding such a calamity would be through the maintenance of firm government controls.

For the longer term, however – as the wartime records of reconstruction planning included in this handbook reveal – there was little party-political agreement over the general desirability, let alone a specific programme, of economic planning.[3] Reconstruction had been a topic of considerable public interest since the summer of 1940 and several administrative innovations had been achieved which were later to be invaluable, such as the establishment of the Economic Section of the Cabinet Office[4] and the Central Statistical Office[5]; but policy had been only weakly co-ordinated in Whitehall by the Reconstruction Problems Committee[6], served by a very small and ineffective Reconstruction Secretariat[7]. With the victory of El Alamein in October 1942 and the publication of the Beveridge Report in December, however, the political climate totally changed. The former lifted the siege mentality that had been enveloping the country and the latter provided the focus through which public pressure could be brought to bear on the government. Reconstruction became for the first time, as has been remarked, 'a matter of first rate importance within Whitehall, worthy of the energies of some of the most powerful politicians and civil servants'.[8]

Both the administration of reconstruction planning and the nature of the resulting White Papers well illustrate the inherent tensions within the wartime coalition. It was not, for instance, the sympathetic welcoming of the Beveridge Report which provided the catalyst for the serious study of reconstruction, but the panic created within both the Conservative Party and the Treasury by the potential cost of the report's social security proposals and its assumption of full employment. Thus it was a Treasury memorandum opposing the report which occasioned the establishment of a new and important ministerial committee, the Reconstruction Priorities Committee[9], which assumed prime responsibility for reconstruction in January 1943. One of its major acts was to set up the Official Steering Committee on Post-war Employment[10] which in turn produced the draft of the 1944 *Employment Policy* White Paper.

Even so powerful a committee, however, was unable to contain the political disputes that discussions of peace-time policy provoked both amongst ministers and within the rank and file of the political parties.[11] Evidence of fundamental policy differences between the two sides of the coalition is provided by the compromise nature of its White Papers, of which the *Employment Policy* White Paper is a prime example. Early intentions that this White Paper should proclaim the government's responsibility for maintaining full employment and that it should lay down the means for achieving it, were not realised. Conservative and Labour leaders simply could not agree on the scale and nature of post-war government interference in the economy and this was matched by similar disagreements among senior officials. The White Paper was thus vague and unspecific in its recommendations, referring simply to the desirability of maintaining 'high and stable employment'. Likewise, it did no more than acknowledge the need for greater industrial efficiency as a precondition for high employment and made only minor reference to the use of fiscal policy as an economic stabilizer.

During the war years, therefore, the centre of British politics shifted to a point at which there was acceptance of a much larger measure of government regulation of the economy than had operated in the 1930s. But this agreement did not amount to a consensus of ideas which crystallized into a broad political programme to which both major parties more or less subscribed. The Conservative Party, while accepting the need for increased government responsibilities, clung to the belief in the primacy of private enterprise and the rule of the market place – how to square need with belief was by no means fully resolved in its political programme. By contrast, the Labour Party (soon to become the government) was committed to what it saw as major social reforms and to the long-term planning of the economy. In its 1945 manifesto, *Let Us Face The Future*, the commitment to planning was unequivocal: '[We shall] plan from the ground up, giving an appropriate place to constructive enterprise and private endeavour in the National Plan'.[12]

The post-war Labour governments regularly reaffirmed their commitment to planning. But what those declarations amounted to in terms of understanding, practice and performance is another matter. The analysis which follows attempts to provide some suggestions which may help to clarify the relationship between aspiration and achievement during this period. In this context the focus will be on the central formulation of economic policy and not on the specific subjects which are covered in detail in the handbook.

What is Economic Planning?

Any attempt to assess post-war economic policy from the standpoint of planning must involve a definition of what constitutes planning as distinct from other forms of political economy. The problem is that an enormous amount has been written on this complex issue. Nevertheless it is possible to provide an adequate definition for our purpose.

At the extreme, economic planning means comprehensive control of the economic system involving a high measure of common, or state, ownership. But in the real world economic planning is not a matter of all or nothing; it is a question of degree. And this necessarily means that there is no clear dividing line between a free market economy on the one hand and a planned economy on the other, since anything which induces a conscious move away from a free competitive market can be described as planning. Thus a more useful distinction is between interventionism and planning. It is, however, more difficult to define this distinction than to indicate its practical effects.

In all settled states a degree of central government direction of, and participation in, economic activity is necessary in order to ensure the provision of essential public goods, such as law enforcement and defence. To argue the contrary is to espouse an Alice-in-Wonderland form of liberal economics. Moreover, central government involvement in the economy can extend beyond the provision of the minimum essential public goods without amounting to what can sensibly be defined as central economic planning. In practical terms, therefore, a distinction can be drawn between interventionism and planning.

Economic interventionism can thus be extended as the state seeks to mitigate the effects of unfettered free markets and as it regulates the day-to-day working of the economy in order to allow the various economic actors (including firms, trade unions, consumers) to pursue their individual objectives according to their relative economic power. The broad aims are to maintain national solvency and to safeguard the means to prosperity as they are commonly understood and accepted. Accordingly, the state can manipulate a variety of regulators (such as taxes, interest rates, exchange rates, the money supply), introduce laws which define limits to economic action (such as patent laws, factory and workshop regulations, monopoly controls), and pursue policies which increase the opportunities and enhance the performance of economic actors – policies which range from those which influence industrial location or make provision for industrial training, to those which seek to provide broader access to welfare, including health and housing. The state may even intervene to the extent that it acquires industries or sectors of industry in the form of public enterprises. But the essential nature of interventionism is preserved so long as the level of economic performance remains substantially the result of choices made by economic actors outside central government; so long as the state itself remains one (even the biggest) of a number of influential economic actors.

Interventionism, on this definition, is clearly a flexible concept. It can incorporate, in the British case, the range which extends from Victorian *laissez-faire* to the late-twentieth-century orthodoxy of the mixed economy. Equally clearly, the applicability of the term is increasingly called into question as the share of national income passing through government hands increases. Indeed, this is the major reason why the Second World War decade poses so strongly the issue of interventionism versus planning, in terms of contemporary politics and in terms of theoretical definition and historical explanation. So how then is planning to be defined?

Planning starts from the position of specifying what should be the outcome of economic activity over a given period (most commonly from one to five years) in terms of targets or quotas. In order to achieve the desired result, a central planning body allocates resources between different industries and sectors of the economy. The degree of control may well extend down to individual firms. Planning also requires the predetermination of consumer choices, even though this may be decided in response to some process for measuring consumer preferences. Consequently, the so-called free market has to be replaced by new mechanisms of control and direction which may or may not involve collaboration or consultation with various economic interests. And all these things will require centrally directed changes in the structure and organization of the economy from its pre-planning state. In short, the key difference between planning and interventionism is that whereas interventionism seeks to use, modify and steer the market mechanism, planning attempts to confront directly its inefficiencies by replacing it with an alternative, predetermined system.

Whilst there can be degrees of planning, the pliability of planning systems is less than that of interventionism for two main reasons. First, planning systems cannot cope with a wide range of consumer choice. On the one hand it becomes increasingly difficult to reconcile choices prior to setting allocations and targets; on the other hand, any attempt to allow wider consumer choice during the planning period itself will tend to undermine the whole system of resource allocation. Secondly, market economies have much more tolerance to the inefficiencies and waste which they create because these are dispersed throughout the system. For example, the common occurrence of bankruptcies, which represent misallocation of resources, rarely threatens the system as a whole. By contrast, waste and inefficiency in a planning system may well threaten its whole existence simply because of the high degree of centralization which exists. In other words, planning requires a higher degree of economic rationality for its satisfactory maintenance than does the alternative interventionist market economy. Nevertheless, planning systems may well be the most effective means of economic organization at certain stages of economic development or – and this is what is especially fascinating about the 1940s in Britain – in conditions of post-war economic reconstruction. The Second World War dramatically demonstrated that planning was within the art of the possible.[13]

Planning in Practice, 1945–51
I

From the outset there was a basic dichotomy in the approach of government to post-war economic planning. Under conditions of shortage and reconstruction targets had to be set, programmes drawn up and systems of implementation put into operation. But working in opposition to this degree of acceptance of the need for planning was the fact that there was no coherent set of principles on which a permanent system of planning could be developed. Little progress had been made in this direction beyond the ideas discussed in the 1930s. There was, too, confusion between planning on the one hand and controls to deal with post-war shortages on the other. The commitment of the Labour government, therefore, was essentially an ideological one. Effective planning required more than simply commitment.

Nationalization was in one sense part of the Labour government's planning programme. The policy involved the idea of controlling strategic parts of the economy. Moreover, implementation of the programme demonstrated a degree of political will and clear responsiveness to strong political pressures, mainly from trade unions. But for virtually all the industries brought into public ownership some form of major state assistance and direction was inevitable because of the enormous long-term economic problems from which they were suffering – problems which had been seriously exacerbated by the unremitting demands of the war. Unfortunately, the new management structures which were developed under nationalization reflected more the administrative preoccupations of civil servants than the commercial needs of the industries concerned.[14] What is more, for all the energy and parliamentary time absorbed by the nationalization programme, it was essentially about ownership rather than control and, as such, was only tenuously linked to the broader issue of planning. The one act of nationalization which appeared to capture the commanding heights – the nationalization of the Bank of England – proved in the longer term to be a kind of Trojan horse. The powerful City establishment was, through its control of the Bank of England (whose organization was left virtually untouched) formally admitted to the centre of economic policy-making.

An important part of the basis of post-war planning at the onset was the *Economic Survey* prepared by the Economic Section of the Cabinet Office in consultation with other departments and committees.[15] The object of the *Survey* was to provide an account of the current position of the economy and to set out government targets for the coming year. The first Survey, for 1946, was a mixture of planning (necessarily influenced by wartime manpower and materials planning) and straightforward regulation. The techniques of national income accounting were very much to the fore. But in the discussion of the Survey in the Ministerial Committee on Economic Planning[16], it soon became clear that peace-time planning faced much more complex problems than was the case in wartime. For example, attempts to restrict supplies of goods for domestic consumption could have adverse effects on the scale and costs of production for exports; and there were hardly any industries which produced solely for export.[17] This Survey was not published for reasons which will be explained later.

Senior civil servants concerned with reconstruction certainly expressed positive views towards peace-time planning. A memorandum from the Cabinet Secretary, Norman Brook, to the Permanent Secretary of the Treasury and chairman of the Official Steering Committee on Economic Development, Edward Bridges, specifically stated that one of the objectives of post-war planning should be the maintenance of full employment.[18] Furthermore, Edward Bridges expressed the view that, 'proposals in the economic and industrial field should be judged, not as isolated projects, but as part of a single national plan'.[19] Yet for all this apparent support, nothing like enough constructive thought was devoted to the machinery of economic planning. Indeed, the report of the Machinery of Government Committee[20] had been made in private because of a lack of administrative and political consensus over future policy, and it was non-committal if not hostile to major innovation. Correspondingly, from the beginning, the post-war administrative structure was largely dictated by the clash of ministerial personality and the vested interests of departments.

Perhaps in an effort to reconcile these attitudes, in 1945 Edward Bridges presented a case for a more integrated approach to planning and envisaged a planning horizon of five years.[21] Whilst he talked in somewhat simplistic terms about changes in the structure of the economic system, the nub of his proposals was for more co-ordinated official control through a high-level steering committee staffed from the Treasury. Moreover, the Treasury would be the agency for transmitting the decisions of this new committee to the Lord President's Committee which was, beneath the Cabinet, the chief ministerial body responsible for economic policy.

It is impossible to be certain whether these proposals reflected any kind of acceptance of the need for planning, though the fact remains that senior civil servants did accept that some form of central regulation and control was essential in face of the enormous problems of post-war reconstruction. At the same time the Treasury was concerned to regain its predominant position within the Civil Service which it had lost during the war, when financial matters had taken second place to the regulation of supplies of personnel and materials. Later evidence will show, however, that a commitment to planning had certainly not become a permanent feature of the department's policy outlook. More immediately, the administrative improvisations of 1945–1946 were not a success. So much so, one of the reasons why the 1946 Economic Survey was never published was the fear that publication might raise a 'clamour for . . . the disclosure of the planning machinery which would cause serious embarrassment to the government'.[22] There is much to suggest, therefore, that in the immediate post-war years senior civil servants judged it useful to employ the rhetoric of planning even if they did not subscribe to its principles.

The basic weakness of the government's early political and administrative approach to planning was made worse by other, independent elements. From the start the trade unions adopted a negative attitude because they were firmly opposed to any kind of manpower planning.[23] Even during wartime, the direction of labour had depended more on wage incentives than on labour controls and, somewhat ironically, a consequence of this fact was that in peace-time it proved difficult to get workers to switch from highly-paid munitions work to lower-paid civilian jobs.[24] The immediate issue, of course, was wage fixing by means of free collective bargaining; but the potentially more explosive issue was the imposition of some form of control over the occupational and geographical distribution of the labour force which would destroy traditional union policies. Furthermore, despite considerable ministerial support for some form of control over labour – from Cripps, for example – the Ministry of Labour was steadfastly opposed to it.[25] An additional and independent obstacle to geographical labour mobility was the acute housing shortage. Somewhat paradoxically, the housing problem provided an excellent opportunity for re-enforcing efforts to introduce central planning. A housing programme could have been used to exercise powerful influence on industrial location and the consequent distribution of labour. Instead, the housing programme was largely developed as a major part of welfare policy to meet needs where they occurred. Only in the cases of coal-mining and agriculture was the programme aimed at encouraging labour mobility.

Another source of resistance to centralized planning was industry itself. In a general sense, this opposition was simply part of the desire amongst businessmen to return to freer market conditions after wartime restrictions and, as such, it was something which could have been incorporated into peace-time planning. But over and above this, certain industries were strongly resistant to government interference because they had already established corporate forms of intra-industry organization which were largely under their control. These developments had arisen in the 1930s through schemes connected with government attempts at promoting or assisting industrial restructuring, or rationalization as it was then the fashion to call it. Industrial boards of one form or another were established – for example, the Cotton Board – and these organizations subsequently became the agencies for regulating industry during the war. Such responsibility substantially enhanced the authority of these bodies and naturally strengthened their determination and capability to retain a controlling position after 1945. Their defence of the interests of particular industries was a major obstacle to national economic planning and to any radical industrial restructuring which that might require.[26]

Such political indecision and popular pressure placed major constraints on the development of the administrative machinery for economic planning from the start, therefore. A succession of committees, for example, directly oversaw the preparation of the *Survey*. Such a constantly changing administrative structure failed to provide a satisfactory focus for planning. Furthermore, it compounded existing serious administrative defects. For instance, no significant reallocation of responsibilities within Whitehall was attempted after the war; each ministry retained control over its traditional area of policy – and thus over the information that was essential to the formulation of policy and over the means of its implementation. One opportunity which was lost was that of transforming the wartime Ministry of Production into an executive ministry of economic planning, as some had hoped;[27] and permanent control over the distribution of physical resources was not accorded to other new ministries, such as the Ministries of Supply and Works[28], which were never even raised to Cabinet status.

The general result was that, in the formulation of economic policy for which it was responsible under the Cabinet, the Lord President's Committee, with its small secretariat[29], was not always fully informed – especially in the area of financial policy where (not only to safeguard budget secrecy) the Treasury[30] remained consistently uncooperative. Further confusion was also caused by the allocation of other areas of policy vital to planning, such as manpower and fuel, to other Cabinet committees (see chart 3). In the implementation of policy, the Lord President's Committee also lacked the administrative muscle to prevent established departments appealing over its head to the Cabinet against unpopular decisions. As Morrison himself admitted later: 'to rely wholly on a committee structure not served by a specially qualified and first-rate staff threw an intolerable load of detail on to Ministers and very senior officials'.[31] Indeed, it epitomized the major misjudgement of the Cabinet's strategy to devolve responsibility for the development of the planning machine (which inevitably had major political repercussions) to the Civil Service, which, itself, had powerful departmental vested interests to defend.

Administrative defects, however, were not the sole cause of administrative failure. As written at the time, 'personalities in the last resort, and not machinery, will make the difference between success and failure. It is a pathetic illusion to suppose that some subtle rearrangements of Cabinet committees, or some general notion of devolution or decentralization, will set everything right'.[32] Administrative efficiency was forestalled by the collective indecision of the Cabinet and the inability of the economic ministers to act 'as a team'.[33] Morrison himself lacked the time, interest and expertise to establish a viable planning machine under the effective control of the Lord President's Committee. He was fully occupied with piloting through Parliament the nationalization legislation, and this was his primary interest. Like Attlee, he did not have instinctive 'feel' for economic policy. For example, it is clear from a speech on planning by Morrison that he did not grasp the need for radical administrative reform if economic planning had any chance of succeeding.[34] The full frailty of the planning machine under Morrison's stewardship was finally exposed by the fuel crisis in the winter of 1946–1947.

II

1947 saw the first serious and sustained attempt, at Cabinet level, to devise adequate administrative machinery for effective economic planning. Reform of the Cabinet committee system had been under consideration for some time.[35] The occasion for its administrative realization was provided by the fuel and convertibility crises in February and August, just as a major readjustment in ministerial responsibilities was required to offset successive challenges to Attlee's leadership, in July by Dalton and in September by Cripps. It would be misleading, however, to give the impression of calm deliberation behind these changes. The hesitancy of the initial moves and the sheer accident of Dalton's enforced resignation in November over the budget leak, which enabled economic and financial policy finally to be combined under Cripps at the Treasury, revealed that the administrative revolution was far from being a carefully planned operation.

There were four elements in the reorganization. First, a new expert body was established in March under the direction of Sir Edwin Plowden, to be known as the Central Economic Planning Staff (C.E.P.S.). Its brief was to co-ordinate the physical aspects of economic planning, 'to develop the long-term plan for the use of the country's manpower and resources' and to ensure the implementation of policy. 'One of the chief gaps in government machinery during the first eighteen months after the war', noted Attlee, 'has been the lack of any organization to see that, even when decisions were taken to put things first, these decisions were made effective'.[36] Initially, it was intended to have planning officers in each department to assist co-ordination, but this degree of organization was never achieved. So far as the long-term plan was conceived, this had often been referred to after 1945 and work had been done on various aspects of long-term forecasting, but nothing formal had been submitted to ministries. In 1947, therefore, long-term planning was a form of invocation rather than any kind of economic programme.

The second element consisted of two initiatives to win greater public support. An Economic Information Unit was set up to co-ordinate publicity and to brief ministers more effectively on economic issues; and the Economic Planning Board[37] was established with the object of involving both sides of industry in the making of policy. Thirdly, ministerial responsibility for economic planning was clarified with the Lord President being relieved of his co-ordinating function. Cripps took over from Morrison and this change was officially recognized in September when he was made Minister of Economic Affairs. He retained this responsibility when, in November, he became Chancellor of the Exchequer on Dalton's resignation. C.E.P.S. and other officials concerned with planning were correspondingly transferred to the Treasury. The final element in the administrative overhaul was a reform of the Cabinet committee structure.

The formal machinery for the administration of economic planning was subject to frequent adjustment between 1947 and 1951. Informal contacts and collaboration often bypassed – and were therefore more important than – formal committee meetings and decisions. Hence, the whole system became exceedingly complex. A detailed description of its operation is provided in the appendix to this chapter. From this it will be seen that a large number of ministerial and official co-ordinating committees continued to dominate economic planning between 1947 and 1949. It further exposes the Labour government's unwillingness to disturb the traditional executive responsibilities of departments within Whitehall. So diverse, indeed, was the system that 'a factual report on major responsibilities' to the Steering Committee for the Economic Organization Enquiry in 1950 stretched to 78 pages. More detailed study of this administrative maze might well reveal that the alleged stress and physical exhaustion which afflicted ministers and civil servants during those years owed much to the fact that they spent a great deal of their time chasing their own tails. There was clearly ample room for simplification, reduced work-load and greater efficiency. But the essential and missing ingredient for achieving it was sufficient political will on the part of the Cabinet to override the vested interests of departments, in particular of the Treasury.[38]

In 1950 the issue of what permanent powers were required for peace-time planning was forced into the open by the impending expiry of the 1945 Supplies and Services (Transitional Powers) Act, under which wartime legislation had been extended for a further five years. The review was given added urgency under the impact of the Korean War. The changes under consideration included an Economic Planning and Full Employment Bill which incorporated new elements of economic planning. No new bill materialized, however, owing to the political uncertainty caused by the government's reduced parliamentary majority after the general election of February 1950 and the need to renew emergency legislation for the duration of the war. Consequently, no new initiatives were attempted before the election of the Conservative government in October 1951.

Economic Planning: Promise and Performance
I

An assessment of post-war attempts at economic planning has to focus on the activities of four main groups: government ministers, civil servants, employers and trade unions. Their combined effect was, ultimately, to reduce to a forlorn hope the confident assertion in the Labour Party's 1945 manifesto that the new government would 'plan from the ground up'.[39] Throughout these years, nevertheless, commitment to the idea of economic planning persisted to produce continuing tension between aspiration and practicality. At the very end of the period, as has been noted, there were even signs – fleeting as it proved – that this tension might be resolved through the planning mechanisms being prepared in a Full Employment Bill. It is this element of continuity, increasingly tenuous though it became, which gives form and coherence to the body of records which are surveyed in this handbook.

II

Morrison, Cripps, Dalton and later Gaitskell and Bevan, were the leading ministers involved in post-war planning, though Bevin exercised considerable indirect influence both as Foreign Secretary and as a long-standing representative of trade union interests. From the beginning these ministers and their subordinates were under enormous pressures of work and these pressures were further intensified by a series of economic crises between 1947 and 1949: the fuel crisis, convertibility, the balance of payments and devaluation. Whilst the claim that these crises were a direct consequence of a lack of planning may not attract much support, there were certain respects in which they obviously reinforced the need and provided the opportunity for longer-term planning. It is equally clear that the government as a whole was unwilling to meet the challenge in this way. On the crucial matter of manpower, for example, the Cabinet rejected proposals by the Ministerial Committee on Economic Planning for easing critical labour shortages by cutting the armed services and supply industries.[40] In reaction to this decision, the secretary of the Lord President's Committee lamented to Edward Bridges: '[there is] a great danger that ministers may go forward with the illusion that they are undertaking economic planning when they are not in fact ready to take any decision which would make economic planning possible'.[41] This comment was somewhat unfair since the Cabinet was aware of being caught between two poles of criticism – on the one side from those who complained that measures of economic planning were not being adopted and, on the other, from those who saw a planned economy as 'inconsistent with British conceptions of personal liberty'.[42] Even so, for Attlee the overriding concern was the lesson to be learned from what he saw as the disastrous pre-war policy of allowing the armed forces to be unduly weakened.[43] In this he had the full support of Bevin. But in both men this attitude revealed an unwillingness to relate foreign policy objectives to economic realities, which was no basis for effective economic planning.

Further evidence of the inconsistent approach to planning by ministers is provided by Morrison and Cripps. Morrison did not consider it necessary to revert to the kind of comprehensive control over fixed investment which had operated during the war. He judged that the main reliance should be placed on the regulation of building licences.[44] A little later Morrison went so far as to indicate that he regarded even building controls as temporary and not as part of any form of long-term planning.[45] Cripps, by contrast, produced a memorandum for the Cabinet (as Minister of Economic Affairs) entitled 'The Framework of Economic Planning'[46]. It was a strong document and made no bones about the fact that what was needed was direct planning and not indicative planning; imports, investment and consumption should all be planned.[47]

By early 1948 Cripps was agreeing with Edwin Plowden that the budget was 'now part of general economic planning'.[48] In this last respect, however, it is very doubtful whether Cripps fully appreciated or, if he did, was prepared to accept, the consequences of integrating financial policy with the detailed requirements of physical planning. It would have required, in particular, the integration of domestic and external financial policy which would almost certainly have resulted in a reduced role for Britain in international affairs generally. Similarly, financial policy would have had to serve planning objectives in ways which would have at least undermined the primacy of the Treasury; a fate which Cripps might have been willing to accept if he kept faith with views he had expressed during the years before he became Chancellor of the Exchequer, but not ones to which his officials would willingly accede. With the advantage of hindsight it can be seen that whatever the hopes and declarations of Cripps and the C.E.P.S., the development of budgetary policy from 1947–48 marked the beginning of the restoration of more orthodox methods of economic regulation.

Cripps's commitment to planning was important because he exercised a dominating influence in government, to a degree which Morrison had not done when he was responsible for economic policy. But by itself Cripps's influence was not enough. Economic planning required the full commitment of the government to a clear set of principles and objectives, whereas the records contain many examples of the kind of ministerial inconsistency cited above. In part, these differences can be explained by the sheer pressures of the economic difficulties which had to be met in the best way possible at the time. In part, also, this lack of consistency reflected a lack of technical understanding.

One area in which this was particularly significant was productivity. There was certainly considerable concern over the issue of productivity which was demonstrated by the establishment of the Anglo-American Council on Productivity, the attention given to it in the *Economic Surveys* and government sponsored publicity.[49] At the same time, however, the government was extremely sensitive to the reaction of industry, not wishing in any way to imply that industry was unduly backsliding or inefficient. For its part, industry (including both employers and unions) was a long way from getting to grips with the problem of low productivity which, although exacerbated by the exigencies of war production, was a long-standing feature of Britain's comparative international standing. Higher productivity could be achieved only through major changes in business organization and management and new forms of industrial relations. Failure to develop a policy for raising productivity in British industry was a central weakness of post-war attempts at economic planning and in the longer-term performance of the British economy generally.[50]

It is somewhat ironic, therefore, that in 1950, when the Labour government was approaching the end of its life, there developed a new sense of understanding of the legislative requirements for economic planning. This change owed much to Gaitskell who, in 1950, became Minister of Economic Affairs and then, later in the same year, Chancellor of the Exchequer. Gaitskell perhaps had a clearer view than any previous minister, with the exception of Cripps, of the nature of economic planning. But whereas Cripps tended to concentrate on the administrative and executive aspects of planning, Gaitskell, possibly because he was an economist, was more concerned with the practical operation of the economy within a planning system.

The form in which these new proposals were made was the Economic Planning and Full Employment Bill, retitled the Full Employment Bill in January 1951, to which reference has already been made.[51] The occasion was the expiry of post-war powers of economic control. There was much discussion amongst ministers on what should replace these controls and considerable opposition from senior officials to their retention. In an attempt to resolve matters Gaitskell was invited to prepare a memorandum on the subject for a ministerial committee.[52] The thrust of Gaitskell's argument was that general control of the economy should be operated through monetary and fiscal policy but that under certain circumstances, and most probably in particular sectors, these methods would have to be supplemented by direct controls. The major powers needed would affect prices, consumer purchases, building materials, imports and the distribution of production between home and foreign markets. Gaitskell was more guarded on powers for controlling public and private investment, manufacturing and the purchase of materials. Furthermore, he was particularly keen to drop reference to economic planning from the Bill: 'people will support controls if they recognize that they can prevent unpleasant things happening, but I doubt if the term economic planning is understood – or if it is, whether it is a popular concept'.[53] The advent of the Korean War made the introduction of the Bill difficult, and the war was certainly used as the reason for delaying it. With the subsequent defeat of the Labour government, attempts at co-ordinated, central economic planning were at an end.

III

When allowance is made for the enormous scale of the economic problems facing ministers and for ministers' ambivalence on the principle of central economic planning, there still remains the question of how far their attitudes and actions were influenced by those on whom they relied for advice and assistance. The official body specifically responsible for providing economic advice was the Economic Section of the Cabinet Office under the direction of James Meade until 1947 and of Robert Hall thereafter.[54] From the outset the Section took the view, understandably so, that it would not be possible to retain wartime labour controls in peace-time. But at the same time the Section appears not to have appreciated the extent to which economic planning required a manpower policy. There was some recognition of the need for a wages policy and Robert Hall believed that there was fairly widespread acceptance among unions and employers of the need for wage restraint.[55] But there was no attempt to develop a longer-term wages policy, largely because there were considerable differences of opinion between economists within the Section.[56] As Meade was later to admit, this was the major failure not just in terms of post-war planning but also in relation to the longer-term management of the economy.[57] Furthermore, the crucial matter of productivity was never the subject of sustained analysis within the Section.

James Meade was a convinced Keynesian, particularly in the sense that he regarded the regulation of aggregate investment and the budget as the major instruments of economic control. The Section was, therefore, particularly concerned with devising counter-cyclical policies. In the field of international trade, Meade was for multilateralism and against bilateralism and tariffs. This implied that there was to be no planning in international trade, other than the promotion of exports. This approach had given rise to some discussion and disagreement during the later stages of the war, but despite opposition from Cripps and Beaverbrook (or maybe because of it) the multilateral approach prevailed.[58] This amounted to a major surrender of planning control since import controls – especially of raw materials – were one of the most effective ways of directing the flow of resources within the economy.[59]

By 1947 earlier doubts in the Economic Section about the nature of economic planning in general, and the long-term plan in particular, were being expressed more strongly because it was felt that there was over-emphasis on the physical allocation of resources thus ignoring the necessary role of the price mechanism for making innumerable adjustments in the economy.[60] The Section therefore placed increasing stress on financial policies and on the use of the price mechanism in conjunction with physical planning.

In 1948 a co-ordinating Committee on Controls and Efficiency was established, under the chairmanship of a senior Treasury official, with the object of pushing hard for general decontrol; and this included getting rid of controls over raw materials.[61] In important respects, therefore, this committee worked in direct opposition to the C.E.P.S. if the latter was intended to carry out an effective and comprehensive planning function. All the while, the Economic Section became more committed to macro-economic management and gave little attention to micro-economic policy.

The C.E.P.S. had ostensibly been established to achieve co-ordination of economic plans emanating from separate ministries. During its early development there was clear endeavour to give the C.E.P.S. independence so that it did not become part of the 'hierarchy of the economic machine'.[62] For its part, the C.E.P.S. aspired to a fairly comprehensive planning role though it was sensitive to the need to reassure industry that it was not seeking powers of direction. Indeed, this was a prime reason why the government appointed someone from industry as the Chief Planning Officer.[63] The C.E.P.S. did not, however, underpin its aims by a carefully considered programme of action. In the crucial area of investment policy, for example, on the one hand it argued for planning but on the other hand it considered that outside the state and public utility sectors decisions had to be left to 'the good sense of industry'.[64]

When, in 1947, the C.E.P.S. became part of the Treasury, the possibilities for planning were strengthened because successful planning had to involve the Treasury, and the most effective way of achieving this was from inside the department. Added to this, a close relationship existed between Edwin Plowden and Cripps who had worked together at the Ministry of Aircraft Production during the war, and Cripps had a high opinion of Plowden. The results of the new arrangement were soon evident and promising, as previously obstructive Treasury officials were far more forthcoming with information, as they knew they had to be.

Shortly afterwards the C.E.P.S. prepared a detailed memorandum, setting out its objectives and functions, for the new Economic Planning Board.[65] But perceptive critics were soon asking how, practically, economic planning was to be carried out, particularly in relation to the existing organization of industry. Beyond this question there was an even broader one of how domestic planning would take account of the new possibilities raised by the Marshall Aid programme. In response, Plowden acknowledged the importance of these issues but he was unable to provide any satisfactory answers.[66] Various ideas were floating around in the C.E.P.S., such as the possibility of indicative planning, but they never solidified into firm lines of action.

It must be borne in mind that the C.E.P.S. had a small staff (17 at the most) and it found it extremely difficult to recruit personnel of sufficiently high calibre. It was staffed mainly by career civil servants. The C.E.P.S. maintained reasonably good relations with the Economic Section, in part because of the good personal relationship between Hall (head of the Section) and Plowden; but it was also because both bodies assumed distinctive roles. As the economist David Butt explained, 'the Economic Section is explicitly a group of professional economists and our task is to give advice to ministers and contribute to official discussions as economists. . . The planning staff on the other hand are explicitly administrative. . . We try to sit outside the hurly-burly of administration and to be somewhat Olympian in our pronouncements, and they go right to the thick of it'.[67] But, of course, this description can be read as administrative impotence rather than strength.

At the end of our period the C.E.P.S. was still talking about its co-ordinating function though in a distinctly downbeat fashion and hedged around with statements about such things as the control of labour in a democratic society, the major preoccupation of rearmament and the need for international co-operation: all of which was a long way from the declared intentions of 1947.[68] Whatever the earlier promise of the close relationship with the Treasury, the attention given by the C.E.P.S. to matters of direct economic planning soon gave way to the traditional Treasury view that economic policy was largely a matter of financial policy.

The formation and implementation of all government policy depended mainly, of course, on the permanent Civil Service. For reasons of space our comments will be confined to the Treasury. Before the war the Treasury had been, without doubt, the dominant department. During the war, however, it had lost its pre-war position because financial matters were firmly controlled and subordinated to the need to secure maximum supplies and the optimum use of personnel and materials. From 1945 to 1948 the Treasury was working its way back to its accustomed role and this may well be the reason why its declared views on economic planning were expressed in flexible terms. In 1946, for instance, the report to the Ministerial Committee on Economic Planning by the Steering Committee under the chairmanship of the permanent secretary of the Treasury, Bridges, hedged its bets by stating that in the development of planning policies: 'we think it is vitally important that nothing should be done to weaken the sense of responsibility of the leaders of both sides of industry'.[69] There was some mention of how productivity gains should be distributed although, typically, nothing on how productivity increases would be achieved. Generally, however, the report was against controls and after considering various options ended up in favour of regulating demands by means of purchase tax.

The Treasury adopted various tactics during this interregnum. Thus Bernard Gilbert, second secretary of the Treasury, argued that planning should be kept apart from general economic policy on the grounds that ' . . . global economic planning is under a cloud at the moment'.[70] When the C.E.P.S. was established the Treasury managed to retain a strong influence over it through the working relationship which existed between Bridges and Brook to whom Plowden reported. The Lord President's Office had fought strongly for the C.E.P.S. to be brought under its supervision, but the battle was lost largely as a result of Morrison's declining credibility as an economic minister.[71]

The convertibility crisis of 1947 provided an ideal opportunity for strengthening Treasury control. Thus Brook argued strongly that there needed to be considerable tightening up of policy-making machinery. But clearly Brook was determined that none of these changes should lead to anything approaching thorough-going economic planning. Accordingly, he soon began to urge the need to play down the emphasis which some ministers were placing on planning because of Britain's clear dependence on the U.S.A. 'with whom the economic power now rests'.[72] In his view, Britain should not upset U.S. sensitivity by talk of planning but should seek to become the U.S.A.'s lieutenant in Western Europe. A little ironically the Marshall Aid programme temporarily increased the importance of the long-term plan (published as the *Long-term Programme* in 1948) since it became the basis for claims made to the O.E.E.C. But, as has been noted, this development did not lead to more comprehensive planning because the *Economic Survey* was emasculated by the virtual elimination of targets, since it was not known how much Marshall Aid would be obtained, and domestic controls generally were being rapidly abandoned. A little earlier, moreover, Bridges and Brook had employed their administrative skills to help ensure that the *Economic Survey* continued to be constructed on a calendar-year basis whereas Treasury budgeting operated on the financial year of April to April.[73] Whilst there was some force in the argument that a separate financial year was important for Treasury confidentiality, the lack of firm co-ordination between the budget and the *Survey* was a critical weakness in any attempt at planning.

These attitudes are not surprising in the light of correspondence between these senior civil servants just two years before. Brook wrote: '[I think that the] planning machinery . . . can be readily developed . . . but we must present this as something new – not funeral bakemeats coldly furnished forth . . . and insofar as they [the directions] are not capable of expressions in terms of financial control, Departments will find it less unusual to receive such directions from the Treasury than from any other source'.[74] *Plus ça change*. . . . Similarly, in its relations with the C.E.P.S. the Treasury would not commit itself to close co-operation but was initially content that the C.E.P.S. should be part of the Cabinet Office where it would be away from the direction of Morrison, the Lord President, and his adviser, Max Nicholson, of whom the Treasury was deeply suspicious. As Bridges put it: 'policy is a matter for the minister', by which he meant the Chancellor of the Exchequer and not the Lord President.[75] It was, nevertheless, thought to be an advantage for Plowden to become a member of the Budget Committee.

During 1948 the Treasury was much more on the offensive. In a series of memoranda and letters to various individuals, the Permanent Secretary defined principles of the department's operations. Fiscal and financial controls were pushed to the fore and in relation to the long-term plan firm emphasis was placed on the principle that the plan, ' . . . should work itself out through the normal process of administration, Treasury control, inter-departmental Ministerial Committees, etc'.[76] This *modus operandi* obviously worked directly against a coherent and centrally directed form of economic planning which was concerned with the allocation of resources and the determination of levels of output between different sectors and industries.

It has been argued that it is hard to discover obstruction by civil servants of ministerial attempts at economic planning.[77] Such a view fails to take account of the unwillingness of ministers to push the policies against a reluctant Civil Service and of the fact that ministers became increasingly exhausted by the pressures of office. More importantly, however, it fails to take account of the intricate and subtle pressures exercised by senior civil servants.

IV

The response of industry to attempts at economic planning was generally lukewarm. In 1947, for example, the Federation of British Industries (F.B.I.) politely accepted what it took to be the government's wish to have an overall plan for the economy, but quickly went on to stress the need for more 'self-government' by industry and the consequent need for a reduction in existing controls.[78] Moreover, both the records surveyed in this handbook and growing evidence from the field of business history indicate that in co-operation with government at various levels (through productivity committees, for example) the clear aim of industry was to limit, and if possible reduce, direct government involvement in its activities.

The T.U.C. was, perhaps not surprisingly, ambivalent on the issue of economic planning. In 1947 it became involved in detailed discussions with the government (through a special committee chaired by the Prime Minister) concerning the establishment of the Planning Board.[79] These discussions brought out the fundamental problem of the role of union representatives on government bodies in relation to the ultimate responsibility of government to govern. This problem was perceived clearly on the union side. The plain fact was that unions were unwilling to accept responsibility for something on which they did not have an equal say with government. Lower level sorting out of problems with civil servants, which was the kind of thing Morrison had in mind and which meant little more than consultation on government terms, would clearly not satisfy the T.U.C.[80] The fundamental political and constitutional constraint on planning, so far as the labour movement was concerned, was thus starkly demonstrated.

Trade unions generally were strongly committed to free collective bargaining, and this had powerful support within government, particularly from Bevin. It is noteworthy that in the discussions on nationalization there were no serious demands for workers' control.[81] Moreover, unions were fully aware that full commitment to economic planning on their part could well require them to accept a strong measure of manpower planning; a possibility which they were determined to avoid. And whilst these attitudes reflected genuine concern to safeguard hard-won democratic freedoms, more fundamentally they were an expression of the innate conservatism of trade unions. One of the misfortunes of post-war Britain was that most union leaders and many industrialists showed a deep resistance to radical economic change.[82] And, most certainly, labour no more than capital looked forward to a planned future.

Economic Planning in Retrospect

The unexpectedly early ending of the Second World War caused some urgent recasting of plans for reconstruction, but the fundamental economic problems remained

15

unchanged. For Britain, in common with other Western European countries, the obstacles to recovery were enormous. In the discussions in the Reconstruction Committee the scale of the task had been fully recognized, but what had not been understood was the extent to which economic reconstruction was but part of the wider need for radical reorganization of British industry. Britain was suffering from chronic industrial problems which stemmed from well before the war. The Second World War, unlike the First, did not provide opportunities for writing-off past mistakes. It made them much worse.[83]

The ideology of planning was strongly stimulated in such conditions. But ideology was not matched by a practical programme of action. In practical terms pressures were intensified by the successive crises of 1947. Leading ministers began to suffer from exhaustion. Civil servants, too, were under great strain. Anything approaching comprehensive planning, therefore, would seem to have been a non-starter. Yet without in any way seeking to denigrate the efforts of ministers or their officials, a strong case can be made that the nature of their burdens was of their own making. In other words, the same amount of effort might well have been more effectively applied.

The key factor in this administrative overloading was the antiquated structure of the Civil Service. In a brilliant contemporary article, Evan Durbin highlighted the cumbersome nature of the Whitehall machine, with its interlocking systems of official departmental committees.[84] In many respects the administrative Civil Service was like the power lathes at work in much of the British engineering industry – remarkable in terms of precision and design and thus a tribute to the skill and ingenuity of its Victorian inventors, but ill-adapted to the needs of the second half of the twentieth century. Decision-making in Whitehall tended to be slow and formulated in carefully refined syntax, as befitted the educational background of the civil servants largely responsible for it. These characteristics are, in themselves, a measure of the formidable difficulties which would face anyone attempting reform.

Senior civil servants, in particular those in the Treasury, naturally had a vested interest in maintaining the *status quo* or, more accurately, in returning to the *status quo ante*. Accordingly, the Permanent Secretary to the Treasury and the Cabinet Secretary, in the persons of Bridges and Brook respectively, showed no inclination to promote economic planning in any way which would alter the structure of government administration. What is perhaps surprising is that leading ministers made no real attempt to modernize the system. In the 1930s Cripps had explicitly argued the case for new forms of executive action to implement planning strategies, but he did not follow this through when he achieved office.[85] Even more surprising is that neither Morrison nor Gaitskell saw the need for radical reform of the Civil Service. Indeed, Gaitskell was almost dismissive of a number of carefully argued proposals for reform made by a former member of the C.E.P.S., reflecting on his experiences in the 1940s. With ministers like these the mandarins had little to fear.[86]

Labour ministers conceived of planning as concentrating on internal policy. External matters – the balance of payments and international finance – were seen as independent factors which to varying degrees limited the government's freedom of action. At the same time the response of ministers to problems tended to be in terms of short-term tactical considerations. In many ways this reaction is understandable because of the crisis nature of many of the difficulties which arose during the period and, moreover, it reflected the natural instincts of politicians. Economic planning required longer-term strategic objectives. But, with or without central planning, tactical decisions needed to be taken in relation to broader strategic objectives, unless the government was willing to allow itself to be driven along by economic forces. Certainly in relation to planning and, it can be argued, in relation to actual economic policy, the Labour governments of 1945 to 1951 did not pursue specific, clear-cut economic objectives. After the declarations of 1945, the government, unconsciously perhaps, settled for *ad hoc* pragmatism, even though its approach to economic policy was still coloured by the idea of economic planning. If this is judged to be a failure then it was a failure of political will.[87]

In political terms, the validity of planning had to be established. The free market system was taken for granted. Thus planning had to prove itself against the growing rhetoric of Keynesian economics with its watchword of managed capitalism. But whilst Keynes – the prophet of *The End of Laissez-Faire* – offered a new framework of political economy, he fell well short of substituting centralized planning for the free market. Individual expectations and many of the principles of the neo-classical market system were central to his analysis. Such an ideology was a formidable obstacle to economic planning. Planning was easily seen as the antithesis of capitalism rather than as something which could be developed within the capitalist system and which might, in certain circumstances and maybe for a limited period, be the means of restoring the system to health and vigour.

The failure of political will combined with administrative obscurantism and the lack of ideological appeal, provide much of the explanation for the abortive nature of planning during the period. By the same token, therefore, planning cannot be seen politically as a lost opportunity. Yet the opportunity was always there. Thus, for example, although the economy achieved external balance in 1948, it was not sustainable in the longer run in relation to the limited size of Britain's official reserves of gold and foreign currency, the level of imports and the still huge dollar deficit. In the same year there was the famous 'bonfire of controls' which meant that growing reliance was placed on the price mechanism as the means of achieving structural change. But the problem with the price mechanism is that it works too slowly to achieve effective structural change in the face of international competition. On the external and internal fronts, therefore, some measure of central planning offered a real but untried alternative. And, as has been noted, in the last months of its life the Labour government was preparing legislation to give force to some planning proposals.

It is the combination of ideological commitment to economic planning and its practical failure as a policy which provides the rationale for the survey of records which follows. Not only are the developments which are covered of major interest in themselves, but also they help to explain the rise to ascendency of the new credo of Keynesianism and the mixed economy. The question remains, however: does the failure of attempts to apply economic planning in the immediate post-war period lie at the heart of Britain's lack-lustre economic performance in the decades which followed? No doubt this is a question upon which many users of this guide will reflect.

Notes

1. John Stuart Mill, *Principles of Political Economy* (Longmans, Green & Co., 1898 edtn), p 128.
2. See for example J. Strachey, *The Theory and Practice of Socialism* (Gollancz, 1936); G.D.H. Cole, *Principles of Economic Planning* (Macmillan, 1935); S. Cripps, *Why this Socialism?* (Gollancz, 1934); H. Dalton, *Practical Socialism For Britain* (Routledge, 1935); E.F.M. Durbin, *Problems of Economic Planning* (Routledge & Kegan Paul, 1949) which is a collection of articles, the earliest on planning having been published in 1935; Mosley's proposals were secret because they were incorporated in a Cabinet document (CAB 24/209, CP (25)211) but the main points leaked out; J.M. Keynes, *The End of Laissez-Faire* (Hogarth Press, 1929); Liberal Party, *Britain's Industrial Future* (Benn, 1928); P.E.P., *Report on the Location of*

Industry (1939) – P.E.P. was founded in 1931; Next Five Years Group, *The Next Five Years: An Essay in Political Agreement* (Macmillan, 1935); H. Macmillan, *Reconstruction: A Plea for a National Policy* (Macmillan, 1933); *ibid., The Middle Way* (Macmillan, 1938).

3. This view contrasts with the quite widely held one that there was growing consensus between the main political parties during the war. Cf. P. Addison, *The Road to 1945* (Quartet, 1977); K.O. Morgan, *Labour in Power 1945–1951* (Oxford University Press, 1984).

4. See Alec Cairncross and Nita Watts, *The Economic Section 1939–1961* (Routledge, 1989), pp 24–39, and also chapter 19 below. Wherever a committee or department of significance to economic planning is mentioned in this introduction, a footnote will guide the reader to the relevant chapter in the handbook, where further administrative details as well as a description or listing of the records can be found.

5. Chapter 8.

6. Chapter 7.1.

7. Chapter 9.

8. Addison, *op. cit.*, p 221.

9. Chapter 7.4.

10. Chapter 7.8.

11. Andrew Chester, 'Planning, the Labour Governments and British Economic Policy 1943–51' (Unpublished Ph.D. thesis, University of Bristol, 1983), chapter 2; J.M. Lee, *The Churchill Coalition* (Batsford, 1980), chapters 2 and 5.

12. The Labour Party, *Let us Face the Future* (1945).

13. The flavour of the contemporary debate on the issue can be gained from E.F.M. Durbin, *op.cit.*; O.S. Franks, *Central Planning and Controls in War and Peace* (Longmans, 1947); F.A. Hayek, *The Road to Serfdom* (Routledge Kegan Paul, 1944); J. Jewkes, *Ordeal By Planning* (Macmillan, 1948); L.C. Robbins, *The Economic Problem in War and Peace* (Macmillan, 1947).

14. An exhaustive account of the programme is provided by Norman Chester, *The Nationalization of British Industry 1945–51* (HMSO, 1975).

15. Alec Cairncross and Nita Watts, *op.cit.*, pp 162–75.

16. Chapter 15.28.

17. T 230/55, Economic Survey Working Party report, 1946, para 39. A detailed analysis of this report is provided by Andrew Chester, *op.cit.*, chapter 4.

18. CAB 21/2215, 4 September 1945.

19. CAB 21/2215, 19 September 1945.

20. Chapter 7.10.

21. CAB 21/2215.

22. T 230/55, 'Economic Survey for 1946'; Draft Memorandum by the Lord President, 22 January 1946.

23. See for example, *79th Annual Report of the TUC* (1947), pp 349–56.

24. CAB 124/800; CAB 124/801.

25. Chapter 14.5; CAB 134/503, MEP(47)1st. See also R. Jones, *Wages and Employment Policy* (Allen and Unwin, 1987), ch.4.

26. See for example Marguerite Dupree (ed.), *Lancashire and Whitehall. The Diary of Sir Raymond Streat, Volume 2. 1939–57* (Manchester University Press, 1987); John Vaizey, *The History of British Steel* (Weidenfeld & Nicolson, 1974), pp 118–49; Steven Tolliday, *Business, Banking and Politics. The Case of British Steel, 1918–1939* (Harvard, 1987), pp 328–44.

27. Alec Cairncross, *Years of Recovery. British Economic Policy 1945–51* (Methuen, 1985), p 50.

28. Chapter 22.7 and 22.9.

29. Chapter 11.

30. Chapter 20.

31. CAB 124/113, memorandum on the history of Lord President's Committee, 27 Aug 1951, p 7.

32. D. Jay *et.al.*, *The Road to Recovery* (Wingate, 1948), p 18.

33. Austin Robinson, 'The Economic Problems of Transition from War to Peace: 1945–49', *Cambridge Journal of Economics*, 10, 1986, p 181.

34. B. Donoughue and G.W. Jones, *Herbert Morrison. Portrait of a Politician* (Weidenfeld and Nicolson, 1973) p 354.

35. P. Hennessy, *Cabinet* (Blackwell, 1986), pp 39–43.

36. T 229/56, 20 March 1947.

37. Chapter 15.12.

38. These attitudes are revealed in Lord Bridges, *The Treasury* (Allen and Unwin, 1964), despite the anodyne style in which the book is written.

39. *Op.cit.*

40. CAB 21/2216, CM(47)8, 16 Jan, 1947; CAB 21/2216, CM(47)9, 17 January 1947.

41. CAB 124/899, M. Nicholson to E.E. Bridges, February 1947.

42. CAB 21/2216, CM(47)9, 17 Jan 1947.

43. *ibid.* See also, A. Bullock, *Ernest Bevin, Foreign Secretary 1945–51* (W.W. Norton & Co., 1983), pp 233–4, 239–41, 244, 322–3, 330, 354, 522–4, 581–2.

44. CAB 132/3, LP(46) 95, 23 April 1946.

45. CAB 132/3, LP(46)133, 13 May 1946.

46. T 229/417, PC(47)11. 'The Framework of Economic Planning'; Memorandum by the Minister for Economic Affairs, 11 November 1947.

47. More generally on investment control see M. Chick, 'Economic Planning, Managerial Decision-Making and the Role of Fixed Capital Investment in the Economic Recovery of the U.K. 1945–55', (unpublished Ph.D. thesis, University of London, 1986).

48. CAB 134/211, E.P.B.(48)12, 'Planning Problems', Memorandum by the Central Economic Planning Staff to the Economic Planning Board, 29 April 1948; see also J.C.R. Dow, *The Management of the British Economy 1945–60* (Cambridge University Press, 1965), p 36, who cites similar comments by Cripps in his 1948 budget speech.

49. *Committee on Industrial Productivity: First Report*, 1948/9, Cmd. 7665; *ibid*; *Second Report*, 1950, Cmd. 7991; The only technical study of the subject made during this period was L.S. Rostas, *Comparative Productivity in British and American Industry* (Cambridge University Press, 1948).

50. See B.W.E. Alford, *British Economic Performance 1945–75* (Macmillan, 1988).

51. T 230/295 first draft of the White Paper on Full Employment.

52. CAB 134/225, EPC(50)9, 'Economic Planning and Liberalism', Memorandum by the Minister of Fuel and Power, 1950.

53. CAB 130/65, GEN 343/1st.

54. See Alec Cairncross and Nita Watts, *op.cit.*

55. See for example, Alec Cairncross (ed.), *The Robert Hall Diaries, 1947–1953* (Unwin Hyman, 1989) p 9.

56. See R. Jones, 'The Wages Problem in Employment Policy 1936–48', (unpublished M.Sc. thesis, University of Bristol, 1984).

57. Frances Cairncross (ed.), *Changing Perceptions of Economic Policy* (Methuen, 1981), pp 259–66, comments by James Meade; J. Meade, *Stagflation. Vol I, Wage Fixing* (Unwin Hyman, 1982).

58. Andrew Chester, *op.cit.*, pp 62–3.

59. See Austin Robinson, *loc.cit.*

60. Alec Cairncross, *Years of Recovery*, *op.cit.*, pp308–9.

61. Chapter 15.4.

62. T 299/417, 17 April 1947; T 229/417, 18 April 1947.

63. Lord Plowden, *An Industrialist in the Treasury: the post-war years* (André Deutsch, 1989).

64. CAB 134/190, IPC(47)9th, meeting of the Investment Programmes Committee, 8 October 1947, chaired by Sir Edwin Plowden.

65. CAB 134/211, EPB(48)12, 29 April 1948. Among other, earlier memoranda which make similar points are T 229/208; T 229/417, PC(47)11.

66. CAB 134/211, EPB(48)16, correspondence between R. Verdon Smith, Edwin Plowden and Geoffrey Ince.

67. T 230/60 Butt to Hall, 28 April 1948.

68. CAB 21/2220, 8 May 1951; T 229/417, 3 November 1951.

69. CAB 134/503, MEP(46)17, 21 December 1946. Wages and Price Policy and Means of Carrying Out Planning Decisions.

70. Cited by Andrew Chester, *op.cit.*, p 161.

71. See CAB 21/2215. See Correspondence between N. Brook and E. Bridges in 1945, PREM 8/642, Extract from Note on Proposals for Strengthening the Staff for Economic Planning, 7 March; CAB 21/2220, N. Brook to J.H. Woods, 7 December 1948; B. Donoughue and G.W. Jones, *op.cit.*, pp 400–25.

72. CAB 21/2244, cited by Andrew Chester, *op.cit.*, p 258.

73. CAB 134/503, MEP(46), 17 June 1946 correspondence between Dalton and J. Meade.

74. CAB 21/2215, N. Brook to E. Bridges, 30 August 1945.

75. T 229/208, E. Bridges to E. Plowden, 24 July 1947.

76. T 229/778, 9 October 1949. The comment was made by E.A. Hitchman, in a draft attempting to summarize a number of memoranda on planning prepared over 1948/49.

77. K.O. Morgan, *op.cit.*, pp 85–6.

78. Andrew Chester, *op.cit.*, p 176. See also CAB 134/211, EPB (48)16, 2 June 1948, letter from R. Verdon Smith to E. Plowden concerning the memorandum prepared for the Economic Planning Board on Planning Problems.

79. T 299/417, 7 May 1949.

80. *Ibid.*

81. Norman Chester, *The Nationalization of British Industry 1945–51*, *op.cit.*, pp 792–96, 844–64.

82. B.W.E. Alford, *op.cit.*, pp 60–73.

83. See B.W.E. Alford, 'Lost Opportunities: British Business and Businessmen During the First World War', in Neil McKendrick and R.B. Outhwaite (eds.), *Business Life and Public Policy* (Cambridge University Press, 1986), pp 205–27.

84. E.F.M. Durbin, *op.cit.*, pp 120–1.

85. Cripps, *op.cit.*

86. Herbert Morrison, 'Economic Planning' in *Public Administration,* 25, 1947, pp 3–9; Hugh Gaitskell 'Labour and Economic Planning', in *Fabian Journal,* 14, 1954, pp 4–11; Robin Marris, *The Machinery of Economic Policy* (Fabian Research Series, 168, 1954). See also, P. Hennessy, *Whitehall* (Secker and Warburg, 1989), especially chapter 4.

87. Cf Alec Cairncross, Years of Recovery, *op.cit.*, pp 499–509; K.O. Morgan, *op. cit.*, pp 492–503.

Appendix: The Administrative Machine

The major administrative changes relevant to economic planning have been identified in the preceding chapter; the evolving responsibilities of particular committees and departments are documented in detail throughout the remainder of the handbook. The purpose of this appendix, therefore, is simply to provide an overview of the administrative machine within Whitehall, as it affected the formulation and implementation of economic planning, so that readers may quickly locate the place of a particular committee or department in the overall administrative structure. It will – as illustrated by the charts – divide the period into four, with the greatest emphasis being placed on the years after 1947. The picture provided, however, can only be a very selective guide to the formal committee structure within Whitehall. The administrative machine was in a constant state of flux throughout the period and, as stated in the preface, the reality of policy-making was that informal contacts were frequently as important as the formal committee structure.

The serious planning of reconstruction, especially as it affected economic planning, commenced in January 1943 in the aftermath of the publication of the Beveridge Report. Until then, post-war policy had been ineffectually handled by the ministerial Reconstruction Problems Committee and its Official Committee on Post-war Internal Economic Problems (see chart 1). Once the maintenance of employment had been made a prime political issue by the Beveridge Report, responsibility for it was immediately transferred to the new Reconstruction Priorities Committee; and it was, for example, its official Steering Committee on Post-war Employment that was responsible for the first draft of the famous 1944 *Employment Policy* White Paper. The importance of this new committee was underlined by its chairman being the Lord President. The Lord President's Committee itself continued to be the effective Cabinet for all day-to-day domestic issues, whilst the future organization of Whitehall – including the organization of its economic departments – remained the separate responsibility of parallel ministerial and official committees on the machinery of government.

The serious discussion of reconstruction initially exacerbated political differences both within the Cabinet and between the political parties. Consequently, in November 1943, Churchill was forced to appoint a non-party Minister of Reconstruction (Lord Woolton) to preside over a new ministerial Reconstruction Committee in which, it was hoped, party differences could be reconciled. The establishment of this committee prompted a major reorganization of the administrative machine (see chart 2). It replaced all the other relevant ministerial committees bar the Lord President's Committee, which continued to be responsible for wartime controls, and the Machinery of Government Committee; and thus it was to the Reconstruction Committee that the draft of the *Employment Policy* White Paper was eventually submitted in January 1944. The new structure encouraged greater harmony until the autumn of 1944, but then political differences – often exploited by Churchill himself – again became predominant. So serious in fact did they become that, on the defeat of Germany in May 1945, Labour ministers were forced by their party to withdraw from government. In Churchill's interim Caretaker Government before the election in July, the responsibilities of the various reconstruction committees were largely concentrated in the Lord President's Committee which reverted to its pre-war name of the Home Affairs Committee.

Between the election of the Labour government and the economic crises of 1947, responsibility for economic planning lay primarily with the Lord President. The responsibility for devising the administrative machinery for the preparation of the annual *Economic Survey* was devolved to Sir Edward Bridges; and he sought to minimise the disruption of Whitehall by entrusting the detailed preparatory work to five working parties to be located in two long-established departments, the Treasury and the Ministry of Labour, and in two wartime creations, the Central Statistical Office and the Economic Section (see chart 3). Their work was co-ordinated by the Official Steering Committee on Economic Development, which had no staff of its own but consisted solely of senior officials from interested departments – who soon proved to have insufficient economic expertise and even less time to devote to so important a task. Political responsibility for the *Economic Survey* was similarly devolved from the Lord President's Committee, which was quickly adjudged too unwieldy for the job, to a succession of smaller ministerial committees under its general control: the Lord President's Industrial Subcommittee, the Ministerial Committee for Economic Planning and finally, during Morrison's illness between January and May 1947, the Committee on Economic Planning under Attlee's chairmanship. The Lord President's Committee had wider responsibilities for economic planning, such as industrial location and controls; and it also adjudicated on disputes within the Materials Committee over the allocation of scarce resources. However, many key responsibilities, which were essential for effective economic planning, continued to lie outside its direct control. These included (as illustrated by chart 3) overseas economic policy, fuel and manpower.

As a result of the fuel crisis of February 1947 and the succeeding economic crises, a major attempt was made to resolve the administrative and political weaknesses that had been exposed in the machinery of economic planning. The most important administrative innovation was the establishment in March 1947 of the Central Economic Planning Staff under Sir Edwin Plowden (see chapter 18). Although its complement of administrative staff was never great, it was to perform over the next few years a wide range of important duties, from the supervision of the drafting of the *Economic Survey* to the general overseeing of the implementation of policy. It effectively replaced the Official Steering Committee on Economic Development, of which Plowden became vice-chairman; and the presence of Plowden and his staff on innumerable committees, dealing with both domestic and international policy, improved the co-ordination of government policy. Most significant of Plowden's co-ordinating responsibilities was his membership of the Budget Committee (20.1); and most significant of his staff's duties was the chairmanship of the Investment Programmes Committee, which had been established during the convertibility crisis and had then been placed on a permanent footing both to advise ministers on investment priorities and to implement their decisions.

Foremost amongst the political innovations in 1947 was the removal from the overworked Lord President of responsibility for economic planning. Originally, it had been intended that Marquand, as Paymaster General, should assume this responsibility but, during Morrison's illness throughout the spring of 1947, Cripps effectively became the 'minister for economic planning'. In September, the position was regularized by his appointment to the new post of Minister of Economic Affairs, with direct responsibility for the C.E.P.S. and a nucleus of officials (under T.L. Rowan) who were responsible for overseeing foreign negotiations, the regional boards for industry and industrial productivity. When Cripps then succeeded Dalton as Chancellor of the Exchequer in November, both sets of advisers were taken with him to the Treasury.

Simultaneously there was a thorough overhaul of the structure of Cabinet committees. A large number of committees was abolished and two particularly powerful new ones created: the Economic Policy Committee and the Production Committee (see chart 4). The Economic Policy Committee formalized the inner cabinet of Attlee, Bevin, Morrison and Cripps, and dealt with all major or urgent domestic and international issues. On the international side, it was served by the Official Committee on Economic Development under Edward Bridges which, as international negotiations intensified in 1949, established the Economic Development Working Group as a subcommittee to deal with urgent matters. On the domestic side, the formulation and implementation of policy was frequently delegated to the Production Committee under Cripps, which one participant has called the 'real nerve centre' of the planning effort.

The reforms of 1947 provided the broad framework for economic planning for the rest of the Labour government; and since the Cabinet committee structure reached its fullest development in 1949 it is perhaps helpful to provide a brief description of it in order to illustrate its sheer complexity (see chart 4). The description is best divided into four interrelated areas: the drafting of the *Economic Survey*, overseas economic policy (including the drafting of the long-term plan), the implementation of policy regarding domestic investment and consumption and, finally, the work of individual departments.

The drafting of the *Economic Survey*, which provided both an account of the current economic position and agreed government targets for the coming year, was primarily the responsibility of the C.E.P.S., the Economic Section and the Central Statistical Office. Through the Economic Survey Working Party (15.15) these three bodies carried out extensive consultation with all the interested ministries and then, having obtained approval from the Official Committee on Economic Development, submitted their draft to ministers. After a further scrutiny by, in turn, the Economic Planning Board, the Economic Policy Committee, the Production Committee and the Cabinet, the *Survey* was finally published in late February or early March. To complicate matters, the drafting and publication of the *Survey* ran parallel with the preparation by the Treasury of the budget, around which the traditional cloak of secrecy was still drawn. Some measure of co-ordination between the two was, however, achieved by the inclusion of the heads of both the C.E.P.S. and the Economic Section on the Treasury's Budget Committee.

The preparation of the annual *Survey* was further complicated by its need to be synchronized with the long-term plan which, after the introduction of the Marshall Plan in 1948, was subsumed in the U.K. programme prepared for the O.E.E.C. Negotiations with the O.E.E.C. were the responsibility of the European Economic Co-operation (London) Committee. The groundwork for the long-term plan, on the other hand, was undertaken by the C.E.P.S.; and the plan itself was collated by the Programmes Committee, which had also to ensure that it did not conflict with short-term measures needed to safeguard the balance of payments. To achieve this aim, the work of two further committees had to be integrated into the planning process: that of the Overseas Negotiations Committee, responsible for bilateral negotiations designed to secure essential imports at minimum cost, and of the Exports Committee.

This myriad of official committees was responsible, through the Official Committee on Economic Development, to the Economic Policy Committee, although whenever necessary each had direct access to ministers. Their administrative procedures were improvised, the demarcation of their responsibilities imprecise, and their encroachment upon traditional departmental responsibilities resented. It was generally agreed, nevertheless, that through Cripps's personal authority, his widespread contacts within government, and a variety of administrative expedients (such as overlapping membership of committees), the system worked reasonably well for domestic policy. By contrast, the linkage between domestic and overseas policy was acknowledged to be very defective and was still giving Bridges cause for serious concern in 1949.

In the implementation of planning policy, the ministerial Production Committee was, as has already been noted, 'the real nerve centre'; and it was the major task of the C.E.P.S. to ensure that its decisions were carried out. To this end, one of its officials chaired the key Investment Programmes Committee, which sought to ensure that departmental investment plans matched available resources and conformed to the Cabinet's economic priorities. The C.E.P.S. also provided secretaries for two other important committees, the Materials and the Fuel Allocation Committees, which attempted to allocate scarce resources in accordance with the priorities established by the Cabinet and the Production Committee. However, despite the involvement of the C.E.P.S. in all three of these committees and the deliberate allocation of the chairmanship of the latter two to the Economic Secretary of the Treasury, co-ordination was often lacking. A further scarce resource, manpower, was treated even less effectively. A Manpower Committee was appointed in March 1949 to make good the defect, but it never actually met until January 1950 (15.30).

The large number of ministerial and official co-ordinating committees, which continued to dominate economic planning in 1949, was indicative of the fact that the traditional executive responsibilities of Whitehall departments had not been seriously disturbed even by the reforms of 1947. Thus it was within these departments that the key to effective economic planning still lay. Two had important co-ordinating as well as executive roles: the Treasury and the Board of Trade (see chapters 20 and 21). Eight others (as identified in chapter 22) had major executive powers, whilst many others – such as the Ministry of Health and the Colonial Office – played important supportive roles. The responsibilities of each were clearly defined in a report to the Steering Committee for the Economic Organization Enquiry in 1950 (15.19).

After 1949, there was only one further major overhaul of the machinery of economic planning, occasioned by the Korean War. The most important change was the replacement of the Official Committee on Economic Development as the main co-ordinating agency by the Economic Steering Committee (15.14), again under the chairmanship of Sir Edward Bridges. This renewed importance for a 'steering' committee of senior officials appeared to be a reversion to the discredited model of the 1945 to 1947 period, before the creation of the C.E.P.S. However, the C.E.P.S. remained to play its own important co-ordinating role through the provision of chairmen for the three committees which – in conjunction with the Materials Committee – dealt with the Korean War's impact on the domestic economy: Manpower (15.30), Raw Materials (15.36) and Productive Capacity (15.7). A final dramatic development occasioned by the war was the creation of a new Whitehall department, the Ministry of Materials (22.6), through the amalgamation of those functions of the Ministry of Supply and the Board of Trade which had been overseen by the Raw Materials Committee.

Administrative Charts

The following charts provide a selective guide to the formal committee structure relevant to economic planning at particular points of time. Ministerial committees have been distinguished from official committees by the use of capital letters. The chapter, or the subsection of the chapter, in which details of a committee's papers can be found has also been noted. To relieve congestion, the word 'committee' has been omitted wherever possible.

CHART 1

**Major committees dealing with the economic aspects of reconstruction,
January – November 1943**

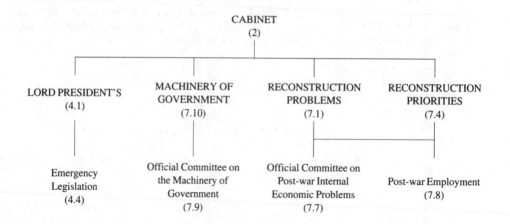

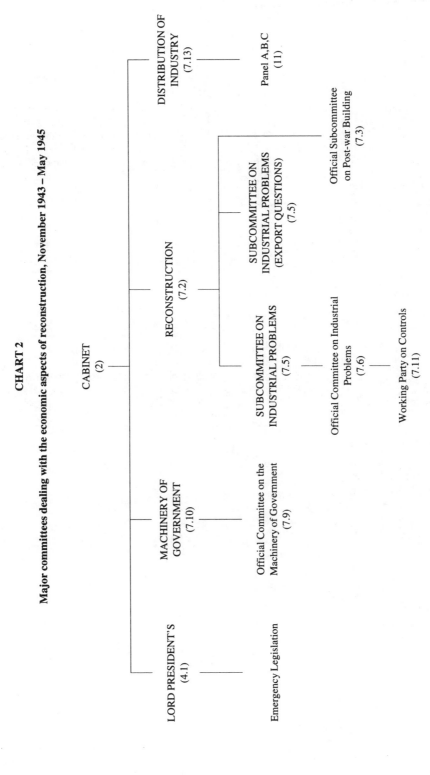

CHART 2

Major committees dealing with the economic aspects of reconstruction, November 1943 – May 1945

CABINET
(2)

LORD PRESIDENT'S
(4.1)

Emergency Legislation

MACHINERY OF
GOVERNMENT
(7.10)

Official Committee on the
Machinery of Government
(7.9)

RECONSTRUCTION
(7.2)

SUBCOMMITTEE ON
INDUSTRIAL PROBLEMS
(7.5)

Official Committee on Industrial
Problems
(7.6)

Working Party on Controls
(7.11)

SUBCOMMITTEE ON
INDUSTRIAL PROBLEMS
(EXPORT QUESTIONS)
(7.5)

Official Subcommittee
on Post-war Building
(7.3)

DISTRIBUTION OF
INDUSTRY
(7.13)

Panel A,B,C
(11)

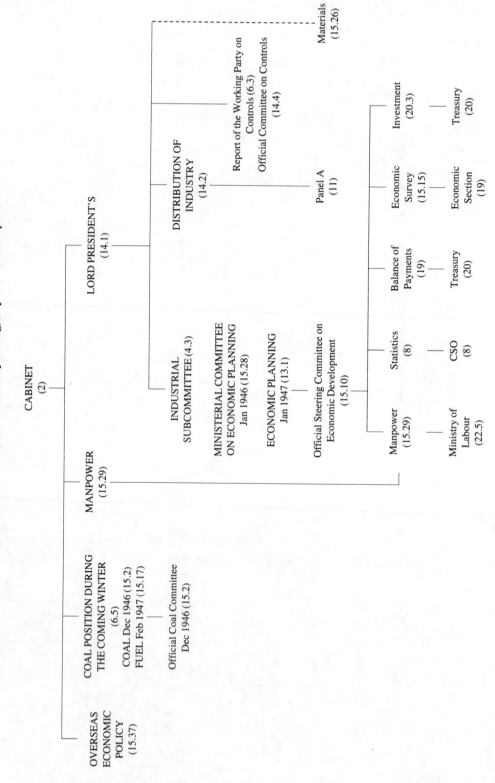

CHART 3

Major committees relevant to economic planning, July 1945–February 1947

CHART 4

Major committees relevant to economic planning, 1949

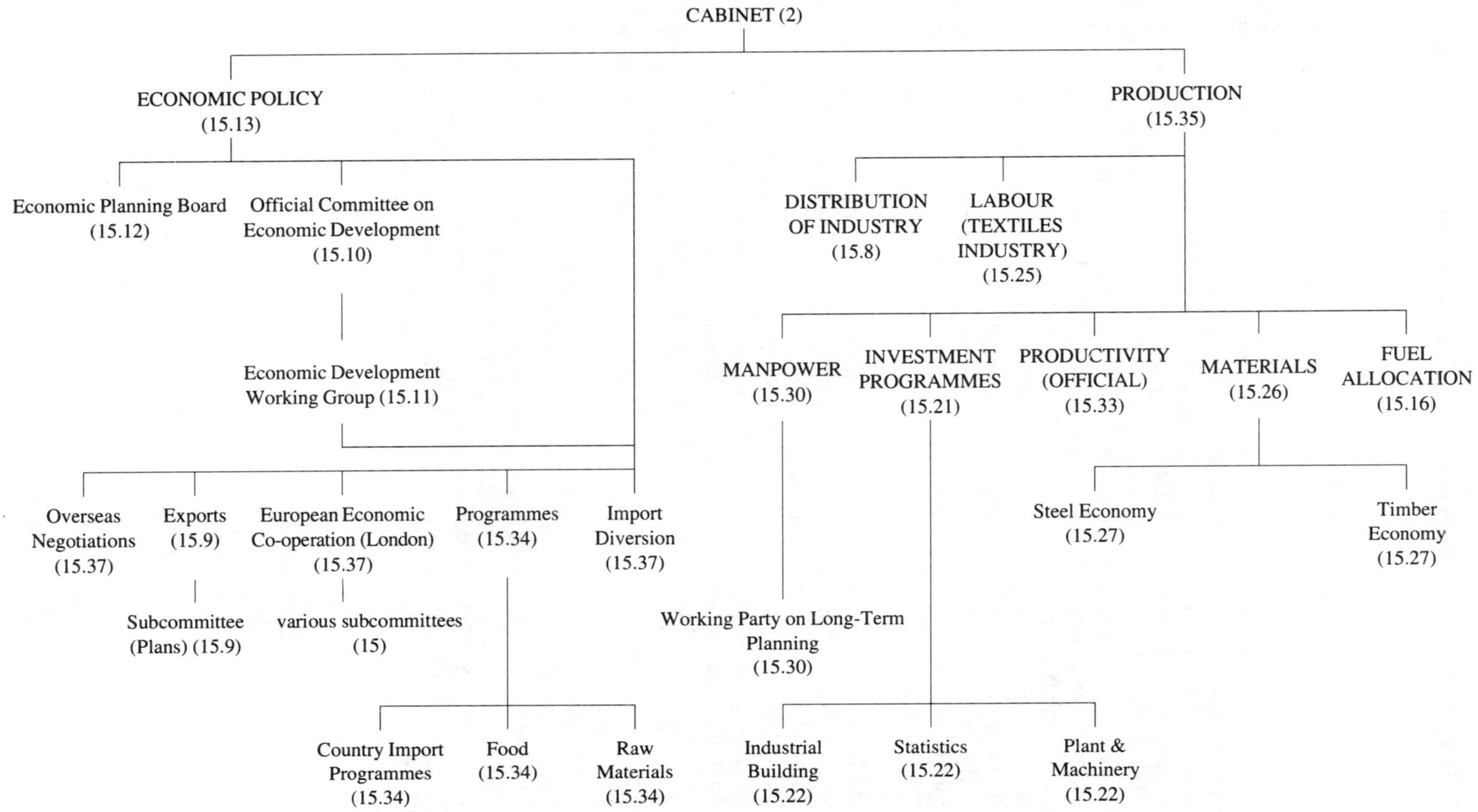

CABINET (2)

ECONOMIC POLICY
(15.13)

PRODUCTION
(15.35)

Economic Planning Board
(15.12)

Official Committee on
Economic Development
(15.10)

Economic Development
Working Group (15.11)

Overseas
Negotiations
(15.37)

Exports
(15.9)

European Economic
Co-operation (London)
(15.37)

Subcommittee
(Plans) (15.9)

various subcommittees
(15)

Programmes
(15.34)

Import
Diversion
(15.37)

Country Import
Programmes
(15.34)

Food
(15.34)

Raw
Materials
(15.34)

DISTRIBUTION
OF INDUSTRY
(15.8)

LABOUR
(TEXTILES
INDUSTRY)
(15.25)

MANPOWER
(15.30)

INVESTMENT
PROGRAMMES
(15.21)

PRODUCTIVITY
(OFFICIAL)
(15.33)

MATERIALS
(15.26)

FUEL
ALLOCATION
(15.16)

Timber
Economy
(15.27)

Steel Economy
(15.27)

Working Party on Long-Term
Planning
(15.30)

Industrial
Building
(15.22)

Statistics
(15.22)

Plant &
Machinery
(15.22)

29

Chapter 2   Cabinet Minutes and Memoranda

The minutes and memoranda of the Cabinet for this period are each divided into two classes. The minutes and memoranda of the wartime coalition (1940–23 May 1945) and the caretaker government (23 May–26 July 1945) are in CAB 65 and CAB 66 respectively. Those for the Labour governments (26 July 1945–23 Feb 1951, 23 Feb 1951–26 Oct 1951) are in CAB 128 and CAB 129. Highly sensitive minutes, which had very restricted circulation in Whitehall, are preserved in separate volumes ('confidential annexes') out of strict chronological sequence. Each class is well indexed and photocopies are available on the open shelves. War Cabinet telegrams, which include communications between the Joint Planning staffs in London and Washington and with British missions in the U.S.A., are classified separately in CAB 105.

The minutes of the Cabinet are usually not very informative. They are brief, and opinions are rarely attributed to individual ministers. Moreover, in Cabinet major debates of political principle were infrequent; and many important issues were not discussed at all either because that was the Prime Minister's intention or because they had been resolved by one of the many Cabinet committees, specifically designed to prevent the overloading of Cabinet. Cabinet memoranda are the better source for individual opinions or departmental views.

The criterion for the selection of documents listed below for the coalition and caretaker governments was to concentrate on reconstruction planning to the exclusion of purely wartime administration. Such administration, however, did set certain precedents for post-war policies and, for this reason, minutes relating to manpower have been identified. For the Labour governments, the selection was somewhat wider in order to provide a broad picture of the context in which economic planning was implemented.

In the minutes cited, reference is made to the complete range of memoranda taken. Not every memorandum may have been directly relevant to economic planning and therefore may not be listed individually in the second half of the chapter.

For a complete list of Cabinet ministers, see D. Butler and G. Butler, *British Political Facts, 1900–85* (1985). Of the many books on the Cabinet, see in particular S.S. Wilson, *The Cabinet Office to 1945* (1975), H. Morrison, *Government and Parliament* (1954), J.P. Mackintosh, *The British Cabinet* (1962) and P. Hennessy, *Cabinet* (1986).

2.1   Cabinet Minutes
1943–July 1945

CAB 65/33   4 Jan–29 March 1943   WM(43)1st–46th.

| 14 Jan | **WM(43)8th:3** | **Social Services – The Beveridge Report.** RP(43)5 The Reconstruction Priorities Committee (CAB 87/12–13) was appointed to consider the report and other substantial claims on expenditure. |
| 12 Feb | **28th** | **The Beveridge Plan.** |

15 Feb	**29th**	**The Beveridge Report.** Consideration of the extent to which post-war problems should be dealt with during wartime.
23 Feb	**34th:2**	**Post-war Building Programme.**
19 Mar	**43th:1**	**Reconstruction – Prime Minister's broadcast.**

CAB 65/34   1 April –29 June 1943   WM(43)47th–90th.

9 Apr	**WM(43)51st:2**	**The budget.**
15 Apr	**56th:1**	**Post-war agricultural policy.** WP(43)103. Discussions with agricultural interests postponed.
4 May	**64th:2**	**Post-war agricultural policy.** WP(43)181.

CAB 65/35   1 July–28 Sept 1943   WM(43)91st–132nd.

1 July	**WM(43)91st:2**	**Post-war agricultural policy.** WP(43)280. War Cabinet against too many post-war commitments.

Manpower was considered at **WM(43)96, 100, 102, 115 and 117.**

CAB 65/36   4 Oct–28 Dec 1943   WM(43)133rd–176th.

14 Oct	**WM(43)140th**	**Reconstruction plans.** (see CAB 65/40).
15 Oct	**141st:1**	**Post-war agricultural policy.** Discussions could now be opened with agricultural interests.
21 Oct	**144th:1**	**Reconstruction plan.** WP(43)465 and 467. Debate over consideration of long-term matters was resumed.
27 Oct	**146th:2**	**Post-war agricultural policy.**
27 Oct	**147th:5**	**Reconstruction plans.** WP(43)476.
9 Dec	**168th**	**Demobilization.** WP(43)494, 543, 548, 553, 556, 560 and 561.
15 Dec	**170th:2**	**Demobilization.** WP(43)494, 543, 548, 553, 556, 560, 561, 564 and 565.

Manpower was considered at **WM(43)164.**

CAB 65/37   11 Jan–29 March 1943   WM(43)6th–46th   Confidential annexes.

CAB 65/38   5 April–21 June 1943   WM(43)48th–87th   Confidential annexes.

CAB 65/39   2 July–8 Sept 1943   WM(43)92nd–126th   Confidential annexes.

CAB 65/40   5 Oct–28 Dec 1943   WM(43)135th–176th   Confidential annexes.

14 Oct	**WM(43)140th**	**Reconstruction Plans.** WP(43)255, 308 and 324. The War Cabinet dealt with the question of whether decisions on reconstruction should be postponed until the post-war financial position was definitely known.

CAB 65/41   3 Jan–28 March 1944   WM(44)1st–42nd.

17 Jan	**WM(44)7th:6**	**Delegated legislation.** WP(44)30.
18 Jan	**8th**	**Reconstruction.** General discussion of progress.
25 Jan	**11th:2**	**Post-war agricultural policy.** WP(44)53.
17 Feb	**22nd:2**	**Demobilization.** WP(44)71, 94, 97 and 106. Anderson expressed less concern with the total cost of demobilization than with its possible inflationary effects and with whether it fitted in with general economic policy.
20 Mar	**36th**	**Reconstruction.** The War Cabinet met alone to discuss Morrison's speech of 19 March in which he had suggested the enactment of general legislation, the details of which would be filled in by delegated legislation. It was agreed that such speeches should not be made in the future since they threatened to break up the coalition.

Manpower was discussed at **WM(44)14 and 22.**

CAB 65/42   3 April–29 June 1944   WM(44)43rd–84th.

4 Apr	**WM(44)44th**	**Water.** Wood suggested that the budget debate would provide an opportunity to give a comprensive review of reconstruction plans.
21 Apr	**54th**	**Budget.**
28 Apr	**59th:2**	**Agricultural policy.** WP(44)218.
19 May	**66th:3,4**	**Employment policy.** WP(44)254 and 256. The War Cabinet decided to retain in the draft White Paper the point that taxes should be changed to maintain employment. In general the White Paper was approved. Publicity for the White Paper was discussed.
22 May	**67th:4**	**Employment policy – publication of White Paper.**
12 June	**75th:7**	**Parliament – debate on the White Paper on employment policy.** The motion to be put down was agreed and it was hoped only two days would be needed for the debate.
13 June	**76th:4**	**Parliament – debate on the White Paper on employment policy.** Slight changes to the motion were made and government speakers were agreed.

Manpower was discussd at **WM(44)48.**

CAB 65/43   3 July–29 Sept 1944   WM(44)85th–129th.

4 July	**WM(44)87th:3**	**Post-war financial commitments and social insurance.** WP(44)353, 356 and 357. General discussion on post-war financial commitments and the importance of increasing the level of export trade.

18 July	**93rd:2**	**Overseas resources and liabilities.** WP(44)360 and 368. The War Cabinet approved a number of proposals to help deal with the problems set out in WP(44)360.
26 July	**96th:2**	**Manpower in the first year after the defeat of Germany.** WP(44)362, 373, 380, 381 and 410. Consideration of the distribution of the estimated 1¾m manpower deficiency.
4 Aug	**101st:4**	**Supplies from North America in Stage II.** WP(44)419 4 Aug.
	102nd:4	**Manpower in the first year after the defeat of Germany.** WP(44)431.
22 Sept	**125th:2**	**Manpower – reallocation between civilian employments in the transitional period.** WP(44)509. The War Cabinet agreed that there should be a statement on the continuance of the economic controls with the publication of Section III of WP(43)509.

Manpower was also discussed at **WM(44)90, 100, 106, 113, 116, 117, 124 and 129.**

CAB 65/44	2 Oct–30 Dec 1944	WM(44)130th–176th.
2 Nov	**WM(44)145th:4**	**Manpower – reallocation between civilian employment during the transitional period.** WP(44)563 and 605.
	:5	**Economic controls in the transition period.** WP(44)604. Discussion on the impression given by the draft statement as to the length of time during which controls should be retained.
7 Nov	**147th:5**	**Controls in the transition period.** WP(44)620 and 623.
16 Nov	**151st:5**	**Distribution of industry.** WP(44)640 and 652. Dalton and Bevin called for measures to prevent regional unemployment.
22 Nov	**154th:2**	**Wages regulation.** WP(44)658. War Cabinet approval for the machinery of post-war wage regulation, based on wages councils.
27 Nov	**158th:6**	**Post-war finance for industry.** WP(44)640 and 652.
4 Dec	**161st:8**	**Parliamentary business.** Discussion of statements to be made on domestic issues in forthcoming debate.
13 Dec	**168th:2**	**Distribution of industry.** WP(44)640 and 652. Renewal of discussion with Dalton amending a number of his proposals. The War Cabinet authorised the drafting of a bill on the lines of WP(44)640.
27 Dec	**174th:5**	**Ministry of Fuel and Power.** WP(44)732. War Cabinet agreed to legislation to allow the Ministry to continue in peace-time.

Manpower was also considered at **WM(44)138, 161, 172 and 173.**

CAB 65/45   3 Jan–27 March 1944   WM(44)1st–40th   Confidential annexes.

CAB 65/46   3 April–27 June 1944   WM(44)43rd–82nd   Confidential annexes.

CAB 65/47   3 July–29 Sept 1944   WM(44)85th–129th   Confidential annexes.

CAB 65/48   2 Oct–30 Dec 1944   WM(44)130th–176th   Confidential annexes.

CAB 65/49   2 Jan–28 Mar 1945   WM(45)1st–37th.

9 Jan	**WM(45)3rd:3**	**Resettlement of men released from the armed forces.** WP(44)602, 700 and 711.
	:4	**Distribution of industry.** WP(45)2. Attached directive by Churchill on the strategic aspects.
25 Jan	**9th:1**	**Munitions production.** WP(45)32 and 34. Agreement for planning purposes on the range of dates for the ending of the German war.
	:2	**Fuel economy.**
	:4	**International Monetary Fund.** WP(45)46.
29 Jan	**12th:6**	**Coal: distribution in the London area.**
31 Jan	**13th:4**	**Coal: distribution in London.**
7 Feb	**15th:2**	**Distribution of industry.** WP(45)78. Consideration of the draft bill by clauses.
	:4	**U.K. stocks.**
9 Feb	**17th:2**	**Munitions production.** Agreement on new planning dates for the end of the German war. Allocations of manpower to be reviewed as the new dates involved a decrease in releases.
13 Feb	**19th:3**	**Reallocation of manpower: treatment of seamen on T.124 agreement.** WP(45)79.
	:5	**Building labour allocation Jan–Mar 1945.** WP(45)90.
16 Feb	**20th:3**	**Coal: coal supply for operational requirements after 30 April 1945.** WP(45)95. Attlee suggested the appointment of a Cabinet committee.
22 Feb	**24th:1**	**Manpower in the first half of 1945.** WP(45)87. See CAB 65/51.
26 Feb	**25th:9**	**Future of the coal industry.**
12 Mar	**29th:5**	**Manpower: labour for the cotton-spinning industry.** WP(45)144.
14 Mar	**30th:1**	**Food.** WP(45)36, 109, 130, 145, 158. Churchill thought that the maintenance of minimum scales of food supply should if necessary take priority over military operations.
15 Mar	**31st:1**	**Housing.** WP(45)161.
	:2	**Food: world supply situation.**
19 Mar	**33rd:2**	**France: Anglo-French financial agreement.** WP(45)169.

21 Mar	**34th:1**	**Commercial policy: views of Canadian government.** WP(45)142, 167, 182.
	:2	**Food: world supply situation.**
22 Mar	**35th**	**Economic controls in the transition period.** During informal discussion of the political situation, the increasing controversy over the continuance of economic control during the transition was noted. Bevin was now pessimistic about the continuation of controls after hostilities in Europe were over. Lyttleton said that the deterioration had not been caused by anything said by leaders of the Conservative Party. Walton and Anderson both agreed that in financial and industrial circles there was no disposition to question the need for retaining the more important of the controls affecting employers during the period of economic instability. Summing up, Churchill said that the press was largely to blame for the deterioration in the political atmosphere on the subject.

CAB 65/50	3 April–18 May 1945	WM(45)38th–62nd.
12 Apr	**WM(45)42nd:1**	**Manpower allocations for 1945.** WP(45)207 and 232. Agreement to take 31 May 1945 as unofficial date on which to base manpower calculations.
	:2	**Manpower.** Reallocation of manpower between civilian employments. Bevin reiterated his concern about the future of labour controls and his inability to effect manpower allocations between the defeat of Germany and that of Japan without such controls.
	:3	**Coal.** WP(45)190.
20 Apr	**47th:1**	**The budget.**
20 Apr	**48th:1**	**Building labour allocations April–June 1945.** WP(45)223.
	:2	**Coal.** WP(45)257 and 262. Acceleration of the release of Class A in the first three months of demobilization.
	:4	**Livestock policy. Measures for increasing home production of pork, bacon and eggs.** WP(45)252.
	:5	**Civil Service. Control of Employment (Civil Servants) Order.** WP(45)211 and 237.
23 Apr	**49th:3**	**Housing. Production agreements, bulk orders and erection of houses by the Ministry of Works.** WP(45)266.
25 Apr	**51st:2**	**Economic controls in the transition period.** WP(45)222. Disagreement over whether to rely on the Emergency Powers (Defence) Acts; general sympathy for the approach in

		WP(45)222 and agreement to consider the draft bill.
4 May	58th:1	**Building. Registration of building work.** WP(45)276.
	:4	**Economic controls in the transition period.** WP(45)222. Churchill was impressed by Morrison's proposals, and the bill was approved in principle.
14 May	61st:4	**Food. World supply situation.** WP(45)291 and 298.
	:7	**Housing. Production agreement, bulk orders and erection of houses by the Ministry of Works.** WP(45)294.
18 May	62nd:6	**Manpower. Reallocation between civilian employment.** There was to be a new Control of Engagement Order covering all employment.

CAB 65/51	2 Jan–28 Mar 1945	WM(45)1st–37th Confidential annexes.
22 Feb	**WM(45)24th:1**	**Manpower in the first half of 1945.** WP(45)87. Agreement that Churchill should issue a directive. Churchill believed that priority should be given first to the army and to munitions production for the European war and then to a reasonable expansion of civilian production, even at the expense of the Japanese war effort.

CAB 65/52	3 Apr–13 Mar 1945	WM(45)39th–60th Confidential annexes.

CAB 65/53	30 May–24 July 1945	CM(45)1st–17th.
11 June	**CM(45)7th:3**	**Coal-mining industry. Future organization.** CP(45)8. Authorization to draft legislation although no further statements would be made before the election.
15 June	8th:3	**Food. Meat supplies for the U.K. and liberated Europe.** CP(45)28 and 29.
	:4	**Food. Labour for the 1945 harvest.** Agreement to make a stronger appeal for volunteers should be made.
	:6	**Coal. The coal situation in N.W. Europe.** CP(45)35.
6 July	11th:3	**Cabinet arrangements.** CP(45)58 and 59.
	:4	**Manpower. Redistribution of manpower in the second half of 1945.** CP(45)53, 61, 62. Agreement, with the improving international situation, to maximize the rate of releases from the forces.
12 July	14th:2	**Manpower.** CP(45)72 and 75. Further review of releases from the forces. Agreement to limit military commitments in Stage II.

	:4	**Coal. Additional bunkering requirements.** CP(45)60 and 66. A small ministerial committee to be set up.
18 July	**15th:4**	**Agricultural policy. Cropping directions and prices of agricultural commodities for the 1946 harvest.** CP(45)81. Approval for the relaxation of compulsory direction of wheat production.
	:5	**Labour for the 1945 harvest.**
	:7	**Supplies of timber.**
20 July	**16th:1**	**Coal. Additional bunkering requirements.** CP(45)85. Endorsement by the ministerial committee of the official report.

CAB 65/54   30 May–20 June 1945   CM(45)1st–10th   Confidential annexes.

CAB 65/55   Sept 1939–May 1945   Index.

Aug 1945–Sept 1951

CAB 128/1   7 Aug–30 Oct 1945   CM(45)18th–47th.

7 Aug	**CM(45)18th:5**	**Parliament.** CP(45)94. Consideration of King's speech.
	:7	**Cotton industry.** CP(45)92.
	:8	**Standing committees of the Cabinet.** Bevin on overseas committees.
9 Aug	**19th:1**	**Parliament.** CP(45)98. Further consideration of King's speech.
10 Aug	**20th:4**	**War production and manpower.** Attlee desired a review on Japan's surrender.
	:5	**Parliament.** Further consideration of King's speech.
16 Aug	**23rd:1**	**Manpower.** CP(45)113 and 114. Agreement on the basis of demobilization.
	:2	**Economic controls in the transition period.** CP(45)111. Agreement that the Supply and Services (Transitional Powers) Bill should be for five years as it was important to establish the principle that the next five years would be a period of transition.
30 Aug	**26th:4**	**Manpower.** Following public criticism the Manpower Committee was to review demobilization.
	:2	**Industrial organization and efficiency.** CP(45)142. Consideration in particular of the composition of the committees to investigate each industry. Cripps felt industry's co-operation was crucial and that the consumer could be best represented by the Board of Trade.

		:3	**Manpower.** CP(45)141. Approval of recommendations to expedite demobilization.
6 Sept	29th:1		**Shipping.** CP(45)135.
11 Sept	30th:4		**Tobacco.** CP(45)154. Agreement to reduce U.S. imports.
13 Sept	31st:4		**Bank of England Bill.** CP(45)167. Consideration in particular of powers to request information from and make recommendations to banks.
19 Sept	33rd:1		**Parliament.** CP(45)158. Consideration of the legislative programme.
		:3	**Prisoners of war.** CP(45)172.
		:4	**Manpower.** Some concern over employment of prisoners of war whilst there was unemployment.
28 Sept	36th:1		**Manpower.** CP(45)191. Agreement on the target for releases from the forces in 1945.
2 Oct	37th		**Organization of government supplies.** CP(45)177, 178, 181, 197. Agreement in principle to maintain the Ministry of Supply.
4 Oct	38th:1		**Expiry of Emergency Powers (Defence) Acts.** CP(45)201.
9 Oct	39th:2		**Housing.** CP(45)208.
		:4	**Dockers' strike.**
15 Oct	41st:1		**Housing.** CP(45)224, 225, 226, 229, 230. Consideration of policy statement and labour shortages.
		:2	**Dockers' strike.**
		:3	**Manpower.** Releases from the army.
16 Oct	42nd:1		**Food.** Agreement to restore fat and cheese rations, and on the Christmas bonus.
		:2	**Dockers' strike.**
		:4	**Electricity and gas industry.** CP(45)217.
22 Oct	44th:1		**The budget.**
		:2	**Women's Land Army.** Approval of the release scheme.
23 Oct	45th:2		**Prisoners of war.** CP(45)219.
26 Oct	46th:1		**Parliament.** Consideration of the Bank of England Bill.
		:3	**Dockers' strike.**
30 Oct	47th:3		**Parliament.** Includes consideration of the Supplies and Services (Transitional Powers) Bill.
		:5	**Food policy and the future of the Ministry of Food.** CP(45)236. Agreement that the ministry should be permanent and that there should be an early announcement on food policy.
		:8	**Parliamentary Labour Party.** On the views of specialist groups.
		:9	**Dockers' strike.**

CAB 128/2   1 Nov–20 Dec 1945   CM(45)48th–65th.

1 Nov	**CM(45)48th:2**	**Prisoners of war.** CP(45)209.
	:6	**Manpower.** CP(45)260. Agreement not to change labour controls at present.
6 Nov	**49th:2**	**Prisoners of war.** CP(45)265.
	:7	**Washington discussions on financial questions and commercial policy.** CP(45)269 and 270.
6 Nov	**50th**	**Washington discussions on financial questions and commercial policy.** See CAB 128/4.
8 Nov	**51st:5**	**Manpower.** CP(45)267. On the release of doctors from the forces.
13 Nov	**52nd:2**	**Agricultural policy.** CP(45)273.
	:3	**Future of the Department of Overseas Trade.** CP(45)271. Agreement that the Secretary would become the Secretary for Overseas Trade, responsible to the President of the Board of Trade alone. He would chair a committee on external economic policy and overseas trade.
20 Nov	**54th:1**	**CP(45)285.** On the demobilization of doctors.
	:2	**Manpower.** CP(45)288. Cabinet was not ready to accept proposals.
	:3	**Housing.** CP(45)274.
	:5	**Tourist traffic from the U.S.** CP(45)284. Agreement to promote tourism.
22 Nov	**55th:4**	**Control of investment.** CP(45)289. Approval of the machinery set out in the Investment (Control and Guarantees) Bill.
27 Nov	**56th:1**	**Naval construction programme.** CP(45)291.
29 Nov	**57th:1**	**Parliament.** Includes ratification of the Bretton Woods Agreement.
	:3	**Washington discussions on financial questions and commercial policy.** CP(45)295, 297, 312. See CAB 128/4.
3 Dec	**58th:1**	**Ratification of Bretton Woods Agreement.** CP(45)319.
	:2	**Washington discussions on financial questions and commercial policy.** See CAB 128/4.
	:5	**Manpower.** CP(45)311, 317, 320, 321. Consideration of releases from the forces.
	:6	**Manpower.** CP(45)314. General support for proposals but the impression should not be given that the Essential Works Orders were being retained only for industries in which it was difficult to retain labour.
	59th	**Washington discussions on financial questions and commercial policy.** See CAB 128/4.
6 Dec	**60th:4**	**National insurance scheme.** CP(45)315 and 323. Concern of Dalton and Morrison over its cost.
	:5	**Prisoners of war.** CP(45)305.

	:6	**Government publicity services.** CP(45)316. Agreement that the Ministry of Information should cease to be a separate department although some central organization was needed.
10 Dec	**61st:2**	**Shipping.** CP(45)299, 324, 325.
13 Dec	**62nd:2**	**National insurance scheme.** CP(45)331. Consideration of the proposal to vary benefit with the level of unemployment.
	:6	**Coal.** CP(45)329 and 337.
20 Dec	**64th:3**	**German prisoners of war.** CP(45)341.
20 Dec	**65th:4**	**Review of budgetary position.** Some concern at the Cabinet's approval of expensive projects without relating them to the general budgetary position.

CAB 128/3	4 Sept–25 Sept 1945	CM(45)28th–35th	Confidential annexes.

CAB 128/4	6 Nov–6 Dec 1945	CM(45)50th–60th	Confidential annexes.

6 Nov	**CM(45)50th**	**Washington discussions on financial questions and commercial policy.** CP(45)269 and 270. Dalton explained the obligations involved in the Bretton Woods Agreement. Concern of some ministers at aims of U.S.A. Dalton set out the situation if the loan was not accepted and agreement to the proposals in CP(45)270.
29 Nov	**57th:3**	**Washington discussions on financial questions and commercial policy.** CP(45)295, 297, 312. Concern of Shinwell and Bevan that the proposals in CP(45)312 were incompatible with the successful operation of a planned economy. However, Attlee felt the preponderant view favoured the proposals.
3 Dec	**58th:2**	**Washington discussions on financial questions and commercial policy.** CP(45)297 and 322. Consideration of latest developments and authorization of Attlee, Dalton and Cripps to make any modification to the draft financial agreement which did not encroach on general principles.
5 Dec	**59th**	**Washington discussions on financial questions and commercial policy.** Further update on negotiations. Despite opposition from Shinwell and Bevan there was general acceptance of the agreement.

CAB 128/5	1 Jan–27 June 1946	CM(46)1st–62nd.	

1 Jan	**CM(46)1st:4**	**World wheat supplies.** CP(45)348.
3 Jan	**2nd:7**	**Gas supplies in London.** Shortage of skilled labour.

	:8	**Manpower.** Progress on releases from the forces.
	:9	**Agricultural wages.**
10 Jan	4th:1	**London Airport (Heathrow).** CP(46)4. Consideration of its financing.
	:4	**Gas supplies in London.** CP(46)5.
15 Jan	5th:1	**Manpower.** Consideration of releases from the forces and munition industries.
	:4	**World wheat supplies.** Consideration of the Washington discussions.
17 Jan	6th:1	**Parliament.** Includes consideration of the Investment (Control and Guarantees) Bill.
	:2	**National Insurance scheme.** CP(46)14. Consideration of varying rates of contribution.
22 Jan	7th:6	**Housing accommodation.**
24 Jan	8th:2	**Coal.** CP(46)20. Consideration of open-cast working in Wentworth Woodhouse Park.
28 Jan	9th:4	**Publication of statistics.** CP(46)23.
	:7	**Demobilization.** CP(46)25.
	:8	**World wheat supplies.**
31 Jan	10th:3	**Meeting of Dominion Prime Ministers.**
	:4	**World supplies of cereals.** CP(46)26, 28, 30, 31, 33. Includes consideration of supplies for U.K. and the extraction rate.
	:5	**Shipping.** CP(46)27.
	:6	**Agricultural wages.** CP(46)29.
7 Feb	13th:2	**Food.**
	:3	**Manpower and the Economic Survey for 1946.** CP(46)32, 35, 40. Morrison felt the document most valuable. As it was on an experimental basis he was against publication. Its recommendations were to be proceeded upon.
	:5	**Timber supplies.** CP(46)41 and 47.
	:6	**Shipping prospects for 1946.** CP(46)27, 36, 42.
	:9	**Agricultural wages.**
11 Feb	14th:4	**Import programmes for 1946.** CP(46)53 and 58. Every effort was to be made to reduce the balance of payments deficit but food imports should be increased.
	:5	**Food.**
14 Feb	15th:6	**German prisoners of war.** CP(46)38.
	:7	**Manpower.** Consideration of the use of foreign labour in essential industries.
	:10	**Clothes rationing.** CP(46)55.
18 Feb	16th:1	**Supplies of rice from Siam.**
	:6	**Defence policy in 1946.** CP(46)65.
	:8	**Government publicity service.** CP(46)54.
25 Feb	18th:7	**Shipbuilding.** CP(46)64.
28 Feb	19th:4	**Financial discussions with Canada.** CP(46)84.
	:8	**World supplies of cereals.** CP(46)80.
4 Mar	20th:4	**World supplies of cereals.** CP(46)80.
	:7	**Shipbuilding.** CP(46)91.

5 Mar	**21st**	**World supplies of cereals.** CP(46)80 and 90.
8 Mar	**22nd:1**	**World supplies of cereals.**
	:6	**Emegency powers.** CP(46)87. See CAB 128/7.
11 Mar	**23rd:10**	**Bulk purchase of cotton.** CP(46)102. Agreement to continue centralized purchase.
	:12	**Tourist traffic from the U.S.** CP(46)66.
14 Mar	**24th:5**	**Strikes in motor industry.**
	:6	**Wages policy.** Disagreement over whether the government should adopt a more positive policy.
25 Mar	**27th:4**	**World food supplies.**
28 Mar	**28th:4**	**Building.** Consideration of brick production.
1 Apr	**29th:8**	**World food supplies.** CP(46)127.
	:10	**Government publicity service.** CP(46)125.
4 Apr	**30th:3**	**Future of the iron and steel industry.** CP(46)120.
	:6	**Food.** Consideration of a reduction in the cheese ration.
8 Apr	**31st:1**	**The budget.**
	:4	**Prosperity Campaign.** CP(46)122. General support for the continuation of the campaign.
10 Apr	**32nd**	**World food supplies.**
11 Apr	**33rd:2**	**Parliament.** CP(46)143. Consideration of the legislative programme 1946–47.
	:5	**Wages policy.** CP(46)130 and 148. General support for the proposed National Industrial Conference. Attlee felt that given full employment policy the government could not leave wages solely to worker and employer organizations. Before any decision, the paper was to be revised in the light of the discussion.
	:6	**Agricultural wages.** CP(46)145 and 146.
12 Apr	**34th**	**World food supplies.**
15 Apr	**35th:2**	**Future of the iron and steel industry.** CP(46)152.
	:3	**Coal.** Reaffirmation of the decision on open-cast working at Wentworth Woodhouse Park.
	:5	**Nationalization of transport.** CP(46)149.
17 Apr	**36th:2**	**World food suplies.** CP(46)159. Acceptance of economy measures.
24 Apr	**37th:2**	**World food supplies.** CP(46)167. Agreement on further economy measures.
29 Apr	**38th:3**	**Import programmes for mid-1946 to mid-1947.** CP(46)168. Approval of the programme and of the aim of achieving a balance between import expenditure and target income on current account in the first half of 1947.
2 May	**40th:2**	**Future of the iron and steel industry.** CP(46)177 and 178.
	:3	**World food supplies.** CP(46)163, 182, 184. Agreement to increase the extraction rate of flour.
	:4	**Railway charges.** CP(46)174.

6 May	**42nd:6**	**Wages policy.** CP(46)179. Despite opposition Shinwell's proposals for a National Industrial Conference were approved.
	:7	**Parliament.** CP(46)143. Consideration of the legislative programme for 1946–47.
7 May	**43rd:2**	**World food supplies.**
9 May	**44th:4**	**Parliament.** CP(46)187.
	:8	**Commercial policy.** CP(46)189.
	:9	**Financial agreement with the U.S.**
	:11	**Prosperity Campaign.**
13 May	**45th:9**	**Financial agreement with the U.S.**
16 May	**48th:3**	**Railway charges.** CP(46)193. Discussion centred on whether it was expedient at present to increase charges.
17 May	**49th**	**World wheat supplies.**
20 May	**50th:2**	**Manpower.** CP(46)126, 138, 194. Consideration of the size of the forces in the transitional period and whether it was practicable for the U.K. to maintain them.
	:3	**Manpower.** CP(46)185.
23 May	**51st:3**	**World food supplies.** CP(46)202 and 203.
27 May	**52nd:3**	**Manpower.** CP(46)206. Approval of the revised scheme to defer call-up of apprentices.
	:5	**World food supplies.** CP(46)200, 201, 209. Agreement on the preparation of bread rationing.
	:6	**Railway charges.** CP(46)205.
30 May	**53rd:1**	**Parliament.** Includes consideration of a White Paper on call-up to the forces.
	:2	**World food supplies.** CP(46)201. Further consideration of bread and feedingstuffs rationing.
17 June	**59th:4**	**World food supplies.**
24 June	**61st:7**	**Coal production.** CP(46)232, 237, 242, 244. Consideration of output, recruitment and conditions of employment. Approval of the five-day week on the understanding that output would not suffer.
	:8	**World food supplies.**
27 June	**62nd:3**	**Bread rationing.** CP(46)247. Approval of proposed scheme.
CAB 128/6	1 July–31 Dec 1946	CM(46)63rd–108th.
1 July	**CM(46)63rd:5**	**Parliament.** Includes consideration of the debate on bread rationing.
4 July	**64th:4**	**Nationalization of transport.** CP(46)225.
	:5	**World food supplies.** CP(46)249.
8 July	**66th:7**	**Petrol rationing.** CP(46)257. Ministerial review agreed.
	:8	**Government publicity service.** CP(46)254.
11 July	**67th:1**	**Agricultural prices.** CP(46)265.

15 July	68th:3	**Import programmes for mid-1946 to mid-1947.** CP(46)266. Approval of some additions.
	:4	**Bread rationing.** Some concern over whether consumers would understand the scheme.
	:5	**Parliament.** CP(46)268. Consideration of the legislative programme 1946–47.
	:7	**Housing.**
18 July	69th:2	**Bread rationing.** Confirmation of decision to introduce rationing.
	:6	**Organization of electricity supply.** CP(46)270.
21 July	70th	**Bread rationing.** See CAB 128/8.
22 July	71st:1	**International economic machinery and U.K. representation in the U.S.** CP(46)215 and 274.
25 July	73rd:6	**Rhodesian railway.** CP(46)282.
	:7	**Timber supplies.** CP(46)277, 291, 294. Need for increased supplies to meet housing programme.
29 July	74th:2	**World food supplies.** 2nd review of world food shortage.
1 Aug	76th:3	**Future of the iron and steel industry.** CP(46)300.
	:4	**Demobilization.** CP(46)312.
	:10	**Germany.** CP(46)316. Consideration of exports of coal from the British zone.
7 Aug	77th:3	**Civil aviation.** CP(46)317. On requirements and possible purchase from the U.S.
	:6	**Persia.** Consideration of relations with the Anglo-Iranian Oil Co.
14 Aug	78th:5	**World food supplies.** CP(46)323.
4 Sept	79th:1	**Repatriation of prisoners of war.** CP(46)325, 327, 332, 335. All departments to assume a reduction of available prisoners.
	:2	**Germany.** CP(46)333. Further consideration of exports of coal from the British zone.
9 Sept	80th:1	**Germany.** Further consideration of coal exports.
	:2	**Bread rationing.** CP(46)336. See CAB 128/8.
	:3	**World food supplies.** CP(46)328 and 339.
	:4	**Argentina.**
12 Sept	81st:1	**Repatriation of prisoners of war.** CP(46)342.
	:2	**Silver coinage.** CP(46)337.
17 Sept	82nd:1	**France.** Dalton set out the basis of financial and commercial discussions.
	:3	**Housing.**
26 Sept	83rd:1	**Textiles for the services.** CP(46)348 and 351.
	:3	**Food.** Consideration of additional meat ration for miners.
3 Oct	84th:5	**International employment policy.** CP(46)364. Agreement that international monetary organizations should co-operate to give effect to international policy for full employment. A small committee of ministers was to monitor

		international discussions on trade and employment.
10 Oct	85th:2	**Parliament.** Includes consideration of the King's speeches.
	:6	**Food.** CP(46)356. Approval of additional meat ration for miners.
15 Oct	86th:1	**Shipping.** CP(46)375.
	:2	**Commercial policy.** CP(46)374.
	:3	**Allocation of excavating machinery.**
21 Oct	89th:3	**Germany.** CP(46)383, 384, 385, 392. Examines the cost of the British zone.
	:4	**Supplies of timber from Germany.** CP(46)388 and 390.
24 Oct	90th:2	**Parliament.** CP(46)387. Consideration of the King's speeches.
	:3	**Legislative programme for 1946–47 session.** CP(46)393.
	:4	**National Service.** CP(46)380. Includes consideration of the effect on the economy.
25 Oct	91st:1	**Food.** CP(46)396.
	:4	**Commercial policy.** CP(46)386. Consideration of economic co-operation with Western Europe.
29 Oct	92nd:2	**Food.** Consideration of supplies from the U.S.
31 Oct	93rd:1	**Parliament.** Includes consideration of legislative programme for 1946–47 session.
	:3	**National Service.** CP(46)380 and 403.
	:5	**Food.** CP(46)399. Agreement to continue bread rationing.
	:6	**Production of ground-nuts in East Africa.** CP(46)402.
4 Nov	94th:5	**Import programme for 1947.** CP(46)401. Dalton set out the drastic action needed on the balance of payments under three heads: strict economy in imports from hard currency countries, no relaxation of the export drive and target, and an intensive study of prospects for improving the trade balance 1947–50. Consideration of whether to abolish petrol rationing. Agreement on the basis for the import programme and export target.
	:6	**Exchange Control Bill.** CP(46)410 and 411. Approval, although some concern at its drastic nature.
7 Nov	95th:2	**International organizations.** CP(46)413, 415, 416.
	:4	**Exchange Control Bill.**
14 Nov	96th:4	**Transport Bill.** CP(46)408 and 420.
	:5	**Fuel supplies for industry.** CP(46)419.
19 Nov	98th:2	**Food.** CP(46)426.
	:4	**Fuel supplies for industry.** CP(46)419, 423, 427. Approval of CP(46)423.

		:5	**Coal.** Consideration of a publicity campaign for increased production.

21 Nov	**99th:2**	**Manpower.** CP(46)421. Approval of negotiations over admission of Poles to civil employment.

25 Nov	**100th:1**	**Manpower.**
	:2	**Germany.**
	:4	**Fuel supplies for industry.**

2 Dec	**102nd**	**Germany.** CP(46)438.

5 Dec	**103rd:3**	**Food.** CP(46)441. Food shortages were increasing because of industrial discontent abroad.
	:4	**Agriculture Bill.** CP(46)435.
	:6	**Manpower.** Consideration of the rate of demobilization.

10 Dec	**104th:6**	**Germany.** CP(46)446. Consideration of exports of coal.

16 Dec	**106th:1**	**Food.** Set out the problems of getting U.S. supplies.
	:2	**Production of textiles.** CP(46)442, 458, 460.
	:3	**Manpower.** Consideration of manning of essential industries.

19 Dec	**107th:5**	**Electricity Bill.** CP(46)459 and 462.
	:6	**Shipping.** CP(46)453.

CAB 128/7   1 Jan–17 June 1946   CM(46)1st–59th   Confidential annexes.

CAB 128/8   21 July–31 Dec 1946   CM(46)70th–108th   Confidential annexes.

21 July	**CM(46)70th**	**World food supplies.** CP(46)286 and 289. Consideration of whether to suspend the introduction of bread rationing or to reduce the extraction rate.

9 Sept	**80th:2**	**Bread rationing.** CP(46)336. Despite Strachey's opposition, agreement that it should continue and that the extraction rate should be reduced as soon as possible.

CAB 128/9   2 Jan–22 May 1947   CM(47)1st–49th.

2 Jan	**CM(47)1st:5**	**Food supplies.**
6 Jan	**2nd:5**	**France.** The French wished to discuss integration.
7 Jan	**3rd**	**Coal and electricity.** CP(47)6, 15, 17, 18. Agreement on certain measures for dealing with the crisis.
8 Jan	**4th:3**	**Food.** CP(47)13 and 21.
13 Jan	**5th:3**	**Production of ground-nuts in East Africa.** CP(47)4 and 10.
16 Jan	**7th:2**	**Economic Survey for 1947.** CP(47)19, 20, 25, 29. The Survey was presented by Cripps in Morrison's absence. It showed a great and increasing gap between requirements and

productive resources. The government had to decide what to curtail or postpone. Cripps stressed that the measures recommended in CP(47)25 represented a concerted plan for closing the gap and were interdependent. The gap would only be fully closed if all measures recommended were adopted.

16 Jan	**8th:2**	**Economic Survey for 1947.** CP(47)19, 20, 25, 29. Appraisal of the general economic situation. The economy was overburdened and adjustments, particularly of manpower, were necessary if the primary objectives of the export target and maintaining essential production for the home market were to be attained. Further action to increase productivity could help to close the gap and remove the need for retrenchment. Consideration of CP(47)25.
17 Jan	**9th:2**	**Economic Survey for 1947.** CP(47)19, 20, 25, 29. Continued consideration of CP(47)25, including the size of the armed forces, and the supply industries. All the measures agreed related to improving the manpower position. A decision to publish a White Paper on the general economic situation was deferred.
21 Jan	**10th:2**	**Defence estimates.** CP(47)33. Disagreement between Dalton and other ministers.
22 Jan	**11th:3**	**Economic Survey for 1947.** Agreement to publish.
28 Jan	**13th:1**	**Defence estimates.** CP(47)33.
	:2	**Commercial policy.** CP(47)35.
	:3	**Food.** CP(47)40.
30 Jan	**14th:3**	**International Trade Organization.** CP(47)44.
	:5	**Economic Survey for 1947.** CP(47)38. Consideration of the increased employment of women and foreign labour, the restriction of entry into non-productive employment and the limitation of weekday sport to ease the manpower position. A small group of ministers were to consider a draft White Paper on the general economic position.
	:6	**Women's Land Army.** CP(47)39.
4 Feb	**16th:1**	**Coal.** Agreement that the N.C.B. should concentrate on the more effective deployment of, rather than an increase in, manpower.
	:2	**Distribution of industry.** Consideration of whether development of light industry in Lancashire was too great.
6 Feb	**17th:3**	**Coal.** CP(47)50. Agreement on proposals to meet the immediate difficulties. Then consideration of further supplies of coal.

7 Feb	**18th:1**	**Coal.** Agreement with Shinwell that drastic cuts in electricity were inevitable.
10 Feb	**19th**	**Coal.** The latest developments. Overriding priority was to be given to the movement of coal on the railways.
11 Feb	**20th:3**	**Coal.** Review and agreement to consider how to monitor the situation.
	:4	**Defence estimate.** CP(47)52.
	:5	**National Service Bill.** CP(47)47.
13 Feb	**21st:1**	**Coal.** Attlee had appointed the Fuel Committee to replace the ministerial Coal Committee.
	:5	**Economic Survey for 1947.** CP(47)53 (revise). Approval of the White Paper, subject to amendments particularly on coal and electricity, and of the lines of Attlee's foreword to the Survey. A popular version was to be published.
14 Feb	**22nd:1**	**Coal.** CP(47)60. Review by Shinwell. Agreement to restrict broadcasting. Unemployment benefit to be paid to those put out of work by fuel cuts.
18 Feb	**23rd:4**	**Coal.** CP(47)61. Consideration of the inducements for coalminers deferred.
20 Feb	**24th:1**	**Parliament.** Includes arrangements for the debate on the economic situation.
6 Mar	**26th:2**	**Parliament.** Consideration of the arguments for the debate on the economic situation.
	:3	**Manpower.** Approval of the arrangements for a review of Civil Service staffs.
	:5	**Electricity Bill.** CP(47)73 and 76.
11 Mar	**27th:4**	**Electricity Bill.** CP(47)73 and 76.
	:5	**Coal.** Consideration of a 5-day week in coal-mining and of importing coal.
13 Mar	**28th:2**	**Prisoners of war.** Includes consideration of their employment.
	:6	**Mid-week sport.** CP(47)86. Approval of the proposals.
18 Mar	**29th:5**	**Expansion of fuel and power resources.** CP(47)92. Approval of the proposals. The Heavy Electrical Plant Committee had been reconstituted by the Minister of Supply.
	:9	**Coal.** Report by Attlee on his meeting with the N.U.M. on attaining the output proposed in the *Economic Survey for 1947.*
20 Mar	**30th:4**	**Parliament: legislative programme for the 1947–48 session.** CP(47)79.
	:5	**Food.** CP(47)94. Decision to increase the sugar ration deferred.
21 Mar	**31st**	**Coal.** Consideration of imports from the U.S.A. and Shinwell to approach the U.S. ambassador.
25 Mar	**32nd:2**	**Mid-week sport.**

	:6	**Coal.** CP(47)103. Rationing was impracticable. Agreement to continue restrictions on use of electricity and gas between certain hours throughout the summer.
	:7	**Coal.** Report on discussions on imports from the U.S.A. and South Africa.
	:8	**Coal: 5-day week.** CP(47)104. Agreement to introduce on the lines of CP(47)104.
27 Mar	33rd:5	**Food.** CP(47)99, 100, 105, 109. Agreement not to increase sugar ration.
	:6	**Coal.** CP(47)108. Shinwell thought it inexpedient to continue the existing restrictions. Conditional approval for revised restrictions in CP(47)108.
1 Apr	34th:1	**Coal.** Consideration of various points likely to be raised in the forthcoming debate on the fuel situation, including imports, domestic fuel rationing and coal allocations for industry.
	:3	**Manpower.** Agreement on the line to be taken on the strength of the armed forces.
	:5	**Town and country planning.** CP(47)110 and 119. Approval of proposed power station at Bankside.
	:9	**Agricultural losses due to floods and winter weather.** CP(47)112, 115, 116. Includes consideration of how to stimulate food production.
3 Apr	35th:5	**National Service Bill.** Agreement to reduce service from 18 to 12 months.
14 Apr	36th:1	**The budget.**
17 Apr	37th:5	**Maintenance of essential supplies and services in an emergency.**
	:6	**Food.** CP(47)122. Agreement not to increase the extraction rate of flour.
	:7	**International Wheat Conference.**
	:8	**Parliament.** CP(47)123 and 124. Consideration of the introduction of iron and steel and gas nationalization bills.
22 Apr	38th:5	**Food.** Reaffirmation that there could be no increase in the flour extraction rate.
	:6	**Manpower.** CP(47)121. Agreement that there could be no substantial reduction of numbers of civil servants whilst rationing and other wartime controls continued; new administrative tasks undertaken in pursuance of government policy.
24 Apr	39th:1	**Home food production in 1947.** CP(47)128. Agreement to spend extra £7m to stimulate home production of crops and milk in 1947. Consideration then of the long term, including houses for agricultural workers.
	:4	**National Service Bill.** CP(47)133.

	:5	**Food.** CP(47)130. Agreement that there should be no change in the sugar or tea rations.
	:6	**Iron and Steel Industry Nationalization Bill.** CP(47)123.
28 Apr	40th:1	**Coal.** Concern of Bevan about the allocations agreed by the Fuel Committee and their impact on the building materials industries.
	:2	**Iron and Steel Industry Nationalization Bill.**
29 Apr	41st:3	**National Service Bill.** CP(47)133.
	:4	**Industrial Organization Bill.** CP(47)131. Resolving of differences between Isaacs and Cripps.
	:5	**Mid-week sport.**
1 May	42nd:2	**Public boards.**
	:4	**Coal.** CP(47)139 and 141. Agreement to increase the allocation for the building materials industry.
	:5	**Timber.** CP(47)136 and 137. On international allocations.
	:6	**Iron and Steel Industry Nationalization Bill.**
6 May	44th:3	**Railway charges and wage claims.** CP(47)145.
	:4	**Wages policy.** CP(47)146.
	:5	**Iron and Steel Nationalization Bill.**
	:7	**Coal.** Statements on strike in Durham.
8 May	45th:1	**Financial relations between the Exchequer and local authorities.** CP(47)142.
15 May	47th:2	**Town and country planning.** A group of ministers under Morrison was to reconsider the Bankside power station.
	:3	**National Service Bill.** CP(47)152.
	:4	**Parliament.** CP(47)151. Approval of the legislative programme for 1947–48.
20 May	48th:3	**Coal.** CP(47)159 and 162. Agreement to continue seeking U.S. imports unless representatives of the European Coal Organization objected.
22 May	49th:2	**Town and country planning.** CP(47)160. Decision to erect Bankside power station reaffirmed.
	:5	**Civil Service.** CP(47)150 and 164. To be a further review of staff economies.

CAB 128/10 23 May–18 Dec 1947 CM(47)50th–96th.

3 June	CM(47)51st:6	**Double summer time.** CP(47)173.
5 June	52nd:2	**Import programme for 1947–48.** CP(47)109, 167, 169, 170. Some ministers felt that the proposed £80m reduction in food imports would adversely affect output. Approval of the proposals in CP(47)169 to stimulate world production of foodstuffs and other essential commodities.

	:3	**Double summer time.**
10 June	53rd:1	**Parliament.** Includes consideration of the Finance and Transport Bills.
	:5	**Development of colonial resources.** CP(47)175 and 176.
17 June	54th:2	**Economic recovery of Europe.** Bevin set out how he intended to initiate the preparation of a European reconstruction plan.
	:4	**Electricity Bill.** CP(47)181.
	:5	**Film remittances.** CP(47)174. Approval of a levy on imported films to reduce dollar expenditure.
19 June	55th:3	**Double day-shift working in factories.** CP(47)180.
	:5	**Economic recovery of Europe.** Bevin gave an account of his discussions in Paris.
	:6	**Trade delegation to Moscow.**
24 June	56th:3	**Economic recovery of Europe.** Bevin's proposed approach to the Foreign Ministers' discussions in Paris.
	:5	**Import programme for 1947–48.** CP(47)109, 167, 170, 172. Consideration of reductions in both the non-food and food import programmes. The programmes of raw materials, goods for industry, consumer goods, tobacco and films in 1947–8 to be reduced as in CP(47)167, subject to possible increased purchases of timber. Food imports were to be reduced by £50m. Every effort was to be made to secure U.S. agreement for a relaxation of the non-discrimination provisions of the Anglo-American Financial Agreement. Preliminary discussion of CP(47)172.
26 June	57th:3	**Import programme for 1947–48.** CP(47)172. Agreement to raise textile exports.
	:5	**Iron and Steel Industry Bill.** CP(47)185.
1 July	58th:3	**Iron and Steel Industry Bill.**
3 July	59th:4	**Wages Policy.** Consideration of the proposed increase in agricultural wages.
8 July	60th:3	**Economic Planning Board.** Bevan complained that the Cabinet had not discussed the Board's constitution before its announcement to the Commons and was particularly critical of the permanent secretaries' membership. It was pointed out that the permanent secretaries were closely concerned with economic planning through the Steering Committee and the new arrangements would, if anything, lighten their burden. The Board's constitution could be revised in the light of experience.
	:4	**Economic recovery of Europe.** CP(47)197. Bevin set out the proposed arrangements.

	:7	**Food.** CP(47)199. Agreement that there should not be the usual seasonal increase in the tea ration.
	:8	**Supplies of carbon black.** With regard to rubber tyres.
	:9	**Transport Bill.**
17 July	62nd:3	**Wages policy.** CP(47)189, 190, 195, 202. Renewed dispute, in particular between Shinwell and Isaacs, over whether there should be a central advisory body. Morrison, Bevan, Dalton and Cripps set out their views. Summing up, Attlee said that the government must have a positive policy but that in other countries state intervention had not always worked. It would be unwise to adopt Shinwell's proposal now but there should be an enquiry into how to deal with claims by workers in socialized industries and local government.
	:4	**Trade delegation to Moscow.**
24 July	64th:2	**Iron and Steel Industry Bill.** CP(47)212.
	:3	**Petrol rationing.** CP(47)206 and 207. Approval of the two papers.
29 July	65th:2	**Balance of payments.** Attlee said that positive action was needed to offset the rapid exhaustion of the U.S. credit. There should be a general discussion and a meeting on 1 August to consider specific proposals. Dalton and Morrison recommended a temporary stop on food imports. Other proposals involved increased production and exports and reduced overseas military expenditure.
31 July	66th:4	**Iron and Steel Industry Bill.** CP(47)215.
1 Aug	67th:1	**Railway charges.** CP(47)214. Approval of increases.
	:2	**Balance of payments.** CP(47)221. Consideration of a wide range of import reductions, overseas and military expenditure and the redistribution of exports. Approval of several proposals, including halt to imports of luxury foods and the search for essential foods from soft currency sources. The aim should be to raise exports to 140% of their 1938 volume in the second quarter of 1948 and to 160% by end 1948.
1 Aug	68th	**Balance of payments.** CP(47)220 and 221. To improve the balance of payments it was agreed: to increase resources for transport of goods, curtail capital investment, expand production by increasing working hours, and increase direction of labour. Departments should have power to take action where production was being impeded by inefficient management.

Bevin, Dalton and Cripps to consider how to negotiate with the U.S. over reducing dollar expenditure as a result of non-discrimination, convertibility obligations and expenditure on the Anglo-American Zone.

5 Aug	**69th:1**	**Supplies and Services (Transitional Powers) Bill.** CP(47)223. Approved.
	:2	**Balance of payments.** CP(47)223, 224, 226. Agreement on increasing production by £100m a year by 1951–52, immediate coal production target, remittances on foreign films, petrol saving, reduced foreign travel allowances and curtailment of capital investment except for export- and import-saving projects. Approval of CP(47)226. Then consideration of government line on dollar resources for the debate on 6 August.
	:3	**Coal.** CP(47)225. N.C.B. should not extend 5–day week to ancillary workers.
7 Aug	**70th:2**	**Balance of payments.** Agreement on statement on the size of the armed forces. Decision on an autumn budget deferred.
	:3	**Anglo-Soviet trade negotiations.**
	:4	**Trade negotiations at Geneva.** OEP(47)29 and 30.
	:6	**Iron and Steel Industry Bill.** CP(47)215.
17 Aug	**71st:1**	**Balance of payments.** CP(47)233. Agreement to limit the convertibility of sterling but to delay action until 19 Aug to allow for discussions with U.S. Attlee was to consider the direction of exports and how to strengthen the inter-departmental machinery for handling balance of payments questions.
	:2	**Coal.** CP(47)232. Agreement to take a firmer line with the miners.
19 Aug	**72nd:1**	**Balance of payments.** Report of discussions in Washington and agreement to postpone the limitation of convertibility for 24 hours.
	:2	**Food.** On the long-term contract for purchase of Australian wheat.
	:3	**Food and raw materials.** Consideration of the future of government bulk purchase.
	:4	**Trade negotiations at Geneva.**
20 Aug	**73rd**	**Balance of payments.** Further reports on Washington negotiations and agreement on the exchange of letters. Some ministers felt that discussions with U.S. should now be at a ministerial level.
25 Aug	**74th:1**	**Coal.** An extension of the working day was still regarded as the most effective method of increasing output.

:2 **Balance of payments.** CP(47)234, 238, 239, 240, 241, 242, 236, 237, 243. Dalton set out immediate effect of the limitation of convertibility. Ministers then considered measures to improve the balance of payments and reduce dollar expenditure. Issues covered included food prices, petrol rationing, gas and electricity prices, colonial production, publicity and the motor industry. Agreement that the Materials Committee should allocate any additional steel supplies to schemes that would benefit the balance of payments. Also any announcement concerning housing should await the completion of the investment programme review. On policy implementation, ministers should personally ensure effective departmental action in conjunction with C.E.P.S. and industry; and N. Brook was to review inter-departmental machinery. On policy formulation Morrison urged greater co-operation between the Treasury and C.E.P.S. whilst Dalton claimed that necessary steps had already been taken. Morrison was authorized to keep the Planning Board fully informed.

9 Sept 75th:3 **Manpower.** CP(47)244 and 248. Approval of CP(47)248 on the Control of Engagement Order and consideration of unproductive employment, Polish Resettlement Corps and housing.

:4 **Housing.** CP(47)249. The report on the priority for rural, mining and development areas was to be considered by a small group of ministers.

:5 **Export programme.** CP(47)250. Despite some protests, it was agreed to give exports overriding priority in steel allocations. The Chancellor of the Exchequer and Paymaster General were to arbitrate on issues which the Materials Committee could not resolve. Collection of scrap was to be reviewed and a joint enquiry to be held with the F.B.I. into machinery for issuing steel to industry.

:6 **Coal.** CP(47)254. The Cabinet refused to modify its views on hours.

:7 **Economic situation.** CP(47)252. Consideration of F.B.I. views.

:8 **International Bank and International Monetary Fund.**

20 Sept 76th:4 **Trade negotiations.** With Argentina.

:5 **Committee on European Economic Co-operation.** CP(47)260.

:7 **Coal.** Shinwell reported on recent events and N.U.M.–N.C.B. negotiations over hours.

	:8	**Balance of payments.** Bevan was reluctant to delay the housing programme until the review of the whole investment programme was complete.
	:9	**Economic Planning Board.** Attlee announced addition of a Treasury representative.
25 Sept	77th:1	**Trade negotiations.** CP(47)266.
	:2	**Proposals for customs unions.**
	:4	**Wages policy.** CP(47)264 and 267. Agreement to submit CP(47)264 to N.J.A.C. after Attlee had seen the T.U.C.
	:5	**Manpower.** CP(47)265. Minister of Labour to have the power to require the registration of those within the ages of control in unproductive employment and unoccupied.
	:6	**Coal.** CP(47)268. Further consideration of the negotiations over hours.
	:7	**Game prices.** CP(47)253. On the removal of price control.
2 Oct	78th:3	**Strength of the armed forces.** CP(47)272. Approval of reductions in CP(47)272 assuming the liquidation of some overseas commitments.
	:4	**Petrol rationing.** CP(47)274. Consideration of allowances for tourists and persons on leave.
	:5	**Steel.** CP(47)269. Marquand explained why the existing scheme for controlling issues of steel had broken down. Approval of proposed new scheme.
9 Oct	79th:2	**Budget.** Dalton now felt that the increased inflationary pressure caused by the measures to reduce imports and increase exports made an autumn budget necessary.
	:4	**International meetings.** CP(47)271.
	:5	**Trade negotiations.** CP(47)278.
	:6	**Economic recovery of Europe: U.S. assistance.** CP(47)279.
	:7	**Food and raw materials.** CP(47)258. Agreement not to reduce bulk purchase.
	:8	**Food.** Approval of a reduced bacon ration.
	:9	**Allocation of resources.** CP(47)273. Cripps was to arrange a review of the existing system of priorities in CP(47)92(revise).
14 Oct	80th:2	**Parliament.** CP(47)281. Consideration of the legislative programme for 1947–48.
	:3	**Parliament.** CP(47)282. Subject to some amendment, the King's speeches were approved.
20 Oct	81st:3	**Balance of payments.** CP(47)283, 291, 293. Dalton set out the dollar situation. Agreement to cut the prospective dollar deficit for 1948 by £175m by reductions in government expenditure, the petroleum programme, and

		imports of manufactured goods, raw materials and food. U.S. tobacco imports were to be suspended.
	:4	**Investment programme.** CP(47)284. Endorsement of recommendations. Approval of a housing programme of 140,000 houses in 1948, with preferential treatment for development areas, continued supervision of the investment programme and a review of the engineering industry's requirements for home and export markets.
23 Oct	82nd:3	**Food.** CP(47)295. Strachey was to report on linking the introduction of a potato distribution scheme with the abolition of bread rationing.
	:4	**Balance of payments.** Bevan questioned the earlier decision to cut food rations following the reduction in the dollar import programme but the cuts were reaffirmed.
30 Oct	83rd:1	**Ministry of Transport.**
	:5	**Registration of street traders.** CP(47)301.
	:7	**Trade negotiations.**
3 Nov	84th:2	**Food.** CP(47)298. Review of wheat and coarse grain supplies, although it was agreed that bread rationing had to continue.
	:3	**Food.** CP(47)295. Approval of the potato distribution scheme.
	:4	**Food.** CP(47)300. Strachey given discretion to effect 25% reduction in manufacturers' use of sugar.
11 Nov	86th:1	**The budget.**
13 Nov	87th:2	**Trade negotiations.** Consideration of the question of publication of the draft charter for the International Trade Organization.
	:5	**Wages policy.** CP(47)303 and 304. Cripps versus Isaacs on the need for a 'positive' policy in line with the requirements of economic planning. Decision deferred but no 'positive' policy was to be advanced in the meeting with the T.U.C. on 17 November.
18 Nov	89th:1	**Allocation of resources.** CP(47)308. Agreement to modify the steel priority system as proposed.
25 Nov	90th:1	**Food.** Approval of increased rations for Christmas.
	:4	**Balance of payments.** CP(47)311. To be a survey of the U.K.'s possible long-term scale of imports, their composition and sources.
27 Nov	91st:7	**Food prices.** CP(47)312. Some concern that price increases would set off a fresh wage cycle, although Cripps pointed out that all the increases were in line with the autumn budget. CP(47)312 to be reconsidered.

2 Dec	**92nd:2**	**Economic affairs.** CP(47)309. Review of the first of a series of periodic reports on the economic situation and suggestion that future ones should cover agriculture and food. Agreement that the publicity for production should be more encouraging.
4 Dec	**93rd:4**	**Government publicity.** On ministerial responsiblity.
11 Dec	**94th:5**	**Food prices.** CP(47)324. Agreement on increases, but they should be spread widely over January to March 1948 and associated with increased availability.
15 Dec	**95th:3**	**Economic affairs.** CP(47)332.
	:4	**Investment programme.** CP(47)329 and 334. Bevan was to discuss with Cripps, Isaacs and Key the safeguarding of labour for the local authority housing programme.
	:6	**White fish industry.** CP(47)325 and 328. A committee of ministers was to re-examine proposals.
18 Dec	**96th:6**	**Oil supplies.** CP(47)330.
	:7	**Trade negotiations.** With Canada.

CAB 128/11   8 Jan–18 Dec 1947   CM(47)4th–96th.   Confidential annexes

CAB 128/12   6 Jan–17 June 1948   CM(48)1st–40th.

6 Jan	**CM(48)1st:1**	**Defence estimates.** CP(48)2. Approval of the manpower ceiling and expenditure.
	:2	**Economic affairs.** CP(48)1. Particular consideration of manpower and employment of Poles.
	:3	**Mid-week sport.** CP(47)338. Agreement on continuation of 1947 restrictions and their possible extension.
	:4	**Summer time.** CP(47)338.
8 Jan	**2nd:2**	**Foreign travel allowances.** CP(48)11.
13 Jan	**3rd:1**	**Food.** CP(48)10. Agreed increase in fats ration.
	:2	**Allocation of resources.** CP(48)13. Agreement to limit the P.M.L. symbol to steel and iron castings and that the Chancellor of the Exchequer could regulate its use.
	:3	**Gas Bill.** CP(48)14.
15 Jan	**4th:1**	**Foreign travel allowances and basic petrol ration.** CP(48)11 and 16. Relaxation of petrol restrictions in the summer was impracticable.
19 Jan	**5th:4**	**Production of ground-nuts in East Africa.** CP(48)18.
22 Jan	**6th:5**	**Economic affairs.** CP(48)19. Consideration of devaluation of the French franc, production, exports, prices and publicity. Concern about

		the consequences of incomplete control over the sterling area's dollar expenditure.
26 Jan	7th:1	**Food.** CP(48)29. Agreement on target for the 1948 potato acreage.
	:2	**Export programme.** CP(48)24. Proposals endorsed.
	:3	**Devaluation of the French franc.**
29 Jan	8th:7	**Wages policy.** CP(48)27 and 28. Concern at increases since mid–1947 and future wage instability. Agreement that Attlee should make an early statement in the Commons.
	:8	**Wages.** Report on the claim of road transport workers.
2 Feb	9th:3	**Wages policy.** CP(48)38. Despite Bevan's opposition, the decision to publish the proposed statement was reaffirmed. Consideration of procedure
	:4	**Steel scrap.** CP(48)33.
5 Feb	11th:2	**Wages policy.** T.U.C. complaint at lack of consultation rejected.
	:4	**Economic affairs.** CP(48)32. Consideration of balance of payments, trade agreements, production and exports.
	:5	**Defence White Paper.** CP(48)34.
16 Feb	14th:1	**Argentina.** Approval of proposed trade agreement.
	:2	**Balance of payments.** CP(48)35, 49, 51. Approval of CP(48)35, as modified by CP(48)51 and the rider that any cut in timber imports would not affect the housing programme.
	:3	**Exports to Canada.** CP(48)48.
19 Feb	15th:3	**Food prices.** Agreement to postpone increases approved on 11 Dec 1947 unless already implemented.
	:4	**Economic affairs.** CP(48)50. Consideration of the balance of payments, production, exports and unemployment in the building industry following the cuts in the investment programme.
	:5	**Wages policy.** CP(48)52, 54, 58, 59. Every effort was to be made to obtain advance information on wage claims. Agreement that departments must be consistent in interpreting paragraph 10 of the *Statement on Personal Incomes, Costs and Prices* and that generally CP(48)54 paragraph 4 should be applied. Report on London road transport workers' claim.
	:6	**Commercial work in Royal Dockyards.** CP(48)26. On the possibilities of ship-breaking for scrap.

23 Feb	16th:3	**Economic Survey for 1948.** CP(48)44 and 60. Agreement against raising the coal production target above 211m tons, despite recommendation of the Economic Planning Board. Agreement not to reduce manpower target for the textile industries. Consideration of the form of the draft survey. Approval of publication subject to agreed revision.
	:4	**Housing programme in 1948 and 1949.** CP(48)56. Approval of additional allocation of timber in 1948 to enable more houses to be started and for the Production Committee to consider the relaxation of other building restrictions.
4 Mar	18th:3	**Parliament.** CP(48)68. Approval of preliminary legislative programme for 1948–49.
	:4	**Economic affairs.** CP(48)67. Consideration mainly of the balance of payments, steel scrap and pig-iron.
8 Mar	20th:2	**European economic co-operation.** CP(48)75. Approval of proposals for the continuing organization.
	:4	**Monopolistic Practices Bill.** CP(48)73.
	:5	**Wages policy.** CP(48)76. Approval of proposals.
11 Mar	21st:1	**Monopolistic Practices Bill.** CP(48)73 and 80.
	:2	**Food.** CP(48)65.
15 Mar	22nd:2	**International Trade Organization.** CP(48)84.
	:4	**Wages policy.** CP(48)74 and 81.
18 Mar	23rd:3	**Investment programme.** CP(48)77 and 87.
	:4	**Economic affairs.** CP(48)85. Consideration of the balance of payments, production, manpower, food, prices and wage rates.
22 Mar	24th:8	**Monopoly (Enquiry and Control) Bill.**
	:9	**Petrol rationing.** CP(48)89 and 90. Approval of a standard petrol allowance, on the understanding that the black market would be dealt with, cuts in rations for goods vehicles and supplementary allowances.
25 Mar	25th:2	**Wages policy: Statement on Personal Incomes, Costs and Prices.** CP(48)97. Report on follow-up action and T.U.C. reaction to the White Paper.
5 Apr	26th:2	**Manpower.** CP(48)100.
	:3	**The budget.**
	:4	**France: balance of payments with the sterling area.** CP(48)101.
	:5	**European economic co-operation.** E.R.P. had been authorized.
	:7	**Employment of disabled persons.**

8 Apr	27th:7	**Steel scrap.** CP(48)99. Agreement on increasing deliveries of booty scrap from Germany.
15 Apr	28th:3	**Economic affairs.** CP(48)105. Consideration of production, external trade and coal exports, prices and finance.
	:4	**Wages policy.** CP(48)106.
	:6	**Appointments to public boards.**
22 Apr	29th:3	**European economic co-operation.** CP(48)109.
29 Apr	30th:5	**Housing programme in 1949.** No announcement to be made yet.
6 May	31st:3	**Steel scrap.** Report on progress of supplies from Germany.
	:4	**France.** Statement by Cripps on French balance of payments.
	:5	**Economic affairs.** CP(48)116. Consideration of production, balance of payments, building and trade negotiations.
	:6	**Coal to oil conversion scheme.** CP(48)119. Approval of proposals.
13 May	32nd:4	**British trade: Philippines.**
27 May	33rd:6	**Economic affairs.** CP(48)125. Consideration of manpower, the coal industry, steel, building, external trade, balance of payments, wages policy and shipbuilding.
3 June	35th:1	**Mr. Hugh Dalton.** Appointed as Chancellor of the Duchy of Lancaster. Includes consideration of the preparation of a 5-year plan for E.R.P.
	:8	**Steel scrap.** CP(48)130. Concern about supplies from Germany.
7 June	36th:4	**Iron and Steel Bill.** CP(48)123, 136, 139.
11 June	38th	**Wages policy.** CP(48)135, 140, 141. How to deal with claims in local authorities and socialized industries.
14 June	39th:4	**European economic co-operation.** Concern at the burden placed on the O.E.E.C. by U.S. demands for statistical information.
	:5	**Iron and Steel Bill.** CP(48)123 and 145.
17 June	40th:2	**Economic affairs.** CP(48)146. Consideration of manpower, production (particularly of coal), external trade, the balance of payments, and financial negotiations with India and Pakistan.
	:3	**International Wheat Agreement.** CP(48)150. Agreement to ratify Cmd. 7382.

CAB 128/13	22 June–22 Dec 1948	CM(48)41st–82nd.
22 June	**CM(48)41st:1**	**Industrial disputes.** On the dock strike.
	:2	**Food.** CP(48)152 and 153. Approval of CP(48)152 on the substitution of bread rationing by bulk flour allocation.
24 June	**42nd:1**	**Industrial disputes.**

	:5	**European economic co-operation.** CP(48)161. Concern about the effect on the U.K. economy of some of the terms for the provision of aid.
25 June	43rd:1	**European economic co-operation.** Update on the negotiations on the draft Economic Co-operation Agreement. Agreement to accept the revised agreement.
	:2	**Industrial disputes.**
28 June	44th:1	**European economic co-operation.** CP(48)167. Approval of the Economic Co-operation Agreement.
	:2	**Industrial disputes.**
	:3	**Iron and Steel Bill.** CP(48)157.
29 June	45th:1	**Industrial disputes.**
1 July	46th:6	**Steel scrap.** CP(48)160 and 164.
5 July	47th:5	**International Wheat Agreement.** CP(48)172. U.K. to withdraw as U.S. Congress had not ratified the agreement.
	:8	**European economic co-operation.** Update on discussions on loans under E.R.P.
8 July	48th:6	**Economic affairs.** CP(48)173. Consideration of production, external trade, balance of payments, retail trade, wages and oil stocks. Cripps, Isaacs and the agricultural ministers were to consider the reform of agricultural wages machinery.
12 July	49th	**Balance of payments.** CP(48)177 and 178. The O.E.E.C. had agreed to allocate aid and to assume that this would total in the first period $4875m, 10% below the original published figure. Consideration of the balance of payments with non-dollar countries and of adjustments to be made to the 1948–49 dollar import programme in view of the expected shortfall.
13 July	50th:1	**Balance of payments.** CP(48)177 and 178. Further consideration of possible savings in the dollar import programme. The removal of bread rationing was reaffirmed.
15 July	51st:4	**Electricity.** CP(48)183. Agreement to publish the Clow Committee report.
19 July	52nd:3	**Iron and Steel Bill.** CP(48)181.
	:4	**Shipping.** CP(48)184.
22 July	53rd:1	**European economic co-operation.** Update on discussions on loans under E.R.P.
	:9	**Economic affairs.** CP(48)186. Consideration of wages, manpower, production and balance of payments.
29 July	55th:1	**Parliament.** CP(48)195. Consideration of the drafts of the King's speeches on the prorogation and opening of Parliament.

	:4	**White fish industry.** CP(48)197. Approval of the proposed legislation.
26 Aug	57th:2	**Preparations for defence.** CP(48)206. Consideration of proposals on manpower and materials.
3 Sept	58th:2	**Preparations for defence.** CP(48)214 and 216.
	:3	**The King's speeches on the prorogation and opening of Parliament.** CP(48)215.
13 Sept	60th:2	**Preparations for defence.** CP(48)221.
30 Sept	62nd:1	**Receipts and expenditure of the British Transport Commission.** CP(48)213.
15 Oct	63rd:4	**Iron and Steel Bill.** CP(48)227 and 229.
18 Oct	64th:1	**Parliament.** CP(48)230 and 235. Approval of the legislative programme for 1948–49.
	:3	**The King's speeches on the prorogation and opening of Parliament.** CP(48)231.
	:5	**Petrol rationing.** CP(48)233. The standard petrol ration to remain unchanged.
	:6	**Iron and Steel Bill.**
22 Oct	65th:4	**Economic affairs.** CP(48)232. Consideration of manpower, production, external trade, prices, wages and bilateral negotiations.
25 Oct	66th:1	**International organizations.** CP(48)241 and 242.
	:2	**Parliament.** Includes consideration of the Iron and Steel Bill.
	:4	**Government information services.** CP(48)199 and 212.
11 Nov	70th:1	**Parliament.** Includes consideration of arrangements for the Iron and Steel Bill.
	:4	**Economic affairs.** CP(48)255. Consideration of manpower, production, building, external trade, balance of payments and prices. Agreement that the Headquarters Building Committee should consider how to check the rise in building costs outside the housing programme.
18 Nov	74th:5	**National service.**
	:9	**Food.** CP(48)266. Approval of increased rations for Christmas.
22 Nov	75th:3	**National service.** CP(48)276. Approval of the extension of national service from 12 to 18 months.
25 Nov	76th:5	**Housing Bill.** CP(48)275 and 279.
2 Dec	77th:3	**Iron and Steel Bill.**
	:6	**Civil Service salaries.** EPC(48)87 and 95. Concern about compliance with the *Statement on Personal Incomes, Costs and Prices*.
6 Dec	78th:4	**National Service Bill.**
9 Dec	79th:6	**Economic affairs.** CP(48)288. Consideration of manpower, production, building, external trade, balance of payments, prices, wage rates

and bilateral negotiations. Isaacs was to
investigate whether improved sickness benefit
had increased absenteeism. Cripps and Wilson
were to consider how to scale down favourable
trade balances with certain soft currency
countries and to secure corresponding
improvement in the balance of payments with
hard currency countries.

13 Dec	**80th:1**	**Argentina.** On meat shipments.
22 Dec	**82nd:4**	**Census of distribution.** CP(48)305.
	:5	**Housing Bill.**

CAB 128/14   5 Mar–6 Dec 1948   CM(48)19th–78th Confidential annexes.

CAB 128/15   12 Jan–30 June 1949   CM(49)1st–43rd.

12 Jan	**CM(49)1st:1**	**Census of distribution.** CP(49)1 and 2. It was argued that economic planning was seriously hampered by the lack of statistics relating to distribution, but that it would be politically unwise to hold the census in the same year as an election. Agreement to delay first census of distribution until 1951.
17 Jan	**4th:1**	**Food.** CP(49)11. Approval of the reduction in the meat ration.
20 Jan	**5th:3**	**Housing Bill.**
	:5	**Economic affairs.** CP(49)13. Consideration of manpower, production, building, external trade, balance of payments, wage rates, relaxations in economic controls.
24 Jan	**6th:1**	**Defence estimates.** CP(49)16. Approval of the estimates for 1949–50, totalling £760m.
3 Feb	**9th:5**	**County Agricultural Executive Committees.**
8 Feb	**10th:3**	**Economic affairs.** Consideration of external trade. Wilson revealed that the provisional estimate of U.K. exports in January was £159m and in volume well in excess of the target for 1949.
10 Feb	**11th:4**	**Defence White Paper.** CP(49)21.
17 Feb	**12th:3**	**Supplementary civil estimates.** Consideration of the main supplementaries: the National Health Service, Food and the Colonies.
21 Feb	**13th:2**	**Economic affairs.** CP(49)30. Consideration of production, food, export trade, balance of payments and prices.
24 Feb	**15th:5**	**European economic co-operation.** CP(49)27. On the preparation of a co-ordinated long-term programme.
28 Feb	**16th:1**	**Cabinet committees.**
	:4	**Economic Survey for 1949.** CP(49)29, 38, 40. Approval of the survey subject to minor amendments including a figure of 795,000 for

		the manpower requirements of the coal industry.
	:5	**Wages policy.** CP(49)28 and 42. General agreement that CP(49)42 disclosed a serious trend. Consideration of the position in particular industries. Discussion on how to prevent a fresh cycle of wage increases.
	:6	**Petrol rationing.** CP(49)41.
8 Mar	18th:1	**International Wheat Agreement.** CP(49)51.
10 Mar	19th:5	**Food.** CP(49)49. Agreement to reduce further the meat ration.
17 Mar	20th:2	**Petrol rationing.** CP(49)41. Approval of the doubling in value of coupons for private cars in summer.
	:5	**Food.** Announcement of the reduced meat ration to be brought forward.
21 Mar	21st:3	**Unauthorized strikes in electricity undertakings.**
24 Mar	22nd:2	**The film industry.** CP(49)66.
28 Mar	23rd:2	**Economic affairs.** CP(49)70. Consideration of manpower, production, external trade, balance of payments, prices, E.R.P. and dollar earnings of colonial commodities.
5 Apr	25th:2	**The budget.**
13 Apr	27th:2	**London dock strike.** CP(49)88 and 89.
	:3	**Food.** CP(49)84.
2 May	31st:4	**Trade with Russia and Eastern Europe.**
	:7	**Wages policy.** Statement by Isaacs on the claim by the N.U.R.
5 May	32nd:8	**Wages policy.** CP(49)96.
12 May	34th:8	**Food.** CP(49)103. Approval of an increase in the meat ration.
16 May	35th:1	**Parliament.** CP(49)104. Approval of the preparation of bills from the 1950 legislative programme.
23 May	37th:1	**National Health Service.** CP(48)302 and 308 and CP(49)105 and 106.
26 May	38th:2	**Dockers' strike.**
30 May	39th:1	**Industrial disputes.** Docks and railways. Publicity matters.
	:3	**Import policy.** CP(49)124. Approval of recommendations for the relaxation of import licensing restrictions.
	:4	**Economic affairs.** CP(49)121. Consideration of manpower, production, building, prices and bilateral negotiations. The Production Committee was to review comprehensively the problem of maintaining employment in the development areas.
	:5	**Resale price maintenance.** CP(49)116.
2 June	40th:3	**The national insurance schemes and sickness absence in industry.** CP(49)85 and 122.

		Agreement to establish a committee to investigate increased absenteeism in coal-mining.
	:4	**Industrial disputes.** CP(49)30.
20 June	**41st:1**	**Industrial disputes.**
	:2	**Iron and Steel Bill.** CP(49)132.
	:3	**Import policy.** CP(49)137. Consideration of parliamentary statements.
23 June	**42nd:3**	**Import policy.** Approval of the deferment of the statement.
30 June	**43rd:1**	**Parliament.** Includes consideration of the timetable for the Iron and Steel Bill.
	:4	**Industrial disputes.**
	:6	**Civil servants and industrial disputes.** CP(49)143.

CAB 128/16	7 July–15 Dec 1949	CM(49)44th–72nd.
7 July	**CM(49)44th:3**	**Industrial disputes.**
	45th:3	**Industrial disputes.**
11 July	:4	**National Dock Labour Board.** CP(49)145.
18 July	**46th:1**	**Sir Stafford Cripps.** During Cripps's illness, Attlee would assume his responsibilities assisted by Wilson and Gaitskell as well as the Financial and Economic Secretaries to the Treasury.
	:6	**National Dock Labour Board.** CP(49)145 and 151.
	:7	**Industrial disputes.**
	:8	**Food.** CP(49)144. There had been some improvement since CP(49)144 had been circulated.
21 July	**47th:2**	**Iron and Steel Bill.**
	:5	**Security of economic and industrial information about the U.K.** CP(49)138.
	:7	**Industrial disputes.**
25 July	**48th:1**	**Industrial disputes.**
	:2	**Meeting of Commonwealth finance ministers.** CP(49)160.
	:3	**The economic situation.** CP(49)158 and 159. Consideration of whether further measures were necessary to halt the drain on reserves before the Washington discussions in September.
27 July	**49th:1**	**Food.** Approval of the proposals for a special issue of rations of animal feedstuffs.
	:4	**Iron and Steel Bill.** CP(49)168.
28 July	**50th:5**	**The economic situation.** CP(49)159. Discussion of the relationship between internal financial policy and the deficit in the U.K. dollar balance of payments. Agreement on the need to educate the public further and to make economies in

government expenditure as long as they did not contradict major policies. The Economic Policy Committee was to consider reductions in government expenditure and how to counter any future inflationary pressure.

29 July	**51st:1**	**Private investment of foreign capital.** EPC(49)74 and 92.
	:2	**The economic situation.** CP(49)165 and 169. Agreement to approach the Canadian government before the September Washington talks. Attlee was to issue a memorandum to ministers on the need for economy in government expenditure. Agreement that, given the comprehensive review of the situation by the Cabinet that week, there should be no emergency Cabinet meetings in August. Attlee should take such decisions as were required.
12 Aug	**52nd:1**	**Wages policy.** CP(49)173. Agreement not to confirm wage increases in the retail distribution trade proposed by Wages Councils.
	:2	**The economic situation.** CP(49)172 and 174. Agreement not to discuss Canada's relations with the sterling area before the Washington discussions.
29 Aug	**53rd:1**	**The economic situation.** CP(49)175. Consideration of forthcoming Washington discussions and general agreement that, if satisfactory understandings could be reached with the U.S., the U.K. should devalue. Then consideration of some external measures which could be taken by the U.K., the U.S. and Canada to meet the dollar crisis. Agreement that public expenditure cuts should not be discussed at Washington. The Cabinet would consider what further measures were required later. Progress of the Washington talks was to be monitored by Attlee, Wilson, Gaitskell and Jay.
	:2	**Wages policy.** Authorization of wage increases in the retail distributive trades vetoed on 12 August.
29 Aug	**54th:5**	**The economic situation.** CP(49)176 and 179. Agreement to attempt to involve the U.S. government in the problem of the sterling balances and to request the suspension of Article 9 of the Anglo-American Loan Agreement. The expansion programme of British oil companies and the continued supply to European countries of sterling oil involving dollar expenditure should be further reviewed.

17 Sept	55th	**The economic situation.** Consideration and amendment of a broadcast talk (annexed) proposed by Cripps, announcing devaluation. Various amendments were agreed.
22 Sept	56th:1	**The economic situation.** Agreement that Parliament should be recalled, Commonwealth countries informed and discussions held with the T.U.C., in particular with regard to wages policy.
26 Sept	57th:1	**Parliament.** CP(49)194. Agreement on the motion for the debate on the economic situation.
	:3	**Wages policy.** CP(49)193. Cripps said that the main purpose of devaluation, to increase U.K. export competitiveness, would be frustrated if there were any serious rise in costs of production, including wages. The government should therefore appeal in the strongest terms for restraint. One possible course was to set up a national tribunal to consider the claims of poorly-paid workers. General agreement on the need for trade unions to accept a voluntary and open-ended wage standstill and to discuss with the T.U.C. how to make the poorly paid a special case. Agreement also of a moderate increase in taxation of distributed profits but of no increase in family allowances. Cripps was to submit proposals on how to increase public understanding of the country's economic situation and the need for restraint.
	:4	**Trade with Canada.**
	:5	**Industrial disputes.**
13 Oct	58th:1	**Economic situation.** CP(49)197. Cripps had planned a major publicity campaign to ensure industry took advantage of the new situation but the Production Committee and representative institutions had expressed reservations. The Cabinet agreed in principle to proceed with an intensive campaign.
	:2	**Iron and Steel Bill.**
18 Oct	59th:1	**Economic situation.** Consideration of the arrangements for handling parliamentary discussion of further proposals for remedying the situation.
	:2	**Economic situation.** Consideration of a parliamentary answer on devaluation.
	:3	**Contracts of service in essential industries.** CP(49)192. Agreement not to revise such contracts as a means of countering unauthorized strikes.
20 Oct	60th:4	**Food.** CP(49)201. Approval of increased rations for Christmas.

21 Oct	**61st:1**	**The economic situation.** Consideration of parliamentary arrangements for the debate on 26–27 October.
	:2	**The economic situation.** CP(49)205. Approval of proposed reductions in the investment programme and government expenditure but rejection of a reduction in the milk subsidy. Agreement that, in announcing the cuts, Attlee should also stress the government's constructive plans, especially increasing productivity. A particular call should be made for longer working hours.
27 Oct	**62nd:4**	**Iron and Steel Bill.** CP(49)211.
	:6	**Economic unification of Europe.** CP(49)203.
3 Nov	**63rd:2**	**Joint consultation in industry.** CP(49)217. Isaacs was to continue his efforts to encourage joint consultation.
	:3	**Cotton industry.** The Production Committee was to consider means of increasing the industry's efficiency.
7 Nov	**64th:1**	**Food.** CP(49)223. Agreement on the increased rations for Christmas.
	:5	**Wages policy.** Concern of Cripps over discussions with the T.U.C.
10 Nov	**65th:2**	**Iron and Steel Bill.**
	:3	**Economic affairs.** CP(49)225. Consideration of manpower, production, external trade, balance of payments, stocks and prices.
	:4	**Government expenditure.** CP(49)216, 221, 228. Morrison felt that a greater impetus was needed to secure more administrative economies. To maximize control over expenditure, the future cost of existing commitments should be reviewed in the light of estimated national income and revenue to assess what each service could expect in the next 3–4 years. Against this the difficulty of making accurate forecasts of future expenditure was stressed. It was decided that Cripps was to submit to the Economic Policy Committee half-yearly forecasts of government expenditure covering the ensuing two years; Attlee was to remind chairmen of Cabinet committees to report on possible savings in public expenditure; and ministers should ensure that government decisions on expenditure were implemented.
14 Nov	**66th:1**	**Oil.**
	:2	**Wages policy.** Report on the line agreed by Cripps, Bevin, Isaacs and Bevan for the forthcoming discussions with the T.U.C. There should be no special treatment for low-paid workers and the standstill should operate for

		preferably more than a year, but with the safety valve that, were the cost of living index to rise by more than 5 or 6 points, wage rates would be reviewed.
	:3	**Production of ground-nuts in East Africa.** CP(49)210, 231, 232.
	:4	**Newsprint.** CP(49)227.
17 Nov	67th:1	**Parliament.** Includes consideration of the Sea Fish Industry Bill.
	:3	**Wages policy.**
24 Nov	68th:3	**Enforcement of financial and economic controls.** Consideration of payment to informers.
	:5	**Receipts and expenditure of the British Transport Commission.** CP(49)239.
	:6	**Wages policy.** CP(49)238.
1 Dec	69th:5	**Parliament.** CP(49)240. Agreement on the legislative programme for 1950.
8 Dec	70th:2	**Industrial Organization and Development Act 1947.** On the Development Council Orders for the woollen and clothing industries.
	:5	**Parliament.** CP(49)243.
12 Dec	71st:2	**Trade with Canada.**
	:3	**Oil and dollars.** Consideration of the proposed abolition of petrol rationing in Australia and its effect on the dollar balance of payments.
	:4	**The film industry.**
15 Dec	72nd:1	**Defence estimates.** CP(49)245. Agreement on a programme for 1950–51 of £780m, on the understanding that if this proved insufficient the balance would be met by supplementary estimates.
	:2	**Electricity strike.**
	:5	**Economic affairs.** CP(49)247.

CAB 128/17	10 Jan–29 June 1950	CM(50)1st–40th.
12 Jan	CM(50)2nd:3	**Local government manpower.** CP(49)252 and CP(50)4.
7 Feb	4th:1	**Agricultural prices.** CP(50)17. Approval of the revised production targets except in regard to wheat acreage. Consideration of whether to negotiate with the N.F.U. deferred.
2 Mar	6th:4	**Iron and Steel Act.** CP(50)21.
	:5	**The King's speech on the opening of Parliament.** CP(50)20.
	:6	**Defence White Paper.** CP(50)19.
3 Mar	7th:2	**The economic situation.** Cripps reported on the situation and the main factors influencing his budget proposals. No record taken.
6 Mar	8th:1	**Agricultural prices.** CP(50)24.

9 Mar	**9th:1**	**Parliament.** Includes consideration of the Iron and Steel Act and the Control of Engagement Order, which it was agreed should be revoked.
	:2	**Agricultural prices.** Agreement to open discussions with the N.F.U. on the basis of an aggregate net income of £250m for farmers in 1950–51.
	:3	**Derationing of animal feedingstuffs.** CP(50)25. Agreement to continue rationing.
	:4	**Housing.** CP(50)29 and 30. Agreement on the desirability of greater flexibility in the granting of licences for the erection of houses for sale.
	:5	**The economic situation.** Agreement not to resume the general discussion of 3 March given the limited time before the budget.
13 Mar	**10th:1**	**Housing programme.** Agreement that there could be no immediate increase, but the Investment Programmes Committee should consider whether some increase in the rate of house-building in 1951 and 1952 was possible.
	:2	**Receipts and expenditure of the British Transport Commission.** CP(50)23. Further disagreements on whether to meet the Commission's deficit on the railways by increasing charges.
	:3	**National Health Service.** CP(50)31. Agreement on a ceiling on expenditure in 1950–51.
16 Mar	**11th:1**	**National Health Service.** Discussion of charges to be resumed prior to the budget.
	:6	**Economic Survey for 1950.** CP(50)28 and 32. Approval, subject to minor amendment.
17 Mar	**12th**	**The economic situation.** CP(50)35. In relation to the budget, Attlee thought it desirable for the Cabinet to discuss whether the government should continue to aim at a substantial budget surplus. No record was made of the discussion on the role of budget policy in the maintenance of full employment without undue inflationary pressure. The broad conclusion, however, was that the Cabinet fully endorsed the approach outlined in CP(50)35.
23 Mar	**14th:4**	**Receipts and expenditure of the British Transport Commission.** Cabinet still could not accept increased charges.
	:5	**Agricultural prices.** CP(50)45. Approval of proposed increases in prices, fertilizer subsidies and extensions of the marginal production scheme.
27 Mar	**15th:5**	**Food.** CP(50)46 and 50. Approval of increased prices for butter and bacon.
30 Mar	**16th:1**	**Parliament.** Includes consideration of the debate on coal and oil supplies, the

		announcement of increased prices for butter and bacon and of Gaitskell's address to the P.L.P. on the *Economic Survey for 1950*.
	:3	**Future of emergency powers.** CP(50)49. Morrison argued that it was unsatisfactory that powers essential to economic planning should be linked so obviously with the continuance of wartime legislation and should rest on so uncertain a basis as an annual renewal. He favoured an economic controls bill which would make permanent the powers required for economic planning. Some ministers expressed doubts about the expediency of such a bill in the existing parliamentary situation. Agreement that the Lord President's Committee should examine what legal form the permanent powers required for planning should take.
	:4	**Economic affairs.** CP(50)47. Consideration of manpower, merchant shipping, wages, production, external trade and balance of payments. Some concern that critics of the *Economic Survey for 1950* had concluded that it marked the end of the planned distribution of manpower.
	:5	**Stocks of animal feedingstuffs.** CP(50)48.
	:6	**The film industry.** CP(50)52.
3 Apr	17th:3	**Gold and dollar reserves.** Report on the position by Cripps.
	:5	**Food.** CP(50)59.
6 Apr	20th:1	**Food.** CP(50)59. Agreement that it would be premature to discontinue the scheme of points rationing.
	:2	**Wages policy.** PC(50)28 and 29. Consideration of increases for manual workers in the gas industry.
17 Apr	21st:1	**The budget.**
	:2	**Housing programme.** CP(50)67. Agreement that for 1950–52 the completion rate should be 200,000 houses a year.
	:3	**Wages policy.** Approval of statement on wages policy which Cripps proposed to make in his budget speech.
20 Apr	22nd:3	**London dock strike.**
	:4	**Socialized industries.** CP(50)60.
21 Apr	23rd	**London dock strike.** CP(50)77.
24 Apr	24th:1	**Receipts and expenditure of the British Transport Commission.** CP(50)76.
	:3	**Wages policy.** CP(50)71.
	:4	**London dock strike.**
25 Apr	25th:1	**London dock strike.**

	:4	**Receipts and expenditure of the British Transport Commission.** CP(50)76. End of price control in restaurants etc.
27 Apr	26th:3	**Sea fish industry.**
	:4	**London dock strike.** CP(50)84.
	:7	**Meals in Establishments Order.** CP(50)72. Approval of revocation.
	:8	**Socialized industries.** CP(50)60.
1 May	27th:1	**London dock strike.**
4 May	28th:4	**Housing.** CP(50)90. Bevan's statement on granting licences for the building of houses for owner-occupiers.
	:5	**Economic affairs.** CP(50)86. Consideration of balance of payments, prices, coal, shipbuilding, development areas, building and textiles.
8 May	29th:1	**Tourist accommodation for 1951.** CP(50)91 and 96.
	:2	**Food.** CP(50)95.
11 May	30th:2	**European Payments Union.** Authorization for the U.K. delegation to the O.E.E.C. to put forward proposals on the lines indicated in EPC(50)51.
	:3	**Parliament.** CP(50)89. Consideration of the legislative programme for 1950–51.
	:4	**Public boards.** CP(50)97.
	:5	**Food.** CP(50)95. Agreement to reduce tea ration.
15 May	31st:1	**Canadian wheat and flour.** CP(50)98 and 102.
	:2	**Agricultural prices.** CP(50)105.
18 May	32nd:4	**Food.** CP(50)111. Agreement to discontinue points rationing.
	:6	**Wages policy.** CP(50)106.
	:7	**House coal.** CP(50)103. Consideration of seasonal price differentials in the south of England.
22 May	33rd:3	**House coal.** CP(50)103. Gaitskell authorized to reduce summer prices and to encourage coal merchants to stockpile for the winter.
2 June	34th	**Integration of French and German coal and steel industries.** Younger set out the state of negotiations. Agreement that the U.K. government should not participate in discussions of the French proposal as set out in the telegram in annex 1 of CP(50)120. If discussions went ahead without U.K., the government's attitude should be publicly explained.
6 June	35th:2	**Industrial disputes.**
15 June	36th:4	**Economic affairs.** CP(50)122. Consideration of the balance of payments, exports, manpower, production, coal. Discussion of how to increase

		total output of coal in the short term by accelerating technical developments.
	:5	**European Payments Union.** Statement by Cripps on negotiations.
	:6	**Iron and Steel Act.** CP(50)112.
19 June	37th:3	**European Payments Union.** Statement by Cripps on negotiations.
	:4	**Trade with Canada.** Statements by Cripps.
22 June	38th:5	**Integration of French and German coal and steel industries.** CP(50)128 and 133. Agreement that a small group of ministers should monitor the situation. Discussion of the line to be taken in Parliament.
27 June	39th:1	**Integration of French and German coal and steel industries.**
	:2	**White fish industry.**
	:3	**Marginal land.** CP(50)135.
29 June	40th:1	**Iron and Steel Act.** CP(50)140.
	:5	**Industrial disputes.** On the strike of Smithfield drivers.

CAB 128/18	3 July–18 Dec 1950	CM(50)41st–87th.
3 July	**CM(50)41st:1**	**Wages policy.** CP(50)151. Approval of Cripps's proposed statement.
	:2	**White fish industry.** CP(50)146 and 147. Agreement on level of subsidy.
	:4	**Industrial disputes.**
4 July	42nd:2	**Integration of French and German coal and steel industries.** CP(50)149, 153, 154.
	:5	**Soap rationing.** CP(50)137.
	:7	**Industrial disputes.**
6 July	43rd:3	**Industrial disputes.** CP(50)158.
10 July	44th:3	**Renewal of emergency powers.** CP(50)166. Agreement to renew emergency powers for a further year given that the Economic Powers Bill could not be introduced before emergency powers lapsed.
	:4	**Industrial disputes.**
	:4	**Involuntary absenteeism in coal-mining industry.** CP(50)161 and 162. Approval of CP(50)162 and agreement that CP(50)161 should not be published.
	:5	**Coal-mining industry.** CP(50)163 and 169. General satisfaction at the progress made by the N.C.B. in promoting technical development. Review of labour relations.
	:7	**Industrial disputes.**
17 July	46th:2	**Korea.** Includes consideration of strategic exports to China.

18 July	47th:2	**Flour extraction rate.** CP(50)144. Approval of CP(50)144 subject to the extraction rate of the national loaf not falling below 80%.
20 July	48th:4	**Newsprint.** CP(50)173.
	:7	**Civil Service salaries.** Agreement to introduce new scales postponed following devaluation.
25 July	50th:2	**Defence expenditure.** Agreement for additional expenditure of £100m. When the defence estimates for 1951–52 were considered additional expenditure would be allowed to enable the U.K. to play its full part under the North Atlantic Treaty.
	:4	**Enquiry into taxation of income.** CP(50)176. Agreement to establish a Royal Commission.
27 July	51st:3	**Permanent economic powers.** CP(50)178. Pointed out that despite the Economic Planning and Full Employment Bill's title it was better suited to the prevention of inflation than the maintenance of full employment. From a longer-term point of view the bill's negative character had political disadvantages. Agreement in principle that permanent economic powers should be secured on the lines suggested but that responsible ministers should consider further powers for inclusion in the bill to promote a positive policy of economic planning and full employment. The timing of the bill's introduction would be considered in the autumn.
	:4	**Economic affairs.** CP(50)177. Consideration of coal production and prices. Concern of Cripps at the current situation.
	:5	**Iron and Steel Act.**
1 Aug	52nd:4	**Defence expenditure.** CP(50)181. Proposal of a new defence programme on the basis of an offer of U.S. assistance. Concern of Bevan at the implications for social services. Approval of CP(50)181.
	:5	**Capital investment programme.** CP(50)184 and 187. Approval of CP(50)187.
11 Aug	53rd	**Defence.** CP(50)188 and 190. Consideration of service pay and agreement to extend national service to two years.
16 Aug	54th:3	**Defence expenditure.** Concern of Shinwell at the delay in re-equipment. Gaitskell explained that little could be done until the amount of U.S. financial aid was determined.
	:4	**Defence.** CP(50)191.
	:5	**Essential services.** Consideration of the risk of sabotage at power stations.
4 Sept	55th:3	**Defence.** Consideration of expenditure and U.S. assistance.

to positive powers of economic planning, further consideration of the government's powers to buy, manufacture and sell commodities was possible as the bill was not to be introduced immediately. Agreement that the existing title of the bill should stand.

	:7	**Industrial disputes.**
2 Nov	70th:1	**Defence.** CP(50)246, 247, 248.
	:3	**Permanent economic powers.** Agreement that the bill should not include powers of labour control. If such powers were ever found necessary, they should form separate legislation.
	:4	**Economic affairs.** CP(50)245. Consideration of manpower, production, building, external trade, balance of payments, prices, wages, E.R.P., raw material shortages, increased cost of living and the coal-mining industry.
6 Nov	71st:1	**Housing programme.**
	:6	**Coal.** CP(50)252, 253, 254, 255, 256. Endorsement of CP(50)252. Appointment of an official committee to assist Noel-Baker in securing inter-departmental co-operation to increase output and to keep under review the impact of prospective supplies on the government's economic plans.
9 Nov	72nd:4	**Christmas food bonuses.** CP(50)258. Approval of increased rations.
	:7	**Defence.** CP(50)246, 247, 248.
16 Nov	74th:3	**Christmas food supplies.**
	:4	**Defence.** CP(50)246, 247, 248. Endorsement of CP(50)246 and 247.
	:5	**Coal.** CP(50)271. Consideration of U.S. imports.
17 Nov	75th:3	**Coal.** CP(50)271. Agreement to import from U.S. and reduce bunkering but that no reduction should be made in the commercial use of lighting or any further cut in exports. Discussion of long-term measures to stimulate output.
20 Nov	76th:2	**Coal.** Approval of a statement to the House of Commons on U.S. imports.
23 Nov	77th:1	**Coal.** Approval of the proposals to reduce exports and restrict U.K. sales of coke.
30 Nov	79th:5	**Food.** CP(50)282. Agreement on size of the meat ration.
	:6	**Wool.** CP(50)295. Agreement to increase maximum price of utility blankets.
4 Dec	81st:1	**Index of retail prices.** CP(50)288. Approval for the reconvening of the Cost of Living Advisory Committee.

	:3	**Coal.** CP(50)285, 287, 290, 299. Consideration of U.S. and Polish imports. Approval of a one million ton cut in exports.
	:4	**Coal.** CP(50)286. Priority for electricity power stations on the understanding that the British Electricity Authority would not build up excessive stocks.
	:5	**Coal.** CP(50)297. Agreement to halt miners joining the forces and on a publicity campaign to stimulate recruitment and to prevent wastage. The N.U.M. was to be approached on the employment of Italian workers.
7 Dec	**83rd:4**	**Production of ground-nuts in East Africa.** CP(50)289.
	:5	**Food.** On the purchase of meat from the U.S.A.
	:7	**Coal.** CP(50)296 and 302. Consideration of open-cast working, exports and supplementary pensions.
	:9	**Industrial disputes.**
11 Dec	**84th:1**	**Industrial disputes.** CP(50)304 and 305.
	:7	**European economic co-operation.**
	:8	**Food.** Report on negotiations with Argentina on meat supplies.
	:9	**Parliament.** Arrangements for the debate on coal.
	:10	**Coal.** CP(50)297 and 302. Agreement not to offer the option of serving in the mines for two years in lieu of national service.
12 Dec	**85th:3**	**Prime Minister's visit to Washington.** Report by Attlee.
14 Dec	**86th:2**	**Housing.** CP(50)314.
	:6	**Summer time in 1951.** CP(50)309.
18 Dec	**87th:1**	**Defence.** Discussion of the U.S. appeal for increased defence effort. Agreement that the U.K. should reply that it had already decided to increase and accelerate its programme and that its implementation was under consideration.
	:2	**Economic affairs.** CP(50)315. Consideration of coarse grains, electricity, external trade.
CAB 128/19	2 Jan–9 July 1951	CM(51)1st–50th.
2 Jan	**CM(51)1st:6**	**Industrial disputes.** CP(50)313, 316, 321.
	:7	**Production of ground-nuts in East Africa.** CP(50)324 and 326.
8 Jan	**2nd**	**Coal.** CP(51)3. Discussions of negotiations with the N.U.M. on wages, lower-paid workers, Saturday working, paid holidays, supplementary pensions, Italian workers and management. Agreement on the government's approach to N.C.B.–N.U.M. negotiations.

15 Jan	3rd:3	**Defence.** Discussion about whether Attlee should make a speech on the impact of the accelerated rearmament programme before the details for increasing the programme and their economic consequences had been considered by Cabinet.
	:4	**Industrial disputes.** CP(51)8 and 9.
	:5	**Coal: economy measures.** CP(50)309 and CP(51)7. Consideration of summer time, mid-week sport, broadcasting and supplementary pensions.
	:6	**Open-cast coal-mining.** CP(51)11.
18 Jan	4th:6	**Defence.**
23 Jan	6th:1	**Food.** CP(51)24. Agreement to reduce the meat ration.
25 Jan	7th:4	**Defence.** CP(51)16, 18, 19, 20, 22, 23, 25, 26, 29, 32. Lengthy discussion of the increased defence programme and appreciation by Gaitskell of the economic consequences of the proposed programme and the measures necessary for its implementation.
25 Jan	8th:2	**Defence.** CP(51)16, 18, 19, 20, 22, 23, 25, 26, 29, 32. Consideration of service manpower, production, works' services, civil defence and defence planning of civil departments. Approval of CP(51)16 on the understanding that shortages might cause delays, so no completion date could be made public. Acceptance of the general economic implications of the programme as outlined in CP(51)20.
29 Jan	10th:1	**Defence.** CP(51)34.
1 Feb	11th:3	**Coal.** CP(51)6 and 12. Approval of the scheme in CP(51)6 for the release of underground miners from the forces.
	:4	**Coal.** Approval of increased prices.
8 Feb	12th:2	**Food.** Report by Gaitskell on negotiations with Argentina.
	:3	**Defence.** CP(51)42.
	:6	**Sulphur.** CP(51)39.
12 Feb	13th:4	**Call-up of agricultural workers.** CP(51)49.
	:7	**Industrial disputes.**
15 Feb	14th:3	**Sulphur.**
	:6	**Resale price maintenance.** CP(51)37.
	:8	**Permanent economic powers.** CP(51)52. Agreement that it was no longer appropriate to proceed with the Full Employment Bill.
22 Feb	15th:2	**Economic affairs.** CP(51)54. Consideration of manpower, coal, steel, textiles, building, wages and balance of payments. The Production Committee was to consider steel output in 1951, the raw materials situation and how to

		increase the supply of timber to the building industry.
	:3	**Industrial disputes.**
1 Mar	16th:6	**Defence.** On the call-up of reservists.
12 Mar	19th:4	**Receipts and expenditure of the British Transport Commission.** CP(51)70.
	:7	**Industrial disputes.** CP(51)75.
15 Mar	20th:3	**Receipts and expenditure of the British Transport Commission.**
19 Mar	21st:2	**Farm price review.** CP(51)80.
	:3	**Retail food prices.** CP(51)79. Approval of £107.6m savings from increased prices of subsidized foodstuffs, although the distribution of these increases was to be reviewed.
	:6	**Receipts and expenditure of the British Transport Commission.** CP(51)85.
22 Mar	22nd:1	**Social services expenditure.** Discussion of Gaitskell's proposals to limit this expenditure. Agreement to a ceiling of £400m on the N.H.S. and charges for dentures and spectacles. Approval of increases in pensions and allowances.
	:4	**Integration of French and German coal and steel industries.** CP(51)83. Approval of proposals.
	:8	**Economic Survey for 1951.** CP(51)77. Approval for publication.
	:9	**Farm price review.**
2 Apr	23rd:3	**Defence.** Statement by Gaitskell on mutual aid.
9 Apr	25th:1	**Food.** Agreement on further negotiations with Argentina.
	:2	**The budget.**
	:3	**Social services expenditure.** Discussion in the light of the budget proposals, with disagreement between Gaitskell and Bevan.
9 Apr	26th	**Social services expenditure.** Resumption of discussions. Bevin reported Attlee's views. After lengthy discussion and the objection of Bevan the Cabinet reaffirmed its decisions of 22 March.
12 Apr	27th:2	**Parliament.** Includes consideration of budget legislation.
16 Apr	28th:2	**Integration of French and German coal and steel industries.** CP(51)108. Agreement to enter discussions regarding the conflict between the Schuman Treaty and Allied control of German heavy industry. There was to be a review of the plan's implications for the U.K. coal and steel industries.
19 Apr	29th:5	**National Coal Board.** CP(51)112. Agreement to double the money which the Minister of Fuel and Power could lend to the N.C.B.

	:8	**Food.** Report on the mission to Argentina.
23 Apr	30th:5	**Organization for European Economic Co-operation.** CP(51)101.
	:4	**Economic affairs.** CP(51)113. Consideration of manpower, production, coal, steel, stocks, internal finance, exports and balance of payments.
3 May	33rd:3	**Socialized industries.** CP(51)121.
	:4	**Coal.** CP(51)118.
7 May	34th:2	**Strategic exports to China.**
10 May	35th:4	**Strategic exports to China.**
	:5	**Parliament.** CP(51)125. Approval of the legislative programme for 1951–52.
	:9	**Retail food prices.** CP(51)126.
22 May	36th:1	**Industrial disputes.** CP(51)124.
28 May	37th:6	**Colonial Development Corporation.** CP(51)141.
29 May	38th:3	**Industrial disputes.**
5 June	40th:2	**Integration of French and German coal and steel industries.** CP(51)147 and 152.
	:5	**Resale price maintenance.** CP(51)149.
11 June	42nd:4	**Supplementary pensions for miners.** CP(51)154.
	:5	**International wheat agreement.** CP(51)156.
18 June	44th:2	**Integration of French and German coal and steel industries.** CP(51)164.
21 June	45th:7	**Raw materials.** Agreement to ask the U.S. to enter negotiations on the stabilization of raw material prices.
25 June	46th:3	**Supplementary pensions for miners.** CP(51)171 and 176.
28 June	47th:4	**Economic affairs.** CP(51)174. Consideration of manpower, production, stocks, internal financial situation and external financial situation.
5 July	49th:6	**Defence.** CP(51)182.
9 July	50th:5	**Coal.** CP(51)189 and 194.

CAB 128/20	12 July–27 Sept 1951	CM(51)51st–60th.
19 July	**CM(51)53rd:5**	**Livestock and meat.** CP(51)202.
	:7	**Information policy.** CP(51)179.
23 July	54th:4	**Industrial disputes.** CP(51)221.
	:6	**British Sugar Corporation.** CP(51)211.
26 July	55th:2	**Profit margins of retail grocers.**
	:4	**Industrial disputes.** CP(51)221 and 224.
	:5	**British Railways.** CP(51)215, 219, 223, 226. Agreement that it would be undesirable to defer the call-up for national service of railway workers.
	:7	**Defence.** CP(51)217.
30 July	56th:3	**European defence and European integration schemes.** CP(51)230.

1 Aug	**57th:1**	**Secretary of the Cabinet.** T. Padmore to replace N. Brook.
	:8	**Hotel accommodation.** Consideration of whether a building licence should be granted for a new hotel in central London.
4 Sept	**58th:1**	**Washington and Ottawa meetings.** CP(51)239.
	:4	**Economic affairs.** CP(51)242 and 243. Consideration of balance of payments and end-item aid, with the U.K.'s deteriorating dollar position.
27 Sept	**60th:5**	**Economic affairs.** CP(51)251. Consideration of balance of payments and U.S. and Canadian loans.
	:7	**The King's speech on the prorogation of Parliament.** CP(51)252.
	:9	**Agricultural prices.** CP(51)253.

CAB 128/21   19 Aug 1949–16 July 1951   Meetings with no circulation record.

19 Aug		**Meeting at Chequers on return of Cripps from Zurich on 19 Aug 1949.**
	:1	**Devaluation.** Despite Cripps's doubts, agreement in principle to devalue. The level was to be considered during the Washington discussions.
	:2	**Measures to accompany devaluation.** Cripps felt further measures were necessary but they should not be of the 'orthodox' variety. Agreement to pursue administrative economies with vigour.
	:3	**Defence.**
	:4	**Wages policy.**
6 Nov	**CM(50)71st**	**Imports.** No serious objection to coal imports but no steps to be taken prior to their consideration by an official committee. 'Measures to prevent a fuel crisis during the winter of 1950–51' – Noel-Baker, Nov 1950, attached.
9 Apr	**CM(51)25th:3**	**Social services expenditure.** As in CAB 128/19.
9 Apr	**26th**	**Social services expenditure.** As in CAB 128/19.
12 Apr	**27th:2**	**Parliament.** Includes consideration of the N.H.S. Bill.
19 Apr	**29th:2**	**N.H.S. Bill.** As in CAB 128/19.

2.2   Cabinet Memoranda
1943–July 1945

CAB 66/33   1 Jan–2 Feb 1943   WP(43)1–50.

12 Jan	**WP(43)18**	**Promises about post-war conditions – Churchill,** 2p. Churchill warned against dangerous optimism over post-war economic conditions.

13 Jan	**21**	**Social Security – Lyttleton,** 1p.

CAB 66/34   2 Feb–11 March 1943   WP(43)51–100.

11 Feb   **WP(43)58**   **Interim report of the Committee on Reconstruction Priorities – The Beveridge Plan,** 10p. RP(43)5 and PR(43)8 showed that in the third year after hostilities there would be insufficient finance for all proposed developments and tax remission. Priorities had to be established. Government spokesmen were to make no firm commitments to the Plan, only to indicate general acceptance of the three assumptions.

15 Feb   **65**   **Beveridge Report – Churchill,** 1p. Post-war government should be allowed a free hand, so there should be a minimum of new legislation and financial commitments before an election.

21 Feb   **75**   **White Paper on training for the building industry – Bevin and Portal,** 1+6p. Any increase in the building labour force should be planned in relation to the long-term construction programme. The programme for ten to twelve years ahead required 1.25m men.

CAB 66/35   9 March–9 April 1943   WP(43)101–150.

10 Mar   **WP(43)103**   **Post-war agricultural policy – Jowitt and the agricultural departments,** 2+16p. Also RP(43)2, IEP(43)3 and USE(43)1. Economic stability in the agricultural industry could be achieved either by continuation of wholesale purchase and influence over internal distribution or by guaranteeing prices by subsidies supported by import regulation and levies.

26 Mar   **127**   **Post-war reconstruction : quarterly survey – Jowitt,** 9+1p appendix. Survey of progress in each field of reconstruction.

CAB 66/36   14 Apr–10 May 1943   WP(43)151–200.

13 Apr   **WP(43)152**   **Post-war agricultural policy – Morrison,** 2p. Discussions with agricultural interests would lead to a commitment before policy had been decided: this was inconsistent with the attitude towards the Beveridge Plan. Policy decisions on such issues should be taken before the end of the war.

29 Apr   **181**   **Post-war agricultural policy – Cranborne, Hudson, R., Johnston and Jowitt,** 2p. Continued absence of any official declaration needed explanation to Parliament.

CAB 66/37   13 May–17 June 1943   WP(43)201–250.

27 May   **WP(43)223**   **The intermediate horizon – Amery,** 3p.
Reconstruction would have to begin once
Germany was defeated even if it meant a return
to party politics.

15 June   **241**   **The two-stage ending of the war and
demobilization, military and civil – Jowitt,** 3p.
A committee should be set up to consider the
implications for industrial policy of anticipated
military requirements after Germany's defeat.

Manpower referred to in **WP(43)219 and 221.**

CAB 66/38   18 June–7 July 1943   WP(43)251–300.

26 June   **WP(43)255**   **The need for decisions – Attlee, Bevin and
Morrison,** 2p. Policy decisions had to be taken
to allow reconstruction plans to proceed. To
permit this the government had to make the
best possible estimate of the post-war economic
situation and to work on that basis rather than
wait until the situation was definitely known.

29 June   **280**   **Motion on post-war agricultural policy –
Hudson, R., and Johnston,** 1p.

29 June   **284**   **The two-stage ending of the war and
demobilization, military and civil – Bevin,** 3p.

Manpower referred to in **WP(43)271, 272, 273,
295, 296.**

CAB 66/39   12 July–4 August 1943   WP(43)301–350.

14 July   **WP(43)308**   **The need for decisions – Churchill covering
Wood,** 1+2p. Wood criticized WP(43)255.
Fiscal or financial devices could not by
themselves secure policy objectives. What was
required was a steady advance over a wide
front of government and industrial policy.

16 July   **316**   **Post-war reconstruction : second quarterly
survey – Jowitt,** 1+12p.

20 July   **324**   **The need for decisions – Attlee, Bevin and
Morrison,** 2p. Disagreement with Wood's
earlier criticisms but agreement that much
valuable work for reconstruction had been
carried out recently.

Manpower referred to in **WP(43)319, 326 and
332.**

CAB 66/40   31 July–16 Sept 1943   WP(43)351–400.

2 Sept   **WP(43)388**   **An expansionist economy – Amery,** 5p. Any
internationally-administered monetary system
would be incompatible with national planning.

CAB 66/41   16 Sept–8 Oct 1943   WP(43)401–450.

| 28 Sept | **WP(43)422** | **Post-war agricultural policy – Hudson, R., Johnston and Morrison**, 4p. Requests the opening of discussions with agricultural interests. |

4 Oct   **432**   **Post-war agricultural policy – Woolton**, 2p. In return for postponing discussions of long-term policy, the government should extend existing guarantees of markets and prices until the end of 1947.

7 Oct   **446**   **Examination of the present system of control in the coal-mining industry and future policy – Lloyd George**, 2p.

Manpower referred to in **WP(43)425 and 448.**

CAB 66/42   11 Oct–2 Nov 1943   WP(43)451–500.

11 Oct   **WP(43)451**   **Draft statement by the Minister of Fuel and Power for the coal debate, 12 October 1943 – Anderson**, 2p.

13 Oct   **455**   **Agricultural prices and post-war policy – Hudson, R., and Johnston**, 1+1p appendix. Agreement with Woolton's proposals for continuing the scheme of guaranteed prices and markets.

13 Oct   **458**   **Post-war agricultural policy – Sinclair and Johnstone**, 5p. Suggests omitting the more controversial matters so that discussions with agricultural industries could begin.

20 Oct   **465**   **Reconstruction plans – Cherwell**, 4p. The only internal decisions which had to be taken were those relating to the transitional period. Long-term solutions should be worked out for submission at an election although non-controversial schemes need not be postponed.

19 Oct   **467**   **War : transition : peace – Churchill**, 2p. Statement of the broad principles which should guide the government's approach to post-war problems.

15 Oct   **470**   **Post-war reconstruction : third quarterly survey – Jowitt**, 16p.

24 Oct   **474**   **Post-war agricultural policy – Attlee**, 2p. Draft directive to agricultural ministers for their forthcoming discussions with agricultural interests.

27 Oct   **476**   **Plans for the transition period – Churchill**, 2p. Proposed arrangements for reviewing such plans.

2 Nov   **494**   **Report of the Demobilization Committee**, 17+3p appendixes.

Manpower referred to in **WP(43)454, 464, 472 and 490.**

CAB 66/43   3 Nov–2 Dec 1943   WP(43)501–550.

26 Nov	**WP(43)538**	**Office of the Minister of Reconstruction –** **Churchill,** 1+5p. Functions of the Minister and his office. Attached minutes of confidential meeting at WM(43)161st which discussed draft of WP(43)538 and decided that the Reconstruction Committee should replace the Reconstruction Priorities Committee and the Reconstruction Problems Committee.
30 Nov	**541**	**Reconstruction Committee – composition and terms of reference – E.E. Bridges,** 1p.
29 Nov	**543**	**Report on demobilization – Portal,** 1p.
2 Dec	**548**	**Demobilization of the Army – Grigg,** 3p.

Manpower referred to in **WP(43)511, 531, 534, 535, 539, 545 and 546.**

CAB 66/44   3 Dec–30 Dec 1943   WP(43)551–592.

3 Dec	**WP(43)553**	**Demobilization and resettlement – Bevin,** 6p.
6 Dec	**556**	**Report on demobilization – Willink and Johnston,** 1p.
17 Dec	**559**	**Anglo-American discussion under Article VII –** **Law,** 1+46p. Revise version.
8 Dec	**560**	**Demobilization and the Navy – Alexander,** 3p.
8 Dec	**561**	**Demobilization – Stanley,** 2p.
14 Dec	**564**	**Demobilization – Bevin,** 2p.
14 Dec	**565**	**Demobilization and the building programme –** **Woolton,** 6+1p appendix.
14 Dec	**566**	**Anglo-American discussion under Article VII :** **commercial policy – Hudson, R.,** 2p. Concern that acceptance of international proposals would prejudice domestic policy.
17 Dec	**571**	**Post-war highway policy – Woolton,** 2+1p appendix. Issue of relating major schemes to a long-term programme of public works.
20 Dec	**576**	**Anglo-American discussions under Article VII** **– Amery,** 3p. Agreement with WP(43)566.

Manpower referred to in **WP(43)578.**

CAB 66/45   3 Jan–24 Jan 1944   WP(44)1–50.

13 Jan	**WP(44)23**	**Employment policy – Cherwell,** 1+3+7+2p appendixes. Two minutes prepared for Churchill: 'Employment policy in the transitional period', 26 October 1943, 'Long-term employment policy', 6 January 1944.

20 Jan	**41**	**The international economic history of the inter-war period – Anderson,** 1+32p. Minute by Hubert Henderson.

CAB 66/46 24 Jan–10 Feb 1944 WP(44)51–100.

25 Jan	**WP(44)53**	**Agricultural policy – E.E. Bridges covering Hudson, R.,** 2p. Letter to Churchill calling for extension of pledge about agricultural prices.
31 Jan	**64**	**Anglo-American discussions under Article VII – Anderson covering the Economic Section,** 3p. Rejoinder to last few pages of Henderson's memorandum WP(44)41.
2 Feb	**71**	**Reallocation of manpower during the transition period between the end of the war in Europe and the end of the war in Japan – Bevin,** 1+3p annex.
5 Feb	**75**	**Anglo-American discussions under Article VII – Law,** 13p. Answers queries from ministers not dealt with in the main report; e.g. in relation to the maintenance of the high level of employment. See WP(43)559(revise).
7 Feb	**81**	**The Washington Conversations on Article VII – Law,** 12+13p annexes.
9 Feb	**94**	**Reallocation of manpower during the transition period between the end of the war in Europe and the end of the war in Japan – Morrison,** 2p.
9 Feb	**95**	**Anglo-American discussions under Article VII – Beaverbrook,** 2p.
9 Feb	**97**	**Reallocation of manpower during the transition period between the end of the war in Europe and the end of the war in Japan – Morrison and Johnston,** 2p.
		Manpower referred to in **WP(44)52 and 85.**

CAB 66/47 11 Feb–6 March 1944 WP(44)101–150.

15 Feb	**WP(44)110**	**Housing in the transition period – Woolton,** 3p. Clear that construction of new houses could not exceed 300,000 in Great Britain in the first two years after end of war with Germany.
16 Feb	**115**	**Coal : report by the Committee on the Organization of the Coal Industry,** 7+1p appendix.
18 Feb	**121**	**Discussions under Article VII of the Mutual Aid Agreement – Committee on External Economic Policy,** 3+3p annex. It would be wrong to accept international conventions which limited domestic agricultural policy among other things.
18 Feb	**122**	**Housing in the transitional period – Wolmer,** 1p.

23 Feb	**129**	**The Washington Conversations : an alternative policy** – Amery, 4p. Supports Henderson's memorandum WP(44)41.
6 Mar	**146**	**Wage structure of the coal-mining industry** – **Lloyd George,** 1p. He wanted proposals in LP(44)47 put before representatives of the Mining Association and the Mineworkers' Federation.

CAB 66/48   7 March–13 April 1944   WP(44)151–200.

16 Mar	**WP(44)162**	**Scheme for reallocation of manpower after the end of hostilities in Europe** – Bevin, 2+3p. Draft White Paper.
29 Mar	**173**	**Manpower for the Japanese War** – **Lyttelton,** 2+4p annexes. War mobilization at the end of 1944 should be 60–65% rather than 75%.
5 Apr	**188**	**Factory-made houses** – Churchill, 2p. Need to maintain steady employment in the building of permanent housing over ten years rather than to have a rush followed by a lull.

CAB 66/49   13 April–11 May 1944   WP(44)201–250.

13 Apr	**WP(44)201**	**Economic policy** – Amery, 1p.
13 Apr	**203**	**Commercial policy** – Hudson, R., 2p.
21 Apr	**217**	**Commercial policy** – Dalton, 2p.
22 Apr	**218**	**Livestock and milk prices** – **Hudson, R., Johnston, Morrison and Llewellin,** 3p. Requests guaranteed prices for these goods until summer 1948.
22 Apr	**219**	**Meeting of Dominion prime ministers** – **Cranborne,** 4+2p annexes. Summary of items to be covered in the meetings. Bevin proposed to outline demobilization scheme and certain plans for post-war employment, in particular the preparation of a 'human budget'. He hoped to secure prime ministers' agreement for similar measures in their own countries.
25 Apr	**224**	**Commercial policy** – Amery, 1p.
25 Apr	**226**	**Arrangements for meetings with Dominion prime ministers** – Churchill, 4p.
25 Apr	**227**	**Commercial policy** – Leathers, 1p.
28 Apr	**232**	**Commercial policy** – Lloyd George, 2p. Concerned about the post-war coal export trade.
1 May	**233**	**Building labour allocations for May and June 1944** – Lyttelton, 1+1p annex.
1 May	**245**	**New construction programme, 1944** – **Alexander,** 4+1p annex.

CAB 66/50   11 May–7 June 1944   WP(44)251–300.

16 May	**WP(44)254**	**Post-war employment** – Woolton, 1+26+3p appendix. Draft White Paper on employment

policy, based on R(44)6. It had the unanimous support of the Reconstruction Committee except for varying tax rates to maintain employment.

16 May	256	**Employment policy: publicity for the White Paper – Bracken,** 1p.
20 May	261	**Town and Country Planning Bill – Morrison, W.,** 3+52p. Draft bill attached.
30 May	280	**Temporary embargo on building – Lyttelton,** 1p.
2 June	291	**Employment – Amery,** 2p. The draft White Paper on employment policy was sketchy in its treatment of expenditure outside the country whether through imports or foreign investment. Its principles required detailed regulation of foreign trade.

Manpower referred to in **WP(44)274.**

CAB 66/51	7 June–27 June 1944	WP(44)301–350.
13 June	**WP(44)310**	**Town and Country Planning Bill – Morrison, W.,** 2+66p. Draft bill attached.
10 June	311	**Town and country planning: the control of land use – Woolton,** 2+13p. Draft White Paper attached.
12 June	317	**Town and Country Planning Bill – Wolmer,** 3p.

Manpower referred to in **WP(44)316.**

CAB 66/52	27 June–20 July 1944	WP(44)351–400.
28 June	**WP(44)353**	**Post-war financial commitments – Anderson,** 5p. Consideration of developments since RP(43)5, PR(43)8, 35, 36 and 97. Commitments were such that there was likely to be a budgetary problem in the early post-war years and that it could not be expected to be lightened over time. It was necessary to look at existing prospective commitments and either take the risk of maintaining them or seek some postponements.
1 July	360	**Our overseas resources and liabilities – Anderson,** 4+14p. Recommends appointment of a ministerial committee to consider exports. 'The problem of our external finance in the transition' – J.M. Keynes, is attached.
4 July	362	**Manpower in the first year after the German armistice. Civil requirements – Bevin and Woolton,** 4+1p appendix. Estimate based on departmental returns.
6 July	373	**Manpower one year after the defeat of Germany. Labour required for munitions – Lyttelton,** 2p. The level of assistance from the U.S.A. and

		Canada would determine capacity to be released.
7 July	379	**Supply of manpower one year after the defeat of Germany – Bevin,** 3p. Figures of estimated manpower assuming the European war finished at the end of 1944. A deficiency of 1.75m was estimated.
7 July	380	**Manpower one year after the defeat of Germany – report by the Chiefs of Staff,** 4+12p annexes. Also COS(44)597(O). Estimated that the minimum service manpower, if all commitments were to be met, was about 3.4m.
14 July	381	**Manpower in the first year after the German armistice – Anderson,** 4p. Suggests a line of approach to close the 1.75m gap.
7 July	384	**Disposal of government-owned factories – Woolton,** 2p. Suggests the Distribution of Industry Committee should be responsible for this.
10 July	386	**Reallocation of manpower during the interim period – Bevin,** 1p. The reallocation scheme should now be announced.

Manpower referred to in **WP(44)375.**

CAB 66/53 21 July–17 August 1944 WP(44)401–450.

25 July	**WP(44)410**	**Agricultural manpower in the first year after the German armistice – Hudson, R., and Johnston,** 2p. While not dissenting from WP(44)381, if anything agriculture required more manpower not less.
25 July	411	**Temporary embargo on building and allocation of building labour – Lyttelton,** 2p. The embargo was lifted.
31 July	419	**Supplies from North America in Stage II – Anderson and Lyttelton,** 3+8p appendix + 16p annexes. 'British requirements after the close of the European war' is appended.
3 Aug	431	**Manpower one year after the defeat of Germany – Churchill,** 4p. Draft directive suggesting ways to reduce the 1.75m gap.
12 Aug	442	**Committee on commercial policy scheme – Churchill,** 1p.
17 Aug	448	**Supplies from North America in Stage II – Anderson and Lyttelton,** 1+9p appendix + 15p annexes. Revision of WP(44)419.

Manpower referred to in **WP(44)423 and 440.**

CAB 66/54 18 August–5 September 1944 WP(44)451–500.

18 Aug	452	**Manpower one year after the defeat of Germany: decisions required from His Majesty's**

		Government – Chiefs of Staff, 4p. A number of decisions had to be made by government before they could make any firm plan of service requirements.
25 Aug	470	**Reallocation of manpower during the interim period – Bevin,** 1p. Concerned at the postponement of publication.
30 Aug	481	**Reallocation of manpower between the forces and civilian employment during the interim period between the defeat of Germany and the defeat of Japan – Bevin,** 1+3p annex. Draft White Paper attached.
31 Aug	482	**The wartime departments – Anderson,** 8p. Report from the ministerial Committee on the Machinery of Government.
		Manpower referred to in **WP(44)453, 463, 465, 467, 471, 487 and 488.**

CAB 66/55 6 September–2 October 1944 WP(44)501–550.

8 Sept	WP(44)509	**Reallocation of manpower between civilian employments during the interim period between the defeat of Germany and the defeat of Japan – Bevin,** 1+7p. Draft White Paper attached.
14 Sept	517	**Munitions production: effects of assumption that the German war ends by 31 December 1944 – Lyttelton,** 2+1p appendix.
14 Sept	518	**Programme reduction procedure – Attlee,** 1+2p annex. Annex by Lyttelton, setting out current procedure.
19 Sept	531	**Town and Country Planning Bill – Morrison, W.,** 1p. Draft statement for Anderson.
28 Sept	545	**Release of capacity from war production – Lyttelton,** 1+2p annex. Draft statement attached.
27 Sept	547	**Town and Country Planning Bill: 1939 standard (clauses 45 and 46) – Morrison, W.,** 3p.

CAB 66/56 3 October–27 October 1944 WP(44)551–600.

5 Oct	WP(44)557	**The Town and Country Planning Bill: 1939 standard – Cripps,** 1p.
10 Oct	563	**Reallocation of manpower between civilian employments during the interim period between the defeat of Germany and the defeat of Japan – Bevin,** 2+7p. Draft White Paper attached, as amended after discussions.
11 Oct	566	**Town and Country Planning Bill, clauses 45 and 46 – Morrison, W.,** 2p.
14 Oct	572	**The aircraft programme – Cripps,** 3+1p appendix.

14 Oct	573	**Release of capacity from munitions production – Lyttelton,** 1+2p. Draft letter to P. Reed of the Mission for Economic Affairs in London.
16 Oct	574	**Publication of statistics about the war effort of the U.K. – Anderson,** 2+2p appendix + 58p. Proof of the revised White Paper attached, covering manpower, home production, shipping and foreign trade, civilian consumption and finance.
18 Oct	575	**The post-war army – Grigg,** 2p.
20 Oct	584	**Two-day shift working in factory employment – Bevin,** 2+1p annex. Need for examination by authoritative committee if industrial disturbance was to be avoided.
23 Oct	586	**Supplies from North America in Stage II – Anderson and Lyttelton,** 1+25+25p annexes. Statement on British requirements from the U.S. for the first year of Stage II, prepared by British negotiators in Washington, is attached.
27 Oct	597	**Release of capacity from munitions production – Lyttelton,** 1+1p annex. Letter to P. Reed, dated 25 October 1944, is attached.
30 Oct	598	**Recruitment to the Civil Service during the reconstruction period – Anderson,** 2+2p annexes + 16p. Draft White Paper attached.
27 Oct	599	**Publication of statistics about the war effort of the U.K. – Anderson,** 1p.
		Manpower referred to in **WP(44)596.**

CAB 66/57   27 October–15 November 1944   WP(44)601–650.

31 Oct	WP(44)602	**Resettlement of men released from the armed forces – Bevin,** 3p.
31 Oct	604	**Economic controls in the transition period – Woolton,** 1+2p appendix. Draft statement, to precede publication of the White Paper on manpower reallocation, is attached.
29 Oct	605	**Reallocation of manpower between civilian employments during the interim period between the defeat of Germany and the defeat of Japan – Sinclair,** 2p. Concerned about the effect of the release of proposals on his department.
3 Nov	620	**Controls in the transition – Churchill,** 2p. As this was a matter which affected general policy, Churchill felt that he should himself answer the arranged parliamentary question. He hoped the War Cabinet would agree to this suggestion instead of the statement approved the day before.
6 Nov	623	**Controls in the transition – Churchill,** 2p. New draft statement which considers the period up

		to the end of the Japanese war or to three years after the European war, whichever came first.
6 Nov	626	**Recruitment to the Civil Service during the reconstruction period – Anderson**, 2+2p annex. Revised preface to the White Paper.
9 Nov	633	**Permanent houses: commencement of building programme – Woolton**, 1p. A specific date should be announced.
11 Nov	635	**The King's speeches on the forthcoming prorogation and opening of Parliament – Attlee**, 1+5p. Dalton wanted to add references to the balanced distribution of industry and the investigation and control of restrictive practices to the list already approved. Drafts of the two speeches are attached.
10 Nov	640	**Legislation on balanced distribution of industry – Dalton**, 2p. Suggested powers to be included in the bill.

CAB 66/58   15 November–22 November 1944   WP(44)651–700.

15 Nov	**WP(44)652**	**Distribution of industry – Beaverbrook and Bracken**, 1p. WP(44)640 gave an unjustified interpretation of the White Paper on employment policy.
16 Nov	658	**Wages regulation: legislation to meet post-war conditions – Bevin**, 2+2p annex. Proposals as agreed by the Reconstruction Committee, although the British Employers' Confederation did not agree to one proposal.
16 Nov	661	**Commercial policy – Anderson**, 4+4p annexes. The agricultural departments felt price stability was crucial to the future of agriculture, even if that involved some degree of protection.
20 Nov	663	**The King's speeches on the forthcoming prorogation and opening of Parliament – Attlee**, 1+5p. Revised draft speeches attached.
21 Nov	668	**Post-war finance for industry – Anderson**, 2+5p annex. Brief description of the Governor of the Bank of England's proposals for banks for small businesses and industrial reorganization. The annex is Appendix A to R(44)6.
21 Nov	673	**Reallocation of manpower between the forces and civilian employment during any interim period between the defeat of Germany and the defeat of Japan – Bevin**, 2p.
23 Nov	679	**The King's speeches on the forthcoming prorogation and opening of Parliament – E.E. Bridges**, 1+5p. Fresh drafts of the speeches.
24 Nov	688	**Reallocation of manpower between the forces and civilian employment during any interim**

period between the defeat of Germany and the
defeat of Japan – **Morrison**, 2p.

CAB 66/59   29 November–19 December 1944   WP(44)701–750.

20 Dec	**WP(44)713**	**Organization of supply – Anderson**, 4p. Report from the ministerial Committee on the Machinery of Government.
7 Dec	**716**	**Legislative programme: 1944–45 session –** **Attlee**, 1+5p annex.
8 Dec	**718**	**Manpower – Bevin**, 6+33p appendixes. It was necessary to re-examine manpower in 1945 on the assumption that the European war would not now end until the middle of the year. Appendixes include the estimated requirements for 1945 if the European war ended by 31 Dec 1944, and a survey of manpower between mid-1939 and mid-1944.
14 Dec	**731**	**11th Report of the Select Committee on National Expenditure – Attlee**, 1p. Reports the conclusions of the Lord President's Committee on LP(44)200.
14 Dec	**732**	**The future of the Ministry of Fuel and Power – Lloyd George**, 2p.
18 Dec	**748**	**Manpower – Cripps**, 1p. WP(44)718 made no mention of the conditional nature of the estimates with regard to the aircraft industry. It was unwise to assume releases greater than in WP(44)572.

Manpower referred to in **WP(44)705, 724, 728 and 729.**

CAB 66/60   19 December 1944–22 January 1945   WP(44)751–769 and
WP(45)1–45.

3 Jan	**WP(45)2**	**Strategic aspects of industrial location – report by the Distribution of Industry Committee**, 2p. Also DI(45)1. Four propositions put forward.
15 Jan	**30**	**U.K. stock position – Attlee**, 1p.
15 Jan	**32**	**The aircraft programme – Sinclair and Cripps**, 2+1p appendix.
12 Jan	**34**	**The assumed date of the end of the war with Germany – Lyttelton**, 2p. It was now necessary to review whether the date should be put back to the end of the year.
17 Jan	**36**	**Post-war contribution of British agriculture to the saving of foreign exchange – Hudson, R., and Llewellin**, 4+3p appendix. Savings in expenditure on imported food which might be achieved by increased home output.

Manpower referred to in **WP(44)751, 755 and 767.**

CAB 66/61   22 Jan–13 Feb 1945   WP(45)46–95.

22 Jan	**WP(45)51**	**Minimum stock of principal imported foods –** Llewellin, 2+10p.
25 Jan	**52**	**The coal position – Lloyd George,** 1+1p. Possible shortage meant that allocations might have to be re-programmed.
25 Jan	**60**	**Raw material imports Jan–June 1945 –** Lyttelton, 2+4p annexes.
24 Jan	**64**	**Combined review of cargo shipping resources – Chiefs of Staff,** 2p.
30 Jan	**69**	**Eleventh report of the Shipping Committee – the Committee,** 3+2p appendix.
30 Jan	**72**	**Negotiations with Sweden: coal – Lloyd George,** 1p.
2 Feb	**77**	**The Washington negotiations on Lend-Lease in the first year of Stage II: report on the deliberations of the Joint Committee appointed by the President and the Prime Minister at the Quebec Conference – J.M. Keynes and R. Sinclair,** 1+12p.
2 Feb	**78**	**Distribution of Industry Bill – Dalton,** 1+1p annex +13p. Draft bill attached.
2 Feb	**79**	**Reallocation of manpower between the forces and civilian employment during any interim period between the defeat of Germany and the defeat of Japan – Bevin,** 1+1p annex. Report by an inter-departmental committee attached.
5 Feb	**80**	**Future of the coal-mining industry – Attlee,** 1p.
12 Feb	**87**	**Manpower in the first half of 1945 – Anderson,** 2p. Recommends that Cabinet should reconsider the whole question.
10 Feb	**90**	**Building labour allocation Jan–Mar 1945 –** Lyttelton, 2+4p appendix.
13 Feb	**95**	**Coal supplies for operational requirements after 30 April 1945 – Lloyd George,** 1p.

CAB 66/62   24 Feb–7 Mar 1945   WP(45)96–145.

24 Feb	**WP(45)96**	**Commercial policy: article VII – Anderson,** 1+7p. Summary report by U.K. officials attached.
24 Feb	**97**	**Commercial policy: article VII – Anderson,** 1+16p annexes. Detailed report.
28 Feb	**109**	**World food supplies – Llewellin,** 2+5p annex. Given the situation it was important that U.K. production rose.
26 Feb	**117**	**Manpower – Churchill,** 2p. Restatement of priorities in the allocation of manpower.
2 Mar	**130**	**World food supplies – Llewellin,** 1p.
7 Mar	**142**	**Commercial policy: views of the Canadian government – E.E. Bridges,** 1+5p annexes.

6 Mar   144   **Labour for the cotton-spinning industry –
                                Lyttelton,** 2p.

7 Mar   145   **U.K. stock levels – Leathers,** 1p.

CAB 66/63   7 Mar–28 Mar 1945   WP(45)146–200.

8 Mar   WP(45)152   **Commercial policy – Churchill,** 1+1p.

12 Mar   158   **Food supplies – Llewellin,** 2p. The food supply
                                situation had deteriorated since WP(45)109
                                and 130.

14 Mar   161   **Housing debate – Woolton,** 1+7p annex. Sets
                                out present state of government organization
                                and intentions.

17 Mar   167   **Commercial policy: views of the Canadian
                                government – Hudson,** 2p.

16 Mar   169   **Anglo-French financial agreement – Anderson,**
                                1p.

19 Mar   176   **Output and labour in the hard coal-mining
                                industry in Greater Germany and the U.K. –
                                Lloyd George,** 3p. Comparison from captured
                                figures.

23 Mar   188   **Output and labour in the hard coal-mining
                                industry in Greater Germany and the U.K. –
                                Wolmer,** 1p.

23 Mar   190   **Coal – Attlee,** 2p. The Lord President's
                                Committee drew Cabinet's attention to the fact
                                that, unless manpower was increased, there was
                                a grave danger of a breakdown of supplies
                                during the forthcoming winter. The early
                                release of miners from the forces was needed.

CAB 66/64   29 Mar–14 Apr 1945   WP(45)201–250.

31 Mar   WP(45)207   **Manpower allocations for the first half of 1945 –
                                Anderson,** 1+2p appendix.

31 Mar   211   **Control of Employment (Civil Servants)
                                Order – Anderson,** 2p.

6 Apr   222   **The legal basis of economic control in the
                                transition period – Morrison,** 2+1p appendix
                                +7p. Draft bill attached. The bill had been
                                prepared as a temporary measure under the
                                direction of the Reconstruction Committee
                                because the purpose of wartime and post-war
                                controls would differ. Renewal would be easier
                                if defence powers were separated from
                                economic powers.

6 Apr   223   **Government building programme. Building
                                labour allocation: April–June 1945 – Lyttelton,**
                                1+2p appendix.

7 Apr   224   **British exports, German industry and
                                reparations – Cherwell,** 5p. Increased exports
                                being more important than reparations, the

		restoration of German industry should be discouraged.
10 Apr	232	**Manpower in the first half of 1945 – Anderson,** 1+2p appendix.
13 Apr	237	**Control of Employment (Civil Servants) Order – Lloyd George,** 1p. The freezing order was leading to increased inefficiency.
14 Apr	250	**Manpower in 1945 – Churchill,** 2p. On the date of the end of the war with Germany and the planning of labour allocations.

CAB 66/65 18 Apr–24 May 1945 WP(45)251–324.

16 Apr	WP(45)252	**Pork, bacon and eggs – Churchill covering Hudson, Leathers and Mabane,** 1+2p. Proposed increase of domestic production.
17 Apr	257	**Release of miners from the armed forces – Bevin,** 2p.
19 Apr	262	**Release of miners from the armed forces: effect on supplies – Lloyd George,** 1p. Adoption of the proposals in WP(45)257 would still leave a 4m ton deficit in the coal budget. Consumption must be reduced.
20 Apr	266	**Production agreements, bulk orders and erection of houses – Sandys,** 1+1p.
24 Apr	268	**British exports, German industry and reparations – Alexander,** 1p. Agreement with WP(45)224.
28 Apr	276	**Registration of building workers – Bevin,** 1p.
10 May	291	**Report of mission to the U.S.A. – Lyttelton and Llewellin,** 1+3+6p annexes. Report of the mission on food supplies.
10 May	292	**Employment of German prisoners of war outside Germany after the cessation of hostilities in Europe – Grigg,** 2+2p.
11 May	294	**Purchase and sale of housing components and houses by the Ministry of Works – Anderson,** 2p.
7 May	297	**Army manpower programme of releases to 30 June 1946 and new requirements to 31 Dec 1945 – Grigg,** 1+6p annex.
12 May	298	**Publication of statistics on the shortage of food – Hudson,** 2p. Recommends publication of the prospective deficiencies in 1945.
15 May	301	**Overseas financial policy in Stage III – Anderson covering J.M. Keynes,** 1+18p.
15 May	302	**Notes on some discussions in the U.S. – Lyttelton,** 2p. Covering coal, textiles, trucks, finance of relief.
17 May	304	**Employment of German prisoners in agriculture – Hudson,** 2p. The only way to reduce the manpower deficit.

16 May		307	**Navy's manpower requirements for the period 1 June to 31 Dec 1945** – Alexander, 4p.
16 May		308	**Future of British coal-mining** – Lloyd George, 1+1p annex.
16 May		309	**Employment of German prisoners of war outside Germany after the cessation of hostilities in Europe** – Wolmer, 1p.
18 May		314	**Release and reconversion of fishing trawlers** – Alexander, 3p.
19 May		316	**Publication of further statistics on the U.K. war effort** – Bracken, 2p.
23 May		321	**R.A.F. manpower: June–Dec 1945** – Sinclair, A., 4p.

CAB 66/66   28 May–25 June 1945   CP(45)1–50.

1 June		**CP(45)8**	**Future organization of coal-mining industry** – Lloyd George, 1+1p annex.
1 June		9	**Labour shortages in building materials industries** – Sandys, 1p. There was a desperate shortage of labour to be rectified in order to produce sufficient materials to provide full employment to returning builders.
4 June		12	**Food and agriculture** – Churchill, 2p.
11 June		29	**U.K. meat position and needs of liberated territories** – Llewellin, 2p.
14 June		35	**Coal situation in N.W. Europe** – Lyttelton, 1+5p. Report of the Potter-Hyndley mission attached.
20 June		43	**Street lighting** – Lloyd George, 1p.

CAB 66/67   28 June–8 Aug 1945   CP(45)51–100.

29 June		**CP(45)53**	**Manpower in the second half of 1945** – Anderson, 5+3p annex +1p appendix. Annex also MP(45)12. Proposals to remedy predicted shortage.
20 June		54	**The new construction programme 1945** – Bracken, 3+2p appendix.
3 July		58	**Programme for July 1945** – Churchill, 2+1p appendix. List of subjects on which he wished to see significant progress.
3 July		59	**Standing ministerial committees of the Cabinet** – Churchill, 1+7p annex. List with terms of reference and composition.
5 July		60	**Coal: additional bunkering requirements** – Lloyd George, 2p.
3 July		61	**Manpower** – Churchill, 1p. Recommends approval of Manpower Committee proposal to increase releases from the Services.
5 July		62	**Manpower** – Churchill, 1p. On the release of women.

7 July	66	**Coal: additional bunkering requirements –** **Leathers,** 2p.
11 July	72	**Manpower in the second half of 1945 –** **Anderson,** 3p. Recommends the acceleration of releases.
11 July	75	**Redistribution of manpower in the second half of 1945 – Macmillan,** 1p.
16 July	81	**Cropping directions and prices of certain agricultural commodities for 1946 harvest –** **Hudson,** 2p.
19 July	85	**Coal: increased bunkering requirements –** **Lyttelton,** 1+8p annexes. Survey of the general coal position by an unofficial working party, arising from CP(45)60 and 66, annexed.
3 Aug	92	**The cotton industry – Cripps,** 2p. Proposed programme to man-up spinning sector, and the longer-term programme for the industry's reorganization.
4 Aug	94	**King's speech on the opening of Parliament –** **Morrison,** 2+2p annex. Draft attached.
8 Aug	96	**Manpower review, 1 June to 31 Dec 1945 –** **Bevin,** 3+2p appendix.
8 Aug	98	**The King's speech on the opening of Parliament – Morrison,** 1+2p. Revised draft.

Aug 1945–Oct 1951

CAB 129/1 8 Aug–5 Sept 1945 CP(45)101–150.

10 Aug	CP(45)105	**The cancellation of war orders – Wilmot,** 2p.
13 Aug	110	**Standing ministerial committees of the Cabinet – Attlee,** 7p. Sets out the terms of reference and membership of the main committees.
14 Aug	111	**Supplies and Services (Transitional Powers) Bill – Chuter Ede,** 1+6p. Draft bill. To allow more time to draft permanent legislation, there were changes to the Coalition Bill concerning exchange control and control over prices and capital issues.
15 Aug	112	**Our overseas financial prospects – Dalton covering J.M. Keynes,** 1+6p annex. Famous memorandum in which Keynes describes Britain's economic position as 'a financial Dunkirk'.
15 Aug	113	**Manpower – Bevin,** 2+3p annex. Recommendations of the Manpower Committee in the light of the Japanese surrender.

15 Aug	**114**	**Manpower in the munitions industries – Cripps,** 2p. Review in light of Japanese surrender.
16 Aug	**116**	**Article VII of the Mutual Aid Agreement: commercial policy – Cripps,** 4p.
16 Aug	**117**	**Raising the school leaving age – Wilkinson,** 1p.
16 Aug	**118**	**Ministerial responsibilities for housing – Attlee,** 2p.
16 Aug	**119**	**Raising of the school leaving age – Westwood,** 1p.
27 Aug	**128**	**Accommodation for prisoners of war – Tomlinson,** 1p. The large scale use of German prisoners for labouring work was jeopardized by accommodation difficulties.
29 Aug	**135**	**Shipping and shipping policy – Barnes,** 4p.
3 Sept	**141**	**Manpower – Bevin,** 1+3p annex +2p appendix. On demobilization.
1 Sept	**142**	**The government plan for encouraging industrial organization and efficiency – Cripps,** 2p. Revision of LP(45)152. The role of the government and the Board of Trade in particular was actively to ensure that private British industry quickly reached and maintained full efficiency. Sets out the plan for the investigation by joint working parties of important export industries. A permanent advisory body was ultimately proposed for each industry.

CAB 129/2   6 Sept–1 Oct 1945   CP(45)151–200.

6 Sept	**CP(45)153**	**Ministerial Oil Committee: membership and terms of reference – E.E. Bridges,** 1p. Also MOC(45)1.
8 Sept	**161**	**Provisional requirements for the post-war armed forces – Alexander, Stansgate and Lawson,** 2+3p annex.
10 Sept	**167**	**Bank of England Bill – Dalton,** 2+4p annex. Draft bill and explanatory memorandum.
14 Sept	**170**	**Naval manpower requirements in June 1946 and programme of releases to that date – Alexander,** 3+1p appendix.
15 Sept	**172**	**The employment of German and Italian prisoners of war in Great Britain – Isaacs,** 6+2p annexes.
18 Sept	**175**	**Army releases and manpower in 1946 – Nathan,** 1+6+3p appendix.
18 Sept	**176**	**R.A.F. manpower: June 1945–30 June 1946 – Stansgate,** 4p.
20 Sept	**177**	**The future of the Ministry of Supply – Nathan,** 2p.
18 Sept	**178**	**The functions of the Ministry of Supply and of aircraft production – Attlee,** 1+3p annexes.

19 Sept	180	**Article VII of the Mutual Aid Agreement: commercial policy – Smith**, 3p.
18 Sept	181	**Organization of government supply – Stansgate**, 2p.
20 Sept	183	**Selling price of houses – Bevan**, 2p. Against the introduction of legislation to control prices.
20 Sept	184	**Ministerial responsibilities for housing – Attlee**, 2p. Arrangements as altered since CP(45)118.
20 Sept	185	**Production and distribution of building materials and components – Attlee**, 3p. Allocation of responsibility.
21 Sept	187	**Manpower in the Civil Service – Attlee**, 1p.
22 Sept	188	**Demobilization – E.E. Bridges covering Lawson**, 1p.
27 Sept	191	**Releases from the forces and supply department work – Bevin**, 3p. Report of the Manpower Committee.
27 Sept	193	**Manpower requirements for agriculture and fisheries in 1946 – Williams**, 4p. Concern at the possibility of a labour shortage.
26 Sept	194	**Anglo-American oil agreement – Shinwell**, 1+3p appendixes.
28 Sept	197	**Future of the Ministry of Supply – Chiefs of Staff**, 2p.

CAB 129/3   1 Oct–26 Oct 1945   CP(45)201–250.

1 Oct	CP(45)201	**Expiry of the Emergency Powers (Defence) Acts – Chuter Ede**, 3+15p. On the amendment to the Supplies and Services (Transitional Powers) Bill and draft of the Emergency Laws (Transitional Provisions) Bill.
6 Oct	208	**Housing – Bevan**, 4p. Proposed general policy statement.
6 Oct	212	**International Labour Conference, Paris, Oct 1945 – Isaacs**, 3p. Sets out subjects on the agenda, including the maintenance of a high level of employment during conversion.
11 Oct	217	**Future of electricity and gas industries – Shinwell**, 1p. It was time the government's intentions on nationalization were announced.
12 Oct	223	**Statistical reports – Attlee**, 2p. Sets out arrangements whereby ministers were to be kept informed of the economic situation by statistical reports. Monthly reports on particular subjects were to go to the responsible ministerial committee, in most cases the Lord President's Committee.
13 Oct	224	**Housing – Bevan**, 5p. Outline of general policy statement.
13 Oct	225	**Labour shortages in building material and component industries – Bevan and Buchanan**, 2p. The situation was deteriorating.

13 Oct	226	**Temporary housing – Tomlinson,** 1+7p. Draft White Paper.
13 Oct	228	**The employment situation – Isaacs,** 4p. Report on the general labour shortage and the development of local pockets of unemployment.
15 Oct	229	**Statement of housing progress – Bevan,** 1p.
15 Oct	230	**Labour shortages in building material and component industries – Isaacs,** 3p. Comments on CP(45)225.
20 Oct	236	**Government controls and food policy – Smith,** 1+1p. Recommends acceptance of LP(45)196 as a statement of the government's long-term food policy and the continuance of a separate Ministry of Food.
20 Oct	239	**The coal position in the coming winter – Shinwell,** 2+1p appendix. Review of the position and of action taken.
25 Oct	248	**Dock strike – Barnes,** 2p.

CAB 129/4	26 Oct–26 Nov 1945	CP(45)251–300.

30 Oct	**CP(45)260**	**Labour controls – Morrison covering the Official Committee on Labour Controls,** 2+9p. Brought to Cabinet on the failure of the Lord President's Committee Industrial Subcommittee to agree on the question of the direction of labour and the control of engagement.
5 Nov	267	**Release of doctors from the armed forces – Chuter Ede and Shawcross,** 4p.
6 Nov	269	**Commercial policy – Cripps,** 2+3p annexes.
6 Nov	270	**Washington financial talks – Dalton,** 2p. On the proposals to be put to the U.S.
7 Nov	271	**The place of the Department of Overseas Trade in the machinery of government – Bevin and Cripps,** 2p. Proposed cutting of link with Foreign Office.
8 Nov	273	**Agricultural policy – Williams, Westwood and Chuter Ede,** 1+3p. Draft announcement of principles.
8 Nov	274	**Progress report on housing, Oct 1945 – Bevan,** 3+2p.
8 Nov	276	**Effects of the dock strike – Barnes,** 1+1p annex.
12 Nov	277	**Public announcement about nationalization proposals – Morrison,** 2+3p.
15 Nov	285	**Release of doctors from the forces – Morrison,** 1+1p annex.
16 Nov	288	**Labour controls – Isaacs,** 2p. Proposed changes following examination following CM(45)48th.
20 Nov	289	**Investment (Controls and Guarantees) Bill – Dalton,** 1+6+2p. Draft bill which was to form

		a vital part of the mechanism for regulating and if need be stimulating investment by means of the Capital Issues Committee and the National Investment Council.
22 Nov	291	**New construction (revised) programme 1945 – Alexander,** 3p.
22 Nov	295	**Commercial policy – Addison,** 2+3p appendixes.
24 Nov	297	**Commercial policy – Cripps,** 2+19p annexes. Draft statement and summary of U.S. proposals for International Trade Organization.
23 Nov	299	**Shipping policy – Barnes,** 7p.

CAB 129/5 24 Nov–31 Dec 1945 CP(45)301–355.

26 Nov	CP(45)305	**The employment of German and Italian prisoners of war in Great Britain – Isaacs,** 5+1p annexes.
4 Dec	306	**Cabinet and committee procedure – Attlee,** 2p. Procedure now that the emphasis was shifting to the detailed preparation and execution of policy.
28 Nov	309	**Tourist Accommodation Committee – E.E. Bridges,** 1p.
28 Nov	311	**Report by the Manpower Committee on releases from the forces – Bevin,** 2p. Sets out changes to alleviate manpower shortages in essential industries.
28 Nov	312	**Washington financial talks – Dalton,** 1+3p. Draft financial agreement.
29 Nov	314	**Labour controls – Bevin and Isaacs,** 2p. Recommends relaxation of controls over direction and engagement but the continuation of the Essential Works Order in some industries.
30 Nov	316	**Government publicity services – Attlee covering various ministers,** 1+18p. On the continuation of the Ministry of Information.
30 Nov	317	**Call-up of men from the building and building materials industry – Buchanan,** 2p.
30 Nov	319	**Bretton Woods Agreement Bill – Dalton,** 1+10p. Draft bill.
30 Nov	320	**Releases from the forces – Bevan,** 2p.
1 Dec	321	**Releases from the forces – Tomlinson,** 1p.
2 Dec	322	**Publicity arrangements for the Washington talks – N. Brook covering the Treasury,** 1+2p.
4 Dec	324	**Shipping policy – Barnes,** 5+1p annex. Follow-up to CP(45)299.
4 Dec	325	**Shipping policy – Alexander,** 1+4p annexes.
8 Dec	329	**Bill for nationalization of coal-mining industry – Shinwell,** 3+40p. Draft bill attached.

6 Dec	330	**Progress report on housing: Nov 1945 – Bevan,** 3+4p.
7 Dec	333	**Standing ministerial committees of the Cabinet – Attlee,** 3p. Sets out the membership and terms of reference of the main committees.
8 Dec	334	**Release of doctors from the Royal Navy – Alexander,** 2p.
10 Dec	337	**Bill for the nationalization of the coal-mining industry – Shinwell,** 1+3p.
11 Dec	338	**U.N. Food and Agriculture Conference, Quebec – Bevin covering Noel-Baker,** 1+2+2p appendixes. Report of the conference.
17 Oct	340	**Committee on External Economic Policy and Overseas Trade – E.E. Bridges,** 1p.
27 Dec	348	**World wheat supplies – Smith,** 3+4p appendixes.
27 Dec	349	**Coal-mining industry: the N.U.M. – Shinwell,** 2p. Sets out the N.U.M. attitude to increased production and recruitment.

CAB 129/6   1 Jan–11 Feb 1946   CP(46)1–50.

1 Jan	**CP(46)1**	**Committee on Socialization of Industries – E.E. Bridges,** 1p.
7 Jan	5	**London gas supplies – Shinwell,** 2p. Difficulties caused by manpower shortages.
15 Jan	14	**National insurance scheme: limitation of unemployment benefit – Griffiths,** 2p.
18 Jan	16	**Progress report on housing: Dec 1945 – Bevan,** 5+17p annexes.
21 Jan	20	**Working of open-cast coal in Wentworth Woodhouse Park – Dalton,** 1+8p appendixes. Issue on which the Lord President's Committee had failed to agree.
25 Jan	23	**Monthly digest of statistics – Morrison,** 2+103p. Proofs of the first volume in the series.
28 Jan	26	**Effect upon the U.K. wheat-flour position of the agreed reduction in shipments to this country during the six months ending 30 June 1946 – Smith,** 7+4p appendixes. Review of the situation and measures to secure reduction.
28 Jan	27	**Shipping requirements for the U.K. food import programme – Smith,** 2p.
28 Jan	29	**Agricultural minimum wage – Williams,** 1+5p. Also LP(46)15.
30 Jan	31	**Home production of wheat and animal feedingstuffs rations in 1946 – Williams and Westwood,** 3p.
30 Jan	32	**Economic Survey for 1946 – Morrison covering Bridges and the Economic Survey Working Party,** 3+2p annex +12+20p appendixes. The survey indicated broadly the claims on the

national resources by departmental programmes and the extent to which they exceeded the aggregate resources available. As it dealt only with 1946 it was not the basis of a long-term plan. The Lord President's Committee Industrial Subcommittee agreed with the Official Steering Committee on Economic Development that it was impossible to maintain the existing defence machine and simultaneously reconvert industry to peace production at the required speed. Attached comments of the Official Steering Committee on the general picture, the release of manpower, the balance of payments, personal consumption and savings, measures to make best use of the civilian labour force, private capital investment and future procedure. Attached survey, based on the summary tables for manpower, balance of payments and national income and expenditure, setting out the background to planning.

1 Feb	35	**Report by the Manpower Committee on the manpower position during 1946 – Bevin,** 4+1p annex. Interim report to assist consideration of CP(46)32. The measures to increase manpower, ensure its better distribution and improve productivity would not wholly close the manpower gap.
31 Jan	36	**The prospects of dry cargo shipping tonnage for 1946 – Barnes,** 4p.
5 Feb	40	**Economic Survey for 1946 – Morrison covering C.S.O. and Economic Section,** 1+1p annex. Analysis of the impact of service cuts proposed in CP(46)35.
4 Feb	41	**Timber for housing – Cripps,** 2+1p appendix. Review of the supply and demand situation of soft wood.
4 Feb	42	**Our foreign shipping relations in the next few months – Barnes,** 3+3p annex.
6 Feb	47	**Timber for housing and for the mines – Westwood and Williams,** 1p. Comments on CP(46)41.
11 Feb	50	**Progress report on housing: Jan 1946 – Bevan,** 3+8p annexes +20p. Draft White Paper housing return for England and Wales.

CAB 129/7   7 Feb–12 Mar 1946   CP(46)51–100.

8 Feb	CP(46)53	**Balance of payments for 1946 – Dalton covering the Balance of Payments Working Party,** 1+6p annex +4p appendixes. Sets out departmental import programmes for 1946 and reviews the

whole balance of payments situation. Dalton recommended the reduction of overseas military expenditure.

8 Feb		**55**	**The clothing ration – Cripps,** 3+1p annex.
8 Feb		**58**	**The overseas deficit – Dalton covering J.M. Keynes,** 1+5p annex. Sets out the situation and policy implications. Keynes was concerned about political and military expenditure overseas and recommended some reduction.
13 Feb		**61**	**Organization of government supply – E.E. Bridges,** 2p. Detailed arrangements following CM(45)37th.
15 Feb		**64**	**Shipbuilding industry – Alexander and Barnes,** 2+3p annex. Note arising out of LP(46)7 and its consideration at LP(46)4th:5.
15 Feb		**65**	**Defence policy in 1946 – Attlee,** 3+9p annex. Includes draft statement relating to defence and service estimates for 1946–47.
14 Feb		**66**	**The accommodation of students and tourists from the U.S. during 1946 – Marquand,** 1+3p appendix.
20 Feb		**71**	**Foreign Labour Committee – E.E. Bridges,** 1p. Also FLC(46)1.
21 Feb		**77**	**Visit to Canada and the U.S., Jan 1946 – Morrison,** 7p.
23 Feb		**78**	**Policy towards Japanese industry – Bevin,** 5p.
22 Feb		**79**	**Policy towards Japanese shipbuilding industry – Bevin,** 2p.
27 Feb		**80**	**World food supplies. Proposed mission to N. America – Morrison,** 2p.
1 Mar		**90**	**Proposed political discussions with U.S. and Canadian governments – Morrison,** 3p. On U.K. and world food supplies.
1 Mar		**91**	**Constitution of Shipbuilding Advisory Committee – Alexander,** 1p.

CAB 129/8	8 Mar–10 Apr 1946	**CP(46)101–150.**	
8 Mar		**CP(46)102**	**Bulk purchase of cotton – Morrison,** 1+4+9p appendix +2p annexes. Also LP(46)55. Report of the Official Committee on Bulk Purchase and covering note by the Lord President's Committee recommending its permanent continuation.
8 Mar		**103**	**Brick production – Westwood, Bevan and Tomlinson,** 3p. Measures to increase labour in the industry.
16 Mar		**114**	**Level of German industry – Bevin covering Hynd,** 1+4+3p annex.
17 Mar		**115**	**Level of German industry – Bevin,** 2p. Comments on CP(46)114.

18 Mar	**116**	**Coal-mining industry: the N.U.M. – Shinwell,** 1+4p appendixes. Twelve-point miners' charter of demands sent to him and his reply.
22 Mar	**117**	**Progress report on housing: Feb 1946 – Bevan,** 5+10p annexes.
28 Mar	**120**	**Future of the iron and steel industry – Wilmot,** 6+1p annex. On nationalization.
22 Mar	**121**	**Call-up to the forces in the transitional period – Bevin,** 3+3p annexes.
25 Mar	**122**	**Prosperity Campaign. Conference of 6 and 7 March with trade union executives and representatives of employers' organizations –** Isaacs, 1+3p annexes. Recommendations arising from the meetings.
27 Mar	**125**	**The Social Survey – Morrison covering the Official Committee on Government Information Services,** 1+2p.
28 Mar	**126**	**Call-up of apprentices – Wilmot,** 2p.
29 Mar	**127**	**Draft White Paper on the world food shortage – Smith,** 1+22p. Draft attached.
3 Apr	**130**	**Wages policy – Morrison covering the Official Working Party on Wages Policy,** 2+8p annex. Also LP(46)71 and W(46)10. Morrison set out the Lord President's Committee general endorsement of the Working Party's recommendations. For the present, reliance must be placed on employers and workers but eventually the government would have to play a more positive role. The Official Working Party recommended the establishment of a permanent National Industrial Conference through which industry could be informed of relevant economic considerations.
4 Apr	**140**	**Call-up to the forces in the transitional period – Morrison covering the Board of Trade,** 1+1p.
8 Apr	**143**	**Major bills from the 1946–47 session – Morrison,** 2+3p annex.
9 Apr	**145**	**Agricultural wages – Isaacs,** 3p. Results of meetings with the National Union of Agricultural Workers, the T.G.W.U. and the N.F.U.
10 Apr	**146**	**Agricultural wages – Williams,** 3p. Comments on CP(46)145.
10 Apr	**148**	**Wages policy – Bevin,** 2p. Comments on CP(46)130.
10 Apr	**149**	**Nationalization of transport – Barnes,** 5+1p appendix.
CAB 129/9	10 Apr–21 May 1946	CP(46)151–200.
10 Apr	**CP(46)151**	**Civilian and commercial requirements for passenger ships during the next six months –** Barnes, 3p.

11 Apr	152	**Future of the iron and steel industry – Bevin,** 2+1p appendix. Draft announcement.
13 Apr	155	**Civilian and commercial requirements for passenger ships during the next six months –** **Barnes,** 1+1p annex. Note of a meeting of officials to consider CP(46)151.
16 Apr	159	**World wheat supplies and their repercussions upon the U.K. position – Smith,** 10+9p appendixes.
6 May	161	**Progress report on housing: Mar 1946 – Bevan,** 5+12p annexes.
23 Apr	167	**Reduction of wheat consumption in the U.K. –** **Smith,** 3+1p appendix. Proposed action and state of discussions with U.S. and Canada.
18 Apr	168	**Import programme for mid-1946 to mid-1947 –** **Dalton covering the Balance of Payments Working Party,** 1+5p annex +11p appendixes. On the basis of the U.S. loan, set out a programme of £600m for the second half of 1946 and of £590m for the first half of 1947.
29 Apr	174	**Proposed increase in charges of controlled railways and London Passenger Transport Board – Barnes,** 4p.
23 Apr	176	**Ministerial Committee on Economic Planning. Composition and terms of reference – E.E. Bridges,** 1p.
29 Apr	177	**Future of the iron and steel industry – Morrison,** 1p.
30 Apr	178	**Future of the iron and steel industry – Wilmot,** 1+4p. Draft White Paper attached.
30 Apr	179	**Constitution of a National Industrial Conference – Morrison and Isaacs,** 2p. Recommended adaptation of N.J.A.C. to meet the proposals in CP(46)130.
30 Apr	182	**U.K. wheat and flour position – Smith,** 2+2p annex.
1 May	183	**U.K. wheat and flour position – Smith covering M. Hutton, the U.K. representative on the Combined Food Board,** 1+8p.
1 May	184	**U.K. wheat and flour position – Williams and Westwood,** 2p.
3 May	185	**Scientific manpower – Morrison covering the Committee on Scientific Manpower,** 1+26p. Draft White Paper.
7 May	189	**Commercial policy – Morrison,** 4+2p annexes.
14 May	193	**Proposed increase in charges of controlled railways and London Passenger Transport Board – Barnes,** 2p.
10 May	194	**Call-up to the forces in the transitional period – Bevin,** 2+4p appendix +4p annexes. Replacement of CP(46)121.

22 May	**199**	**Questions of procedure for ministers – Attlee,** 1+9p.
21 May	**200**	**Supplies of home-grown wheat – Williams and Westwood,** 2p.

CAB 129/10   24 May–2 July 1946   CP(46)201–250.

24 May	**CP(46)201**	**Rations of feedingstuffs – Williams and Westwood,** 3+1p appendix.
22 May	**202**	**Report on mission to the U.S. and Canada – Morrison,** 1+3+7p annexes. With regard to world food supplies.
22 May	**203**	**World food supplies: Lord President's Mission – Morrison,** 1+7p. Draft statement to the Commons.
23 May	**205**	**Proposed increase in charges of controlled railways and London Passenger Transport Board – Barnes,** 2+1p.
24 May	**206**	**Call-up to the forces in 1947 and 1948 – Bevin,** 2+4p annex. On the deferring of the call-up of apprentices and revised proof of draft White Paper attached.
25 May	**209**	**Supply position of wheat and flour for the period from 1 May to 31 Oct 1946 – Smith,** 5+5p appendixes.
30 May	**214**	**Prospects of dry cargo shipping tonnage for 1946 – Barnes,** 3p.
24 June	**215**	**Notes on some overseas economic and publicity problems – Morrison,** 2p. Wider issues arising from his mission.
1 July	**225**	**Nationalization of transport – Morrison,** 4+2p appendixes.
17 June	**232**	**Output, recruitment and conditions of employment in the coal-mining industry – Shinwell,** 4+3p annex. Despite manpower limitations the situation seemed to be improving and the worst was over. The main problem was how to attract labour. 'The present outlook for coal production and the action proposed to relieve the demand of next winter on available coal supplies' attached.
17 June	**233**	**Statistical reports – Attlee,** 2p. Revision of CP(45)223.
19 June	**237**	**Output, recruitment and conditions of employment in the coal-mining industry – Isaacs,** 2p. On the question of the five-day week and increased holidays.
20 June	**242**	**Output, recruitment and conditions of employment in the coal-mining industry – Morrison,** 2p. The annex to CP(46)232 showed the situation was very grave and suggested the

		need for further measures to increase recruitment.
22 June	244	**The five-day week in the coal-mining industry – Shinwell**, 1+2p. Text of his proposed statement at the N.U.M. annual conference.
26 June	247	**Rationing of bread and other cereals – Strachey**, 3+4p appendixes. Arrangements for and recommendations to introduce bread rationing.
2 July	249	**Canadian wheat contract – Strachey**, 2p.

CAB 129/11   28 June–30 July 1946   CP(46)251–300.

1 July	CP(46)254	**The Social Survey – Morrison**, 2p.
4 July	257	**Petrol rationing – Shinwell**, 3+2p annex. Recommends abolition once the U.S. loan was approved.
9 July	265	**Agricultural prices: special review – Williams, Westwood and Chuter Ede**, 5+4p appendixes.
12 July	266	**U.S. dollar expenditure – Dalton**, 2+2p annex. A small increase in dollar expenditure could be afforded.
10 July	268	**Legislative programme, 1946–47 session – Morrison and Greenwood**, 2+2p annex.
15 July	270	**Organization of electricity supply – Shinwell**, 3p.
16 July	274	**Overseas economic and publicity problems – Bevin covering Lord Inverchapel**, 2+3p appendix. On the organization of British representation in Washington.
17 July	277	**Timber for housing – Bevan**, 2p. The urgent need for imports had to be recognised.
19 July	286	**Canadian wheat supplies – Strachey**, 1+5p.
20 July	289	**Canadian wheat supplies – N. Brook covering Strachey**, 1+1p. Revised draft public statement.
22 July	291	**Supplies of softwood – Cripps**, 3p. Sets out the present position with regard to CP(46)277.
23 July	294	**Exports of timber from Germany and Austria to the U.K. – Hynd**, 4+2p annex.
25 July	297	**Location of power stations – Shinwell**, 3p. With regard to the strategic aspect.
30 July	300	**Iron and steel. Establishment of interim control board – Wilmot**, 2p.

CAB 129/12   27 July–20 Sept 1946   CP(46)301–350.

29 July	CP(46)307	**Location of power stations – De Freitas**, 2+3p. Strategic arguments against the siting of a station at Poplar.
30 July	309	**Full employment in Germany before the war – Morrison covering Economic Section**, 4p. Review of lessons to be learnt.

30 July	312	**The size of the R.A.F. at the end of 1946 – De Freitas**, 1+3p. In relation to manpower.
31 July	316	**Exports of coal from the British zone of Germany – Hynd**, 2p.
2 Aug	317	**Civil aircraft requirements – Wilmot and Winster**, 4+8p annexes.
29 Aug	325	**Repatriation of German prisoners from the U.K. – Edwards, N.**, 3p. Deals only with manpower implications.
30 Aug	327	**Repatriation of German prisoners of war – Nathan**, 2+2p appendixes. Revised version.
2 Sept	332	**Repatriation of German prisoners from the U.K. – Collick**, 2p. Agreement with CP(46)325.
2 Sept	333	**German coal – Greenwood**, 3p.
3 Sept	335	**Repatriation of German prisoners of war – E.E. Bridges covering Bevin**, 1+1p annex.
6 Sept	336	**Bread rationing – E.E. Bridges covering Strachey**, 1+3p annex. Memorandum to Attlee recommending derationing.
6 Sept	337	**Silver – Dalton**, 1+1p.
5 Sept	338	**Increases in buying and selling prices of tin – Wilmot**, 4p.
10 Sept	342	**Repatriation of German prisoners of war – Greenwood**, 4+11p annexes.
11 Sept	344	**Civil aircraft requirements – Attlee**, 1+3p annex +1p appendixes.
18 Sept	348	**Clothing and textiles for the services – Cripps**, 2p.

CAB 129/13   24 Sept–29 Oct 1946   CP(46)351–400.

24 Sept	**CP(46)351**	**Clothing and textiles for the services – Nathan**, 2p.
24 Sept	355	**Full employment in the Soviet Union – Morrison covering the Economic Section**, 1+2p. It was difficult to derive lessons from so different an economy.
8 Oct	356	**Importation of Danish meat – Morrison covering Strachey and Williams**, 1+1+6p annex. Also LP(46)237.
26 Sept	357	**Cabinet committees – Attlee**, 3p. Attempt to reduce ministers' committee work.
30 Sept	364	**International employment policy – Morrison covering the Treasury, Economic Section and Board of Trade**, 1+3p. Summary of the technical brief for the U.K. delegation to forthcoming international discussions.
8 Oct	370	**Proposed inter-governmental shipping organization – Barnes**, 4p.
18 Oct	372	**War Office requirements of land – Bellinger**, 2+3p appendix.

29 Oct	**403**	**Introduction of a permanent scheme of national service – Isaacs**, 3p.
29 Oct	**404**	**The King's speech on the opening of Parliament – Attlee**, 1+2p. Revised draft.
30 Oct	**405**	**German food supplies – Hynd**, 1+5p annexes.
1 Nov	**408**	**Transport Bill – Barnes**, 12+1p appendix +124p. Draft bill.
30 Oct	**409**	**War Office requirements of agricultural land for training purposes – Williams**, 2p.
31 Oct	**410**	**Exchange Control Bill – Soskice**, 2p. Felt it was too drastic.
31 Oct	**411**	**Exchange Control Bill – Dalton**, 2+44+5p. Draft bill and draft White Paper attached.
8 Nov	**417**	**Timber for housing – Bevan**, 3p. Need to increase supplies.
11 Nov	**419**	**Winter fuel supplies for industry – Shinwell**, 1+8+2p annex. Shinwell did not believe all the apprehensions justified, nor that the compulsory scheme suggested would secure the savings contemplated.
12 Nov	**420**	**Transport Bill – Morrison**, 3p.
12 Nov	**421**	**Admission of Poles to civilian employment – Isaacs**, 2p. Attempts to speed up the process.
15 Nov	**423**	**Proposals for supplying industry with fuel during the winter – Shinwell**, 4p.
15 Nov	**427**	**Fuel requirements for the iron and steel industry – Wilmot**, 2p.
15 Nov	**428**	**Legislation in the 1945–46 session – Morrison and Greenwood**, 1+2p annexes.
25 Nov	**431**	**Civil Service manpower – Attlee**, 1p. Proposed committee to control the size of government departments.
26 Nov	**433**	**Proposed inter-governmental shipping organization – Barnes**, 3p.

CAB 129/15   27 Nov–30 Dec 1946   CP(46)435–468.

27 Nov	**CP(46)435**	**Agriculture Bill – Williams**, 3+6p appendix +106p. Draft bill attached providing for guaranteed prices and assured markets.
5 Dec	**441**	**Impending food difficulties – N. Brook covering Strachey**, 1+1+2p. Draft statement to the Commons.
7 Dec	**442**	**The clothing ration – Cripps**, 4p.
7 Dec	**446**	**Exports of coal from Germany – Hynd**, 3p.
10 Dec	**453**	**Shipping policy – Barnes**, 4+3p annexes.
13 Dec	**458**	**Clothes rationing – Addison**, 2p.
14 Dec	**459**	**Electricity Bill – Shinwell**, 7+73p. Draft bill attached.
14 Dec	**460**	**Clothes rationing – Pethick-Lawrence**, 1p.
17 Dec	**462**	**Electricity Bill – Griffiths**, 1p.
30 Dec	**467**	**Defence Committee – Attlee**, 1p.

CAB 129/16   4 Jan–5 Feb 1947   CP(47)1–50.

4 Jan	**CP(47)4**	**E. Africa ground-nuts scheme – Strachey,** 5p.
3 Jan	**6**	**Coal and electricity – Shinwell,** 3p. Reviews the situation and asks for guidance on whether to increase supplies to power stations at the expense of industry or permit power stations to cut off electricity supply to specified works for specified times.
4 Jan	**10**	**E. African ground-nut project – Strachey,** 2p. Covering note to CP(47)4.
3 Jan	**11**	**Middle East oil – Bevin and Shinwell,** 1+7p. Factual note on its importance to Britain.
5 Jan	**15**	**Coal and electricity – Barnes,** 2p. Response to CP(47)6 on transport difficulties.
6 Jan	**17**	**Coal and electricity – Morrison,** 2p. Concern at repercussions of fuel shortage on the economy. Recommendations on immediate problems.
6 Jan	**18**	**Coal and electricity – Cripps,** 2p. Proposed changes to the priority arrangements.
7 Jan	**19**	**Economic Survey for 1947 – Morrison covering the Economic Survey Working Party,** 1+19+8p appendixes. Chapter 1 – Introduction; Chapter 2 – Resources and demands; Chapter 3 – The balance between income and expenditure; Chapter 4 – Current manpower trends, in particular, shortages; Chapter 5 – General summary and issues for decision. Appendix – Manpower at Sept 1946 and a statistical appendix. Based on tables of national income and expenditure, the balance of payments, manpower supplies and requirements, and the forecast of manpower distribution, the survey revealed a gap in income, manpower and raw materials.
7 Jan	**20**	**Economic Survey for 1947 – Morrison covering the Official Steering Committee on Economic Development,** 1+16p. Also MEP(46)16. Steering Committee report on the survey setting out the serious nature of the situation and proposed remedies. Until ministers considered the whole matter and took their decisions it was impossible to suggest the lines of the White Paper.
7 Jan	**21**	**Wheat purchases in Turkey – Strachey,** 1+4p annexes.
10 Jan	**25**	**Economic Survey for 1947 – Ministerial Committee on Economic Planning,** 6p. Agreement with the Steering Committee's analysis and acceptance of its recommendations subject to some qualification, particularly in relation to the

		balance of payments, manpower, coal, power, steel, building, agriculture. Sets out the basic lines for the White Paper.
14 Jan	29	**Economic Survey for 1947. Proposed postponement of the raising of the school leaving age – Wilkinson,** 3p. Criticism of CP(47)25.
18 Jan	33	**Defence estimates 1947/48 – Alexander,** 2+13p annexes +7+6p annexes. Also DO(47)4 and 5. Includes consideration of defence production and of manpower requirements.
18 Jan	35	**Proposal for a study of the possibilities of close economic co-operation with our western European neighbours – Bevin,** 2p. Redraft of CP(46)386.
28 Jan	38	**Employment of women – Isaacs,** 1+4p. Effect of scheme for the direction of women as proposed at the Ministerial Committee on Economic Planning.
27 Jan	39	**The Women's Land Army – Williams,** 4p. Recommends its abolition from Oct 1948 and possibly sooner.
26 Jan	40	**Food supplies – N. Brook,** 1+2p. Letter from Strachey to Attlee with regard to CP(46)396.
29 Jan	44	**International Trade Organization – Cripps,** 1p.
30 Jan	46	**Consultation with the T.U.C. – Attlee,** 3p. Guidance for ministers.
31 Jan	47	**National Service Bill – Isaacs,** 1+4p annex.
5 Feb	50	**Dislocation of coal supplies through transport difficulties – Shinwell,** 2p. Review of the situation and measures taken. Sets out the proposals for reducing supplies, which he opposed at present.

CAB 129/17   5 Feb–21 March 1947   CP(47)51–100.

7 Feb	CP(47)52	**Statement relating to defence – Alexander,** 1+12p. Proof of the White Paper.
12 Feb	53	**White Paper on the economic situation – Attlee,** 1+25p. Revise version. Second revise draft. Chapter 1 – Economic planning; Chapter 2 – Review of period July 1945–Dec 1946; Chapter 3 – The situation in 1947; Chapter 4 – Conclusion.
12 Feb	58	**Fuel Committee – N. Brook,** 2p.
13 Feb	60	**Unemployment benefit: three-day waiting period – Griffiths,** 2+1p annex. Consideration in relation to lay-offs caused by electricity cuts.
16 Feb	61	**Inducements for coal-miners – Strachey,** 2p. Proposal for increased rations.
1 Mar	73	**Electricity Supply Nationalization Bill – Shinwell,** 3p.

4 Mar	76	**Electricity Supply Nationalization Bill –** **Barnes,** 1p.
12 Mar	79	**Preparation of legislation for the 1947–48** **session – Greenwood,** 3+3p annexes.
12 Mar	84	**Transport Bill limitation on 'Licences' – Barnes,** 3+1p annex.
12 Mar	86	**Mid-week sporting events – Chuter Ede,** 4p. Recommendations arising out of meetings of responsible ministers.
12 Mar	87	**Government publicity – Attlee,** 1p. Responsibilities of Cripps in Morrison's absence, particularly on economic issues.
20 Mar	92	**Expansion of fuel and power resources – Attlee,** 1p. Revise version. Priority in manpower and materials was to be given to fuel and power industries as far as was possible.
18 Mar	94	**Report on food discussions in N. America –** **Strachey,** 7p.
21 Mar	99	**Food supplies for the U.K. – Strachey,** 2+7p annex. Attached report on nutrition of British people and the need to improve diet.
21 Mar	100	**Exhaustion of the dollar credit – Dalton,** 2p. Sets out the extent and reasons for the drain. It was necessary to sustain the export drive and severely limit the import programme. No increased food supplies from dollar sources should be permitted.

CAB 129/18	21 Mar–15 May 1947	CP(47)101–150.
22 Mar	**CP(47)103**	**Gas and electricity rationing scheme – Shinwell,** 2+3p annex. Sets out progress of the Fuel Committee on the summer ration scheme for households.
21 Mar	104	**Introduction of five-day week in mining** **industry – Shinwell,** 1+2+5p. Attached letter from the N.C.B.
24 Mar	105	**Food supplies for the U.K. – Edwards, J.,** 2p.
26 Mar	108	**Domestic fuel rationing – Shinwell,** 2+1p annex. Draft statement on the continuation of existing restrictions throughout the summer.
26 Mar	109	**The need for a positive balance of payments** **policy – Shinwell,** 5p. Concern at the frittering away of the U.S. loan and inability to agree with recommendations in CP(47)100 on increased exports and reduced dollar imports. A new approach was required.
26 Mar	110	**Power station at Bankside – Dalton,** 2p. Brought to Cabinet because of disagreement at the Lord President's Committee.
27 Mar	115	**Equipment required for the restoration of** **flooded farm land – Attlee,** 1p. All possible

		assistance was to be given in making allocations.
31 Mar	119	**Power station at Bankside – Noel-Baker**, 2p. On the strategic aspects.
10 Apr	121	**Civil Service manpower – Civil Service Manpower Committee**, 5+7p annex. Report reviewing future demand and possible cuts.
11 Apr	122	**Wheat supplies – Strachey**, 3+1p annex. Review of proposals to safeguard flour distribution.
14 Apr	123	**Proposed scheme for public ownership of sections of the iron and steel industry – Wilmot**, 3+18p appendixes. Also SI(M)(47)13.
14 Apr	124	**Nationalization of gas – Shinwell**, 6+1p annex.
10 Apr	125	**Anglo-Iranian Oil Co. – McNeil**, 1+1p.
18 Apr	128	**Home production of food in 1947 – Williams**, 7+2p appendix. Appreciation of food losses and remedial measures.
19 Apr	130	**Ration changes – Strachey**, 2p.
1 Apr	131	**The Industrial Organization Bill – Isaacs**, 3p. Brought to Cabinet because of the inability of Isaacs and Cripps to agree.
25 Apr	132	**Proposed scheme for public ownership of sections of the iron and steel industry – Wilmot**, 4p.
22 Apr	133	**The National Service Bill – Alexander**, 3p.
26 Apr	136	**International allocation of timber – Cripps**, 5p.
26 Apr	137	**International allocation of timber – Cripps**, 1+2p.
28 Apr	139	**Coal: allocations to industry – N. Brook**, 1+5p annexes. Also FC(47)80. Proposed allocations for 1 June to 31 October 1947.
29 Apr	141	**Fuel allocations to building materials industries – Bevan, Westwood and Key**, 2+1p appendix. Concern at the impact of FC(47)80.
29 Apr	142	**Financial relations between the Exchequer and local authorities – Dalton, Bevan and Westwood**, 3+1p appendix.
3 May	145	**Adjustment of railway fares and charges, and claims for reduced hours and increased wages – Barnes**, 4p.
5 May	146	**Development of national arbitration machinery – Morrison and Isaacs**, 1p. Proposed examination of the possibility of a central arbitral body.
15 May	150	**The numbers and cost of the Civil Service – Dalton**, 2+1p appendix.

CAB 129/19	12 May–8 July 1947	CP(47)151–200.
12 May	**CP(47)151**	**Legislative programme: 1947–48 session – Morrison and Greenwood**, 2p.

15 May	152	**National Service Bill – Alexander**, 3p.
17 May	159	**Coal imports – Shinwell**, 3+2p appendix. On approaching the European Coal Organization.
21 May	160	**Power station at Bankside – Morrison**, 2p.
18 May	162	**Coal imports – McNeil**, 3p.
19 May	163	**Level of German industry – Bevin**, 1+2p annex.
29 May	166	**Report on the fourth session of the Economic and Social Council – McNeil**, 1+1p.
28 May	167	**Import programme 1947–48 – Dalton**, 2+7+13p appendixes. Proposed programme.
2 June	169	**Planning for expansion – Morrison**, 3p. CP(47)167 showed that it was essential to create new sources of supply otherwise planning would come to nothing and economic crises appear. Need to assist other countries to increase world production.
31 May	170	**Import programme 1947–48 – Strachey**, 7+7p appendixes. Sets out the repercussions of a reduction of hard currency food imports 1947/48 by £80m as proposed in CP(47)167. Recommends a reduction of only £25m.
2 June	172	**Textile exports and the clothing ration – Cripps**, 3p. Proposals for increased exports and resulting maintenance of existing rations.
2 June	173	**Double summer time – Attlee**, 5p.
9 June	174	**Film remittances – Cripps**, 3p. On the reduction of dollar expenditure.
6 June	175	**Development of colonial resources – Creech Jones**, 3p.
8 June	176	**E. African ground-nut scheme – Strachey**, 3p.
8 June	177	**Production of foodstuffs and raw materials in the Colonies – Creech Jones**, 4+2p appendix.
13 June	180	**Double day-shift working in factory employment – Isaacs**, 3+52p annexes. Proof of the Brierly Committee White Paper.
13 June	181	**Electricity Supply Nationalization Bill – Shinwell**, 3p.
23 June	185	**Reorganization of the iron and steel industry – Morrison**, 2+12p appendix. Also SI(M)(47)25.
23 June	188	**European reconstruction and the U.S. offer – Bevin**, 3+5p annexes. Report of his trip to Paris in relation to the Marshall speech.
30 June	189	**A national wages policy – Shinwell**, 2+7p annex. Also LP(46)255. Repeat of his proposals for a national wages authority.
3 July	190	**Development of national arbitration machinery – Isaacs**, 5+7p. Opposed to CP(47)189.
8 July	195	**National wages policy – Isaacs**, 2+4p annex. Also LP(46)259. Reiteration of his criticisms of LP(46)255. Concern that Shinwell's proposals would destroy the responsibility of both sides of industry.

5 July	**197**	**Foreign ministers' talks on Marshall offer – Bevin**, 2p.
7 July	**199**	**Tea ration – Strachey**, 4p.

CAB 129/20   10 July–5 Sept 1947   CP(47)201–250.

14 July	**CP(47)202**	**National wages policy – Morrison**, 4+5p annex. Reviews previous ministerial discussions and recommends acceptance of CP(47)190.
18 July	**206**	**Reduction of petrol consumption – Shinwell**, 3p.
18 July	**207**	**Reduction of petrol consumption – Barnes**, 2p.
22 July	**210**	**Economic recovery of Europe: German coal output, etc. – Bevin**, 1+5p appendix. Despatch to Washington ambassador.
21 July	**212**	**Reorganization of the iron and steel industry – Morrison and Wilmot**, 3p.
28 July	**214**	**Adjustment of charges of controlled railway companies – Barnes**, 1+7p annexes. Also LP(47)120 and 125.
28 July	**215**	**Reorganization of the iron and steel industry – Morrison and Wilmot**, 2p.
30 July	**220**	**National crisis scheme for increasing production – Isaacs**, 1+2p annex. The only short-term means of increasing production of dollar-earning and dollar-saving goods was the lengthening of hours.
30 July	**221**	**Balance of payments – Dalton**, 7p. Review of position and proposed remedies to increase productivity, curtail import expenditure and review overseas commitments. Queries whether there should be legislation similar to the Emergency Powers (Defence) Act 1940.
4 Aug	**223**	**Balance of payments – Dalton**, 1+5p annexes. Draft Bill annexed. This provided new powers under existing legislation.
4 Aug	**224**	**Statement on food imports for Parliamentary debates on 6 Aug 1947 – Strachey**, 2p.
4 Aug	**225**	**Extension of the five-day week to the ancillary undertakings of the N.C.B. – Shinwell**, 2+2p annexes. Summary of N.C.B. – N.U.M. negotiations.
4 Aug	**226**	**Overseas military commitments and size of the armed forces – Attlee**, 3p. On the scale of reduction.
5 Aug	**227**	**Balance of payments and convertibility – Dalton**, 3+4p annex. Review of dollar expenditure during the past year and the drain on resources.
6 Aug	**228**	**Development of new sources of food supply – Strachey**, 5p.
9 Aug	**230**	**The trade negotiations at Geneva – Attlee**, 2p.
13 Aug	**231**	**Investment Programmes Committee – N. Brook**, 2p.

5 Sept		**250**	**The export programme – Cripps,** 8+13p. Sets out the revised programme aimed at increasing the volume of exports over the 1938 level by 140% by mid-1948 and 160% by end-1948.
CAB 129/21	5 Sept–17 Oct 1947		CP(47)251–290.
5 Sept		**CP(47)252**	**Economic recovery: views of the F.B.I. – Morrison,** 1+17p annexes. Includes 'Industry and the way to recovery' – F.B.I.
8 Sept		**253**	**Game prices – Strachey,** 2p. From aspect of price control.
8 Sept		**254**	**Proposed extension of hours in the coal-mining industry – Shinwell,** 3p.
12 Sept		**255**	**Inter-departmental organization for handling balance of payments questions – N. Brook,** 1+3p. Approval of new machinery of official committees, setting up the Overseas Negotiations Committee, the Exchange Requirements Committee, the Exports Committee. Planning was to be left to the C.E.P.S.
6 Sept		**256**	**Report on the fifth session of the Economic and Social Council – McNeil,** 1+1p annex.
15 Sept		**258**	**Government bulk purchase of foodstuffs and raw materials – Attlee,** 1+2p annexes +2p appendix. Two memoranda by Cripps and Strachey attached on whether to reduce bulk purchase.
19 Sept		**260**	**Report of the Committee on European Economic Co-operation – Bevin covering the committee,** 1+46p. Chapter 1 – Historical introduction; Chapter 2 – The European Recovery Programme; Chapter 3 – The production effort; Chapter 4 – Internal financial monetary stability; Chapter 5 – Economic co-operation; Chapter 6 – Import requirements; Chapter 7 – The problem of payment; Chapter 8 – Conclusions. The report, in response to the Marshall proposals, stressed that aid in 1948 was essential. The deficit with the American continent was forecast to last until 1951.
23 Sept		**264**	**Interim report of the Working Party on Stabilization of Wages – Isaacs,** 1+6+3p annexes. Report and annexed draft statement for discussion at the N.J.A.C. Sets out further possible steps to prevent increases in wages or other costs.
24 Sept		**265**	**Unproductive employments – Isaacs,** 2p. Manpower Committee recommended compulsory registration of all those unoccupied within the ages of control.
24 Sept		**266**	**The tariff negotiations at Geneva – Cripps,** 5+7p annexes.

the extent of U.S. aid and immediate action necessary to close the gap and protect reserves.

16 Oct | 284 | **Report of the Investment Programmes Committee – Cripps covering the committee,** 2+49p annexes. Also IPC(47)9. The Production Committee, the Official Steering Committee on Economic Development and the Economic Planning Board all agreed to the proposed reductions. The Steering Committee questioned whether they went far enough. 'Report of the I.P.C.' – C.E.P.S. and Economic Section annexed.

16 Oct | 286 | **The King's speeches on the prorogation and opening of Parliament – Attlee,** 1+5p. Revised drafts.

21 Oct | 287 | **Inter-departmental organization for handling balance of payments questions – Attlee,** 1+2+1p annex. The appointment of Cripps as Minister of State for Economic Affairs led to some changes to CP(47)255. The terms of reference and composition of the official committees affected set out in the annex.

18 Oct | 288 | **Cabinet business and procedure – Attlee,** 3+3p appendix. Sets out revised ministerial responsibilities including Cripps's assumption of responsibility for economic planning from Morrison. His primary duties were to co-ordinate domestic and overseas economic policy; with Dalton, to advise Cabinet on balance of payments policy and to submit to it a general economic plan for achieving the production required to meet the nation's needs; and to co-ordinate and supervise the execution of the production programmes under the approved economic plan. 'Interdepartmental organization for economic planning' appended. Sets out the hierarchy in the consideration of economic planning from the Cabinet to the official level.

17 Oct | 289 | **The food import programme 1947/48 from hard currency countries – Strachey,** 3+4p. The cuts agreed on 1 Aug 1947 could not be effected yet because of time considerations, long-term contracts and the nutritional aspect.

CAB 129/22   17 Oct–31 Dec 1947   CP(47)291–343.

17 Oct | CP(47)291 | **Dollar programme in 1948 – Strachey,** 4+2p annex. Consequences of a further £75m of cuts in dollar food purchases.

18 Oct | 293 | **Dollar programme in 1948: nutritional implications of proposed cuts in food imports – Strachey,** 1p.

16 Dec	**330**	**Oil supplies – Barnes and Gaitskell,** 6p. Request for Cabinet approval of PC(47)24 and 26.
10 Dec	**332**	**Fortnightly economic report – Cripps,** 1+6p.
13 Dec	**334**	**Priority for building labour – Cripps,** 2p. Recommends endorsement of Key's proposal to limit W.B.A. priority to a very small number of projects.
19 Dec	**338**	**Mid-week sport and summer time in 1948 – Chuter Ede and Woodburn,** 1+2p. Also PC(47)21.
22 Dec	**340**	**European recovery programme – Cripps,** 1+7p annex. Statement by O. Franks on the Marshall Plan at the Economic Planning Board on 11 December 1947.

CAB 129/23   1 Jan–26 Jan 1948   CP(48)1–30.

1 Jan	**CP(48)1**	**Fortnightly economic report – Cripps,** 1+9p.
2 Jan	**2**	**Defence estimates 1948/49 – Alexander,** 1+4+3p appendixes. Also DO(47)97.
7 Jan	**10**	**Fats ration – Strachey,** 2p.
5 Jan	**11**	**Tourist travel – Cripps,** 1+9p appendixes. Two memoranda by the Overseas Negotiations Committee on whether tourist travel should be resumed. Possible arrangements appended.
9 Jan	**13**	**Allocation of resources: priority system for materials other than steel and for components – Cripps,** 2+3p annex. No change except the P.M.L. symbol should apply only to steel and iron casting.
9 Jan	**14**	**Gas Bill – Gaitskell,** 4+95p. Draft attached.
13 Jan	**16**	**The basic petrol ration – Shinwell,** 3p. Against its restoration.
14 Jan	**18**	**E. African ground-nut scheme – Strachey,** 4+9p. Draft White Paper on progress to end November 1947.
15 Jan	**19**	**Fortnightly economic report – Cripps,** 1+5p.
20 Jan	**22**	**Scottish affairs – Woodburn,** 1+6p. Draft White Paper including economic issues.
22 Jan	**24**	**Textile exports and the home clothing ration – Cripps,** 3p. The export target should be reduced owing to the steel shortage and, whilst the home ration should be maintained, forward planning should assume some reduction.
23 Jan	**25**	**The scrap position and outlook – Strauss,** 5p.
29 Jan	**26**	**Ship-breaking and other commercial work in the Royal Dockyards – Viscount Hall,** 4p.
23 Jan	**27**	**Past and prospective wages movements – Isaacs,** 2+6p annex +7p appendixes. Sets out the trend of wages from 1939 to end-1947 and its likely immediate future.

23 Jan	**28**	**Wages policy – Isaacs**, 4+3p appendix. He recommended as a more positive wages policy a statement setting out principal economic considerations to be borne in mind in wage negotiations. Draft statement to be discussed with the T.U.C. attached.
23 Jan	**29**	**Potato supplies – Strachey**, 3+2p appendix.

CAB 129/24 27 Jan–20 Feb 1948		CP(48)31–60.
28 Jan	**CP(48)32**	**Fortnightly economic report – Cripps**, 1+8p.
30 Jan	**33**	**Scrap from ship-breaking – Strauss**, 3p.
2 Feb	**34**	**Defence White Paper – Alexander**, 1+13p. Revised proof copy.
5 Feb	**35**	**1948 dollar position – Cripps**, 2+8+6p annexes. Includes the views of the Official Steering Committee on Economic Development and the Economic Planning Board. Sets out the main factors which made the situation look grave in the short and long term.
30 Jan	**38**	**Statement on personal incomes, costs and prices – Morrison**, 1+6p annex. Draft of the White Paper as revised and agreed with Isaacs.
19 Feb	**44**	**Economic Survey for 1948 – Cripps**, 2+52p. Chapter 1 – The fundamental economic problems of 1948; Chapter 2 – The balance of payments in 1948; Chapter 3 – Critical sectors at home; Chapter 4 – Capital development in 1948; Chapter 5 – Manpower, national income and consumption; Chapter 6 – The means of implementing plans for 1948; Chapter 7 – Conclusions. Appendixes on the fulfilment of the objectives of the *Economic Survey for 1947* and the *Statement on Personal Incomes, Costs and Prices*. The survey was based on the expectation of Marshall Aid. Two questions still required decisions: the coal target for 1948 and objectives of the textile industries.
10 Feb	**48**	**Exports to Canada – Wilson, H., covering the Export Committee**, 1+9+2p annex. Report on the probable level in 1948.
11 Feb	**49**	**1948 dollar position – Strachey**, 5+6p appendixes. Sets out the nutritional consequences of the cuts in food imports proposed in CP(48)35.
16 Feb	**50**	**Fortnightly economic report – Cripps**, 1+4+2p appendix +5p.
14 Feb	**51**	**1948 dollar position – Attlee**, 2p. Sets out the recommendations of the Economic Policy Committee on CP(48)35 and 49.
16 Feb	**52**	**Information regarding wages negotiations – Isaacs**, 1p.

17 Feb	54	**Statement on Personal Incomes, Costs and Prices: enquiries received by government departments under paragraph 10 – Isaacs**, 2p. Suggested rules for enquiries on whether wage increases could be passed on in prices.
18 Feb	56	**The housing programmes in 1948 and 1949 – Cripps**, 2p. Recommendation of an increased allocation of timber during 1948.
18 Feb	57	**Machinery for furthering the project for a Western Union – Bevin**, 3p.
18 Feb	58	**Statement on Personal Incomes, Costs and Prices: enquiries received by government departments under paragraph 10 – Wilson, H.**, 2p. Criticism of CP(48)54, proposing alternative machinery.
18 Feb	59	**Statement on Personal Incomes, Costs and Prices: agricultural prices – Williams**, 1+3p annex. Agreement with CP(48)54 except on the special review.
20 Feb	60	**Economic Survey for 1948 – Isaacs**, 1+2p annex. Comments in particular on the cotton manpower target and manpower developments in 1947.

CAB 129/25   23 Feb–18 Mar 1948   CP(48)61–90.

23 Feb	CP(48)61	**Overseas military expenditure – Cripps and Alexander**, 2p. On the need to be consistent with balance of payments policy.
4 Mar	63	**Composition and terms of reference of the Information Services Committee – N. Brook**, 1p.
4 Mar	65	**Overseas ration scales of the services – Alexander**, 4p.
28 Feb	67	**Fortnightly economic report – Cripps**, 1+4+6p appendix.
27 Feb	68	**Preparation of legislation for the 1948–49 session – Morrison**, 3+3p annex.
3 Mar	73	**Monopolistic Practices Bill – Wilson, H.**, 2+1p annex +11p. Draft bill.
6 Mar	75	**European economic co-operation – Bevin and Cripps covering the London Committee**, 3+6+2p annex on whether there should be closer links with Europe on top of E.R.P.
4 Mar	76	**Statement on Personal Incomes, Costs and Prices: follow-up action – Isaacs**, 2+1p annex. Proposals for distribution.
5 Mar	77	**Services accommodation in the U.K. – Alexander**, 2+1+4+3p.
9 Mar	80	**Monopolistic Practices Bill – Wilson, H.**, 4p. Developments since CP(48)73.

12 Mar	84	**Havana Trade Conference – Wilson, H.,** 6+31p appendixes.
15 Mar	85	**Fortnightly economic report – Cripps,** 1+5+6p appendix.
16 Mar	87	**Service accommodation in the U.K. – Bevan,** 2p. It should be seen as part of the general housing programme.
18 Mar	89	**The report of the Russell Vick Committee on the black market in petrol – Gaitskell,** 2+2p annex. Recommends acceptance of the Committee's proposals which are annexed.
18 Mar	90	**Petrol rationing – Gaitskell,** 4p.

CAB 129/26   17 Mar–5 May 1948   CP(48)91–120.

18 Mar	CP(48)92	**Production of potatoes in allotments and gardens – Woodburn and Williams,** 2p.
19 Mar	93	**Monopolistic Practices Bill – Morrison,** 3+13+1p annex. Draft Monopoly (Enquiry and Control) Bill.
19 Mar	94	**Film agreement – Wilson, H.,** 1+1p annex.
24 Mar	97	**Statement on Personal Incomes, Costs and Prices: follow-up action – Isaacs,** 1+3p annexes. Outcome of discussions with the T.U.C.
1 Apr	98	**The second meeting of the Committee on European Economic Co-operation held in Paris from 15–18 Mar – Bevin,** 2+1+1p annex. Report.
6 Apr	99	**Iron and steel scrap – Strauss,** 4+5+15p appendixes. First interim report of the Scrap Investigation Committee attached.
3 Apr	101	**French balance of payments deficit – Cripps** covering the Overseas Negotiations Committee, 1+11p.
13 Apr	105	**Fortnightly economic report – Cripps,** 1+10p.
12 Apr	106	**Claims for wage increases by employees of local authorities and socialized industries – Isaacs,** 1p.
19 Apr	107	**Havana Trade Conference – Wilson, H.,** 1+5p annexes. Summary.
21 Apr	109	**European Economic Co-operation – Bevin,** 2p. Account of developments in Paris.
22 Apr	110	**Sixth session of the Economic and Social Council of the U.N. – Bevin,** 1+3p.
4 May	116	**Fortnightly economic report – Cripps,** 1+9p.
5 May	119	**Coal/oil conversion – Cripps,** 3p. Given the oil supply position, recommendation that only the most economically valuable schemes should be introduced and the railway conversion scheme abandoned.

CAB 129/27   24 May–14 June 1948   CP(48)121–150.

20 May	**CP(48)123**	**Iron and Steel Bill – Strauss**, 7+13p appendixes +50p. Draft bill attached.
25 May	**125**	**Fortnightly economic report – Cripps**, 1+13p.
26 May	**130**	**Scrap from Germany – Strauss**, 2+1p appendix. Progress on increased deliveries.
29 May	**135**	**Wage claims in the public sector – Cripps**, 2p.
2 June	**136**	**Iron and Steel Bill – Morrison**, 2p.
3 June	**137**	**European Recovery Programme: committee organization – N. Brook**, 1+1p. Review of inter-departmental organization in light of the establishment of the O.E.E.C.
2 June	**139**	**Iron and Steel Bill – Addison**, 3p.
4 June	**140**	**Wage claims by employees of socialized industries and local authorities – Isaacs**, 2p.
8 June	**141**	**Wage claims in the public sector – Isaacs**, 2p.
9 June	**144**	**Dry cargo shipping prospects in the light of the U.S. Economic Co-operation Act – Barnes**, 4p.
10 June	**145**	**Iron and Steel Bill – Strauss**, 3p.
14 June	**146**	**Fortnightly economic report – Cripps**, 1+9p.
14 June	**150**	**International Wheat Agreement – Strachey**, 2+21p. Cmd. 7382 attached.

CAB 129/28   17 June–19 July 1948   CP(48)151–190.

17 June	**CP(48)152**	**Grain supplies for the U.K. 1948–49 – Strachey**, 3+5p annex +3p appendixes. Recommends derationing of bread.
18 June	**153**	**Grain supplies for the U.K. 1948–49 – Williams**, 3p. Support for most of CP(48)152.
18 June	**154**	**Arrival in the U.K. of Jamaican unemployed – Creech Jones**, 3p.
22 June	**157**	**Iron and Steel Bill – Strauss**, 2p.
23 June	**160**	**Scrap Investigation Committee: final report – Strauss covering the Committee**, 3+16p +2p appendixes.
23 June	**161**	**Economic consequences of receiving no European Recovery Programme Aid – Cripps**, 3+11p. Report made the previous March setting out how drastic the consequences would have been.
25 June	**164**	**Exports of commercial scrap from Germany – Strauss**, 5+1p appendix.
29 June	**166**	**Dock strike – N. Brook**, 1+2+8p. Correspondence between Chuter Ede and Attlee.
27 June	**167**	**Economic Co-operation Agreement between His Majesty's Government and the U.S. government – N. Brook**, 1+13+3p. Draft White Papers on E.C.A. and most-favoured-nation treatment for W. Germany.
27 June	**168**	**London dock-workers' strike – Edwards, N.**, 3p.

1 July	172	**International Wheat Agreement – Strachey,** 3+6p.
6 July	173	**Economic report – Cripps,** 1+10p.
6 July	175	**E. African ground-nuts scheme – Strachey,** 5p.
9 July	177	**Import programme: July 1948–June 1949 – Cripps,** 3+11p annex. Report by officials seeking (1) authority for the programmes and statistics to be submitted to the O.E.E.C. in relation to E.R.P. and (2) decisions on purchases during the next twelve months. Programmes were based on the maintenance of reserves and concentrated on the movement towards viability. A further reduction of £50–£100m in dollar imports was necessary.
9 July	178	**Summary of material to be submitted to the O.E.E.C. – Cripps,** 1+11p annex. Sets out and contrasts the 'budget' and 'requirements' programmes.
15 July	181	**Iron and Steel Bill – Morrison,** 1+5p.
13 July	183	**Electricity peak load problem – Gaitskell,** 3+3p appendix. Includes summary of the Clow Committee report on transferring non-industrial demand from peak periods. Load-spreading was necessary since the generating station building programme could not be fulfilled because of the steel shortage.
20 July	186	**Economic report – Cripps,** 1+8p.
19 July	188	**Anti-inflationary measures in the Colonies – Creech Jones,** 2p.

CAB 129/29	22 July–15 Oct 1948	CP(48)191–230.
30 July	CP(48)193	**E.R.P. information policy – Attlee,** 1+4p.
26 July	195	**King's speeches on the prorogation and opening of Parliament – Morrison,** 1+8p annexes. Draft.
27 July	197	**Report of the Committee on the White Fish Industry – Morrison,** 5p.
27 July	198	**Reorganization of the white fish industry – Woodburn and Williams,** 2p.
4 Aug	199	**Cost of information services – Cripps,** 1+2p annex.
4 Aug	200	**Legislation in the 1947–48 session – Morrison,** 1+2p.
24 Aug	206	**Preparations for defence – Attlee,** 6+15p annexes.
28 Aug	212	**Information services: staff – Cripps,** 1+1p annex.
30 Aug	213	**Receipts and expenditure of the British Transport Commission – Barnes,** 6+1p appendix. A deficit was likely if charges were held down artificially.

30 Aug	**214**	**Preparations for defence: suspension of releases** – **Alexander,** 1+6p. Report by a working party.
1 Sept	**215**	**The King's speeches on the prorogation and opening of Parliament: Sept 13 and 14 1948** – **Cripps,** 1+8p. Revised drafts.
2 Sept	**216**	**Preparations for defence: suspension of releases** – **Shinwell,** 3p.
7 Sept	**217**	**The King's speeches on the prorogation and opening of Parliament** – **Cripps,** 1+4p. Revised drafts.
8 Sept	**218**	**Rice supplies: S.E. Asia** – **Bevin,** 1+4+1p annex.
11 Sept	**221**	**Draft statement on preparations for defence** – **Alexander,** 1+5p. Draft for Morrison.
1 Oct	**227**	**Iron and Steel Bill** – **Strauss,** 4+82p. Draft bill attached.
11 Oct	**229**	**Iron and Steel Bill** – **Morrison,** 2p.
15 Oct	**230**	**Legislative programme: 1948–49 session** – **Morrison,** 2+2p annex.

CAB 129/30 15 Oct–16 Nov 1948 CP(48)231–270.

15 Oct	**CP(48)231**	**The King's speeches on the prorogation and opening of Parliament** – **Morrison,** 1+3p. Further drafts.
14 Oct	**232**	**Economic report** – **Cripps,** 1+15p.
15 Oct	**233**	**Petrol rationing** – **Gaitskell,** 3+1p appendix.
14 Oct	**234**	**Reparations and the E.R.P.** – **Bevin,** 3+8p annexes.
15 Oct	**235**	**Motorways Bill** – **Barnes,** 4+1p annex. Question of introduction, given restrictions on capital investment and impact on railway revenue.
18 Oct	**236**	**Bizonal scrap exports** – **Bevin and Strauss,** 2+5+2p. Cmd. 7538 attached.
20 Oct	**240**	**The King's speeches on the prorogation and opening of Parliament** – **Attlee,** 1+3p. Revised drafts.
21 Oct	**243**	**Loans by the Economic Co-operation Administration** – **Cripps,** 1+1p annex.
22 Oct	**245**	**Seventh session of the E.C.O.S.O.C. of the U.N.** – **Bevin,** 1+1p.
9 Nov	**255**	**Economic report** – **Cripps,** 1+12p.
8 Nov	**259**	**Reparations and the E.R.P.** – **Bevin,** 2+4p annexes.
11 Nov	**266**	**Christmas food bonus** – **Strachey,** 1p. It was impossible to do much this year.

CAB 129/31 16 Nov–31 Dec 1948 CP(48)271–309.

18 Nov	**CP(48)273**	**Acquisition of land and buildings for the public service** – **Cripps,** 3p.
18 Nov	**275**	**Housing Bill** – **Bevan,** 2p.

18 Nov	276	**National service – Alexander**, 3+28p annexes. Also CSO(48)125 and GEN 254/1. Review of the future size of the forces and proposal to increase national service to 18 months.
23 Nov	279	**Housing Bill – Addison**, 2p.
25 Nov	282	**Cost of new schemes in men and money – Attlee**, 2p. This was an important consideration for any new or increased administrative commitment.
26 Nov	283	**Commonwealth consultation – Attlee**, 2+2p annex.
29 Nov	284	**Committees on Civil Service Manpower – N. Brook**, 1p. To be disbanded with the Treasury resuming full responsibility.
6 Dec	288	**Economic report – Cripps**, 1+15p.
6 Dec	291	**Acquisition of land and buildings for the public service – Key**, 3p.
7 Dec	294	**Acquisition of land for agriculture and forestry – Williams**, 2p.
13 Dec	302	**National Health Service – Bevan**, 3p. Progress report including costs.
20 Dec	303	**Reparations and the E.R.P. – Bevin**, 3+9p annexes.
20 Dec	305	**Census of distribution – Wilson, H.**, 2+3p. Consideration of the first year for the census.
29 Dec	308	**The National Health Service – Woodburn**, 3p.

CAB 129/32   Part 1   6 Jan–2 Feb 1949   CP(49)1–20.

6 Jan	**CP(49)1**	**Census of distribution – Wilson, H.**, 4+2p. Concern at possible delay.
6 Jan	2	**Census of distribution – Dalton**, 1p. Against a starting date of 1950 on political grounds.
14 Jan	11	**Meat ration – Strachey**, 2p. Recommended reduction.
17 Jan	13	**Economic report – Cripps**, 1+7+3p appendix +8p. Appendix on the relaxation of economic controls in 1948.
20 Jan	16	**Defence estimates 1949–50 – Alexander**, 2+6p annex. Also DO(48)83.

CAB 129/32   Part 2   8 Feb–4 Mar 1949   CP(49)21–40.

8 Feb	**CP(49)21**	**Statement on defence – Alexander**, 1+16p. Draft White Paper.
15 Feb	27	**European Economic Co-operation. The European long-term programme – Cripps** covering the European Economic Co-operation Committee, 3+21+12p appendix. Cripps broadly agreed with the Official Committee on Economic Development and the Economic Planning Board on the report. Sets out the

		programme for Europe and its impact on the U.K. and the U.K.'s long-term programme.
15 Feb	28	**Wage movements in 1948 – Isaacs,** 3+6p annex +6p appendixes. Summary with forecasts. Experience in 1948 had shown that wages, profits and the cost of living were inextricably interdependent.
16 Feb	29	**Economic Survey for 1949 – Cripps,** 1+53p. Proof of the White Paper arising out of the drafts put before the Production Committee, the Official Committee on Economic Development and the Economic Planning Board. Part 1 – Progress in 1948; Part 2 – Prospects for 1949; Part 3 – The tasks for 1949. Appendix on capital investment in 1949, on the lines of the 1948 White Paper on *Capital Investment*.
17 Feb	30	**Economic Survey for 1949 – Cripps,** 1+3p annex. Amendments to CP(49)29.
25 Feb	40	**Economic Survey for 1949 – Isaacs,** 2p. Sets out the implications of changing the forecasts for coal-mining labour.

CAB 129/33   Part I   25 Feb–14 Mar 1949   CP(49)41–59.

25 Feb	**CP(49)41**	**The petrol ration – Gaitskell,** 2p.
25 Feb	42	**Wage movements in 1948 – Isaacs,** 2p. Update on developments since CP(49)28. Wage stability could not be assured.
8 Mar	49	**Meat ration – Strachey,** 5+3p appendixes. Recommendation to reduce the ration, with appreciation of 1949 prospects.
4 Mar	51	**International Wheat Agreement – Strachey,** 3+4p annex. Sets out outstanding problems in the final stages of negotiations.
7 Mar	54	**Composition and terms of reference of the Manpower Committee – N. Brook,** 2p.

CAB 129/33   Part II   9 Mar–23 Mar 1949   CP(49)60–70.

11 Mar	**CP(49)63**	**The first year's work of the Overseas Food Corporation – Strachey,** 5p.
15 Mar	66	**The film industry – Wilson, H.,** 4p.
24 Mar	68	**Demobilization clothing for national servicemen – Alexander,** 5p.
23 Mar	70	**Economic report – Cripps,** 1+14p.

CAB 129/34   24 Mar–13 May 1949   CP(49)71–110.

11 Apr	**CP(49)83**	**Overseas economic development: committee organization – N. Brook,** 2p. Reorganization of official committees.

9 Apr	**84**	**The meat ration – Strachey**, 1p. No need for decision yet.
12 Apr	**88**	**The London dock strike – Chuter Ede**, 2p.
12 Apr	**89**	**The London dock strike – Isaacs**, 3+1p annex +1p appendix.
29 Apr	**95**	**Questions of procedure for ministers – Attlee**, 1+10p.
28 Apr	**99**	**Report on the internal financial position of the U.K. – Cripps**, 1+8p. Report by the U.K. to the O.E.E.C., setting out the problem of maintaining internal financial stability, the measures taken to maintain it, their impact and future action for 1949.
9 May	**103**	**The meat ration – Strachey**, 2p.
9 May	**104**	**Preparation of legislation for the 1950 session – Morrison**, 2+1p appendix.
6 May	**105**	**The National Health Service – Bevan**, 3+1p appendix. Sets out the need for more money.
10 May	**106**	**The National Health Service – Woodburn**, 2p.
12 May	**107**	**Eighth session of the Economic and Social Council of the U.N. – Bevin**, 1+3p annex.

CAB 129/35   18 May–13 July 1949   CP(49)111–150.

10 May	**CP(49)114**	**The Havana Charter for an international trade organization – Wilson, H.**, 4+4p annexes.
19 May	**116**	**Report of the Committee on Resale Price Maintenance – Cripps covering Edwards, J.**, 1+3p annex +3p appendixes.
25 May	**121**	**Economic report – Cripps**, 1+15p.
31 May	**122**	**Effect of new sickness and injury benefits upon absenteeism in coal mines – Gaitskell**, 4p.
28 May	**124**	**Import licensing restrictions – Cripps**, 3p. Recommends reduction of controls because of the advantage to the domestic economy.
1 June	**130**	**Railway disputes – Barnes**, 2+5p annexes.
10 June	**132**	**Iron and Steel Bill: date of implementation – Strauss**, 2p.
18 June	**137**	**Liberalization of trade – Wilson, H.**, 2+4p annexes. Draft statement.
6 July	**144**	**Meat: sources of supply other than Argentina – Strachey**, 7p. There were few alternatives.
6 July	**145**	**The dock labour industry and the National Dock Labour Board – Barnes**, 3+7p annexes.
8 July	**148**	**The London dock strike – Shawcross**, 4p.

CAB 129/36   Part I   15 July–8 Aug 1949   CP(49)151–171.

15 July	**CP(49)151**	**The dock labour industry and the National Dock Labour Board – Isaacs**, 3p.
21 July	**158**	**The dollar situation – Attlee**, 3p. Sets out the latest information. For some time the U.K.

would be in heavy deficit on current account with a consequent drain on reserves.

21 July	159	**The economic situation – Morrison,** 4p. Any economic adjustment should not injure progress on essential policies and provoke a political crisis. He identified three to four distinct dangers: inflation; the external problem; public expenditure; and, related to this, manpower and the Civil Service.
21 July	160	**Meeting of Commonwealth finance ministers – Wilson, H.,** 2+3p annex. There had been a notable identity of views. Sets out resulting recommendations on a long-term economic policy, positive steps to increase dollar earnings of the sterling area and to reduce dollar expenditure, emergency action to reduce the dollar drain and the machinery for continuing consultation.
21 July	163	**The London dock strike: emergency powers – Shawcross,** 2p.
27 July	165	**The dollar crisis: interim measures which might be taken either by the U.S. or Canada – Wilson, H.,** 4p. Sets out the points which either could be or have been raised.
26 July	168	**Iron and Steel Bill: parliamentary timetable – Strauss,** 2p.
27 July	169	**Trade relations with Canada – Wilson, H.,** 1+3+1p annex.
4 Aug	170	**Government expenditure – Attlee,** 2p. There should be a review to reduce civil expenditure by 5%.

CAB 129/36   Part II   11 Aug–10 Oct 1949   CP(49)172–200.

11 Aug	**CP(49)172**	**The dollar situation: Canada – Attlee,** 1+5p. Draft memorandum for Canadian authorities on current difficulties and long-term relations.
8 Aug	173	**Retail trade wages – Isaacs,** 3+3p appendixes.
11 Aug	174	**The dollar situation: Canada's attitude – N. Brook,** 1+4p. Note of a meeting between Attlee, Addison and U.K. High Commissioner for Canada.
23 Aug	175	**The economic situation: Washington talks – Gaitskell,** 1+12+6p appendixes. Draft brief for forthcoming ministerial talks.
18 Aug	176	**Oil and dollars – Gaitskell,** 4+12p annex +15p appendixes. Means of reducing the dollar deficit on oil by increasing British companies' production. Report by an official working party attached.
24 Aug	178	**The investment programme – Wilson, H.,** 1+6+1p. Interim report attached, covering

			measures to counter any inflationary pressure, in particular by reducing investment. However, this would necessitate major changes of policy.
24 Aug		179	**Sterling balances of the sterling area – Wilson, H., covering the Treasury,** 1+4+1p annex.
29 Aug		185	**The economic situation: Washington talks –** Cripps, 1+12+6p appendixes. Revision of CP(49)175.
31 Aug		186	**The economic situation: Washington talks: value of short-term measures – Cripps,** 1+3p. Evaluation by the Treasury of various short-term measures to impress on U.S. and Canada.
12 Sept		188	**The future of multilateral international economic co-operation – Wilson, H.,** 1+8p. Summary of Anglo-American relations in commercial policy since the war and possible developments.
14 Sept		189	**Ninth session of the Economic and Social Council of the U.N. – Attlee,** 1+2p.
20 Sept		191	**The Washington discussions, 7–12 Sept 1949 –** Cripps, 4+10p appendixes. Report on the discussions and each part of the communiqué.
19 Sept		192	**Contracts of service in essential industries – Isaacs,** 2p.
23 Sept		193	**Wages policy – Cripps and Isaacs,** 4p. The input of devaluation would be wasted if costs, of which wages were the largest item, seriously increased. A wages standstill for at least nine months, although the T.U.C. could ask for a review after three, was necessary. There should be no general escape clause. Under pressure one might have to be allowed but it should not be linked to a specific increase in the cost of living index. Suggested means of dealing with the low paid.
23 Sept		194	**Special sittings: terms of government motion – Morrison and Cripps,** 1p. With regard to the debate on devaluation.
28 Sept		195	**Iron and Steel Bill: hiving off – Strauss,** 3p.
6 Oct		197	**The economic situation: publicity to industry – Cripps,** 1+2p.

CAB 129/37   Part I   11 Oct–19 Oct 1949   CP(49)201–210.

11 Oct		CP(49)201	**Christmas food bonus – Strachey,** 1p.
25 Oct		203	**Proposals for the economic unification of Europe – Bevin and Cripps,** 4+8p annexes. U.K. policy with regard to the O.E.E.C. and the Council of Europe.
20 Oct		205	**Reduction of investment programme and government expenditure – Attlee,** 4p. Report of the Economic Policy Committee's

consideration of EPC(49)102 and 111. Were devaluation to succeed, the pull of the home market would have to be restricted as well as positive steps taken to increase production and productivity. Sets out the Economic Policy Committee's measures to reduce capital investment by £140m and government expenditure by £116.5m. Cripps wanted larger cuts in the latter.

18 Oct	**208**	**European policy – Bevin**, 7p.
19 Oct	**210**	**Annual report and accounts of the Overseas Food Corporation 1948–49 – Strachey**, 1+158p. Draft White Paper setting out progress which would shock and disappoint many.

CAB 129/37   Part II   19 Oct–22 Nov 1949   CP(49)210–238.

19 Oct	**CP(49)210**	Last five pages of the White Paper. See CAB 129/37 part I.
19 Oct	**211**	**Iron and Steel Bill – Strauss**, 2+1p appendix.
26 Oct	**216**	**Government expenditure – Attlee**, 2p. Need for departments to ensure the implementation of cuts.
28 Oct	**217**	**Development of joint consultation – Isaacs**, 1+2p annex +1p appendix. Also NJC 66.
27 Oct	**219**	**Prison officers' pay – Chuter Ede**, 2p.
1 Nov	**220**	**Stabilization of salaries and wages in the N.H.S. – Woodburn and Bevan**, 2+1p appendix.
8 Nov	**221**	**Public expenditure – Morrison**, 3p. The burden on the Chancellor of the Exchequer had to be reduced. It was important to ensure that all possible economies were implemented although the obstacles to more economical administration should not be underestimated. One possible solution would be to plan government expenditure for a number of years ahead, for example with regard to social services.
3 Nov	**223**	**Christmas food bonuses – Strachey**, 1p.
4 Nov	**225**	**Economic report – Cripps**, 1+16p.
8 Nov	**227**	**Size of daily newspapers and periodicals – Wilson, H.**, 3p.
8 Nov	**228**	**Public expenditure – Cripps**, 2p. Comments on CP(49)221. Big savings required the examination not just of administration but of policy. Despite the difficulties, proposed to make forecast of expenditure twice a year.
11 Nov	**231**	**The East African ground-nuts scheme – Strachey**, 10+4+4p appendixes. Proposals for future development.
11 Nov	**232**	**The East African ground-nuts scheme – Creech Jones**, 1p. Agreement with CP(49)231 that the scheme should continue.

22 Nov	**238**	**Retail trade wages – Isaacs,** 3+4p annexes.

CAB 129/37   Part III   21 Nov–17 Dec 1949   CP(49)239–252.

21 Nov	**CP(49)239**	**Finances of the British Transport Commission –** **Barnes,** 3+2p annexes.
28 Nov	**240**	**Legislative programme: 1950 session –** **Morrison,** 2+3p annexes.
5 Dec	**243**	**The King's speech on the prorogation of** **Parliament – Morrison,** 1+3p annex.
8 Dec	**245**	**Defence estimates 1950–51 – Attlee,** 4+14p annexes +10p appendixes. Also DO(49)66.
12 Dec	**246**	**The King's speech on the prorogation of** **Parliament – Attlee,** 1+3p annex. Revised draft.
10 Dec	**247**	**Economic report – Cripps,** 1+12p.
17 Dec	**252**	**Local government manpower – Cripps covering** **the Local Government Manpower Committee,** 1+30p. First report on economies.

CAB 129/38   2 Jan–27 Mar 1950   CP(50)1–50.

9 Jan	**CP(50)4**	**Local government manpower – Bevan,** 2+1p appendix.
25 Jan	**12**	**Legislation in the 1948–49 session – Morrison,** 1+2p annexes.
26 Jan	**14**	**National Health Service: charges for** **prescriptions – Bevan,** 2p.
2 Feb	**17**	**Agricultural prices and feedingstuffs rationing –** **Chuter Ede, Woodburn and Williams,** 6p. Sets out the subjects requiring Cabinet decisions.
27 Feb	**19**	**Statement on defence 1950 – Alexander,** 1+13p. Draft White Paper.
1 Mar	**20**	**The King's speech on the opening of** **Parliament – Morrison,** 1+2p.
1 Mar	**21**	**Iron and Steel Act – Strauss,** 2+1p annex.
2 Mar	**23**	**British Transport Commission: proposed** **increase of charges – Barnes,** 3+22+10p. Reports of the railways and dockers and canals transport tribunals.
2 Mar	**24**	**1950 farm price review – Chuter Ede, Williams** **and McNeil,** 6p. Sets out the basis for opening discussions with the N.F.U.
2 Mar	**25**	**The derationing of animal feedingstuffs –** **Chuter Ede, Williams and McNeil,** 2p.
3 Mar	**26**	**The King's speech on the opening of** **Parliament – Attlee,** 1+2p. Revise text.
7 Mar	**28**	**Economic Survey for 1950 – Cripps,** 1+31p. Draft White Paper. First draft originally considered by the Production Committee. Part I – Developments in 1949; Part II – Prospects for 1950; Part III – Production, investment and consumption. Appendix – capital investment in 1950.

7 Mar	29	**Housing: local authorities' waiting lists – Bevan,** 1+3p. Draft statement.
7 Mar	30	**Housing: licences for erection of new houses –** **Bevan,** 1p.
10 Mar	31	**National Health Service (England and Wales):** **control of expenditure – Bevan,** 11p.
14 Mar	32	**The Economic Survey for 1950 – Cripps,** 1+7p annexes. Sets out the recommendations of the Production Committee covering Marshall Aid, fuel and power, steel, manpower direction, food consumption and Scottish investment. Also revised conclusion.
13 Mar	34	**Cabinet committees – N. Brook,** 1+3p. Reconstitution of main ministerial standing committees.
15 Mar	35	**Budget policy – Cripps,** 1+3p. Treasury paper on whether the budget should aim at a large surplus, given the suggestion by some that, so long as the budget above the line was balanced, taxation could be reduced.
21 Mar	45	**Farm price review 1950 – Chuter Ede, Williams and McNeil,** 3p. Decisions arising from discussions to date.
22 Mar	46	**Retail food price increases – Webb,** 2p. Recommended increases on the basis of a subsidy ceiling of £410m.
24 Mar	47	**Economic report – Cripps,** 1+17p.
27 Mar	48	**U.K. stocks of animal feedingstuffs – Strachey,** 2p.
27 Mar	49	**Future of emergency powers – Morrison,** 2p. The Lord President's Committee needed guidance from Cabinet. He recommended the drafting of legislation to provide permanent powers for economic control and price regulation.
24 Mar	50	**Retail food price increases – Webb,** 2p.

CAB 129/39   20 Mar–10 May 1950   CP(50)51–100.

28 Mar	CP(50)52	**Provision of additional funds for the National Film and Finance Corporation – Wilson, H.,** 2p.
29 Mar	53	**National Health Service – Cripps,** 2p. Need for decisions further to CM(50)10th:3.
30 Mar	56	**National Health Service (England and Wales) –** **Bevan,** 2p. Against charges.
31 Mar	57	**National Health Service (Scotland) – McNeil,** 4+1p appendix.
1 Apr	59	**Points rationing – Webb,** 2p. Proposed ending.
31 Mar	60	**Efficiency and public accountability of socialized industries – Morrison,** 5+1p annex.
13 Apr	67	**The Housing Programme (England and Wales) – Bevan,** 2p. On the restoration of the cut in the programme.

12 May	**110**	**Proposed Franco-German coal and steel authority** – **Attlee,** 1p. An official committee of senior officials under E.E. Bridges was to be established to collect information and to advise ministers on the scheme, distinguishing between a European scheme and one involving U.K.
15 May	**111**	**Points rationing** – **Webb,** 2p. Recommends its ending.
17 May	**112**	**Implementation of the Iron and Steel Act, 1949** – **Strauss,** 2+4p annexes.
19 May	**114**	**Conversations with Mr. Acheson of 9 and 10 May** – **Bevin,** 6+11p annexes. Includes Anglo-U.S. relations and the economic situation.
22 May	**115**	**Conversations with Mr. Schuman and Mr. Acheson on 11, 12 and 13 May** – **Bevin,** 4+4p annexes. Includes European economic integration.
26 May	**119**	**Canadian wheat flour** – **Cripps, Gordon Walker and Webb,** 2+1p appendix.
2 June	**120**	**Integration of French and German coal and steel industries** – **committee of officials,** 2+3 annexes. Before negotiations could open the U.K. had to accept the communiqué. The economic arguments were inconclusive and therefore the key issue was political. The report recommended rejection as, following the decision to develop the Atlantic community, sovereignty might be even further infringed. Reasons for rejection must be carefully explained.
12 June	**122**	**Economic report** – **Cripps,** 1+13p.
13 June	**124**	**Control of Civil Service numbers** – **Cripps,** 2+1p annex.
20 June	**128**	**Integration of Western European coal and steel industries** – **N. Brook covering committee of officials covering its working party,** 1+6+37+2p. Also FG(WP)(50)38. Report of the working party examining (i) the case for concerted international action on economic grounds and (ii) the functions and constitution appropriate to an international authority which the U.K. could join.
21 June	**133**	**Integration of Western European coal and steel industry: debate in the House of Commons** – **N. Brook,** 1p.
23 June	**135**	**Marginal land** – **Chuter Ede, Williams and McNeil,** 2+8p. Report by the Agricultural Output Committee attached.
28 June	**137**	**Soap rationing** – **Webb,** 2p. Recommended derationing.

27 June	**140**	**Implementation of the Iron and Steel Act, 1949 – Strauss**, 3p.
28 June	**143**	**Illegal strikes – Shawcross**, 2p.
27 June	**144**	**Flour extraction rate – Webb**, 1+4p annex +3p appendix.
1 July	**146**	**White fish industry: short-term remedies – Williams and McNeil**, 1p. Assistance to the industry prior to the White Fish Industry Board becoming effective.
30 June	**147**	**Fish: encouragement of sales – Webb**, 3p.
1 July	**149**	**Integration of Western European coal and steel industries – committee of ministers**, 4p. Report of the committee established in CM(50)38th to consider U.K. proposals. The decision was dependent on the body's constitution.

CAB 129/41   30 June–30 Aug 1950   CP(50)151–200.

30 June	**CP(50)151**	**Wages policy – Cripps**, 1+5p annexes. Copy of the T.U.C. statement to affiliated unions on wages policy, 28 June 1950, and draft Commons statement annexed.
3 July	**153**	**Integration of Western European coal and steel industries: Commonwealth implications – Gordon Walker**, 3p.
1 July	**154**	**Integration of Western European coal and steel industries: defence implications – Shinwell**, 4p.
3 July	**155**	**Economic action arising out of the Korean conflict – Younger**, 2p. On sanctions etc.
3 July	**157**	**Control of strategic exports to China and North Korea – Younger**, 2p.
5 July	**158**	**The Smithfield strike – Chuter Ede**, 3+2p appendix.
7 July	**161**	**Involuntary absenteeism in the coal-mining industry – Attlee covering the Lidbury Committee**, 1+9+5p appendix. Report of the Committee attached.
11 July	**162**	**Report of the Lidbury Committee on Involuntary Absenteeism – Noel-Baker**, 4p. Comments on CP(50)161.
11 July	**163**	**Short-term measures to increase coal production – Noel-Baker**, 6p. Little more could be done to increase mechanization and miners were working well, so output could not much exceed the lower limits set in the Economic Survey.
7 July	**166**	**Renewal of emergency powers – Morrison**, 1p. Recommends renewal for a further year since any legislation giving permanent economic powers was unlikely to be passed in time and would only cover part of the field of powers required.

12 July	**169**	**General labour relations in the coal-mining industry – Isaacs**, 3+1p appendixes. Strikes had increased in number but decreased in length.
18 July	**173**	**Supplies of newsprint – Wilson, H.**, 5+3p annexes.
21 July	**176**	**Inquiry into the taxation of income – Cripps**, 3p. Proposal to establish a Royal Commission.
21 July	**177**	**Economic report – Cripps**, 1+13p.
25 July	**178**	**Permanent economic powers – Morrison**, 2+20p. Draft bill covering economic controls and price regulation attached. The bill in effect made permanent the powers conferred on ministries by defence regulations and other emergency measures. Its powers were negative although Morrison said there was much potential for purposive direction. Further positive powers could be included in the bill or a preamble drafted to emphasize the indispensability of the powers for the type of economic planning needed to secure full employment and general well-being of the country. Then sets out procedure for the bill. It had been brought to Cabinet to decide whether, or when, it should be submitted to Parliament.
31 July	**181**	**Defence requirements and U.S. assistance – Cripps**, 4+3p annexes. Sets out information as requested by U.S., concluding that the programme would be impossible without U.S. aid which was not tied to dollar purchases. Asking for approval of defence expenditure of £950m per year net over the next three years which would require no reduced government expenditure, increased taxation, or reduced investment.
24 July	**184**	**Capital investment programme: sewerage and sewage disposal works – Bevan**, 2p.
28 July	**187**	**The capital investment programme: outstanding points – Cripps**, 3+1p appendix. Recommends endorsement of the Production Committee decision on the programme for manufacturing industry in 1951 and 1952 and its distribution as recommended by the Investment Programmes Committee, thereby rejecting CP(50)184.
9 Aug	**188**	**Service manpower requirements – Shinwell**, 4p.
10 Aug	**190**	**Regular recruiting and re-engagements: proposals for increased pay, etc. – Shinwell**, 2+6p annex.
4 Sept	**198**	**Claims on Germany – Bevin**, 5p.
4 Sept	**199**	**Control of German industry – Bevin**, 3+2p annex.

CAB 129/42   31 Aug–26 Oct 1950   CP(50)201–250.

31 Aug	**CP(50)201**	**Restriction of exports to eastern Europe and China** – **Shinwell,** 3+1p appendix.
8 Sept	203	**Employment of national servicemen** – **Strachey,** 2p.
9 Sept	204	**Control of exports to eastern Europe and communist Asia** – **Shinwell,** 2p.
15 Sept	208	**East African ground-nut scheme : report of the Kongwa Working Party** – **Webb,** 3p.
16 Sept	209	**Export of two machine tools to Poland** – **Wilson, H.,** 3+3p annexes.
25 Sept	213	**Kongwa Working Party report** – **Webb,** 2+10p annex. Copy of report annexed.
6 Oct	220	**New York meetings: (i) foreign ministers' conferences; (ii) North Atlantic Council; and (iii) U.N. General Assembly** – **Bevin,** 4p.
11 Oct	224	**Legal action in connection with unofficial strikes** – **Shawcross,** 2p.
12 Oct	226	**The King's speech at the prorogation of Parliament** – **Morrison,** 1+2p annex.
12 Oct	227	**The King's speech on the opening of Parliament** – **Morrison,** 1+2p annex.
12 Oct	228	**Legislative programme for 1950/51 session** – **Morrison,** 2+3p annexes.
17 Oct	230	**The Economic Planning and Full Employment Bill** – **Bevan,** 3p. Report from his subcommittee of the Production Committee on the positive powers needed to allow departments to buy, sell and manufacture goods for civilian use.
16 Oct	231	**Proposal to transfer the British Sugar Corporation to public ownership** – **Webb,** 2+3p annex +2p appendix.
16 Oct	233	**Efficiency and public accountability of the socialized industries** – **Morrison,** 2p.
20 Oct	237	**The King's speech on the opening of Parliament** – **Morrison,** 1+2p. Revised draft.
21 Oct	239	**The King's speech on the prorogation of Parliament** – **Attlee,** 1+3p. Revised draft.
24 Oct	241	**The British Sugar Corporation** – **Webb,** 1p.
26 Oct	243	**The King's speech on the opening of Parliament** – **Attlee,** 1+2p.
27 Oct	245	**Economic report** – **Cripps,** 1+15p.
30 Oct	246	**The finance of defence** – **Attlee,** 1p.
30 Oct	247	**Finance of defence** – **N. Brook covering Cripps and Bevin,** 8+4p annexes. Also DO(50)91. Nitze exercise with regard to a full programme of £3600m.
30 Oct	248	**Size and shape of the armed forces 1951/1954** – **N. Brook covering Shinwell,** 1+1+5+9p annexes. Also DO(50)81.

CAB 129/43   31 Oct–30 Dec 1950   CP(50)251–326.

2 Nov	**CP(50)252**	**Exports of coal – Gaitskell,** 1p. Sets out the decisions of the Production Committee with regard to CP(50)255 and 256.
3 Nov	253	**Importance of coal exports and foreign relations of the U.K. – Bevin,** 2p.
3 Nov	254	**Coal supplies: outlook for the period 1951–1955: possible methods of increasing production – Noel-Baker,** 4p.
3 Nov	255	**Coal supplies in the winter 1950/51 – N. Brook covering Noel-Baker,** 1+2p.
3 Nov	256	**Coal supplies in the winter 1950/51 – N. Brook covering Noel-Baker,** 1+2+1p annex.
4 Nov	257	**Wages in the coal-mining industry – Noel-Baker,** 2+6p annexes.
6 Nov	258	**Christmas bonuses – Webb,** 3p.
8 Nov	265	**Legislation in the 1950 session – Morrison,** 1+1p annex.
14 Nov	271	**Coal emergency measures – Noel-Baker,** 3+3+8p annexes. Attached report on the coal situation by the Official Coal Committee. Recommends a reduction in bunkering and the importation of coal from U.S.
29 Nov	281	**Coal situation: Opposition criticism – Noel-Baker,** 4+2p.
29 Nov	282	**Argentine trade negotiations and the meat ration – Webb,** 3p.
28 Nov	285	**Coal emergency measures: imports and exports – Noel-Baker,** 3p. Necessary to decide at that time whether to cut exports again.
28 Nov	286	**Coal: priority for power stations – Noel-Baker,** 3p. Increased imports were only the first step. Special measures sought to safeguard the power stations.
28 Nov	287	**Coal exports – Gaitskell,** 1+3p. Attached report by the Overseas Negotiations Committee.
1 Dec	288	**Interim index of retail prices – Isaacs,** 3p. Recommended the recall of the Cost of Living Advisory Committee.
30 Nov	289	**The future of the East African ground-nut scheme – Griffiths and Webb,** 10+17p annexes.
29 Nov	290	**Purchase of Polish coal – Gaitskell,** 1+2p. Report by the Overseas Negotiations Committee attached.
30 Nov	291	**Wages policy: the British system – Isaacs,** 4p. The British system of collective bargaining might be illogical but it worked in practice and should not be changed.
30 Nov	292	**Wages policy: systems in operation in certain foreign countries – Isaacs,** 2+11p appendix.

		Sets out the system in countries where there was some element of central control.
21 Nov	295	**Prices of utility wool blankets – Wilson, H.,** 2p.
1 Dec	296	**Coal emergency measures: open-cast – Noel-Baker,** 1+1p. Fifth report by the chairman of the Official Coal Committee attached.
1 Dec	297	**Manpower for the mines – Noel-Baker,** 6+9p annexes. Two reports by the Official Coal Committee on supplementary pensions and manpower, recruitment and wastage attached.
6 Dec	298	**Development of coal-mining in Africa and other overseas territories – Griffiths and Gordon Walker,** 1+2p annex.
2 Dec	299	**Coal: shipping for imports – Gaitskell,** 1+2p. Memorandum by the chairman of the Official Coal Committee attached.
5 Dec	301	**Supplementary pensions for miners – Morrison,** 2p.
5 Dec	302	**Coal emergency measures – Noel-Baker,** 3p. Progress report setting out the problems for winter 1950–51 and 1951.
11 Dec	309	**Summer time in 1951 – Chuter Ede,** 2p.
13 Dec	313	**Conditions of employment and national arbitration order: dispute between Kemsley Newspapers Ltd. and members of the *Daily Graphic* and Kemsley Newspapers (London) Chapels of the N.U.J. – Isaacs,** 2p.
13 Dec	314	**Housing – Bevan and McNeil,** 2p.
14 Dec	315	**Economic report – Gaitskell,** 1+13p.
29 Dec	324	**Future of the East African ground-nut scheme – Gaitskell,** 4+2p appendix.
30 Dec	326	**Future of the East African ground-nut scheme – Webb,** 2+5p. Draft White Paper.

CAB 129/44   1 Jan–9 Mar 1951   CP(51)1–75.

5 Jan	CP(51)3	**Negotiations with the N.U.M. about wages, holidays with pay and supplementary pensions – Noel-Baker,** 3+1p annex.
9 Jan	6	**Coal-miners: release of volunteers from the armed forces – Noel-Baker,** 2+1p.
10 Jan	7	**Economy in the use of coal: further measures – Noel-Baker,** 1+2p appendix. Also extract of OCC(51)9th. Recommends reconsideration of extending summer time, stopping broadcasting after 11 p.m. and restricting mid-week sport.
12 Jan	11	**Open-cast coal – Noel-Baker,** 2+9p annexes. Recommends increased programme for the next five years and the lifting of the ban on the import of U.S. excavators. Third report of the Working Party on Open-cast Coal Production of the Official Coal Committee annexed.

13 Jan	12	**Coal-miners: proposal to release volunteers from the armed forces** – Shinwell, 2p. Critical of CP(51)6.
12 Jan	16	**Defence programmes 1951–54** – Chiefs of Staff, 2+16p annex. On the acceleration of defence preparations.
19 Jan	20	**Economic implications of the defence proposals** – Gaitskell, 13p. Sets out the expenditure on preparations although no account was taken of price increases. The new proposals were an increase in, rather than an acceleration of, the defence programme. Since aid was not inevitable, the maintenance of external financial strength was as important as ever. Sacrifices had to be made on current consumption rather than burdening the future.
23 Jan	22	**Supply of national servicemen to meet the needs of the forces** – Isaacs, 1+4p annex. Also DO(51)1.
23 Jan	23	**Supply of national servicemen to meet the needs of the forces** – Williams and McNeil, 2p. Against the suggested end to the deferment of the call-up of agricultural workers.
22 Jan	24	**Argentine negotiations and the meat ration** – Webb, 4p.
19 Jan	25	**Defence programmes 1951/54** – Shinwell, 3p. Comments on CP(51)16. Agreement in principle to the need to increase the armed forces but some of the proposals were too drastic and politically unacceptable.
19 Jan	26	**Recall of class 'Z' reservists** – Strachey, 5p.
23 Jan	29	**Supply of national servicemen to meet the needs of the forces** – Shinwell, 2p. It was impossible to give agricultural workers complete immunity.
24 Jan	32	**Increased defence expenditure** – Attlee, 2p. Provisional views on the proposals of the Defence Committee.
28 Jan	34	**Statement on defence** – Attlee, 1+10p. Draft for comments.
31 Jan	35	**Inter-relation between farm prices, retail food prices and food subsidies** – Gaitskell, 3+5p appendixes. Sets out how subsidies on home-produced goods benefitted both producers and consumers.
1 Feb	36	**Defence programme** – Attlee, 4p. Sets out how outstanding points were to be resolved and the machinery for ensuring the programme's execution.
1 Feb	37	**Resale price maintenance** – Dalton and Wilson, H., 4+10p appendix. Final report of the Official

		Working Party on Resale Price Maintenance appended.
6 Feb	39	**Sulphur – Wilson, H.,** 3+4p annex. Problems of supply and possible action.
6 Feb	42	**Call-up of reservists – Shinwell,** 4p.
9 Feb	49	**Call-up of agricultural workers – Isaacs,** 2p. Points outstanding after discussions between agricultural ministers and the Minister of Defence and Secretary of State for War.
13 Feb	52	**Full Employment Bill – Morrison,** 2p. Since it was desirable to knit together positive and negative powers into a coherent whole, ministers had felt the emphasis of the bill should be on full employment not economic planning. Circumstances had changed considerably since October with the defence programme requiring the maintenance of a number of emergency powers. New permanent controls could lead to confusion and thus endanger full employment. It was therefore recommended that the Full Employment Bill should not be introduced in present circumstances but the Cabinet might wish the ministerial committee to continue its drafting.
15 Feb	54	**Economic report – Gaitskell,** 1+13p.
6 Mar	70	**British Transport Commission: financial position – Barnes,** 4+8p. On the question of increasing charges.
13 Mar	71	**Post Office tariffs – Edwards, N.,** 5p.
CAB 129/45 9 Mar–30 May 1951		CP(51)76–150.
15 Mar	CP(51)77	**Economic Survey 1951 – Gaitskell,** 1+33p. Chapter 1 – Impact of rearmament; Chapter 2 – Prospects for output; Chapter 3 – The balance of payments; Chapter 4 – National income and expenditure; Conclusions. The draft survey had been prepared by the C.E.P.S. in conjunction with the Economic Section and apart from the section on coal had been agreed at the official level. Concentrates on the changed circumstances brought about by rearmament.
15 Mar	79	**Retail prices of subsidized foodstuffs – Gaitskell and Webb,** 3+2p appendix. Sets out proposed price increases to maintain the ceiling of £410m.
16 Mar	80	**Annual review under part I of the Agricultural Act 1947 – Gaitskell,** 4+4p annexes.
17 Mar	85	**British Transport Commission: financial position – Barnes,** 1+2p. Draft statement.

19 Mar	88	**Duties of the Lord Privy Seal and the Lord President of the Council** – Attlee, 2p. Redistribution of functions on Bevin and Addison taking the positions.
20 Mar	90	**Post Office tariffs** – Edwards, N., 2p.
19 Apr	101	**Swedish proposal for the amalgamation of the Organization for European Economic Co-operation (O.E.E.C.) and the Council of Europe** – Morrison, 2p.
17 Apr	112	**Borrowing powers of the N.C.B.** – Noel-Baker, 2p. Recommends increased borrowing limit to enable reorganization on the basis of *Plan for Coal*.
18 Apr	113	**Economic report** – Gaitskell, 1+13p.
20 Apr	114	**Persian oil** – Morrison, 4+1p annex.
27 Apr	118	**Economy in the consumption of coal** – Noel-Baker, 4p. Recommendations to expedite progress.
1 May	121	**Parliament and the socialized industries** – Chuter Ede, 2p.
21 May	124	**Manchester dock strike: unloading of raw materials** – Chuter Ede, 2+1p annex.
5 May	125	**Preparation of legislation for the 1951–52 session** – Chuter Ede, 2+3p annex. Assumes the Full Employment Bill would not be proceeded with at present.
7 May	126	**Retail food prices** – Gaitskell and Webb, 2p.
9 May	129	**Persian oil** – Morrison, 1+3p.
18 May	136	**Information Services Committee: ministerial responsibility and committee structure** – N. Brook, 2p.
24 May	138	**U.N. Economic and Social Council: report on the twelfth session** – Morrison, 2p.
24 May	141	**Colonial Development Corporation: debate on the annual report** – Dugdale, 1p.
24 May	143	**Ministerial duties** – Attlee, 1p. Sets out the duties of the Lord Privy Seal on the replacement of Bevin by Stokes, including responsibility for the Materials Department.
29 May	149	**Resale price maintenance** – Shawcross, 5+7p annex.
CAB 129/46 1 June–24 July 1951		CP(51)151–225.
31 May	**CP(51)152**	**Schuman Treaty** – Gaitskell covering the Economic Steering Committee, 1+6p annex. Also EPC(51)44.
7 June	154	**Supplementary pensions for miners: restriction to underground workers** – Noel-Baker, 2p.
18 June	168	**Control of delegated legislation** – Chuter Ede, 3+5p annexes.

20 June	**169**	**Low-cost housing – McNeil,** 2p. On the reduction of cost by reducing facilities and size.
20 June	**170**	**Validity of emergency acts – Chuter Ede,** 2p. They were being tested in the courts. There could be problems with import duties and some price controls.
22 June	**171**	**Supplementary pensions for miners – Noel-Baker,** 2+1p annex.
23 June	**174**	**Economic report – Gaitskell,** 1+15p.
22 June	**176**	**Supplementary pensions for miners – Summerskill,** 3p.
26 June	**179**	**Information policy – Gordon Walker,** 3p. Need for a new campaign as the rearmament programme would not be possible without public support.
27 June	**182**	**Staff for defence work – Gaitskell,** 2+1p annex.
3 July	**189**	**Manpower for the mines – Noel-Baker,** 4p. Increased consumption had outstripped increased production. Proposals to supplement manpower, which was the main short-term remedy.
6 July	**192**	**Persia: ruling of the Hague Court – Morrison,** 1+5p.
5 July	**194**	**Manpower for the mines: withdrawal of ex-miners from the armed forces – Shinwell,** 3p. Against the proposal in CP(51)189.
11 July	**200**	**Persia – Morrison,** 4+7p annexes.
16 July	**202**	**Livestock and meat: slaughtering policy – Dalton,** 4p.
23 July	**204**	**Merchandise marks – Shawcross,** 2p.
13 July	**206**	**General enquiry into supplementary pension schemes – Alexander,** 2+2p appendixes.
18 July	**210**	**Exports to Persia – Shawcross,** 3p.
19 July	**215**	**The manpower position on the British Railways – Barnes,** 1+5p annex. There had been serious problems in the movement of freight owing to an acute shortage in certain essential grades of staff. Recommendation of their deferment from national service.
20 July	**217**	**Service works programme: provision of staff – Shinwell,** 4+3p appendixes.
20 July	**219**	**National service of railwaymen – Robens,** 2p. It was impossible to make the concession requested in CP(51)215.
20 July	**221**	**The future of the Conditions of Employment and National Arbitration Order – Robens,** 3+12p.
23 July	**223**	**The manpower on the British Railways – Shinwell,** 2p. Support for CP(51)219.
24 July	**224**	**The future of the Conditions of Employment and National Arbitration Order – Soskice,** 3p.

CAB 129/47   24 July–26 Oct 1951   CP(51)226–267.

24 July	CP(51)226	**Railway manpower and winter coal supplies –** **Noel-Baker,** 1p. Support for Barnes to ensure coal supplies.
27 July	230	**The European defence effort and European integration schemes – Morrison,** 3p.
16 Aug	236	**Council of Europe – Bevin,** 2+7p annexes.
3 Sept	237	**The manpower position in the British Railways – Barnes,** 2p. Again requesting deferment.
13 Aug	238	**German defence contribution: economic and financial implications – Attlee,** 1+8p annex. Report by the Mutual Aid Committee annexed.
30 Aug	239	**Washington and Ottawa meetings: review of British policy – Attlee,** 10+2p annexes. Included economic questions.
3 Sept	241	**Persia: Sterling Control Order – Gaitskell,** 4p.
3 Sept	242	**The balance of payments position – Gaitskell,** 3p. The deterioration of the dollar deficit was rapidly eating into reserves.
3 Sept	243	**Supplies of finished military equipment from the U.S. – Shinwell,** 4p.
	245	**Long-term financial prospects of the British Transport Commission – Barnes,** 6+1p annexes.
13 Sept	246	**The coal transport situation – Noel-Baker,** 2p. Urged acceptance of CP(51)237.
14 Sept	247	**The manning of the Civil Defence Corps and fire service – Chuter Ede and McNeil,** 3p.
14 Sept	248	**Manpower requirements of the police at the outset of any major war – Chuter Ede and McNeil,** 2p.
17 Sept	249	**The manpower position on the British Railways – Isaacs,** 2p. Still against deferment.
25 Sept	251	**Report on discussions in Washington and Ottawa on balance of payments and defence questions – Gaitskell,** 3+18p annexes. Report on discussions and memorandum on U.K. balance of payments position handed to U.S. annexed.
25 Sept	252	**The King's speech on the prorogation of Parliament – Chuter Ede,** 1+3p annex.
24 Sept	253	**Agricultural wages and prices – Williams,** 2p.
25 Sept	254	**Locomotive contract for Persia – Shawcross,** 2p.
25 Sept	255	**Manpower for the mines – Noel-Baker,** 2+3p annexes. Recommends the import of large coal for the house coal market. Annexes set out the manpower and house coal situations.
26 Sept	257	**The oil dispute with Persia – Morrison,** 11+2p annex.
2 Oct	259	**The King's speech on the prorogation of Parliament – Attlee,** 1+3p. Revised draft.

5 Oct	**362**	**Manpower: measures to deal with labour supply – Isaacs,** 6+1p appendix. Review of the position and proposed measures for allocating manpower to defence, exports and other essential production and services.
22 Oct	**266**	**Bilateral and tripartite talks in Washington and Atlantic Council meeting in Ottawa 10th–20th Sept 1951 – Morrison, Gaitskell and Shinwell,** 14p. Includes consideration of the financial aspects of defence.

Chapter 3 Cabinet Office Registered Files

CAB 21 contains the working papers of Cabinet Office officials on a wide variety of subjects. It includes copies of the Prime Minister's minutes, and briefs for both the Prime Minister and the Lord President. It is particularly important for background information on the establishment and subsequent history of many Cabinet committees; and on disputes between ministers arising from the minutes of those committees and of the Cabinet itself. Supplementary files originating in the Cabinet Office are in CAB 104.

CAB 21

771 **Agriculture policies.** (1/5/7 part 2) Sept 1942–Feb 1945. Includes papers on reconstruction and post-war policy, and documents on Churchill's opposition to internal commitments which prejudiced international settlements.

779 **War Cabinet organization: central executive government of Great Britain.** (41/6C part 1) Jan 1942–May 1946.

822 **Cabinet committees: composition and terms of reference.** (7/2/3 part 3) January 1941–July 1945. Includes papers on the reorganization of September 1943. Gap to May 1945, then papers leading to CP(45)59 and others on arrangements for the caretaker government.

823 **Organization of Cabinet committees.** (7/2/3 part 4) July 1945–Jan 1946. Includes discussion on the organization under Labour and outlines the principal committees and the resulting Cabinet memoranda.

824 **Lord President's Committee.** (7/2/31 part 1) June 1940–Mar 1945. On its composition and functions.

938 **Select Committee on National Expenditure: report on fuel and power.** (30/1/2/10) May–June 1943.

940 **Functions and organization of the Economic Section.** (13/6/17 part 2) 1939–June 1941.

962 **Anglo-Russian trade relations.** (14/3/11 part 1) Oct 1937–July 1944.

985 **U.S. Lend-Lease for munitions in Stage II.** (14/13/15/4) Sept 1944–Oct 1945. Papers on financial negotiations and commercial policy with U.S., including preparatory meetings, 23 and 31 August 1945. Includes some papers by J.M. Keynes.

1084 **Cabinet Office war book: functions of the Cabinet Secretariat.** (19/1/5 part 1) Feb 1940–Sept 1944. Includes E.E. Bridges' memoranda on Cabinet Secretariat since 1904.

1108 **Ministry of Supply organization and functions etc.** (19/6/41 part 4) Aug 1939–Oct 1945. Includes consideration in 1945 of future organization.

1147–1148 **Manpower policy in the transitional stage from war to peace.** (19/9/163 parts 1 and 2).

1147   July 1943–July 1944. Papers relating to the Committee on Demobilization and the two-stage ending of the war, including draft reviews of the manpower position in 1944 and in the first year after the German armistice.

1148   Aug 1944–July 1945. Further papers on manpower in 1944, one year after defeat of Germany and in the two halves of 1945. Some correspondence relating to the Manpower Committee.

1159   **Defence (general) post-war policy.** (19/10/87 part 6) Dec 1943–Nov 1945.

1194   **Ministerial Oil Committee: general correspondence.** (19/11/142 part 1) Feb–Dec 1944.

1217   **Government legislative programmes session 1943–44.** (27/8/1 part 7) Aug 1943–Sept 1944.

1220   **Government pledge not to introduce controversial legislation.** (27/8/9) Sept–Oct 1942.

1224   **Legislation: submission of bills to the War Cabinet before being introduced in Parliament.** (27/8/23) Feb–Sept 1945.

1225   **Defence regulations: 1. legislative measures to be taken at the end of hostilities 2. revocation of.** (27/8/24 part 1) Jan 1944–Nov 1945. Includes papers on the legal position concerning post-war retention and reviews of which should be kept.

1229   **Publication of statistics, etc. Removal of security ban at the end of hostilities in Europe.** (28/1/5 part 1) May–July 1945.

1235   **Demobilization scheme: return of troops to U.K.: transport arrangements.** (29/11/32) Mar–Oct 1945.

1241   **Shipping Committee: general correspondence.** (29/12/75 part 2) Jan–Dec 1945. Various papers on shipping policy including Jay on the need for a long-term plan for shipping and shipbuilding.

1247   **Commercial policy.** (30/22/43) Nov 1944–Mar 1945. Papers, including one by L.C. Robbins, on Article VII and a report by U.K. officials on the discussions.

1249   **Industry: reconversion from war to peace-time production.** (30/31/3) Sept 1944–Feb 1945. Includes meeting of ministers, 7 September 1944, a paper by Sir Robert Sinclair and correspondence between Lyttelton and Dalton.

1365   **War Cabinet Office: statistical and economic sections, reorganization of.** (48/48 part 1) Nov 1940–Mar 1941.

1419   **Britain's wartime economic organization. Information for the U.S.A.** (S50/24/16) May 1938–Oct 1944.

1515   **Office of the Minister of Production.** (51 part 3) Jan 1942–Nov 1943. Includes papers on the relationship with the Board of Trade.

1579   **Economic Section organization and functions.** (55) Jan–Mar 1941.

1583   **Committee on Reconstruction Problems: composition and functions.** (56/1 part 2) Nov 1940–Feb 1943.

1586   **Reconstruction problems: ministerial responsibility and procedure.** (56/2) Feb 1941–Dec 1943.

1588   **Committee on Reconstruction Priorities: miscellaneous correspondence.** (56/5/2) Jan–Nov 1943. Includes papers on its establishment, J.E. Meade on the maintenance of employment and E.E. Bridges' recommendation to postpone consideration of 'The need for decisions' until after 20 July 1943.

1589	**Official Committee on Post-war Internal Economic Problems: production of a Cease-fire book.** (56/13) Oct 1942–Mar 1945. Includes papers on 'The need for decisions', October 1943, and Churchill's directive on the plans for the transition period and R(44)45.
1590–1593	**Cease-fire (Europe) book. Correspondence with government departments.** (56/13/1 parts 1–4) Jan 1944–May 1945.
1594	**Cease-fire (Europe) book: arrangements for VE Day.** (56/13/2) Mar–May 1945.
1595	**Cease-fire (Europe) book: public announcements.** (56/13/9) Aug 1944–May 1945.
1615	**Agriculture prices.** (1/3/5 part 2) Aug 1940–Jan 1947.
1616	**Agriculture policy.** (1/5/7 part 3) June 1946–1947. Copies of drafts of the Agriculture Bill and the final Act, Cmd. 6996. Little correspondence.
1617–1618	**Food policy and agriculture marketing.** (1/5/47 parts 1 and 2) Apr 1948–May 1950. Includes papers of the Food Policy Working Party and the Food Distribution Committee.
1621	**Members of the Cabinet and composition of the government.** (4/1/3 part 3) May 1945–July 1951.
1646	**Briefing of ministers on economic subjects.** (4/1/67) Aug 1950–Nov 1951. C.E.P.S. was no longer to assist various offices in briefing on economic subjects. Economic Section was available if required.
1672	**Cabinet documents: procedure regarding the issue of: to Sir Leslie Rowan** (4/3/324) Oct 1949–July 1951. Includes a weekly letter from N. Brook to L. Rowan in Washington on relevant issues such as economic questions considered by Cabinet and the Economic Policy Committee.
1690	**Economic development in the colonies.** (6/15/25 part 1) Jan–May 1948.
1701–1702	**Organization of Cabinet committees.** (7/2/3 part 5 and 6).
1701	May 1946–June 1947. Includes lists of various committees and their members, CP(46)357, and correspondence on the overhaul of the system to reduce ministers' workload.
1702	July 1947–January 1950. Further lists, proposals to abolish certain committees and correspondence on the reorganization following Cripps's appointment as Minister for Economic Affairs including consideration of the Economic Planning (later renamed Economic Policy) Committee. Correspondence on making the Economic Secretary, rather than E.N. Plowden, chairman of the Materials, Fuel Allocations and Distribution of Industry Committees. Much less after 1947.
1703	**Cabinet committee book.** (7/2/3/1) Sept 1945–Dec 1950. Correspondence on revision, and partial drafts of the book which set out committees' terms of reference and membership.
1704	**Cabinet economic committees: preparation of, guide to, by J.D. Peek.** (7/2/3/4) Feb 1946–Sept 1950. Composition and terms of reference of various committees with list of official committees and the GEN series, May 1949, leading to the guide, June 1949, and revised, Sept 1950, giving terms of reference, composition, secretaries, and including an organization chart.

1709 Lord President's Committee: composition and terms of reference. (7/2/31 part 2) Aug 1945–Mar 1950.

1710–1712 Lord President's Committee: general correspondence. (7/2/31/3 parts 1–3) Jan 1944–July 1951. Papers on a variety of economic subjects. CAB 21/1712 has less relevant material but does include papers on the Economic Powers Bill and the manufacture of goods for civilian use in government-owned establishments.

1713 Materials Committee: composition and terms of reference. (7/2/46 part 1) Nov 1945–May 1950. Includes papers on the 1946 rearrangement and the discussion between N. Brook and E.N. Plowden on its relationship with C.E.P.S. Gap from Jan 1948 to Mar 1950.

1714 Official Committee on Food Supplies from South East Asia and Certain Other Countries: composition and terms of reference. (7/2/50) Feb 1946–May 1950.

1715 Committee on Overseas Economic Policy: composition and terms of reference. (7/2/61) Oct 1946–Oct 1947.

1716 Coal Committee: composition and terms of reference. (7/2/63) July–Dec 1946. Correspondence on the overlap with other committees leading to the eventual formation of the smaller Coal Committee.

1719 Overseas economic development: committee organization. (7/2/66/4) Jan 1944–Jan 1950.

1720 Fuel Committee: composition and terms of reference. (7/2/73) Feb 1947–Apr 1950. Papers on its establishment and a possible official committee.

1721 Paymaster General: membership of Cabinet committees and issue of Cabinet documents to. (7/2/76) Mar 1947–Apr 1949. Papers relating to Marquand's responsibilities concerning economic planning in early 1947 and the replacement of the Ministerial Committee on Economic Planning during Morrison's illness by *ad hoc* meetings under Attlee.

1724 Economic Policy Committee: composition and terms of reference. (7/2/82 part 1) Oct 1947–July 1951. Papers on its establishment and membership.

1725 Production Committee: general correspondence. (7/2/83/3 part 1) Oct 1947–Apr 1949. Includes papers on capital investment, accommodation for miners and agriculture workers, winter transport, mid-week sport, building and various materials.

1726 Legislation Committee: composition and terms of reference. (7/2/87 part 2) Feb 1942–Mar 1950.

1730 Food Distribution Committee: composition and terms of reference. (7/2/103) May 1948.

1736 1. Committee on the Census of Distribution.
2. Committee on Census of Production. (7/3/9) May 1945–Jan 1949.

1740 Balance of payments: 1. Overseas Negotiations Committee 2. Export Committee 3. Exchange Requirements Committee: composition and terms of reference. (7/3/21 part 1) Aug–Sept 1947. Papers on the machinery dealing with balance of payments leading to CP(47)255 and 287 and the establishment of the three committees. Later papers on changes in membership etc.

1741 Overseas Negotiations Committee Working Party: general papers etc. (7/3/21/2) Jan–Nov 1949.

1743   **Committee on the Machinery of Government: composition and terms of reference.** (7/4/33) June 1942–July 1950. Papers relating to the ministerial committee and its reconstitution in 1946.

1744   **Distribution of Industry Committee: composition and terms of reference.** (7/4/67) July 1944–Mar 1951. Papers on the establishment of the 1944 and 1946 committees. Includes discussion between N. Brook and Jay.

1745   **Housing: ministerial responsibility: composition and terms of reference of housing committees.** (7/4/83) Oct 1944–Aug 1947.

1759   **Conference on financial and economic aid to Europe held in Paris: June 1947 (General Marshall, Secretary of State for U.S., Plan)** (9/42) June 1947–Nov 1950. Includes a paper on developments following Marshall's speech, documents relating to the Paris conference and the Washington discussions October/November 1947, the London Committee report on Marshall Aid, and the establishment of the O.E.E.C.

1761   **The London Conference: May 1950: Sir Norman Brook's papers.** (9/62/13) April–May 1950. On Anglo-U.S. relations, N.A.T.O. etc.

1802   **Customs unions: consultation with Commonwealth.** (10/4/35) Aug 1947–Feb 1951.

1806   **Commonwealth consultation: economic planning.** (10/4/44) July 1948–Apr 1950. Papers relating to the Working Party on Sterling Area Planning and the Commonwealth's position in regard to long-term planning for the O.E.E.C. Also on the transfer of economists between Britain and Australia, and papers for the 1948 Commonwealth prime ministers' conference.

1830   **Conference of Commonwealth finance ministers (July 1949) on gold and dollar reserves (telegrams).** (10/4/62) June–Aug 1949.

1831   **Committee on Commonwealth Economic Affairs: general.** (10/4/63 part 1) Aug 1949–May 1952.

1832   **Conference of Commonwealth finance ministers on gold and dollar reserves (July 1949): general papers.** (10/4/66) July–Aug 1949.

1856   **Inter-departmental Committee on Resettlement in Employment of Members of the Forces: general correspondence and miscellaneous papers.** (12/4/77) Jan 1947–Oct 1948. Attached annex on Inter-service Committee on the Recognition of Regular Service Tradesmen by Trade Unions.

1860–1864   **Ceiling strength of the armed forces.** (12/4/94 parts 1–5) Jan 1943–Aug 1950. Includes various papers on the size of the armed forces, the defence budget and national service. CAB 21/1863 includes the Harwood Report, with comments.

1868   **Sterling area negotiations.** (13/3/7) Feb 1946–May 1950. Includes papers on the 1949 Sterling Area Conference.

1869   **Control of key prices.** (13/6/44) Dec 1940–Oct 1949. Little after 1941, although one 1949 brief on oil prices.

1870   **Contracts expiring at the end of the war.** (13/6/48) Apr 1945–Oct 1952. Includes consideration of the legal definition of the end of the war.

1873–1874   **Germany: post-war development of industry and export trade.** (14/2/107 parts 2 and 3) 1946–48.

1927–1928   **Policy towards Japanese industry.** (14/19/29 parts 1 and 2) Dec 1945–June 1948.

1962–1963   **European Economic Committee: general correspondence.** (14/31/163 parts 1 and 2).

     1962   December 1944–Dec1949: Papers relating to the O.E.E.C. and the long-term programme.

     1963   June 1949–Sept 1951: Papers relating to the O.E.E.C., E.R.P. appropriations, E.P.U. internal financial stability and the liberalization of trade.

1984   **Economic sanctions against Persia.** (14/41/9) July–Sept 1951.

1992   **Foreign Office: establishment of an economic and industrial planning staff.** (15/4/3) Jan 1944–Nov 1946.

1998   **Committee on Machinery of Government: general correspondence.** (15/34/37) Aug 1942–June 1949.

2010   **Government departments: functions and ministerial responsibilities.** (15/34/61/3 part 1) Mar 1946–Dec 1951. Various briefs and reviews of departments for the Government Organization and Machinery of Government Committees.

2011   **Government information services.** (15/36/2 part 1) Sept 1945–Mar 1952.

2021   **Production of bricks.** (16/3/13 part 1) Jan–June 1946. Papers and briefs relating to the brick shortage and means of increasing labour in the industry. Notes of meetings of the Inter-departmental Committee on Brick Making.

2023   **Housing: informal meetings of ministers.** (16/3/20) Oct 1945–June 1946. Minutes of meetings.

2024–2025   **Building Controls Committee: general correspondence.** (16/3/24 parts 1 and 2) Mar 1948–Dec 1949. Minutes, memoranda and correspondence relating to particular cases including its report (BCC(48)6).

2026   **Future policy towards the building industry. Meetings of ministers to consider: general correspondence etc.** (16/3/28) Nov 1948–May 1951. Papers, including the report, of the Working Party on Future Policy Towards the Building Industry (GEN 320).

2040–2041   **India: trade questions.** (18/4/1-2) Jan 1947–Dec 1949.

2051   **Ministry of Supply organization and functions, etc.** (19/6/41 part 5) Apr 1951–Mar 1952. Papers on the ministry's reorganization and notes on its civil functions regarding the engineering industry.

2058–2059   **Government surplus stores. Plans for disposal (Cmd. 6539).** (19/6/702 parts 1 and 2) June 1944–Aug 1946.

2060   **Service requirements and stocks of civilian-type equipment in short supply in the civilian market, enquiry into.** (19/6/708) May 1946–Jan 1950.

2061–2065   **Defence Committee enquiry into service requirements and stocks of civilian-type equipment in short supply in the civilian market (Professor Plant's report).** (19/6/708/1–5) June 1946–Mar 1947.

2069–2071   **Compulsory military service: post-war policy.** (19/9/154 parts 1– 3) Aug 1945–Oct 1948. Papers on manpower allocations and service requirements, call-up during the transition and papers leading up to the National Service Bill.

2073   **Manpower policy in the transitional stage from war to peace.** (19/9/163 part 3) Aug 1945–Oct 1946. Papers on the release from munitions and the forces, reviews of the manpower situation, and papers relating to the Manpower Committee and the Manpower Working Party.

2074   **Civil Service Manpower Committee: miscellaneous papers.** (19/9/166) Nov 1946–Nov 1947. Includes the Hamilton Report on the regional organization of Trade and Industry Departments' possible overlap of functions.

2095   **Preparation of defence estimates (1947–49).** (19/10/203 part 2) Dec 1948–July 1950.

2104   **Defence programme: economic implications.** (19/10/239/4 part 1) Sept 1948–Jan1951. Includes notes and briefs relating to GEN 333/1 and on how the Cabinet should consider the programme.

2105   **Oil: Anglo-American discussions on.** (19/11/136) June 1944–Mar 1947.

2106   **Oil: planning of oil resources.** (19/11/138 part 1) Jan 1947–July 1948. Includes papers of the Official Oil Committee (OOC).

2107   **Ministerial and Official Oil Committees: general correspondence** (19/11/142 part 2) Sept 1945–Oct 1950. Various briefs and notes for meetings etc.

2109   **Labour: wages and hours etc.: collective bargaining: meeting of the T.U.C. officials, Drapery Joint Industrial Council and ministers.** (21/1/13) Sept 1947–Mar 1948. Includes record of deputation from the T.U.C. to Attlee, 1 October 1947, and reaction of Isaacs and Attlee. Note of further T.U.C. meetings with ministers, 11 Feb 1948 and 23 Mar 1948.

2111   **International Labour Conferences.** (21/6/1 part 2) Nov 1941–Dec 1949.

2129–2131   **Revocation of defence regulations.** (27/8/24 parts 2–6) Feb 1946–Oct 1951. Papers relating to the Emergency Legislation Committee (EL), reviews of defence regulations and the duration of emergency powers. Annex attached to CAB 21/2131 contains miscellaneous acts and statutory instruments.

2132   **Duration of emergency acts.** (27/8/24/1 part 1) Mar 1944–Oct 1950.

2133   **Legislation Committee: general correspondence.** (27/8/28 part 1) Apr 1942–Nov 1949.

2136–2137   **Government legislative programme session 1947/1948: Treasury.** (27/8/51 parts 1 and 2) Feb 1947–Nov 1949.

2139   **Government legislation: preparation of bills.** (27/8/65 part 1) Nov 1947–June 1949.

2144   **Parliament etc.: continuation of emergency legislation (Cmd. 8069).** (27/8/132 part 1) Dec 1949–Nov 1950. Papers on the future of emergency powers after December 1950. Papers on the drafting of the bill, and relating to GEN 324 and GEN 343. Also includes papers on powers for operating economic controls, the E.C.O.S.O.C. full employment resolution and the draft White Paper on full employment, Nov 1950.

2145   **Legislation: statutory instruments.** (27/8/163) Nov 1950–Nov 1953.

2147   **Review of Parliamentary control of delegated legislation: general.** (27/8/167) Apr–June 1951.

2159   **Publication of monthly statistical digest.** (28/1/5) July 1945–Oct 1951.

2160   **Publication of annual statistical abstract.** (28/1/7) June 1947–Jan 1948.

2188   **Publication of Cabinet documents: post-war contribution of British agriculture to the saving of foreign exchange.** (28/2/96) Feb–May 1947. Mention in public of figures in WP(45)36 leading to Cmd. 7072.

2190   **Use of official information etc.: Economic studies and the problems of government: lecture by Sir John Anderson.** (28/2/99) Jan 1947–July 1948. Note by the Economic Section on the Monnet Plan, discussions with Monnet, and notes and correspondence in relation to Anderson's Stamp Memorial Lecture including one on the problems of economic planning in a free society.

2198   **U.K. import programmes.** (29/12/59 part 3) June 1942–Feb 1950. Includes some consideration of shipping but little after the war.

2199   **Balance of payments: follow-up action.** (30/1/18) Aug–Oct 1947. Includes relevant Cabinet and GEN 179 minutes and memoranda on action to be taken following the convertibility crisis.

2200   **Balance of payments committee's procedure.** (30/1/19) Nov 1947–Nov 1948. Procedural arrangements for the Overseas Negotiations and Exchange Requirements Committees.

2201   **European trade: relaxation of import restrictions.** (30/1/22) May 1949–July 1950. Includes briefs on import licensing, economic planning and liberalization, and the Stikker Plan.

2202   **Trade Negotiations Committee: international trade discussions.** (30/3/13) Feb 1946–July 1951.

2205   **Trade etc.: machinery for analysing and interpreting economic statistics.** (30/12/6) Dec 1947. Cripps was keen for increased interpretation of statistics.

2206   **Committee on Overseas Economic Information: statistical information about economic conditions from foreign countries.** (30/12/7 part 1) Jan 1945–Nov 1947.

2207   **Coal industry: general.** (30/18 part 1) Sept 1945–Jan 1947. Mainly in relation to nationalization.

2208–2210   **Electricity: proposals for socialization.** (30/20/12 parts 1–3) Nov 1945–Dec 1948.

2211   **Electricity consumers' consultative machinery.** (30/20/12/3) June 1948–Jan 1951.

2212   **Electricy general and miscellaneous questions.** (30/20/12/6) Dec 1946–June 1951. Includes papers on generating capacity, efficiency and hydro-electric schemes.

2213   **Electricity: North of Scotland Hydro-electric Board: appointments etc.** (20/12/8) Apr 1948–July 1951.

2214   **Electricity: North of Scotland Hydro-electric Board: functions etc.** (30/20/12/9 part 1) Dec 1942–June 1949. Includes the White Papers of the Board's Annual Reports and construction schemes.

2215   **Preparations for national economic plans.** (30/22/32 part 1) Aug 1945–Nov 1946. Includes E.E. Bridges's circular on economic planning, with comments, including those by the Economic Section and N. Brook; J.P.R. Maud on the role of the Treasury; and E.E. Bridges's circular of 6 September 1945 and the resulting meeting, 12 September which led to his memorandum 'Planning of economic development' for ministers. Also Economic Section and C.S.O. on national income in 1946, 1947 and 1948, Ministry of Health circular to local authorities on capital expenditure, the Economic Survey for

1946 with related papers, and the Economic Section on capital development and future organization of the iron and steel industry.

2216   **U.K. general economic position (Cmd. 7046 and Cmd. 7344).** (30/22/32 part 2) Dec 1946–Apr 1948. Includes relevant Cabinet minutes and memoranda leading to the 1947 and 1948 Surveys, brief for ministers for meeting with the T.U.C., 7 May 1947, and J.E. Meade and F.W. Paish 'Aggregate supply and demand at the end of 1948', *London and Cambridge Economic Service Bulletin* xxvi (1948).

2217   **Outline history of central organization for economic policy (1919–47).** (30/22/35) 1947. Unsigned paper with extract of O. Franks, *Central Planning and Control in War and Peace.*

2218   **Cabinet: decisions on economic matters 'progressing'.** (30/22/36) September 1947–March 1948. Proposal for a fortnightly progress report.

2219   **Information Division of the Treasury: duties and functions of.** (30/22/38) Oct 1947–Dec 1950. Papers and meetings on the functions of the Economic Information Unit set up in 1947, on the Economic Bulletin and the Unit's transfer to the Treasury in 1950.

2220   **Organization for economic planning.** (30/22/41) Oct 1947–Oct 1951. Papers relating to the appointment of the Minister of Economic Affairs and the public announcement of details of economic planning machinery. Various notes on the central economic planning organization, in particular on the balance of payments machinery and handling E.R.P. questions, C.E.P.S. May 1951, and a draft paper on the co-ordination of economic policy. October 1951.

2221   **Economic Policy Committee: general correspondence.** (30/22/46 part 1) May 1948–Aug 1951. Includes various briefs, correspondence between Attlee and the Ministers of Fuel and Power, Food, Supply and Works, July 1951, on price controls, and discussions with Australians on economic planning.

2222   **Investment programmes: general.** (30/22/48 part 1) July 1948–December 1951. Papers relating to the annual programmes, steel allocations, departmental replies to the E.N. Plowden circular on the reduction of capital investment, October 1949, and the resulting revised investment programmes for 1950, and civil investment in 1952 and 1953.

2223   **The state of the nation in November 1951.** (30/22/71) Dec 1951–June 1952. Paper setting out the position on the change of government with resulting correspondence.

2224   **Regional organization.** (30/31/2) Feb 1945–July 1946. Includes consideration of the future of regional boards.

2241   **Transport: increase in railway freight rates and dock and canal charges.** (31/7/3) Sept 1948–Mar 1951.

2242   **Briefs for ministers' speeches.** (32/87 part 2) Oct 1938–Sept 1950. Includes draft passages on the impact of the defence programme on the U.K. economy in 1950.

2243–2250   **Prime Minister's briefs.** (32/87/1 parts 1–8) Jan 1947–Dec 1951. Miscellaneous briefs on papers for various committees, including Cabinet, the Economic Policy Committee and the Fuel Committee.

2260–2262   **Miscellaneous briefs for the Lord President.** (32/289 parts 1–3) Oct 1945–Mar 1950.

2260   October 1945–November 1946: Includes Economic Section briefs on various subjects, including centralized purchasing, the import programme, national wages policy, and monthly statistical reports.

2261   Jan 1947–July 1948: Economic Section and E.M. Nicholson briefs, including ones on agriculture, wages, building programme, coal and the world dollar shortage.

2271   **Ministry of Materials: formation and functions etc. (44/99)** March 1951–July 1954. Proposals for the new ministry submitted to Attlee, April 1951, with drafts of the resulting bill.

2273   **Offices of the War Cabinet: distribution of duties. (48B part 3)** Oct 1943–Oct 1944. Includes a chart of the central executive government of Great Britain.

2276   **War Cabinet conclusions: carrying out of, policy. (48/36)** Sept 1939–Mar 1950. Very little after 1943.

2277–2281B   **Prime Minister's minutes. (48/37/1 parts 1–6).** Minutes on miscellaneous subjects to various ministers.

2277   Sept 1945–Dec 1946. M194/45–M482/46.

2278   Jan–Dec 1947. M1/47–M438/47.

2279   Jan–Dec 1948. M1/48–M213/48.

2280   Jan–Dec 1949. M1/49–M295/49.

2281A   Jan–Dec 1950. M1/50–M152/50.

2281B   Jan–Dec 1951. M1/51–M98/51.

2283   **C.S.O (H. Campion) organization and functions. (48/49)** Apr 1941–Mar 1950. Paper on work and organization of C.S.O., March 1943, and various notes thereafter including Cripps requesting a review of statistical services, 1950.

2285   **Report of the mission appointed to enquire into the production and transport of vegetable oils and oil seeds produced in the West African colonies. (48/50/7)** Aug 1946.

2295   **Committee on Reconstruction Problems: Inter-departmental Committee on Social Insurance and Allied Services (report by Sir William Beveridge) (Cmd. 6404 and Cmd. 6405). (56/5)** July 1941–Mar 1944. Includes J.E. Meade's comparison of the White Paper on *Employment Policy* with Beveridge's *Full Employment in a Free Society.*

2297   **Industrial reconversion: ministerial responsiblity. (56/31)** October 1943–June 1946. Papers arising from WP(43)476 and leading on to R(44)45. Economic Section note on regional industrial problems in the transition, April 1945 and April 1946.

2310   **Socialized industries ministerial committee: general correspondence. (78/4/1)** June 1948–Aug 1951.

2311   **Socialization: general. (78/4/2 part 1)** Jan 1948–Mar 1951.

2312   **Socialization: enquiries for information about socialized industries. (78/4/3)** Apr 1948–May 1951.

2313   **Socialization: overseas experience. (78/4/4)** Dec 1945–Apr 1951.

2314   **Socialization: circularization of material of general interest to socialized boards: items. (78/4/6)** Mar 1948–Oct 1950.

2321   **Socialization: membership of government advisory bodies. (78/4/14)** Dec 1947–Mar 1951.

2322   **Socialization: meeting with chairmen of boards, summer 1950: efficiency and public accountability and pensions. (78/4/15)** May–Oct 1950.

2327	**Socialization: relations of boards with ministers and government departments.** (78/4/31) June 1948–January 1951.
2329	**Socialization: organization: general.** (78/4/34) May 1946–June 1951.
2330–2331	**Socialization: checks on efficiency.** (78/4/35 parts 1 and 2) Feb 1947–Dec 1950.
2332	**Socialization: productivity.** (78/4/37) Sept 1948–May 1949.
2333	**Socialization: charges, prices, etc.** (78/4/39) Jan 1949–Sept 1951.
2338	**Socialization: annual report and accounts.** (78/4/45) Nov 1948–July 1951.
2339	**Gas: proposals for socialization.** (78/7/1) November 1946–Jan 1949.
2340–2344	**Transport and socialization: proposals for.** (78/8 parts 1–5) Sept 1945–Sept 1948.
2345–2348	**Transport charges, prices etc.** (78/8/5 parts 1–4) Apr 1946–July 1950.
2349	**Transport: general and miscellaneous questions.** (78/8/6) May 1946–Apr 1951.
2350	**Transport: Transport Commission and executives appointments etc.** (78/8/12 parts 1 and 2) Apr 1946–Oct 1951.
2352–2353	**Aviation: proposals for socialization.** (78/9/1 parts 1 and 2) Nov 1945–Jan 1947.
2354	**Aviation: aerodromes.** (78/9/7 part 1) Jan 1945–May 1951.
2355	**Aviation: London airport.** (78/9/15) Feb 1945–Jan 1951.
2357	**Aviation: air corporations: organization.** (78/9/17) Jan 1948–Apr 1951.
2358	**Aviation: air corporations: relations with ministers and government departments.** (78/9/18) Jan 1948–July 1950.
2359–2365	**Iron and steel: proposals for socialization.** (78/10 parts 1–7) Oct 1945–Apr 1951.
2367	**Socialization: National Health Service Bill.** (78/19/1) May 1949–June 1952.
2368	**Defence and economic policy: committee structure.** (80) August 1950–Sept 1951. Papers on the review of committee structure with rearmament, including departmental comments leading to ES(50)1.
2369	**Economic and defence co-ordination: progress report.** (80/10) Nov 1950–Dec 1951. Weekly reports.
2473	**Home Affairs Committee: composition and terms of reference.** (7/2/1 part 2) Mar–July 1945. Includes papers on co-ordination of reconstruction and *ad hoc* committees.
2475	**Housing (Official) Committee: composition and terms of reference.** (7/2/10) June–July 1945. Includes papers on housing programme, controls and labour supply.
2480	**Committee on External Economic Policy and Overseas Trade: composition and terms of reference.** (7/2/28) July 1944–Nov 1946. Papers on the establishment of the Overseas Economic Policy Committee (OEP), the future of the Department of Overseas Trade and the establishment of the committee itself (E), its winding up and replacement by the new Overseas Economic Policy Committee.
2482	**Ministerial Committee on Socialization of Industries: composition and terms of reference.** (7/2/32/1) Jan 1946–May 1951.
2483	**Socialized industries: working party constitution etc.** (7/2/32/2) Nov 1948–Jan 1950.

2484 **Ministerial Committees on Home and Overseas Information Services: composition and terms of reference.** (7/2/51 part 1) March 1946–Dec 1947.

2488 **Sub-committee on Distribution of Industry: composition and terms of reference.** (7/2/55) Mar 1946–Apr 1947. Consideration of the machinery for the development areas leading to the sub-committee's establishment.

2489 **Official Committee on Economic Development Working Group: composition and terms of reference.** (7/2/66/5) Mar 1949–Oct 1950. Papers on the reorganization of external economic policy committee structure leading to the working group's establishment.

2492 **Official Oil Committee: composition and terms of reference.** (7/2/72 part 1) Jan 1944–Oct 1950.

2493 **Production Committee: Sub-committee on Manufacture in Government-Controlled Establishments of Goods for Civilian Use: general correspondence.** (7/2/83/5) July–October 1950. Includes papers on positive powers to be included in the Full Employment Bill.

2497 **Defence (Transition) Committee: Manpower Sub-committee: composition and terms of reference.** (7/2/102) Jan 1948–Mar 1950.

2500 **Productivity (Official) Committee: composition and terms of reference.** (7/2/113) Aug 1948–Mar 1951. Papers on its establishment arising from the review by Government Organization Committee. Includes a report on the promotion of industrial productivity.

2501 **Manpower Committee (Official): composition and terms of reference.** (7/2/119 part 1) December 1948–May 1951. Papers on the discussions leading to the committee's establishment.

2505 **Committee on the Control of Investment: composition and terms of reference.** (7/2/131) May 1949–July 1950. Papers on its establishment, note of the meeting, 25 May 1949, on the powers for operating economic controls and extract of the Second Secretaries' meeting, 31 May 1949.

2506 **Official Committee on Powers for Operating Economic Controls: composition and terms of reference.** (7/2/132) May–July 1949. Note of a meeting, 25 May 1949, on powers and extract of the Second Secretaries' meeting, 31 May 1949, leading to BC(49)1.

2507 **Committee on Commonwealth Economic Affairs: composition and terms of reference.** (7/2/133) Aug 1949–Nov 1951.

2508 **Committee on Development Charges: composition and terms of reference.** (7/2/136) Nov 1949.

2509 **Committee on Distribution and Marketing: composition and terms of reference.** (7/2/144) Mar–Apr 1950. Includes interim report of the Food Distribution Committee (FD(48)18).

2512 **Raw Materials Committee: composition and terms of reference.** (7/2/161) Oct 1950–Dec 1951. Papers on its establishment, changes of membership and changes following the establishment of the Ministry of Materials.

2513 **Cabinet Committee on the Hotel Industry: composition and terms of reference.** (7/2/163) Nov–Dec 1950.

2514 **Ministerial Committee on Fuel Economy: composition and terms of reference.** (7/2/174) Feb–Sept 1951. Includes *ad hoc* meeting, 9 February 1951, on fiscal inducement to saving fuel and Noel-Baker's

	proposal for a ministerial committee, with comments, leading to its establishment (CFE).
2515	**National economy in war: consultation with U.S.A.** (13/6/53/1 part 1) Mar–Sept 1950. Some minutes and memoranda of GEN 317 and GEN 317A.
2562	**Foreign Office: proposed Economic Intelligence Department.** (15/4/4) Mar–Dec 1944.
2635	**Geographical distribution of war production.** (19/10/23 part 3) Nov 1940–Nov 1944.
2636	**Distribution of industry.** (19/10/23 part 4) Mar–Aug 1946. Includes papers on public utility projects and their consideration by Panel A, and strategic aspects of the policy.
2653	**Industrial disputes: docks.** (21/10/2 part 1) June 1948–June 1950.
2654	**Papers prepared on the assumption that a Conservative government was formed after the general election October 1951.** (27/3/3) Oct–Nov 1951. Includes a review of Conservative policy, T.L. Rowan on the deteriorating economic position and other papers on the amalgamation of the Ministry of Food and the Ministry of Agriculture and Fisheries, the Commonwealth conference, defence, co-ordination of economic policy and the implications of supervisory ministers for Cabinet structure.
2655–2658	**Emergency Business Committee: miscellaneous papers.** (27/4/11 parts 1–4) May–July 1945.
2666–2671	**The King's speeches on the prorogation and opening of Parliament.** (27/6/1 parts 9–14) Sept 1943–Nov 1946.
2718	**Composition etc. of committees.** (48/21 part 5) May 1945–Jan 1945. Covers various committees and the Cabinet Committee Book.
2730	**Leakage of information: Iron and Steel Bill.** (S50/10/10/3) June 1948–June 1949.
2758	**Coal industry: general and miscellaneous questions.** (78/5/12) July 1948–Feb1951. Includes papers on the quality of the coal, domestic solid fuel appliances, transport for miners and various addresses by Viscount Hyndley.
2759	**Coal industry: human factors.** (78/5/13) February 1948–Mar 1951. Includes papers on industrial productivity, involuntary absenteeism, correspondence between Noel-Baker and Morrison on man management in the industry, and note of the meeting between the N.C.B. and the Ministries of Labour and Fuel and Power on personnel management, 22 January 1951.

Chapter 4 Lord President's Committee (Wartime)

Set up in 1940 and became the major committee co-ordinating domestic policy. In July 1945 took over the function of the Reconstruction Committee, see CAB 87/5–10; and temporarily renamed Home Affairs Committee (HA). Received regular reports on manpower, the coal and food situation, stocks of food, raw materials etc. Papers after December 1945 continue in CAB 132.

Terms (1940) (i) to keep continuous watch on behalf of the War Cabinet over the general trend of economic development (ii) to concert the work of the economic committees and to deal with any differences not requiring reference to the War Cabinet (iii) to deal with any residual matters and with special questions which arise from time to time.

(July 1945) (i) to consider, and where necessary to advise the Cabinet on, all questions of domestic policy not specifically assigned to other committees including questions of post-war reconstruction (ii) to keep under review the general trend of our economic development.

(Aug 1945) (i) to consider questions of internal economic policy and to keep under review the general trend of our economic development (ii) to deal, as required, with other questions of domestic policy not specifically assigned to other committees.

Members (1943) Ld President (ch.); Ch. of Exchequer; Home Sec.; Ld Privy Seal; S./ S. Dominions; Mins. of Labour & N.S., Production, Supply, Without Portfolio. (Sept 1943) Pres. Bd Education, Paymaster-Gen. replace Ld Privy Seal, Min. of Supply. (Nov 1943) Min. of Reconstruction replaces Min. Without Portfolio.

(July 1945) Ld President (ch.); Ch. of Exchequer; Home Sec.; Ld Privy Seal; Pres. Bd Trade; Min. of Prod.; S./S. Scotland; Min. of Labour & N.S.; Paymaster-Gen. (Aug 1945) Added: Mins. of Agriculture & Fish, Food, Fuel & Power, Supply & Air Prod., War Transport. (Mar 1950) Mins. of Civil Aviation, Education, Health, Nat. Insurance, Town & Country Planning and Ch. D. Lancaster replace Pres. Bd Trade and Mins. of Agriculture & Fish, Food, Fuel & Power, Supply & Air Prod., and Transport.

Secs. J.P.R. Maud (Ld Pres. O.) and W.S. Murrie (Cab. O.).

4.1 Meetings and Memoranda

CAB 71/11 Meetings 1 January–31 December 1943 LP(43)1st–77th.

8 Jan	**LP(43)2nd**	**Cost of living index.** LP(43)4. Acceptance of LP(43)4.
18 Jan	**4th**	**The building industry: post-war training and entry into the industry.** LP(43)12. Whilst sympathetic to LP(43)12 the practicability of the construction programme must be assured.
29 Jan	**8th:1**	**Coal: production and consumption.** LP(43)20.

2 Mar	13th:2	**Concentration and transfer of production.** LP(43)39.
5 Mar	14th:7	**Agricultural prices: calculation of aggregate net income from farming.** LP(43)34.
19 Mar	17th:2	**Cost of living index.** LP(43)56 and 58.
9 Apr	24th:2	**Agricultural production. Quarterly report.** LP(43)73.
	:4	**Review of the economic position.** LP(43)55, 57 and series 'A' statistical digest.
7 May	31st:2	**Building: functions of the Ministry of Works.** LP(43)95.
14 May	33rd:2	**Rail transport.** LP(43)98.
21 May	34th:5	**Coal: production and consumption in the coal year 1942/43.** LP(43)110.
9 June	38th:1	**Government building programme.** LP(43)130.
	:2	**Building: functions of the Ministry of Works.** LP(43)129 and 131.
22 June	40th	**Coal.** LP(43)139. The industry's reorganization, concentration, the limitations of the present system of control, manpower, the 1943–44 coal budget, an output bonus and the Harriman Mission's report.
25 June	41st:3	**Post-war employment.** LP(43)143. Compulsory military service, the control of labour, financial assistance to transferred workers, the reinstatement of ex-service personnel in employment, financial assistance to unemployed ex-service personnel and the giving of preference in employment to ex-servicemen and women.
2 July	43rd:2	**Agricultural wages and prices.** LP(43)154.
9 July	47th:4	**Industry: monopolistic and restrictive practices.** LP(43)164. The Board of Trade to submit a memorandum to the Reconstruction Priorities Committee.
16 July	49th:4	**Coal: production and consumption in 1943–44.** LP(43)172.
28 July	52nd:3	**Cost of living.** LP(43)183. Minutes are in the confidential annex attached.
20 Aug	55th:2	**Coal: manpower.** LP(43)191.
17 Sept	57th:1	**Manpower: post-war control.** LP(43)206. The reinstatement of ex-service personnel in employment.
	:2	**Manpower: post-war control.** LP(43)203. Resettlement of the demobilized.
	:3	**Agricultural prices: calculation of aggregate net income from farming.** LP(43)196.
29 Sept	59th:3	**Coal: output bonus.** LP(43)214.
	:4	**Coal: general situation.**
6 Oct	60th:1	**Coal: budget for 1943/44.** LP(43)222.
	:2	**Coal.** LP(43)219. The appointment of a ministerial committee to consider long-term

proposals for the industry was to be
recommended to the War Cabinet.

12 Oct	**62nd:2**	**Agricultural prices.** LP(43)220.
12 Nov	**69th:1**	**Coal: finance of the coal-mining industry.** LP(43)229.
19 Nov	**70th:1**	**Coal: manpower.** LP(43)252.
3 Dec	**73rd:5**	**Retail trade.** LP(43)266.
13 Dec	**75th:1**	**Coal: budget for 1943–44.** LP(43)263 and 276.
	:2	**Coal: finance of the coal-mining industry.** LP(43)275.
	:5	**Cost of living index.** The Ministry of Labour was concerned about an unofficial study by Rowntree.
17 Dec	**76th:2**	**Food: proposed long-term contracts for meat.** LP(43)279.
	:3	**Agricultural policy.** LP(43)285.
31 Dec	**77th:3**	**Coal: consumption and production.** LP(43)295.

CAB 71/12   Memoranda   1 January–24 May 1943   LP(43)1–119.

6 Jan	**LP(43)4**	**Cost of living index – Wood,** 3p. Simplification of the calculations proposed.
13 Jan	**9**	**Statistical studies relating to industrial efficiency – Anderson,** 2p.
14 Jan	**12**	**White Paper on training for the building industry – Bevin and Portal,** 5p.
26 Jan	**20**	**The prospects of coal production and consumption. Coal year 1 May 1943 to 30 April 1944 – Lloyd George,** 9p.
22 Feb	**34**	**Calculation of the aggregate net income from farming – Anderson covering the Ministry of Agriculture and Fisheries,** 2+1p.
25 Feb	**39**	**Concentration and transfer of production – Bevin, Lyttleton and Dalton,** 2p.
12 Mar	**56**	**Review of policy on subsidies and prices – Anderson,** 6p. Report by the Treasury reviewing the success of the stabilization policy.
17 Mar	**57**	**Quarterly survey of the general economic situation – Anderson covering the Economic Section,** 10p. Primarily concerned with manpower and shipping.
6 Apr	**76**	**United States assistance to the United Kingdom import programme – Leathers,** 4p.
15 Apr	**83**	**Revocation of licences – Woolton,** 2p.
29 Apr	**95**	**The position and functions of the Ministry of Works – Portal,** 6p. Lists Ministry's functions and controls over industry.
3 May	**98**	**Restriction of rail traffic – Leathers,** 5p.
17 May	**110**	**Coal production and consumption in the coal year 1 May 1942 to 30 April 1943 – Lloyd George,** 4p.

Manpower referred to in **LP(43)104** and **115.**

CAB 71/13 Memoranda 25 May–27 September 1943 LP(43)120–216.

28 May	**LP(43)125**	**Review of war legislation – Anderson,** 4p. Consideration of emergency powers felt to be necessary post-war.
5 June	**129**	**Government building programme – E.E. Bridges covering the Treasury,** 3p.
7 June	**130**	**Government building programme – Portal,** 3p. Single ministerial direction needed to secure greater efficiency and more effective use of labour.
7 June	**131**	**Concentration of government building – Portal,** 2p.
17 June	**139**	**Coal: progress report on the operation of the White Paper scheme – Lloyd George,** 8p.
22 June	**143**	**Questions relating to post-war employment on which early decision is now required – Bevin,** 5p. Departmental planning and organization for resettlement required immediate decisions on certain issues.
30 June	**154**	**Agricultural wages and prices – Hudson,** 3p.
7 July	**164**	**Enquiry into monopolies – Dalton,** 3p.
13 July	**172**	**Coal requirements, 1943–44 – Lloyd George,** 5p. Provisional statement of the coal budget given.
24 July	**183**	**Cost of living index –Wood,** 3p.
18 Aug	**191**	**Labour supply for coal-mining – Bevin and Lloyd George,** 5p. Need for immediate action and for plans to increase the labour force in 1944–45.
25 Aug	**196**	**Calculation of the aggregate net income from farming – Anderson covering the Ministry of Agriculture and Fisheries,** 1+1p.
14 Sept	**206**	**Reinstatement on demobilization – Bevin,** 2p.
28 Sept	**213**	**Composition of the committee – E.E. Bridges,** 1p.

Manpower also referred to in **LP(43)184** and **200.**

CAB 71/14 Memoranda 1 October–31 December 1943. LP(43)217–302.

4 Oct	**LP(43)219**	**Examination of the present system of control in the coal-mining industry and future policy – Lloyd George,** 4p. Recommendation that committees were needed to consider both the present and post-war organization of the industry.
4 Oct	**220**	**Agricultural prices – Hudson, R. and Johnston,** 4p.
4 Oct	**221**	**Agricultural prices – Morrison,** 5p.

4 Oct	222	**Revised coal budget, 1943–1944 – Lloyd George,** 3p.
13 Oct	229	**Financial position of the coal industry – Lloyd George,** 3+3p appendixes.
12 Nov	252	**Compulsory drafting to coal-mining – Bevin,** 4+2p appendix.
18 Nov	255	**Composition of the committee – E.E. Bridges,** 1p.
29 Nov	264	**Period of paid furlough for service personnel on demobilization – Bevin,** 3p.
30 Nov	266	**Retail trade – Dalton,** 2p.
6 Dec	274	**Price of gas – Lloyd George,** 4p.
6 Dec	275	**Financial position of the coal industry – Lloyd George,** 4p.
10 Dec	276	**Coal supply position (revised consumption estimates) – Lloyd George,** 2p. Revised version.
8 Dec	277	**Retail trade –Woolton, Dalton and Mabane,** 1p. Continuance of retail licencing through the transitional period, but not permanently, recommended.
10 Dec	279	**Long term contracts for meat – Mabane,** 4+1p appendix.
9 Dec	281	**Arrangements for regular weekly meetings – Attlee,** 1p.
11 Dec	282	**Survey of the general economic position – Economic Section,** 19p. Manpower, shipping, raw materials, food and standards of consumption are covered.
14 Dec	285	**Long-term meat contracts – Hudson, R. and Johnston,** 2p.
22 Dec	293	**Regulation of wages and conditions of employment. Legislation to meet post-war requirements – Bevin,** 4p. Further powers required to prevent the disintegration of voluntary machinery in certain industries once state support was removed.

CAB 71/15   Meetings   7 January–29 December 1944   LP(44)1st–59th.

7 Jan	**LP(44)1st:1**	**Coal: transport facilities.** LP(44)1 and 3.
	:3	**Exports: prices of United Kingdom exports to the colonies.** LP(43)292.
	:5	**Review of the economic situation.** LP(43)282.
14 Jan	**3rd:3**	**Clothing: relaxation of restrictions on men's suits.** LP(44)6.
28 Jan	**5th:1**	**Cost of living index.** LP(44)14.
	:2	**Cost of living index.** LP(44)15. The committee endorsed LP(44)15.
	:6	**Production: publication of statistics of absenteeism.**
4 Feb	**6th:2**	**Location of industry: placing of additional load in designated areas.** LP(44)23.

	:3	**Coal.** LP(44)19, 20 and 26.
	:4	**Prices.** LP(44)25.
11 Feb	7th:3	**Supplies of raw materials in the transition period.** LP(44)28.
	:4	**Statistics: publication of export figures.** LP(44)29. No decision.
25 Feb	10th:2	**Release of requisitioned factory premises.** LP(44)40.
3 Mar	11th	**Consumption.** LP(44)43.
6 Mar	12th	**Coal.** LP(44)47.
24 Mar	14th:1	**Coal.**
31 Mar	15th:4	**Agricultural credit.** LP(44)60. Anderson recommended that the Agricultural Mortgage Corporation should be made ready to resume its operations.
	:5	**Cost of living index.** No action to be taken.
28 Apr	21st:1	**Control of Employment (Civil Servants) Order.** LP(44)72.
5 May	23rd:1	**Coal: publication of coal statistics.** LP(44)83.
12 May	25th:1	**Registration of builders and contractors.** LP(44)84.
	:2	**Housing: priority for labour and materials.** LP(44)87.
19 May	26th:2	**Registration of builders and contractors.** LP(44)88.
26 May	27th:2	**Labour supply in designated areas.** LP(44)98.
	:3	**Civil service.** LP(44)89. The Treasury wanted a larger release from the armed forces of persons with administrative experience.
9 June	29th:2	**Control of Employment (Civil Servants) Order.** LP(44)72. Lloyd George was concerned that, because so many of his staff were temporary, he could not guarantee successful administration by his department.
23 June	32nd:2	**Coal.** Finance of the coal-mining industry.
	:3	**Coal: budget for the years 1943–44 and 1944–45.** LP(44)109.
14 July	36th:4	**Home food production.** LP(44)120.
28 July	38th:1	**Control of Employment (Civil Servants) Order.** LP(44)132.
	:2	**Coal: the price of coke.** LP(44)129.
4 Aug	40th:5	**Agriculture. Publication of agricultural statistics.** LP(44)123.
11 Aug	41st:2	**Production. Absenteeism in industry.** LP(44)138.
22 Sept	45th:1	**Statistics: publication of export figures.** LP(44)149.
3 Oct	46th:4	**Agriculture: publication of agricultural statistics.** LP(44)159.
6 Oct	47th:1	**Statistics.** LP(44)162 and 163. The committee agreed in principle to the publication of

statistics about the war effort of the U.K. on
the lines of LP(44)163.

	:2	**Statistics: publication of export figures.** LP(44)161. Acceptance of proposals.
	:3	**Agriculture: publication of agricultural statistics.** LP(44)164.
13 Oct	**48th:2**	**Coal: position in Stage II.** LP(44)165.
20 Oct	**49th:5**	**Home food production.** LP(44)170.
27 Oct	**50th:3**	**Unauthorized disclosure of information.** LP(44)169.
28 Nov	**54th:1**	**Agricultural prices.** LP(44)192.

Manpower was considered at **LP(44)22nd, 42nd, 43rd** and **49th.**

CAB 71/16   Memoranda   3 January–7 June 1944   LP(44)1–100.

3 Jan	**LP(44)1**	**Transport of coal – Leathers,** 3p.
5 Jan	**3**	**Transport facilities for coal – Lloyd George,** 3+1p annex.
24 Jan	**14**	**The cost of living index in 1944 – Anderson,** 4p. The base level at which prices should be stabilized should be increased, if stabilization policy was not to become unaffordable.
24 Jan	**15**	**The present position in regard to the make-up of the official cost of living index – Treasury,** 6p. The present index should be retained for the duration of the war and then revised.
26 Jan	**19**	**Estimates of coal production and consumption for 1943–44 – Attlee,** 3+1p.
29 Jan	**23**	**Placing of additional load in designated areas – Lyttleton,** 1+3p annexes.
31 Jan	**25**	**Price control of consumer goods – Dalton,** 3+5p appendix. Review of existing arrangements and the likely post-war situation.
2 Feb	**26**	**Facilities for coal stocking at and near collieries – Lloyd George,** 2+1p appendix.
5 Feb	**28**	**Supplies of raw materials in the transition period – Lyttelton,** 3p. It was hoped that shortages of material would not impose any serious handicap on industry in the transition period.
7 Feb	**29**	**Publication of export figures – Dalton,** 1p.
22 Feb	**40**	**Release of requisitioned factory premises – Dalton,** 2p.
29 Feb	**43**	**Comparison of food consumption levels in the United Kingdom, the United States and Canada – Llewellin,** 3+13p appendixes.
3 Mar	**47**	**Proposals for the overhaul of the wage structure of the coal-mining industry – Lloyd George,** 4p.
24 Mar	**60**	**Agricultural credit – Hudson, R. and Johnston,** 1+1p. Two papers. See R(44)62 and 63.

22 Apr	72	**Control of Employment (Civil Servants) Order** – Anderson, 4p.
3 May	83	**Publication of coal statistics** – Lloyd George, 1p.
4 May	84	**Registration of builders and contractors** – Portal, 2p.
11 May	87	**Priorities for labour and materials for the housing programme** – Willink, Johnston and Portal, 2p.
15 May	88	**Registration of builders and contractors** – Portal, 2p.
16 May	89	**Shortage of government administrative staff** – Anderson, 3p.
24 May	95	**Control of Employment (Civil Servants) Order** – Alexander and Grigg, 3p.
24 May	98	**Labour supply in designated areas** – Lyttelton, 2p.
3 June	99	**Control of Employment (Civil Servants) Order** – Anderson, 3p.

Manpower referred to in **LP(44)79.**

CAB 71/17 Memoranda 7 June–28 September 1944 LP(44)101–158.

21 June	**LP(44)109**	**The coal budget for the United Kingdom. Coal years 1943–44 and 1944–45** – Lloyd George, 6p.
17 July	123	**Publication of agricultural statistics** – Hudson, R., Johnston and Morrison, 2+7p appendixes.
	129	**The financial condition of the coke industries and its bearing on coke prices** – Lloyd George, 8+6p appendixes.
26 July	132	**Control of Employment (Civil Servants) Order** – Anderson, 2p.
16 Sept	149	**Publication of export figures** – Dalton, 1+1p annex. Publication was necessary in order to allow industrialists to plan the post-war export trade.

CAB 71/18 Memoranda 27 October–29 December 1944 LP(44)159–211.

27 Sept	**LP(44)159**	**Publication of agricultural statistics** – Hudson, R., 2p.
3 Oct	161	**Publication of export figures** – Dalton, 2p.
4 Oct	162	**Proposed publication of statistics about the war effort of the United Kingdom** – Anderson, 2p.
4 Oct	163	**Proposed publication of statistics about the war effort of the United Kingdom** – E.E. Bridges, 51p. Draft White Paper by the C.S.O.
5 Oct	164	**Publication of agricultural statistics** – Hudson, R. and Johnston, 1p.
9 Oct	165	**The coal position in Stage II** – Lloyd George, 2+5p annexes.

13 Oct	**169**	**Unauthorized disclosures of proceedings of the Lord President's Committee and the Reconstruction Committee – Attlee and Woolton,** 1+2p annex. See R(44)171.
23 Nov	**192**	**Agricultural prices – Hudson, R., Johnston and Morrison,** 7+2p appendix.
1 Dec	**196**	**Revised coal budget, 1944–45 – Lloyd George,** 2p.
29 Dec	**211**	**Price control in the transition period: proposed amendment of the Goods and Services (Price Control) Act, 1941 – Dalton,** 2p. In the transition, prices should be fixed by directions to individual firms as well as for classes of goods.

Manpower referred to in **LP(44)171** and **183.**

CAB 71/19   Meetings   10 January–14 December 1945   LP(45)1–47.

10 Jan	**LP(45)1st:1**	**Price control in the transition period.** LP(44)211. Committee approved LP(44)211 and the proposal for a National Mark for certain utility goods.
	:3	**Consumption. Comparison of food consumption levels in the United Kingdom, the United States, Canada and Australia.** LP(45)1.
12 Jan	**2nd:2**	**United Kingdom stock position.** LP(45)12.
26 Jan	**5th:2**	**Coke. The coke supply position.** LP(45)13.
16 Feb	**8th:3**	**Coal.** LP(45)40.
	:4	**Price control in the transition period: proposed amendment of the Goods and Services (Price Control) Act, 1941.** LP(45)37.
	:5	**Distribution of industry: list of development areas.** Amended to include Pembroke.
22 Feb	**9th:1**	**Coal: operational requirements.** LP(45)41. Prospects for the next coal year should be urgently reviewed.
23 Feb	**10th:1**	**Cement prices.** LP(45)39. Bevin wanted longer-term price settlement.
2 Mar	**11th:1**	**Wages: wages of agricultural and other rural workers.** LP(45)42.
	:2	**Agriculture: food production programme and related manpower requirements.** LP(45)45 and 52. Agreement that the appendix to LP(45)45 provided realistic targets for the level of food production in 1945–46 and 1946–47.
7 Mar	**13th**	**Agricultural prices.** LP(45)55 and 56. Consideration related to the cost of living index and the stabilization policy.
21 Mar	**16th:2**	**Coal: production and consumption.** LP(45)54 and 61. Anderson felt that the general problem of manpower allocation and the prospect of a

breakdown in coal supplies during the winter of 1945–46 were two separate problems.

	:3	**Coal prices.** LP(45)64.
23 Mar	17th:1	**Fertilisers: requirements for the three years 1945–48.** LP(45)67.
29 Mar	18th:3	**Fish: post-war production and distribution of white fish.** LP(45)66, 68, 77 and 81.
13 July	25th:1	**Work of the committee in the immediate future.** Review of forthcoming subjects.
	:2	**Highway policy: estuarial crossings.** HA(45)7.
20 July	26th:4	**Publication of statistics.** LP(45)122.
17 Aug	27th:1	**Composition and terms of reference of the committee.** LP(45)129. Morrison's views on future work.
	:2	**Supplies of coal for gas works.** LP(45)133.
21 Aug	28th:3	**Allocation of building labour.** LP(45)131. Tomlinson's proposals were temporarily accepted but the whole position to be reviewed.
	:4	**Supplies of coal for gas works.**
24 Aug	29th:1	**Future of the regional boards and the National Production Advisory Council.** LP(45)145. Regional boards were to become strictly advisory.
	:5	**Food: present position and prospects for the winter 1945–46.** LP(45)142.
31 Aug	30th:5	**Industrial organization and efficiency.** LP(45)152. The committee generally agreed with LP(45)152 but the Cabinet must decide.
7 Sept	31st:3	**Survey of the general economic position.** LP(45)138, 139 and 148. Consideration of the machinery of planning, the maintenance of employment and essential services during the period of demobilization and reconversion, the domestic implications of the world food situation, the implications of the coal shortage and the control of inflation.
18 Sept	33rd:1	**Civil Service: staffing position.** LP(45)169 and 176.
2 Oct	35th:2	**Nationalization of the coal-mining industry.** LP(45)179.
	:4	**Coal.** LP(45)178, 184 and 191. Morrison felt that the coal problem, after housing, threatened to be the most serious source of social distress. A coherent and practical plan of attack was needed.
5 Oct	36th:1	**Labour controls.** LP(45)187. Agreement that an official committee should consider the issue.
	:2	**National building programme.** LP(45)180 and 192. Labour ceilings approved, provided that they would be reviewed, once experience had been gained.
12 Oct	37th:1	**Food. World shortage.** LP(45)181, 182 and 189.

	:2	**Food: long-term food policy.** LP(45)196.
19 Oct	38th:1	**Future meetings of the committee.**
	:3	**Employment and unemployment statistics.** LP(45)198. Publication of a monthly manpower statement was deferred until January 1946.
	:7	**Future of the electricity and gas industries.** CP(45)217 and LP(45)202. Dalton felt that it was important that each nationalized industry should have its own plans for periods of stagnation. These should be drawn up.
1 Nov	40th:1	**Iron and steel.** LP(45)212.
	:4	**Agricultural policy.** LP(45)216.
	:7	**Mr. John Maud.**
9 Nov	42nd:1	**Employment and unemployment statistics.** Isaacs and Attlee disagreed with LP(45)38th:3. The committee decided to publish the statements from October 1945.
	:3	**Coal-mining Industry (Nationalization) Bill.** LP(45)227.
	:4	**Nationalization proposals.** LP(45)222, 228, 233 and 234.
16 Nov	43rd:6	**Investment (Control and Guarantees) Bill.** LP(45)236. Morrison felt that the draft White Paper overstated the significance of the legislation. It was agreed that no White Paper should be published.
23 Nov	44th:5	**Coal-mining Industry (Nationalization) Bill.** LP(45)238.
7 Dec	46th:6	**Incentives, restrictions and controls.** LP(45)253 and 259.
14 Dec	47th:1	**Building: removal of embargo on new works in the London civil defence region.** LP(45)260.
	:2	**Remuneration of members of boards to operate socialized industries.** LP(45)257 and 264.

Manpower was discussed at **LP(45)2nd** and **3rd.**

CAB 71/20   Memoranda   2 January–22 May 1945   LP(45)1–107.

2 Jan	LP(45)1	**Comparison of food consumption levels in the United Kingdom, the United States, Canada and Australia** – Hudson, R., 2+7p appendix.
10 Jan	11	**Labour supply position in Greater London** – Bevin, 3p.
11 Jan	12	**United Kingdom stock position** – Lyttelton and Leathers, 1p.
11 Jan	13	**The coke supply position** – Lloyd George, 4p.
12 Jan	15	**Labour supply position in Greater London (fuel and power industries)** – Lloyd George, 1p.
17 Jan	17	**Attendance at meetings** – Attlee, 1p. The aim of the committee was to relieve the burden on

the War Cabinet. This was impossible if important ministers were missing.

13 Feb	37	**Price control in the transition period: proposed amendment of the Goods and Services (Price Control) Act, 1941 – Dalton,** 2p.
14 Feb	40	**Coal supplies for S.H.A.E.F. up to 30 April 1945 – Lloyd George,** 2p.
21 Feb	41	**Coal supplies for S.H.A.E.F. and the Mediterranean – Leathers and Lloyd George,** 3p.
23 Feb	42	**Wages of agricultural and other rural workers – Hudson, R.,** 1p.
23 Feb	45	**Food production programme – Hudson, R.,** 1+2p appendix.
27 Feb	52	**Manpower in agriculture during 1945 and succeeding years – Hudson, R.,** 3p. Concerned that the manpower for post-war agriculture may be insufficient.
2 Mar	55	**Review of agricultural prices, February 1945 – Hudson, R., Johnston and Morrison,** 2+1p appendix +2p annex.
2 Mar	56	**Calculation of the aggregate net income from farming – Attlee covering the Ministry of Agriculture and Fisheries,** 2+7p appendix. Written in consultation with the Department of Agriculture for Scotland and the C.S.O.
9 Mar	61	**Budget for the coal year 1945–46 – Lloyd George,** 4+2p annexes.
19 Mar	66	**Post-war production and distribution of white fish – Hudson and Johnston,** 3+10p appendix. Report of the inter-departmental Committee on the Post-war Regulation of Fisheries, 29 November 1941, is attached.
19 Mar	67	**Fertiliser requirements for 1945–46, 1946–47 and 1947–48 – Hudson, R., Johnston and Morrison,** 2+1p appendix.
19 Mar	68	**Post-war production and distribution of white fish – Llewellin,** 2p.
26 Mar	75	**Post-war production and distribution of white fish – Alexander,** 2p.
26 Mar	77	**Post-war production and distribution of white fish – Morrison,** 2p. Expressed general concern that producing industries might organize themselves on the basis of restricted supplies and maintained prices which in total would jeopardize expansion and full employment.
28 Mar	81	**Post-war production and distribution of white fish – Hudson, R.,** 2p.

CAB 71/21   Memoranda   5 July–1 October 1945   LP(45)108–189.

5 July	**LP(45)108**	**Membership in terms of reference – E.E. Bridges,** 1p.

12 July	**114**	**Highway policy: estuarial crossings – Leathers,** 1p.
14 July	**118**	**Interim report of the Committee on the Future of the White Fish Industry – the Committee,** 5p.
17 July	**122**	**Publication of statistics – Anderson,** 2p. The aim was to publish as many statistics as possible in order to gain the co-operation of industry.
25 July	**127**	**Survey of the general economic situation – Economic Section,** 18+6p appendixes. Charts the main features expected as the economy moved from Stage I to Stage II, by considering the size of the aggregate demand for the national product, the size of the national product and the problems of the gap between the two. Two dangers were perceived: inflation and tardy reconversion. Exports and coal supplies were the two main priorities.
14 Aug	**129**	**Composition and terms of reference – E.E. Bridges,** 1p.
14 Aug	**131**	**National building programme, August to December, 1945 – Tomlinson,** 2+2p appendixes.
14 Aug	**134**	**The control of land use – Silkin,** 3+7p appendixes.
15 Aug	**137**	**'Nat and Rat' – Morrison,** 1+5p. Article from *The Economist*, 4 August 1945, is attached.
16 Aug	**138**	**Survey of the general economic position – Morrison covering the Economic Section,** 1+18+6p appendixes. See LP(45)127.
18 Aug	**139**	**Survey of the general economic position: supplementary note – Morrison covering the Economic Section,** 2p. Supplementary to LP(45)138 taking into account the defeat of Japan.
18 Aug	**142**	**Present food position and prospects for the winter of 1945–46 – Smith,** 9p.
21 Aug	**145**	**The future of the regional boards and of the National Production Advisory Council – Cripps,** 4p. Recommends modifications.
22 Aug	**148**	**Survey of the general economic position – Morrison,** 1p. There were five main points requiring discussion by the committee: (a) domestic measures leading to the restoration of the balance of payments; (b) measures for large-scale demobilization and industrial reconversion; (c) domestic implications of the world food situation; (d) implications of the coal shortage and (e) controls and restraints necessary to prevent inflation.
27 Aug	**152**	**The government's plan for encouraging industrial organization and efficiency – Cripps,**

| 26 Sept | 185 | **Vocational training for demobilized personnel – Isaacs,** 3p. |
| 29 Sept | 187 | **Labour controls – Isaacs,** 2+6p appendixes. Recommends their continuance subject to certain relaxations and review in January 1946. |

CAB 71/22 Memoranda 1 October–27 December 1945 LP(45)190–267.

1 Oct	LP(45)190	**Nationalization of the coal-mining industry, colliery-owned railway wagons – Barnes,** 1p.
1 Oct	191	**Transport situation during winter 1945–46 – Barnes,** 2p.
2 Oct	192	**Proposals for the control of the national building programme – Tomlinson,** 4p. Proposes two priority classes of building and the machinery for policy implementation.
3 Oct	193	**The future of the Royal Ordnance factories – Wilmot,** 3p.
10 Oct	195	**Future of the road haulage organization – Barnes,** 3p.
10 Oct	196	**Government controls and food policy – Smith,** 5+2p appendix. Sets out long-term objectives.
10 Oct	197	**Shipping policy – Barnes,** 1p.
10 Oct	198	**The publication of employment and unemployment statistics – Isaacs,** 1p. Also MP(45)138.
18 Oct	202	**Future of transport – Barnes,** 1p.
25 Oct	209	**Labour controls – Morrison covering the official committee,** 8+2p appendixes. Consideration of the impact of the relaxation of labour controls on a co-ordinated scheme of controls. Conflict between what was politically practical and economically desirable.
24 Oct	210	**The future of economic controls – Cripps and Wilmot,** 4p. Proposals to relieve short-term problems.
24 Oct	211	**Progress of the export trade – Cripps,** 2+3p appendixes. First of a new monthly series of reports.
25 Oct	213	**Distribution of Industry Act, 1945 – Cripps,** 3+3p annex.
29 Oct	216	**Agricultural policy – Williams, Westwood and Ede,** 8+3p. The proposed system of assured markets should be announced.
2 Nov	222	**Nationalization of gas and electricity industries – Shinwell,** 2p.
7 Nov	227	**Nationalization of the coal-mining industry – Shinwell,** 2p.
7 Nov	228	**Future of the iron and steel industry – Wilmot,** 5p. Of three options public ownership was recommended.

7 Nov	233	**Future organization of transport services and shipping – Barnes,** 2p. Proposal to bring essential transport services under public ownership.
8 Nov	234	**Nationalization proposals: public announcement – Morrison,** 3p. Draft announcement.
14 Nov	236	**Investment (Control and Guarantees) Bill – Dalton,** 3+6p. Draft bill and White Paper attached, setting out roles of the Capital Issues Committee and National Investment Council.
21 Nov	238	**Coal-mining Industry (Nationalization) Bill – Shinwell,** 4+32p. Draft bill attached.
20 Nov	240	**Acquisition of Land (Authorization Procedure) Bill – Bevan and Fraser,** 3p.
28 Nov	253	**Supply of consumer goods for coal-miners – Shinwell,** 1p. Proposal to increase the range of consumer goods in mining communities to reduce absenteeism.
3 Dec	257	**Remuneration of chairmen and members of boards set up to operate socialized industries and undertakings – Dalton,** 2p.
5 Dec	259	**Incentives, restrictions and controls – Morrison,** 2p. Austerity had a deadening influence on morale and enterprise. Controls had to be shown to be necessary.
5 Dec	260	**New building in the London civil defence region – Tomlinson,** 1p. Proposal to lift embargo.
5 Dec	263	**Method of appointment to boards operating socialized industries and undertakings – Morrison covering the official committee on socialized industries,** 1+2p.
6 Dec	264	**National Coal Board. Salaried members – Shinwell,** 2p.

4.2 Home Affairs (Industrial) Subcommittee

Set up on formation of the caretaker government to replace the Industrial Problems and Export Questions Subcommittees of the Reconstruction Committee and the Distribution of Industry Committee, see CAB 87/14–15, 94. Superseded by the Industrial Subcommittee (CAB 71/27), see immediately below.

Terms (a) to consider the problems of the reconversion of industry from war to peace and other problems of industrial reconstruction (b) to keep under review the progress of preparations for the promotion of export trade (c) to supervise and control the development and execution of government policy for securing the balanced distribution of industry, as outlined in Chapter III of Cmd. 6527: and, in particular, to consider (i) such questions as may be submitted to it relating to projects for new industrial development, (ii) such issues as may be submitted to it regarding the allocation of government factories, and (iii) such applications as may be referred to it for the grant of facilities to individual firms to undertake preparatory work with a view to the post-war expansion of civil production.

Members   Ld President (ch.); Ch. of Exchequer; Pres. Bd Trade; Mins. of Labour & N.S., Production and co-opted ministers.

Secs.   M.T. Flett and A.N. Coleridge (Ld Pres. O.).

CAB 71/26   Meetings and Memoranda   5 July–25 July 1945   HA(I)(45)1st and HA(I)(45)1–4.

Meeting

25 July	**HA(I)(45)1st:1**	**Composition and terms of reference.** HA(I)(45)1.
	:2	**Export prospects: overseas trade in the second quarter of 1945.** HA(I)(45)4.
	:3	**Allocation of Desborough Works, High Wycombe.** HA(I)(45)3.
	:4	**Inter-departmental machinery for handling industrial problems.** HA(I)(45)2.

Memoranda

5 July	**HA(I)(45)1**	**Membership and terms of reference – E.E. Bridges,** 2p. The subcommittee replaced the Distribution of Industry Committee and the Industrial Problems and Industrial Problems (Export Questions) Subcommittees of the Reconstruction Committee.
6 July	2	**Inter-departmental machinery for handling industrial problems – Woolton,** 3p.
23 July	3	**Allocation of Desborough Works, High Wycombe – Lyttleton,** 1+2p.
23 July	4	**Export prospects: overseas trade in the second quarter of 1945 – Lyttleton,** 2+2p. Selected export targets should be made.

4.3   Industrial Subcommittee

Set up in September 1945, see CAB 129/1, CP(45)110.   Ends April 1946, see CAB 132/3, LP(46)101.

Terms   (Sept 1945)   (a) to consider the problems of the reconversion of industry from war to peace and other problems of industrial reconstruction,   (b) to keep under review the development of the export trade,   (c) to supervise and control the development and execution of government policy for securing the balanced distribution of industry, as outlined in Chapter III of Cmd. 6527; and, in particular, to consider   (i) such questions as may be submitted to it relating to projects for new industrial development,   (ii) such issues as may be submitted to it regarding the allocation of government factories and   (iii) such applications as may be referred to it for the grant of facilities to individual firms to undertake preparatory work with a view to the expansion of civil production. (Dec 1945) (d) to determine such issues as may be referred to them in connection with the distribution and use of storage space and the disposal of surplus stores. See CAB 129/5, CP(45)333.

Members Ld President (ch.); Ch. of Exchequer; Pres. Bd Trade; Min. of Labour & N.S. with other ministers co-opted, especially Mins. of Supply & Air Prod., Works after Dec 1945.

Secs. M.T. Flett and A.N. Coleridge (Ld Pres. O.).

CAB 71/27 Meetings and Memoranda 11 September 1945–26th April 1946
LP(I)(45)1st–LP(I)(46)4th and LP(I)(45)1–LP(I)(46)23.

Meetings

11 Sept	**LP(I)(45)1st:1**	Future of the economic controls. LP(45)162. Consideration of their general role in the immediate post-war period.
	:2	**Easing of control and reversion from public to private purchase in minor raw materials.** LP(45)154. Approval of LP(45)154.
	:3	**Export control.** LP(45)160.
	:4	**Wartime controls: proposed government publication.** Morrison suggested the publication of a paper showing the success of controls during the war.
29 Oct	**2nd:1**	**Labour controls.** LP(45)209. The subcommittee were unable to reach agreement. Demobilization, however, should be speeded up, with no favourable treatment of any particular industry. In the long run an adequate supply of labour to essential industries must be based on a revision of the wages structure.
	:2	**Advisory service on production efficiency.** LP(I)(45)2. Approval of proposals.
8 Nov	**3rd:1**	**Economic controls.** LP(45)210. Approval of LP(45)210, and of a standing committee of senior officials to review controls.
	:2	**Employment situation.** LP(I)(45)5.
	:3	**Distribution of Industry Act, 1945: (Wrexham and Wigan).** LP(45)213. The two areas should be designated development areas.
	:4	**Development areas: recent progress.** LP(45)170.
	:5	**Development areas: basic services.** LP(I)(45)6.
12 Nov	**4th:1**	**Development areas.** LP(45)170 and LP(I)(45)6.
	:2	**Exports.** LP(45)211 and LP(I)(45)4.
1 Jan	**LP(I)(46)1st:2**	**Distribution of industry.** LP(I)(45)11.
7 Feb	**2nd:2**	**The employment situation.** LP(I)(46)6. Morrison saw no prospect of mass unemployment for several years.

	:3	**Allocation of raw materials to firms in the development areas.** LP(I)(46)2, 7, 8 and 9. Supplies of raw materials should be increased to firms in areas which could absorb labour. In exceptional cases, production departments must accept the neccessity of discriminating in favour of firms in these areas even if supplies of the raw material in question were not increasing.
	:4	**Distribution of industry: Greater London.** LP(I)(46)4.
12 Feb	**3rd:3**	**Elimination of 'backyard' or 'slum' factories.** LP(I)(46)5.
12 Mar	**4th:1**	**Distribution of industry.** LP(I)(46)16.
	:4	**Development areas: recent progress.** LP(I)(46)14.

Memoranda

15 Sept	**LP(I)(45)1**	**Composition and terms of reference** – E.E Bridges, 2p.
24 Oct	**2**	**Advisory service on production efficiency** – Cripps, 3p. Proposal to continue this wartime service.
24 Oct	**4**	**Development of the export trade** – Cripps, 4p. Since it was intended to plan the domestic economy the export trade should also be planned. Specific targets for each market were impractical, but investment, labour supply and production programmes at home could be planned to fit output to the export targets deemed necessary for the attainment of a suitable balance of payments.
13 Oct	**5**	**The employment situation** – Isaacs, 4p. See CP(45)228.
26 Oct	**6**	**The improvement of basic services in the development areas** – Cripps covering Panel A of the Official Committee on the Distribution of Industry, 3+7p appendixes.
11 Dec	**9**	**Expansion of terms of reference to include storage and disposals questions** – E.E Bridges, 1p.
18 Dec	**11**	**Distribution of industry** – Cripps covering Panel A, 1+1p.
10 Jan	**LP(I)(46)1**	**Economic Survey for 1946** – Dalton, 1+3+32p. See CP(46)32, also ED(46)1.
18 Jan	**2**	**Allocation of raw materials to industries in development areas** – Isaacs, 2p. Policy should be to bring work to the workers, rather than *vice versa*.

22 Jan	4	**Distribution of industry: industrial building projects in Greater London – Cripps covering Panel A,** 1+6p.
23 Jan	6	**The employment and unemployment situation –** Isaacs, 4+5p appendix. Review of the situation, which was to be carried out quarterly. It showed the acute manpower shortage.
28 Jan	7	**Allocation of raw materials to food manufacturers in development areas – Smith,** 3p. Opposes LP(I)(46)2.
28 Jan	8	**Allocation of raw materials to industries in unemployment areas – Cripps,** 3p.
29 Jan	9	**Allocation of raw materials to industries in development areas – Westwood,** 1p. Strongly supports LP(I)(46)2.
22 Feb	14	**Progress in the development areas – Cripps covering Panel A,** 1+7+1p appendix.
28 Feb	16	**Distribution of industry – Cripps covering Panel A,** 1+2p.
7 Mar	17	**The improvement of basic services in the development areas – Cripps,** 2+7p. Inter-departmental reports on physical development and development areas attached.
8 Mar	19	**Employment and unemployment situation –** Isaacs, 5+7p appendixes. Progress report.
1 Apr	22	**Supplies of fuel to industry – Belcher,** 3p.
26 Apr	23	**Termination of the industrial subcommittee –** E.E. Bridges, 1p. See LP(46)101.

4.4 Committee on Emergency Legislation

Set up in CAB 75/15, HPC(43)19th:3. Committee co-ordinates departmental working parties. Replaced by Emergency Legislation Committee, CAB 134/206–208.

Terms (a) to review the whole of war legislation, including the Defence Regulations and other subordinate legislation, and to consider which parts of this legislation could be dispensed with immediately after the cessation of hostilities (i) in Europe and (ii) in other theatres of war; which parts could be dispensed with at various stages in the period of transition from war to peace; and which parts should be continued, with or without modification, until it can be decided by the government of the day whether they should be embodied in permanent legislation

(b) to consider what legislative authority will be needed for the exercise of the emergency powers required during the transitional period beginning with the cessation of hostilities in Europe; and, in particular, whether that authority could be secured, at any rate in the initial stages, by so adapting the Emergency Powers (Defence) Acts and other wartime Acts that they would be appropriate to the conditions obtaining in the period immediately following the end of the war.

Members C. Schuster (Ld Chanc. O., ch.); A. Maxwell (H.O.); H. Hamilton (Scot.); B.W. Gilbert (Try); G. Ram (Parl. C.); A. Hurst (Recon.); N. Brook (War Cab. O.) with others co-opted for security and public order; production; supply and labour.

Secs. H.S. Kent (Parl. C.), A. Johnson (Recon.).

CAB 71/29   Meetings and Memoranda   24 July 1943–12 December 1944
EL(43)1st–EL(44)5th & EL(43)1–EL(44)22.

Meetings

19 Apr	**EL(44)3rd:1**	**Interim report on review of defence regulations.** EL(44)9.
6 Sept	**4th:1**	**GEN 24/6: draft Emergency Powers (Transitional Provisions) Bill.**
12 Dec	**5th:2**	**Proposals for revocation or retention of regulations made or amended between 1 Jan and 31 Aug 1944.** EL(44)19.
	:3	**Legislative authority for continuance of emergency powers.** EL(44)22.
	:4	**Draft of Supplies and Services (Transitional Powers) Bill.** EL(44)20.

Memoranda

24 July	**EL(43)1**	**Terms of reference, composition and procedure – E.E. Bridges,** 2p.
17 Aug	**4**	**Statistics – G. Schuster,** 1p. Also attached:
3 Sept	**EL(S)(43)1**	**Statistics of post-war employment policy – J.R.N. Stone,** 4p. Sets out statistics felt to be required.
22 Oct	**2**	**First interim report: statistics required in connection with post-war employment policy – the Statistics Subcommittee,** 11p. See EC(43)17.
18 Feb	**EL(44)5**	**Review of defence regulations setting out proposals for revocation or retention – H.S. Kent and A. Johnston,** 104p.
24 Mar	**6**	**Proposals regarding the duration of emergency acts – H.S. Kent and A. Johnston,** 23p.
5 Apr	**9**	**Draft of interim report. Review of defence regulations – the committee,** 7p.
4 May	**12**	**Interim report: review of defence regulations – the committee,** 5p.
4 May	**13**	**Review of defence regulations setting out proposals for revocation or retention – the committee,** 104p.
15 Aug	**17**	**Duration of recent defence regulations – H.S. Kent and A. Johnston,** 1+5p.
22 Sept	**18**	**Legislative authority for continuance of emergency powers – H.S. Kent and A. Johnston,** 3+5p. Draft bill attached.
30 Sept	**19**	**Proposals for revocation or retention of regulations made or amended between 1 Jan and 31 Aug 1944 – H.S. Kent and A. Johnston,** 6p.

13 Oct	20	**Draft of Supplies and Services (Transitional Powers) Bill – H.S. Kent and A. Johnston covering G. Schuster,** 1+1p appendix. Letter from Schuster to the Reconstruction Committee attached.
30 Nov	22	**Legislative authority for continuance of emergency powers – H.S. Kent and A. Johnston,** 3+4p annexes.

CAB 71/30   Meetings and Memoranda   6 March–31 December 1945
EL(45)1st–5th and EL(45)1–24.

Meetings

1 Aug	**EL(45)2nd**	**Supplies and Services (Transitional Powers) Bill.** EL(45)10.
10 Aug	3rd	**Supplies and Services (Transitional Powers) Bill.** EL(45)12.
7 Sept	4th	**Legislative authority for continuance of emergency powers.** EL(45)16.
21 Sept	5th	**Emergency Laws (Transitional Provisions) Bill.** EL(45)16.

Memoranda

5 May	**EL(45)4**	**Revocation of defence regulations at the end of hostilities in Europe – H.S. Kent and A. Johnston,** 1p.
5 May	5	**Revocation of defence regulations at the end of hostilities in Europe – H.S. Kent and A. Johnston,** 1+10p. Draft Order in Council.
1 June	6	**Revocation of defence regulations – H.S. Kent and A. Johnston,** 1+2p.
4 June	7	**Duration of recent defence regulations – H.S. Kent and A. Johnston,** 1+3p.
17 July	8	**Proposals for revocation or retention of regulations made or amended between 1 Sept 1944 and 1 June 1945 – H.S. Kent and A. Johnston,** 4p.
17 July	9	**Revocation of defence regulations – H.S. Kent and A. Johnston,** 1+14p. Departmental observations on EL(45)6.
31 July	10	**Supplies and Services (Transitional Powers) Bill – H.S. Kent and A. Johnston,** 1p. Need to consider enlargement of bill's scope concerning restrictive practices in industry and to replace other proposed legislation, including the Exchange Control and Capital Issues Bill and the Goods and Services (Price Control) (Amendment) Bill.
3 Aug	11	**Supplies and Services (Transitional Powers) Bill – H.S. Kent and A. Johnston covering A. Maxwell,** 1+3+2p. Minute to the Lord

President with the results of the consideration
of the issues raised in EL(45)10.

8 Aug	**12**	**Supplies and Services (Transitional Powers) Bill – H.S. Kent and A. Johnston**, 1+6p. Revised draft bill.
11 Aug	**13**	**Revocation of defence regulations at the end of hostilities in all theatres of war – H.S. Kent and A. Johnston**, 1p.
14 Aug	**14**	**Supplies and Services (Transitional Powers) Bill – H.S. Kent and A. Johnston**, 1+6p. Draft bill as it went to Cabinet.
24 Aug	**15**	**Legislative authority for continuance of emergency powers – H.S. Kent and A. Johnston**, 2p.
5 Sept	**16**	**Legislative authority for continuance of emergency powers – H.S. Kent and A. Johnston**, 3+8p.
13 Sept	**17**	**Revocation of defence regulations at the end of hostilities in all theatres of war – H.S Kent and A. Johnston**, 1+5p. Draft Order in Council.
14 Sept	**18**	**Emergency Laws (Transitional Provisions) Bill – H.S. Kent and A. Johnston**, 2+12p. Draft bill.
27 Sept	**19**	**Emergency Laws (Transitional Provisions) Bill – H.S. Kent and A. Johnston**, 1+15p. Revised draft bill.
26 Sept	**20**	**Emergency Laws (Transitional Provisions) Bill – H.S. Kent and A. Johnston**, 1+18p. Draft as it went to the Legislation Committee.
1 Nov	**21**	**Note by the joint secretaries – H.S. Kent and A. Johnston**, 1+15p. Draft Orders in Council for when the Supplies and Services (Transitional Powers) Bill passes into law.
24 Nov	**22**	**Supplies and Services (Transitional Powers) Bill – H.S. Kent and A. Johnston**, 1+15p. Revised Orders in Council.
31 Dec	**24**	**Emergency Laws (Transitional Provisions) Bill – H.S. Kent and A. Johnston covering the Home Office**, 2+1+21p.

Chapter 5   Miscellaneous Standing Committees (Wartime)

This chapter covers the papers of seven permanent Cabinet committees, from five record classes, CAB 75, CAB 77, CAB 92, CAB 97 and CAB 98. They have been selected from the many committees dealing with wartime administration because they cover issues relevant to economic planning after 1945 (and in some cases continued for a short period under the Labour government). Several of the committees deal with Anglo-American relations. For related papers on the Joint American Secretariat see CAB 110, and of the British Joint Staff Mission see CAB 122 and CAB 138.

5.1   Home Policy/Legislation Committee

It was originally intended that the Home Policy Committee should be one of the two main wartime committees dealing with the home front. In February 1942, the Lord President took over its chairmanship; and business hitherto assigned to its Home Front and Social Services Section was transferred to the Lord President's Committee. This left only the Legislative Section, so the committee was renamed the Legislation Committee. Its papers after 1945 are in CAB 134/323–40.

Terms (July 1945)   To keep the government's legislative programme under review and to undertake on behalf of the Cabinet a detailed examination of all draft bills and of Orders in Council under the Defence Acts.

Members (Feb 1942)   Ld President (ch.); Ld Chancellor; Home Sec.; Fin. Sec. (Try); S./S. Overseas Trade; English and Scottish law officers.
   (July 1945)   Ld Chancellor (ch.); Home Sec.; Min. of Information; Fin. Sec. (Try); A.-G.; Ld Advocate; Solicitor-Gen.; Solicitor-Gen. of Scotland.
   (Aug 1945)   Ld Privy Seal (ch.); Ld Chancellor; Home Sec.; S./S. Dominions (as leader of the House of Lords); S./S. Scotland; Fin. Sec. (Try); A.-G.; Ld Advocate; Solicitor-Gen.; Solicitor-Gen. of Scotland; Chief Whip. The Lord President (as leader of the House of Commons) might also attend.

Sec.   R.B. Howorth (Cab. O.)   (1944) W.S. Murrie (Cab. O.).

CAB 75/15	Meetings	12 Jan–14 Dec 1943 HPC(43)1st–33rd.
16	Memoranda	1 Jan–1 May 1943 HPC(43)1–68.
17	Memoranda	6 May 1943–4 Feb 1944 HPC(43)69–141.
18	Meetings	11 Jan–19 Dec 1944 HPC(44)1st–40th.
19	Memoranda	3 Jan–30 June 1944 HPC(44)1–59.
20	Memoranda	5 July–30 Dec 1944 HPC(44)60–98.
21	Meetings	9 Jan–17 Dec 1945 HPC(45)1st–34th. See CAB 75/22–3 for the legislation considered.
22	Memoranda	5 Jan–8 June 1945 HPC(45)1–61. Includes the Distribution of Industry Bill.

23 Memoranda 8 June–14 Dec 1945 HPC(45)62–137. Includes papers on the Supplies and Services (Transitional Powers), Bank of England, Building Materials and Housing, Investment (Control and Guarantees), and Bretton Woods Agreement Bills as well as the continuance of emergency powers and price control legislation. Also reviews and progress reports on the annual legislative programme.

5.2 Ministerial Oil Committee

Originally set up in March 1943 in connection with the Washington oil discussions, reporting in May (see CAB 66/50, WP(44)269). It was not active again until its reconstitution under the Labour government in 1945 (see CAB 129/2, CP(45)153), when it considered, among other subjects, Anglo-American discussions on oil and the Petroleum Board.

Terms (Sept 1945) To consider and advise the Cabinet as may be necessary on such questions as may from time to time be referred to it.

Members (Sept 1945) Ld President (ch.); 1st Ld Admiralty; Mins. of Fuel & Power, W. Transport, State (F.O.); Fin. Sec. (Try); Parl. Sec., Bd Trade; Parl. Under S./S. India and Burma.

Secs. G. Laithwaite (Cab. O.) and K.L. Stock (Fuel & P.)

CAB 77/15	Meetings and Memoranda 28 Mar–26 May 1944 MOC(44)1st–7th and MOC(44)1–12.	
30	Meetings and Memoranda 6 Sept–4 Dec 1945 MOC(45)1st–4th and MOC(45)1–9.	

5.3 Joint War Production Staff

Established by the Ministry of Production in 1942 to co-ordinate production for war.

CAB 92/40	Meetings and Memoranda 1943 JWPS(43)1st–10th and JWPS(43)1–64.
41	Meetings and Memoranda 1944 JWPS(44)1st–8th and JWPS(44)1–41. Includes consideration of reconversion and manpower requirements, and reciprocal aid.
42	Meetings and Memoranda 1945 JWPS(45)1st–8th and JWPS(45)1–41. Includes consideration of the planning date of the end of the war with Germany, Lend-Lease in Stage III and raw materials in short supply.
129	Meetings and Memoranda 1946 JWPS(46)1st–7th and JWPS(46)1–19. Mainly on production programmes and estimates.

5.4 Committees on Manpower

Both a ministerial and an official committee were appointed as a result of a meeting of ministers (see CAB 78/18, GEN 26/1st) in November 1943 to deal with the annual manpower allocations. Once the official committee had reported (MP(43)3, also see CAB 66/43, WP(43)539) in November 1943, it was disbanded; but the ministerial committee continued and covered requirements, allocations, reviews, and releases from the forces. Agricultural manpower received considerable attention. For later papers see CAB 134/509.

Official Committee:

Terms A provisional manpower allocation for the year 1944 should be worked out, as a matter of urgency, on hypothesis (a) set out in paragraph 5 of WP(43)490, namely, that *for the purposes of manpower plans* departments should work on the *assumption* that Germany will be defeated by the end of 1944 and should concentrate on the measures necessary to bring our greatest striking power to bear in that year. In presenting the picture on this assumption, an indication should be given of what our situation would be in 1945, if manpower plans for 1944 had been made on hypothesis (a) and in the event that war with Germany continued after the end of 1944.

Members R. Sinclair (Prod., ch.); R. Weeks (War O.); G. Dunn (Adm.); C. Courtney (Air); N. Brook (Cab. O.); E. I. Jacob (Cab. O.); G. Ince (Lab. & N.S.).

Secs. S.R. Dennison (Ec. Sect.) and A. Reeder (Lab. & N.S.).

Ministerial Committee:

Terms To consider the broad principles involved in this investigation and give such guidance as may be necessary to the official committee.
   (July 1945) To submit to the Cabinet periodical reviews of the manpower position and proposals for the redistribution of manpower.
   (Aug 1945) See CAB 134/509.

Members Ch. of Exchequer (ch.); Mins. of Labour & N.S., Production; Paymaster-Gen.
   (July 1945) Ch. of Exchequer (ch.); Pres. Bd Trade; Min. of Labour & N.S.; Paymaster-Gen.
   (Aug 1945) See CAB 134/509.

Secs. N. Brook (Cab. O.).
   (July 1945) W.S. Murrie (Cab. O.) and S.R. Dennison (Ec. Sect.).
   (Aug 1945) See CAB 134/509.

   CAB 92/104   Meetings and Memoranda   8 Nov 1943–21 Dec 1945
                 MP(43)1st–6th, MP(44)1st–10th, MP(45)1st–14th and
                 MP(43)1–6, MP(44)1–7 and MP(45)1–67.

5.5 Committee on Lend-Lease

Consists of the papers of the Lend-Lease Committee (Washington) in 1943 and various papers on Lend-Lease matters in 1944-45.

>CAB 97/73   Memoranda only   15 Jan 1943–4 July 1945   LL(43)1–43, LL(44)1–68, LL(45)1–17.

5.6 Informal Committee on the Combined Boards

Dealt mainly with the wartime work of the Combined Boards responsible for the co-ordination of production and supply in the U.K. and the U.S.A. In 1946 the committee considered the possible establishment, on the abolition of the boards, of a joint economic secretariat for the exchange of information between the two countries.

>CAB 97/130   Meetings and Memoranda   3 Jan 1944–26 Apr 1946 ICB(44)1st–9th, ICB(45)1st–5th, ICB(46)1st–2nd and ICB(44)1–8, ICB(45)1–12 and ICB(46)1–10.

5.7 Committee on the King's Speeches

The committee was appointed annually as a small group of senior ministers to draft the speeches which formally announced the government's legislative programme for the forthcoming parliamentary year. The first draft considered by the Cabinet is always included. For later papers see CAB 134/467–468.

Terms   To prepare and submit to the War Cabinet a draft of the King's speeches on the prorogation and opening of Parliament.

Members (1943) Ld President (ch.); For. Sec.; S./S. Dominions; S./S. Air; Pres. Bd. Education; Min. of Labour & N.S.
  (1944) Deputy P.M.; Mins. of Labour & N.S., Information, Education; S./S. Dominions; S./S. Air.
  (June 1945) For. Sec.; Ld Chancellor; S./S. Colonies; Min. of Labour & N.S.; 1st Ld Admiralty.
  (1946) Ld President (ch.); Ld Privy Seal; Ch. of Exchequer; S./S. Dominions; Chief Whip.
  (1947) Ld President (ch.); For. Sec.; Ch. of Exchequer; Min. of Ec. Affairs; Ld Chancellor; Home Sec.; Chief Whip.

Sec. (June 1945) W.S. Murrie (Cab. O.).

>CAB 98/3   Meetings and Memoranda   10 Nov 1939–10 Oct 1947 KS(39)1st, KS(40)1st–2nd, KS(41)1st–2nd, KS(42)1st–2nd, KS(43)1st–2nd, KS(44)1st–3rd, KS(45)1st–2nd, KS(46)1st–2nd, KS(47)1st–2nd and KS(39)1–3, KS(41)1–3, KS(42)1–5, KS(43)1–6, KS(44)1–7, KS(45)1–6, KS(46)1–7, KS(47)1–6.

5.8   Departmental Committee on the White Fish Industry

Set up under Woolton to consider the state of the industry.

CAB 98/43   Meetings May 1945   WFI(45)1st–2nd.

Chapter 6 *Ad Hoc* Cabinet Committees (Wartime)

6.1 Committee on Agricultural Policy

The ministerial committee was set up on 15 October 1943 by the War Cabinet (see CAB 65/36, WM 141(43):1) and its directive (CAB 66/42, WP(43)474) approved on 27 October, see CAB 65/36, WM 146(43):2.

Terms To draw up the terms of a draft directive to guide the agricultural ministers in their forthcoming discussions with the representatives of the industry.

Members Ld President (ch.); Ld Privy Seal; S./S. Scotland; Min. of Agriculture & Fish; Paymaster-Gen.

Secs. E.E. Bridges (Cab. O.) and P. Allen (H.O. & H.S.).

CAB 78/15 Meeting and Memoranda 18 October–21 October 1943 GEN 20/1st, GEN 20/1–3 and WP(43)474.

Meeting
20 Oct	**GEN 20/1st**	Untitled. GEN 20/1. GEN 20/1 was to be revised.

Memoranda
18 Oct	**GEN 20/1**	**Draft directive to the agricultural ministers – E.E. Bridges,** 1+4p. Directive for forthcoming discussions with representatives of the industry.
21 Oct	2	**Revised draft directive to the agricultural ministers – Attlee,** 1+3p.
21 Oct	3	**Revised draft directive to the agricultural ministers – Attlee,** 1p. To be submitted to the War Cabinet.
		WP(43)474 attached.

6.2 Committee on the Publication of Statistics

An informal official committee called by E.E. Bridges, which considered and supported the immediate publication of statistics which would provide a general picture of the war effort. There were no formal terms of reference or membership.

Members E.E. Bridges (Cab. O., ch.).

Sec. R.F. Fowler (Cab. O.).

CAB 78/23   Meetings only   31 August–15 September 1944   GEN 42/1st–2nd.

31 Aug	**GEN 42/1st**	Untitled. General agreement in favour of a White Paper, providing a general picture of the war effort. Annex of provisional outlines, 'Statistics relating to the war effort of the UK', 2p, is attached.
15 Sept	**2nd**	Untitled.

6.3   Committee on the Report of the Working Party on Controls

Set up in September 1945 to consider the report by the Reconstruction Committee's Official Subcommittee on Industrial Problems: Working Party on Controls (see CAB 87/89). Its report (CAB 71/21, LP(45)162) was discussed at the Industrial Subcommittee of the Lord President's Committee, see CAB 71/27, LP(I)(45)1st:1. It was then asked in October to consider the future of labour controls (see CAB 71/19, LP(45)36th) and its report (CAB 71/22, LP(45)209) was discussed by the Industrial Subcommittee on 29 October, see CAB 71/27, LP(I)(45)2nd. It was superseded by the Official Committee on Controls (CAB 132/58).

Members   B.W.Gilbert (Try, ch.); W. Palmer (B.T.); L. Scott (Air P.); W.G. Nott-Bower (Fuel & P.); A.S. Le Maitre (Adm.); P.D. Proctor (Try); A.E. Feavearyear (Food); A.J. Manson (Supply); G. Turner (Supply); H.D. Hutchinson (Supply); R.H. Tolerton (W. Transport); A. Johnston (Ld Pres. O.); M.G. Smieton (Lab & N.S.); J.E. Meade (Ec. Sect.); A.J. Filer (Works); R. Hughes (Adm.).

Sec.   A.N. Coleridge (Ld Pres. O.).

CAB 78/37   Meetings and Memoranda   4 Sept–23 Oct 1945   GEN 87/1st–2nd, GEN 87/1–5 and LP(45)209.

Meetings

6 Sept	**GEN 87/1st**	Untitled. GEN 87/1. Agreement that an amended paper should go to the Industrial Subcommittee of the Lord President's Committee.
23 Oct	**2nd**	**Economic controls.** GEN 87/3 and 4. No minutes issued.

Memoranda

4 Sept	**GEN 87/1**	**Report of the Working Party on Controls,** 19+10p appendixes. See EC(45)12.
12 Oct	**2**	**Economic controls – Office of the Lord President covering Dalton,** 1+4p. Consideration of controls in the period 6–9 months ahead.
20 Oct	**3**	**Economic controls – Office of the Lord President,** 1+10+2p appendix. Draft of a report by officials dealing with labour controls, which became the basis of LP(45)209.

20 Oct	4	**Economic controls – Office of the Lord President covering Dalton, Duncan and Cripps,** 1+5p. Revision of GEN 87/2, entitled 'The future of economic controls'.	
22 Oct	5	**Economic controls – Office of the Lord President,** 1+9+2p appendix. Revised draft of GEN 87/3.	

LP(45)209 attached.

6.4   Committee on Government Controls and Food Policy

Set up in September 1945 to consider the range of controls needed for a long-term food policy and the future of the Ministry of Food. Its report (CAB 71/22, LP(45)196) was discussed at the Lord President's Committee on 12 October 1945, see CAB 71/19, LP(45)37th:2.

CAB 78/38   Memoranda only   19 September–5 October 1945   GEN 92/1–3 and LP(45)196.

19 Sept	**GEN 92/1**	**Government controls and food policy – Llewellin,** 4p.	
28 Sept	2	**Government controls and food policy – Ministry of Food,** 4p.	
5 Oct	3	**Government controls and food policy – Llewellin,** 5+3p appendix. Draft announcement attached.	

LP(45)196 attached.

6.5   Committee on the Coal Position during the Coming Winter

Set up in October 1945 to deal first with the winter of 1945–46 and then to prepare for the winter of 1946–47, see CAB 71/19, LP(45)35th:4. It was served by an official committee (15.2). At the 8th meeting in November 1946 Dalton reported that, in response to his complaint that the Lord President's Committee was duplicating its work, Attlee had recommended the committee's supersession by a smaller body. Accordingly, the Coal Committee was set up on 9 December 1946 (CAB 134/62).

Terms   To discuss plans for dealing with the serious situation which threatened to arise and to arrange for the co-ordination of departmental action for this purpose.

Members   Ch. of Exchequer (ch.); Mins. of Fuel & Power, Supply, Transport, Lab. & N.S.   (July 1946)   Parl. Sec., Bd Trade added.

Sec.   M.T. Flett (Ld Pres. O.)   (Oct 1946) J.H. Lidderdale (Ld Pres. O.) replaced Flett.

CAB 78/38   Meetings and Memoranda   4 October 1945–21 November 1946   GEN
          94/1st–8th and GEN 94/1–25.

4 Oct	**GEN 94/1st**	Untitled. The committee was to discuss plans and co-ordinate departmental action, whilst Lloyd George was to constitute an inter-departmental committee of senior officials. 'Action to meet the coal situation during the coming winter', 5p, is attached.
3 Dec	**2nd**	Untitled. GEN 94/1. Lloyd George was reasonably optimistic of getting through the winter without crisis, provided there was no severe weather or transport breakdown. He and Leathers were concerned about the possibility of the latter.
25 Mar	**3rd**	Untitled. GEN 94/2. No immediate need for the ministerial or official committee to meet as they had successfully fulfilled their functions.
1 Aug	**4th:1**	**The coal budget for 1946–47.** GEN 94/5, 6, 7, 8 and LP(46)199 and 201. Shinwell said that the measures in GEN 94/8 would reduce the coal deficit from 9.5m to 4.5m tons. The committee considered measures to bridge the gap.
16 Sept	**5th**	**Progress report from the official committee.** GEN 94/9. Shinwell said that the revised coal budget could not be presented until the beginning of October.
22 Oct	**6th:1**	**Coal prospects for the coming winter.** GEN 94/11. Dalton referred to a minute from Attlee about the disturbing prospects shown in GEN 94/11. Shinwell felt there was no call for immediate cuts. The committee agreed to bridge the gap by drawing up global allocations for the remainder of the coal year and selective cuts on industrial consumers in line with weekly fluctuations in coal production. Shinwell was to submit a further appreciation on the lines of GEN 94/11 before the end of the year.
	:2	**Report of the official committee.** GEN 94/12.
	:3	**Manpower problems affecting coal.** GEN 94/13.
	:4	**Transport.** GEN 94/10. Barnes was still worried by the shortage of locomotives and wagons. Drastic action needed.
6 Nov	**7th:1**	**The transport problem.** GEN 94/15, 16 and 18. Barnes and Shinwell judged that the situation was grave. Dalton concluded that there were a number of remedial actions available.
	:2	**Excavators and crawler tractors.** GEN 94/17.

	:3	**Allocation of coal to industry.** The scheme put before the Emergency Committee of the N.P.A.C.I. was not considered as it would be discussed at the Lord President's Committee.
21 Nov	8th:1	**Transport of coal.** GEN 94/19, 20, 21, 24 and 25. Attlee had decided that the present committee should be replaced by a subcommittee of the Lord President's Committee to monitor progress.
	:2	**5th report of the official committee.** GEN 94/23.
	:3	**Recruitment of the unemployed.** GEN 94/22.

Memoranda

29 Nov	GEN 94/1	**Progress report – Lloyd George,** 5p.
18 Mar	2	**Progress report – Lloyd George,** 3p.
6 Apr	3	**Adjournment of ministerial and official committees until October, 1946 – M.T. Flett,** 1+2p. Letter from Dalton to Morrison, 'Coal situation during the winter', 30 March 1946, and one from Attlee to Dalton, 2 April 1946, are attached.
24 July	4	**Ministerial Committee on Coal during the Coming Winter – M.T. Flett,** 1p.
29 July	5	**Report by the official committee – M.T. Flett covering the official committee,** 1+3p. Notes of a meeting of the official committee are attached.
30 July	6	**Extra rations for underground miners – Shinwell,** 2p.
31 July	7	**2nd report of the official committee – M.T. Flett covering the official committee,** 1+3p. Notes of a meeting of the official committee on 29 July 1946.
31 July	8	**Revised budget for the coal year 1946/47 – Shinwell,** 1+4p.
12 Sept	9	**3rd report of the official committee – M.T. Flett covering the official committee,** 1+5p.
17 Oct	10	**Transport of coal – Barnes,** 2p.
17 Oct	11	**Revised appreciation of coal prospects in the year 1946/47 – Shinwell,** 4p. A gap of 3.5m tons was now expected. Effects of measures to increase output and decrease consumption should be known by Christmas.
18 Oct	12	**4th report of the official committee – J.H. Lidderdale covering the official committee,** 1+4p.
17 Oct	13	**The coming winter – Isaacs,** 5+5p appendixes. Concerned with certain manpower problems.
24 Oct	14	**Change in secretaryship – J.H. Lidderdale,** 1p.
2 Nov	15	**Rail transport. Problem on coal – Shinwell,** 2+1p annex. Increasing concern with rail

		transport, since the coal budget was based on an effective distribution to points of consumption. A number of remedies suggested.
4 Nov	16	**Transport position – Barnes,** 2p. Review of problems with rail transport.
6 Nov	18	**Transport position: additional note – Barnes,** 1p. Summary of the problems facing distribution from open-cast workings.
9 Nov	19	**Loss of deep-mined production and coal stocked owing to railway difficulties – J.H. Lidderdale,** 1+1p. First of a series of weekly statements from the Ministry of Fuel and Power.
15 Nov	20	**Loss of deep-mined production and coal stocked owing to railway difficulties – J.H. Lidderdale,** 1+1p.
18 Nov	21	**Transport of coal – J.H. Lidderdale covering the official committee,** 1+2p. If all coal production was to be moved it could be only at the expense of other traffic. The Lord President's Committee should therefore decide.
19 Nov	22	**Recruitment of the unemployed – Isaacs,** 4+2p appendixes.
19 Nov	23	**5th report by the official committee – J.H. Lidderdale covering the official committee,** 1+2p.
19 Nov	24	**Use of road transport – Barnes,** 1p.
21 Nov	25	**Loss of deep-mined production and coal stocked owing to railway difficulties – J.H. Lidderdale,** 1+1p.

6.6 Working Party on Incentives to Production

Set up in December 1945 after discussion at the Lord President's Committee of memoranda by Shinwell and Morrison on the need to boost general morale and that of coal-miners in particular, see CAB 71/19, LP(45)46th:6. There was no fixed membership. Its report (CAB 132/2, LP(46)105) in general opposed the Ministry of Fuel and Power's proposals but in May 1946 Shinwell secured the diversion of consumer goods to mining areas (see CAB 132/1, LP(46)15th:3 and 17th:5).

Terms To examine whether a scheme of inducements for coal-miners and other priority groups should be prepared on the lines proposed by the Ministry of Fuel and Power in LP(45)253.

Members E.M. Nicholson (Ld Pres. O., ch.).

Sec. A.N. Coleridge (Ld Pres. O.).

CAB 78/39 Meetings and Memoranda 12 December 1945–30 April 1946 GEN 105/1st–2nd and GEN 105/1–5.

Meetings

| 17 Dec | **GEN 105/1st** | Untitled. GEN 105/1. |
| 11 Feb | **GEN 105/2nd** | **Incentive schemes for underground miners.** GEN 105/2. |

Memoranda

12 Dec	**GEN 105/1**	**Incentives to production – Office of the Lord President,** 2p. Suggested terms of reference.
27 Jan	**GEN 105/2**	**Incentive schemes and schemes to increase production through improving civilian morale –** **Ministry of Fuel and Power,** 8+2p annex.
31 Jan	**3**	**Incentives to production – Ministry of Works,** 1p.
5 Apr	**4**	**Incentives to production – E.M. Nicholson,** 1+7p. Draft report.
30 Apr	**5**	**Incentives to production – report of the official working party,** 4+4p annex. The Ministry of Fuel and Power wanted to put an incentive scheme before ministers. Others found the scheme bad in principle. It could prejudice the prosperity drive and had insuperable administrative problems.

Chapter 7   Reconstruction Committees

7.1   Reconstruction Problems Committee

Set up in 1941 as the major ministerial committee planning reconstruction. Consideration of the long-term implications of the Beveridge Report was devolved in January 1943 to the Reconstruction Priorities Committee (CAB 87/12–13). Both committees were disbanded in November 1943 with their domestic responsibilities being assumed by the Reconstruction Committee (CAB 87/5–10). It was served by the Official Committee on Post-war Internal Economic Problems (CAB 87/57).

Terms (1942) (a) to arrange for the preparation of practical schemes of reconstruction, to which effect can be given in a period of, say, three years after the war. These plans should have as their general aim the perpetuation of the national unity achieved in this country during the war, through a social and economic structure designed to secure equality of opportunity and service among all classes of the community (b) to prepare a scheme for a post-war European and world system, with particular regard to the economic needs of the various nations, and to the problem of adjusting the free life of small countries in a durable international order. The committee was also to take over the functions of the Committee on Economic Aspects of Reconstruction Problems (CAB 87/64), which was dissolved.

Members (Feb 1942) Paymaster-Gen. (ch.); Ch. of Exchequer; Foreign Sec.; Mins. of Labour & N.S., Health, S./S. Scotland; Pres. Bd Education; Sec. Overseas Trade; (Feb 1943) Min. Town and Country Planning added.

Secs. A. Hurst (Cab. O.).

CAB 87/3   Meetings and Memoranda   5 Jan–26 Oct 1943   RP(43)1st–10th and RP(43)1–30.

Meetings

27 Jan	**RP(43)2nd**	**Post-war Agricultural Policy.** RP(43)2, 7 and 8. Agreed, with dissent from Attlee, Bevin and Johnstone, to ask for War Cabinet authorization to open discussions on the lines of RP(43)2.
15 Apr	**5th:1**	**Planning and internationalism.** RP(43)16.
8 July	**7th:2**	**Post-war export trade.** RP(43)25.
26 Oct	**10th:2**	**Post-war highway policy.** RP(43)27 and 30.

Memoranda

5 Jan	**RP(43)2**	**Post-war agricultural problems – A. Hurst covering the agricultural departments,** 4+16p. See WP(43)103, also IEP(43)3 and USE(43)1. Covering note different from WP(43)103.
11 Jan	**5**	**The financial aspect of the social security plan – Wood covering the Treasury,** 2+6p. In light of

200

future uncertainties and other commitments the Treasury was concerned lest a firm commitment to Beveridge was made when it could not be afforded. An order of priority was required.

14 Jan	**6**	**Official Committee on Beveridge Report : report,** 24+10p appendixes.
16 Jan	**7**	**Post-war agricultural policy – Attlee, 4p.** RP(43)2 concentrated on maintaining agricultural land as productive at the expense of concern with production of food for the people.
19 Jan	**8**	**Post-war agricultural policy – Amery, 4p.** Criticizes RP(43)7 as too short-term and concurs with RP(43)2.
10 Feb	**15**	**Note by secretary, A. Hurst, 1p.**
12 Feb	**16**	**Planning and internationalism – Amery, 2p.** Questions the compatibility of the two.
11 Mar	**19**	**Stabilization policy – Jowitt covering the Treasury and the Board of Trade, 1+6+7p.** See PR(43)16. Not discussed by the Committee.
25 May	**24**	**Post-war housing policy – Official Committee on post-war Internal Economic Problems,** 10+31p appendixes. Also IEP(43)24. There were a number of requirements if there were to be a large long-term programme of house-building, including a reduction in building costs and the re-entry of private initiative into the industry. Appendixes include IEP(42)23, 27, 65 and IEP(43)2.
15 June	**25**	**Report on the recovery of export markets and the promotion of export trade – Dalton covering Johnstone, 2+60p.** Review of the whole problem of the discussions with industries. Includes a series of recommendations relating to both the short- and the long-term international and domestic aspects.
20 July	**27**	**Post-war highway policy – Leathers, 8+17p** appendixes. Also IEP(43)38.
9 Sept	**28**	**Scott Report – Jowitt, 1+1+7+21p appendixes.** Also IEP(43)39.

7.2   Reconstruction Committee

On the appointment of a Minister of Reconstruction (Lord Woolton) in November 1943 the committee was established as the major ministerial committee to handle all questions of reconstruction on the home front, replacing the Reconstruction Problems Committee (CAB 87/3) and the Reconstruction Priorities Committee (CAB 87/12–13), see CAB 66/43, WP(43)541. It was specifically excluded from dealing with international, financial, economic or commercial policy and questions of priorities covered by the

Production Council. Owing to pressure of work, a ministerial subcommittee was delegated to deal with certain industrial and export questions (CAB 87/14–15). The committee was served by several official committees including ones on post-war building and industrial problems (CAB 87/11, 17–18, 89). It ended with the dissolution of the national government in May 1945.

Terms The committee is responsible, under the War Cabinet, for dealing with the following matters (i) formulating government policy on the Social Security Scheme (ii) reviewing all major reconstruction schemes from the point of view of (a) any issues of principle involved; (b) the claims which these projects are likely to make on the Exchequer (iii) dealing with questions of principle arising out of the work of the Minister of Reconstruction in reviewing the whole range of preparations for the transitional period.

Members Min. of Reconstruction (ch.); Ld President; Ch. of Exchequer; Mins. of Labour & N.S., Production, Education, Without Portfolio; Home Sec.; Paymaster-Gen.; Postmaster-Gen. (Dec 1944) Lds Cranborne, Listowel to attend so they could explain policy to House of Lords.

Secs. N. Brook (Recon.) (Jan 1945) J.P.R. Maud (Recon.).

CAB 87/5 Meetings 20 Dec 1943–26 June 1944 R(43)1st–R(44)50th.

20 Dec	**R(43)1st:1**	**Future of aircraft production.** PR(43)98, R(43)3, 7. Need for planning and government control if the engineering industry were to be kept substantially larger than pre-war. Woolton felt it would be helpful if the problems of the switch-over of industry from war to peace could be kept under review by a smaller body of ministers.
3 Jan	**R(44)1st:2**	**Wages policy – post-war regulation of wages and conditions of employment.** LP(43)293. Bevin authorized to open talks with the Joint Consultative Committee.
21 Jan	**8th**	**Post-war employment.** R(44)6. Agreement to issue statement at earliest possible date and general discussion on first three chapters. Bevin concerned that the report did not afford a sufficient basis for a plan for curing post-war unemployment.
28 Jan	**11th**	**Post-war employment. Location of industry.** R(44)6, 22, 23. Discussion of chapter V of R(44)6. The majority were inclined to feel that positive action to restrict further development in certain areas was impracticable.
31 Jan	**12th:1** **:2**	**Post-war housing.** R(44)18, 19, 20, 25. Agreed that government should maintain subsidies and should assist local authority purchase of land although aware it might lead to a loss of food production.

4 Feb	**13th:2**	**Post-war employment.** R(44)6 and 27. General view that some form of legislation for the control of restricted practices was required but further consideration was necessary before making any decisions.
14 Feb	**15th:3**	**Industry: reconstruction problems.** R(44)31.
	:4	**Membership of the committee.**
21 Feb	**16th**	**Post-war employment.** R(44)6 and 28. Consideration of sections (ii) and (iii) of chapter VI of R(44)6, and proposals for an industrial development board and for finance for both small businesses and industrial re-equipment.
25 Feb	**17th**	**Post-war employment.** R(44)6. Consideration of section (v) of chapter VI and chapter VII. Agreement that while the White Paper demands some reference to trade unions' restrictive practices it should emphasize that these were largely confined to periods of high unemployment and would disappear if employment were at a high level. Also agreed that a group of officials should be engaged continuously on statistical aspects of employment policy.
28 Feb	**18th**	**Future of the electricity industry.** R(44)3, 17, 21, 32, 33. Detailed discussion of proposals in R(44)3.
27 Mar	**27th:6**	**Agricultural credit.** R(44)62 and 63. Papers to go to the Lord President's Committee.
	:7	**Problems of the transitional period.** R(44)45.
12 Apr	**30th**	**Post-war employment : location of industry.** R(44)58, 60 and 72. General feeling that the President of the Board of Trade should be the minister responsible for the balanced distribution of industry. If there was to be public ownership of an industry it should be on the merits of the case and not because it was in a particular area.
17 Apr	**32nd**	**Post-war housing.** R(44)75, 76, 78. Consideration of the cost of post-war building.
19 Apr	**33rd**	**Future meetings of the committee.** As pressure of work prevented weekly meetings detailed consideration of draft white papers was to be left to officials and settled by Woolton.
24 Apr	**34th:1**	**Post-war building : report of the subcommittee.** R(44)49, 67, 77, 80.
	:3	**Post-war employment : restrictive practices in industry.** R(44)65. Confidential annex attached. Consideration related solely to employment aspects not as to whether such practices were anti-social. Attlee's suggested alternative to R(44)65 was accepted as the

			general line of approach. It was agreed that the White Paper should contain only a brief and general reference to the government's intentions here.
8 May	**36th**		**Employment policy : draft of White Paper.** R(44)93. Discussion on order of chapters and then of each paragraph.
9 May	**37th**		**Employment policy : draft of White Paper.** R(44)93. Continuation of discussion of draft by paragraphs.
15 May	**38th**		**Post-war employment : draft White Paper.** R(44)98. Disagreement over variation of taxation. The issue was to be brought to the attention of the War Cabinet.
31 May	**41st:1**		**Highways : acquisition of land.** R(44)89.
	:2		**Capital issues : post-war control.** R(44)83 and 90. Consideration of the post-war Capital Issues Committee and the position of local authorities in the financial market.
5 June	**43rd:1**		**Housing policy.** R(44)108.
	:2		**Housing : private enterprise after the war.** R(44)109.
	:3		**Housing : provision of flats.** R(44)84.
12 June	**46th:1**		**Social insurance : draft White Paper.** R(44)104, 114, 117. There was some discussion of the assumption of 8½% unemployment.
26 June	**50th:1**		**Emergency legislation : review of defence regulations.** R(44)94.
	:2		**Emergency legislation : legislative authority for continuance of emergency powers.** R(44)95, 107, 119, 121, 127. Issue of whether new powers should be taken after the end of the war in Europe or after the Japanese war. No decision.
	:3		**Housing : private enterprise in post-war housing.** R(44)126.

CAB 87/6   Meetings   3 July–20 Dec 1944   R(44)51st–80th.

3 July	**R(44)51st:2**	**Post-war building : size of labour force.** R(44)112, 122, 128.
10 July	**52nd:1**	**Shipbuilding industry.** R(44)53 and 92. Discussion on which department should be responsible for the industry.
	:3	**Housing : private enterprise in post-war housing.** R(44)130. Approval of proposals for subsidies but Attlee and Bevin asked for their grave misgivings about the effect of the proposed subsidy on private house-building to be put on record.
28 Aug	**56th:2**	**Demobilization : interim report on release from the forces.** R(44)140 and 146.

6 Sept	**58th:1**	**Wages policy : post-war regulation of wages and conditions of employment.** R(44)141. Proposals approved.
8 Sept	**59th**	**Housing.** R(44)149 and 153. Willink felt there should be no reduction in the proportion of post-war new building resources allocated to housing, i.e. two-thirds, and that it might have to be increased.
11 Sept	**60th:1**	**Post-war employment : restrictive practices.** R(44)145, 151, 154, 155, 156. Agreement that there should be legislation for a statutory tribunal of enquiry.
	:2	**The cotton industry.** R(44)152.
14 Sept	**61st**	**The cotton industry.** R(44)152 and 159. Confidential annex attached. Agreed proposal of a Cotton Spinning Board should not be put to the industry. Further government help was conditional on the leaders of the industry putting their own house in order.
18 Sept	**62nd**	**Demobilization : remuneration during the period of paid furlough.** R(44)162.
25 Sept	**64th:3**	**Building : procedure of securing consent.** R(44)160. Agreed there was a need to simplify existing procedure.
9 Oct	**66th:1**	**Emergency legislation : legislative authority for continuance of emergency powers.** R(44)169. No decision reached on continuing debate.
	:2	**Iron and steel : future of the iron and steel industry.** R(44)150 and 166. Rejection of the proposal in R(44)6 for an independent comprehensive enquiry.
20 Oct	**67th:3**	**Family allowances : provision of school meals.** R(44)172. School building had to be curtailed at that time because labour was needed elsewhere. Priority would be given as soon as possible.
23 Oct	**68th**	**Finance for industry.** R(44)132 and 174. Line agreed for the next stage of Anderson's talks with the Governor of the Bank of England.
6 Nov	**70th:1**	**Wages policy : pace for regulation of wages and conditions of employment.** R(44)182. Approval of proposals.
16 Nov	**72nd**	**Finance for industry.** R(44)132 and 174. Update on talks with the Governor of the Bank of England. Agreement that he should be encouraged to proceed with negotiations.
27 Nov	**74th:3**	**Restrictive practices.** R(44)187.
28 Nov	**75th:2**	**Future of the electricity industry.** R(44)196.
4 Dec	**76th:1**	**Restrictive practices.** R(44)187.
18 Dec	**79th:1**	**Procedure of the committee.** Cranborne or Listowel to attend meetings so that government

			policy could be explained to the House of Lords.
20 Dec		**80th**	**Electricity supply.** R(44)3, 199, 200 and 207.

CAB 87/7   Memoranda   30th Nov 1943–31 March 1944   R(43)1–R(44)71.

30 Nov	**R(43)1**	**Composition and terms of reference – E.E. Bridges,** 1p. Also WP(43)541.
29 Nov	2	**Note by the Chancellor – Anderson covering the Government Actuary,** 1+10p. Revision of estimates for financing the Beveridge Plan.
1 Dec	3	**The future of aircraft production – Dalton,** 2p. Need to consider locational aspects and contraction of war industries.
2 Dec	4	**Capital expenditure after the war – N. Brook covering the C.S.O.,** 5+2p appendixes. In part a complement to PR(43)35.
6 Dec	6	**Post-war building programme. Control in the immediate post-war period – Woolton,** 2p. An official committee to consider the programme for the first two years after the end of the war in Europe. He suggested terms of reference and membership.
14 Dec	7	**Supplementary note on the future of aircraft production – Cripps,** 2p.
10 Jan	**R(44)3**	**Report of the Sub-committee on the Future of the Electricity Industry – Lloyd George covering the report,** 1+23+10p appendixes. See CAB 87/4.
3 Jan	4	**Procedure for discussing problems at the switch-over of industry from war to peace – Woolton,** 1p. Reports that Churchill has decided against a subcommittee at present and instead would have informal discussions with a nucleus of himself, Bevin, Cripps and Dalton.
11 Jan	6	**Post-war employment – Woolton covering the Steering Committee on Post-war Employment,** 65+13p appendixes. The report was the forerunner of the White Paper (Cmd. 6527). It was seen by the official committee as an exposition of a general economic argument and a study of its practical application to the industrial and financial problems of the country. Chapter I – Introductory, Chapter II – Control of Aggregate Demand, Chapter III – Wages and Prices, Chapter IV – Mobility of Labour, Chapter V – Location of Industry, Chapter VI – Industrial Efficiency, Chapter VII – General, Chapter VIII – Conclusion and Note of Dissent by Professor Robbins – restrictive development in industry. Appendix A –

		Finance for small businesses and for reorganization. Appendix B – Statistics required in connection with post-war employment policy – first interim report of the Subcommittee on Post-war Statistics of the Emergency Legislation Committee.
20 Jan	17	**The future of electricity – Lloyd George,** 3p.
22 Jan	18	**Post-war housing – Woolton,** 6p. Need for assistance to local authorities to help building get under way in the first two years after the end of the war in Europe.
22 Jan	19	**Advanced preparation of housing sites – Portal, Willink and Johnston,** 2p. Housing should have immediate priority over the use of land for other purposes.
24 Jan	20	**Post-war housing – Hudson,** 2p. Against R(44)19 unless the Ministry of Agriculture and Fisheries had a chance to consider each particular case.
25 Jan	21	**Report of the Subcommittee on the Future of the Electricity Industry – Dalton,** 2p.
27 Jan	22	**Location of industry – Cripps,** 5p. Comments on R(44)6 Chapter V. Can only deal with depressed areas within a framework of a general industrial policy.
27 Jan	23	**Location of industry – Johnstone,** 2p. Suggestion of subsidy of £1 a week to wages in certain regions for a period of ten years.
29 Jan	25	**Advanced preparation of housing sites – Lloyd George,** 1p.
2 Feb	26	**Suggested procedure for discussion at meeting of Friday 4th February, 1944 – Woolton,** 1p. Format for consideration of R(44)6 Chapter VI.
3 Feb	27	**Restrictive developments in industry – Cripps,** 2p. Committee not sufficiently restrictive and the standard set in Robbins's note of dissent in R(44)6 should be the minimum.
3 Feb	28	**Industrial efficiency – Cripps,** 2p. Note prepared in his department on Chapter VI of R(44)6 questioning need for an Industrial Commission in main industries.
10 Feb	31	**Inter-departmental organization to deal with problems of industrial reconstruction – Woolton,** 1+3+3p appendix. Suggested ministerial and official committees to deal with various aspects of the issue.
23 Feb	32	**Future of electricity – Johnston,** 2p.
25 Feb	33	**The future of electricity. Recommendations received from associations of the industry – Lloyd George,** 6p.

8 Mar	**42**	**Government and the major industries – Cripps,** 2p. Again questions the idea of an Industrial Commission as it would break existing direct contact with major industries and would be a return to a situation not substantially different from pre-war. General measures were not sufficient alone to achieve full employment and such contacts with the main industries were crucial for its success.
14 Mar	**45**	**Problems of the transitional period – Woolton,** 1+48p. Departments, in accordance with WP(43)476, sent returns setting out their problems in the transition. These had now been updated.
15 Mar	**49**	**Report of the Subcommittee on Post-war Building – Woolton covering the subcommittee,** 17+3p appendixes. Cannot devise a better scheme of control than that suggested by Portal in PR(43)54. Report proposed that a third of labour available for new building during the first two years of the transition should be allocated to new building other than houses.
17 Mar	**53**	**The shipbuilding industry – Alexander,** 4p. Should aim at a long-term steady load on the industry rather than a fluctuating demand.
22 Mar	**58**	**Post-war employment: location of industry –** **Woolton,** 2+4p. Draft statement on government policy entitled 'The Balanced Distribution of Industry'. In formulation there had been some difficulties over whether the government in the last resort should operate factories and also over the administrative arrangements.
22 Mar	**59**	**Government and the major industries – Portal,** 2p. Refers to the Board of Trade as the responsible department for contact with industry.
24 Mar	**62**	**Agricultural Mortgage Corporation – Hudson,** 1p. Also LP(44)60.
24 Mar	**63**	**Agricultural credit – Johnston,** 1p. Also LP(44)60.
29 Mar	**65**	**Restrictive practices – Dalton and Jowitt,** 5+14p appendixes. Proposals for dealing with the issue, preferring registration to prohibition. Letter from Johnstone to Woolton, 21 April 1944 attached.
30 Mar	**66**	**Post-war employment: location of industry –** **Cripps,** 2p. Did not believe R(44)58 would be effective in preventing structural unemployment and there was a need for greater government action.
30 Mar	**67**	**Post-war building programme – Butler,** 2p.

31 Mar 69 **Government and the major industries – Cripps,** 3p. A general trade department responsible for major industries cannot undertake a full employment policy effectively.

CAB 87/8 Memoranda 7 April–28 June 1944 R(44)72–129.

7 Apr **R(44)72** **The balanced distribution of industry –** **Morrison, W.,** 3p.

14 Apr 77 **Report of the Subcommittee on Post-war** **Building – Woolton,** 1p. The committee should consider whether the present control of building should be extended. Should priority be given to building other than housing?

14 Apr 78 **House-building costs – Portal,** 1+2p.

15 Apr 80 **Report of the Subcommittee on Post-war** **Building – Dalton,** 1p. The committee was yet to make the allocation of labour for new building other than housing.

19 Apr 83 **Capital issues control after the war – Anderson,** 4p. Clear need for continuation of the control for some time.

1 May 89 **Acquisition of land for road works – Leathers,** 1p.

1 May 90 **Borrowing by local authorities after the war –** **Anderson,** 2+10p. Attached Treasury memorandum proposed that local authorities could borrow only from the Local Loans Fund, supplied by funds from the Treasury.

3 May 92 **Shipbuilding – Leathers,** 3p. General agreement with R(44)53.

3 May 93 **Employment policy – Woolton and Anderson,** 1+16p. Attached draft White Paper, though not quite complete.

9 May 94 **Interim report of Emergency Legislation** **Committee – Woolton covering the committee,** 1+5+104p annex. Also EL(44)12 and 13. Review of defence regulations setting up proposals for revocation or retention.

9 May 95 **Legislative authority for continuance of** **emergency powers – Woolton,** 1+4p.

13 May 98 **Employment policy. Draft White Paper –** **Woolton,** 1+18p.

30 May 107 **Legislative authority for continuance of** **emergency powers – Morrison,** 3p. Feels that there should be legislation at the end of hostilities in Europe.

1 June 109 **Private enterprise in housing after the war –** **Willink,** 4+2p appendixes. Sees it having a large role even if not in the first two years of the transition.

2 June	**112**	**The long-term post-war building programme –** **Cherwell**, 2p. Concern that building labour force of 1.25m will not be kept busy for the whole of the ten-year period of the programme once arrears have been made good.
8 June	**117**	**Social insurance and allied services. Financial comparisons of government proposals and the Beveridge Plan – Anderson covering the Government Actuary,** 1+5p.
9 June	**119**	**Legislative authority for continuance of emergency powers – Bevin,** 3p. Disagrees with R(44)107.
13 June	**121**	**Legislative authority for continuance of emergency powers – Duncan,** 1p.
13 June	**122**	**The long-term post-war building programme – Portal, Willink and Johnston,** 2p. Disagreement with R(44)112.
20 June	**126**	**Private enterprise in housing after the war –** **Willink,** 3p. Concerns subsidy arrangements and discussions with building societies.
20 June	**127**	**Legislative authority for the continuance of emergency powers – Hudson,** 1p. Supports proposals in R(44)119.
23 June	**128**	**Long-term post-war building programme –** **Johnstone,** 3p. R(44)122 did not remove the uneasiness expressed by Cherwell.

CAB 87/9   Memoranda   4 July–30 Dec 1944   R(44)130–211.

4 July	**R(44)130**	**Private enterprise in housing after the war –** **Willink,** 3p.
20 July	**132**	**Finance for small industrial firms – Anderson,** 2p.
4 Aug	**140**	**Reallocation of manpower between the forces and civilian employment during the interim period between the defeat of Germany and the defeat of Japan – Bevin,** 1+3p annex plus 3p appendix. Attached interim report by Inter-departmental Committee on the Release from the Forces and Civil Defence Services. Appendix – draft White Paper on reallocation of manpower between the armed forces and civilian employment during any interim period between the defeat of Germany and the defeat of Japan.
17 Aug	**141**	**Wages regulation. Legislation to meet post-war requirements – Bevin,** 2+5p. Agreement with the British Employers' Confederation and the T.U.C. should be possible on the basis of attached note.
24 Aug	**145**	**Restrictive practices – Woolton,** 2p. Proposes an independent tribunal and that the

government should define forms of such
practices if such a body were to be effective.

25 Aug	146	**Reallocation of manpower between the forces and civilian employment during Stage II – Lyttleton,** 1p.
30 Aug	149	**London housing – Morrison,** 2p.
2 Sept	150	**Iron and steel industry – Dalton,** 2p. Should take up suggestion in R(44)6 of an enquiry into the industry.
2 Sept	151	**Restrictive practices – Dalton,** 2+2p appendix. Supports R(44)145 but against the suggestion of a departmental committee to examine forms of such practices.
2 Sept	152	**The cotton industry – Dalton,** 3+3p annex. Recommends the establishment of a Cotton Spinning Board as the sole buyer of raw cotton and sole seller of yarn.
5 Sept	153	**Housing policy – Woolton,** 3p. Committee should have a general discussion on the subject and suggested a housing subcommittee.
7 Sept	154	**Restrictive practices – Morrison,** 4p. Sees the issue as a test case of how far inter-party agreement could go in the field of economic policy. As a compromise he suggests that the government should adopt positive measures to secure the operation of effective competition in those industries whose members feel well-being would be better preserved by that means rather than by centralized arrangements.
8 Sept	155	**Restrictive practices – Dalton,** 1+1p. Tentative heads of a bill on restrictive practices.
8 Sept	156	**Restrictive practices – N. Brook,** 1+2+3p. Attached proceedings of a meeting between Eden and a deputation of Conservative M.P.s and the memorandum they presented to him.
13 Sept	159	**Cotton industry – Johnstone,** 3p. Doubts about R(44)152.
20 Sept	160	**Simplification of procedure for securing consents to building developments – Woolton,** 3+8+11p appendixes. Attached report of the conference on this subject.
15 Sept	162	**Reallocation of manpower between the forces and civilian employment during the interim period between the defeat of Germany and the defeat of Japan – Woolton,** 2p.
26 Sept	166	**Iron and steel industry – Duncan,** 4p. Against an enquiry into the industry. Governmental supervision during the transition.
5 Oct	169	**Draft of Supplies and Services (Transitional Powers) Bill – Woolton,** 1+1+6p draft bill. Also EL(44)20. Prepared by Emergency Legislation Committee to help the Reconstruction

		Committee decide whether a bill dealing with powers of economic control during the transition should be introduced at the end of hostilities in Europe, or at a later stage.
13 Oct	171	**Unauthorized disclosures of proceedings of the Lord President's Committee and the Reconstruction Committee – Attlee and Woolton,** 1+2p annex by Churchill. Also LP(44)169.
18 Oct	172	**School meals in relation to family allowances – Butler,** 2p. Special priority needed after housing for school-building if promise about school meals were to be kept.
19 Oct	174	**Finance for industry – Anderson,** 7p. Update on latest developments and suggests acceptance of the proposals of the Governor of the Bank of England.
21 Oct	175	**Post-war food policy – Hudson,** 2+8p annex. Draft White Paper on food policy.
25 Oct	182	**Wages regulation : legislation to meet post-war conditions – Bevin,** 3+4p annex. Follow-up to R(44)141. The British Employers' Confederation were not completely in agreement with the proposals.
14 Nov	187	**Post-war employment: restrictive practices – Woolton,** 1+5+2p appendix. Draft heads of a bill by Maxwell Fyfe attached dealing with restrictive practices and monopolies, including definitions of forms of such practices.
24 Nov	196	**The future of the electricity industry – Morrison,** 2p. Unwarranted delay in report by Anderson on its financial aspects.
2 Dec	199	**Public utility corporations – Woolton and Anderson,** 1+31+12p appendixes. Report of the Official Committee. The terms of reference had been broadened from consideration of the financial aspects of the future of the electricity industry to include all public utility corporations and their relationships to the state.
2 Dec	200	**Future of electricity in the North of Scotland district – Johnston and Lloyd George,** 2p.
18 Dec	207	**Future of the electricity industry – Woolton,** 2p.
19 Dec	209	**Highway policy – Leathers,** 3p.
	210	Circulated as **R(45)8.**

CAB 87/10   Meetings and Memoranda   1 Jan–7 May 1945   R(45)1st–18th and R(44)1–15.

Meetings

8 Jan	**R(45)1st:1**	**Highway policy.** R(44)209, R(45)2 and 4.

29 Jan	**6th:1**	**Post-war building programme.** R(45)8, 17, 20. Sandys invited to appoint an official committee to consider the needs of particular areas in determining the regional allocation of building labour in the transition.
	:2	**Restrictive practices : international cartels.** R(45)16.
5 Feb	**8th:1**	**Restrictive practices.** R(45)16. After some discussion the committee agreed that proposals in the paper should be submitted to the War Cabinet.
26 Feb	**10th**	**Demobilization : releases in Class B.** R(45)27, 29, 30.
9 Apr	**14th**	**Electricity supply : future procedure.** R(45)38. Confidential annex attached. Ministry of Fuel and Power was not to open talks and was to keep it under study until a future date because of lack of agreement over proposals.
30 Apr	**17th**	**Iron and steel.** R(45)36. Again disagreement over issue of private or public ownership.

Memoranda

3 Jan	**R(45)2**	**Highway policy: Forth Road Bridge –** **Johnstone,** 2p. Argues for construction on the grounds of economic solvency of the area.
3 Jan	**4**	**Highway policy – Dalton,** 2p.
16 Jan	**8**	**Requirements and priorities for post-war building work other than housing – Woolton and Sandys,** 2+3p appendix. Sets out in terms of expenditure (at 1939 prices) and of manpower, the estimated requirements of departments in respect of work by the building industry against the expected labour force. Less than 50% would be met and therefore there was a need for priorities. A tentative allocation of building labour for the first year after end of hostilities is attached.
23 Jan	**10**	**Electricity reorganization: extent of municipal enterprise – Lloyd George,** 1+3+2p. Appendixes by the Electricity Commissioners.
24 Jan	**16**	**Post-war employment: restrictive practices –** **Maxwell Fyfe,** 3+2p appendixes. Revised draft of heads of bill.
25 Jan	**17**	**Priorities for post-war building work –** **Morrison, W.,** 3p. Concern with lack of consideration of special needs of certain regions in allocations.
25 Jan	**18**	**International cartels – Woolton,** 1+3p. Attached memorandum by Anderson.
27 Jan	**20**	**Requirements and priorities for post-war building work for Home Office services –**

		Morrison, 3p. Does not accept his allocation in R(45)8.
5 Feb	26	**Future of electricity – Lloyd George,** 2+4p. Attached heads of bill.
16 Feb	27	**Release from the forces in the interim period. Block releases in Class B – Bevin,** 3+3+1p appendix. Report by the chairman of the Inter-departmental Committee on the Release from Forces and Civil Defence Services.
21 Feb	28	**Future of electricity – Anderson,** 2p.
22 Feb	29	**Release of manpower for the food trades – Llewellin,** 2p.
23 Feb	30	**Release from the forces in the interim period. Block releases in Class B – Lyttelton,** 1p.
6 Apr	36	**Iron and steel – Duncan and Dalton,** 1+40+79p appendixes. Report on the iron and steel industry by officials of the two departments attached. Expressed concern with ensuring that the industry plays its full part in the post-war economy in increasing export trade and maintaining full employment.
20 Mar	37	**Electricity reorganization: rural electrification – Crookshank,** 1+2p.
24 Mar	38	**Electricity reorganization – Woolton,** 1p. While the scheme in R(45)26 seemed reasonable he wondered whether the government should introduce such legislation at this stage in its life or whether the scheme in R(45)26 would be the right one.

7.3 Subcommittee on the Control of Post-war Building

Set up in December 1943 to continue the work on building by the Reconstruction Priorities Committee (CAB 87/12). It ceased to function after drafting a report in March 1944 which, submitted to the Reconstruction Committee (CAB 87/7, R(44)49), was discussed in April 1944 (CAB 87/5, R(44)34th:1).

Terms (a) to represent within what limits the licensing of building operations would be practical and, on stated assumptions as to the limits of cost up to which building would be permitted without a licence, to establish the probable demand for licensed and unlicensed work respectively on maintenance and repair (b) to estimate, on stated assumptions regarding the amount of labour required for essential maintenance and repair work and for new building work other than housing, what number of habitable homes could be made available by the end of the first two years by reconditioning and by new construction (c) to establish the probable level of costs of new house construction as affected by the factors involved in (a) and (b) above.

Members F.R. Robinson (Works, ch.); J.C. Wrigley (Health); W.S. Murrie (Scot.); G.C. Veysey (Lab. & N.S.); K.S. Dodd (T. & C. Plan.); H.B. Usher (Try); M.F. Rowe (War Damage C.) (Dec 1943) G.A. Duncan (Prod.) added.

Secs. J.G. Orr (Works) and P. Callard (Recon.).

CAB 87/11   Meetings and Memoranda   6 Dec 1943–2 March 1944
R(B)(43)1st–R(B)(44)12th and R(B)(43)1–R(B)(44)8.

Meetings

15 Dec	**R(B)(43)1st**	Untitled. PR(43)54. Basic assumptions considered.
17 Dec	**2nd**	Untitled. Consideration of the building programme for the first three post-war years.
21 Dec	**3rd**	Untitled. Progress of the committee's work and examination of terms of reference.
30 Dec	**4th**	Untitled. R(B)(43)12, 14, 15. It was agreed that the total demand for maintenance in the first two post-war years should be £390m.
4 Jan	**R(B)(44)1st**	Untitled. R(B)(43)11, 16, R(B)(44)1.
11 Jan	**2nd**	Untitled. PR(43)44 and 54. Estimate of available labour for new construction during the transition and restriction of demand for maintenance work by licensing related to rateable value.
14 Jan	**3rd**	Untitled. R(B)(44)1 and PR(43)54. Allocation of available labour between housing and other new works was discussed along with the factors influencing post-war costs.
18 Jan	**4th**	Untitled. R(B)(44)2 and PR(43)54. Consideration of the output of employed men and the rate of housing construction, and the licensing of both maintenance work and non-house property expenditure.
21 Jan	**5th**	Untitled. Continued discussion of the licensing limit for maintenance work. Draft report considered.
25 Jan	**6th**	Untitled. Outstanding issues in the first section of the draft report were discussed. 'Control of post-war building' – H.B. Usher, 25 Jan 1944, 1p is attached.
28 Jan	**7th**	Untitled. Drafting amendments to the report.
7 Feb	**8th**	Untitled. 'The draft report – first revision of the introduction, Part I and Part II', 8 Feb 1944, 15p is attached.
10 Feb	**9th**	Untitled. Draft amendments.
18 Feb	**10th**	Untitled. Draft amendments.
25 Feb	**11th**	Untitled. R(B)(44)8(draft). An incomplete version of the draft report, R(B)(44)8(1st revise), 28 Feb 1944, 20+1p appendix is attached.
29 Feb	**12th**	Untitled. Final approval of the report.

Memoranda

6 Dec	**R(B)(43)1**	**Composition and terms of reference – N. Brook,** 1p.

14 Dec	2–8	**Notes by joint secretaries.** Covering notes to extracts of minutes and memoranda respectively: PR(43)44, PR(43)15th, PR(43)54, 56, 61, 63 and PR(43)20th. The papers themselves are not included.
16 Dec	9	**Composition of the subcommittee – N. Brook,** 1p.
16 Dec	10	**Future building programme – joint secretaries covering Davson and Purdie,** 1+2p. Also AC 17. Paper submitted to the Advisory Council of the Building and Civil Engineering Industries.
20 Dec	11	**The post-war problem of the War Damage Commission – joint secretaries covering M.E. Rowe,** 1+4p.
21 Dec	12	**Tentative allocation of labour – joint secretaries covering C.T. Every,** 1+3p. Explained the allocation of available labour by the Ministry of Works in PR(43)44.
21 Dec	13	**New construction in the transitional period – joint secretaries covering J.C. Wrigley and W.S. Murrie,** 1+2p.
28 Dec	14	**Definition of essential works of maintenance and repair – joint secretaries covering the Department of Health for Scotland,** 1+2p.
29 Dec	15	**Arrears of maintenance – joint secretaries covering I.I. Bowen,** 1+1p.
30 Dec	16	**Factors tending to prevent inflation of building costs – joint secretaries covering D.N. Chester and C.T. Every,** 1+2p.
4 Jan	R(B)(44)1	**Factors influencing the level of post-war building costs – joint secretaries covering D.N. Chester,** 4p.
18 Jan	2	**The output of labour – joint secretaries covering the Ministries of Health and Works,** 1+2p.
20 Jan	3	**Rating – joint secretaries covering the Ministry of Health,** 3p.
9 Feb	4	**The output of labour (Scotland) – Department of Health for Scotland and the Ministry of Works,** 1+2p.
21 Jan	5	**Rating (Scotland) – joint secretaries covering the Department of Health for Scotland,** 1+1p.
8 Feb	6	**Rateable values and probable expenditure – joint secretaries covering D.N. Chester,** 1+2p.
17 Feb	7	**Revised labour figures – joint secretaries,** 1+3p. Revision of some of the estimates made in PR(43)44.
23 Feb	8	**Draft report – second revision,** 34+3p appendixes. Draft version.
2 Mar	8	**Continuation of draft report,** 1+25+5p appendixes. First revise version.

9 Mar   **8**   **Report,** 17+3p appendixes. Final version. See
                                         R(44)49.

7.4 Reconstruction Priorities Committee

Set up in January 1943 during the political and administrative controversy occasioned
by the Beveridge Report. Two agendas were drafted to focus the committee's work
(PR(43)14, 37). It was the first committee to consider seriously the overall cost of future
government commitments and the need to determine priorities in the light of estimates
of post-war national income and expenditure. It appointed two committees: the Sheepshanks Committee on the detailed implementation of the Beveridge Report (PIN 8/
1–2) and the Steering Committee on Post-war Employment (see CAB 87/63). The
committee was served by the Official Committee on Post-war Internal Economic
Problems (CAB 87/57) and was superseded in November 1943 by the Reconstruction
Committee (CAB 87/5–10).

Terms   To consider the Beveridge Report, together with the general review of other
substantial claims to financial assistance set out in the Chancellor of the Exchequer's
memorandum (CAB 87/3, RP(43)5).

Members   Ld President (ch.); Mins. of Labour & N.S., Production, Without Portfolio;
Ch. of Exchequer; Ld Privy Seal. Other ministers to attend when relevant.
   (Sept 1943) Ch. of Exchequer (ch.); Ld President; Home Sec.; S./S. Dominions; Pres.
Bd Education; Postmaster-Gen.; Mins. of Production, Without Portfolio.

Secs.   E.E. Bridges and N. Brook (Cab. O.)

CAB 87/12   Meetings 22 Jan–8 Nov 1943   PR(43)1st–31st.

22 Jan	**PR(43)1st**	Untitled. RP(43)5, 6, PR(43)2. Discussion of the post-war financial setting of any scheme of social security.
28 Jan	**2nd:1**	**Post-war building programme.** LP(43)12 and IEP(43)2. The committee agreed, subject to Wood's acceptance, that the post-war building programme required a labour force of 1.25m. It would take three years to reach this level at which it would remain for ten years.
5 Feb	**4th**	**Beveridge Report on Social Services.** RP(43)6. Consideration of various matters related to the report, including the maintenance of employment.
9 Feb	**5th:2**	**Draft interim report on the Beveridge Plan.** PR(43)9. Cost of measures proposed.
10 Feb	**6th:1**	**General financial position.** PR(43)9. Discussion of the paper continued.
	:2	**Completion of the report.** Anderson was to amend the draft report and then submit it to the War Cabinet.

23 Feb	7th:1	**The Beveridge Plan: arrangements for working out a detailed plan of social insurance.** PR(43)15. It was agreed that departments would work out the parts of the scheme for which each was responsible but that there would be a small central staff working under Jowitt and the committee.
	:2	**Future procedure of the committee.** PR(43)14. Approval of Anderson's proposals.
7 Apr	8th:2	**Beveridge Report on Social Services: suggested plan of work.** PR(43)19.
17 May	9th:1	**Beveridge Report on Social Services: safeguards against abuse of unemployment benefit.** PR(43)22. Bevin said that because the scheme was based on the assumption of 8% unemployment it was important that unemployment was prevented from getting any greater. If necessary this should be achieved by state action.
31 May	11th	**Maintenance of employment, and continuation of stabilization policy after the war.** PR(43)16, 17, 26, 28, 29, 30. Wood felt that PR(43)26 went too far towards treating unemployment as a single problem for which one solution could be found. Bevin and Dalton were also concerned with the problem of increasing labour mobility. There was general acknowledgement of the need to take all practical steps to stimulate investment when a depression began and to continue stabilization during the transition, which required the maintenance of controls and rationing.
13 July	13th:1	**Post-war employment.** PR(43)37 and 39. Anderson's proposals were approved. It was agreed that the resulting official steering committee should report to the committee by the end of October.
	:2	**Location of industry.** PR(43)38. Agreement that the Board of Trade's proposed statement should be deferred.
	:3	**Post-war national income.** PR(43)35. Wood felt that a gratifying majority of those involved in the discussions on PR(43)35 had agreed on an estimate of net national income in 1948 of £6,800m. Personally, he was prepared to work to an estimate of £7,000m.
	:4	**Post-war income and taxation.** PR(43)36. Decisions deferred.
30 July	15th:2	**Post-war building programme.** PR(43)44. Portal pointed out the need to regulate labour on maintenance work if the programme of new building was to be carried out.

20 Sept	**20th:2**	**Post-war building programme.** PR(43)54, 56, 61, 63. Anderson pointed to the clear need for a plan for the control of building during the first two years after hostilities ended.
11 Oct	**23rd:7**	**Post-war employment.** Anderson informed the committee that the Official Steering Committee on Post-war Employment could not now report until mid-November.
29 Oct	**28th:3**	**Social insurance and allied services: rates of benefit.** PR(43)87.
1 Nov	**29th:3**	**Social insurance and allied services: rates of benefit.** PR(43)87. Anderson was asked to arrange for the Government Actuary to recalculate the financial commitments involved in the Beveridge Plan.
5 Nov	**30th:1**	**Social insurance and allied services: training period.** PR(43)91. Proposals accepted.

CAB 87/13   Memoranda   18 Jan–10 Nov 1943   PR(43)1–98.

18 Jan	**PR(43)1**	**Committee on Reconstruction Priorities – E.E. Bridges,** 1p.
20 Jan	**2**	**The social security plan – Morrison,** 3p. There would be more than enough money to finance the Beveridge Plan.
5 Feb	**8**	**Supplementary notes on the financial aspects of the social security plan – Wood covering the Treasury,** 1+8p. Follow-up to RP(43)5, giving the background to the estimates in that paper.
7 Feb	**9**	**Draft interim report on the Beveridge Plan – the committee,** 9p.
13 Feb	**12**	**Views of the British Employers' Confederation – E.E. Bridges covering the British Employers' Confederation,** 1+20p. Considers aspects of the Beveridge Plan. With regard to employment policy, the Confederation felt that international and other factors outside the country's control might largely determine the position.
11 Feb	**13**	**The Beveridge Plan: interim report – the committee,** 10p. See WP(43)58.
9 Feb	**14**	**Future procedure of the committee – Anderson,** 1p. Need for a background paper on the future work of the committee.
22 Feb	**15**	**Social security: future procedure – Morrison,** 2p. Suggestions to ensure future satisfactory progress.
3 Mar	**16**	**Stabilization policy – Jowitt covering the Treasury and the Board of Trade,** 5+1p appendix and 6+1p appendix. Also RP(43)19 and IEP(43)11. This includes two papers (a) 'Continuance of the policy of stabilization' –

Treasury. The control and direction of consumption by means of firm control of both prices of staple goods and wage levels was necessary to prevent a dangerous price boom. The maintenance of high taxation and voluntary saving would also be required; (b) 'Control of industrial prices' – Board of Trade. Consideration of the controls necessary in the industrial field to hold prices during the transition and thereafter.

27 Mar	17	**Stabilization policy – Stanley,** 3p. Stabilization in relation to the colonies.
2 Apr	19	**Beveridge Report. Suggested plan of work –** **Jowitt,** 1+2p appendixes. Main subjects still to be tackled listed and allocated between departments.
18 May	26	**Maintenance of employment – Economic** **Section,** 14+13p appendixes. Survey of the problems involved in order to indicate some of the ways in which they could be solved. International as well as national aspects are considered. The single ultimate objective was seen to be the maintenance of the total volume of demand at a high level. The paper does assess immediate post-war problems but is more concerned with the general perspective of the likely long-term situation. It suggests eight areas which require more detailed study. The appendixes relate to unemployment and investment in the inter-war years, international comparison of national incomes in the 1930s, the importance of visible exports in the United Kingdom national income and possible schemes of controlling consumption.
27 May	28	**Maintenance of employment – Wood,** 3p. The role of financial and budgetary devices in this field was overestimated in PR(43)26; moreover it concentrated on a situation of declining demand, which would not be the problem facing Britain at the end of the war. He recommended that the committee should determine its views on the policy of stabilization and the maintenance of controls in the transition before detailed discussion of PR(43)26.
27 May	29	**Maintenance of employment in depressed areas** **– Dalton,** 2p. Maintenance of aggregate demand was an insufficient cure since it required labour mobility. Some national control over industrial location was also essential.

28 May   **30**   **Maintenance of employment – Morrison,** 3p. It was wrong to hold back discussion of the maintenance of employment.

25 June   **35**   **Estimate of the national income – Wood covering the Treasury,** 1+15p. Written with assistance from the Economic Section and the C.S.O. It considered the six main factors which were thought likely to affect the size of the national income. It was agreed, with dissent from J.M. Keynes and H. Henderson, that in 1948 the net national income would lie in the range of £6,700m–£6,900m.

25 June   **36**   **Post-war national income and taxation – Wood,** 3p. Changed circumstances meant that there was an estimated surplus of £525m a year as against £325m a year previously assumed. However, the likely strong pressure for tax remission meant that there should be no change of view towards new commitments from that in RP(43)5.

7 July   **37**   **Post-war employment. Proposals for further studies – Anderson,** 5p. There were six subjects which were in need of enquiry and which should be carried out by departments under the direction of a steering committee.

9 July   **38**   **Post-war employment and the location of industry – Jowitt covering the Committee on Post-war Internal Economic Problems,** 1+9p. Also IEP(43)27(final). Post-war reconstruction offered a unique opportunity to make major changes in the location of industry. There was disagreement between the Board of Trade and the rest of the committee over the proposal to announce that companies contemplating new factory provision should notify the Board of Trade before entering into definite commitments.

10 July   **39**   **Maintenance of employment – Wood,** 1p. A list of subjects requiring consideration had been in the process of preparation, but this had been made unnecessary by PR(43)37.

22 July   **44**   **Post-war building programme – Portal,** 5+2p appendixes. Consideration of the issues requiring decisions in relation to the building programme for the first two post-war years. Statement showing the provisional estimate of the size of the post-war programme in the first two, and the subsequent ten, years is attached.

29 July   **47**   **Committee on Post-war Employment – E.E. Bridges,** 1p. This was the steering committee referred to in PR(43)37.

2 Sept	**50**	**Location of industry and its control – Dalton,** 4+3p appendixes. Concern about the possibility of black spots of unemployment during the transitional period and suggestion of ministerial committee to consider this.
9 Sept	**54**	**Post-war building programme – Portal,** 3p. Consideration of priorities in the programme.
13 Sept	**56**	**Post-war building programme – Brown,** 2p. PR(43)54 did not give enough provision for new housing.
15 Sept	**61**	**Post-war building programme – Johnston,** 2p. The post-war distribution of building labour should not be based on the pre-war position.
17 Sept	**63**	**Post-war building programme – Hudson,** 2p. Inadequate provision for the agricultural industry in PR(43)54.
20 Sept	**64**	**Sanctions applicable to the recalcitrant or work-shy following the exhaustion of unemployment insurance benefit – Bevin,** 4p.
29 Sept	**68**	**Composition of the committee – E.E. Bridges,** 1p. Changes caused by the death of Wood.
6 Oct	**71**	**Social insurance. Period of unemployment benefit – Bevin,** 3p. Benefit should not last too long if there was no likelihood of re-employment in the same industry.
27 Oct	**87**	**Social insurance: rates of benefit – Anderson,** 1+1p appendix. Concern about the tendency to estimate a higher all-round standard of benefits than could be maintained with confidence.
1 Nov	**91**	**Training benefit – Bevin,** 3p. The aim of such schemes was to increase labour mobility.
9 Nov	**97**	**New services and commitments after the war – Anderson,** 2p. The estimate of £100m for new commitments might prove an underestimate.
10 Nov	**98**	**The future of aircraft production – Cripps,** 6p. If the engineering industry was to be larger than pre-war some measure of government planning and control was necessary.

7.5 Ministerial Subcommittee on Industrial Problems

Appointed in February 1944, see CAB 87/5, R(44)15th:3. It was responsible for regional policy until July 1944, when it was superseded by the Distribution of Industry Committee (CAB 87/94), and for exports until August 1944 (see CAB 87/14–15). It was served by an official subcommittee (CAB 87/17–18) and was disbanded on the dissolution of the coalition government in May 1945. Its work was continued by a ministerial subcommittee of the Home Affairs Committee which, after August 1945, became the Industrial Subcommittee of the Lord President's Committee (CAB 71/26–7).

Terms To deal with the problem of the switch-over of industry from war to peace and other problems of industrial reconstruction, under the general direction of the Reconstruction Committee.

Members Min. of Reconstruction (ch.); Mins. of Labour & N.S., Production; Pres. Bd Trade; and ministers of the three Supply Departments when issues concerned industries engaged in munitions production.

Secs. J. Jewkes (Recon.) (Feb 1945) A.N. Coleridge (Recon.)

CAB 87/14   Meetings and Memoranda   20 April–20 Dec 1944   R(I)(44)1st–8th and R(I)(44)1–21.

Meetings

29 June	**R(I)(44)2nd**	**Export trade prospects.** R(I)(44)5 and 6. Agreement that priority should be given to export firms as soon as possible to enable them to prepare for the transition.
31 July	**3rd:1**	**Balanced distribution of industry.** R(I)(44)7.
	:2	**Post-war trade.** R(I)(44)10.
29 Sept	**4th**	**Economic controls in the transition.** R(I)(44)16. General view that it was not enough to rely on any single group of controls. It was important that the government kept the initiative in this field. A statement was required to show what the government had in mind.
16 Oct	**5th**	**Economic controls: draft of White Paper.** R(I)(44)18. Woolton was to prepare a short draft statement.
27 Oct	**6th**	**Economic controls in the transition period.** R(I)(44)19. It was agreed that an oral statement would be better than a White Paper.
13 Dec	**7th**	**Refugee industrialists.** R(I)(44)12 and 14.
20 Dec	**8th**	**Machine tools: control and disposal.** R(I)(44)20. Proposals approved.

Memoranda

20 Apr	**R(I)(44)1**	**Composition and procedure** – Woolton, 1p.
23 June	**5**	**Post-war exports** – **Dalton,** 1+4+23p annexes. Long-term prospects of British industry – Board of Trade, attached, which showed that prospects were bleak. Annexes relate to the Board of Trade estimate and export prospects, recent observations by representatives of British industries on foreign competition, the effect on British trade of overseas industrialization and the industrialization of Japan.
15 June	**6**	**Long-term prospects of British industry** – **Johnstone,** 2p. Preparation for the post-war export trade was of national importance in order to help firms plan for that time.

8 July	**7**	**The balanced distribution of industry: inter-departmental machinery – Woolton,** 3p. Outline of organization to control policy as laid down in the White Paper on *Employment Policy*, with new ministerial and official committees to deal with the policy of industrial distribution.
8 July	**8**	**Measures to promote exports and industrial efficiency – Dalton,** 2p. A series of measures to meet the problem posed in R(I)(44)5.
20 July	**10**	**Facilities for preparatory work for the expansion of the export trade – Woolton,** 1+3p. Report by the official committee, attached, deals with the procedure for advising departments responsible for controls on the facilities to be given to selected firms to prepare for the expansion of their exports.
25 July	**12**	**Refugee industrialists – Woolton,** 1+1p annex. Letter from Johnstone to Woolton, 3 July 1944, attached.
28 July	**13**	**Preparatory work for expansion of export of heavy electrical plant – Lloyd George,** 1p.
11 Aug	**14**	**Refugee industrialists – Morrison,** 3p.
22 Aug	**15**	**Inter-departmental machinery for the development of government policy on I. balanced distribution of industry and II. exports – Woolton,** 1+4p. I. Suggestion of terms of reference and membership for the ministerial and official committees on the distribution of industry. II. Churchill had decided that it was not necessary to have a committee to deal with exports yet and so the Ministerial Subcommittee on Industrial Problems was to deal with the question.
18 Sept	**16**	**Economic controls in the transition – Woolton** covering the official subcommittee, 2+9+11p appendixes. Also R(IO)(44)21. This suggests that the Ministerial and Official R(I) Subcommittees were the most appropriate focus and clearing house at present for discussions of all questions relating to the course of economic control during the transition. The appendixes go through each type of control in more detail. At some later stage it was felt there should be a study of this issue on the assumption that the war against Japan would last for less than two years.
28 Sept	**17**	**Economic controls in the transition – Cripps,** 2p. Measures should be taken to avoid unemployment in the engineering industry during the transition. The government should

		retain its full powers and the machinery of control.
12 Oct	**18**	**Control of economic resources in the transition period – Woolton,** 1+17p. Draft White Paper attached, although yet to be decided if it should be published in this or some other form. Decision on this urgently required as it was holding back publication of the White Paper on the reallocation of manpower between civilian employment. It was concerned with the regulation of economic resources other than manpower, although it was felt impossible to give details of application or to look beyond a year after the end of hostilities in Europe.
26 Oct	**19**	**Economic controls in the transition – Woolton,** 1+3p. Draft statement attached.
14 Dec	**20**	**Control and dispersal of machine tools – report by the official subcommittee,** 3+1p appendix. The removal of individual licensing had been agreed by the official subcommittee with the exception of the Ministry of Labour who had asked for the matter to be put before the ministerial subcommittee.
18 Dec	**21**	**Manufacture of goods formerly imported – report by the official subcommittee,** 4+11p appendixes. A number of industries with potential for home manufacture was considered.

CAB 87/15   Meetings and Memoranda   3 Jan–12 June 1945   R(I)(45)1st–7th and R(I)(45)1–15.

Meetings

3 Jan	**R(I)(45)1st**	**Manufacture of goods formerly imported.** R(I)(44)21. Anderson pointed out that the original concentration had been on goods from Germany but that goods from hard currency countries should now be looked at.
7 Feb	**2nd**	**Future of the light metal fabricating industry.** R(I)(45)1.
12 Feb	**3rd**	**Future of the regional organization and regional boards.** R(I)(45)2. It was felt there should be a gradual development of regional boards towards an advisory form.
21 Feb	**4th:1**	**Disposal of machine tools.** R(I)(45)3.
	:2	**Tin plate industry.** R(I)(45)6.
7 Mar	**5th:1**	**Industrial management.** R(I)(45)4.
	:2	**Future of the light metal fabricating industry.** R(I)(45)5 and 7.
5 Apr	**6th:1**	**The tin plate industry.** R(I)(45)8.
	:2	**The motor industry.** R(I)(45)9 and 11. It was decided that a working party of officials should

		make a thorough examination of the industry and recommend steps to secure an increased export trade.
14 May	7th:2	**Future of the clock and watch industry.** R(I)(45)13. This was related to the question of the manufacture of goods formerly imported.
	:3	**Future of the light metal fabricating industry.** R(I)(45)10.
12 June	*ad hoc*:2	**The building materials industry: combines and price rings.** H(45)31.

Memoranda

19 Jan	R(I)(45)1	**Future of the light metal fabricating industry – Cripps and Dalton,** 1+5+3p appendixes.
2 Feb	2	**The future of the regional organization and regional boards – report by the official subcommittee,** 6p. Only concerned with the transitional period.
5 Feb	3	**Disposal of machine tools – report by the official subcommittee,** 3+3p appendix.
6 Feb	4	**Industrial management – Dalton,** 2+6+4p appendix. Report on industrial management by a committee of three of his business advisers is attached. It recommends the establishment of a British Institute of Management to be financed initially by the government.
12 Feb	5	**Future of the light metal fabricating industry – Bevin,** 2p. Suggests a national corporation to run the industry.
15 Feb	6	**Redundancy of plant in the tin plate industry – Dalton,** 2p.
28 Feb	7	**The future of the light metal fabricating industry – Cripps,** 7p.
9 Mar	8	**Redundancy of plant in the tin plate industry – Dalton,** 1p.
21 Mar	9	**Post-war resettlement of the motor industry – report by the official subcommittee,** 7+5p appendix.
22 Mar	10	**The future of the light metal fabricating industry – report by the ministerial subcommittee,** 3p.
3 Apr	11	**Motor car industry – Cherwell,** 2+1p. The industry was crucial to Britain's export prospects.
10 Apr	12	**Arrangements for the holding of patents and the development and commercial testing of inventions – Anderson,** 5p.
3 May	13	**Enquiry into the future of the clock and watch industry – Cripps,** 2+1+13+6p appendixes.
6 June	15	**The development and commercial testing of new products and processes – Hudson,** 2p.

Ministerial Subcommittee on Industrial Problems (Export Questions)

In August 1944, Churchill deferred a Cabinet decision (CAB 65/43, WM(44)93rd:2) to establish a new committee on the post-war export trade and instructed that separately-constituted meetings of the Subcommittee on Industrial Problems should deal with the issue. They ended in May 1945.

Members   As the Subcommittee on Industrial Problems, with Ch. of Exchequer or Fin. Sec. (Try), and Sec., Overseas Trade.

Secs.   J. Jewkes (Recon.) and G. Parker (B.T.)   (March 1945) A.N. Coleridge (Recon.) replaced Jewkes.

CAB 87/14   Meetings and Memoranda   31 Aug–14 Dec 1944   R(IE)(44)1st–3rd and R(IE)(44)1–10.

Meetings

14 Sept	**R(IE)(44)1st:2**	**Export policy in the transition period.** R(IE)(44)3.
21 Nov	**2nd:1**	**Facilities to prepare for expansion of civil production.** R(IE)(44)4 and 6.
	:2	**Export targets.**
	:3	**Measures to increase facilities for British exports.** R(IE)(44)8.
	:4	**Coal export trade.** R(IE)(44)5. This question would be reconsidered after the publication of the Reid Committee report.
13 Dec	**3rd**	**Export credit guarantees.** R(IE)(44)9.

Memoranda

31 Aug	**R(IE)(44)1**	**Ministerial committee on exports – Woolton,** 2p.
12 Sept	**3**	**Export policy in the transition period – Dalton,** 1+8p. Departmental paper attached considering the problem of encouraging the will to export and the direction of exports to the most desirable markets.
4 Oct	**4**	**Facilities to prepare for the expansion of civil production – Dalton,** 1+4p. Progress report, to 1 Oct 1944, from Panel C of the Official Distribution of Industry Committee.
11 Nov	**5**	**The future of the coal export trade – Lloyd George,** 3p.
11 Nov	**6**	**Facilities to prepare for the expansion of civil production – Dalton,** 1+2p. Second progress report, to 10 Nov 1944.
11 Nov	**7**	**Export targets – Dalton,** 2+1p appendix. Indication given of the export prospects and an estimate of the export level in year two of Stage II of various industries.

17 Nov	**8**	**Measures designed to increase facilities for British exports – Dalton,** 1+2p. Until there was sufficient capacity and labour available it was futile to start a new export drive.
1 Dec	**9**	**Export credit guarantees – Dalton,** 2+4p. Draft bill attached.
15 Dec	**10**	**Facilities to prepare for the expansion of civil production – Dalton,** 1+1p. Progress report, to 14 Dec 1944.

CAB 87/15   Meetings and Memoranda   18 Jan–1 June 1945   R(IE)(45)1st–3rd and R(IE)(45)1–7.

Meetings

20 Mar	**R(IE)(45)1st:1**	**Export targets.**
	:2	**Coal processing.** R(IE)(45)2.
	:3	**Facilities for the expansion of civil production.** R(IE)(44)10 and R(IE)(45)1 and 4.
25 Apr	**2nd**	**Exports to India and the rest of the Empire.** R(IE)(45)5. Some disagreement with Amery's views.
14 May	**3rd**	**Export targets.** R(IE)(45)3 and 7. General agreement that the time was not right for a widely-publicized export drive.

Memoranda

18 Jan	**R(IE)(45)1**	**Facilities to prepare for the expansion of civil production – Dalton,** 1+1p. A further progress report, to 15 Jan 1945.
9 Mar	**2**	**Coal processing – Lloyd George,** 3+2p annex.
30 Mar	**3**	**Export targets – Dalton,** 2+4p annex. Export prospects of a number of industries considered.
15 Mar	**4**	**Facilities to prepare for the expansion of civil production – Dalton,** 1+1p. Progress report, to 4 March 1945.
6 Apr	**5**	**Exports to India and the rest of the Empire – Amery,** 2p.
19 Apr	**6**	**Report of the Technical Advisory Committee on Coal-mining – Lloyd George covering the committee,** 1+149p. Cmd. 6610.
5 May	**7**	**Export targets – Lyttelton,** 2+2p appendix. Challenges Dalton's generalizations as they were based on a narrow field of industries.
1 June	**–**	**Finance of post-war supplies to Russia – Office of the Lord President covering Dalton and Lyttelton,** 1+3p.

7.6   Official Subcommittee on Industrial Problems

Appointed in February 1944 with the ministerial Subcommittee on Industrial Problems (see CAB 87/5, R(44)15th:3) and augmented after April 1944 by a working party on controls (CAB 87/93), and after July 1944 by an informal subcommittee on regional organization (CAB 134/311–313). It was disbanded in June 1945.

Terms (i) to consider matters remitted to it for examination by the Reconstruction Committee or the Ministerial Subcommittee on Industrial Problems (ii) to review from time to time the work being done by Departments on the industrial problems of the transitional and post-war periods with a view to ensuring that adequate progress is made on all major questions.

Members N. Brook (Recon., ch.); B.W. Gilbert (Try); J.H. Woods (Prod.); G. Myrddin Evans (Lab. & N.S.); O.S. Franks (Supply); W. Palmer (B.T.) (March 1945) J.P.R. Maud replaced Brook. Representatives of Adm., Air P., Supply to attend when munitions industry discussed.

Secs. P. Callard (Recon.) (June 1944) A.M. Seed (Recon.) (Jan 1945) A.N. Coleridge (Recon.).

CAB 87/17 Meetings and Memoranda 1 Mar–15 Dec 1944 R(IO)(44)1st–22nd and R(IO)1–R(IO)(44)34.

Meetings

7 Mar	**R(IO)(44)1st:1**	**Service requirements for the Japanese war.** R(IO)(44)2.
	:2	**Facilities for experimental work of post-war significance.** R(IO)(44)4.
3 Apr	**2nd**	**Economic control in the transition period.** R(IO)(44)3. Small working party of officials set up to consider the issue.
18 Apr	**3rd:1**	**Facilities for experimental work of post-war significance.** R(IO)(44)6.
	:2	**Manufacture in this country of goods formerly imported.**
	:3	**Cease-fire.** R(IO)(44)5. Consideration of the issue of a Cease-fire book.
10 May	**4th:1**	**Material and equipment programme for permanent houses.** R(IO)(44)8. Agreement that bulk purchase was not essential for a successful housing programme.
	:2	**Future use of the regional organization.** Suggestion of an informal working party to consider the issue.
30 May	**5th**	**White Paper on employment policy.** R(IO)(44)9. Consideration of the balanced distribution of industry, the distribution of labour and the transition from war to peace.
7 June	**6th**	**Production changes affecting employment.** R(IO)(44)10. The committee felt that before making any commitments more information was needed on the degree of labour control which would exist and the extent of consultation with industry required during the transition.

13 June	7th:1	**Arrangement of meetings.** Weekly meetings to be held.
	:2	**White Paper on employment policy: chapter II Preparatory measures.** R(IO)(44)11. Discussion of the White Paper by paragraphs.
20 June	8th	**White Paper on employment policy: chapter II Preparatory measures.** R(IO)(44)11. Discussion continued.
4 July	9th:1	**Balanced distribution of industry: White Paper on employment policy: paragraph 30 Administrative arrangements.** R(IO)(44)12. Agreement that a new official committee, if necessary meeting in separate panels, should deal with this question.
	:2	**Facilities for work of post-war significance.**
11 July	10th	**Facilities for work of post-war export significance: administrative machinery for consideration of applications.** R(IO)(44)13. Agreement that ministers should be asked to authorize an announcement by the Board of Trade that, while such facilities could not be granted at present, applications would be considered as soon as circumstances allowed.
18 July	11th:1	**Production changes affecting employment.** R(IO)(44)15. Agreement in principle that the Ministry of Labour should consult with production departments about such changes in the period after the end of hostilities in Europe.
	:2	**Future use of the regional organization.** Agreement that there should be an informal working party, but with its terms of reference different from those suggested in R(IO)(44)4th:2.
	:3	**Facilities for preparatory work for the export trade: administrative machinery.** R(IO)(44)14 and 16. Draft report with minor amendments approved.
1 Aug	12th:1	**Future use of the regional organization.** R(IO)(44)17. Revised terms of reference for the working party.
	:2	**White Paper on employment policy: chapter II Preparatory measures.** R(IO)(44)18. Consideration of draft statement showing the inter-relation of certain committees and the general pattern of inter-departmental machinery for dealing with industrial questions.
29 Aug	13th	**Economic controls following the end of hostilities in Europe.** R(IO)(44)19. A number of amendments were made to the report. There was some discussion of further action required in this field.

5 Sept	**14th**	**Reconversion arrangements.** R(IO)(44)20.
26 Sept	**15th:1**	**White Paper on employment policy: chapter II Preparatory measures.**
	:2	**Manufacture in this country of goods formerly imported.** R(IO)(44)22. J.E. Meade said that restriction of imports for three to five years, followed thereafter by protection of some goods by subsidy, would be compatible with the lines of proposed commercial policy.
	:3	**Economic controls following the end of hostilities in Europe.** R(IO)(44)19. The War Cabinet decision to reduce the assumed length of the war against Japan from two years to eighteen months would not greatly affect R(IO)(44)21. However, the case for maintaining controls would have to rest less upon the labour shortage and more upon the need to ensure that production was in accordance with government priorities.
3 Oct	**16th**	**Future use of the regional organization.** R(IO)(44)23.
17 Oct	**17th**	**Reconversion arrangements: briefing ministers for the debate in the House of Commons.** R(IO)(44)24. Departments were to prepare statements on the various items included in R(IO)(44)24.
24 Oct	**18th:1**	**Future use of the regional organization.** R(IO)(44)23 and 26. W. Palmer said that the Board of Trade had not yet decided the form and scope of their post-war field organization.
3 Nov	**19th**	**Reconversion arrangements.** R(IO)(44)27. Consideration of the briefing of ministers for the Reconstruction Joint Advisory Council and for the debate in the House of Commons.
8 Nov	**20th**	**Machine tools.** R(IO)(44)28.
28 Nov	**21st:1**	**Manufacture in this country of goods formerly imported.** R(IO)(44)32.
	:2	**Machine tools.** R(IO)(44)31. Agreement in principle to remove individual licensing system for such tools, although the Ministry of Labour was concerned about the problems this would cause with regard to economic controls during the transition.
15 Dec	**22nd:1**	**Future of the regional organization and regional boards.** R(IO)(44)34. Agreement on regional organization but not on the regional boards.
	:2	**Post-war resettlement of the motor industry.** R(IO)(44)33. Approval of recommendation of an inter-departmental committee. Consideration of the industry's future.

Memoranda

1 Mar	**R(IO)1**	**Terms of reference and procedure – N. Brook,** 2p.
1 Mar	**R(IO)2**	**Service requirements for the Japanese war and their effect on the switch-over of industry from war to peace – N. Brook,** 4p. The Joint War Production Staff was estimating labour required for munitions and it would then be possible for the subcommittee to consider the civil side, although detailed planning could not be carried very far until individual firms could be told whether, or at what stage, they would be free to undertake civil production.
2 Mar	**R(IO)(44)3**	**Economic control during the transition – N. Brook,** 8p. Some controls might require strengthening but equally those that were unnecessary should be removed. However, in many cases it was impossible to resolve the issue of retention until it was known whether the control was needed as part of a permanent post-war apparatus.
1 Mar	**4**	**Facilities for experimental work of post-war significance – Board of Trade,** 3p.
6 Mar	**5**	**Action relating to industry and employment to be completed within seven to fourteen days of the conclusion of hostilities in Europe – N. Brook,** 1+3+4p appendix. Issue of whether there should be a government Cease-fire book.
27 Mar	**6**	**Facilities for experimental work of post-war significance – Board of Trade,** 3p.
2 May	**7**	**Economic control in the transition period – P. Callard covering the Raw Materials Department of the Ministry of Supply,** 1+2+1+4+10p annex. Three papers attached on (a) controls which are likely to be required two years after the German armistice, assuming that occurs at the end of 1944 and that the Japanese operations continue throughout the two-year period, (b) main raw materials of which there is unlikely to be a shortage in the transition period, (c) list of raw material regulations and other control measures which it is expected could be withdrawn soon after the armistice with Germany.
8 May	**8**	**Material and equipment programme for permanent houses – P. Callard covering the Board of Trade,** 1+3p. Consideration of the degree of central control required even if there were to be no bulk purchase scheme.
26 May	**9**	**Employment policy – N. Brook,** 1+31p. White Paper on *Employment Policy* (Cmd. 6527) attached.

3 June	10	**Production changes affecting employment – Ministry of Labour,** 2p.
10 June	11	**Employment policy – N. Brook,** 1+3p. 'White Paper on employment policy, chapter II. Preparatory measures' is attached. Considers the measures suggested in paragraphs 14 and 16 of the White Paper and the state of progress on each.
1 July	12	**The balanced distribution of industry – N. Brook,** 2+3p. Draft memorandum on the inter-departmental organization to control the administration of policy set out in paragraph 30 of the White Paper on *Employment Policy* is attached.
7 July	13	**Facilities for work of post-war significance – A.N. Seed covering the Board of Trade,** 1+3p.
13 July	14	**Facilities for preparatory work for the expansion of the export trade – N. Brook,** 1+3p. Draft report attached.
14 July	15	**Production changes affecting employment – Ministry of Labour,** 2+3p. 'Labour controls in the interim period', a note by the Ministry of Labour to the Informal Committee on Controls, 28 Jan 1944, is attached.
17 June	16	**Facilities for preparatory work for the expansion of the export trade – N. Brook,** 1+3p. Revised draft of R(IO)(44)14 which, after amendment, became R(I)(44)10.
27 July	17	**Informal Subcommittee on Regional Organization: revised terms of reference – N. Brook,** 1+1p.
28 July	18	**Industrial problems of the transition period. Administrative arrangements – N. Brook,** 1+3+1p appendix.
22 Aug	19	**Economic controls following the end of hostilities in Europe – report by the working party,** 13+26p appendixes. This deals primarily with the controls needed in the first six to twelve months after the end of hostilities in Europe. Some general system of controls must continue to operate. The major controls are then considered individually. The appendixes cover various controls in greater detail and are mainly written by the responsible department.
2 Sept	20	**Arrangements for conversion of industrial capacity to civilian needs – N. Brook,** 2p.
18 Sept	21	**Economic controls in the transition – report of the Official Subcommittee on Industrial Problems,** 9+11p appendixes. Redraft of R(IO)(44)19. See R(I)(44)16.

13 Sept	22	**Manufacture of goods formerly imported. Clocks and watches – A.M. Seed covering the report of the working party,** 1+8+9p appendixes.
29 Sept	23	**Future use of the regional organization – A.M. Seed covering the report of the informal subcommittee,** 1+9p.
14 Oct	24	**Briefing of ministers on the forthcoming debate on reconversion – Board of Trade and Ministry of Production,** 1+2p annex.
19 Oct	25	**Reconversion: briefing of ministers – N. Brook,** 1+1p annex +4p appendix. Memorandum submitted to the National Joint Advisory Council by the T.U.C., Federation of British Industries and the British Employers' Confederation, is attached.
20 Oct	26	**Future use of the regional organization – N. Brook,** 2p. List of questions which he thinks the committee should consider following the request from the Official Committee on the Machinery of Government for the committee's views.
1 Nov	27	**Reconversion: briefing of ministers for meeting of Reconstruction Joint Advisory Council – N. Brook,** 4+16p appendix.
3 Nov	28	**Machine tools – N. Brook covering the Committee on the Disposal of Machine Tools,** 1+6p. Report of the committee attached.
	29	**Note by the Ministry of Aircraft Production on the report of Sir William Palmer's Committee on the Disposal of Machine Tools,** 2p.
20 Nov	30	**Reconversion: brief for meeting of the Reconstruction Joint Advisory Council – N. Brook,** 1+35p. Brief attached.
23 Nov	31	**Control and disposal of machine tools – Ministry of Supply,** 2+1p annex.
23 Nov	32	**Manufacture in this country of goods formerly imported – N. Brook,** 1+3+9p appendixes. Draft report attached.
9 Dec	33	**Post-war resettlement of the motor industry –A.M. Seed covering the Informal Committee on the Post-war Resettlement of the Motor Industry,** 1+8p. Report of the informal committee.
13 Dec	34	**Regional organization – N. Brook,** 1+5p. Draft report.

CAB 87/18 Meetings and Memoranda 2 Jan–4 June 1945 R(IO)(45)1st–10th, R(IO)(45)1–18 and R(I)(45)2, 3 and 9.

Meetings

5 Jan	**R(IO)(45)1st:1**	**Machine tools.** R(IO)(44)28 and R(IO)(45)1.

	:2	**Manufacture in this country of goods formerly imported.**
16 Jan	2nd:1	**Future of the regional organization and regional boards.** R(IO)(45)3. Decision that a report should be submitted to ministers.
	:2	**Disposal of machine tools.** R(IO)(45)2 and 4. As a result of R(IO)(45)4, R(IO)(45)2 needed to be redrafted.
30 Jan	3rd:1	**Economic controls in the transition.** R(IO)(45)6. Agreement that there should be an informal working party to re-examine the proposals for the working of economic controls in the early part of the transition if the war against Japan lasted for less than eighteen or even six months.
	:2	**Manufacture in this country of goods formerly imported.**
13 Feb	4th:1	**Regional organization.** The subcommittee was informed of the ministerial decision at R(I)(45)2nd.
	:2	**Economic controls in the transition.** Confirmation that the review should go ahead.
17 Feb	5th	**Post-war resettlement of the motor industry.** R(IO)(45)9.
13 Mar	6th	**Post-war resettlement of the motor industry.** R(IO)(45)10.
10 Apr	7th:1	**Manufacture of goods formerly imported.** R(IO)(45)12 and 14.
	:2	**War potential industries.** R(IO)(45)12. Working party set up to consider the issue.
	:3	**Future business.**
24 Apr	8th	**Economic controls.** R(IO)(45)11, 13, 15. The Board of Trade was trying to reduce the use of export licensing in Stage II to a minimum. It hoped that by bulk licensing of machinery it would be able to safeguard priorities in Stage II.
15 May	9th	**Work of the subcommittee in Stage II.** List of subjects on which the subcommittee was to receive papers. Agreement that the subcommittee was a useful forum for the discussion of the industrial problems of the transition.
29 May	10th:1	**Agricultural machinery and implements.** R(IO)(45)16.
	:2	**Modifications of controls** R(IO)(45)17.

Memoranda

2 Jan	**R(IO)(45)1**	**Disposal of machine tools – Ministry of Supply,** 1p.
8 Jan	**2**	**Disposal of machine tools – N. Brook,** 1+1+5p appendix. Draft report for the ministerial subcommittee.

12 Jan	3	**Regional organization** – N. Brook, 1+7p. Revised draft report.
13 Jan	4	**Disposal of machine tools** – N. Brook, 3p. Revised draft report and letter from G. Turner.
17 Jan	5	**Regional organization** – N. Brook, 1p. Revision of paragraph 12 of R(IO)(45)3.
25 Jan	6	**Economic controls in the transition** – N. Brook, 1p. He felt the need to review progress on questions raised in R(IO)(44)21 and suggested a number of issues for immediate consideration.
6 Feb	7	**Disposal of machine tools** – A.N. Coleridge, 1p. The draft report had been amended and submitted to ministers as R(I)(45)3.
6 Feb	8	**The future of the regional organization and regional boards** – A.N. Coleridge, 1p. The draft report had been amended and submitted to ministers as R(I)(45)2.
24 Feb	9	**Post-war resettlement of the motor industry** – A.N. Coleridge, 1+7p.
6 Mar	10	**Post-war resettlement of the motor industry** – **J.P.R. Maud covering the Official Committee on the Post-war Resettlement of the Motor Industry**, 1+6+5p appendix. Draft report by the official committee.
22 Mar	11	**Economic controls: possible use of trade associations** – **Raw Materials Department of the Ministry of Supply**, 6p.
5 Apr	12	**Manufacture of goods formerly imported** – **Board of Trade**, 3+16p appendixes. Enquiries carried out in a number of relevant industries.
6 Apr	13	**Economic controls: engineering industries** – **Board of Trade**, 4p.
7 Apr	14	**Manufacture of goods formerly imported: photographic film base** – **Ministry of Aircraft Production**, 4+2p appendix.
9 Apr	15	**Control of consumer goods industries and promotion of exports** – **Board of Trade**, 3+3p annex. Progress report on the Board of Trade's plans for the control of essential and non-essential civilian goods.
22 May	16	**Agricultural machinery and implements** – **Ministry of Agriculture and Fisheries**, 7+4p appendixes. The Board of Trade and the Ministry of Agriculture and Fisheries considered that only by encouraging North American firms to establish production plants could the country hope to get an efficient industry on modern lines.
22 May	17	**Modifications of controls** – **A.N. Coleridge covering the Board of Trade**, 1+2p.

4 June	**18**	**Modifications in controls – A.N. Coleridge covering the Raw Materials Department of the Ministry of Supply, 1+4p.**

Appended to file: R(I)(45)2, 3 and 9.

7.7   Official Committee on Post-war Internal Economic Problems

Appointed in 1941, to report to the Reconstruction Problems Committee (CAB 87/3) and, after January 1943, the Reconstruction Priorities Committee when appropriate (CAB 87/12). It was the main forum for debate on employment policy until the formation of the Steering Committee on Post-war Employment (CAB 87/63), attended by economists within Whitehall and receiving Meade's initial proposal for employment policy in October 1941 (CAB 87/54, IEP(41)3). It was disbanded in November 1943 on the creation of the Reconstruction Committee (CAB 87/5–10).

Terms   (a) to formulate the chief problems of post-war internal economic policy   (b) to arrange for the preparation of memoranda on these problems   (c) to formulate for ministers the considerations which should be borne in mind in framing policy.

Members   (1942) A. Hurst (Paymaster-Gen., ch.); Q. Hill (Paymaster-Gen.); R. Hopkins or W. Eady (Try); C. Hurcomb (W. Transport); F.W. Leggett (Lab. & N.S.); A. Overton (B.T.); H. Hamilton (Scot.); H. French (Food); G. Whiskard (Works); D. Fergusson (M.A.F.); F.W. Leith Ross (Chief Ec. Adv.).   (Feb 1943) G. Whiskard (T. & C. Plan.); F.P. Robinson (Works).

Sec.   A. Baster (Paymaster-Gen. O.).

CAB 87/57   Meetings and Memoranda   1 Jan–17 Nov 1943   IEP(43)1st–21st and IEP(43)1–43.

Meetings

1 Jan	**IEP(43)1st:1**	**Post-war agricultural policy.** IEP(42)67 and 69.
	:3	**The stabilization issue.** IEP(42)24, 55, 62 and minutes of IEP(42)22nd. IEP(42)62 was to be redrafted.
12 Feb	**2nd:2**	**The policy of stabilization.** IEP(43)9. After slight amendment IEP(43)9 was to be submitted to the Reconstruction Problems Committee.
	:3	**Industrial reconstruction.** IEP(43)6.
	:4	**Revival of peace-time production.** IEP(43)8.
9 Apr	**7th:1**	**Future work of the committee.** It was confirmed that papers could go to either the Reconstruction Problems Committee or the Reconstruction Priorities Committee.
	:3	**Post-war housing.** IEP(42)65 and IEP(43)2. The problems for the committee in this field were set out.
14 Apr	**8th**	**Post-war housing.** IEP(42)65.

23 Apr	**9th**	**Post-war housing.** IEP(43)17. There was a problem in asking local authorities to prepare a housing programme for longer than one year before the location of industry policy had been settled. IEP(43)17 was to be redrafted.
7 May	**10th**	**Post-war housing policy.** IEP(42)23, 27, 65, IEP(43)2, 19.
18 May	**11th**	**Post-war housing policy.** IEP(42)23, 27, 65, IEP(43)2, 20.
25 May	**12th:2**	**Future work of the committee.** IEP(43)21. Suggestion that each department should submit a statement of the order of priority adopted in tackling reconstruction questions.
25 June	**13th:1**	**Location of industry.** IEP(43)25. The Board of Trade could not agree to housing necessarily taking precedence over all industrial building in the immediate post-war period.
	:2	**Bulk purchase under the housing programme.** IEP(43)26.
2 July	**14th**	**Location of industry.** IEP(43)25. Agreement that IEP(43)25 should be replaced by a new paper.
8 July	**15th**	**Location of industry.** IEP(43)27. Agreement that IEP(43)27 should be submitted to Jowitt for the Reconstruction Priorities Committee.
3 Sept	**18th:1**	**Report of Production Departments Subcommittee.** IEP(43)33.
10 Sept	**19th**	**Post-war highway policy.** IEP(43)30 and 38. A. Hurst said that consideration of the subject should be divided between (a) finance, and priority to be accorded to various schemes and (b) executive machinery.
1 Oct	**20th**	**Post-war highway policy.** IEP(43)38 and 41. Issue of whether the covering note for ministers should deal principally with long-term or short-term issues.
15 Oct	**21st:1**	**Post-war highway policy.** IEP(43)42. Agreement that after slight amendment IEP(43)42 should be submitted to the Reconstruction Problems Committee.
	:2	**Times of meetings.**

Memoranda

18 Jan	**IEP(43)2**	**The economic background of the post-war building and constructional programme – A. Baster,** 1+11p. Final version, as revised for submission to Jowitt. The programme allowed for 4.5m houses to be built in ten years in Great Britain. As it offered long-term employment it was hoped it would result in a sense of responsibility from both management and workers.

5 Jan	**3**	**Post-war agricultural problems – A. Baster covering the agricultural departments,** 4+16p. Also RP(43)2, USE(43)1 and see WP(43)103. The covering note differs from these other papers.
4 Feb	**6**	**Industrial reconstruction – A. Baster covering the Board of Trade,** 1+1+8p annexes. Transition of production to civilian goods requires care. The paper sets out those responsible in the Board of Trade and various aspects of the subject.
5 Feb	**8**	**Departmental studies – A. Baster covering the Board of Trade,** 1+16p. 'The revival of peace-time production and maintenance of a due balance between production for the home market and for export' – H. Clay, 14 Aug 1942, is attached.
9 Feb	**9**	**Continuance of the policy of stabilization – Treasury,** 14+3p appendix. Revised draft of IEP(42)62.
20 Feb	**10**	**Membership of the committee – A. Baster,** 1p.
5 Mar	**11**	**Untitled – A. Hurst covering the Treasury and the Board of Trade,** 5+1p appendix and 6+1p appendix. 'The continuance of the policy of stabilization' – Treasury and 'The control of industrial prices' – Board of Trade. Also RP(43)19 and see PR(43)16.
22 Apr	**17**	**Post-war housing policy** – unsigned, 11p. Draft memorandum.
4 May	**19**	**Post-war housing policy** – unsigned, 20p. Redraft of IEP(43)17.
15 May	**20**	**Post-war housing policy – the official committee,** 28p. Redraft of IEP(43)17.
11 May	**21**	**Future work of the committee: priorities – A. Baster covering Jowitt,** 2p. Jowitt concerned at the slow progress in reaching decisions on reconstruction.
21 May	**23**	**New member of the committee – A. Baster,** 1p.
27 May	**24**	**Post-war housing policy – official committee,** 1+10+31p appendixes. Appendixes include IEP(42)23, 27, 65 and IEP(43)2. See RP(43)24.
15 June	**25**	**Location of industry – A. Baster covering an interim report by the Board of Trade,** 7p. The report had been written on the assumption that the cure of localized unemployment would be an essential feature of post-war policy. Surveys of the relevant areas were being undertaken.
22 June	**26**	**Bulk purchase under the housing programme and its relation to the location of industry – A. Baster covering the Board of Trade,** 10p. In the interest of employment policy it was important that government should control the placing and

		the timing of orders necessary to fulfil the housing programme.
8 July	27	**Location of industry – the official committee,** 7+2p appendix. Final version of the interim note. See PR(43)38.
4 Aug	29	**Reports of the Acquisition of Land Subcommittee on the Uthwatt Report on Compensation and Betterment – A. Baster covering the Subcommittee on the Acquisition of Land,** 1+15+23p appendixes and 36p.
9 Aug	30	**Local government reform and post-war highway policy – A. Baster covering the Reconstruction Problems Committee,** 1+5p. Minutes of RP(43)8th.
25 Aug	33	**The disposal of surplus stocks of raw materials, manufactured goods and machinery, factories and storage premises – A. Baster covering the production departments subcommittee,** 10p. Interim report of the subcommittee.
7 Sept	38	**Post-war highway policy – A. Baster covering Leathers,** 1+8+17p appendixes. See RP(43)27.
29 Sept	41	**Post-war highway policy – the official committee,** 7p. Draft covering note.
16 Oct	42	**Post-war highway policy – P. Callard covering the official committee,** 1+8p. Final version of the covering note. See RP(43)30.

7.8   Steering Committee on Post-war Employment

Appointed by the Reconstruction Priorities Committee in July 1943, see CAB 87/12, PR(43)13th:1, this official committee produced the basis for the first draft of the *Employment Policy* White Paper (Cmd. 6527). Its report was submitted to the Reconstruction Committee in January 1944 (CAB 87/7, R(44)6) and initially discussed on 21 January (CAB 87/5, R(44)8th). From the end of November, during Hopkins's illness, the committee was chaired by Barlow.

Terms   (a) to map out the field of enquiry and to assign the various parts to the Departments primarily concerned   (b) to keep in touch with the progress of the work and to receive the reports of the Departments as the various studies are completed   (c) to bring together the results of these enquiries into a single comprehensive report for submission to the Reconstruction Priorities Committee.

Members   R. Hopkins (Try, ch.); T.W. Phillips (Lab. & N.S.); A. Hurst (Recon.); J.A. Barlow (Try) or W. Eady (Try); A. Overton (B.T.); L. Robbins (Ec. Sect.).

Secs.   W.L. Gorrell-Barnes (Cab. O.) and D.N. Chester (Cab. O.).

CAB 87/63   Meetings and Memoranda   30 July 1943–10 Jan 1944
EC(43)1st–EC(44)1st and EC(43)1–31 and R(44)6.

Meetings

30 July	**EC(43)1st:1**	**General work of the committee.**
	:2	**Timetable.** Report required by 31 October.
	:3	Untitled. Discussion of amendment of list in PR(43)47 of subjects to be considered.
	:4	Untitled. Division of subjects among departments.
	:5	Untitled. General method of approach. Departments should regard themselves as primarily concerned with the long-term or 'normal' economic conditions.
20 Oct	**2nd**	Untitled. Agreement with general approach suggested by R. Hopkins. No figure of unemployment was to be given as a target and the efficacy of potential measures was to be considered in only the broadest terms. 'Note for consideration of the Steering Committee' – R. Hopkins, undated, 3p, is attached.
21 Oct	**3rd:1**	**Procedure.**
	:2	**Mobility of labour.** EC(43)1, 7, 11.
22 Oct	**4th:1**	**Mobility of labour.** EC(43)1 and 11.
	:2	**Restrictive practices.**
25 Oct	**5th**	**Restrictive practices in industry.** EC(43)3 and 8.
26 Oct	**6th:1**	**Restrictive practices in industry.** EC(43)3 and 8. Consideration in particular of the manner in which questions raised should be treated in the report. Agreement that, since aspects other than employment were involved, which the committee did not have time to consider, it would not be possible to formulate definite proposals.
	:2	**General support of trade.** EC(43)4 and 15. The Board of Trade felt that measures to maintain aggregate demand and control structural dislocation would not be successful unless industry were sufficiently efficient to stand up to foreign competition.
27 Oct	**7th:1**	**General support of trade.** EC(43)4 and 15. Discussion of powers required by industrial boards and preliminary consideration of an industrial commission.
	:2	**Future procedure.**
28 Oct	**8th**	**General support of trade.** EC(43)3 and 4. General agreement that there was a need for some semi-independent body to investigate cases where it was believed that restrictive practices were operating against the national interest.

29 Oct	**9th**	**General support of trade.** EC(43)4. Consideration of the functions of an industrial commission and the possibility of financial assistance to industry. Agreement that there was a case for granting subsidies for re-equipment of selected industries.
30 Oct	**10th:1**	**General support of trade.** EC(43)4. Agreement that some form of financial assistance for amalgamation of industry was required.
	:2	**Location of industry.** EC(43)5 and 13.
1 Nov	**11th**	Untitled. EC(43)6 No.1. L.C. Robbins felt that EC(43)6 No.1 badly misrepresented the Economic Section in places and was unacceptable in others, in particular on structural unemployment, the stabilization of industry and deficit financing. In reply, W. Eady felt that neither PR(43)26 nor any published work adequately discussed the practical questions of how to translate broad principles into practice and felt that Robbins was being more cautious than the original Economic Section paper.
2 Nov	**12th:1**	**Financial policy and the maintenance of employment.** L.C. Robbins recommended the use of total public investment as a compensatory factor to offset changes in private investment and possibly in consumption. He put forward the Section's views on the necessary administrative machinery.
	:2	**Planning and timing of public investment.** EC(43)6 No.2 and EC(43)14. The subject was to be approached on the basis of what was practicable rather than what was necessary to compensate for fluctuations in demand.
3 Nov	**13th:1**	**Planning and timing of public investment.** EC(43)6 No.2 and EC(43)14. Agreement that central powers over the capital expenditure of local authorities were sufficient to reduce it in times of high employment. In times of low employment central government would neither reduce its own expenditure nor exhort local authorities to do so, thereby removing one of the traditional obstacles to the maintenance of local authority capital expenditure in such times.
	:2	**Control and timing of private investment.** EC(43)6 No.3 and EC(43)10.
4 Nov	**14th**	**Control and timing of private investment.** EC(43)6 No.3 and EC(43)10. Discussion on the need and practicability of reducing the rate

		of interest below 3%, the use of subsidies and tax remission to stimulate private investment.
5 Nov	15th	**Regulation of consumption.** EC(43)6 No.4 and EC(43)16. Discussion of a scheme to vary social security contributions to control consumption.
6 Nov	16th	Untitled. Consideration of the form which the committee's report might take, in particular the treatment of the sections on general characteristics of the post-war world and on wages and prices in relation to employment policy.
8 Nov	17th	Untitled. EC(43)5, 13, 18, 19, 21. Discussion on the location of industry.
9 Nov	18th	**Location of industry.** EC(43)19 and 21.
10 Nov	19th	**Location of industry.** Discussion based on draft statement prepared by R. Hopkins, not included.
12 Nov	20th	Untitled. Location of industry discussed on the basis of a revised note by R. Hopkins, not included.
13 Nov	21st	**Location of industry.** EC(43)5. Hopkins to revise again his draft statement.
15 Nov	22nd:1	**Location of industry.** EC(43)5. The secretaries were instructed on how the proposals in EC(43)5 should be dealt with in the first draft of the report.
	:2	**Cost of employment measures.**
16 Nov	23rd:1	**Location of industry.** Agreement that during the transition there would be a need for some official regional machinery to keep the central machinery informed of local conditions, possibly to settle minor questions and to act as a link between national policy and local opinion.
	:2	**Deficit financing.**
17 Nov	24th:1	**Deficit financing.** L.C. Robbins was invited to write two pieces on the budgetary implications of employment policy for the draft report.
	:2	**Industrial efficiency and employment.**
18 Nov	25th	**Variation of social security contribution.** EC(43)24, 27, 28.
19 Nov	26th:1	**Variation of social security contribution.** EC(43)24, 27, 28. Substantial agreement that the Economic Section's scheme was a valuable aid to the maintenance of purchasing power. There seemed to be no insuperable administrative difficulties although it could not be introduced immediately.
	:2	**Location of industry.** Discussion of the draft report.

25 Nov	27th:1	**Post-war prospects of the coal industry.** EC(43)20.
	:2	**The post-war prospects of the United Kingdom cotton industry.** EC(43)25.
	:3	**Hire purchase of consumer goods.** EC(43)26. Consideration of a state hire purchase corporation.
26 Nov	28th	**Draft report.** EC(O)(43)2 and 4. Amendments to the draft report.
29 Nov	29th	**Draft report: industrial efficiency and employment.** EC(O)(43)3(revise). Amendments.
10 Jan	EC(44)1st	Untitled. EC(O)(44)3. Final proof of the report considered. Reference made to a large number of informal meetings to consider the draft report but no record was circulated of them.

Memoranda

15 Oct	EC(43)1	**The mobility of labour and structural unemployment – Ministry of Labour,** 4p. The solution to structural unemployment lay not only in increased labour mobility but more importantly in securing an adequate distribution and diversification of light and developing industry.
15 Oct	2	**Restrictive practices affecting entry of workers into new trades – Ministry of Labour,** 4+11p appendixes. Such practices had to be considered industry by industry to see if they were incompatible with full employment policy.
15 Oct	3	**Restrictive practices in industry – Board of Trade,** 4+3p annex. The post-war policies for the maintenance of employment, increased output and the control of monopoly should be closely linked. Fresh legislation would be needed.
15 Oct	4	**General support of trade – Board of Trade,** 15+9p annexes. Measures were required which not only helped to achieve full employment, but also led to a higher level of efficiency, so as to be able to increase the competitiveness of exports. Proposals for industrial boards and an industrial commission, tax remission and subsidies, and government assistance for research were made. Annex includes a paper on finance for industry.
18 Oct	5	**Location of industry – Board of Trade,** 17+25p annexes. Written in consultation with the Ministry of Labour, the Ministry of Town and Country Planning and the Scottish Office.

While a successful location policy was vital, first consideration must be given to the increased efficiency of industry and in particular the stimulation of the export industries. Development areas and restricted areas were considered and a location board to advise the Board of Trade proposed. Annexes deal with the results of the Board of Trade's location surveys, location of industry inducements and wartime production of importance to development areas.

16 Oct   **6**   **Note by W.L. Gorrell-Barnes and D.N. Chester covering the Treasury and the Inland Revenue,** 1+13+4+2+3+2p. Five papers included: (1) 'The maintenance of employment. Prefatory note' – Treasury. Treasury's general views of PR(43)37. Highly critical of PR(43)26, attacking its views on structural unemployment, the stabilization of investment and the use of deficit financing. (2) 'Planning and timing of public investment' – Treasury. Examination of how far the tendency of public investment to decline in the wake of private activity could be arrested or reversed and the practical considerations which were involved. (3) 'Control and timing of private investment' – Treasury. Consideration of the proposals in PR(43)26, especially monetary policy and the creation of public finance corporations. (4) 'Variation of social security contributions' – Treasury. Practical rather than economic aspects assessed. (5) Note by the Inland Revenue. Consideration of the proposal in PR(43)26 of specific tax privileges to help capital development at particular times.

18 Oct   **7**   **Mobility of labour and structural unemployment** – Economic Section, 2p. Two further points in relation to EC(43)1.

18 Oct   **9**   **Maintenance of employment** – Economic Section, 4p. Consideration of the three areas of difference between it and the Treasury. Criticizes, as unduly pessimistic, the Treasury's rejection of virtually all of its proposals to stabilize aggregate demand.

19 Oct   **10**   **Control and timing of private investment** – Economic Section, 3p. Substantial agreement with the Treasury over public finance corporations and the Inland Revenue argument against the use of income tax as a means of subsidizing investment in a depression. Suggests instead a straight subsidy on private capital expenditure. The Treasury case against

the use of monetary policy in the early post-war years was strong but not unanswerable.

18 Oct	11	**1. Post-war resettlement scheme 2. Transitional scheme – Ministry of Labour,** 3p.
20 Oct	12	**Maintenance of employment – Board of Trade,** 4p. Comments on EC(43)6 No.1. Agreement in particular with proposals regarding structural unemployment and the danger that the post-war level of investment might be too high; but the Treasury's conclusions and its general attitude on budgetary policy were unacceptable.
20 Oct	13	**Location of industry – Economic Section,** 5p. Policy should be considered in the light of town and country planning as well as full employment principles because depressed areas would not be as important as in the inter-war period.
20 Oct	14	**Planning and timing of public investment – Economic Section,** 5p. Comments on three aspects of EC(43)6 No.2: (a) the objectives of public investment policy; (b) the prospects of attaining these objectives with pre-war powers and organizations; and (c) desiderata regarding new powers and planning organization.
20 Oct	15	**General support of trade – Economic Section,** 6p. Concern that some of the Board of Trade's proposals in EC(43)4 would lead to more monopoly and restrictive practices.
23 Oct	16	**Variation of social security contributions – Economic Section,** 4+1p annex. Despite some problems, the scheme seemed the most efficient and practical of the various proposals for affecting consumption.
22 Oct	17	**Statistics required in connection with post-war employment policy – W.L. Gorrell-Barnes and D.N. Chester covering the Subcommittee on Post-war Statistics of the Emergency Legislation Committee.** 11p. First interim report of the subcommittee. Also EL(S)(43)2. Suggestions aimed mainly towards the period of 'normal' peace-time conditions. Legislation for collection of statistics was needed. An outline of the statistics required is given.
2 Nov	18	**Location of industry – Ministry of Town and Country Planning,** 11p. Background considerations. Indicates how, in the short-term, planning operations could contribute to full employment.
4 Nov	19	**Location of industry – Ministry of Aircraft Production,** 3p. Agreement with the Board of Trade that efficiency should be the first

priority. Suggestion that industrial development should be considered as a problem of particular industries not areas.

6 Nov	20	**Export prospects for the coal industry – Ministry of Fuel and Power,** 2+4p. 'Survey of production and export of coal from the United Kingdom since 1913' – Ministry of Fuel and Power, 29 Sept 1943, is attached.
6 Nov	21	**Location of industry – Ministry of Supply,** 4p. Sceptical of many features of EC(43)5. Increasing efficiency was of overwhelming importance.
8 Nov	22	**Restrictive practices in industry – W.L. Gorrell-Barnes and D.N. Chester covering replies sent to the Board of Trade,** 3p. Comments from officials on EC(43)3.
10 Nov	23	**Location of industry – Ministry of Works,** 2p. The favouring of firms in development areas in the building programme could lead to problems because of the shortage of building labour.
11 Nov	24	**Variations in social security contributions – Economic Section,** 3p. Subtitled 'Interval between a change in the unemployment percentage and the consequent change in the value of the weekly social insurance stamp'.
11 Nov	25	**Post-war prospects of the United Kingdom cotton industry – Board of Trade,** 4p.
12 Nov	26	**Hire purchase of consumer goods – Board of Trade,** 13p. Consideration of the use of hire purchase to help iron out cyclical fluctuations and whether, as suggested by the Minister of Labour in RP(42)20, there should be a national hire purchase corporation.
12 Nov	27	**Variations in social security contributions – Economic Section,** 3p. Subtitled 'Effect on possible deficit of the social insurance fund'.
12 Nov	28	**Variations in social security contributions – Economic Section,** 1+1p. Subtitled 'Illustrations of the working of a hypothetical scheme, 1923–1938'.
17 Nov	29	**Location of industry – A.S. Le Maitre,** 2p. There was an important link between Admiralty work and the development areas.
22 Nov	30	**National expenditure, income and employment – Economic Section,** 2+3p. Three charts, aiming to illustrate the effect of changes in the general level of aggregate money expenditure upon the general level of employment, are attached. They show: (a) movements in money income, real income and employment in the U.K., 1924–28; (b) fluctuations in money income,

real income and employment around their trends, 1924–28; and (c) from *The Economist* of 7 Jan 1939, the effect of these movements upon employment in particular regions.

20 Dec   31   **Variability of post-war investment – Economic Section,** 3p. Estimate, on the basis of figures in appendix D of PR(43)26, appendix II of PR(43)44 and R(43)4, of the amount by which post-war total public investment might be varied to offset fluctuations in the general level of national expenditure.

Appended to file – **R(44)6.**

CAB 87/70   Memoranda only   9 Nov 1943–8 Jan 1944   EC(O)(43)1–EC(O)(44)3
and R(44)6.

9 Nov   **EC(O)(43)1**   **Industrial efficiency and employment – W.L. Gorrell-Barnes and D.N. Chester,** 1+14p. First draft of chapter VI of R(44)6 excluding its introduction, to be written by A. Overton and L.C. Robbins.

11 Nov   2   **Labour and employment – W.L. Gorrell-Barnes and D.N. Chester,** 1+9p. Draft of part of chapter IV of R(44)6.

25 Nov   3   **Industrial efficiency and employment – W.L. Gorrell-Barnes and D.N. Chester covering the Board of Trade,** 1+13p. Revise version. Redraft of chapter VI of R(44)6.

13 Nov   4   **The need for information and planning – W.L. Gorrell-Barnes and D.N. Chester,** 3p. Draft of part of chapter VII of R(44)6.

17 Nov   5   **The control of aggregate demand – W.L. Gorrell-Barnes and D.N. Chester,** 1+7p. Draft of chapter II of R(44)6.

1 Dec   6   **Note by the joint secretaries – W.L. Gorrell-Barnes and D.N. Chester covering L.C. Robbins,** 1+8+10p. Two draft sections of chapter I of R(44)6 on 'The international background' and 'The problems of the transitional period'.

3 Dec   7   **Note by joint secretaries – W.L. Gorrell-Barnes and D.N. Chester,** 1+7p. Draft of part of chapter II of R(44)6 on 'Control of consumption'.

4 Dec   8   **Industrial efficiency and employment – W.L. Gorrell-Barnes and D.N. Chester,** 1+19p. Redraft of EC(O)(43)3(revise) paragraphs 1–49.

17 Dec   9   **Location of industry – W.L. Gorrell-Barnes and D.N. Chester,** 1+9p. Revise version. Draft of chapter V of R(44)6.

14 Dec	10	**Industrial efficiency and employment – W.L. Gorrell-Barnes and D.N. Chester covering A. Hurst,** 10p. Redraft of chapter VI of R(44)6.
16 Dec	11	**Wages and prices – W.L. Gorrell-Barnes and D.N. Chester covering L.C. Robbins,** 1+4p. Draft of chapter III of R(44)6.
18 Dec	12	**Budgetary implications – W.L. Gorrell-Barnes and D.N. Chester covering L.C. Robbins,** 1+3p. Draft of part of chapter II of R(44)6.
21 Dec	13	**Introductory paragraphs – W.L. Gorrell-Barnes and D.N. Chester,** 1+11p. Draft of chapter I of R(44)6.
21 Dec	14	**Control of aggregate demand – W.L. Gorrell-Barnes and D.N. Chester,** 1+5p. Draft of part of chapter II.
22 Dec	15	**The education of public opinion – W.L. Gorrell-Barnes and D.N. Chester,** 1+1p. Draft of part of chapter VII of R(44)6.
24 Dec	16	**Draft report – W.L. Gorrell-Barnes and D.N. Chester,** 1p. A copy is not attached.
1 Jan 1944	17	**Note by joint secretaries – W.L. Gorrell-Barnes and D.N. Chester,** 1+4p. Draft of a chapter listing subjects requiring ministerial decisions which was to form the basis of chapter VIII of R(44)6.
4 Jan	EC(O)(44)1	**Note by joint secretaries – W.L. Gorrell-Barnes and D.N Chester,** 1+3p. Redraft of part of chapter I of R(44)6.
4 Jan	2	**Note by joint secretaries – W.L. Gorrell-Barnes and D.N. Chester,** 1p. Covering note to a redraft of the section on budgetary considerations agreed by W. Eady and L.C. Robbins but not attached.
8 Jan	3	**Note by joint secretaries – W.L. Gorrell-Barnes and D.N. Chester,** 1p. Covering note to the final proof of the report which is not attached.

Appended to the file is **R(44)6.**

7.9   Official Committee on the Machinery of Government

Appointed in November 1942 to report to the ministerial Committee on the Machinery of Government (CAB 87/73–75), see CAB 87/73, MG(42)1st:3. It considered, amongst other aspects of the central machinery of government, the possible role of an economic general staff. For a full list of its responsibilities see CAB 87/73, MG(42)1st:4. The nucleus committee was joined, whenever necessary, by other officials acting in an individual capacity. D. Foot, Parliamentary Secretary of the Ministry of Economic Warfare, attended between July and September 1943.

Terms   As ministerial committee (CAB 87/73–75).

Members   J.A. Barlow (Try, ch.); R. Ward (Ed.); P. Liesching (B.T.).   (Dec 43) N. Brook (Recon.) added.

Secs.   (July 43) B.D. Fraser (Try), R.M.J. Harris (Cab. O.) and E.C.S. Wade (Cab. O.).   (Dec 43) Wade withdrew.   (Nov 44) Harris withdrew.

CAB 87/71   Meetings   19 Nov 1942–31 May 1945   MGO 1st–MGO 83rd.

19 Nov	**MGO 1st**	Untitled. Division of subjects between departments.
23 Nov	**2nd**	Untitled. Anderson outlined the task of the official committee.
3 Dec	**3rd**	Untitled. Evidence of A.D.K. Owen.
11 Dec	**4th**	Untitled. Evidence of D. Fergusson.
16 Dec	**5th**	Untitled. Evidence of E.E. Bridges and N. Brook.
30 Dec	**6th**	Untitled. Evidence of H. Wilson.
5 Feb	**8th**	Untitled. Evidence of T. Gardiner.
10 Mar	**9th**	Untitled. Evidence of F. Stewart.
31 Mar	**10th**	Untitled. Evidence of J.P.R. Maud.
15 Apr	**12th**	Untitled. Evidence of Lord Hankey.
28 May	**13th**	Untitled. Evidence of C. Hurcomb.
	14th	No record.
7 June	**15th**	Untitled. Evidence of H. Laski.
10 June	**16th**	Untitled. Evidence of F. Tribe.
11 June	**17th**	Untitled. Evidence of F. Leith-Ross.
18 June	**18th**	Untitled. Evidence of G. Crowther, editor of *The Economist*.
15 July	**20th**	Untitled. Evidence of L.C. Robbins.
29 July	**21st**	Untitled. Evidence of D. Fergusson.
9 Aug	**22nd**	Untitled. Continued evidence of D. Fergusson.
13 Sept	**23rd**	Untitled. Evidence of Lord Solbury and Reid.
15 Sept	**24th**	Untitled. Evidence of A. Street.
16 Sept	**25th**	Untitled. Evidence of W.A. Robson.
23 Sept	**27th**	Untitled. Evidence of T. Baxter and S. Foster.
12 Oct	**28th**	Untitled. Evidence of W. Beveridge.
12 Oct	**29th**	Untitled. Continued evidence of W. Beveridge.
20 Oct	**30th**	Untitled. Evidence of A. Robinson.
29 Oct	**31st**	Untitled. Evidence of Miss M. Curtis and H. Wilson-Smith.
3 Nov	**32nd**	Untitled. Continued evidence of A. Street.
12 Nov	**34th**	Untitled. MGO 30. Non-departmental organizations were discussed. MGO 30 to be redrafted.
4 Dec	**35th**	**Distribution of government business.**
10 Dec	**36th:1**	**Machinery of government in Scotland. MGO 33 and MG(43)10.**
	:2	**Distribution of government business.**
7 Jan	**38th**	**Distribution of government business.**
10 Jan		Consideration of transport and fuel and power.

14 Jan	**39th**	**Distribution of government business.** Consideration of transport.
1 Feb	**40th**	**Distribution of government business.** MGO 38 and 39. Consideration of questions raised by departmental replies to the Prime Minister's directive regarding the preparation of plans for the transitional period (WP(43)476). Ministry of Food's future considered.
8 Feb	**41st**	**Future of the Ministry of Information and its functions.** Evidence of C. Radcliffe.
14 Feb	**42nd**	**Distribution of government business.** Discussion with C. Hurcomb and F. Tribe of the future location of responsibility for fuel and power policy.
17 Feb	**43rd**	**Organization of supply after the war.** MGO 40.
7 Mar	**44th**	**Organization of supply after the war.** MGO 40.
18 Mar	**46th**	**Distribution of government business.** Consideration of draft paper on the wartime departments.
23 Mar	**47th**	**Organization of supply.** Consideration of draft chapter for the report on the distribution of government business.
4 Apr	**48th**	**Organization of supply.** Redraft of chapter.
12 Apr	**49th**	**Distribution of government business.** The Ministry of Information's future.
27 Apr	**50th**	**Departmental responsibility for external economic relations.** MGO 44 and 48. Discussion with W. Eady and D. Waley, primarily on the future of the Department of Overseas Trade.
28 Apr	**51st**	**Departmental responsibility for external economic relations.** MGO 44 and 48. Discussion with A. Overton.
2 May	**52nd**	**Departmental responsibility for external economic relations.** MGO 44 and 48. Discussion with Col. C.G. Vickers and A. Mullins.
3 May	**53rd**	**Departmental responsibility for external economic relations.** MGO 44 and 48. Consideration with N.V. Ronald of the Foreign Office scheme for economic relations and economic intelligence sections.
12 May	**54th**	**Departmental responsibility for external economic relations: the position of the Export Credits Guarantee Department.** Discussion with F. Nixon.
19 May	**55th**	**Departmental responsibility for external economic relations: the future of the Department of Overseas Trade and the commercial, diplomatic and trade commissioner services.** Discussion with F.T. Ashton and G. Watkin.

9 June	**56th**	**Distribution of government business: external economic relations.** Consideration of draft chapter.
14 June	**57th**	**Distribution of government business: external economic relations.** Consideration continued.
12 Oct	**60th:1**	**Distribution of government business: responsibility for metalliferous mining.** MGO 11 and 54.
	:2	**Functions of the Cabinet secretariat.** MGO 55. A comprehensive report on the central organization of government would be more useful to ministers than self-contained appreciations of the Treasury and the Cabinet secretariat.
16 Nov	**63rd:1**	**Organization of supply.**
	:2	**Distribution of government business: industrial safety, health and welfare.** MGO 58.
24 Nov	**64th**	**Distribution of government business: industrial safety, health and welfare.** MGO 58. Discussion with H. Emmerson.
29 Nov	**65th**	Untitled. MGO 24. Discussion about MGO 24 with W. Fisher and H. Creedy.
30 Nov	**66th**	**Non-departmental organizations.** Consideration of the draft.
5 Dec	**67th:1**	**Distribution of government business: industrial safety, health and welfare.** Discussion with W. Garett.
	:2	**Functions of the Cabinet secretariat.** Comments on MGO 55.
8 Dec	**68th**	**Non-departmental organizations.** Consideration of the draft report.
13 Dec	**69th**	**Non-departmental organizations.** Consideration of draft alternatives for sections of the report.
18 Jan	**71st:2**	**Distribution of government business: industrial health, safety and welfare.**
15 Mar	**78th**	**The roles of the Treasury and the Cabinet secretariat.** Consideration of the draft report.
20 Mar	**79th**	**The roles of the Treasury and the Cabinet secretariat.** Consideration of the draft report continued.
17 May	**82nd**	**The centre of the government machine.**
31 May	**83rd**	**The centre of the government machine.** Report to be submitted to the chairman of the ministerial committee.

CAB 87/72 Memoranda 25 Jan 1943–1 Oct 1945 MGO 1–74.

25 Jan	**MGO 1**	**Notes on the role of the economist in the future machinery of government – L.C. Robbins,** 9p. Opposes an economic general staff, but argues for the continuation of a body like the

		Economic Section possibly including civil servants as well as academic economists.
2 Feb	2	**Role of the economist in the future machinery of government – H. Wilson,** 2p. Comments on MGO 1, arguing for an equivalent to the Stamp survey.
4 Feb	3	**Role of the economist in the future machinery of government – H. Henderson,** 2p. MGO 1 under-estimated the problems of peace-time.
23 Feb	5	**Role of the economist in the future machinery of government – D. Fergusson,** 4p. Opposes a central body of economists.
11 Mar	7	**Role of the economist in the future machinery of government – G. Gater,** 3p. Supports MGO 1.
9 Apr	9	**Role of the economist in the future machinery of government – J.M. Keynes,** 4p. In support of a small central body of economists to advise a committee or minister charged with the responsibility of co-ordinating economic policy and to consider changes in the economic outlook.
27 Apr	11	**Distribution of business among the departments – F. Tribe,** 6p. The Ministry of Fuel and Power's future.
17 Apr	14	**Role of the economist in the future machinery of government – A. Overton,** 1p. Argues for an economic adviser in each department and a senior economist, supported by a few younger ones, at the centre.
18 May	15	**Role of the economist in the future machinery of government: first report by the committee of officials,** 10p. Draft report for the ministerial committee.
21 June	21	**Distribution of business among the departments: machinery of government in the field of industry and commerce – P. Liesching,** 9p. Post-war role of the Board of Trade.
4 Aug	22	**The post-war functions of the Board of Trade – Dalton,** 3p. Largely in agreement with MGO 21, but the Board of Trade should be responsible for all price regulation, and perhaps for an industrial budget and economic planning. The wartime practice of an inner Cabinet, with the President of the Board of Trade co-ordinating industrial departments, should be continued.
11 Aug	23	**Statisticians in the government service – J.M Keynes,** 4p. Largely in support of the draft report of the Council of the Royal Statistical Society but considered it did not go far enough.

27 Aug	24	**The role of the Treasury – Treasury, 12p.** Subtitled 'The functions of the Treasury in relation to general financial control and to the control and management of the Civil Service'. The restoration of peace was likely to increase the need for greater co-ordination, forethought and financial planning.
8 Sept	25	**Role of the economist: first report of the official committee, 12p.** Revision of MGO 15.
15 Oct	28	**The role of the Treasury – J.A. Barlow, 5p.** Consideration of various comments received on MGO 24.
10 Nov	30	**Non-departmental organizations – D. Foot, 1+4p.**
15 Nov	32	**The role of the economist in the machinery of government – report by the official committee, 10p.** See MG(43)12.
18 Jan	37	**Distribution of government business – report by the official committee, 10p.** See MG(44)2.
26 Jan	38	**Distribution of government business: food and agriculture and fisheries – B.D. Fraser and R.M.J. Harris covering H. French and D. Foot, 5+3p.**
27 Jan	39	**Distribution of government business – B.D. Fraser and R.M.J. Harris, 4p.** Work to be done by the official committee.
3 Feb	40	**Organization of supply after the war – B.D. Fraser and R.M.J. Harris covering B. Gilbert, 1+4+6p appendixes+6p.**
26 Feb	42	**Organization of supply after the war – B.D. Fraser and R.M.J. Harris covering A. Street and J. Woods, 1+3+4+13p appendixes.**
3 Mar	43	**Organization of supply in peace and war – B.D. Fraser and R.M.J. Harris covering Brig. E.I.C. Jacob, 1+16p.**
3 Mar	44	**Departmental responsibility for external economic relations – B.D. Fraser and R.M.J. Harris covering the Treasury, 1+3p.** Written by officials without reference to ministers, it recommended the machinery to be left as it was, with reliance placed on inter-departmental co-operation.
24 Apr	47	**Distribution of government business: further report by the official committee, 14+1p** appendix. Deals with the wartime departments, ie Food, Home Security, Fuel and Power and Information.
22 Apr	48	**Departmental responsibility for external economic relations – B.D. Fraser and R.M.J. Harris covering replies to MGO 40, 1+11p.**

254

25 Apr	49	**Distribution of government business: further report by the official committee,** 12p. Deals with the organization of supply.
6 May	50	**Departmental responsibility for external economic relations – B.D. Fraser and R.M.J. Harris covering the Department of Overseas Trade,** 1+16+1p appendix. Written in 1935.
12 May	52	**Departmental responsibility for external economic relations – B.D. Fraser and R.M.J. Harris covering Col. Vickers,** 1+5p.
14 July	53	**Distribution of government business: further report by the official committee,** 8p. Deals with external economic relations and recommends the continuation of the Department of Overseas Trade.
23 Aug	54	**Distribution of government business: responsibility for metalliferous mining – B.D. Fraser and R.M.J. Harris,** 5p. Includes letters from A. Overton, F. Tribe and O. Franks.
19 Sept	55	**Functions of the Cabinet secretariat – B.D. Fraser and R.M.J. Harris,** 1+18+3p appendix.
23 Oct	58	**Distribution of government business: industrial safety, health and welfare – B.D. Fraser and R.M.J. Harris,** 2+18p.
12 Nov	59	**The role of the Treasury – B.D. Fraser,** 1+18p annex. Replies to MGO 24 and a continuation of MGO 28.
3 Jan	61	**Non-departmental organizations – Treasury covering report by the committee,** 2+44+4p appendixes.
14 Apr	71	**The future of the Development Commission – report by the official committee,** 2p.
June	74	**The centre of the government machine – report by the official committee,** 7+15p. See MG(45)16.

7.10   Committee on the Machinery of Government

Appointed in November 1942, see CAB 65/27, WM(42)117th:2 and CAB 66/32, WP(42)578, partly in response to demands that peace-time Cabinets should largely consist of 'super' ministers with no departmental responsibilities. It was consciously seen as a counterpart to the 1918 Haldane Committee on the Machinery of Government. It reserved for itself consideration of the general distribution of government functions, the role of 'super' ministers, composition and size of the Cabinet, and any consequent implications for departmental or collective responsibility. Other issues were delegated to the Official Committee on the Machinery of Government (CAB 87/71-72). The original intention was to publish a report but owing to the break-up of the coalition, the two reports which were drafted were restricted to use within the Civil Service (CAB 87/75, MG(45)11, 16).

Terms To consider the machinery of government and to report what changes in the organization and functions of the central executive are desirable to promote efficiency under post-war conditions.

Members (1942) Ld President (ch.); Ld Privy Seal; Ch. of Exchequer; S./S. Colonies; Home Sec.
(Sept 43) Ch. of Exchequer (ch.); Home Sec.; Ld Chancellor; S./S. Colonies; Min. of Air Prod. (Nov 43) Min. of Recon., Postmaster-Gen. added.
(July 45) Ch. of Exchequer (ch.); Ld President; S./S. Colonies; Ld Chancellor; Postmaster-Gen.

Secs. T. Padmore (Try) and E.C.S. Wade (Cab.O.) (Sept 43) B.D. Fraser (Try) and R.M.J. Harris (Cab.O.).

CAB 87/73   Meetings 12 Nov 1942–23 Nov 1944   MG(42)1st–MG(44)22nd

12 Nov	**MG(42)1st:1**	**Scope of enquiry.**
	:2	**Terms of reference.** The committee to decide its own terms of reference.
	:3	**Official staff.**
	:4	**Subjects of enquiry.** Division of subjects between the ministerial and official committees.
9 Dec	**2nd:1**	**Terms of reference.** MG(42)1. Terms agreed.
	:2	**Studies by officials.**
	:3	**Distribution of the functions of government and the role of the supervising minister.** MG(42)2.
29 Dec	**3rd:1**	**Plan of work of the official group.** MG(42)3. A. Barlow explained that the intention of approaching individuals was merely to obtain a starting point for the enquiry.
	:2	**Distribution of the functions of government and the role of the supervising minister.** MG(42)2, 3 and 5. Reinforcement of the tentative conclusion of the previous meeting that the concept of a supervising minister was useful and workable as a permanent feature, only so far as was exemplified in the working of the present Lord President with the Lord President's Committee and the Minister of Home Security with the Civil Defence Committee.
25 Jan	**MG(43)1st:1**	**House of Commons debate on the organization and control of the Civil Service.** MG(43)1.
	:2	**The distribution of the functions of government and the role of the supervising minister.** MG(42)2, 3, 5 and MG(43)2.
22 Mar	**2nd:1**	**Standing committees of the Cabinet.** MG(43)2 (revise). A number of amendments were made.
	:2	**Distribution of business among the departments.** MG(43)3. Agreement that the

		official committee should make a provisional study.
	:3	**Ministerial responsibility.** MG(42)5 and 7.
22 Apr	3rd:1	**The home Civil Service after the war.** MG(43)4. Approval of Wood's proposals.
27 Sept	4th	**Standing committees of the Cabinet.** MG(43)2 (second revise). Discussion with Eden. He was, like the committee, against the use of supervising ministers. He then considered three alternative systems of standing committees suggested in MG(43)2 (second revise).
7 Oct	5th:1	**Post-war responsibility for employment policy.** MG(43)7 and 8. The committee agreed that the Ministry of Labour should collect the fullest possible intelligence bearing on the employment situation. Post-war, it should discharge more positive functions in relation to employment policy, along the lines indicated in MG(43)7.
2 Dec	6th:1	**The role of the economist in the machinery of government.** MG(43)12. Agreement with the report that a central economic section should be retained as part of the Cabinet secretariat.
	:3	**Review of committee's work.**
6 Dec	7th	**Staffing of the Civil Service in the immediate post-war period.** MG(43)13.
16 Dec	8th:2	**Staffing of the Civil Service in the immediate post-war period.** MG(43)13 and 18.
22 Dec	9th	**Staffing of the Civil Service in the immediate post-war period.** The First Civil Service Commissioner was present.
29 Dec	10th:1	**Staffing of the Civil Service in the immediate post-war period.** MG(43)13, 20 and 21.
	:2	**Standing committees of the Cabinet.** MG(43)2 (2nd revise).
6 Jan	MG(44)1st	**Demobilization of the Ministry of Economic Warfare.** MG(43)11 and MG(44)1.
2 Mar	6th	**Standing committees of the Cabinet.** MG(43)2 (2nd revise).
3 May	8th:1	**Training of Civil Servants.** MG(44)10.
	:2	**Future business of the committee.**
	:3	**Distribution of government business: organization of supply.** MG(44)9.
18 May	9th:2	**Distribution of government business: the war-time departments.** MG(44)8.
25 May	10th	**Distribution of government business: the war-time departments.** MG(44)8. Leathers and Lloyd George both agreed with MG(44)8 on the future of the Ministry of Fuel and Power.

257

22 June	12th	Distribution of government business: the future of the Ministry of Information and Government Publicity. MG(44)8, 12 and 13. Discussion with Eden and Bracken.
29 June	13th:1	Staffing of the Civil Service in the immediate post-war period. MG(44)16.
	:2	Distribution of government business: organization of supply. MG(44)9.
13 July	15th:2	Distribution of government business: the war-time departments: the Ministry of Food. MG(44)8. Discussion with Hudson, Johnstone and Llewellin.
18 July	16th	Distribution of government business: organization of supply. MG(44)9.
27 July	17th:3	Training of civil servants. MG(44)18.
5 Sept	18th	Distribution of government business: external economic relations. MG(44)20. Agreement that the post of Secretary to the Department of Overseas Trade should be retained.
24 Oct	19th	Distribution of government business: organization of supply. MG(44)9 and 25.
26 Oct	20th	Civil Service: structure of the administrative class. MG(44)26.
2 Nov	21st:1	Staffing of the Civil Service in the immediate post-war period.
23 Nov	22nd:1	Distribution of government business: organization of supply. MG(44)9, 27 and 28.

CAB 87/74   Memoranda   17 November 1942–27 December 1944
MG(42)1–MG(44)29.

17 Nov	MG(42)1	Note by the Chairman – Anderson, 2p. Alternative terms of reference suggested.
3 Dec	2	Note by the secretaries – T. Padmore and E.C.S. Wade, 1+6p. 'The distribution of the functions of government and the role of the supervising minister' is attached. Issues felt to require consideration.
24 Dec	3	Plan of work of official group – T. Padmore and E.C.S. Wade, 4p. Scope and method of the official committee's work.
23 Dec	4	The supervising minister – T. Padmore and E.C.S. Wade covering the Cabinet secretariat and the Ministry of Production, 1+4+4+3p. Three memoranda attached: (a) 'The Lord President's Committee' – Cabinet secretariat. Review of the development of the functions of the Lord President and his committee since the committee's formation in June 1940; (b) 'Co-ordinating functions of the Minister of Home Security' – Cabinet secretariat;

		(c) 'Relations between the Ministry of Production and the three supply departments' – informal note by the Ministry of Production.
28 Dec	5	**Ministerial responsibility – Anderson,** 9p. The historical development and nature of individual and collective ministerial responsibility.
31 Dec	6	**Note by the Chairman – Anderson covering Attlee,** 4p. Sets out the issues which Attlee would like the committee to consider.
31 Dec	7	**Collective responsibility – Simon,** 6p.
6 Jan	MG(43)1	**Memorandum by Wood,** 3+1p annex.
18 Jan	2	**Standing committees of the Cabinet – Anderson,** 9p. Suggestion of areas where standing committees could be useful and their possible membership.
12 Mar	2	**Standing committees of the Cabinet – Anderson,** 4+3p appendix. Revise version.
16 Apr	2	**Standing committees of the Cabinet – Anderson,** 5+3p appendix. Second revise version, putting forward various alternatives.
12 Mar	3	**Distribution of business among the departments – Anderson.** 2p.
8 Apr	4	**The home Civil Service after the war – Wood,** 6+30p appendix. The appendix is a preliminary study carried out under Crookshank.
22 June	7	**Post-war responsibility for employment policy – Bevin,** 3p. A single department would be needed after the war to keep an overview of , and constant watch on, the employment situation. It should be the Ministry of Labour. This would require the adaptation of the department's organization from the purpose of alleviating unemployment to the initiation of measures to prevent it.
4 Aug	8	**Post-war responsibility for employment policy – Dalton,** 3p. Largely in agreement with MG(43)7 although the Ministry of Labour could not initiate measures to increase employment.
29 Sept	9	**Composition of the committee – T. Padmore and E.C.S. Wade,** 1p.
2 Nov	11	**Demobilization of the Ministry of Economic Warfare – Anderson,** 3+17+7p annexes. Report by Lord Finlay's Committee attached.
15 Nov	12	**The role of the economist in the machinery of government – report by the official committee,** 10p. Also MGO 32. All witnesses before the committee had agreed that economists had an important contribution to make to policy formulation. The report recommends the

retention of the Economic Section. Its function would be to receive and appraise economic intelligence; to cover by its own researches any gaps in this intelligence; to make or to procure specific studies in those spheres which are not covered by any one department; and to present co-ordinated and objective pictures of the economic situation as a whole, and of the economic aspects of projected government policy.

29 Nov	14	**Composition of the committee – T. Padmore and E.C.S. Wade,** 1p.
5 Dec	16	**Survey of the work of the committee – T. Padmore and E.C.S. Wade,** 1+3p appendix.
4 Jan	MG(44)1	**Demobilization of the Ministry of Economic Warfare – Anderson,** 3p. Issue of whether economic intelligence should be attached to the Cabinet secretariat rather than to the Foreign Office.
8 Jan	2	**Distribution of government business – Anderson covering the official committee,** 1+10p. Also MGO 37. The principles on which the official committee are working and the first chapter, on transport, of its report.
24 Apr	8	**Distribution of government business – Anderson covering the official committee,** 14+1p appendix. Also MGO 47.
25 Apr	9	**Distribution of government business – Anderson covering the official committee,** 12p. Also MGO 49.
2 June	12	**The future of the Ministry of Information and government publicity – Morrison,** 5p. Stresses the importance of public relations work for the government.
6 June	13	**The future of the Ministry of Information and government publicity – Crookshank,** 3p. Against the collating of public opinion as a part of governmental machinery.
15 July	20	**Distribution of government business – Anderson covering the official committee,** 1+8p. Also MGO 53.
21 Oct	25	**Organization of supply – Alexander and Sinclair,** 3p.
20 Nov	27	**Organization of supply – Anderson,** 4p.
21 Nov	28	**Organization of supply – Cripps,** 5p.

CAB 87/75   Meetings and Memoranda   10 Jan–8 Nov 1945   MG(45)1st–12th and MG(45)1–24.

Meetings

12 Feb	**MG(45)3rd:1**	**The post-war Cabinet.** MG(45)5. Consideration of the post-war size of the Cabinet.

15 Mar	**4th:1**	**Non-departmental organizations. MG(45)3 and** 6.
	:2	**Future work of the committee.**
22 Mar	**5th:1**	**Non-departmental organizations. MG(45)3, 6** **and 8.**
	:2	**The wartime departments. MG(45)7.**
2 May	**6th:1**	**Non-departmental organizations.**
	:2	**Future work of the committee.**
	:3	**Cabinet organization. MG(45)11.** Draft approved with minor amendments.
10 May	**8th:2**	**Future of the Development Commission.** MG(45)10.
10 Oct	**9th:1**	**Work of the committee. MG(45)15 and 19.** MG (45)19 was endorsed. Discussion of the possible terms of a bill to meet various points in MG(45)15.
18 Oct	**10th**	**The centre of the government machine.** MG(45)16. General approval of the report but an updated version of the paper should be prepared.
8 Nov	**12th:2**	**Ministers (Transfer of Powers) Bill. MG(45)24.**

Memoranda

10 Jan	**MG(45)1**	**Organization of supply – Anderson covering W.** **Freeman,** 1+3p annex.
22 Jan	**2**	**Administration of Wales and Monmouthshire –** **report by the official committee,** 1+7+1p appendix. Also MGO 64.
23 Jan	**3**	**Non-departmental organizations – Anderson** **covering D. Foot covering the official committee,** 1+4+44+4p appendix. Also MGO 61.
2 Feb	**5**	**The post-war Cabinet – Anderson.** 4+3p appendixes. The committee should consider the size of the post-war Cabinet before deciding in favour of a system of standing Cabinet committees. It was hoped that the Cabinet's size would be about 20 for which there were 41 candidates.
8 Feb	**6**	**Non-departmental organizations – Anderson,** 2p.
19 Mar	**7**	**The future of the wartime departments –** **Anderson,** 1p. Churchill had agreed that the main features of the committee's recommendations should be taken as assumptions for planning purposes.
20 Mar	**8**	**Non-departmental organizations: the consumer** **interest – Anderson,** 1+3p appendix.
16 Apr	**10**	**The future of the Development Commission –** **Anderson covering the official committee,** 1+2p. Also MGO 71.
16 Apr	**11**	**The post-war Cabinet – Anderson,** 1+4+2p appendixes. Draft memorandum to the War

Cabinet, based on MG(43)2(2nd revise) and MG(45)5. It considered supervising ministers, the Cabinet committee system and the optimum size of the post-war Cabinet.

5 July	**14**	**Membership and terms of reference – E.E. Bridges,** 1p.
1 Oct	**15**	**Work of the committee – B.D. Fraser,** 1+3p. Summary of progress and outstanding issues.
1 Oct	**16**	**Centre of the government machine – Morrison** covering the official committee, 1+7+33p appendixes. Also MGO 74. Appendixes consider the role of the Treasury, the functions of the Cabinet secretariat and the functions of the Private Office at No. 10.
6 Oct	**19**	**Work of the committee – Morrison,** 2p. A comprehensive report on the coalition government's views was no longer possible and he now opposed publication.
7 Nov	**24**	**Ministers (Transfer of Powers) Bill – Morrison** covering E.E. Bridges and G. Ram, 1+4+3p.

7.11 Official Subcommittee on Industrial Problems: Working Party on Controls

Appointed in January 1945, see CAB 87/18, R(IO)(45)3rd:1. Its purpose was to re-examine proposals in CAB 87/17, R(IO)(44)21 concerning economic controls in the transitional period following revision by the Chiefs of Staff of the assumptions concerning the length of the Japanese war. Its report was considered by an *ad hoc* committee of senior officials in September 1945 (CAB 78/37, GEN 87/1st).

Terms To define the position that would arise if the Japanese war were to last for a shorter period than eighteen months after the end of the war with Germany and, in particular, if it were to last for so short a time as six months after that date.

Members A. Johnston (Recon., ch.); P.D. Proctor (Try); M.G. Smieton (Lab. & N.S.); A.J. Manson (Supply); R. Hughes (Adm.); R.F. Kahn (Prod.); H.G. Lindsell (Supply); W.A. Downey (Air P.); R.L. Cohen (B.T.); D.N. Chester (Ec. Sect.).

Sec. A.N. Coleridge (Recon.)

CAB 87/89 Meetings and Memoranda 20 Feb–4 Sept 1945 EC 1st–EC(45) 6th and EC 1–EC(45)12.

Meetings

20 Feb	**EC 1st**	**Terms of reference.** R(IO)(44)21. The committee was to consider the year after the defeat of Germany, assumed to be 30 June 1945.
7 Mar	**2nd:1**	**Release of manpower from munitions industries.** EC 1.

	:2		**Distribution of the working population.**
10 Apr	3rd:1		**Absorption of labour. EC 4.** The figures in EC 3 and EC 4 implied a shortage, not a surplus, of labour in the first quarter of 1946.
	:2		**Supply prospects for raw materials. EC 2.**
	:3		**Reasons for maintaining controls. R(IO)(44)21.** Consideration of the means by which the objectives in R(IO)(44)21 were to be achieved. More detail was required.
9 Aug	EC(45)4th		**Draft report. EC(45)8. Amendments.**
29 Aug	5th:1		**Revised draft of report. EC(45)8(revise).**
	:2		**Submission of report.**
4 Sept	6th		**Draft of report (final). EC(45)11.** The report was to be discussed by senior officials on 6 September 1945. See CAB 78/37.

Memoranda

3 Mar	EC 1		**The release of manpower from the munitions industries – A.N. Coleridge covering E.A.G. Robinson,** 1+3+3p appendix. Informal estimates.
16 Mar		2	**Supply prospects for raw materials – A.N. Coleridge covering the Raw Materials Department of the Ministry of Supply,** 1+2p. Estimates for March 1946.
29 Mar		3	**The release of manpower from the forces and the munitions industries – E.A.G. Robinson,** 1+1p. Revised estimates.
5 Apr		4	**Absorption of labour – A. Johnston,** 1+1p. Estimates of the additional labour that could be absorbed by industries and services in the first quarter of 1946.
17 May		5	**Note by the chairman – A. Johnston,** 1p. Request for amendments to R(IO)(44)21 to update it as a statement of controls policy for the first six to twelve months of Stage II.
18 May		6	**Board of Trade controls should the Japanese war end six months after the German war – Board of Trade,** 3p. This change of assumptions required no substantial alteration in the technique of Board of Trade controls.
nd		7	**Labour controls at the end of the Japanese war – Ministry of Labour,** 2p. Consideration of each main type of labour control, although their continuation was largely a political decision.
15 Aug	EC(45)8		**Revised draft report – A. Johnston,** 1+32p. The report had been recast to deal with the problems of the next six months now that the war against Japan was over.
11 Aug		9	**Note by the chairman – A. Johnston,** 1+4p. Amendments to the draft report, submitted by the Ministry of Labour.

27 Aug	**10**	**Suggested amendments to draft report – A. Johnston,** 1+10p.
31 Aug	**11**	**Second revised draft of report – A. Johnston,** 1+20+10p appendixes.
4 Sept	**12**	**Report – the working party.** 19+10p appendixes. Also GEN 87/1. Analysis of the likely situation and the role which economic controls could play generally and in particular fields. Controls should continue to deal with scarcities. Even where individual controls seemed ineffective they could be useful as part of an integrated system.

7.12 Committee on the Organization of the Coal Industry

Set up in October 1943 to prepare for a House of Commons debate on 12–13 October 1943, see CAB 65/36, WM(43)137th:6. A draft statement was submitted to Cabinet (CAB 66/42, WP(43)451) and the committee ended in February 1944 having completed a report which deliberately avoided the issue of nationalization (CAB 66/47, WP(44)115).

Terms   To consider the question of improvements to the wartime machinery for the operational control of the coal-mining industry.

Members   Ch. of Exchequer (ch.); Mins. of Lab. & N.S., W. Transport, Fuel & P.; Paymaster-Gen.

Secs.   E.E. Bridges (Cab. O.) and W.L. Gorrell Barnes.   (Nov 1943) D.N. Chester (Cab. O.) replaced Bridges.

CAB 87/93   Meetings and Memoranda   8 Oct 1943–12 Feb 1944
CI(43)1st–CI(44)1st, CI(43)1 – CI(44)2 and WP(43)451 and
WP(44)115.

Meetings

8 Oct	**CI(43)1st**	Untitled. The assumption of full government control would not be an effective remedy for any weaknesses in the existing organization so long as the industry's post-war organization was uncertain.
11 Oct	**2nd**	Untitled. Draft statement by the Minister of Fuel and Power is attached.
18 Nov	**3rd**	Untitled. CI(43)1 and 2. Rejection of proposal to increase rations for miners.
1 Feb	**CI(44)1st**	Untitled. CI(44)1.

Memoranda

8 Nov	**CI(43)1**	**Causes and remedies of the decline in the output of coal – Lloyd George,** 5+3p appendixes. The

		only complete solution to the problem of falling output was a state takeover.
16 Nov	2	**Note by the Minister of Fuel and Power – Lloyd George,** 1+16p. Correspondence between the Ministry of Fuel and Power and the M.F.G.B. is attached.
18 Jan	CI(44)1	**Progress report on discussions with the coal-mining industry (Dec 43/Jan 44) – Lloyd George,** 4p.
12 Feb	2	**Note by the Chancellor of the Exchequer – Anderson,** 1+10p. Draft report attached. There were no definite proposals needing War Cabinet approval.

7.13 Distribution of Industry Committee

The appointment of the committee was requested in July 1944 by the Reconstruction Committee's ministerial Subcommittee on Industrial Problems to implement chapter III of the *Employment Policy* White Paper. Its terms of reference were announced by Lord Woolton in August (see CAB 87/14, R(I)(44)3rd and R(I)(44)15). The chairmanship was temporarily given to Bevin 'in a personal capacity' although the Board of Trade had departmental responsibility for policy. An official committee was appointed, divided into three panels: Panel A, general questions of industrial distribution and projects for new industrial development; Panel B, government factories; Panel C, facilities to prepare for the expansion of civil production. For their terms of reference and membership, see CAB 87/14, R(I)(44)15.

Terms (a) to supervise and control the development and execution of government policy for securing the better distribution of industry as outlined in Chapter III of Cmd. 6527 (b) to consider such questions as may be submitted to them relating to projects for new industrial development (c) to determine such issues as may be submitted to them regarding the allocation of government factories (d) to consider any applications which may be referred to them for the grant of facilities to individual firms to undertake preparatory work with a view to the post-war expansion of civil production.

Members Min. of Lab. & N.S. (ch.); Pres. Bd Trade; Mins. of Production, Town and Country Planning; S./S. Scotland. Mins. of Agriculture & Fish, War Transport, Works, Fuel & Power, and the three Supply ministers to be co-opted when necessary.

Sec. W.L. Gorrell Barnes (Cab. O).

CAB 87/94   Meetings and Memoranda   6 Sept 1944–17 May 1945
            DI(44)1st–DI(45)3rd and DI(44)1–DI(45)21.

Meetings

| 3 Oct | DI(44)1st:1 | **Development areas.** DI(44)2. A provisional list of development areas was accepted. |
| | :2 | **Balanced distribution of industry.** DI(44)4. It was agreed that the regional committees on the |

		distribution of industry should be attached to the regional boards.
	:3	**Strategic aspects of industrial location.**
	:4	**Distribution of industry and expansion of civil production.**
	:5	**Disposal of machine tools.**
	:6	**Terms of disposal of government factories.** DI(44)3.
12 Oct	**2nd:2**	**Conversion of steel industry from war to peace production.**
31 Oct	**3rd:1**	**Curtailment of fabricated light metal production.** DI(44)7.
	:2	**Legislation of balanced distribution of industry.** DI(44)8. Dalton outlined the main features of the bill. Power to build factories, secure land compulsorily, etc. outside the development areas in appropriate cases, was approved.
30 Nov	**4th:2**	**Strategic aspects of industrial location.** DI(44)9 and 12. General agreement with Bevin's view that the factories which had been constructed during the war in relatively safe areas and away from larger centres of population should be kept open.
21 Feb	**DI(45)1st:1**	**Strategic aspects of industrial location.** DI(45)3.
14 Mar	**2nd:1**	**Production and employment in West Cumberland.** DI(45)10, 11, 14.
	:2	**Production and employment in Northern Ireland.** DI(45)9, 12, 13.
29 Mar	**3rd**	**Production and employment in Northern Ireland.** DI(45)16. Discussion with the Prime Minister of Northern Ireland and his ministers.

Memoranda

6 Sept	**DI(44)1**	**Composition and terms of reference – E.E. Bridges,** 2+4p.
25 Sept	**2**	**Development areas – Dalton,** 1+2p. Four core development areas were proposed: the main industrial belt of Scotland and Dundee, Tyneside and County Durham, West Cumberland and industrial South Wales and Monmouthshire.
25 Sept	**3**	**Terms of disposal of government factories – Dalton,** 1+2p. Draft statement by Panel B attached.
30 Sept	**4**	**Regional machinery – Bevin,** 3p. Sets out the chief features of the proposed regional distribution of industry committees. They should be independent rather than committees of the regional boards and responsible to the Board of Trade and not the Ministry of Production.

26 Oct	7	**Curtailment of fabricated light metal production – Cripps,** 2+5p. Note of the Planning Committee (Programme Reduction) Subcommittee on Light Metals Curtailment attached.
27 Oct	8	**Legislation on the balanced distribution of industry – Dalton,** 3p. Proposals for legislation resulting from the White Paper on *Employment Policy.* The Board of Trade should have powers to build factories on individual or collective sites for sale or lease, to establish and finance trading estates, to acquire land compulsorily or by agreement, and to clear sites for industrial development. Firms should also be required to notify the Board of Trade of any proposal to build or extend a factory above a certain size.
10 Nov	9	**Strategic aspects of industrial location – Lyttelton,** 1+1p appendix. Sets out four propositions agreed by the Joint War Production Staff on the size, dispersion and location of armament industries.
28 Nov	12	**Strategic aspects of industrial location – Morrison, W,** 2p. DI(44)9 needed qualification.
5 Dec	13	**Strategic aspects of industrial location – Bevin,** 1+2p. Draft report, accepting DI(44)9 subject to the reservations in DI(44)12.
11 Dec	14	**Strategic aspects of industrial location – Bevin,** 1p.
20 Dec	15	**Strategic aspects of industrial location – Bevin,** 3p. Revised draft report.
3 Jan	DI(45)1	**Strategic aspects of industrial location – report by the committee,** 2p. See WP(45)2.
19 Jan	2	**Future of the light metal fabricating industry – Cripps and Dalton,** 1+5+3p appendix. See R(I)(45)1.
3 Feb	3	**Strategic aspects of industrial location – W.L. Gorrell-Barnes,** 2p. Directive by Churchill with regard to the four propositions attached.
8 Feb	4	**Future of the light metal fabricating industry – W.L. Gorrell-Barnes covering the Ministerial Subcommittee on Industrial Problems,** 1+4p. See R(I)(45)2nd.
12 Mar	13	**Production and employment in Northern Ireland – Dalton,** 2p.
21 Mar	15	**Production and employment in Northern Ireland – W.L. Gorrell-Barnes covering the Home Office,** 1+3p. Production and employment in Northern Ireland – W.L. Gorrell-Barnes covering the Home Office, 1+4p.

		Memorandum as sent to Northern Ireland ministers.
23 Mar	**17**	**Production and employment in Northern Ireland – W.L. Gorrell-Barnes,** 2p. Correspondence between Bevin and Woolton, dated 15 March and 20 March 1945 attached.
30 Mar	**18**	**Production and employment in Northern Ireland – W.L. Gorrell-Barnes,** 1+5p annexes.
6 Apr	**19**	**Production and employment in Northern Ireland – W.L. Gorrell-Barnes,** 1+1p annex. Note of a meeting held on 4 April 1945 between Bevin, G. Martin and B. Gardner.
2 May	**20**	**Strategic aspects of industrial location – W.L. Gorrell-Barnes covering the Joint War Production Staff,** 1+2p annex.
17 May	**21**	**Inter-departmental consultation on location of industry – Hudson, R.,** 2p. Believes that his department is not being consulted sufficiently.

7.14 Other Committees Relevant to Economic Planning

CAB 87/4 Subcommittee on the Future of the Electricity Industry

Set up to consider alternative schemes of ownership and to report its findings to the Reconstruction Problems Committee (CAB 87/3). It replaced and considered the work of the Subcommittee on the Electricity Industry (CAB 87/105–106).

Chairman Lloyd George.

Sec. A.F. James.

Meetings and Memoranda 13 Apr–30 Dec 1943 RP(ES)(43)1st–14th and RP(ES)(43)1–36(final).

CAB 87/19 Reconstruction Joint Advisory Council

Set up late in 1942 to engage both sides of industry in the discussion of important reconstruction issues. In 1943 it took, amongst others, papers by the T.U.C. on control in the post-war transition and by the Board of Trade on the reconstruction approach to industry. With the appointment of Woolton as Minister of Reconstruction meetings became rarer and papers were no longer submitted. In 1944 the White Paper on *Employment Policy* was considered and, in 1945, the transition from war to peace.

Terms (Feb 1943) To secure a mutual exchange of views between representatives of labour and industry and the Minister Without Portfolio on important issues of general

policy arising out of post-war reconstruction. The discussions of the co
without prejudice to any discussions, arranged on the initiative of tl
concerned, with representatives of labour and industry for the purpose of
particular problems arising out of post-war reconstruction.

Members   Min. Without Portfolio (ch.); J. Brown, G. Chester, W. Citrine, A.
G. Gibson, G.W. Thomson and G. Woodcock (all T.U.C.); H.F. Brand, C. Crav ...u
J. Forbes Watson (all B.E.C.); D. Gorden, G. Nelson and G. Locock (all F.B.I.)   (Feb
44) Woolton (ch.).

Sec.   Q. Hill (Cab. O.).

Minutes and Memoranda   1942–Jan 1945   RJ(42)1st, RJ(43)2nd–5th, RJ(44)1st–2nd,
RJ(45)1st and RJ(42)1, RJ(43)2–13.

CAB 87/95   Committee on External Economic Policy

Set up in February 1944 to report to Cabinet on the line to be taken in commercial
policy negotiations with parts of the Commonwealth. It reported later that month (see
CAB 66/47, WP(44)121).

Terms   To determine, in the light of the discussions in the War Cabinet as summarized
by the Prime Minister, the attitude to be taken by U.K. officials in the forthcoming
discussions with official representatives of the Dominions and India, over the whole
field of the Washington conversations under Article VII.

Members   Ch. of Exchequer (ch.); Mins. of Production, State (F.O.); Ld Privy Seal;
Pres. Bd Trade; Paymaster-Gen.

Secs.   E. Rowe Dutton (Try) and E.E. Bridges (Cab. O.)

Minutes and Memoranda   Feb 1944   EEPO(44)1st–6th and EEP(44)1–3.

CAB 87/96   Committee on Demobilization

Set up by the Cabinet (CAB 65/35, WM(43)111th:2) in August 1943, it submitted its
report in November (CAB 66/42, WM(43)494).

Terms   To carry out a general survey of our demobilization plans on the basis of a
two-stage ending of the war.

Members   Min. Without Portfolio (ch.); Parl. Secs. of Home, Supply, Education, War
Transport, Economic Warfare; Fin. Sec.

Secs.   A Hurst (Cab. O.) and Q. Hill (Cab. O.).

Chapter 8   Central Statistical Office

Prior to the war, the collection of statistics was extremely poor. This situation was partly changed by the establishment of the Stamp Survey and the Prime Minister's Statistical Branch (see D.N. Chester (ed.) *Lessons of the War Economy* (1951) chapter 4). However, the most significant development came in January 1941 when a separate Central Statistical Office was established. The objective was to provide an authoritative source of statistical information, which was to be available to ministers and departments generally but divorced from the business of providing advice on particular policies. Although the C.S.O. remained small it led to a revolution in the collection, reconciliation and presentation of statistics, in particular of current statistics.

A large part of its work related to the *Monthly Digest of Statistics*, its annual counterpart and other similar publications. With regard to economic planning, it was important in the formulation of national income statistics and the resulting annual process of national income estimation and the production of the *Economic Survey*. Indeed, a member of the C.S.O. chaired the National Income Forecasts Working Party (CAB 134/520–522); and, after the White Paper on *Employment Policy* (Cmd. 6527) had identified the need for better statistical information, a Working Party on Statistics for Employment Policy (CAB 108/124–126) was established under a C.S.O. chairman.

The C.S.O. had a far less direct role in economic planning than that of the Economic Section and C.E.P.S. Its members normally only served on technical committees or as technical experts on policy committees. They were specifically not involved in policy formulation. Thus, while the Chief Planning Officer and the Director of the Economic Section were, or became, permanent members of the main official economic committees, such as the Official Steering Committee on Economic Development (CAB 134/186–193) and the Budget Committee (T 171), the same was not true of the Director of the C.S.O.

8.1   Meetings and Memoranda

CAB 108

1–3	**Statistical digest Series A (statistics relating to the economic situation).**
1	Apr 1942–Dec 1943. 1–21.
2	Jan–Dec 1944. 22–33.
3	Jan–Dec 1945. 34–43.
15–19	**Statistical digest Series C (statistics relating to manpower).**
15	Mar–Dec 1943. 1–10.
16	Jan–Dec 1944. 11–22.
17	Jan–Dec 1945. 23–33.
18	Jan–Dec 1944. Supplements to issues 13–22.
19	Jan–Sept 1945. Supplements to issues 23–30.
21–24	**Statistical digest Series D (statistics relating to production and manpower).**
21	Jan–Dec 1943. 22–33.
22	Jan–Dec 1944. 34–45.

270

23	Jan–Sept 1945. 46–54.
24	Jan 1941–Feb 1943. Supplements to Series D.
26–28	**Statistical digest Series E (statistics relating to import problems).**
26	Jan–Dec 1943. 21–32.
27	Jan–Dec 1944. 33–44.
28	Jan–Aug 1945. 45–52.
35–38	**C.S.O. memoranda. CS(S)series.** All include monthly reports on stocks of food and animal feedingstuffs for the Lord President's Committee, and on statistics in relation to the forces, iron and steel and imports.
35	Jan–Dec 1943. CS(S)(43)1–91.
36	Jan–Dec 1944. CS(S)(44)1–88. Includes memoranda on the allocation of manpower, post-war housing statistics and appreciation of appendix C and other statistics used in Beveridge's *Full Employment in a Free Society.*
37	Jan–July 1945. CS(S)(45)1–65. From April 1945 includes statistical reports on housing. Other memoranda relate to statistics for employment policy and agricultural machinery.
38	Aug–Dec 1945. CS(S)(45)66–103. Includes memoranda on the net national income in 1946, 1947 and 1948, house-building costs, the report of the Working Party on Statistics for Employment Policy, and from November 1945 a monthly series of statistical reports on reconversion.
85	**Inter-departmental Committee on Non-food Consumption Levels in the U.K., U.S. and Canada.** July 1944–Apr 1945. NFC(44)1st–2nd and NFC(44)1–4, NFC(45)1–6 and the committee's report to the Combined Production and Resources Board.
86–88	**C.S.O. Memoranda CSO(RM) series.** Monthly series on U.K. statistics on raw materials and finished products (excluding munitions). Continued in CAB 108/147.
86	Sept–Dec 1944. CSO(RM)(44)1–4.
87	Jan–May 1945. CSO(RM)(45)1–5.
88	June–Oct 1945. CSO(RM)(45)6–9.
90–95	**Statistical reports series A (statistics relating to the economic situation).** Monthly series covering the main sectors of the economy. Discontinued in July 1951 and replaced by *Economic Trends* apart from the section on stocks which was already contained in the supplement to the *Monthly Digest of Statistics.*
90	Jan–Dec 1946. Nos. 44–55.
91	Jan–Dec 1947. Nos. 56–67.
92	Jan–Dec 1948. Nos. 68–79.
93	Jan–Dec 1949. Nos. 80–91.
94	Jan–Dec 1950. Nos. 92–103.
95	Jan–July 1951. Nos. 104–110.
96–101	**Statistical reports series C (statistics relating to manpower).**
96	Jan–Dec 1946. Nos. 34–45.
97	Jan–Dec 1947. Nos. 46–57.
98	Jan–Dec 1948. Nos. 58–69.
99	Jan–Dec 1949. Nos. 70–81.
100	Jan–Dec 1950. Nos. 82–93.
101	Jan–Dec 1951. Nos. 94–105.

102–103	**Statistical reports series D (statistics relating to housing).** Earlier reports appeared under the CS(S) series up to CS(S)(46)2. The series was discontinued after September 1947 and incorporated into the building section of the *Monthly Digest of Statistics*.
102	Feb–Dec 1946. Nos. 10–20.
103	Jan–Sept 1947. Nos. 21–29.
106–111	**Supplements to the *Monthly Digest of Statistics*.** Statistics formerly in series B but discontinued December 1945.
106	Mar–Dec 1946. Nos. 1–12.
107	Jan–Dec 1947. Nos. 13–24.
108	Jan–Dec 1948. Nos. 25–36.
109	Jan–Dec 1949. Nos. 37–48.
110	Jan–Dec 1950. Nos. 49–60.
111	Jan–Dec 1951. Nos. 61–72.
112–117	**C.S.O. Memoranda. CS(S) series.** All files include monthly statements of stocks of food and animal feedingstuffs for the Lord President's Committee (after October 1947 the Production Committee).
112	Jan–Dec 1946. CS(S)(46)1–38. Includes statistical reports on housing and on reconversion until May 1946. Also memoranda on preliminary estimate of national income of 1945, statistics required for progressing the import programme, and minutes of meetings on full costs of capital expenditure and building labour figures.
113	Jan–Dec 1947. CS(S)(47)1–47. Includes selected weekly statistics of U.K. production, and papers on: the recording of information on a reserve of investment projects, changes in productivity in British industry, the index of production, the fortnightly economic report and the Committee on Overseas Economic Information Statistical Subcommittee.
114	Jan–Dec 1948. CS(S)(48)1–38. From Sept 1948 includes monthly appreciation of price movements for the Wages and Price Policy Committee and also monthly statistics on petroleum products. Other memoranda cover the fourth U.S.S.R. five-year plan, statistics of employment on export orders, index of production and the classification of imports for the Statistical Working Group of the Programmes Committee.
115	Jan–Dec 1949. CS(S)(49)1–48. Includes further monthly appreciation of price movements and of statistics on petroleum products. Other memoranda cover the report on statistics of employment on export orders, the trend of production in non-agricultural industry 1946–49, the fourth U.S.S.R. five-year plan, the family budget enquiry, a comparison of the index of production with changes of employment 1946–49, production and employment in the first half of 1946, and statistics of saving and employment in public and private enterprise.
116	Jan–Dec 1950. CS(S)(50)1–30. Includes monthly statistics on petroleum products. Other memoranda cover statistics of exports of building materials, sample enquiry on private capital expenditure, recent changes in production per man, the new family budget survey, equitable sharing of the burden of defence, the extent of the public sector of the economy in recent years, rearmament statistics, and the economic history of manpower 1945–50.

117   Jan–Dec 1951. CS(S)(51)1–30. Includes memoranda on statistical report on rearmament, post-war trends in normal hours, overtime and short-term working in manufacturing industry, economic history 1945-51, the introduction of new food price index numbers and the index of the cost of building.

118   **Inter-departmental Committee on Estimates of Balance of Payments.** Jan 1945–Nov 1946. CSO(BP)(45)1st–2nd, CSO(BP)(46)1st and CSO(BP)(45)1–2.

118   **Working Party on Capital Expenditure Sample Survey.** Dec 1950–Dec 1951. CSO(CE)(51)1st–2nd, CSO(CE)(50)1–2, CSO(CE)(51)1–40.

119–121   **Inter-departmental Committee on Industrial Classification.**

119   1945-58 Meetings. CS(IC)(45)1st–9th, (46)1st–11th, (47)1st–7th, (48)1st–3rd, (49)1st–3rd, (50)1st–3rd, (52)1st.

120   May 1945–Dec 1946. Memoranda. CS(IC)(45)1–10, (46)1–16.

121   Jan 1947–Dec 1951. Memoranda. CS(IC)(47)1–14, (48)1–6, (49)1–2, (50)1, (52)1–2, (54)1–5. For its report see CAB 134/190, ED(47)29.

122–123   **Inter-departmental Committee on Industrial Classification Working Party.**

122   Oct 1946–Dec 1947. Meetings. CS(IC)(W)(46) 1st–12th, (47)1st–43rd.

123   Oct 1946–Oct 1947. Memoranda. CS(IC)(W)(46)1–5, (47)1–13.

124–126   **Working Party on Statistics for Employment Policy.**

124   1945–59. Meetings. ES(W)(45)1st–11th, (46)1st–9th, (47)1st–5th, (48)1st, (49)1st–2nd.

125   July 1945–Oct 1949. Memoranda. ES(W)(45)1–20, (46)1–3(revise), (47)1–8, (48)1–5, (49)1–11. Established as a result of a meeting under E.E. Bridges, 1 June 1945, to prepare a revise version of CS(S)(45)39 on departmental responsibilities for collecting statistics and to examine the statistics required. Includes its report (ES(W)(45)20).

126   Jan 1950–May 1955. Memoranda. ES(50)1–3.

127–128   **Working Party on Statistics for Employment Policy Subcommittee on Budget Enquiries.**

127   1947–59. Meetings. ES(W)(BE)(47)1st–6th, (50)1st–9th, (51)1st–4th.

128   October 1947–January 1953. Memoranda. ES(W)(BE)(47)1, (50)1–12, (51)1–12.

129   **Working Party on Statistics for Employment Policy.** Aug–Sept 1945. ES(W)(O)(45)1–4. Includes E.E. Bridges on capital expenditure statistics, action arising out of meetings of the working party, and draft reports on departmental responsibility for approaches to industry, and statistical demands upon industry.

130   **Working Party on Statistics for Employment Policy Subcommittee on Prices.** 1949–58. Minutes and memoranda.

134   **Working Party on Farm Incomes and Prices.** July–Dec 1950. CSO(FP)(50)1st–12th and CSO(FP)(50)1–29. Includes papers on data used for agricultural price reviews and the calculation of the annual aggregate net national income of U.K. farmers. Includes its report (CSO(FP)(50)29.)

141   **National Income Committee.** 1946–57. CSO(NI)(46)1st–2nd.

142–146   **Committee on the Censuses of Production and Distribution.**

142   1947–58. Meetings. CSO(PD)(47)1st–9th, (48)1st–6th, (49)1st, (50)1st–4th, (51)1st.

143   Jan–July 1947. Memoranda. CSO(PD)(47)1–22.

144   July–Sept 1947. Memoranda. CSO(PD)(47)23–31.

145   Sept–Oct 1947. Memoranda. CSO(PD)(47)32–36.

146   1948–60. Memoranda. CSO(PD)(48)1–14, (49)1, (50)1–7, (51)1–2.

147   **C.S.O. Memoranda, CSO(RM) Series.** October 1945–February 1946. CSO(RM)(45)10–12 and (46)1. Continuation from CAB 108/88.

148   **Revising Committee on the Trade Accounts.** 1946–61. CSO(TA)(46)1st–2nd, (47)1st–2nd, (48)1st, (49)1st–3rd, (50)1st, (51)1st–2nd and CSO(TA)(48)1–3, (49)1–2, (50)1, (51)1–3.

167   **C.S.O. staff meetings.** August 1941–June 1945. SM(41)1st–4th, (42)1st–4th, (43)1st, (45)1st. Includes consideration of post-war staffing of C.S.O., full employment policy, forecasting national income and expenditure, estimate of balance of payments, publication of statistics and the industrial classification.

8.2   Correspondence and Papers

CAB 139 contains the correspondence and papers arising from the C.S.O.'s work on the various committees and in the preparation of publications specified in CAB 108. Many files are not yet open. It includes files on statistical organization (5–6, 121–122, 128, 131, 175–176, 181, 456); statistics of various commodities; unemployment (28–29, 31); national income (30, 37–42, 242–310, 417–421); the balance of payments (43–45, 297–299, 444); manpower (49–55, 301–302, 311–326, 408–412); productivity and efficiency (67, 105–106, 327); imports (73–74, 305); the industrial classification (107–110, 518–519); the census of and index of production (112–116, 328); statistics for employment policy (123–127, 174, 191–192); reconstruction (139–144); economic surveys (162–172, 402); economic planning (173); capital expenditure, including the Investment Programmes Committee (204–241); rearmament (332–334); building (345–348); reports on the economic situation (354–356, 413); prices (367–377); the O.E.E.C. (403–404); and economic trends (432–434). See also CAB 141.

8.3   Selected Working Papers

CAB 141 contains the files generated by the correspondence and papers in CAB 139. Each is related to particular files in that class, e.g. pieces 1–22 are the working papers on coal and relate to CAB 139/10. Other subjects covered include iron and steel (23–40); non-ferrous metals (41–47); paper (48–50); raw materials in general (51); stocks (53–57); wages index (67); balance of payments (71–77); employment survey (83–87); ship-building (111–120); imports (121–124, 144); absenteeism (130–131, 145); building (132–140); and labour (142–143).

Chapter 9   Reconstruction Secretariat

The secretariat was originally established under Arthur Greenwood as Minister Without Portfolio; and from 1942 served Sir William Jowitt as both Paymaster General and Minister Without Portfolio. It acted as a co-ordinating centre for all interested departments and such bodies as the R.I.I.A. and the Nuffield College Social Reconstruction Survey. CAB 117 covers the period to November 1943, when a new reconstruction secretariat was established under Lord Woolton (CAB 124), and consists of the papers and correspondence of the various ministerial and official committees dealing with reconstruction.

CAB 117

7-12	**Official Committee on Post-war Internal Economic Problems: plan of work.** (53/1/4-7, 10-11) Nov 1941–Nov 1943. Covering the Treasury, Ministry of Health, Board of Trade, and Ministries of Agriculture and Fisheries, War Transport and Food.
19	**Post-war priorities.** (53/1/4/25) May–Oct 1943.
22-24	**Office Council.** (53/1/11/1 and 2, parts 1 and 2) Mar 1941–May 1943.
22	Minutes R(21)1–63.
23	Memoranda RC 1–80.
24	Memoranda RC 81–140. Includes RC 140. The present state of reconstruction, by Q. Hill, 4 May 1943.
26	**Post-war programme of the building industry: demarcation of duties between Ministers of Works and Planning and Minister of Health.** (53/1/27) Dec 1942–July 1943.
27	**Government pledges: post-war policy.** (53/1/34) Oct 1942–July 1943. Papers on various commitments made during the war, Ministries of Reconstruction 1917–19 and 1941–Jan 1943.
27-29	**Agriculture policies.** (53/2/1 parts 1 and 2) Apr 1941–Feb 1944.
29	Jan 1943–Feb 1944. Includes ministerial correspondence on post-war policy leading to WP(43)103.
40-41	**Economic demobilization: analysis of post-war experience (1918).** (53/3/1/1 parts 1 and 2).
40	(Professor Tawney) Feb 1941–Aug 1943. Includes papers by Tawney on the abolition of economic controls 1918–21, M. Dobb on decontrol of industry 1918–20, W.T. Corlett on external relations and J. Robinson on housing policy.
41	(Professor Pigou) Sept 1941–Aug 1943. Includes correspondence with J.H. Clapham, A.P. Pigou, and M. Dobb and drafts of Pigou's *The Economic History of Great Britain* from the Armistice in November 1918 to the abandonment of the gold standard.
41	**Post-war disposal of surplus equipment.** (53/3/4) May 1941–Nov 1943.
43-44	**Post-war industrial organization.** (53/3/11 parts 1 and 2) Jan 1941–Dec 1943.
47	**Economic reconstruction: Mr. George Schicht.** (53/3/41) Feb 1942–Mar 1943.

51   **Official Committee on Post-war External Economic Problems and Anglo-American Co-operation: composition and terms of reference.** (53/4/3) May 1941–May 1943.

55   **British and U.S. trade policies in Latin America.** (53/4/3/3) May 1941–Jan 1943.

61   **Anglo-American economic co-operation: Mutual Aid Agreement 1942: discussions under Article VII.** (53/4/3/17) Mar 1942–June 1943.

65   **Post-war Export Trade Committee (Mr. Harcourt Johnstone).** (53/4/15) Dec 1941–June 1944. Includes drafts of the committee's report on the recovery of export markets and the promotion of export trade, and note of a meeting, September 1943, with Lord Riverdale and M. Mackenzie of the F.B.I. on the effect of present restrictions on post-war export trade.

67-68   **Post-war commercial policy.** (53/4/20 parts 1 and 2) Mar 1942–July 1943.

67   Mar 1942–Feb 1943. Includes L.C. Robbins on alternative commercial policies, with comments, including those of H.D. Henderson and J.M. Keynes, plus papers relating to A. Hurst's report on post-war commercial policy, with comments and amendments.

68   Jan–July 1943. Papers relating to Washington discussions.

69   **Monopolies and restrictive practices.** (53/4/25) Sept 1942–Nov 1943.

71   **Proposals for an international clearing union.** (53/4/26) Aug 1942–Oct 1943. Papers on the alternative U.S. proposal for a stabilization fund and U.K. proposal for an international clearing union. Includes some papers by J.M. Keynes.

76   **International conference in the U.S.A.** (53/4/35) June–Nov 1943. Mainly telegrams on the discussions on post-war commercial policy and Article VII.

125   **Post-war building, housing and hire purchase programme: memorandum by the Minister of Labour (E. Bevin)** (53/8/34) May 1942–Dec 1943. Ministerial correspondence on RP(42)20 and papers leading to RP(43)24.

138   **Location of industry: machinery for the control of.** (53/9/3 part 2) Mar 1941–Feb 1944.

141   **Inter-departmental Committee on Demobilization: composition and terms of reference.** (53/10/1) Jan 1941–Oct 1942.

142   **Final report of the Inter-departmental Committee on the Machinery of Demobilization.** (53/10/1/2) Oct 1942–Oct 1943. Includes copy of the second report of the committee under A. Hurst and resulting correspondence.

144   **Post-war resettlement.** (53/10/7) June 1941–Mar 1943.

153   **Two stage demobilization: correspondence etc.** (53/10/30) May–June 1943. Papers relating to WP(43)241.

154   **Demobilization and resettlement: post-war employment.** (53/10/32) May–Dec 1943.

157   **Nuffield College Social Reconstruction Survey.** (53/12/2) Dec 1940–Dec 1943.

166   **Nuffield College Survey Progress Reports.** (53/12/2/13) Mar 1941–June 1943.

168   **Nuffield College Survey: report on the location of industry.** (53/12/2/20) Jan 1942–May 1943.

177   **Post-war reconstruction: P.E.P. (Political and Economic Planning).** (53/12/5) Jan 1941–Sept 1943. Related correspondence.

178   **Rotary International.** (53/12/8) May 1941–Oct 1943. Includes various publications and resulting correspondence on reconstruction.

179   **West Midland Group on Post-war Reconstruction and Planning.** (53/12/9) January 1941–August 1943.

182   **Joint Committee of Chatham House, Nuffield College Social Reconstruction Survey and the Institute of Statistics International Joint and International Research Committees.** (53/12/19) Jan 1941–May 1943. Papers arising from their work.

183   **Reconstruction Committee (City Council of Birmingham).** (53/12/20) Feb 1942–Mar 1943.

199   **Post-war reconstruction problems: F.B.I.** (53/13/69) May 1942–Feb 1943. Includes F.B.I. pamphlet on reconstruction and 'The Future of Export Trade' by Glenday.

200   **Post-war use of hostels (Minister of Labour).** (53/13/71) May 1942–Mar 1943.

203   **Establishment of the Reconstruction Joint Advisory Council.** (53/13/115) Sept 1942–Feb 1943.

204   **R.J.A.C.: correspondence in connection with the third meeting 31 March 1943.** (53/13/116) Feb–May 1943.

205   **R.J.A.C. fourth meeting: correspondence and paper in connection with.** (53/13/117) Apr–July 1943.

206   **Lord Southwood's motion in the House of Lords July 21st.** (53/13/133) July 1943. Motion on the need for plans to deal with unemployment through international reconstruction, with draft reply.

207   **R.J.A.C. fifth meeting November 9 1943: correspondence and papers in connection with.** (53/13/135) Sept–Dec 1943. Papers on its future with the appointment of the Minister of Reconstruction, including correspondence between Jowitt and Woolton.

209   **Government policy and public opinion.** (53/14/5) Jan 1941–Oct 1943.

210   **Publicity: Ministry of Information.** (53/14/24) Sept 1941–July 1943.

237   **The international regulation of primary products.** (53/18/6) Aug 1942–Apr 1943. Includes papers by F. Leith-Ross, R.F. Harrod and J.M. Keynes.

238   **Scottish Advisory Council on Reconstruction.** (53/19/2) Sept 1941–Aug 1944.

240   **Electricity distribution.** (53/22/1) Aug 1941–Sept 1943.

241   **Electricity: correspondence with electric power and light authorities and companies.** (53/22/3) Jan 1943–Nov 1944.

244   **British Embassy Washington: information received from.** (53/23/1/1) Dec 1940–Dec 1943.

245   **Information sent for transmission to the U.S. government: exchange of information with the U.S.** (53/23/1/2) Feb 1941–Aug 1943.

246   **Dominion governments exchange of information.** (53/23/2) June 1941–Aug 1943.

247   **Canada: information received from.** (53/23/2/1/1) Apr 1941–Aug 1943. Includes reports on governmental organization and policy in the U.K. for post-war reconstruction, and on wartime economic controls and controls for the transition to peace by M. Cohen.

248   **Information received from South Africa.** (53/23/2/2/1) Oct 1941–Feb 1943.

Chapter 10 Lord President's Private Office and Secretariat

10.1 Various Ministers' Files

CAB 118 consists of a collection of mainly 'private office' files of Neville Chamberlain, Sir John Anderson and Clement Attlee largely during their periods as Lord President of the Council. Those of Attlee also cover his period as Deputy Prime Minister as well as Lord President 1943–45, and include two files of the papers of Arthur Greenwood as Lord Privy Seal 1945–47. The class includes correspondence with other ministers: Bevin (21, 62); Bracken (22); Cripps (23); Morrison (60); and Churchill (75). There are also files on food and agricultural policy (12); demobilization (31); WP(43)255 ('The need for decisions') (33); post-war and reconstruction (73).

10.2 Lord President's Secretariat

CAB 123 consists of the registered, and a few unregistered, files of the Lord President's Office between 1940 and 1945, and reflects the work of the Lord President's Committee and its subcommittees (CAB 71). Most of the files relate to immediate wartime domestic issues but there are some relevant to reconstruction and post-war policy. These include files on the employment of prisoners and Europeans (7–8); wartime and post-war coal policy (17–33); social security and economic problems of the reconstruction period (43); the Beveridge Report (45); the Reconstruction Joint Advisory Council (49); post-war location of industry policy (60); rationing (74–81); U.K. imports (85–92); export policy (94); Article VII discussions (96); manpower (100–120); post-war building (123); the reconversion of industry (140); post-war commercial policy (221); post-war employment policy (229); the continuation of economic controls (231); and the functions of the Minister of Reconstruction (238). For files opened after 1945 see CAB 124.

Chapter 11 Lord President's Secretariat

CAB 124 contains the papers of the reconstruction secretariat following Woolton's appointment as Lord President in the caretaker government in May 1945 (for earlier papers see, respectively, CAB 117 and CAB 123). They contain major files on the planning of reconstruction, including drafts of the 1944 *Employment Policy* White Paper, and on post-war economic planning for which the Lord President was primarily responsible between 1945 and 1947 (see in particular 890–903, 1079–80, 1166–7). There are further files on the powers of the Minister of Reconstruction (436, 438) and on the committees dealing with reconstruction (361–2, 599).

The class also contains the papers of several committees related to economic planning, including: the Ministerial Committee on Demobilization (502–4); the Inter-departmental Committee on the Balanced Distribution of Industry, Panel A (642–61) and Panel B (664–8); the Informal Working Party on Economic Controls (685–7); and the Balance of Payments Working Party (1043–4).

CAB 124

1	**Confidential record of a Cabinet discussion on the Prime Minister's minute of 25 Nov 1943 setting up the office of the Minister of Reconstruction.** (1) Nov–Dec 1943. Note of a meeting following WM(43)161st to consider a draft of WP(43)538 and the terms of reference for the Reconstruction Committee. Correspondence on the exclusion of the Ministry of Food.
3	**Lord President's speech at Preston 6 Nov 1949.** (2/01) Oct–Nov 1949. Drafts of speech on the economic situation following devaluation.
5	**Lord President's speech at Oxford University Club 22 Apr 1950.** (2/04) Apr–June 1950. Drafts of speech on socialized industries and public accountability.
6	**Correspondence in connection with the setting up of the Subcommittee on Post-war Building. Composition and terms of reference.** (3) Aug 1943–Jan 1944. Correspondence including the division of departmental responsibility for building.
43	**Housing: demarcation of functions between the Minister of Health and the Minister of Works.** (5) Dec 1942–July 1946. Papers on post-war building responsibilities.
53–54	**Duration of emergency legislation.** (6/06A and B) Feb 1950–Feb 1951. Papers on the future of emergency powers, defence regulations and notes for the debate on transitional powers.
55–56	**Legislative programme session 1950/51.** (6/09A and B) Mar 1950–Mar 1951.
56	July 1950–Mar 1951. Some papers relating to the Currency and Bank Notes Bill.
55–62	**Government departments' transition plans. Reply to the Prime Minister's directive WP(43)476.** (7/1–3) Nov–Dec 1943. Arranged alphabetically by ministry.

Attlee, summary of the White Paper for Churchill, brief and draft
statement to the War Cabinet for Woolton and notes on the
international implications.

215A   **Draft White Paper on employment policy: amendments.** (27/13)
Feb–May 1944. Comments on the drafts by J.M. Fleming, R.
Hopkins, W. Eady (including his analysis of Keynes's views),
Cherwell, the Ministry of Labour and various other papers.

215B   **Action to be taken on the White Paper on employment policy.**
(27/17) May–Aug 1944. Drafts and redrafts of R(IO)(44)11 with
comments and extracts from the relevant meetings. Papers mainly
concerned with chapter II.

216   **Nuffield College private conference: employment policy.** (27/24) Mar
1944–Jan 1945. Report of the 13th and 16th conferences and part
of the report on full employment with a published summary of the
Beveridge Plan.

217   **Northern Industrial Group. Memoranda on the White Paper on
Employment Policy.** (27/26) Nov 1944–Feb 1945. Memorandum
from a group representing both sides of industry in the North East
on likely industrial problems and legislation needed to implement
the White Paper. Subsequent correspondence.

218–223   **The employment situation.** (27/29 parts I–VI) Oct 1945–Dec 1947.
218   Oct 1945–Feb 1946. Papers including briefs by J.E. Meade and
correspondence between Morrison, Smith and Wilmot on the
increased allocation of resources to areas where unemployment was
appearing. Correspondence between Morrison and Attlee on
unemployment in certain areas and remedial action with tables of
local unemployment.

219   Feb–June 1946. Correspondence between Morrison and Attlee on
the allocation of raw materials to firms in unemployment areas and
related papers by Jay and the Board of Trade.

220   June–July 1946. Papers on specific cases, the direction of building
labour to factory construction in development areas, Westwood's
concern at the possible increase of unemployment in Scotland and
a reading list on employment policy for Morrison.

221   Oct–Dec 1946. Includes draft note of a meeting, Dec 1946, on
statistics for employment policy with representatives of both sides
of industry in an attempt to obtain co-operation.

222   Dec 1946–May 1947. Includes reports on unemployment resulting
from electricity cuts and Wilson on whether Merseyside should be
made a development area.

223   June–Dec 1947. Mainly cuttings, but includes a paper on the
prospects for the West of Scotland if allocations were made on a
pre-war basis.

224   **North East coast and post-war planning. Correspondence between
Mr. Peat, the Ministry of Supply and Viscount Ridley.** (29) Nov
1943–Feb 1945. Report on the situation in North East factories,
Oct 1943, and correspondence on reconstruction and post-war
planning. Includes a copy of the Northern Industrial Group
memorandum (see CAB 124/217).

242   **Capital expenditure after the war.** (43) Dec 1943–Oct 1945. Includes
comments on R(43)4 in relation to employment. Little after early
1944.

243   **Correspondence with the Minister of Reconstruction on the export trade, etc.** (45) Jan 1944–Apr 1945. Various correspondence from industry on exports, particularly of engineering and steel, and the need for exporters to know what government policy was going to be.

251–259   **Committee on Emergency Legislation.**

   251   Terms of reference, composition and procedure. (61) Mar 1943–June 1944. Includes papers on the reliance of employment policy statistics on emergency powers which would lapse post-war and the machinery for considering selective relaxation of wartime legislation.

   254   Defence (General) Regulations 1939 part V (61/1/2) Nov 1943–Jan 1944.

   255   Defence (General) Regulations 1939 part III (policy) (61/3) Nov–Dec 1947. List of regulations with comments on their future.

   257   Defence Regulation 55. (61/6) July 1942–Jan 1944.

   259   Future structure of emergency legislation (61/10) Nov 1943–Mar 1944. Copy of GEN 24/2 and correspondence arising.

260   **Case for the law officers (emergency legislation).** (61/13) Jan 1944–Jan 1946. Copy of GEN(44)24/1 on the duration and scope of emergency legislation and resulting papers.

261   **Emergency legislation. Order in Council to be made at Stage A.** (61/14) Mar 1944–Feb 1946. Draft for changing or revoking defence regulations.

262–268   **Supplies and Services (Transitional Powers) Bill.** (61/18 parts I–VII).

   262   Sept 1944–May 1945. Drafts and papers relating to the relevant Emergency Powers (Transitional Provision) and Supplies and Services (Transitional Powers) Bills.

   263   May–Oct 1945. Further drafts of the bill, including possible inclusion of restrictive practices in industry, exchange control and capital issues.

   264   Oct 1945–Apr 1946. Draft Orders in Council on the bill and resulting correspondence.

   265   Briefs for the second reading. Sept–Oct 1945.

   266   Price regulation. Nov 1945. Draft Order in Council with regard to defence regulation 55AB.

   267   Supplies and Services (Extended Purposes) Act 1947. Aug 1947.

   268   Supplies and Services (Extended Purposes) Act 1947. Oct 1947–Dec 1949. Sets out the orders since the Act. Then gap to Dec 1947.

270   **Contracts expiring at the end of the war in Europe.** (61/21) Apr–June 1945.

271   **Retention of regulations noted for revocation at or before Stage C and required after Feb 1946.** (61/23) Aug 1945–Dec 1946. Includes EL(45)15 and 16, the relevant extract of EL(45)4th and comments arising.

272–274   **Emergency Laws (Transitional Provisions) Bill.** (61/24 parts I–III) Sept 1945–Nov 1948.

275   **Emergency Legislation Committee. Ministers (Transfer of Powers) Bill.** (61/25) Aug 1945–May 1946. Papers relating to the future of wartime departments.

290   **Shipbuilding yards on the River Tyne. Representations by boroughs of Tynemouth, Jarrow and Wallsend re the opening of disused shipyards on the Tyne.** (63) Dec 1943–May 1945.

291–292   **Prefabricated houses.** (64 parts I and II) Mar 1943–Mar 1948.

293   **Newsprint.** (69/01) July 1950–Feb 1951. On supplies.

294   **Paper supplies.** (69/02) Nov 1950–Jan 1951.

297   **North Wales post-war industrial reconstruction.** (92) Nov 1943–June 1948. Representations from regional bodies and reports on post-war development.

298   **North Wales post-war development.** (92/1) Aug 1944–Mar 1947. Papers leading to consideration of making North Wales a development area.

299   **Proposed discussion with the members of the Reconstruction Joint Advisory Council and the Minister of Reconstruction on the White Paper on Employment Policy.** (93/1) May 1944–May 1945. Joint statement by the F.B.I., the B.E.C. and the T.U.C. on the transition from war to peace. Notes for meetings of the N.J.A.C. and the N.P.A.C.I.

318   **London and Home Counties Joint Electricity Authority. Post-war reconstruction of electricity supply services.** (97) Jan–June 1944.

319   **Welsh Reconstruction Advisory Council. Observations by departments on first interim report.** (98/1) Mar–Oct 1944.

320   **The Bristol Channel ports.** (98/6) Oct 1944–Feb 1947. Papers on proposed developments arising out of the interim report of the Welsh Reconstruction Advisory Council. Little after mid–1945.

324   **South Wales Regional Council of Labour. Full employment for the people of Wales.** (98/8) Aug–Oct 1946. Request by the Regional Council of Labour for a meeting with Morrison. Verbatim reports of meetings between ministers and Welsh M.P.s on unemployment in Wales and Monmouth, July 1946, and between Morrison and the South Wales Regional Council of Labour, Sept 1946.

336–341   **Discussion regarding the cotton industry.** (137 parts I–VI).

336   Jan 1944–June 1945. Report of the Cotton Board Committee on post-war problems and resulting comments and meetings. J. Jewkes on the reorganization of the cotton industry. Report of the cotton textile mission to the U.S.A. Mar–Apr 1944.

337   Aug 1945–Mar 1946. Mainly copies of Materials Committee minutes and memoranda.

338   Mar–June 1946. Papers relating to centralized and bulk purchase of cotton and to the Raw Cotton Buying Commission.

339   July–Dec 1946. Relevant Materials Committee minutes and memoranda, draft of the Cotton (Centralized Buying) Bill and further papers on the Raw Cotton Buying Commission.

340   Dec 1946–Mar 1948. Includes some relevant Materials Committee minutes and memoranda and Prosperity Campaign (Official) Committee papers (PC(O)C). Also some papers on the Cotton (Centralized Buying) Bill, the draft Cotton Industry Development Council Order 1948 and manning up the industry.

341   Mar 1948–Jan 1951. Further Materials Committee minutes and memoranda, note of a deputation to Attlee from the industry, Mar 1948, papers on the productivity campaign and criticism of the Raw Cotton Buying Commission.

342   **Suggestions and enquiries received on the cotton industry, etc.** (137/6) Dec 1943–May 1946.

343–344   **Central purchase and the control of the cost of distribution of building materials.** (146 parts I and II).

343   Jan–Nov 1944. Papers on the central purchase of housing materials and the standardization and bulk purchase of fitments. Minutes and memoranda of the Reconstruction Committee on Housing (R(H)).

344   Oct 1944–July 1945. Further minutes and memoranda of the committee and its successor, the Housing Committee (H), with notes on the supply of components for houses during the transition.

345   **Reduction of cost of foodstuffs. Address given by Mr. Harry Ferguson to delegates to the International Food Conference held at Hot Springs.** (152) June 1943–Aug 1944.

346   **Inter-departmental organization to deal with problems of industrial reorganization.** (161) Jan–Feb 1944. Includes full details of inter-departmental committees on industrial questions.

347   **Enlarging the scope of departmental committees to cover the problems of the transitional and post-war period.** (161/1) Jan–Apr 1944.

348–350   **Future use of the regional organization.** (161/2 parts I–III).

348   Jan 1944–June 1945. Some minutes and memoranda of the Reconstruction Committee's Official Subcommittee on Industrial Problems and its informal subcommittee on regional organization, particularly in relation to the transition.

349   Aug 1945–Nov 1947. Papers leading to LP(46)17, and a few papers of the Regional Organization Committee (ROC). Minutes of a conference of chairmen of the regional boards for industry and of district committees with Morrison, June 1947. The Hamilton Report on Regional Organization of Trade and Industrial Departments.

350   Dec 1947–Feb 1951. Change of ministerial responsibility for regional boards with changes in their constitution and function. Chart of the organization of a typical Ministry of Fuel and Power region. Some circulars of the Regional Procedure (Industrial) Committee (RP(I)), including the establishment of a Treasury committee to co-ordinate information for the boards and to direct their procedure.

351   **Investigation by Paymaster General of the working of regional boards and district committees.** (161/6) June–Nov 1947. Note of a conference of the chairmen of regional boards and district committees with Morrison, June 1947. Regional board circulars 1/1–14. Notes of regional visits by the Paymaster General and his draft reports leading to LP(47)122.

354–356   **Storage and disposals.** (179 parts I–III) Dec 1943–Apr 1948.

354   Dec 1943–June 1945. Includes some minutes and memoranda of the Inter-departmental Committee on the Disposal of Surpluses (CDS).

357–358   **Report of Sir William Palmer's Committee on Disposal of Government Surpluses.** (179/1 parts I and II) Oct 1944–Dec 1946. Copy of the report on the disposal of machine tools with resulting minutes and memoranda of the Reconstruction Committee's Official Subcommittee on Industrial Problems.

359–360   **Surplus stores held by the service departments.** (179/2 parts I and II) May 1946–Jan 1947.

361–362   **Records of committees dealing with reconstruction matters.** (180 parts I and II).

482	**Draft White Paper on housing.** (315/45) Mar–Apr 1945. On post-war objectives.
485	**Housing costs.** (315/64) Nov 1945–Dec 1946. Papers on the control of costs and ministerial concern at their level.
486	**The extent of the Minister of Reconstruction's responsibility for co-ordinating departmental action on the post-war problems of industry.** (323/3) Nov 1944–Mar 1945. Note of a meeting of permanent secretaries and subsequent notes on ministerial responsibility for switch-over of industry from war to peace.
487–489	**Note on statistical assumptions used in reconstruction papers to Cabinet committees.** (328 parts I–III).
487	Jan–Oct 1944. Drafts of a note setting out by subjects the papers written and their respective assumptions to minimize inconsistencies.
488	Oct 1944–June 1945. Completed note covering decisions bearing on reconstruction policy, Oct 1944, with permanent secretaries' comments and the record of a subsequent meeting, Jan 1945.
489	Feb–Apr 1945. Revision with comments.
500	**Major St. Clare Grondana. Plans for price stabilization.** (344) July 1942–June 1945. Various publications by Grondana, resulting correspondence and comments.
501	**Raw materials stock position in 1944 – correspondence with the C.S.O.** (346) Dec 1943–Nov 1945. Review to see if supplies were sufficient for the transition.
502–504	**Ministerial Committee on Demobilization.** (350/1–3) Nov 1942–Dec 1945. Working papers and correspondence of the committee (DC), the report (DC(43)18(final)) and its consideration by Cabinet.
505	**Demobilization. Correspondence on civil defence services and home guard.** (353) July 1941–Apr 1945.
506	**Demobilization. War Office calculations.** (355) Oct 1943.
510	**Deferred demobilization.** (361) Oct–Nov 1943.
511	**Demobilization of building labour.** (363) Nov 1943–May 1945. Estimates of numbers involved and of manpower requirements.
516	**Future arrangements for determining manpower allocation.** (381) Feb–Mar 1944. Papers on the proposed inter-departmental organization.
517	**Suggestions and ideas on reconstruction problems forwarded by engineering associations.** (402) Jan 1944–June 1945.
518	**(A) Memorandum on the Esparta paper-making industry of Great Britain. (B) Memorandum on post-war policy for the paper and board-making industry.** (403) Feb–June 1944. Representations from the Paper-makers' Association.
519–520	**Post-war export trade: suggestions, memoranda, etc.** (404 parts I and II) Jan 1944–Mar 1946. Correspondence and various pamphlets by industrial associations.
521–522	**Post-war position of commerce and shipping.** (406 parts I and II) Dec 1943–Mar 1948. Correspondence and various papers by the General Council of British Shipping, the Chamber of Shipping of the U.K. and the Liverpool Steamship Owners' Association. Includes a survey of post-war shipping problems and opportunities.

523   **Post-war reconstruction in the clothing industry. Report, suggestions, etc.** (409) Jan 1944. Report by the Council of Clothing Trade Associations.

528   **(A) The training of scientists.**
(B) Release of scientists from the forces. (413/4) May 1945–Jan 1947.

560   **Legislative programme 1945–1946.** (424/2) Oct–Nov 1945.

561–564   **Legislative programme for the 1946–47 session.** (424/3 parts I–IV) Dec 1945–Apr 1947. Proposed list with related correspondence and working papers.

565   **Subordinate legislation.** (424/4) Feb 1946–Nov 1947.

566   **Proposal that the number of reconstruction committees should be reduced.** (435) Dec 1944–Feb 1945. Correspondence between Lyttelton and Woolton on the number of committees and postponing controversial legislation.

567–576   **Post-war agricultural policy.** (448 parts I–V and VIII–XII). Apr 1943–June 1949. The major series of files on policy including papers arising out of Cabinet memoranda, such as WP(43)103 and WP(45)36, and the work of the Lord President's Committee. Amongst the subjects covered: the application of scientific principles to agriculture, P.L.P. views on the food production campaign, the 1947 Agriculture Act and other relevant legislation, the Agricultural Expansion Programme and the work of the Committee on Agricultural Output (AD). In addition there are papers and reports of speeches by Addison and Williams.

577   **N.F.U. Agricultural machinery.** (448/5 part I) July 1946–Aug 1947. Interim review of requirements by the N.F.U. Correspondence between Williams and Morrison and further correspondence on departmental responsibility.

578   **The Agricultural Mortgage Corporation Limited. Agricultural credits.** (448/7) Mar 1944–Mar 1948. Notes on its formation and history. Correspondence by ministers, including Williams, Addison, Morrison and Dalton.

580   **Correspondence between the Minister of Health and the Minister of Reconstruction as to whether the return of evacuated firms to London might afford any substantial relief in the matter of rural housing.** (457) Jan 1943–May 1944.

582   **The post-war international settlement and the U.K. balance of payments.** (464) Jan 1944. Memorandum by J.E. Meade to Woolton on the U.K. position under the proposed Washington arrangements should there be a U.S. slump.

583   **National Federation of Registered House Builders. Proposals, memoranda and correspondence on post-war housing.** (465) Feb–Oct 1944.

584   **Nuffield College report on distribution and location of industry on the North East coast.** (469) Dec 1943–Mar 1944. Copy of the report and covering note.

585   **Report of the Subcommittee on Control of Post-war Building.** (475) Mar 1944–Feb 1945. Proof copy of the report (R(B)(44)8(final)) with comments leading to R(44)49 and further Reconstruction

Committee papers. D.N. Chester on the different estimates of post-war housing.

588–590   Allocation of manpower for 1945. (499/1 parts I–III).

588   Mar–May 1944. Papers and correspondence on the attempt to formulate a rough estimate of the supply and demand for labour in the first year after the end of the war with Germany. Includes consideration of a tentative manpower budget for 1945.

589   May–Sept 1944. Further notes on manpower one year after the end of the war with Germany, as presented to Cabinet. Some consideration of how to reduce the manpower gap. N. Brook to Woolton emphasizing the importance of the manpower budget to reconstruction planning.

590   Sept 1944–Aug 1945. WP(44)509 and resulting comments, including consideration of need for a revised manpower budget for 1945. Ministry of Labour survey of manpower mid–1939 to mid–1944 and estimated supply of manpower 1945. Relevant Cabinet minutes and memoranda. Note of an informal meeting of officials, August 1945, to define issues for ministerial consideration. Papers leading to a detailed manpower budget up to end June 1946.

591–594   Defence policy. (499/6 parts I–IV) Apr 1945–Dec 1948. Includes papers relating to the National Service Bill and post-war defence policies.

599   Committees concerned with reconstruction problems. (563) Sept 1942. See CAB 124/361.

600   The system of motor car taxation and its effect on our export trade. (568) Mar 1943–Aug 1945. Correspondence with industrial associations and articles in motor magazines.

601   Post-war housing. (570/3) Nov 1943–July 1944.

606   General transport policy. (612 part I) Apr 1944–Sept 1945. Papers on the co-ordination of inland transport and plans for the transition period.

607–608   Future of the road haulage organization. (612/6 parts I and II) Aug 1945–Nov 1949. Papers particularly on whether there should be a return to competition prior to nationalization. Only cuttings after April 1946.

609   Transport Bill: points raised by various bodies. (612/15) Dec 1946–Mar 1948.

610–611   Railways. (615 parts I and II) Mar 1944–Mar 1949. Correspondence and papers on the Railway (London Plans) Committee report, future policy and railways during the fuel crisis.

612   Railway charges and claims for increased wages and shorter hours. (615/3) Mar 1944–Aug 1947. Only press cuttings prior to April 1946. Thereafter papers by the Ministry of Transport and Barnes on increased charges with comments, particularly from the Lord President's Committee.

613   Capital issues control after the war. (622) Nov 1942–May 1947. Outline and drafts of the initial memorandum on guidance to the committee on U.K. issues and related papers leading to Cmd. 6645.

615   Cornish metalliferous mining. Memorandum by the Cornish Tin Mining Advisory Committee. (640) July 1941–Dec 1944. Memorandum on post-war reconstruction and related correspondence.

617   **The preparation of post-war projects. The consideration of possible improvements to the principal waterways.** (650/1) Apr–Nov 1944. Ministry of War Transport on the relationship between employment policy and the preparation of such schemes.

618–619   **Highway policy.** (668 parts I and II).

618   May 1944–July 1945. Includes papers on the acquisition of land for roadworks and estimates of post-war roads and traffic.

619   Aug 1945–Sept 1948. Copy of the Trunk Roads Bill and its amendment. Notes on relevant memoranda of the Lord President's Committee and its Distribution of Industry Committee, including papers on highways and development areas.

625   **Proposals on the brewing trade. Proposed deputation to the Minister of Reconstruction.** (715) May–Sept 1944. Correspondence and record of a meeting, Sept 1944.

626–627   **Post-war resettlement of the motor industry.** (720 parts I and II).

626   Nov 1943–May 1946. Includes relevant minutes and memoranda of the Reconstruction Committee's Official Subcommittee on Industrial Problems report (R(I)(45)9). Some papers on standardization of models and its impact on demand.

627   June 1946–July 1950. Further papers on standardization. Others on supply of cars to the Empire. Little after Aug 1947.

629   **Post-war Resettlement of the Motor Industry Working Party.** (720/2) Mar–July 1945. Papers on its establishment and work on how to increase exports.

630–631   **Closer control of building in the post-war period.** (721 parts I and II). April 1944–Feb 1948. Papers on various labour and financial controls including those covered by the Supplies and Services (Transitional Powers) Act, 1947.

632–634   **Post-war building programme.** (722 parts I–III).

632   Nov 1943–July 1945. Includes regular issues by the Official Committee on Housing on outstanding questions.

633   July 1945–Dec 1946. Papers on building labour, direction and suggestions by Attlee to redeploy labour.

634   Jan 1947–Mar 1950. Correspondence between Key and Morrison on licensing and papers on training following the August 1947 cuts. Then gap to 1950.

635   **Building executives.** (722/1) Apr–June 1945. Consideration of a ministerial or official committee to co-ordinate building requirements and departmental responsibilities.

636   **Wages and output in the building industry.** (722/2) Nov 1946–Sept 1947.

637–639   **The Social Survey.** (728/1 parts I and II and annex I) Dec 1945–Dec 1948.

637   Dec 1945–May 1947. Includes some papers on demobilization and employment.

638   Dec 1946–Dec 1948. Includes papers on manpower and preliminary results of the Survey of Knowledge and Opinion about the Economic Situation.

639   Reports including some Surveys of Knowledge and Opinion of the Economic Situation.

640–641   **Balanced distribution of industry: inter-departmental machinery.** (741 parts I and II). Mar 1944–June 1945. Minutes and memoranda of the Reconstruction Committee's Ministerial and Official Subcommittees on Industrial Problems and resulting correspondence. Minutes and memoranda of the Cabinet following WP(44)640 leading to drafts of the Distribution of Industry Bill.

641   June 1945. Notes on the bill and for Woolton's speech.

642–651   **Inter-departmental Committee on the Balanced Distribution of Industry. Panel A.** (741/1 parts I–X). Some minutes and memoranda are not in numerical order.

642   July 1944–May 1945. Correspondence on membership. Then minutes and memoranda to BDI(A)15th and BDI(A)22.

643   Apr–Sept 1945. To BDI(A)23rd and BDI(A)31/1.

644   Aug–Nov 1945. To BDI(A)34th and BDI(A)31/4.

645   Nov 1945–Jan 1946. To BDI(A)40th and BDI(A)43(revise).

646   Jan–May 1946. To BDI(A)52nd and BDI(A)55.

647   May–Sept 1946. To BDI(A)59th and BDI(A)58.

648   Aug–Oct 1946. To BDI(A)70th and BDI(A)64.

649   Oct 1946–Jan 1947. To BDI(A)83rd and BDI(A)70.

650   Jan–Dec 1947. To BDI(A)125th and BDI(A)95.

651   Jan–June 1948. To BDI(A)149th.

652–661   **Inter-departmental Committee on the Balanced Distribution of Industry: Panel A: building cases.** (741/2 parts I–X).

652   Nov 1944–May 1945. Applications for approval of new building work. Cases 1–162.

653   May–July 1945. Cases 163–320.

654   Aug–Oct 1945. Cases 321–541.

655   Oct–Dec 1945. Cases 542–699.

656   Dec 1945–Feb 1946. Cases 700–898.

657   Jan–Apr 1946. Cases 899–1099.

658   May–Oct 1946. Cases 1100–1327.

659   Nov 1946–Mar 1947. Cases 1328–1426(revise).

660   Mar 1947–Jan 1948. Cases 1427–1669.

661   Jan–July 1948. Cases 1670–1797.

662–663   **Distribution of Industry Committee: papers and correspondence.** (741/4 parts I and II).

662   Aug 1944–Feb 1945. Papers leading to R(I)(44)15 on how to implement policy. Then correspondence on the committee's role with memoranda and papers on the strategic/air defence consideration.

663   Feb–Oct 1945. Papers following WP(45)78 on the Distribution of Industry Bill, with explanatory note. Some correspondence on N. Ireland.

664–668   **Official Committee on the Balanced Distribution of Industry: Panel B: allocations of government-owned factories.** (741/6 parts I–V).

664   June–Nov 1945. Minutes and memoranda BDI(B)10th–12th and BDI(B)158–325.

665   Nov 1945–May 1946. BDI(B)13th–14th and BDI(B)326–556.

666   May–Oct 1946. BDI(B)15th–18th and BDI(B)560–834.

667   Nov 1946–Oct 1947. BDI(B)19th–23rd and BDI(B)836–1199.

668   Oct 1947–July 1948. BDI(B)28th and BDI(B)1200–1402.

669–675   **The development areas.** (741/8 parts I–VII).

669   July–Oct 1945. Copy of the Neal Report on the Physical Development of the Development Areas and resulting papers.

670 Nov 1945–Feb 1946. Includes ministerial correspondence on basic services and some minutes and memoranda of the Ministry of Town and Country Planning Inter-departmental Group on the Physical Development of the Development Areas (PDDA).

671 Jan–Apr 1946. Further memoranda of the inter-departmental group, correspondence between Morrison, Cripps and Fraser on responsibility for policy and Westwood on Lanarkshire. Some notes on progress.

672 Apr–June 1946. Mainly minutes and memoranda of the Lord President's Committee Distribution of Industry Committee.

673 June–Oct 1946. Further minutes and memoranda of the committee and correspondence between Barnes, Morrison and de Freitas.

674 Oct 1946–Apr 1947. Further minutes and memoranda of the committee with a few Panel A papers.

675 Apr 1947–May 1950. Further minutes and memoranda of the committee with a few Panel A papers.

676 **Scottish industrial planning.** (741/19) July 1946–Mar 1948. Papers by various bodies on industrial development and employment in Scotland.

677 **Scottish development areas.** (741/23) Sept 1946–Dec 1950. Includes some minutes and memoranda of the Lord President's Distribution of Industry Committee and papers on attracting new industries and on the Highlands.

678–681 **Future of controls.** (761 parts I–IV).

678 Feb 1942–May 1944. Various papers on controls during the transition, including labour controls, with a draft report by the Working Party on Economic Controls on controls following the end of hostilities in Europe. A few papers of the Informal Committee on Controls.

679 May–July 1944. Further papers of the Informal Committee, including drafts of its report with comments and amendments.

680 Aug–Sept 1944. Further comments and amendments leading to the revised report (R(IO)(44)19). J. Jewkes on the problems if the war ended sooner than assumed.

681 Sept 1944–Jan 1945. Comments on R(IO)(44)21. J.E. Meade on the role of financial controls. Meeting, Oct 1944, and later papers on purchase tax.

682–683 **Economic controls during the transition period.** (761/2 parts I and II).

682 July–Sept 1944. Report of the Working Party on Economic Controls on controls following the end of hostilities in Europe and draft reports of the Informal Committee on Controls leading to R(IO)(44)21.

683 Oct 1944. Further minutes and memoranda of the Reconstruction Committee's Official Subcommittee on Industrial Problems on economic controls.

684 **Draft of White Paper on economic control.** (761/3 part I) Sept–Oct 1944. Drafts of the unpublished White Paper and related papers arising out of R(IO)(44)21.

685–687 **Economic controls during the transition period. Informal working party.** (761/7 parts I–III).

685   Sept 1944–May 1945. Correspondence and papers of the Working Party on Economic Controls (EC), established out of R(IO)(44)21. See CAB 87/89.

686   May–Sept 1945. Drafts of the working party's report and related correspondence leading to EC(45)12 and the establishment of a new working party (GEN 87). See CAB 87/89 and CAB 78/37.

687   Sept–Oct 1945. Some minutes and memoranda of the new committee and draft of LP(45)210. See CAB 78/37. J.E. Meade on the nature of controls.

688–690   Economic controls: notification to R(IO) secretariat of substantial modification. (761/8 parts I–III) Feb 1945–Apr 1948. Notes on modifications leading to regular papers for the Home Affairs Committee's Official Committee on Industrial Problems (IO), then circulars by the Lord President's Office (OC). Includes some monthly bulletins on conservation and substitution of raw materials by the Raw Materials Department.

691   **Working Party on Economic Controls: controls in remainder of Stage II.** (761/9) May–July 1945. Copy of EC5 and resulting correspondence. See CAB 87/89.

692   **Labour controls.** (761/12) Oct 1945–Feb 1947. Memoranda and minutes of various committees on the relaxation of labour controls leading to the Cabinet decision of 1 Nov 1945 and Isaacs's disagreement resulting in CP(45)288. Note of a meeting, 16 Oct 1945, on possible means for preventing workers taking unproductive employment in the distributive trades.

693–694   Incentives to production. (761/14 parts I and II).

693   Dec 1945–May 1946. Minutes and memoranda, correspondence and drafts of the report of the Working Party on Incentives to Production (GEN 105) leading to LP(46)105.

694   May 1946–Oct 1950. Minutes and memoranda of the Lord President's Committee arising out of LP(46)105. Little after August 1947.

695   **The problem of price control during the transition period.** (771) June–July 1944. Papers arising out of a Treasury note, then a subsequent meeting, 17 July 1944.

699   **National Savings publicity.** (794/1) Oct 1947–July 1948. Part I – Minutes and related notes of a meeting, 19 Nov 1947, on the Lord President's role. Correspondence on the possibility of enlisting the leader of the opposition to help the savings movement and correspondence with Churchill's help. Part II – pamphlets and advertisements on savings.

702   **The position of refugee industrialists in Great Britain.** (851) July–Dec 1944.

703   **The possibility of wider use of the services of the British Federation of Commodity and Allied Trade Associations by Government departments.** (852) July 1944–Aug 1945. Correspondence with Johnstone and papers and notes of meetings on the future of bulk purchase and government trading arrangements.

704–707   The coal-mining industry: prospects and efficiency. (856 parts I–IV).

704   Aug 1943–Apr 1945. Report of the Combined Production and Resources Board's London Coal Committee's U.S. Coal Mission with comments by Ministries of Fuel and Power and Works. Papers

on increasing U.K. production and notes on the coal position in Stage II.

705   Apr–July 1945. Report of the Reid Committee (Cmd. 6610) and CP(45)8 with comments and correspondence.

706   July 1945–July 1946. Attlee to Isaacs on intensifying efforts to increase manpower to increase winter production and to Wilmot on increasing machinery supplies. Jay on the coal crisis. Economic Section recommendation that miners should not have a five-day working week without accepting foreign labour. Discussion of whether problems were due to ministerial weaknesses or N.U.M. intransigence.

707   July 1946–Jan 1947. Papers on recruitment and minimizing the impact of the crisis.

708   **Coal and its uses. Inquiry as to the Government's post-war policy.** (856/3) Mar 1944–Mar 1945. Papers on encouraging the use of British fuel for transport purposes to save dollars.

709   **Correspondence on the coal industry.** (856/4) July 1944–Jan 1946.

710   **The profitable exportation of the by-products of coal.** (856/5) Jan 1945–Oct 1946. Correspondence between Churchill and Woolton on desirability of exporting non-profitable manufactures other than coal leading up to R(IE)(45)2 with comments.

711   **Summary of Mr. Robert Foot's report on the coal industry.** (856/6) Jan–Apr 1945.

712   **Limitations on the N.C.B.'s commercial activities overseas.** (856/7/1) Jan–June 1948.

713   **Incentives for coal-miners.** (856/8) Oct 1945–Apr 1948. On non-financial incentives, such as increased rations.

714–720   **The coal position in the coming winter.** (856/9 parts I–VII).

714   Oct–Dec 1945. Some minutes and memoranda of the Ministerial and Official Committees on the Coal Situation during the Coming Winter (GEN 94 and CS respectively) and related papers.

715   Dec 1945–Aug 1946. Further minutes, memoranda and papers of both committees. Attlee to Isaacs, June 1946, on increasing manpower. Jay on the coal crisis.

716   Sept–Nov 1946. Further minutes, memoranda and papers of both committees.

717   Nov–Dec 1946. Further minutes, memoranda and papers of the ministerial committee, including correspondence between Barnes, Attlee and Dalton on the committee structure.

718   Nov 1946–Jan 1947. Papers relating to the replacement of the ministerial committee by the larger Coal Committee (CAB 134/62) and arrangements for the establishment of an Official Coal Committee (CAB 134/62). Papers relating to both committees. Includes Attlee on coal allocations and Barnes on accommodation for railwaymen. Consideration of the new scheme of fuel allocations as a means of manning up undermanned industries. Statistical note on the industry and the transport situation.

719   Jan–Feb 1947. Statistical summaries of the coal and transport positions. Papers on the early closing down of the B.B.C. and other measures to save fuel. Consideration of measures to improve transport position. Includes first meeting of the Official Coal

Committee Subcommittee on the Transport and Distribution of Coal (CC(T)).

720 Apr 1946–Feb 1947. Minutes by Attlee to ministers on means of reducing fuel consumption and their replies. Correspondence on the replacement of the Ministerial Committee on Coal during the Coming Winter by the new Coal Committee. Some papers on the more long-term prospects for coal.

721 **Publicity arrangements for the coal-mining industry.** (856/13) July 1946–June 1948. Papers relating to the coal production drive.

722 **Coal for bunkering British ships.** (856/14) Dec 1946–May 1947.

723–736 **Fuel Committee: fuel situation.** (856/16 parts I–XIV). Feb 1947 – June 1948. Most pieces include minutes and memoranda of the Fuel Committee (FC) and reports on the fuel situation and the transport of coal.

726 Includes W.L. Gorrell-Barnes on the 1947–48 coal budget.

727 Feb–Mar 1947. Includes notes on fuel policy 1947–48 and measures to reduce consumption.

728 Mar 1947. Includes correspondence on reducing domestic household supplies of solid fuel. Consideration of the import of coal.

729 Mar 1947. Includes a brief for Attlee's meeting with the N.U.M. and related papers. Consideration of restrictions on electricity and gas and their possible revision.

730 Mar–Apr 1947. Papers on the allocation of coal to industry and on coal imports, particularly from the U.S.A.

731 Apr 1947. Further papers on the import of coal from the U.S.A. and on allocations for industry.

732 Apr–May 1947. Papers on further work of the committee and the Lord President's membership.

733 May–June 1947. Papers on a five-day week. Dalton and Attlee on coal imports.

734 June–July 1947. Papers on coal prospects and the balance of payments, and statistics on the coal situation.

735 July–Nov 1947. Some N.P.A.C.I. memoranda.

736 Aug 1947–June 1948. Review of prospects for 1947–1948 and of coal target prospects for 1948. Re-organization of the committees on fuel.

737 **Recruitment for the coal mines.** (856/17) Oct 1946–July 1948. Includes relevant minutes and memoranda of the Fuel Committee, including papers on the disagreement between Isaacs and Gaitskell on labour shortages as the cause of the coal crisis.

738 **The N.C.B.'s arrangements for the purchase of American coal.** (856/24) June 1947.

739 **Accommodation for miners.** (856/25) Mar–Dec 1947.

740 **The extension of the five-day week to the ancillary undertakings of the N.C.B.** (856/27) July–Aug 1947.

741 **Appeal to miners for greater output.** (856/28) July 1947–Jan 1948. Discussions with the N.U.M. on the extension of hours and their resistance. Meeting of ministers on the appeal, Aug 1947. Papers on absenteeism. Includes a number of minutes by Attlee.

742 **The Lord President's speech to the miners at Durham on July 26 1947.** (856/30) July 1947. First draft and comments on the speech which emphasized the realities of the coal problem.

Economic Section on views of the Ministries of Labour and Fuel and Power. Consideration of whether the N.J.A.C. or the J.C.C. was a suitable body to consider wages policy in relation to government plans. See CAB 132/88.

784   Nov 1946–Aug 1947. Includes W.L. Gorrell-Barnes's concern at the handling of wages policy by the Official Steering Committee on Economic Development. Correspondence between E.M. Nicholson and C.A. Lidbury on the lack of published papers on wages policy.

785–787   **National Industrial Conference.** (950/2 parts I–III).

785   Apr–Nov 1946. Papers on its constitution in the form of a revised N.J.A.C., Joint Advisory Council, notes from Morrison's speech to the first meeting and comments on it. Minutes of some meetings.

786   Nov 1946–Jan 1947. Drafts of the White Paper on *Economic Considerations Affecting Relations between Workers and Employers* (Cmd. 7018).

787   June 1947–Nov 1949. Further minutes and memoranda of the N.J.A.C. and including a draft paper for the T.U.C. on the economic situation and an update on the 1947 Economic Survey part III.

788   **The methods by which reconstruction enquiries were made during the last war and their results.** (959) July–Oct 1944.

789–791   **Future of the iron and steel industry.** (969 parts I–III) Sept 1944–June 1947. Various papers on the industry's reorganization, including some Economic Section discussion papers, Materials Committee memoranda and notes of meetings between ministers and the British Iron and Steel Federation.

792   **Future of the iron and steel industry. Correspondence etc., with the British iron and steel industry.** (969/1) Mar 1944–Mar 1945.

793   **Nationalization of the iron and steel industry. Information for the Canadian press.** (969/5) Aug 1946.

794–798   **Steel supplies and steel allocations.** (969/10 parts I–V) June 1946–Dec 1949. Mainly Materials Committee minutes and memoranda including some on the revision of the steel priority scheme. Also correspondence, including some between Gaitskell and Morrison (CAB 124/796) on allocations.

799–800   **Arrangements for the conversion of industrial capacity to civilian needs.** (796 parts I and II).

799   Aug 1944–July 1945. Includes ministerial correspondence on the release of particular types of manpower and production. Mainly papers relating to the switch-over of industry from munitions to civil production, including a note of a meeting of ministers, Sept 1944. Note on the winding up of Panel C of the Balanced Distribution of Industry Committee.

800   July–Dec 1945. Two factual reports on reconversion in Stage II as it progressed.

801–802   **Plans for increasing the supplies of clothing and domestic furniture and utensils for the civilian population.** (978 parts I and II).

801   Sept 1944–May 1945. Action resulting from an enquiry by Churchill.

802   Oct 1945–Jan 1950. Papers on the reduction of service clothing contracts and on clothing rations.

803   **The difficulty of the Daimler Co. in acquiring suitable post-war premises.** (989) Sept–Oct 1944.

805–806 **Manufacture in this country of goods formerly imported.** (994 parts I and II).

805 Apr 1944–Feb 1945. Review of possible goods and resulting correspondence following consideration by the Reconstruction Committee's Industrial Subcommittee, in particular clocks, watches and agricultural machinery.

806 Aug–Dec 1945. Further correspondence.

817 **Reports on post-war reconstruction.** (1039) Oct 1944. Includes T.U.C. Interim Report on Post-war Reconstruction.

822 **Hotels and Restaurants Association deputation received by the Minister of Reconstruction 17 Oct 1944.** (1057) Sept 1944–Jan 1945.

823 **Deputation from the City Council of Birmingham.** (1058) Oct–Nov 1944. Papers and record of the meeting, Nov 1944, particularly on the balanced distribution of industry proposals.

824 **Brief for ministers for the meeting of Reconstruction Joint Advisory Council and debate in the House of Commons.** (1068) Sept 1944–Feb 1945.

825 **Long-term policy for milk production.** (1071/1) Apr 1944–Mar 1945.

826 **Reconstruction achievement.** (1076) Oct 1944–Feb 1945. Notes setting out the achievements of the Ministry of Reconstruction's first year.

827 **Proposals for improving industrial management.** (1080) Aug 1944–Mar 1945. Includes proposed establishment of a British Institute of Management.

828 **Public Utility Corporation.** (1081) Dec 1944. R(44)199 and comments on it.

829–830 **Reconstruction pamphlet.** (1103 parts I and II) Oct 1944–May 1946. Suggested outline and drafts of a government pamphlet.

831 **Sir William Beveridge's book *Full Employment in a Free Society*. Some appreciations and comments.** (1120) Nov 1944–Jan 1945. Draft and final copy of EC(S)(44)20 comparing the book with the White Paper on *Employment Policy* and CS(S)(44)78 on the equations underlying Appendix C of the book.

854 **Informal discussion between the Minister of Reconstruction and the Executive of the British National Committee of the International Chamber of Commerce, Feb 8 1945.** (1193) Nov 1944–Feb 1945.

855 **Visit of Lord Woolton to Wolverhampton to open an exhibition dealing with the post-war development of the town.** (1195) Jan 1944–Mar 1945.

856 **Future of the light metal fabricating industry.** (1196) Oct 1944–June 1945.

858–859 **Allocation of wood-working capacity.** (1208 parts I and II) Feb–Sept 1945. Notes on the resettlement of the industry leading to GEN 86/1.

860–861 **Government building programme: building labour allocation.** (1209 parts I and II) Sept 1944–Sept 1947. Includes Jay on priorities for building labour.

866 **Redundant plant in the tin plate industry.** (1218) Feb–June 1945. Includes relevant minutes and memoranda of the Reconstruction Committee's Ministerial Industrial Subcommittee.

867 **Proposed report on public opinion on reconstruction to be prepared by Wartime Social Survey.** (1236) Dec 1944–Feb 1945.

872–874   **Use of foreign labour in Great Britain.** (1301 parts I–III) Dec 1945–Oct 1949. Mainly minutes and memoranda of the Foreign Labour Committee and its successor, the Labour Committee.

875   **Employment of aliens in defence establishments.** (1301/2) May–Aug 1949.

876–877   **Lord President's Committee.** (1341 parts I and II).

    876   July 1945–June 1947. Arrangements for the committee post-election and the need for co-ordination with other committees. Briefs for meetings. Progress report on implementation of the committee's conclusions.

    877   June 1947–Dec 1948. Further reports of the implementation of conclusions. Some ministerial correspondence and notes on meetings.

890–903   **Central planning of economic development.** (1381 parts I–XIV).

    890   July–Nov 1945. Correspondence between Morrison and Cripps on the Economic Section joining the Board of Trade. Papers on whether the Section should be part of a planning general staff and on the production of an economic survey. Outline of the machinery to be set up for planning, Sept 1945, as circulated by E.E Bridges for comments by departments, and discussed at a meeting, 12 Sept 1945. E.E. Bridges's circular, Oct 1945, on the establishment of the Steering Committee and its working parties. Draft of ED(45)1, with comments of Mayhew, and consequent meeting, 29 Sept.

    891   Oct–Dec 1945. Drafts of a paper by E.E. Bridges for the Lord President's Committee Industrial Subcommittee on the machinery for economic planning. Jay's comments on ED(45)1, draft heads of a public announcement on the organization of economic planning, with comments, including Jay's. Preview of manpower in 1946 by the Ministry of Labour and papers on the exchange of information between working parties.

    892   Dec 1945. Draft of the Economic Survey for 1946 with comments, including W. Eady's, leading to ED(45)5. C.H. Secord on the implementation of economic policy.

    893   Dec 1945–Feb 1946. Notes on statistics for employment policy, on the implementation of policy for a meeting, 7 Jan 1946, and the technique of economic control. Copy of the Survey for 1946 with drafts of covering note for ministers with comments by Dalton, Cripps and Isaacs. J.E. Meade on planning after the survey. Correspondence on long-term planning (EC(S)(46)9).

    894   Feb–Apr 1946. Further notes and comments on the Economic Survey for 1946, draft of the 1946–47 Survey, drafts of ESWP(46)3 and statement on the national situation, May 1946, by the conference of employers.

    895   Apr–June 1946. Includes memoranda of the Official Steering Committee on Economic Development, the report by the Statistics Working Party and Economic Section views on the lack of representation of basic industries in planning.

    896   June–Nov 1946. Correspondence on whether the Economic Survey should be on a financial or calendar year basis and its integration with the budget. Draft paper on the means of implementing planning decisions for the Steering Committee. Meeting of Morrison and officials, Oct 1946, on the progress of the Steering Committee on

Economic Development. Paper for a working party on policy for the production campaign publicity.

897   Nov–Dec 1946. Includes preliminary views on form and content of White Paper on planning. Draft memorandum on bottlenecks in production. Comments on memorandum on the basis for further publicity on increased production. Memorandum on opportunities for M.P.s to familiarize themselves with industrial production problems at home and abroad. Correspondence on Foreign Office representation on Committee on Economic Development and Ministerial Committee on Economic Planning. Paper on distribution of labour force. Full agenda for meeting of Steering Committee on Economic Development, 9 Dec. Copy of Economic Survey for 1947. Draft summary of paper on manpower and basic supplies.

898   Dec 1946–Jan 1947. Includes Economic Survey for 1947 and covering memorandum, together with related comments and correspondence. Notes for revised report on employment policy and investment programme. Notes for Defence Committee on reduction in direct manpower requirements for the armed forces. Draft N.J.A.C. White Paper on economic considerations affecting relations between employers and workers.

899   Jan–Feb 1947. Includes rough draft of report on Britain's productivity in 1946 with suggested revisions. Revised proof copies of economic White Paper, plus a popular edition of its text (*The battle for output 1947*) prepared by the C.O.I. Organization of work for Economic Review, 1948–1951.

900   Feb–Aug 1947. Central Office of Information. Includes notes for parliamentary questions on economic planning and on publicity for the economic White Paper. Memorandum by the Lord President on planning for expansion and draft of speech on manpower and economic planning. Notes on economic information and opinion surveys and on the proportion of administrative workers in industry.

901   Sept 1947–June 1948. Statement by the Board of Trade on production for August and September. Copies of Labour Party pamphlet, *ABC of the crisis* and *Economic bulletin, 2.* Trades Union Congress, *Interim report on the economic situation* (1947). Draft of 1948 Economic Survey and various notes on it. Some copies of fortnightly economic reports. Note on fall in prices in the USA.

902   Mar–June 1948. Includes copies of *The 1948 Short Economic Survey* (pamphlet) and *Our Money* (booklet). Some fortnightly economic reports and notes on the economic recovery programme.

903   July–Nov 1948. Includes some fortnightly economic reports. Notes on a deputation from the Executive Committee of the Trades Union Congress to the Chancellor of the Exchequer. Draft Economic Survey for 1948–1952. Notes on the long-term plan.

904–910   **Prosperity campaigns.** (131/4 parts I–VII).

904   Feb–May 1946. Correspondence on the recommendations of the Official Committee on the Prosperity Campaign (PC(OC)) and some of its minutes. Notes for and report of the production conference, 22 Mar 1946. C.A. Lidbury on new incentives for production and resulting correspondence.

905   May–July 1946. Further minutes of the official committee and notes for prosperity conferences. Jay on the economic situation.

906   July–Oct 1946. Further minutes of the official committee. Proofs of campaign pamphlet and the notes for the Lord President's press conference.

907   Oct–Nov 1946. Further minutes and memoranda of the official committee and of the Official Committee on Home Information Services.

908   Nov 1946–Jan 1947. Further minutes and memoranda of the official committee and of the Official Committee on Home Information Services. Consideration of the future and administration of the drive. *The Battle of Output – Report on Production in 1946* – C.O.I.

909   Jan–Apr 1947. Consideration of the publication of the C.O.I. pamphlet, speeches by Cripps and Dalton, minutes and memoranda of the official committee, copy of the T.U.C. production pamphlet *Down to Brass Tacks* and paper by N.F. Newsome on the winter 1947–48 plan for averting a complete industrial breakdown.

910   Apr–Dec 1947. Further minutes and memoranda of the official committee, copy of the C.O.I. publication *Production for Britain*, and other government publications emphasizing the need to increase output and exports. Includes a survey of reactions to the production drive.

915–916   **Socialization of industries: general questions.** (1400 parts I and II) Sept 1945–June 1947.

917   **Nationalization of industries: public announcements.** (1400/1) Oct–Nov 1945.

918–919   **Committee of Enquiry on Socialization of Industries.** (1400/2 parts I and II) Nov 1945–Aug 1948. Includes minutes, memoranda and correspondence of the Official Committee on Socialization of Industries (SI(O)).

927   **Nationalization proposals: points raised by various bodies.** (1400/6) Dec 1945–June 1950.

928–929   **Workers' assistance in the management of socialized industries.** (1400/8 parts I–III) Feb–July 1946.

931   **The efficiency of nationalized enterprise.** (1400/15) Dec 1946–June 1947. Includes a paper by R.H. Thornton with resulting correspondence.

933   **The Public Accounts Committee and the accounts of public boards.** (1400/19 part I) Dec 1946–Dec 1947.

937   **Organization of socialized industries.** (1400/24) July 1947–May 1949.

938   **Application of government dispersal policy to nationalized industries.** (1400/25) Apr 1947.

939–940   **Parliamentary enquiries concerning nationalized industries.** (1400/ 26 parts I and II) May 1947–Aug 1948.

944–946   **Taking stock.** (1400/29 parts I–III) July 1947–May 1949. On socialized industries and their relations with government.

947   **Meeting between ministers and chairmen of boards to discuss the organization of socialized industries.** (1400/29/1) Mar–May 1948.

950   **Price policy of socialized boards.** (1400/34) Dec 1945–Dec 1948.

951   **Methods of dealing with criticisms of socialized industries.** (1400/ 64) June–Nov 1949.

952–956   **Stocks. Monthly reports on the food situation and the position of raw materials and petroleum products in the U.K.** (1401 parts I–V) Aug 1945–Jan 1950. Briefs on reports for the Lord President and later the Production Committee.

957–976   **World food position.** (1401/1 parts I–XX) Oct 1945–Dec 1949. Reviews of the world and U.K. food situation, measures to increase agricultural production and reduce consumption. Some minutes and memoranda of the Committee on Food Supplies (WFS) and papers on rationing.

983   **The future of the Ministry of Supply and Aircraft Production.** (1410) Aug 1945–Feb 1946. Includes official report on organization of government supplies.

985–996   **Post-war organization of government publicity.** (1421 parts I–XII) Sept 1945–Nov 1949. Review of government information services and the future of the Ministry of Information. Includes minutes and memoranda and related correspondence of GEN 85, the Official Committee on Government Information Services (GIS) and the Official Committee on Home Information Services. Also some monthly progress reports by the C.O.I.

1004–1005   **Home information services.** (1421/7 parts I and II) Apr 1946–Feb 1949. Minutes and memoranda of the Ministerial and Official Committees on Home Information Services.

1033   **Dispersal of population and industry throughout the Commonwealth.** (1447/1) Nov 1947–Feb 1948.

1038   **Reduction in home service ration scales.** (1458) Oct 1945–Mar 1948.

1043–1044   **Balance of Payments Working Party.** (1510/2 parts I and II).

1043   Jan 1946–Mar 1947. Some minutes and memoranda of the working party (BPWP), Cabinet minutes and memoranda, and briefs for the ministerial committees on balance of payments.

1044   Mar–June 1947. BPWP(47)1 and resulting comments on its proposed reduction in imports, including criticism of the Treasury line by Economic Section and E.M. Nicholson. R.W.B. Clarke on balance of payments 1948–51. Correspondence and briefs for ministers on action to avert the crisis and talks with the U.S.

1045–1049   **Balance of payments crisis.** (1510/3 parts I–V).

1045   May–Aug 1947. Includes an article by Jay on the dollar situation, briefs and telegrams for the Lord President and minutes and memoranda of GEN 179.

1046   Aug 1947. Includes minutes and memoranda of GEN 179 and the Cabinet, and various briefs and telegrams from Washington.

1047   Aug–Oct 1947. Further minutes and memoranda of GEN 179 and the Cabinet. Papers on proposed remedial action, including ones by Morrison, Wilson, H., Cripps, Attlee and the Economic Planning Board.

1048   Oct 1947–May 1949. Further minutes and memoranda as well as some of the Overseas Negotiations Committee on the 1948 dollar programme. Comments on this and balance of payments statistics. Notes for Chancellor's press conference on the balance of payments and of his speech. Little after March 1948.

1049   Apr 1948–July 1949. Papers on U.K. balance in the post-transitional period and the impact of the war on the balance of payments. Includes relevant briefs.

1050–1055   **European Recovery Programme.** (1510/4 parts I–V).

    1050   June 1947–Mar 1948. Telegrams and briefs on European reconstruction and the Marshall statement, in particular for Bevin. Briefs on GEN 191 papers and on the Economic Survey 1948 and E.R.P. Official summary of the report for the Committee on European Economic Co-operation and various telegrams.

    1051   Apr–July 1948. Various resolutions and acts of the Committee on European Economic Co-operation at Paris and of the Council of the O.E.E.C. Draft statement on U.S. bilateral agreement leading to Cmd. 7447.

    1052   July–Nov 1948. Some minutes and memoranda of the Commonwealth Liaison Committee (CLC), the London Committee (ER(L)) and GEN 258. Also includes a few briefs.

    1053   Dec 1948–Jan 1949. Minutes and memoranda of GEN 258, GEN 258A and GEN 258C.

    1054   Jan–Feb 1949. Further minutes and memoranda of GEN 258A and GEN 258C.

    1055   Feb–Apr 1949. Further minutes and memoranda of GEN 258A and GEN 258C.

1060–1061   **Mid-week football and dog racing, and their effect on working time.** (1592 parts I and II) Feb 1946–Mar 1951. Various papers on the restriction of mid-week sport.

1079–1080   **Planning for expansion.** (1730 parts I and II).

    1079   Nov 1945–Aug 1947. C.H. Secord on a central economic staff and E.M. Nicholson on the difficulties of planning and allocation, Nov 1945. Then gap to March 1947, when E.E. Bridges proposed strengthening the planning staff. Draft paper by Morrison on planning, minutes of a meeting of May 1947 on the new planning machinery and steel problems, with resulting correspondence on the establishment of the Planning Board. Views of Marquand on planning. S.C. Leslie on publicity.

    1080   Sept 1947–Jan 1949. EPB(47)11 and related correspondence. Little after November 1947.

1081   **Central planning organization.** (1730/1) May 1947–June 1948. Papers on the establishment of the Economic Information Unit and the appointment of S.C. Leslie. Correspondence on the size of his and Plowden's salaries. Membership of the Economic Planning Board and its announcement. E.E. Bridges's proposals for strengthening the staff for economic planning.

1082   **Publicity on expansion of supplies.** (1730/2) June–Dec 1947.

1083–1086   **Development of colonial resources. Overseas Resources Development Bill.** (1731 parts I–IV) Mar 1947–Nov 1948.

1090–1092   **East African ground-nuts scheme.** (1731/15 parts I–III) Oct 1946–Aug 1949.

1093–1097   **Committee on Industrial Productivity.** (1732/4 parts I–V).

    1093   Mar–Nov 1947. Includes some minutes and memoranda of the Advisory Council on Scientific Policy (SP) and papers on the relationship between productivity and research and industrial morale.

    1094   Nov 1947–Jan 1948. Papers on industrial morale and transfer of responsibility for productivity from Morrison to Cripps.

1095   Jan–May 1948. Correspondence of the committee, and drafts of its report leading to CIP(48)18.

1096   May–Dec 1948. Draft progress report and comments leading up to EPB(48)14. Revised membership and terms of reference of the committee and its various panels and review of its future work.

1097   May 1949–Oct 1950. Further papers on future work, final report (CIP(50)8) and dissolution.

1099   **E.C.A. assistance for colonial development.** (1732/15/14) Oct 1949–May 1950.

1108   **Building applications for newspapers.** (1799) Oct 1948–July 1950.

1110   **Control of government expenditure.** (1811 part I) Apr 1949–Jan 1950. Treasury circular on supplementary estimates, Morrison, Aug 1949, on possible cuts in public expenditure and Attlee's circular on possible cuts.

1111   **Machinery of government and government organization committees.** (7/01) Mar 1945–May 1951. Briefs relating to the work of the Machinery of Government Committee and various pieces relating to the Government Organization Committee. Copy of Anderson's Romanes Lecture.

1112–1113   **Lord President's Office.** (7/03 parts A and B).

1112   July 1945–Nov 1950. Various papers on the office's role, including discussions on lightening Morrison's load, May 1947 overlap with C.E.P.S., and its revised functions after September 1947.

1113   Feb–Oct 1951. Draft article on the work of the Lord President 1945–50.

1115   **Departmental responsibility for mining and quarrying.** (7/04 part A) May 1948–Apr 1950.

1116   **Cabinet and Cabinet committees.** (7/07A) Aug 1945–May 1951. Views of Morrison, Aug 1945, on various committees and later administrative papers.

1118   **Controls.** (7/010) July 1949–Feb 1951. Some papers relating to the Government Organization Committee (GOC), notes and briefs on building controls, final report to the President of the Board of Trade on the examination of controls, April 1950, and draft paper by Morrison on economic controls and the public.

1121   **Lord President's Office speeches.** (7/018 part A) Aug 1948–May 1950. Correspondence about Morrison's speeches and a few transcripts.

1134–1135   **Briefs for Cabinet meetings.** (7/7/01 parts A and B) Feb 1946–Oct 1951. Includes briefs on coal, allocation of resources, rearmament and the 1951 Economic Survey.

1139–1140   **Briefs for the Economic Policy Committee.** (7/7/02 parts A and B) Oct 1947–July 1951. Includes briefs on the livestock expansion programme, Marshall Aid, wages policy, economic planning and liberalization, the reduction of capital investment, national income forecasts, the proposed White Paper on full employment and trade and sterling negotiations.

1147   **Briefs for miscellaneous ministerial committees.** (7/7/05 part A) July 1946–May 1951.

1166–1167   **Central planning of economic development.** (10/01 parts A and B).

1166   Jan–Dec 1949. Includes proofs of the 1949 Survey, briefs on economic reports and reports on the internal financial situation. E.M. Nicholson on the problems to be faced.

1167   Jan 1950–Mar 1952. Notes for Morrison on economic policy. Proof of the 1950 Economic Survey and briefs on it, economic reports and reports on the internal financial situation, and papers on budgetary policy and the committee structure for defence and economic policy.

1168–1169   **Investment programme.** (10/02 A and B).

1168   May 1949–Apr 1951. Minutes and memoranda of the Official Committee on the Control of Investment (CCI). Briefs on reports and correspondence between Stokes and Morrison on the relationship between investment and inflation.

1169   Nov 1951–1954. Very little before 1952.

1179   **Balance of payments.** (10/1/01 part A) July 1949–Apr 1951. Drafts of Morrison's paper CP(49)159 on the economic situation. Mainly briefs on the gold and dollar position.

1181   **Dollar expenditure.** (10/1/02 part A) Feb 1947–July 1951. Papers on the restriction of dollar expenditure. Gap Nov 1947–Mar 1949 and then reviews of the dollar position and briefs. Little after November 1949.

1182   **Bretton Woods Agreement.** (10/1/03) Feb 1945–Apr 1948.

1183   **Sterling area development.** (10/1/04 part A) Oct 1948–Dec 1950. Some minutes and memoranda of the Sterling Area Development Working Party (SADWP).

1184–1186   **Revaluation of the sterling/dollar exchange rate.** (10/1/07 parts A–C).

1184   Aug–Oct 1949. Briefs and papers relating to Washington negotiations leading to devaluation with notes on consequent measures. Includes correspondence between Bevan and Attlee on administrative economies.

1185   Oct 1949. Notes for Morrison's speech in the Economic Debate and notes on 'The Right Road for Britain'.

1186   Nov 1949–Feb 1950. Correspondence between Cripps and Morrison on the economy drive and copy of a speech by Morrison, Nov 1949.

1187–1188   **National Health Service.** Jan 1948–Mar 1951. Includes papers on possible economies and the control of expenditure.

1194–1195   **Labour – strikes.** (17/02 parts A and B) Aug 1946–Feb 1951.

1196   **Unofficial strikes.** (17/08) Sept–Dec 1950. Includes some papers on wages policy, one by Gaitskell with comments by E.M. Nicholson.

1197   **Labour – wages policy.** (17/1/01) Apr 1948–July 1952. Includes correspondence between Bevin and Cripps. Other papers and briefs on wages policy also included.

1200   **The state and private enterprise.** (61/01A) Aug 1948–May 1951. D.N. Chester on the nationalized industries, Wilson, H., on the state and private industry, with Attlee's comments and note of consequent meeting, May 1950.

Chapter 12   Private Papers

CAB 127 contains the private papers of various ministers and officials. The holdings for each individual vary considerably in size, but there is a subject index for the whole class. Amongst the relevant files are:

Cripps papers: Files on 1942 correspondence on reconstruction matters (72); correspondence with various departments (84); letters received on his appointment as Minister for Economic Affairs (112); and personal correspondence (117–154).

Jowitt papers: Files on planning in 1942 (164, 169, 172); reconstruction of the electricity supply industry (165); post-war agricultural policy (170); general correspondence (171); central machinery for planning (176); post-war policy proposals for the steel industry (179); note on reconstruction to Beaverbrook (182); and the post-war organization of transport (189).

Cherwell papers: All files have been retained except one on the 1952 currency crisis (202).

H. Dale papers: One file on the post-war fishing industry (229).

E.E. Bridges papers: Files on commercial policy (263); oil and Anglo-American discussions (273); and world food supplies (279). See also T 273.

Gordon Walker papers: Files on the information services.

N. Brook papers: One file on the Dalton budget leak of November 1947 (340).

Chapter 13 *Ad Hoc* Cabinet Committees (Post-war)

CAB 130 contains the records of *ad hoc* ministerial and official committees, normally called to draft a paper or to consider a particular problem. It was rare for either formal terms of reference or membership to be laid down. The most important committees in relation to economic planning have been listed but other committees have simply been noted in 13.11, with descriptive comments where necessary.

13.1 Committee on Economic Planning

The ministerial committee, under Attlee's chairmanship, dealing with economic planning whilst meetings of the Ministerial Committee on Economic Planning (CAB 134/503) were suspended owing to Morrison's illness and before the creation of C.E.P.S. (T 229) and the Economic Planning Board (T 229/26–36, CAB 134/210–214).

CAB 130/17   Minutes and Memoranda   31 Jan–7 Mar 1947   GEN 169/1st–2nd and GEN 169/1–3.

Meetings

4 Feb	**GEN 169/1st**	Untitled. GEN 169/1, 2, 3. Consideration of GEN 169/1 with regard to the fuel and manpower situation. Amendments agreed.
7 Mar	**2nd**	Untitled. Consideration of E.E. Bridges's note on points requiring ministerial consideration before the debate on the economic situation. These included co-operation with industry, fuel and power allocations (and their use to control the distribution of manpower), raw material allocations, and various economies in manpower. Agreement with his proposals for strengthening central government staff for economic planning but also on the need to associate both sides of industry with the work. This could best be provided by a Planning Board.

Memoranda

31 Jan	**GEN 169/1**	**Draft Economic White Paper – E.E. Bridges,** 1+19p. First draft of ED(47)6. A short description of the purposes and machinery of planning, a review of the period mid-1945 to Dec 1946 and analysis of the situation in 1947 and of the government's policy for dealing with it.

31 Jan	2	**Economic planning – E.E. Bridges covering the Official Steering Committee on Economic Development**, 1+5+3p appendix. See ED(47)13. Draft M.E.P. paper on changes in productivity in British industry.
3 Feb	3	**Economic planning – E.E. Bridges**, 4p. Various points in GEN 169/1 needing ministerial guidance.

13.2   Balance of Payments: Import Programme

CAB 130/19   Meetings and Memoranda   28 Apr–18 Sept 1947   GEN 179/1st–15th and GEN 179/1–30.

Meetings

12 May	**GEN 179/1st**	**Import programme for 1947–48.** BPWP(47)1 (revise). Review of the effect of the proposed change in the food cuts. General review of the import programme and whether to approach the U.S.
16 May	**2nd**	**Import programme for 1947–48.** GEN 179/2(revise). Consideration of nutritional aspects.
13 June	**3rd**	**World dollar shortage, European rehabilitation and U.K. import programme 1947–48.** GEN 179/6 and 7. The meetings were no longer official and were now ministerial. Agreement to approach the U.S. immediately on Marshall's proposals for European rehabilitation and the world dollar shortage. Then consideration of the import programme.
17 June	**4th**	**Economic recovery of Europe and American aid.** GEN 179/8, 9, 10. Approval of Bevin's line in his talks with the French. Consideration of the non-discrimination provisions of the Anglo-American Financial Agreement and how to inform the U.S. of import cuts. Agreement to make no announcement of measures to remedy the U.K. foreign exchange position before the U.S. had been informed.
28 July	**5th:1**	**Anglo-Soviet trade talks.** GEN 179/16.
	:2	**Balance of payments.** GEN 179/14. Suggestions by Bevin to remedy the situation without drastic import cuts. Dalton and Morrison supported cuts in overseas expenditure.
	:3	**Balance of payments and the International Trade Organization.** GEN 179/15.
28 July	**6th:1**	**Anglo-Soviet trade talks.**
	:2	**Balance of payments.** GEN 179/14 and 17. Further consideration of import cuts. Bevin

		proposed an Emergency Powers Act to arm the government with all the powers it might need to deal with the situation.
30 July	7th:1	**Balance of payments in the International Trade Organization.**
	:2	**Balance of payments.** Consideration of a draft of CP(47)221 and the detailed proposals therein.
4 Aug	8th:1	**Film remittances.**
	:2	**Food imports.** GEN 179/18. Agreement that it would be impossible to avoid stating that reduction would be made in purchases from hard currency sources. To avoid ration cuts it was essential that stocks should not be reduced to dangerous levels.
	:3	**Coal production.** Agreement on the target for Sept 1947–May 1948.
	:4	**Supplies and Services (Transitional Powers) Bill.** Consideration of draft bill.
5 Aug	9th	**Anglo-Soviet trade talks.**
8 Aug	10th	**Balance of payments in the International Trade Organization.**
8 Aug	11th	**Balance of payments in the International Trade Organization negotiations.** GEN 179/20.
11 Aug	12th	**Balance of payments.** GEN 179/21. Consideration of the constitution of the mission to Washington, the general approach, scarce currency and Germany.
13 Aug	13th	**Balance of payments.** GEN 179/22.
20 Aug	14th	**Balance of payments.** Meeting called by Morrison to consider the adjustments required following the decision to limit convertibility. Agreement that some measures must be announced immediately to impress the critical situation upon the public.
21 Aug	15th	**Balance of payments.** Review of the various suggestions made at GEN 179/14 for further adjustments of the national economy.

Memoranda

28 Apr	**GEN 179/1**	**Import programme 1947–48 – Dalton covering the Treasury,** 1+9+13p appendixes. Also BPWP(47)1(revise). Sets out the crisis in the external financial position and an immediate plan to cut imports and increase exports, with proposals for the long term.
15 May	2	**Import programme for 1947–48 – Official Steering Committee on Economic Development,** 5+2p annex. Revise version. Comments on GEN 179/1, in particular in relation to raw materials imports, food imports and discussion with the U.S.

17 May	3	**Import programme for 1947–48 – Official Steering Committee on Economic Development,** 6+5p annexes. Revise version. Revision of GEN 179/2(revise).
4 June	4	**Discussions with Mr. Clayton – Dalton,** 1+10+14p appendixes. Brief for the forthcoming discussions, setting out the U.K.'s foreign exchange position since Dec 1945. TN(P)(47)61 and 66 appended.
6 June	5	**Economic recovery of Europe and American aid – Bevin,** 1+2+2p annex. Sets out proposed way to approach the U.S.
9 June	6	**World dollar shortage – unsigned,** 7p. Notes for information of ministers of suggested lines of action.
11 June	7	**Discussions with Mr. Clayton – Dalton,** 1+5p. Redraft of GEN 179/4 paras. 1–24.
16 June	8	**Economic recovery of Europe and American aid – E. Bevin,** 1+1p. Text of telegram to H.M. Ambassador, Washington.
16 June	9	**Economic recovery of Europe and American aid – E. Bevin,** 1+2p. Note to be used as the basis of his discussions with the French.
16 June	10	**Brief for Mr. Marshall – Dalton,** 1+6p. Statement of the U.K. foreign exchange position and the world dollar shortage.
24 June	11	**Discussions with Mr. Clayton – Dalton,** 1+6p. Statistical tables on the dollar situation.
24 June	12	**Discussions with Mr. Clayton – E.E. Bridges,** 1+3p. Note of discussions between officials and Mr. Clayton and Mr. Douglas.
25 June	13	**Discussions with Mr. Clayton – E.E. Bridges,** 1+6p. *Aide memoire* for Bevin informally agreed by U.K. officials and Mr. Clayton for their meeting the next day.
25 July	14	**Balance of payments – Dalton,** 2p. Sets out the deteriorating situation, the need to reduce substantially the import programme and net government expenditure overseas, and the need to increase exports. There should also be discussions on convertibility and non-discrimination with the U.S.
26 July	15	**Balance of payments and the I.T.O. – Cripps,** 3p. Consideration of the line to be taken by the U.K. delegation on the I.T.O. negotiations, given the possible problems on non-discrimination due to the dollar shortage.
29 July	16	**Anglo-Soviet trade talks – Cripps,** 1+2p. Note of discussions.
29 July	17	**The dollar position – Dalton,** 1+5p. Factual statement.

5 Aug	18	**Statement on food imports for parliamentary debate on 6 Aug 1947 – Strachey,** 2p. Sets out draft statement.
5 Aug	19	**Capital investment – Morrison covering E.N. Plowden,** 1+1p. Sets out the proposed principles of the investment review.
8 Aug	20	**International Trade Organization negotiations: non-discrimination obligations – Wilson, H.,** 4p.
8 Aug	21	**Balance of payments – Dalton,** 1+2p. Note on the proposed approach, timing and arrangements of the Washington talks.
13 Aug	22	**Balance of payments – N. Brook,** 4p. Notes on the procedure to be followed in implementing the decisions announced by Attlee in the House of Commons on 6 Aug 1947.
18 Aug	23	**Supplies and Services (Extended Purposes) Act, 1947 – N. Brook,** 1p.
27 Aug	24	**Balance of payments: temporary increase in working hours – Isaacs,** 1p. On the possibilities of approaching dollar-earning and dollar-saving industries, and basic industries on a temporary increase in hours of work.
2 Aug	25	**Subordinate instruments under defence regulations – N. Brook,** 1p.
29 Aug	26	**Balance of payments – N. Brook,** 6p. Progress in implementing the decisions announced by Attlee, updating GEN 179/22.
5 Sept	27	**Balance of payments – N. Brook covering the Ministry of Supply,** 1+3p. Consideration of the policy implications of concentrating engineering production on products for export.
5 Sept	28	**Representations by the F.B.I. – N. Brook,** 5+8p annex. Note of a meeting between ministers and the F.B.I. representatives to consider *Industry and the way to recovery* by the F.B.I.
13 Sept	29	**Representations by the F.B.I. – N. Brook,** 1+4p annexes. Correspondence between Morrison and Sir Clive Baillieu arising from the meeting of 5 Sept 1947.
18 Sept	30	**Balance of payments – N. Brook,** 4p. Update of GEN 179/26 on progress in implementing the decisions announced by Attlee.

13.3 Investment Programmes Review

An official committee, under N. Brook's chairmanship, which recommended the establishment of the Investment Programmes Committee on a permanent basis (see CAB 134/437–442).

CAB 130/27   Meeting only   31 Oct 1947   GEN 200.

31 Oct	**GEN 200**	Untitled. CP(47)284. Discussion of the Investment Programmes Committee report and agreement on the need for, and rough terms of reference of, a small standing committee to assume the work of the Investment Working Party. The Board of Trade was to consider the amalgamation of Panel A regional organizations with regional building committees and the simplification of the Headquarters Building Committee approval procedure.

13.4   European Economic Co-operation Committee

Working Party on the Long-term Programme

An annual working party reporting to the main committee (CAB 134/232–254). The minutes and memoranda of the working party, omitted from this listing, refer to the long-term programmes of other individual European countries. Also included in this file are the minutes and memoranda of the European Economic Co-operation Committee Country Long-term Programme Subcommittee (GEN 250/SC) which also considered the programmes of other individual countries.

CAB 130/41   Meetings and Memoranda   16 Sept–18 Nov 1948
GEN 250/1st–10th and GEN 250/1–33.

Meetings

16 Sept	**GEN 250/1st:1**	**Independent bilateral discussions on the long-term programme.**
	:2	**Fields of activity.**
27 Oct	**2nd**	**Estimated balance of payments with France and its dependent overseas territories in 1952/53. GEN 250/1.**
30 Sept	**3rd:1**	**Production of seeds in Europe for the U.K.**
	:2	**Bilateral talks with France. GEN 250/2.**
	:3	**Long-term activity of the O.E.E.C. in the field of food and agriculture. ER(L)(48)102.**
11 Oct	**4th:1**	**Arrangements for the study of the long-term plans of other participating countries.**
	:2	**Meeting of the five finance ministers.**
	:3	**Discussion with the Norwegians.**
13 Oct	**5th:1**	**Balance of payments with Netherlands and the Netherlands East Indies in 1952/53. GEN 250/4.**
26 Oct	**7th:1**	**Timetable.**
	:2	**Pattern of trade with Western Europe. GEN 250/10.**
29 Oct	**8th:3**	**Timetable.**
12 Nov	**10th:1**	**Future work.**

Memoranda

24 Sept	**GEN 250/1**	**Estimated 1952/53 balance of payments with France and its dependent overseas territories –**

		T.A.G. Charlton and A.K. Ogilvy-Webb covering the Programmes Committee, 1+3+3p. See P(48)31st and P(48)57 annex.
30 Sept	2	Bilateral talks with France on the long-term programme – A.K. Ogilvy-Webb and E.J. Beaven, 1+4p.
9 Oct	3	Bilateral talks with France on the long-term programme – A.K. Ogilvy-Webb and E.J. Beaven, 1+5+6p.
8 Oct	4	Estimated balance of payments with the Netherlands and the Netherlands East Indies in 1952/3 – A.K. Ogilvy-Webb and E.J. Beaven, 1+7p annexes.
25 Oct	10	Trade between Western Europe and the Sterling Area – A.K. Ogilvy-Webb and E.J. Beaven covering the Board of Trade, 1+2p.
25 Oct	11	Future programme of work – E.A. Hitchman, 2p.
2 Nov	19	Anglo-Danish bilateral discussions – H. Ellis-Reece, 2p.
8 Nov	27	Copy of a letter from Mr. Ellis-Reece to Mr. Playfair, 1+4+2p annexes.

13.5 European Economic Co-operation Committee

Working Group on Long-term Programmes

An official working group, under T.L. Rowan, to consider various issues arising out of the O.E.E.C. report. It was served by a Statistical Working Group (CAB 130/42). Other minutes and memoranda relate to the long-term programmes of other countries.

CAB 130/42 Minutes and Memoranda   12 Nov 1948–18 Jan 1949
GEN 258/1st–9th and GEN 258/1–23.

Meetings

12 Nov	GEN 258/1st:1	1949/50 and long-term programmes.
16 Nov	2nd:1	The long-term and 1949/50 programmes.
	:2	Procedure for handling programmes. GEN 258/2.
	:3	European viability in 1952/3. GEN 258/1.
	:4	Publication of the O.E.E.C. report.
18 Nov	3rd:4	Next steps on the long-term programme and the programme for 1949/50.
25 Nov	5th:2	The Sterling Area and the O.E.E.C. GEN 258/4.
29 Nov	6th:1	Discussions between the Chancellor of the Exchequer and the French Prime Minister on the long-term programme. GEN 258/12.
	:2	Viability of Western Europe. GEN 258/7.
30 Nov	7th:1	Viability of Western Europe in 1952/3. GEN 258/7.

2 Dec	**8th**	**Technical aspects of the long-term programme.** LTWG(48)88 and ER(P)(48)117.
20 Dec	**9th:1**	**O.E.E.C. report on the long-term programme.**
	:2	**Future work on the long-term programme in Paris and London.** GEN 258/18.
	:3	**U.K. long-term programme: questionnaire by the O.E.E.C. secretariat.** ER(P)(48)117.

Memoranda

15 Nov	**GEN 258/1**	**European viability in 1952/3 – D.J.B. Robey, A.K. Ogilvy-Webb and E.J. Beaven covering the Economic Section,** 1+7+9p.
15 Nov	**2**	**Procedure for handling programmes – R.W.B. Clarke,** 3p.
22 Nov	**4**	**The Sterling Area and the O.E.E.C. – Treasury,** 3p.
	5	**Effect upon the U.K. of French 1952/3 programme – A.K. Ogilvy-Webb and E.J. Beaven covering the Programmes Committee,** 1+3p. Second revised version.
24 Nov	**7**	**Viability of Western Europe 1952/53 – T.A.G. Charlton, A.K. Ogilvy-Webb and E.J. Beaven covering Economic Section,** 1+9+16p addendum.
24 Nov	**9**	**Policy for bilateral discussions with the French and other O.E.E.C. countries on long-term programmes – T.A.G. Charlton, A.K. Ogilvy-Webb and E.J. Beaven,** 1+3p.
30 Nov	**10**	**Economic problems of Western Europe – A.K. Ogilvy-Webb and E.J. Beaven covering E.A.G. Robinson,** 1+11p.
4 Dec	**12**	**Discussions between the Chancellor and M. Queuille on the long-term programme – officials,** 6p. Revised version.
7 Dec	**15**	**Consideration of the long-term programme report – T.A.G. Charlton, A.K. Ogilvy-Webb and E.J. Beaven,** 1p.
13 Dec	**16**	**The longer-term problems of co-operation – D.J.B. Robey, A.K. Ogilvy-Webb and E.J. Beaven covering the French delegation to the O.E.E.C.,** 1+7p.
10 Dec	**17**	**The balance of payments in 1952/3 – D.J.B. Robey, A.K. Ogilvy-Webb and E.J. Beaven covering the Italian delegation to the O.E.E.C.,** 1+4p.
14 Dec	**18**	**Future work on the long-term programme in Paris and London – D.J.B. Robey, A.K. Ogilvy-Webb and E.J. Beaven covering T.L. Rowan,** 1+2p.
29 Dec	**19**	**O.E.E.C. long-term programmes – D.J.B. Robey, A.K. Ogilvy-Webb and E.J. Beaven covering the Foreign Office,** 1+4p.

4 Jan	20	**European viability – D.J.B. Robey, A.K. Ogilvy-Webb and E.J. Beaven covering R.W.B. Clarke, 1+6p.**
5 Jan	21	**Arrangements for future work – D.J.B. Robey, A.K. Ogilvy-Webb and E.J. Beaven covering E.A. Hitchman, 1+4p.**
14 Jan	22	**Commitments of the O.E.E.C. and remits to governments contained in the interim long-term report – Foreign Office, 1+9p.**
18 Jan	23	**Steel – D.J.B. Robey and A.K. Ogilvy-Webb and E.J. Beaven covering the Ministry of Supply, 1+4p.**

Working Groups on Long-term Programmes Group 'C' (U.K.)

The working group, under E.A. Hitchman, to consider revision of the U.K. long-term programme in the light of developments since 1 October. It was served by the Working Group on Co-ordination of Investment (CAB 130/42, GEN 258/C/I).

CAB 130/42   Meetings and Memoranda   7 Jan–30 Nov 1949   GEN 258/C/1st–9th and GEN 258/C/1–22.

Meetings

10 Jan	**GEN 258/C/1st:1**	**Constitution of sub-group 'C' (U.K.). GEN 258/C/1.**
	:2	**Work of the sub-group.**
17 Jan	2nd:1	**Coal estimates in the U.K. long-term programme.** GEN 258/C/3.
	:2	**Oil estimates in the U.K. long-term programme.** GEN 258/C/4.
	:3	**Raw cotton imports in the 1952/53 programme.** GEN 258/C/2.
28 Jan	3rd:1	**Balance of payments 1952/53. GEN 258/C/8.** Agreement to reduce the forecast dollar deficit.
	:2	**Coal estimates in the long-term programme.** GEN 258/C/6.
29 Jan	**4th**	**Section I of the report.**
4 Feb	**5th**	Untitled. GEN 258/C/11.
11 Feb	**6th**	Untitled. GEN 258/C/11(revise), 12, 13, 14.
29 Mar	**7th**	Untitled. ER(L)(49)96. On Eire agriculture.
13 Apr	**8th**	Untitled. GEN 258/C/19.
20 May	**9th**	Untitled. GEN 258/C/20.

Memoranda

7 Jan	**GEN 258/C/1**	**Constitution of the sub-group 'C' (U.K.) E.A. Hitchman, 1p.**
14 Jan	2	**Raw cotton imports in the 1952/3 programme – R.L. Marris and J. Downie covering the Board of Trade, 1+4p.**

13 Jan	3	**Coal estimates in the U.K. long-term programme – Ministry of Fuel and Power,** 2p.
14 Jan	4	**Oil estimates in the U.K. long-term programme – Ministry of Fuel and Power,** 1p.
14 Jan	5	**Future level of activity in the cotton industry – R.L. Marris and J. Downie covering the Board of Trade,** 1+9+3p appendixes.
27 Jan	6	**Coal estimates in the U.K. long-term programme – Ministry of Fuel and Power,** 1p.
28 Jan	7	**Draft report of sub-group 'C': section 1 – R.L. Marris and J. Downie,** 1+3p.
27 Jan	8	**Revision of 1952–53 balance of payments – Programmes Committee,** 9+5p annex. The situation was worse than originally thought.
1 Feb	9	**Report of sub-group 'C' – R.L. Marris and J. Downie,** 1+13+1p annex. Revision of the long-term programme considered under two headings: production and investment programmes and balance of payments estimates.
1 Feb	10	**Copper and the long-term programme: estimated world availabilities in 1952/3 and possible division of supplies between the U.K. and other participants – R.L. Marris and J. Downie covering the Statistical Working Group,** 1+5p.
3 Feb		**Addendum. Wool and the long-term programme: estimated world availabilities in 1952/3 and possible division of supplies between the U.K. and other participants – R.L. Marris and J. Downie covering the Statistical Working Group,** 1+4p.
10 Feb	11	**Eire – R.L. Marris and J. Downie,** 1+7+1p. Revise version.
10 Feb	12	**Egg and bacon prices – R.L. Marris and J. Downie,** 1p.
10 Feb	13	**Coarse grain for Eire – Treasury,** 3p.
11 Feb	14	**Coarse grain for Eire – Ministry of Agriculture and Fisheries,** 2p.
17 Feb	15	**Egg imports from Eire – R.L. Marris and J. Downie covering the Ministry of Agriculture and Fisheries,** 1+2+1p.
16 Mar	16	**Amendments to the U.K. investment programme in the light of the resolution of the Ministerial Consultative Committee – E.A. Hitchman,** 1p.
23 Mar	17	**Eire long-term programme – Ministry of Food,** 2p.
25 Mar	18	**Eire trade statistics – Commonwealth Relations Office,** 1+3p.
1 Apr	19	**U.K. long-term programme – R.L. Marris and J. Downie covering the Programmes Committee,** 1+3+4p appendix. The closer the analysis the

		more serious the prospective difficulties of achieving viability appeared.
12 May	20	**Safeguarding the U.K.'s supplies of U.K. commodities in the long-term – A.K. Ogilvy-Webb and R.L. Marris** covering the working party, 1+14+8p appendix.
25 Oct	21	**The co-ordination of investment – A.K. Ogilvy-Webb covering R. Willis**, 1+3p. On surplus production and inefficient producers.
3 Nov	22	**Future policy on co-ordination of investment – Ministry of Fuel and Power**, 4p.

13.6   Economic Situation

Ministerial committee under Attlee which considered the impact of devaluation, in particular of wages and prices.

CAB 130/53   Meeting and Memoranda   13 Sept–16 Sept 1949   GEN 298/1st and GEN 298/1–5.

Meeting

14 Sept	**GEN 298/1st:1**	**Wages, prices and profits.** GEN 298/1. Agreement on policy in these three fields following devaluation.
	:2	**Action on rise of wheat prices.** GEN 298/2 and 4. Consideration of the price of bread and of the extraction rate for flour.
	:3	**Statutory standstill on prices.** GEN 298/3. Agreement there should be no such standstill.
	:4	**Future procedure.**

Memoranda

13 Sept	**GEN 298/1**	**Wages, prices and profits – A. Johnston** covering the Working Party on Wages, Prices and Profits, 1+6+2p appendix.
13 Sept	2	**Action on rise of wheat prices – A. Johnston**, 1+4p. Telegrams from Bevin and Cripps on increasing the price of bread.
13 Sept	3	**Statutory standstill on prices – Treasury**, 2p. On the possibilities of a one-month standstill.
14 Sept	4	**Action on rise of wheat prices – A. Johnston**, 1+1p. Telegram from Cripps to Attlee.
16 Sept	5	**Action on rise of wheat prices – A. Johnston**, 1p.

13.7   Official Committee on Economic Planning and Full Employment Bill

Committee responsible for drafting the bill, with particular reference to positive powers to manufacture, purchase and sell goods. Ceased to function once the bill was dropped, see CAB 128/19, CM (51)14th:8. See also CAB 130/65, GEN 343, immediately below.

CAB 130/60   Meetings and Memoranda   9 June 1950–6 Feb 1951   GEN 324/1st–7th and GEN 324/1–17 and one *ad hoc* meeting.

Meetings

9 June	**GEN 324/1st:1**	**Economic Powers Bill.** Adequacy of powers and consideration of whether there should be separate price control legislation.
11 July	**2nd:1**	**Economic Powers Bill.** GEN 324/1.
22 Nov	**3rd**	**Economic Planning and Full Employment Bill.** GEN 324/4.
8 Dec	**4th:1**	**Control of undertakings.**
	:2	**Positive powers.**
	:3	**Powers to control production, distribution and consumption.** GEN 324/5 and 7.
	:4	**Parliamentary control.** GEN 324/4 and 6.
10 Jan	**5th:1**	**Charges orders.** GEN 324/9.
	:2	**Stimulation of investment.** GEN 324/8. Some Treasury concern at the proposals.
	:3	**Reserve of works.**
	:4	**Powers to manufacture, purchase and sell goods.** GEN 324/10.
	:5	**Strategic material.**
	:6	**Price control.**
	:7	**Future work of the committee.**
17 Jan	**6th:1**	**Parliamentary control.** GEN 324/11.
	:2	**Revised draft of the bill.** GEN 324/8.
nd	***ad hoc***	**Powers to manufacture, purchase and sell goods.** GEN 324/10, GEN 324/5th:4 and note by G.W. Penn 20 Jan 1951.
2 Feb	**7th**	**Full Employment Bill.** GEN 324/12, 14, 15, 16.

Memoranda

4 July	**GEN 324/1**	**Revised draft of the bill** – G.W. Penn, 1+20p. Draft economic powers bill attached.
12 July	**2**	**Points arising on the bill** – B.W. Gilbert, 2p.
17 Nov	**3**	**Note by the Treasury** – E.G. Compton, 1+35p. Note covering CP(50)178 and the Economic Planning and Full Employment Bill, CP(50)230, GEN 343/2 and GEN 343/1st.
20 Nov	**4**	**Note by the Treasury** – E.G. Compton, 2+1p annex. Sets out the issues to be discussed.
25 Nov	**5**	**Powers to control production, distribution and consumption** – G.W. Penn covering H.S. Kent, 1+2p. Revised draft of part of the bill.
5 Dec	**6**	**Parliamentary control** – H.S. Kent, 4p.
7 Dec	**7**	**Powers to control production, distribution and consumption** – H.S. Kent, 4p.
22 Dec	**8**	**Revised draft of the bill** – G.W. Penn, 1+22p. Draft attached.
28 Dec	**9**	**Charges orders** – Treasury, 2p.
9 Jan	**10**	**Powers to manufacture, purchase and sell goods** – Treasury, 1+3+2p. Collection of

		information recorded by earlier committees. It appeared there was scope for a further official study.
16 Jan	11	**Parliamentary control – H.S. Kent,** 1+4p. Draft report.
12 Jan		**Powers to manufacture, purchase and sell goods – G.W. Penn,** 1p.
27 Jan	12	**Positive directions to industry – Board of Trade,** 3p. An *ad hoc* subcommittee was to consider the question of government powers to manufacture, purchase and sell goods.
20 Jan		**Powers to manufacture, purchase and sell goods. Points for consideration – G.W. Penn,** 1+3p. List of points from the Board of Trade on such powers.
31 Jan	13	**Reserve of works – F.F. Turnbull,** 1+5p. Working party endorsed conclusion of the report of the Committee on the Control of Investment that the Full Employment Bill should empower local authorities to establish financial reserves for maintenance work and in special cases for new capital works.
30 Jan	14	**Further revised draft of the Full Employment Bill – G.W. Penn,** 1+28p. Draft attached.
31 Jan	15	**Report to ministers – G.W. Penn,** 1+30p annex. Draft report.
1 Feb	16	**Price control – S.J. Page covering the Working Party on Price Policy in the Socialized Industries,** 1+2p.
6 Feb	17	**Report – G.W. Penn,** 1+28+13+7p appendixes. Draft of bill and of committee's report. Bill now included positive powers.

13.8 Committee on the Economic Planning and Full Employment Bill

Ministerial committee under Morrison to review the work of the official committee on positive powers (see CAB 130/60, GEN 324 immediately above). It recommended that the bill should be dropped owing to the possible confusion of permanent legislation with emergency powers necessitated by the Korean War, and ceased to function thereafter.

CAB 130/65 Meetings and Memoranda 7 Nov 1950–21 Feb 1951 GEN 343/1st–2nd and GEN 343/1–5.

Meetings

10 Nov	**GEN 343/1st**	**Economic and Full Employment Bill.** GEN 343/2 and CP(50)178 and 230. Consideration of both negative and positive powers and

		whether the bill should promote full employment or economic planning.
9 Feb	**2nd**	**Full Employment Bill.** GEN 343/4. Agreement that the bill should not be introduced at the present time.

Memoranda

7 Nov	**GEN 343/1**	**Composition of the committee – N. Brook,** 1p.
9 Nov	**2**	**Economic Planning and Full Employment Bill – Gaitskell,** 5p. Summary of the points at issue and his recommendations. Proposes that full employment should be the basis of the bill and that it should involve two types of power: those to restrict and those to expand demand.
23 Nov	**3**	**Composition of the committee – A. Johnston,** 1p.
6 Feb	**4**	**Revised draft of the bill – Gaitskell,** 1+20p annex +29p. Also GEN 324/17. Report of the official committee and draft of the bill.
21 Feb	**5**	**Memorandum by the Minister of Works – Stokes,** 1p. Comments on socialized industries and preparation of work to counter slump.

13.9   Materials (Allocation) Committee

Steel Working Group

Official working group under F.F. Turnbull (C.E.P.S.) to review the steel allocation scheme for the Materials (Allocation) Committee (CAB 134/486).

CAB 130/66   Meetings and Memoranda   19 Mar–23 Apr 1951   GEN 361/1st–3rd and GEN 361/1–3.

Meetings

19 Mar	**GEN 361/1st**	**Home distribution control for general steel.** Arising out of PC(51)32.
13 Apr	**2nd:1**	**Steel allocation scheme.**
	:2	**Priority scheme for steel.**
20 Apr	**3rd:1**	**Home distribution control for general steel.**
	:2	**Steel allocation scheme.**
	:3	**Priority scheme for steel.**

Memoranda

10 Apr	**GEN 361/1**	**Home distribution control for general steel – F.F. Turnbull,** 5+1p.
18 Apr	**2**	**Note by the secretary – C.D. Smith,** 1+6p appendixes. Revise draft schemes for steel allocation and priority.

| 23 Apr | 3 | **Note by the secretary – C.D. Smith covering the working group,** 1+3+8p appendixes. Report on steel allocation. |

13.10   Working Party on Economic Prospects for 1952

Working party of deputy secretaries or their equivalents, under W. Strath (C.E.P.S.) with J. Atkinson (Cab. O.) as secretary, see CAB 134/266, ES(51)53. It received memoranda from relevant departments on different aspects of the existing and future economic situation. These memoranda were incorporated into a final report to the Economic Steering Committee (CAB 134/266, ES(51)57(final)).

CAB 130/71   Meetings and Memoranda   21 Sept–24 Oct 1951   GEN 380/1st–2nd
and GEN 380/1–12.

Meetings

5 Oct	**GEN 380/1st:1**	**Production prospects for 1952.** GEN 380/5.
	:2	**Wages and prices.**
16 Oct	**2nd**	**Draft report on economic prospects for 1952.** GEN 380/2, 3, 4, 5, 6, 7, 8, 9. Comments and agreed revisions.

Memoranda

21 Sept	**GEN 380/1**	**Composition and terms of reference – W. Strath,** 1+6p annexes. Annex A also ES(51)53. Annex B – note of a meeting, 11 Sept 1951, to consider ES(51)53 and to obtain agreement on the best way of preparing the general economic review.
24 Sept	2	**Inland transport problems – J.A. Atkinson covering the Ministry of Transport,** 1+5p.
27 Sept	3	**Steel supplies – J.A. Atkinson covering the Ministry of Supply,** 1+2p.
27 Sept	4	**Coal supplies – J.A. Atkinson covering the Ministry of Fuel and Power,** 1+7+1p annex.
4 Oct	5	**Production prospects for 1952 – J.A. Atkinson covering C.E.P.S.,** 5+2p appendix. See NIF(WP)(51)16.
18 Oct	7	**Draft report on economic prospects for 1952 – J.A. Atkinson,** 1+29p. Revise version.
15 Oct	8	**Restriction of production of consumer goods for home consumption – J.A. Atkinson,** 1+13+39p annexes. Also CPC(51)58 and MP(51)9.
15 Oct	9	**Investment in 1951 and 1952 – J.A. Atkinson covering F.F. Turnbull,** 1+8+14p appendixes. See ES(51)61.
13 Oct	10	***Ad hoc* meeting on transport facilities on 13 Oct 1951,** 2p. Consideration of economic prospects for 1952, with particular reference to coal imports.

18 Oct	11	*Ad hoc* **meeting on U.K. exports on 12 Oct 1951,** 3p.
24 Oct	12	**Report on economic prospects for 1952 – J.A. Atkinson covering the working party,** 1+1+18p. See ES(51)57.

13.11 Other Committees relevant to Economic Planning

The number of meetings and memoranda of the following committees can be determined by their GEN number. Hence the second committee held only one meeting (GEN 126/1st) and received one memorandum (GEN 126/1).

CAB 130/8　　　**Manpower Employed on Supplies and Equipment for the Forces at the end of 1945.**
GEN 114/1st　16 Jan 1946.

CAB 130/10　　**Extra Rations for Underground Miners.**
GEN 126/1st and GEN 126/1　27 Mar–3 Apr 1946.

Release of Bricklayers from the Forces.
GEN 129/1st　2 Apr 1946.

CAB 130/11　　**Working Party on Catering, Holiday and Tourist Services.**
GEN 137/1st–5th and GEN 134/1–19　7 May–11 Nov 1946.

Working Party on the Recruitment of Polish Miners.
GEN 137/1st–5th and GEN 137/1–3　6 June–7 Aug 1946.
Leading to the report to the Lord President's Committee (LP(46)173).

CAB 130/13　　**Location of Public Utility Projects.**
GEN 142/1st　12 July 1946.

Canadian Wheat Supplies.
GEN 144/1st　20 July 1946.

Home and Overseas Information Services.
GEN 149/1st–3rd　3 Oct 1946–17 Jan 1951.

Timber Supplies from Germany.
GEN 153/1st and GEN 153/1　23–24 Oct 1946.

CAB 130/16　　**Fuel Supplies for Industry for this Winter.**
GEN 161/1st–3rd and GEN 161/1–2　26 Nov 1946–14 Jan 1947.
A ministerial committee which considered Shinwell's original proposals and their later revision.

CAB 130/17　　**Electricity Generating Capacity.**
GEN 172/1st　10 Mar 1947.

CAB 130/19   **White Fish Industry.**
GEN 177/1st–2nd and GEN 177/1–8   11 Apr–15 July 1947.

CAB 130/20   **Proposed Erection of a Power Station at Bankside.**
GEN 182/1st   21 May 1947.
Arose out of CM(47)47th.

CAB 130/21–6   **European Economic Co-operation (London).**
   21   GEN 188/1st–37th   8 July–4 Dec 1947.
   22   GEN 188/38th–80th   12 Dec 1947–2 June 1948.
   23   GEN 188/1–70   7 July–4 Oct 1947.
   24   GEN 188/71–136   6 Oct 1947–18 Feb 1948.
   25   GEN 188/137–184   19 Feb–13 Apr 1948.
   26   GEN 188/185–236   13 Apr–5 June 1948.
Until 17 July 1947 entitled the European Reconstruction (London Committee). It was set up under R.W.B. Clarke (Treasury) as a subcommittee of the Official Steering Committee on Economic Development (CAB 134/186–193). Its purpose was to prepare the U.K. case to be submitted to Paris, and the case to be submitted to Washington later in 1947 when the bilateral negotiations took place between the U.S. and the various European countries. In addition it co-ordinated the instructions to be given to the Paris committees. The subcommittee's papers continue in CAB 134/232–54 with its development into a committee. The papers of some of its working parties are also in this class.

CAB 130/27   **Official Committee on the Civil Supply Functions of the Ministry of Works and the Ministry of Supply.**
GEN 189/1st and GEN 189/1   22 July–16 Oct 1947.

European Economic Co-operation Committee of Ministers.
GEN 191/1st–2nd and GEN 191/1–7   16 July–8 Aug 1947.

Expansion of Oil Refinery Capacity.
GEN 193/1st   2 Aug 1947.

Discussions with Eire Ministers.
GEN 194/1st–6th and GEN 194/1–4   17 Sept 1947–20 June 1948.

Sterling Area Conference.
GEN 195/1st–6th and GEN 195/1–6   18 June–29 Oct 1947.

Definition of Functions of the Colonial Development Corporation and the Overseas Food Campaign.
GEN 196/1st   10 Oct 1947.

The 1948 Dollar Programme.
GEN 197/1st and GEN 197/1   11–14 Oct 1947.

Exchange Requirements Committee: Working Parties on Purchases of Rice and Services Oil Requirements.
GEN 199/1st–2nd   29 Oct–1 Dec 1947.

CAB 130/28   **European Economic Co-operation (London): Working Party on U.K. Aid Policy.**
GEN 202/1st–11th and GEN 202/1–18   14 Nov–18 Dec 1947.

European Economic Co-operation (London): Economic Commission for Europe Working Party.
GEN 204/1st–9th and GEN 204/1–40   10 Dec 1947–4 June 1948.

CAB 130/29   **European Economic Co-operation (London): Working Party on Conditions Affecting the Use of Supplies under the European Recovery Programme.**
GEN 207/1st and GEN 207/1–5   22 Dec 1947–12 Feb 1948.

European Economic Co-operation (London): Working Party on Stockpiling.
GEN 208/1st–4th and GEN 208/1–15   30 Dec 1947–28 May 1948.

European Economic Co-operation (London): Executive Committee.
GEN 209/1st–33rd and GEN 209/1–65.
Under R.W.B. Clarke.

CAB 130/31–3   **European Economic Co-operation (London): Subcommittee on Programmes.**
31   GEN 212/1st–8th and GEN 212/1–30   12 Jan–22 Apr 1948.
32   GEN 212/31–44   14 Feb–24 Feb 1948.
33   GEN 212/45–75   23 Feb–10 May 1948.
The subcommittee, under H.T. Weeks (C.E.P.S.), was set up in accordance with GEN 188/105 (CAB 130/24), (also EPC(47)33, see CAB 134/215), to develop, in consultation with the Exchange Requirements Committee, the Export Committee, the Investment Programmes Committee, and the Overseas Negotiations Committee, the programme of U.K. requirements under E.R.P.; to examine the effect of E.R.P. on the general economic future of the U.K., including home investment and exports; to consider what export commitments to other participants we should be prepared to make; and to prepare an estimate of U.K. balance of payments under E.R.P. during the period 1 April 1948 to 30 March 1949. Papers tend to relate to particular commodities. A working party was set up (CAB 130/31, GEN 212/2nd) to consider the economic consequences of receiving no E.R.P. aid and reported in March 1948 (CAB 130/33, GEN 212/54).

CAB 130/34   **European Economic Co-operation (London): Subcommittee on Supplies.**
GEN 213/1st–15th and GEN 213/1–18   12 Jan–8 Mar 1948.

White Fish Industry.
GEN 214/1st–5th and GEN 214/1–13   13 Jan–20 July 1948.

Overseas Negotiations Committee: Working Party on Exports of Finished Steel.
GEN 215/1   14 Jan 1948.

Supply of Materials to the Hostel Programme.
GEN 216/1st   13 Jan 1948.

CAB 130/35   **European Economic Co-operation (London): Subcommittee on Supplies: Working Party on Accounting Procedure.**
GEN 217/1st–10th and GEN 217/1–11   16 Jan–4 June 1948.

The Statement on Personal Incomes, Costs and Prices.
GEN 218/1st   30 Jan 1948.

European Economic Co-operation (London): Subcommittee on Programmes: Working Party on Economic Consequences of E.R.P.
GEN 219/1st–8th and GEN 219/1–7   2 Feb–15 Mar 1948.

CAB 130/37   **Monopolistic Practices Bill.**
GEN 224/1st   16 Mar 1948.

Economic Relations with Eire.
GEN 225/1st–2nd   22 Mar–1 Apr 1948.

Food Policy.
GEN 232/1st   11 May 1948.

European Economic Co-operation (London): Working Party on the Draft Anglo-U.S. Bilateral Agreement.
GEN 234/1st–2nd and GEN 234/1–3   23 May–9 June 1948.

CAB 130/38   **European Economic Co-operation: Working Party on the Supervision of Efficient Use.**
GEN 236/1st–3rd and GEN 236/1–3   4–15 June 1948.
On the efficient use of external aid and indigenous resources.

Preparation for Meeting of Commonwealth Prime Ministers.
GEN 237/1st–5th and GEN 237/1–7   15 June–4 Oct 1948.
Includes consideration of the long-term programme for E.R.P.

The Place of Agriculture in the National Economy.
GEN 238/1st   15 June 1948.

CAB 130/40   **Working Party on Non-Dollar Balance of Payments.**
GEN 247/1st–2nd and GEN 247/1–4   12 Aug–7 Oct 1948.

Working Party to Prepare Briefs on the General Economic Situation for the Commonwealth Prime Ministers' Meeting.
GEN 248/1st–5th and GEN 248/1–25   9 Aug–4 Oct 1948.

CAB 130/41   **The Size of the Armed Forces in the Years 1949, 1950 and 1951.**
GEN 254/1st–4th and GEN 254/1–2   25 Oct–17 Nov 1948.

Productivity in the Socialized Industries.
GEN 255/1st   1 Nov 1948.

CAB 130/44   **Long-term Programme for Europe.**
GEN 263/1st   3 Dec 1948.

European Economic Co-operation Committee: Export of Strategic Materials to Russia and Eastern European Countries.
GEN 265/1–3   22 Dec 1948–8 Mar 1949.

CAB 130/45   **Working Party on Security of Economic and Industrial Information about the U.K.**
GEN 275/1st–4th and GEN 275/1–6   18 Feb–30 May 1949.

CAB 130/46   **Programmes Committee Working Party on Commodities (1949/50 Programme).**
GEN 283/1st–3rd and GEN 283/1   4–13 April 1949.

European Economic Co-operation Committee: Working Party on Reports on Internal Finances.
GEN 290/1–18   1 June–19 July 1949.

CAB 130/47   **Programmes Committee: Working Party on Imports of Dollar Cotton.**
GEN 292/1st–5th and GEN 292/1–11   27 May–26 Aug 1949.

CAB 130/48–51 **Working Party on the Oil Expansion Programme.**
48   GEN 295/1st–69th   10 June 1949–6 Apr 1951.
49   GEN 295/1–31   9 June–29 Nov 1949.
50   GEN 295/32–70   29 Nov 1949–12 Apr 1950.
51   GEN 295/71–114   5 Apr 1950–23 May 1951.
The working party of officials was set up (see CAB 134/220, EPC(49)17th:2) to make a comprehensive examination of the oil position in the light of the oil expansion programme. An urgent report was to be produced on the consequences of the programme for the dollar and overall balance of payments, and the long-term oil requirements of the U.K. and the sterling area.

CAB 130/52   **Working Party on the Oil Expansion Programme: Subcommittee on U.K. Consumption (General).**
GEN 295/A/1st–3rd and GEN 295/A/1–8   11 July–23 Aug 1949.

Working Party on the Oil Expansion Programme: Oil Working Party.
GEN 295/A/1st–12th and GEN 295/A/1–9   5 July 1951–29 Jan 1952.
Set up to examine the impact on the U.K. of losing Persian oil.

Working Party on the Oil Expansion Programme: Subcommittee on U.K. Consumption (Road and Rail).
GEN 295/B/1st–14th and GEN 295/B/1–33   7 July–8 Sept 1949.

CAB 130/53   **Commonwealth Finance Ministers' Conference Working Party.**
GEN 297/1st–4th and GEN 297/1–22   4–11 July 1949.

CAB 130/54–5   **Programmes Committee: Committee of Four.**
       54   GEN 299/1–36   28 Apr–14 Nov 1950.
       55   GEN 299/1st–34th   27 Sept 1949–15 Nov 1950.
Initially a Committee of Three, comprising C.T. Saunders (ch, C.S.O.), H.A. Turner (C.E.P.S.) and M. Stevenson (Try), was formed on the basis of P(49)119 (see CAB 134/617), to save the time of the full Programmes Committee. It examined the 1949/50 dollar import programme to ensure that it was in line with the criteria agreed by the Programmes Committee and to establish the implications of making any reductions in the programme. In October 1949, J.A. Jukes (Ec. Sect.) joined and it became the Committee of Four. The committee began to consider the import programme for future years. At that time, A.C. Sparks (Try) replaced C.T. Saunders as chairman, although the latter remained a member, with M. Stevenson leaving. In May 1950 D.A.V. Allen (C.E.P.S.) and M.F.W. Hemming (Ec. Sect.) replaced H.A. Turner and J.A. Jukes respectively.

CAB 130/56   **Iron and Steel Bill.**
GEN 302/1st–2nd   31 Oct–7 Nov 1949.

Ad hoc Inter-departmental Committee on U.S. Investment in the Sterling Area.
GEN 303/1st–5th and GEN 303/1–22   1 Nov 1949–28 Feb 1950.

Customs Union.
GEN 304/1st   14 Nov 1949.

CAB 130/57   **Preparations for Meetings of Commonwealth Officials on Economic Affairs in Colombo January 1950.**
GEN 305/1st–6th and GEN 305/1–33   25 Nov–31 Dec 1949.

Wool Textile Industry Development Council Order.
GEN 308/1st   5 Dec 1949.

CAB 130/58   **European Economic Co-operation Committee: Working Party on Manpower.**
GEN 312/1st   9 Jan 1950.

Working Party on 1950–1951 O.E.E.C. Submissions of Other Participants.
GEN 313/1st–5th and GEN 313/1–31   9 Jan–14 Apr 1950.

Strikes at Electricity Generating Stations.
GEN 314/1st and GEN 314/1   19 Jan–24 Jan 1950.

Farm Price Review.
GEN 315/1st and GEN 315/1   14 Mar–15 Mar 1950.

Transport Charges.
GEN 316/1st   21 Mar 1951.

CAB 130/59   **National Economy in War.**
GEN 317/1st–7th and GEN 317/1–14   21 Mar–11 Oct 1950.
Associated with this committee was the Working Party on
Financial and Economic Relations with the U.S. and other [sic]
Commonwealth Countries, which received a memorandum on the
history of the U.K. balance of payments in World War II (GEN
317/A/5).

Future Policy towards the Building Industry.
GEN 320/1st–4th and GEN 1–11   25 Apr 1950–5 Apr 1951.

CAB 130/60   **Proposals for the Integration of Western European Coal and Steel
Industries.**
GEN 322/1st–4th and GEN 322/1–10   11 May–27 July 1950.
In May 1950 a meeting (GEN 322/1st) decided to appoint an
official committee to consider the proposals (see CAB 134/293).
A group of ministers under Cripps (Ch. of Exchequer) was then
appointed in accordance with CM(50)38th:5 (CAB 128/17) to
examine, on the basis of the report (CP(50)128, see CAB 129/40)
of the Official Working Party (see CAB 134/294–7) set up by the
official committee, the economic implications of proposals for the
integration of the coal and steel industries of Western Europe; to
keep in touch with the progress of international discussions
proceeding in Paris on the subject; and to report to the Economic
Policy Committee.

CAB 130/61   **Working Party on Long-term Economic Relations with Japan.**
GEN 326/1st–8th and GEN 326/1–13   26 June 1950–22 Feb
1951.

CAB 130/62   **Working Group on the O.E.E.C. Third Report.**
GEN 328/1st–11th and GEN 328/1–20   4 July 1950–15 Mar
1951.

East-West Trade.
GEN 330/1st and GEN 330/1   17 July–19 July 1950.

CAB 130/63   **Working Group on Briefs for the Commonwealth Meeting on
General Economic and Trade Questions.**
GEN 332/1st–6th and GEN 1–11   9 Aug–18 Sept 1950.

Meetings of Ministers (Defence and National Economy).
GEN 333/1st–2nd and GEN 1–4   7–22 Sept 1950.
Includes memorandum on the economic impact of increased
defence expenditure (GEN 333/1).

CAB 130/64   **Decontrol of Apples and Softwood Buying.**
GEN 335/1st and GEN 335/1   14 Sept–15 Sept 1950.

Proposed International Tin Agreement.
GEN 339/1st   24 Oct 1950.

CAB 130/65 **Briefs for the Prime Minister's Visit to Washington.**
GEN 347/1–2   3–4 Dec 1950.

Socialization of Industries Committee: Subcommittee on Relations with Workers in Socialized Industries.
GEN 349/1st–7th and GEN 349/1–11   29 Dec 1950–10 May 1951.

Defence Production Programme.
GEN 351/1 and GEN 351/1st   6 Jan 1950.

Working Party on Cereal Feedingstuffs Supplies.
GEN 352/1st–2nd and GEN 352/1–7   1 Jan–8 Feb 1951.

Coal.
GEN 353/1st   26 Jan 1951.
Review of allocation of coal to industry as requested in PC(51)4.
See CAB 134/650.

CAB 130/66 **Expenditure on the Social Services.**
GEN 357/1st and GEN 357/1–2   14 Mar–15 Mar 1951.

Exemption of Utility Goods from Purchase Tax.
GEN 358/1st and GEN 358/1   14 Mar–16 Mar 1951.

CAB 130/67 **Persian Oil.**
GEN 363/1st–25th and GEN 363/1–14   1 May–11 Oct 1951.

CAB 130/68 **Programmes Committee: Statistical Group.**
GEN 364/1st–5th and GEN 364/1–6   9 May–21 May 1951.

CAB 130/69 **Relations with Workers in the Socialized Industries.**
GEN 372/1st–2nd   28 June–9 July 1951.

CAB 130/71 **Working Party on Fuel Economy.**
GEN 378/1st–5th and GEN 378/1–15   18 Aug 1951–9 Jan 1952.
See CAB 134/97.

Programmes Committee: Statistical Group.
GEN 381/1st–7th   25 Sept–2 Oct 1951.

Manpower for the Mines and Railways.
GEN 381/1st   5 Oct 1951.

Iron Ore.
GEN 384/1st   11 Oct 1951.

Chapter 14 Lord President's Committee (Post-war)

For papers before 1946, see CAB 71/1–22. The committee remained the major committee co-ordinating domestic policy, although it lost the main responsibility for economic policy in October 1947 to the Economic Policy and Production Committees (CAB 134/215–230 and CAB 134/635–652). As the committee responsible for the legislative programme, however, it retained an interest in such issues as building and economic controls where fresh legislation was needed.

Between 1945 and October 1947, many of its economic responsibilities were delegated to its Industrial Subcommittee (CAB 71/26–27), the ministerial Committee on Economic Planning (CAB 134/503) and the Official Steering Committee on Economic Development (CAB 134/186–193). For Morrison's views on economic planning at this time, see *Public Administration*, XXV (1947) pp 3–9.

It received regular statistical reports.

Terms As CAB 71/11.
(Oct 1947) To deal with questions of domestic policy outside the economic field which are not specifically assigned to other Committees.

Members As CAB 71/11 (March 1947) Paymaster-Gen. added (April 1947) Ld Privy Seal added.
(Oct 1947) Ld President (ch.); Ch. of Exchequer (or Fin. Sec.); Home Sec.; S./S. Scotland; Mins. of Defence, Labour & N.S., Health, Education, Food, Town & Country Planning, Nat. Insurance; Ch. D. Lancaster. (Feb 50) Min. of Civil Aviation replaced Min. of Defence.

Secs. W.S. Murrie (Cab. O.), E.M. Nicholson (Ld Pres. O.) and A. Johnson (Ld Pres. O.). (Oct 1948) J.H. Lidderdale (Ld Pres. O.) and J.A.R. Pimlott (Cab. O.) replaced Murrie. (Dec 1949) Lidderdale left. (June 1951) D. Le B. Jones (Ld Pres. O.) added.

14.1 Meetings and Memoranda

CAB 132/1 Meetings 11 January–20 December 1946 LP(46)1–42.

11 Jan	LP(46)1st:2	Coal: working of open-cast coal on the Wentworth Woodhouse estate. LP(46)3 and 4. To go to Cabinet.
	:3	Publication of statistics. LP(46)5.
18 Jan	2nd:1	National building programme. LP(46)8.
	:2	Housing subsidies. LP(46)9 and 10. Consideration of a House Building Corporation.

25 Jan	3rd:3	**Agriculture: agricultural minimum wage.** LP(46)15 and 19.
1 Feb	4th:3	**Regional organization.** LP(46)17.
	:5	**Shipbuilding industry.** LP(46)7.
8 Feb	5th:2	**Highway policy.** LP(46)22, 23, 30. Morrison and Dalton agreed that to maintain maximum flexibility specific commitments should not be made. This would help with employment policy.
15 Feb	6th:1	**Highway policy: Forth Road Bridge.** LP(46)37.
	:3	**Housing: application of the Essential Work Order to permanent houses.** LP(46)29.
	:4	**Town and country planning: Greater London planning:** LP(46)32.
22 Feb	7th:3	**Housing: application of the Essential Work Order to permanent houses.** Agreement that the Essential Work Order could be used for the building of new factories, factory reconversion and permanent housing.
	:4	**Employment of unemployed men in development areas on building work.** LP(46)38.
1 Mar	8th:5	**Town and country planning.** LP(46)50.
8 Mar	9th:1	**Agricultural prices: February 1946 review.** LP(46)54 and 56.
	:2	**Bulk purchase of cotton.** LP(46)55. Continuation recommended.
	:4	**Distribution of industry.** LP(I)(46)16.
15 Mar	10th:5	**Progressing of schemes in the Scottish development area.** LP(46)58 and 60.
	:6	**Census of distribution.** LP(46)62.
29 Mar	11th:3	**Wages policy.** LP(46)71. Consideration of a National Industrial Conference. General agreement was that the report represented all that could be done at present but, in future, government would probably have to play an increasingly positive role.
	:5	**Employment and unemployment situation and improvement of basic services in the development areas.** LP(I)(46)17 and 19. Morrison was to organize a ministerial committee to review progress.
5 Apr	12th:3	**New towns.** LP(46)79.
	:5	**Road haulage organization.** LP(46)74 and 83.
12 Apr	13th:2	**New Towns Bill.** CP(46)142 and LP(46)90.
	:3	**New towns.** LP(46)79 and 88.
	:4	**Town and country planning: portable cost of works payments.** LP(46)80.
	:5	**Supplies of fuel to industry.** LP(I)(46)22. Approval of regional advisory machinery.
3 May	15th:2	**Distribution of industry.** Detailed work was to be delegated to the Distribution of Industry Subcommittee.

	:3	**Incentives to production.** LP(46)105. Disagreement on whether LP(46)105 had concentrated unduly on the export of consumer goods. Some ministers wanted to increase domestic supply as an incentive to production.
10 May	16th:1	**Disposal of surplus stores and derequisitioning of industrial and other premises.** LP(46)106.
	:2	**Control of investment and statistics for employment policy.** LP(46)95 and 96.
	:3	**Recruitment of labour to undermanned industries.** LP(46)89. Greater direction of labour considered.
	:5	**Agricultural wages.** LP(46)98, 108, 111, 112. The recent increase in the agricultural minimum wage should be prevented from causing wage increases elsewhere.
17 May	17th:1	**Prices of products of coal carbonization.** LP(46)110.
	:3	**Road haulage organization.** LP(46)116.
	:5	**Incentives to production.** Consumer goods were now being diverted to miners' areas. It was to be announced that miners had not previously had their fair share, not that they were getting an increased share.
24 May	18th:1	**National building programme.** LP(46)121.
	:4	**Controls.** LP(46)113. Approval of the report.
31 May	19th:2	**Agricultural prices and wages.** LP(46)129.
	:3	**Report of the Cotton Industry Working Party.** LP(46)136.
4 June	20th:2	**Disposal of surplus stores and service holdings of building and civil engineering equipment.** LP(46)131, 132 and 139.
	:3	**Export group and industrial organization.** LP(46)126 and 140.
	:4	**Cotton Buying Commission.** LP(46)141.
6 June	21st:3	**Supplies of soap and linseed oil.** LP(46)144.
21 June	22nd:1	**Regulation of race meetings in the interests of production.** LP(46)148.
	:2	**Coal.** CP(46)232, 237, 242.
28 June	23rd:1	**Wages policy.** Consideration of the National Industrial Conference.
	:3	**Methods of purchase of non-ferrous metals.** LP(46)154. Disagreement over the reopening of the London Metal Exchange.
	:7	**Cotton Buying Commission.** LP(46)153.
5 July	24th:2	**Direction of building labour.** LP(46)165, 170, 171. Approval of LP(46)165, although there was doubt over the proposals' effectiveness.
	:3	**Agricultural policy.** LP(46)155.
	:4	**Agricultural prices.** LP(46)162.
12 July	25th:5	**Iron and steel.** LP(46)168. All ministers to scrutinize their requirements.

	:6	**Diversion of labour to industries of national importance.** LP(46)175 and MEP(46)8. Concern that overproduction of non-essentials was preventing the necessary diversion.
	:7	**Disposal of surplus stores and derequisitioning of factory premises.** LP(46)172.
17 July	26th:1	**Price control of building materials.** LP(46)178.
	:2	**Cost of living index.** LP(46)181.
	:4	**Resettlement training scheme.** LP(DI)(46)39.
19 July	27th:1	**Agricultural prices.**
	:2	**Coal situation.** LP(46)158. Some improvement reported. It would not be possible to see the prospects for winter until September.
	:3	**Recruitment for the coal-mining industry.** To be considered by the ministerial Coal Committee.
	:4	**Marginal production in agriculture.** LP(46)163.
	:7	**Iron and steel prices, and coke prices.** LP(46)187.
	:9	**Agricultural policy.** LP(46)188.
26 July	28th:2	**Economic Survey for 1946/47.** MEP(46)5, 7, LP(46)175. Discussion of the country's economic prospects and whether the government had adequate powers to implement its plans.
	:3	**Wages policy.** LP(46)186, 190, 192. Disagreement between Isaacs and Shinwell over the degree of government intervention.
	:4	**Exchange Control Bill.** LP(46)197.
	:5	**Cotton Buying Commission: compensation to cotton merchants and their staff.** LP(46)193. Proposals accepted.
12 Aug	29th:2	**Co-ordination of the building and civil engineering programme.** LP(46)198. Proposals accepted.
	:3	**Transfer from the Board of Trade to the Ministry of Supply of functions relating to the price control of engineering consumer goods.** LP(46)203. Proposals accepted.
	:7	**Motorways Bill.** LP(46)191. Proposals accepted.
	:8	**Farm prices.** LP(46)210.
	:9	**Importation of fresh fruit and vegetables.** LP(46)211.
	:11	**Cost of living index figure.** LP(46)216.
	:12	**Regulation of sport in the interests of coal production.** LP(46)218. Proposals accepted.
20 Sept	30th:3	**Economic controls.** A review of the adequacy of economic controls over essential materials was arranged.
	:4	**Disposal of government surplus stores.** LP(46)225.
27 Sept	31st:1	**Agricultural machinery.** LP(46)226.

	:2	**Restrictive practices.** LP(46)202. Outline proposals approved.
	:4	**Civil engineering equipment.** LP(46)229. An official committee was to examine the overall position.
	:8	**Statistical review: coal.** LP(46)231. A vigorous publicity campaign calling for greater effort from miners was required.
4 Oct	32nd:1	**Business of the committee.** CP(46)357.
	:2	**National building programme.** LP(46)236.
	:3	**Raw Cotton Buying Commission.** LP(46)235. Proposals approved.
11 Oct	33rd:1	**Administration of Wales and Monmouthshire.** LP(46)241 and 244.
	:2	**Industry and employment in Scotland.** Agreement for a White Paper.
	:3	**Disallowance of unemployment benefit on refusal of suitable employment.** LP(46)239.
18 Oct	34th:1	**Timber: supplies of timber and plywood, prices, allocation and controls.** LP(46)246, 247 and 249.
	:2	**Industrial Organization Bill.** LP(46)252.
25 Oct	35th:1	**Steel supplies.** LP(46)250. Agreement to continue present allocation procedure.
	:2	**Aluminium supplies.** LP(46)248.
1 Nov	36th:1	**Disposal of government surplus stores.** LP(46)254 and 261.
	:2	**Wages policy.** LP(46)255 and 259. Debate between Shinwell and Isaacs over whether the National Joint Advisory Council was an adequate instrument for correcting wage differentials whilst preventing a general wage increase.
	:3	**Cost of living index figure.** LP(46)260.
8 Nov	37th:2	**Agricultural prices.** LP(46)257.
	:3	**Fuel allocations to industrial consumers in the winter of 1946/47.** LP(46)265 and 267. A revised scheme of allocation to be prepared.
22 Nov	38th:2	**Steel supplies: end uses of steel sheets.** LP(46)272.
	:3	**Rail transport.** LP(46)269, 270, 274, 275.
	:6	**Cotton industry: grants for re-equipment of cotton spinning mills.** LP(46)271. Cripps could see no alternative to nationalization if the suggested scheme failed.
	:7	**Control of Employment (Civil Servants) Order.** LP(46)264.
29 Nov	39th:1	**Disposal of government surplus stores.** LP(46)276.
	:2	**Steel supplies: end uses of steel.** LP(46)278. Agreement that there should be no change of allocations for the last quarter of 1946.

6 Dec	**40th:1**	**Fishing Industry Bill.** LP(46)283 and 284.
	:2	**Building industry: wages and output.** LP(46)282. A group of ministers was to consider the more effective use of and possible supplements to existing building controls.
	:3	**Cost of living index figure.** LP(46)285. The Cost of Living Advisory Committee to report on revising the index.
13 Dec	**41st**	**Fishing Industry Bill.** LP(46)283 and 284. Disagreement over ownership of the industry, given its importance in the economy.
20 Dec	**42nd:4**	**Raising the school leaving age.** LP(46)287 and 295. If this was to be achieved education required a higher priority in the building programme. A decision was deferred until the Economic Survey for 1947.
	:5	**Building priority for hospitals and allied purposes.** LP(46)291 and 294.
	:6	**Industrial restrictions on voluntary recruitment.** LP(46)293. Consideration was postponed until the Economic Survey for 1947.

CAB 132/2 Memoranda 2 January–22 March 1946 LP(46)1–69.

7 Jan	**LP(46)3**	**The working of open-cast coal on the Wentworth Woodhouse Estate** – Shinwell, 2p.
8 Jan	**4**	**Wentworth open-cast working** – Silkin, 2p.
7 Jan	**5**	**Publication of statistics** – Dalton, 1p.
8 Jan	**7**	**Shipbuilding industry** – Alexander and Barnes **covering the Shipbuilding Committee**, 5+12p. The report estimated how far the probable demand over the next 10 years would fully employ labour and capacity.
8 Jan	**8**	**National building programme. Labour demands and proposed ceilings for quarters ending 31 March and 30 June 1946** – Tomlinson, 2+3p appendixes.
15 Jan	**9**	**Housing subsidies** – Bevan, 3+2p appendix.
16 Jan	**10**	**Revision of housing subsidies: Scotland** – Westwood, 4+2p appendix.
22 Jan	**15**	**Agricultural minimum wage** – Williams, 5+2p appendix. Concern about long-term labour supply in agriculture.
22 Jan	**17**	**Regional organization** – Dalton covering the Treasury, 1+8+5p appendixes.
24 Jan	**19**	**Agricultural minimum wage** – Isaacs, 1p.
4 Feb	**22**	**Highway programme** – Barnes, 4+3p appendix.
4 Feb	**23**	**Highway communications in the development areas** – Barnes, 2+7p appendix.
5 Feb	**29**	**Application of the essential work order to permanent housing** – Isaacs, 2p.
6 Feb	**30**	**Highway programme** – Westwood, 1p.

8 Feb	**32**	**Greater London planning – Silkin**, 5p.
13 Feb	**37**	**Forth Road Bridge – Westwood**, 2p.
13 Feb	**38**	**Employment of unemployed men in the development areas on building work – Isaacs**, 2p. All that was practicable was being done.
4 Mar	**52**	**Future of the iron and steel industry – Wilmot covering the British Iron and Steel Federation and the Ministry of Supply**, 2+27+11+1p annex +4p.
5 Mar	**54**	**Review of agricultural prices, Feb 1946 – Williams, Westwood and Ede**, 2+7p annex +3p appendix. The world food situation made it impossible to assume the continued application of the principle of a declining trend in prices.
6 Mar	**55**	**Bulk purchase of cotton – Cripps**, 4+9+2p annexes. Cripps recommended continuing the present system, against the advice of the Bulk Purchase Official Committee.
7 Mar	**56**	**1946 review of agricultural prices – Summerskill**, 2p.
13 Mar	**58**	**Progressing of scheme in the Scottish development area – Cripps**, 1p.
14 Mar	**60**	**Progressing of scheme in the Scottish development area – Westwood**, 2p.
13 Mar	**62**	**Census of distribution – Cripps**, 2+1p annex +1p appendix.

CAB 132/3   Memoranda   23 Mar–18 June 1946   LP(46)70–150.

27 Mar	**LP(46)71**	**Wages policy – Morrison covering the Official Working Party on Wages Policy**, 1+8p. Also W(46)10(final). The report outlined the existing constitutional machinery, reviewed the tendencies in wage settlements which might conflict with short- and long-term employment policy and proposed a permanent link between government and both sides of industry in a National Industrial Conference.
26 Mar	**74**	**Future of the road haulage organization – Barnes**, 4p.
29 Mar	**79**	**New towns – Silkin**, 4p.
5 Apr	**80**	**'Portable' cost of works payments – Silkin**, 10p.
3 Apr	**81**	**Training of building craftsmen – Isaacs and Tomlinson**, 4p.
3 Apr	**83**	**Future of the road haulage organization – Smith**, 2p.
10 Apr	**88**	**Finance of new town development – Silkin**, 1+4p.
9 Apr	**89**	**Problem of recruiting labour in certain undermanned industries of national importance – Isaacs covering the Official**

		Labour Co-ordinating Committee, 1+4+2p appendix. The report did not deal with wage inducements but recommended long-term measures specific to each industry.
23 Apr	95	**Control of investment – Morrison covering the Investment Working Party**, 1+4p. Also ED(46)5(final). The report proposed measures to postpone, during 1946, less essential investment in areas of labour shortage. It recommended a £150 million reduction in gross investment subject to the revised economic survey. Eight priority classes of investment are given.
23 Apr	96	**Statistics for employment policy – Morrison covering the Working Party on Statistics for Employment Policy**, 1+25+3p. Lists all information available or required for an integrated system.
23 Apr	97	**Economic planning – W.S. Murrie covering the Ministerial Committee on Economic Planning**, 1+4p. Copy of the minutes of GEN 115/2nd.
25 Apr	98	**Agricultural wages legislation – Williams**, 4p.
26 Apr	100	**Composition and terms of reference of Distribution of Industry Subcommittee – E.E. Bridges**, 1p. Also LP(DI)(46)1.
26 Apr	101	**Termination of the Industrial Subcommittee – E.E. Bridges**, 1p. Also LP(I)(46)23.
30 Apr	104	**Building labour in the development areas – Belcher covering Panel A**, 1+3p.
30 Apr	105	**Incentives to production – Morrison covering the Official Working Party on Incentives to Production**, 1+4+4p annex. Also GEN 105/5. Despite the opposition of the rest of the working party, the Ministry of Fuel and Power wanted the scheme of inducements for coal-miners put before ministers.
2 May	106	**Disposals and derequisitioning of industrial premises: progress report for the months of March and April, 1946 – W. Lindsell**, 3+1p appendix.
2 May	108	**Agricultural wage increases – Williams**, 2p.
7 May	110	**Coal carbonization – Shinwell**, 4p.
8 May	111	**Report on agricultural wages – Morrison covering the Official Working Party on Wages**, 1+4p. Also W(46)16(final). The machinery for wage settlement in agriculture should be as similar as possible to that in industry.
9 May	112	**Agricultural wage increases – Isaacs**, 4p.
13 May	113	**Controls – Morrison covering the Official Committee on Controls**, 7p. Also OC(46)6(final) and 11(final). Both papers recommended that controls should be kept to

a minimum but that the continued need for
some controls should be publicized.

14 May	116	**Future of road haulage organization – Barnes**, 3p.
18 May	121	**National building programme: labour demands and proposed ceilings for quarters ending 30 June 1946 and 30 September 1946 – Tomlinson**, 1+3p annexes.
21 May	125	**Centralized purchase of rubber – Marquand covering the Official Bulk Purchase Committee**, 1+5p.
22 May	126	**Trade associations, export groups and future industrial organizations – Belcher**, 4p. Recommends the establishment of central bodies of employers and employees which could represent each industry's views to the government and jointly improve efficiency.
28 May	131	**Surplus stores held by the War Department – Bellenger**, 2+3p annex +3p corrigenda.
31 May	132	**Service holdings of buildings and civil engineering equipment – W.S. Murrie**, 2+4p annex.
30 May	136	**Report of the Cotton Industry Working Party: parliamentary statement – W.S. Murrie**, 1+2p.
30 May	139	**Disposal of surplus stores and derequisitioning of industrial premises: progress report for May, 1946 – W. Lindsell**, 2+6p appendix.
31 May	140	**State trading in exports – Marquand covering the Committee on External Economic Policy and Overseas Trade**, 1+1p. Extract from CP(46)215.
31 May	141	**Cotton Buying Commission – Marquand**, 3p.
4 June	144	**Supplies of soap and linseed oil – Strachey**, 3p.
14 June	148	**Regulation of greyhound racing in the interests of coal production – Ede**, 2p.
17 June	149	**Overseas economic situation – N. Brook covering the Economic Section**, 1+5+17p appendix. From the present course of exports it could be hoped that equilibrium in the U.K.'s current external payments would be attained by mid-1947.

CAB 132/4   Memoranda   18 June–24 Sept 1946   LP(46)151–233.

25 June	LP(46)153	**Cotton Buying Commission – Marquand**, 2p.
25 June	154	**Report on the centralized purchase of non-ferrous metals – Morrison covering the Bulk Purchase Committee**, 6+2p annex.
25 June	155	**Agricultural policy – Williams**, 3+7p appendix.
2 July	162	**Agricultural prices: special review – Williams, Westwood and Ede**, 3+10p.

1 July	163	**Marginal production in agriculture – Williams, Westwood and Ede,** 2+5p.
1 July	165	**Direction of building labour to work on factory construction in the development areas – Isaacs and Tomlinson,** 2p. To increase employment, recommends direction of men under 50.
3 July	168	**Iron and steel position – Wilmot,** 3p.
3 July	170	**Direction of building labour to work on factory construction in the development areas – Bevan,** 1p. No objection to LP(46)165 but he did not think it would be effective.
4 July	171	**Direction of building labour to urgent government building work – Wilkinson,** 1p. Agreement with LP(46)165.
8 July	172	**Disposal of surplus government stores and derequisitioning of factory premises used for storage: progress report for June, 1946 – W. Lindsell,** 3+1p appendix.
10 July	173	**Recruitment to the coal-mining industry – Gaitskell covering the working party,** 1+4+2p annexes. Necessary action already in hand.
8 July	175	**Diversion of labour to industries of national importance – Isaacs,** 4p. Recommends the use of persuasion rather than more forceful means.
10 July	178	**Price control of building materials – Tomlinson,** 2+5p appendixes.
11 July	181	**Proposed revision of the cost of living index figure – Isaacs,** 2+2p annex.
16 July	186	**Wage increases in agriculture and related industries – Williams,** 1p. Doubts if the recommendations of LP(46)111 will be successful but agrees that they must be tried.
16 July	187	**Iron and steel prices: coke prices – Wilmot,** 6p.
16 July	188	**Agricultural policy – Williams and Westwood,** 4p.
18 July	190	**Wage increases in agriculture and related industries – Barnes,** 2p.
19 July	191	**Motorways – Barnes,** 3p.
24 July	192	**Trend of wages, costs and prices – Isaacs covering the Official Working Party,** 1+8+2p appendixes. Two problems faced the government: the maintenance of overall stability and the need for selective wage changes to benefit undermanned industries whilst retaining overall stability.
22 July	193	**Centralized purchase of cotton. Compensation to cotton merchants and their staffs – Cripps,** 4p.
23 July	197	**Exchange Control Bill – Dalton,** 2p.
24 July	198	**Co-ordination of building and civil engineering programme – Tomlinson,** 3p. Recommends a

standing headquarters building committee and more long-term building programmes.

26 July	201	**Supplies of goods in mining districts – Cripps** covering the consumer needs officers, 1+7p.
26 July	202	**Restrictive practices – Cripps,** 3p. Legislative proposals.
26 July	203	**Price control of non-food consumer goods: proposed transfer of functions under the Ministers of the Crown (Transfer of Functions) Act, 1946 – Cripps,** 2p.
27 July	204	**Marketing of agricultural products and fish. Division of responsibility between the Ministry of Food and Agricultural and Fisheries Departments – Williams, Westwood and Ede,** 5+5p appendix.
28 July	206	**Marketing and processing of home-produced foodstuffs – Strachey,** 2p.
31 July	208	**Analysis of unemployment benefit statistics with special reference to the refusal of suitable employment – Griffiths,** 2+3p appendixes.
30 July	210	**Farm prices – Williams,** 2+3p appendix.
30 July	211	**Importation of fresh fruit and vegetables – Strachey,** 3+1p appendix.
30 July	216	**Proposal to reconstitute the Cost of Living Advisory Committee – Isaacs,** 4p.
30 July	218	**Regulation of sport in the interests of coal production – Ede,** 1p.
17 Sept	225	**The disposal of government surplus stores – Woodburn,** 3+1p appendix. Progress report.
23 Sept	226	**Agricultural machinery – Williams,** 5+1p appendix.

CAB 132/5   Memoranda   25 Sept–27 December 1946   LP(46)234–299.

26 Sept	LP(46)235	**Raw Cotton Buying Commission – Cripps,** 2p.
30 Sept	236	**National building programme: labour demands and proposed ceilings for quarters ending 30 Sept 1946, 31 Dec 1946 and 31 Mar 1947,** 1+2p appendixes.
2 Oct	239	**Disqualification for unemployment benefit on the grounds of refusal of suitable employment – Isaacs and Griffiths,** 2+5p appendixes.
7 Oct	241	**Administration of Wales and Monmouthshire – Morrison,** 1+56+22p appendix. Draft White Paper attached.
9 Oct		**Administration of Wales and Monmouthshire – Morrison,** 1+2p annex.
10 Oct	247	**Supplies of timber and plywood – Cripps,** 1+6p appendixes.
14 Oct	248	**The control of aluminium – Wilmot,** 3p.
16 Oct	249	**Timber: allocation and control machinery – Cripps,** 3p.

14 Oct	250	**Steel supplies – Ministry of Supply,** 5+7p appendixes. Given continued shortages, the allocation system should perhaps be changed.
14 Oct	252	**Industrial Organization Bill – Cripps,** 4+4p appendixes. The bill would allow the Board of Trade to establish a body to help stimulate industrial efficiency.
18 Oct	254	**Disposal of government surplus stores – Woodburn,** 3p. Progress report.
22 Oct	255	**A proposed national wages policy – Shinwell,** 9p. See CP(47)190.
4 Nov	257	**Agricultural prices – Williams,** 3+2p appendix.
29 Oct	259	**National wages policy – Isaacs,** 6p. See CP(47)195.
28 Oct	260	**Proposal to reconstitute the Cost of Living Advisory Committee – Isaacs,** 1p.
28 Oct	261	**Disposal of government surplus stores – Woodburn,** 1p. Supplementary progress report.
18 Nov	264	**Control of Employment (Civil Servants) Order – Dalton,** 2p.
5 Nov	265	**Coal. Allocations to industrial consumers, winter 1946–47 – Belcher,** 1+2+2p annexes. Also NPACI(46)41.
7 Nov	267	**Fuel: allocations to industrial consumers, winter 1946–47 – W.S. Murrie covering the Board of Trade and the Ministry of Fuel and Power,** 1+2p. Points raised at N.P.A.C.I.
16 Nov	269	**Rail transport situation – Barnes,** 5+3p annexes. Measures to prevent a recurrence of the previous winter's difficulties.
18 Nov	271	**The cotton industry – Cripps,** 2p.
18 Nov	272	**End uses of steel sheet – Morrison,** 2+9p appendix.
18 Nov	273	**Transport and coal – Dalton,** 3p. Official report attached.
20 Nov	274	**Rail transport situation: railway locomotives and wagons – Wilmot,** 3p.
23 Nov	276	**The disposal of government surplus stores – Woodburn,** 3+1p appendix. Progress report.
25 Nov	278	**End uses of steel – Morrison,** 2+8p.
3 Dec	282	**Wages and output in the building industry – Isaacs and Tomlinson,** 3p.
2 Dec	283	**Fishing Industry Bill – Williams and Westwood,** 4p.
4 Dec	284	**Fishing Industry Bill – Strachey,** 2+3p annex.
3 Dec	285	**Revision of the cost of living index – Morrison,** 1+5p annex +1p appendix.
9 Dec	286	**Coal Committee composition and terms of reference – N. Brook,** 1p. Also CC(46)1.
16 Dec	291	**Building priority for hospitals and allied purposes – Bevan,** 2p.

16 Dec	**293**	**Industrial restrictions on voluntary recruitment – Manpower Working Party,** 3p.
19 Dec	**294**	**Building priority for hospitals and allied purposes – Tomlinson,** 2p.
24 Dec	**298**	**The marketing of home-produced foodstuffs – Morrison covering the Economic Section,** 8+3p annex. Section felt that planning should be based on the 'optimistic' assumption of high demand for domestic agricultural produce. The assumption underlying this was that unemployment would not normally rise above 5%.
27 Dec	**299**	**Fishing Industry Bill – Isaacs,** 3p.

CAB 132/6   Meetings   10 Jan–12 Dec 1947   LP(47)1st–29th.

10 Jan	**LP(47)1st:2**	**Preparation of investment projects by public authorities.** LP(47)4. Dalton believed there to be a risk of serious deflationary pressure within a measurable time. He wanted a circular to local authorities and departments to be sent, urging the greatest possible preparation of suitable investment projects.
	:3	**Building industry: wages and output.** LP(47)8. Morrison thought that the government could not leave the discussion to employers and trade unions as suggested by Isaacs. The committee decided that the Health Ministers and the Minister of Works should meet representatives of both sides of the industry.
17 Jan	**2nd:2**	**Raw materials.** LP(47)11 and 12.
	:5	**Accommodation for nationalized industries.** LP(47)10.
	:6	**Control of building operations.** LP(47)9.
	:7	**Building industry: wages and output.**
24 Jan	**3rd:1**	**Shipping policy.** CP(46)453 and LP(47)15.
	:2	**Agriculture.** LP(47)16, 19, 20, 21, 23.
	:4	**Building industry: wages and output.**
	:5	**Hours and conditions of work of road passenger transport workers in London.** LP(47)24.
4 Feb	**4th:2**	**Disposal of government surplus stores.** LP(47)25.
	:3	**Agriculture: principles governing the annual review of agricultural prices.** LP(47)20 and 23.
7 Feb	**5th:3**	**Disposal of government surplus stores.**
21 Feb	**6th:3**	**Restrictive practices by supervisory boards.** LP(47)1.
28 Feb	**7th:2**	**Agricultural prices.** LP(47)34.
7 Mar	**8th:1**	**Restrictive practices.** LP(47)38.
	:2	**Distribution policy.** LP(47)35.
14 Mar	**9th:1**	**Cost of living index figure.** LP(47)46. Publication of interim report authorized.

	:3	**Statistical review.** LP(47)42, 45, 49. Dalton said that Attlee was concerned at the low level of food stocks.
21 Mar	**10th:1**	**Disposal of government surplus stores.** LP(47)52.
	:2	**Fishing Industry Bill.** LP(47)31 and 51. Strachey was concerned that if the government sought to control too many industries, it would not exercise control effectively.
	:3	**Business of the committee.**
28 Mar	**11th:1**	**National building programme for 1947–48.** LP(47)50, 53, 54, 55, 58, 59, 61, 66. A number of ministers felt that the supply of building materials rather than labour should form the basis of the programme. Key and Gaitskell were to consider changes to LP(47)61 to ensure that the programme took full account of material allocations.
	:2	**Functions of food and agriculture departments in relation to the marketing of agricultural products.** LP(47)62 and 63.
	:3	**Food distribution policy.** LP(47)64.
25 Apr	**12th:1**	**National building programme for 1947/48.** LP(47)50, 53, 54, 55, 58, 59, 61, 66, 75. The committee agreed to the proposals in LP(47)75.
	:2	**Timber: supplies of softwood in 1947/48.** LP(47)71.
	:4	**Steel supplies: allocations to the engineering industries.** LP(47)73 and 77.
	:5	**Industry and employment in Scotland: draft White Paper.** LP(47)72.
2 May	**13th:1**	**Railway fares and charges: claims for increased wages and shorter hours and Central Arbitration Tribunal.** Agreement that national economic policy was not being sufficiently considered in wage claims. A Central Arbitration Tribunal would rectify this.
16 May	**14th:3**	**Statistical review.** LP(47)82 and 83. Barnes renewed request for a general discussion reviewing the whole internal economic situation.
	:4	**Wages policy: claims of railway workers for increased wages and shorter hours.** Shinwell felt that the government would have to intervene more directly but it was agreed that there should be no shift from the line decided at Cabinet on 6th May 1947.
23 May	**15th:1**	**Steel supplies.** LP(47)87, 88, 90. Discussion on steel allocations. Morrison, Dalton, Gaitskell with the help of E.N. Plowden, were to review allocations for the third quarter of 1947.

6 June	**16th:2**	**Claims of railway workers for increased wages and shorter hours.**
	:3	**Wages policy.** LP(47)92. Isaacs had changed his mind from LP(47)13th:1 and now opposed a central arbitral body. Cripps and Shinwell disagreed and were asked to write a joint memorandum.
20 June	**18th:1**	**Steel supplies.** LP(47)98. Agreed not to change priorities but the position should be reviewed before allocating for the fourth quarter of 1947.
27 June	**19th:1**	**Supply of goods and equipment for non-government services.** LP(47)101.
	:3	**Claim for reduced hours and increased wages by railway trade unions.**
4 July	**20th:1**	**Economic Survey.** Morrison felt that the forthcoming survey provided an opportunity to discuss the general home economic situation.
11 July	**21st:3**	**Shipping and shipbuilding.** LP(47)102(revise).
18 July	**22nd:1**	**Railway fares and charges: claims of railway workers for higher wages and shorter hours.**
25 July	**23rd:1**	**Organization of building research.** LP(47)126. Morrison recommended an enquiry into the structure and organization of the building industry on the lines of the Reid Report. Key was to arrange this.
	:2	**Agricultural production programme – 1948–51.** LP(47)119 and 124.
	:3	**Extension of five-day week to ancillary undertakings of the N.C.B.** LP(47)127.
	:4	**Regional boards and district committees.** LP(47)122 (written in minutes as 112 but a typing error).
	:5	**Railway fares and charges.** LP(47)120, 121, 125.
	:6	**Coal prices.**
8 Aug	**24th:1**	**Agricultural production programme 1948/51.** LP(47)137.
12 Aug	**25th:2**	**Coal prices.** LP(47)144.
	:3	**White fish industry.** LP(47)129 and 133. Approval of Barnes's recommendations. Strachey should raise any objections in the Cabinet if he was not happy.
	:6	**Housing programme.** LP(47)143 and 145. Morrison said the Planning Staff should not be bound by prior decisions on the housing programme when formulating detailed proposals for the curtailment of investment.
	:7	**Petroleum board.** LP(47)123.
31 Oct	**27th:2**	**Administration of Wales and Monmouthshire: annual White Paper.** LP(47)60.

CAB 132/7   Memoranda   1 Jan–5 May 1947   LP(47)1–83.

1 Jan	**LP(47)1**	**Restrictive practices by supervisory board –** **Cripps covering the Supervisory Board's** **Committee,** 1+6+1p appendix. Final report.
6 Jan	**4**	**Preparation of investment projects by public** **authorities – Dalton covering the Investment** **Working Party,** 2+7p. Dalton saw this as the first stage in the use of planned investment to offset slumps. It emphasized that vague aggregate proposals were insufficient. Clearly formulated plans should be in the most advanced state of preparation possible. This was to be explained in the circular to local authorities for capital expenditure programmes in 1947–48 and 1949–50 by the Ministry of Health and the Scottish Office.
8 Jan	**8**	**Meeting with representatives of the National** **Executive of the National Federation of Building** **Trade Operatives – Isaacs,** 2+4p annex. A note of the meeting of 16 December 1946 is annexed.
9 Jan	**9**	**Control of building operations – Ede,** 1+2p annex. Note of a meeting of officials to consider the effectiveness of building controls.
11 Jan	**10**	**Nationalized industries – Tomlinson.** 4p. Proposal of co-ordinating machinery between the Ministry of Works and the nationalized industries with regard to the erection of buildings.
8 Jan	**11**	**Raw materials – Cripps covering the Raw** **Materials Subcommittee of N.P.A.C.I.,** 2+4p appendix. Also NPACI(46)3. Proposed modification of the present distribution system to make each industry the responsibility of one government department. Each steel user was to obtain his allocation in bulk from one parent department.
13 Jan	**12**	**Report of N.P.A.C.I. Subcommittee on Raw** **Materials (steel) – Wilmot,** 2p. The proposals in LP(47)11 were already largely in operation.
13 Jan	**13**	**Coal supplies to industry – Cripps,** 1+2p appendix +2p annex. Revised arrangements for the supply of coal to individual firms as decided by Cabinet.
20 Jan	**15**	**Shipping policy – Barnes,** 4+2p annexes.
18 Jan	**16**	**Farm labour and rural housing – Williams,** 3p. The chief restriction on agricultural production in the next few years was the shortage of labour. Recruitment suffered from the shortage and low standard of housing. The committee should

consider ways of accelerating the rural housing campaign.

19 Jan	19	**Actual earnings of agricultural workers – Williams, Westwood, Ede and Isaacs,** 2+2p appendix.

19 Jan — 20 — **Methods of price fixing in agriculture and other industries – Williams, Westwood and Ede,** 1+5p appendix. Comparison of the principles of price control by the Board of Trade with the annual agricultural reviews is appended.

20 Jan — 21 — **Future production of food in the U.K. – Williams, Westwood, Ede and Strachey,** 2+7p appendix. Tentative programme of home food production for the next three to four years, requiring a labour force substantially in excess of that then expected.

22 Jan — 23 — **Price adjustments following wage increases – Official Steering Committee on Economic Development,** 3p. Recommends that the government announce that wage increases would not necessarily be wholly reflected in increased prices; but opposes any arbitrary ceiling, such as the 80% figure suggested by the Board of Trade.

17 Feb — 31 — **Fishing industry bill – Strachey,** 7+3p annexes. Alternative proposals to LP(46)283.

24 Feb — 34 — **Agricultural prices – Williams, Westwood and Ede covering an official report,** 2+9p annex +1p appendix.

25 Feb — 35 — **Distribution policy – Cripps,** 3p. Proposals for increasing efficiency in the distributive trades, especially of manpower.

1 Mar — 38 — **Restrictive practices – Cripps,** 1+1p annex. Draft statement for the debate on the Economic Survey annexed.

10 Mar — 46 — **Interim report – Isaacs covering the Cost of Living Advisory Committee,** 1+3+2p appendixes. See Cmd.7077.

14 Mar — 50 — **National building programme for financial year 1947–48 – Official Steering Committee on Economic Development,** 4+1p appendix. Also ED(47)23. The demands of fuel and power should be met in full and those of industry as fully as possible. The housing allocation should be revised downwards except for the provision of new houses for miners, agricultural workers and other key workers.

14 Mar — 51 — **Fishing Industry Bill – Williams and Westwood,** 2+4p appendix. Reply to LP(47)31.

15 Mar — 52 — **The disposal of government surplus stores – Woodburn,** 2p. Progress report.

17 Mar	53	**National building programme for financial year 1947–48 – Tomlinson,** 2p. Unhappy with his department's allocation.
17 Mar	54	**Ministry of Works building programme – Key,** 3+2p appendix. Requires guidance on the cuts necessitated by LP(47)50.
17 Mar	55	**National building programme for financial year 1947–48 – Edwards, J.,** 4p. Concern about the impact of LP(47)50 on the housing programme.
19 Mar	58	**National building programme for financial year 1947–48 – Westwood,** 2p. Also concerned about the housing programme.
19 Mar	59	**National building programme for financial year 1947–48 – Williams,** 2p. Food production should on no account be impaired.
24 Mar	61	**National building programme for financial year 1947–48 – Key,** 6+2p appendixes. Given shortages of various building materials there was no practical alternative to LP(47)50.
25 Mar	62	**Marketing of agricultural products and the demarcation of departmental responsibilities – Strachey,** 7p. The government should accept liability for assuring a market for the whole output of the guaranteed price commodities, provided changing requirements were taken into account when fixing minimum and actual prices.
25 Mar	63	**Marketing of agricultural products and the demarcation of departmental responsibilities – Westwood and Williams,** 3p. In general agreement with LP(47)62.
25 Mar	64	**Food distribution policy – Strachey,** 3p.
26 Mar	65	**Note by the secretary – W.S. Murrie,** 1p.
27 Mar	66	**National building programme for financial year 1947–48 – Cripps,** 2p. LP(47)61 pressed for the highest priority in coal allocation for building material industries. Given other priorities, the result would be disastrous for the rest of industry.
16 Apr	71	**Softwood supply position July 1947 to June 1948 – Cripps,** 4+1p appendix.
18 Apr	72	**White Paper on industry and employment in Scotland – Westwood,** 1+92p. Draft White Paper, designed as supplement to the Economic Survey for 1947, is attached.
18 Apr	73	**Steel allocations to the engineering industries – Wilmot,** 4p. Unless there were substantial increases in the third and fourth quarters of 1947 there was no chance of reaching targets set, especially for exports.
21 Apr	75	**National building programme for 1947/48 – Key and Gaitskell,** 4p. While labour ceilings were

		needed in the short term, the building programme should be more closely related to material allocations.
22 Apr	77	**Steel for the agricultural engineering industry – Williams**, 2p. Without increased allocations for the rest of 1947 it would be impossible to meet both food production targets and export demands.
23 Apr	78	**Change in membership – W.S. Murrie**, 1p.
23 Apr	79	**Food situation in the U.K. – Strachey**, 1+3+1p appendix. The reports were to become quarterly rather than monthly unless significant changes arose.

CAB 132/8   Memoranda   9 May–31 Dec 1947   LP(47)84–172.

20 May	**LP(47)87**	**Steel allocations: period III 1947 – Gaitskell**, 9+7p appendixes. Sets out allocations and the principles behind them.
19 May	88	**Allocations of steel to transport – Barnes**, 2p. Asking for increased allocation.
21 May	90	**Steel and timber for shipbuilding – Hall and Barnes**, 4p.
23 May	91	**Claim for reduced hours and increased wages by railway trade unions – Barnes**, 2p.
3 June	92	**Development of national arbitration machinery – Isaacs**, 6+10p appendixes. The risk to the present machinery was too great from a central arbitral body. Reliance should continue to be placed on publicizing the economic position.
12 June	98	**Steel allocations: period III – Morrison and Dalton**, 2p. Results of the review of the allocations. The general priority position was to be looked at before period IV allocations were made.
17 June	101	**Supply of goods and equipment for non-governmental services – Key**, 3p.
8 July	102	**Prospects of U.K. shipping and shipbuilding industry over the next two or three years – Barnes**, 3+6p annex. Revise version.
14 July	118	**The rise in wages since 1939 and the effect of cost of living subsidies – Isaacs**, 1+1p. Grounds for thinking that, since the war, subsidies had become less important in wage negotiations.
15 July	119	**Requirements of the agricultural production programme for 1948–51 – Williams**, 5+4p appendixes. Revision of the programme in LP(47)21 taking account of the losses owing to the weather and labour shortages.
21 July	122	**Regional boards and district committees – Marquand**, 5+6p appendixes. Recommends

their retention. The grievances of non-official members, who had lost executive responsibility since the war, should be allayed.

21 July	123	**Demerging of the Petroleum Board – Gaitskell,** 3p.
24 July	124	**Agricultural prices: special review, 1947 – Williams,** 2p.
23 July	129	**White fish industry – Barnes,** 2+4p appendix. Also GEN 177/6. Report of Official Committee on the Restrictive Practices by Supervisory Boards is attached.
28 July	133	**White fish industry – Strachey,** 3p. Disagrees with the proposals in LP(47)129.
28 July	134	**Distribution of fruit and vegetables – Strachey,** 4p. Recommends applying his proposals in LP(47)133 to these areas.
4 Aug	137	**Expansion of agricultural and fisheries production in the U.K.: report of officials – Williams,** 2+14+8p appendixes. By 1951/2 it was technically possible to increase agricultural output by £100m over 1946/7, but only if all necessary resources and incentives were applied.
8 Aug	143	**Housing programme – Bevan and Fraser,** 4+1p appendix.
9 Aug	144	**Coal prices – Gaitskell,** 3+5p appendix.
11 Aug	145	**Supplies for the housing programme – Belcher,** 1p. Detailed proposals for reducing capital investment projects should be decided before any agreement on the housing programme, for which housing ministers proposed materials should be guaranteed, was made.
13 Aug	146	**Outstanding matters before the committee – E.M. Nicholson,** 1p.
23 Sept	152	**Steel prices – Wilmot,** 2p.
9 Oct	156	**Reconstitution of the committee – N. Brook,** 1p.
28 Oct	160	**Annual White Paper on Wales – Morrison** covering the heads of government offices in Wales and Monmouth, 1+70+21p appendixes. Draft attached.

CAB 132/9   Meetings   16 Jan–3 Dec 1948   LP(48)1st–18th.

19 Mar	**LP(48)4th:2**	**Town and Country Planning Act: regulations on development charges.** LP(48)20.
	:3	**Agriculture (Miscellaneous Provisions) Bill.** LP(48)17.
23 Apr	6th:7	**Licensing bill.** LP(48)26 and 37.
	:8	**New towns.** LP(48)32 and 35.
30 Apr	7th:1	**New towns.** LP(48)32 and 35.
23 July	13th:4	**New town at Bracknell.** LP(48)65.

24 Sept	**14th:1**	**Food distribution policy. LP(48)71 and 77.** Agreement on proposals on retail trade.
	:2	**Annual White Paper on Wales. LP(48)72.**
	:3	**New towns in South Wales. LP(48)73.**
26 Nov	**17th:3**	**New town development corporations. LP(48)82** and 86.
	:4	**Agricultural Marketing Bill. LP(48)87.**
3 Dec	**18th:1**	**Town and country planning. LP(48)88.**

CAB 132/10   Memoranda   9 Jan–20 Dec 1948   LP(48)1–91.

16 Mar	**LP(48)17**	**Agriculture (Miscellaneous Provisions) Bill –** **Woodburn and Williams,** 2p.
17 Mar	**20**	**Regulations on the development charges –** **Woodburn and Silkin,** 2+2p appendix.
7 Apr	**26**	**Licensed premises in new towns: question of** **state management – Woodburn and Silkin,** 4p.
17 Apr	**32**	**New town programme: proposals for a new town** **at Pitsea-Laindon, Essex – Silkin,** 5p.
19 Apr	**34**	**The resettlement of members of the forces –** **Isaacs,** 2+13p. A report by an inter-departmental Committee on Resettlement in Employment is attached.
20 Apr	**35**	**New towns in Scotland – Woodburn,** 1+3p appendixes. Progress report.
9 June	**–**	**Membership of the committee – W.S. Murrie,** 1p.
20 July	**65**	**Proposal for a new town at Bracknell,** **Berkshire – Silkin,** 4p.
16 Sept	**71**	**Interim report – Morrison covering the Food** **Distribution Committee,** 1+9p. Recommends freedom of competition in the retail food trade. However, the Ministry of Food should consider nationalizing appropriate sections of the wholesale food trade.
18 Sept	**72**	**Annual White Paper on Wales – Morrison,** 1+64p. Draft report.
20 Sept	**73**	**New towns in South Wales – Silkin,** 4p.
23 Sept	**77**	**Announcement of the interim report of the Food** **Distribution Committee – Strachey,** 4+2p annex. Draft statement attached.
10 Nov	**82**	**Paid membership of new town development** **corporations – Silkin,** 4p.
17 Nov	**86**	**Paid membership of new town development** **corporations – Woodburn,** 2p.
17 Nov	**87**	**Agricultural Marketing Bill – Brown, G.,** 2p.
23 Nov	**88**	**Town and Country Planning Acts 1947 –** **Woodburn and Silkin,** 1+2p annex. Report on the workings of the acts by the chairman of the Central Land Board.

CAB 132/11   Meetings   14 Jan–16 Dec 1949   LP(49)1st–22nd.

18 Mar	**LP(49)6th:2**	**New towns in Cheshire.** LP(49)19 and 21.
25 Mar	**7th:2**	**Peterlee new town.** LP(49)28.
13 May	**11th:3**	**Agriculture Act.** LP(49)38.
15 July	**15th:3**	**New town at Corby.** LP(49)56.
	:4	**Loss of agricultural land.** LP(49)57 and 60. Agreement that planning departments should make every effort to reduce claims on good agricultural land.
	:6	**Agricultural housing.** LP(49)58.
	:7	**Procedure for securing approval for new buildings.** LP(49)62. Agreement to establish a working party to study the simplification of procedures for obtaining official consent in connection with building, so as not to discredit the planning machinery.
22 July	**16th:1**	**Defence (finance) regulations.** LP(49)64.
	:5	**Peterlee new town.** LP(49)63.
28 Oct	**18th:1**	**Annual White Paper on Wales.** LP(49)75.
9 Dec	**21st:2**	**Building controls.** LP(49)85. Bevan argued that controls should not be sacrificed without reason, while Morrison felt that needless inconvenience to citizens would discredit planning.
	:6	**The finance of new town development.** LP(49)91.
	:7	**New towns: Houston.** LP(49)90.
16 Dec	**22nd:1**	**Agricultural marketing schemes.** LP(49)93 and 96. To go to Cabinet.

CAB 132/12   Memoranda   5 Jan–20 May 1949   LP(49)1–43.

18 Feb	**LP(49)15**	**Charges at industrial hostels** – Isaacs, 3p.
15 Mar	**19**	**Proposals for developments in Cheshire: a new town at Congleton and development by Manchester at Mobberley** – Silkin, 3p.
17 Mar	**21**	**Proposals for developments in Cheshire: a new town at Congleton and developments by Manchester at Mobberley** – Williams, 3+2p appendixes.
23 Mar	**28**	**Peterlee new town** – Silkin, 4p.
21 Apr	**38**	**Smallholdings: part IV of the Agriculture Act 1947** – Williams, 3+61p. First report of the Smallholdings Advisory Council is attached. Aimed at the creation of small farming units to provide agricultural workers with opportunities for advancement.

CAB 132/13   Memoranda   23 May–14 Dec 1949   LP(49)44–96.

11 July	**LP(49)56**	**Corby new town** – Silkin, 2p.

12 July	57	**Loss of agricultural land – Williams and Silkin,** 5+1p annex.
12 July	58	**Agricultural housing – Bevan and Williams,** 2p. General priority for agricultural workers no longer necessary.
13 July	60	**Encroachment on agricultural land in Scotland –** **Woodburn,** 3p.
12 July	62	**Difficulties experienced by farmers who wished** **to erect small buildings – Addison,** 1p. Number of forms excessive.
19 July	63	**Peterlee Working Party – Silkin,** 2+4p appendix.
19 July	64	**Defence (finance) regulations – Hall,** 2p. Recommends permanent legislation to replace the three regulations remaining.
20 Oct	75	**Annual White Paper on Wales – Morrison,** 1+71p. Draft White Paper.
30 Nov	85	**Building controls – Morrison,** 1+8p annexes. While the machinery was complex, previous reviews had concluded that little simplification could be obtained by altering the machinery or the relevant authorities. It was better to change the requirements of the Town and Country Planning Act.
6 Dec	90	**New town at Houston – Woodburn,** 2p.
6 Dec	91	**The finance of new town development – Cripps,** 1+6p annex +3p appendixes. Paper on the capital cost of new towns and the extent to which they might be a continuing burden on the Exchequer is attached.
13 Dec	92	**Finance of new town developments in Scotland –** **Woodburn,** 3+1p appendix.
14 Dec	93	**Hops marketing scheme – Wilson covering the** **Official Committee on Restrictive Practices by** **Supervisory Boards,** 6+11+4p appendix. Also SB 18.
14 Dec	96	**Tomatoes and cucumbers marketing scheme –** **Wilson covering the Official Committee on** **Restrictive Practices by Supervisory Boards,** 8+5+2p appendix. Also SB 21.

CAB 132/14   Meetings   20 Jan–8 Dec 1950   LP(50)1st–19th.

20 Jan	**LP(50)1st:1**	**Finance of new town development in Scotland.** LP(49)92.
	:6	**Proposed housing site for Nottingham at** **Clifton.** LP(50)5.
	:7	**New towns in South Wales.** LP(50)4.
24 Mar	**2nd:6**	**Working party report on the building industry.** LP(50)6. Morrison said that the committee's concern was limited. It was agreed that the report should be published. However, a

statement should be prepared giving the government's case since the report suggested that the industry's deficiencies were owing to government policy and not the industry's own inefficiency and the urgent need to reduce its costs.

31 Mar	**3rd:1**	**Loss of agricultural land.**
	:3	**Miscellaneous Financial Provisions Bill.** LP(50)18.
21 Apr	**4th:1**	**Merchandise marks.** LP(50)23.
	:2	**Emergency powers.** LP(50)1, 10, 16, 21. Morrison said that permanent legislation would be necessary. There was general agreement with LP(50)16 on the extent of the long-term powers but the committee did not agree that economic controls should not be used to direct industry and commerce in a positive sense.
	:3	**Domestic food production.** LP(50)22.
	:5	**Local Government (Scotland) Bill.** LP(50)19. Pointed out that central control of local authority borrowing was essential to the government control of capital investment.
19 May	**6th:4**	**Government controls and the public.** LP(50)33. Morrison and Wilson agreed on the need to adjust controls in the light of changing conditions. Agreement that ministers should review the situation and machinery of control periodically and consider the need for an external inspector of controls in each department.
25 May	**7th:2**	**Restoration of iron ore workings.** LP(50)35.
	:3	**Restoration of pre-war trade practices.** LP(50)34.
16 June	**8th:3**	**Statistics of Trade Act, 1947.** LP(50)37, 43 and 48.
	:5	**Loan sanctions in London.** LP(50)46.
23 June	**9th:2**	**Wool marketing scheme.** LP(50)52.
	:3	**Loss of agricultural land: more intensive use of playing fields.** LP(50)42.
7 July	**11th:1**	**Marginal land.** LP(50)135.
14 July	**12th:3**	**Working party on the building industry.** LP(50)57. Proposals approved.
	:5	**Marginal land.**
21 July	**13th:3**	**Permanent economic powers.** LP(50)65. It was suggested that if there was some mention of economic planning it could be called the Economic Planning and Full Employment Bill. The general view was that the bill should be permanent, not limited to seven or ten years, and that the Lord President should be responsible for its parliamentary progress.

	:4	**Revocation of defence regulations 58A and 80B.**
28 July	14th:1	**Land acquisition in the City of London.** LP(50)64.
29 Sept	15th:5	**Compulsory purchase of land: quick procedure.** LP(50)76.
	:7	**Annual White Paper on Wales.** LP(50)80.
	:8	**Forestry: acquisition of land.** LP(50)78 and 81.
3 Nov	17th:3	**Amendment to the Town and Country Planning Act 1947.** LP(50)90 and 91. Proposals approved.
24 Nov	18th:1	**Council for Wales and Monmouthshire: memorandum.** LP(50)92.

CAB 132/15   Memoranda   3 Jan–26 June 1950   LP(50)1–53.

3 Jan	LP(50)1	**Duration of emergency legislation – Morrison covering the Emergency Legislation Committee,** 1+1+24p. Also EL(50)1. Consideration of permanent powers but little mention of economic controls.
16 Jan	4	**New towns in South Wales – Silkin,** 3p.
16 Jan	5	**Proposed housing site for Nottingham – Silkin,** 2p.
20 Mar	6	**Building industry – Stokes covering the Working Party on the Building Industry,** 5+89p. Decline in productive efficiency compared with the inter-war period was attributed to: (a) a vast building programme begun by government with inadequate planning; (b) the disturbance caused by subsequent efforts to balance the programme and drastic revisions of the capital investment programme; and (c) the scarcity of raw materials.
14 Feb	10	**Duration of emergency statutes – Morrison covering the Emergency Legislation Committee,** 1+7p.
27 Mar	16	**Economic controls: long-term powers – Morrison covering the Committee on Economic Controls,** 1+16+2p annex. Sets out the powers likely to be required in the long term for operating controls on prices, production, consumption, centralized purchase, labour, and import and export licensing. The powers were largely negative. If more purposeful direction was required, a fundamentally different approach from using the surviving controls would be necessary. With the increasing supply of raw materials it would be possible in the foreseeable future to abandon their allocation (with a few exceptions due to the balance of payments) and rely increasingly on budgetary policy.

29 Mar		18	**Miscellaneous Financial Provisions Bill – Jay,** 3p.
3 Apr		19	**Local Government (Scotland) Bill – McNeil,** 1p.
6 Apr		21	**Future of emergency powers – Morrison,** 2p. The Emergency Legislation Committee should proceed with the drafting of permanent legislation covering economic controls and price regulation.
14 Apr		22	**Domestic food production – Williams and McNeil,** 2+27p. Report of the departmental committee attached.
19 Apr		23	**Merchandise marks – Webb,** 3p.
1 May		26	**Date of coming into operation of statutes –** Morrison covering the official committee, 1+7p.
8 May		33	**Government controls and the public – Morrison,** 4p. Proposes machinery to remove unnecessary controls wherever possible so that the public would be more likely to accept those required for long-term planning.
17 May		34	**Restoration of Pre-war Trade Practices Act 1942 – Isaacs,** 2p.
25 May		37	**Statistics of Trade Act, 1947, Amending Bill –** Wilson, 2p.
12 June		42	**Loss of agricultural land: more intense use of playing fields – Dalton,** 2p.
13 June		43	**Statistics of Trade Act, 1947, Amending Bill –** Shawcross, 1p.
14 June		46	**Loan sanctions in London – Bevan,** 1p. Minister of Health to become the sanctioning authority.
14 June		48	**Statistics of Trade Act, 1947, Amending Bill –** Wheatley, 2p.
21 June		52	**Wool marketing scheme – Wilson covering the Official Committee on Restrictive Practices by Supervisory Boards,** 1+4p annex +1p appendix. Also SB 24.

CAB 132/16 Memoranda 27 June–20 Dec 1950 LP(50)54–102.

8 July	LP(50)57		**Building Industry Working Party report – Jay covering the Government Organization Committee,** 1+7+2p appendix. Consideration of recommendations affecting the machinery of government.
14 July		61	**Revocation of defence (general) regulations 58A and 80B – Isaacs,** 1+1p annex.
18 July		64	**Land acquisition policy in the City of London –** Dalton, 2p.
18 July		65	**Permanent economic powers – Morrison,** 1+6+20p. Draft bill covering both economic controls and price regulation is attached.
31 Aug		71	**Release of requisitioned premises – Stokes covering the inter-departmental Committee on**

		Priority of Release of Requisitioned Premises, 2+5+3p appendix. Progress report.
19 Sept	76	Compulsory purchase of land: quick procedure – Bevan, 1p.
21 Sept	78	Forestry: acquisition of land – Williams, 2p.
25 Sept	80	Annual White Paper on Wales – Morrison, 1+74p. Draft White Paper attached.
26 Sept	81	Forestry: acquisition of land – McNeil, 2p.
26 Oct	90	Amendment to the Town and Country Planning Act, 1947 – Dalton, 1p.
31 Oct	91	Town and country planning proposed amending bill – McNeil, 1p.
16 Nov	92	Memorandum by the Council for Wales and Monmouthshire (Cmd. 8060) – Morrison, 2+9p annex. Includes proposals to reduce unemployment.

CAB 132/17   Meetings   12 Jan–27 July 1951   LP(51)1st–18th.

9 Feb	**LP(51)4th:2**	Use of requisitioning powers.
16 Feb	**5th**	Requisitioning and acquisition of land for defence. LP(51)11.
16 Mar	**8th:1**	Use of requisitioning powers. LP(51)16.
	:3	Control over capital issues. LP(51)17. General approval of LP(51)17 although there could be no legislation until the 1951–52 session.
6 Apr	**9th:1**	Requisitioning and acquisition of land for defence. LP(51)19.
20 Apr	**10th:2**	Increase in value of agricultural land. LP(51)23.
22 June	**14th:2**	Wages Councils Act: weekly payments of statutory remuneration.
6 July	**16th:1**	Proposed advisory committee on employment of elderly persons. LP(51)39.
20 July	**17th:3**	Expansion of existing towns. LP(51)44.
27 July	**18th:6**	Hops marketing scheme. LP(51)52.

CAB 132/18   Memoranda   10 Jan–26 Sept 1951   LP(51)1–63.

14 Feb	**LP(51)11**	Use of emergency powers in connection with the defence works programme – Shinwell, 4p.
1 Mar	16	Service and supply departments' requirements of office accommodation – Stokes, 2p.
9 Mar	17	Borrowing (Control and Guarantees) Act Amendment Bill, 1951 – Jay, 2p. Two minor amendments proposed.
27 Mar	19	Acquisition of land for defence and essential civilian needs – Morrison covering the Official Working Party, 1+7p.
6 Apr	23	Increase in value of agricultural land – Ede, Williams and McNeil, 3p.
22 May	35	Wages Councils Act: weekly payments of statutory remuneration – Ministry of Labour, 2p.

27 June	**39**	**The appointment of an advisory committee on the employment of elderly persons** – Isaacs, 2p.
17 July	**44**	**Expansion of existing towns** – Dalton, 2p.
24 July	**52**	**Hops marketing scheme** – Shawcross covering the Official Committee on Restrictive Practices by Supervisory Boards, 2+5p. Also SB 36.
3 Aug	**56**	**Continuance of emergency acts** – Morrison covering T. Sheepshanks, 1+4p. Also EL(51)5.
19 Sept	**62**	**Report of government action in Wales and Monmouthshire for the year ended 30 June 1951** – Ede, 1+79p.

14.2 Distribution of Industry Subcommittee

Set up by the Lord President's Committee in March 1946 in accordance with Attlee's wish to expedite the execution of plans for the development areas, see CAB 132/1, LP(46)11th:5. Distribution of industry policy had previously been the responsibility of the Lord President's Industry Subcommittee (CAB 71/26–27). One of the committee's roles was to adjudicate on individual cases before Panel A (see 7.13), where that panel's authority was uncertain or agreement had proved impossible. It reported, when necessary, to the Lord President's Committee and was superseded in October 1947 by the Distribution of Industry Committee (CAB 134/130–132), when the Lord President's Committee lost its economic responsibilities.

Terms To supervise the development and execution of the government's policy for securing a balanced distribution of industry and in particular to review the progress made in dealing with the problems of the development areas.

Members Ch. of Exchequer (ch.); Mins. of Lab & N.S., Supply, Town & Country Planning; S./S. Scotland; Parl. Secs. of B.T., Transport. (April 1947) Paymaster-Gen. added and Jt Parl. Sec., Supply replaced Min. of Supply.

Secs. M.T. Flett (Ld Pres. O.) and R.J.W. Stacy (B.T.). (Oct 1946) T.M. Wilson (Ld Pres. O.) replaced Flett.

CAB 132/21 Meetings 1 May–11 Dec 1946 LP(DI)(46)1st–13th.

1 May	**LP(DI)(46)1st:1**	**Terms of reference.** LP(DI)(46)1.
	:2	**Progress in development areas.** LP(DI)(46)2, 3 and LP(I)(46)17.
	:3	**Future meetings.**
15 May	**2nd:2**	**Requisitioned factory space still held in development areas by the government departments.** LP(DI)(46)7.
	:3	**The training of building labour in development areas.** LP(46)81, 104, LP(DI)(46)8. Proposals in LP(46)104 approved.
	:4	**Ministry of Transport depot at Rumney.** LP(DI)(46)5.

	:5	**Houses for key workers in development areas.** LP(DI)(46)9.
	:6	**Machinery for site clearance.**
23 May	3rd:2	**New towns.** LP(DI)(46)12, 13, 17. Approval for two new towns and another one in principle.
	:3	**Demolition of houses, etc., for road works.** LP(DI)(46)16.
29 May	4th:1	**Allocation of raw materials to firms in unemployment areas.** LP(DI)(46)6 and 15. No more precise general rules could be laid down but no representation from firms in unemployment areas were to be rejected without ministerial authority.
	:2	**Creation of new brickworks and the use of imported trucks in the development areas.** LP(DI)(46)10.
	:3	**Release of Ministry of Food storage space in development areas.** LP(DI)(46)14. One depot was to be converted into a factory.
	:4	**Iron and steel factories in Lanarkshire and Renfrewshire.** LP(DI)(46)11.
	:5	**Factory space occupied by supply departments in development areas.** LP(DI)(46)20.
	:6	**Future location of Short Brothers.** LP(DI)(46)19. Movement to Belfast approved.
4 June	5th	**Estimated cost of establishing new towns.** LP(DI)(46)22, 23, 24. Generally in favour of three new towns at Chipping Ongar, Harlow and Hemel Hempstead, provided they were properly co-ordinated with other policies, including employment policy. The cost of their transport facilities should be established.
26 June	6th:1	**The employment situation.** LP(DI)(46)25 and 29. Both Isaacs and Dalton agreed that the situation was largely satisfactory.
	:2	**Improvement of basic services in development areas.** LP(DI)(46)21.
	:3	**Employment in connection with forestry in the development areas.** LP(DI)(46)27.
	:4	**Training of building craftsmen in development areas.** LP(DI)(46)28. Isaacs said that the scheme was going well.
	:5	**Major road schemes.** LP(DI)(46)26.
10 July	7th:1	**New towns.** LP(DI)(46)30 and 37. Cost and timing of new towns' transport facilities discussed. New towns in the West Riding of Yorkshire and South Wales approved in principle.
	:2	**Factory building: progress for the period ended 31 May 1946.** LP(DI)(46)33. Progress was satisfactory.

	:3	**Provision of employment for women and girls in South Wales.** LP(DI)(46)34.
	:4	**Clearance of storage space in Scotland.** LP(DI)(46)32.
	:5	**Housing in the development areas: key workers' houses.** LP(DI)(46)35. General agreement that the Board of Trade should use its powers under the 1945 Distribution of Industry Act to build some houses.
	:6	**Messrs. Wiggins, Teape and Co. (1919) Ltd.** LP(DI)(46)36.
31 July	8th:1	**Location of government industrial establishments.** LP(DI)(46)41.
	:2	**New towns.** LP(DI)(46)44 and 45.
	:3	**Allocation of raw materials in unemployment areas.** LP(DI)(46)40, 43, 46, 47.
	:4	**Employment situation on Merseyside.** LP(DI)(46)48.
	:5	**Economic position in Lewis and Harris.** LP(DI)(46)49.
	:6	**Clearance of derelict land in development areas.** LP(DI)(46)38.
	:7	**Houses for key workers.** LP(DI)(46)50. Agreement that such housing should be secured by use of the Board of Trade's powers if the Ministry of Health agreed that this would expedite matters.
	:8	**Factory building in development areas.** LP(DI)(46)42, 51, 55.
	:9	**Iron and steel factories in Lanarkshire.** LP(DI)(46)52.
	:10	**Water supply, sewerage and sewerage disposal in development areas.** LP(DI)(46)53.
	:11	**Supplies of gas and electricity in development areas.**
	:12	**Financial assistance to firms setting up in development areas.**
	:13	**Ross factory development by C.W.S. at Taffs Well.** LP(DI)(46)54.
	:14	**Construction of forest roads.** LP(DI)(46)56.
11 Sept	9th:1	**Emergency training centres.** LP(DI)(46)62.
	:2	**Lewis Burger's factory expansion.** LP(DI)(46)58.
	:3	**Water supply, sewerage and sewerage disposal in development areas.** LP(DI)(46)60.
	:4	**Housing of managerial staff.** LP(DI)(46)59.
	:5	**Recruitment in agriculture of unemployed men and women from the development areas.** LP(DI)(46)61.
	:6	**Basic services in the Scottish development area.** LP(DI)(46)63. Situation satisfactory.

	:9	**Employment and unemployment situation.** LP(DI)(46)66 and 86.
	:10	**Allocation of cloth to garment makers in unemployment areas.** LP(DI)(46)73.
27 Nov	**12th:1**	**Employment and unemployment situation.** LP(DI)(46)66, 86, 96 (revise). Discussion of further steps to improve the employment position in the development areas. The general feeling was that cuts in the supplies of materials to these areas should be minimized since they might extinguish new industries.
	:2	**Progress in clearance in derelict land in development areas.** LP(DI)(46)95.
	:3	**Development of Welwyn Garden City and Hatfield.** LP(DI)(46)93, 97, 101.
	:4	**Building programme in South Wales.** LP(DI)(46)98. Dalton said that the fundamental aim was to press forward with factory development until there was no unemployment in development areas.
	:5	**Restoration of prosperity of the South Wales ports: free ports.** LP(DI)(46)99. Agreed no case for a free port.
11 Dec	**13th:1**	**Development area policy.** LP(DI)(46)100. Discussion of need for more state action.
	:2	**Development of Welwyn Garden City and Hatfield.** LP(DI)(46)97, 101, 102. There was some feeling that too much was being done on new towns and that there was over-concentration on London.

CAB 132/22   Memoranda   26 Apr–31 Dec 1946   LP(DI)(46)1–109.

26 Apr	**LP(DI)(46)1**	**Composition and terms of reference of Distribution of Industry Subcommittee – E.E. Bridges,** 1p. Also LP(46)100.
25 Apr	2	**Progress in the development areas – Belcher,** 5+13p appendixes. Recommends concentration on the completion of schemes already planned.
30 Apr	3	**Requirements of the development areas – Dalton,** 3p. Sets out thirteen questions to be considered.
8 May	4	**Requirements of the development areas – Civil Lord of the Treasury,** 2p. Not circulated.
10 May	5	**Ministry of Transport depot at Rumney, near Cardiff – Strauss,** 1p.
10 May	6	**Allocation of materials to development area firms – Dalton covering Jay,** 1+2p. Recommends that, even when total supplies of materials are not increasing, departments should divert a small quota from areas of labour

		shortage to areas where extra employment could be generated.
13 May	7	**Amount of requisitioned factory space still held in development areas by the services and other departments – W. Lindsell,** 2p.
13 May	8	**Training of building trade craftsmen in the development areas – Isaacs and Tomlinson,** 3p. Progress report.
13 May	9	**Houses for key workers in development areas – Belcher,** 2p.
21 May	10	**Creation of new brickworks and the use of imported bricks in development areas – Tomlinson,** 1+2p appendix.
24 May	11	**Iron and steel factories in Lanarkshire – Wilmot,** 6p.
13 May	12	**Establishment of new towns – Silkin,** 7p.
15 May	13	**New towns in Scotland – Westwood,** 3+1p.
21 May	14	**Release of permanent storage space in development areas – Smith,** 2p.
20 May	15	**Allocation of raw materials to firms in unemployment areas – Belcher,** 2+4p. The effect of policy was small but it was hoped to increase it by greater discrimination in favour of unemployment areas, as supplies of raw materials increased.
20 May	16	**Demolition of houses, etc., for road works – Barnes,** 2p.
21 May	17	**New towns – Dalton covering Jay,** 1+3p. There were two aspects to this policy: (a) redistribution of labour to areas of labour shortage from those with a surplus; (b) decongestion of population from large-scale overgrown areas. To attain the former it was necessary to control the latter strictly, so that facilities in new towns were reserved for firms from congested areas.
22 May	18	**Ministry of Food oil hardening plant at Dowlais – Belcher covering panel B,** 1+2p annex.
26 May	19	**Future location of Short Bros. (Rochester and Bedford) Ltd., and of Short and Harland Ltd. – Wilmot,** 6p.
26 May	20	**Factory space in the development areas not in use for productive purposes – Wilmot,** 2+2p appendixes. Supplement to LP(DI)(46)11.
29 May	21	**The improvement of basic services in the development areas – Belcher,** 2+4p appendix. Recommendations by panel A on the third report of the Inter-departmental Group on the Physical Development of the Development Areas.
31 May	22	**Estimated capital cost to public funds of establishing new towns – Silkin,** 2+2+2p

appendixes. He was convinced that the creation of every new town would save public money.

2 June	23	**Capital cost to public funds of the development of a new town in Scotland – Westwood**, 2+2p appendix.
2 June	24	**Prospective expenditure on transport facilities in the London area – Barnes**, 2+1p annex. He envisaged expenditure of £150m on railways alone.
12 June	25	**The employment and unemployment situation – Isaacs**, 1+3p annex +9p appendixes. Quarterly report. Reconversion was going well but there were still problems with the development areas, especially South Wales.
13 June	26	**Programme for major road schemes in development areas – Barnes**, 3p.
14 June	27	**Employment in connection with forestry in the development areas – Williams and Westwood covering the Forestry Commission**, 1+4p.
15 June	28	**Training of building trade craftsmen in development areas – Isaacs and Tomlinson**, 2p. Progress report.
15 June	29	**The definition of an unemployment area – Isaacs**, 2p. The definition included all development areas and other areas where registered unemployment among insured persons was 5% and there was no reason to think that level was temporary. 5% was chosen because it was roughly twice the national percentage at that time.
23 June	30	**Divergence between estimated capital cost of developing a new town at East Kilbride and of developing a town of similar size in the London region – Westwood**, 1+2p.
27 June	31	**Clearance of War Office stores from Barrhead depot – M. Flett**, 1p.
3 July	32	**Clearance of space in Scotland – W. Lindsell**, 3+1p annex.
5 July	33	**Factory building progress for the period ending 31 May 1946 – Belcher**, 1+4p. First bi-monthly report.
7 July	34	**Provision of employment for women and girls in the South Wales development area – Belcher**, 2+7p.
8 July	35	**Housing: general progress, priority centres, key workers – Bevan**, 2+2p appendixes. The decision to give factories equal priority to housing in development areas inevitably meant slower progress.
6 July	36	**Wiggins Teape and Co. (1919) Ltd.: proposal for factory extension at Woodburn Green, Buckinghamshire – Belcher**, 2p.

7 July	37	**Cost of providing transport facilities for new towns – Barnes,** 2+5p annex. Officials had not compared closely the relative costs of unplanned dispersal of London as against Silkin's proposals, since the problem was more one of timing and priorities than of comparative costs.
8 July	39	**Progress report on the resettlement training scheme – Isaacs,** 6+1p appendix.
9 July	40	**Unemployment areas – Strachey,** 3p. Improvization needed because hard and fast rules could not be applied to food industries.
17 July	41	**Location of government industrial establishments – Dalton,** 3p.
24 July	42	**Proposal to modernize and extend the Round Oak Steel Works, Brierley Hill, Staffordshire – Belcher,** 2p.
25 July	43	**Allocation of raw materials to firms in unemployment areas – Belcher,** 1+3p annex. Progress report.
28 July	44	**Establishment of new towns – Silkin,** 3p. Progress report.
26 July	45	**New towns in Scotland – Westwood,** 3p. Progress report.
26 July	46	**Allocation of raw materials by the Ministry of Supply to firms in unemployment areas – M. Flett covering the Ministry of Supply,** 1p. Extract of a letter pointing out that opportunities were limited.
29 July	47	**Allocation of raw materials to unemployment areas – Tomlinson,** 1p.
28 July	48	**Employment situation on Merseyside – Belcher covering the Inter-departmental Committee on Unemployment during the Period of Reconversion,** 1+7+10p annexes. Long-term plans were being drawn up but it would be eighteen months before they would have any real impact. Action needed to solve the short-term problem.
29 July	49	**Economic position of the island of Lewis and Harris – Fraser,** 6+5p appendixes. Recommends immediate public works and the island's scheduling as a development area.
29 July	50	**Building of houses for key workers in development areas – Tomlinson,** 2p. Existing procedure was quicker than provision under the Distribution of Industry Act, 1945.
28 July	51	**Factory building progress for the period ending 30 June 1946 – Belcher,** 1+3p.
27 July	52	**Iron and steel factories in Lanarkshire and Renfrewshire – Wilmot,** 2p.

26 July	53	**Water supply, sewerage and sewerage disposal in development areas – Bevan,** 4+3p appendixes.
27 July	54	**Co-operative Wholesale Society: possible factory development at Taffs Well – Silkin,** 2p.
29 July	55	**Proposal to reconstruct and extend the Sound City Film Studios, Shepperton, Middlesex – Belcher,** 2p.
30 July	56	**Construction of forest roads – Isaacs,** 3p.
16 Aug	57	**The Army Training School at Beachley – M. Flett covering Lawson,** 1+1p.
6 Sept	58	**Lewis Berger and Sons Ltd.: proposal for a factory extension at Chadwell Heath, Essex – Belcher,** 2p.
6 Sept	59	**Housing of managerial staff – Belcher,** 2p.
8 Sept	60	**Water supply, sewerage and sewerage disposal in development areas – Bevan,** 2+2p appendix.
9 Sept	61	**Arrangements to be made to stimulate the recruitment to the agricultural industry of suitable unemployed men and women from the development areas – Edwards, N.,** 5p.
9 Sept	62	**Emergency Training Centres – Edwards, N.,** 1p.
10 Sept	63	**Basic services in the Scottish development area – Fraser,** 2p. Progress report.
12 Sept	64	**Unemployment figures for development areas – Edwards, N.,** 1+1p.
10 Sept	65	**Factory building. Progress in development areas – Belcher,** 1p.
17 Sept	66	**The employment and unemployment situation – Edwards, N.,** 1+3p annex +7p appendixes. Quarterly report.
1 Oct	67	**Acquisition of land for roads – Barnes,** 1+4p. Consideration of how to quicken the process.
4 Oct	68	**Barry Moor Works and International Alloys factory at Cardiff – Wilmot,** 1p.
8 Oct	69	**Allocation of raw materials to firms in unemployment areas – Tomlinson,** 1p. Progress report.
10 Oct	70	**Construction of forest roads – Isaacs,** 2+3p appendix.
11 Oct	71	**Restoration of the prosperity of the South Wales ports – Barnes,** 3+7p annexes. Long-term prospects were hopeful but action required in the short term.
12 Oct	72	**Geographical maps of the development areas – R.J.W. Stacy and J.H. Lidderdale covering the Board of Trade location of industry planning room,** 1+6p. Maps of each area.
12 Oct	73	**Allocation of cloth to garment makers in unemployment areas – Belcher,** 2p.
16 Oct	74	**Crawley Aircraft and Precision Tool Co. Ltd.: proposal for a factory extension at London Road, Crawley, Sussex – Wilmot,** 2p.

17 Oct	75	**Establishment of new towns at Mobberley and Aycliffe** – Silkin, 3p. Asking for committee's general approval.
21 Oct	76	**Employment in the separate areas of the South Wales and Monmouthshire development area** – Belcher, 2+12p. Sets out position in different parts of the development area.
20 Oct	77	**Steel factories in development areas** – Wilmot, 1+6p. Letter to Cripps, with note of a meeting with deputation from the British Constructional Steelwork Association attached.
21 Oct	78	**Proposals by Messrs. G.W. King Ltd. to erect an extension of 14,450 sq. ft. to their factory at Fairview Road, Stevenage** – Belcher, 3p.
21 Oct	79	**Proposal to extend Ford Motor Company's works at Dagenham, Essex** – Belcher, 3p.
19 Oct	80	**Roofing materials for factory building** – Wilson, H., 1p.
24 Oct	81	**Change of secretaryship** – T.M. Wilson, 1p.
21 Oct	82	**Employment on Merseyside** – Belcher, 1+9p annex +1p appendix. Progress report by the Inter-departmental Committee on Unemployment during the Period of Reconversion.
21 Oct	83	**Germiston and Rutherglen** – Belcher, 2p.
21 Oct	84	**Unemployment areas** – Strachey, 3p. Supply shortages had limited his ability to help these areas.
24 Oct	85	**Release of Ministry of Food storage space in development areas** – Strachey, 1p.
21 Oct	86	**The unemployment situation** – Isaacs, 1+4p annex +16p appendixes. Supplement to LP(DI)(46)66.
28 Oct	87	**Building programme for the South Wales development area (excluding Pembroke)** – T.M. Wilson covering the Ministry of Works, 1+1p. Sets out the number of skilled and unskilled workers required.
28 Oct	88	**Allocation of raw materials to firms in unemployment areas** – Belcher, 1+5p annex. Progress report. Scope for action remained limited.
29 Oct	89	**Allocation of raw materials to firms in unemployment areas** – Wilmot, 2p. Progress report on industries for which he was responsible.
1 Nov	90	**Long-term aspects of employment in the South Wales and Monmouthshire development area** – Silkin, 1+3p. Consideration of some of the longer-term problems arising out of LP(DI)(46)76.

1 Nov	91	**Factory building programme in the development areas for the period ending 30 Sept 1946 – Belcher,** 1+2p appendix. Progress report.
4 Nov	92	**Note by the Minister of Labour and National Service on a memorandum by the Parliamentary Secretary to the Board of Trade on employment in the separate areas of the South Wales and Monmouthshire development area – Isaacs,** 1p.
21 Nov	93	**Development of Welwyn Garden City and Hatfield – Tomlinson,** 1p.
4 Nov	94	**New towns in mining areas – Westwood,** 3+1p appendix.
11 Nov	95	**Progress in the clearance of derelict land in development areas – Belcher,** 3p.
15 Nov	96	**The employment and unemployment situation – Isaacs,** 4p. Revise version.
13 Nov	97	**Development of Welwyn Garden City and Hatfield – Silkin,** 2p.
22 Nov	98	**Building programme in the South Wales development area (excluding Pembroke) – Tomlinson covering the Headquarters Building Committee,** 1+3+2p annexes.
25 Nov	99	**Restoration of prosperity at the South Wales ports: free ports – Dalton,** 1p.
25 Nov	100	**Development area policy – Fraser,** 3p. Concern that present policy would not solve male unemployment at least in the Scottish development area. The state should enter into production in development areas.
26 Nov	101	**Development of Welwyn Garden City and Hatfield – Belcher,** 2p.
5 Dec	102	**Development of Welwyn Garden City and Hatfield – Silkin,** 2p.
8 Dec	103	**Electricity and gas in the development areas – Gaitskell,** 4+4p appendixes.
9 Dec	104	**Labour supply for forest roads construction scheme – Isaacs,** 1p.
10 Dec	105	**The employment and unemployment situation – Isaacs,** 1+3p annex +5p appendixes. Progress report.
12 Dec	106	**Recruitment of inexperienced unemployed workers for employment in agriculture – Isaacs,** 2+1p appendix. Progress report.
16 Dec	107	**Ennerdale scheme: progress report – Bevan,** 2p.
23 Dec	108	**Balloon barrage site, Fazakerly – Belcher covering de Freitas,** 1+1p.
31 Dec	109	**Employment in the separate areas of the South Wales and Monmouthshire development areas – Belcher,** 2p.

CAB 132/23   Meetings   15 Jan–24 Sept 1947   LP(DI)(47)1st–14th.

15 Jan   **LP(DI)(47)1st:1**   **Employment and unemployment situation.**
LP(DI)(46)105.

:2   **Employment in the separate areas of the South Wales and Monmouthshire development area.** LP(DI)(46)109.

:3   **Recruitment of inexperienced unemployed for employment in agriculture.** LP(DI)(46)106.

:4   **Electricity and gas in the development areas.** LP(DI)(46)103.

:5   **Restriction of new factory building and extensions in London.** LP(DI)(47)2 and 7.

:6   **Proposal by Shell Co. to erect new buildings at Watford.** LP(DI)(47)1.

:7   **Proposal by Watts-Hilger-Swift Group to erect a new factory at Grange Hill Estate, Essex.** LP(DI)(47)5 and 6.

:8   **Balloon barrage site, Fazakerly.** LP(DI)(46)108.

:9   **Ennerdale scheme.** LP(DI)(46)107.

:10   **Progress in clearance of derelict land in development areas.** LP(DI)(47)3.

:11   **Labour supply for forest roads construction.** LP(DI)(46)104.

5 Feb   **2nd:1**   **Factory building progress in development areas.** LP(DI)(47)8, 13, 17, 18. The subcommittee was dissatisfied with department's apparent lack of initiative and co-ordination. There should be closer scrutiny of licence applications for buildings other than factories and housing.

:2   **Housing of managerial staff and key workers in development areas.** LP(DI)(47)11.

:3   **Building labour in South Wales.** LP(DI)(47)4.

:4   **New town proposals.** LP(DI)(47)12.

:5   **Application by Star Aluminium Co. to extend factory at Wolverhampton.** LP(DI)(47)9 and 14.

:6   **Application by Jaguar Cars Ltd. to extend factory at Coventry.** LP(DI)(47)15.

:7   **Barry Moor works.** LP(DI)(47)10.

:8   **Labour supply for forest roads construction scheme.** LP(DI)(47)16.

26 Feb   **3rd:1**   **Restriction of new factory building and extensions in London.** LP(DI)(47)2 and 21.

:2   **Linwood Factory, Paisley.** LP(DI)(47)24.

:3   **Proposal by Watts-Hilger-Swift Group to erect new factory in Essex.** LP(DI)(47)5 and 6. Wilmot felt this to be the most important case to come before the subcommittee. The production of the leading firm in its field, with the possibility of exports to the United States, could be delayed if it were forced to go to a

		new town. The subcommittee agreed to the proposed construction in Essex.
	:4	**Application by Fromson Construction Co. to build a factory at Colnbrook, West Middlesex.** LP(DI)(47)19 and 20.
	:5	**Proposal to locate Gas Research Board establishment at Beckenham.** LP(DI)(47)22.
	:6	**Proposal by Shell Refining and Marketing Co. to erect new buildings at Watford.** LP(DI)(47)1 and 27.
	:7	**Proposed extension to Firth Vickers Stainless Steels Ltd., Sheffield.** LP(DI)(47)23 and 28.
	:8	**Restoration of the prosperity of the South Wales ports.** LP(DI)(47)26.
	:9	**Clearance of derelict land in development areas.** LP(DI)(47)25.
	:10	**Steel for factories at St. Helens, Auckland.**
19 Mar	4th:1	**Proposed expansion at Coventry by Jaguar Cars Ltd.** LP(DI)(47)15 and 37.
	:2	**Principles to be applied in considering industrial building projects in the Greater London area.** LP(DI)(47)35.
	:3	**Employment on Merseyside.** Statement by Wilson, H. that the situation was far less hopeful than expected. Consideration of whether Merseyside should become a development area.
	:4	**Factory building in the development areas.** LP(DI)(47)30, 31, 32, 33, 34. Delays were not due to a labour shortage but there might be difficulties once the material situation improved. Discussion then centred on steel supplies and why factory building in development areas was not on the priority list of steel allocations.
2 Apr	5th:1	**Membership of the subcommittee.**
	:2	**Factory building in development areas.** Dalton reported on his talk with Cripps on measures to remedy the situation.
	:3	**Houses for key workers in industry in West Cumberland development area.** LP(DI)(47)29.
	:4	**Economic position of the island of Lewis and Harris.** LP(DI)(47)36. Consideration of whether it should be scheduled as a development area.
	:5	**Recruitment of unemployed workers for agriculture.** LP(DI)(47)38.
	:6	**Labour supply for forest roads construction.** LP(DI)(47)39.
24 Apr	6th:1	**Government-financed factory building in the development areas.** LP(DI)(47)42. Belcher wished to correct steel makers'

misapprehension that steel for development areas was no longer important because it did not have priority for factory building there.

	:2	**Employment prospects in the Scottish development areas** LP(DI)(47)41. The subcommittee recognized that the existing programme was not adequate.
	:3	**Allocation of raw materials to employment areas.** LP(DI)(47)40.
	:4	**Road works in West Cumberland and smaller schemes elsewhere.** LP(DI)(47)45.
	:5	**Use of trainees in mobile labour force.** LP(DI)(47)43.
	:6	**Embargo on carriage by rail of steel for Wales.** LP(DI)(47)46.
1 May	7th	**Steel for development area factories.** LP(DI)(47)49 and 51. The timetable of factory building in development areas could not be adhered to and so a separate sub-allocation of steel for such building should be made.
8 May	8th:1	**Industrial building in development areas: regional progress meetings.** LP(DI)(47)47.
	:2	**Location of projects for modernization and development of sheet and tin plate production in South Wales.** LP(DI)(47)54.
	:3	**Proposal by Mulliners to extend their premises at Birmingham.** LP(DI)(47)48.
	:4	**Clearance of derelict land in development areas.** LP(DI)(47)52.
	:5	**Proposal by Courtaulds Ltd. to establish a fundamental research institute in Central London.** LP(DI)(47)53.
	:6	**Proposal by Johnson Matthey and Co. to extend their factory in Enfield, Middlesex.** LP(DI)(47)55.
4 June	9th:1	**Location of projects for modernization and development of steel and tin plate industry in South Wales.** LP(DI)(47)54, 58, 59. Wilmot disagreed with Cripps that industry should be guided to particular districts within development areas.
	:2	**Progress of government-financed factory building schemes in development areas.** LP(DI)(47)60.
	:3	**Bulk allocations of materials to industrial estates.**
	:4	**Proposal by Courtaulds Ltd. to establish a fundamental research site in Central London.**
18 June	10th:1	**Labour for forest roads and forest work generally.** LP(DI)(47)63.

		:2	**Progress of government-financed factory building schemes in development areas.** LP(DI)(47)60.
		:3	**Proposal by Standard Telephones and Cables Ltd. to extend premises at Footscray.** LP(DI)(47)56. Approved, but some ministers felt too many cases were being recommended for exceptional treatment.
		:4	**Army Training School at Beachley.** LP(DI)(47)64.
		:5	**Application by Star Aluminium Co. to extend factory at Wolverhampton.** LP(DI)(47)61.
2 July	11th:1		**Employment and unemployment situation.** LP(DI)(47)62. Isaacs felt that a good recovery had been made from the fuel crisis and that development area policy was bearing fruit. Marquand agreed that, with unemployment at 2.2%, full employment as defined by Beveridge had been attained. Further increases in production could only be achieved by increased productivity. This view was supported by other ministers although material shortages were also identified as a serious impediment to increased production.
		:2	**Proposals for increasing employment in the Scottish development area.** LP(DI)(47)65.
		:3	**Proposal to erect factory at Loughton, Essex, by Baird and Tatlock Ltd., and Hopkin and Williams Ltd.** LP(DI)(47)67.
		:4	**Proposal to erect factory at Crayford, Kent, by F. Braby and Co. Ltd.** LP(DI)(47)68.
30 July	12th:1		**Allocation of raw materials to unemployment areas.** LP(DI)(47)44, 57, 65, 76, 77.
		:2	**Progressing of steel and supplies of glass and lead in development area factories.** LP(DI)(47)71(revise) and 88.
		:3	**Development of light industries in Lancashire and North Cheshire.** LP(DI)(47)74.
		:4	**Unemployment in Merseyside.** LP(DI)(47)78. Merseyside not to be scheduled as a development area.
		:5	**Recruitment of unemployed for agriculture.** LP(DI)(47)69.
		:6	**Watson and Sons Electro-medical Ltd.** LP(DI)(47)66.
		:7	**Rotary Hoes Ltd., East Hordon.** LP(DI)(47)75.
6 Aug	13th:1		**Factory proposal: Roy Feddon Ltd.** LP(DI)(47)94.
		:2	**New towns.** LP(DI)(47)80, 84, 91, 92.
		:3	**Unemployment situation.** LP(DI)(47)93.
		:4	**Factory building in development areas.** LP(DI)(47)95.

	:5	**Economic position of the island of Lewis and Harris.** LP(DI)(47)89.
	:6	**Panel A approvals in the Greater London area.** LP(DI)(47)79.
	:7	**Clearance of derelict land in development areas.** LP(DI)(47)90.
	:8	**Factory erection proposal: J. Lyons and Co.** LP(DI)(47)70.
	:9	**Factory erection proposal: Scaffolding Ltd.** LP(DI)(47)86.
	:10	**Factory creation proposal: Goodyear Tyre and Rubber Co.** LP(DI)(47)82.
	:11	**Factory proposals: Daily News Ltd., Daily Express Newspapers Ltd., Kemsley Newspapers Ltd.** LP(DI)(47)83.
	:12	**Star Aluminium Co.** LP(DI)(47)85.
24 Sept	**14th:1**	**Factory erected at Stockton-on-Tees by Northern Trading Estates Ltd., for Le Tourneau (GB) Ltd.** LP(DI)(47)100.
	:2	**Provincial freight markets.** LP(DI)(47)97.
	:3	**Watson and Sons (Electro-medical) Ltd.** LP(DI)(47)101.
	:4	**Government orders in textile areas.** LP(DI)(47)99.

CAB 132/24   Memoranda   2 Jan–24 Sept 1947   LP(DI)(47)1–102.

2 Jan	**LP(DI)(47)1**	**Proposal by Shell Refining and Marketing Co. Ltd., to erect new buildings on the Munden Estate, Watford – Belcher**, 2p.
9 Jan	**2**	**Restriction of new factory building and extensions in London – Tomlinson**, 3p. Recommends that Panel A should operate more rigorous control.
9 Jan	**3**	**Progress in clearance of derelict land in the development areas – Belcher**, 2p.
10 Jan	**4**	**Building labour in South Wales – Isaacs and Tomlinson**, 1+4p.
13 Jan	**5**	**Proposal by the Watts-Hilger-Swift Group to erect a new factory at the Grange Hill Estate, Essex – Belcher**, 3p.
14 Jan	**6**	**Proposal by the Watts-Hilger-Swift Group to erect a factory at Grange Hill, Essex – Woodburn**, 2p.
14 Jan	**7**	**Restriction of new factory building and extensions in London – Belcher**, 1p.
25 Jan	**8**	**Factory building programme in development areas – Tomlinson**, 3+6p appendixes. Labour shortages suggested: (a) too much factory building work had been started; (b) closer control was needed in development areas over the various types of building.

27 Jan	**9**	**Application of the Star Aluminium Co. for a licence to extend their factory at Wolverhampton – Isaacs**, 2p.
28 Jan	**10**	**Barry Moor Works, South Wales – Wilmot**, 1p.
29 Jan	**11**	**Housing of managerial staff and key workers in development areas – Belcher**, 3p.
1 Feb	**12**	**New town proposals – Silkin**, 7p. Full statement of proposals, with estimates of the labour and materials necessary.
3 Feb	**13**	**Factory building programme in the development areas for the period ending 31 December 1946 – Belcher**, 2+3p appendix.
3 Feb	**14**	**Application by the Star Aluminium Co. for a licence to extend their factory at Wolverhampton – Shinwell**, 2p.
3 Feb	**15**	**Proposal by Jaguar Cars Ltd. to extend their premises at Swallow Road, Coventry – Belcher**, 3p.
3 Feb	**16**	**Labour supply for forest roads construction scheme – Williams and Westwood covering the Chairman of the Forestry Commission**, 1+2p. Progress report.
3 Feb	**17**	**Factory building progress in development areas – Belcher**, 1p. Criticism of LP(DI)(47)8. The committee should consider methods of ensuring that comparatively modest claims were fully met.
3 Feb	**18**	**Factory building progress in the development areas – Isaacs**, 2p. Criticism of implication in LP(DI)(47)8 that delay was due to a shortage of building labour.
5 Feb	**19**	**Application of the Fromson Construction Co. of Canada for a licence to build a new factory at Colnbrook, West Middlesex – Silkin**, 3p.
17 Feb	**20**	**Fromson Construction Co. – Belcher**, 2p.
17 Feb	**21**	**Report of Panel A on approvals of industrial building in the Greater London area – Cripps covering Panel A**, 2+3+1p appendix. Cripps did not think that more restrictive principles could be adopted without detriment to industrial efficiency.
17 Feb	**22**	**Proposal by the Gas Research Board to adapt the Abbey School buildings, Beckenham, Kent, for use as a central research unit – Belcher**, 3p.
18 Feb	**23**	**Proposed extension to Firth Vickers Stainless Steel Ltd. Sheffield – Noel-Baker**, 2p.
22 Feb	**24**	**Ministry of Supply Factory, Linwood Road, Paisley (760,000 sq. ft.) – Belcher**, 3p.
21 Feb	**25**	**Progress in clearance of derelict land in the development areas – Belcher**, 2p.

22 Feb	26	**Restoration of the prosperity of the South Wales ports – Strauss,** 1+5p appendixes. Progress report.
21 Feb	27	**Proposal by Shell Refining and Marketing Co. Ltd. to erect central laboratories on the Munden Estate, Watford – Gaitskell,** 2p.
25 Feb	28	**Firth Vickers Stainless Steels Ltd. – Belcher,** 2p.
28 Feb	29	**West Cumberland development area: houses for key workers in industry – Bevan,** 2p.
3 Mar	30	**Progress of factory building in the English development areas – Wilson,** 1+12+15p annexes. Questions the value of trading estates and recommends urgent examination of steel supply.
5 Mar	31	**Report by the Parliamentary Secretary of the Ministry of Labour on enquiry into delays in factory building in the South Wales and Monmouthshire development area – Edwards, N.,** 3+8p appendix.
18 Mar	31	**Delays in factory building in the South Wales and Monmouthshire development area – Edwards, N.,** 1+1p. Includes some amendments to LP(DI)(47)30.
6 Mar	32	**Factory building in the Scottish development area – Fraser,** 5p. Means of overcoming delays.
10 Mar	33	**Factory building in the development area – Belcher,** 1p.
10 Mar	34	**A report on the progress of Treasury-financed factory building schemes in the development areas – Belcher,** 3+1p appendix. Progress report followed by consideration of the most critical material shortages.
10 Mar	35	**Principles to be applied in considering individual building projects in the Greater London area – Cripps covering Panel A,** 1+2p. Draft report.
12 Mar	36	**Economic position on the island of Lewis and Harris – Fraser covering Panel A,** 2+4p.
14 Mar	37	**Proposal by Jaguar Cars Ltd. to extend their premises at Swallow Road, Coventry – Wilmot,** 2p.
25 Mar	38	**Recruitment of unemployed workers for agriculture – Westwood and Williams,** 3p.
29 Mar	39	**Labour supply etc. for forest roads construction scheme – Westwood and Williams,** 2p. Progress report.
8 Apr	40	**Unemployment areas – Strachey,** 3p. Third report.
21 Apr	41	**Employment prospects in the Scottish development area – Fraser,** 4p. Describes employment prospects and measures taken to

let factories to firms predominantly employing men. Questions whether existing policy should not be supplemented by direct government production.

22 Apr	42	**Report on the progress of government-financed factory building schemes in development areas – Belcher,** 1+1p.
22 Apr	43	**Use of trainees in mobile labour force – Key,** 2p. Mobile forces of building labour, employing a high proportion of trainees, were not the most efficient or rapid way to counteract the expected building labour shortage in South Wales.
22 Apr	44	**Allocation of raw materials to firms in unemployment areas – Wilmot,** 1p. Preferential treatment for development of unemployment areas should continue but the importance of the end product should also be considered.
22 Apr	45	**Road schemes in West Cumberland and smaller schemes elsewhere – Barnes,** 2p. Progress report.
21 Apr	46	**Factory building in development areas – Strauss and Belcher,** 2p. Background to the embargo on steel supplies for Wales carried by rail.
23 Apr	47	**Industrial building in the development areas – Belcher,** 1p.
24 Apr	48	**Proposal by Messrs. Mulliners Ltd. to extend their premises at Bordesley Green, Birmingham – Wilmot,** 3p.
28 Apr	49	**Steel for development area factories – Marquand,** 3p. A drastic overhaul and reduction of authorizations were needed if deliveries were to match allocations.
29 Apr	50	**Changes in membership – T.M. Wilson,** 1p.
30 Apr	51	**Steel for development area factories – Belcher,** 1p. In agreement with LP(DI)(47)49 except with regard to the progressing of structural steel.
5 May	52	**Clearance of derelict land in the development areas – Belcher,** 4p. Progress report.
5 May	53	**Proposal by Courtaulds Ltd. to establish a fundamental research institute in Central London – Belcher,** 2p.
6 May	54	**Scheme for the modernization and development of the steel and tin plate industry in South Wales – Belcher covering the chairman of Panel A,** 1+3p.
6 May	55	**Johnson Matthey and Co. Ltd.: proposal for an extension to a factory at Brimsdown, Enfield, Middlesex,** 3p.
8 May	56	**Proposal by Standard Telephones and Cables Ltd. to extend their premises at Footscray,**

		Kent – Leonard, 2p.
20 May	57	**Allocations of raw materials to firms in unemployment areas – Edwards, N.,** 2p. In contrast to LP(DI)(47)44, he felt that existing arrangements for the allocation of raw materials for manufacture, as opposed to factory construction, were sufficient.
20 May	58	**Location of projects for the modernization and development of sheet and tin plate production in South Wales – Belcher,** 3p.
28 May	59	**Location of projects for the modernization and development of sheet and tin plate production in South Wales – Wilmot,** 6p.
3 June	60	**Report on the progress of government-financed factory building schemes in the development areas – Cripps,** 1+1p.
3 June	61	**Application by Star Aluminium Co. to extend factory at Wolverhampton – Leonard,** 3p.
11 June	62	**The employment and unemployment situation – Isaacs,** 1+3p annex +7p appendixes. Covers two quarters as the previous report had been cancelled due to the electricity crisis.
12 June	63	**Labour supply for forest roads and forest work generally – Westwood and Williams,** 3p. Progress report.
16 June	64	**The Army Training School at Beachley – Bellinger,** 3p.
25 June	65	**Proposals for increasing employment in the Scottish development area – Fraser,** 4p. Further proposals.
11 July	66	**Watson and Sons Electro-medical Ltd. – Belcher,** 3p.
28 June	67	**Baird and Tatlock (London) Ltd. and Hopkin and Williams Ltd. proposal to erect a factory at Loughton, Essex – Belcher,** 2p.
30 June	68	**F. Braby & Co. proposal to erect a factory at Crayford, Kent – Belcher,** 1p.
7 July	69	**Recruitment of unemployed workers for agriculture – Fraser,** 2p.
11 July	70	**J. Lyons and Co., Cadby Hall – Belcher,** 3p.
25 July	71	**Steel, cement, lead and glass for factory building in development areas – Belcher covering H.M. Fraser,** 1+3p. Revise version. H.M. Fraser believed the chief obstacle to reasonable progress was the Prime Minister's list of priorities, which excluded factory building in development areas.
12 July	72	**Expansion of oil refinery capacity in the United Kingdom – Belcher,** 5p.
15 July	73	**Progress of privately-financed factory building schemes in the development areas – Key,** 1+2p appendix.

12 July	74	**The development of light industries in Lancashire and North Cheshire – Belcher**, 2p. Development considered to be excessive.
12 July	75	**Rotary Hoes Ltd., East Hornden – Belcher**, 2p.
12 July	76	**Allocation of raw materials to unemployment areas: general policy – Belcher**, 2p. Increased raw material shortages made preferential treatment more difficult but such short-term shortages should not unduly influence policy. Once acute material shortages had disappeared there would still be a manpower problem.
12 July	77	**Progress report on allocation of raw materials to unemployment areas – Belcher**, 1+3p annex.
17 July	78	**Unemployment on Merseyside – Cripps**, 3+11p appendixes. Against scheduling Merseyside or any more regions as a development area at present.
18 July	79	**Panel A approvals in the Greater London area January-June, 1947 – Belcher covering Panel A**, 1+1p.
19 July	80	**New town proposals in the provinces – Silkin**, 4p. Three new towns proposed.
19 July	81	**Expansion of oil refinery capacity in the U.K. – Noel-Baker**, 1+1p annex.
21 July	82	**The Goodyear Tyre and Rubber Co. Ltd.: proposal for an extension to their factory at Wolverhampton – Belcher**, 2p.
21 July	83	**Daily News Ltd. (*News Chronicle* and *Star*); Daily Express Newspapers Ltd. (*Daily Express* and *Sunday Express*); Kemsley Newspapers Ltd. (*Daily Sketch, Daily Graphic* and *Sunday Chronicle*) – Belcher**, 1p.
22 July	84	**New town at East Kilbride – Westwood**, 1p.
22 July	85	**Star Aluminium Co. – Leonard**, 1p.
23 July	86	**Proposal by Scaffolding (Great Britain) Ltd. to establish a new building in Mitcham, Surrey – Belcher**, 1p.
23 July	87	**Expansion of oil refinery capacity in the U.K. – Shinwell**, 3p.
24 July	88	**Lead sheet and pipe for factories in development areas – Leonard**, 1p.
26 July	89	**Economic position of the island of Lewis and Harris – Fraser**, 1p.
26 July	90	**Clearance of derelict land in the development areas – Belcher**, 2p. Progress report.
26 July	91	**New town at Welwyn-Hatfield – Silkin**, 1p.
28 July	92	**New town proposal for Durham – Williams**, 2p. Conflict between the development of the new town and the use of the land for agriculture.
30 July	93	**Unemployment in the development areas – Edwards, N.**, 1+11p appendix. Omitting the period of the fuel crisis, unemployment in the

development areas had been improving, relative to the country as a whole, since June 1946.

30 July	94	**Roy Fedden Ltd., Stoke Orchard, near Cheltenham – Belcher**, 2p.
5 Aug	95	**Report on the progress of government- and privately-financed building schemes in the development areas – Belcher and Key**, 1+3p appendixes.
16 Aug	96	**Factory building in development areas – Strauss and Belcher**, 1p. Concerned with the embargo on the movement of steel for factory building in South Wales.
29 Aug	97	**Provincial freight rate – Marquand**, 2+2p appendix.
13 Sept	98	**Compulsory acquisition of factory premises in development areas – Fraser**, 1p. This was legally acceptable and should be used where factories were empty.
15 Sept	99	**Government orders in textile manufacturing areas – Marquand**, 1p.
22 Sept	100	**Factory erected at Stockton-on-Tees by the North Eastern Trading Estates Ltd. for Le Tourneau (Great Britain) Ltd. – Cripps**, 2p.
23 Sept	101	**Watson and Sons Electro-medical Ltd. – Marquand**, 2p.
24 Sept	102	**The employment and unemployment situation – Isaacs**, 1+3p annex +5p appendixes. Quarterly report.

14.3   Committee on Industrial Productivity

Set up in Dec 1947 following agreement between Isaacs, Cripps and Morrison that there should be a committee on industrial efficiency to consider problems affecting industrial morale, productivity and the machinery for handling them. The committee was to supplement the work of the Advisory Council on Scientific Policy (see CAB 132/64–69). Most of its work was to be conducted through panels which were constituted as required to report on particular aspects of the subject. Those established covered human factors (see CAB 132/31–35), imports substitution (see CAB 132/39–41), which later became the Natural Resources (Technical) Committee (see T 229/872), technical information services (see CAB 132/44–46) and technology and operational research (see CAB 132/47–48). A working party was also established in Feb 1948 to assist the committee and any of its panels (see CAB 132/49–50). The committee was essentially a temporary organization and was wound up in July 1950 as it was felt there was little more it could constructively do. It wrote two reports for the Economic Planning Board (T 229/827–829) and maintained links with the Productivity (Official) Committee and the Anglo-American Council on Productivity. See also CAB 124/1093–1097.

Terms   To advise the Lord President of the Council and the Chancellor of the Exchequer on the form and scale of research effort in the natural and social sciences, which will best assist an early increase in industrial productivity and further to advise on the manner in which the results of such research can best be applied.

Members H. Tizard (ch.); S. Zuckerman (Birmingham Univ., dep. ch.); W. Stanier (Supply); G. Schuster (British Institute of Management Council); A. King (Ld Pres. O.); E. Appleton (D.S.I.R.); H. Weeks (C.E.P.S.); R.L. Hall (Ec. Sect.); E.M. Nicholson (Ld Pres. O.); G.B. Blaker (Try); J. Tanner (Amalgamated Engineering Union); T. Williamson (National Union of General and Municipal Workers); C. Gibb (C.A. Parsons & Co. Ltd.); W.T. Griffiths (Mond Nickel Co. Ltd.); J. Neill (North Eastern Marine Engineering Co. Ltd.). (April 1949) E.M. Amphlett for Neill and W.B. Beard for Tanner.

Sec. E.D.T. Jourdain (Ld Pres. O.).

CAB 132/28 Meetings and Memoranda 30 Jan–24 Nov 1948 CIP(48)1st–8th and CIP(48)1–31.

Meetings

4 Feb	**CIP(48)1st:1**	**Terms of reference and composition.** CIP(48)1.
	:2	**Technology and operational research.** CIP(48)2.
	:3	**Import substitution.** CIP(48)4.
	:4	**Human factors affecting productivity.** CIP(48)3.
	:5	**Technical information services.** CIP(48)5.
	:6	**Working party.** CIP(48)6.
	:7	**Report from the Economic Planning Board.** CIP(48)7.
24 Mar	**2nd:1**	**Textile weaving industry.** CIP(48)11.
	:2	**Cotton spinning industry.** CIP(48)13.
	:3	**Automatic control and instrumentation.** CIP(48)10.
	:4	**Report from the Panel on Human Factors.** CIP(48)9.
	:5	**Report from the Panel on Technical Information Services.** CIP(48)12.
12 May	**3rd:1**	**Report by the chairman of the Imports Substitution Panel.** CIP(48)15 and 16.
	:2	**Interim progress report.** CIP(48)18 and 19. Agreement that a summary of progress should be forwarded to the Economic Planning Board.
	:3	**Textiles.** CIP(48)13 and 17.
	:4	**Scientific instrument industry.** CIP(48)14. Agreement that expansion of the industry was of importance to national productivity.
26 May	**4th:1**	**Matters arising from the minutes of the third meeting.** CIP(48)10 and 20(revise).
28 July	**5th:1**	**Oral statements by chairmen of panels.**
	:2	**Operational research.** CIP(48)21 and 25.
	:3	**University research projects.** CIP(48)22, 23, 24.
4 Oct	**6th:1**	**Matters arising from minutes of the fifth meeting.**
	:2	**Future work of the committee.** CIP(48)27 and 28.

	:3	Future meetings. E. Appleton to be acting chairman.
27 Oct	7th:1	Minutes of the sixth meeting.
	:2	Statements by chairmen of panels.
	:3	Sulphuric acid. CIP(48)29.
	:4	Statement by Dr. King. Report on his visit to the U.S.A.
24 Nov	8th:1	Matters arising from the minutes of the seventh meeting.
	:2	Oral statement by chairmen of panels.
	:3	The work of the Industrial Research Associations in relation to productivity. CIP(48)30.

Memoranda

30 Jan	CIP(48)1	Terms of reference and composition of committee – E.D.T. Jourdain, 2+1p addendum.
2 Feb	2	Panel on Technology and Operational Research – E.D.T. Jourdain, 2p.
3 Feb	3	Panel on Human Factors affecting Productivity – E.D.T. Jourdain, 1p.
30 Jan	4	Panel on Import Substitution – E.D.T. Jourdain, 2p.
31 Jan	5	Panel on Technical Information Services – E.D.T. Jourdain, 2p.
2 Feb	6	Formation of working party – A. King, 1p.
31 Jan	7	Report from the Economic Planning Board – E.D.T. Jourdain, 2p. Sets out the industries and problems which the Board felt should be tackled first.
6 Mar	8	Steel economy – H. Tizard covering the Panel on Imports Substitution, 1+4p.
16 Mar	9	Report from the Panel on Human Factors – E.D.T. Jourdain covering the Panel, 1+2+8+21p appendixes.
22 Mar	10	Automatic control and instrumentation – E.D.T. Jourdain covering the Industrial Electronics Panel, 1+14+14p appendixes.
19 Mar	11	Cotton weaving industry – E.D.T. Jourdain covering the Cotton Manufacturing Commission, 1+63p. Interim report.
20 Mar	12	Report from the Panel on Technical Information Services – E.D.T. Jourdain covering the Panel, 1+2p.
22 Mar	13	Report from the Panel on Technology and Operational Research – E.D.T. Jourdain covering the Panel, 1+9+8p appendixes.
6 May	14	The British Scientific Instrument Industry – E.D.T. Jourdain covering the Ministry of Supply, 1+4p.

8 May	15	**Report on paper-making materials – E.D.T. Jourdain covering the Panel on Imports Substitution,** 1+10p.
11 May	16	**Report by Chairman of Imports Substitution Panel – E.D.T. Jourdain covering S. Zuckerman,** 1+3p.
10 May	17	**Textiles – E.D.T. Jourdain covering W. Stanier,** 1+1p.
7 May	18	**Interim progress report – E.M. Nicholson,** 2+6+1p annex.
11 May	19	**Midlands Advisory Council on Productivity – E.M. Nicholson,** 1+6p annexes.
25 May	20	**The place of agriculture in the national economy – E.D.T. Jourdain covering S. Zuckerman,** 1+11p. Revise version. Stresses the importance of an expanded agricultural programme as a means of substituting imports.
22 July	21	**Principles and practices of operational research – E.D.T. Jourdain covering the Working Party on the Principles and Practices of Operational Research,** 1+44+19p appendixes. Also CIP(TR)(48)10(revise).
21 July	22	**A study of productivity in the wool textile industry – E.D.T. Jourdain covering J. Cohen,** 1+2p.
21 July	23	**Research projects at Birmingham University – E.D.T. Jourdain covering Professor T.U. Matthew,** 1+3p.
27 July	24	**University research projects – E.D.T. Jourdain covering A. King,** 1+1p.
26 July	25	**Operational research – E.D.T. Jourdain,** 1+3p. Summary of CIP(48)21.
6 Aug	26	**Depredations of rabbits – E.D.T. Jourdain covering S. Zuckerman,** 1+2+4+1p annex +1+2p. Also CIP(IS)(48)43(revise) and 51. Includes a note by E.M. Nicholson, 'Rabbits and the balance of payments'.
20 Sept	27	**Future work of the committee – E.D.T. Jourdain covering H. Tizard,** 1+4+2p appendix. Recommends preparation of a report.
20 Sept	28	**Recent developments at national level – E.D.T. Jourdain covering G.B. Blaker,** 1+3p. Mainly on the establishment and membership of the Anglo-American Council on Productivity.
21 Oct	29	**Report on sulphuric acid – E.D.T. Jourdain covering the Panel on Imports Substitution,** 1+14p. Amended version, 9 Nov.
17 Nov	30	**The work of the Industrial Research Associations in relation to productivity – E.D.T. Jourdain covering D.S.I.R.,** 1+9+17p appendixes. See OP(48)10 annex 10(a).

20 Nov	**31**	**Anglo-American Council on Productivity –**
		E.D.T. Jourdain covering the Council, 1+7p.
		Published report of the Council.

CAB 132/29   Meetings and Memoranda   21 Jan–14 Dec 1949   CIP(49)1st–8th
and CIP(49)1–32.

Meetings

26 Jan	**CIP(49)1st:1**	**Annual report. CIP(49)2.**
	:2	**Human Factors Panel. CIP(49)1.**
23 Feb	**2nd:1**	**Appointment of deputy chairman.**
	:2	**Annual report. CIP(49)4.** Detailed consideration.
	:3	**Consumption of electrical energy. CIP(49)6.**
1 Mar	**3rd:1**	**Annual report. CIP(49)4.** Detailed examination.
	:2	**Carbon black. CIP(49)5.**
	:3	**Coal saving.**
27 Apr	**4th:1**	**Changes in membership.**
	:2	**Minutes of the previous meeting. CIP(49)5 and 10.**
	:3	**Coal saving. CIP(49)12 and 13.**
	:4	**Work of the Research Associations in relation to productivity.**
25 May	**5th:1**	**Minutes of the previous meeting.**
	:2	**Tanning materials. CIP(49)14.**
	:3	**Panel on Imports Substitution. CIP(49)16.**
	:4	**Panel on Technical Information Services. CIP(49)17.**
	:5	**Future programme. CIP(49)18.**
	:6	**Measurement of productivity.**
22 June	**6th:1**	**Matters arising from the minutes of the previous meeting.**
	:2	**Nutritional requirements for industrial work. CIP(49)21.**
	:3	**Nitrogenous fertilizers. CIP(49)22.**
	:4	**Standardization. CIP(49)23.**
16 Sept	**7th:1**	**Matters arising from the minutes of the previous meeting.**
	:2	**Contribution of the Research Associations to industrial productivity. CIP(49)25.**
	:3	**Measurement of productivity. CIP(49)26.**
	:4	**Consumption of electrical energy. CIP(49)27.**
26 Oct	**8th:1**	**Minutes of the previous meeting.**
	:2	**Future work of the committee. CIP(49)28.**
	:3	**Scientific and technical library facilities. CIP(49)29.**

Memoranda

21 Jan	**CIP(49)1**	**Report on the work of the Panel on Human Factors – G. Schuster,** 1+4p.

22 Jan	2	**Draft annual report – E.D.T. Jourdain,** 1+25p. Draft of CIP(49)4.
8 Feb	3	**The American trade unions and productivity – E.D.T. Jourdain covering A. King,** 1+6+18p appendixes.
17 Feb	4	**Annual report (2nd draft) – E.D.T. Jourdain,** 1+35p. Draft of CIP(49)9.
21 Mar	5	**Carbon black – E.D.T. Jourdain,** 1+6p. Revise version.
17 Feb	6	**Consumption of electrical energy – H. Tizard,** 1p.
4 Mar	7	**Annual report – E.D.T. Jourdain,** 1p. Administrative arrangements.
11 Mar	8	**Changes in membership – E.D.T. Jourdain,** 1p.
17 Mar	9	**Annual Report (3rd draft) – E.D.T. Jourdain,** 1+30+4p appendix. Draft of CIP(49)10.
4 Apr	10	**First report – E.D.T. Jourdain covering the Committee,** 1+31p. See Cmd. 7665.
7 Apr	11	**Change in membership – E.D.T. Jourdain,** 1p.
20 Apr	12	**Coal saving – H. Tizard,** 1p.
21 Apr	13	**Coal saving – E.D.T. Jourdain covering H. Roxbee-Cox,** 1+6p.
19 May	14	**Tanning materials – S. Zuckerman covering the Panel on Imports Substitution,** 1+8p.
23 May	15	**Parliamentary debate on productivity – E.D.T. Jourdain,** 1+34p. See Parliamentary Debates House of Commons Volume 464 columns 2147–2212 (13 May 1949). Includes the debate on the Committee on Industrial Productivity's first report.
23 May	16	**Panel on Imports Substitution – S. Zuckerman,** 4p. Sets out proposed future work.
21 May	17	**Panel on Technical Information Services – A. King,** 2p. Proposed future work.
19 May	18	**Future programme – H. Tizard,** 2p.
24 May	19	**Anglo-American Council on Productivity – E.D.T. Jourdain covering the Council,** 1+12p. Report of the second session of the council.
15 June	20	**British and American cotton textile industries – E.D.T. Jourdain covering the Director of the British Cotton Industry Research Association,** 1+2p.
16 June	21	**Nutritional requirements for industrial work – E.D.T. Jourdain covering the Scientific Adviser of the Ministry of Food,** 1+9p annexes.
20 June	22	**Nitrogenous fertilizers – S. Zuckerman,** 2+6p annex +1p appendix.
21 June	23	**Standardization – E.D.T. Jourdain,** 2p.
12 Aug	24	**Standardization – simplification and specialization – E.D.T. Jourdain covering the Anglo-American Council on Productivity,** 1+3p.

15 Aug	25	**The contribution of research associations to industrial productivity and production – E.D.T. Jourdain covering B. Lockspeiser,** 1+6p.
7 Sept	26	**Productivity measurement – E.D.T. Jourdain covering L.O. Russell,** 1+2+79p appendixes. 'Indices of productivity' and 'Measurement of the effectiveness of the productive unit', both by the British Institute of Management, attached.
12 Sept	27	**Consumption of electrical energy – E.D.T. Jourdain covering H. Roxbee-Cox,** 1+2p.
19 Oct	28	**The future work of the committee – E.D.T. Jourdain covering G.B. Blaker,** 1+4p. Proposes the committee's abolition.
19 Oct	29	**Report on scientific and technical library facilities – E.D.T. Jourdain covering the Panel on Technical Information Services,** 1+3+15+8p appendixes.
14 Dec	30	**Publication of the results of industrial research – E.D.T. Jourdain covering the Study Group of the Panel on Technical Information Services,** 1+7+3p appendixes.
14 Dec	31	**Arrangements for the ninth meeting – H. Tizard,** 1p.
14 Dec	32	**Tin mining in the U.K. – E.D.T. Jourdain covering the Panel on Imports Substitution,** 1+2p

CAB 132/30   Meetings and Memoranda   17 Jan–24 July 1950   CIP(50)1st–2nd and CIP(50)1–12.

Meetings

25 Jan	**CIP(50)1st:1**	**Matters arising from the minutes of the previous meeting.** CIP(49)30 and 31.
	:2	**Magnesium.** CIP(50)1.
	:3	**Draft report of committee.** CIP(50)4.
	:4	**Panel on Human Factors.**
	:5	**Panel on Import Substitution.** CIP(50)2.
24 May	**2nd**	**Further consideration of the draft of the committee's second report.** CIP(50)6, 7, 8, 9. Continued reservations particularly from E.M. Amphlett.

Memoranda

17 Jan	**CIP(50)1**	**Magnesium – E.D.T. Jourdain covering the Panel on Imports Substitution,** 1+3p.
21 Jan	2	**Panel on Imports Substitution: change of name – S. Zuckerman,** 1p.
20 Jan	3	**Human Factors Panel – E.D.T. Jourdain,** 1p.
23 Jan	4	**Draft report – E.D.T. Jourdain,** 1+22p. Draft of CIP(50)5.

23 Feb	5	**Report of the committee (second draft) – E.D.T. Jourdain,** 1+4+3p appendix. Draft of CIP(50)6.
29 Mar	6	**Report of the committee (third draft) – E.D.T. Jourdain,** 1+6+3p annexes.
15 Apr	7	**Report of the committee – H. Tizard,** 1+4p appendixes. Sets out the disagreement of E.M. Amphlett and W. Griffiths to CIP(50)6, in particular on the continuation of the Human Factors Panel.
9 May	8	**Report of the committee – E.D.T. Jourdain covering E.M. Amphlett,** 1+1p. Criticisms of the two versions of the final paragraphs of the second report in CIP(50)7.
23 May	9	**Report of the committee – E.D.T. Jourdain,** 1+2p. Revised version.
6 June	10	**Report of the committee (fourth draft) – E.D.T. Jourdain,** 1+7+3p annexes.
17 June	11	**Report of the committee – E.D.T. Jourdain covering the committee,** 1+7+3p annexes. As submitted to ministers.
24 July	12	**Second report of the committee – E.D.T. Jourdain covering the committee,** 1+10p. See Cmd. 7991.

14.4 Official Committee on Controls

Committee on the Report of the Working Party on Controls (CAB 78/37), see CAB 71/27, LP(I)(45)3rd. It was terminated in November 1946 because modifications to controls were being agreed inter-departmentally without reference to the committee and more general issues were being handled by the Official Steering Committee on Economic Development (CAB 134/186–193).

Terms To keep under review the working of the controls over labour, raw materials, production and prices, with a view to ensuring that all these controls are used as an integrated whole for the general purposes approved by Ministers, and to report to the subcommittee as necessary.

Members E.M. Nicholson (Ld Pres. O., ch.); T. Sheepshanks (Try); G.S. Owen (B.T.); J.H. James (Adm.); E.A. Hitchman (Lab. & N.S.); A.F. Hemming (Fuel & P.); W. Strath (Supply); R.H. Tolerton (W. Transport); A.E. Feavearyear (Food); H.N. de Villiers (Works); J.E. Meade (Ec. Sect.).

Sec. A.N. Coleridge (Ld Pres. O.).

CAB 132/58 Meetings and Memoranda 5 Dec 1945–14 Nov 1946
OC(45)1st–OC(46)3rd and OC(45)1–OC(46)29.

Meetings

10 Dec	**OC(45)1st:1**	**Composition and terms of reference.** OC(45)1.

	:2	**Review of controls.** Brief synopsis by each ministry.
	:3	**Notification of changes in controls.** Departments were to inform the secretariat of any substantial modifications.
9 Jan	**OC(46)1st:1**	**Sponsoring authority guide.**
	:2	**Panel A.**
	:3	**Review of controls.** OC(45)3, 4, 5, 6 and OC(46)2, 3. Discussion of each paper. Consideration of labour controls postponed.
17 Jan	**2nd:1**	**Identity cards.**
	:2	**Building costs.**
	:3	**Transport restrictions on bricks.**
	:4	**Essential Works Order.** The Ministry of Labour view was that the onus was upon departments to justify their retention in each industry.
	:5	**Review of controls.** OC(46)1 and 4.
	:6	**Form of report.**
	:7	**Store control.**
24 Jan	**3rd:1**	**Essential Works Order.**
	:2	**First draft report.** OC(46)6. Annex with revisions attached.

Memoranda

5 Dec	**OC(45)1**	**Composition and terms of reference – E.M. Nicholson,** 1p.
11 Dec	2	**Review of controls – A.N. Coleridge,** 2p. Draft form for departments.
27 Dec	3	**Controls exercised by the Admiralty –** Admiralty, 2p.
27 Dec	4	**Controls exercised by the Ministry of Works –** Ministry of Works, 1+6+3p appendix.
31 Dec	5	**Controls exercised by the Ministry of Labour –** Ministry of Labour, 2+4p appendix.
31 Dec	6	**Controls exercised by the Ministry of Food –** Ministry of Food, 4+7p appendixes.
1 Jan	**OC(46)1**	**Fuel and power controls – Ministry of Fuel and Power,** 4p.
4 Jan	2	**Controls exercised by the Ministry of Supply and Aircraft Production – Ministry of Supply and Aircraft Production,** 8p.
4 Jan	3	**Transport controls – Ministry of War Transport,** 3p.
16 Jan	4	**Controls exercised by the Board of Trade –** Board of Trade, 4+6p appendix.
31 Jan	5	**Panel A – E.M. Nicholson,** 1+1p.
7 Feb	6	**First report – official committee,** 8p. Final version. See LP(46)113.

4 Feb–19 Mar	**7–10**	**Modifications in controls – A.N. Coleridge covering the Raw Materials Department at the Ministry of Supply.** Series of memoranda reporting any change in material controls.
9 Apr	**11**	**First report – official committee,** 2p. Final version. See LP(46)113.
5 Apr	**12**	**Modifications in controls – A.N. Coleridge covering the Metals Division of the Ministry of Supply,** 1+1p.
12 Apr–11 June	**13–17**	**Modifications in controls – J.H. Lidderdale covering the Raw Materials Department of the Board of Trade.** Further memoranda in the series.
18 June	**18**	**Controls affecting the Ministry of Education – J.H. Lidderdale covering Wilkinson and Morrison,** 1+1p.
21 June–25 Oct	**19–28**	**Modifications in controls – J.H. Lidderdale covering the Raw Materials Department of the Board of Trade.** Further memoranda in the series.
4 Nov	**29**	**Winding up of the committee – E.M. Nicholson,** 1+1p annex.

CAB 132/88   Meetings and Memoranda   7 Feb–8 May 1946   W(46)1st–7th and W(46)1–16.

Meetings

14 Feb	**W(46)1st**	Untitled. W(46)1 and 2. Agreed that every effort should be made to find the means of limiting the overall increase of wages, modifying wage differentials (to help redistribute manpower) and maximizing supply of labour, without resort to wage fixing by government.
28 Feb	**2nd**	Untitled. W(46)3. Form of the report agreed.
20 Mar	**3rd**	Untitled. W(46)5, 6, 7, 8.
25 Mar	**4th**	Untitled. W(46)10.
1 Apr	**5th**	Untitled. W(46)9 and 11. Agreed to consider further co-ordination of agricultural with general industrial wage policy.
15 Apr	**6th**	Untitled. W(46)12. Form and initial agenda of the National Industrial Conference agreed.
6 May	**7th**	Untitled. Consideration of draft report on agricultural wages.

Memoranda

7 Feb	**W(46)1**	**Composition and terms of reference – E.M. Nicholson,** 1p.
9 Feb	**2**	**Wages policy – Ministry of Labour,** 1+7p. Against any change in the wage fixing structure, preferring government guidance to government control.

25 Feb	3	**Wages policy – Economic Section,** 11p. The present system of wage bargaining should not be radically changed, but the government should act to ensure that relative wages could be altered without a general wage increase.
15 Mar	4	**Wages and conditions in socialized industries – C.H. Secord,** 1+3p. Also SI(M)(46)6.
15 Mar	5	**First report – C.H. Secord covering the Ministry of Labour,** 1+3p. Basis of first section of the report.
16 Mar	6	**First report – C.H. Secord covering the Economic Section,** 1+5p. Basis for second section.
13 Aug	7	**First report – C.H. Secord covering E.M. Nicholson,** 1+4p. Basis for final section.
19 Mar	8	**Stabilization policy – Treasury,** 3p. It was still felt to play an important role.
19 Mar	9	**Agricultural wages problems – Ministry of Agriculture and Fisheries,** 6p. Sets out special problems for wages policy in the industry.
26 Mar	10	**First report – Official Working Party,** 8p. Final version. See CP(46)130. Also LP(46)71.
29 Mar	11	**Agricultural wages problems – Ministry of Labour,** 2p. Comments on W(46)9.
13 Apr	12	**Constitution of a National Industrial Conference – M.D. Tennant and C.H. Secord,** 2p.
23 Apr	13	**Constitution of a National Industrial Conference – E.M. Nicholson,** 1+2p. Draft report.
2 May	14	**Constitution of a National Industrial Conference – C.H. Secord,** 1+2p. Revised draft. See CP(46)179.
2 May	15	**Regional differences in wage rates – C.H. Secord covering the Economic Section,** 4+2p appendix.
8 May	16	**Report on agricultural wages – Official Working Party,** 4p. Final version. See LP(46)111.

14.5   Industrial Subcommittee:

Official Working Party on Wages Policy

Set up in February 1946, see CAB 71/27, LP(I)(45)2nd:1. Two of its reports (CAB 132/3, LP(46)71 and 111) were discussed by the Lord President's Committee in March and May 1946 (CAB 132/1, LP(46)11th:3 and 16th:5). The former, with its recommendation of a National Industrial Conference, was discussed in full Cabinet (CAB 128/5, CM 33(46)5) and at the Cabinet's request revised proposals were submitted (CAB 129/8, CP(46)179) which led on 6 May to the Cabinet's agreement to establish a N.I.C. (see CAB 128/5, CM 42(46)6).

Terms   To examine the wages structure of industry . . . with a view to framing proposals for a wages policy.

Members   E.M. Nicholson (Ld Pres. O., ch.); T. Sheepshanks (Try); H.C. Emmerson (Lab. & N.S.); R.M. Nowell (B.T.); J.E. Meade (Ec. Sect.); D. Jay (P.M.O.). A.F. Hemming (Fuel & P.), S.S. Wilson (W. Transport) to attend when nationalized industries discussed.

Secs.   M.D. Tennant (Lab. & N.S.) and C.H. Secord (Ld Pres. O.).

CAB 132/88   Meetings and Memoranda   7 Feb–8 May 1946   W(46)1st–7th and W(46)1–16.

Meetings

14 Feb	**W(46)1st**	Untitled. W(46)1 and 2. Agreed that every effort should be made to find the means of achieving the objectives of limiting the overall increase of wages, modifying wage differentials to help redistribute manpower and maximizing supply of labour without resort to wage fixing by government.
28 Feb	**2nd**	Untitled. W(46)3. Form of the report agreed.
20 Mar	**3rd**	Untitled. W(46)5, 6, 7, 8.
25 May	**4th**	Untitled. W(46)10.
1 Apr	**5th**	Untitled. W(46)9 and 11. Agreed to consider further co-ordination of agricultural wage policy with general industrial wage policy.
15 Apr	**6th**	Untitled. W(46)12. Form and initial agenda of the National Industrial Conference agreed.
6 May	**7th**	Untitled. Consideration of draft report on agricultural wages.

Memoranda

7 Feb	**W(46)1**	**Composition and terms of reference – E.M. Nicholson**, 1p.
9 Feb	**2**	**Wages policy – Ministry of Labour**, 1+7p. Against any change in the wage fixing structure, preferring government guidance to government control.
25 Feb	**3**	**Wages policy – Economic Section**, 11p. While not wishing to change the present system of wage bargaining radically, it was felt that the government could play a more positive role to ensure that relative wages could be altered without a general upward movement in wages.
15 Mar	**4**	**Wages and conditions in socialized industries – C.H. Secord**, 1+3p. Also SI(M)(46)6.
15 Mar	**5**	**First report – C.H. Secord covering the Ministry of Labour**, 1+3p. Basis of first section of the report.
16 Mar	**6**	**First report – C.H. Secord covering the Economic Section**, 1+5p. Basis for second section.

13 Aug	7	**First report – C.H. Secord covering E.M. Nicholson,** 1+4p. Basis for final section.
19 Mar	8	**Stabilization policy – Treasury,** 3p. It was still felt to play an important role.
19 Mar	9	**Agricultural wages problems – Ministry of Agriculture and Fisheries,** 6p. Sets out special problems for wages policy in the industry.
26 Mar	10	**First report – official working party,** 8p. Final version. See CP(46)130. Also LP(46)71.
29 Mar	11	**Agricultural wages problems – Ministry of Labour,** 2p. Comments on W(46)9.
13 Apr	12	**Constitution of a National Industrial Conference – M.D. Tennant and C.H. Secord,** 2p.
23 Apr	13	**Constitution of a National Industrial Conference – E.M. Nicholson,** 1+2p. Draft report.
2 May	14	**Constitution of a National Industrial Conference – C.H. Secord,** 1+2p. Revised draft. See CP(46)179.
2 May	15	**Regional differences in wage rates – C.H. Secord covering the Economic Section,** 4+2p appendix.
8 May	16	**Report on agricultural wages – official working party,** 4p. Final version. See LP(46)111.

Chapter 15   Miscellaneous Standing Committees

15.1   Committee on Exports

Set up in September 1947 (see CAB 129/21, CP(47)255), although terms of reference and membership were not agreed until 21 October 1947 (see CAB 129/21, CP(47)287). It generally reported to the Official Steering Committee on Economic Development (see CAB 134/186–193), but when action was urgently required it had direct access to ministers. It worked in conjunction with the Overseas Negotiations Committee (see CAB 134/46–48 and 555–587) and the Exchange Requirements Committee (see CAB 134/45 and 258–261) and was served by a Board of Trade working party, code WP(E), see BT 64/2959. For later papers see CAB 134/166–169.

Terms   a) to stimulate production for export and to determine and progress the targets; b) to assist the Overseas Negotiations Committee in increasing the availability of commodities which are of special importance to the conclusion of particular trade agreements, and to devise administrative measures to ensure that for the purpose of such agreements exports of particular goods can be guaranteed or directed to particular countries.

Members   B.T. representative (ch.); G.S. Owen (B.T., vice–ch.); R.W.B. Clarke (Try); J.H. James (Adm.); E.A. Hitchman (Lab. & N.S.); A.F. Hemming (Fuel & P.); E. Bowyer (Supply); E.A. Seal (Works); H.J. Johns (M.A.F.); H. Weeks (C.E.P.S.); R.L. Hall (Ec. Sect.). R. Makins (F.O.), C.G.L. Syers (C.R.O.), G.H. Baxter (C.R.O.), G. Clauson (Col. O.), W. Johnston (Burma O.), J. Hutt (Food), W. Graham (Transport) could also attend when relevant.   (Nov 1947) J.R.C. Helmore (B.T.) becomes chairman.

Sec.   G.M. Wilson (Cab. O.).

CAB 134/44   Meetings and Memoranda   19 Sept–30 Dec 1947   BP(E)(47)1st–10th and BP(E)(47)1–36.

Meetings

19 Sept	BP(E)(47)1st:1	**Terms of reference and scope of the committee.** Yet to be decided.
	:2	**General questions arising out of the memorandum by the President of the Board of Trade on the export programme (CP(47)250).**
	:3	**Export of Southern Rhodesian coal to the Argentine.**
	:4	**Automobile industry: coal and export position.**
	:5	**Exports of aircraft.**
	:6	**Exports of government surplus stores.**
	:7	**Direction of exports.**
	:8	**Arrangements for future meetings.**

30 Sept	**2nd:1**	**Terms of reference.** Yet to be agreed. Suggested that the committee should initially consider the production side of U.K. exports and any questions of Empire production which were put to it.
	:2A	**Oral reports by the Board of Trade, Ministry of Supply, Ministry of Food and Ministry of Works on the progress of export targets.**
	:2B	**Assistance by merchants' organizations to the achievement of export targets.**
	:3	**Regional organization of the export drive.** Regional committees to be set up.
	:4	**Fuel supplies for export firms.**
	:5	**Export of Southern Rhodesian coal to the Argentine.** BP(E)(47)4 and 5.
	:6	**Export target for textile machinery.** BP(E)(47)2.
	:7	**Direction of exports.** BP(E)(47)3.
	:8	**Manpower for exports.** BP(E)(47)1.
14 Oct	**3rd:1**	**Matters arising from previous minutes.**
	:2	**Southern Rhodesian coal.**
	:3	**Export of surplus stores.** BP(E)(47)8.
	:4	**Packaging.** BP(E)(47)6.
	:5	**Progress report and targets from the Ministry of Works.** Nothing could be resolved until the capital investment programme was settled.
	:6	**Progress report on export targets from the Admiralty.**
	:7	**Progress report on export targets from the Ministry of Food.**
	:8	**Progress reports on export targets from the Ministry of Supply.**
	:9	**Progress reports from the Board of Trade.**
	:10	**Royal Ordnance factories.**
21 Oct	**4th:1**	**Working Party on Export Targets.** Agreement to set up a working party to consider progress reports, talks with industries and difficulties with the achievement of the targets.
	:2	**Matters arising from previous minutes.**
	:3	**Market information.** BP(ON)(47)11.
	:4	**Risk of inability to deliver.** BP(E)(47)9.
	:5	**Exports of small aircraft.** BP(ON)(47)10.
	:6	**Progress report on export targets by the Ministry of Supply.**
	:7	**Progress report on export targets from the Ministry of Works.**
	:8	**Progress report on export targets from the Board of Trade.**
6 Nov	**5th:1**	**Matters arising from previous minutes.**
	:2	**Matters arising from the minutes of the Working Party.** BP(E)(47)13 and 16.
	:3	**Export availability of key items for bilateral negotiations.** BP(E)(47)17.

	:4	**Textile machinery. BP(E)(47)18.**
	:5	**Merchants' organizations assistance in the achievement of export targets. BP(E)(47)12.**
	:6	**Association of trade unions with discussion on export targets. BP(E)(47)15.**
	:7	**Frustrated exports.**
13 Nov	6th:2	**Unrequited exports and the direction of exports.**
	:3	**Sisal and manilla.**
	:4	**Whisky.**
	:5	**Government trading organization. BP(E)(47)23.**
	:6	**Association of trade unions with discussions of export targets. BP(E)(47)15.**
	:7	**Exports of pottery–making machinery. BP(E)(47)21.**
	:8	**Wool exports in 1948. BP(E)(47)22.** To be considered by the Overseas Negotiations Committee.
21 Nov	7th:1	**Availabilities of capital goods.**
	:2	**Frustrated exports.**
	:3	**Automobile industry.**
	:4	**Southern Rhodesian coal.**
	:5	**Whisky.**
	:6	**Matters arising from the minutes of the third meeting of the Working Party on Exports. BP(E)(47)25.**
	:7	**Government trading organization.** Consideration deferred until J.R.C. Helmore had discussed it with the chairman of the Overseas Negotiation Committee.
	:8	**Assistance by merchants to the achievement of export targets.**
	:9	**Sisal.**
	:10	**Export of furniture. BP(E)(47)20.**
4 Dec	8th:1	**Packaging.**
	:2	**Government trading organization.**
	:3	**Sisal.**
	:4	**Colonial import policy.**
	:7	**Export prospects for certain dollar-earning commodities. BP(E)(47)29.**
	:8	**Motor vehicles exports for 1948. BP(E)(47)30.**
11 Dec	9th:1	**Colonial import policy.**
	:2	**Hard and soft currencies. BP(E)(47)31.**
	:3	**Export prospects for certain dollar-earning commodities.**
	:4	**Export of building materials. BP(E)(47)32.**
22 Dec	10th:1	**Exports of Singer sewing machines. BP(E)(47)36.**
	:2	**Revised export programme. BP(E)(47)34.** Amendments made.
	:3	**Minutes of the fourth meeting of the Working Party. BP(E)(47)35.**

Memoranda

26 Sept	**BP(E)(47)1**	**Outline of the arrangements for placing in employment workers covered by the Control of Engagement Order – Ministry of Labour and National Service, 2p.**
27 Sept	**2**	**Textile machinery industry – Ministry of Supply, 2p.**
27 Sept	**3**	**Direction of exports – G.M. Wilson covering the Board of Trade, 1+5p. Direction should be as limited and flexible as possible.**
29 Sept	**4**	**Comparative financial value of exports of chrome, copper and coal resulting from the provision of 550 wagons and 19 locomotives to Southern Rhodesia – G.M. Wilson covering the Treasury, 1+1+2p.**
29 Sept	**5**	**Locomotives and wagons for Southern Rhodesia – G.M. Wilson covering the Ministry of Supply, 1+2p.**
6 Oct	**6**	**Packaging – G.M. Wilson covering the Board of Trade, 1+1p.**
8 Oct	**7**	**Priorities in overseas negotiations – G.M. Wilson covering the chairman of the Overseas Negotiations Committee, 1+3p. Also BP(ON)(47)24.**
13 Oct	**8**	**Export of surplus stores from the United Kingdom – G.M. Wilson covering the Ministry of Supply, 1+1+5p appendixes.**
13 Oct	**9**	**Risks of inability to deliver exports – G.M. Wilson covering the Treasury, 1+2p.**
17 Oct	**10**	**Exports of small aircraft – G.M. Wilson covering the Ministry of Supply, 1+1p.**
17 Oct	**11**	**The provision of information about tariff changes and import licensing restrictions in overseas countries – Board of Trade, 1p.**
30 Oct	**12**	**Assistance to new exporters from merchants' organizations and others – G.M. Wilson covering the Board of Trade, 1+5p.**
1 Nov	**13**	**Minutes of the first meeting of the Committee on Exports Working Party – G.M. Wilson, 1+6p. Also WP(E)(47)1st.**
3 Nov	**14**	**Exports of Finnish steel in 1948 – G.M. Wilson covering the Board of Trade, 1+3+1p. Also BP(ON)(47)72.**
5 Nov	**15**	**Association of trade unions with discussions on export targets – G.M. Wilson covering the Board of Trade, 1+2p.**
5 Nov	**16**	**Minutes of the second meeting of the Committee on Exports Working Party – G.M. Wilson, 1+5p. Also WP(E)(47)2nd.**
5 Nov	**17**	**Export availability of key items for bilateral negotiations – G.M. Wilson covering the Board of Trade, 1+6+4p annexes.**

5 Nov	18	**Textile machinery industry – G.M. Wilson covering the Ministry of Supply and the Board of Trade,** 1+1+1p.
6 Nov	19	**Appointment of chairman – G.M. Wilson,** 1p.
11 Nov	20	**Exports of furniture – G.M. Wilson covering the Board of Trade,** 1+2p.
12 Nov	21	**Exports of pottery-making machinery – G.M. Wilson covering the Board of Trade,** 1+1p.
12 Nov	22	**Wool exports in 1948 – G.M. Wilson covering the Board of Trade,** 1+1+2p appendix.
12 Nov	23	**State trading organization – G.M. Wilson covering the Treasury,** 1+4+5p annexes. Compensation Trading and I.T.O. – Board of Trade, and State Trading Organization Report of Treasury Working Party – Ministry of Food and the Economic Section, annexed.
12 Nov	24	**Progress report on export achievement – G.M. Wilson,** 1+2p. First monthly report.
19 Nov	25	**Minutes of the third meeting of the Committee on Exports Working Party – G.M. Wilson,** 1+3p. Also WP(E)(47)3rd.
24 Nov	26	**Guaranteed deliveries of capital goods – G.M. Wilson covering Strauss,** 1+3p. Also BP(ON)(47)100. Letter to Cripps.
2 Dec	27	**Frustrated exports – G.M. Wilson covering the Board of Trade,** 1+4p.
2 Dec	28	**Progress report on export achievement – G.M. Wilson covering the Board of Trade,** 1+2p. Also BP(ON)(47)125.
3 Dec	29	**Export prospects for certain dollar-earning commodities – G.M. Wilson covering the Board of Trade,** 1+2+1p annex.
3 Dec	30	**Motor vehicles exports for 1948 – G.M. Wilson covering the Ministry of Supply,** 1+2+2p appendix.
6 Dec	31	**Hard and soft currencies – Treasury,** 3p. Categorization into ultra-hard, hard, worthwhile and soft currencies.
10 Dec	32	**Contribution of basic building materials industries to the export drive – Ministry of Works,** 2+3p appendix. Summary of meetings with the main industries which have export potential.
10 Dec	33	**Minister of Supply's statement to the Engineering Advisory Council on 3 Dec 1947 – G.M. Wilson covering the Ministry of Supply,** 1+1p.
19 Dec	34	**Revised export programme – J.R.C. Helmore,** 1+6+5p. Draft report for submission to the Production Committee, containing forecasts for the level of exports at mid- and end-1948.

20 Dec	**35**	**Minutes of the fourth meeting of the Working Party on Exports – J.G. Marsh,** 1+4p. Also WP(E)(47)4th.
30 Dec	**36**	**Exports of Singer sewing machines – G.M. Wilson covering the Ministry of Supply,** 1+2p.

15.2 Coal Committee

Set up on 9 December 1946 (see CAB 132/5, LP(46)285) as a smaller committee to replace the ministerial Committee on the Coal Position during the Coming Winter (see CAB 78/38, GEN 94). It was assisted by the Official Coal Committee (see immediately below) and was replaced in February 1947 by the Fuel Committee (CAB 134/272-275).

Terms To ensure that all necessary action is taken to secure the maximum production and most efficient distribution of coal and to bridge any gap between supply and demand.

Members Ch. of Exchequer (ch.); Mins. of Fuel & Power, Labour & N.S., Transport.

Secs. J.H. Lidderdale (Ld Pres. O.) and M.C.T. Grieve (Fuel & P.).

CAB 134/62   Meetings and Memoranda   8 Dec 1946–12 Feb 1947   CC(46)1st – CC(47)2nd and CC(46)1 – CC(47)13.

Meetings

18 Dec	**CC(46)1st:1**	**Setting up of the Committee and of the Official Committee.** CC(46)1 and 4.
	:2	**First report of the Official Committee.** CC(46)6. Shinwell gave his views on the general situation. Dalton on the role of the Official Committee.
	:3	**Loss of deep-mined production and coal stocked owing to railway difficulties.** CC(46)2, 3, 5.
	:4	**Future work of the committee.**
	:5	**Chairman of the previous Official Committee.**
6 Jan	**CC(47)1st:1**	**Coal and electricity.** CP(47)6 and 15. Agreement on measures to recommend to Cabinet to alleviate the coal crisis, including the increase of deliveries to power stations at the expense of industry.
	:2	**Statistics on the transport of coal.** CC(47)1.
10 Jan	**2nd:1**	**Second report of the Official Committee.** CC(47)5.
	:2	**Recruitment of men in N. Ireland.** CC(47)3.
	:3	**Monthly statistical report for Nov 1946.** CC(47)2.
	:4	**Statistics of transport of coal.** CC(47)4.

Memoranda

9 Dec	**CC(46)1**	**Composition and terms of reference – N. Brook,** 1p. Also LP(46)286.
2 Dec	**2**	**Loss of deep-mined production and coal stocked owing to railway difficulties – J.H. Lidderdale covering the Ministry of Fuel and Power,** 1+1p.
11 Dec	**3**	**Loss of deep-mined production and coal stocked owing to railway difficulties – J.H. Lidderdale covering the Ministry of Fuel and Power,** 1+1p.
14 Dec	**4**	**Composition of the Official Committee – N. Brook,** 1p. Also CC(O)(46)1.
14 Dec	**5**	**Loss of deep-mined production and coal stocked owing to railway difficulties – J.H. Lidderdale covering the Ministry of Fuel and Power,** 1+1p.
15 Dec	**6**	**First report of the Official Committee – J.H. Lidderdale covering the Official Committee,** 1+3p. Also CC(O)(46)2. Review of situation.
22 Dec	**7**	**Loss of deep-mined production and coal stocked owing to railway difficulties – J.H. Lidderdale covering the Ministry of Fuel and Power,** 1+1p.
4 Jan	**CC(47)1**	**Transport of coal – J.H. Lidderdale covering the Ministry of Fuel and Power,** 1+1p. Statement for four weeks ending 28 Dec 1946 on the loss of deep-mined coal output due to transport difficulties and changes in the amount of coal in stock.
8 Jan	**2**	**Monthly statistical report (coal) for November 1946 – Shinwell,** 1+2p. Also LP(47)6.
7 Jan	**3**	**Recruitment of men in N. Ireland for work in the coal mines in Great Britain – Isaacs,** 1p.
8 Jan	**4**	**Transport of coal – J.H. Lidderdale covering the Ministry of Fuel and Power,** 1+1p. Update of CC(47)1.
9 Jan	**5**	**Second report of the Official Committee – J.H. Lidderdale covering the Official Committee,** 1+4p. CC(O)(47)1. Reviews the action taken to implement Cabinet decisions.
15 Jan	**6**	**Transport of coal – J.H. Lidderdale covering the Ministry of Fuel and Power,** 1+1p. Update of CC(47)4.
18 Jan	**7**	**Monthly statistical report (coal) for Dec 1946 – Shinwell,** 1+2p. Also LP(47)18.
22 Jan	**8**	**Transport of coal – J.H. Lidderdale covering the Ministry of Fuel and Power,** 1+1p. Further update.
29 Jan	**9**	**Transport of coal – J.H. Lidderdale covering the Ministry of Fuel and Power,** 1+1p. Update.
30 Jan	**10**	**Transport of coal: a general survey – Barnes,** 1+6p. General statement of the problem of the movement of coal. Consideration of the immediate and long-term remedies.

5 Feb	**11**	**Transport of coal – J.H. Lidderdale covering the Ministry of Fuel and Power,** 1+1p. Further update.
7 Feb	**12**	**Third report of the Official Committee – J.H. Lidderdale covering the Official Committee,** 1+3p. Also CC(O)(47)9. Deals with the revised scheme, the supply of solid fuel to industrial firms and the progress of measures both to improve transport and to convert industry and railways from coal to oil.
12 Feb	**13**	**Transport of coal – J.H. Lidderdale covering the Ministry of Fuel and Power,** 1+1p. Update.

Official Coal Committee (1946–1947)

Set up on 9 December 1946 (see CAB 132/5, LP(46)286) to work under the Coal Committee (see immediately above). It was itself served by two Ministry of Fuel and Power Subcommittees on the Transport and Distribution of Coal and on Coal/Oil Conversion and Mining Supplies.

Terms As Coal Committee (see immediately above).

Members D. Fergusson (Fuel & P., ch.); G.S. Owen (B.T.); A.F. Hemming (Fuel & P.); J.M. Glen (Lab. & N.S.); A.F. Barnes (Supply); C.A. Birtchnell (Transport).

Sec. M.C.T. Grieve (Fuel & P.).

CAB 134/62   Meetings and Memoranda   14 Dec–7 Feb 1947
CC(O)(46)1st–CC(O)(47)3rd and CC(O)(46)1-CC(O)(47)9

Meetings

14 Dec	**CC(O)(46)1st:1**	**Setting up of the Official Committee and two subcommittees.**
	:2	**Progress report to Ministerial Committee.**
8 Jan	**CC(O)(47)1st:1**	**Fuel situation before the Cabinet and action arising therefrom. D. Fergusson's views.**
	:2	**Transport of coal.**
	:3	**Coal/oil conversion.**
	:4	**Future coal requirements.**
	:5	**Mining machinery.**
	:6	**Electricity consumption.**
	:7	**Report to the Ministerial Committee.**
23 Jan	**2nd:1**	**Fuel allocation scheme: progress report.**
	:2	**Transport of coal. CC(O)(47)3, 4, 5.**
	:3	**Coal/oil conversion: progress report. CC(O)(47)2.**
5 Feb	**3rd:1**	**Fuel allocation scheme: progress report. CC(O)(47)8.**
	:2	**Transport position.**

	:3	**Public utilities.**
	:4	**Coal for hotels. CC(O)(47)6.**
	:5	**Transport of coal: forward position.**
	:6	**Coal/oil conversion programme: power stations.**
	:7	**Coal/oil conversion programme for industry. CC(O)(47)7.**

Memoranda

14 Dec	**CC(O)(46)1**	**Composition of the Official Committee – N. Brook, 1p. Also CC(46)4.**
15 Dec	**2**	**First report of the Official Committee – J.H. Lidderdale covering the Official Committee, 1+3p. See CC(46)6.**
9 Jan	**CC(O)(47)1**	**Second report of the Official Committee – J.H. Lidderdale covering the Official Committee, 1+4p. See CC(47)5.**
21 Jan	**2**	**Coal/oil conversion – M.C.T. Grieve covering the Ministry of Fuel and Power, 1+1+2p. Progress report.**
21 Jan	**3**	**Transport of coal – Ministry of Supply, 1p.**
21 Jan	**4**	**Austerity locomotives in Europe – Ministry of Transport, 1p.**
21 Jan	**5**	**Coal in transit. Tightening up embargoes to ensure coal movements – Ministry of Transport, 1p.**
4 Feb	**6**	**Coal for hotels – Board of Trade, 2p.**
4 Feb	**7**	**Coal/oil conversion programme for industry – Ministry of Fuel and Power, 2+3p. Progress report.**
4 Feb	**8**	**Supply of coal to industry – Board of Trade, 2p. Progress report on revised allocations introduced on 20 Jan 1947.**
7 Feb	**9**	**Third report – J.H. Lidderdale covering the official committee, 1+3p. See CC(47)12.**

15.3 Committee on Control of Investment

Set up on 31 May 1949 by the Production Committee, see CAB 134/640, PC(49)14th.

Terms To make a comprehensive review of the powers and administrative machinery required in the long term for the control of capital investment.

Members P.D. Proctor (Try, ch.); R.W. Burkett (B.T.); W. Strath (C.E.P.S.); R.F. Bretherton (Ec. Sect.); B. Barnes and P. Chantler (Fuel & P.); F.L. Edwards (Health); H.R. Smith (Scot.); V.P. Harries (Supply); C.A. Birtchnell (Transport); E.F. Muir (Works). (Aug 1949) I. Wild replaces Birtchnell.

Secs. P. Vinter (C.E.P.S.) and P.J. Moorhouse (Cab. O.) (Aug 1949) C.D. Smith (C.E.P.S.) replaces Vinter.

CAB 134/63   Meetings and Memoranda   21 June–5 Sept 1949   CCI(49)1st–8th and CCI(49)1–11.

Meetings

27 June	**CCI(49)1st**	**Control of investment: general discussion.** CCI(49)2. P.D. Proctor set out his views. It was agreed to consider (a) control in a period of continuing shortages, (b) control in the advent of a recession.
11 July	**2nd:1**	**Analysis of building licences issued and building work authorized.** CCI(49)3. General feeling that permanent building controls were needed.
	:2	**Control of investment in a trade recession.** Consideration of the state of preparations and the potential degree of control of investment by government departments, local authorities, socialized industries, private enterprise and individuals.
18 July	**3rd**	**The relation of financial and physical methods of influencing investment to physical controls.** Views of departments most directly concerned with the administration of taxation.
26 July	**4th**	**Draft report.** CCI(49)4.
15 Aug	**5th**	**Draft report.** CCI(49)4.
24 Aug	**6th**	**Draft report.** CCI(49)7.
30 Aug	**7th**	**Draft report.** CCI(49)7.

Memoranda

21 June	**CCI(49)1**	**Composition on terms of reference – N. Brook,** 1p.
24 June	**2**	**Note by the chairman – P.D. Proctor,** 1p. Sets out basis for general discussion.
9 July	**3**	**Analysis of building licences issued and building work authorized – Ministry of Works,** 1+7p.
23 July	**4**	**Draft report,** 6p.
22 July	**5**	**Control of investment – P. Vinter and P.J. Moorhouse covering V.P. Harries and F.L. Edwards,** 1+3p.
29 July	**6**	**Control of building investment by financial ceilings – E.F. Muir,** 3+1p appendix.
19 Aug	**7**	**Draft report (revise) – P. Vinter and P.J. Moorhouse,** 1+10p.
17 Aug	**8**	**Membership of the committee – P. Vinter and P.J. Moorhouse,** 1p.
31 Aug	**9**	**Draft report (second revise) – P.J. Moorhouse and C.D. Smith,** 1+16p.

1 Sept	**10**	**Note by the chairman – P.D. Proctor,** 1+4p. Suggested amendment to the second revise report.
5 Sept	**11**	**Note by the joint secretaries – P.J. Moorhouse and C.D. Smith,** 1+18p. Final version of the report. See PC(49)95.

15.4 Committee on Controls and Efficiency

Set up by the inter-departmental Wages and Price Policy Committee, see T 223/57, WPP(48)3rd:1.

Terms To consider the economic questions arising out of the operation of controls in the light of papers remitted to them (WPP(48)5) and to present an interim report to the Wages and Price Policy Committee before the end of July 1948 on how they propose the questions should be handled.

Members B.W. Gilbert (Try, ch.); E.A. Hitchman (C.E.P.S.); R.L. Hall (Ec. Sect.); D.C.V. Perrett (Food); E.B. Bowyer (Supply); P.D. Proctor (Try); J.R.C. Helmore (B.T.); H.N. de Villiers (Works).

Secs. J.R.C. Dow (Ec. Sect.) and M.E. Hill (B.T.)

CAB 134/89 Meetings and Memoranda 4 June–1 Dec 1948 CE(48)1st–11th and CE(48)1–24.

Meetings

25 June	**CE(48)1st**	**Work of the committee.** CE(48)1, 2, 3. Agreement to look at goods most likely to be immediately hit by a depression.
1 July	**2nd**	**Control of the footwear industry.** CE(48)6.
6 July	**3rd:1**	**Controls affecting electric cookers and fires and water tanks.** CE(48)9.
	:2	**Controls affecting the production of radios.** CE(48)8.
	:3	**Work of the committee.**
15 July	**4th:1**	**Controls affecting furniture.** CE(48)11.
	:2	**Controls affecting jam and marmalade.** CE(48)12.
	:3	**Work of the committee.**
21 July	**5th**	**Report of the committee.** CE(48)13.
29 July	**6th**	**Interim report.**
8 Oct	**7th**	Untitled. CE(48)16 and 17. Consideration of alternatives to material allocation schemes.
9 Nov	**8th:1**	**Controls of chocolate and sugar confectionery.** CE(48)21.
	:2	**Lead allocations.** CE(48)20.
	:3	**Work of the committee.**
16 Nov	**9th:1**	**Control of paper supplies.** CE(48)23.
	:2	**Controls over timber supplies.** CE(48)24.

	:3	**Work of the committee.**
23 Nov	**10th:1**	**Working of the steel distribution scheme.** CE(48)22.
	:2	**Alternatives to materials allocation.** CE(48)21.
	:3	**Work of the committee.**
1 Dec	**11th**	**The programming of raw materials imports in connection with relaxations of controls.** Analysis of the position under Board of Trade control.

Memoranda

21 June	**CE(48)1**	**Formation of Deputy Secretary's committee –** **E.E. Bridges,** 1p. Also WPP(48)6.
4 June	2	**Controls and efficiency – E.E. Bridges,** 1+6p annexes. Also WPP(48)5. Annexes by J.H. Woods and R.L. Hall identifying the main issues.
21 June	3	**Minutes of a meeting held in Sir Edward Bridges's room on 15 May 1948,** 2p. Also WPP(48)3rd. Bridges's views on the main issues.
24 June	4	**Note by the joint secretaries – M.E. Hill and J.C.R. Dow,** 1p.
30 June	5	**Controls in the food industries – M.E. Hill and J.C.R. Dow,** 1+21p annexes. Views of the food industry's council.
29 June	6	**Control of the footwear industry – M.E. Hill and J.C.R. Dow,** 1+1p.
1 July	7	**The impact of deflation – M.E. Hill and J.C.R. Dow,** 1+5+2p appendixes. See EC(S)(48)25.
3 July	8	**Control in the radio industry – M.E. Hill and J.C.R. Dow covering the Ministry of Supply,** 1+2p.
5 July	9	**Control of electric cookers and water tanks –** **M.E. Hill and J.C.R. Dow covering the Ministry of Works,** 1+1p.
5 July	10	**Shopping trends – M.E. Hill and J.C.R. Dow covering the Board of Trade,** 1+10+2p appendixes. Analysis for the period May–June 1948.
10 July	11	**Control of the furniture industry – M.E. Hill and J.C.R. Dow,** 1+2p.
14 July	12	**Controls affecting jam and marmalade – M.E. Hill and J.C.R. Dow covering the Ministry of Food,** 1+2p.
20 July	13	**Draft outline of interim report – M.E. Hill and J.C.R. Dow,** 1+6p. See EC(S)(48)27.
27 July	14	**Draft interim report – M.E. Hill and J.C.R. Dow,** 1+10p.
3 Aug	15	**Interim report – M.E. Hill and J.C.R. Dow covering the committee,** 1+9p.

29 Sept	16	**Note of a meeting held in Sir Edward Bridges's room on Monday 16 Aug,** 1+2p.
29 Sept	17	**Interim report on controls and efficiency – J.C.R. Dow covering E.E. Bridges,** 1+1p. Also WPP(48)11.
21 Oct	18	**Material allocations: questions for consideration – M.E. Hill and J.C.R. Dow,** 1+2p. Revise version.
2 Nov	19	**The alternatives to allocations for industrial materials – Economic Section,** 5p. Also EC(S)(48)33(revise).
5 Nov	20	**Lead allocations – M.E. Hill and J.C.R. Dow covering the Ministry of Supply,** 1+3p.
8 Nov	21	**Controls over chocolate and sugar confectionery – M.E. Hill and J.C.R. Dow covering the Ministry of Food,** 1+3p.
8 Nov	22	**Report of the Joint Committee on the Working of the Steel Distribution Scheme – M.E. Hill and J.C.R. Dow covering the Joint Committee,** 1+8p. Also SDS(48)36.
12 Nov	23	**Licensing control of paper supplies – M.E. Hill and J.C.R Dow covering the Board of Trade,** 1+2p.
13 Nov	24	**Licensing control of timber supplies – M.E. Hill and J.C.R. Dow covering the Board of Trade,** 1+2+1p.

15.5 Committee on Economic Controls

Set up in July 1949 to work in liaison with the Emergency Legislation Committee (see CAB 134/206–208), which was making a comprehensive review of existing emergency powers. It established two working parties on controls over production and over consumption.

Terms To consider what powers are likely to be required in the long term for operating economic controls on prices; production; consumption; centralized purchase; labour; and import and export licensing.

Members B.W. Gilbert (Try, ch.); W. Strath (C.E.P.S.); J.R.C. Helmore (B.T.); E.B. Bowyer (Supply); E.G. Harwood (Food); R.F. Bretherton (Ec. Sect.); A. Johnston (Cab. O.). H. Crow (Scot.), J. Hancock (Adm.), P. Chantier (Fuel & P.), E.S. Foster (Transport), E.F. Muir (Works) and F. Grant (M.A.F.) could also attend when relevant.

Secs. E.J. Beaven (Cab. O.) and M.E. Johnston (Try).

CAB 134/95 Meetings and Memoranda 9 July 1949–3 Mar 1950 CEC(49)1st–CEC(50)2nd and CEC(49)1–CEC(50)3.

Meetings
| 20 July | **CEC(49)1st:1** | Terms of reference. |

	-	:2	**The work of the committee.** CEC(49)1. Agreement to consider only negative and restrictive controls.
11 Nov		**2nd:1**	**Control of labour.** CEC(49)4.
		:2	**Controls on import and export licensing.** CEC(49)7.
		:3	**Controls on consumption, production and prices.** CEC(49)5, 6, 8.
13 Jan	**CEC(50)1st**		**Draft report.** CEC(49)9. Consideration of possible legislation.
1 Feb	**2nd**		**Draft report on economic controls.** CEC(50)1.

Memoranda

9 July	**CEC(49)1**	**Composition and terms of reference – B.W. Gilbert,** 1p.
2 Sept	2	**Appointment of working parties and other arrangements for the conduct of further reviews – M.E. Johnston and E.J. Beaven,** 1p.
13 Sept	3	**Appointment of working parties and other arrangements for the conduct of further reviews – M.E. Johnston and E.J. Beaven,** 1p. H. Beer to report on price control.
28 Sept	4	**Controls over labour – M.E. Johnston and E.J. Beaven covering the Ministry of Labour,** 1+2p. Consideration of whether or not they should be permanent.
24 Oct	5	**Price control – M.E. Johnston and E.J. Beaven covering H. Beer,** 1+5+2p appendixes. Sets out the objective and basis of long-term price control.
26 Oct	6	**Controls over consumption – M.E. Johnston and E.J. Beaven covering the Treasury,** 1+5+3p appendixes. Consideration of powers likely to be required after 1950.
27 Oct	7	**Import and export licensing controls – Board of Trade,** 3p.
9 Nov	8	**Controls over production – M.E. Johnston and E. J. Beaven covering the Working Party on Controls over Production,** 1+5+3p appendix. Also CEC(P)(49)11.
30 Dec	9	**Report by the committee – M.E. Johnston and E. J. Beaven,** 1+12+3p annex. First draft.
25 Jan	**CEC(50)1**	**Report by the committee – M.E. Johnston and E. J. Beaven,** 1+15+2p annex. Revised version.
17 Feb	2	**Report by the committee – E.J. Beaven and M.E. Johnston,** 1+21+2p annex. Final draft. Analysis of the extent to which reliance could be placed on financial as opposed to physical controls.

| 3 Mar | 3 | **Report by the committee – E.J. Beaven and M.E. Johnston,** 1+23+3p annex. Final draft as amended after discussion with relevant permanent secretaries. |

15.6 Ministerial Committee on Fuel Economy

Established in anticipation of a fuel crisis over the winter of 1951/2. Its work was related to that of the official Working Party on Fuel Economy (CAB 130/71, GEN 378).

Terms To consider what further measures can be taken (i) to promote the greater use of insulation and of improved solid-fuel appliances in buildings of all kinds (and especially in buildings belonging to government departments, nationalized industries and local authorities) and (ii) to increase the supply of insulation material, improved solid-fuel appliances and individual fuel-saving equipment.

Members Ld Privy Seal (ch.); Ec. Sec. (Try); Parl. Secs. Local Govt., Education, Fuel & Power, Transport, Supply, Works.

Sec. R. Gedling (Cab. O.).

CAB 134/97 Meeting and memoranda 23 Aug–17 Oct 1951 CFE(51)1st and CFE(51)1–3.

Meeting

| 5 Sept | **CFE(51)1st** | Fuel economy. CFE(51)2. |

Memoranda

23 Aug	**CFE(51)1**	**Terms of reference and composition – N. Brook,** 1p.
31 Aug	**2**	**Fuel efficiency – Ministry of Fuel and Power,** 6p.
17 Oct	**3**	**The use of improved domestic solid-fuel burning appliances – R. Gedling,** 2p. Also GEN 378/12.

15.7 Committee on Productive Capacity

Set up as a result of departmental consultations following discussions at the Economic Steering Committee, see CAB 134/263, ES(50)4th:2. It took over some functions from the Exports Committee (see CAB 134/166–169). It worked in conjunction with the Manpower Committee (see CAB 134/511–512) and the Raw Materials Committee (see CAB 134/658–661), with a chairman common to all three, and the Materials (Allocation) Committee (see CAB 134/485–486). In December 1951 its work was assumed by the Manpower Committee.

Terms To advise the Economic Steering Committee on the use of productive capacity, and to co-ordinate departmental action to avoid or resolve differences arising from the competing demands on productive capacity of exports, civil requirements, and the defence production programme.

Members   E.A. Shillito (C.E.P.S., ch.); J.H. Hancock (Adm.); D.H. Lyal (B.T.); D.M.B. Butt (Ec. Sec.); A.M. Jenkins (C.E.P.S.); G. Wheeler (M.O.D.); M. Smieton (Lab. & N.S.); L.H. Robinson (Supply); G.P. Humphreys-Davis (Try).

Secs.   P.G. Oates (Cab. O.) and A. Savage (Cab. O.)   (June 1951) C.J. Felton (Cab. O.) replaced Oates.

CAB 134/114   Meetings   8 Feb–30 Nov 1951   CPC(51)1st–26th.

8 Feb	**CPC(51)1st:1**	**New productive capacity for defence.**
	:2	**Limitation of civil output in the metal-using industries.** Agreement to form a working party.
	:3	**Increase in exports of consumer goods.**
19 Feb	**2nd:1**	**Machine tools.** CPC(51)3.
	:2	**Limitation of civil output in the metal-using industries.** CPC(51)4.
	:3	**Increase in exports of consumer goods.** CPC(51)2.
6 Mar	**3rd:1**	**Machine tools.** CPC(51)7.
	:2	**Tanks: Leyland agency factory.**
20 Mar	**4th**	**Limitation of civil output in the metal-using industries.** CPC(51)10.
5 Apr	**5th:1**	**Location of new capacity for defence.**
	:2	**Capacity in the textile industry.**
	:3	**Machine tools.**
	:4	**Limitation of civil output in the metal-using industries.** CPC(51)10(2nd revise).
	:5	**Regional organization: functions regarding competing demands on productive capacity.**
13 Apr	**6th**	**Limitation of civil output in the metal-using industries: raw materials and production controls and their effect on the labour supply.** CPC(51)11. General agreement that the support of industry was necessary for any system of control and that co-operation was dependent on the system's equity.
3 May	**7th:1**	**Machine tools.**
	:2	**Manpower requirements of the Royal Ordnance factories, Swynnerton and Radway Green.** CPC(51)17.
29 May	**8th:1**	**Limitation of civil output in the metal-using industries.** Reaction of the Economic Steering Committee to CPC(51)10(final) given.
	:2	**Machine tools for defence.** CPC(51)22.
	:3	**New building in connection with the defence programme.** CPC(51)23. Agreement on the need to avoid such building.

7 June	**9th:1**	**Transfer of labour within firms to defence or other essential work.** CPC(51)24. Agreement that, experimentally, regional controllers of the Ministry of Labour and regional officers of other departments should confer to agree a common approach to firms.
	:2	**Rotax Ltd.: Hemel Hempstead.** CPC(51)25.
8 June	**10th**	**Textile requirements for the defence programme.** CPC(51)26 and 27.
15 June	**11th:1**	**Rotax Ltd.: Hemel Hempstead.**
	:2	**Textile requirements for the defence programme: canvas.** CPC(51)26.
21 June	**12th:1**	**Transfer of labour within firms to defence or other essential work.** CPC(51)29.
	:2	**Textile requirements for the defence programme: canvas.** CPC(51)26 and 30.
3 July	**13th**	**Defence programme: labour requirements at Coventry.** CPC(51)31 and 32.
5 July	**14th:1**	**Textile requirements for the defence programme.** CPC(51)34.
	:2	**Defence programme: labour requirements at Coventry.** CPC(51)36.
13 July	**15th:1**	**Rotax Ltd.: Hemel Hempstead.**
	:2	**Labour requirements for the defence programme at Coventry.**
	:3	**Control of manufacture and supply.** CPC(51)13 and 35.
	:4	**Machine tools for defence.** CPC(51)37.
20 July	**16th:1**	**Machine tools for defence.** CPC(51)37.
	:2	**Canvas requirements for the British railways.** CPC(51)38.
	:3	**Canvas requirements for the defence programme.** CPC(51)39 and 40.
23 Aug	**17th:1**	**Jute supplies for the defence programme.** CPC(51)51.
	:2	**Canvas for the defence programme.** CPC(51)52.
	:3	**Canvas and jute: high level approach to industry.** CPC(51)45.
27 Aug	**18th:1**	**Labour situation in the Coventry area in relation to the defence programme.** CPC(51)53.
	:2	**Labour requirements for the defence programme.** CPC(51)50 and 54.
13 Sept	**19th**	**Restriction of production of goods for home consumption.** CPC(51)56 and 58. See MP(51)3rd.
21 Sept	**20th:1**	**Labour situation in the Preston, Chorley and Blackburn area in relation to the defence programme.** CPC(51)57.
	:2	**Expansion of production of British Timken Ltd.** CPC(51)59.
26 Sept	**21st:1**	**Labour situation in the Coventry area in relation to the defence programme.** CPC(51)62.

	:2	**Production and distribution of nylon.** CPC(51)61.
4 Oct	**22nd:1**	**Labour requirements for the Royal Ordnance factory, Swynnerton.** CPC(51)65.
	:2	**Jute supplies for the defence programme.**
	:3	**Transfer of labour within firms to defence or other essential work.**
	:4	**Machine tools for defence.**
	:5	**Measures to alleviate the labour situation in the Chorley, Preston and Blackburn area and in the Coventry area.**
23 Oct	**23rd:1**	**Cotton drill and denim.** CPC(51)70.
	:2	**Machine tools for defence.** CPC(51)72.
15 Nov	**24th:1**	**Marconi Wireless Telegraph Co. Ltd.** CPC(51)79 and 80.
	:2	**Labour situation in the Redditch area in relation to the defence programme.** CPC(51)77.
	:3	**Labour situation in the Cricklewood area in relation to the defence programme.** CPC(51)78.
	:4	**Expansion of production of British Timken Ltd.**
16 Nov	**25th**	**Report on the labour situation in the Coventry area in relation to the defence programme.** CPC(51)81.
30 Nov	**26th:1**	**Report on the labour situation in the Coventry area in relation to the defence programme.** CPC(51)81(revise).
	:2	**Report on the labour situation in the Chorley, Preston and Blackburn area in relation to the defence programme.** CPC(51)83.

CAB 134/115 Memoranda 1 Feb–28 Sept 1951 CPC(51)1–66.

1 Feb	**CPC(51)1**	**Terms of reference and composition** – N. Brook, 2p.
13 Feb	**2**	**U.K. export target** – **Board of Trade**, 1p. Exposition of approach used.
15 Feb	**3**	**Machine tools for £4,700m defence programme**– **Ministry of Supply**, 4+3p appendixes.
9 Feb	**4**	**Limitation of civil output in the metal-using industries** – **A.M. Jenkins**, 2+11p.
26 Feb	**5**	**Tanks: Leyland agency factory** – **Ministry of Supply**, 2p.
1 Mar	**6**	**Tanks: Leyland agency factory** – **Ministry of Labour**, 2+1p.
3 Mar	**7**	**Machine tools** – **E.A. Shillito**, 1+5p. Draft report.
9 Mar	**8**	**Machine tools for defence** – **E.A. Shillito**, 1+8p. Second draft of the interim report. Draft of ES(51)22.
10 Mar	**9**	**Creation of additional capacity for machine tool production** – **Ministry of Supply**, 2+1p.

26 Apr	10	**Limitation of civil output in the metal-using industries – interim report of the committee,** 9+3p appendixes. Final version. See ES(51)31.
7 Apr	11	**Raw material and production controls and their effect on labour supply – Ministry of Labour,** 3p. Raises the question of how far raw material controls, needed because of scarcity of metals, should help secure transfer of labour.
18 Apr	12	**Regional organization: functions regarding repeated demands on productive capacity – P.G. Oates and A. Savage covering the Board of Trade,** 1+4p. General guidance to regional boards of industry concerning defence and exports.
18 Apr	13	**Limitation of supplies – Board of Trade,** 3p. Consideration of the wartime Limitation of Supplies Orders. See CPC(51)35.
20 Apr	14	**Machine tools for defence – P.G. Oates and A. Savage,** 1p. Outcome of ES(51)22.
27 Apr	15	**Regional organization: function in regard to competing demands on productive capacity – Admiralty,** 1p.
28 Apr	16	**Controls over non-ferrous metals – Ministry of Supply,** 4p. Consideration of how far controls in this field could assist the transfer of labour.
1 May	17	**Manpower requirements of Royal Ordnance factory, Swynnerton – E.A. Shillito,** 1+2p.
4 May	18	**Labour requirements at the Royal Ordnance factories, Swynnerton and Radway Green – E.A. Shillito,** 1+4p. See EPC(51)50.
10 May	19	**Shortage of materials: effect on production – Ministry of Supply,** 2p. Examples of shortages leading to underemployment.
15 May	20	**Labour requirements of the Royal Ordnance factories at Swynnerton and Radway Green – P.G. Oates and A. Savage,** 1p. Economic Policy Committee comments.
16 May	21	**Ministry of Supply regional organization: functions regarding competing demands on productive capacity,** 2p.
23 May	22	**Supply of machine tools for defence programme– Ministry of Supply,** 4+5p appendixes.
22 May	23	**New building in connection with the defence programme – Board of Trade,** 1+3+3p appendix. Sets out applications for industrial development certificates.
28 May	24	**Transfer of labour within firms to defence work– Ministry of Labour,** 2+1p appendix. Suggested arrangements for avoiding clashes between priorities for labour.

2 June	25	**Rotax Ltd.: Hemel Hempstead – Board of Trade,** 3p. Conflict of defence needs with distribution of industry policy.
4 June	26	**Final report of the Working Party on Textile Requirements for the Defence Programme – Board of Trade,** 2+7+1p.
2 June	27	**Jute goods for the defence programme – Board of Trade,** 3p.
9 June	28	**Requests for economic information by U.S. agencies – W. Strath,** 1+2p. See RM(51)137. Also MAC(51)82 and JWPC(51)71.
27 June	29	**Transfer of labour within firms to defence work– Ministry of Labour,** 2p. Revise version. Draft letter to regional controllers.
19 June	30	**Canvases used in agriculture – Ministry of Agriculture and Fisheries,** 1p.
30 June	31	**Labour requirements for defence programmes at Coventry – Ministry of Supply,** 3p.
29 June	32	**Statistics on the employment position in Coventry – Ministry of Labour,** 1+2p.
28 June	33	**Change in secretariat –** unsigned, 1p.
29 June	34	**Canvas and the defence programme – Board of Trade,** 5p.
29 June	35	**Control of manufacture and supply – Board of Trade,** 4+2p. Continuation of CPC(51)13 with regard to the reintroduction of wartime control.
6 July	36	**Proposed production of aero engines by Standard Motor Co. Coventry – E.A. Shillito,** 1+6p. Final version. Report by the committee.
27 July	37	**Machine tools for defence – A. Savage and C.J. Felton covering the Ministry of Supply,** 1+6+1p. Revise version.
17 July	38	**Textile requirements for the defence programme: canvas – A. Savage and C.J. Felton covering the Railway Executive,** 1+1p.
17 July	39	**Canvas requirements for the defence programme – Ministry of Defence,** 4+2p appendix. appendix.
18 July	40	**Revised estimate of supply possibilities – Board of Trade,** 2p. In relation to canvas.
24 July	41	**Labour requirements for the defence programme at Coventry – E.A. Shillito,** 3p. Final version. *Ad hoc* Working Party of senior regional officials of departments concerned with Coventry.
24 July	42	**Short-time and overtime working in the manufacturing industries at March 1951 – Ministry of Labour,** 1+2+2p. Information from employers.
24 July	43	**Machine tools for defence – E.A. Shillito,** 1+2p.
27 July	44	**Canvas requirements for the defence programme – E.A. Shillito,** 1p.

30 July	45	**Canvas and jute supplies for the defence programme – A. Savage and C.J. Felton,** 1p.
31 July	46	**Proposed production of aero engines at Coventry – A. Savage and C.J. Felton,** 1p.
7 Aug	47	**Labour requirements for the defence programme in the Preston, Chorley and Blackburn area – E.A. Shillito,** 1+3p. Final version. *Ad hoc* Working Party of senior regional officials to be established.
4 Aug	48	**Machine tools for defence – E.A. Shillito,** 1p.
10 Aug	49	**Restriction of production of goods for home consumption – E.A. Shillito covering a note of an** *ad hoc* **meeting on 9 Aug 1951,** 1+3p. See MP(51)6.
16 Aug	50	**Labour requirements for the defence programme – Ministry of Supply,** 2+4p. Revised version. version.
18 Aug	51	**Jute goods and defence programme – Ministry of Materials,** 2p.
17 Aug	52	**Canvas for defence – E.A. Shillito,** 2p.
22 Aug	53	**Labour position in the Coventry area – C.J. Felton covering the** *ad hoc* **Working Party of senior regional representatives,** 1+27+30p appendix. Working Party report.
27 Aug	54	**Labour requirements for the defence programme – Admiralty,** 1p.
31 Aug	55	**Building projects in the Coventry zone – A. Savage and C.J. Felton covering the Ministry of Works,** 1+1p.
7 Sept	56	**The manpower position and measures to deal with the labour supply – Ministry of Labour,** 1+9+2p appendix. MP(51)8.
10 Sept	57	**Labour situation in the Preston, Chorley and Blackburn area – A. Savage and C.J. Felton covering the** *ad hoc* **Working Party of senior regional representatives,** 1+35+14p appendixes.
10 Sept	58	**Restriction of production of goods for home consumption – A. Savage and C.J. Felton covering the Working Party,** 1+8+40p annexes. See MP(51)9.
17 Sept	59	**British Timken Ltd.: Coleshill, Warwicks. – Board of Trade,** 3+2p appendix. Conflict of defence needs with distribution of industry policy.
14 Sept	60	**Regional surveys of areas with heavy labour demands for the defence programme – A. Savage and C.J. Felton,** 1+3p.
17 Sept	61	**Production and distribution of nylon yarn – Board of Trade,** 2p.
19 Sept	62	**Labour situation in the Coventry area in relation to the defence programme – A. Savage and C.J. Felton,** 1+5p. Draft report.

19 Sept	**63**	**Ministry of Supply labour requirements in the north west – Ministry of Supply,** 2+1p. Prefaced by note by the Secretary – A. Savage, 1p.
24 Sept	**64**	**Regional surveys of areas with heavy labour demands for the defence programme – A. Savage and C.J. Felton,** 1p. Amendments to CPC(51)60.
26 Sept	**65**	**Labour requirements at Royal Ordnance factory Swynnerton – Ministry of Labour and Ministry of Supply,** 2p.
28 Sept	**66**	**Labour situation in the Chorley, Preston and Blackburn area – note of an *ad hoc* meeting on 25 Sept 1951,** 3p.

CAB 134/116   Memoranda   3 Oct–1 Dec 1951   CPC(51)67–84.

3 Oct	**CPC(51)67**	**Local surveys of the labour situation in relation to the defence programme – A. Savage and C.J. Felton,** 1+4p annexes. Revise version. Terms of reference for further surveys of Coventry and the Chorley, Preston and Blackburn areas.
15 Oct	**68**	**Production and distribution of nylon yarn – Board of Trade,** 2p.
15 Oct	**69**	**Labour situation in the Coventry and Chorley, Preston and Blackburn areas – note of an *ad hoc* meeting on 11 Oct 1951,** 4p.
19 Oct	**70**	**Report on cotton drill and denim – Ministry of Supply,** 2p.
16 Oct	**71**	**Restriction of production of goods for home consumption – A. Savage and C.J. Felton,** 1+11+2p appendix +9p annex. See MP(51)11.
19 Oct	**72**	**Machine tools for the defence programme – Ministry of Supply,** 5p.
19 Oct	**73**	**Labour situation in the Chorley, Preston and Blackburn area – A. Savage and C.J. Felton covering the working party,** 1+8+25p appendix +19+32p appendix. First and second supplementary reports.
19 Oct	**74**	**Reports on the labour situation in the Coventry area and in the Chorley, Preston and Blackburn area – A. Savage and C.J. Felton,** 1p.
26 Oct	**75**	**Labour situation in the Coventry area – A. Savage and C.J. Felton,** 2+2+15+32p. Supplementary report.
	76	Not issued.
7 Nov	**77**	**Labour situation in the Redditch area – A. Savage and C.J. Felton covering a working party,** 1+22+12p appendix.
8 Nov	**78**	**Labour situation in the Cricklewood area – A. Savage and C.J. Felton covering a working party,** 1+46+31p appendixes.

12 Nov	79	**Labour situation in the Chelmsford area – A. Savage and C.J. Felton covering a working party,** 1+24+24p appendixes.
13 Nov	80	**Marconi Wireless Telegraph Co. Ltd. – Board of Trade,** 2p. Conflict of defence needs with distribution of industry policy.
19 Nov	81	**Labour situation in the Coventry area in relation to the defence programme – A. Savage and C.J. Felton covering the Committee,** 1+9p. Revise version. See ES(51)69.
23 Nov	82	**Machine tools for the defence programme – Ministry of Supply,** 4p.
1 Dec	83	**The labour situation in the Chorley, Preston and Blackburn area – A. Savage and C.J. Felton covering the Committee,** 1+10p. See ES(51)70.
1 Dec	84	**Note by the Secretary of the Cabinet – N. Brook,** 1p.

15.8   Distribution of Industry Committee

On the reconstitution of the government in October 1947, the Minister of State for Economic Affairs assumed responsibility for what had previously been a Subcommittee of the Lord President's Committee. For earlier papers and terms of reference, see CAB 132/21–24.

Members   Paymaster-Gen. (ch.); Fin. Sec. (Try); Jt Parl. U./Sec., Scotland; Parl. Secs., Bd Trade and Mins. of Labour & N.S., Supply, Town & Country Planning, Transport, Works.   (Dec 47) Econ. Sec. (Try, ch.); Paymaster-Gen. and Fin. Sec. (Try) no longer members.
   (March 1950) Pres. Bd Trade (ch.); Jt Parl. U./Sec., Scotland; Parl. Secs., Mins. of Labour & N.S., Supply, Town & Country Planning, Transport, Works. Fin. Sec. (Try) to attend when necessary.

Secs.   D.F. Hubback (Cab. O.) and C.T. Plumb (B.T.).   (Feb 1948) B. Hirst (B.T.) replaces Plumb. (March 1948) A.R.W. Bavin (Cab. O.) replaces Hubback.   (July 1948) A.R. Bunker (Cab. O.) replaces Bavin.   (Jan 1949) P.V. Collyer (Cab. O.) replaces Bunker.   (May 1949) N. Craig (B.T.) replaces Hirst.   (Dec 1949) P.J. Moorhouse (Cab. O.) replaces Collyer.

CAB 134/130   Meetings and Memoranda   10 Oct 1947–14 Dec 1948
             DI(47)1st–DI(48)6th and DI(47)1–DI(48)37.

Meetings

3 Nov	**DI(47)1st**	**The future of the Blaenavon Co.** DI(47)3.
12 Dec	**2nd:1**	**Prestressed concrete. Pilot scheme at Iver.** DI(47)10.

	:2	**Location of projects for modernization and development of steel and tin plate industry in South Wales** DI(47)9.
	:3	**Labour supply for forest roads and forest work generally.** DI(47)7 and 11.
	:4	**Proposals by the Gas Research Board to adapt the Abbey School buildings, Beckenham, Kent, for use as a central research unit.** DI(47)8.
	:5	**Report on the progress of government and privately financed factory building schemes in the development areas.** DI(47)4.
	:6	**Panel A approvals in the Greater London area, Jan to Sept 1947.** DI(47)5.
	:7	**Clearance of derelict land in the development areas.** DI(47)6.

13 Jan	DI(48)1st:1	**Coltness Foundry, Newmains, Lanarkshire.** DI(48)4.
	:2	**Future of the Blaenavon Co.** DI(48)1 and 5.
	:3	**Proposals of the de Havilland Aircraft Co. for extension at Hatfield.** DI(48)2 and 3.
12 Feb	2nd:1	**Public works schemes in the Merseyside area.** DI(48)7 and 11. Approval of Jay's proposal that, provided there was no substantial use of scarce materials, the continuation of public works schemes should be re-examined.
	:2	**Proposal by the General Electric Co. to extend their premises at Witton, Birmingham.** DI(48)10.
	:3	**Future of the Blaenavon Co.**
4 Mar	3rd:1	**The incidence of new industrial projects inside and outside the development areas.** DI(48)13(revised).
	:2	**Effects of new investment programme on factory building and the provision of key workers' houses.** DI(48)15.
	:3	**Report on the progress of government and privately financed factory schemes in the development areas.** DI(48)12.
	:4	**Unemployment position in Lewis and Harris.** DI(48)9.
	:5	**Proposal by M.B. Foster and Sons to erect a factory at Brentford.**
	:6	**Proposal by the General Electric Co. to extend their premises at Witton, Birmingham.**
14 Apr	4th:1	**The General Electric Co. valve factory, Shaw.**
	:2	**De Havilland Aircraft Co., Hatfield.**
	:3	**Review of industrial building.** DI(48)18.
	:4	**The effects of the new investment programme on factory building in the development areas.** DI(48)19.

	:5	**Public works and areas of heavy unemployment.** DI(48)17. Ministry of Works to collect information about public works delayed by cuts in capital investment, which could help to relieve unemployment.
18 June	**5th:1**	**Location of houses for additional workers required at Margam.** DI(48)20.
	:2	**Location of the aircraft industry in the United Kingdom.** DI(48)22.
	:3	**Expansion of the factory of Vauxhall Motors Ltd., Luton.** DI(48)23.
	:4	**Gas Research Board Centre at Beckenham.** DI(48)24.
	:5	**General Electric Co. valve factory, Shaw: labour requirements.** DI(48)25.
	:6	**Report on the progress of factory building in the development areas.** DI(48)21.
	:7	**White Paper on the development areas.**
14 Dec	**6th**	**The Ford Motor Co.: proposals for expansion.** DI(48)35, 36, 37. Issue of efficiency against planning. It was argued that to agree to the proposal would strike at the whole basis of the distribution of industry policy. The majority were against the application but it was to go to the Production Committee.

Memoranda

10 Oct	**DI(47)1**	**Note by Secretary of the Cabinet – N. Brook,** 1p.
8 Nov	**2**	**Development area policy – Jones,** 2p. Against the Ministry of Works using 'advanced' factories as a means of providing employment in development areas.
31 Oct	**3**	**The future of the Blaenavon Co. – Belcher,** 3p.
13 Nov	**4**	**Report on the progress of government and privately financed factory building schemes in the development areas – Belcher and Durbin,** 2+3p appendix.
13 Nov	**5**	**Panel A approvals in the Greater London area Jan–Sept 1947 – Belcher,** 1+1p.
18 Nov	**6**	**Clearance of derelict land in the development areas – Belcher,** 2p. Progress report.
17 Nov	**7**	**Labour supply for forest roads and for forest work generally – Woodburn and Williams,** 3p. Also IPC(WP)(47)61. Progress report.
22 Nov	**8**	**Proposal by the Gas Research Board to adapt the Abbey School buildings, Beckenham, Kent for use as a central research unit – Belcher covering the Department of Scientific and Industrial Research.**

26 Nov	9	**Scheme for the modernization and development of sheet and tin plate production in South Wales – Jones,** 3+6p annex.
3 Dec	10	**Proposal to erect a pilot plant at Iver to manufacture prestressed concrete – Key,** 2p.
5 Dec	11	**Forest roads – C.T. Plumb and D.F. Hubback,** 1+2p.
16 Dec	12	**Modernization of steel and tin plate industry in South Wales – Marquand,** 2p.
17 Dec	13	**The employment and unemployment situation – Isaacs,** 1+5p annex and 8p appendixes. Report for third quarter of 1947.
30 Dec	14	**Changes in membership – N. Brook,** 1p.
1 Jan	DI(48)1	**The future of the Blaenavon Co. – Belcher,** 3p.
3 Jan	2	**Proposal by the de Havilland Aircraft Co. to erect a new assembly shed at Hatfield, Herts. – Belcher,** 2p.
3 Jan	3	**The expansion of the de Havilland Aircraft Co. at Hatfield, Herts. – Belcher,** 4p.
7 Jan	4	**Coltness foundry, Newmains, Lanarkshire – Jones,** 2p.
8 Jan	5	**Future of the Blaenavon Co. – Jones,** 1+6p annex.
22 Jan	6	**Panel A approvals in the Greater London area Jan-Dec 1947 – Belcher,** 1+1p.
5 Feb	7	**Public works schemes in the Merseyside area – Jay,** 5+12p appendixes. Call for cautious reduction of investment in Merseyside and parts of other development areas.
5 Feb	8	**Change of secretary – D.F. Hubback,** 1p.
9 Feb	9	**Unemployment position in Lewis and Harris – Fraser,** 2p.
10 Feb	10	**Proposal by the General Electric Co. Ltd. to extend their premises at Witton, Birmingham – Belcher,** 2p.
10 Feb	11	**Unemployment on Merseyside: views of North-West Regional Board for Industry – D.F. Hubback,** 1p.
19 Feb	12	**Report on the progress of government and privately financed factory building schemes in the development areas – Belcher and Durbin,** 2+3p appendix.
18 Feb	13	**The incidence of new industrial projects inside and outside the development areas – Durbin,** 2+1p annex. Revised version. In absolute and relative terms development areas were receiving highly preferential treatment.
19 Feb	14	**Proposal by M.B. Foster & Sons, Brentford, to erect a factory at Brentford – Belcher,** 2p.

24 Feb	15	**Effects of the new investment programme on factory building and the provision of key workers' houses – Durbin, 3p.**
9 Mar	16	**Change in secretariat – A.R. Bavin and B. Hirst, 1p.**
23 Mar	17	**Public works schemes in areas of high unemployment – Edwards, N., 1+2p appendix.**
24 Mar	18	**Review of industrial building – Durbin, 2+2p appendix.**
7 Apr	19	**The effects of the new investment programme on factory building in the development areas – Belcher, 2+1p annex.**
7 May	20	**Location of houses for additional workers required at Margam – King, 3p.**
18 May	21	**Report on the progress of government and privately financed factory building schemes in the development areas – Belcher and Durbin, 2+3p appendixes.**
5 June	22	**Location of the aircraft industry in the U.K. – Freeman, 2+5p appendixes +1p corrigendum.**
8 June	23	**Expansion of the factory of Vauxhall Motors Ltd., Luton – Jones, 2p.**
9 June	24	**The Gas Research Board Centre at Beckenham – Belcher, 1p.**
15 June	25	**General Electric Co. valve factory at Shaw – Belcher, 2p.**
29 June	26	**Employment in completed factories in the Scottish development area – Belcher, 3+2p appendix.**
28 June	27	**Expansion of the factory of Vauxhall Motors Ltd., Luton – A.R.W. Bavin and B. Hirst, 1+1p annexes.**
20 July	28	**Change in secretariat – A.R. Bunker and B. Hirst, 1p.**
21 July	29	**Employment in government and privately financed factories completed since the war in development areas and unemployment in these areas – Belcher, 3p.**
21 July	30	**Progress made in the allocation of Grenfell factories – Belcher, 2p.**
24 July	31	**Panel A approvals in the Greater London area 1 Jan – 30 June 1948 – Belcher, 1+2p.**
6 Aug	32	**White Paper on distribution of industry policy – Belcher, 1+33+12p appendixes. Draft of Cmd. 7540.**
10 Sept	33	**Report on the progress of government and privately financed factory building schemes in the development areas – Board of Trade and Ministry of Works, 1+3p appendixes.**
18 Nov	34	**Report on the progress of government and privately financed factory building schemes in**

		the development areas – **Belcher and Lord Morrison,** 2+3p appendixes.
10 Dec	35	**The Ford Motor Co. Proposals for expansion – Bottomley covering the Chairman of Panel A,** 1+2p.
10 Dec	36	**Proposed expansion of the Ford Motor Co., Dagenham – King,** 2p.
10 Dec	37	**Ford Motor Co.'s proposals for expansion – Fraser,** 2p.

CAB 134/131 Meetings and Memoranda 17 Jan–30 Dec 1949 DI(49)1st–6th and DI(49)1–26.

Meetings

3 Feb	**DI(49)1st:1**	**Report on the progress of government and privately financed factory building schemes in the development areas.** DI(48)33 and 34.
	:2	**Merseyside development area.** DI(49)1.
	:3	**Industrial and unemployment position in Portsmouth.** DI(49)2, 5, 6.
	:4	**Unemployment in the development areas.** DI(49)3. Concern at the level of unemployment. While welcoming an investigation, Jay pointed out that unemployment in the areas was very low in relation to pre-war years and that there was also a shortage of certain classes of labour. Therefore building more new factories was not the solution.
8 Mar	**2nd:1**	**Ford Motor Co.: proposals for expansion.**
	:2	**Location of the aircraft industry.** DI(49)4.
	:3	**Employment in the coal and tin plate industries.**
	:4	**Direction of increased production for the services to Merseyside and Clydeside.**
	:5	**Extension of Easter road maintenance scheme to Portsmouth.**
	:6	**Report on factory building schemes.**
5 May	**3rd**	**Certificates granted under the Town and Country Planning Acts, 1947 in period 1 July – 31 Dec 1948.** DI(49)10. General discussion of the future of the distribution of industry policy and the balance between its long-term economic objectives and the short-term economic needs of the balance of payments. Agreement that development areas should not be tested as strictly as the rest of the country for their contribution to the balance of payments.
2 June	**4th:1**	**Rotary Hoes Ltd., East Hordon, Essex: proposals for expansion.** DI(49)13. No agreement between advocates of short- and long-term objectives.

	:2	**Proposed expansion of Harris Lebus Ltd., Tottenham.** DI(49)14.
	:3	**Employment position in South Wales and Monmouthshire.** DI(49)11 and 12.
	:4	**New industrial projects: location approvals more favourable to the development areas.** DI(49)15.
20 July	5th:1	**Maintenance of employment in the development areas.** PC(49)72.
	:2	**Location of new oil refineries.**
	:3	**Remploy and Grenfell factories.** DI(49)16.
	:4	**Unemployment in the development areas.**
	:5	**Employment position in South Wales and Monmouthshire.** DI(49)17, 18, 21.
	:6	**Measures to help development and unemployment areas.** DI(49)19.
	:7	**Procedure for dealing with applications for industrial development certificates in the Greater London and Greater Birmingham areas.** DI(49)20.
	:8	**Hawker Aircraft Ltd.: accommodation at Squires Gate.**
22 Sept	6th:1	**Maintenance of employment in the development areas (legislation).** DI(49)22. Consideration of possible further legislation.
	:2	**Champion Sparking Plugs, Feltham.** DI(49)23.
	:3	**Leavesden airfield: de Havilland Engine Co.** DI(49)24.

Memoranda

24 Jan	DI(49)1	**Merseyside development area – Bottomley,** 1+2p appendix.
21 Jan	2	**The industrial and unemployment position in Portsmouth – Bottomley,** 2p.
17 Jan	3	**Unemployment in the development areas – Edwards, N.,** 1+1p appendix. The committee should consider urgently further steps to improve the situation in parts of development areas. Urgent need for further help for specific districts within the areas.
21 Jan	4	**Location of the aircraft industry – Freeman,** 1+4p annex.
27 Jan	5	**The industrial and unemployment position in Portsmouth – P.V. Collyer and B. Hirst covering Major Bruce,** 1+1+1p addendum. Correspondence with Jay.
11 Feb	6	**(a) factory approvals (b) Portsmouth – P.V. Collyer and B. Hirst covering Jay,** 1+1p.
2 Mar	7	**Report on the progress of government and privately financed factory building schemes in the development areas – Belcher and Lord Morrison,** 1+3p appendixes.

420

4 Mar	**8**	**Ford Motor Co.'s proposals for expansion –** **Belcher**, 3+8p annexes.
17 Mar	**9**	**List of areas where unemployment is most** **severe – P.V. Collyer and B. Hirst**, 1+1p.
2 May	**10**	**Certificates granted under the Town and** **Country Planning Acts, 1947 in period 1 July –** **31 Dec 1948 – Belcher**, 2+6p appendix. Any apparent weakening of power to steer industry to development areas was due to changed economic circumstances rather than to the new procedures.
26 May	**11**	**Employment position in South Wales – Jay,** 1+8p annexes. Proposals of Welsh Labour M.P.s.
30 May	**12**	**Unemployment in Wales and Monmouthshire –** **Belcher**, 2p. Against Welsh Labour M.P.s' proposals but agreed that a review was needed.
30 May	**13**	**Rotary Hoes Ltd., East Hordon, Essex:** **proposals for expansion – Belcher**, 3p. See PC(49)64.
30 May	**14**	**Proposed expansion of Harris Lebus Ltd.,** **Tottenham – King**, 4p.
30 May	**15**	**Measures to secure a geographical distribution** **of new industrial projects more favourable to the** **development areas – Belcher**, 2p. Need to concentrate on positive rather than negative action.
21 June	**16**	**Employment position in South Wales –** **Edwards, N.**, 2p.
30 June	**17**	**Afforestation in South Wales – Williams**, 2p.
1 July	**18**	**Employment position in South Wales and** **Monmouthshire – Callaghan**, 3+1p appendix.
16 July	**19**	**Measures to help development and** **unemployment areas – Belcher**, 2p. Industry was now, in general, unwilling to plan for an expansion unless assured of prospects of economic success over the long term. Need to help firms already established in development areas and to secure a better distribution of government or government-sponsored projects.
16 July	**20**	**Procedure for dealing with applications for** **industrial development certificates in the** **Greater London area – Belcher**, 1p.
6 July	**21**	**Employment position in South Wales and** **Monmouthshire – Robens**, 2p.
17 Sept	**22**	**Maintenance of employment in the development** **areas. Proposed amendments to the Distribution** **of Industry Act, 1945 – Belcher**, 5p. Proposal to pay for the cost of removals, training and moving key workers. Power of compulsory acquisition in certain cases was also proposed.

17 Sept	23	**Champion Sparking Plugs Co. Ltd. – Belcher,** 2p.
17 Sept	24	**Leavesden Airfield: de Havilland Engine Co. –** **Belcher,** 3p.
1 Nov	25	**The placing of government contracts with firms** **in development areas – Freeman,** 1+2p.
30 Dec	26	**Change in secretariat – P.V. Collyer and N.** **Craig,** 1p.

CAB 134/132 Meetings and Memoranda   21 Jan–7 Oct 1950   DI(50)1st–3rd and DI(50)1–11.

Meetings

26 Jan	**DI(50)1st:1**	**Certificates granted under the Town and** **Country Planning Act, 1 July 1948 – 30 June** **1949.** DI(50)3.
	:2	**New oil refinery projects: Caltex Ltd. and** **Vacuum Oil Co. Ltd.** DI(50)1 and 4.
	:3	**Report on the progress of government and** **privately financed factory building schemes in** **the development areas.** DI(50)2.
5 Apr	**2nd:1**	**Morris Motors Ltd., Cowley.** DI(50)6.
	:2	**Industrial expansion in Coventry.** BDI(B)1643 and BDI(A)167.
28 June	**3rd:1**	**Certificates granted under the Town and** **Country Planning Acts in the period 1 July – 31** **Dec 1949.** DI(50)7. Discussion turned on the adequacy of present powers for controlling distribution of industry.
	:2	**Industrial expansion in Coventry.** DI(50)8.
	:3	**Proposed expansions by D.R. Collins Ltd. and** **Matlow Bros.** DI(50)9.

Memoranda

21 Jan	**DI(50)1**	**New oil refinery projects – Belcher,** 3+4p appendixes.
20 Jan	2	**Report on the progress of government and** **privately financed factory building schemes in** **the development areas – Belcher and Lord** **Morrison,** 2+3p appendixes.
21 Jan	3	**Certificates granted under the Town and** **Country Planning Act, 1 July 1948 – 30 June** **1949 – Belcher,** 1+5p appendix. No doubt that the production drive, with its emphasis on increased efficiency and reduced costs, had further discouraged industrialists from setting up new enterprises away from existing plant. Panel A concluded that under present conditions it was difficult to put any tighter brake on developments in Greater London.
25 Jan	4	**New oil refinery projects – Callaghan,** 2p.
31 Mar	5	**Composition of the committee – N. Brook,** 1p.

1 Apr	**6**	**Morris Motors Ltd., Cowley – Wilson, H., 2+2p** appendix.
15 June	**7**	**Certificates granted under the Town and Country Planning Acts, 1 July – 31 Dec 1949 – Wilson, W.,** 1+4 appendix.
17 June	**8**	**Industrial expansion at Coventry – Wilson, H.,** 2+7p appendixes.
27 June	**9**	**Proposed expansions of D.R. Collins Ltd. and Matlow Bros. Ltd. – Wilson, H.,** 1+4p appendixes.
16 Sept	**10**	**Report on the progress of government and privately financed factory building schemes in the development areas – P.J. Moorhouse and N. Craig,** 1+6p annex.
7 Oct	**11**	**Dispersal of nationalized boards – Jay covering the Official Committee on Dispersal from London of Headquarter Government Offices,** 1+6p.

15.9   Committee on Exports (1948–1951)

For earlier papers, terms of reference and membership, see CAB 134/44. The change in chairmanship in March 1949 from the Second Secretary (Home) of the Board of Trade to the Second Secretary (Overseas) reflected the shifting emphasis of the committee's work from the securing of production for export to markets and selling. In February 1951 its responsibilities for production were assumed by the Committee on Productive Capacity (see CAB 134/114–116) and for distribution by both the Overseas Negotiations Committee (see CAB 134/555–587) and the Commonwealth Economic Affairs Committee (see CAB 134/90–94).

Members   (March 1948)   R.K. McGregor and H. Trevelyan new representatives for F.O. and B.T.   (Nov 1948)   J. Hensley new representative for M.A.F.   (Jan 1949) T. Brockie new representative for Works.   (March 1949) S.L. Holmes (B.T.) new chairman.   (1949) W.T. Garnett new representative for C.R.O.

Secs.   G.M. Wilson (Cab. O.), J.G. March (B.T.) and E.M. Gwyer (B.T.).   (Feb 1948) E.J. Beaven (Cab. O.) replaced Wilson and March.   (June 1948) D. Caplan (B.T.) replaced Gwyer.   (Aug 1948) M. Bannister (B.T.) replaced Caplan.   (Feb 1950) E.I.J. MacPherson (B.T.) replaced Bannister.   (Aug 1950) R.S. Buer (Cab. O.) replaced Beaven.   (Sept 1950) M. Dalton (B.T.) replaced MacPherson.   (Oct 1950) M.M. du Merton (Cab. O.) replaced Buer.

CAB 134/166   Meetings   8 Jan–22 Nov 1948   E(48)1st–17th.

8 Jan	**E(48)1st:1**	**Canada.** E(48)3.
	:2	**Hard and soft currencies.** E(48)4.
	:3	**Singer sewing machines.** E(48)6.
	:4	**Revised export targets.** E(48)5.

		:5	**Minutes of the fourth meeting of the Working Party of the Committee on Exports.** BP(E)(47)35.
15 Jan	2nd:1		**Hard and soft currencies.** E(48)9. Amendments made to the paper.
		:2	**Singer sewing machines.** E(48)7.
22 Jan	3rd:1		**Canada.**
		:2	**Hard and soft currencies.** The committee had to take all possible steps to implement the policy in E(48)9(revise) because of the increasingly serious dollar deficit.
		:3	**Exports to Belgium.** E(48)12.
		:4	**Singer sewing machines.** No decision reached.
		:5	**Frustrated exports: mechanical lighters.** E(48)10.
		:6	**Revised export targets.** Consideration of their publication in the Economic Survey.
29 Jan	4th:1		**Frustrated exports: mechanical lighters.**
		:2	**Revised export targets: publication in the Economic Survey.** To be further considered.
		:3	**France.**
		:4	**Canada.**
		:5	**Singer sewing machines.**
		:6	**Exports containing gold.** E(48)13. Working Party to be convened.
		:7	**Supplies for the Greek army.**
		:8	**Exports of whisky.**
5 Feb	5th:1		**France.**
		:2	**Exports to Canada.** E(48)14.
		:3	**Singer sewing machines.**
		:4	**Aerodrome contracts.**
		:5	**Aluminium houses.**
		:6	**Price variation guarantees.**
12 Feb	6th:1		**Supply of small canal vessels to Canada.**
		:2	**Progress report on exports to the U.S.A.** E(48)14.
		:3	**Action necessary after bilateral negotiations.** E(48)17.
		:4	**Exports to Italy.** E(48)19.
		:5	**Exports to Switzerland and Liechtenstein.** E(48)18.
		:6	**Steel for export in industry.** E(48)16.
26 Feb	7th:1		**Singer sewing machines.** E(48)28.
		:2	**Exports to the U.S.A.** E(48)26.
		:3	**Publicity for Export Promotions Department.** Working Party to be set up.
4 Mar	8th:1		**Purchase of rationed textiles and clothing by overseas visitors.**
		:2	**Export programme.** E(48)29. Agreement to reconsider the programme when figures for the first quarter of 1948 were available.
		:3	**Export of aluminium houses.** E(48)27.

	:4	**Argentine agreement.** E(48)22.
	:5	**Exports to the Netherlands.** E(48)21.
	:6	**Exports of cement.** E(48)25.
	:7	**Supply of aerodrome equipment abroad.** E(48)23.
	:8	**Frustrated exports.** E(48)30. Subject to Treasury agreement on the import for re-export scheme, the Board of Trade was to implement E(48)30.
22 Mar	9th:1	**Points arising from the previous minutes.**
	:3	**Export targets.** E(48)35. To be revised in the light of the discussion and certain revised estimates.
	:4	**Poland.** E(48)33.
	:5	**Belgium.** E(48)36.
	:6	**Denmark.** E(48)37.
	:7	**Finland.** E(48)38.
22 Apr	10th:1	**Belgium.**
	:2	**Allocation of steel for the export of building components.** E(48)42.
	:3	**British antique dealers' fair in Toronto.** E(48)45.
29 Apr	11th:1	**Canada.**
	:2	**Export of capital goods.**
	:3	**Belgium and the Belgian monetary area.** E(48)48.
	:4	**Progress report for March 1948.** E(48)47.
3 June	12th:1	**Frustrated exports.**
	:2	**Belgium.** E(48)48.
	:3	**Desirable and less desirable markets.**
	:4	**Meetings of the Exports Committee.**
	:5	**Iceland.** E(48)49.
	:6	**Norway.** E(48)56.
	:7	**Progress reports.** E(48)57 and 58.
	:8	**Export programme 1948.** E(48)52, 59 and 60. Need for some revision as the estimate of total U.K. exports was higher than the sum of forecasts for exports to individual countries.
14 June	13th:1	**U.S.A. progress report.**
	:2	**Co-ordination of programmes.** Regular meetings of the chairmen to co-ordinate the work of the London, Overseas Negotiations, Programmes and Exports Committees.
	:3	**Canada: progress report.** E(48)62.
	:4	**Spain.** E(48)63.
26 July	14th:1	**Points arising from previous minutes.**
	:2	**Work of the committee in relation to long-term Economic Survey 1948–1952.** Subcommittee to prepare a programme of further study to establish how to improve exports over the four-year period, changing the destination of exports, the commodities exported and production for export.

	:3	**Economic relations with non-dollar non-participating countries.**
	:4	**Anglo-Brazilian trade agreement.** E(48)69(revise).
	:5	**Exports to the Belgian Congo.** E(48)70.
	:6	**Exports to the U.S.A.** E(48)68, 71, 72. Working party to consider how the government might assist merchanting organizations in the U.S.A. Agreement to keep the progress of exports to the U.S.A. under close review.
	:7	**Report on overseas trade.** ROOT(48)1 and 2. New monthly report on overseas trade.
	:8	**Poland.** E(48)73.
23 Aug	15th:1	**Minutes of the fourteenth meeting.**
	:2	**Balance of payments 1948/52.** E(48)80. Consideration of each recommendation of the report.
	:3	**Development of tourism.** E(48)82.
	:4	**Italy.** E(48)81.
	:5	**Switzerland.** E(48)78 (wrongly typed as ON(48)78).
	:6	**Export of dogs to the U.S.A.** E(48)77.
	:7	**Argentina.**
20 Sept	16th:1	**Export quotas for silk.** E(48)88.
	:2	**Export target for 1949.** The Subcommittee (Plans) should consider what the President of the Board of Trade should say at his press conference. Emphasis was to be given to the 160% increase in the value of exports from 1938 compared to the figure of 150% shown in the long-term balance of payments statement.
	:3	**Subcommittee (Plans).** E(48)90.
	:4	**Canada.** E(48)85.
	:5	**India and Pakistan.** E(48)83.
	:6	**Exports to the U.S.A.** E(48)89.
22 Nov	17th:1	**Minutes of the sixteenth meeting.**
	:2	**Guidance of exports of capital goods.**
	:3	**Export targets 1949.** E(48)93 and 100.
	:4	**Exports to the U.S.A.** E(48)92.
	:5	**Exports to India and Pakistan.** E(48)98.
	:6	**France.** E(48)94.
	:7	**Portugal.** E(48)102.
	:8	**Denmark.** E(48)95 (revise).
	:9	**Argentina.** E(48)99 and 101.
	:10	**Development of the O.E.E.C. affecting exports to Europe.** E(48)103.

CAB 134/167   Memoranda   1 Jan–30 Dec 1948   E(48)1–107.

1 Jan	E(48)1	**Distribution of exports of capital goods – G.M. Wilson covering the Ministry of Supply.** 1+1+3p annexes.

5 Jan	2	**Monthly progress report on export achievement – G.M. Wilson covering the Board of Trade,** 1+2p. Also ON(48)6.
7 Jan	3	**Canada – J.R.C. Helmore,** 1+4p. Extract from BP(ON)(47)69th:1.
7 Jan	4	**Hard and soft currencies – G.M. Wilson,** 1+3p. Extract from ON(48)1st:1.
6 Jan	5	**Revised export targets (final report) – E.M. Gwyer,** 5+5p. Revision of BP(E)(47)34.
6 Jan	6	**Singer sewing machines – Treasury,** 3+3p.
12 Jan	7	**Singer sewing machines – G.M. Wilson covering the Ministry of Labour and National Service,** 1+1p.
14 Jan	8	**Singer sewing machines – G.M. Wilson covering the Board of Trade,** 1+2p.
16 Jan	9	**Hard and soft currencies – G.M. Wilson,** 1+5+7p annex. Revise version. Also ON(48)40(revise). Classification of markets into six categories.
20 Jan	10	**Frustrated exports: mechanical lighters – Board of Trade,** 2p.
29 Jan	11	**Desirable and less desirable markets – G.M. Wilson,** 1+4+4p annexes. Revision of E(48)9.
21 Jan	12	**Exports to Belgium – Board of Trade,** 2p.
26 Jan	13	**Exports containing gold – Treasury,** 3p.
2 Feb	14	**Exports to Canada – J.R.C. Helmore,** 1+12+3p annex +1p appendix. Final version.
6 Feb	15	**Monthly report on export progress – G.M. Wilson covering the Board of Trade,** 1+2p.
9 Feb	16	**Steel for exporting industries – Ministry of Works,** 2p.
10 Feb	17	**Action necessary when bilateral negotiations are concluded – Board of Trade,** 2p.
10 Feb	18	**Exports to Switzerland and Liechtenstein – Board of Trade,** 3+3p appendixes.
11 Feb	19	**Exports to Italy – Board of Trade,** 2+5p appendixes.
13 Feb	20	**Change of secretariat – unsigned,** 1p.
17 Feb	21	**Exports to the Netherlands,** 2+4p appendix.
21 Feb	22	**Argentine agreement – Board of Trade,** 3p.
19 Feb	23	**Supply of aerodrome equipment abroad – E.J. Beaven covering the Board of Trade,** 1+2p.
9 Feb	24	**Bilateral availabilities – Ministry of Supply,** 4+20p. Also ON(48)85.
23 Feb	25	**Export of cement – E.J. Beaven covering the Board of Trade,** 1+2p.
5 Mar	26	**Exports to the U.S.A. – J.R.C. Helmore,** 1+6+10p appendix. Final version, as submitted to the President of the Board of Trade. Estimate of expected levels in 1948 and consideration of steps to increase exports.

24 Feb	27	**Export of aluminium houses – E.J. Beaven covering the Board of Trade**, 1+3p.
25 Feb	28	**The Singer organization in the U.K. – Treasury**, 2+1p.
1 Mar	29	**Export programme 1948 – Board of Trade**, 2+1p. Draft programme.
2 Mar	30	**Frustrated exports – Board of Trade**, 3p.
4 Mar	31	**Change of membership – E.J. Beaven**, 1p.
4 Mar	32	**Monthly report on export progress – E.J. Beaven covering the Board of Trade**, 1+1p. Also ON(48)121.
15 Mar	33	**Anglo-Polish trade talks. The understanding of June 1947 – Board of Trade**, 4+16p annexes.
17 Mar	34	**Export prices in 1948 – E.J. Beaven**, 1+2p. Also WP(E)(48)1st.
2 Apr	35	**Export targets for end–1948 – E.J. Beaven**, 1+2+7p. Final version. Revised targets on the basis of an increase in the volume of U.K. exports of 150% above 1938 instead of the original target of 160%.
18 Mar	36	**Belgium – Board of Trade**, 2p.
18 Mar	37	**Denmark – Board of Trade**, 2p.
18 Mar	38	**Finland – Board of Trade**, 2+2p appendix.
20 Mar	39	**Progress report on U.K. exports Feb 1948 – J.R.C. Helmore**, 1+2+3p. First of new series of reports concentrating on certain important markets.
14 Apr	40	**Procedure for following up bilateral negotiations – E.J. Beaven covering the chairman of the Overseas Negotiation Committee and J.R.C. Helmore**, 1+2p. Also ON(48)163.
31 Mar	41	**Price control – E.J. Beaven covering the Subcommittee on Prices of the Official Committee on Economic Development**, 1+2p. Also ED(SP)(48)1. Draft report on price control and exports.
6 Apr	42	**Allocations of steel for exports of building components 1948 – Ministry of Works**, 1+1p.
8 Apr	43	**Monthly report on export progress – E.J. Beaven covering the Board of Trade**, 1+1p. Also ON(48)158.
10 Apr	44	**Export targets for end–1948 – E.J. Beaven**, 1+2+7p. Schedule of revised targets is to be published.
14 Apr	45	**Proposed British antique dealers' fair and exhibition in Toronto – Board of Trade**, 2p.
21 Apr	46	**Exports to Belgium and Belgian Congo – E.M. Gwyer**, 1+6p.
24 Apr	47	**Progress report on U.K. exports March 1948 – Board of Trade**, 1+3p.

18 May	**48**	**Exports to the Belgian monetary area – J.R.C. Helmore,** 2+8+2p appendixes. Revise version. Also ON(48)207.
1 May	**49**	**Iceland – Board of Trade,** 2p.
1 May	**50**	**Price control – J.R.C. Helmore,** 2p. Comments on E(48)41.
5 May	**51**	**Monthly report on export progress – E.M. Gwyer covering the Board of Trade,** 1+1p. Also ON(48)189.
11 May	**52**	**Revised export programme 1948. Statistical analysis – E.M. Gwyer,** 2+2+13p annexes.
17 May	**53**	**Exports to Canada – J.R.C. Helmore,** 1p.
20 May	**54**	**Exports to Canada – E.M. Gwyer,** 1+2p.
21 May	**55**	**Progress report on Switzerland – E.M. Gwyer,** 1+1p.
28 May	**56**	**Norway – Board of Trade,** 2+3p appendix.
26 May	**57**	**Progress report on exports of U.K. produce to certain important markets April 1948 – Board of Trade,** 2+3p.
1 June	**58**	**Report of export progress: Jan–Apr 1948 – Board of Trade,** 1+3p.
1 June	**59**	**Revised export programme 1948 – Board of Trade,** 4p. Analysis of the points arising from the new programme.
1 June	**60**	**Revised export programme 1948 – J.R.C. Helmore,** 2p. Action taken as a result of E(48)52.
8 June	**61**	**Change in secretariat – E.J. Beaven,** 1p.
18 June	**62**	**Exports to Canada – J.R.C. Helmore covering the committee,** 2+4+10p annex. Revise version. Progress report.
11 June	**63**	**Spain – Board of Trade,** 4+5p annexes.
15 June	**64**	**Exports to the U.S.A. – J.R.C. Helmore,** 1p.
24 June	**65**	**Report on export progress: Jan–May 1948 – Board of Trade,** 1+3p.
24 June	**66**	**Progress report on exports of U.K. produce to certain important markets May 1948 – Board of Trade,** 2+3p.
25 June	**67**	**Revised export programme to Norway – Board of Trade,** 1+1p.
29 June	**68**	**Progress report in export programmes to the U.S.A., Jan–May 1948 – Board of Trade,** 1+2p.
7 July	**69**	**Trade and payments agreement with Brazil – D. Caplan and E.J. Beaven covering the Board of Trade,** 1+4+3p annexes.
6 July	**70**	**Belgian Congo – Board of Trade,** 2p.
6 Aug	**71**	**Quarterly report on exports to the U.S.A. – D. Caplan and E.J. Beaven,** 1+6+6p annexes. Final version.
21 July	**72**	**Exports to the U.S.A. – D. Caplan and E.J. Beaven,** 1+1p. Supplement to E(48)62.

22 July	**73**	**Supplementary Anglo-Polish agreement about an exchange of miscellaneous goods – D. Caplan covering the Board of Trade,** 1+2+7p.
23 July	**74**	**Report on overseas trade: May – D. Caplan and E.J. Beaven,** 1+2p.
24 July	**75**	**Exports to the U.S.A. – D. Caplan and E.J. Beaven,** 1+2p.
30 July	**76**	**Denmark – D. Caplan covering the Board of Trade,** 1+1+5p appendixes.
5 Aug	**77**	**Exports to the U.S.A.: dogs – D. Caplan,** 1+2+1p annex.
9 Aug	**78**	**Progress report on Switzerland – D. Caplan covering the Board of Trade,** 1+2+1p appendix.
16 Aug	**79**	**Change in secretariat – E.J. Beaven and M. Bannister,** 1p.
18 Aug	**80**	**Balance of payments 1948/52 – E.J. Beaven and M. Bannister covering the Subcommittee on Visible Exports,** 1+8p. Interim report indicating the programme of further study requested at E(48)14th:2.
18 Aug	**81**	**Exports to Italy – E.J. Beaven and M. Bannister covering the Board of Trade,** 1+2+8p annexes +1p addendum.
19 Aug	**82**	**Development of tourism: 1949/52 – E.J. Beaven and M. Bannister covering the Board of Trade,** 1+7p.
1 Sept	**83**	**Exports to India and Pakistan – E.J. Beaven and M. Bannister covering the Board of Trade,** 1+7+7p annexes.
30 Aug	**84**	**Report by the Subcommittee on Visible Exports – E.J. Beaven and M. Bannister covering S.L. Holmes,** 2p. Covering note to E(48)80.
1 Sept	**85**	**Canada – J.R.C. Helmore,** 4+16p annexes +1p addendum. Record of discussions with Canadian officials. JCH/CAN/1–7, detailed records of the discussions, annexed.
7 Sept	**86**	**Progress report on Argentina – E.J. Beaven and M. Bannister,** 1+1p.
9 Sept	**87**	**Denmark – Board of Trade,** 1+1p appendix.
16 Sept	**88**	**Export quota for silk goods – Board of Trade,** 2p.
11 Sept	**89**	**Exports to the U.S.A. – E.J. Beaven and M. Bannister covering the Board of Trade,** 1+4+1p annex.
17 Sept	**90**	**Subcommittee (Plans) – E.J. Beaven and M. Bannister,** 1p.
21 Sept	**91**	**Export targets 1949 – E.J. Beaven and M. Bannister covering the Board of Trade,** 1+2+8p annexes. Sets out end-1949 targets resulting from discussions with production departments.

30 Sept	**92**	**Exports to the U.S.A. – E.J. Beaven and M. Bannister covering N. Blond,** 1+7p. Report from Washington.
1 Oct	**93**	**Export targets 1949 – J.R.C. Helmore,** 2+2+1p annex. Sets out recommendations of the Subcommittee (Plans), and a draft brief for the President of the Board of Trade. Revised summary of export targets for the end of 1948 and 1949 is annexed.
1 Oct	**94**	**France – Board of Trade,** 2+1p annex.
6 Nov	**95**	**Anglo-Danish trade agreement – E.J. Beaven and M. Bannister covering the Board of Trade,** 1+2p. Revise version.
5 Oct	**96**	**Subcommittee (Plans) – E.J. Beaven and M. Bannister,** 1p.
6 Oct	**97**	**Export targets 1949 – J.R.C. Helmore covering J. Stafford,** 1+1p appendix +1p annex. Objection to E(48)93.
8 Oct	**98**	**Exports to India and Pakistan – Board of Trade,** 2+3p annex.
18 Oct	**99**	**Exports to Argentina and Brazil – Ministry of Supply,** 2p.
25 Oct	**100**	**Export targets 1949 – E.J. Beaven and M. Bannister,** 1+2+2p annexes. Press statement on export targets.
6 Nov	**101**	**Exports to the Argentine – Board of Trade,** 6+7p annexes.
9 Nov	**102**	**Exports to Portugal – Board of Trade,** 2+1p annex.
11 Nov	**103**	**Developments in the O.E.E.C. affecting exports to Europe – Board of Trade,** 4+3p annexes.
17 Nov	**104**	**Change of membership – E.J. Beaven and M. Bannister,** 1p.
3 Dec	**105**	**Exports to the U.S.A. – E.J. Beaven and M. Bannister covering the Research Institute of America,** 1+3p. Article on Britain's push for U.S. markets.
22 Dec	**106**	**The Singer organization in the U.K. – Treasury,** 2+3p.
30 Dec	**107**	**Exports of newsprint – Board of Trade,** 3p.

CAB 134/168   Meetings and Memoranda   14 Jan–30 Dec 1949   E(49)1st–7th and E(49)1–82.

Meetings

17 Jan	**E(49)1st:1**	**Minutes of sixteenth meeting.**
	:2	**The Singer organization in the U.K.** E(48)106.
	:3	**Export of newsprint.** E(48)107.
	:4	**Responsibility for work in connection with overseas negotiations.** E(49)3.
	:5	**Sweden.** E(49)1.
	:6	**Switzerland.** E(49)4.

	:7	**Yugoslavia.** E(49)5.
	:8	**Diversion of exports to North America.** E(49)2.
30 May	2nd:1	**Export targets end-1949.** E(49)19.
	:2	**Bizone: prospects of foreign trade.** E(49)22.
	:3	**Supplies for ships' shops.** E(49)23.
	:4	**Guidance on export destinations.** E(49)28.
	:5	**Expansion of exports to North America.** E(49)25 and 32. New permanent independent body needed to assist expansion.
	:6	**Canada.** E(49)31.
11 July	3rd:1	**Exports to Canada.** E(49)33, 40, 42. Analysis of possible measures to increase exports.
	:2	**Persia.** E(49)37.
	:3	**Argentina.** E(49)41.
	:4	**Dollar Export Board.** E(49)35 and 36.
	:5	**Guidance on export destinations: Italy.** E(49)34.
18 July	4th:1	**Exports to the U.S.A.** Report by N. Blond.
	:2	**Dollar Exports Board.** E(49)35 and 36.
	:3	**Exports to Canada.** E(49)42, 43, 46, 48.
	:4	**Commonwealth finance ministers' conference.**
8 Aug	5th:1	**Minutes of the fourth meeting.**
	:2	**Report of the U.K. clothing mission on exports to Canada.** E(49)52.
	:3	**U.K. consulting engineers and Canada.** E(49)53.
	:4	**Discrimination by industry in favour of Canadian orders.** E(49)54.
	:5	**Action taken by the Ministry of Health to stimulate interest in the Canadian market.** E(49)55.
	:6	**Exports to dollar account countries.**
7 Nov	6th:1	**Exports to dollar account countries in Central and South America.** E(49)68. Agreement on need to increase exports.
	:2	**Follow-up action on trade opportunity in North America.** E(49)64.
	:3	**Report by the parliamentary secretary to the Ministry of Supply on his visit to Canada.** E(49)69.
	:4	**New dollar drive facilities offered by the Export Credits Guarantee Department.** E(49)70.
	:5	**Report on the work of the Frustrated Exports Panel.** E(49)62.
	:6	**Revaluation and the Dollar Exports Board.** E(49)67.
	:7	**International trade fairs in the U.S.A.** E(49)71.
13 Dec	7th:1	**Trade fairs in the U.S.A.**
	:2	**Report by the joint parliamentary secretary to the Ministry of Supply on his visit to Canada.** E(49)78.
	:3	**Export of cement to Canada.** E(49)74.
	:4	**Canadian Dollar/Sterling Trade Board.** E(49)72.

:5   **New dollar drive facilities.** E(49)73.
:6   **Discussions in Washington on U.S. customs procedure.** Extract from a letter by Ministry of Supply to Board of Trade, annexed.

Memoranda

14 Jan   **E(49)1**   **Sweden – Board of Trade**, 3+9 appendixes +1p addendum.

2   **The possibility of further diversion of exports to North America – E.J. Beaven and M. Bannister covering the Subcommittee (Plans),** 1+6+2p annex. Report recommended the intensification of existing policy.

13 Jan   3   **Responsibility for work in connection with overseas negotiations – E.J. Beaven and M. Bannister covering the Board of Trade,** 1+3p. Sets out the procedure for consultation with industry.

13 Jan   4   **Switzerland – E.J. Beaven and M. Bannister covering the Board of Trade,** 1+3+11p annexes. Also E(P)(48)15.

14 Jan   5   **Yugoslavia – Board of Trade**, 2+3p.

19 Jan   6   **Exports to the U.S.A. and Canada – E.J. Beaven and M. Bannister,** 1p.

20 Jan   7   **Denmark – Board of Trade**, 2+4p appendixes.

22 Jan   8   **Membership of the committee – E.J. Beaven and M. Bannister,** 1p.

31 Jan   9   **Norway – Board of Trade**, 2+3p appendixes.

31 Jan   10   **Exports to the U.S.A. and Canada – E.J. Beaven and M. Bannister,** 1+2p. Progress report.

2 Feb   11   **Export of whisky – E.J. Beaven and M. Bannister covering the Ministry of Food,** 1+2p. Also E(P)(49)6.

5 Feb   12   **Finland – Board of Trade**, 2+6p appendixes +2p addendum.

9 Feb   13   **Spain – Board of Trade**, 1+2+1p addendum.

15 Feb   14   **Anglo-Polish trade and finance agreement Jan 1949 – Board of Trade,** 4+2p annexes +26p. Cmd. 7628 attached.

25 Feb   15   **Exports to Italy – E.J. Beaven and M. Bannister covering the Board of Trade,** 1+2+7p appendixes.

25 Feb   16   **France – E.J. Beaven and M. Bannister covering the Board of Trade.** 1+2+2p annex.

7 Mar   17   **Trade with Switzerland – Board of Trade,** 2p.

8 Mar   18   **Anglo-Netherlands trade arrangement 1949 – Board of Trade,** 3+9p annexes.

8 Mar   19   **Export targets: end-1949 – Board of Trade,** 1+1+6p. Schedule of revised export targets.

16 Mar   20   **Trade with Western Germany Jan–June 1949 – E.J. Beaven and M. Bannister covering the Board of Trade,** 1+2+4p appendix.

31 Mar	**21**	**Change of chairmanship – E.J. Beaven and M. Bannister,** 1p.
12 Apr	**22**	**Prospects of the foreign trade of the bizone – Board of Trade,** 1+5+7p.
8 Apr	**23**	**Supplies for ships' shops – Board of Trade,** 3+2p.
7 Apr	**24**	**Trade with Western Germany – Board of Trade,** 2+1p appendix.
11 Apr	**25**	**Expansion of exports to North America – S.L. Holmes,** 2+3p annexes. Recent developments.
13 Apr	**26**	**Review of exports to Egypt in 1949 – Board of Trade,** 2+2p.
14 Apr	**27**	**Change of membership – E.J. Beaven and M. Bannister,** 1p.
21 Apr	**28**	**Guidance of export destinations – E.J. Beaven and M. Bannister,** 1+3+2p appendixes. Restatement of policy in a more simplified form than the paper, 'Desirable and less desirable markets', issued in Jan 1948.
29 Apr	**29**	**Portugal – Board of Trade,** 2+3p annexes +1p addendum.
3 May	**30**	**Iceland – Board of Trade,** 2+5p appendixes.
5 May	**31**	**Report by the Chairman of the Association of Consulting Engineers on his visit to Canada – E.J. Beaven and M. Bannister covering G.K. Bell,** 1+6+1p appendix.
6 May	**32**	**North American export drive. Conference held by the President of the Board of Trade and industry on 26 Apr 1949 – Board of Trade,** 1+27p annexes. Report of the conference annexed.
30 Apr	**33**	**Exports to Canada – E.J. Beaven and M. Bannister,** 6+5p annexes +1p addendum.
2 June	**34**	**Memorandum of guidance on export destinations. Supplementary note on Italy – E.J. Beaven and M. Bannister,** 1+1p.
13 June	**35**	**Dollar Exports Board – E.J. Beaven and M. Bannister,** 1+5p. Manifesto of the Board.
23 June	**36**	**Operations of the Dollar Exports Board,** 2p. Arrangements for the examination with individual industries of the problems and prospects of increasing exports to North America.
8 July	**37**	**Persia – Board of Trade,** 5+45p appendixes +9p addendum.
2 July	**38**	**Anglo-Spanish trade and payments negotiations June 1949 – Board of Trade,** 4+7p appendixes.
4 July	**39**	**Anglo-Swedish trade negotiations June 1949 – Board of Trade,** 3+7p appendixes.
2 July	**40**	**Exports to Canada – S.L. Holmes,** 1p.
4 July	**41**	**Argentina – Board of Trade,** 2+5p annex.

8 July	**42**	**Exports to Canada – E.J. Beaven and M. Bannister covering Wilson, H.,** 1+2+7p annexes. Extract from EPC(49)65 and minutes of a meeting of ministers and officials on exports to Canada and the U.S.A., 6 July 1949, annexed.
13 July	**43**	**Exports to Canada – E.J. Beaven and M. Bannister covering Wilson, H.,** 1+21+9p annexes. Report on his trade mission to Canada.
13 July	**44**	**Exports to Canada – E.J. Beaven and M. Bannister,** 1+3p. Note of a meeting 24 June 1949, with D. Harvey, Director of Import Division, Canadian Ministry of Trade and Commerce.
15 July	**45**	**Exports to Canada. Acceleration of Canadian orders – E.J. Beaven and M. Bannister,** 1p.
15 July	**46**	**Exports to Canada. Discrimination in favour of dollar-earning firms – E.J. Beaven and M. Bannister,** 4+2p. Summary of the reports from the Production Department on measures taken.
15 July	**47**	**Norway – Board of Trade,** 1+1p appendix.
15 July	**48**	**Information for potential exporters about possible openings in dollar markets – Board of Trade,** 2p.
20 July	**49**	**Fourth meeting of the Anglo-Italian Economic Committee July 1949 – Board of Trade,** 3+12p annexes.
22 July	**50**	**Memorandum of guidance on export destinations. Supplementary note on Japan – E.J. Beaven and M. Bannister,** 1+1p.
26 July	**51**	**Scheduling of dollar-earning firms – E.J. Beaven and M. Bannister,** 1p.
3 Aug	**52**	**Exports to Canada. Report of the U.K. clothing mission – E.J. Beaven and M. Bannister covering the U.K. clothing mission,** 1+4p. Extract from the report on marketing concerning the representation of the industry and sales promotion in Canada.
4 Aug	**53**	**U.K. consulting engineers and Canada – Board of Trade,** 2p.
5 Aug	**54**	**Exports to Canada. Discrimination by industry in favour of Canadian orders – E.J. Beaven and M. Bannister,** 3p. Summary of departmental progress reports on talks with industry.
5 Aug	**55**	**Exports to Canada. Action taken to stimulate interest in the Canadian market – Ministry of Health,** 2+3p appendix.
8 Aug	**56**	**Anglo-Brazilian trade agreement – Board of Trade,** 3+1p.

16 Aug	57	**Compensation or barter trading with North America – E.J. Beaven and M. Bannister covering the working group of the Subcommittee (Plans),** 1+2+2p annexes. Also E(P)(49)17. Report on preconditions for favourable consideration of applications for additional imports from the U.S.A. and Canada in return for additional exports to those countries.
18 Aug	58	**Price comparisons in Canada – Board of Trade,** 1+9p. Schedules of comparative prices for Canadian, U.S. and U.K. goods, illustrating that in order to increase dollar earnings, U.K. manufacturers had to reduce prices.
18 Aug	59	**The dollar drive. Activities of the Export Credits Guarantee Department – Exports Credits Guarantee Department,** 3p.
24 Aug	60	**Trade with Western Germany 1 July 1949–30 June 1950 – Board of Trade,** 5p.
13 Sept	61	**The dollar drive. Purchase tax remission as an incentive to export to dollar markets – E.J. Beaven and M. Bannister covering G.H. Andrew,** 1+4p. Also E(P)(49)19. Report on a possible scheme.
20 Sept	62	**Report on the work of the Frustrated Exports Panel – E.J. Beaven and M. Bannister,** 2+2p.
19 Sept	63	**New sterling/dollar exchange rate: export trade – E.J. Beaven and M. Bannister,** 1+2p.
1 Oct	64	**Follow-up action on trade opportunities in North America which have been brought to the notice of British industry – Board of Trade,** 2p.
3 Oct	65	**Persia – E.J. Beaven and M. Bannister covering the Commercial Counsellor in Tehran,** 1+1p.
5 Oct	66	**Anglo-Czechoslovak trade and financial agreement Sept 1949 – unsigned,** 2+2p.
12 Oct	67	**Revaluation and the work of the Dollar Exports Board – E.J. Beaven and M. Bannister covering the Dollar Exports Board,** 1+2p. Statement addressed to trade organisations.
20 Oct	68	**Exports to dollar account countries in Central and South America – E.J. Beaven and M. Bannister covering the Board of Trade,** 1+1+5+8p appendixes.
24 Oct	69	**Report by the Joint Parliamentary Secretary, Ministry of Supply, on his visit to Canada – E.J. Beaven and M. Bannister covering Freeman,** 1+9+26p appendixes.
1 Nov	70	**New dollar drive facilities – E.J. Beaven and M. Bannister covering the Export Credits Guarantee Department,** 1+5p.
4 Nov	71	**International trade fairs in the U.S.A.: participation by British industries – Board of Trade,** 2+2p appendix.

16 Nov	**72**	**The Canadian Dollar/Sterling Trade Board –** **Board of Trade,** 1+4p annexes.
17 Nov	**73**	**New dollar drive facilities – E.J. Beaven and M.** **Bannister covering the Dollar Exports Board,** 1+1p. Memorandum given to manufacturing organizations commending the improved services of the Export Credits Guarantee Department.
23 Nov	**74**	**Export of cement to Canada – Ministry of** **Works,** 2p.
29 Nov	**75**	**Discussions in Washington on U.S. customs** **procedures – Board of Trade,** 3p.
5 Dec	**76**	**Trade arrangement between certain sterling area** **countries and occupied Japan – Board of Trade,** 2p.
6 Dec	**77**	**Anglo-Portuguese negotiations Nov 1949 –** **Board of Trade,** 2+14p annexes.
7 Dec	**78**	**Report by the joint parliamentary secretary to** **the Ministry of Supply on his visit to Canada.** **Points arising and action taken – Ministry of** **Supply,** 3p.
16 Dec	**79**	**Future meetings of the committee – E.J. Beaven** **and M. Bannister,** 1p.
20 Dec	**80**	**Anglo-Swedish negotiations Nov/Dec. 1949 –** **Board of Trade,** 2+14p annexes.
23 Dec	**81**	**Exports to Italy – Board of Trade,** 2+2p annex.
30 Dec	**82**	**Report on the tour of the U.K. by representatives** **of the Canadian technical press Oct/Nov 1949 –** **Ministry of Supply,** 1+5+6p appendixes.

CAB 134/169   Meetings and Memoranda   2 Jan 1950–13 Feb 1951   E(50)1st–3rd, E(50)1–43 and E(50)1–5.

Meetings

27 Feb	**E(50)1st:3**	**Anglo-Yugoslav trade agreement 1949.** E(50)1.
	:4	**Norway.** E(50)2.
	:5	**Exports to Austria.** E(50)3.
	:6	**Exports to France.** E(50)5.
	:7	**Denmark.** E(50)6.
	:8	**Canadian Dollar/Sterling Trade Board.**
	:9	**New dollar drive facilities.**
	:10	**Discussions in Washington on U.S. customs** **procedure.**
	:11	**Exports to the U.S.A.** E(50)4. Consideration of each individual recommendation in E(50)4.
	:12	**The dollar export drive as seen from** **Washington.**
15 May	**2nd:1**	**Exports to the U.S.A.**
	:2	**U.S. restrictions on the import of goods for** **federal products.**
	:3	**Board of Trade sample room.**
	:4	**Export of aircraft to North America.** E(50)10.

	:5	**Argentina: status as an export market.** E(50)15.
	:6	**Changes in export prices since devaluation.** E(50)16.
2 Aug	**3rd:1**	**Exports to the U.S.** E(50)19.
	:2	**Persia.** E(50)24.

Memoranda

2 Jan	**E(50)1**	**Anglo-Yugoslav trade agreement 1949 – Board of Trade,** 2+4p annexes.
6 Feb	**2**	**Norway – Board of Trade,** 3+4p appendixes.
11 Feb	**3**	**Exports to Austria – Board of Trade,** 2+2p annex.
14 Feb	**4**	**Exports to the U.S. – E.J. Beaven and M. Bannister,** 1+5p. Recommendations and extracts from EPC(50)4.
18 Feb	**5**	**Exports to France – Board of Trade,** 4+3p appendixes.
20 Feb	**6**	**Denmark – Board of Trade,** 2+6p appendixes.
17 Mar	**7**	**Finland – Board of Trade,** 2+7p appendixes.
21 Mar	**8**	**Anglo-Polish negotiations Jan–Mar 1950 – Board of Trade,** 2+2p appendix.
30 Mar	**9**	**India – E.I.J. MacPherson and E.J. Beaven covering the Board of Trade,** 1+3+3p.
4 Apr	**10**	**Export of aircraft to North America – E.I.J. MacPherson and E.J. Beaven,** 1+1p.
12 Apr	**11**	**Argentina – E.I.J. MacPherson and E.J. Beaven covering the Board of Trade,** 1+3p.
12 Apr	**12**	**Switzerland – unsigned,** 2p.
13 Apr	**13**	**Indonesia – Board of Trade,** 2+6p appendixes +2p addendum.
13 Apr	**14**	**U.K. trade and payments agreement with Paraguay – Board of Trade,** 2p.
3 June	**15**	**Guidance on export destinations. Argentina – E.J. Beaven and E.I.J. MacPherson,** 1+1+4p. Revise version.
10 May	**16**	**Changes in export prices since devaluation – E.I.J. MacPherson and E.J. Beaven covering the Board of Trade,** 1+3+3p appendixes. Summary of information on average prices of exports to all markets and of exports to North America.
24 May	**17**	**Exports to French North Africa – Board of Trade,** 2p.
8 June	**18**	**Exports to Holland – Board of Trade,** 2+6p appendix.
21 June	**19**	**Progress report on exports to the U.S.A. – E.J. Beaven and E.I.J. MacPherson,** 2+1p annex.
27 June	**20**	**Anglo-Czech negotiations: June 1950 – Board of Trade,** 2+2p appendix.
29 June	**21**	**Anglo-Spanish trade and payments negotiations: June 1950 – Board of Trade,** 3+6p appendixes.

4 July	22	**Sweden – Board of Trade,** 2+3p appendix.
5 July	23	**Norway – Board of Trade,** 1+1p appendix.
28 July	24	**Report on progress of trade with Persia – Board of Trade,** 6+4p appendixes.
26 July	25	**Anglo-Mexican negotiations: June 1950 – Board of Trade,** 3p.
27 July	26	**Anglo-Italian negotiations – Board of Trade,** 4+8p annexes.
18 Aug	27	**Status of Argentina as an export market – A.N. Halls and E.I.J. MacPherson,** 1+2p. Note sent to employers' organizations.
23 Aug	28	**Barter or compensation trading with North America – Board of Trade,** 2+1p appendix.
28 Aug	29	**Review of the U.K. export trade with Persia – R.S. Buer and M. Dalton covering J.R.C. Helmore,** 1+4p. Also ON(50)195.
25 Aug	30	**Export guidance – Board of Trade,** 1+1p. Draft statement about the effect of a European Payments Union on Europe as an export market.
30 Aug	31	**Report of the U.K. industrial mission to Pakistan 1950 – R.S. Buer and M. Dalton,** 1+87p. Also CEA(50)50. As published.
2 Sept	32	**Information about the Canadian market – Board of Trade,** 4+12p appendixes.
13 Sept	33	**Review of steel exports – J.R.C. Helmore covering the Board of Trade,** 1+2+1+p.
23 Sept	34	**U.K./Brazilian trade agreement 1950/51 – Board of Trade,** 4+11p annexes.
28 Sept	35	**Export policy and the new defence programme – R.S. Buer and M. Dalton,** 1+1p. Extract from the Board of Trade Journal, 30 Sept 1950.
3 Oct	36	**Anglo-German trade agreement 1950 – Board of Trade,** 3+11p.
9 Oct	37	**E.C.G.D. progress report on the dollar drive – R.S. Buer and M. Dalton covering the E.C.G.D.,** 1+6+16p appendixes.
10 Oct	38	**Anglo-Portuguese trade – Board of Trade,** 2+3p.
18 Oct	39	**Distribution of steel exports – Board of Trade,** 2+2p. Letter from the British Iron and Steel Federation proposing to maintain the current distribution pattern of finished steel exports, attached.
20 Oct		**Change in secretariat – M.M. du Merton,** 1p.
6 Nov	40	**Barter or compensation trading with North America – Board of Trade,** 1+2p annex. Revision of procedures in E(49)57.
21 Nov	41	**Anglo-Swiss trade and financial discussions – Board of Trade,** 1p.
16 Dec	42	**Sterling area trade arrangement with Japan 1950–51 – Board of Trade,** 4+3p appendix.

30 Dec	**43**	**Anglo-Swedish trade negotiation Nov/Dec 1950 – Board of Trade,** 2+11p annexes.
1 Jan	**E(51)1**	**Italy – Board of Trade,** 2+8p annex.
3 Jan	**2**	**Norway – Board of Trade,** 2+2p annex.
18 Jan	**3**	**Prefabricated buildings – Board of Trade,** 1p.
25 Jan	**4**	**Exports to France and French North Africa – Board of Trade,** 3+7p appendixes.
13 Feb	**5**	**Winding up of the committee – J.R.C. Helmore,** 1p.

Subcommittee (Plans) on Visible Exports

Set up in Sept 1948, see CAB 134/166, E(49)16th:3, following a report from the Subcommittee on Visible Exports recommending means by which U.K. exports could be increased to 150% of their 1938 volume as called for by the long-term Economic Survey (see CAB 134/167, E(48)80). It became a Board of Trade committee in Dec 1949.

Terms   To review (1) export forecasts to 1952   (2) levels of industry forecast in the balance of payments and their implications   (3) the competitive power of the U.K.'s exports   (4) productivity in the major export industries   (5) the development of new products for export   (6) methods of export promotion   (7) problems and possibilities of export guidance   (8) incentives for export.

Members   J.R.C. Helmore (B.T., ch.); M.T. Flett (Try); L.P. Thompson-McCausland (Bank of Eng.); R.L. Hall (Ec. Sect.); A.V. Francis (C.E.P.S.); L.H. Robinson (Supply); G.S. Owen, K. McGregor, D. Caplan, A.K. Cairncross (all B.T.).

Secs.   E.J. Beaven (Cab. O.) and M.M. Bannister (B.T.).   (Dec 1949) Beaven left.

CAB 134/170   Meetings and Memoranda   25 Sept–20 Dec 1948   E(P)(48)1st–9th and E(P)(48)1–17.

Meetings

28 Sept	**E(P)(48)1st:1**	**Circulation of subcommittee papers.** Lists departmental representatives on the subcommittee.
	:2	**1949 export targets.** E(48)91. Consideration in general and of some in detail. See E(48)93.
	:3	**Work of the subcommittee.** E(P)(48)1.
4 Oct	**2nd**	**Exports to the U.S.A.** E(48)89. Consideration of the means of increasing exports.
11 Oct	**3rd:1**	**Export targets 1949.** E(48)97. Consideration of the price assumptions behind the 1949 targets.
	:2	**Control of exports: Ministry of Supply goods.** E(P)(48)2. Consideration of the criteria for the export of capital goods and available methods of control.

	:3	**Machinery, Plant and Appliances Order.** E(P)(48)3.
	:4	**Engineering consultants in Canada.**
18 Oct	**4th:1**	**Distribution of capital goods exports.** E(P)(48)4. Consideration of the scope of possible controls.
	:2	**Export of cars to the U.S.A.** E(P)(48)6.
	:3	**Methods of increasing exports to the U.S.A.**
	:4	**Long-term trend of exports to the U.S.A.** E(P)(48)5.
8 Nov	**5th:1**	**Belgium.**
	:2	**Exports to the U.S.A.: textiles.** E(P)(48)7.
22 Nov	**6th:1**	**Exports of capital goods to India and Pakistan.** E(P)(48)9.
	:2	**Exports to Canada.** E(P)(48)8.
29 Nov	**7th:1**	**Exports to Belgium and the Belgian Congo.** E(P)(48)10 and 12.
	:2	**Distribution of exports of capital goods.** E(P)(48)11.
	:3	**Exports of cars.**
13 Dec	**8th:1**	**Exports to Canada in 1949: textiles.** E(P)(48)13.
	:2	**Exports to the U.S.A.: food and drink.** E(P)(48)14.
	:3	**Exports of machinery and vehicles to the U.S.A. in 1952/53.** E(P)(48)7.
	:4	**Singer sewing machines.**
20 Dec	**9th:1**	**Exports of vehicles to the U.S.A.** Target for 1952/53 agreed.
	:2	**Exports of motor cars in 1949.** E(P)(48)17.
	:3	**Exports to Canada: pottery, carpets, cutlery, glassware.** E(P)(48)13.
	:4	**Exports to Canada: cotton piece-goods.**
	:5	**Switzerland.** E(P)(48)15.

Memoranda

25 Sept	**E(P)(48)1**	**The work of the subcommittee (Plans) – J.R.C. Helmore,** 2p. Sets out the eight main areas envisaged in E(48)80.
6 Oct	2	**Control of exports: Ministry of Supply goods – E.J. Beaven and M. Bannister,** 1+10p annexes. Papers by the Board of Trade, Ministry of Supply and T.L. Rowan relating to the control and guidance of the export of capital goods.
8 Oct	3	**Machinery, Plant and Appliances Order – Ministry of Supply,** 2p.
14 Oct	4	**Distribution of exports of capital goods – J.R.C. Helmore,** 2p. Sets out the conclusions reached in E(P)(48)3rd:2.
14 Oct	5	**Exports to the U.S.A.: long-term trends – Board of Trade,** 2+4+3p. March 1948 paper on the U.S. and world trade, attached.

18 Oct	6	Exports of principal car manufacturers – E.J. Beaven and M. Bannister covering the Ministry of Supply, 1+1p.
4 Nov	7	Exports to the U.S.A. (long-term targets) – Board of Trade, 1+2p. Targets for 1952/3, deliberately set high as a basis for discussion with production departments.
12 Nov	8	Exports to Canada – J.R.C. Helmore covering the Board of Trade, 1+3+1p.
19 Nov	9	Exports of capital goods to India – Board of Trade, 2+5p annexes.
26 Nov	10	U.K. exports to the Belgian Congo – Board of Trade, 4p.
26 Nov	11	The distribution of exports of capital goods – Ministry of Supply, Board of Trade and Treasury, 4p. Consideration of how far the Ministry of Supply should guide exports of engineering products.
27 Nov	12	Exports to the Belgian monetary area – Board of Trade, 2+2p.
4 Dec	13	Exports to Canada in 1949 – E.J. Beaven and M. Bannister covering the Board of Trade, 1+1+1p.
8 Dec	14	Exports to the U.S.A.: food and drink – Ministry of Food, 2p.
15 Dec	15	Switzerland – Board of Trade, 3+14p annexes.
16 Dec	16	Exports to the Belgian Congo – E.J. Beaven and M. Bannister covering the Board of Trade, 1+1p.
16 Dec	17	Exports of motor cars in 1949 – E.J. Beaven and M. Bannister, 1+1p.

CAB 134/171   Meetings and Memoranda   3 Jan–31 Dec 1949   E(P)(49)1st–13th and E(P)(49)1–25.

Meetings

3 Jan	E(P)(49)1st:1	Guidance of exports in relation to the U.K.'s balance of payments in 1949.
	:2	Quarterly reports on exports to hard currency markets. Agreement to continue reports on a periodical basis.
10 Jan	2nd:1	Desirable and less desirable markets. E(P)(49)2. Qualified approval of memorandum.
	:2	Exports to North America. E(P)(49)1 and addendum.
17 Jan	3rd	Exports to Canada in 1949/50: engineering products and vehicles. E(P)(48)13.
24 Jan	4th:1	Exports to North America.
	:2	Financial incentives to export. E(P)(49)4.
1 Feb	5th:1	Minutes of E(P)(49) fourth meeting.
	:2	Exports to North America. E(P)(49)8 and 9.
	:3	Exports of whisky. E(P)(49)6.

	:4	**Exports of domestic pottery to the U.S.A. and Canada.** E(P)(49)5.
28 Feb	**6th:1**	**Exports to Belgium and the Belgian Congo.** E(P)(49)7.
	:2	**Exports of motor cars in 1949.** E(P)(49)11.
21 Mar	**7th:1**	**Exports of machinery to Germany.**
	:2	**Steel for cars.**
	:3	**Co-ordination of advertising in the U.S.A.** E(P)(49)10.
	:4	**Exports to India.** E(P)(49)12.
13 Apr	**8th**	**U.K. export programme 1949/50.** E(P)(49)13.
20 July	**9th:1**	**Compensation or barter trading with North America.** E(P)(49)14.
	:2	**Incentives to exporters.** E(P)(49)4 and 15.
25 July	**10th:1**	**Utility incentive to exports to North America.** E(P)(49)16. Agreement that the scheme was impracticable and that the rebate of purchase tax on exports to North America should be further considered.
	:2	**Incentives to exporters.** E(P)(49)15.
8 Aug	**11th:1**	**Compensation or barter trading.** E(P)(49)17.
	:2	**Portuguese requirements of engineering goods and equipment for development of the port of Beira.**
22 Aug	**12th:1**	**Matters arising from previous minutes.**
	:2	**Scheduling of dollar-earning firms.** E(P)(49)18.
	:3	**Remission of purchase tax.** E(P)(49)19. Agreement that there were considerable problems.
	:4	**Activities of the Export Credits Guarantee Department.** E(49)59.
	:5	**Capacity available to meet an increased volume of orders from dollar markets.** E(P)(49)20.
	:6	**U.K. consulting engineers in Canada.** E(49)53.
22 Sept	**13th**	**Effect of the change in the sterling/dollar rate on exports to hard currency markets.** Considered in relation to price policy, incentives to export, future levels of exports to the dollar markets and productive capacity. '1949/50 dollar export forecast' – Board of Trade, annexed.

Memoranda

7 Jan	**E(P)(49)1**	**Exports to North America. Draft report for the Balance of Payments Working Party** – E.J. Beaven and M. Bannister, 1+7p+2p addendum. See E(49)2.
10 Jan	**2**	**Destinations for exports** – Treasury, 2+1p. Revised and simplified directions to exporters.
13 Jan	**3**	**Reports on the possibility of further diversion of exports to North America** – E.J. Beaven and

		M. Bannister covering J.R.C. Helmore, 1+1p. Covering note to E(49)2.
19 Jan	4	**Financial incentives to export – E.J. Beaven and M. Bannister,** 1+9p. Consideration of various expedients.
19 Jan	5	**Export of domestic pottery to the U.S.A. and Canada – Board of Trade,** 4+1p annex.
27 Jan	6	**Export of whisky – Ministry of Food,** 2p.
27 Jan	7	**Export to Belgium and the Belgian Congo – Board of Trade,** 3+2p annex.
31 Jan	8	**Export targets for North America – Board of Trade,** 1+1p.
31 Jan	9	**Development of exports to North America – E.J. Beaven and M. Bannister covering the Board of Trade,** 1+1+5p appendixes. Considers the basis of increased government encouragement and assistance.
11 Feb	10	**Co-ordination of advertising in the U.S.A. – Board of Trade,** 2p.
25 Feb	11	**Export of motor cars in 1949 – Ministry of Supply,** 2+1p.
18 Mar	12	**Exports to India – E.J. Beaven and M. Bannister covering the Board of Trade,** 1+4+3p annexes.
7 Apr	13	**U.K. export programme 1949–1950 – E.J. Beaven and M. Bannister covering the Board of Trade,** 1+2+4+2p. Examination of the programme to help the Programmes Committee in revising the U.K. programme for the O.E.E.C.
16 July	14	**Compensation or barter trading with North America – Board of Trade,** 1+3p appendix.
16 July	15	**The dollar export drive. Incentives to exporters – E.J. Beaven and M. Bannister,** 2+2p. Sets out schemes in operation or under consideration with limited incentives for particular industries.
22 July	16	**Incentives to exporters. A utility incentive to export of textiles and clothing to North America – E.J. Beaven and M. Bannister covering the Board of Trade,** 1+2p.
5 Aug	17	**Compensation or barter trading with North America – Working Group,** 2+1p annex. Report on how to deal with applications relating to additional imports from, in return for additional exports to, the U.S.A. and Canada. Also E(49)57.
12 Aug	18	**Scheduling of dollar-earning firms – E.J. Beaven and M. Bannister,** 3+2p annexes.
19 Aug	19	**Purchase tax remission as an incentive to exporters – G.H. Andrew,** 4p. Consideration of problems.

19 Aug	20	**Capacity available to meet an increased volume of orders from dollar markets – E.J. Beaven and M. Bannister,** 2p.
30 Aug	21	**Dollar drive. Activities of the Export Credits Guarantee Department – E.J. Beaven and M. Bannister covering M. Stevenson,** 1+1p.
14 Nov	23	**Indian import licensing policy – Board of Trade,** 2p.
23 Nov	24	**Export targets – Board of Trade,** 4p. Revision of export tables to remove confusion between export targets and export programmes.
31 Dec	25	**Change of secretary – E.J. Beaven and M. Bannister,** 1p.

15.10   Official Steering Committee on Economic Development

On the election of the Labour government in 1945, Attlee asked E.E. Bridges to obtain officials' views on the machinery for the co-ordination of economic planning. His consultations concluded with an *ad hoc* meeting on 12 September 1945, and on 19 September 1945 he issued a minute (subsequently approved by ministers) authorizing the establishment of the committee as an inter-departmental committee of permanent secretaries, or their equivalent (see T 273/298). It became the main official body co-ordinating economic policy and was initially guided by five working parties, dealing with statistics (see CAB 108/124–126), balance of payments (see T 230/11, T 236/308), manpower (see CAB 134/510), economic development (see T 230/54–60) and investment (see T 161/1297/S53555/01–02). Ministerial responsibility for the committee was exercised through the Industrial Subcommittee of the Lord President's Committee (see CAB 71/27) which was reconstituted in January 1946 as the Ministerial Committee on Economic Planning (see CAB 134/503). With the creation of the C.E.P.S. in 1947, the committee's role became mainly one of giving formal approval of reports before submission to ministers. It consequently met irregularly and, in November 1947, was renamed the Official Committee on Economic Development.

There were two further developments. In April 1949 the reorganization of the committee structure dealing with overseas economic development resulted in the committee's responsibility for the co-ordination of the work of the Committee on Colonial Development (see CAB 134/64–67), Commonwealth Economic Development (see CAB 134/96), Middle East (Official) Committee (see CAB 134/499–502) and Far East (Official) Committee (see CAB 134/277–291), see CAB 129/34, CP(49)83. For this purpose, smaller meetings of the committee could be organized, which were to be known as the Official Committee on Economic Development (Overseas) (see CAB 134/194–195). In May 1949 the Economic Development Working Group (see CAB 134/202–203) was set up and frequently took urgent economic policy matters which could not wait for a meeting of the full committee. The Official Committee on Economic Development was finally replaced by the Economic Steering Committee in October 1950 (see CAB 134/263–266).

Terms   (June 1949) To advise the Chancellor of the Exchequer on all questions of internal or external economic policy and, generally, on the use to be made of the nation's economic resources.

Members E.E. Bridges (Try, ch.); B.W. Gilbert (Try), J.H. Woods (B.T.), J.P.R. Maud (Ld Pres. O.), J.E. Meade (Ec. Sect.), G. Ince (Lab. & N.S.), O.S. Franks (Supply).   (Nov 1945) E.M. Nicholson (Ld Pres. O.) replaces Maud.

  (June 1949) E.E. Bridges (Try, ch.); B.W. Gilbert (Try); W. Eady (Try); H. Wilson-Smith (Try); T.L. Rowan (Try); E.N. Plowden (C.E.P.S.); J.H. Woods (B.T.); E.M. Nicholson (Ld Pres. O.); R.L. Hall (Ec. Sect.); G. Ince (Lab. & N.S.); A. Rowlands (Supply); D. Fergusson (Fuel & P.); R. Makins (F.O.).

Secs. M.T. Flett (Ld Pres. O.) and P.D. Proctor (Try).

CAB 134/186   Meetings and Memoranda   12 Sept–21 Dec 1945
              ED(45)1st–3rd, ED(45)1–6 and an *ad hoc* meeting.

Meetings

12 Sept	***ad hoc*:1**	**Planning of economic development.** Consideration of the use of existing administrative machinery rather than the creation of a large central economic staff.
	:2	**General points.**
	:3	**Main Steering Committee.** Consideration of membership.
	:4	**Working parties.** Five working parties agreed: Economic Development, Statistics, Public and Private Investment, Balance of Payments and Manpower.
	:5	**Ministerial responsibility.**
14 Nov	**ED(45)1st:1**	**Economic plan for 1946.** Form of draft plan and working parties agreed.
	:2	**Publicity for the work of planning.** Agreement that there should be some public statement.
	:3	**Progress report to ministers.** ED(45)2.
	:4	**Economic planning.** Comments on an Economic Section memorandum, probably ED(45)1.
18 Dec	**2nd:1**	**Draft plan for 1946.** ED(45)3, 5, 6. Amendments made.
	:2	**Statistics for employment policy.** ED(45)4. Paper approved.
	:3	**Publicity for economic planning.** Morrison, H. sought to delay any statement.
21 Dec	**3rd**	**Economic plan for 1946.** Agreement to submit to Morrison, H.

Memoranda

7 Nov	**ED(45)1**	**Economic Planning – M.T. Flett covering the Economic Section,** 1+10p. Sets out the section's general views on planning. It should be concerned with the overall position, not individual industries, and based on broad categories of demand upon the community's reserves. Production could not be rigidly fixed

if there was to be any consumer choice. Target national income and total national expenditure should be estimated, albeit based on an examination of real resources, such as manpower. The degree of uncertainty in each forecast should be made explicit and the plan kept flexible, so long as the appropriate level of demand was maintained.

8 Nov	2	**Draft progress report – M.T. Flett,** 3p. Includes summary of E.E. Bridges's note 'Planning of Economic Development Co-ordinating Machinery', giving the membership of the ministerial committee, the composition of the official steering committee and of the working parties.
4 Dec	3	**Manpower during the calendar year 1946 – M.T. Flett covering the Ministry of Labour,** 1+5+5p appendixes. Also MP(O)(45)1(revise). Estimates the size and nature of the manpower gap expected at the end of 1946.
13 Dec	4	**Report of the Working Party on Statistics for employment policy,** 18+7p annexes. See LP(46)96.
12 Dec	5	**Economic Survey for 1946 – M.T. Flett covering the Economic Survey Working Party,** 1+15+22p appendixes. First draft based on three tables of manpower requirements and supply, the current balance of payments and receipts and national income and expenditure. All showed deficits and measures were suggested to reduce the size of the inflationary gap, estimated at £470m.
17 Dec	6	**Economic Survey for 1946. Illustrative diagrams – M.T. Flett covering the C.S.O.,** 1+4p.

CAB 134/187   Meetings   15 Mar–19 Dec 1946   ED(46)1st–16th.

15 Mar	**ED(46)1st:1**	**Statistics for employment policy.** ED(45)4 and ED(46)2.
	:2	**Publicity for planning estimates.** ED(46)4. Form of the White Paper agreed.
	:3	**First report of the Investment Working Party.** ED(46)3. Consideration of question of investment cuts.
9 Apr	**2nd:1**	**Railway extensions in the London area.** ED(46)8.
	:2	**Draft White Paper on the Economic Survey for 1946–47.** ED(46)9. Timing of publication discussed.
25 June	**3rd:1**	**Economic Survey for 1946–1947.** ED(46)13. Discussed distribution of manpower.

	:2	**Publicity for the economic work of planning.** Agreement to prepare an Economic Survey for the financial year 1947–48.
4 July	4th:1	**Measures to safeguard the national economy.**
	:2	**Economic Survey for 1946–47.** ED(46)16 and 17. Growing concern about the winter's electricity supply.
	:3	**Central approach to industry on statistics for economic planning.** ED(46)12.
11 July	5th:1	**Economic Survey for 1946–1947.** ED(46)18. Final approval.
	:2	**Productivity.**
1 Oct	6th:1	**Departmental responsibility for censuses of Production and Distribution.** ED(46)25.
	:2	**Economic Survey: regrouping of industries.** ED(46)28.
	:3	**Statistics for employment policy: timing of the central approach to industry.**
	:4	**Information for the National Joint Advisory Council.** ED(46)26.
	:5	**Controls over essential materials.** ED(46)27.
8 Oct	7th:1	**Information for the National Joint Advisory Council.** ED(46)29.
	:2	**Means of implementing planning decisions.** ED(46)22. E.E. Bridges and J.E. Meade gave their views on economic planning. Discussion of the control of labour.
	:3	**Controls over essential materials.**
15 Oct	8th:1	**White Paper on Economic Planning.** ED(46)24. Consideration of ED(46)24 as a useful basis for a report to ministers.
	:2	**Prosperity campaign publicity.** ED(46)30.
8 Nov	9th:1	**Planning White Paper.** ED(46)32(revise). To be submitted after amendment to ministers.
	:2	**Wages and price policy.** ED(46)34.
18 Nov	10th:1	**Wages and price policy.** ED(46)34.
	:2	**Cost of living index number.** ED(46)37.
25 Nov	11th:1	**Revision of the cost of living index.** ED(46)40.
	:2	**Draft White Paper for the National Joint Advisory Council.** ED(46)41.
	:3	**Wages and price policy.**
27 Nov	12th	**Draft White Paper for the National Joint Advisory Council.** ED(46)41.
2 Dec	13th:1	**Revision of the cost of living index.** ED(46)44.
	:2	**Distribution of the labour force.** ED(46)42.
	:3	**Wages and price policy.**
	:4	**Price controls.**
9 Dec	14th:1	**Wages and price policy.** ED(46)47.
	:2	**Economic Survey for 1947.** ED(46)46.
12 Dec	15th:1	**Economic Survey for 1947.** ED(46)46.
	:2	**Wages and price policy.**

19 Dec	**16th:1**	**Wages and price policy, and implementation of planning decisions.**
	:2	**Economic Survey for 1947.** ED(46)50.
	:3	**Scheme for the direction of the work of the Census Office.** ED(46)49.

CAB 134/188 Memoranda 10 Jan–12 Oct 1946 ED(46)1–30.

10 Jan	**ED(46)1**	**Economic Survey for 1946 – E.E. Bridges covering the Economic Survey Working Party,** 3+12+20p. See CP(46)32. Also LP(I)(46)1.
6 Mar	**2**	**Statistics for employment policy – M.T. Flett,** 1+3p. How to approach industry.
13 Mar	**3**	**First report of the Investment Working Party – M.T. Flett covering the Investment Working Party,** 1+4+6+2p. Also IWP(46)1 and INV/WP(46)4(revise). Examination of the broad categories of investment and the way to approach the 10% reduction thought necessary in the 1946 Economic Survey.
13 Mar	**4**	**Publicity for planning estimates – P.D. Proctor and M.T. Flett,** 3p. Consideration of a national income and expenditure budget forecast.
28 Mar	**5**	**First report of the Investment Working Party – E.E. Bridges covering the Investment Working Party,** 1+4p. Final version. Revision of ED(46)3. See LP(46)96.
28 Mar	**6**	**Statistics for employment policy – E.E. Bridges,** 3p. Final version. See LP(46)96.
21 Mar	**7**	**References to economic planning in the House of Commons debate on manpower 27th–28th February – M.T. Flett,** 1+5p.
1 Apr	**8**	**East and West extensions of the central London railway and the electrification of the Liverpool Street–Shenfield line of the London and North Eastern Railway – Barnes,** 2p.
3 Apr	**9**	**Draft White Paper of the Economic Survey for 1946–47 – P.D. Proctor and M.T. Flett covering the Economic Survey Working Party,** 1+14+10p appendixes. Skeleton draft.
8 Apr	**10**	**Economic Survey for 1946–47. Interim report by the Economic Survey Working Party – M.T. Flett covering the Working Party,** 1+17+21p appendixes. Shows how the decisions so far taken had affected the demand on national resources.
27 Apr	**11**	**Draft White Paper on Economic Survey for 1946–47, M.T. Flett covering the Steering Committee,** 1+3+6+4p appendix. See MEP(46)3.
25 May	**12**	**Central approach to industry on statistics for full employment and economic planning – P.D.**

		Proctor and M.T. Flett covering the Working Party on Statistics for Employment Policy, 1+1+4p. Also ES(W)(46)2(revise). Proposed method of approach.
3 June	13	**Economic Survey for 1946/7 – M.T. Flett covering the Economic Survey Working Party,** 1+1+28+13p appendixes. Also ESWP(46)6. Report of the Working Party.
13 June	14	**Prosperity Campaign material for leaflet – P.D. Proctor and M.T. Flett,** 1+4p. Document as approved.
20 June	15	**Economic Survey for 1946/47: corrigenda – M.T. Flett,** 2p.
2 July	16	**Economic Survey for 1946–47. Final revise – P.D. Proctor and M.T. Flett covering the Economic Survey Working Party,** 1+15+13p appendixes.
2 July	17	**Economic Survey for 1946–47 – P.D. Proctor and M.T. Flett,** 1+4p. Draft covering note.
10 July	18	**Economic Survey for 1946–1947. Revised submission to ministers – P.D. Proctor and M.T. Flett,** 1+5p.
11 July	19	**Economic Survey for 1946/47 – E.E. Bridges,** 4p. See MEP(46)7. Final version of submission to ministers.
11 July	20	**Economic Survey for 1946/47 – report by the Economic Survey Working Party,** 15+13p appendixes. See MEP(46)5.
26 July	21	**Wages policy – M.T. Flett covering the Official Working Party on Trends of Wages, Costs and Prices,** 1+8+2p. See LP(46)192.
12 Aug	22	**Means of implementing planning decisions – E.E. Bridges,** 2p. Steering Committee had been asked to examine and report to the Lord President's Committee on the weapons available for planning. Bridges felt the review should cover (a) controls applicable to labour and materials, (b) fiscal policy and differential taxation and (c) wages policy and the control of prices and profits.
20 Aug	23	**Future work of the Committee – M.T. Flett,** 4p. Sets out progress on ten aspects of the Steering Committee's work.
4 Sept	24	**The period to be covered by the annual White Paper on Economic Planning – P.D. Proctor and M.T. Flett covering a working party,** 1+5p. Issue of whether it should be concerned with the financial year or the calendar year.
25 Sept	25	**Departmental responsibility for the collection of statistics required for the censuses of Production and Distribution – P.D. Proctor and M.T. Flett covering the Working Party on Statistics for**

		Employment Policy, 1+8+9p appendixes. Also ES(W)(46)3(revise).
27 Sept	**26**	**Draft economic review for the National Joint Advisory Council – P.D. Proctor and M.T. Flett covering the Office of the Lord President,** 17p.
25 Sept	**27**	**Controls over essential raw materials – P.D. Proctor and M.T. Flett,** 1p.
27 Sept	**28**	**Regrouping of industries – C.S.O.,** 2p. Industries reclassified to reflect the grouping used in national income and expenditure analysis.
7 Oct	**29**	**Revised draft economic review for the National Joint Advisory Council – unsigned,** 14p. Covers the supply and distribution of manpower, the disposition of the national income and the balance between supply and demand.
12 Oct	**30**	**Prosperity Campaign publicity – P.D. Proctor and J.A.R. Pimlott covering Prosperity Campaign (Official) Committee,** 1+3+2p annex. Asking for guidance from the Steering Committee on its future approach.

CAB 134/189   Memoranda   23 Oct–21 Dec 1946   ED(46)31–52.

23 Oct	**ED(46)31**	**Economic Planning – P.D. Proctor and J.A.R. Pimlott covering Morrison, H.,** 1+11p. Address to the Institute of Public Administration. See *Public Administration*, vol. XXV (1947).
5 Nov	**32**	**Planning White Paper – P.D. Proctor and J.A.R. Pimlott covering E.E. Bridges,** 4p. Revise version. Agreement on period to be covered.
1 Nov	**33**	**Basis for further publicity on increased production – P.D. Proctor and J.A.R. Pimlott covering a Working Party,** 1+7p.
6 Nov	**34**	**Wages and price policy – E.E. Bridges,** 3p. Possible agenda for a general discussion, starting with the objectives of wages policy.
7 Nov	**35**	**Basis for further publicity on increased production – P.D. Proctor and J.A.R. Pimlott,** 1p.
13 Nov	**36**	**Planning White Paper – P.D. Proctor and J.A.R. Pimlott covering E.E. Bridges,** 1+4p. See MEP(46)12.
13 Nov	**37**	**Cost of living index – P.D. Proctor and J.A.R. Pimlott covering the Economic Section,** 1+6+12p appendixes. Consideration of impact of abandoning stabilization.
15 Nov	**38**	**Basis for further publicity on increased production – P.D. Proctor and J.A.R. Pimlott,** 1+7p. Revision of ED(46)33.

15 Nov	39	**Cost of living index number – Ministry of Labour,** 2p. Index needed revision if it were to be widely accepted.
22 Nov	40	**Revision of the cost of living index – P.D. Proctor and J.A.R. Pimlott,** 1+3p.
22 Nov	41	**Draft White Paper for the National Joint Advisory Council – P.D. Proctor and J.A.R. Pimlott,** 1+6p.
22 Nov	42	**Distribution of the labour force – P.D. Proctor and J.A.R. Pimlott covering the Office of the Lord President,** 1+7+1p annex. Problems of implementing this policy once manpower controls had been abolished.
27 Nov	43	**Draft White Paper for the National Joint Advisory Council – P.D. Proctor and J.A.R. Pimlott,** 1+7p. Revision of ED(46)41.
28 Nov	44	**Revision of the cost of living index – P.D. Proctor and J.A.R. Pimlott,** 1+5+1p appendix. Revision of ED(46)40. Draft of LP(46)285.
11 Dec	45	**Draft White Paper for the National Joint Advisory Council – J.D. Proctor and J.A.R. Pimlott,** 1+7p. Revise version. Draft of MEP(46)14.
6 Dec	46	**Economic Survey for 1947 – P.D. Proctor and J.A.R. Pimlott covering the Economic Survey Working Party,** 1+33+16p appendixes. Four sections deal with an examination of total resources and demand, the various ways of reducing the perceived inflationary gap, specific difficulties and a summary of all the problems raised in the survey.
6 Dec	47	**Wages policy – P.D. Proctor and J.A.R. Pimlott covering the Board of Trade Committee on Improvements in Undermanned Industries,** 1+19+17+6+2+7+4p. Reports on the causes of undermanning and the impact of wages policy on it in the coal, cotton, iron foundries, agriculture and brick industries.
11 Dec	48	**National building programme for the next five years – P.D. Proctor and J.A.R. Pimlott covering the Headquarters Building Committee,** 1+3+2p appendix.
16 Dec	49	**Scheme for the direction of the work of the Census Office – P.D. Proctor and J.A.R. Pimlott covering P.D. Proctor,** 1+4p.
18 Dec	50	**Economic Survey for 1947 – P.D. Proctor and J.A.R. Pimlott covering the Economic Survey Working Party,** 1+20+8p appendixes. Draft survey.
21 Dec	51	**Economic Survey for 1947 – report of the Economic Survey Working Party,** 20+8p appendixes. See MEP(46)15.

21 Dec   **52**   **Wages and price policy and means of carrying out planning decisions – report by the Steering Committee**, 11p. See MEP(46)17.

CAB 134/190   Meetings and Memoranda   15 Jan–17 Dec 1947   ED(47)1st–10th and ED(47)1–53.

Meetings

17 Jan	**ED(47)1st:1**	**Price adjustments following wage increases.** ED(47)1 and 4. Agreement with approach suggested by E.E. Bridges.
	:2	**Productivity.** ED(47)2.
	:3	**Economic White Paper.** ED(47)3.
24 Jan	**2nd:1**	**Employment of women.** ED(47)10.
	:2	**Draft Economic White Paper.** ED(47)6.
	:3	**Report on production in 1946.** ED(47)9.
	:4	**Productivity.** A revised version of ED(47)2 was agreed.
	:5	**Wages and price policy.** ED(47)8.
29 Jan	**3rd:1**	**Economic White Paper.** ED(47)14.
	:2	**The Social Survey.** ED(47)7.
	:3	**Changes in productivity in British industries.** ED(47)13.
2 Feb	**4th:1**	**Draft Economic White Paper.** ED(47)15.
	:2	**Restriction of the entry of labour into non-productive employments.** Consideration of possible measures to divert labour in the absence of powers of direction.
	:3	**Overseas Economic Survey.** The Official Committee on Overseas Economic Information to edit OEP(47)6 for publication.
26 Feb	**5th:1**	**Limitation of weekday sporting events.** ED(47)16.
	:2	**Survey of Overseas Economic Information.** ED(47)17. Agreement not to publish.
	:3	**Debate on the economic situation and future business of the committee.** ED(47)11, 12, 18. Confidential annex attached. Discussion of the basis of allocations, wages policy and planning machinery.
3 Mar	**6th:1**	**Building programme for the financial year 1947–48.** ED(47)19.
	:2	**Debate on the economic situation.** ED(47)20. Consideration of (a) co-operation with industry, (b) fuel and power allocations, (c) allocation of manpower, (d) wages and conditions of service, and (e) planning machinery.
30 Apr	**7th:1**	**Future procedure for exchange of insurance books.** ED(47)28.
	:2	**Index of production.** ED(47)24.

	:3	**Study of productivity in British industry.** ED(47)27.
	:4	**Planning statistics.** ED(47)26.
	:5	**Current and future work of the committee.** ED(47)30. Discussion on the limitations of any survey for 1948 produced in the early autumn. The future of the committee in relation to the work of Sir Edwin Plowden and the Economic Planning Board had to be decided.
30 July	8th:1	**Future of price control: factual statement.** ED(47)34.
	:2	**Applications for increased prices on account of fuel shortage.** ED(47)38.
	:3	**Price adjustments following wage increases.** ED(47)40.
	:4	**Economic Survey 1948/51.** ED(47)39. Agreement to circulate to the Economic Planning Board.
	:5	**Changes in output per head in 1946.** ED(47)35.
	:6	**Balance of payments equilibrium at end of 1951.** ED(47)42.
13 Oct	9th	**Report of the Investment Programmes Committee.** IPC(47)9. Consideration of each departmental programme and future supervision of the overall investment programme.
17 Dec	10th	**Economic Survey for 1948.** ED(47)53. Consideration of the draft and the procedure to be followed.

Memoranda

16 Jan	ED(47)1	**Report to Official Steering Committee on price adjustments following wage increases – Subcommittee on Prices,** 6+4p appendix. Consideration of the principles and application of the Board of Trade 80% price sanction.
15 Jan	2	**Changes in productivity in British industry – Board of Trade,** 5+2p appendix. The first attempt at measuring productivity in Britain.
15 Jan	3	**Covering note – E.E. Bridges,** 1+12p. Draft Economic White Paper. Experimental paper in four parts covering the aim of economic planning in a democratic society and the limitations attendant, the methods adopted in preparing the paper, an account of economic development from mid-1945 to the end of 1946 and the prospects for 1947.
16 Jan	4	**Price adjustments following wage increases – J.A.R. Pimlott covering the Agricultural Departments,** 1+5p.

16 Jan	5	**Draft Economic White Paper – Economic Section,** 1+2p. Suggestions for the section dealing with 1947.
21 Jan	6	**Draft Economic White Paper – E.E. Bridges,** 1+7+14p addendum. Revision of parts of ED(47)3.
21 Jan	7	**The Social Survey – E.M. Nicholson covering the C.S.O.,** 2+4p. How the Social Survey could help to improve estimates of consumer expenditure and give up-to-date information on changes of demand.
22 Jan	8	**Wages and prices policy – E.E. Bridges,** 1+6p. See MEP(47)4. Redrafted to deal with long-term objectives of wages policy.
22 Jan	9	**Britain's production in 1946 – E.M. Nicholson,** 2+22p. Draft outline for publication of the main achievements of the production drive.
22 Jan	10	**Economic Survey for 1947. Employment of women – Ministry of Labour,** 5p.
23 Jan	11	**The Monnet Plan. Anglo-French discussions in Paris: January 1947 – J.A.R. Pimlott covering J.E. Meade,** 1+8+8p annexes. Impressions of their discussions. Analysis by J.E. Meade of French planning.
23 Jan	12	**The Monnet Plan – J.A.R. Pimlott,** 1+14p. Amended version of published article. See *The Economist,* 14 Dec 1946.
23 Jan	13	**Changes in productivity in British industry – E.E. Bridges,** 1+5+3p. Redraft of ED(47)2.
28 Jan	14	**Draft Economic White Paper – E.E. Bridges,** 1+15p. Draft of concluding section.
31 Jan	15	**Draft Economic White Paper. Draft covering note – E.E. Bridges,** 1+4p.
17 Feb	16	**Regulation of mid-week sport – Home Office,** 4+3p appendix.
21 Feb	17	**Survey of overseas economic situation – E. Rowe-Dutton covering the Economic Section,** 1+6+25p appendix +4p annex. Also OEP(47)6.
25 Feb	18	**Items 4 and 6 of the agenda for ED(47)5th meeting. Item 4: debate on the economic situation: preparation of material. Item 6: future business of the committee – J.E. Meade,** 5p. Suggestions in relation to (a) the progressing of the programme as laid down in the White Paper, (b) allocation of fuel and power, (c) the balance of payments, (d) incentives and inducements, in particular prices, profit margins, taxes and wage rates, (e) the development of contacts with both sides of industry and (f) work on a more long-term survey and consideration of action to deal with effects of a world economic slump.

28 Feb	**19**	**Building and civil engineering labour demands and ceilings for the financial year 1947–48 – P.D. Proctor and J.A.R. Pimlott covering the Investment Working Party,** 5p. Also INV WP(47)4.
28 Feb	**20**	**Debate on the economic situation – E.E. Bridges,** 1+6p. Consideration of the effect of the fuel crisis and short-term policy.
4 Mar	**21**	**Limitation of mid-week sporting events – P.D. Proctor and J.A.R. Pimlott,** 1+2+4p annexes. See FC(47)32.
4 Mar	**22**	**Debate on the economic situation – Steering Committee,** 7p. Redraft of ED(47)20.
6 Mar	**23**	**National building programme for financial year 1947–48 – Steering Committee,** 4+1p appendix.
31 Mar	**24**	**Index of production – E.E. Bridges,** 2p.
8 Apr	**25**	**Index of production – P.D. Proctor and J.A.R. Pimlott,** 1p.
28 Apr	**26**	**Planning statistics – E.E. Bridges,** 2+17p annexes. The statistics required to monitor the progress of economic planning.
24 Apr	**27**	**Study of productivity in British industry – C.S.O. and Board of Trade,** 3p. Proposed lines of enquiry.
25 Apr	**28**	**The exchange of insurance books – C.S.O.,** 1+3p. Also ES(W)(47)4.
7 May	**29**	**Standard industrial classification – E.E. Bridges,** 1+2+4p appendix. Also CS(IC)(47)6. Proposals for a classification for use by all government departments.
27 Apr	**30**	**Current and future work of the committee – E.E. Bridges,** 2p.
8 May	**31**	**Membership of the committee – P.D. Proctor and J.A.R. Pimlott,** 1p.
3 June	**32**	**Progress of reconversion. Report for April and May – Board of Trade,** 1+7p.
7 June	**33**	**Economic Survey for 1947. Progress record, June 1947 – C.S.O.,** 2p.
12 June	**34**	**Future of price control: factual statement – A. Kilroy,** 2+2+37p appendixes. Paper from the Subcommittee on Prices. It proposed a step-by-step approach with regular reference back to the Steering Committee, since the subject was so large.
21 June	**35**	**Changes in output per head in 1946 – P.D. Proctor and J.A.R. Pimlott covering the Board of Trade,** 1+2+3p appendix. Update of ED(47)27.
30 June	**36**	**Economic Survey for 1947. Progress Record No. 2 – C.S.O.,** 2p.
3 July	**37**	**Economic Survey for 1947. Progress Record No. 2 – C.E.P.S.,** 3p. Comments on ED(47)36.

18 July	**38**	**Report on applications for increased prices on account of fuel shortage** – A. Kilroy, 1+3p. Also ED(SP)(47)16.
21 July	**39**	**Economic Survey for 1948–51** – C.E.P.S., 1p. Sets out the proposed procedure.
26 July	**40**	**Price adjustments following wage increases** – J.H. Woods, 3p.
27 July	**41**	**Future of price control: factual statement** – J.A.R. Pimlott, 1+5p. Letter from H. Emmerson to E.E. Bridges, 19 Nov 1946.
28 July	**42**	**Balance of payments equilibrium by end-1951** – London Committee (European Economic Co-operation), 2+1p appendix.
31 July	**43**	**Statement on production for June and July** – Board of Trade, 1+8+1p appendix. Also NPACI(47)74.
7 Aug	**44**	**Balance of payments equilibrium by end-1951** – P.D. Proctor and J.A.R. Pimlott, 1+4p.
8 Aug	**45**	**Economic Survey for 1947. Progress Record No. 3** – C.S.O., 4p.
5 Sept	**46**	**Economic Survey for 1947. Progress Record No. 4** – C.S.O., 4p.
26 Sept	**47**	**Statement on production for Aug and Sept** – Board of Trade, 1+8+9p appendixes. Also NPACI(47)81.
9 Oct	**48**	**Investment programmes** – P.D. Proctor covering the Investment Programmes Committee, 1+2+14+32p. See CP(47)284. Also IPC(47)9.
11 Oct	**49**	**Change in secretariat**, 1p.
12 Oct	**50**	**Report of the Investment Programmes Committee** – P.D. Proctor covering the Ministry of Health, 1+3p.
	51	Not issued.
26 Nov	**52**	**Change in title of committee** – P.D. Proctor and J.G. Stewart, 1p. 'Steering' was to be dropped.
12 Dec	**53**	**Economic Survey for 1948** – P.D. Proctor and J.G. Stewart, 1+51+3p appendix.

CAB 134/191 Meetings and Memoranda   26 Jan–23 Nov 1948   ED(48)1st–6th and ED(48)1–11.

Meetings

29 Jan	**ED(48)1st**	**1948 dollar position.** ED(48)1.
5 Feb	**2nd**	**Economic Survey for 1948.** ED(48)2. Consideration chapter by chapter.
15 June	**3rd**	**Changes in productivity in British industries.** ED(48)3. Agreement that the work should go to ministers and could be published.
12 July	**4th:1**	**Balance of payments forecasts for the long-term economic survey.** ED(48)4.
	:2	**Long-term balance of payments plan.** ED(48)5.

457

20 July	**5th**	**Capital investment in 1949: report by the Investment Programmes Committee.** ED(48)6. General discussion on the main principles and then more detailed consideration.
10 Sept	**6th:1**	**The long-term programme.** ED(48)8.
	:2	**1949–50 programme.** ED(48)9. Discussion of principles.

Memoranda

26 Jan	**ED(48)1**	**1948 dollar position – E.E. Bridges covering a working party,** 1+11+9p annexes. See EPB(48)3.
2 Feb	**2**	**Economic Survey for 1948 – P.D. Proctor and J.G. Stewart,** 1+46p. See EPB(48)5.
4 June	**3**	**Changes in productivity in British industries – Board of Trade,** 5+2p appendix. Update of ED(47)2.
8 July	**4**	**1948/52 balance of payments forecasts programmes – E.N. Plowden,** 3+26p appendix. Draft of EPB(48)21.
9 July	**5**	**Long-term balance of payments plan – E.E. Bridges covering C.E.P.S.,** 1+2p.
16 July	**6**	**Report on capital investment in 1949 – J.G. Stewart covering the Investment Programmes Committee,** 1+87+9p. See PC(48)93. Also IPC(48)8 and EPB(48)23.
28 July	**7**	**Change in membership – J.G. Stewart,** 1p.
7 Sept	**8**	**The long-term plan – J.G. Stewart,** 1+4p annex +42+4p addendum. See EPC(48)79. Also ER(L)(48)91 and EPB(48)26.
8 Sept	**9**	**1949/50 programme – Programmes Committee,** 15+2p appendix. Also P(48)46 (revise).
12 Oct	**10**	**Economic Survey for 1949 – E.E. Bridges covering C.E.P.S.,** 1+2p.
23 Nov	**11**	**Review of European long-term programmes – E.E. Bridges,** 1p.

CAB 134/192 Meetings and Memoranda 7 Jan–28 Dec 1949 ED(49)1st–9th and ED(49)1–25.

Meetings

13 Jan	**ED(49)1st**	**Economic Survey for 1949: first draft.** ED(49)1 and 2. Differences from the 1948 Survey explained. Consideration by paragraphs.
9 Feb	**2nd**	**European long-term programme.** ED(49)3 and 4.
21 Feb	**3rd**	**Economic Survey for 1949.** ED(49)5.
12 May	**4th**	**U.K. revised 1949/50 import programme.** ED(49)8.
23 May	**5th**	**Report on capital investment 1950–52.** ED(49)10. Consideration of the total programme and individual programmes.

11 Oct	6th	**The Council of Europe and the O.E.E.C.** ED(49)14 and 14 addendum.
17 Oct	7th	**The dollar programme for the period July 1949 to Dec 1950.** ED(49)15, 16, 17.
25 Nov	8th	**Closer economic association between Scandinavia and the sterling area.** ED(49)20. General agreement to favour any such proposals.
5 Dec	9th:1	**Balance of payments in 1950.** ED(49)22.
	:2	**Submission to the O.E.E.C. on the U.K. position in 1950/51.** ED(49)23 and 24. General agreement that presentation of a programme involving such substantial increases in U.K. reserves presented serious difficulties. Nevertheless, the building up of the reserves was an essential part of the programme.

Memoranda

7 Jan	**ED(49)1**	**Economic Survey for 1949: first draft – G.M. Wilson covering the Economic Survey Working Party,** 1+65p. See EPB(48)35.
10 Jan	2	**Economic Survey for 1949: first draft – G.M. Wilson,** 2p. Extract from EPB(49)1st.
4 Feb	3	**The U.K. long-term programme and European viability – G.M. Wilson covering the European Economic Co-operation Committee,** 1+28+8p appendixes. See CP(49)27. Also EPB(49)6.
8 Feb	4	**The U.K. long-term programme and European viability – G.M. Wilson,** 1+6p. Extract from a meeting of the European Economic Co-operation Committee, 7 Feb 1949.
16 Feb	5	**Economic Survey for 1949 – E.E. Bridges,** 1+38+15p appendix. Also EPB(49)9. First proof.
24 Feb	5	**Economic Survey for 1949 – E.E. Bridges,** 1+48+16p appendix. See CP(49)29. Revised proof.
1 Apr	6	**Revision of the draft Economic Survey for 1948–52 – E.E. Bridges covering C.E.P.S.,** 1+1p. Administrative arrangements.
28 Apr	7	**Additional functions of the Committee – E.E. Bridges,** 2p. Also ED(OS)(49)1.
6 May	8	**U.K. revised 1949/50 programme – R.W.B. Clarke covering the Programmes Committee,** 1+13+4p annex +12p addenda. Also ER(L)(49)146. Draft of EPC(49)52.
10 May	9	**Economic Development Working Group – E.E. Bridges,** 2p. Also ED(W)(49)1.
13 May	10	**Report on capital investment 1950–52 – G.M. Wilson covering the Investment Programmes**

		Committee, 1+88+10p appendix. See PC(49)59. Also IPC(49)3 and EPB(49)13.
19 May	11	**Educational building programme 1950–1952 – Ministry of Education**, 2p. Criticism of the reductions proposed in ED(49)10.
25 July	12	**Revision of the draft Economic Survey for 1948/52 – E.E. Bridges**, 1p. Proposes suspension of the revision.
6 Oct	13	**Economic Survey for 1950 – E.E. Bridges covering C.E.P.S.**, 1+1p. Administrative arrangements.
6 Oct	14	**The Council of Europe and the Organization for European Economic Co-operation – G.M. Wilson covering the European Economic Co-operation Committee**, 1+10+2p addendum.
14 Oct	15	**Financial and economic relations with Canada – G.M. Wilson and D.J.B. Robey**, 1+10+9p annexes. Draft of EPC(49)118.
14 Oct	16	**The 1950 dollar programme – G.M. Wilson and D.J.B. Robey covering the Programmes Committee**, 1+11+30p appendixes. See EPB(49)19.
15 Oct	17	**1949/50 dollar imports and the Commonwealth Finance Ministers' Meeting – Working Group of the Commonwealth Economic Affairs Committee**, 3p. Implications and difficulties resulting from acceptance of ED(49)16.
14 Oct	18	**The Council of Europe and the O.E.E.C. – G.M. Wilson and D.J.B. Robey covering the European Economic Co-operation Committee**, 1+10+4p annex. Also ER(L)(49)275.
19 Oct	19	**The dollar programme for July 1949 to Dec 1950 – E.E. Bridges covering the Programmes Committee**, 2+8+22p appendixes.
24 Nov	20	**Closer economic association between Scandinavia and the sterling area – E.A. Hitchman**, 1+23p annexes. Annexes include a draft of EPC(49)151 and EPB(49)23.
24 Nov	21	**The future of intra-European payments – G.M. Wilson and D.J.B. Robey covering the Subcommittee on Intra-European Trade and Payments**, 1+9+10p appendixes.
29 Nov	22	**Balance of payments in 1950 – G.M. Wilson and D.J.B. Robey covering the Programmes Committee**, 1+7+38p appendix. Draft of EPC(49)157.
30 Nov	23	**Submission to the O.E.E.C. on the U.K. position in 1950/51 – G.M. Wilson and D.J.B. Robey covering the Programmes Committee**, 1+50+9p appendixes. Draft of EPC(49)158.
3 Dec	24	**Submission to the O.E.E.C. on the U.K. position in 1950/51 – E.A. Hitchman**, 2p.

| 22 Dec | 25 | **Economic Survey for 1950 – G.M. Wilson and D.J.B. Robey covering the Economic Survey Working Party,** 1+57+7p addendum. See EPB(49)24. |

CAB 134/193   Meetings and Memoranda   4 Jan–7 July 1950   ED(50)1st–4th and ED(50)1–5.

Meetings

6 Jan	**ED(50)1st**	**Economic Survey for 1950.** ED(49)25. Agreement that the publicized version should be shorter and should emphasize action needed in 1950.
23 Feb	**2nd**	**Draft Economic Survey for 1950.** ED(50)2.
27 Apr	**3rd**	**Capital investment in 1951 and 1952.** ED(50)4. Agreement to recommend the higher programme although it had serious implications for budgetary policy and also restricted some desirable investment.
7 July	**4th**	**Balance of payments for 1950/51.** ED(50)5.

Memoranda

4 Jan	**ED(50)1**	**Change in secretariat – G.M. Wilson and D.J.B. Robey,** 1p.
20 Feb	2	**Economic Survey for 1950: draft for publication – P.J. Moorhouse,** 1+36+16p appendix.
1 Apr	3	**Change in secretariat – M.M. du Merton and P.J. Moorhouse,** 1p.
25 Apr	4	**Capital investment in 1951 and 1952 – F.F. Turnbull covering the Investment Programmes Committee,** 1+69+2p appendix. See EPC(50)47. Also IPC(50)2.
30 June	5	**Balance of payments for 1950–51 – M.M. du Merton and R.B. Marshall covering the Programmes Committee,** 1+6+78p annexes. Also P(50)25 and EPB(50)15. Draft of EPC(50)73.

15.11   Official Committee on Economic Development

Working Group

The size of the Official Committee prevented it from meeting regularly and so, in May 1949, the Working Group was set up to enable leading officials to keep a continuous watch over official committees working within the Official Committee's terms of reference, to handle any urgent problems raised by their chairman and to advise the Chancellor of the Exchequer directly, see CAB 134/192, ED(49)9. Its chairmanship was normally devolved from the Permanent Secretary of the Treasury to another Treasury official. Despite its terms of reference, it concentrated largely on overseas issues. It was dissolved, during the major administrative reorganization of October 1950, at the first meeting of the Economic Steering Committee, see CAB 134/263, ES(50)1st:1.

Terms To deal with problems within the terms of reference of the Official Committee on Economic Development, as required.

Members Perm. Sec., Try (ch.); all Second Secs., Try; E.N. Plowden (C.E.P.S.); Perm. Secs. or Deputy Secs. of B.T., F.O., Ec. Sect.

Secs. G.M. Wilson (Cab. O.) and C.H.W. Hodges (Try). (Dec 1949) E.J. Beaven (Cab. O.) replaced Wilson. (June 1950) D.J. Atherton (C.E.P.S.) replaced Hodges. (Sept 1950) R.S. Buer (Cab. O.) replaced Beaven. (Oct 1950) D.O. Henley (C.E.P.S.) replaced Atherton.

CAB 134/202   Meetings and Memoranda   10 May–31 Dec 1949   ED(W)(49)1st–13th and ED(W)(49)1–19.

Meetings

17 May	**ED(W)(49)1st**	**Possible import licensing relaxations and the intra-European payments scheme.** ED(W)(49)3.
23 May	**2nd**	**Import licensing relaxation.** ED(W)(49)4 and 5.
1 June	**3rd**	**Economic policy in a recession.** ED(W)(49)6.
15 June	**4th**	**Programme of work.** ED(W)(49)2.
12 July	**5th**	**Import prices and the dollar shortage.** ED(W)(49)7. Agreement on the need for more information.
18 July	**6th**	**European import relaxations and non-discrimination.** ED(W)(49)8.
18 Oct	**7th**	**Relaxation of import restrictions: action by other O.E.E.C. countries.** ED(W)(49)9.
1 Nov	**8th**	**Matters arising out of the Washington communiqué.** ER(L)(49)274.
10 Nov	**9th:2**	**Report on sterling balances.** ED(W)(49)11.
	:3	**Matters arising from the last meeting.**
	:4	**European integration.** ED(W)(49)10.
	:5	**Customs Union Study Group.**
15 Nov	**10th**	**Imports of machinery from dollar sources.** ED(W)(49)12.
29 Nov	**11th:1**	**Report on dual price policy.** ED(W)(49)14.
	:2	**Sterling balances.**
	:3	**Brief on integration for Sir Leslie Rowan.**
6 Dec	**12th:1**	**Substitution of sterling for dollar oil.**
	:2	**U.S. customs procedure.** E(49)75.
13 Dec	**13th:1**	**Incentives for dollar exports.** ED(W)(49)15. Agreement that positive inducements could alone boost exports in the short term. Arrangements made to review possible measures.
	:2	**Washington tripartite discussion in relation to the Anglo-Canadian Continuing Committee.** ED(W)(49)16.

Memoranda

10 May	**ED(W)(49)1**	**Economic Development Working Group – E.E. Bridges,** 2p. See ED(49)9.

17 May	2	**Methods of work and timing of meetings – E.M. Plowden**, 1p. The Working Group should keep a continuous watch over all economic policy but not attempt particular studies.
16 May	3	**Report of the Working Party on Import Licensing Relaxations – G.M. Wilson and C.H.W. Hodges covering the Working Party,** 1+4+1+24+35p appendix. Also ILC/ILR/36(final).
19 May	4	**Report on import licensing relaxations – G.M. Wilson and C.H.W. Hodges covering the Treasury,** 1+5+2p annexes. Implications for the balance of payments.
20 May	5	**Draft report for the E.P.C. on import policy – G.M. Wilson and C.H.W. Hodges covering the Board of Trade,** 1+5+3p annex. Draft of EPC(49)55.
27 May	6	**Economic policy in a recession – G.M. Wilson and C.H.W. Hodges covering the Economic Section,** 1+11p. See EPB(49)14. Draft of EPC(49)64.
6 July	7	**Import prices and dollar shortage – Board of Trade,** 4p.
16 July	8	**European import relaxations and non-discrimination – Board of Trade,** 4+1p annex.
14 Oct	9	**Relaxation of import restrictions. Action by other O.E.E.C. countries – Board of Trade,** 3p.
7 Nov	10	**European integration: matters arising following the Paris meetings – E.A. Hitchman,** 3+3p.
8 Nov	11	**Report of the Working Party on Sterling Balances – G.M. Wilson and C.H.W. Hodges covering the Working Party,** 1+15+61p addenda. See EPC(49)137.
4 Nov	12	**Imports of machinery from dollar sources – Programmes Committee,** 4+1p appendix.
23 Nov	13	**Licensing policy for imports of machinery from dollar sources – G.M. Wilson and C.H.W. Hodges,** 1p.
28 Nov	14	**Dual price policy – E.A. Hitchman,** 1+8+1p appendix. See EPB(49)22. Draft of EPC(49)155.
9 Dec	15	**Incentives for dollar exports – Board of Trade,** 2+12p appendix. Progress report.
9 Dec	16	**Washington tripartite discussions in relation to the Anglo-Canadian Continuing Committee – G.M. Wilson and C.H.W. Hodges covering T.L. Rowan,** 1p. Extract of a letter to E.A. Hitchman.
2 Jan	17	**Fritalux – G.M. Wilson and C.H.W. Hodges covering the European Economic Co-operation Committee,** 1+7p.
31 Dec	18	**Western Germany in relation to European Regional Groups – G.M. Wilson and C.H.W.**

Hodges covering the European Economic Co-operation Committee, 1+1+4p. Also ER(L)(49)335.

31 Dec   **19**   **Change in secretariat – G.M. Wilson and C.H.W. Hodges,** 1p.

CAB 134/203   Meetings and Memoranda   3 Jan–2 Oct 1950   ED(W)(50)1st–10th and ED(W)(50)1–31.

Meetings

3 Jan   **ED(W)(50)1st**   **Fritalux.** ED(W)(49)17 and 18.

10 Jan   **2nd:1**   **Dual pricing.** ED(W)(50)3 and 5.

:2   **U.S. investment in the sterling area.** ED(W)(50)1.

:3   **Incentives for dollar export drive.** ED(W)(50)2 and 4.

3 Feb   **3rd**   **E.C.A. loan for the development of the Rhodesias.** ED(W)(50)9.

7 Mar   **4th**   **Economic relationships with the U.S.A.** ED(W)(50)11.

14 Mar   **5th:1**   **Incentives for dollar exports.** ED(W)(50)13. Rejection of a differential tax.

:2   **Tariff ceiling for Europe.** ED(W)(50)8.

14 Mar   **6th:1**   **Sterling balances in South East Asia.** ED(W)(50)17.

:2   **Economic relations with the U.S.A.** ED(W)(50)15.

21 Mar   **7th:1**   **Dollar retention scheme.** ED(W)(50)13 and 20. A report to be drafted on the conflicting views expressed.

:2   **Dollar export policy.** ED(W)(50)19.

:3   **Economic dispute between India and Pakistan.** ED(W)(50)18.

3 May   **8th**   **Sterling oil/dollar oil: reply to U.S. memo.** ED(W)(50)22.

15 May   **9th**   **Sterling oil/dollar oil: proposal by Standard Oil Co. of New Jersey.** ED(W)(50)25.

12 Sept   **10th**   **Building and construction work for the defence programme.** ED(W)(50)30.

Memoranda

5 Jan   **ED(W)(50)1**   **Report on U.S. investment in the sterling area – E.J. Beaven and C.H.W. Hodges covering the Working Party,** 1+37+12p annexes. Also GEN 303/18(final).

6 Jan   **2**   **Incentives for dollar exports – Board of Trade,** 1+7p. Draft interim report on financial incentives.

9 Jan   **3**   **Note by the chairman of the London Committee – E.A. Hitchman,** 2p. London Committee's views on ED(W)(50)5.

9 Jan   **4**   **Report on incentives by the Dollar Export**

		Board – E.J. Beaven and C.H.W. Hodges covering C. Weir, 1+7p.
9 Jan	5	Dual pricing – E.J. Beaven and C.H.W. Hodges covering the Working Party on Dual Prices of the European Economic Co-operation Committee, 1+15+11p annexes. Also GEN 301/8. Draft of EPC(50)1.
11 Jan	6	Dual price policy – E.J. Beaven and C.H.W. Hodges covering E.N. Plowden and the Working Party, 1+4+15+11p annexes. See EPC(50)1.
14 Jan	7	Fritalux – E.J. Beaven and C.H.W. Hodges, 1+7p. Also ER(L)(50)10.
30 Jan	8	Suggested tariff ceiling for Europe – E.J. Beaven and C.H.W. Hodges covering the Trade Negotiations Committee, 1+13+3p annexes.
30 Jan	9	E.C.A. loan for the development of the Rhodesias – E.A. Hitchman, 3p.
14 Feb	10	Proposed dollar loan for development in the Rhodesias – E.J. Beaven and C.H.W. Hodges covering E.N. Plowden and Cripps, 1+2p.
3 Mar	11	Economic relationships with the U.S.A. – E.N. Plowden covering T.L. Rowan, 1+4p. Letter to E.A. Hitchman, 14 Feb 1950.
9 Mar	12	Progress report on Washington oil talks – E.J. Beaven and C.H.W. Hodges covering V.S. Butler and M. Stevenson, 1+1p.
10 Mar	13	Incentives for dollar exports – Board of Trade, 1+1+6p annex +9+4p appendixes +2p. Reports by the Working Parties on Differential Taxation for the Dollar Exporter, Dollar Retention Incentive Scheme and F.E.C.C. Machinery and Business Visits to North America.
11 Mar	14	Better knowledge about the sterling area – E.N. Plowden covering the Economic Information Unit, 1+2p. Proposals for the education of U.S. public opinion.
14 Mar	15	Fundamental discussions with the U.S.A. – Treasury, 2+5p.
16 Mar	16	Economic relationships with the U.S.A.: interim reply to Sir Leslie Rowan – E.J. Beaven and C.H.W. Hodges covering E.A. Hitchman, 1p.
15 Mar	17	Sterling balances and South East Asia – E.J. Beaven and C.H.W. Hodges covering Working Parties on the Sterling Area and on Development in South and South East Asia, 1+8p. Also ED(SA)(50)14(revise) and SA(50)10(revise).
15 Mar	18	The economic dispute between India and Pakistan – E.J. Beaven and C.H.W. Hodges covering a working party, 1+4+33p annexes.

16 Mar	19	**Dollar export policy – J.H. Woods, 1+5p.** Summary of progress and issues outstanding.
18 Mar	20	**Dollar retention scheme: Commonwealth reactions – E.J. Beaven and C.H.W. Hodges covering the Colonial Office, 1+2p.**
22 Mar	21	**Incentives for dollar exports: dollar retention scheme – E.N. Plowden, 1+5p.**
5 May	22	**Sterling oil/dollar oil: reply to U.S. memorandum – C.H.W. Hodges and E.J. Beaven covering the Oil Working Party, 1+14+19p annexes. Final version. Also GEN 295/79(final).**
28 Apr	23	**U.K. and U.S. memoranda on sterling oil/dollar oil problem – E.J. Beaven and C.H.W. Hodges, 1+19p annexes.**
8 May	24	**Sterling oil/dollar oil: submission to ministers – E.J. Beaven and C.H.W. Hodges covering E.N. Plowden, 1+2p.**
12 May	25	**Sterling oil/dollar oil: proposal by Standard Oil Co. of New Jersey – E.J. Beaven and C.H.W. Hodges covering the Oil Working Party, 1+8p. See EPC(50)54.**
20 May	27	**Housing for dollar export workers – C.E.P.S., 3p.**
25 May	28	**Housing for dollar export workers – E.J. Beaven and C.H.W. Hodges covering E.N. Plowden, 1+1p. Letter to J. Wrigley.**
5 June	29	**Change in secretariat – E.J. Beaven, 1p.**
8 Sept	30	**Building and construction work for the defence programme – R.S. Buer and D.J. Atherton, 1+4+1p appendix. Also IPC(WP)(50)114.**
2 Oct	31	**Change of secretary – unsigned, 1p.**

15.12 Economic Planning Board

Set up on 7 July 1947, having been announced during the House of Commons debate on the economic situation 10–12 March 1947 (see *Parl. Deb.* 5th Series vol 434). It was intended to be a forum for discussion between the two sides of industry and the production departments and, in contrast to the N.J.A.C. of the Ministry of Labour and the N.P.A.C.I. of the Board of Trade, to be a small committee on which industrial representatives could comment on policy documents before their submission to ministers. The Government was unsuccessful in its original aim of limiting each side of industry to two representatives as was the T.U.C. in its demand for ministers rather than civil servants to attend.

The Board was not a conspicious success. Meetings, which were initially intended to be fortnightly, were infrequent and often cancelled at short notice. In a crisis, the Board had little opportunity to participate in decisions. In 1949 in particular, dissension was rife with Cunningham and Verdon Smith threatening resignation over the inadequacies of economic policy (see E.N. Plowden's Note for Record, January 1950, in T 229/644) and Rowlands complaining that the minutes ignored officials' views (see his correspondence with Plowden, 22 November–2 December, in T 229/647). The Board was maintained, however, even after the fall of the Labour government, both to prevent the political furore that might attend its abolition and in the belief that each side, if only indirectly, benefited from the discussions.

Chairmanship of the Board was normally devolved from the Lord President to E.N. Plowden as Chief Planning Officer. The other members, to act as individuals rather than representatives, were three nominees of the Federation of British Industries and the British Employers' Confederation; three nominees of the T.U.C.; the permanent secretaries of the Board of Trade, Ministry of Labour and National Service and Ministry of Supply; three members of C.E.P.S. and the director of the Economic Section. At the request of the industrial representatives, a Treasury representative was added after September 1947, in effect replacing one of the C.E.P.S. representatives.

The Board's minutes and memoranda for 1947 are in the papers of C.E.P.S (T 229/26–36). A major statement on planning by C.E.P.S was submitted to the Board and discussed in July 1948 (see CAB 134/211, EPB(48)12 and CAB 134/210, EPB(48)8th:4). For its papers after 1951, see CAB 134/877–881.

Terms   To advise His Majesty's Government on the best use of our economic resources, both for the realization of a long-term plan and for remedial measures against our immediate difficulties.

Members   Ld President (ch.); E.N. Plowden (C.E.P.S.); R.L. Hall (Ec. Sect.).
Employers' representatives: Sir W. Coates, Sir G. Cunningham, W.R. Verdon Smith. (Jan 1949) C.B. Clegg replaced Coates.
T.U.C. representatives: A. Naesmith, J. Tanner, H.V. Tewson. (Jan 1949) L. Evans replaced Naesmith.
Perm. Secs.: J.H. Woods (B.T.), G. Ince (Lab. & N.S.), A. Rowlands (Supply).
C.E.P.S.: A.S. Le Maitre, H.T. Weeks, F.W. Smith. (Nov 1947) Le Maitre left and not replaced. (July 1948) E.A. Hitchman replaced Weeks. (Nov 1948) Smith left. (Nov 1949) W. Strath replaced Hitchman.
Treasury: (Sept 1947) B.W. Gilbert.

Secs.   S.Bodington (C.E.P.S) and J.A.R. Pimlott (Lord Pres. O.). (1947) J.G. Stewart (Cab. O.) replaced Pimlott. (Nov 1947) D.A.V. Allen (C.E.P.S.) replaced Bodington. (Jan 1949) D.J.B. Robey (Cab. O.) replaced Stewart. (Jan 1950) P.V. Collyer (Cab. O.) replaced Robey. (March 1950) M.M. du Merton (Cab. O.) replaced Collyer. (Oct 1950) D.O. Henley (C.E.P.S) replaced Allen. (March 1951) A. Savage (Ag.) replaced du Merton. (Aug 1951) J.A. Atkinson (Nat. I.) replaced Savage.

CAB 134/210   Meetings   22 Jan–16 Dec 1948   EPB(48)1st–16th.

22 Jan	**EPB(48)1st:1**	**Minutes of last meeting.**
	:2	**Report by Working Party on Textile Exports.** EPB(48)1.
	:3	**The human factor in industrial productivity.** EPB(48)2 and 4. Agreement on industries to be investigated.
	:4	**Distribution of iron and steel.** EPB(47)31.
28 Jan	**2nd**	**1948 dollar position.** EPB(48)3. Explanation of the report by T.L. Rowan and qualified agreement. Import programmes to be

		maintained in the expectation of adequate Marshall Aid.
5 Feb	3rd:1	**Minutes of last meeting.**
	:2	**Economic Survey for 1948 (draft for publication).** EPB(48)5. Consideration by chapters of questions of principle.
4 Mar	4th:1	**Minutes of the previous meeting.**
	:2	**Supplies and requirements of steel.** EPB(48)6.
	:3	**Steel for shipbuilding.** EPB(48)7.
1 Apr	5th:1	**Attendance.**
	:2	**Reserve of works.** EPB(48)8. Agreement on the nature of such a reserve.
	:3	**Chancellor's press conference: future policy** EPB(48)9.
	:4	**Invitation to attend the British Industries Fair.**
15 Apr	6th:1	**Draft interim report of Colonial Development Working Party.** EPB(48)10.
	:2	**Work of the Economic Information Unit.** EPB(48)11.
3 June	7th	**Progress report of the Committee on Industrial Productivity.** EPB(48)14. General discussion followed by consideration of report.
1 July	8th:1	**Membership of the Board.**
	:2	**E.R.P.** EPB(48)19.
	:3	**Interim report of the Sterling Area Working Party.** EPB(48)20.
	:4	**Planning problems.** EPB(48)12, 16, 18. Survey by E.A.G.R. Robinson. Agreement on the need for flexibility and more information about private capital investment.
7 July	9th:1	**Long-term economic survey: balance of payments forecasts.** EPB(48)21. Endorsement of paper although some of the assumptions were adjudged optimistic.
21 July	10th:1	**Capital investment 1949.** EPB(48)23. General agreement to accord priority to dollar-earning and dollar-saving industries.
	:2	**Changes in productivity in British industry 1946/47.** EPB(48)24.
	:3	**The long-term demand for steel in the U.K.** EPB(48)22.
5 Aug	11th	**The draft Economic Survey for 1948–52.** EPB(48)25. Consideration by chapter.
13 Sept	12th:1	**The long-term plan.** EPB(48)26. Agreement that the plan was courageous rather than optimistic.
21 Oct	13th:1	**Report of the Colonial Development Working Party.** EPB(48)27.
	:2	**Grass production and conservation.** EPB(48)28.
4 Nov	14th:1	**Membership of the Board.**
	:2	**Progress of the O.E.E.C.** Outline of recent developments.

2 Dec	**15th:1**	**Agricultural programme: organization of discussion.** EPB(48)17, 28, 29, 30, 31, 32.
	:2	**Feedingstuffs and grassland improvement.** EPB(48)17, 28, 29, 31.
	:3	**Fertilizer supplies.** EPB(48)31.
	:4	**Survey of agricultural expansion programme.** EPB(48)30. General approval.
16 Dec	**16th:1**	**Viability of Western Europe in 1952/53.** EPB(48)33.
	:2	**Long-term programme of the bizone of Germany.** EPB(48)34. Concern over possible consequences for U.K. plans.

CAB 134/211   Memoranda   14 Jan–30 Dec 1948   EPB(48)1–35.

14 Jan	**EPB(48)1**	**Report by Working Party on the Increase of Textile Exports – J.G. Stewart and D.A.V. Allen covering the Working Party,** 1+24+2p appendixes.
17 Jan	**2**	**The human factor in industrial productivity – Lord President's Office,** 1+3p appendix.
26 Jan	**3**	**1948 dollar position – J.G. Stewart and D.A.V. Allen covering an official working party.** 1+11+9p annexes. Revision of forecast for 1948 made in CP(47)283. Series of recommendations to increase reserves.
20 Jan	**4**	**The human factor in industrial productivity – C.E.P.S.,** 2p.
2 Feb	**5**	**Economic Survey for 1948 – J.G. Stewart and D.A.V. Allen,** 1+46p. First draft for publication.
27 Feb	**6**	**Supplies and requirements of steel – C.E.P.S.,** 8p. Also IPC(WP)(48)38. Outline of the possible distribution in 1949 of an extra 950,000 tons.
27 Feb	**7**	**Steel for shipbuilding – C.E.P.S.,** 3p. Also IPC(WP)(46)38. Programme for the next two to three years.
24 Mar	**8**	**Reserve of works – J.G. Stewart and D.A.V Allen,** 1+4p. Recommendations for a reserve to offset unemployment caused by a shortage of raw materials.
30 Mar	**9**	**Chancellor's press conferences: future policy – J.G. Stewart and D.A.V. Allen covering the Economic Information Unit,** 1+2p. Need for conferences with employers and employees to stimulate increased production.
10 Apr	**10**	**Draft interim report – Colonial Development Working Party,** 17+17p appendixes.
10 Apr	**11**	**The work of the Economic Information Unit – Economic Information Unit,** 4p.

29 Apr	**12**	**Planning problems – C.E.P.S.**, 6p. It was now necessary to look to more long-term than immediate issues.
8 May	**13**	**Note by the chairman – E.N. Plowden**, 1p.
26 May	**14**	**Progress report by the Committee on Industrial Productivity – E.M. Nicholson**, 3+6p. Number of issues on which the committee sought guidance.
1 June	**15**	**Work in hand – J.G. Stewart and D.A.V Allen**, 1p.
2 June	**16**	**Planning problems – J.G. Stewart and D.A. Allen covering W.R. Verdon Smith**, 1+6p. Asks what the relationship of the domestic economy to the wider issue of the political and economic stability of Europe was. Notes by E.N. Plowden and G. Ince attached.
14 June	**17**	**Home produced feedingstuffs from grassland – J.G. Stewart and D.A.V. Allen**, 1+7p. Note circulated by Sir William Coates.
12 June	**18**	**Planning problems – J.G. Stewart and D.A.V. Allen covering Sir William Coates**, 1+4p.
28 June	**19**	**E.R.P. – E.A. Hitchman**, 2+5p annex.
29 June	**20**	**Interim report of the Sterling Area Working Party – J.G. Stewart and D.A.V. Allen covering the Working Party**, 1+7+15p appendixes. Report on major development schemes in the non-colonial part of the sterling area in relation to calls on capital resources.
3 July	**21**	**Long-term Economic Survey: balance of payments forecasts – J.G. Stewart and D.A.V Allen**, 1+25p. Also ED(48)4. Drafts of the appropriate sections.
15 July	**22**	**The long-term demand for steel in the U.K. – J.G. Stewart and D.A.V. Allen covering the Working Party**, 1+5+12p appendixes. Estimate of demand in the 1950s to be used in the planning of steel supplies.
16 July	**23**	**Report on capital investment in 1949 – J.G. Stewart and D.A.V. Allen covering the Investment Programmes Committee**, 1+87+9p appendixes. See PC(48)93. Also ED(48)6 and IPC(48)8.
13 July	**24**	**Changes in productivity in British industry, 1946/47 – J.H. Woods**, 2+6p. Summary of available information, refuting the general belief that there had been a substantial post-war decline in productivity.
29 July	**25**	**Draft Economic Survey for 1948/52 – J.G. Stewart and D.A.V. Allen covering C.E.P.S.**, 1+41p. Identifies the problems which would confront any attempt to establish a viable U.K. economy free from foreign aid.

7 Sept	26	**U.K. 1952–53 balance of payments and production plans. Programme for submission to the O.E.E.C. – C.E.P.S.,** 4+4p annex +42p. See EPC(48)79. Also ED(48)8 and ER(L)(48)91.
15 Oct	27	**Report of the Colonial Development Working Party – J.G. Stewart and D.A.V. Allen covering the working party,** 1+18+25p appendixes. See EPC(48)92.
14 Oct	28	**Grass production and conservation – J.G. Stewart and D.A.V. Allen covering the Agricultural Output Committee,** 1+7+4p appendixes. See PC(48)150 Appendix II. Also AD(48)17.
26 Nov	29	**Feedingstuffs subsidies – Agricultural Output Committee,** 9+1p appendix. Also AD(48)25. Consideration of their removal.
26 Nov	30	**Survey of agricultural expansion programme – Agricultural Output Committee,** 13+1p appendix. See PC(48)150. Also AD(48)24.
27 Nov	31	**Report of the inter-departmental Working Party on Fertilizer Supplies – the Working Party,** 4+13p annexes.
26 Nov	32	**Material supplies for the grassland improvement scheme – C.E.P.S.,** 1p.
9 Dec	33	**Viability of Western Europe in 1952/53 – J.G. Stewart and D.A.V. Allen covering the Economic Section,** 1+16+13p appendixes. Summarizes the general features of the long-term programmes of the O.E.E.C. countries and identifies problems requiring future attention.
10 Dec	34	**The long-term programme of the bizone of Germany – J.G. Stewart and D.AV. Allen,** 1+6p. Report by officials.
30 Dec	35	**Economic Survey for 1949. First draft – J.G. Stewart and D.A.V. Allen covering the Economic Survey Working Party,** 1+65p. Also ED(49)1. Draft of PC(49)8.

CAB 134/212   Meetings and Memoranda   3 Jan–31 Dec 1949   EPB(49)1st–10th and EPB(49)1–25.

Meetings

6 Jan	**EPB(49)1st**	**Economic Survey for 1949: first draft.** EPB(48)35. Amendments agreed.
11 Feb	**2nd:1**	**The U.K. long-term programme and European viability.** EPB(49)6. General agreement on the paper except for proposals on coal production and steel investment.
	:2	**Report of the Imports Diversion Committee.** EPB(49)4.

21 Feb	**3rd:1**	**Economic Survey for 1949.** EPB(49)9. General discussion followed by detailed consideration.
	:2	**Future meetings of the Board.** No dates agreed.
19 May	**4th**	**Capital investment 1950/52.** EPB(49)13. General agreement with the paper, although it was felt that manufacturing industry should be safeguarded from any cuts.
2 June	**5th**	**Economic policy in a recession.** EPB(49)14. Report to be redrafted.
7 July	**6th**	**The dollar situation.** EPB(49)15.
28 Sept	**7th**	**Tripartite economic discussions in Washington.** Report by E.N. Plowden and R.L. Hall.
6 Oct	**8th**	**The internal financial situation and adjustment of exchange rates.** EPB(49)18. Recommendations of the Board to ministers, in particular to counter the resurgence of inflationary pressure.
20 Oct	**9th**	**The revised dollar import programme.** EPB(49)19. General agreement with the paper, although there was some concern at the proposed reduction of imports of raw materials.
17 Nov	**10th:1**	**Membership of the Board.**
	:2	**Ministerial meetings in Paris.** EPB(49)21.
	:3	**The reduction of capital investment in 1950.** EPB(49)20. Endorsement of proposed cuts but opposition to any reduction in depreciation allowances. Some concern that the cuts were inadequate and should be more selective.

Memoranda

3 Jan	**EPB(49)1**	**Change in secretariat – D.A.V. Allen and D.J.B. Robey,** 1p.
21 Jan	**2**	**Meetings in February – D.A.V. Allen and D.J.B. Robey,** 1p.
21 Jan	**3**	**Report for 1948 – D.A.V. Allen and D.J.B. Robey,** 1+4p. Report on subsequent action taken on questions discussed by the Board during 1948.
28 Jan	**4**	**Report of the Imports Diversion Committee to the Chief Planning Officer – the Committee,** 5+28p appendixes. Also ID(49)4. Consideration of the extent to which the proposed £100m diversion could be secured by 1952/53.
31 Jan	**5**	**Membership of the Economic Planning Board – D.A.V. Allen and D.J.B. Robey,** 1p.
4 Feb	**6**	**The U.K. long-term programme and European viability – D.A.V. Allen and D.J.B. Robey covering the European Economic Co-operation Committee,** 1+28+8p appendixes. See CP(49)27. Also ED(49)3.

4 Feb	7	**Meetings in February – D.A.V. Allen and D.J.B. Robey,** 1p.
8 Feb	8	**Security of documents – D.A.V. Allen and D.J.B. Robey,** 1p.
16 Feb	9	**Economic Survey for 1949 – D.A.V. Allen and D.J.B. Robey,** 1+38+15p appendix. See CP(49)29. Also ED(49)5. First proof.
	10	Not issued.
27 Apr	11	**The U.K. long-term programme and the Commonwealth – D.A.V. Allen and D.J.B. Robey,** 1+8+12+34p appendixes. Attached report by Sub-group B of the European Economic Co-operation Committee.
29 Apr	12	**Future meetings – D.A.V. Allen and D.J.B. Robey,** 1p.
13 May	13	**Report on capital investment 1950–52 – D.A.V. Allen and D.J.B. Robey covering the Investment Programmes Committee,** 1+88+10p appendix. See PC(49)59. Also ED(49)10 and IPC(49)3.
27 May	14	**Economic policy in a recession – D.A.V. Allen and D.J.B. Robey covering an official working party,** 1+11p. Also ED(W)(49)6. Draft of EPC(49)64.
29 June	15	**The dollar situation – E.N. Plowden,** 1+9p. Description of the general situation and steps taken by ministers. The rapidity of developments had prevented prior consultation with the Board.
20 July	16	**Recommendations to governments by Commonwealth Finance Ministers – D.A.V. Allen and D.J.B. Robey,** 1+6p.
26 Aug	17	**Tripartite talks in Washington – D.A.V. Allen and D.J.B. Robey,** 1+4+12p annex +15p appendixes +6+1p appendix +13+6p appendixes. See CP(49)175, 176, 178.
30 Sept	18	**The internal financial situation and the adjustment of exchange rates – D.A.V. Allen and D.J.B. Robey covering C.E.P.S. and the Economic Section,** 1+6+4p appendix. Appendix also EPC(49)93. Recommends reduced government expenditure and capital investment to counter inflationary pressure.
14 Oct	19	**The revised dollar import programme – D.A.V. Allen and D.J.B. Robey covering the Programmes Committee,** 1+11+30p appendixes. Also ED(49)16. Proposed import programme following devaluation.
11 Nov	20	**The reduction in capital investment in 1950 – D.A.V. Allen and D.J.B. Robey covering the Investment Programmes Committee,** 1+18p. See EPC(49)135. Also IPC(49)6.

14 Nov	21	Ministerial meeting in Paris of the O.E.E.C., the Council of Europe and the Brussels Treaty Powers: the economic integration of Europe – E.N. Plowden, 3+15p annexes. Summary of developments.
28 Nov	22	Dual price policy – D.A.V. Allen and D.J.B. Robey covering the European Economic Co-operation Committee, 1+8+1p appendix. Also ED(W)(49)14. Draft of EPC(49)155.
28 Nov	23	Closer economic association between Scandinavia and the sterling area – D.A.V. Allen and D.J.B. Robey covering the Steering Committee on Economic Development, 1+6p. See EPC(49)151.
21 Dec	24	The Economic Survey for 1950 – D.A.V. Allen and D.J.B. Robey covering the Economic Survey Working Party, 1+57+7p addendum. Also ED(49)25. First draft for ministers.
31 Dec	25	Review of agricultural expansion programme – D.A.V. Allen and D.J.B. Robey covering the Agricultural Output Committee, 1+13+1p appendix. Also AD(49)18(revise). Tentative suggestions concerning the pattern of agriculture after 1952/53.

CAB 134/213 Meetings and Memoranda 5 Jan–14 Dec 1950 EPB(50)1st–15th and EPB(50)1–20.

Meetings

5 Jan	EPB(50)1st:1	New Year Honours List.
	:2	Economic Survey for 1950. EPB(49)24. Criticism of survey's failure to give a clear picture of the state of the national economy. Some doubted whether a survey should be published.
5 Jan	2nd	Review of the agricultural programme. EPB(49)25.
16 Feb	3rd	Economic Survey for 1950: draft publication. EPB(50)2. Agreement to recommend publication.
6 Apr	4th	Report on a visit to Australia and New Zealand. EPB(50)6.
20 Apr	5th	Distribution scheme. EPB(50)8. Agreement to abolish the allocation of steel (except sheet steel and tin plate) in the home market provided the export situation was safeguarded. Allocation was disliked as a planning instrument since its success was dependent on the creation of an artificial shortage.
28 Apr	6th	Capital investment in 1951 and 1952. EPB(50)7. Consideration of the proposals for individual sectors.

4 May	7th	**Capital investment in 1951 and 1952.** EPB(50)7 and 9. Consideration of whether to adopt the higher or lower programme.
19 June	8th:1	**Capital investment in 1951 and 1952.**
	:2	**The Schuman proposals for an international coal and steel authority in Western Europe.** EPB(50)12 and 13. Agreement on the U.K.'s approach.
6 July	9th	**Balance of payments for 1950/51.** EPB(50)15. Endorsement of the estimated trend in the paper.
20 July	10th:1	**Preparation of the third annual report of the O.E.E.C.** Statement by D.B. Pitblado.
	:2	**Inflation in the U.K. and Australia.** EPB(50)11.
	:3	**Emigration from the U.K. to the Commonwealth.** EPB(50)10.
	:4	**Date of next meeting.**
14 Sept	11th:1	**Changed date of meeting.**
	:2	**Economic impact of increased defence expenditure.** EPB(50)16. Agreement that it would be inadvisable to allow defence production to be held up for the balance of payments or for other reasons.
	:3	**Date of next meeting.**
22 Sept	12th	**Labour in relation to defence production.** EPB(50)17.
19 Oct	13th	**The economic aspects of defence: recent discussions in the U.S.A.** Statement by W. Strath.
2 Nov	14th:1	**The international problem in raw materials.** EPB(50)18. Agreement that international discussion was imperative.
	:2	**Internal allocation of materials.** Discussion deferred.
16 Nov		**Conclusions of a meeting called by E.N. Plowden to discuss the winter coal budget.** Unnumbered meeting to advise industrial members of the Board of the situation over the coming winter. Agreement on the need for the measures proposed.
14 Dec	15th	**Economic prospects for 1951.** EPB(50)20. Consideration in particular of the assumed rate of productivity and the proposed external surplus of £100m.

Memoranda

6 Jan	**EPB(50)1**	**Change of secretariat** – D.A.V. Allen, 1p.
9 Feb	2	**Economic Survey for 1950; draft for publication** – D.A.V. Allen and P.V. Collyer, 1+37+15p addendum. To be rewritten for ministers. Draft of CP(50)28.

23 Feb	3	Recommendations to ministers – D.A.V. Allen and P.V. Collyer, 1p. Draft of EPB(50)4.
6 Mar	4	Economic Survey for 1950: submission to ministers – D.A.V. Allen and P.V. Collyer covering E.N. Plowden, 1p. See PC(50)17.
24 Mar	5	Change of secretariat – D.A.V. Allen, 1p.
31 Mar	6	Report on a visit to Australia and New Zealand – D.A.V. Allen and M.M. du Merton covering W. Strath, 1+31+5p appendixes.
14 Apr	7	Report on capital investment in 1951 and 1952 – D.A.V. Allen and M.M. du Merton covering the Investment Programmes Committee, 1+69+2p appendixes. Also IPC(50)1. Draft of EPC(50)47, ED(50)4 and IPC(50)2.
14 Apr	8	Steel distribution scheme – D.A.V. Allen and M.M. du Merton covering the Ministry of Supply, 1+2+1p appendix. Sets out the existing situation.
1 May	9	The financing of the investment in 1951 and 1952 – D.A.V. Allen and M.M. du Merton, 1+7+4p appendix. Report by officials on the growth of national resources anticipated and the amount of personal savings required if the levels of investment in EPB(50)7 were to be achieved without inflation.
26 May	10	Emigration from the U.K. to the Commonwealth – D.A.V. Allen and M.M. du Merton covering the Commonwealth Relations Office and the Ministry of Labour, 1+10+3p annex.
26 May	11	Inflation in the U.K. and Australia – D.A.V. Allen and M.M. du Merton, 1+4+4p annex. Analysis contrasting the U.K.'s balance of payments deficit and Australia's surplus, while both were suffering from inflation.
16 June	12	Schuman proposals for an international coal and steel authority in Western Europe – D.A.V. Allen and M.M. du Merton covering the Working Party on the Proposed Franco-German Coal and Steel Authority, 1+13+7p annexes. Also FG(50)3 and FG(WP)(50)38.
17 June	13	Constitutional problems involved in a supra-national authority as envisaged by M. Schuman – Foreign Office, 1+8+6p annex. Also FG(50)4 and FG(WP)(50)40.
28 June	14	Draft corrigendum to EPB(50)7th meeting conclusion 3 (capital investment in 1951 and 1952) – D.A.V. Allen and M.M. du Merton, 1p.
30 June	15	Balance of payments for 1950–51 – D.A.V. Allen and M.M. du Merton covering the Programmes Committee, 1+6+78p annexes. See EPC(50)73. Also ED(50)5 and P(50)25.

9 Sept	**16**	**Economic impact of increased defence expenditure – D.A.V. Allen and M.M. du Merton,** 1+34p. Report by officials dealing with broad changes to be expected in the balance of payments and the internal financial position.
19 Sept	**17**	**Skilled labour for the defence programme – D.A.V. Allen and M.M. du Merton covering the Ministry of Labour,** 1+2p. Sets out the proposed procedure and considerations with regard to skilled labour situation.
19 Oct		**Change of secretary,** 1p. Unnumbered paper.
27 Oct	**18**	**The international problem in raw materials – E.N. Plowden covering the Economic Section,** 1+5p.
	19	Not issued.
13 Dec	**20**	**Economic prospects for 1951 – E.N. Plowden covering officials,** 1+24p. Review of prospects and problems consequent to rearmament.

CAB 134/214 Meetings and Memoranda 12 Jan–13 Dec 1951 EPB(51)1st–10th and EPB(51)1–16.

Meetings

18 Jan	**EPB(51)1st:1**	**Demand for and supply of steel up to 1953.** EPB(51)1.
	:2	**The economic implications of the defence proposals.** EPB(51)2.
15 Feb	**2nd**	**Long-term economic relations with Japan.** EPB(51)3.
12 Mar	**3rd**	**First draft of the Economic Survey for 1951.** EPB(51)5.
5 Apr	**4th**	**Capital investment in 1951, 1952 and 1953.** EPB(51)6. Agreed recommendations for ministers.
2 May	**5th:1**	**Steel allocation.** EPB(51)7.
	:2	**Suggested high level approach to the U.S. authorities on raw materials.** EPB(51)8.
7 June	**6th:1**	**Report on the visit to the U.S.A. by Sir Edwin Plowden and Mr. Robert Hall.** EPB(51)12.
	:2	**Long-term raw materials prospects.** EPB(51)10.
	:3	**Sulphur and sulphuric acid production.** EPB(51)11.
21 June	**7th**	**The balance of payments in 1951/52.** EPB(51)13. Review of prospects and recommendations.
26 July	**8th**	**Defence production and the general economic situation.** EPB(51)14. The Board were particularly concerned about the supply of labour for defence and other essential production, and a shortage of electricity and certain raw materials.
22 Nov	**9th:1**	**Statement by the Chancellor of the Exchequer.**

	:2	**Economic outlook for 1951.** EPB(51)15.
	:3	**The work of the Temporary Committee of the North Atlantic Treaty Council.**
13 Dec	**10th**	**Urgent economic problems.** EPB(51)16. Agreed recommendations to the Chancellor.

Memoranda

12 Jan	**EPB(51)1**	**Demand and supply of steel up to 1953 – D.O. Henley and M.M. du Merton covering the Ministry of Supply,** 1+6+3p appendix. Estimates likely shortage of steel.
17 Jan	**2**	**The economic implications of the defence proposals – E.N. Plowden,** 1+17p. See CP(51)20.
9 Feb	**3**	**Long-term relations with Japan – E.N. Plowden covering the Official Working Party,** 1+26+26p annexes. Also ES(51)7 and GEN 326/11(final).
13 Mar		**Change of secretary,** 1p. Unnumbered paper.
	4	Not issued.
7 Mar	**5**	**Economic Survey for 1951 – E.N. Plowden covering C.E.P.S. and Economic Section,** 1+37+22p appendixes. Also ES(51)20. First draft.
21 Mar	**6**	**Report on capital investment in 1951, 1952 and 1953 – D.O. Henley and A. Savage covering the Investment Programmes Committee,** 1+73+2p appendix. See PC(51)49. Also ES(51)24 and IPC(51)1.
27 Apr	**7**	**Steel allocation – Working Party of the Materials (Allocation) Committee,** 4+6p appendixes. See M(51)21.
27 Apr	**8**	**Approach to the U.S. authorities on raw materials – E.N. Plowden,** 1+17+5p appendix +6p addenda. Also RM(51)101(final). Arguments to be used to ensure adequate supplies.
1 May	**9**	**Report on capital investment in 1951, 1952 and 1953 – E.N. Plowden,** 3p. Note to the Chancellor covering comments by the Economic Planning Board and the Economic Steering Committee.
31 May	**10**	**Long-term raw materials prospects – D.O. Henley and A. Savage covering the Economic Section,** 1+6+2p appendix. Considers the possibility of permanent shortages.
31 May	**11**	**Sulphur and sulphuric acid – D.O. Henley and A. Savage covering the Board of Trade,** 1+7+1p appendix +1p addendum.
1 June	**12**	**Report on visit to the U.S.A. – E.N. Plowden and R.L. Hall,** 4p.
15 June	**13**	**Balance of payments for 1951–52 – D.O. Henley and A. Savage covering the Programmes**

		Committee, 1+8+28p annex +5p appendix. See EPC(51)63. Also ES(51)40.
20 July	14	**Defence production and the general economic situation – E.N. Plowden covering C.E.P.S.,** 1+10p. Progress report.
3 Aug		**Change of secretary, 1p.** Unnumbered paper.
3 Sept		**Membership of the Economic Planning Board – D.O. Henley and J.A. Atkinson, 1p.** Unnumbered paper.
19 Nov	15	**Report on the economic outlook for 1952 – D.O. Henley and J.A. Atkinson,** 1+17p. Identifies areas requiring ministerial guidance.
7 Dec	16	**Urgent economic problems – D.O. Henley and J.A. Atkinson covering C.E.P.S.,** 1+8+2p annex. Recommended means of reconciling the defence programme with the maintenance of both the external balance and capital investment.

15.13 Economic Policy Committee

Set up during the administrative reorganization of October 1947 to replace the Lord President's Committee as the major ministerial committee dealing with domestic economic policy, see CAB 129/21, CP(47)280. It also assumed responsibility for overseas policy from the Committee on Overseas Economic Policy (CAB 134/541). The initial intention was to entitle it the Economic Planning Committee, see CAB 21/1724. It was designed to be a small body of senior ministers dealing only with issues of major policy but over time, and despite considerable efforts, its membership and agenda widened. It remained, however, the main body below Cabinet which discussed Marshall Aid, devaluation, full employment policy and the economic consequences of rearmament whilst the Production Committee (which had been set up concurrently) dealt with more detailed aspects of policy. A surprising omission from formal membership until March 1950 was Harold Wilson as President of the Board of Trade.

It was served by the ministerial Subcommittee on the Location of Defence Projects (CAB 134/231) and various official committees, in particular the Official Steering Committee on Economic Development (CAB 134/186–193) and the Economic Steering Committee (CAB 134/263–266). Its later papers are in CAB 134/841–855.

Terms   (a) to exercise on behalf of the Cabinet a general oversight over the work of economic policy in relation to both external and internal questions   (b) to reconcile, subject to the Cabinet, conflicts between the needs of our foreign trading and the requirements of our internal economy   (c) to consider questions of external economic policy;   (Nov 1950) to exercise a general oversight over economic policy, both external and internal; and, in particular, to ensure a proper balance between investment and military demands on the national economy.

Members   Prime Min. (ch.); Ld President; Foreign Sec.; Ch. of Exchequer; Min. of Ec. Affairs (until Nov 1947); Ld Privy Seal.   (March 1948) Mins. of Defence and Health added.   (June 1948) Ch. D. Lancaster added.   (March 1950) Min. of Town and Country Planning, Pres. Bd Trade and Min. of Ec. Affairs replaced Min. of

Defence. (Nov 1950) Min. of Defence added. (June 1951) Min. of Lab. & N.S. replaced Min. of Health.

Sec. N. Brook (Cab. O.).

CAB 134/215 Meetings and Memoranda 9 Oct–30 Dec 1947 EPC(47)1st–15th and EPC(47)1–37.

Meetings

9 Oct	**EPC(47)1st:1**	**Procedure of the committee.** Statement by Attlee.
	:2	**Balance of payments: general survey.**
	:3	**Balance of payments situation: recommendations of the Economic Planning Board.** EPC(47)2. General agreement with the recommendations and discussion on the control of inflation.
27 Oct	**2nd:1**	**Wages policy.** EPC(47)4.
	:2	**Rationing of consumption of dollar imports.** EPC(47)5.
	:3	**Food supplies from the colonies.** EPC(47)3.
31 Oct	**4th:3**	**Collection of scrap metal.**
3 Nov	**5th**	**Dollar aid from the U.S.A.** EPC(47)8 and 9.
7 Nov	**6th**	**Customs unions.** EPC(47)11.
11 Nov	**7th:1**	**Eire: trade negotiations.**
	:2	**Canada: trade negotiations.** EPC(47)13.
	:3	**Tobacco: purchases from Canada.**
	:5	**Argentina: trade negotiations.**
17 Nov	**8th**	**Argentina: trade negotiations.** EPC(47)15.
21 Nov	**9th:1**	**Petroleum Board.** Gaitskell to seek agreement with the oil companies for its continuation.
	:2	**Livestock expansion programme.** EPC(47)17 and 20.
	:3	**Balance of payments with non-dollar countries in 1948.** EPC(47)18.
	:4	**Tourist traffic.**
	:5	**Production for export.** A comprehensive review to be arranged.
1 Dec	**10th:1**	**Canada: trade negotiations.** EPC(47)24.
	:2	**Russia: trade negotiations.**
11 Dec	**13th:1**	**Trade negotiations: non-discrimination obligations.** EPC(47)28.
	:2	**Russia: trade negotiations.**
16 Dec	**14th:1**	**Canada: trade negotiations.** EPC(47)30.
30 Dec	**15th:1**	**International trade organization: control of quantitative restrictions.** EPC(47)37.
	:2	**International Wheat Agreement.** EPC(47)29.
	:4	**Argentina: trade negotiations.**

Memoranda

9 Oct	**EPC(47)1**	**Composition and terms of reference –** N. Brook, 1p.

17 Oct	2	**Balance of payments situation: recommendations of the Economic Planning Board** – N. Brook, 1+10p annexes. Paper on the economic position by C.E.P.S. (EPB(47)10) and resulting recommendations of the Board.
22 Oct	3	**Food supplies from the colonies** – Cripps covering C.E.P.S., 1+2p annex.
23 Oct	5	**The rationing of dollar imports** – Cripps, 1+2p annex. Scheme to ration semi-luxuries involving dollar expenditure.
31 Oct	7	**Dollar aid** – Cripps covering M.I. Hutton, 1+7p annex.
3 Nov	8	**U.S. dollar aid** – N. Brook, 1+2p.
3 Nov	9	**U.S. dollar aid** – N. Brook, 1+3p. Background to EPC(47)8.
5 Nov	10	**U.S. dollar aid** – N. Brook, 1+3p. Telegram from Washington on discussions attached.
6 Nov	11	**Customs unions: interim report of the Inter-departmental Study Group** – N. Brook, 1+8p annex +6p appendix.
6 Nov	12	**U.S. dollar aid** – N. Brook, 1+4p annexes.
7 Nov	13	**Negotiations with Canada** – Cripps covering the Overseas Negotiations Committee, 1+7+7p annexes.
10 Nov	14	**Economic Information Unit** – N. Brook, 2p. Sets out the unit's functions.
14 Nov	15	**Negotiations with Argentina** – Cripps covering the Overseas Negotiations Committee, 1+10+8p annexes.
15 Nov	16	**Claim for increased wages in the coal-mining industry** – Isaacs, 1+4p annex. Sets out the implications of allowing the increase.
18 Nov	17	**Livestock expansion programme** – Chuter Ede, Johnston and Williams, 3+4p appendix.
18 Nov	18	**1948 non-dollar balance of payments plan** – Cripps, 2+7p. Recommendations of officials.
19 Nov	20	**Livestock expansion programme** – Strachey, 4p.
26 Nov	21	**Bilateral negotiations with Portugal** – Cripps, 2+3p annex.
1 Dec	24	**Negotiations with Canada** – N. Brook covering the Overseas Negotiations Committee, 1+7+11p annexes.
3 Dec	27	**Profits and dividends** – Isaacs, 4p. Limitation of both recommended.
9 Dec	28	**Non-discrimination obligations** – Cripps covering the Board of Trade, 1+3+1p annex.
9 Dec	29	**International Wheat Agreement** – Strachey, 3+8p appendix.
15 Dec	30	**Negotiations with Canada** – Cripps, 3p.
18 Dec	32	**Potatoes, flour and dried fruit** – Strachey, 4p.
23 Dec	33	**European Recovery Programme** – N. Brook covering the London Committee on European

		Economic Co-operation, 1+3+30p appendixes. Recommended policy towards E.R.P.
29 Dec	34	**Marshall Aid. Undertakings on U.K. internal finance – Cripps**, 1+4p annex. The position of the budget in relation to internal financial policy.
27 Dec	35	**Feedingstuffs rations – Strachey**, 3p.
29 Dec	36	**Livestock expansion programme – Chuter Ede, Johnston and Williams**, 2p.
29 Dec	37	**International trade conference. Prior approval for quantitative restrictions – Wilson**, 7+3p annex.

CAB 134/216   Meetings   5 Jan–14 Dec 1948   EPC(48)1st–40th.

5 Jan	**EPC(48)1st:1**	**Livestock expansion programme.** EPC(47)35 and 36.
	:2	**International Trade Organization: control of quantitative restrictions.**
9 Jan	**2nd:1**	**E.R.P.** EPC(47)33 and 34 and EPC(48)2 and 4.
	:2	**Economic Survey for 1948.** EPC(48)1. Approval of the survey as a basis for departmental planning subject to raising the manpower target for the coal-mining industry.
	:3	**Oil production.** EPC(48)3.
22 Jan	**4th**	**Denmark: trade negotiations.** EPC(48)9.
27 Jan	**5th:1**	**Wages policy.** EPC(48)11. Concern at probable effects of accepting the passenger transport workers' claim.
	:3	**Livestock expansion programme.** EPC(48)10.
10 Feb	**6th:1**	**Wages policy.** Discussion of the line to be taken with the T.U.C. on the White Paper on personal incomes.
	:3	**Argentina: trade negotiations.**
13 Feb	**7th:1**	**Restrictions on public banquets.**
	:2	**Balance of payments: 1948 dollar position.** CP(48)35 and 49. Subject to certain modifications, agreement that CP(48)35 should be submitted to Cabinet.
27 Feb	**8th:1**	**International Wheat Agreement.** EPC(48)13.
	:2	**Economic Survey for 1948.**
4 Mar	**9th:1**	**E.R.P.: continuing organization.** EPC(48)15. Discussion centred on the political and economic implications of the policy of European economic co-operation.
	:2	**Rice supplies.** EPC(48)14.
11 Mar	**10th:1**	**International Trade Organization.** EPC(48)16.
	:2	**Cinematograph films.**
23 Mar	**11th:1**	**E.R.P.: supply of information to the U.S. authorities.** EPC(48)19.
23 Mar	**12th:1**	**U.K. organization for E.R.P.** EPC(48)21.

	:2	**Livestock expansion programme. EPC(48)39.**
	:3	**Eire: trade negotiations. EPC(48)23.**
	:4	**France: unrequited exports from the sterling area.**
9 Apr	13th:1	**U.K. – Canadian wheat agreement. EPC(48)27 and 28.**
	:3	**Future of North German timber control.** EPC(48)22.
	:4	**Direction of exports to hard currency markets.**
	:5	**France: balance of payments with sterling area.**
	:6	**European policy: Joint International Committee of Movements for European Unity.**
20 Apr	14th:1	**Wages policy: government industrial employees.** EPC(48)32.
	:2	**Petroleum Board.** EPC(48)30.
22 Apr	15th	**Iron and Steel Bill.** Morrison to inform the Parliamentary Labour Party that the bill would be introduced during the present parliament.
3 May	17th:1	**Price policy.** EPC(48)20 and 36.
	:2	**Wages claims.** EPC(48)50. Attached annex on increases in claims since the end of March.
13 May	19th	**E.R.P.: U.K. import programme.** EPC(48)38 and 39. Endorsement of the principles behind the initial programme.
3 June	20th:1	**Russia: trade negotiations.** EPC(48)43.
	:2	**Spain: trade negotiations.** EPC(48)46.
	:4	**E.R.P.: draft economic co-operation agreement between the U.K. and the U.S.A.**
8 June	21st	**E.R.P.: draft economic co-operation agreement between the U.K. and the U.S.A.** EPC(48)48 and 49.
11 June	22nd	**E.R.P.: draft economic co-operation agreement between the U.K. and the U.S.A.**
15 June	23rd:1	**Eire: trade negotiations.** EPC(48)47, 50 and 52.
	:2	**Customs unions.** EPC(48)34 and 37.
	:4	**Balance of payments: import saving.**
	:5	**European economic co-operation.**
21 June	24th:1	**India and Pakistan: financial negotiations.**
	:2	**E.R.P.: draft economic co-operation agreement between the U.K. and the U.S.A.** EPC(48)55 and 56.
22 June	25th:1	**European economic co-operation.** EPC(48)53 and 54.
	:2	**Eire: trade negotiations.**
24 June	26th	**E.R.P.: draft economic co-operation agreement between the U.K. and the U.S.A.** EPC(48)59.
6 June	27th:1	**European economic co-operation.**
	:3	**Industrial productivity.** EPC(48)42. Some concern at the slowness of movements.
9 July	28th:1	**Coal prices.** EPC(48)64 and 65.
	:2	**European economic co-operation: U.K. coal exports.** EPC(48)62 and 63. Concern that

		figures given to the O.E.E.C. prejudged future coal allocations.
16 July	29th:1	**European economic co-operation.**
	:2	**Wages policy: government industrial employees.** EPC(48)69 and 70.
	:3	**E.R.P.: prospective balance of payments in 1952.** EPC(48)66 and 68. Acceptance of the forecast in the annex to EPC(48)66.
27 July	30th:1	**Oil production.** EPC(48)45, 67, 72, 74.
	:2	**The clothing ration.**
10 Sept	31st:1	**Argentina: trade negotiations.** EPC(48)80.
	:2	**European customs union.** EPC(48)78.
14 Sept	32nd	**E.R.P.: balance of payments and production programmes for 1952/53.** EPC(48)79, 82, 83.
16 Sept	33rd:1	**E.R.P.** EPC(48)81 and 85.
	:2	**Anglo-Canadian economic relations.** EPC(48)84.
2 Nov	34th:1	**Poland: trade and financial negotiations.** EPC(48)90.
	:2	**Yugoslavia: trade negotiations.**
9 Nov	35th:1	**Civil Service manpower.** EPC(48)91. Agreement to rely on existing methods of control.
	:2	**Size and circulation of newspapers.** EPC(48)94.
	:3	**Price policy: sliding scale wage agreements.** EPC(48)89.
23 Nov	36th	**Section 117(d) of the U.S. Foreign Assistance Act.** EPC(48)97 and 98.
25 Nov	37th:1	**Canada: trade negotiations.** EPC(48)103 and 105.
	:2	**E.R.P.: the next steps on the long-term programme and the programme for 1949/50.** EPC(48)100.
	:3	**E.R.P.: publication of long-term programme.** EPC(48)99.
	:4	**The French long-term programme.** EPC(48)102.
3 Dec	39th:1	**E.R.P.: publication of the long-term and 1949/50 programmes.** EPC(48)107.
	:2	**The French long-term programme.**
14 Dec	40th:2	**European economic co-operation: the long-term programme of the Anglo-American zone of Germany.** EPC(48)101, 106, 109.

CAB 134/217   Memoranda   23 Dec 1947–1 June 1948   EPC(48)1–44.

3 Jan	**EPC(48)1**	**Economic Survey for 1948 – Cripps,** 4p. Copy of the Survey (EPB(47)30) prefixed. Note stressing the gravity of the situation.
5 Jan	**2**	**European Recovery Programme – Bevin,** 1p.

6 Jan	3	**Oil supply situation – Gaitskell covering the Official Oil Committee,** 2+3+7+6p appendix. Also OOC(47)16.
8 Jan	4	**The next meeting of the Committee on European Economic Co-operation – N. Brook covering the London Committee,** 1+3+2p annex.
12 Jan	5	**Wagon repairs – Cripps covering P. Mills,** 1+4+2p appendix.
21 Jan	9	**Negotiations with Denmark – Cripps covering T.L. Rowan,** 1+2p.
23 Jan	10	**Livestock expansion programme – Chuter Ede, Johnston and Williams,** 2+1p appendix.
23 Jan	11	**Wage claims in the road passenger transport industry – Isaacs covering the Committee on Wages and Conditions of Employment,** 1+2+2p appendixes.
3 Feb	12	**India and Pakistan: sterling balance negotiations – Cripps,** 3p.
26 Feb	13	**International Wheat Agreement – Strachey,** 1+11+3p annex.
16 Feb	14	**Rice supplies – Bevin covering the Official Committee on Food Supplies from South East Asia,** 2+6p annex.
2 Mar	15	**E.R.P.: the continuing organization – N. Brook covering the London Committee,** 1+6+2p annex.
8 Mar	16	**Havana Trade Conference – Cripps and Wilson,** 4p.
5 Mar	17	**Additional members of the Committee – N. Brook,** 1p.
19 Mar	19	**E.R.P.: programmes to be transmitted to the U.S. authorities – N. Brook covering the London Committee,** 1+3+5p annexes.
18 Mar	20	**Price policy – Cripps covering E.E. Bridges,** 1+4+1p appendix. Sets out the main issues arising from the White Paper on Personal Incomes and the appeal to the F.B.I.
19 Mar	21	**U.K. organization for handling E.R.P. – Attlee,** 3p.
20 Mar	22	**The future of the North German Timber Control – Wilson,** 3p.
22 Mar	23	**Price of live cattle imported from Eire – Cripps covering the Overseas Negotiations Committee,** 1+3p annex.
25 Mar	24	**European Recovery Programme Aid 1948–52 – Cripps covering the Treasury,** 1+3+1p appendix. Tentative estimate of likely situation.
3 Apr	25	**Draft charter of the continuing organization – N. Brook covering the London Committee,** 1+1+2+15p annexes.
4 Apr	26	**Arms for Latin America – Bevin,** 6+2p appendix.

6 Apr	27	**U.K.-Canadian Wheat Contract – Strachey,** 3+3p annex.
8 Apr	28	**U.K.-Canadian Wheat Agreement – Gordon Walker,** 2+1p annex.
9 Apr	29	**The Dominions and E.R.P. – N. Brook covering the London Committee,** 1+2p. Arrangements to keep Dominions informed.
12 Apr	30	**De-merging of the Petroleum Board – Gaitskell,** 2p. Companies now wanted it dissolved. Gaitskell accepted.
12 Apr	31	**Convention of European Economic Co-operation – N. Brook covering the London Committee,** 1+1+8p. Revised draft text of the convention setting up the O.E.E.C. and draft resolution on its functions.
16 Apr	32	**Wages of government industrial employees – Cripps,** 1+4p. Factual note by officials on the nature of claims and the relevant considerations.
19 Apr	33	**Conditions of aid under E.R.P. – N. Brook covering the London Committee,** 1+2+5p annexes.
23 Apr	34	**Customs union – Wilson covering the Inter-departmental Study Group on Customs Unions,** 1+10+3p annexes.
27 Apr	36	**Price policy after 6 Apr 1948 – Cripps covering E.E. Bridges,** 1+5p. Consideration of the budget's impact.
11 May	37	**European customs union – N. Brook,** 1p. Prefix to EPC(48)37.
8 May	37	**Report on the study of a European Customs Union – Wilson covering the European Customs Union Study Group,** 4+5p annex.
10 May	38	**Prospects under E.R.P. – Cripps,** 3+14p annexes. Consideration of the import policy during E.R.P.
11 May	39	**E.R.P.: food supplies – Strachey,** 3p.
18 May	41	**Registration and publication of trade and payments agreements – Cripps covering the Overseas Negotiations Committee,** 1+2p annex.
21 June	42	**Progress report from the Committee on Industrial Productivity – Morrison and Cripps covering the Committee,** 1+5p annexes. Also PC(48)77.
31 May	43	**Further negotiations with the U.S.S.R. – Cripps and Wilson,** 4+9+4p annexes. Also ON(48)212(revise).

CAB 134/218   Memoranda   1 June–14 July 1948   EPC(48)45–68.

1 June	**EPC(48)45**	**The dollar element in oil – Cripps and Gaitskell,** 3+6+9p appendixes. The possibilities for reducing the dollar drain.

2 June	46	**Anglo-Spanish trade and payments negotiations – Cripps covering T.L. Rowan,** 1+2+1p annex.
2 June	48	**Draft economic co-operation agreement between the U.K. and the U.S.A. – N. Brook covering the London Committee,** 1+4+9+29p annexes.
7 June	49	**Draft bilateral agreement between the U.K. and the U.S.A. – N. Brook covering the Foreign Office,** 1+2p.
9 June		**Membership of the committee – N. Brook,** 1p. Unnumbered paper.
11 June	50	**Trade negotiations with Eire – Cripps covering the Overseas Negotiations Committee,** 1+9+4p appendixes.
12 June	52	**Trade negotiations with Eire – N. Brook covering T.L. Rowan,** 1+3+3p appendix.
18 June	53	**European economic co-operation – N. Brook covering the European Economic Co-operation Committee,** 1+11+13p annexes.
18 June	54	**European economic co-operation – Cripps,** 1p. Disagreement with part of EPC(48)53.
19 June	55	**Draft economic co-operation agreement between the U.K. and the U.S.A. – N. Brook,** 1+15p.
19 June	56	**Draft economic co-operation agreement between the U.K. and the U.S.A. – N. Brook covering T.L. Rowan,** 1+5+3p annexes. Report on latest developments.
22 June	57	**Draft economic co-operation agreement between the U.K. and the U.S.A. – N. Brook,** 1+12+1p annex.
23 June	58	**Projects for European Economic Co-operation – N. Brook covering the European Economic Co-operation Committee,** 1+1+3p.
24 June	59	**Draft economic co-operation agreement between the U.K. and the U.S.A. – N. Brook covering the Official Working Party on the Bilateral Agreement,** 1+4p. Progress report on negotiations.
7 July	62	**E.R.P. coal exports for fiscal year 1948/49 – Gaitskell,** 2p.
8 July	63	**Coal and coke exports: 1948–49 – Cripps covering the European Economic Co-operation Committee,** 1+3p.
8 July	64	**Adjustments in inland coal prices – Gaitskell,** 3+1p annex. Adjustments to correct the balance between supply and demand of various qualities of coal.
8 July	65	**Coal for the railways – Barnes,** 2p. Concern that proposals in EPC(48)64 would be bad for the railways and basic industries.
9 July	66	**1948/52 balance of payments programmes – Cripps covering C.E.P.S.,** 3+18p appendix.

Need for decision on the basis on which the programmes should be formulated.

13 July	**67**	**Review of oil situation – Gaitskell,** 2+7+1p appendix. Also OOC(48)10.
14 July	**68**	**1948/52 balance of payments programmes – Cripps,** 1+1p. Comments by the Steering Committee on Economic Development.

CAB 134/219   Memoranda   14 July–31 Dec 1948   EPC(48)69–116.

14 July	**EPC(48)69**	**Government industrial wages – Cripps,** 1+5p annex +4p appendixes.
15 July	**70**	**Government industrial employees – Isaacs,** 1p. Alternative to EPC(48)69.
15 July	**71**	**Interim report by the Sterling Area Development Working Party – Cripps covering the Working Party,** 1+3+7p appendixes.
19 July	**72**	**The oil expansion programme – Cripps and Gaitskell,** 4p.
23 July	**74**	**Oil – Cripps and Gaitskell,** 3p. Summary of the position and recommendations.
29 July	**75**	**Submission of long-term programme to the O.E.E.C. – N. Brook,** 1+1p. Possibility of discussing the programme with Commonwealth prime ministers before submission to the O.E.E.C.
14 Aug	**76**	**Submission of 1948/52 and 1949/50 programmes to the O.E.E.C. – S.E.V. Luke,** 1p. Timetable of work.
7 Sept	**78**	**European customs union – Cripps covering the European Economic Co-operation Committee,** 1+6+13p annexes.
7 Sept	**79**	**Balance of payments and production programmes for 1952–53 for submission to the O.E.E.C. – Cripps,** 5+42p. Also ED(48)8, EPB(48)26 and ER(L)(48)91. Draft long-term programme forecasting considerable improvement in the situation, although success was dependent on factors outside U.K. control. Chapter I – introductory, chapter II – general policies, chapter III – major industrial plans, chapter IV – investment in the U.K., chapter V – development of overseas territories, chapter VI – forecast of balance of payments and level of activity in 1952–53, chapter VII – conclusions.
9 Sept	**80**	**Trade negotiations: Argentina – Cripps covering the Overseas Negotiations Committee,** 1+19p annex.
14 Sept	**81**	**1949–50 programme – Cripps,** 2+13p annex.
10 Sept	**82**	**Food consumption level proposed for the next four years – Strachey,** 10+24p appendixes.

Concern over the level of food consumption proposed by the planning departments. So small an increase in the basic rations would be bad politically. A higher level of food consumption should be aimed for since the forecast underlying the proposals was defective.

10 Sept	83	**Publication of documents submitted to the O.E.E.C. – Cripps covering T.L. Rowan,** 1+3p.
13 Sept	84	**Anglo-Canadian economic relations – Cripps,** 3+1p annex.
15 Sept	85	**1948–49 programme – Cripps,** 2+16p annexes.
13 Oct	86	**Discussions in Ottawa and Washington – Cripps,** 2+5p annex +3p appendixes.
1 Nov	89	**Price policy and sliding scale wage agreements – Cripps,** 1+1p annex. Also WPP(48)14.
1 Nov	90	**Trade and financial negotiations with Poland – Cripps covering the Overseas Negotiations Committee,** 1+5+2p appendix.
1 Nov	91	**Civil Service manpower – Cripps,** 4+5p annex. Letter sent to Attlee.
3 Nov	93	**Official talks with Australia and New Zealand on long-term economic planning and development – Cripps,** 3p. Account of discussion centering around the balance of payments.
6 Nov	94	**Size and circulation of newspapers – Wilson,** 3+1p annex.
10 Nov	96	**Delay in recoveries against E.R.P. allotments – Cripps,** 1+6p.
16 Nov	97	**Section 117(d) of the U.S. Foreign Assistance Act – Noel-Baker,** 3+14p annexes.
20 Nov	98	**Section 117(d) of the U.S. Foreign Assistance Act – Mayhew,** 3p.
23 Nov	99	**Publication of the long-term programme – Cripps,** 2p. Recommendation to publish the programme as sent to Paris.
20 Nov	100	**The next steps on the long-term programme and the programme for 1949–50 – Cripps,** 4p. Progress of work on the O.E.E.C. long-term programme and the problems so far identified.
22 Nov	101	**Long-term programme of the bizone of Germany – Cripps,** 2+13p annexes.
22 Nov	102	**French long-term programme – Mayhew,** 3p. Revise version. Review of the programme and proposals in relation to Anglo-French economic co-operation.
20 Nov	103	**Trade negotiations with Canada – Cripps,** 4p.
22 Nov	105	**Forthcoming food negotiations with Canada – Strachey,** 2p.
23 Nov	106	**Long-term programme of the bizone of Germany – Wilson,** 1p. Programme's potential

		conflict with the U.K.'s own export programme.
1 Dec	107	**E.R.P.: publication of the long-term programme – Cripps,** 1+3p. Draft foreword to the White Paper.
11 Dec	109	**The long-term programme of the bizone of Germany – Cripps,** 2+8p annex.
7 Dec	110	**The long-term programme for Europe – Cripps,** 4p. Outstanding features of individual countries' programmes and their implications for the U.K. and sterling area.
31 Dec	113	**Canadian wheat negotiations – Cripps and Strachey,** 6+2p appendix.

CAB 134/220   Meetings   3 Jan–14 Dec 1949   EPC(49)1st–52nd.

3 Jan	**EPC(49)1st:1**	**Canadian Wheat Agreement.** EPC(48)113.
13 Jan	**2nd**	**International Wheat Agreement.** EPC(49)2. General support for U.K. participation.
18 Jan	**3rd:1**	**Argentina: trade negotiations.** EPC(49)3.
26 Jan	**5th:2**	**The O.E.E.C.: U.K. policy and proposals for structure.** EPC(49)6. Consideration of the desirable extent of U.K. participation.
21 Feb	**6th:1**	**International Wheat Agreement.** EPC(49)9.
	:2	**European Economic Co-operation: European long-term programme.** CP(49)27 and EPC(49)8. General agreement to approach integration with caution.
24 Feb	**7th:1**	**Yugoslavia: trade negotiations.** EPC(49)11.
	:2	**Russia: trade negotiations.** EPC(49)10.
	:3	**Proposed international tin agreement.** EPC(49)13, 14, 15.
11 Mar	**8th:1**	**Tariff policy.** EPC(49)16. Powers to impose duties on Commonwealth goods should not be sought.
24 Mar	**9th:1**	**Coal-oil conversion programme.** EPC(49)25. No new conversions would be authorized until the long-term oil policy had been decided.
	:3	**Proposed international tin agreement.** EPC(49)19 and 23.
	:4	**Anglo-Canadian Continuing Committee on Trade and Economic Affairs.** EPC(49)12 and 21.
	:5	**European Economic Co-operation: programme for second quarter of 1949.** EPC(49)22 and 24.
29 Mar	**10th:2**	**Size and circulation of newspapers.** EPC(49)26.
	:3	**Argentina: trade negotiations.** EPC(49)28 and 29.
1 Apr	**11th:2**	**Yugoslavia: trade negotiations.**
	:3	**Argentina: trade negotiations.** EPC(49)32.
	:4	**Import policy.** EPC(49)30.

		:5	**Expansion of exports to North America.** EPC(49)31 and 32.
		:6	**Proposed international tin agreement.**
11 Apr	12th:3		**Tariff negotiations at Annecy.** EPC(49)34.
		:4	**U.K.-Canada trade relations.**
20 Apr	13th:1		**Wages policy.** EPC(49)38. Draft statement for Attlee by Isaacs attached.
		:2	**International Bank's request for a negative pledge.**
25 Apr	14th:1		**U.K.-Canada trade negotiations.** EPC(49)40 and 43.
		:3	**Argentina: trade negotiations.**
		:4	**U.K. balance of payments.** Statement by Cripps on the size of the dollar deficit in the second quarter of 1949 and by Wilson on the difficulty of maintaining sales in the U.S.A.
10 May	15th:3		**Argentina: trade negotiations.** EPC(49)49.
		:4	**Purchase of maize and oil-cake for stock.** EPC(49)46 and 48.
		:5	**Proposed three-year bacon agreement with Holland.** EPC(49)45 and 47.
12 May	16th		**Argentina: trade negotiations.** EPC(49)51.
18 May	17th:1		**Intra-European trade and payments.**
		:2	**European economic co-operation: the revised U.K. programme for 1949–50.** EPC(49)52 and 53. Marked deterioration in the dollar situation since the original programme. Consideration by various ministers of the impact of the report on their respective departments.
24 May	18th:1		**Licensing of shipbuilding orders.**
		:2	**Future of the shipbuilding industry.** Concern at the possibility of increased unemployment, which should be further examined by Barnes and Hall.
		:4	**Food supplies and the communist threat.** EPC(49)54.
26 May	19th:1		**Production of silage and dried grass.** EPC(49)39.
		:2	**Import licensing relaxation.** EPC(49)55.
1 June	20th		**Yugoslavia: trade negotiations.** EPC(49)58.
15 June	21st:1		**International Wheat Agreement.** EPC(49)60.
		:2	**Yugoslavia: trade negotiations.**
		:3	**Intra-European trade and payments.** EPC(49)56.
		:4	**Tariff policy.** EPC(49)62.
		:5	**U.K. balance of payments.** EPC(49)61. H. Wilson-Smith reported on the Washington discussions.
24 June	22nd:1		**U.K. balance of payments.** EPC(49)66. Approval of the paper.
		:2	**Economic policy in a recession.** EPC(49)64. No decisions were necessary then but at some stage

		the committee would have to consider the policy to be adopted in a recession.
27 June	**23rd**	**Intra-European trade and payments.** EPC(49)68 and 69.
1 July	**24th:1**	**Intra-European trade and payments.**
	:2	**U.K. balance of payments.** EPC(49)72. Report by O. Franks of his discussions in Washington. Consideration of possible measures to alleviate the dollar situation, including devaluation.
1 July	**25th:1**	**U.K. balance of payments.** EPC(49)32. Further consideration followed by discussion of the form of statement to be made in Parliament.
	:2	**Oil and dollars.** EPC(49)71.
5 July	**26th:1**	**U.K. balance of payments.** EPC(49)70.
	:2	**Food: changes in ration scales.**
7 July	**27th**	**U.K. balance of payments.** EPC(49)73 and 75. Agreement on the need to consider long-term solution whilst discussing the immediate problem. Consideration of how to seek agreement on future relations between the sterling and dollar areas.
12 July	**28th:1**	**General economic situation.** EPC(49)76 and 77.
	:2	**U.K. balance of payments.** EPC(49)78 and 80. Approval of measures to help the dollar situation.
	:3	**Conference of Commonwealth finance ministers.** EPC(49)79.
22 July	**29th:1**	**Russia: trade negotiations.** EPC(49)85.
	:2	**Tin plate.** EPC(49)81.
	:3	**U.S. strategic stockpile of tin.** EPC(49)82.
26 July	**30th:1**	**Development of aluminium production within the Commonwealth.** EPC(49)77 and 83.
	:2	**Import policy.** EPC(49)89. Consideration of suggestions by Wilson.
	:3	**Price reduction.** EPC(49)87 and 90.
22 Sept	**31st**	**Import policy.** EPC(49)97. Relaxation of import controls considered.
10 Oct	**32nd**	**Internal financial situation.** EPC(49)102 and 107.
12 Oct	**33rd:1**	**Argentina: trade negotiations.** EPC(49)109.
	:2	**Internal financial situation.** EPC(49)102 and 110. Consideration of the extent of the inflationary situation and of possible remedial action.
14 Oct	**34th**	**Internal financial situation.** EPC(49)111. Consideration of proposed cuts in public expenditure including the introduction of prescription charges.
14 Oct	**35th**	**Internal financial situation.** EPC(49)111. Further discussion, including cuts in capital investment.

17 Oct	**36th:2**	**Internal financial situation.** EPC(49)111 and 112. Further consideration of cuts.
18 Oct	**37th**	**Oil prices.** EPC(49)113.
20 Oct	**38th**	**Internal financial situation.** EPC(49)111. Further consideration.
21 Oct	**39th:1**	**Clothes rationing.**
	:2	**Financial and economic relations with Canada.** EPC(49)118.
	:3	**Dollar import programme.** EPC(49)117 and 119. Agreement on a $1200m import programme for 1950.
	:4	**The tea ration and restoration of the London Tea Market,** EPC(49)108.
8 Nov	**40th:1**	**Wages policy.** Consideration of the strategy for forthcoming discussions with the T.U.C. Economic Committee.
	:2	**Financial and economic relations with Canada.** EPC(49)123 and 124.
	:3	**U.N. Food and Agriculture Organization: proposal for international commodity clearing house.** EPC(49)120.
	:5	**Replacement of South London tramways.** EPC(49)84.
	:6	**Export of home-produced eggs for dollars.** EPC(49)122.
10 Nov	**41st**	**Coal export prices.** EPC(49)125, 129 130. The N.C.B. were to give the government adequate advance notice of future alterations to the contract price.
16 Nov	**43rd:1**	**Development of tourism.** EPC(49)88, 96, 131.
	:2	**Third round of multilateral tariff negotiations under the General Agreement on Tariffs and Trade.** EPC(49)128.
	:3	**Commonwealth sugar policy.** EPC(49)116.
	:4	**International Wheat Agreement.**
	:5	**Gas Act: compensation.** EPC(49)136.
18 Nov	**44th:2**	**Sterling balances.** EPC(49)137.
	:3	**Financial and economic relations with Canada.** EPC(49)138, 144, 146.
	:4	**Commonwealth sugar policy.** EPC(49)116.
18 Nov	**45th:2**	**Wages policy.** Consideration of the best time to meet employers' organizations.
22 Nov	**46th:1**	**Capital investment in 1950.** EPC(49)135, 139, 141, 142. Consideration of the individual programmes recommended by the Investment Programmes Committee where there was disagreement from the relevant department.
25 Nov	**47th:2**	**International Wheat Agreement.** EPC(49)145.
	:3	**Transfer of Canadian ships to U.K. registry.** EPC(49)147.
29 Nov	**48th:2**	**Tin plate.** EPC(49)103.

1 Dec	**49th:1**	**Closer economic association between Scandinavia and the sterling area.** EPC(49)151.
	:2	**Financial and economic relations with Canada.** EPC(49)154.
7 Dec	**50th:1**	**Dual prices.** EPC(49)155.
	:2	**Commonwealth sugar policy.** EPC(49)156.
	:3	**Oil.**
13 Dec	**51st:1**	**European economic co-operation: submission to the O.E.E.C. on the U.K. position in 1950–51.** EPC(49)158 and 167.
	:2	**U.K. balance of payments.** EPC(49)157.
	:3	**Argentina: trade negotiations.** EPC(49)163.
14 Dec	**52nd:1**	**Commonwealth sugar policy.**
	:2	**Public Works Loan Board.** EPC(49)164.

CAB 134/221 Memoranda 1 Jan–17 May 1949 EPC(49)1–54.

10 Jan	**EPC(49)2**	**International Wheat Agreement – Strachey,** 8+12p appendix.
13 Jan	**3**	**Negotiations with Argentina – Cripps covering the Overseas Negotiations Committee,** 1+6p annex.
25 Jan	**6**	**Our policy to the O.E.E.C. and our proposals for its structure – Bevin and Cripps,** 4p.
17 Feb	**8**	**European long-term programme: food implications – Strachey,** 6p. Concern over the proposed revision of food consumption levels from those in CP(49)27.
17 Feb	**9**	**International Wheat Agreement – Strachey,** 7+6p annexes.
22 Feb	**10**	**Negotiations with Russia – Cripps covering the Overseas Negotiations Committee,** 1+6+1p annex +3p appendix.
22 Feb	**11**	**Negotiations with Yugoslavia – Cripps covering the Overseas Negotiations Committee,** 1+7p.
17 Feb	**12**	**The Anglo-Canadian Continuing Committee on trade and economic affairs – Cripps covering the U.K. members of the Committee,** 1+7+6p annex.
19 Feb	**13**	**Proposed international tin agreement – Wilson covering the Commodity Policy Subcommittee of the Trade Negotiations Committee,** 1+8+8p appendixes.
19 Feb	**14**	**Proposed international tin agreement – Creech Jones,** 2p.
22 Feb	**15**	**Proposed international tin agreement – Strauss,** 2p.
4 Mar	**16**	**Tariff policy – Wilson,** 1+3+1p annex. Question of increased duties on Commonwealth imports.
10 Mar	**18**	**Tariff policy – Strachey,** 1p.
14 Mar	**19**	**Proposed international tin agreement – Bevin,** 2+3p appendixes.

14 Mar	20	**European economic co-operation. Ministerial Consultative Group – Cripps**, 1+4p annexes. Results of meetings 4th–8th March 1949.
21 Mar	22	**E.R.P. programme for second quarter – Cripps**, 3p. Measures to reduce the carry-over of dollar aid.
17 Mar	23	**International tin agreement – Creech Jones**, 2+2p appendixes.
22 Mar	24	**E.R.P. programme for second quarter: food purchases – Strachey**, 7+1p appendix. Proposal to use the carry-over to improve food consumption levels.
21 Mar	25	**Coal/oil conversion – Gaitskell**, 2p.
25 Mar	26	**Size of newspapers – Wilson**, 3p.
26 Mar	28	**Negotiations with Argentina – Cripps covering the Overseas Negotiations Committee**, 1+8p.
26 Mar	29	**Argentine negotiations – Cripps covering Stokes**, 1+1p.
29 Mar	30	**Import policy – Cripps and Wilson**, 3p. Only general statements should be made pending a detailed enquiry into import licensing.
29 Mar	31	**Expansion of exports to North America – Wilson**, 7p. Proposals for a new dollar export drive. The overall balance of payments problem seemed solved.
31 Mar	32	**Coal for Argentina – Gaitskell**, 3p.
31 Mar	33	**Expansion of exports to North America – Wilson**, 4p. The 1948 programme and the prospects for 1949 of the main export groups.
4 Apr	34	**Tariff negotiations at Annecy – Wilson**, 2+3p.
14 Apr	38	**Personal incomes, costs and prices – Cripps**, 1+1p annex. The importance of continuing wage restraint was vital. A statement by Attlee, rather than another White Paper, recommended.
20 Apr	39	**Grass drying – Woodburn and Williams**, 4+11p appendix. Also AD(48)17.
22 Apr	40	**Canada – Cripps**, 5+13p annexes. Suggested approach to the latest discussions.
5 May	45	**Proposed three-year agreement on bacon with Holland – Strachey**, 5+1p appendix.
5 May	46	**Purchase of maize and oil-cake for stocks – Strachey**, 2p.
7 May	47	**Proposed three-year bacon agreement with Holland – Jay**, 2p.
7 May	48	**Purchase of maize and oil-cake for stocks – Jay**, 2p.
9 May	49	**Argentine trade negotiations – Jay**, 1+2p.
11 May	51	**Argentine trade negotiations – Jay covering the Overseas Negotiations Committee**, 1+2p.
13 May	52	**The revised U.K. programme for 1949–50 – Jay covering E.E. Bridges covering the Programmes**

Committee, 1+2+13+14p annexes. Steering
Committee on Economic Development
comments on the suitability of the revised
programme and the U.K.'s submission to the
O.E.E.C., and on the report's recommendation
of import cuts.

16 May   53 **Revised U.K. programme for 1949–50 –
Strachey,** 11p. Concern that the
recommendations in EPC(49)52
underestimated public dissatisfaction with
consumption levels.

17 May   54 **Food supplies and the communist threat –
Strachey,** 2+7p annex. Working party report
on the effect of the spread of communism on
world supplies.

CAB 134/222   Memoranda   24 May–11 Oct 1949   EPC(49)55–110.

24 May **EPC(49)55** **Import licensing relaxations – Cripps,** 6+4p
annex. Recommended measures arising from
the Working Party Report on Import Licensing
Relaxations, summary annexed.

14 June   56 **Conditions for liberalization of trade in Europe –
Cripps,** 2+10p.

28 May   58 **Yugoslav negotiations – Cripps covering the
Overseas Negotiations Committee,** 1+11+2p
appendix. Also ON(49)181(revise).

2 June   59 **Food: the next twelve months – Strachey,** 9+2p
annex. Survey of prospects and their political
implications.

2 June   60 **International Wheat Agreement – Strachey,**
3+22p. Cmd. 7680 attached.

11 June   61 **The dollar drain – Cripps,** 2p. Explanation of
the reasons for the worsening position. Sharp
action would soon be needed.

10 June   62 **Tariff policy – Wilson,** 3+1p annex.

16 June   63 **Report on a visit to the U.S.A. in June 1949 by
Sir Henry Wilson-Smith and Mr. R.L. Hall –
Cripps covering R.L. Hall and H. Wilson-
Smith,** 1+7+5p annexes.

21 June   64 **Economic policy in a recession – Cripps covering
officials,** 1+9p annex. Two main dangers to full
employment: a threat to U.K. dollar raw
materials supplies owing to the U.S. depression
and a general decline in demand for U.K.
exports.

23 June   65 **Exports to Canada – Wilson,** 3+21+9p annexes.
Report on his trade mission to Canada.

22 June   66 **The dollar situation – Cripps,** 11+8p appendix.
Measures recommended included a halt on all
new dollar commitments except the most
urgent.

22 July	89	**European import relaxations and non-discrimination – Wilson,** 5+5p annexes.
23 July	90	**Proposed arbitrary reduction in retail prices –Strachey,** 3p. Against the proposal in EPC(49)87 with regard to food.
13 Aug	91	**Signs of disinflation – Jay covering the Economic Section,** 1+4p. Report on the internal financial situation for May and June.
27 July	92	**U.S. private direct investment – Wilson,** 1+6+2p annexes.
2 Sept	93	**Inflationary pressure – Wilson covering the Economic Section,** 1+4p. Also EPB(49)18. Report on the internal financial situation for June and July. The title of these reports had been changed to be more appropriate to the situation being described.
9 Sept	94	**Conclusion of the Tariff Negotiations Act at Annecy – Wilson,** 2+1p annex.
20 Sept	96	**Shipping space for North Atlantic tourists –Barnes,** 4p.
20 Sept	97	**Relaxation of import controls – Cripps and Wilson,** 8+31p annexes. Suggested relaxations to be applied to all soft currency countries.
4 Oct	101	**Inflationary pressure – Cripps covering the Economic Section,** 1+3p. Report for July and August.
5 Oct	102	**The internal financial situation, Sept 1949 –Cripps,** 4p. Estimate of the inflationary situation having taken account of devaluation. To return to the position envisaged in the April budget, savings of £300m were necessary.
6 Oct	103	**Tin plate – Isaacs and Strauss,** 1p.
6 Oct	104	**Devaluation: effects on some public accounts –Cripps covering the Treasury,** 1+2p annex.
6 Oct	105	**American press and radio comment on devaluation – Cripps covering the Washington Embassy,** 1+4p annex.
7 Oct	106	**Report on visit to Canada – Wilson and Strauss covering Freeman,** 1+9+1p appendix. Written before devaluation.
8 Oct	107	**Internal financial situation: views of the Economic Planning Board – Cripps,** 1p.
11 Oct	108	**The tea ration and the restoration of the London Tea Market – Strachey,** 7+2p annex.
11 Oct	109	**Economic relations with Argentina – Cripps covering the Overseas Negotiations Committee,** 1+1+12p. Also ON(49)328(revise).
11 Oct	110	**The internal financial situation – Cripps,** 2p. Supplement to EPC(49)102.

CAB 134/223   Memoranda   12 Oct–19 Dec 1949   EPC(49)111–168.

12 Oct	EPC(49)111	**Measures necessary to combat inflation –** **Cripps,** 13p. Domestic consumption had to be reduced by £280m p.a. to return to the budget situation and to take advantage of devaluation. Equal cuts in capital investment and government expenditure proposed and set out.
15 Oct	112	**The internal financial situation: summary of decisions reached so far – Cripps,** 2p.
15 Oct	113	**Oil prices – Cripps and Gaitskell covering officials,** 1+7p. Question of the selling prices of oil produced by British companies after devaluation.
15 Oct	114	**Public reaction to devaluation – Cripps covering the Central Office of Information,** 1+1p annex.
15 Oct	116	**Commonwealth sugar policy – Strachey covering the Ministry of Food,** 2+7+1p appendix.
19 Oct	117	**Dollar import programme – Cripps,** 3p.
19 Oct	118	**Financial and economic relations with Canada – Cripps,** 11+11p annexes.
20 Oct	119	**Dollar import programme: views of the Economic Planning Board – Cripps,** 1p.
2 Nov	120	**Food and Agriculture Organization of the U.N. – Strachey,** 9+5p.
4 Nov	122	**Export of home-produced eggs for dollars – Strachey,** 3p.
4 Nov	123	**Financial and economic relations with Canada – Addison covering the High Commissioner,** 1+2+2p addendum.
4 Nov	124	**Financial and economic relations with Canada – Cripps,** 1+9p. Report by U.K. officials on discussions with Canadian officials 24–27 Oct 1949.
5 Nov	125	**Price of coal exported to Denmark – Cripps covering the Overseas Negotiations Committee,** 1+2+1p.
7 Nov	126	**European Economic Co-operation. Council of the O.E.E.C. and Ministerial Consultative Group – Cripps,** 1+3+9p annexes. Report of meetings 28 Oct–2 Nov 1949.
9 Nov	127	**Reopening of the London Metal Exchange and dissolution of the Combined Tin Committee – Cripps,** 4p.
8 Nov	128	**Third round of the multilateral tariff negotiations under the General Agreement on Tariffs and Trade – Wilson,** 1+5p annex.
8 Nov	129	**Price of coal exported to Denmark – Strachey,** 4p.
9 Nov	130	**Coal export prices – Gaitskell,** 2p. Disagreement with EPC(49)129.

10 Nov	**131**	**Development of tourism – Wilson,** 2+10p annex.
11 Nov	**133**	**Inflationary pressure – Cripps covering the Economic Section,** 1+4p. Report for August and September.
14 Nov	**135**	**Capital investment in 1950 – Cripps covering the Investment Programmes Committee,** 1+18p. Also EPB(49)20 and IPC(49)6. Programme on the basis of the £140m reduction, with all the cuts to be made effective by the end of 1950.
15 Nov	**136**	**Gas Act: compensation – Cripps and Gaitskell,** 4p.
14 Nov	**137**	**Sterling balances – Cripps,** 2+15+32p appendixes +16p pamphlet. Includes the recommendations of the Steering Committee on Economic Development Working Group and the report of the Working Party on Sterling Balances. 'The Sterling Area' – P. Bareau, attached.
14 Nov	**138**	**Financial and economic relations with Canada – Noel-Baker,** 1+2p annexes.
17 Nov	**139**	**1950 programme for blitzed cities – Silkin,** 2+1p appendix. Sets out the consequences of the suspension of work recommended in EPC(49)135.
19 Nov	**141**	**Capital investment in 1950 – Cripps,** 2+1p annex. Views of the Economic Planning Board annexed. Stricter criteria for departmental support of applications to the Capital Issues Committee recommended.
16 Nov	**142**	**Reductions in the rate of capital investment – Key covering the Headquarters Building Committee,** 1+12p. Report on methods to reduce miscellaneous building and civil engineering investment, and the effect of general cuts in investment on the building, building materials, and civil engineering industries.
18 Nov	**143**	**The new role of North America – Cripps,** 1+6p. Address by the Deputy Governor of the Bank of Canada, on the need for North America to increase imports.
17 Nov	**144**	**Financial and economic relations with Canada – Cripps,** 1+2p.
23 Nov	**145**	**International Wheat Agreement: proposed accession of Germany and Japan – Strachey,** 7+3p appendix.
18 Nov	**146**	**Financial and economic relations with Canada – N. Brook covering the Canadian Prime Minister,** 1+2p. Message to Attlee.
23 Nov	**147**	**Transfer of Canadian ships to U.K. registry – Cripps and Barnes,** 4p.

23 Nov	**148**	**Financial and economic relations with Canada –** **N. Brook covering Attlee and Cripps,** 1+3p annexes.
24 Nov	**149**	**Report by the Economic Co-operation** **Administration on European dollar earnings –** **Cripps,** 1+3p. Extracts from the report attached.
26 Nov	**151**	**Closer economic association between** **Scandinavia and the sterling area – Cripps** **covering the Steering Committee on Economic** **Development,** 1+6p. Also EPB(49)23.
29 Nov	**153**	**Financial and economic relations with Canada –** **N. Brook covering the High Commissioner,** 1+4p.
30 Nov	**154**	**Financial and economic relations with Canada –** **Cripps,** 3p.
5 Dec	**155**	**Dual prices – Cripps covering the Working** **Party on Dual Prices,** 1+8+6p appendixes.
5 Dec	**156**	**Commonwealth sugar policy,** 2+4p.
7 Dec	**157**	**Balance of payments in 1950 – Cripps covering** **the Programme Committee,** 1+5p. Recommended basis on which the balance of payments policy should be formulated with an increasing role for indirect measures of control. Includes the comments of the Steering Committee on Economic Development.
7 Dec	**158**	**Submission to the O.E.E.C./E.C.A. on the U.K.** **position in 1950–51 – Cripps covering E.E.** **Bridges,** 1+5+35+7p appendixes. Report concentrated on the balance of payments and the dollar problem but also covered the internal situation.
10 Dec	**159**	**A new scheme for intra-European payments –** **Cripps,** 1+3p.
10 Dec	**160**	**Development of aluminium production within** **the Commonwealth sterling area – Strauss,** 3+5p appendixes.
9 Dec	**161**	**Financial and economic relations with** **Canada – Cripps,** 1+1p.
10 Dec	**162**	**Inflationary/disinflationary symptoms – Cripps** **covering the Economic Section,** 1+3+6p appendix. Report on November.
10 Dec	**163**	**Argentina – Cripps covering the Overseas** **Negotiations Committee,** 1+9+4p appendixes.
12 Dec	**164**	**Public Works Loans Board – Cripps,** 4+2p appendix. Consideration of measures to check marked acceleration of loans to local authorities.
12 Dec	**165**	**Import policy – Cripps covering the Working** **Party on Import Licensing Relaxations,** 2+6+14p annexes. Also ER(L)(49)339 and ILC/ ILR 58.

| 12 Dec | **167** | **Submission to the O.E.E.C. on the U.K. position in 1950–51 – Cripps**, 1p. |
| 19 Dec | **168** | **Anglo-Yugoslav negotiations – Bevin**, 2p. |

CAB 134/224   Meetings   5 Jan–21 Dec 1950   EPC(50)1st–32nd.

5 Jan	**EPC(50)1st:1**	**International Wheat Agreement.** EPC(50)3.
	:4	**Commonwealth sugar policy.** EPC(50)6.
9 Jan	**2nd:2**	**Exchequer subsidy on animal feedingstuffs.** EPC(50)7 and 8. Agreement on the withdrawal of subsidy, except for that on fertilizers.
	:3	**Export of home-produced eggs for dollars.**
12 Jan	**3rd:1**	**Dual prices.** EPC(50)1.
	:2	**Expansion of exports to North America.** EPC(50)4. Consideration of the use of controls and incentives. Development of aluminium production within the Commonwealth sterling area. EPC(49)160 and EPC(50)12.
17 Jan	**4th:1**	**Oil.** EPC(59)15, 16, 17, 19.
	:2	**Capital investment in 1950.** EPC(50)14. Consideration of the programme for the blitzed cities, central London and the fuel and power industries.
	:3	**Third round of the multilateral tariff negotiations under the General Agreement on Tariffs and Trade.** EPC(50)11.
19 Jan	**5th:3**	**Economic planning and liberalization of trade.** EPC(50)9. Gaitskell believed that it was not practicable to maintain full employment without a slight excess of money incomes. This required the retention of physical, as well as financial, controls in order to prevent inflation. The liberalization of trade, in order to ensure Marshall Aid and co-operation from certain European countries, might also undermine the whole system of controls. Cripps agreed that care had to be taken but that compromise with free economies was required.
	:4	**European Economic Co-operation: ministerial meetings in Paris.** EPC(50)20 and 21.
	:5	**Newsprint: size of newspapers.**
24 Jan	**6th**	**Closer economic association between Scandinavia and the sterling area.** EPC(50)23.
7 Mar	**7th:2**	**European Payments Union.** EPC(50)31.
14 Mar	**8th**	**Argentina: trade negotiations.** EPC(50)34.
17 Mar	**9th:1**	**Proposed international tin agreement.** EPC(50)35.
	:2	**Commonwealth wool conference.** EPC(50)36.
24 Mar	**10th:1**	**Commonwealth sugar policy.** EPC(50)38.
	:2	**Newsprint: size of newspapers.** EPC(50)39.
12 May	**12th:1**	**European Payments Union.** EPC(50)41. Update.

	:2	**National income and expenditure.** EPC(50)46 and 52. Cripps explaincd that if government expenditure was on the level in EPC(50)52 there could be no net reduction in taxation over the coming two years even on the more favourable productivity assumption. Bevan was concerned that intrinsically desirable and important capital investment projects were being constantly frustrated by the fear of inflation, while expansion of production in the private sector continued.
	:3	**Capital investment in 1951 and 1952.** EPC(50)47. Agreement that capital investment in 1951 and 1952 should be related to the higher programme in EPC(50)47 on condition that the programme represented an absolute ceiling. Increases in one part of the programme had to be matched by cuts in another.
16 May	13th:1	**European Payments Union.** Update.
	:2	**Integration of French and German coal and steel industries.** Statement by Cripps on the approach which should be adopted.
	:3	**Sterling and dollar oil: discussions with U.S. oil companies.** EPC(50)54.
	:5	**Dual prices.** EPC(50)43.
23 May	14th:1	**Sterling and dollar oil: discussions with U.S. oil companies.** EPC(50)56.
	:2	**Integration of French and German coal and steel industries.** EPC(50)55.
	:3	**International tin agreement.** EPC(50)53.
25 May	15th:2	**Integration of French and German coal and steel industries.** Statement by Bevin.
	:3	**European Payments Union.**
	:4	**Sterling and dollar oil: discussions with U.S. oil companies.** EPC(50)59.
20 June	16th:1	**Development of aluminium in the sterling area.** EPC(50)62.
	:3	**The dollar retention incentive scheme.** EPC(50)64. Agreement that it was inopportune to introduce incentives suggested in EPC(50)64.
	:5	**Restoration of the London Tea Market.** EPC(50)65. Agreement should reopen.
4 July	17th:1	**European Payments Union.**
	:2	**The Stikker plan.** EPC(50)68. Rejection of plan.
13 July	18th:1	**Balance of payments for 1950–51.** EPC(50)73, 74, 75. Approval of the dollar import programme.
	:2	**Financial and economic relations with Canada.** EPC(50)74.

	:4	**Applications made by the National Farmers Union to withdraw certain tariff commitments under the General Agreement on Tariffs and Trade.**
20 July	**19th**	**Third report of the O.E.E.C.** EPC(50)78.
28 July	**20th:1**	**Government trading losses for 1948–49.** EPC(50)79.
	:2	**Integration of Western European coal and steel industries.** EPC(50)81.
	:4	**Withdrawal of tariff commitments.** EPC(50)80.
15 Sept	**21st:1**	**Meeting of Commonwealth ministers on economic and trade questions.** EPC(50)90 and 91.
29 Sept	**22nd:1**	**Building and construction work for the defence programme.** EPC(50)95.
	:2	**Reversion of softwood to private trade.** EPC(50)96.
	:3	**Wool.** EPC(50)98 and 99.
	:4	**Supplies of plasterboard liner for the building industry.** EPC(50)97.
17 Oct	**23rd**	**Purchase of coarse grains from the U.S.S.R.** EPC(50)106.
19 Oct	**24th:1**	**Australian meat agreement.** EPC(50)102.
	:3	**Supplies of raw cotton from the U.S.A.** Statement by Wilson.
	:4	**Proposed international tin agreement.** EPC(50)107.
	:5	**Seventh session of the Customs Union Study Group.** EPC(50)108.
	:6	**Tariff commitments under the General Agreement on Tariffs and Trade (G.A.T.T.).** EPC(50)103 and 104.
31 Oct	**25th:3**	**Meeting of Commonwealth ministers on economic and trade questions.** EPC(50)109 and 110.
7 Nov	**26th:1**	**Agricultural wages and prices.** EPC(50)113.
	:2	**Trade agreement with Pakistan.** EPC(50)114.
10 Nov	**27th:1**	**Suspension of Marshall Aid.** EPC(50)115.
	:2	**White Paper on full employment.** EPC(50)116. Agreement on need for a White Paper. A draft layout to be prepared.
	:3	**European grain discussions.** EPC(50)117.
24 Nov	**28th:1**	**East–West trade.** EPC(50)123.
5 Dec	**29th**	**Raw materials.** EPC(50)125 and 126. Shortages were owing to U.S. action. Agreement to prohibit inessential uses of raw materials and to consider urgently the reintroduction of machinery to allocate scarce raw materials.
12 Dec	**30th:1**	**The dollar programme for 1951.** EPC(50)127.
	:2	**Effect of shipping shortage on the softwood position.** EPC(50)130.

18 Dec	**31st:1**	**Wages and prices and full employment.** EPC(50)124 and CP(50)291 and 292. Gaitskell argued it was time to choose between laissez–faire and permanent intervention in wage negotiations. General agreement to set up a Wages Advisory Service.
	:2	**White fish imports,** EPC(50)133 and 134.
	:3	**European grain discussions.**
	:4	**Tariff-making machinery.** EPC(50)128.
21 Dec	**32nd:3**	**Availability of dry cargo shipping.** EPC(50)137.
	:4	**The coal situation.** EPC(50)138. Consideration of means to increase supplies to the home market and to reduce inessential demand.

CAB 134/225 Memoranda 10 Jan–12 May 1950 EPC(50)1–53.

10 Jan	**EPC(50)1**	**Dual price policy – Cripps covering E.N. Plowden,** 1+4+26p. Also ED(W)(50)6.
3 Jan	**3**	**International Wheat Agreement: proposed accession of Germany and Japan – Strachey,** 9p.
30 Dec	**4**	**Exports to the U.S.A. – Wilson,** 19+16p annexes. Report on his recent trip and resulting recommendations.
4 Jan	**6**	**Commonwealth sugar policy – Creech Jones,** 5+1p appendix.
5 Jan	**7**	**The subsidy on animal feedingstuffs and the agricultural expansion programme – Chuter Ede, Woodburn and Williams,** 2+4+1p appendix +12+1p appendix. Also AD(49)17(revise) and 18(revise). Recommendation that feedingstuff subsidies should be eliminated on an overall basis, not item by item.
6 Jan	**8**	**Agricultural expansion programme: views of the Economic Planning Board – Cripps,** 1p.
7 Jan	**9**	**Economic planning and liberalization – Gaitskell,** 6p. There was a risk that the government would be drawn unconsciously towards decontrol in particular by the O.E.E.C. countries and the E.C.A. over the so-called liberalization of European trade. This was undesirable as the deliberate use of physical controls to supplement the price mechanism was the distinguishing feature of British socialist planning. Also decontrol would lead to either a balance of payments crisis or deflation.
7 Jan	**10**	**A new scheme for intra-European payments – Cripps,** 3p.
10 Jan	**11**	**Third round of tariff negotiations under the General Agreement on Tariffs and Trade – Wilson,** 3p.

10 Jan	12	**Development of aluminium production within the Commonwealth sterling area – Creech Jones**, 2p.
11 Jan	13	**The dollar crisis 1949: an analysis of movements in the sterling area gold and dollar accounts in the second and third quarters – Cripps**, 4+4p appendix.
13 Jan	14	**Reductions in capital investment – Cripps**, 2+4+1p appendix. Recommendations for fuel and power industries and damage.
14 Jan	15	**Oil negotiations in Washington – Cripps and Gaitskell**, 5p.
14 Jan	16	**Petrol rationing in Australia – Cripps**, 1+8p annexes.
14 Jan	17	**Australian petrol rationing. Mr Menzies's telegram to the Prime Minister – Gaitskell**, 2p.
16 Jan	19	**Petrol rationing in Australia – S.E.V. Luke**, 1+5p annex.
17 Jan	20	**Meetings of the O.E.E.C. ministers in Paris – Cripps**, 8p.
18 Jan	21	**Article by M. P.H. Spaak in the *Daily Telegraph* – S.E.V. Luke**, 1+2p. Summary of the article of 17 Jan 1950.
19 Jan	22	**Full employment – Cripps covering the Economic Section**, 1+8p. Summary of U.N. report on national and international measures to achieve full employment.
21 Jan	23	**Economic co-operation with the Scandinavian countries (Uniscan) – Cripps**, 1+7+4p appendix.
3 Feb	25	**Internal economic situation – Cripps covering the Economic Section**, 1+2+6p appendix. Also EC(S)(50)8. Report for January.
3 Feb	26	**Aluminium production in the Gold Coast – Creech Jones**, 1+6+1p appendix.
6 Feb	27	**Full employment – Cripps covering an inter-departmental working party**, 1+1+12p. Also NIFE(50)2 and EC(S)(50)15. Response to the U.N. report.
10 Feb	28	**Proceedings at the meetings of O.E.E.C. ministers in Paris – Cripps**, 7+4p annex.
2 Mar	30	**Composition of the Committee – N. Brook**, 1p.
3 Mar	31	**European Payments Union – Cripps**, 4+14+5p appendix. Sets out five ways in which U.K. interests might be imperilled.
4 Mar	32	**Full employment – Cripps covering J.M. Fleming**, 1+10+1p annex. Report on the fifth session of the U.N.'s Economic and Employment Commission at which the full employment report was discussed.

8 Mar	**34**	**Trade negotiations with the Argentine 1950 – Cripps covering the Overseas Negotiations Committee,** 1+11+3p annexes.
13 Mar	**35**	**Proposed international tin agreement – Wilson covering the Commodity Policy Subcommittee of the Trade Negotiations Committee,** 1+2p.
13 Mar	**36**	**Commonwealth Wool Conference – Wilson,** 1+6p.
16 Mar	**37**	**Internal economic situation – Cripps covering the Economic Section,** 1+1+5p appendix. Report for February.
21 Mar	**38**	**West Indies sugar – Griffiths,** 6+2p appendix.
22 Mar	**39**	**Size of newspapers – Wilson,** 2p.
4 Apr	**42**	**The O.E.E.C. mission to Washington – Bevin,** 1+2+7p.
24 Apr	**43**	**Dual prices – Cripps covering chairman of the London Committee,** 1+4p.
27 Apr	**44**	**Fundamental discussions with the U.S. – Cripps,** 3+10p annexes.
9 May	**46**	**Forecast of national income and expenditure – Cripps,** 5+7p appendix. Also NIF(WP)(50)28. From the forecast, Cripps concluded that, even if the rate of productivity continued to increase, there was a considerable (but not insurmountable) danger of inflation.
5 May	**47**	**Capital investment in 1951 and 1952 – Cripps covering the Investment Programmes Committee,** 1+69+2p appendix. Also ED(50)4 and IPC(50)2. Sets out a higher and a lower programme. The lower, involving drastic cuts, was based on forecasts of what was financially feasible, whilst the higher was designed to meet the needs of all the individual programmes required to implement existing policy.
2 May	**48**	**The Commonwealth meetings on oil – Noel-Baker,** 2+6+4p annexes.
9 May	**49**	**Reductions in capital investment: blitzed cities – Cripps,** 1+3p.
6 May	**50**	**Capital investment in 1951 and 1952: views of the Economic Planning Board and the Official Committee on Economic Development – Cripps,** 4p.
10 May	**51**	**European Payments Union – Cripps,** 1+2p annex.
10 May	**52**	**Forecast of supply expenditure – Cripps,** 1p. Forecast up to 1952–53.
12 May	**53**	**The proposed international tin agreement – Wilson covering the Commodity Policy Subcommittee of the Trade Negotiations Committee,** 1+9+1p annex.

CAB 134/226   Memoranda   15 May–16 Oct 1950   EPC(50)54–106.

15 May	EPC(50)54	**Sterling oil/dollar oil problems: proposal by the Standard Oil Co. of New Jersey** – N. Brook **covering the Economic Development Working Group,** 1+3+8p annex. Also ED(W)(50)25 and 26.
19 May	55	**Integration of French and German coal and steel industries** – Bevin and Cripps, 1+2p. Interim report by an official committee on possible effects on the U.K. attached.
22 May	56	**Oil negotiations** – Noel-Baker, 4p. Recommended end of petrol rationing.
22 May	57	**Proposed Franco-German coal and steel authority** – unsigned, 1+2p. Translation of the French foreign minister's communiqué.
25 May	59	**Petrol rationing and the Jersey proposal** – **Cripps and Noel-Baker,** 2p.
2 June	61	**Internal economic situation** – Cripps covering the Economic Section, 1+2+7p appendix. Also EC(S)(50)28. Report for April.
12 June	62	**Development of aluminium production in the sterling area** – Griffiths and Strauss, 5p.
26 May	64	**The dollar retention incentive scheme** – Wilson, 2+9p annex +4p appendix +3p annex. Report by inter-departmental working group attached. Wilson doubted the value of all such schemes.
15 June	65	**Proposal to reopen the London Tea Auctions** – **Webb,** 4+11p appendixes.
16 June	66	**Internal economic situation** – Cripps covering the Economic Section, 1+2+7p appendix. Report for May.
16 June		**Secretarial arrangements** – N. Brook, 1p.
23 June	67	**Report on a visit to the U.S. in May and June by Sir Henry Wilson-Smith and Mr. R.L. Hall, and on a short visit to Canada by Sir Henry Wilson-Smith** – Cripps covering H. Wilson-Smith and R.L. Hall, 1+6+5p annexes.
1 July	68	**The Stikker Plan** – Cripps covering the London Committee, 1+14+4p annex.
8 July	69	**Favourable results of petrol derationing** – **Younger,** 1p.
5 July	70	**Canada and the dollar-sterling problem** – **Wilson covering J.S. Duncan,** 1+18p.
6 July	71	**Cotton industry mission to Japan** – Wilson, 1+4p.
8 July	73	**Balance of payments 1950-51** – O.C. Morland **covering the Programmes Committee,** 1+6+78p annexes. Report for July 1950 – June 1951. Policy should be designed to secure the internal balance of the economy and to expand exports not just to the dollar area.

10 July	74	**Financial and economic relations with Canada** – Cripps, 1+2+8p.
10 July	75	**Balance of payments for 1950–51** – Cripps, 1+3p annexes. Views of the Economic Planning Board and the Official Committee on Economic Development.
31 July	76	**Forecast of supply expenditure** – Cripps, 2p. Further forecast on the lines of EPC(50)52 emphasizing need for economy.
10 July	77	**Applications by the National Farmers Union and others to withdraw tariff commitments entered into under the General Agreement on Tariffs and Trade** – Wilson, 4+1p annex.
18 July	78	**The O.E.E.C. third report** – Cripps covering the London Committee, 1+1+3p annex +9p. Report of the Working Group on the preparation of the U.K. memo to the O.E.E.C. attached.
24 July	79	**Internal economic situation** – Cripps covering the Treasury, 1+2+10p appendixes. On government trading losses.
24 July	80	**Notification of intention to consider withdrawals of tariff commitments under the General Agreement on Tariffs and Trade** – Wilson, 4+3p appendix.
24 July	81	**Integration of Western European coal and steel industries** – Cripps, 1+9p annexes.
25 July	84	**Internal economic situation** – Cripps covering the Economic Section, 1+3+7p appendix. Also EC(S)(50)34(revise). Report for June.
9 Aug	85	**Internal financial situation** – Gaitskell covering the Economic Section, 1+2+7p appendix. Also EC(S)(50)38. Report for July.
10 Aug	86	**Convertibility and non-discrimination** – Gaitskell, 1+3p.
13 Sept	90	**Meeting of Commonwealth ministers on trade questions** – Wilson, 2p.
14 Sept	91	**Commonwealth dollar expenditure** – Gaitskell, 5p.
2 Sept	93	**Internal financial situation** – Gaitskell covering the Economic Section, 1+1+7p appendix. Also EC(S)(50)43. Report for August.
14 Sept	95	**Building and construction work for the defence programme** – Gaitskell covering the Economic Development Working Group and the Investment Programmes Committee, 1+6p annexes +1p appendix. Also IPC(WP)(50)114.
27 Sept	96	**Reversion of softwood to private trade. Proposal for public and private buy zones** – Wilson, 2p.
27 Sept	97	**Supplies of plasterboard liner for the building industry** – Wilson, 2p.
26 Sept	98	**Wool: U.S. and Commonwealth discussions** – Wilson, 5+4p appendix.

27 Sept	99	**Future for wool joint organization – Wilson**, 2p.
12 Oct	101	**Internal financial situation – Jay covering the Economic Section**, 1+4+7p appendix. Also EC(S)(50)46. Report for September.
14 Oct	102	**Australian meat contract – Webb**, 3+1p appendix.
16 Oct	103	**Tariff commitments under the General Agreement on Tariffs and Trade which conflict with applications from the National Farmers Union for higher duties on fruit pulps etc. – Wilson**, 4+1p annex.
16 Oct	104	**Tariff commitments under the General Agreement on Tariffs and Trade which conflict with applications from the National Farmers Union for higher duties on seeds – Wilson**, 4p.
16 Oct	106	**Purchase of coarse grains from the U.S.S.R. – O.C. Morland covering K. Anderson**, 1+4+3p. Letter to Jay.

CAB 134/227   Memoranda   16 Oct–20 Dec 1950   EPC(50)107–138.

16 Oct	EPC(50)107	**The proposed international tin agreement – Wilson**, 2+7+2p appendixes +7p annex.
17 Oct	108	**Seventh session of the Customs Union Study Group. Instructions to be given to the U.K. delegation – Wilson**, 5+15p annexes.
25 Oct	109	**Financial discussions with Commonwealth ministers Sept 1950 – Gaitskell**, 7p.
27 Oct	110	**Commonwealth ministers' meeting on general economic and trade questions – Wilson**, 2p.
2 Nov	112	**Composition and terms of reference – N. Brook**, 1p.
3 Nov	113	**Agricultural wages and prices – Williams**, 6+2p appendix. Question of whether there should be a special review.
3 Nov	114	**Trade agreement with Pakistan – Wilson**, 1+5p appendix +4p annex.
7 Nov	115	**Suspension of E.R.P. – Bevin and Gaitskell covering the Mutual Aid Committee**, 1+4p.
8 Nov	116	**White Paper on full employment – Gaitskell**, 1p. Recommends the preparation of a draft White Paper to highlight lessons learnt since 1944.
9 Nov	117	**European grain discussions – Webb**, 3p.
11 Nov	118	**Argentine trade negotiations – Gaitskell covering the Overseas Negotiations Committee**, 1+5p.
18 Nov	119	**Internal economic situation – Gaitskell covering the Economic Section**, 1+3+7p appendix. Also EC(S)(50)54. Report for October.
21 Nov	120	**Prices of utility wool blankets – Wilson**, 2p.

1 Dec	**124**	**Wages and prices and full employment –** **Gaitskell**, 8p. Sets out the problems with the present system of wage settlement and summarizes possible alternatives in preparation for a meeting with the T.U.C.
2 Dec	**125**	**Raw materials – Gaitskell**, 1+5+11+8p annexes. Also ES(50)22. Sets out the action taken and suggests additional measures. The two main issues were: whether to intensify control and restrict inessential end uses of scarce materials, and whether to seek a long-term agreement with Commonwealth countries on the purchase of the whole wool clip.
2 Dec	**126**	**Raw materials – Strauss**, 1+3p.
8 Dec	**127**	**The dollar programme for 1951 – Gaitskell** **covering E.E. Bridges and the Programmes** **Committee**, 1+2+7+13p appendixes. Comments of the Official Committee on Economic Development on the report's recommendations, including the programme of $1,551m.
8 Dec	**128**	**Tariff-making machinery – Wilson**, 5+5p annexes.
8 Dec	**129**	**Gordon Gray report – Gaitskell covering the** **Economic Section**, 1+11p. Summary of the report to the U.S. President on foreign economic policies.
9 Dec	**130**	**Effect of shipping shortage on the softwood** **position – Wilson**, 2p.
11 Dec	**131**	**Effect of shipping shortage on the coal import** **position – Noel-Baker**, 3+1p annex. Recommends priority for coal in the first quarter of 1951.
14 Dec	**132**	**European grain discussions – Webb**, 2p.
15 Dec	**133**	**White fish imports – Gaitskell covering the** **London Committee**, 1+6+12p annexes.
15 Dec	**134**	**White fish imports – Williams and McNeil**, 3+1p appendix.
18 Dec	**137**	**Availability of dry cargo shipping – Barnes**, 4p.
20 Dec	**138**	**Coal – Noel-Baker**, 7+6p annexes. Decisions required before Christmas to avert possible fuel crisis.

CAB 134/228 Meetings 16 Jan–31 July 1951 EPC(51)1st–19th.

16 Jan	**EPC(51)1st:1**	**Availability of dry cargo shipping.** EPC(51)1.
	:2	**Coal.** EPC(51)2.
	:3	**Future of the Wool Joint Organization.** EPC(51)3.
2 Feb	**2nd**	**Food prices in 1951–52.** EPC(51)4 and 9 and CP(51)35.

27 Feb	**4th:1**	**Annual review of the agricultural industry.** EPC(51)14 and 17.
	:2	**Shipping for the U.K. bulk import programmes.** EPC(51)15.
	:3	**Allocated raw materials: restrictions on use.** EPC(51)16.
9 Mar	**5th:1**	**Television.** EPC(51)19.
	:2	**Full employment standard.** EPC(51)20. Paper accepted with minor amendments.
	:3	**Production of raw materials in the Colonial Empire.** EPC(51)18.
	:5	**National Institute of Houseworkers.** CP(51)66 and 69.
21 Mar	**6th:1**	**Procedure for special reviews.** EPC(51)21.
	:2	**Agricultural wage regulations.** EPC(51)23.
	:3	**Tariff-making machinery.** EPC(51)27.
	:5	**Tank production: Leyland agency factory.** EPC(51)26.
	:6	**Shortage of non-ferrous metals.** EPC(51)28.
	:8	**Sterling area imports from the dollar area.** EPC(51)24.
3 Apr	**7th:1**	**Machine tools for defence.** EPC(51)33.
	:5	**G.A.T.T. conference at Torquay.**
	:6	**Persian oil.**
17 Apr	**8th:3**	**Future of the Wool Joint Organization.** EPC(51)36.
	:4	**Trade talks with Cuba.** EPC(51)39.
	:5	**Draft White Paper on the agricultural price review for 1951.** EPC(51)38.
26 Apr	**9th**	**Stocks of raw material for steel making.** EPC(51)42 and 42 addendum.
15 May	**10th:1**	**Trade talks with Cuba.** EPC(51)47 and 49.
	:2	**Draft White Paper on the agricultural price review for 1951.** EPC(51)45.
	:3	**Labour requirements for Royal Ordnance factories at Swynnerton and Radway Green.** EPC(51)50.
	:4	**Control of factory and storage space.** EPC(51)40.
	:5	**Wage increases and the price sanction.** EPC(51)48. Agreement on departmental response to enquiries as to whether wage increases could be passed on as higher prices.
30 May	**11th:1**	**Trade talks with Cuba.** EPC(51)53.
	:2	**Proposed meeting of Commonwealth ministers concerned with supply and production.** EPC(51)52.
12 June	**12th:1**	**U.K. export objective.** EPC(51)55 and 56.
	:2	**The defence programme and material supplies.** EPC(51)57 and 58. No special priority supplies of steel for fuel and power industries.

26 June	13th:2	**Control of factory and storage premises.** EPC(51)60.
	:3	**Russian timber contract.** EPC(51)66.
	:5	**Economic policy and raw material prices.** EPC(51)61, 65, 68. Continuing support for subsidy policy.
3 July	14th:1	**Balance of payments for 1951–52.** EPC(51)63. A satisfactory balance of payments and increased exports were again of the highest priority.
	:2	**Economic policy.** EPC(51)65. Continuation of EPC(51)13th:5. Ministers should publicize the need for controls over prices and profits. Gaitskell was to announce government proposals to check the increase in the cost of living, in particular price controls.
10 July	15th:1	**Shipping for the U.K. bulk import programme.** EPC(51)67.
	:3	**Revision of iron and steel prices.** EPC(51)70.
	:4	**Consultation with the U.S. on raw material prices: wool.** EPC(51)71.
18 July	16th:1	**U.K.–Canada Continuing Committee on trade and economic affairs.** EPC(51)78.
	:2	**Purchase tax on utility-type imports.** EPC(51)76.
	:4	**Sterling area commodity prices.** EPC(51)81.
19 July	17th:1	**Price control.** EPC(51)84 and 86. Approval of further proposals.
	:2	**Retail grocers' margins.** EPC(51)73.
	:3	**Import cuts.** EPC(51)63 and 79.
24 July	18th:1	**Schuman Plan.** EPC(51)85.
	:2	**Proposed meeting of Commonwealth supply ministers.** EPC(51)87.
	:3	**Revision of iron and steel prices.** EPC(51)88.
31 July	19th:1	**Special review procedure and wage regulation in agriculture.** EPC(51)95.
	:2	**Meat supplies and animal feedingstuffs.** EPC(51)94 and 96.
	:4	**Development of aluminium production in the sterling area.** EPC(51)89.
	:5	**Machine tools for defence.** EPC(51)91.
	:6	**Steel exports.** EPC(51)90, 98, 99 and PC(51)98. Agreement to limit exports in the third quarter of 1951.
	:7	**Restriction of production on goods for home consumption.** EPC(51)97.
	:8	**Imports of coal.** EPC(51)92.

CAB 134/229 Memoranda 12 Jan–8 May 1951 EPC(51)1–50.

12 Jan	**EPC(51)1**	**Availability of dry cargo shipping – Barnes,** 1+2+2p appendix.

5 Jan	2	**Coal exports: further reduction – Noel-Baker covering the Official Coal Committee,** 1+3p. Acceptance of the Committee's recommendation to deter reductions.
5 Jan	3	**Future of the Wool Joint Organization – Wilson,** 3+2p annex.
10 Jan	4	**Food prices during 1951–52 – Webb,** 5p. Paper to be the basis of a consideration of the whole problem of the cost of living and wages spiral.
17 Jan	5	**The economic and social policies of the governments of Australia and New Zealand – Gordon Walker,** 1+9+4p annex.
18 Jan	7	**International tin conference 1950 – Griffiths and Strauss,** 1+5p. Report by the U.K., British Colonial and Dependent Territories Delegations.
23 Jan	8	**Composition of the Committee – N. Brook,** 1p.
25 Jan	9	**Food prices during 1951–52 – Williams,** 2p. Criticism of EPC(51)4.
9 Feb	12	**Tariff preferences and the Torquay negotiations – Wilson,** 5+1p annex.
24 Feb	14	**Farm price review 1951 – Williams and McNeil,** 3p.
23 Feb	15	**Shipping for the U.K. bulk dry cargo import programmes – Barnes,** 1+5p.
23 Feb	16	**Allocated raw materials: restrictions on use – Gaitskell covering the Treasury,** 1+5p. Line to be taken by the U.K. in negotiations with the U.S.A.
23 Feb	17	**Annual review under Part I of the Agriculture Act 1947 – Gaitskell covering the Agricultural Output Committee,** 1+1+12+3p appendixes.
26 Feb	18	**Production of raw materials in the colonial Empire – Griffiths,** 5+12p appendixes.
27 Feb	19	**Television – Gaitskell,** 4p. Issue of whether transmitting stations should be built given the economic situation.
1 Mar	20	**Full employment standard – Gaitskell,** 2+1p annex. Proposal of a standard of 3%.
7 Mar	21	**Proposal for special reviews of farm prices – Williams,** 4p.
8 Mar	23	**Agricultural wage regulation – Williams,** 1+11p annex +1p appendix.
12 Mar	24	**Sterling area imports from the dollar area – Gaitskell,** 2+1p annex.
14 Mar	26	**Tank production: Leyland agency factory – Wilson,** 4p. Officials were unable to agree on the factory location.
14 Mar	27	**Tariff-making machinery – Wilson,** 3p.
18 Mar	28	**Non-ferrous metal shortages and their effect on rearmament and the economy – Strauss,** 5+7p

appendixes. Serious prospective shortages required high level representation to the U.S.A.

19 Mar	32	**Meat supplies – Webb**, 3p.
27 Mar	33	**Machine tools for defence – Gaitskell covering the Committee on Productive Capacity**, 1+7p. Also ES(51)22. Interim report on machine tools and industrial capacity.
3 Apr	36	**Future of the Wool Joint Organization – Wilson**, 3p.
13 Apr	38	**Draft White Paper on the agricultural price review for 1951 – Gaitskell, Williams, McNeil and Webb**, 1+1+16+6p appendixes. Also ES(51)28. Draft attached.
14 Apr	39	**Trade talks with Cuba – Wilson**, 4+3p annex.
17 Apr	40	**Control of factory and storage premises – Wilson**, 3p.
23 Apr	41	**Sulphur and sulphuric acid – Wilson**, 1+9p annexes.
24 Apr	42	**Stocks of raw materials for steel making – Strauss**, 1+1+2p addendum. Draft statement.
24 Apr	43	**Impact of the defence programme on civilian building projects – Gaitskell covering the Headquarters Building Committee**, 1+1+5p appendix. No adverse impact yet, but gathering problems.
27 Apr	44	**Schuman Plan. Reply to the French invitation to hold discussions with H.M.G. – Gaitskell covering the Working Party on Proposed Franco-German Coal and Steel Authority**, 1+1+8p. Also ES(51)29 and FG(WP)(51)14(revise).
3 May	45	**Draft White Paper on the agricultural price review for 1951 – Williams**, 1+17p. Revised draft attached.
7 May	46	**Defence production: conversations with Mr. Charles Wilson – Gaitskell**, 1+3+4p.
8 May	47	**Trade talks with Cuba – Shawcross**, 3p.
8 May	48	**Wages increases and the prices sanction – Shawcross and Webb**, 5p. Prices sanction was now unmanageable as wage restraint had broken down.
7 May	49	**Trade talks with Cuba – Griffiths**, 2p.
8 May	50	**Labour requirements at the Royal Ordnance factories, Swynnerton and Radway Green – Gaitskell covering the Official Committee on Productive Capacity**, 1+4p. Also CPC(51)18. Conflict of labour demands of the Royal Ordnance factories with production of pottery for export.

CAB 134/230   Memoranda   17 May–30 July 1951   EPC(51)51–99.

17 May	**EPC(51)51**	**U.K. submission for the Nitze exercise –** **Gaitskell,** 1+16p. 'The burden of defence on the U.K.' attached.
25 May	**52**	**Proposed meeting of Commonwealth ministers concerned with supply and production – Gordon Walker,** 7+2p annex.
28 May	**53**	**Trade talks with Cuba: visit of Secretary for Overseas Trade to the West Indies – Shawcross,** 3+7p annex +1p appendix.
31 May	**55**	**U.K. export objective – Gaitskell and Shawcross,** 1+6+10p appendixes.
5 June	**56**	**Imports and exports in January–April 1951 – Gaitskell and Shawcross,** 1+4+3p annexes.
8 June	**57**	**The fuel and power requirements of the defence programme – Noel-Baker,** 3+2p annex. Fuel and power should be given higher priority than in EPC(51)58.
8 June	**58**	**The defence programme and material supplies – Gaitskell,** 5p. Recommends the preparation of plans for further detailed allocation of steel and non-ferrous metals. In the interim the Defence Order system for certain defence contracts and preferential treatment for selected civil orders should be introduced.
8 June	**60**	**Control of factory and storage premises – Gaitskell,** 3p.
18 June	**61**	**Price policy on raw material imports – Gaitskell and Stokes covering an official working party,** 1+5p.
19 June	**62**	**Sterling area imports for the dollar area: first quarter 1951 – Gaitskell,** 1+1p appendix.
22 June	**63**	**Balance of payments for 1951–52 – Gaitskell covering the Programmes Committee,** 1+3+8+29p annex +5p appendixes. Also EPB(51)13 and ES(51)40. Note by E.N. Plowden covering the comments of the Economic Steering Committee and the Economic Planning Board and the report itself, setting out measures to prevent a balance of payments crisis within the next few years.
22 June	**65**	**Economic policy – Gaitskell,** 11p. Recommends pegging import prices through international commodity agreements, price control, credit policy, subsidies, wages and dividends policy, and revaluation.
25 June	**66**	**Russian timber contract – Bottomley,** 2p.
27 June	**67**	**Shipping for the U.K. bulk dry cargo import programme – Barnes,** 1+3p. Third report of the official committee.

26 June	68	**Raw materials prices. Proposed discussion in Washington – Gaitskell and Stokes,** 1+2p.
3 July	69	**Subcommittee on the Location of Defence Projects. Terms of reference and composition – N. Brook,** 1p.
6 July	70	**Revision of iron and steel prices – Strauss,** 6+2p annexes.
7 July	71	**Raw materials discussion in Washington. Wool – Stokes,** 1+11+8p appendixes.
10 July	73	**Retail grocers' margins – Webb,** 2p.
16 July	76	**Pruchase tax on utility-type imports – Shawcross,** 7+1p annex.
16 July	78	**U.K.–Canada Continuing Committee on trade and economic affairs – Gaitskell covering U.K. members,** 2+12+7p annexes.
16 July	79	**Import cuts – Gaitskell covering the Programmes Committee,** 1+6+1p annex. Recommended cuts for 1951–52.
17 July	80	**Import programme 1951–52 – Webb,** 2p. Disagreement with the reduction in food imports proposed in EPC(51)79.
16 July	81	**Sterling area commodity prices – Gaitskell covering the Treasury,** 1+3+3p appendix.
17 July	82	**U.K. tin purchases – Stokes,** 3p.
17 July	84	**Proposals in regard to prices, profits, production and distribution – Shawcross,** 11p. Proposed action on price control and restrictive practices.
17 July	85	**Report by the Economic Steering Committee on the Schuman Plan – Gaitskell covering the Economic Steering Committee,** 1+4+50+23p appendixes +48p. Also ED(51)45 and FG(WP)(51)30(final). Includes a report by an official working party on the plan.
18 July	86	**Price controls – Gaitskell,** 4+2p annex. Means of tightening up controls.
20 July	87	**Proposed meeting of Commonwealth ministers concerned with supply and production – Gordon Walker,** 3+2p annexes.
20 July	88	**Revision of iron and steel prices – Strauss,** 2+10p appendix.
26 July	89	**Development of aluminium production in the sterling area – Griffiths and Stokes,** 3+5p annexes.
26 July	90	**Steel exports and colonial requirements – Griffiths,** 3p.
27 July	91	**Machine tools for defence – Gaitskell covering E.A. Shillito covering the Ministry of Supply,** 1+1+6p.
27 July	92	**Imports of coal – Noel-Baker,** 5p. Grave danger of a shortage of large coal which only imports could remedy.

27 July	94	**Meat supplies – Webb,** 5+8p appendix +3p annex. Prospects to 1955 and resulting proposals.
27 July	95	**Special review procedure and wage regulation in agriculture – McNeil and Williams covering an official working party of the Agricultural Output Committee,** 2+10p. Also ES(51)51.
27 July	96	**Animal feedingstuffs – McNeil and Williams,** 2+3p appendix.
28 July	97	**Restriction of production of goods for home consumption – Gaitskell,** 2p. Need to consider restriction of such production and discouragement of labour from entering inessential industries.
30 July	98	**Exports of steel – Shawcross,** 4+2p.
30 July	99	**Steel exports and colonial requirements – Gaitskell,** 2p.

15.14   Economic Steering Committee

Set up by Attlee in the administrative reorganization of October 1950, occasioned by the Korean War rearmament programme, to co-ordinate the work of all official committees considering the economic consequences of defence expenditure (as detailed in ES(50)1). It was therefore responsible for ensuring the co-ordination of civil and military demands on the economy, in particular the consequences of the immediate and medium-term defence programmes and Britain's membership of N.A.T.O.

It replaced the Official Committee on Economic Development and its Working Group (CAB 134/186–193, 202–203) and played a far more active role than that committee. It also took over the work of the informal group on the National Economy in War Committee and that of the whole Committee when it was disbanded in April 1951 (CAB 130/59, GEN 317). It was served by a Subcommittee on Prices.

It reported to the Economic Policy Committee (CAB 134/215–230) and the Production Committee (CAB 134/635–652). Its later papers are in CAB 134/884–889.

Terms   (i) to report to the Economic Policy Committee on questions of internal or external policy, and generally on the use to be made of the nation's economic resources   (ii) to advise ministers on the economic implications of defence policy and on the means of meeting defence requirements.

Members   E.E Bridges (Try, ch.); E.N. Plowden (C.E.P.S., dep. ch.); B.W. Gilbert (Try); H. Parker (M.O.D.); G. Ince (Lab. & N.S.); J.H. Woods (B.T.); A. Rowlands (Supply); R. Makins (F.O.); N. Brook (Cab. O.); D. Fergusson (Fuel & P.); E.M. Nicholson (Ld Pres. O.); R.L. Hall (Ec. Sect.).

Secs.   O.C. Morland (Cab. O.) and J.A. Atkinson (Cab. O.).

CAB 134/263   Meetings and Memoranda   17 Oct–23 Dec 1950   ES(50)1st–10th and ES(50)1–30.

Meetings

| 26 Oct | **ES(50)1st:1** | **Constitution, procedure and programme of work.** ES(50)1. |

	:2	**Defence statistics.** ES(50)2.
	:3	**Materials in short supply.** ES(50)4.
	:4	**Allied economic mobilization.** ES(50)3. Agreement on administrative arrangements.
	:5	**The finance of defence. DO(50)91.**
	:6	**Requirements of the service departments for works staffs.**
2 Nov	2nd:1	**Committee structure.**
	:2	**Fuel supply outlook.** ES(50)5. An official committee to be set up.
	:3	**Requests for U.S. assistance in the form of end-items.** ES(50)6.
	:4	**Meeting with representatives of the F.B.I.**
	:5	**Placing of orders under the defence programme.**
9 Nov	3rd	**International discussion of raw material questions.** ES(50)7.
16 Nov	4th:1	**Raw materials outlook.** ES(50)8.
	:2	**Defence and shortages.** ES(50)9.
22 Nov	5th	**Raw materials.** ES(50)14. Recommendation for discussions with France prior to those with the U.S.A.
23 Nov	6th:1	**Statistical report on rearmament.** ES(50)15. To be quarterly reports.
	:2	**Information to industry on rearmament.**
	:3	**Germany's industrial contribution to Western European defence.** ES(50)12.
	:4	**Gordon Gray report.** ES(50)13.
13 Nov	7th:1	**Korea.**
	:2	**Measures for dealing with raw material shortages.** ES(50)17.
	:3	**Information to industry about the defence programme.** The Treasury to consider the advisability of a public statement on the government's intention to proceed with the £3,600m defence programme.
	:4	**Imports of coal: shipping difficulties.** An inter-departmental committee to be appointed.
	:5	**Placing of defence orders in Europe.**
	:6	**Purchase of machine tools from the U.S.A.**
7 Dec	8th:1	**Dollar programme for 1951.** ES(50)25. Agreement on recommendations to ministers.
	:2	**Full employment standard.** ES(50)24. Ministers to be advised to seek the opposition's agreement on the standard, which they recommended should be a ceiling of 4%.
	:3	**N.A.T.O. and the Commonwealth.** ES(50)23.
14 Dec	9th:1	**Requests from overseas governments and international bodies for technical experts.** ES(50)19 and 27.
	:2	**Increased placing of defence orders in Europe.** ES(50)26.

15 Dec	**10th**	**The economic outlook and the general balance of payments in 1951.** ES(50)28 and 29. Agreement on advice to ministers, particularly on the consequences of not reaching the assumed 4% increase in industrial production.

Memoranda

17 Oct	**ES(50)1**	**Official committees dealing with defence and economic policy** – N. Brook, 3+4p annexes.
24 Oct	**2**	**Defence statistics** – E.E. Bridges, 1p. Need for regular information on the progress of rearmament.
24 Oct	**3**	**Allied economic mobilization** – O.C. Morland and J.A. Atkinson, 2p.
25 Oct	**4**	**Materials in short supply** – E.N. Plowden and R.L. Hall, 2p. Recommends a review of administrative procedure and policy.
31 Oct	**5**	**The fuel supply outlook** – D. Fergusson, 6p. Supplies appeared insufficient to meet the increasing industrial activity planned to 1955 and the defence programme would accentuate the shortage. A fuel crisis could occur that winter.
1 Nov	**6**	**Requests for U.S. assistance in the form of end-items** – Treasury, 1p.
9 Nov	**7**	**International discussion of raw material questions** – F.F. Turnbull, 3p.
14 Nov	**8**	**The raw materials outlook** – F.F. Turnbull, 6+5p annex. Also RM(50)9(final). General survey concluding that the U.S.A. had to modify its present policies, including stock-piling, if substantial shortages were to be avoided.
14 Nov	**9**	**Defence and shortages** – Board of Trade, 2p. Urgent need for something more than *ad hoc* solutions.
15 Nov	**10**	**Preparation of general economic reports** – E.E. Bridges, 1p. Four were to be prepared in the next few months.
15 Nov	**11**	*Plan for Coal* – **D. Fergusson covering the N.C.B.,** 1+76p. Draft plan.
20 Nov	**12**	**Germany's industrial contribution to Western European defence** – Foreign Office, 1+9+16p annexes.
20 Nov	**13**	**Report to the President on foreign economic policies** – R.L. Hall covering the Economic Section, 1+11p. Also EC(S)(50)55. Summary of the Gordon Gray report.
22 Nov	**14**	**Raw materials** – O.C. Morland and J.A. Atkinson, 1+8+2p annex. Revise version. Also RM(50)23. Draft brief for Gaitskell's meetings with the French.

21 Nov	**15**	**Report on rearmament – C.S.O.,** 6+6p appendix. Progress report.
22 Nov	**16**	**Raw materials – O.C. Morland and J.A. Atkinson,** 1+2p. Draft covering note for ES(50)14(revise).
23 Nov	**17**	**Measures for dealing with raw material shortages – F.F. Turnbull,** 1+7p. Also RM(50)20. Report on measures for internal and international allocation.
23 Nov	**18**	**Raw materials – O.C. Morland and J.A. Atkinson,** 1+10+2p annex. Also RM(50)24. Final version of ES(50)14(revise) and 16.
27 Nov	**19**	**Requests from overseas governments and international bodies for technical experts – Ministry of Labour,** 3p.
28 Nov	**20**	**White Paper on full employment – E.E. Bridges,** 1p. To be prepared by C.E.P.S., in consultation with the Economic Section assisted by a small working party under R.L. Hall, for possible publication in spring 1951.
30 Nov	**21**	**Imports of coal: shipping difficulties – E.N. Plowden,** 1p.
2 Dec	**22**	**Report on the raw materials situation – E.E. Bridges,** 5+19p annexes. Issue of intensifying controls and restricting inessential end uses of scarce materials. Report by the Raw Materials Committee on the shortage of principal raw materials and probable consequences for the U.K. and extracts from reports on U.K. and U.S. internal remedies.
4 Dec	**23**	**N.A.T.O. and the Commonwealth – O.C. Morland and J.A. Atkinson,** 1+18+4p annex.
5 Dec	**24**	**Full employment standard – E.E. Bridges,** 2+2+3p appendix. Recommendation of a ceiling of 4% unemployment at the seasonal peak.
5 Dec	**25**	**The dollar programme for 1951 – R.W.B. Clarke,** 1+10+16p appendixes. Also T(50)43. Draft of EPC(50)127.
5 Dec	**26**	**Increased placing of defence orders in Europe – Treasury,** 5+1p appendix.
6 Dec	**27**	**Requests from overseas governments and international bodies for technical experts – Ministry of Education,** 3p.
9 Dec	**28**	**U.K. general balance of payments for 1951 – R.W.B. Clarke covering the Programmes Committee,** 7+17p appendix +13p annexes. Also P(50)45. A balance of the current account should be the basis of policy during the period of worsening terms of trade and rearmament.

13 Dec	29	**Economic outlook for 1951 – O.C. Morland and J.A. Atkinson,** 1+21p. See EPB(50)20. Also EC(S)(50)60.
23 Dec	30	**Economic implications of rearmament to colonial territories – Colonial Office,** 3+7p annexes.

CAB 134/264   Meetings and Memoranda   11 Jan–22 Nov 1951   ES(51)1st–24th and ES(51)1–16.

Meetings

11 Jan	**ES(51)1st:1**	**Economic implications of rearmament to colonial territories.** ES(50)30.
	:2	**Requests from overseas governments and international bodies for technical experts.**
25 Jan	2nd:1	**Third report of the O.E.E.C.** ES(51)2. Problems for the defence programme needed highlighting.
	:2	**Economic policy towards Europe.** ES(51)1.
	:3	**Economic Survey for 1951.** ES(51)3.
	:4	**Enquiries of government departments by U.S. officials.**
8 Feb	3rd:1	**Arms production in Europe.** ES(51)5.
	:2	**Comprehensive reimposition of price controls.** ES(51)6. General agreement with paper but controls should be restored or introduced only when the need arose.
15 Feb	4th:1	**Report on rearmament.** ES(51)8.
	:2	**Export policy in relation to negotiations on raw materials with the U.S.A.** ES(51)9 and 10.
	:3	**Long-term economic relations with Japan.** ES(51)7.
22 Feb	5th:1	**Report on development of economic controls.** ES(51)13. Agreement such reports should be regular and also cover voluntary controls and informal agreements with industry.
	:2	**Financial co-operation with the U.S.A. and the Commonwealth in a total war.** NEW(51)2.
	:3	**Wage increases and the prices sanction.** ES(51)12. Need to draw ministers' attention to the problems faced by production departments.
23 Feb	6th:1	**Annual review under Part I of the Agricultural Act, 1947.** ES(51)15.
	:2	**Supplies of cereal feedingstuffs.** ES(51)11.
1 Mar	7th:1	**Procedure for U.S. assistance in the form of end-items.** ES(51)16.
	:2	**Objectives of the Nitze exercise.** ES(51)17.
	:3	**Report on rearmament.** ES(51)8. A. Rowlands concerned with slow resolution of conflicts between defence and civil requirements.
5 Mar	8th	**Future raw materials policy.** ES(51)18 and 19.

12 Mar	9th	**Economic Survey for 1951.** ES(51)20. Consideration in detail.
15 Mar	10th:1	**Machine tools for defence.** ES(51)22.
	:2	**Anglo-U.S. economic relations: statement by Sir Oliver Franks.**
5 Apr	11th:1	**Development of economic controls.** ES(51)23.
	:2	**Raw materials position in Washington.** Progress report by Viscount Knollys.
12 Apr	12th:1	**Capital investment in 1951, 1952 and 1953.** ES(51)24. Approval of an estimated 5% increase in the building industry's productivity followed by consideration of individual programmes.
	:2	**Impact of the defence programme on civilian building projects.** ES(51)26.
	:3	**Technical manpower for the defence programme.** ES(51)27.
	:4	**Draft White Paper on the agricultural price review for 1951.** ES(51)28.
24 Apr	13th	**Schuman plan: implications for the U.K.** ES(51)29 and 30.
1 May	14th:1	**Raw materials: discussions with the U.S.A.** ES(51)32 and 34.
	:2	**Shipment of iron ore.**
24 May	15th:1	**Limitation of civil output in the metal-using industries.** ES(51)31.
	:2	**The U.K. export objective.** ES(51)37. It was too soon to consider either revising the planning assumption that production in 1951 would be more than 4% above 1950 or abandoning the objective of balancing the external accounts.
	:3	**Report on the economic situation in the U.S.A.**
14 June	16th:1	**Report on rearmament.** ES(51)36. The report in future would consider the impact of rearmament on the civilian economy.
	:2	**Australian wartime production of food and raw materials.** ES(51)39.
21 June	17th:1	**Future raw materials policy.** ES(51)41.
	:2	**Balance of payments for 1951–52.** ES(51)40 and 43. Agreement to advise ministers the situation was serious and likely to worsen, necessitating precautionary measures.
28 June	18th:1	**Supply organization in the Middle East in the event of war.** ES(51)42.
	:2	**Australian wartime production of food and raw materials.** ES(51)44.
	:3	**Raw materials discussions in Washington.** Update by Viscount Knollys.
9 July	19th	**The Schuman Treaty.** ES(51)45.
13 July	20th	**East/West trade.** ES(51)47.
25 July	21st	**Service production programme 1951/54.** ES(51)49 and JWPC/P(51)72(final).

Agreement to advise ministers that the economic departments considered that the J.W.P.C. programme implied a greater impact on the economy than had been envisaged when the £4,700m programme had been approved. The economy was not so well able to support the defence programme as had been earlier expected.

11 Oct	**22nd:1**	**The bargaining strength of the U.K. in respect of exports to the rest of the independent sterling Commonwealth.** ES(51)50.
	:2	**Economic outlook for 1952.** ES(51)53.
	:3	**Quarterly report on rearmament.** ES(51)52. General view that the paper was superseded by the report on economic prospects in 1952.
25 Oct	**23rd:1**	**Report on economic prospects for 1952.** ES(51)57, 59, 60, 61, 62, 63, 64, 65. ES(51)57 was to be redrafted by C.E.P.S. to identify more clearly possible courses of action.
22 Nov	**24th:1**	**Manpower in a future war.** ES(51)68. Agreement that the deficiency of manpower revealed in the report brought out the urgent need to reconsider the estimated requirements on which it was based.
	:2	**The labour situation in the Coventry area in relation to the defence programme.** ES(51)69.

Memoranda

23 Jan	**ES(51)1**	**Policy towards Europe – O.C. Morland covering the Treasury and Board of Trade,** 1+7p.
23 Jan	**2**	**Third report of the O.E.E.C. – O.C. Morland and J.A. Atkinson,** 1+24+16p appendixes. Review of economic development in 1950 and prospects for 1951.
24 Jan	**3**	**Economic Survey for 1951 – E.N. Plowden,** 2p. Timetable for preparation.
30 Jan	**4**	**Agricultural Output Committee – O.C. Morland and J.A. Atkinson,** 1+1p.
5 Feb	**5**	**Arms production in Europe – H. Parker,** 3p.
6 Feb	**6**	**Comprehensive reimposition of price controls – Subcommittee on Prices,** 5+4p annexes. ES(SP)(51)5. General review recommending the selective imposition of lapsed or new controls.
6 Feb	**7**	**Long-term economic relations with Japan – E.N. Plowden covering the Working Party on Long-term Economic Relations with Japan,** 1+4+22+26p annexes.
13 Feb	**8**	**Report on rearmament – C.S.O.,** 4+8p appendix. Progress report.
13 Feb	**9**	**General line to be taken by the U.K. in negotiations with the U.S.A. on raw materials**

allocations, with particular reference to export policy – E.N. Plowden covering C.E.P.S, 1+4p. Also RM(51)54.

14 Feb	**10**	**O.E.E.C. harmonization of raw material control** – E.A. Shillito, 1+4p. Also RM(51)32(final).
16 Feb	**11**	**Supplies of cereal feedingstuffs – Chairman of the Agricultural Output Committee covering the Working Party on Cereal Feedingstuffs Supplies,** 1+10+5p appendix.
20 Feb	**12**	**Wage increases and the prices sanction –** Subcommittee on Prices, 4p. Also ES(SP)(51)6.
20 Feb	**13**	**Reports on development of economic controls –** E.N. Plowden, 1p. Request from T.L. Rowan for monthly reports to be sent to Washington.
20 Feb	**14**	**Export policy in relation to negotiations on raw materials with the U.S.A.** – O.C. Morland and J.A. Atkinson, 1+1p. Also RM(51)54. E.E. Bridges submission to Gaitskell on ES(51)9.
21 Feb	**15**	**Annual review under Part I of the Agricultural Act, 1947 – Chairman of the Agricultural Output Committee,** 1+27+5p appendixes.
26 Feb	**16**	**Report on the procedure for U.S. assistance in the form of end-items – Chairman of the Mutual Aid Committee,** 5+4p annexes.

CAB 134/265 Memoranda 27 Feb–19 June 1951 ES(51)17–43.

27 Feb	**ES(51)17**	**Objectives of the Nitze exercises – E.A. Hitchman,** 1+6p annexes. The Mutual Aid Committee could not agree on whether to seek aid from the U.S.A. in terms of specific goods for the defence programme or general support.
1 Mar	**18**	**Future raw materials policy – E.N. Plowden,** 1+4p. See PC(51)31. Also RM(51)75.
3 Mar	**19**	**The raw materials situation. Progress report no. 1: February 1951 – R.S. Buer covering the Raw Materials Committee,** 1+2+26p annexes. See PC(51)29. Also RM(51)52(final).
7 Mar	**20**	**Economic Survey for 1951 – E.N. Plowden,** 1+37+22p appendix. See EPB(51)5.
8 Mar	**21**	**Note of an *ad hoc* meeting on the forthcoming discussions in Washington on tin, held on Wednesday 7 March 1951 at 3.30 p.m.,** 3p. Also RM(51)69.
12 Mar	**22**	**Machine tools for defence – E.A. Shillito covering the Committee on Productive Capacity,** 1+7p. See EPC(51)33.
21 Mar	**23**	**Development of economic controls – O.C. Morland and J.A. Atkinson covering the Economic Section,** 1+1+12p appendixes. First

in a series of quarterly reports with monthly supplements.

2 Apr   **24**   **Capital investment in 1951, 1952 and 1953 – E.N. Plowden covering the Investment Programmes Committee**, 1+73+2p appendix. See PC(51)49. Also EPB(51)6 and IPC(51)1.

5 Apr   **25**   **Reorganization of committees concerned with defence and economic questions – N. Brook**, 2p. Also NEW(51) 4 and DTC(51)15.

6 Apr   **26**   **Impact of the defence programme on civilian building projects – H.C. Emmerson covering the Headquarters Building Committee**, 1+2+4p. Review of regional building committees' reports.

6 Apr   **27**   **Technical manpower for the defence programme – H.C. Emmerson covering the Headquarters Building Committee**, 1+6p. See PC(51)52.

7 Apr   **28**   **Draft White Paper on the agricultural price review for 1951 – Chairman of the Agricultural Output Committee**, 2+15+5p appendixes. See EPC(51)38.

20 Apr   **29**   **Schuman Plan – Working Party on Proposed Franco-German Coal and Steel Authority**, 8p. See EPC(51)44. Also FG(WP)(51)14(revise).

23 Apr   **30**   **Schuman Plan Treaty: summary of provisions – O.C. Morland and J.A. Atkinson covering the Working Party on Proposed Franco-German Coal and Steel Authority**, 1+13p. Also FG(WP)(51)11(2nd revise).

26 Apr   **31**   **Limitation of civil output in the metal-using industries – Committee on Productive Capacity**, 9+3p appendixes. Also CPC(51)10(final). Interim report.

27 Apr   **32**   **High-level approach on raw materials to the U.S. authorities – F.F. Turnbull**, 2+2+17+5p appendix +5p addendum. Also RM(51)101(final).

2 May   **33**   **Development of economic controls: supplementary report for March and April 1951 – O.C. Morland and J.A. Atkinson covering the Economic Section**, 1+2p.

30 Apr   **34**   **Economic expansion and raw materials supply – C.E.P.S.**, 5+4p annex. The free world's expansion plans were incompatible with potential supply. U.S. reaction was vital.

8 May   **35**   **High-level approach on raw materials to the U.S. authorities – O.C. Morland and J.A. Atkinson**, 1+18+5p appendix +6p annexes. Also RM(51)119. Revision of ES(51)32.

22 May   **36**   **Report on rearmament – C.S.O.**, 5+8p appendix. Progress to the end of March.

22 May	37	**U.K. export objective – C.E.P.S. covering Board of Trade**, 1+9+14p appendixes. Measures to increase exports of consumer goods.
8 June	38	**Development of economic controls: supplementary report for May 1951 – O.C. Morland and J.A. Atkinson covering the Economic Section**, 1+2p.
12 June	39	**Australian wartime production of food and raw materials – Commonwealth Relations Office**, 2+2p.
15 June	40	**Balance of payments for 1951–52 – R.W.B. Clarke**, 1+8+36p annex +5p appendixes. See EPC(51)63. Also EPB(51)13.
18 June	41	**Future raw materials policy – Raw Materials Committee**, 5+5p appendix. See PC(51)78. Also RM(51)127(final).
18 June	42	**Supply position in the Middle East in the event of war – Foreign Office**, 3p.
19 June	43	**Balance of payments for 1951–52 – E.N. Plowden**, 2p. Possible measures to improve the situation. Whilst the balance of payments since 1950 had been of secondary importance it was now once again a major problem.

CAB 134/266   Memoranda   26 June–17 Dec 1951   ES(51)44–73.

26 June	ES(51)44	**Australian wartime production of food and raw materials – E.N. Plowden covering the Working Party**, 1+7+2p annex.
3 July	45	**The Schuman Treaty – E.N. Plowden covering the Working Party on the Schuman Treaty**, 1+50+23p appendixes +48p. See EPC(51)85. Also FG(WP)(51)30(final).
6 July	46	**Development of economic controls Jan–June 1951 – O.C. Morland and J.A. Atkinson covering the Economic Section**, 1+1+10p appendixes.
12 July	47	**East/West trade – Foreign Office covering the U.K. delegation to the tripartite talks**, 2+6+18p annexes. See EPC(51)75.
24 July	48	**Bank/Fund: 6th annual meeting – Treasury**, 1+2+11+6p appendix +3+4+9p. Also US/GEN(51)1, 2, 3 and US/BF(51)6. Briefs for the meeting.
24 July	49	**Service production programme 1951–54 – Ministry of Defence**, 1+18+1p annex. Also JWPC/P(51)72.
31 July	50	**The bargaining strength of the U.K. in respect of exports to the rest of the independent sterling Commonwealth – Commonwealth Economic Affairs Committee**, 5+4p appendix.

3 Aug	51	**Report of the Official Working Party on Special Price Review Procedure and Weight Regulation in Agriculture – D.E. Vandepeer,** 1+10p. See EPC(51)95.
22 Aug	52	**Quarterly report on rearmament – C.S.O.,** 7+9p appendix.
7 Sept	53	**Economic outlook for 1952 – W. Strath,** 2p. Review needed owing to poor position of present balance of payments.
10 Sept	54	**Development of economic controls July and August 1951 – O.C. Morland and J.A. Atkinson covering Economic Section,** 1+2p.
13 Sept	55	**Review of invisible receipts and expenditure – Treasury,** 1+2p.
18 Sept	56	**Review of invisible receipts and expenditure – O.C. Morland and J.A. Atkinson,** 1p.
29 Oct	57	**Report on economic prospects for 1952 – O.C. Morland and J.A. Atkinson covering C.E.P.S.,** 1+18p. Final version. Part I – Present trends in the economic situation: the growth and balance of production, the balance of payments, manpower, wages and prices, consumer demand, summary and conclusions. Part II – Possible remedies: (a) measures to reduce the general strain, (b) action on specific weaknesses, (c) the external gap, (d) conclusions. Concludes that internal and external gaps will not be fully closed even if ministers adopt suggested remedies. If the defence programme were implemented at the pace planned, the external gap could not be closed without substantial U.S. support. Officials needed immediate guidance.
19 Oct	58	**Development of economic controls July–Sept 1951 – O.C. Morland and J.A. Atkinson covering the Economic Section,** 1+1+10p appendixes.
19 Oct	59	**Balance of payments for 1952 – O.C. Morland and J.A. Atkinson covering the Programmes Committee,** 1+12+8p annex +10p appendix. Six-monthly review in three parts: (a) appraisal of the present situation and the possible course of events in 1952; (b) the considerations which called for immediate action; (c) discussion of possible lines of remedial action. Measures suggested would reduce the deficit to £150m–200m p.a.; further reductions would cause serious damage to the economy or international complications.
19 Oct	60	**Report on U.K. export prospects – O.C. Morland and J.A. Atkinson covering the Board of Trade,** 1+11+4p appendix. Sets out the

		estimated level of export earnings and the problems hindering expansion.
19 Oct	61	**Report on investment in 1951 and 1952 – O.C. Morland and J.A. Atkinson covering the Investment Programmes Committee,** 1+8+14p appendixes. Also IPC(51)5 and GEN 380/9. Review of 1951 and prospects for 1952. Given the overload, the report recommended the review of all starting dates to become effective before mid-January and to suspend until then approval of new starting dates for work in 1952. The programme for 1952 and 1953 should be reviewed as soon as possible.
19 Oct	62	**Report on the restriction of the production of goods for home consumption – O.C. Morland and J.A. Atkinson,** 1+7+32p annexes. Sets out measures to release 160,000 workers and resources for defence and export production.
24 Oct	63	**Report on invisible receipts and expenditure – O.C. Morland and J.A. Atkinson covering the Treasury,** 1+9+52p appendixes. Assessment of invisibles' contribution to closing the balance of payments gap.
22 Oct	64	**Report on exports of key commodities in 1952 – O.C. Morland and J.A. Atkinson covering the Overseas Negotiations Committee,** 1+14+10p annexes. Also ON(51)137(second revise). Sets out the level of exports necessary to meet commitments.
22 Oct	65	**Report on manpower problems – O.C. Morland and J.A. Atkinson covering the Ministry of Labour,** 1+5+1p appendix. Review of the existing situation, current and possible future measures, including labour supply inspection and the control of engagement.
23 Oct	66	**Allocation of steel – F.F Turnbull,** 7+7p annexes. Also M(51)64. Proposals for allocation of general steel.
24 Oct	67	**Statistical estimates for general steel consumption in 1952 – O.C. Morland and J.A. Atkinson covering C.E.P.S.,** 1+3+3p annexes. Also M(51)61.
12 Nov	68	**Manpower in a future war – Manpower Committee,** 5p. Also MP(51)12(final). Interim report.
19 Nov	69	**Labour situation in the Coventry area in relation to the defence programme – E.A. Shillito,** 1+9p. Also CPC(51)81(revise).
1 Dec	70	**The labour situation in the Preston–Chorley–Blackburn area – E.A. Shillito,** 1+10p. Also CPC(51)83(revise).

6 Dec	**71**	**Labour situation in the Preston–Chorley–Blackburn area – O.C. Morland and J.A. Atkinson,** 1p.
18 Dec	**72**	**Quarterly report on rearmament – C.S.O.,** 7+8p appendix.
17 Dec	**73**	**Development of economic controls Oct–Nov 1951 – O.C. Morland and J.A. Atkinson covering the Economic Section,** 1+1+3p appendixes.

15.15 Economic Survey Working Party

Set up in 1945 as one of the working parties serving the Official Steering Committee on Economic Development (CAB 134/186–193) to draft the annual economic survey. Under the chairmanship of R.L. Hall (Ec. Sect.). Membership was fluid and drawn mainly from the Economic Section, C.S.O. and, after 1947, C.E.P.S. The minutes of the one formal meeting in 1948 are in T 230/144 and other working papers can be found in T 230 and CAB 139.

CAB 134/267   Memoranda only   23 Apr–30 Dec 1948   ESWP(48)1–21.

nd	**ESWP(48)1**	**Long-term forecasts of British foreign trade and the pattern of British industry** – unsigned, 1p. Method of approach.
23 Apr	**2**	**Working population, productivity and the national income. The general economic background of the 1950s** – P. Jeffries, 1+25p. Also LDS(WP)(48)6.
24 Apr	**3**	**Corrigenda to Tables V and VI of ESWP(48)2** – unsigned, 1p. Revise version.
30 Apr	**4**	**U.K. exports in the early 1950s** – P. Jeffries, 1+12p. Summary of pre-war trends in world trade, the impact of the war and the possible pattern in the early 1950s.
	5	Not issued.
14 May	**6**	**The scale of investment programmes in the 1950s** – P. Jeffries, 1+8p. Revise version. Estimate of investment capability in 1952.
18 May	**7**	**Exports of cotton piece-goods 1952 forecast** – P. Jeffries covering the Board of Trade, 1+4p.
18 May	**8**	**Exports of woollen and worsted piece-goods 1952 forecast** – P. Jeffries covering the Board of Trade, 1+3p.
4 June	**9**	**The elasticity of demand for British exports** – P. Jeffries, 1+7+1p appendix.
4 June	**10**	**Competitive power devaluation and U.K. long-term export prospects** – P. Jeffries covering the Board of Trade, 1+2p.
4 June	**11**	**Estimates of shipping earnings** – P. Jeffries, 1+3p.

4 June	**12**	**The dollar balance of the rest of the sterling area – P. Jeffries,** 1+3p.
4 June	**13**	**Forecast of U.K. earnings in 1952 by areas – P. Jeffries,** 1+4p.
5 July	**14**	**Long-term economic survey: balance of payments forecasts – P. Jeffries,** 1+25p. See EPB(48)21. Also ED(48)4.
nd	**15**	**Draft Economic Survey for 1948–1952 – C.E.P.S.,** 41p. See EPB(48)25.
	16	Not issued.
11 Nov	**17**	**Economic Survey for 1949 – D.M.B. Butt,** 1+25p. Preliminary drafts with sections on progress in 1948, prospects for 1949, investment in 1949, manpower and national income and expenditure.
16 Nov	**18**	**Economic Survey for 1949 – D.M.B. Butt and J. Downie,** 1+9p. Preliminary draft sections on textiles and problems for 1949.
10 Dec	**19**	**Economic Survey for 1949 – R.L. Hall,** 1+38p +20p addendum. Drafts of sections.
10 Dec	**20**	**Tables for the Economic Survey for 1949 – D.M.B. Butt and J. Downie,** 1+19p.
30 Dec	**21**	**Economic Survey for 1949 first draft – D.M.B. Butt and J. Downie,** 2+65p. See EPB(48)35. Also ED(49)1.

CAB 134/268   Memoranda only   23 Mar–22 Dec 1949   ESWP(49)1–20.

23 Mar	**ESWP(49)1**	**Revision of the draft Economic Survey for 1948–1952 – R.L. Hall,** 1p. To be revised for the Official Committee on Economic Development.
28 Apr	**2**	**Existing material of long-term economic prospects – Secretary,** 14+1p annex.
4 May	**3**	**The working population in 1952 – J. Downie covering D.R.F. Turner,** 1+1p.
5 May	**4**	**Productivity 1948–52 – J. Downie covering C.E.P.S.,** 1+6+2p appendix. Questioning increase in productivity assumed in the long-term survey.
11 May	**5**	**Draft outline for the Economic Survey for 1952 – secretary,** 8p.
25 May	**6**	**Weights used for calculating average productivity increase in ESWP(49)4 – J. Downie covering C.E.P.S.,** 1+1p.
14 June	**7**	**Long-term export forecast – Board of Trade,** 37p. Notes on various commodities.
23 June	**8**	**The U.S.A. in world trade – J. Downie covering the Board of Trade,** 1+7+4p appendix.
24 June	**9**	**Effect of price changes on the long-term balance of payments – J. Downie,** 1+11p.

29 June	**10**	**Economic Survey for 1952 – J. Downie**, 1+20p. Drafts of chapters 1–3.
4 July	**11**	**Western Germany: trade in 1952/53 – J. Downie covering the Board of Trade**, 1+3p.
22 July	**12**	**Note by the Chairman – R.L. Hall covering J. Downie**, 1+1+19+1p. Suspension of work on the 1952 Survey.
5 Aug	**13**	**Estimates of consumer demand 1938–52 – J. Downie covering C.E.P.S.**, 1+41p. Primarily an exercise in methodology.
5 Oct	**14**	**Arrangements for the Economic Survey for 1950 – R.L. Hall**, 2p.
2 Nov	**15**	**Economic Survey for 1950 – J. Downie and J. Kelley**, 1+21p. Draft outline.
17 Nov	**16**	**Economic Survey for 1950 – R.L. Hall**, 1p. Administrative arrangements.
9 Dec	**17**	**Economic Survey for 1950 – J. Downie and J. Kelley**, 1+28+18p addenda. Drafts of various sections.
16 Dec	**18**	**Economic Survey for 1950 – J. Downie and J. Kelley**, 1+12+9p addenda. Draft of balance of payments sections.
16 Dec	**19**	**Economic Survey for 1950 – J. Downie and J. Kelley**, 1+11p. Draft of longer-term balance of payments section.
22 Dec	**20**	**Economic Survey for 1950 – R.L. Hall**, 1+57+8p addenda. See EPB(49)24. Also ED(49)25.

15.16   Fuel Allocations Committee

Set up by the Fuel Committee in June 1947 to deal with the detailed allocation of coal and coke to industry, see CAB 134/272, FC(47)18th:4 and CAB 134/273, FC(47)86. It continued after the dissolution of the Fuel Committee in October 1947 and reported to the Production Committee thereafter, although it was virtually inoperative after January 1948. To ensure co-ordination with the Materials Committee (CAB 134/475–486), it always had the same chairman – Gaitskell, Marquand and then Jay – and the secretariat was drawn from the C.E.P.S. There was no fixed membership, only a set number of representatives from relevant departments, and it was formally wound up in April 1950.

Terms   (i) to make specific allocations to industry from the global allotment made by the Fuel Committee. This was the most important function but it would be premature to consider this question until figures were available   (ii) to determine the basis on which these allocations should be made. It would be convenient to take as a starting point the paper which had been prepared by F.G. Lee   (iii) to deal with any immediate problems arising out of the summer scheme – e.g. questions of principle, differences on deliveries etc. In addition the Committee would be required to undertake the allocation of coke to industry.

(Oct 1947) To frame a detailed coal budget for industry in conformity with the broad allocations laid down by the Production Committee and, on the basis of this budget, to determine the amounts of coal to be made available for particular industries.

Members Parl. Sec., Min. Fuel & P. (ch.); official representatives of B.T. (two), Mins. of Supply (four), Food (two), Fuel & P. (three), Works, N.C.B. (two), C.E.P.S. (two), Ec. Sect., Materials Committee. (Oct 1947) Paymaster-Gen. chairman. (Dec 1947) Ec. Sec. (Try) chairman.

Secs. H.L. de Bourcier (Fuel & P.), R.E. France (C.E.P.S.) and H. Scholes (Fuel & P.). (Nov 1947) E.R. Brett (Fuel & P.) replaced Scholes.

CAB 134/270 Meetings and Memoranda 19 June 1947–20 Dec 1948
FAC(47)1st–FAC(48)2nd and FAC(47)1–FAC(48)10.

Meetings

19 June	**FAC(47)1st**	Untitled. FC(47)86.
10 July	**2nd:1**	**Grouping of industry. FAC(47)1.**
	:2	**Form of statistical information. FAC(47)2.**
	:3	**Relation of allocation to fuel efficiency.** FAC(47)3.
	:4	**Additional coal allocations for the operation of private electrical generating plant. FAC(47)4.**
	:5	**Industrial allocation scheme. FAC(47)5.**
	:6	**Allocation of coal to meet expansions.** FAC(47)6. Gaitskell favoured a reserve of coal.
	:7	**Report of Fuel Committee and material for publication.**
21 July	**3rd:1**	**Adjustments in the winter scheme of allocations.** FAC(47)9.
	:2	**Fuel allocations to mid-winter plans. FAC(47)8.**
	:3	**Supply of coal for the manufacture of soda ash.**
	:4	**Industrial coke allocations. FAC(47)7.**
6 Aug	**4th:1**	**Priorities for iron and steel.** Ministry of Supply proposal for priority allocations.
	:2	**Discussions with chairmen of regional boards and the N.P.A.C.I.** Both bodies emphasized the need for an adequate margin to meet contingencies.
	:4	**Coal for industry, winter 1947/48.** **Requirements, probable availability, and provisional allocations. FAC(47)10 and 13.**
22 Aug	**5th:1**	**Winter scheme for industry: discussions with the N.P.A.C.I.**
	:2	**Plan B.**
	:3	**Coke budget: winter 1947/48. FAC(47)14.**
	:4	**The machinery for securing equitable distribution of coal supplies among industrial consumers. FAC(47)16.**
	:5	**Private generation of electricity. FAC(47)15.**
	:6	**Composition of the miscellaneous item in Table II of Appendix to FAC(47)10. FAC(47)17.**

23 Sept	6th:1	**Industrial allocations: timing of scheme.** Awaiting decision from the Fuel Committee on the overall allocation for industry.
	:2	**Priority in supplies of coke and coal for the iron and steel industry.** FAC(47)18. Priority agreed for the remainder of the summer.
	:3	**Revised coke budget: winter 1947/48.** FAC(47)20.
	:4	**Coal for industry: winter 1947/48.** FAC(47)24. Agreement that the plan was broadly workable.
	:5	**Winter coal scheme: publicity.** FAC(47)21.
	:6	**Liaison between the coal and coke programming authorities.** FAC(47)22.
	:7	**Operation of machinery for securing equitable distribution.** FAC(47)23.
29 & 30 Sept	7th:1	**Memoranda submitted to the Fuel Committee.** FC(47)130 and 131.
	:2	**Matters arising from the last meeting.**
	:3	**Coke budget: winter 1947/48.** FC(47)131.
	:4	**Coal for industry: winter 1947/48.** FC(47)130 and FAC(47)25. Consideration of allocations under Plan B.
	:5	**Miscellaneous.** Statements attached showing revised requirements of industrial A consumers and the allocations under Plans B and C.
2 Oct	8th:1	**Coal for industry: winter 1947/48.** Agreement to use Plan B.
	:2	**Reserves for industry other than iron and steel.** Agreement to reduce allocations under Plan B to industrial A consumers.
	:3	**Instructions for regional boards.** FAC(47)26.
11 Nov	9th:1	**Reports on consultations with the N.P.A.C.I.**
	:2	**Coal supplies for industry: winter 1947/48.** FAC(47)29, 30, 31.
	:3	**Coke supplies for industry: winter 1947/48.** FAC(47)32.
	:4	**Statistics.** IR11, 11a and 12 – coal and IR11 – coke.
23 Dec	10th:1	**Instructions for regional boards.** FAC(47)33 and 36.
	:2	**Export requirements and their effect upon the winter allocations.** FAC(47)34.
	:3	**Conversion from oil to coal.** FAC(47)35.
	:4	**Coke for industry, winter 1947/48.**
	:5	**Statistics.** IR11, 11a, 11b, 12, 13, 14, 15 – coal and IR11 – coke.
26 Jan	FAC(48)1st:1	**Coke.** FAC(48)1.
	:2	**Coal allocation scheme: summer 1948.** FAC(48)2. Agreement on the alterations to be recommended.

	:3	**Statistics.** IR11, 11a, 11b, 12, 13, 14, 15 – coal and IR11 – coke.
	:4	**Exports.** Agreement to export some of the industrial reserve.
20 Dec	**2nd:1**	**Coal stocks for industry: level planned for April 1949.** FAC(48)9.
	:2	**Estimates of coal consumption by industry in 1949.** FAC(48)10.
	:3	**Instructions to regional boards.**

Memoranda

9 July	**FAC(47)1**	**Groupings of industry and responsibility of departments – Ministry of Fuel and Power,** 2+4p appendix. Suggested classification of industry attached.
8 July	**2**	**Form of statistical information – Ministry of Fuel and Power,** 2+5p annexes.
8 July	**3**	**Industrial coal allocations and fuel efficiency – Ministry of Fuel and Power,** 3p. Consideration of bonuses in allocations to fuel-efficient firms.
8 July	**4**	**Private generation of electricity – Ministry of Fuel and Power,** 2p.
8 July	**5**	**Fuel supplies to industry during the winter – Board of Trade and Ministry of Fuel and Power,** 9p. Proposed scheme for allocations to industry, adjustable if supplies varied from estimates. It followed closely the plan prepared by F. Lee, the previous April.
8 July	**6**	**Allocation of coal to meet expansions since last summer – Board of Trade,** 2+2p appendix.
19 July	**7**	**Industrial coke allocations – Ministry of Fuel and Power,** 3p.
21 July	**8**	**Fuel allocations to industry: winter plans – Gaitskell,** 3p. Draft of FC(47)113.
21 July	**9**	**Adjustments in the winter scheme of allocations – Ministry of Fuel and Power,** 2p.
5 Aug	**10**	**Coal for industry, winter 1947/48: comparison of requirements and probable availability – Ministry of Fuel and Power,** 5+7p appendix.
31 July	**11**	**Summary of reports from Regional Fuel Allocation Committees – Board of Trade,** 3p.
21 July	**12**	**Supply of coal for the manufacture of soda ash – Board of Trade,** 2p.
1 Aug	**13**	**Estimated weekly consumption requirement – Ministry of Fuel and Power,** 1p.
20 Aug	**14**	**Coke budget: winter 1947/48 – Ministry of Fuel and Power,** 5+4p appendix. Estimate of the gap between demand and supply with proposals to close it.
15 Aug	**15**	**Private generation of electricity – Ministry of Fuel and Power,** 1p.

12 Aug	**16**	**The machinery for securing equitable distribution of coal supplies among industrial consumers** – N.C.B., 2p.
20 Aug	**17**	**Composition of the miscellaneous item in table 2 of appendix to FAC(47)10** – Ministry of Fuel and Power, 3p.
6 Sept	**18**	**Priority in supplies of coal and coke for the iron and steel industry** – secretariat covering the Ministry of Supply, 1+3+7p appendixes.
nd	**19**	**Coal for industry: winter 1947/48** – Ministry of Fuel and Power. No copy available.
22 Sept	**20**	**Revised coke budget: winter 1947/48** – Ministry of Fuel and Power, 5+2p appendix.
22 Sept	**21**	**Winter coal scheme: publicity** – Board of Trade, 2p.
17 Sept	**22**	**Liaison between the coal and coke programming authorities** – N.C.B., 1p.
19 Sept	**23**	**Operation of machinery for securing equitable distribution** – N.C.B., 3p. Investigation of the summer industrial allocation scheme.
19 Sept	**24**	**Coal for industry: winter 1947/48** – N.C.B., 3+3p appendixes. Examination of practicability of the scheme agreed at FAC(47)5th.
26 Sept	**25**	**Stocks held by industrial A consumers at 30 Aug 1947** – Ministry of Fuel and Power, 2+6p appendix.
1 Oct	**26**	**Coal supplies to industry, winter 1947/48. Instructions for regional boards** – secretariat, 1+5+5p appendix. Draft circular.
6 Oct	**27**	**Coal supplies to industry, winter 1947/48** – secretariat, 1+5+4+5p. See FAC(47)130 and 131.
9 Oct	**28**	**Note by Secretary of the Cabinet** – N. Brook, 1p.
6 Nov	**29**	**Instructions for regional boards** – secretariat, 1+6+5p annex. RB Circ.1/31.
10 Nov	**30**	**The winter coal budget 1947/48** – N.C.B., 3+3p annex. Review of coal availability and commitments for the four weeks beginning 3 Nov 1947.
10 Nov	**31**	**Coal for industry: winter 1947/48 for meeting a shortfall** – unsigned, 6+1p annex.
6 Nov	**32**	**Instructions for regional boards** – secretariat, 1+5+1p appendix. RB Circ.1/34.
29 Nov	**33**	**Instructions for regional boards** – secretariat, 1+1p. Amendment to FAC(47)32.
16 Dec	**34**	**Export requirements and their effect upon the winter fuel allocation scheme** – Ministry of Fuel and Power, 2p.
16 Dec	**35**	**Conversion from oil to coal** – Ministry of Fuel and Power, 2p.

17 Dec	**36**	**Instructions for regional boards – secretariat,** 1+2p. RB Circ.1/38.
30 Dec	**37**	**Note by Secretary of the Cabinet – N. Brook,** 1p.
22 Jan	**FAC(48)1**	**Coke – Ministry of Fuel and Power,** 3+1p annex. Outlook for supplies.
24 Jan	**2**	**Coal allocation scheme: summer 1948 – Ministry of Fuel and Power,** 4p. Provisional consideration.
18 Feb	**3**	**Note by the secretariat,** 1+1p. N.C.B.'s budget summary for four weeks.
18 Mar	**4**	**Note by the secretariat,** 1+1p. N.C.B.'s budget summary.
14 Apr	**5**	**Note by the secretariat,** 1+1p. Budget summary.
29 May	**6**	**Note by the secretariat,** 1+4p. Budget summary.
16 June	**7**	**Note by the secretariat,** 1+3p. Budget summary.
10 Aug	**8**	**Note by the secretariat,** 1+1p. Budget summary.
17 Dec	**9**	**Coal stocks for industry: level planned for April 1949 – Ministry of Fuel and Power,** 4+1p annex.
16 Dec	**10**	**Estimates of coal consumption by industry in 1949 – Ministry of Fuel and Power,** 7p.

15.17 Fuel Committee

Set up, under official pressure, in the crisis of February 1947 to co-ordinate overall fuel and power policy and thereby to replace the more narrowly-defined Coal Committee (CAB 134/62), see CAB 129/17, CP(47)58. During the crisis the committee 'virtually put in commission' the office of Minister of Fuel and Power (see P.M. Williams (ed.), *The Diary of Hugh Gaitskell*, p 29) and, with Attlee as chairman, few decisions had to be referred to the full Cabinet. The committee authorized immediate emergency measures and considered problems of future supply, including imports from the U.S.A., as well as receiving regular reports on the nature and consequences of the fuel situation (CAB 134/275).

It was initially served by the Official Coal Committee (CAB 134/62) and delegated matters of a special urgency to an executive subcommittee consisting of the President of the Board of Trade and the Ministers of Fuel & Power, Labour & National Service, and Transport. In June 1947 it delegated work to the Fuel Allocations Committee (CAB 134/270) before being dissolved during the administrative reorganization of October 1947, see CAB 129/21, CP(47)280.

Terms (a) to keep the fuel situation under review and to authorize or recommend to the Cabinet such action as may be required to meet further developments (b) to supervise the preparation of plans for avoiding a similar crisis in the winter of 1947–48 and to consider the relation of such plans to the long-term measures for the reorganization of the coal-mining and electricity industries.

Members Prime Min. (ch.); Ch. of Exchequer; Pres. Bd Trade; Mins. of Labour & N.S., Fuel & Power, Transport. Others who might attend included Permanent Secs. of Mins. of Fuel & P., Transport, chairman of the N.C.B., the C.E.B. and deputy chairman

Railway Exec. Committee. (March 1947) Paymaster-Gen. added. (May 1947) Ld President added.

Secs. N. Brook (Cab. O.), and J.H. Lidderdale (Ld Pres. O.).

CAB 134/272 Meetings 12 Feb–1 Oct 1947 FC(47)1st–23rd.

12 Feb	**FC(47)1st:1**	**Work of the committee.** Statement by Attlee.
	:2	**Fuel situation.** Agreement on many measures to improve the situation.
14 Feb	2nd:1	**Fuel situation.** FC(47)2. Consideration of daily reports from the Ministries of Fuel and Power and Transport. Agreement on further remedial measures.
	:2	**Restrictions of electricity consumption.** FC(47)3 and 4. Proposals approved.
	:3	**Industrial consumption of electricity.**
	:4	**Import of coal into the U.K.**
	:5	**Public statement.**
	:6	**Future procedure.**
18 Feb	3rd:1	**Review of the situation.** Consideration of further daily reports on the fuel, transport and unemployment situations.
	:2	**Fuel supplies for industry.** FC(47)6, 7, 9. Both the F.B.I. and the T.U.C. preferred Plan A and this was approved.
21 Feb	4th:1	**Fuel situation.** Consideration of further reports.
	:2	**Summer time.**
	:3	**Staggering of hours of work.**
	:4	**Generating plant.**
24 Feb	5th:1	**Ideal Home Exhibition.**
	:2	**Electricity supply.** Attlee felt that, in considering the long-term fuel position, steps to balance the demand and supply of electricity should be planned.
	:3	**Gas supplies.**
	:4	**Longer-term coal problems.** FC(47)8, 10, 14, 15.
	:5	**Deputation from the N.U.M.** FC(47)13. Agreement that any increase in wages for miners should be linked to increased production.
25 Feb	6th:1	**Review of the situation.** Consideration of further reports.
	:2	**The staggering of hours of work.**
	:3	**Domestic and non-industrial fuel rationing.** FC(47)16.
	:4	**Restoration of B.B.C. services.** FC(47)18.
	:5	**Coal for Eire.**
27 Feb	7th:1	**Restoration of electricity supply to industry.**
	:2	**Deputation from the N.U.M.**
28 Feb	8th:1	**Ideal Home Exhibition.**

	:2	**Fuel situation.** FC(47)28. Further reports considered.
	:3	**Coal for the railways.** FC(47)19 and 27.
	:4	**Domestic and non-industrial electricity restrictions.** FC(47)22.
	:5	**Greyhound racing.** FC(47)21.
	:6	**Domestic and non-industrial fuel rationing.** FC(47)16.
3 Mar	**9th:1**	**Review of the situation.** Further report considered.
	:2	**Longer-term coal problems.** FC(47)10 and 25.
	:3	**Coal stocks.** Agreement on minimum stock levels.
	:4	**Coal/oil conversion.**
4 Mar	**10th:1**	**Domestic and non-industrial electricity restrictions.** FC(47)29. Agreement to lift some restrictions.
	:2	**Staggering of hours of work.** A committee to be set up under the N.J.A.C. to examine shift working.
	:3	**Coal budget for the summer of 1947.** FC(47)10, 31, 34. D. Fergusson explained that the figure of 18.1m tons for stocks in FC(47)34 was on the same basis as the 15m tons agreed at FC(47)9th. This was rejected and the 15m tons figure was reaffirmed. Consideration of measures to close the summer deficit of 13.3m tons.
	:4	**Limitation of mid-week sporting events.** FC(47)32.
7 Mar	**11th:1**	**Summer time.**
	:2	**Domestic and non-industrial electrical restrictions.** FC(47)39. Agreement on the form of the scheme of non-industrial restrictions on consumption.
	:3	**Coal budget for the summer of 1947.** FC(47)37. Approved in principle.
	:4	**Domestic and non-industrial fuel rationing.** FC(47)16 and 36. Agreement to defer decision on summer restrictions until the summer budget had been discussed with the N.U.M.
	:5	**Miners in the forces.**
	:6	**Solid fuel allocation to industry.**
	:7	**Saving of coal by the railways.** Agreement on 10% cut in the level of summer services.
7 Mar	**12th:1**	**Review of the situation.** Further reports considered.
	:2	**Electricity generating capacity.** FC(47)12, 20, 26, 30.
	:3	**Auxiliary generating sets.**
	:4	**Coal/oil conversion.** FC(47)30.
	:5	**Staggering of hours of work.** FC(47)35.

14 Mar	13th:1	**Fuel situation.** FC(47)42. Further reports considered.
	:2	**Domestic consumption of solid fuel.**
	:3	**Coal for the railways.**
	:4	**Transport of coal.** FC(47)23, 33, 40.
	:5	**Restoration of B.B.C. services.** FC(47)46.
	:6	**Imports of foreign coal.** FC(47)43, 45, 47.
20 Mar	14th:1	**Import of coal.** To be taken up with the U.S.A.
	:2	**Domestic and non-industrial fuel rationing.** FC(47)48 and 50. Agreement that a compulsory rationing scheme as in FC(47)36 should be introduced.
	:3	**Staggering of hours of work.**
	:4	**Coal and coke for Malta, Gibraltar and Bermuda.** FC(47)49.
2 Apr	15th:1	**Heavy electrical plant.** FC(47)53 and 59.
	:2	**Staggering of hours of work.** FC(47)60.
	:3	**Allocation of solid fuel to industry.** FC(47)61 and 64. Agreement to increase coal supplies to industry on the basis of FC(47)61. Shinwell dissented on the grounds that it would jeopardize stock building and risk breakdown that winter.
	:4	**Production of calcium carbide.** FC(47)62.
	:5	**Housing for miners.** FC(47)38, 55, 58.
	:6	**Export of coal to Eire.** FC(47)56.
	:7	**Transport of coal.** FC(47)54 and 57.
	:8	**Saving of coal by the railways.**
	:9	**Domestic and non-industrial fuel rationing.**
16 Apr	16th:1	**Restoration of B.B.C. services.** FC(47)79.
	:2	**Proposals by the N.U.M.** FC(47)67 and 75.
	:3	**Import of coal.** FC(47)70.
21 Apr	17th:1	**Domestic and non-industrial fuel restrictions.** FC(47)71 and 74.
	:2	**Domestic consumption of solid fuel.** FC(47)78.
	:3	**Allocation of solid fuel to industry.** FC(47)68 and 80.
	:4	**Mining machinery and coal/oil conversion.** FC(47)72 and 73.
	:5	**Conversion of generating stations to oil burning.** FC(47)76.
	:6	**Auxiliary generating plant.** FC(47)77.
	:7	**Import of coal.** FC(47)69.
6 June	18th:1	**Prospects for the summer.** FC(47)88, 90, 91, 95. Agreement that the cost of U.S. coal, imported in the third quarter of 1947, should be absorbed in that of indigenous coal but the extra overall cost should not be passed on to the consumer.
	:2	**Coal allocations.** FC(47)93, 94, 95. Agreement to increase allocations to the iron and steel industry subject to availability.

	:3	**Coke shortage.** FC(47)92.
	:4	**Fuel Allocation Committee.**
	:5	**Street lighting.** FC(47)81.
	:6	**Coal/oil conversion programme.** FC(47)89 and 96.
	:7	**Auxiliary generating sets.** FC(47)83.
	:8	**Staggering of working hours.**
11 July	19th:1	**Procedure.** Morrison wanted officials to handle certain matters given the large number of memoranda.
	:2	**Budget for the remainder of the coal year.** FC(47)102, 103, 104.
	:3	**Estimates of output and exports for the Marshall discussions.** FC(47)98.
	:4	**Recruitment.** FC(47)85 and 95.
	:5	**Accommodation for miners.** FC(47)99.
	:6	**Coal washeries.** FC(47)87.
	:7	**Mining equipment and coal/oil conversion.** FC(47)100.
	:8	**Transport of coal** FC(47)84 and 106. E.N. Plowden was to investigate the probable economic effects of an overriding priority for coal traffic next winter.
	:9	**Staggering of working hours.** FC(47)101.
	:10	**Weekly publication of coal output figures.** FC(47)105 and 107.
	:11	**Proposed new power station at Woolwich.** FC(47)100.
18 July	20th:1	**Transport of coal.**
	:2	**Electricity supply for 1947/1948 and subsequent years.** FC(47)109.
	:3	**Heavy electrical plant.** FC(47)100.
	:4	**Single summer time.**
	:5	**Economies in domestic consumption of gas and electricity.** FC(47)108.
	:6	**Staggering of work hours.** FC(47)110.
	:7	**New sinkings.**
24 July	21st:1	**Increased coal production and exports to Eire.** FC(47)111, 114, 115, 116. Increasing pressure on the U.K. to start exporting. Consideration of the measures in FC(47)111 to increase production and an agreement that the first step was to meet the N.U.M.
	:2	**Domestic and non-industrial gas and electricity restrictions.** FC(47)112. Shinwell opposed restriction by price disincentive. Agreement in favour of voluntary restrictions.
	:3	**Fuel allocations to industry: winter plans.** FC(47)113. Approval, subject to certain safeguards to meet any shortfall.

25 Aug	**22nd:1**	**Recruitment to the coal-mining industry.** FC(47)119 and 122. Discussion of N.U.M. proposals.
	:2	**Extension of five-day week for ancillary workers in the coal-mining industry.** FC(47)123.
	:3	**Fuel allocations for industry.** Despite Shinwell's disagreement supplies to particular firms from the pool were increased.
1 Oct	**23rd:1**	**Fuel situation.** Consideration of further reports.
	:2	**Coal budget for winter of 1947/48.** FC(47)128 and 130. Agreement that any restrictions should fall on non-industrial consumers. Agreement on the basis of allocations to industry with the 3.05m ton gap being met from de-stocking and coal/oil conversion.
	:3	**Coke budget for winter of 1947/48.** FC(47)131. Approved.
	:4	**Coal/oil conversion.** FC(47)133.
	:5	**Transport prospects.** Covering the period 1948/51.
	:6	**Turn-round of wagons.** FC(47)134.
	:7	**Export of locomotives and wagons.** FC(47)129.
	:8	**Staggering of hours of work.** FC(47)137.

CAB 134/273   Memoranda   12 Feb–5 June 1947   FC(47)1–96.

12 Feb	**FC(47)1**	**Fuel Committee – N. Brook**, 2p. See CP(47)58.
13 Feb	**2**	**Unloading and return of coal wagons – N. Brook** covering Isaacs, 1+2p annex. Two letters.
13 Feb	**3**	**Broadcasting during restricted hours – Listowel**, 1p.
14 Feb	**4**	**Consumption of electricity generated by oil or water power – Shinwell**, 1p.
17 Feb	**5**	**Note by secretary – N. Brook**, 1p. Statement sent to Attlee by the National Union of Manufacturers.
18 Feb	**6**	**Report by the Inter-departmental Committee on the Removal of Electricity Restrictions on Industry – Shinwell**, 1+5+2p annexes.
18 Feb	**7**	**Coal stocks of industrial undertakings – Cripps**, 3p.
17 Feb	**8**	**Plans for avoiding a fuel crisis in the winter of 1947–48 – Attlee**, 6p. Sets out proposed general strategy. Suggested measures to increase manpower in the industry, curtail consumption and to prepare an allocation scheme for industry, although the aim was to match demand and supply with no reduction of industrial supplies. The main issue was the level of winter stocks.
18 Feb	**9**	**Coal stocks of industrial undertakings – Shinwell**, 2p.

20 Feb	10	**Coal prospects for the next three years – D. Fergusson,** 1+14+2p appendix. The problem arose because industrial consumption was outstripping production regardless of exports. It was no longer possible to draw on stocks. A large gap existed and possible measures to reduce consumption were suggested. The situation would improve over the next two coal years and by 1949/50 it was estimated there would be surplus production for export.
21 Feb	11	**Stocking and supplying of power stations – Ministry of Fuel and Power,** 2p. Progress report.
21 Feb	12	**Heavy electrical plant – Wilmot,** 1+4p.
21 Feb	13	**Note by secretary – N. Brook,** 1+2p. N.U.M. proposals.
21 Feb	14	**Coal position: 1947/48 – Shinwell,** 4+2p annexes. Estimated deficit of 19m tons. Output could be increased in the next six months only by additional manpower, increased effort and reduced absenteeism, but even then there must be drastic reduction of consumption.
22 Feb	15	**Recruitment for coal-mining – Isaacs,** 3+1p appendix. Action taken by the Ministry of Labour as proposed in FC(47)8 and matters requiring further guidance.
22 Feb	16	**Domestic and non-industrial fuel rationing – Shinwell,** 1+7+5p annexes. Rationing scheme drawn up by the Board of Trade to effect maximum savings that summer.
22 Feb	17	**Transport during the next coal year – Barnes,** 1p. Preliminary survey.
24 Feb	18	**Restoration of B.B.C. services – Listowel,** 2p.
26 Feb	19	**Coal for the railways for the period between now and Easter – Shinwell,** 2p.
27 Feb	20	**North of Scotland Hydro-electric Board's constructional schemes – Westwood,** 3p.
27 Feb	21	**Greyhound racing – Shinwell,** 1p.
27 Feb	22	**Domestic and non-industrial electricity restrictions – Shinwell covering the Interdepartmental Committee on the Continuance of Restrictions on Non-industrial Users of Electricity,** 1+3+1p annex.
27 Feb	23	**Coastal movement of coal in the coal year 1947/48 – Barnes,** 2p.
27 Feb	24	**Coal for bunkering British ships – Barnes,** 2p.
27 Feb	25	**Coal production – Shinwell covering the N.C.B.,** 1+1+6p. General policy and suggested production targets.
28 Feb	26	**Electricity prospects in the next few years – N. Brook covering the Chairman of the Central Electricity Board,** 1+3+4p annexes. Review of the shortage of generating plant.

28 Feb	27	**Coal for the railways for the period between now and Easter – Barnes**, 2+2p appendix. Disagreement with FC(47)19.
28 Feb	28	**Coal deliveries and stocks – Ministry of Fuel and Power**, 1+2p annex.
4 Mar	29	**Domestic and non-industrial electricity restrictions – Shinwell**, 1+1p annex. Recommended lifting of restrictions from commerce.
3 Mar	30	**Power stations electrical generating plant – Shinwell**, 2+2p. Note on conversion of boilers to oil firing.
3 Mar	31	**Coal budget for the summer of 1947 – Attlee**, 2p. Estimated summer gap of 8.5m tons.
3 Mar	32	**Limitation of mid-week sporting events – Official Steering Committee on Economic Development**, 2+4p annexes. Also ED(47)21.
3 Mar	33	**Inland transport during the coal year 1947–48 – Barnes**, 3p. Drastic steps necessary to ensure sufficient supplies of materials, especially steel and timber, if the railways were to meet likely demand.
4 Mar	34	**Coal required during the coming summer for consumption and stock building – Ministry of Fuel and Power**, 2+1p annex. Need to build stocks to prevent serious dislocation next winter. This required summer consumption to be reduced by 14.4m tons.
4 Mar	35	**Transfer of the industrial electricity load to the night period – Isaacs**, 3p.
5 Mar	36	**Restriction of non-industrial gas and electricity consumption – Shinwell**, 8+2p annex. Sets out the alternatives for reducing such consumption by purchase taxes, prohibitions or rationing schemes.
6 Mar	37	**Coal budget for the summer of 1947 – Attlee**, 2p. There was still a deficit of 8.8m tons. While some increased output could be hoped for, minimum allocations which firms could be certain of receiving should be worked out.
5 Mar	38	**Assessment of the accommodation position within ten miles of the deep coal-mine pit heads – Isaacs and Wilmot**, 2+5p appendixes.
6 Mar	39	**Domestic and non-industrial electricity restrictions – N. Brook covering Shinwell**, 1+1p annex.
7 Mar	40	**Accommodation for railwaymen in London – Barnes**, 2p.
8 Mar	41	**Gas industry requirements for plant, etc. – Shinwell**, 2p. Request for top priority for raw materials required.

8 Mar	42	**Monthly statistical report (coal) for January 1947** – Shinwell, 2+2p annex. Also LP(47)45.
11 Mar	43	**Importing coal from the U.S.A.** – N. Brook covering Shinwell, 1+3p annex.
12 Mar	44	**Coal production** – Shinwell, 1+12p. Supplements to FC(47)25 by the N.C.B. on manpower, coal production and the supply of colliery materials and equipment.
13 Mar	45	**Imports of foreign coal** – Shinwell, 4p. Consideration of possible sources.
12 Mar	46	**Restoration of B.B.C. services** – Listowel, 2p.
13 Mar	47	**Import of coal into the U.K.** – McNeil, 2p.
17 Mar	48	**Restrictions on the consumption of gas and electricity for domestic and non-industrial purposes** – Shinwell, 2+1p annex. Sets out the proposed summer voluntary ration scheme.
18 Mar	49	**Coal and coke for Malta, Gibraltar and Bermuda** – Shinwell, 2p.
19 Mar	50	**Restrictions on the consumption of gas and electricity for domestic and non-industrial purposes** – Isaacs, 2p. Against FC(47)48.
24 Mar	51	**Membership of the Committee** – N. Brook, 1p.
26 Mar	52	**Continuance of restriction on the entry of men from Eire** – Chuter Ede and Isaacs, 1p.
28 Mar	53	**Heavy electrical plant** – Wilmot, 3p. Progress report.
31 Mar	54	**Effect of the five-day week in the coal-mines on transport** – Barnes, 3p. Suggestions to ease the increased strain.
31 Mar	55	**Accommodation for miners** – Bevan, 2+1p appendix.
31 Mar	56	**Export of U.K. coal and coke to Eire** – Shinwell, 2p.
1 Apr	57	**Policy relating to the export of main line steam locomotives and wagons** – Cripps, 3p.
31 Mar	58	**Accommodation for miners** – Westwood, 3+1p appendix.
31 Mar	59	**Approval of generating station sites and quality of coal supplied** – Shinwell, 3p.
31 Mar	60	**Spreading the industrial electricity load** – Cripps, 1+3p appendix. Progress report on arrangements.
1 Apr	61	**Allocation of solid fuel to industry** – Cripps, 2p. Proposed certain immediate increase of deliveries.
31 Mar	62	**Calcium carbide and coal** – Cripps, 3p.
1 Apr	63	**North of Scotland Hydro-electric Board's constructional schemes** – Westwood, 2+3p appendixes.
1 Apr	64	**Coal for industry** – Shinwell, 2p. Disagreement with FC(47)61.
9 Apr	65	**Calcium carbide and coal** – Westwood, 1p.

12 Apr	66	**Monthly statistical report (coal) for February 1947 – Shinwell,** 2+2p appendix. Also LP(47)70.
14 Apr	67	**Proposals by the National Executive Committee of the N.U.M. – N. Brook and J.H. Lidderdale,** 1+2p. Letter from A.L. Horner.
14 Apr	68	**Allocation of solid fuel to industry – Shinwell,** 1p. Had started to implement the committee's decision to increase the allocation to industry at the expense of stockbuilding for power stations and domestic and miscellaneous consumption. He still felt there were serious risks with the power stations.
20 Apr	69	**Imports of coal from the U.S.A. – Attlee,** 1p.
15 Apr	70	**Imports of coal from the U.S.A. and Poland – Shinwell,** 4+2p appendix.
18 Apr	71	**Restrictions on the domestic and non-industrial (commercial) use of gas and electricity – Shinwell,** 1+3+2p appendix. Proposed summer restrictions.
14 Apr	72	**Progress report – Shinwell,** 2p. Update on coal/oil conversion.
15 Apr	73	**Mining machinery and equipment and coal/oil conversion – Wilmot,** 2p. Progress report.
21 Apr	74	**Restrictions on domestic and non-industrial (commercial) use of gas and electricity – Isaacs,** 2+5p appendix. Criticism of the proposal in FC(47)71 to abandon existing restrictions.
15 Apr	75	**Control of Engagement Order in agriculture – Williams,** 2p.
16 Apr	76	**Report by the Minister of Fuel and Power, in the light of recommendations made by the Heavy Electrical Plant Committee, on the extent to which it would be practicable to arrange for the conversion of generating stations from coal to oil burning as an emergency matter before next winter,** 2+6p annexes.
16 Apr	77	**Auxiliary generating plant – Shinwell,** 1p. Report on its impact on alleviating electrical supply difficulties.
16 Apr	78	**Reduction of domestic coal (ration) as a contribution to the industrial coal shortage – Shinwell,** 2p. Further cut would not benefit industry.
16 Apr	79	**Restoration of B.B.C. services – Listowel,** 1p.
17 Apr	80	**Coal for industry during the summer – Cripps,** 3p. A cut of a third in industrial consumption would be disastrous. Industry should receive the same quantity of coal as the previous summer, although this involved some risk.
2 May	81	**Street lighting – N. Brook covering Chuter Ede, Shinwell and Barnes,** 1+1p.

2 May	**82**	**Monthly statistical report (coal) for March 1947 – Shinwell,** 2+2p appendix. Also LP(47)82.
6 May	**83**	**Auxiliary generating sets for use in factories – Wilmot,** 2p.
14 May	**84**	**Locomotive and wagon position – Barnes,** 2p.
15 May	**85**	**Absorption of additional workers in the coal-mining industry – Shinwell,** 2p. Summary of N.C.B. survey of manpower capacity.
9 June	**86**	**Industrial allocations scheme – N. Brook,** 1+2p annex. Sets out the procedure of allocation and the work of the new Fuel Allocations Committee.
21 May	**87**	**Coal washeries – Shinwell,** 2p.
27 May	**88**	**Import of coal – Barnes,** 1p.
2 June	**89**	**Coal/oil conversion target – Shinwell,** 6p.
2 June	**90**	**Imports of coal from the U.S.A. – Shinwell,** 2p.
4 June	**91**	**Preliminary report of the effect of the five-day week on the coal output during the present summer – Shinwell,** 5p. Encouraging developments.
4 June	**92**	**Coke shortage – Shinwell,** 3p.
4 June	**93**	**Coal and coke allocations for the summer – Cripps,** 2p. Given the optimistic tone of FC(47)91 and 95, increased allocations to iron and steel industry proposed.
4 June	**94**	**Fuel supplies for the iron and steel industry in the summer months – Wilmot,** 3p. The industry should get priority.
4 June	**95**	**Coal supplies and coal requirements in the present winter – Shinwell,** 4+2p appendix. Agreement that allocations to the iron and steel programme should be increased.
5 June	**96**	**Coal/oil conversion – Shinwell,** 2p.

CAB 134/274 Memoranda 27 June–26 Sept 1947 FC(47)97–137.

27 June	**FC(47)97**	**Progress of recruitment in coal-mining industry – Shinwell,** 1+4+5p appendixes.
1 July	**98**	**Estimates of coal output and exports for the Marshall discussions in Paris – Shinwell,** 2p. Provision of estimates rather than targets.
1 July	**99**	**Accommodation for miners – Bevan covering the Inter-departmental Committee on Housing for Miners,** 1+3+2p appendix. Progress report.
3 July	**100**	**Production of heavy electrical plant, coal-mining machinery and equipment, and coal/oil conversion equipment for the railways – Wilmot,** 4p. Progress report.
3 July	**101**	**Staggering of working hours – Isaacs,** 3+7p appendixes.

4 July	**102**	**Output of coal from the mines during the coal year 1947/8: provisional forecast prepared in the light of the experience of the five-day week gained during the first two months since operation** – Shinwell, 2+6+2p appendix.
8 July	**103**	**Provisional coal budget for the coal year 1947–48** – Shinwell, 10+2p appendix. Summer supplies appeared to be sufficient to meet demand and to increase stocks adequately. The Fuel Allocations Committee should assume that industrial demand next winter could be met in full although an allocation scheme should be held in reserve.
4 July	**104**	**Coke budget for the coke year 1947/48** – Shinwell, 1+3p. First ever coke budget.
4 July	**105**	**Weekly publication of coal output figures** – Shinwell, 2p. Preference for monthly figures.
5 July	**106**	**Transport prospects for the next winter** – Barnes, 4p. It would only be possible to move all the coal with substantial embargoes on other freight, maintenance of other restrictions and the sufficient supply of materials to transport.
3 July	**107**	**Weekly publication of coal output** – Morrison, 2p. Recommends weekly publication.
15 July	**108**	**Economies in domestic consumption of gas and electricity** – Shinwell, 4p. Voluntary effort was the only practicable policy.
16 July	**109**	**Electricity supply for 1947–48 and subsequent years** – Shinwell, 2p. Estimate of the deficit with demand up to 1950/51.
17 July	**110**	**Spreading the industrial electricity load** – Isaacs, 2+7p appendixes. Draft statements.
23 July	**111**	**Increased coal production** – Morrison, 2p. Proposals to maximize output for the next two winters.
22 July	**112**	**Restriction of domestic consumption of gas and electricity** – Shinwell, 2+3p annex. Unable to recommend schemes annexed, based on price disincentives and past consumption.
22 July	**113**	**Coal allocations to industry: winter plan** – Gaitskell, 1+3p annex. Sets out principles of allocation scheme.
22 July	**114**	**Revised estimates of coal output and exports for the Marshall discussions in Paris** – Shinwell, 2p. Increase in export availability since FC(47)98.
24 July	**115**	**Development work in hand and projected by the N.C.B.** – Shinwell covering the N.C.B., 1+1+7p appendixes.
24 July	**116**	**Increased coal production** – Bevin, 1p.

28 July	**117**	**The N.U.M. – A. Johnston covering the Secretary of the N.U.M.,** 1+1p annex. Letter to Attlee.
1 Aug	**118**	**Imports of U.S. coal fourth quarter 1947 – Shinwell,** 2p. Against further imports. Attached: Imports of U.S. coal fourth quarter 1947 – W.S. Murrie, 1p; and Imports of U.S. coal fourth quarter 1947 – N. Brook, 1p. The committee had agreed there should be no more U.S. imports.
7 Aug	**119**	**Suggestions by the N.U.M. for improving recruitment to the coal-mining industry – Isaacs,** 2+4p appendix.
7 Aug	**120**	**Proposal that a list of ex-miners in other industries be drawn up – Isaacs,** 2p. Against the proposals. Attached: Proposal that a list of ex-miners in other industries be drawn up – N. Brook, 9 Aug 1947, 1p; and Proposal that a list of ex-miners in other industries be drawn up – N. Brook, 21 Aug 1947, 1p. Committee had agreed there should be no list.
12 Aug	**121**	**Electricity supply for 1947–48 and subsequent years – Shinwell,** 1+2p. Review by the C.E.B. of probable operating conditions during the winter 1947/48 attached.
18 Aug	**122**	**Recruitment to the coal-mining industry – Shinwell,** 4+3p annexes. Comments on FC(47)119.
22 Aug	**123**	**Extension of five-day week to ancillary workers in the coal-mining industry – Isaacs,** 1+6p annexes.
28 Aug	**124**	**Increased coal output – N. Brook,** 1+8p. Note of a meeting with the N.C.B. and the N.U.M. on 30 July 1947 attached.
28 Aug	**125**	**Hours of work in the coal-mining industry – N. Brook,** 1+2+5+1p annex. Notes of two meetings on 21 Aug 1947 with the N.C.B. and the N.U.M.
15 Sept	**126**	**Plant and equipment for coal-mining – N. Brook covering C.E.P.S.,** 1+4p. Interim report on improving the supply.
22 Sept	**127**	**Setting up of Official Committee – N. Brook,** 1p. Also FC(O)(47)1.
27 Sept	**128**	**Revised provisional coal budget for the winter 1947/48 – Shinwell,** 5+1p appendix. Revision of FC(47)103.
nd	**129**	**Working Party on the Export of Wagons and Locomotives – Cripps, Wilmot and Barnes,** 2p.
27 Sept	**130**	**Coal allocations to industry: winter 1947/48 – Gaitskell,** 4+1p appendix. Also FAC(47)27. Three plans on the alternative assumptions that (a) the requirements of industry be met in

full; (b) the lowest deficit (2.36m tons in FC(47)128) be met wholly by industry; (c) supplies to industry be reduced by a further 2m tons. (C) should be kept in reserve, leaving (a), (b) or some compromise between them.

27 Sept	**131**	**The coke budget: winter 1947/1948** – Shinwell, 1+2+1p appendix. Also FAC(47)27.
	132	Not issued.
26 Sept	**133**	**Coal/oil conversion** – Shinwell, 2p. Progress report.
30 Sept	**134**	**Turn-round of wagons** – Barnes, 2p.
	135	Not issued.
26 Sept	**136**	**Transport prospects 1948–51** – Barnes, 3p. Action necessary to prevent breakdown.
26 Sept	**137**	**Progress of arrangements to spread the industrial load** – Isaacs covering the chairman of the Electricity Subcommittee of the Joint Consultative Committee, 1+2p annex.

CAB 134/275   Fuel Committee Reports   12 Feb–1 Oct 1947.

FUEL SITUATION   12 Feb–1 Oct 1947 Nos. 1–38. Daily reports for February, twice weekly for March and fortnightly thereafter.

TRANSPORT   14 Feb–30 Apr 1947 Nos. 1–14. Twice weekly reports in February and March and thereafter fortnightly.

UNEMPLOYMENT   13 Feb–13 Mar 1947 Nos. 1–8. Twice weekly in February and thereafter weekly on unemployment resulting from cuts in electric power.

15.18   Foreign Labour Committee

Set up in February 1946 (see CAB 128/5, CM(46)15th:7) and replaced in the administrative reorganization of October 1947 by the Labour Committee (CAB 134/469). It was served by the Official Committee on the Employment of Poles.

Terms   To examine, in the light of the existing manpower shortage, the possibility of making increased use of foreign labour, particularly in essential industries which are now finding special difficulty in recruiting labour.

Members   Ld Privy Seal (ch.); Home Sec.; S./S. Scotland; Mins. of Labour & N.S., Agriculture & Fish, Fuel & Power, Health; Parl. Sec., B.T.; Parl. U./Sec., Foreign Affs. (April 1947) Min. Without Portfolio (ch.); with Ld Privy Seal becoming member.

Sec.   J.A. Drew (Cab. O.).

CAB 134/301   Meetings and Memoranda   20 Feb 1946–8 Oct 1947   FLC(46)1st–FLC(47)3rd and FLC(46)1–FLC(47)29.

Meetings

14 Mar	**FLC(46)1st**	Untitled. FLC(46)2. General discussion on the use of foreign labour in particular industries facing manpower shortages.
3 Apr	**2nd:2**	**Italian labour.**
	:3	**Poles. FLC(46)3.**
23 May	**3rd:1**	**Progress of schemes in hand. FLC(46)8.**
31 July	**4th:1**	**Progress in placing members of the Polish forces in employment pending the formation of a Polish resettlement corps. FLC(46)9.**
	:2	**Importation of Italian foundry workers. FLC(46)10.**
	:3	**Future of Working Party on the Recruitment of Polish Miners.**
26 Sept	**5th:1**	**Employment of the Polish forces in the U.K. FLC(46)13.**
7 Nov	**6th:1**	**Polish resettlement corps: accommodation problems. FLC(46)15.**
	:2	**Employment of Poles. FLC(46)16.**
27 Nov	**7th:1**	**Accommodation for Poles. FLC(46)17 and 19.**
	:2	**Importation of Italian foundry workers. FLC(46)18.**
10 Dec	**8th:1**	**Employment of Poles. FLC(46)21.**
	:2	**Recruitment of displaced persons for the cotton spinning mills. FLC(46)20.**
14 Feb	**FLC(47)1st**	**Recruitment of displaced persons. FLC(47)4.**
26 Feb	**2nd**	**Recruitment of foreign labour. FLC(47)6.** Proposals rejected.
14 May	**3rd:1**	**Incentives for prisoners of war. FLC(47)16.**
	:2	**The recruitment of European volunteer workers. FLC(47)17.**

Memoranda

20 Feb	**FLC(46)1**	**Foreign Labour Committee – E.E. Bridges, 1p.** See CP(46)71.
1 Mar	**2**	**Preliminary questions for consideration – Greenwood, 5p.**
13 Mar	**3**	**Employment of members of the Polish forces in Great Britain – Isaacs, 3p.**
4 May	**5**	**Employment of foreign labour – Isaacs, 3p.**
14 May	**7**	**The trend of population – J.A. Drew covering the Royal Commission on Population, 1+3p annex +3p.**
22 May	**8**	**Employment of foreign labour – Isaacs, 4p.** Progress report.
9 July	**9**	**Progress in placing members of the Polish forces in employment pending the formation of the resettlement corps – Isaacs, 2p.**

19 July	10	**Importation of Italian foundry workers – Isaacs and Wilmot**, 1p.
19 Sept	13	**Employment of the Polish forces in the U.K.: results of action taken prior to the formation of the Polish resettlement corps – Edwards, N.,** 7p.
2 Nov	15	**Polish resettlement corps: accommodation problems: erection of new accommodation – Isaacs**, 5p.
5 Nov	16	**Employment of the Polish resettlement corps – Isaacs**, 5+2p annexes.
18 Nov	17	**Accommodation for members of the Polish resettlement corps – Isaacs**, 3+4p appendix.
22 Nov	18	**Importation of Italian foundry workers – J.A. Drew covering Isaacs**, 1+2p.
25 Nov	19	**Employment of Poles – Isaacs covering the Official Committee on the Employment of Poles**, 2+4p annex. 1st report.
5 Dec	20	**Recruitment of displaced persons for the cotton spinning mills – Belcher**, 2p.
6 Dec	21	**Employment of Poles – Isaacs covering the Official Committee on the Employment of Poles**, 2+3p. 2nd report.
3–29 Jan	FLC(47)1–3	**Employment of Poles – Isaacs covering the Official Committee on the Employment of Poles.** 3rd–5th reports.
12 Feb	4	**Recruitment of displaced persons – Isaacs**, 4p.
13 Feb	5	**Employment of Poles – Isaacs covering the Official Committee on the Employment of Poles**, 1+2p. 6th report.
25 Feb	6	**Recruitment of foreign labour – Greenwood**, 4p. The extent to which foreign labour could be recruited and placed throughout industry rather than relying on particular industries should be examined.
25 Feb	7	**Employment of Poles – Isaacs covering the Official Committee on the Employment of Poles**, 1+3+2p. 7th report.
5 Mar	8	**Proposal to increase proportion of training facilities for Poles in coal-mining – Isaacs**, 2p.
10 Mar	10	**Recruitment of labour from among displaced persons in Europe – Isaacs**, 2p. 1st progress report.
11–25 Mar	10–11	**Employment of Poles – Isaacs covering the Official Committee on the Employment of Poles.** 8th and 9th reports.
1 Apr	12	**Recruitment of labour from among displaced persons – Isaacs**, 2p. 2nd progress report.
8–23 Apr	13–14	**Employment of Poles – Isaacs covering the Official Committee on the Employment of Poles.** 10th and 11th reports.
23 Apr	15	**Change in membership – J.A. Drew**, 1p.

2 May	**16**	**Incentives for prisoners of war – Williams**, 3+1p appendix.
8 May	**17**	**Recruitment of European volunteer workers from the British zones of Germany and Austria – Isaacs**, 3+4p. Progress report.
9 May–15 July	**18–22**	**Employment of Poles – Isaacs covering the Official Committee on the Employment of Poles.** 12th–16th reports.
31 July	**23**	**Recruitment of E.V.W.s (Westward Ho!) – Isaacs**, 3p. Progress report.
7 Aug	**24**	**Employment of Poles in engineering – Isaacs**, 2p.
8 Aug–9 Sept	**25–27**	**Employment of Poles – Isaacs covering the Official Committee on the Employment of Poles.** 17th–19th reports.
1 Oct	**28**	**Incentives for prisoners of war – Williams**, 2p.
8 Oct	**29**	**Employment of Poles – Isaacs covering the Official Committee on the Employment of Poles,** 1+2p. 20th report.

15.19   Government Organization Committee

Steering Committee for Economic Organization Enquiry

Set up in December 1949 to consider both the co-ordination of economic policy (with the exception of ministerial committees) and departmental machinery for the implementation of policy, see CAB 134/308, GOC(49)4th:2. Work was delegated to the Economic Organization Working Group (T 222/324–346 and 565–568). Its papers after 1951 are in CAB 134/906.

Terms   To supervise a comprehensive enquiry into 'Government organization at all levels in the field of economic affairs, trade and industry.'

Members   E.E. Bridges (Try, ch.); E.N. Plowden (C.E.P.S.); J. Woods (B.T.); H. Emmerson (Works); A. Rowlands (Supply); D. Fergusson (Fuel & P.); G. Turner (War); F. Lee (Food); J.R. Simpson (Try).

Sec.   L. Petch (Try) and R.J.P. Hewison (Cab. O.).

CAB 134/314   Minutes and Memoranda   20 Jan 1950–8 Oct 1951
　　　　　　　GOC(SC)(50)1st–GOC(SC)(51)1st and
　　　　　　　GOC(SC)(50)1–GOC(SC)(51)5.

Meetings

25 Jan	**GOC(SC)(50)1st**	**Conduct of the enquiry.** GOC(SC)(50)1, 2, 3.
29 June	**2nd**	**Progress of the enquiry.** GOC(SC)(50)5 and 6.
13 July	**GOC(SC)(51)1st**	**Progress of the enquiry.** GOC(SC)(51)1,2,3,4.

Memoranda

20 Jan	**GOC(SC)(50)1**	**Note by secretary – L. Petch,** 1+5p. Sets out possible approach.
24 Jan	**2**	**Enquiry into government organization in the field of economic affairs, trade and industry – L. Petch covering H. Emmerson,** 1+1p. Should start with central economic planning since there was an agreed document on this, i.e. the White Paper on Employment Policy. It was necessary to decide whether one body should be responsible for planning and then consider departmental contacts with industry.
24 Jan	**3**	**Enquiry into government organization in the field of economic affairs, trade and industry – L. Petch covering F. Lee,** 1+2p. The views of experienced outsiders should be sought.
15 Feb	**4**	**Note by the chairman – E.E. Bridges covering J.R. Simpson,** 1+6p. Scheme of work.
9 June	**5**	**Note by the joint secretaries – L. Petch and R.J.P. Hewison covering C.E.P.S.,** 1+7p. 'Essential functions of government in the economic field' attached.
16 June	**6**	**Progress of the enquiry – J.R. Simpson,** 2+14p appendix.
14 Feb	**GOC(SC)(51)1**	**Contacts between government departments and industry and business – E.E. Bridges covering the working group,** 1+15+32p appendixes. First interim report. Consideration of the production authority system.
26 Feb	**2**	**Contacts between government departments and industry and business – N. Brook,** 3p. Comments on GOC(SC)(51)1.
7 July	**3**	**Progress of the enquiry – E.E. Bridges,** 2p.
10 July	**4**	**Factual report on major responsibilities – E.E. Bridges covering the Working Group,** 1+14+5p appendix.
8 Oct	**5**	**Factual report on major responsibilities – E.E. Bridges covering the Working Group,** 1+14+64p appendixes. Second interim report. Report on the allocation and co-ordination of departmental responsibility for economic activities. The appendixes describe the organization for handling important areas of policy.

15.20 Home Affairs Committee

Official Committee on Industrial Problems

Set up in July 1945 under the caretaker government to replace the Reconstruction Committee's Official Subcommittee on Industrial Problems (CAB 87/17–18), see CAB

71/26, HA(I)(45)2. Under the Labour government its work on controls was taken over by the Official Committee on Controls under the Lord President's Committee (CAB 132/58).

Terms (a) to consider matters remitted to it for examination by the Home Affairs Committee or the Home Affairs (Industrial) Subcommittee (b) to keep under review the work being done by departments on the industrial problems of the transitional and post-war periods with a view to ensuring that adequate progress is made on all major questions.

Members J.P.R. Maud (Ld Pres. O., ch.); B.W. Gilbert (Try); W. Palmer (B.T.); J.H. Woods (Prod.); G. Myrrdin Evans (Lab. & N.S.).

Sec. A.N. Coleridge (Ld Pres. O.).

CAB 134/376 Meeting and Memoranda 20 June 1945–7 Jan 1946 IO(45)1st and IO(45)1–7.

Meeting

10 July	**IO(45)1st:1**	**Future of the scientific instrument industry.** IO(45)2.
	:2	**Modification in controls.**

Memoranda

13 July	**IO(45)1**	**Composition and terms of reference – J.P.R. Maud,** 1p.
20 June	**2**	**Future of the scientific instrument industry – Lord President's Office covering the working party on the scientific instrument industry,** 1+10+1+8+54p appendixes. Also SOI(44)47.
3 July	**3**	**Modifications of controls – Lord President's Office covering the Board of Trade,** 1+2p.
6 July–7 Aug	**4–7**	**Modifications of controls – Memoranda by Raw Materials Department of the Ministry of Supply,** 1+11p.
29 Aug		**Modifications in controls – Lord President's Office covering the Ministry of Aircraft Production and the Raw Materials Department of the Ministry of Supply.**
8 Sept–7 Jan 1946		**Modifications in controls – Lord President's Office covering the Raw Materials Department of the Ministry of Supply.** Further unnumbered memoranda of amendments to controls.

15.21 Investment Programmes Committee

Set up in August 1947 as a subcommittee of the Official Steering Committee on Economic Development to draw up a detailed plan to curtail capital investment programmes, other than those contributing to export or import savings, see CAB 128/10, CM(47)68th:2 and CAB 129/20, CP(47)231. Reconstituted as a standing committee in December 1947 to maintain a continuous survey of investment, see CAB 128/10, CM(47)81st:4 and CAB 129/22, CP(47)322.

It replaced the larger and ineffective Investment Working Party (T 161/1297). Its papers were prepared by the Investment Programmes Committee Working Party (CAB 134/444–457) and it was served by three subcommittees on plant and machinery, investment statistics and industrial building (CAB 134/443). Its decisions were implemented by the Ministry of Works' Headquarters Building Committee (T 229/674). Its work provoked political controversy for two major reasons: first, the lack of co-ordination between its programmes and the allocations of the Materials Committee (despite the secretariat of both committees being members of the C.E.P.S.) and, secondly, the suspicion that strategic decisions especially concerning housing were being taken in effect by officials. Its later papers are in CAB 134/982.

Terms (i) to review the size of the total investment programme, both building and plant and machinery, and to make proposals as to the extent to which the programmes of departments require modification (ii) to obtain from departments a statement of the steps necessary to carry out these proposals and of their effect on their programmes (iii) to submit a comprehensive review to ministers (iv) to supervise methods of controlling and reducing the total programme through labour ceilings, expenditure limits, material supplies, licences or any other methods which are necessary (v) to make proposals as to the relative priorities which departments should observe in dealing with existing and new projects.

(Dec 1947) (i) to draw up general investment priorities, this to include the impact on U.K. supplies of the investment programmes of the colonies and of British overseas oil schemes (ii) to approve departmental investment programmes and in the light of them to draw up national investment programmes (iii) to consider departmental building labour ceilings submitted by the Headquarters Building Committee and, if necessary, to propose revision of the balance between different departments (iv) to have general oversight of all investment programmes (v) to approve major projects for capital investment above £500,000 in value (including both building and plant); the committee to have power to raise or lower this figure in the light of experience. (March 1948) Section (v) deleted.

Membership E.N. Plowden (C.E.P.S., ch.); P.D. Proctor (Try); E.F.Muir (Works); L.B. Hutchinson (Supply); E.A. Hitchman (Labour & N.S.); G.H. Andrew (B.T.); D.M.B. Butt (Ec. Sect.); J. Stafford (C.S.O.); H.T. Weeks (C.E.P.S.); E.A.G. Robinson (C.E.P.S.).

(Dec 1947) H.T. Weeks (C.E.P.S., ch.); P.D. Proctor (Try); R.L. Hall (Ec. Sect.); W. Strath (C.E.P.S.); E.F. Muir (Works); L.B. Hutchinson (Supply); A.K. Cairncross (B.T.). (April 1948) W. Strath (ch.). (Jan 1949) V.P. Harries (Supply) replaced Hutchinson, R.F. Bretherton (Ec. Sect.) replaced Hall. (Nov 1949) F.F. Turnbull (C.E.P.S., ch.) replaced Strath. (Dec 1950) F.C. How (Supply) replaced Harries. (Oct 1951) M.W. Bennitt (Works) replaced Muir, R.F. Bretherton (now Materials) remained member.

Secs. F.R.P. Vinter (Try) and J.G. Stewart (Cab. O.). (Dec 1947) J.L. Croome (C.E.P.S.) replaced Stewart. (Feb 1948) A.R.W. Bavin (Cab. O.) replaced Croome. (Dec 1948) P.J. Moorhouse (Cab. O.) replaced Bavin. (July 1950) E. Jones (C.E.P.S.) replaced Vinter. (Oct 1951) C.D. Smith (C.E.P.S.) replaced Jones.

CAB 134/437 Meetings and Memoranda 14 Aug–30 Dec 1947 IPC(47)1st–31st and IPC(47)1–12.

Meetings

15 Aug	**IPC(47)1st**	**Plant, machinery and vehicles.** IPC(47)1. Agreement to discuss the requirements of certain industries with departments concerned.
18 Aug	**2nd**	**Generating plant programme.** Consideration of possible reductions.
20 Aug	**3rd:1**	**List of industries and services using plant and machinery.** IPC(47)3.
	:2	**Housing programme.**
25 Aug	**4th:1**	**Agricultural building programme.** IPC(47)4.
	:2	**Agricultural machinery.**
27 Aug	**5th**	Untitled. IPC(WP)(47) 1 and 13. Consideration of the education investment programme.
28 Aug	**6th:1**	**Housing.** IPC(WP)(47)2 and 4. To achieve the labour targets existing contracts would have to be cancelled and work even stopped on some houses already begun.
	:2	**New towns.**
	:3	**Health services: hospitals, sewerage and water supply.**
29 Aug	**7th:1**	**Home Office services.** IPC(WP)(47)5.
	:2	**Scottish Home Department services.**
29 Aug	**8th:1**	**Plant requirements of the building materials industries.** IPC(WP)(47)11.
1 Sept	**9th:1**	**Control of plant and machinery.**
	:2	**Proposals for control of investment put forward by Sir Graham Cunningham at a meeting of the Planning Board.** Proposal impracticable at least until the government had decided on existing cuts.
	:3	**Distribution of building cuts.**
	:4	**Form of committee's report.** Agreement that the report should cover the relationship between the volume of investment and inflation and deflation, an analysis of investment, an overall target and individual targets for each department, the expected results of proposed cuts, and their consequences for the building industry.
2 Sept	**10th**	**Ministry of Transport programme.**
2 Sept	**11th:1**	**Ministry of Supply direct building programme.**
	:2	**Ministry of Supply sponsored schemes.**
	:3	**Board of Trade schemes.**
3 Sept	**12th:1**	**Ministry of Works direct building work.** IPC(WP)(47)10.
	:2	**Ministry of Works civil licensing ceiling.** IPC(WP)(47)9.
4 Sept	**13th**	**Post Office investment programme.** IPC(WP)(47)20.
5 Sept	**14th:1**	**Electricity programme.**
	:2	**Coal.** IPC(WP)(47)22.

	:3	**Petroleum. IPC(WP)(47)22.**
	:4	**Gas industry. IPC(WP)(47)22.**
9 Sept	**15th:1**	**Admiralty civil licence building work.** IPC(WP)(47)30.
	:2	**Merchant shipping programme.** IPC(WP)(47)24.
9 Sept	**16th**	**Civil aviation investment programme.** IPC(WP)(47)29.
10 Sept	**17th:1**	**Investment programmes of the service departments. IPC(WP)(47)31, 32, 33.**
	:2	**R.A.F. rehabilitation centre, Leatherhead.**
12 Sept	**18th:1**	**Ministry of Food investment programme.** IPC(WP)(47)34.
15 Sept	**19th:1**	**New towns. IPC(WP)(47)35.**
	:3	**Departmental building labour ceilings.** IPC(WP)(47)42.
17 Sept	**20th**	**Investment in plant and machinery (Board of Trade and Ministry of Supply). IPC(WP)(47)45.** Consideration in relation to the export target for machine tools.
17 Sept	**21st**	**Investment in plant and machinery (Ministry of Food and Ministry of Works). IPC(WP)(47)45.**
18 Sept	**22nd:1**	**Timing of the committee's report.**
	:2	**Investment in plant and machinery (Ministry of Agriculture and Fisheries).**
19 Sept	**23rd:1**	**New towns. IPC(WP)(47)35.**
	:2	**Building programme. IPC(WP)(47)47.** Consideration to prevent the labour force being greater than the material resources available for its use.
29 Sept	**24th**	**Draft report. IPC(WP)(47)52.**
30 Sept	**25th**	**Draft report. IPC(WP)(47)52.**
1 Oct	**26th**	Untitled. Further consideration of the draft report. Agreement that the committee should reconsider whether, even after the proposed cuts, the programme was too large.
4 Oct	**27th**	Untitled. IPC(WP)(47)52(revise). Approval of report with amendments.
3 Dec	**28th:1**	**Forest roads. IPC(WP)(47)61.** Agreement on reductions in the workforce to be recommended to the Distribution of Industry Committee.
	:2	**Construction work at Prestwick Airport.** IPC(WP)(47)63.
	:3	**Southern Railway colour–light signalling.** IPC(WP)(47)62.
8 Dec	**29th:1**	**Southern Railway colour–light signalling.** IPC(WP)(47)62.
	:2	**Composition and terms of reference. IPC(47)11.**
	:3	**Maximum building labour forces.**
	:4	**Review of industrial building. IPC(WP)(47)64.**

	:5	**I.C.I. capital and special maintenance programme. IPC(WP)(47)65.**
16 Dec	**30th:1**	**Review of industrial building.**
	:2	**Capital programmes of local authorities.** IPC(WP)(47)66. Agreement that the Ministry of Health should not collect details of prospective capital expenditure from local authorities, but the authorities should be reminded of the importance of having reserves of works in a maximum state of readiness.
	:3	**Procedure for the submission of projects.** IPC(WP)(47)67.
30 Dec	**31st:1**	**Bairnswear Ltd., new worsted spinning mill at Worksop. IPC(WP)(47)68.**
	:2	**Review of industrial building and factory building statistics.**
	:3	**Merthyr Tydfil bypass road.**
	:4	**Government research and experimental stations.**
	:5	**Report on Marshall Aid.**

Memoranda

14 Aug	**IPC(47)1**	**Composition and terms of reference – F.R.P. Vinter and J.G. Stewart,** 1p.
15 Aug	2	**Note by joint secretaries – F.R.P. Vinter and J.G. Stewart,** 1+3+2p annexes. Letter sent to departments on the investment review.
19 Aug	3	**List of industries and services using plant and machinery – C.S.O.,** 1+3p appendix +1p addendum.
20 Aug	4	**Building manpower ceilings – J.G. Stewart and F.R.P. Vinter covering the Ministry of Agriculture,** 1+3p.
20 Aug	5	**Analysis of approvals by Panel A and Regional Distribution of Industry Panels – J.G. Stewart and F.R.P. Vinter covering the Board of Trade,** 1+23p.
22 Aug	6	**Review of investment programme – J.G. Stewart and F.R.P. Vinter,** 1+2p. Letter to departments on plant and machinery.
25 Aug	7	**Housing programme – J.G. Stewart and F.R.P. Vinter,** 1p.
27 Aug	8	**Review of the investment programme. Meetings with departments – J.G. Stewart and F.R.P. Vinter,** 1p. Progress report.
8 Oct	9	**Report – the committee,** 11+3+32p appendixes. See CP(47)284. Also EPB(47)17 and ED(47)48.
7 Nov	10	**Analysis of approvals by Panel A and Regional Distribution of Industry Panels – J.G. Stewart and F.R.P. Vinter covering the Board of Trade,** 1+20p.

5 Dec	11	Composition and terms of reference – N. Brook, 2p.
19 Dec	12	Procedure for the submission of projects costing £500,000 and upwards – H.T. Weeks, 2+1p appendix.

CAB 134/438   Meetings 6 Jan–31 Dec 1948   IPC(48)1st–72nd.

6 Jan	IPC(48)1st:1	Capital programmes of local authorities. IPC(WP)(48)2.
	:2	Iron and steel programmes. IPC(WP)(48)1.
	:3	Petroleum development programmes.
13 Jan	2nd:1	Capital programmes of local authorities. IPC(WP)(48)5.
	:2	Petroleum development programmes.
	:3	Industrial buildings ban.
	:4	Expansion of caustic soda production by I.C.I. Ltd. IPC(WP)(48)3.
	:5	Metropolitan Water Board supply main, Kempton to Cricklewood. IPC(WP)(48)4.
	:6	Procedure for the submission of programmes. IPC(WP)(48)7.
	:7	Marshall Aid and investment programmes. IPC(WP)(48)6.
20 Jan	3rd:1	New turbo shop for G.E.C. at Witton, Birmingham. IPC(WP)(48)9.
	:2	New plant for British Petroleum Chemicals Ltd., Grangemouth.
	:3	New factory for Norfolk Film Base Ltd., Norwich. IPC(WP)(48)11.
	:4	Review of industrial building.
27 Jan	4th:1	The effect of the European Recovery Programme on investment programmes. IPC(WP)(48)14.
	:2	Information available on the progress of new construction. IPC(WP)(48)8.
	:3	Government research and experimental stations.
	:4	Maximum building labour forces.
	:5	Synthetic soap plant at Stanlow refinery. IPC(WP)(48)12.
10 Feb	5th:1	Canteen building schemes. IPC(WP)(48)13 and 15.
	:2	Exemptions from industrial ban.
	:3	Reserve of works. IPC(WP)(48)16. Consideration of possible modification to Treasury rules governing loan sanctions to local authorities.
	:4	Railway coaching stock. IPC(WP)(48)18.
17 Feb	6th:1	Clayton Aniline Co. Ltd. IPC(WP)(48)19.
	:2	Loughton–Epping railway electrification. IPC(WP)(48)22.
	:3	Railway coaching stock.

	:4	**Information required about capital projects.** IPC(WP)(48)21.
	:5	**Capital investment cuts on docks.**
24 Feb	7th:1	**Fylde Water Board trunk main.** IPC(WP)(48)23.
	:2	**Note by Mr. Cairncross.** Three problems to consider: (a) the frustration of the average businessman over controls; (b) the kind of project the committee should favour; (c) the schemes the committee should look at.
27 Feb	8th:1	**Electricity Commission: new generating station plant.** IPC(WP)(48)25 and 29.
	:2	**The scale of industrial building and the steel allocation.** IPC(WP)(48)33. Agreement to bring to the attention of the Economic Secretary, Treasury, the discrepancies between steel allocation and manpower ceilings before the next meeting of the Materials Committee.
2 Mar	9th:1	**Steel and the investment programme.**
	:2	**Monsanto Chemicals Ltd.: new factory at Newport, Monmouthshire.** IPC(WP)(48)26.
	:3	**I.C.I. proposals for expanding alkali production.** IPC(WP)(48)30.
	:4	**Murgatroyd's Saltworks Ltd.: project for the production of salt, caustic soda and chlorine at Sandbach, Cheshire.** IPC(WP)(48)31.
	:5	**Reserve of works.** IPC(WP)(48)16 and 32. Consideration of the nature and state of preparedness of anti-cyclical public works.
9 Mar	10th	**Capital investment programme.** IPC(WP)(48)24, 38, 39.
16 Mar	11th:1	**Investment digest.** IPC(WP)(48)45.
	:2	**Incidence of investment cuts in dock and road programmes in development areas and on Merseyside.** IPC(WP)(48)36 and 37.
	:3	**Expansion of the cement industry.** IPC(WP)(48)43.
	:4	**Capital investment programme.**
	:5	**Reserve of works.** IPC(WP)(48)46. Detailed consideration.
23 Mar	12th:1	**Alkali production: expansion of capacity.** IPC(WP)(48)47.
	:2	**Investment digest.** IPC(WP)(48)45.
	:3	**Capital investment programme.** Discussion of plans for the review of capital investment.
	:4	**Educational building in 1948.** IPC(WP)(48)48.
24 Mar	13th	**Capital investment programme 1949.** IPC(48)5. Discussion on preparation of departmental programmes.
31 Mar	14th	**Capital investment programme 1949.** IPC(48)5. Discussion with departmental representatives

		of programmes for industrial building, defence, agriculture and fuel and power.
1 Apr	15th	**Capital investment programme 1949.** IPC(48)5. Similar discussion on housing, town and country planning, Home Office, Post Office, B.B.C. and transport.
13 Apr	16th:1	**Reduction in the labour force of highway authorities.** IPC(WP)(48)44.
	:2	**Public works schemes in areas of heavy unemployment.** DI(48)17. Preference for a higher rate of unemployment than that recommended by the Ministry of Labour before any easement of investment cuts in areas of heavy unemployment.
	:3	**Relations with socialized industries.** IPC(WP)(48)49.
	:4	**Capital investment programme 1949.** IPC(WP)(48)40. Agreement that the review should be guided by the main material limiting factors on capital investment, i.e. timber, steel and exports rather than building labour and money value.
20 Apr	17th:1	**Labour for Home Office building and civil engineering work.** IPC(WP)(48)51.
	:2	**B.B.C. building programme.** IPC(WP)(48)50.
	:3	**Modernization and expansion of the artificial fibre industry.** IPC(WP)(48)41.
20 Apr	*ad hoc*	**Electricity programme.**
4 May	18th:1	**The load of work on the building industry.** IPC(WP)(48)58. Consideration of the effect of investment cuts on employment in the industry.
	:2	**Steel in 1949.** IPC(WP)(48)54.
	:3	**Timber supplies in 1949.** IPC(WP)(48)55.
	:4	**Plant and machinery in 1949.** IPC(WP)(48)57.
6 May	19th:1	**Post Office capital investment programme: 1948–1952.** IPC(WP)(48)66.
	:2	**B.B.C. capital investment programme: 1948–1952.** IPC(WP)(48)70.
	:3	**Deep water quays: Leith.**
10 May	20th	**Merchant shipping capital investment programme: 1947–1951.**
11 May	21st:1	**Ministry of Works capital investment programme 1949: government building.** IPC(WP)(48)83.
	:2	**Ministry of Works investment programme 1949–52: miscellaneous building.** IPC(WP)(48)82.
	:3	**Ministry of Labour employment exchange and regional office, Manchester.** IPC(WP)(48)61.
12 May	22nd:1	**Housing programme for England and Wales 1948/52.** IPC(WP)(48)62.

	:2	**Housing programme 1948/52: Scotland.** IPC(WP)(48)68.
13 May	23rd:1	**Educational building 1947–1952: England and Wales.** IPC(WP)(48)79.
	:2	**Educational building 1947–52: Scotland.** IPC(WP)(48)65.
18 May	24th:1	**Steel development programme 1948/52.** IPC(WP)(48)63.
	:2	**Capital investment: iron foundries.**
19 May	25th	**Capital investment 1947–52: agriculture.** IPC(WP)(48)67 and 69.
20 May	26th:1	**Road programme 1948/1952.** IPC(WP)(48)64.
	:2	**Road vehicle programme 1948/52.** IPC(WP)(48)97.
21 May	27th:1	**Capital investment 1947–52: Admiralty sponsored industries.** IPC(WP)(48)77.
	:2	**Capital investment 1947–52: building materials and components industries.** IPC(WP)(48)81.
	:3	**Capital investment 1947–52: Board of Trade.** IPC(WP)(48)89.
	:4	**Capital investment 1947–52: Ministry of Supply.** IPC(WP)(48)72.
	:5	**Capital investment 1947–52: Ministry of Food.** IPC(WP)(48)90.
	:6	**Labour allocation for the provision of grain storage.** IPC(WP)(48)96.
	:7	**Ministry of Food labour force 1948.** IPC(WP)(48)95.
24 May	28th:1	**Capital investment 1947–52: home departments.** IPC(WP)(48)71 and 91.
	:2	**Capital investment 1947–1952: fisheries.** IPC(WP)(48)93 and 94.
	:3	**Capital investment 1947/1952: collection of statistics.**
	:4	**Board of Trade capital investment programme.** IPC(WP)(48)89.
	:5	**1951 exhibition.**
25 May	29th	**Capital investment 1947–52: defence.** IPC(WP)(48)74, 76, 80, 84, 88.
26 May	30th:1	**Capital investment 1947/1952: British Electricity Authority.** IPC(WP)(48)52.
	:2	**Capital investment 1947/1952: North of Scotland Hydro-electric Board.** IPC(WP)(48)71.
27 May	31st	**Capital investment 1947/52: health services (other than housing).** IPC(WP)(48)73 and 75.
28 May	32nd:1	**Capital investment 1947/52: petroleum industry.** IPC(WP)(48)87.
	:2	**Capital investment 1947/52: coke ovens.**
	:3	**Capital investment 1947/52: British Electricity Authority.**

31 May	**33rd:1**	**Capital investment 1947–52: ports and inland waterways.** IPC(WP)(48)102.
	:2	**Capital investment 1947–52: railways and London Transport road services.** IPC(WP)(48)98.
1 June	**34th:1**	**Capital investment 1947/1952: open-cast coal.** IPC(WP)(48)108.
	:2	**Capital investment 1947/1952: National Coal Board.** IPC(WP)(48)85.
4 June	**35th**	**Capital investment 1947/52: civil aviation.** IPC(WP)(48)60.
7 June	**36th**	**Capital investment 1947/1952: Northern Ireland.** IPC(WP)(48)100.
8 June	**37th:1**	**Capital investment 1947/1952: Forestry Commission.** IPC(WP)(48)92.
	:2	**Expansion of dyestuffs production.** IPC(WP)(48)99.
9 June	**38th**	**Capital investment 1947–1952: commercial building.**
10 June	**39th:1**	**Capital investment 1947/52: coating industry.** IPC(WP)(48)105.
	:2	**Capital investment 1947/52: tar distilling.** IPC(WP)(48)106.
	:3	**Capital investment 1947/52: gas industry.** IPC(WP)(48)86.
	:4	**Ministry of Fuel and Power investment programmes: relative priorities.**
14 June	**40th**	**Capital investment 1949: Ministry of Food.** IPC(WP)(48)109.
15 June	**41st**	**Supply of materials in 1949.**
	:1	**Steel.**
	:2	**Cast iron.** IPC(WP)(48)113.
	:3	**Refractories.** IPC(WP)(48)114.
	:4	**Timber.** IPC(WP)(48)112.
	:5	**Bricks.**
	:6	**Cement.**
16 June	**42nd**	**Merchant shipbuilding programme.** IPC(WP)(48)104.
18 June	**43rd**	**Capital investment 1947–52: statistics.** IPC(WP)(48)129.
21 June	**44th**	**Capital investment 1949: supply of materials.** IPC(WP)(48)129. Consideration of the contrasting requirements of the tentative steel budget and current allocations by the Materials Committee; and of particular sectors of investment in the light of their estimated demand for timber and steel.
29 June	**45th:1**	**Capital investment 1949.** Resumed consideration of the report's main principles.
	:2	**Future meetings.**

30 June	**46th:1**	**Capital investment 1949: draft report: appendixes on iron and steel and railway programmes.** IPC(WP)(48)118 and 136.
	:2	**Capital investment 1949: timber supplies.**
	:3	**Capital investment 1949: steel supplies.**
1 July	**47th**	**Capital investment 1948/49: building and civil engineering labour.** IPC(WP)(48)148.
1–2 July	**48th:1**	**Capital investment 1949: draft report: appendixes on ports, harbours and inland waterways; road vehicles; shipbuilding; gas and tar distilling industries; electricity; housing; education; health services; home departments; defence services.** IPC(WP)(48)110, 119, 120, 121, 125, 130, 134, 135, 139, 140.
	:2	**Capital investment 1949: steel supplies.**
5 July	**49th**	**Capital investment 1949: draft report: appendixes on petroleum; coke; coal; electricity (main transmission and distribution and North of Scotland Hydro-electric Board); Post Office, B.B.C.** IPC(WP)(48)116, 126, 131, 134, 141, 149.
6 July	**50th**	**Capital investment 1949: draft report: appendixes on industrial investment; miscellaneous building; government building.** IPC(WP)(48)124, 142, 144.
7 July	**51st:1**	**Capital investment 1949: draft report: appendixes on plant and machinery; civil aviation.** IPC(WP)(48)137 and 150.
	:2	**Capital investment 1949: presentation of report.**
	:3	**Great Exhibition centenary.**
8 July	**52nd**	**Capital investment 1949: draft report: appendixes on agriculture; forestry; roads; Northern Ireland.** IPC(WP)(48)122, 133, 143, 145.
9 July	**53rd:1**	**Capital investment 1949: draft report.**
	:2	**Capital investment 1949: steel supplies.**
10 July	**54th:1**	**Steel: 1948 allocations.**
	:2	**Capital investment 1949: draft report part 2.** IPC(WP)(48)110(revise), 118(revise), 120(revise), 126(revise), 134(revise), 135(revise), 139(revise), 149(revise), 151.
12 July	**55th:1**	**Capital investment 1949: draft report part 1.**
	:2	**Capital investment 1949: draft report part 2.** IPC(WP)(48)116(revise), 119(revise), 121(revise), 122(revise), 124(revise), 125(revise), 133(revise), 137(revise), 140(revise), 141(revise), 142(revise), 143(revise), 144(revise), 145(revise), 154, 155.
	:3	**Great Exhibition centenary.** IPC(WP)(48)152.
13 July	**56th**	**Capital investment 1949: draft report.** IPC(WP)(48)136(revise), 156, 157.

3 Aug	57th:1	**Capital investment 1949: report of the Investment Programmes Committee (IPC(48)8): steel requirements for the coal industry.** First of a series of detailed discussions, lasting until 11 August, to reconsider the draft report at the Production Committee's request.
	:2	**Capital investment 1949: report of the Investment Programmes Committee (IPC(48)8): steel requirements for the electricity industry.**
	:3	**Capital investment 1949: report of the Investment Programmes Committee (IPC(48)8): steel requirements for the oil industry.**
5 Aug	58th	**Capital investment 1949: report of the Investment Programmes Committee (IPC(48)8): steel requirements for the transport industry.**
9 Aug	59th	**Capital investment 1949: report of the Investment Programmes Committee (IPC(48)8): steel requirements for the coal, electricity and transport industries.**
11 Aug	60th:1	**Capital investment 1949: report of the Investment Programmes Committee (IPC(48)8): steel requirements for the electricity industry.** IPC(WP)(48)162.
	:2	**Capital investment 1949: report of the Investment Programmes Committee (IPC(48)8): steel requirements for the coal, electricity and transport industries.** IPC(WP)(48)147, 160, 161, 163, 164. Lines of a supplementary report agreed.
	:3	**Capital investment 1949: steel allocation for the North of Scotland Hydro-electric Board's programme.**
16 Aug	61st	**Supplementary report on capital investment in 1949.** Consideration of a first draft.
16 Aug	62nd	**Long-term survey (1948–52): section on investment.**
3 Sept	63rd:1	**Film industry programme 1948–50.** IPC(WP)(48)158.
	:2	**Programme of research establishments for associations assisted by the Department of Scientific and Industrial Research.** IPC(WP)(48)159.
	:3	**Draft report for the O.E.E.C. 1949/50: section on investment.** IPC(WP)(48)166.
14 Sept	64th:1	**Sulphuric acid.** IPC(WP)(48)167.
	:2	**Future work and meetings of the committee.**
	:3	**School building in Northern Ireland.** IPC(WP)(48)169.

	:4	**Recovery of steel scrap from disused tramway tracks.**
	:5	**Film industry programme 1948–50.** IPC(WP)(48)170.
	:6	**Analysis of approvals by Panel A and regional distribution of industry panels.** IPC(WP)(48)168.
	:7	**Steel controls and investment programming. W.** Strath gave his first reactions to the steel allocation scheme with regard to investment programming.
	:8	**Capital investment 1948–1952.** IPC(WP)(48)171.
	:9	**Capital investment 1949.** IPC(48)10.
21 Sept	65th:1	**Future work on investment programmes.** IPC(WP)(48)172. Approval of the general programme in the memorandum.
	:2	**Steel controls and investment programming.** IPC(WP)(48)173. Agreement that, even if the steel allocation scheme were abandoned, it might be necessary to control the major steel-using programmes by steel 'ceilings' in addition to financial control.
	:3	**Capital investment 1948/52.** IPC(WP)(48)171.
12 Oct	66th:1	**Factory building statistics: inclusion of information on costs.**
	:2	**Publication of information on capital investment in 1949.**
	:3	**Scottish housing programme.**
	:4	**Capital investment in the colonies.**
	:5	**Capital investment 1948/52.** IPC(WP)(48)180.
	:6	**Capital investment 1950.** IPC(WP)(48)181.
9 Nov	67th:1	**Economic Survey for 1949: appendix on capital investment** IPC(WP)(48)186.
	:2	**Proposal for a return of private capital expenditure.**
16 Nov	68th:1	**Warehouses at ports.** IPC(WP)(48)178.
	:2	**The chemical industry.**
	:3	**The fertiliser industry.** IPC(WP)(48)185.
	:4	**Sulphuric acid.** IPC(WP)(48)167.
	:5	**Ammonia and nitric acid.** IPC(WP)(48)177.
	:6	**The plastics industry.** IPC(WP)(48)179.
7 Dec	69th:1	**Electricity investment programmes.** IPC(WP)(48)187.
	:2	**Scottish housing.** IPC(WP)(48)191.
21 Dec	70th:1	**Forestry.** IPC(WP)(48)200.
	:2	**Economic Survey for 1949: appendixes on capital investment.** IPC(WP)(48)204.
	:3	**Programme of work on the 1950 investment programme.**
22 Dec	71st	**Road programme 1950/52.** IPC(WP)(48)197.

31 Dec	**72nd:1**	**Estimated timber supplies in 1950.** IPC(WP)(48)189.
	:2	**Aluminium.**
	:3	**Public works schemes.** Consideration of scheduling Newcastle as an area in which cuts in public works could be relaxed.

CAB 134/439   Memoranda   20 Jan–15 Dec 1948   IPC(48)1–15.

20 Jan	**IPC(48)1**	**Departmental liaison with the committee –** **F.R.P. Vinter and J.L. Croome,** 1+1p.
18 Feb	**2**	**Note by the joint secretaries – F.R.P. Vinter and** **J.L. Croome,** 1p.
25 Feb	**3**	**Change in secretariat – F.R.P. Vinter and** **A.R.W. Bavin,** 1p.
20 Mar	**4**	**Change in the committee's terms of reference –** **F.R.P. Vinter and A.R.W. Bavin,** 1p.
20 Mar	**5**	**Investment programme 1949 – F.R.P. Vinter** **and A.R.W. Bavin covering E.N. Plowden,** 1+6p. Circular to permanent heads of departments.
8 Apr	**6**	**Capital investment programme 1949:** **investment in plant and machinery – note of a** **meeting on 6 Apr 1948,** 2p. Consideration of how to collect information for the 1949 programme.
29 Apr	**7**	**Change of chairman – F.R.P. Vinter and J.** **Downie,** 1p.
16 July	**8**	**Report on capital investment 1949 – Investment** **Programmes Committee,** 87+9p appendixes. See PC(48)93. Also ED(48)6 and EPB(48)23.
1 Sept	**9**	**Capital investment 1949. Supplementary** **report – Investment Programmes Committee,** 6+10p annex. Concerned with additional claims from certain industries.
8 Sept	**10**	**Capital investment 1949 – F.R.P. Vinter and** **A.R. Bunker,** 1+2p. Extracts of PC(48)15th and 16th.
28 Oct	**11**	**Investment review 1950 – F.R.P. Vinter and** **A.R. Bunker covering E.N. Plowden,** 1+5p. Circular to permanent heads of department.
12 Nov	**12**	**Estimated gross fixed investment 1948 and** **1949 – F.R.P. Vinter and A.R. Bunker,** 1+2p.
12 Nov	**13**	**Note by the joint secretary – F.R.P. Vinter,** 1p.
22 Nov	**14**	**Departmental liaison with the committee –** **F.R.P. Vinter,** 1+1p. Revised list of IPC(48)1.
15 Dec	**15**	**Change in secretariat – F.R.P. Vinter and P.J.** **Moorhouse,** 1p.

CAB 134/440   Meetings and Memoranda   4 Jan–20 Dec 1949   IPC(49)1st–76th and IPC(49)1–11.

Meetings

| 4 Jan | **IPC(49)1st** | **Steel supplies.** Consideration of the possibility of a steel shortage. |

5 Jan	**2nd:1**	**General Post Office.** IPC(WP)(48)225. Confidential annex attached.
	:2	**British Broadcasting Corporation.** IPC(WP)(48)205.
7 Jan	**3rd:1**	**Civil aviation.** IPC(WP)(48)192 and 193.
	:2	**Statistical summary.**
10 Jan	**4th**	**North of Scotland Hydro-electric Board.** IPC(WP)(48)203 and IPC(WP)(49)3.
11 Jan	**5th:1**	**Road vehicles.** IPC(WP)(48)211 and IPC(WP)(49)2.
	:2	**Education.** IPC(WP)(48)201 and IPC(WP)(49)1.
13 Jan	**6th**	**Housing.** IPC(WP)(48) 190 and 206. Confidential annex attached setting out the provisional conclusion on the housing investment programme.
14 Jan	**7th:1**	**Agriculture.** IPC(WP)(48)196 and 202.
	:2	**Agricultural machinery.** IPC(WP)(48)210.
	:3	**Development Fund.**
17 Jan	**8th:1**	**Coal (open-cast).** IPC(WP)(48)213.
	:2	**Coal (National Coal Board).** IPC(WP)(48)212.
18 Jan	**9th:1**	**Shipbuilding.** IPC(WP)(48)224.
	:2	**Ports and inland waterways.** IPC(WP)(49)5.
19 Jan	**10th:1**	**Electricity.** IPC(WP)(48)216.
	:2	**Estimates of investment.** IPC(WP)(49)8 and 9.
20 Jan	**11th:1**	**Oil.** IPC(WP)(48)217.
	:2	**Electricity.**
21 Jan	**12th**	**Board of Trade investment programme 1950.** IPC(WP)(48)226.
24 Jan	**13th:1**	**Ministry of Supply investment programme 1950.** IPC(WP)(49)4.
	:2	**Machine tools.** IPC(WP)(49)12.
25 Jan	**14th**	**Aluminium.** IPC(WP)(49)10, 13, 18.
26 Jan	**15th:1**	**Estimates of investment.** IPC(WP)(49)22 and 23.
	:2	**Housing programme for England and Wales.**
	:3	**Aluminium.**
3 Feb	**16th:1**	**The motor industry.** IPC(WP)(49)14.
	:2	**The aircraft industry.** IPC(WP)(49)15.
	:3	**The ball and roller bearing industry.** IPC(WP)(49)7.
	:4	**The non-ferrous metals (excluding aluminium) industry.** IPC(WP)(49)16.
4 Feb	**17th:1**	**Synthetic detergent materials.** IPC(WP)(48)222.
	:2	**Sulphuric acid.** IPC(WP)(49)17.
7 Feb	**18th:1**	**D.S.I.R. building programme 1949/52.** IPC(WP)(48)195.
	:2	**Ministry of Works: government building.** IPC(WP)(49)19.

8 Feb	**19th:1**	**Cement and bricks and other building materials.** IPC(WP)(48)209 and 220.
	:2	**Gas.** IPC(WP)(48)215.
9 Feb	**20th**	**Building in the newspaper industry.** IPC(WP)(49)32.
10 Feb	**21st**	**Health services.** IPC(WP)(48)190 and 207.
11 Feb	**22nd**	**Iron and Steel Board: steel development programme.** IPC(WP)(49)28.
14 Feb	**23rd**	**Railways.** IPC(WP)(49)26 and 28 (revise).
15 Feb	**24th:1**	**Admiralty works programme at home.** IPC(WP)(48)230.
	:2	**Plant and machinery for naval shore establishments.** IPC(WP)(48)229.
	:3	**War Office.** IPC(WP)(49)29.
	:4	**Air Ministry.** IPC(WP)(49)30.
16 Feb	**25th:1**	**Food.** IPC(WP)(48)194 and IPC(WP)(49)20, 21, 24.
	:2	**Plant and Machinery Subcommittee.**
17 Feb	**26th:1**	**Ministry of Works: licensed building work.** IPC(WP)(48)221.
	:2	**Home Office.** IPC(WP)(49)6.
	:3	**Scottish Home Department.** IPC(WP)(48)203.
18 Feb	**27th:1**	**Northern Ireland investment programme.**
	:2	**Integration of European investment programmes.**
22 Feb	**28th:1**	**Building labour.** Consideration of the probable size of the building labour force in 1950–52, likely bottle-necks and factors affecting productivity.
	:2	**Contractors' plant.**
25 Feb	**29th**	**Synopsis for draft report on capital investment 1950/52.** IPC(WP)(49)40.
3 Mar	**30th:1**	**Coke ovens.** IPC(WP)(48)214 and IPC(WP)(49)31.
	:2	**Refractories.** IPC(WP)(49)11.
4 Mar	**31st**	**Continuing commitments.** IPC(WP)(49)35 and 45. Agreement that the committee should examine the suggested distribution of investment and that the report should make recommendations on the distribution between the broad fields of investment; alternative programmes within the totals for each group should also be incorporated in the report. Each investment group was then discussed.
9 Mar	**32nd:1**	**Productivity in the building industry.** IPC(WP)(49)48. Need for further consideration.
	:2	**Changes in stocks in 1947 and 1948 and prospective changes in 1950/1952.** IPC(WP)(49)51.
	:3	**New towns 1950/52.**

10 Mar	33rd	**Industrial investment programmes.** IPC(WP)(49)52 and 55. Consideration of the prospective programmes despite concern over estimates' accuracy.
11 Mar	34th	**National resources available for investments.** IPC(WP)(49)53. Qualified agreement on the level of gross investment at home in 1952 which could be assumed.
17 Mar	35th	**Draft report on investment 1952.** Agreement on the extent by which gross fixed investment in 1952 would increase.
18 Mar	36th	**Scottish building programme. Manpower budget 1949–1952.** IPC(WP)(49)44.
21 Mar	37th	**Oil investment programme.** IPC(WP)(49)50.
22 Mar	38th	**Hospital services: revised programme.** IPC(WP)(49)54.
23 Mar	39th	**Control of investment.** General discussion, centering on nationalized industries, of future means of controlling investment.
24 Mar	40th:1	**Draft section of the report (part II).** IPC(WP)(49)57.
	:2	**Share of the national resources available for investment 1952.** IPC(WP)(49)63.
25 Mar	41st:1	**Supplies of plant and machinery 1950–52.** IPC(WP)(49)62.
	:2	**Division of the increase in investment 1948–52. between building and plant.** IPC(WP)(49)65.
	:3	**Division of investment for 1952.** IPC(WP)(49)58. Examination of the individual programmes.
30 Mar	42nd:1	**Television.**
	:2	**General discussion on the division of investment programmes in 1952.** IPC(WP)(49)58. Continuation of examination of individual programmes.
1 Apr	43rd	**Draft report.** IPC(WP)(49)63 and 69.
5 Apr	44th:1	**Investment programme 1950.** IPC(WP)(49)66 and 73. Examination of the estimates of individual programmes.
	:2	**Draft report.** IPC(WP)(49)72.
7 Apr	45th	**Draft report (part II).** IPC(WP)(49)72.
8 Apr	46th	**Draft report (part I).** IPC(WP)(49)69(revise).
11 Apr	47th	**Draft report (part II).** IPC(WP)(49)72.
12 Apr	48th	**Draft report (part II).** IPC(WP)(49)72.
13 Apr	49th	**Draft report (part II).** IPC(WP)(49)72.
20 Apr	50th	**Draft report (part I).** IPC(WP)(49)69(revise).
21 Apr	51st:1	**Gross investment 1948–1952.** IPC(WP)(49)76. A number of modifications to programmes were made.
	:2	**Draft report (part I).** IPC(WP)(49)69(second revise).
22 Apr	52nd	**Draft report (part II).**

26 Apr	**53rd:1**	**Division between building and plant.** IPC(WP)(49)79. Agreement that the building industry was likely to face more difficulties.
	:2	**Housing.** IPC(WP)(49)72.
	:3	**Unprogrammed investment.** IPC(WP)(49)72 and 75.
	:4	**Hard coke.** IPC(WP)(49)72.
	:5	**General discussion.** Allocation to each member of responsibility for the final examination of specific sectors of part II of the report.
27 Apr	**54th**	**Draft report.**
28 Apr	**55th**	**Draft report (part I).** IPC(WP)(49)69(third revise).
28 Apr	**56th**	**Draft report (part II).** IPC(WP)(49)72 addenda.
29 Apr	**57th**	**Draft report (part II).** IPC(WP)(49)72 addenda.
5 May	**58th**	**Draft report.**
16 May	**59th:1**	**Investment and trade recession.** IPC(WP)(49)80. General agreement with the paper and consideration of how to approach industry.
	:2	**Investment in 1949: contributions to the United Kingdom programme for 1949/50 for the O.E.E.C.** IPC(WP)(49)81.
28 June	**60th:1**	**Industrial building.** IPC(WP)(49)82. Agreed extension of the criteria under which licences could be issued.
	:2	**Report on capital investment 1950/52.**
	:3	**Investment statistics.**
26 July	**61st:1**	**Reserve of works.** IPC(WP)(49)87. Agreement on the nature of future discussions with the departments sponsoring investment.
	:2	**Load on the building industry.** IPC(WP)(49)84.
	:3	**Industrial building.** IPC(WP)(49)85, 86, 88.
13 Sept	**62nd:1**	**Licensed building schemes to avoid unemployment.** IPC(WP)(49)90. Approval of the paper.
	:2	**Ports and roads investment programme 1950.** IPC(WP)(49)93.
	:3	**Value of industrial building work in 1948 and the first half of 1949.** IPC(WP)(49)92. Agreement to examine the statistical basis of the building programmes of manufacturing industry and to consider the implications for the wider building programme.
20 Sept	**63rd**	**Ports and roads investment programmes 1950.** IPC(WP)(49)93 and 94.
19 Oct	**64th:1**	**Changes in stocks in 1948.** IPC(WP)(49)95.
	:2	**Industrial building.** IPC(WP)(49)96. Departments were to re-examine their arrangements for ensuring that the rate of licensing accorded with the rate of work authorized by ministers.

26 Oct	**65th**	**General review of departmental views on the proposed cuts in the 1950 investment programme.**
26 Oct	**66th:1**	**Industrial and miscellaneous building investment.** Ministry of Supply's reaction to suggested cuts.
	:2	**Investment in plant and machinery.** Ministry of Supply's reaction to suggested cuts.
27 Oct	**67th:1**	**Housing.**
	:2	**Water supply, sewerage, hospital services and miscellaneous services.**
28 Oct	**68th**	**Transport investment programme 1950.** Consideration of the Ministry of Transport's views on proposed cuts.
28 Oct	**69th:1**	**Electricity.** Consideration of the reductions of investment in the fuel and power group of industries.
	:2	**North of Scotland Hydro-electric Board.**
	:3	**Coal (deep-mined).**
	:4	**Petroleum.**
	:5	**Gas.**
29 Oct	**70th**	**Reductions in the 1950 investment programme in manufacturing industry.** The reduced programme of industrial building was agreed.
1 Nov	**71st**	**Draft report on proposed cuts in the investment programme 1950.** Concern at embarrassment to departments if they were obliged to implement the report, although generally stronger deflationary action could lessen this.
1 Nov	**72nd**	**Draft report on proposed cuts in the investment programme 1950.**
4 Nov	**73rd**	**Draft report on proposed cuts in the investment programme 1950.**
5 Nov	**74th**	**Draft report.** (First revise). Agreement to examine estimates of industrial building before proposals were put to ministers.
7 Nov	**75th**	**Education investment programme 1950.** IPC(WP)(49)98.
24 Nov	**76th:1**	**Investment programmes 1951 and 1952.** IPC(WP)(49)100. Approval that departments should submit programmes on two bases.
	:2	**Fuel and power investment programme 1950.** IPC(WP)(49)101.

Memoranda

8 Jan	**IPC(49)1**	**Membership of the committee – F.R.P. Vinter and P.J. Moorhouse, 1p.**
17 Jan	**2**	**Membership of the committee – F.R.P. Vinter and P.J. Moorhouse, 1p.**
13 May	**3**	**Report of the committee – F.R.P. Vinter and P.J. Moorhouse covering the committee,**

		1+88+10p appendix. See PC(49)59. Also ED(49)10 and EPB(49)13.
21 July	4	**Capital investment 1950/52 – F.R.P. Vinter and P.J. Moorhouse,** 1+3p. Extracts from PC(49)17th and PC(49)84.
3 Nov	5	**Capital investment 1950 – Investment Programmes Committee,** 7+25p appendixes. Draft report.
10 Nov	6	**Capital investment 1950 – Investment Programmes Committee,** 17+1p. See EPC(49)135. Also EPB(49)20.
18 Nov	7	**Change of chairman – F.R.P. Vinter and P.J. Moorhouse,** 1p.
28 Nov	8	**Investment review 1951–1952 – F.R.P. Vinter and P.J. Moorhouse covering E.N. Plowden,** 1+3p. Letter to permanent heads of departments.
7 Dec	9	**Investment Statistics Subcommittee – F.R.P. Vinter and P.J. Moorhouse,** 1p. Also IPC(IS)(49)1.
9 Dec	10	**Capital investment 1950 – F.R.P. Vinter and P.J. Moorhouse,** 1p. Comments of the Economic Policy Committee on IPC(49)6.
20 Dec	11	**Investment review 1951–1952 – F.R.P. Vinter and P.J. Moorhouse,** 1p.

CAB 134/441   Meetings and Memoranda   3 Jan–21 Dec 1950   IPC(50)1st–47th and IPC(50)1–7.

Meetings

3 Jan	**IPC(50)1st:1**	**Investment review 1951–52: how much investment?** IPC(WP)(49)105. Agreement that the volume of investment in 1951 should be roughly equal to that at the reduced rate for 1950, although the ultimate level of investment in 1951 would depend on the success of the export drive.
	:2	**Stocks.** IPC(WP)(49)103 and 104.
	:3	**Net fixed investment before and after the war.** IPC(WP)(49)109.
	:4	**Investment in the United Kingdom and in the U.S.A. 1948.** IPC(WP)(49)106.
	:5	**Future timetable.**
10 Jan	**2nd:1**	**Ports and inland waterways 1951/52.** IPC(WP)(50)8.
	:2	**Industrial building at the end of 1950.** IPC(WP)(50)7. General agreement with the report, but there was a fear that too much precision on this small section of the programme would be attempted.
10 Jan	**3rd:1**	**Educational investment 1951 and 1952.** IPC(WP)(50)14 and 15.

	:2	**Forestry Commission 1951/52.** IPC(WP)(50)16.
13 Jan	4th:1	**Gas industry investment programme 1951/52.** IPC(WP)(50)9.
	:2	**New towns.** Agreement that the committee should consider such a programme of capital investment.
16 Jan	5th:1	**Post Office and telephone services: investment review 1951–1952.** IPC(WP)(50)6.
	:2	**British Broadcasting Corporation: investment review 1951/52.** IPC(WP)(50)21.
18 Jan	6th:1	**Housing investment review for England and Wales 1951 and 1952.** IPC(WP)(50)5.
	:2	**Scottish housing investment review 1951 and 1952.** IPC(WP)(49)110.
	:3	**Health services: investment review 1951 and 1952.** IPC(WP)(49)112 and IPC(WP)(50)5.
20 Jan	7th:1	**Road investment review 1951/2.** IPC(WP)(50)18.
	:2	**Water supply and sewerage investment review 1951/2.** IPC(WP)(49)111 and IPC(WP)(50)5.
23 Jan	8th	**Agricultural investment 1948/52.** IPC(WP)(50)1 and 26.
25 Jan	9th	**British Electricity Authority investment review 1951/2.** IPC(WP)(50)10 and 33.
26 Jan	10th:1	**Investment for food industries 1951 and 1952.** IPC(WP)(50)4.
	:2	**Investment in Board of Trade industries 1951 and 1952.** IPC(WP)(50)24.
31 Jan	11th:1	**Home department's investment programme 1948/52.** IPC(WP)(50)3 and 17.
	:2	**North of Scotland Hydro-electric Board.** IPC(WP)(50)3.
1 Feb	12th:1	**War Office investment 1950/52.** IPC(WP)(50)28.
	:2	**Admiralty capital investment 1950/52.** IPC(WP)(50)19 and 38.
	:3	**Air Ministry: investment review 1951/52.** IPC(WP)(50)34.
	:4	**Ministry of Supply direct and assisted schemes, excluding housing: investment review 1951/52.** IPC(WP)(50)32.
	:5	**Capital investment in civil defence 1951/52.**
2 Feb	13th:1	**Open-cast coal 1951/52.** IPC(WP)(50)29.
	:2	**Deep-mined coal: investment review 1951/52.** IPC(WP)(50)12.
3 Feb	14th:1	**Government building: investment review 1951/52.** IPC(WP)(50)35.
	:2	**Department of scientific and industrial research: investment programme 1951/52.** IPC(WP)(50)27.

6 Feb	15th	**Commercial and public service vehicles.** IPC(WP)(50)23.
7 Feb	16th:1 (revise)	**Iron and steel: investment 1951/52.** IPC(WP)(50)36.
	:2	**New towns.** IPC(WP)(50)40 and 41.
	:3	**Blitzed cities.**
8 Feb	17th:1	**Civil aviation: investment programme for 1951 and subsequent years.** IPC(WP)(50)31.
	:2	**Building labour prospects.** The Ministries of Labour and Works outlined the position in the industry.
9 Feb	18th	**Northern Ireland.** IPC(WP)(50)2.
10 Feb	19th	**Supplies of capital equipment 1949/52.** IPC(WP)(50) 46. Consideration of their impact on the possible level of investment.
13 Feb	20th	**The railways: capital investment 1951/52.** IPC(WP)(50)42 and supplement.
14 Feb	21st:1	**The Ministry of Supply investment programme for sponsored industries 1951 and 1952.** IPC(WP)(50)37.
	:2	**Investment programme of the Ministry of Works sponsored industries 1951 and 1952.** IPC(WP)(50)39.
	:3	**Investment programme of the Admiralty sponsored industries 1951 and 1952.** IPC(WP)(50)22.
16 Feb	22nd	**Investment of merchant shipping 1951/52.** IPC(WP)(50)43.
22 Feb	23rd	**Investment review in miscellaneous building 1951/52.** IPC(WP)(50)47.
27 Feb	24th:1	**Level of investment 1951/52.** Agreement to submit to ministers two programmes: (1) a lower programme consistent with the financial estimates in NIF(WP)(50)12; and (2) a higher programme reflecting the level of capital investment which the committee now considered desirable in the light of present policy.
	:2	**Coke oven investment programme.** IPC(WP)(50)13.
1 Mar	25th	**Capital investment in petroleum 1951/52.** IPC(WP)(50)11 and 60.
3 Mar	26th	**Capital investment in universities 1951/52.** IPC(WP)(50)57.
6 Mar	27th	**Proposals for fixed investment 1951/52.** IPC(WP)(50)65 and 66. Consideration of the programmes for fuel and power, roads, road vehicles, ports, Post Office and agriculture.
7 Mar	28th	**Proposals for fixed investment 1951/52.** IPC(WP)(50)66. Consideration of programmes for agriculture, manufacturing industry, health and local services, Home Office and the B.B.C.

8 Mar	**29th**	**Proposals for fixed investment 1951/52.** IPC(WP)(50)66. Consideration of programmes for education, defence and government building.
13 Mar	**30th:1**	**Draft sections of part II of the report.** IPC(WP)(50)69, 70, 72, 73, 76, 77, 80, 81, 85, 86, 87, 91, 92.
	:2	**Miscellaneous investment.** Agreement on the level of investment for the reduced and the desirable programme.
15 Mar	**31st**	**Draft sections of part II of the report.** IPC(WP)(50)71, 74, 75, 82, 93, 94, 95, 96, 97, 98, 99, 100, 103.
20 Mar	**32nd**	**Draft sections of the report.** IPC(WP)(50)78, 79, 83, 84, 88, 89, 90, 106.
21 Mar	**33rd**	**Draft chapters of part I of the report.** IPC(WP)(50)106 and addendum.
23 Mar	**34th:1**	**Draft sections of the report.** IPC(WP)(50)72(revise), 75(revise), 76(revise), 77(revise), 82(revise), 85(revise).
	:2	**Building labour in Scotland in relation to the capital investment programmes.** IPC(WP)(50)104.
27 Mar	**35th:1**	**Miscellaneous investment.** Agreement on the level to be included in the two programmes.
	:2	**Draft sections of the report.** IPC(WP)(50)106 addendum and 106(revise).
29 Mar	**36th:1**	**Building labour in Scotland.** IPC(WP)(50)104.
	:2	**Draft report.**
1 Apr	**37th**	**Draft report (part I).** IPC(WP)(50)106.
19 Apr	**38th**	**Report on capital investment 1951 and 1952.** IPC(50)1. Meeting of all departments affected by the report. Consideration of part II of the report, programme by programme.
5 June	**39th**	**New building work in manufacturing industry 1951 and 1952.** IPC(WP)(50)109. Agreement on the basis for the division of the money available for investment in new building for manufacturing industry in 1951 and 1952.
6 June	**40th**	**New building work in manufacturing industry 1951 and 1952.** Consideration of the division of the sums for investment in new building in manufacturing industry in 1951 and 1952 as agreed by the Production Committee (PC(50)8th:1). Confidential annex setting out the division attached.
31 Aug	**41st**	**Impact of the defence programme on capital investment.** Generally felt that no immediate cut in the investment programme was necessary. Any difficulties should be met through the regional administration of the building programme.

6 Dec	**42nd**	**Petroleum: investment programme 1951/1954.** IPC(WP)(50)134. Corrigenda attached.
8 Dec	**43rd**	**Commercial and public service vehicles.** IPC(WP)(50)127 and supplement.
13 Dec	**44th**	**Merchant shipping investment 1951 and 1952.** IPC(WP)(50)138.
15 Dec	**45th**	**Electricity investment programme 1951/54.** IPC(WP)(50)132.
20 Dec	**46th:1**	**Housing: investment review 1952/53.** IPC(WP)(50)126 and 146.
	:2	**North of Scotland Hydro-electric Board: investment review 1952/54.** IPC(WP)(50)137 addendum 1.
	:3	**Home department investment programme (excluding civii defence) 1948/54.** IPC(WP)(50)124 and 137.
21 Dec	**47th**	**Agricultural investment 1949/54.** IPC(WP)(50)142 and 143.

Memoranda

14 Apr	**IPC(50)1**	**Capital investment 1951 and 1952 – F.R.P. Vinter and P.J. Moorhouse covering the committee,** 1+69+2p appendix. See EPB(50)7. Draft of IPC(50)2.
25 Apr	**2**	**Capital investment 1951 and 1952 – F.R.P. Vinter and P.J. Moorhouse,** 1+69+2p appendix. See EPC(50)47. Also ED(50)4.
1 June	**3**	**Capital investment 1951 and 1952 – F.R.P. Vinter and P.J. Moorhouse,** 1+2p annex. Revised table of gross fixed investment 1948–52 as approved by ministers.
5 Oct	**4**	**Annual investment review – E. Jones and P.J. Moorhouse,** 1+3p. Annual circular by E.N. Plowden to permanent heads of department.
17 July	**5**	**Note by the joint secretaries – F.R.P. Vinter and R.B. Marshall,** 1p.
19 Oct	**6**	**Investment review 1951–1952 – E. Jones and P.J. Moorhouse,** 1p.
20 Dec	**7**	**Change of membership** – unsigned, 1p.

CAB 134/442   Meetings and Memoranda   4 Jan–20 Dec 1951   IPC(51)1st–42nd and IPC(51)1–7.

Meetings

4 Jan	**IPC(51)1st**	**Steel development programme.** IPC(WP)(50)152.
5 Jan	**2nd**	**Educational investment 1952/54.** IPC(WP)(50)135 and 141.
9 Jan	**3rd:1** (revise)	**Water supply and sewerage 1951–1954.** IPC(WP)(50)126 and 147.
	:2	**Miscellaneous local government services.** IPC(WP)(50)126.

	:3	Health services. IPC(WP)(50)126 and 148.
	:4	New towns. IPC(WP)(50)122.
	:5	New building of business centres of provincial blitzed cities. IPC(WP)(50)150.
10 Jan	4th	Ports and inland waterways: investment review 1952/54. IPC(WP)(50)136.
12 Jan	5th	Northern Ireland capital investment review 1951/54. IPC(WP)(50)119.
18 Jan	6th	Roads investment programme 1952/54. IPC(WP)(50)151.
23 Jan	7th:1	British Broadcasting Corporation: capital investment programme 1951/54. IPC(WP)(51)10.
	:2	Post Office: programme of capital investment 1952/54. IPC(WP)(50)118.
24 Jan	8th	Ministry of Civil Aviation: capital investment programme for 1952 and subsequent years. IPC(WP)(50)120.
26 Jan	9th:1	Gas investment programme 1951/54. IPC(WP)(50)131.
	:2	Investment review 1952/1954: miscellaneous building. IPC(WP)(51)12.
30 Jan	10th:1	Open-cast coal capital investment programme 1951/54. IPC(WP)(50)130.
	:2	Deep-mined coal capital investment programme 1951–54. IPC(WP)(50)129.
31 Jan	11th	Railways and London Transport garages etc.: capital investment programme 1952/54. IPC(WP)(51)2.
1 Feb	12th:1	Department of Scientific and Industrial Research building programme 1951–54. IPC(WP)(50)145.
	:2	Government building investment proposals 1952–53. IPC(WP)(51)14.
	:3	Civil defence capital investment programme 1951–54. IPC(WP)(50)124 addendum and 137 second addendum.
5 Feb	13th:1	Capital investment in Ministry of Supply sector of industry. IPC(WP)(51)1.
	:2	Supplies of capital equipment. Consideration of likely supplies in 1951.
	:3	Future supplies of railway wagons.
	:4	Coal plant and machinery.
6 Feb	14th:1	Capital investment in the Board of Trade sponsored industries 1951–54. IPC(WP)(50)121.
	:2	Ministry of Food investment programme 1952/54. IPC(WP)(50)154.
	:3	Review of investment in Admiralty sponsored industries. IPC(WP)(50)140.
7 Feb	15th:1	Capital investment in Ministry of Works sponsored industries. IPC(WP)(51)13.

	:2	**Supplies of building material.**
	:3	**Building productivity and costs.** IPC(WP)(51)24. Agreement on anticipated increase in productivity for 1951.
	:4	**Building labour prospects.** Description of likely situation in 1951.
9 Feb	16th:1	**Ministry of Supply investment review 1950–54: direct and assisted schemes (excluding housing).** IPC(WP)(51)7 and 26.
	:2	**Coke oven investment programme 1951–54.** IPC(WP)(50)133 and addendum.
12 Feb	17th:1	**Capital and repair expenditure on fixed naval assets on plant and machinery for naval shore establishments.** IPC(WP)(50)125 and 139 and IPC(WP)(51)25.
	:2	**War Office programme.** IPC(WP)(50)144 and IPC(WP)(51)25.
	:3	**Air Ministry investment review.** IPC(WP)(50)149 and IPC(WP)(51)25.
13 Feb	18th	**Report for 1951–54.** IPC(WP)(51)18, 20, 27, 28. General discussion of fundamental issues and preliminary decisions to permit the preparation of individual programmes.
16 Feb	19th	**Level of investment 1951–1953.** IPC(WP)(51)34. Consideration of the extent to which it would be possible to close the gap between investment resources available and departmental requirements.
19 Feb	20th:1	**Control of investment in plant and machinery.** Assuming that the impact of the defence programme upon the supply of capital goods was divided equally between the home and export markets, departmental programmes for 1952 could not be fully met. About half of the gap could be closed by the normal methods of restricting investment by government departments and nationalized industries, but some means would have to be found to restrict investment by manufacturing industries as well. Consideration of possible means.
	:2	**Levels of investment 1952 and 1953.**
21 Feb	21st	**Report for 1951–54.** IPC(WP)(51)35, 36, 40. Consideration of cuts in department investment programmes suggested by C.E.P.S. Agreement on the level of increase in productivity in the building industry on which the report should be based.
26 Feb	22nd:1	**Supply of investment goods.** Consideration of the level of increase in productivity in the metal goods industry on which the report should be based.
	:2	**Part 2 of the report.** IPC(WP)(51)41.

28 Feb	**23rd:1**	**Part 2 of the report.** IPC(WP)(51)41 addendum and second addendum.
	:2	**Demand for investment.** IPC(WP)(51)38.
	:3	**Part 1 of the report.** IPC(WP)(51)36(revise), 38, 42, 43.
2 Mar	**24th:1**	**Part 2 of the report.** IPC(WP)(51)41 third and fourth addenda.
	:2	**Control of plant and machinery.**
5 Mar	**25th**	**Part 1 of the report.** IPC(WP)(51)45.
7 Mar	**26th**	**Part 1 of the report.** IPC(WP)(51)45(revise).
9 Mar	**27th:1**	**Part 1 of the report.** IPC(WP)(51)45(second revise).
	:2	**Part 2 of the report.**
3 Apr	**28th**	**Capital investment 1951, 1952 and 1953.** IPC(51)1. Consideration of the total investment programme and individual programmes by all departments concerned.
29 Nov	**29th**	**Building capacity 1952.** IPC(51)5. Consideration of need for cuts in the building programme.
3 Dec	**30th:1**	**Housing.** IPC(WP)(51)57 and 74.
	:2	**Water supply and sewerage.** IPC(WP)(51)57 and 76.
	:3	**New towns.** IPC(WP)(51)59 and 67.
	:4	**Blitzed cities.** IPC(WP)(51)58.
4 Dec	**31st:1**	**Manufacturing industry.** IPC(WP)(51)61 and 64. Consideration of the consequences of reducing civil investment in building by £80m at 1950 prices and of investment in engineering products by £100m p.a. at 1950 factory prices.
	:2	**Miscellaneous investment: Board of Trade and Ministry of Food sectors.** IPC(WP)(51)64.
5 Dec	**32nd:1**	**Health services.** IPC(WP)(51)69 and 70.
	:2	**Manufacturing industry: Ministry of Health.** IPC(WP)(51)69.
	:3	**Agriculture and fisheries.** IPC(WP)(51)72, 73, 89.
6 Dec	**33rd:1**	**Control of investment in plant and machinery.** Consideration of the available means of control by the Ministry of Supply.
	:2	**Road vehicles.** IPC(WP)(51)62.
6 Dec	**34th:1**	**Civil aviation.** IPC(WP)(51)53.
	:2	**Home departments (excluding civil defence).** IPC(WP)(51)54 and 80.
7 Dec	**35th:1**	**Ports and inland waterways.** IPC(WP)(51)97.
	:2	**Roads.** IPC(WP)(51)71.
	:3	**Miscellaneous investment: Ministry of Transport.** IPC(WP)(51)66.
10 Dec	**36th:1**	**Iron and steel investment programme.** Ministry of Supply set out the consequences of reducing investment in plant and machinery in the industry by £5m.

	:2	**Steel production prospects.**
	:3	**Ships.** IPC(WP)(51)96.
	:4	**Manufacturing industry: Admiralty.** IPC(WP)(51)90.
10 Dec	37th:1	**Post Office.** IPC(WP)(51)52.
	:2	**British Broadcasting Corporation.** IPC(WP)(51)77.
	:3	**Education.** IPC(WP)(51)78 and 79.
11 Dec	38th:1	**Railways.** IPC(WP)(51)98.
	:2	**North of Scotland Hydro-electric Board.** IPC(WP)(51)56.
	:3	**Miscellaneous building.** IPC(WP)(51)95.
11 Dec	39th:1	**Gas.** IPC(WP)(51)68.
	:2	**Electricity.** IPC(WP)(51)75.
	:3	**Coal.** IPC(WP)(51)99.
13 Dec	40th	**Draft report to ministers.**
15 Dec	41st:1	**Government building.** IPC(WP)(51)93.
	:2	**Draft report to ministers.**
20 Dec	42nd	**Defence investment programme for 1952 other than for the services and Ministry of Supply (direct).** IPC(WP)(51)55, 80 addendum, 101.

Memoranda

17 Mar	IPC(51)1	**Capital investment 1951, 1952 and 1953 – E. Jones and P.J. Moorhouse covering the committee,** 1+73+4p appendix. See PC(51)49. Also EPB(51)6, ES(51)24.
5 Sept	2	**Capital investment 1951, 1952 and 1953 – P.J. Moorhouse,** 3p. Modifications in the programme made by the Steering Committee and the Production Committee.
2 Oct	3	**Membership of the committee – P.J. Moorhouse,** 1p.
4 Oct	4	**Manufacturing industry in new towns – P.J. Moorhouse and C.D. Smith,** 2p. Arrangements for the licensing of an additional £1m for industrial projects.
29 Oct	5	**Report on investment 1951 and 1952 – P.J. Moorhouse and C.D. Smith covering F.F. Turnbull,** 1+6+10p appendixes. Draft of ES(51)61.
16 Nov	6	**Annual investment review – P.J. Moorhouse and C.D. Smith covering E.E. Bridges,** 1+6p. Annual circular to all departments.
17 Dec	7	**Civil investment 1952 – P.J. Moorhouse and C.D. Smith covering the committee,** 1+9+11p annexes. See C(51)45.

15.22 Investment Programmes Committee

Industrial Building Subcommittee

Set up by the Investment Programmes Committee in November 1949 with its joint secretary as chairman, see CAB 134/440, IPC(49)74th.

Terms To examine in conjunction with the departments concerned and the Central Statistical Office, the existing estimates of the amount of industrial building done in the past years, in 1949, and in 1950, together with the corresponding rates of licensing; to prepare agreed estimates; and to report to the committee.

Members F.R.P. Vinter (C.E.P.S., ch.); C.D. Smith (C.E.P.S.); P. Redfern (C.S.O.); A.W.T. Ellis (Works); R.W. Burkitt (B.T.); H.V. Lupton (Supply); J. Hancock (Adm.); J.N. Brailsford (Food).

Sec. P. Cousins (C.E.P.S.).

CAB 134/443   Meetings and Memoranda   10 Dec 1949–19 Jan 1950
              IPC(IB)(49)1st and IPC(IB)(49)1–IPC(IB)(50)2.

Meetings

16 Dec	**IPC(IB)(49)1st**	**Draft report on industrial building.** IPC(IB)(49)2.

Memoranda

10 Dec	**IPC(IB)(49)1**	**Composition and terms of reference – P. Cousins, 1p.**
12 Dec	**2**	**Draft report on industrial building – F.R.P. Vinter, 1+4p.**
18 Jan	**IPC(IB)(50)1**	**Industrial building at the end of 1950 – F.R.P. Vinter, 5+1p appendix. See IPC(WP)(50)7.**
19 Jan	**2**	**Industrial building at the end of 1950 – P. Cousins, 1+1p. Extract from IPC(50)2nd.**

Investment Statistics Subcommittee

In the report of the Investment Programmes Committee on capital investment in 1950 (CAB 134/440, IPC(49)6), it was recommended that the committee should be authorized to collect from departments information about the progress of investment and the implementation of the cuts. The recommendation was endorsed by the Chancellor of the Exchequer (CAB 134/223, EPC(49)141) and approved by the Economic Policy Committee in November 1949 (CAB 134/220, EPC(49)46th).

Terms To collect, in accordance with the instructions of the Economic Policy Committee, statistics and information about investment programmes, and to prepare periodical reports for the Investment Programmes Committee showing, in particular, the extent to which the revised rates of investment approved by the Economic Policy Committee on 22 November 1949 have been achieved.

Members H. Campion (C.S.O., ch.); F.R.P. Vinter (C.E.P.S.); C.D. Smith (C.E.P.S.); S. Hays (Supply); A.B. Moore (Works); F.J. Atkinson (Ec. Sect.); P. Redfern (C.S.O.).

Sec. P. Cousins (C.E.P.S).

CAB 134/443 Meetings and Memoranda 7 Dec 1949–21 Sep 1950
IPC(IS)(49)1st–IPC(IS)(50)1st and IPC(IS)(49)1–IPC(IS)(50)3.

Meetings

20 Dec	**IPC(IS)(49)1st**	**Statistics and information about investment programmes.** IPC(IS)(49)1.
3 July	**IPC(IS)(50)1st**	Untitled. IPC(IS)(50)2. Two-page annex attached.

Memoranda

7 Dec	**IPC(IS)(49)1**	**Composition and terms of reference –** P. Cousins, 1p. Also IPC(49)9.
12 Dec	**2**	**Progress of fixed investment in the first half of 1949** – P. Cousins covering C.E.P.S., 1+6+6p appendixes. See IPC(WP)(49)97.
30 Jan	**IPC(IS)(50)1**	**Draft plan of work** – P. Cousins, 1+1p.
23 June	**2**	**Fixed investment statistics** – C.S.O., 5p.
21 Sept	**3**	**Returns of investment in the public sector** – C.S.O., 2+4p appendix.

Plant and Machinery Subcommittee

Set up in February 1949, see CAB 134/440, IPC(49)25th:2.

Terms To advise and report in conjunction with the departments concerned, on the statistics of plant and machinery generally, with particular reference to supplies for home investment.

Members Representatives of C.E.P.S. (ch.), Ec. Sect., B.T., Supply.

Secs. F.R.P. Vinter (C.E.P.S.) and C.D. Smith (C.E.P.S.).

CAB 134/443 Meetings and Memoranda Feb 1949 IPC(PM)(49)1st and IPC(PM)(49)1–2.

Meeting

22 Feb	**IPC(PM)(49)1st**	**Home investment in plant and machinery.** IPC(PM)(49)1 and IPC(WP)(49)34 and 39.

Memoranda

Feb	**IPC(PM)(49)1**	**Home investment in plant and machinery** – C.E.P.S., 4p.

23 Feb	2	**Composition and terms of reference of the Subcommittee – F.R.P. Vinter and C.D. Smith,** 1p.

15.23 Investment Programmes Committee

Working Party

CAB 134/444 Memoranda only 25 Aug–23 Dec 1947 IPC(WP)(47)1–70.
Items 1–40 contain many memoranda in response to IPC(47)2 and IPC(WP)(47)12 entitled 'Review of the Investment Programme' by individual departments with a covering note by the joint secretaries (J.G. Stewart and F.R.P. Vinter). The titles of these memoranda have been shortened to 'Review', followed by the name of the relevant department.

25 Aug	**IPC(WP)(47)1**	**Review – Ministry of Education,** 1+5+2p appendix.
23 Aug	2	**Review – Ministry of Health,** 1+4p.
26 Aug	3	**The investment programme – J.G. Stewart and F.R.P. Vinter,** 1+2p. Extract from EPB(47)4th.
27 Aug	4	**Review – Department of Health for Scotland,** 1+2p.
27 Aug	5	**Review – Home Office,** 1+5p.
27 Aug	6	**Review – Scottish Home Department,** 1+1p.
28 Aug	7	**Review – Ministry of Supply,** 1+4p.
28 Aug	8	**Review – Board of Trade,** 1+4p.
28 Aug	9	**Review – Ministry of Works,** 1+2p. In regard to the civil licensing ceiling.
29 Aug	10	**Review – Ministry of Works,** 1+3+8p appendixes. In regard to its direct ceiling on labour.
28 Aug	11	**Priority for plant and machinery – Ministry of Works,** 2p. Alternative procedure suggested.
29 Aug	12	**Review of investment programme – J.G. Stewart and F.R.P. Vinter,** 1+2+3p appendix. Letter to relevant departments about the plant and machinery classifications.
2 Sept	13	**Review – Scottish Education Department,** 1+2+1p appendix.
30 Aug	14	**Review – Ministry of Transport,** 1+2+14p annex. Excluding plant and machinery and schemes under £100,000.
1 Sept	15	**Review – Scottish Office,** 1+1+2p. In regard to the North of Scotland Hydro-electric Board.
1 Sept	16	**Requirements of plant and machinery – Ministry of Transport,** 3p.
1 Sept	17	**Minor schemes (under £100,000) – Ministry of Transport,** 2p.

3 Sept	**18**	**Investment in building work for agriculture –** **J.G. Stewart and F.R.P. Vinter,** 1+2p. Draft for report.
2 Sept	**19**	**Problems of reducing the building programme –** **J.G. Stewart and F.R.P. Vinter.** 1+4p. Draft for report.
3 Sept	**20**	**Review – Post Office,** 1+2p.
4 Sept	**21**	**The Health Departments' building** **programme – J.G. Stewart and F.R.P. Vinter,** 1+5p. Draft for report.
4 Sept	**22**	**Review of investment programmes – J.G.** **Stewart and F.R.P. Vinter,** 1+5p annexes +3p appendixes. Notes on gas and petroleum industries and the N.C.B.
3 Sept	**23**	**Ministry of Education building programme –** **J.G. Stewart and F.R.P. Vinter,** 1+3p. Draft for report.
5 Sept	**24**	**Merchant shipbuilding programme – J.G.** **Stewart and F.R.P. Vinter covering the** **Admiralty,** 1+1p.
6 Sept	**25**	**Review – Scottish Office,** 1+1+4p.
5 Sept	**26**	**Review – Ministry of Food,** 1+1p.
5 Sept	**27**	**Review – Admiralty,** 1+2p.
5 Sept	**28**	**Ministry of Supply investment programme –** **J.G. Stewart and F.R.P. Vinter,** 1+2p.
6 Sept	**29**	**Review – Ministry of Civil Aviation,** 1+6p.
8 Sept	**30**	**Review of investment programmes – F.R.P.** **Vinter,** 1+3p. Related to the Admiralty civil licence building work.
8 Sept	**31**	**Review – Admiralty,** 1+6p.
9 Sept	**32**	**Review – War Office,** 1+1+3p.
9 Sept	**33**	**Review – Air Ministry,** 1+3p.
9 Sept	**34**	**Review – Ministry of Food,** 1+1+2p.
10 Sept	**35**	**Minutes of IPC(47)6th meeting held on the 28** **Aug 1947 – J.G. Stewart and F.R.P. Vinter,** 1+2p.
10 Sept	**36**	**Review – Board of Trade,** 1+2p.
10 Sept	**37**	**Review – Ministry of Fuel and Power,** 1+2p.
10 Sept	**38**	**Review – G.P.O.,** 1+2p.
11 Sept	**39**	**Review – Ministry of Transport,** 1+4p.
11 Sept	**40**	**Review – Ministry of Agriculture and Fisheries,** 1+1p.
12 Sept	**41**	**Problems of reducing the building programme –** **J.G. Stewart and F.R.P. Vinter covering the** **Scottish Office,** 1+2p. Comments on IPC(WP)(47)19.
11 Sept	**42**	**Building labour ceilings – F.R.P. Vinter,** 1+1p.
12 Sept	**43**	**Meetings of the committee – F.R.P. Vinter,** 1p.
13 Sept	**44**	**Distribution of building labour force – F.R.P.** **Vinter covering the Ministry of Works,** 1+1+1p. Statement on the distribution between new work, adaptations and maintenance.

15 Sept	45	**Review of investment programmes – F.R.P. Vinter,** 1+4p. Letter about forthcoming meeting on plant and machinery investment in private enterprise.
15 Sept	46	**Review of investment programmes – F.R.P. Vinter,** 1p. There was to be a meeting on investment in agricultural machinery.
17 Sept	47	**Building programme – F.R.P. Vinter covering P.D. Proctor,** 1+4p. Suggestions about the nature of the report.
20 Sept	48	**Meetings of the committee – F.R.P. Vinter,** 1p.
22 Sept	49	**Merchant shipbuilding programme – F.R.P. Vinter and R.J.E. Taylor covering the Economic Section,** 1+2p. Assesses possible impact on foreign exchange earning.
26 Sept	50	**Home investment in road transport vehicles – J.G. Stewart and F.R.P. Vinter,** 1+4p. Attached note of informal meeting.
24 Sept	51	**Meetings of the committee on the draft report – J.G. Stewart and F.R.P. Vinter,** 1p.
26 Sept	52	**Draft report – J.G. Stewart and F.R.P. Vinter,** 1+15+46p appendixes. General recommendations on future investment control, with the individual programmes set out in the appendixes.
29 Sept	53	**Meetings of the committee – F.R.P. Vinter,** 1+2p.
29 Sept	54	**Electricity generating station programme and hydro-electric schemes – J.G. Stewart and F.R.P. Vinter,** 1+5p. Note of informal meeting.
30 Sept	55	**Gas industry programme – J.G. Stewart and F.R.P. Vinter,** 1+3p. Note of informal meeting.
30 Sept	56	**Ministry of Transport programmes: railway requirements – J.G. Stewart and F.R.P. Vinter,** 1+5p. Note of informal meeting.
29 Sept	57	**Discussion on shipbuilding programme – J.G. Stewart and F.R.P. Vinter,** 1+3p. Note of meeting.
	58	Not issued.
1 Oct	59	**Coal and petroleum programmes – J.G. Stewart and F.R.P. Vinter,** 1+4p. Note of informal meeting.
24 Oct	60	**Meetings of the committee – J.G. Stewart and F.R.P. Vinter,** 1+1p. Update of IPC(WP)(47)53.
29 Nov	61	**Forest roads – F.R.P. Vinter and J.L. Croome covering Woodburn and Williams,** 1+3p. See DI(47)7.
29 Nov	62	**Southern Railway colour-light signalling (Battersea – Coulsdon section) – F.R.P. Vinter and J.L. Croome covering the Ministry of**

		Transport, 1+4p. Appeal against postponement.
29 Nov	63	**Strengthening of runways at Prestwick Airport – Ministry of Civil Aviation**, 2p.
4 Dec	64	**Review of industrial building projects – Ministry of Works**, 2+8p appendixes.
3 Dec	65	**Imperial Chemical Industries' capital and special maintenance programme – F.R.P. Vinter and J.L. Croome covering I.C.I.**, 1+4+4p appendixes.
9 Dec	66	**Capital programmes of local authorities – Ministry of Health**, 2+14p appendixes. Consideration of need for a new circular.
12 Dec	67	**Procedure for submission of projects – F.R.P. Vinter and J.L. Croome**, 1+2+1p appendix. Draft circular on the procedure for the submission of projects over £500,000.
15 Dec	68	**Bairnswear Ltd.: new worsted spinning wheel at Worksop – Board of Trade**, 2p.
19 Dec	69	**Control of building programme – F.R.P. Vinter and J.L. Croome covering the Ministry of Works**, 1+5+10p appendixes. Also RPO 41. Issued for guidance of regional building committees.
23 Dec	70	**Forest roads – J.L. Croome**, 1+1p. Extract from DI(47)2nd.

CAB 134/445   Memoranda only   2 Jan–15 Apr 1948   IPC(WP)(48)1–51.

2 Jan	**IPC(WP)(48)1**	**Iron and steel programme – J.L. Croome and F.R.P. Vinter covering the Iron and Steel Board**, 1+3p. Review of programme.
5 Jan	2	**Capital programmes for local authorities – J.L. Croome and F.R.P. Vinter covering the Ministry of Health**, 1+1+1p annex. Draft letter to local authorities following decision at IPC(47)30th.
7 Jan	3	**Expansion of caustic soda production by I.C.I. at Hillhouse near Fleetwood – Board of Trade**, 3p.
7 Jan	4	**Metropolitan Water Board supply main, Kempton to Cricklewood – J.L. Croome and F.R.P. Vinter**, 1p.
12 Jan	5	**Capital programmes of local authorities – P.D. Proctor**, 1p. Redraft of IPC(WP)(48)2.
8 Jan	6	**The impact of Marshall Aid on investment programmes – F.R.P. Vinter and J.L. Croome**, 1+4p. Consideration of impact, particularly on housing, machinery and steel.
8 Jan	7	**Procedure on the submission of programmes – F.R.P. Vinter and J.L. Croome covering the Ministry of Transport**, 1+1p.

10 Jan	8	**Information available concerning the progress of new construction – Ministry of Works,** 1+4p.
10 Jan	9	**New turbo-shop for G.E.C. at Witton, Birmingham – J.L. Croome and F.R.P. Vinter covering the Ministry of Supply,** 1+3p.
13 Jan	10	**British Petroleum Chemicals Ltd., Grangemouth – Board of Trade,** 4p.
13 Jan	11	**Norfolk Film Base Ltd. – Board of Trade,** 4p.
16 Jan	12	**Synthetic soap plant at Stanlow refinery – F.R.P. Vinter and J.L. Croome covering the Ministry of Fuel and Power,** 1+1p.
16 Jan	13	**Building schemes for canteens – J.L. Croome and F.R.P. Vinter covering the Ministry of Supply,** 1+1+2p appendix.
25 Jan	14	**The effect of Marshall Aid on investment programmes – H.T. Weeks,** 5p. Contrasts the effect if there were no aid and if aid were on the scale anticipated.
24 Jan	15	**Building schemes for canteens – Ministry of Labour,** 2p.
29 Jan	16	**Reserves of works – J.L. Croome and F.R.P. Vinter,** 1+10p. Circulation of four papers from the investment working party: INV WP(47)1 revise, INV (Panels)(46)1, 6, 12. A fresh approach to the socialized industries was now necessary.
3 Feb	17	**Procedure for the submission of projects – F.R.P. Vinter and J.L. Croome covering H.T. Weeks and J.R.C. Helmore,** 1+1p. Correspondence relating to IPC(47)12.
2 Feb	18	**Construction of railway coaching stock in 1948 – Ministry of Transport,** 1+1+4+2p appendix.
9 Feb	19	**Clayton Aniline Ltd.: project for the production of dyestuffs intermediates – F.R.P. Vinter covering the Board of Trade,** 1+2p.
9 Feb	20	**Cases considered by Priorities Subcommittee for exemption from the industrial ban up to end of January 1948 – E.F. Muir,** 2+2p appendix.
12 Feb	21	**Information required about capital projects – F.R.P. Vinter covering the Economic Section,** 1+2p. Suggests the general information thought necessary for consideration of particular projects.
Feb	22	**Submission for approval of capital investment projects – Ministry of Transport,** 3+1p annex. Concerned with electrification between Loughton and Epping.
13 Feb	23	**Fylde Water Board: construction of trunk main – F.R.P. Vinter covering the Ministry of Health,** 1+3+3p.

13 Feb	24	**Note by Mr. Cairncross – F.R.P. Vinter covering A.K. Cairncross,** 1p. The committee should take stock of its work and consider the more general consequences of present controls over investment.
16 Feb	25	**Electricity Commission: new generating station plant – E.G. McKenzie covering the Electricity Commission,** 1+7p.
19 Feb	26	**Monsanto Chemicals Ltd.: new factory at Newport, Mon. – F.R.P. Vinter covering the Board of Trade,** 1+2p.
20 Feb	27	**The effects of the new investment programme on factory building and the provision of key workers' houses – F.R.P. Vinter covering Durbin,** 1+2p.
21 Feb	28	**Steel for building – F.R.P. Vinter covering E.F. Muir,** 1+3+9p appendixes. Also ECP 53. Circulated for consideration with IPC(WP)(48)24. Sets out the problems of the Priorities Subcommittee of the Headquarters Building Committee.
23 Feb	29	**Electricity generating station programme – F.R.P. Vinter covering the Ministry of Fuel and Power,** 1+2+5p appendix.
25 Feb	30	**Alkali production. Expansion of capacity – Board of Trade,** 4+8p appendixes.
21 Feb	31	**Murgatroyd's Salt Works Ltd.: project for the production of salt, caustic soda and chlorine at Sandbach, Cheshire – Board of Trade,** 3p.
28 Feb	32	**The material requirements involved in certain types of project – Ministry of Works,** 1+3p. Detailed examination of requirements from one example each of hospitals, schools, factories, offices, roads and sewers.
25 Feb	33	**The scale of industrial building and the steel allocation – F.R.P. Vinter and A.R.W. Bavin covering A.K. Cairncross,** 1+2p. Concern that the effective limit on factory building was steel allocation, fixed independently of the committee. Allocations for industrial building did not tally with the committee's manpower ceilings.
26 Feb	34	**Analysis of approvals by Panel A and regional distribution of industry panels – F.R.P. Vinter covering the Board of Trade,** 1+20p.
4 Mar	35	**Road programme 1948–49 – Ministry of Transport,** 1+2p appendixes.
4 Mar	36	**Incidence of cuts in road programme in development areas and on Merseyside – Ministry of Transport,** 2+4p appendixes.

4 Mar	37	**Incidence of cuts in dock programme in development areas and on Merseyside – Ministry of Transport,** 2p.
2 Mar	38	**Steel and the investment programme – H.T. Weeks covering the C.E.P.S.,** 1+14p annexes. Three papers attached EPB(48)6, 7, and 'The oil companies' expansion programme'.
5 Mar	39	**Programme of work on capital investment – H.T. Weeks,** 3+4p appendix. Considers the possibility of developing standards for non-comparable investment projects.
9 Apr	40	**Capital investment programme for 1949 – J. Downie and F.R.P. Vinter,** 3p. Considers the main factors on which the committee should operate and the limits to global investment planning.
12 Apr	41	**Modernization and expansion schemes. Rayon and other artificial fibres – Board of Trade,** 9+6p appendixes.
7 Mar	42	**Reservoir for Liverpool – F.R.P. Vinter and A.R.W. Bavin covering the Ministry of Health,** 1+3p.
9 Mar	43	**The expansion of the cement industry – Ministry of Works,** 2+3p annexes.
8 Apr	44	**Reduction in the labour force of highway authorities – Ministry of Transport,** 2p.
13 Mar	45	**Investment digest – F.R.P. Vinter and A.R.W. Bavin,** 1+28p. Mock-up of the statistical digest on investment. The covering note to IPC(WP)(48)41 attached.
12 Mar	46	**Reserve of works – H.T. Weeks covering the C.E.P.S.,** 1+4+10p annexes. General review. Consideration of the possibility of a shortage of material becoming the main factor in causing unemployment. Assesses the reserves of works available and the types of work for inclusion in the programme. Annexes include INV WP(47)1 revise, INV(Panels)(46)1, 6 and 12, which was also circulated as LP(DI)(46)22.
16 Mar	47	**Alkali production. Expansion of capacity – Board of Trade,** 2p.
19 Mar	48	**Educational building in 1948 – Ministry of Education,** 2p.
5 Apr	49	**Relations with socialized industries – E.F. Muir,** 3p. Proposals concerning their programmes.
13 Apr	50	**B.B.C. building programme – F.R.P. Vinter and A.R.W. Bavin covering the B.B.C.,** 1+3+1p annex.
15 Apr	51	**Review of the investment programme. Home Departments' labour ceiling – Home Office,**

2+4p appendixes. Letter from F.A. Newsam to E.N. Plowden.

CAB 134/446   Memoranda only   21 Apr–22 May 1948   IPC(WP)(48)52–81.

22 May	**IPC(WP)(48)52**	**British Electricity Authority investment programme 1948–52 – Ministry of Fuel and Power,** 1+1p.
21 Apr	53	**Northern Ireland building programme – F.R.P. Vinter and J. Downie covering the Ministry of Works,** 1+2+1p appendix.
29 Apr	54	**Steel 1949 – F.R.P. Vinter and J. Downie covering C.E.P.S.,** 1+3p. Review of likely supply situation.
27 Apr	55	**Timber supplies in 1949 – J. Downie covering the Board of Trade and the C.E.P.S.,** 1+3+2p. Review of likely situation with C.E.P.S. comments attached.
3 May	56	**Changes in the value of stocks in 1946 and 1947 – C.S.O.,** 3p.
28 Apr	57	**Plant and machinery in 1949 – Board of Trade and Ministry of Supply,** 2p. Examines possible effect on investment of probable export targets for 1949 and of the supply of steel to the engineering industry.
27 Apr	58	**The load of work on the building industry – E.F. Muir,** 2+2p. Estimates effect of cut in approvals of building work resulting from the White Paper on Capital Investment in 1948.
23 Apr	59	**Northern Ireland building programme – F.R.P. Vinter and J. Downie,** 1+4p. Note of a meeting of the Northern Ireland Official Building Committee, 14 Apr 1948.
28 Apr	60	**Civil aviation capital investment programme 1949 – Ministry of Civil Aviation,** 1+19p.
27 Apr	61	**Ministry of Labour employment exchange and regional offices, Aytoun Street, Manchester – F.J. Root,** 2p.
29 Apr	62	**Housing programme for England and Wales 1948–52 – Ministry of Health,** 3+2p appendix.
28 Apr	63	**Steel development programme – F.R.P. Vinter and J. Downie covering the Iron and Steel Board,** 1+7+11p appendix.
7 May	64	**Road programme for 1948–52 – Ministry of Transport,** 2+6p appendix.
29 Apr	65	**Scottish Education Department: capital investment programme – F.R.P. Vinter and J. Downie covering the Scottish Education Department,** 1+4p.
28 Apr	66	**Post Office capital investment programme 1948–52 – F.R.P. Vinter and J. Downie covering the Post Office,** 1+3+7p appendix.

4 May	67	Investment programme 1947–52 – Ministry of Agriculture and Fisheries, 2+2+8p appendix.
5 May	68	Capital investment programme 1949. Housing: Scotland – F.R.P. Vinter and A.R.W. Bavin covering the Department of Health for Scotland, 1+5+1p annex.
6 May	69	Investment programme 1949. Agriculture: Scotland – F.R.P. Vinter and A.R.W. Bavin covering the Department of Agriculture for Scotland, 1+1+5p appendix.
30 Apr	70	British Broadcasting Corporation: investment programme for 1949 – F.R.P. Vinter and J. Downie covering the B.B.C., 1+1+3p appendixes.
5 May	71	Capital investment programme 1949. Scottish Home Department – F.R.P. Vinter and A.W.R. Bavin covering the Scottish Home Department, 1+2+8p.
30 Apr	72	Ministry of Supply investment programme – Ministry of Supply, 6p.
5 May	73	Capital investment programme 1949. Health services: Scotland. Water supplies and general sanitation: Scotland – F.R.P. Vinter and A.R.W. Bavin covering the Department of Health for Scotland, 1+5+3+4p appendix.
6 May	74	Capital investment programme 1949. Army works services at home – F.R.P. Vinter and A.R.W. Bavin covering the War Office, 1+2+1p.
22 May	75	Investment programme for 1949. Ministry of Health non-housing services – Ministry of Health, 8+10p appendix.
6 May	76	Capital investment programme 1949. Plant and machinery for naval shore establishments – F.R.P. Vinter and A.R.W. Bavin covering the Admiralty, 1+1p.
6 May	77	Capital investment programme 1949. Admiralty sponsored industries – F.R.P. Vinter and A.R.W. Bavin covering the Admiralty, 1+1+1p.
5 May	78	Capital investment programme 1949. Merchant shipbuilding – F.R.P. Vinter and A.R.W. Bavin covering the Admiralty, 1+2+1p.
10 May	79	The educational building programmes 1949–1952 – Ministry of Education, 7+3p appendixes.
6 May	80	Capital investment programme 1949. Naval works and building – F.R.P. Vinter and A.R.W. Bavin covering the Admiralty, 1+4+4p.
6 May	81	Capital investment programme 1949. Building materials and components industries – F.R.P. Vinter and A.R.W. Bavin covering the Ministry of Works, 1+8+7p appendix.

CAB 134/447 Memoranda only 6 May–16 July 1948 IPC(WP)(48)82–129.

6 May	**IPC(WP)(48)82**	**Capital investment programme 1949. Ministry of Works: miscellaneous building – F.R.P. Vinter and A.R.W. Bavin covering the Ministry of Works, 1+2p.**
6 May	**83**	**Capital investment programme 1949. Ministry of Works: government building – F.R.P. Vinter and A.R.W. Bavin covering the Ministry of Works, 1+3+10p appendixes.**
20 May	**84**	**Air Ministry investment programme for 1949 – F.R.P. Vinter and A.R.W. Bavin covering J.H. Barnes, 1+1+2+3p.**
26 May	**85**	**National Coal Board programme 1948–52 – Ministry of Fuel and Power, 2+1p.**
3 June	**86**	**Gas industry investment programme, 1948–52 – Ministry of Fuel and Power, 1+1p.**
22 May	**87**	**Petroleum industry investment programme 1948–52 – Ministry of Fuel and Power, 2+3p.**
10 May	**88**	**Investment programme 1949 – Ministry of Defence, 1p.**
14 May	**89**	**Capital investment programme 1949 – F.R.P. Vinter and A.R.W. Bavin covering the Board of Trade, 1+9+2p appendix.**
19 May	**90**	**Capital investment programme 1949–52 – Ministry of Food, 2+1p appendix.**
13 May	**91**	**Review of the investment programme. Home Departments' investment programme 1947/52 – Home Office, 3+27p.**
1 June	**92**	**Capital investment 1949. Forestry Commission – F.R.P. Vinter and A.R.W. Bavin covering the Forestry Commission, 1+1+3p.**
11 May	**93**	**Capital investment programme 1949. Fisheries: England and Wales – F.R.P. Vinter and A.R.W. Bavin covering the Ministry of Agriculture and Fisheries, 1+3p.**
13 May	**94**	**Capital investment programme 1949. Fisheries: Scotland – F.R.P. Vinter and A.R.W. Bavin covering the Scottish Home Department, 1+9p.**
19 May	**95**	**Capital Investment in 1948 (Cmd. 7268). Ministry of Food maximum labour force June 1948, 11,000 – December 1948, 8,000 – Ministry of Food, 3p.**
19 May	**96**	**Labour force required for the provision of grain storage – Ministry of Food, 3+3p appendixes.**
18 May	**97**	**Road vehicle programme for 1948–52 – Ministry of Transport, 3+3p.**
28 May	**98**	**British Transport Commission programme for 1948–52 – Ministry of Transport, 1+10p.**
20 May	**99**	**Expansion of dyestuffs production – Board of Trade, 4+4p appendix.**

25 May	100	**Capital investment programme 1949: Northern Ireland – F.R.P. Vinter and A.R.W. Bavin covering the Northern Ireland Department,** 1+2+2+17p appendixes.
27 May	101	**Analysis of tonnages estimated for completion to overseas order in the report on merchant shipbuilding IPC(WP)(48)78 – Admiralty,** 1+1p annex.
28 May	102	**Ports and inland waterways programme for 1947–52 – Ministry of Transport,** 3+31p appendixes.
28 May	103	**Analysis of approvals by Panel A and regional distribution of industry panels – F.R.P. Vinter and A.R.W. Bavin covering the Board of Trade,** 1+11p.
31 May	104	**Capital investment 1949: shipbuilding programme – F.R.P. Vinter and A.R.W. Bavin covering the Admiralty and the Ministry of Transport,** 1+4+1p.
8 June	105	**Coking industry programme 1948–52 – Ministry of Fuel and Power,** 3p.
8 June	106	**Tar distilling programme 1948–52 – Ministry of Fuel and Power,** 1+1p.
1 June	107	**Contract labour for transport – Ministry of Transport,** 3p.
28 May	108	**Open-cast coal investment programme 1948–52 – Ministry of Fuel and Power,** 1+1p.
3 June	109	**Capital investment programme 1949 – Ministry of Food,** 16p.
8 June	110	**Draft report: appendix on housing in Great Britain,** 5p. Revise version.
7 June	111	**British Electricity Authority investment programme 1948–52 – Ministry of Supply,** 1+4p. Supplementary note.
9 June	112	**Timber supplies in 1949 – Board of Trade,** 2p.
11 June	113	**Cast iron pipes of the type used in gas, water and drainage schemes – Ministry of Supply,** 2p.
11 June	114	**Silica bricks for the carbonizing industries – Ministry of Supply,** 2p.
9 June	115	**Capital investment 1947–52: ports and canals – F.R.P. Vinter and A.R.W. Bavin covering the Ministry of Transport,** 1+2p appendixes.
9 July	116	**Draft report: appendix on the Post Office investment programme,** 3+1p. Revise version.
9 June	117	**National Coal Board investment programme 1948–1952 – Ministry of Fuel and Power,** 2+2p appendix. Supplementary note.
8 July	118	**Draft report: appendix on iron and steel development programme,** 4p. Revise version.
9 July	119	**Draft report: appendix on educational investment programmes,** 6p. Revise version.

| 9 July | 120 | **Draft report: appendix on Home Departments' investment programme,** 3p. Revise version. |

9 July   120   **Draft report: appendix on Home Departments' investment programme,** 3p. Revise version.

9 July   121   **Draft report: appendix on defence services,** 4p. Revise version.

9 July   122   **Draft report: appendix on agriculture and fisheries,** 6p. Revise version.

16 June   123   **Petroleum industry programme 1948–1952 – Ministry of Fuel and Power,** 1+4p. Supplementary note.

10 July   124   **Draft report: appendix on Ministry of Works: direct government building work,** 5p. Revise version.

9 July   125   **Draft report: appendix on investment programmes for ports and inland waterways,** 3p. Revise version.

7 July   126   **Draft report: revised appendix on British Broadcasting Corporation,** 2p. Revise version.

15 June   127   **Capital investment 1949: British Broadcasting Corporation – F.R.P. Vinter and A.R.W. Bavin covering the B.B.C.,** 1+2p.

15 June   128   **Production of public service and goods vehicles – Ministry of Supply,** 3p.

16 June   129   **Capital investment 1947–52: statistics – C.S.O.,** 5+7p. Departmental returns from circular of 26 May 1948.

CAB 134/448   Memoranda only   17 June–1 Oct 1948   IPC(WP)(48)130–180.

17 June   **IPC(WP)(48)130**   **Draft report: appendix on health services.** 5p.

17 June   131   **The hard coke investment programme – F.R.P. Vinter and A.R.W. Bavin,** 3p.

18 June   132   **The proportions of steel used for various purposes (equipment and buildings for industry, housing, consumer goods, etc.) – C.E.P.S.,** 2+2+1p appendix. Estimate to establish whether the existing pattern of distribution was desirable on economic, political and social grounds.

9 July   133   **Draft report: appendix on forestry,** 3+1p annex. Revise version.

9 July   134   **Draft report: appendix on electricity investment programme,** 6p. Revise version.

8 July   135   **Draft report: appendix on investment programme for gas industry,** 4p. Revise version.

12 July   136   **Draft report: appendix on railways investment programmes,** 6p. Revise version.

9 July   137   **Draft report: appendix on civil aviation,** 5p. Revise version.

25 June   138   **Approximate distribution of cement by end users June 1947 – F.R.P. Vinter and A.R.W. Bavin covering the Ministry of Works,** 1p.

8 July	**139**	**Draft report: appendix on road vehicles,** 4p. Revise version.
9 July	**140**	**Draft report: appendix on shipbuilding,** 4p. Revise version.
12 July	**141**	**Draft report: revised appendix on the coal industry,** 6p. Revise version.
12 July	**142**	**Draft report: appendix on miscellaneous building,** 2p. Revise version.
10 July	**143**	**Draft report: appendix on Northern Ireland,** 8p. Revise version.
10 July	**144**	**Draft report: appendix on industrial investment,** 9p. Revise version.
9 July	**145**	**Draft report: appendix on roads,** 3p. Revise version.
28 June	**146**	**A.R.P. building – Ministry of Works,** 1p.
10 Aug	**147**	**London Transport omnibuses: increases in route mileage and number of passengers carried – F.R.P. Vinter and A.R. Bunker covering the British Transport Commission,** 1+1+1p addendum.
29 June	**148**	**Investment in 1949: building and civil engineering labour demands – F.R.P. Vinter and A.R.W. Bavin,** 1+2p.
9 July	**149**	**Draft report: appendix on petroleum industry investment programme,** 5p. Revise version.
5 July	**150**	**Draft report: appendix on plant and machinery – F.R.P. Vinter and A.R.W. Bavin,** 1+4p.
7 July	**151**	**Draft report: appendix on investment programme for hard coke,** 3p.
7 July	**152**	**Great Exhibition centenary – F.R.P. Vinter and A.R.W. Bavin covering E.M. Nicholson,** 1+10p. Also GEC(48)18 and 21.
8 July	**153**	**Report on capital investment in 1949 – F.R.P. Vinter and A.R.W. Bavin,** 1p. Arrangements for consideration of draft.
10 July	**154**	**Draft report: appendix on water supply and sewerage,** 2p.
10 July	**155**	**Draft report: appendix on health services,** 4p.
12 July	**156**	**Draft report: appendix on building and civil engineering labour,** 4p.
12 July	**157**	**Draft report: appendix on supplies of raw materials in 1949 (steel, timber, cement, bricks, cast iron pipes),** 6p.
21 July	**158**	**Film industry building programme 1948–1950 – Board of Trade,** 10+4p appendix.
28 July	**159**	**Programme of research establishments for associations assisted by the Department of Scientific and Industrial Research – Board of Trade,** 3+7p appendix.

10 Aug	**160**	**Steel requirements for highways during 1949 – F.R.P. Vinter and A.R. Bunker covering the Ministry of Transport,** 1+5p.
10 Aug	**161**	**Steel allocation for the coal industry for 1949 – F.R.P. Vinter and A.R. Bunker covering the Ministry of Fuel and Power,** 1+2+3p.
10 Aug	**162**	**Steel requirements for the electricity industry during 1949 – F.R.P. Vinter and A.R. Bunker covering the Ministry of Fuel and Power,** 1+3+2p addendum.
10 Aug	**163**	**Public service vehicles: numbers of double-deckers and single-deckers to be provided during 1949 – F.R.P. Vinter and A.R. Bunker covering the Ministry of Transport,** 1+1p.
10 Aug	**164**	**Production of public service vehicles during 1949: division between double-deckers and single-deckers – F.R.P. Vinter and A.R. Bunker covering the Ministry of Supply,** 1+4p.
27 Aug	**165**	**Draft of supplementary report on capital investment in 1949,** 4+10p annex. Revise version. Consideration of recommendations in the main report, referred back by the Production and Economic Policy Committees.
2 Sept	**166**	**Draft report for the O.E.E.C. 1949/50: section on investment – C.E.P.S.,** 5p.
26 Aug	**167**	**Sulphuric acid: production, materials, requirements and development – Board of Trade,** 5+5p appendixes.
2 Sept	**168**	**Analysis of approvals by Panel A and regional distribution of industry panels – F.R.P. Vinter and A.R. Bunker covering the Board of Trade and the C.S.O.,** 1+11+5p.
8 Sept	**169**	**School building in Northern Ireland – F.R.P. Vinter and A.R. Bunker covering the Ministry of Education in Northern Ireland,** 1+3p.
13 Sept	**170**	**Film industry investment programme for 1948/50 – F.R.P. Vinter and A.R. Bunker covering a note of the meeting,** 1+2p.
8 Sept	**171**	**Capital investment 1948–1952 – F.R.P. Vinter and A.R. Bunker covering the C.S.O.,** 1+1+1p. Sets out the estimated value of gross fixed investment by users.
17 Sept	**172**	**Future work on investment programmes – C.E.P.S.,** 5+2p annex. Sets out work under four headings: improving investment programmes; difficulties in interpreting decisions; timing of investment decisions; deciding the long-term balance of investment.
23 Sept	**173**	**Steel controls and investment programming – C.E.P.S.,** 2p. Consideration of how to control investment were steel controls to be abolished.

20 Sept	**174**	**Recovery of steel scrap from disused tramway tracks – F.R.P. Vinter and A.R. Bunker covering the Iron and Steel Board,** 1+2p.
27 Sept	**175**	**Fuel and power and iron and steel research building programmes – F.R.P. Vinter and A.R. Bunker,** 1+3p.
20 Sept	**176**	**Steel requirements for the electricity industry – F.R.P. Vinter and A.R. Bunker covering the Ministry of Fuel and Power,** 1+2p.
27 Sept	**177**	**Ammonia and nitric acid: production, requirements and developments – Board of Trade,** 3p.
30 Oct	**178**	**Privately owned port warehousing accommodation – Board of Trade,** 4+1p appendix.
1 Oct	**179**	**The plastics industry: raw materials, requirements, production and developments – Board of Trade,** 7+18p appendixes.
1 Oct	**180**	**Capital investment 1948–1952 – C.S.O.,** 3p. Supplementary note on the basis of certain figures in IPC(WP)(48)171.

CAB 134/449	Memoranda only	8 Oct–30 Dec 1948 IPC(WP)(48)181–230.
8 Oct	**IPC(WP)(48)181**	**Investment review 1950 – C.E.P.S.,** 7+1p. Sets out programme of work and the likely problems to be faced.
22 Oct	**182**	**Capital investment review 1950 – F.R.P. Vinter and A.R. Bunker covering a note of a meeting,** 1+4p. Consideration of the work required.
22 Oct	**183**	**Electricity investment programme – F.R.P. Vinter and A.R. Bunker covering F.W. Smith,** 1+11+6p appendixes.
26 Oct	**184**	**The proposal for a return on private capital expenditure – Economic Section,** 2p. Recommends the early introduction of such returns including projected as well as past investment.
3 Nov	**185**	**The fertilizer industry: requirements, raw materials, production and developments – Board of Trade,** 7+15p appendixes.
Nov	**186**	**Economic Survey for 1949: appendix on investment – C.E.P.S.,** 1+45p. Draft covering all the individual programmes dealt with in part II of IPC(48)8, except industrial investment and plant and machinery.
22 Nov	**187**	**Electricity investment programmes – F.R.P. Vinter covering F.W. Smith and the Working Party on the Programmes of the Minister of Fuel and Power's Steering Committee on Generating Station Extensions,** 1+3+3+7p.

24 Nov	188	Analysis of approvals by Panel A and regional distribution of industry panels – F.R.P. Vinter covering the Board of Trade, 1+9p.
25 Nov	189	Estimated supplies of timber 1950 – Raw Materials Department, Board of Trade, 2p.
16 Dec	190	Investment programme for 1950. Housing services – Ministry of Health, 5+9p appendix +3p addenda.
1 Dec	191	Scottish housing – F.R.P. Vinter covering Woodburn, 1+3p. Extract of letter to Cripps.
15 Dec	192	Revised civil aviation investment programme for 1950 and subsequent years – Ministry of Civil Aviation, 3+5p appendix +6+1p appendix +3p.
15 Dec	193	Civil aviation augmented investment programme for London Airport, Northolt and Renfrew for 1949 – Ministry of Civil Aviation, 6p.
Dec	194	Capital investment programme 1950–2 – Ministry of Food, 18+2p appendixes.
15 Dec	195	Department of Scientific and Industrial Research building programme 1949–52 – D.S.I.R., 5+2p appendixes.
13 Dec	196	Review of investment programme 1947–1952 – Ministry of Agriculture and Fisheries, 2+2+10p appendixes.
14 Dec	197	Road programme for 1950–1952 – Ministry of Transport, 2+6p.
15 Dec	198	Estimated steel supplies 1950 – F.R.P. Vinter and P.J. Moorhouse covering J.C. Carr, 1+1p.
15 Dec	199	Fisheries (England and Wales): investment programme 1950 – F.R.P. Vinter and P.J. Moorhouse covering the Ministry of Agriculture and Fisheries, 1+1p.
15 Dec	200	Forestry Commission: investment programme 1950 – F.R.P. Vinter and P.J. Moorhouse covering the Forestry Commission, 1+2p.
15 Dec	201	Scottish Education Department: investment programme 1950 – F.R.P. Vinter and P.J. Moorhouse covering the Scottish Education Department, 1+1p.
13 Dec	202	Investment programme 1947–52 – Department of Agriculture for Scotland, 1+5p.
15 Dec	203	Scottish Home Department: investment programme 1950 – F.R.P. Vinter and P.J. Moorhouse covering the Scottish Home Department, 1+19p.
16 Dec	204	Economic Survey for 1948: investment appendixes – F.R.P. Vinter and P.J. Moorhouse, 1+35p. Revised appendixes for the survey.
16 Dec	205	British Broadcasting Corporation: investment programme 1950 – F.R.P. Vinter and P.J. Moorhouse covering the B.B.C., 1+1+1p.

16 Dec	206	Scottish housing: investment programme 1950 – F.R.P. Vinter and P.J. Moorhouse covering the Department of Health for Scotland, 1+3+7p.
16 Dec	207	Scottish health services, water supplies and general sanitation programme: investment programme 1950 – F.R.P. Vinter and P.J. Moorhouse covering the Department of Health for Scotland, 1+2+1p.
16 Dec	208	Northern Ireland: investment programme 1950 – F.R.P. Vinter and P.J. Moorhouse covering the Northern Ireland Departments, 1+48p.
Dec	209	Supplies of cement and bricks in 1950 – Ministry of Works, 2p.
20 Dec	210	Production plans and investment needs of the agricultural engineering industry – Ministry of Agriculture and Fisheries, 4+10p appendixes.
17 Dec	211	Road vehicle programme for 1950–52 – Ministry of Transport, 2+1p.
18 Dec	212	Investment review 1950: revised National Coal Board investment programme 1948–52 – Ministry of Fuel and Power, 3+3p.
17 Dec	213	Investment review 1950: revised open-cast coal investment programme 1948–52 – Ministry of Fuel and Power, 1+1p.
21 Dec	214	Investment review 1950: revised coke oven programme 1948–52 – Ministry of Fuel and Power, 2+2p.
23 Dec	215	Investment review 1950: revised gas industry investment programme 1948–52 – Ministry of Fuel and Power, 2+1p.
31 Dec	216	Investment review 1950: revised British Electricity Authority programme 1948–1952 – Ministry of Fuel and Power, 2+2p.
18 Dec	217	Investment review 1950: revised oil investment programme 1948–1952 – Ministry of Fuel and Power, 1+6p.
30 Dec	218	Investment review 1950: tar distilling investment programme 1948–52 – Ministry of Fuel and Power, 1p.
	219	Not used.
21 Dec	220	Ministry of Works: capital investment programme 1950–1952. Building materials and components industries – Ministry of Works, 2p.
21 Dec	221	Ministry of Works: capital investment programme 1950–1952. Licensed building work (excluding building materials and components industries) – Ministry of Works, 4p.
18 Dec	222	Synthetic detergent materials: production, raw materials, requirements and developments – Board of Trade, 6+1p appendix.

21 Dec	223	**Admiralty sponsored industries: investment programme 1950 – F.R.P. Vinter and P.J. Moorhouse covering the Admiralty, 1+1+1p.**
21 Dec	224	**Merchant shipbuilding: investment programme 1950 – F.R.P. Vinter and P.J. Moorhouse, 1+3+4p annexes.**
21 Dec	225	**Post Office investment programme 1950 – F.R.P. Vinter covering the Post Office, 1+2+4p.**
5 Jan	226	**Board of Trade investment programme 1950 – Board of Trade, 7+1p.**
30 Dec	227	**Analysis of industrial building Jan–Sept 1948 – F.R.P. Vinter and P.J. Moorhouse, 1+18p.**
	228	Not used.
29 Dec	229	**Plant and machinery for naval shore establishments: investment in 1950 and subsequent years – F.R.P. Vinter and P.J. Moorhouse covering the Admiralty, 1+1p.**
29 Dec	230	**Admiralty works programme at home – F.R.P. Vinter and P.J. Moorhouse covering the Admiralty, 1+4p.**

CAB 134/450   Memoranda only   1 Jan–16 Feb 1949   IPC(WP)(49)1–31.

3 Jan	**IPC(WP)(49)1**	**Educational building programme 1950 to 1952 – Ministry of Education, 3+1p appendix.**
1 Jan	2	**Road vehicle programme for 1950–52 – Ministry of Transport, 1p. Supplementary memorandum.**
Jan	3	**North of Scotland Hydro-electric Board: 1949 programme – F.R.P. Vinter and P.J. Moorhouse, 1+14p.** Papers relating to further discussions of the 1949 programme.
1 Jan	4	**Ministry of Supply investment programme 1950 – Ministry of Supply, 8p.**
14 Jan	5	**Capital investment in 1950. Ports and inland waterways – Ministry of Transport, 2+12p appendixes.**
19 Jan	6	**Home Office: investment programme 1950–1952 – F.R.P. Vinter and P.J. Moorhouse covering the Home Office, 1+62+1p addendum.**
10 Jan	7	**The ball- and roller-bearing industry – Ministry of Supply, 4p.**
6 Jan	8	**Estimates of gross fixed capital investment – C.S.O., 2p.**
6 Jan	9	**Statistics submitted for the 1950 programme – C.S.O., 1+1p.**
12 Jan	10	**North Borneo aluminium scheme – F.R.P. Vinter and P.J. Moorhouse covering the Ministry of Supply, 1+2+3p.**
11 Jan	11	**The refractories industry – Ministry of Supply, 4+5p.**

10 Jan	12	**The machine tool industry – Ministry of Supply,** 3+2p annex.
12 Jan	13	**The aluminium industry – Ministry of Supply,** 6+4p appendixes.
12 Jan	14	**The motor industry – Ministry of Supply,** 5+1p appendix.
12 Jan	15	**The aircraft industry – Ministry of Supply,** 2+5p annexes.
11 Jan	16	**The non-ferrous metals (excluding aluminium) industry – Ministry of Supply,** 3+2p appendix.
12 Jan	17	**Sulphuric acid. Industrial usage and forecast of demand – Board of Trade,** 1+1p.
18 Jan	18	**Primary aluminium: production in the Commonwealth sterling area – F.R.P. Vinter and P.J. Moorhouse covering the working party,** 1+10p.
19 Jan	19	**Ministry of Works: government building: investment programme 1950 – F.R.P. Vinter and P.J. Moorhouse covering the Ministry of Works,** 1+2+7p appendixes.
Jan	20	**Capital investment programme 1950–52. Baking and yeast industries – Ministry of Food,** 5p.
Jan	21	**Capital investment programme 1950–52. Oils and fats industry – Ministry of Food,** 15p.
24 Jan	22	**Investment table for the Economic Survey – C.S.O.,** 1p.
24 Jan	23	**Requirements of steel and building labour – C.S.O.,** 2p.
Jan	24	**Capital investment programme 1950–1952. Brewing and malting: whisky distilling – Ministry of Food,** 5p.
28 Jan	25	**Report of the Colonial Development Working Party – F.R.P. Vinter and P.J. Moorhouse covering the working party,** 1+18+25p appendixes. Revised version of the report.
9 Feb	26	**British Transport Commission programme for 1950–1952 – Ministry of Transport,** 2+17p.
Feb	27	**Capital investment programme 1950–52. Milk and milk products industries – Ministry of Food,** 6+5p.
9 Feb	28	**Iron and Steel Board: steel development programme – F.R.P. Vinter and P.J. Moorhouse covering the Iron and Steel Board,** 1+3+1p.
11 Feb	29	**War Office works programme – F.R.P. Vinter and P.J. Moorhouse covering the War Office,** 1+1p.
11 Feb	30	**Air Ministry works programme – F.R.P. Vinter and P.J. Moorhouse covering the Air Ministry,** 1+1p.

16 Feb	31	**Investment review 1950. Revised coke oven programme 1948–52 – Ministry of Fuel and Power,** 2+2p.

CAB 134/451   Memoranda only   3 Feb–21 Apr 1949   IPC(WP)(49)32–65.

nd	IPC(WP)(49)32	**Building in the newspaper industry – Board of Trade,** 5+3p.
3 Feb	33	**Post Office engineering stores – F.R.P. Vinter and P.J. Moorhouse covering the Post Office,** 1+4p.
3 Feb	34	**Supplies of machinery for home manufacturing industry 1937, 1946 and 1948 – F.R.P. Vinter and P.J. Moorhouse covering the Board of Trade,** 1+3+8+5p appendix.
10 Feb	35	**Departmental investment programmes 1948–1952 – C.S.O.,** 1+7p. Estimates of actual investment in 1948 and requirements for 1949–52 as stated by departments.
10 Feb	36	**Road passenger services (excluding London Transport and those with five or fewer vehicles) – F.R.P. Vinter and P.J. Moorhouse covering the Ministry of Transport,** 1+2p.
Feb	37	**Capital investment programme 1950–52. Sugar and allied industries – Ministry of Food,** 16p.
11 Feb	38	**Railways investment programme – F.R.P. Vinter and P.J. Moorhouse,** 1+1p.
15 Feb	39	**Production, supplies to home market and exports of machinery 1938, 1947, 1948 – Ministry of Supply,** 5+1p.
22 Feb	40	**Synopsis for draft report on capital investment 1950–1952 – C.E.P.S.,** 6p.
Feb	41	**Capital investment programme 1950–52. Cereal products industries – Ministry of Food,** 3p.
3 Mar	42	**Potential export markets for agricultural tractors and agricultural machinery 1952/53 – Ministry of Supply and Ministry of Agriculture and Fisheries,** 2+1p.
26 Feb	43	**Ministry of Health: non-housing services investment programme (supplementary note on water and sewerage) – F.R.P. Vinter and P.J. Moorhouse covering W.H. Howes,** 1+2p.
1 Mar	44	**Scottish building programme. Manpower budget 1949 to 1952 – F.R.P. Vinter and P.J. Moorhouse covering the Ministry of Works,** 1+2+3p.
2 Mar	45	**Continuing commitments – C.E.P.S.,** 2+4p annexes. Analysis of how far departmental programmes for 1952 represented continuing commitments.
3 Mar	46	**Steel deliveries, requirements and allocations – C.S.O.,** 1+2p.

7 Mar	47	**Commitments for new works in 1950 – F.R.P. Vinter and P.J.Moorhouse, 1+3p.**
5 Mar	48	**Productivity in the building industry – Ministry of Works, 1+11p annex.**
4 Mar	49	**The paint industry. Raw materials, requirements, production and developments – Board of Trade, 4+7p appendixes.**
7 Mar	50	**Investment review 1950. Oil investment programme 1949–52 – Ministry of Fuel and Power, 4+5p annexes.** Supplementary memorandum.
7 Mar	51	**Changes in stocks in 1947 and 1948 and prospective changes in 1950–2 – Economic Section, 8p.** Estimate of the impact of changes in the value of stocks on total investment in 1946 and 1947 and forecast of probable changes in 1950–52.
8 Mar	52	**Industrial investment programmes – F.R.P. Vinter and P.J. Moorhouse, 1+6p.** Summary of available information in the spheres of the Ministries of Supply (excluding iron and steel) Food and Board of Trade.
10 Mar	53	**The share of national resources available for investment – Economic Section and C.E.P.S., 8p.** Concern that, while the long-term programme presented to the O.E.E.C. provided for a distinct increase in home consumption per head, such an increase could not take place unless the resources used in home investment in 1952 fell below the 1948 level.
12 Mar	54	**Investment programme for 1950. Hospital services: revised programme (England and Wales) – Ministry of Health, 5+7p appendix.**
8 Mar	55	**Investment in plant and machinery – C.E.P.S. and C.S.O., 3p.**
17 Mar	56	**Investment programme for 1950. Medical supplies industries – Ministry of Health, 2+6p appendixes.**
15 Mar	57	**Note by the secretariat – F.R.P. Vinter and P.J. Moorhouse, 1+29.** First draft of sections relating to coal, North of Scotland Hydro-electric Board, gas, roads, ports and inland waterways, civil aviation, water supply and sewerage, education and government building.
23 Mar	58	**Division of investment programmes in 1952 – F.R.P. Vinter and P.J. Moorhouse, 3+3p.** Sets out the implications of the decisions reached at IPC(49)35th and suggests further proposals to restrict the total increase in investment between 1948 and 1952 to £200m.

16 Mar	**59**	**Iron and Steel Board: ore prospects – F.R.P. Vinter and P.J. Moorhouse covering the Iron and Steel Board,** 1+2p.
16 Mar	**60**	**Iron and Steel Board progress report – F.R.P. Vinter and P.J. Moorhouse covering the Iron and Steel Board,** 1+3p.
18 Mar	**61**	**Productivity in the building industry – A.K. Cairncross and A.W.T. Ellis,** 2p.
21 Mar	**62**	**Supplies of plant and machinery 1950–1952 – C.S.O. and Ministry of Supply,** 4p.
1 Apr	**63**	**The share of national resources available for investment in 1952 – Economic Section,** 7p. Revise version. Consideration of the financial, as opposed to physical, limits to investment in 1952, if inflation were to be avoided.
22 Mar	**64**	**Port facilities for monster tankers – Ministry of Transport and Ministry of Fuel and Power,** 2+1p.
22 Mar	**65**	**Division of the increase in investment 1948/52 between building and plant – F.R.P. Vinter and P.J. Moorhouse,** 1+1p annex.

CAB 134/452   Memoranda only   23 Mar 1949–5 Jan 1950   IPC(WP)(49)66–112.

23 Mar	**IPC(WP)(49)66**	**Investment requirements 1950 – F.R.P. Vinter and P.J. Moorhouse,** 1+3p. Table of requirements.
23 Mar	**67**	**Merchant shipbuilding: investment programme 1950 – Ministry of Transport,** 2+3p appendixes.
30 Mar	**68**	**Timber economy in housing – F.R.P. Vinter and P.J. Moorhouse,** 1+4p. Correspondence between A.K. Cairncross, R.I. Michaels and E.F. Muir.
26 Apr	**69**	**Draft report (part 1) – the committee,** 48p. Third revise version. Part dealing with the overall programme.
2 Apr	**70**	**Capital investment programme 1950–52. Oils and fats industry – Ministry of Food,** 2p. Supplementary memorandum.
1 Apr	**71**	**Home Office: investment programme 1950–52 – F.R.P. Vinter and P.J. Moorhouse covering W.S. Murrie,** 1+2+4p.
1 Apr	**72**	**Draft report (part 2): sections on individual programmes – F.R.P. Vinter and P.J. Moorhouse covering the committee,** 1+118p.
1 Apr	**73**	**Investment in 1950 – F.R.P. Vinter and P.J. Moorhouse,** 2+1p. Suggests levels of investment in main investment groups in relation to the likely supply of raw materials and manpower.
8 Apr	**74**	**Changes in stocks – Economic Section,** 1+6p. New estimate of changes in 1948,

606

		distinguishing between the effects of physical changes and price movements.
13 Apr	75	**Unprogrammed investment – C.S.O.,** 2p.
19 Apr	76	**Estimated gross fixed investment 1948–1952 – F.R.P. Vinter and P.J. Moorhouse covering the C.S.O.,** 1+2p. New estimates.
25 Apr	77	**Building and civil engineering labour in Scotland. Appendix to draft report – the committee,** 3p.
2 May	78	**Standard stocks and types of locomotives, carriages and wagons – F.R.P. Vinter and P.J. Moorhouse covering the Railway Executive,** 1+8+1p.
25 Apr	79	**Division of recommendations between building and plant – F.R.P. Vinter, P.J. Moorhouse and the C.S.O.,** 1+2p.
12 May	80	**Investment policy in a recession – F.R.P. Vinter ad P.J. Moorhouse covering the Economic Section,** 1+4p. Suggests objectives of investment policy and possible measures to maintain purchasing power.
13 May	81	**Draft report on investment – F.R.P. Vinter and P.J. Moorhouse covering the committee,** 1+10p. Report on investment in 1949/50.
21 June	82	**Note by the joint secretaries – F.R.P. Vinter and P.J. Moorhouse covering J.R.C. Helmore,** 1+1+3p. Concerned with moves by the London County Council to replace industrial premises with housing schemes.
2 July	83	**New factory buildings approved – C.S.O.,** 1+2p.
4 July	84	**The load on the building industry – F.R.P. Vinter and P.J. Moorhouse covering E.F. Muir,** 1+1+4p.
6 July	85	**Board of Trade sponsored building – F.R.P. Vinter and P.J. Moorhouse covering R.W. Burkitt,** 1+2+7p appendixes +3p.
July	86	**Review of capital investment for first half of 1949 – Ministry of Food,** 2+1p.
19 July	87	**Reserve of works – F.R.P. Vinter and P.J. Moorhouse,** 1p.
22 July	88	**Analyses of industrial building 1949 (Board of Trade and Ministry of Supply) – unsigned,** 1+3p appendixes.
28 July	89	**Economic policy in a recession – F.R.P. Vinter and P.J. Moorhouse,** 1+4p. Extracts from EPC(49)64.
24 Aug	90	**Licensing of building schemes to avoid unemployment – E.F. Muir,** 2p.
29 Aug	91	**New factory buildings approved – C.S.O.,** 1+3p. Continuation of IPC(WP)(49)83.

7 Sept	92	**Report on the volume of industrial building and manufacturing industry in 1948 and the first half of 1949** – unsigned, 3p.
7 Sept	93	**Note by the joint secretaries – F.R.P. Vinter and P.J. Moorhouse covering Barnes,** 1+2+3p. Letters from Barnes to Cripps about the 1950 investment programmes for ports and roads.
19 Sept	94	**Ports and roads investment programmes in 1950 – F.R.P. Vinter and P.J. Moorhouse,** 1+5+2p. Note of an official meeting on 15 Sept 1949 between the Treasury and the Ministry of Transport.
6 Oct	95	**Changes in stocks in 1948 – F.R.P. Vinter and P.J. Moorhouse covering the C.E.P.S.,** 1+14p.
14 Oct	96	**Estimates of the value of work done on new industrial building – E.F. Muir,** 2+6p appendix.
17 Oct	97	**Progress of fixed investment in the first half of 1949 – C.E.P.S. and the C.S.O.,** 6+6p appendixes. Also IPC(IS)(49)2.
5 Nov	98	**Educational investment programme for 1950 – Ministry of Education,** 3+1p appendix.
Oct	99	**Capital investment 1949 and 1950 – Ministry of Food,** 1p.
22 Nov	100	**Note by the chairman – F.F. Turnbull,** 1+2p. Draft letter to permanent heads of departments about the forthcoming investment review.
23 Nov	101	**Note by the joint secretaries – F.R.P. Vinter and P.J. Moorhouse covering P. Chantler,** 1+1p. Letter about projected further cuts in fuel and power investment programmes in 1950.
13 Dec	102	**New factory buildings approved – C.S.O.,** 1+2p. Continuation of IPC(WP)(49)83 and 91.
15 Dec	103	**Investment in stocks – F.R.P. Vinter and P.J. Moorhouse covering the C.E.P.S.,** 1+16p. Revision of IPC(WP)(49)95.
15 Dec	104	**Stocks in 1949 – F.R.P. Vinter and P.J. Moorhouse covering the C.E.P.S.,** 1+2+2p.
16 Dec	105	**Investment review 1951–1952 – F.R.P. Vinter and P.J. Moorhouse covering the Economic Section,** 1+13p. Consideration of the question of the proper rate of investment.
16 Dec	106	**Investment in the U.K. and U.S.A. in 1948 – F.R.P. Vinter and P.J. Moorhouse covering the Economic Section,** 1+2p.
16 Dec	107	**Note by the joint secretaries – F.R.P. Vinter and P.J. Moorhouse,** 1p.
16 Dec	108	**Inquiry into capital investment by private industry – F.R.P. Vinter and P.J Moorhouse,** 1+1p.
23 Dec	109	**Net fixed investment before and after the war – C.E.P.S.,** 2+2p appendix.

29 Dec		**110**	**Scottish housing: investment review 1951–1952 – Department of Health for Scotland,** 4p.
31 Dec		**111**	**Investment review 1951–1952. Water supply and sewerage – Department of Health for Scotland,** 2p.
5 Jan		**112**	**Scottish health services: investment review 1951–52 – Department of Health for Scotland,** 1p.

CAB 134/453   Memoranda only 4 Jan–9 Feb 1950   IPC(WP)(50)1–47.

4 Jan	**IPC(WP)(50)1**		**Review of investment programme 1948–52 – Department of Agriculture for Scotland,** 2+2p.
9 Jan		**2**	**Northern Ireland: investment review 1951–52 – F.R.P. Vinter and P.J. Moorhouse covering the Northern Ireland departments,** 1+28p.
6 Jan		**3**	**Investment review 1951–1952. General services, fisheries, hydro-electricity and peat development – Scottish Home Department,** 2+4p appendixes.
Jan		**4**	**Review of capital investment programme 1951 and 1952 – Ministry of Food,** 13+4p appendixes.
12 Jan		**5**	**Investment review 1951–1952 – Ministry of Health,** 9p.
10 Jan		**6**	**The Post Office: investment review 1951–52 – F.R.P. Vinter and P.J. Moorhouse covering the Post Office,** 1+8+3p.
4 Jan		**7**	**Industrial building at the end of 1950 – F.R.P. Vinter,** 5+1p appendix. Also IPC(IB)(50)1.
6 Jan		**8**	**Ports and inland waterways – Ministry of Transport,** 3+5p appendixes.
6 Jan		**9**	**Investment review 1951–1952. Gas industry programme – Ministry of Fuel and Power,** 1+1p.
5 Jan		**10**	**Investment review 1951–1952. British Electricity Authority programme – Ministry of Fuel and Power,** 2+3p.
6 Jan		**11**	**Investment review 1951–52. Petroleum investment programme – Ministry of Fuel and Power,** 2+3p annexes.
5 Jan		**12**	**Investment review 1951–1952. National Coal Board investment programme (excluding coke ovens) – Ministry of Fuel and Power,** 3+1p.
6 Jan		**13**	**Coke oven investment programme – Ministry of Fuel and Power,** 3+5p.
6 Jan		**14**	**Scottish education: investment review 1951–52 – Scottish Education Department,** 4+3p appendixes.
10 Jan		**15**	**Educational investment in 1951 and 1952 – Ministry of Education,** 6+3p appendixes.

10 Jan	16	Forestry Commission: investment review 1951–52 – F.R.P. Vinter and P.J. Moorhouse covering the Forestry Commission, 1+2p.
7 Jan	17	Review of the investment programme. Home Departments' investment programme 1948/52 – Home Office, 1+14p.
7 Jan	18	Investment review 1951–52. Road programmes – Ministry of Transport, 4+4p.
10 Jan	19	Plant and machinery for naval shore establishments: investment review 1951–52 – F.R.P. Vinter and P.J. Moorhouse covering the Admiralty, 1+1p.
9 Jan	20	Fisheries – England and Wales: investment review 1951–52 – F.R.P. Vinter and P.J. Moorhouse covering the Ministry of Agriculture and Fisheries, 1+1p.
10 Jan	21	British Broadcasting Corporation investment review 1951–52 – F.R.P. Vinter and P.J. Moorhouse covering the B.B.C., 1+1+1p.
16 Jan	22	Admiralty sponsored industries: investment review 1951–52 – F.R.P. Vinter and P.J. Moorhouse covering the Admiralty, 1+2p.
13 Jan	23	Investment review 1951–52: Public service and commercial goods vehicles programmes – Ministry of Transport, 2+1p.
Jan	24	Capital investment in Board of Trade sponsored industries in 1951 and 1952 – unsigned, 13+12p appendixes.
11 Jan	25	Gross fixed investment 1948–50 – F.R.P. Vinter and P.J. Moorhouse,1+1p.
19 Jan	26	Review of investment programme 1948–1952 – Ministry of Agriculture and Fisheries, 3+11p annexes.
18 Jan	27	Department of Scientific and Industrial Research building programme 1951–1952 (revised) – 1+2p.
17 Jan	28	War Office works programme – War Office, 1+2p.
17 Jan	29	Investment review 1951–1952. Open-cast coal investment programme – Ministry of Fuel and Power, 1+1p.
19 Jan	30	Investment review 1951–1952. Tar distilleries and benzole refineries programme – Ministry of Fuel and Power, 1p.
30 Jan	31	Civil aviation investment programme for 1951 and subsequent years – F.R.P. Vinter and P.J. Moorhouse covering the Ministry of Civil Aviation, 1+16p.
24 Jan	32	Ministry of Supply direct and assisted schemes, excluding housing: investment review 1951–52 – F.R.P. Vinter and P.J. Moorhouse

		covering the Ministry of Supply, 1+3+2p appendixes.
20 Jan	33	**British Electricity Authority generating plant –** F.R.P. Vinter and P.J. Moorhouse covering the Ministry of Fuel and Power, 1+8+8p.
30 Jan	34	**Air Ministry: investment review 1951–52 –** F.R.P. Vinter and P.J. Moorhouse covering the Air Ministry, 1+1+2p.
30 Jan	35	**Ministry of Works: government building generally: investment review 1951–1952 –** F.R.P. Vinter and P.J. Moorhouse covering the Ministry of Works, 1+3+6p appendixes.
26 Jan	36	**Steel development programme –** F.R.P. Vinter and P.J. Moorhouse covering the Ministry of Supply, 1+3p.
26 Jan	37	**Industrial works sponsored by the Ministry of Supply (excluding iron and steel) –** unsigned, 3+4p appendixes.
30 Jan	38	**Admiralty naval works at home investment programme –** F.R.P. Vinter and P.J. Moorhouse covering the Admiralty, 1+2p.
10 Feb	39	**Investment review 1951–1952 – Ministry of Works,** 2p. On the Ministry's sponsored industries.
2 Feb	40	**New towns in Scotland – Department of Health for Scotland,** 2+1p appendix.
3 Feb	41	**Investment review 1951–1952. New towns – Ministry of Town and Country Planning,** 3+4p appendixes.
8 Feb	42	**Investment review 1951–1952. Railways – British Transport Commission,** 3+52+3p.
Feb	43	**Investment in merchant shipping 1951 and 1952 –** unsigned, 2+3p annexes.
2 Feb	44	**Gross fixed investment 1948–52 – F.R.P. Vinter and P.J. Moorhouse,** 1+2p. Information available to 31 Jan 1950.
3 Feb	45	**Total investment in 1951–1952 – F.R.P. Vinter and P.J. Moorhouse covering the Economic Section,** 1+9p. Estimate of investment possible without damaging the external balance or increasing inflation.
4 Feb	46	**Supplies of capital equipment 1949–1952 –** F.R.P. Vinter and P.J. Moorhouse covering the Ministry of Supply, 1+3p.
9 Feb	47	**Investment review 1951–1952. Miscellaneous building licensed by Ministry of Works without sponsorship – Ministry of Works,** 2p.

CAB 134/454   Memoranda only   10 Feb–30 Mar 1950   IPC(WP)(50)48–105.

10 Feb	**IPC(WP)(50)48**	**Changes in building costs and in prices of plant and machinery – C.S.O.,** 1p.

11 Feb	49	**Investment in vehicles – Economic Section**, 4p.
13 Feb	50	**Investment review of 1951–1952. British Electricity Authority programme – Ministry of Fuel and Power**, 2p. Supplementary note.
30 Mar	51	**The leather industry. Raw materials, requirements, production, exports and capital developments – Board of Trade**, 7+5p appendixes.
4 Apr	52	**The dyestuffs industry – Board of Trade**, 5+3p appendixes.
1 Mar	53	**The salt industry. Production, requirements and developments – Board of Trade**, 3+2p appendixes.
24 Mar	54	**The timber trade – Board of Trade**, 7+3p appendixes.
24 Mar	55	**The rubber industry – Board of Trade**, 6+12p appendixes.
16 Feb	56	**Educational investment in 1951 and 1952 – Ministry of Education**, 3+7p.
27 Feb	57	**Building programme for universities, 1951 – F.R.P. Vinter and P.J. Moorhouse covering the University Grants Committee**, 1+7+1p.
22 Feb	58	**Railway wagons – F.R.P. Vinter and P.J. Moorhouse**, 1p.
23 Feb	59	**Investment in vehicles – V.P. Harries**, 2p.
24 Feb	60	**The oil expansion programme – F.R.P. Vinter and P.J. Moorhouse covering the Ministry of Fuel and Power**, 1+6+24p appendixes. Also GEN 295/49.
24 Feb	61	**Hospitals building – F.R.P. Vinter and P.J. Moorhouse**, 1+1p.
27 Feb	62	**Gross fixed investment 1950 and 1951 (programme B) – F.R.P. Vinter and P.J. Moorhouse**, 1+2p.
28 Feb	63	**Investment review 1951–1952. Gas industry programme – Ministry of Fuel and Power**, 5+5p appendix. Supplementary note.
3 Mar	64	**Open-cast coal investment programme – F.R.P. Vinter and P.J. Moorhouse covering F.F. Turnbull**, 1+2p.
2 Mar	65	**Gross fixed investment 1948–1952 – C.S.O.**, 1+6p.
3 Mar	66	**Proposals for fixed investment 1951 and 1952 – F.R.P. Vinter**, 1+2p. Sets out proposals on two bases: austere, which would be financially possible; and desirable, which would meet existing policies.
4 Mar	67	**Softwood timber supplies in 1951 – F.R.P. Vinter and P.J. Moorhouse**, 1+3+1p.
4 Mar	68	**Electricity programme – F.R.P. Vinter and P.J. Moorhouse covering the committee**, 1+5+2p.
10 Mar	69	**Draft report : deep-mined coal**, 3p.

10 Mar	70	**Draft report: open-cast coal,** 1p.
10 Mar	71	**Draft report: hard coke,** 2p.
22 Mar	72	**Draft report: revised section on electricity – British Electricity Authority,** 5p. Revise version.
10 Mar	73	**Draft report: electricity – North of Scotland Hydro-electric Board,** 2p.
13 Mar	74	**Draft report: gas,** 2p.
22 Mar	75	**Draft report: revised section on petroleum,** 2p. Revise version.
22 Mar	76	**Draft report: revised section on railways,** 4p. Revise version.
22 Mar	77	**Draft report: revised section on roads,** 2p. Revise version.
17 Mar	78	**Draft report: road vehicles,** 3p.
17 Mar	79	**The 1951/1952 proposals – F.F. Turnbull,** 2p. Proposed cuts in recommended and reduced programmes.
10 Mar	80	**Draft report: ports,** 2p.
10 Mar	81	**Draft report: inland waterways,** 1p.
22 Mar	82	**Draft report: revised section on civil aviation,** 3p. Revise version.
15 Mar	83	**Investment 1948–52 – F.R.P. Vinter and P.J. Moorhouse,** 1+1p. Sets out the committee's proposals to 14 Mar 1950.
15 Mar	84	**Draft report: shipping,** 3p.
22 Mar	85	**Draft report: revised section on agriculture,** 2p. Revise version.
10 Mar	86	**Draft report: fisheries,** 1p.
10 Mar	87	**Draft report: forestry,** 1p.
16 Mar	88	**Draft report: iron and steel,** 3p.
30 Mar	89	**Draft report: revised section on manufacturing industry,** 4p. Revise version.
30 Mar	90	**Draft report: revised section on new houses,** 4p. Revise version.
10 Mar	91	**Draft report: water supply and sewerage,** 2p.
10 Mar	92	**Draft report: health services,** 2p.
11 Mar	93	**Draft report: education,** 4p.
14 Mar	94	**Draft report: universities,** 2p.
10 Mar	95	**Draft report: home departments,** 2p.
14 Mar	96	**Draft report: British Broadcasting Corporation,** 2p.
10 Mar	97	**Draft report: miscellaneous local services (England and Wales),** 1p.
13 Mar	98	**Draft report: defence,** 3p.
14 Mar	99	**Draft report: government building,** 3p.
13 Mar	100	**Draft report: Northern Ireland,** 2p.
31 Mar	101	**Draft report: miscellaneous investment,** 3p.
23 Mar	102	**Report on non-ferrous metal industry – F.R.P. Vinter and P.J. Moorhouse covering the Ministry of Supply,** 1+3p.
13 Mar	103	**Draft report: Post Office,** 2p.

15 Mar	**104**	**Building labour in Scotland in relation to the capital investment programmes – F.R.P. Vinter and P.J. Moorhouse covering W.V. Wastie,** 1+2+8p.
17 Mar	**105**	**Scottish Education Department: investment review 1951–52 – F.R.P. Vinter and P.J. Moorhouse covering the Scottish Education Department,** 1+6p.

CAB 134/455   Memoranda only   17 Mar–21 Dec 1950   IPC(WP)(50)106–154.

17 Mar	**IPC(WP)(50)106**	**Draft report: part 1 – F.R.P. Vinter and P.J. Moorhouse,** 1+31p. Latest drafts of chapters 1–8 of part 1.
23 Mar	**107**	**Estimated supplies of investment goods 1948/ 52 – F.R.P. Vinter and P.J. Moorhouse covering the C.S.O.,** 1+1p.
22 Apr	**108**	**Domestic pottery – Board of Trade,** 7+5p appendixes.
1 June	**109**	**New building work in manufacturing industry in 1951 and 1952 – F.F. Turnbull,** 4p.
1 June	**110**	**Capital investment in 1951 and 1952 – F.R.P. Vinter and P.J. Moorhouse,** 1+1p annex. Revised table of gross fixed investment 1948–52 showing programmes for 1951 and 1952 as finally approved by ministers.
15 Aug	**111**	**Manufacturing industry (new building) – C.D. Smith,** 1p.
16 Aug	**112**	**Investment control in Sweden – F.F. Turnbull and R.F. Bretherton,** 12p.
21 Aug	**113**	**Quarterly estimates of gross fixed investment – C.S.O.,** 2p.
5 Sept	**114**	**Report on building and construction work for the defence programme – F.F. Turnbull,** 4+1p appendix. Revise version. Consideration of the consequences of additional building work in terms of the capacity of the building industry and availability of materials.
12 Oct	**115**	**Socialized industries and national investment policy – F.F. Turnbull,** 2p. The Investment Programmes Committee was to consider how to use socialized industries as a more effective instrument of investment policy. Ministers were concerned that officials were not giving this sufficient consideration.
17 Oct	**116**	**Note by the joint secretaries – E. Jones and P.J. Moorhouse,** 1+2p. Correspondence between the Scottish Office and F.F. Turnbull.
21 Oct	**117**	**Quarterly estimates of fixed investment – C.S.O.,** 1p.
14 Dec	**118**	**Post Office programme of capital investment 1952–1954 – E. Jones and P.J. Moorhouse covering the G.P.O.,** 1+5+1+2p addendum.

4 Dec	119	**Northern Ireland: capital investment review 1951–1954 – E. Jones and P.J. Moorhouse covering the Northern Ireland departments,** 1+28p.
3 Jan	120	**Civil aviation investment programme for 1952 and subsequent years – E. Jones and P.J. Moorhouse covering the Ministry of Civil Aviation,** 1+21p.
16 Dec	121	**Capital investment in Board of Trade sponsored industries in 1951, 1952, 1953 and 1954 –** unsigned, 14+27p appendixes.
16 Dec	122	**Investment review. New towns – Ministry of Town and Country Planning,** 3+2p appendixes.
29 Nov	123	**Investment review 1951–1952: Forestry Commission – E. Jones and P.J. Moorhouse covering the Forestry Commission,** 1+2p.
1 Dec	124	**Review of the investment programme. Home Office investment programmes 1948/54 – Home Office,** 1+20+5p addendum.
8 Dec	125	**Investment review – Admiralty,** 2+2p.
5 Dec	126	**Investment review 1952–53: housing –** unsigned, 10p.
30 Nov	127	**Investment review 1952–54. Public service and commercial goods vehicles programmes (home civil demand – excluding N. Ireland) – Ministry of Transport,** 2+1+4p supplements.
29 Nov	128	**Criteria for investment in manufacturing industry – E. Jones and P.J. Moorhouse covering the Economic Section,** 1+3p. Consideration of revision of committee's July 1948 criteria to give defence top priority.
6 Dec	129	**Annual investment review. National Coal Board investment programme 1951–54 (excluding coke ovens) – Ministry of Fuel and Power,** 4+6p appendixes.
12 Jan	130	**Annual investment review. Open-cast coal investment programme 1951–54 – Ministry of Fuel and Power,** 2+1p annex.
2 Dec	131	**Annual investment review. Gas investment programme 1951–54 – Ministry of Fuel and Power,** 6+22p annexes.
4 Dec	132	**Annual investment review. Electricity investment programme 1951–54 – Ministry of Fuel and Power,** 4+2p annexes.
12 Dec	133	**Annual investment review. Coke oven investment programme 1951–54 – Ministry of Fuel and Power,** 3+1p annex +2p addendum.
29 Nov	134	**Annual investment review. Petroleum investment programme 1951–54 – Ministry of Fuel and Power,** 4+1p annex.
11 Dec	135	**Educational investment 1952–1954 – Ministry of Education,** 6+1p appendix.

19 Dec	**136**	**Investment review 1952–54. Ports and inland waterways – Ministry of Transport,** 3+4p appendixes.
7 Dec	**137**	**Investment review 1952–1954. General services (including peat development) and fisheries – Scottish Home Department,** 2+2p appendix +9p addenda.
5 Dec	**138**	**Investment in merchant shipping 1951 and 1952 – unsigned,** 2+5p appendix.
12 Dec	**139**	**Annual investment review. Plant and machinery for Naval Shore Establishments – Admiralty,** 1p.
7 Dec	**140**	**Annual investment review. December 1950: Admiralty sponsored industries – E. Jones and P.J. Moorhouse covering the Admiralty,** 1+2p.
5 Dec	**141**	**Scottish education: investment review 1948–1954 – Scottish Education Department,** 10p.
8 Dec	**142**	**Review of investment programme 1949–1954 – Ministry of Agriculture and Fisheries,** 3+10p appendixes.
7 Dec	**143**	**Review of investment programme 1948–54 – Department of Agriculture for Scotland,** 2+2p.
6 Dec	**144**	**War Office works programme – War Office,** 1+1p.
1 Dec	**145**	**Department of Scientific and Industrial Research building programme 1951–1954 – unsigned,** 2+2p.
7 Dec	**146**	**Investment review 1951–1952. Housing (Scotland) – Department of Health for Scotland,** 2p.
7 Dec	**147**	**Investment review 1951–1952. Water supply and sewerage (Scotland) – Department of Health for Scotland,** 2p.
7 Dec	**148**	**Investment review 1951–1952. Scottish health services – Department of Health for Scotland,** 2p.
14 Dec	**149**	**Investment review 1951–1952 – Air Ministry,** 1+2p.
12 Dec	**150**	**Annual investment review. Allocation for rebuilding of business centres of provincial blitzed cities – Ministry of Town and Country Planning,** 3+1p.
12 Dec	**151**	**Investment review 1952–54. Road programmes – Ministry of Transport,** 5+8p appendixes.
15 Dec	**152**	**Steel development programme: estimates as at 1 Dec 1950 – E. Jones and P.J. Moorhouse covering the Iron and Steel Division of the Ministry of Supply,** 1+4p.
18 Dec	**153**	**Fisheries. England and Wales: capital investment programme – E. Jones and P.J.**

| | | Moorhouse covering the Ministry of Agriculture and Fisheries, 1+1+1p. |
| 21 Dec | **154** | **Capital investment programmes 1952, 1953 and 1954 – Ministry of Food**, 17+6p appendixes. |

CAB 134/456   Memoranda only   3 Jan–22 Oct 1951   IPC(WP)(51)1–50.

3 Jan	**IPC(WP)(51)1**	**Capital investment in Ministry of Supply (manufacturing industry sector)** – unsigned, 3+1p.
11 Jan	**2**	**Investment review 1952–4. British Transport Commission. Railways and London Transport garages, etc.** – British Transport Commission, 2+8+36+2+4+1p supplement.
10 Jan	**3**	**Coke oven investment programme** – E. Jones and P.J. Moorhouse covering the Ministry of Fuel and Power, 1p.
15 Jan	**4**	**Iron and steel industry development programme 1951/54** – E. Jones and P.J. Moorhouse covering H.G. Lindsell, 1+1+2p.
15 Jan	**5**	**Building programme for univerisities 1952** – University Grants Committee, 4p.
16 Jan	**6**	**The rate of return on some National Coal Board investments** – E. Jones and P.J. Moorhouse covering the Economic Section, 1+2+1p annex.
18 Jan	**7**	**Ministry of Supply investment review 1950–1954. Direct and assisted schemes excluding housing** – Ministry of Supply, 3+3p.
19 Jan	**8**	**Annual maintenance figure for the Health Services** – E. Jones and P.J. Moorhouse covering W.H. Howes, 1+1p.
20 Jan	**9**	**Electricity capital investment 1950/54** – E. Jones and P.J. Moorhouse covering the British Electricity Authority, 1+2p.
20 Jan	**10**	**British Broadcasting Corporation: capital investment programme 1951–54** – E. Jones and P.J. Moorhouse, 1+4+1p.
20 Jan	**11**	**Home Office capital investment programmes for 1951 and 1952** – E. Jones and P.J. Moorhouse covering W.S. Murrie, 1+1p.
22 Jan	**12**	**Investment review 1952–1954. Miscellaneous building** – Ministry of Works, 3p.
22 Jan	**13**	**Investment review 1952–54. Sponsored industries: the building materials and the building and civil engineering industries** – Ministry of Works, 2+1p.
22 Jan	**14**	**Investment proposals 1952–1953. Government building generally** – Ministry of Works, 2+1+4p appendixes.
23 Jan	**15**	**Ports and inland waterways: investment review 1952/54** – E. Jones and P.J. Moorhouse, 1p.

24 Jan	16	**Quarterly estimates of investment goods supplied to the home market** – C.S.O., 1p
26 Jan	17	**Petroleum: investment programme 1951/54** – E. Jones and P.J. Moorhouse covering V.S. Butler, 1+1+1p annex.
26 Jan	18	**Building priority for defence purposes** – E. Jones and P.J. Moorhouse covering E. Jones and A.W.T. Ellis, 1+3p. Review of the scheme's progress.
6 Feb	19	**Investment in new farm buildings** – E. Jones and P.J. Moorhouse covering G.S. Dunnett, 1+1+1p.
30 Jan	20	**Prices of investment goods** – E. Jones and P.J. Moorhouse covering the Economic Section, 1+1p. Proposals to stop departments having a free hand to exceed the money values of their investment quotas to the extent they have deemed prices to have risen.
1 Feb	21	**Capital investment: ports and inland waterways** – E. Jones and P.J. Moorhouse covering the Ministry of Fuel and Power, 1+1p.
2 Feb	22	**Shoreham harbour scheme** – E. Jones and P.J. Moorhouse, 1p.
2 Feb	23	**Electricity capital investment 1950–1954** – E. Jones and P.J. Moorhouse covering the British Electricity Authority, 1+2p.
5 Feb	24	**Building productivity and costs** – E. Jones and P.J. Moorhouse covering the Economic Section, 1+1p.
9 Feb	25	**Defence building programme** – E. Jones and P.J. Moorhouse, 1+4p.
8 Feb	26	**Defence programme: revised Ministry of Supply building requirements** – E. Jones and P.J. Moorhouse covering the Ministry of Supply, 1+1+2p.
9 Feb	27	**The report for 1951–1954** – F.F. Turnbull, 3p. Main issues underlying the report which required discussion.
12 Feb	28	**Limits to total investment in 1952 and 1953** – E. Jones and P.J. Moorhouse covering the Economic Section, 1+6p.
15 Feb	29	**Railway Executive investment programme: wagons** – E. Jones and P.J. Moorhouse, 2p.
15 Feb	30	**Supplies of capital equipment 1950–51** – E. Jones and P.J. Moorhouse covering the Ministry of Supply, 1+2p.
15 Feb	31	**London Transport Executive: investment in works costing less than £500,000** – E. Jones and P.J. Moorhouse covering the London Transport Executive, 1+2p.
15 Feb	32	**Demand for investment and resources available** – F.F. Turnbull, 1+1p. Estimate of gap

between total demands and resources on the assumptions of 4% and 5% increase p.a. in building productivity.

17 Feb	**33**	**Capital and repair expenditure 1948–54 –** C.S.O., 3+6p.
15 Feb	**34**	**Level of investment 1951–53 – E. Jones and P.J. Moorhouse,** 1+2p. Proposed programme.
16 Feb	**35**	**Draft report (first edition) – F.F. Turnbull,** 3p.
22 Feb	**36**	**Draft chapter on the finance of investment – E. Jones and P.J. Moorhouse covering the Economic Section,** 1+5p. Revise version.
19 Feb	**37**	**Home Office revised civil defence programme – E. Jones and P.J. Moorhouse covering the Home Office,** 1+4+3p.
20 Feb	**38**	**Draft report: chapter 4 – F.F. Turnbull,** 5p. The demand for investment.
22 Feb	**39**	**Capital investment in the Board of Trade's sponsored industries – E. Jones and P.J. Moorhouse,** 2p.
22 Feb	**40**	**Draft chapter on the supply of investment goods – E. Jones and P.J. Moorhouse covering the Economic Section,** 1+4p. Revise version.
23 Feb	**41**	**Part 2 of the report – E. Jones and P.J. Moorhouse,** 1+25+36p addenda. Individual programmes.
26 Feb	**42**	**Draft report: chapter 4 – F.F. Turnbull,** 5p. Special problems requiring decisions by ministers.
27 Feb	**43**	**Part 1 of the report – E. Jones and P.J. Moorhouse,** 1+16p. Further chapters on the supply of investment and proposals for 1951, 1952 and 1953.
28 Feb	**44**	**Government building: Ministry of Works investment programme – E. Jones and P.J. Moorhouse covering the Ministry of Works,** 1+1p.
8 Mar	**45**	**Part 1: general report – E. Jones and P.J. Moorhouse,** 1+36+2p addendum. Second revise version.
7 Apr	**46**	**The B.B.C. investment programme 1951–54 – E. Jones and P.J. Moorhouse covering the B.B.C.,** 1+1+1p.
8 May	**47**	**Investment in medical supplies industry – P.J. Moorhouse covering J. Parkin,** 1+2+4p appendixes.
6 Oct	**48**	**Investment 1950–1952 – C.E.P.S.,** 7+11p appendixes. Review and recommendations.
16 Oct	**49**	**Investment in 1951 and 1952 – C.D. Smith covering F.F. Turnbull,** 1+8+14p appendixes. Report sent to the Working Party on Economic Prospects for 1952.

22 Oct	**50**	**Annual investment review – C.D. Smith covering F.F. Turnbull,** 1+3p. Letter to department liaison officers concerning the next review.

CAB 134/457   Memoranda only   20 Nov–19 Dec 1951   IPC(WP)(51)51–101.

20 Nov	**IPC(WP)(51)51**	**Investment review 1952–1953 – P.J. Moorhouse and C.D. Smith,** 1p.
3 Dec	**52**	**Post Office annual investment review – G.P.O.,** 5+1p.
30 Nov	**53**	**Civil aviation investment programme for 1952 and 1953 – Ministry of Civil Aviation,** 1+6+6p appendixes +7+2p appendixes.
4 Dec	**54**	**Investment review 1949–1953. General services (including peat development) and fisheries – Scottish Home Department,** 2+2p appendixes.
14 Dec	**55**	**Civil defence: Scottish Home Department – P.J. Moorhouse and C.D. Smith covering the Scottish Home Department,** 1+2+2p.
5 Dec	**56**	**North of Scotland Hydro-electric Board investment review – P.J. Moorhouse and C.D. Smith covering the Scottish Home Department,** 1+1+2p.
30 Nov	**57**	**Investment review 1952–53–54 –** unsigned, 10p. Deals with housing, water supply and sewerage and miscellaneous local government services.
28 Nov	**58**	**Annual investment review. Allocation for rebuilding of business centres of provincial blitzed cities – Ministry of Housing and Local Government,** 2p.
30 Nov	**59**	**Investment review. New towns – Ministry of Housing and Local Government,** 3+2p appendixes.
3 Dec	**60**	**Forestry Commission investment programme for 1952/3 – Forestry Commission,** 1+1p.
5 Dec	**61**	**Investment review 1952/53 – Ministry of Materials,** 3+7p appendixes.
28 Nov	**62**	**Investment review 1952–53. Public service and commercial goods vehicles programmes (home civil demand – excluding Northern Ireland) – Ministry of Transport,** 2+1p.
	63	Not issued.
30 Nov	**64**	**Capital investment in Board of Trade sponsored industries 1949–1953,** 11+12p appendix.
1 Dec	**65**	**Building programme 1952–53 – Department of Scientific and Industrial Research,** 2+2p.
7 Dec	**66**	**Investment review 1952–1953. Miscellaneous investment programme – Ministry of Transport,** 2+1p.
29 Nov	67	**New towns in Scotland. Capital investment 1951–52–53–54 – Department of Health for Scotland,** 1+2p.

6 Dec	68	**Investment review 1952–1953. Draft gas industry investment programme 1951–1955 – Ministry of Fuel and Power,** 2+3p annexes.
28 Nov	69	**Investment review 1952/53 – Ministry of Health,** 12p.
28 Nov	70	**Investment review 1952/53. Scottish health services – Department of Health for Scotland,** 4p.
6 Dec	71	**Investment review 1952–53. Roads programme – Ministry of Transport,** 6+10+1p corrigenda.
28 Nov	72	**Review of investment programme 1949–1953 – Ministry of Agriculture and Fisheries,** 3+9p appendixes.
29 Nov	73	**Review of investment programme 1949–53 – Department of Agriculture for Scotland,** 4p.
28 Nov	74	**Investment review 1952–53. Housing (Scotland) – Department of Health for Scotland,** 2p.
7 Dec	75	**Investment review 1952–1953. Draft electricity investment programme – Ministry of Fuel and Power,** 3+6p annexes.
30 Nov	76	**Investment review 1952 and 1953. Water supply and sewerage (Scotland) – Department of Health for Scotland,** 2p.
5 Dec	77	**The B.B.C. investment programme – P.J. Moorhouse and C.D. Smith,** 1+2+1+3p addendum.
4 Dec	78	**Educational investment 1952–54 – Ministry of Education,** 5+2p appendix.
30 Nov	79	**Scottish education: investment review 1948–1954 – Scottish Education Department,** 7p.
1 Dec	80	**Review of the investment programme. Home Office investment programmes 1948/54 – Home Office,** 1+16+6p addenda.
	81	Not issued.
14 Dec	82	**Housing – P.J. Moorhouse and C.D. Smith covering the Ministry of Housing and Local Government,** 1+3p.
	83	Not issued.
3 Dec	84	**Investment in manufacturing industry – Ministry of Supply,** 2+1p annex. Covering those industries sponsored by the Ministry of Supply (excluding iron and steel).
11 Dec	85	**Northern Ireland investment programme – P.J. Moorhouse and C.D. Smith covering the Northern Ireland Departments,** 1+3+28p.
8 Dec	86	**Capital investment programmes (revised) 1952 and 1953 – Ministry of Food,** 3+6p appendixes.
30 Nov	87	**Investment review 1952 and 1953 – Admiralty,** 1p. On naval works.

29 Nov	88	**Investment review 1952 and 1953 – P.J. Moorhouse and C.D. Smith,** 1p. Administrative arrangements.
30 Nov	89	**Fisheries: England and Wales – P.J. Moorhouse and C.D. Smith covering the Ministry of Agriculture and Fisheries,** 1+2+1p.
4 Dec	90	**Manufacturing industry: Admiralty sponsored industries – Admiralty,** 2p.
1 Dec	91	**War Office works programme at home – War Office,** 1+1p.
30 Nov	92	**Annual investment review. University building – University Grants Committee,** 5p.
3 Dec	93	**Investment review 1952–1953. Government building – Ministry of Works,** 3+1p.
3 Dec	94	**Investment review 1952–1953. Manufacturing industries – Ministry of Works,** 2p.
3 Dec	95	**Investment review 1952–1953. Miscellaneous building – Ministry of Works,** 2p.
5 Dec	96	**Annual investment review. Merchant shipping – Admiralty and Ministry of Transport,** 5+3p appendixes.
5 Dec	97	**Investment review in 1952–53. Ports and inland waterways – Ministry of Transport,** 3+4p appendixes.
10 Dec	98	**Investment review 1952–53. Railways and London Transport garages etc. – British Transport Commission,** 3+3+1+3+3+4p.
11 Dec	99	**Investment review 1952–53. Draft N.C.B. colliery investment programme – Ministry of Fuel and Power,** 3+4p appendixes.
	100	Not issued.
19 Dec	101	**Civil defence investment programme for 1952 – P.J. Moorhouse and C.D. Smith,** 1+2p.

15.24 Labour Committee

Set up in the reorganization of October 1947 to handle manpower questions generally and therefore replace the Foreign Labour Committee (CAB 134/301), see CAB 129/21, CP(47)280. Discontinued with the reorganization of manpower committees in March 1949, see CAB 129/33 part 1, CP(49)54.

Terms (a) to consider problems connected with the redeployment of labour in pursuance of approved economic policy (b) to consider the use of foreign labour and problems arising therefrom.

Members Min. Economic Affs. (ch.); Home Sec.; S./S. Scotland, War; Mins. of Labour & N.S., Agriculture & Fish, Fuel & Power, Works. (Dec 1947) Ec. Sec. (Try) added.

Sec. J.A. Drew (Cab. O.). (July 1948) J.G. Stewart (Cab. O.).

CAB 134/469   Meetings and Memoranda   9 Oct 1947–13 July 1948   LC(48)1st–4th and LC(47)1–LC(48)11.

Meetings

5 Jan	**LC(48)1st:1**	**The manpower situation.** LC(47)3 and LC(48)3.
	:2	**Regular employment in agriculture in 1948.** LC(47)5.
	:3	**Seasonal employment in agriculture.** LC(47)4, 7, 8 and LC(48)2.
	:4	**Reorganization of the Women's Land Army.** LC(47)2.
13 Feb	**2nd:1**	**Polish Resettlement Corps.** LC(48)4.
	:2	**Employment of prisoners of war in agriculture.**
	:3	**Employment of European volunteer workers on seasonal work in agriculture.**
14 Apr	**3rd**	**Discharge of the Polish armed forces.** LC(48)7.
8 July	**4th:1**	**Winding up of the Polish Resettlement Corps.** LC(48)9.
	:2	**Employment of ex-members of the Polish armed forces.** LC(48)8 and 10.
	:3	**Employment of foreign labour in military installations.** LC(48)11.

Memoranda

9 Oct	**LC(47)1**	**Labour Committee – N. Brook,** 1p.
10 Oct	**2**	**The repatriation of prisoners of war in the U.K. –** **Bevin,** 1+2p.
1 Dec	**3**	**The manpower situation – Isaacs,** 5+1p annex. Sets out steps taken to overcome the problem of undermanned industries without running down other essential industries.
5 Dec	**4**	**Seasonal labour requirements in agriculture –** **Woodburn,** 2p.
6 Dec	**5**	**Report on agricultural labour supply –** **Woodburn and Williams,** 4+2p appendix. Consideration of how to close the gap estimated for 1948.
8 Dec	**6**	**Seasonal labour requirements in agriculture in** **England and Wales – Williams and Isaacs,** 4p.
19 Dec	**7**	**Seasonal labour requirements in agriculture in** **England and Wales – Chuter Ede,** 1p.
23 Dec	**8**	**Seasonal labour requirements in agriculture –** **Key,** 1p.
30 Dec	**9**	**Change in membership – J.A. Drew,** 1p.
1 Jan	**LC(48)1**	**Seasonal labour requirements in agriculture in** **England and Wales – Isaacs,** 2p.
1 Jan	**2**	**Employment of women in agriculture –** **Williams,** 2p.
2 Jan	**3**	**The manpower situation at end October 1947 –** **Isaacs,** 2p. Supplement to LC(47)3.
30 Jan	**4**	**Polish Resettlement Corps – Isaacs,** 4p.

17 Feb	**5**	**Seasonal employment in agriculture – Isaacs,** 1p. Issue of the increased use of European volunteer workers.
6 Mar	**6**	**Employment of prisoners of war in agriculture – Woodburn,** 1p.
7 Apr	**7**	**Discharge of the Polish armed forces – Isaacs,** 2p.
25 May	**8**	**Employment of ex-members of the Polish armed forces – Isaacs,** 2p.
17 June	**9**	**Winding up of the Polish Resettlement Corps – Isaacs,** 4p.
5 July	**10**	**Employment of ex-members of the Polish armed forces – Isaacs,** 1p. Addendum to LC(48)8.
5 July	**11**	**Employment of foreign labour in military installations – Shinwell,** 3p.
13 July		**Change in secretariat – Unsigned,** 1p.

15.25   Labour (Textile Industries) Committee

Set up by the Production Committee in January 1948 to help the export drive, see CAB 134/636, PC(48)2nd:4. It was served by two regional committees, one for cotton based in Manchester (set up in February 1948) and the other for wool and worsted based in Leeds (set up in May 1948). It made three reports to the Production Committee in April 1948, July 1948 and March 1950 (CAB 134/638, PC(48)53, 94 and CAB 134/645, PC(50)27), before being formally disbanded in April 1950. The final report concluded that substantial increases in labour supply, production and exports had been achieved mainly by wage rises but also by an improvement in the industries' reputation through publicity and by better welfare provision. This was taken as evidence that, even in a period of full employment, the labour force in undermanned industries could be increased by voluntary methods.

Terms   On behalf of the Production Committee, to concert and progress measures for maintaining an adequate supply of labour for the textile industries and securing the most productive use of labour in those industries.

Members   Parl. Sec., Min. of Lab. & N.S. (ch.); Ec. Sec. (Try); Parl. Secs. of Mins. of Health, Bd Trade, Works; Joint Parl. Sec., Min. of Supply.

Sec.   J.G. Stewart (Cab. O.) and H.W. Morris (B.T.).   (June 1949) S.E.V. Luke (Cab. O.) replaced Stewart.

CAB 134/471   Meetings   2 Feb–10 Nov 1948   L(TI)(48)1st–11th.

2 Feb	**L(TI)(48)1st:1**	**Composition and terms of reference.** L(TI)(48)1.
	:2	**Increase of textile exports.** L(TI)(48)2 and 3. Concentration on cotton because it contributed most to exports to hard currency countries and had the greatest labour problems. A regional board should be established to consider local problems.

9 Feb	**2nd:1**	**Exemption of the cotton industry from the staggered hours scheme.** The N.J.A.C. had rejected.
	:2	**Deferment of call-up of cotton operatives.** L(TI)(48)8.
	:3	**Publicity campaign.** L(TI)(48)7.
	:4	**Provision of day nurseries in the textile areas.** L(TI)(48)6.
	:5	**Improvement of welfare and working conditions in cotton spinning mills.** L(TI)(48)9.
	:6	**Analysis of the labour requirements of the cotton industry town by town.** L(TI)(48)10.
	:7	**Chairmanship of the regional committee.**
26 Feb	**3rd:1**	**Recruitment of women operatives to the auxiliary forces.**
	:2	**Oral statement by the chairman on his visit to Lancashire.**
	:3	**Progress made by the regional committee.** L(TI)(48)11 and 14.
	:4	**Analysis of the labour requirements of the cotton industry, town by town, on the basis of the labour required to meet the revised export targets.** L(TI)(48)12.
	:5	**Hostel requirements.** L(TI)(48)13.
	:6	**Direction of labour.** Progress report on the provision of amenities in cotton mills is annexed.
24 Mar	**4th:1**	**Day nurseries.**
	:2	**Matters arising from the minutes of the previous meeting.**
	:3	**Importation of workers from Europe.**
	:4	**Possibility of diverting labour from other industries in the cotton areas to the cotton industry.** L(TI)(48)16 and 19.
	:5	**Progress of the regional committee.** L(TI)(48)18 and 20.
	:6	**Employment in the cotton industry and the Control of Engagement Order.** L(TI)(48)17.
	:7	**Publicity.** L(TI)(48)21.
	:8	**Redeployment.**
	:9	**Wool industry.**
	:10	**Report to the Production Committee.**
14 Apr	**5th:1**	**Redeployment. Consideration of the Cotton Manufacturing Commission's interim report on wages and organization of work.**
	:2	**Report to the Production Committee.** L(TI)(48)28. Detailed consideration.
	:3	**Statistics: monthly report by the Board of Trade.** BTSP(48)1.
	:4	**Progress of the regional committee.** L(TI)(48)26 and 30.
	:5	**Progress as to factory amenities.** L(TI)(48)22.

	:6	**Release of service accommodation.** L(TI)(48)23.
	:7	**Female labour for the textile area.** L(TI)(48)24.
	:8	**Machinery supplies.** L(TI)(48)25.
	:9	**Establishment of the cotton industry outside Lancashire.** L(TI)(48)27.
	:10	**Wool industry.** L(TI)(48)29.
5 May	**6th:1**	**Publicity.**
	:2	**Report to the Production Committee.** L(TI)(48)31 and 33.
	:3	**Progress made by the regional committee.** L(TI)(48)32 and 37.
	:4	**Gratuities for government employees entering the textile industry.** L(TI)(48)35.
	:5	**Hostel accommodation for textile workers.** L(TI)(48)36.
4 June	**7th:1**	**Discussion with Sir Raymond Streat, Chairman of the Cotton Board.** He considered that the committee overestimated short-term effects of redeployment.
	:2	**Provision of nurseries.**
	:3	**Woollen and worsted industries.**
10 June	**8th:1**	**Labour supply for the cotton industry.** L(TI)(48)44 and 50. Consideration of recruitment and estimation of labour requirements. Agreement not to alter the labour target in the Economic Survey (1948).
	:2	**Progress of the regional committee (Manchester).** L(TI)(48)41 and 47.
	:3	**Productivity in the cotton spinning industry.** L(TI)(48)45.
	:4	**Placings and vacancies outstanding in the cotton industry.** L(TI)(48)43.
	:5	**Publicity for the cotton industry campaign.** L(TI)(48)40.
	:6	**Woollen and worsted industry.** L(TI)(48)38, 39, 42, 49.
	:7	**Survey of women in industry.** L(TI)(48)46.
13 July	**9th:1**	**Progress of the regional (Manchester) committee.** L(TI)(48)51 and 54.
	:2	**Monthly statistical report of the cotton industry.** BT(S)(P)(C)(48)3.
	:3	**Progress of the regional (Leeds) committee.** L(TI)(48)53 and 57.
	:4	**Statistics of the worsted and woollen industry.** BTSP(W)(48)2.
	:5	**Export industries and housing policy.** L(TI)(48)55.
	:6	**Recruitment of foreign workers for the cotton industry.** L(TI)(48)52.
	:7	**Publicity for the cotton production campaign.** L(TI)(48)56.

	:8	**Publicity arrangements for ministers to address meetings and for a survey among cotton operatives.** L(TI)(48)59.
	:9	**Assisted travel scheme for the cotton industry.** L(TI)(48)60.
	:10	**Draft second interim report to the production committee.** L(TI)(48)58. Amended to emphasize positive action taken. Letter to Edwards, N. from G.B. Fielding, Director of the Cotton Spinners' and Manufacturers' Association and A.E. Naesmith, Secretary of the Northern Counties Textile Trades Federation.
12 Oct	10th:1	**Membership of the committee.** L(TI)(48)75.
	:2	**Progress of the regional (Manchester) committee.** L(TI)(48)62, 67, 72.
	:3	**Labour recruitment and redeployment in the cotton industry.** L(TI)(48)73, 74, 76. Disagreement with L(TI)(48)73 and 76 but agreement with L(TI)(48)74 that publicity should be switched from emphasizing recruitment to productivity.
	:4	**Statistics of the cotton industry.** BTS(P)(C)(48)4 and 5.
	:5	**Publicity in the cotton production campaign.** L(TI)(48)66.
	:6	**Textile machinery supplies.** L(TI)(48)68.
	:7	**Progress of the regional (Leeds) committee.** L(TI)(48)65, 69, 71.
	:8	**Statistics of the wool industry.** BTS(P)(W)3, 4, 5.
	:9	**West Riding textile publicity campaign.** L(TI)(48)63 and 70.
	:10	**Report to the Production Committee.** L(TI)(48)61 and 64.
10 Nov	11th:1	**Redeployment.** L(TI)(48)73 and 82. Agreement that the Cotton Board should be the responsible body.
	:2	**Arrangements for dealing with shortages of mill accessories for the cotton textile industry.** L(TI)(48)83.
	:3	**Supply of foreign workers for the textile industries.**
	:4	**Publicity for the cotton production campaign.** L(TI)(48)79.
	:5	**Statistics of the cotton industry.** BTSP(C)(48)6 and 7.
	:6	**Progress of the regional committee.** L(TI)(48)77 and 84. On wool.
	:7	**Statistics of the wool industry.** BTSP(W)(48)6.
	:8	**West Riding textile publicity campaign.** L(TI)(48)78.

	:9	Survey of conditions in woollen and worsted mills in the south-west region. L(TI)(48)80.
	:10	Market prospects for the cotton industry.
	:11	Wages in the wool industry.
	:12	Hostel accommodation.

CAB 134/472   Memoranda   26 Jan–20 May 1948   L(TI)(48)1–41.

26 Jan	L(TI)(48)1	Composition and terms of reference – J.G. Stewart and H.W. Morris, 1p.
28 Jan	2	Report by the Working Party on the Increase of Textile Exports – J.G. Stewart and H.W. Morris covering Cripps covering the Working Party, 1+3+24+2p appendixes. See PC(48)9.
28 Jan	3	Report by the Working Party on the Increase of Textile Exports – J.G. Stewart and H.W. Morris covering Edwards, N., 1+1p. See PC(48)13.
29 Jan	4	Report by Mrs. Barbara Castle M.P. on a visit to Lancashire 6 – 10 Jan, 4p.
2 Feb	5	Membership of the committee – J.G. Stewart and H.W. Morris, 1p.
5 Feb	6	Note by parliamentary secretary of the Ministry of Health – Edwards, J., 2+2+1p appendix.
6 Jan	7	Publicity campaign for the cotton industry 1948 – Edwards, N., 4+3p appendixes.
5 Feb	8	Deferment of calling-up of young men in the cotton industry – Edwards, N., 2p.
5 Jan	9	Progress in improving welfare and working conditions in cotton spinning mills – Edwards, N., 1p.
9 Feb	10	Analysis of the labour requirements of the cotton industry, town by town – Belcher, 1+1p.
23 Feb	11	Progress made by the regional committee – J.G. Stewart and H.W. Morris covering the regional labour (cotton industry) committee – north-west region, 1+1+1+4+12p.
24 Feb	12	Analysis of the labour requirements of the cotton industry, town by town, on the basis of the labour required to meet the revised export targets – Belcher, 1+1p.
24 Feb	13	Hostel requirements for workers for the textile industries – Durbin, 2p.
25 Feb	14	Progress made by the regional committee – J.G. Stewart and H.W. Morris covering the regional labour (cotton industry) committee – north-west region, 1+4p.
5 Mar	15	Use of hutting for day nurseries – Edwards, J., 1p.
12 Mar	16	Possibility of reducing numbers of women employed by industries competing for labour with cotton mills – H.N. Grundy, 11p.

9 Mar	**17**	**Employment in the cotton industry and the Control of Engagement Order 1947 – Edwards, N.,** 2p.
10 Mar	**18**	**Progress made by the regional committee – J.G. Stewart and H.W. Morris covering the regional labour (cotton industry) committee – north-west region,** 1+6+6p.
12 Mar	**19**	**Allocation of materials to industries other than textiles in the textile areas – J.G. Stewart and H.W. Morris,** 1+3p. Note of a meeting chaired by Jay, 8 Mar 1948. Consideration of whether steel allocation could reduce other industries' labour demands.
19 Mar	**20**	**Progress made by the regional committee – J.G. Stewart and H.W. Morris covering the regional labour (cotton industry) committee – north-west region,** 1+6p.
23 Mar	**21**	**Publicity for the cotton production campaign – Edwards, N.,** 3+10p. Publicity subcommittee of the regional labour committee in Manchester had been established.
24 Mar	**22**	**Progress as to factory amenities, etc. – Edwards, N., covering the chief inspector of factories,** 1+4+1p.
1 Apr	**23**	**Minutes of a discussion at the Treasury on 25 Mar 1948 – J.G. Stewart and H.W. Morris,** 1+2p. Also EAC(48)19. On hostel accommodation.
1 Apr	**24**	**Female labour for the textile areas – J.G. Stewart and H.W. Morris,** 1+4+2p annexes +1p Treasury circular.
5 Apr	**25**	**Progress of the official working party on textile machinery supplies – J.G. Stewart and H.W. Morris,** 1+4+3p. First interim report and minutes of a meeting.
5 Apr	**26**	**Progress made by the regional committee – J.G. Stewart and H.W. Morris covering the regional labour (cotton industry) committee,** 1+5p.
8 Apr	**27**	**Establishment of the cotton industry outside Lancashire – Belcher,** 2+2p appendixes.
9 Apr	**28**	**Draft report to the Production Committee,** 1+8+1p appendix +1p addendum. Draft of L(TI)(48)31.
12 Apr	**29**	**Labour requirements of the wool textile industry by areas – Belcher,** 3+1p appendix.
10 Apr	**30**	**Progress made by the regional committee – J.G. Stewart and H.W. Morris covering the regional labour (cotton industry) committee,** 1+7+8p.
20 Apr	**31**	**Interim report – the committee,** 7+2p appendixes. See PC(48)53.

24 Apr	32	**Progress made by the regional committee – J.G. Stewart and H.W. Morris covering the regional labour (cotton industry) committee,** 1+7+8p.
26 Apr	33	**Report to the production committee – J.G. Stewart and H.W. Morris,** 1+1p. Extract of PC(48)8th.
6 May	34	**Survey of conditions in cotton weaving factories – Edwards, N. covering the chief inspector of factories,** 1+3p.
1 May	35	**Gratuities to government employees entering the textile industries – Jay,** 1p.
3 May	36	**Report – Durbin,** 1+1p. Probable rate of provision of hostel accommodation.
1 May	37	**Progress made by the regional committee – J.G. Stewart and H.W. Morris covering the regional labour (cotton industry) committee,** 1+4+12p.
12 May	38	**Progress of the regional labour (woollen and worsted industry) committee – J.G. Stewart and H.W. Morris covering the committee,** 1+4+6p.
19 May	39	**Appointment of regional committee for the woollen industry – Edwards, N.,** 1+9p appendixes.
19 May	40	**Publicity for the cotton production campaign – J.G. Stewart and H.W. Morris,** 1+6p. Bulletin on progress of the production drive in the industry.
20 May	41	**Progress made by the regional committee – J.G. Stewart and H.W. Morris covering the regional labour (cotton industry) committee,** 1+6+3p.

CAB 134/473   Memoranda   26 May–30 Dec 1948   L(TI)(48)42–91.

26 May	**L(TI)(48)42**	**Publicity campaign for the woollen and worsted industry – Edwards, N.,** 4p.
26 May	43	**Placings and vacancies outstanding in the cotton industry – Edwards, N.,** 2p.
26 May	44	**Future rate of recruitment of foreign workers for the textile industries – Edwards, N.,** 1p.
29 May	45	**Short note on productivity in the cotton spinning industry – Belcher,** 2p.
29 May	46	**Survey on women in industry – J.G. Stewart and H.W. Morris covering the Social Survey,** 1+3+5p. Extract of a report on 1947.
31 May	47	**Progress made by the regional committee for the cotton industry – J.G. Stewart and H.W. Morris covering the regional labour (cotton industry) committee,** 1+6+1p.
1 June	48	**Emergency hostels: Oldham/Rochdale and Burnley/Nelson districts – J.G. Stewart and H.W. Morris,** 1+1p. See PC(48)11th. Also EAC(48)31.

2 June	**49**	**Progress made by the regional committee for the woollen and worsted industry – J.G. Stewart and H.W. Morris covering the regional committee,** 1+5+11p.
9 June	**50**	**Recruitment of foreign workers for the textile industries – J.G. Stewart and H.W. Morris,** 1+2p. Also EAC(48)32. Note of a meeting, 8 June 1948.
15 June	**51**	**Progress made by the regional committee for the cotton industry – J.G. Stewart and H.W. Morris,** 1+7+19p.
16 June	**52**	**Recruitment of foreign workers for the cotton industry – J.G. Stewart and H.W. Morris covering Edwards, N.,** 1+1p.
24 June	**53**	**Progress made by the regional committee for the woollen and worsted industry – J.G. Stewart and H.W. Morris,** 1+5+4p.
29 June	**54**	**Progress made by the regional committee for the cotton industry – J.G. Stewart and H.W. Morris,** 1+7+4p.
29 June	**55**	**Export industries and housing policy – J.G. Stewart and H.W. Morris covering H. Grundy,** 1+1p. More manpower meant a need for more houses.
6 July	**56**	**Publicity for the cotton production campaign – J.G. Stewart and H.W. Morris,** 1+9p. The campaign.
8 July	**57**	**Progress made by the regional committee for the woollen and worsted industry – J.G. Stewart and H.W. Morris,** 1+4+7p appendixes.
9 July	**58**	**Draft second interim report to the Production Committee – J.G. Stewart and H.W. Morris,** 1+4+4p appendixes. Draft of L(TI)(48)61.
9 July	**59**	**Publicity: arrangements for ministers to address meetings and for a survey among cotton operatives – Edwards N.,** 2+2p appendix.
10 July	**60**	**Assisted travel scheme for the cotton industry – Belcher,** 2p.
19 July	**61**	**Second interim report – the committee,** 5+4p appendixes. See PC(48)94.
22 July	**62**	**Progress made by the regional committee for the cotton industry – J.G. Stewart and H.W. Morris,** 1+6+6p.
26 July	**63**	**West Riding textile publicity campaign – J.G. Stewart and H.W. Morris,** 1+12p. First of a series of bulletins on the woollen industry's production drive.
28 July	**64**	**Second report to the Production Committee – J.G. Stewart and H.W. Morris,** 1+1p. Extract from PC(48)16th.

30 July	65	**Progress made by the regional committee for the woollen and worsted industry – J.G. Stewart and H.W. Morris,** 1+4+6p.
9 Aug	66	**Publicity for the cotton production campaign – J.G. Stewart and H.W. Morris,** 1+10p. Bulletin and progress.
17 Aug	67	**Progress made by the regional committee for the cotton industry – J.G. Stewart and H.W. Morris,** 1+8+5p.
25 Aug	68	**Progress of the official working party on textile machinery supplies – J.G. Stewart and H.W. Morris,** 1+1p. Extract of PC(48)70.
30 Aug	69	**Progress made by the regional committee for the woollen and worsted industry – J.G. Stewart and H.W. Morris,** 1+6+2p.
9 Sept	70	**West Riding textile publicity campaign – J.G. Stewart and H.W. Morris,** 1+11p.
27 Sept	71	**Progress made by the regional committee for the woollen and worsted industry – J.G. Stewart and H.W. Morris,** 1+5+11p.
29 Sept	72	**Progress made by the regional committee for the cotton industry – J.G. Stewart and H.W. Morris,** 1+6+8p.
1 Oct	73	**Productivity in the cotton manufacturing industry: letter from Mr. Moelwyn Hughes – Edwards, N. covering L.H. Hornsby,** 1+2p annex +5p appendixes. Envisages a change of emphasis from recruitment to productivity.
6 Oct	75	**Membership of the Committee – J.G. Stewart and H.W. Morris,** 1p.
7 Oct	76	**Redeployment and recruitment in the cotton industry – Jay,** 2p. Urges continuation of the recruitment drive.
20 Oct	77	**Progress made by the regional committee for the woollen and worsted industry – J.G. Stewart and H.W. Morris,** 1+5+4p.
21 Oct	78	**West Riding textile publicity campaign – J.G. Stewart and H.W. Morris,** 1+8p.
26 Oct	79	**Publicity for the cotton production campaign – J.G. Stewart and H.W. Morris,** 1+12p. Bulletin on the cotton production drive.
3 Nov	80	**Survey of conditions in the woollen and worsted mills in the south-west region – Edwards, N.** covering the factory inspectorate, 1+1p annex.
3 Nov	81	**Progress made by the regional committee for the woollen and worsted industry – J.G. Stewart and H.W. Morris,** 1+3+2p.
5 Nov	82	**Redeployment in cotton mills – Edwards, N.** covering H.N. Grundy, 1+4p.
6 Nov	83	**Arrangements for dealing with reported shortages of accessories for the cotton textile industry – J.H. Jones,** 2p.

5 Nov	84	**Recruitment for the women's services – J.G. Stewart and H.W. Morris covering the War Office,** 1+1p. Letter about L(TI)(48)77.
18 Nov	85	**Cotton industry conference at Harrogate – Wilson,** 4p.
4 Dec	86	**Progress made by the regional committee for the woollen and worsted industry – J.G. Stewart and H.W. Morris,** 1+5+10p.
4 Dec	87	**Cotton industry conference at Harrogate – J.G. Stewart and H.W. Morris,** 1+1p. Extract from PC(48)24th.
6 Dec	88	**Statutory basis of the wage system in the cotton industry – J.G. Stewart and H.W. Morris,** 1+3p. Note of a meeting, 25 Nov 1948.
10 Jan	89	**The Scottish wool textile industry – Board of Trade,** 1+2+3p annex. Revise version.
20 Dec	90	**The Cotton Board trade letter – J.G. Stewart and H.W. Morris,** 1+8p. Replacement of the bulletin on the cotton production drive.
30 Dec	91	**Progress made by the regional committee for the cotton industry – J.G. Stewart and H.W. Morris,** 1+7+14p.

CAB 134/474   Meetings and Memoranda   5 Jan 1949–18 Apr 1950
L(TI)(49)1st–L(TI)(50)1st and L(TI)(49)1–L(TI)(50)4.

Meetings

2 Feb	**L(TI)(49)1st:1**	**Long-term prospects for the cotton industry.** Consideration of an unnumbered Board of Trade paper.
	:2	**Redeployment.** L(TI)(48)85, 87, 88. Progress report by H.N. Grundy.
	:3	**Progress of the regional (Manchester) committee.** L(TI)(48)91.
	:4	**Shortage of card clothing.** L(TI)(49)4.
	:5	**Cotton Board trade letter.** L(TI)(48)90.
	:6	**Statistics for the cotton industry.** BTSP(C)(48)8.
	:7	**Public opinion in the Lancashire cotton towns.** L(TI)(49)5.
	:8	**Allocation of European volunteer workers between the cotton and wool industries.** L(TI)(49)3. Allocation approved.
	:9	**Regional (Leeds) committee: progress report.** L(TI)(48)86 and L(TI)(49)1.
	:10	**Scottish wool textile industry.** L(TI)(48)89(revise).
	:11	**West Riding textile publicity campaign.**
	:12	**Statistics of the woollen and worsted industry.** BTSP(W)(48)7.
1 Mar	**2nd:1**	**Redeployment in the wool industry.** L(TI)(49)8.

		:2	**Progress of the regional (Leeds) committee.** L(TI)(49)6.
		:3	**Progress of the south-western region working party for the woollen and worsted industry.** L(TI)(49)9.
		:4	**Statistics of the wool industry.** BTSP(W)(48)9.
		:5	**Redeployment in the cotton industry.** Progress report by E.M. Gray.
		:6	**Recruitment of foreign workers for the cotton industry.**
		:7	**The Cotton Board trade letter.** L(TI)(49)7.
		:8	**Statistics of the cotton industry.** BTSP(C)(48)10.
		:9	**Progress of the regional (Manchester) committee.**
4 May	3rd:1		**Imports of Pirn winding machinery.** L(TI)(49)17.
		:2	**Day nurseries for the textile industries.**
		:3	**Long-term prospects of the wool industry.** L(TI)(49)11.
		:4	**Progress of the regional (Leeds) committee.** L(TI)(49)14.
		:5	**West Riding textile publicity campaign.** L(TI)(49)12.
		:6	**Statistics of the wool industry.** BTSP(W)(49)1.
		:7	**Progress of the regional (Manchester) committee.** L(TI)(49)13.
		:8	**Cotton Board trade letters.** L(TI)(49)10 and 15.
		:9	**Statistics of the cotton industry.** BTSP(C)(49)1 and 2.
		:10	**Production and manpower targets for 1949.** L(TI)(49)16.
		:11	**Publicity for the textile industries.** L(TI)(49)18.
8 Dec	4th:1		**Economy in government expenditure.**
		:2	**Day nurseries in the textiles areas.** L(TI)(49)22.
		:3	**Implications on production and employment of revised dollar import programme.** L(TI)(49)32 and 33. L(TI)(49)16 assumed plentiful raw materials, which was no longer valid for cotton. Continued recruitment agreed.
		:4	**Publicity for the textile industries.** L(TI)(49)34 and 35.
		:5	**Wool industry: training within industry.** L(TI)(49)23.
		:6	**Progress of the regional (Manchester) committee.** L(TI)(49)26.
		:7	**Cotton Board trade letters.** L(TI)(49)20, 24, 27, 30, 31.
		:8	**Statistics of the cotton industry.** BTSP(C)(49)3, 4, 5, 6, 7, 8, 9.
		:9	**Progress of the regional (Leeds) committee.** L(TI)(49)25 and 29.

	:10	**West Riding publicity campaign.** L(TI)(49)21 and 28.
	:11	**Statistics of the wool industry.** BTSP(W)(49)2, 3, 4, 5, 6, 7, 8, 9.
	:12	**Future work of the Committee.** Edwards, N. felt the continuation of the regional committees should be reviewed.
	:13	**Retirement of Mr. H.N. Grundy.**
26 Jan	L(TI)(50)1st:1	**Draft report to the Production Committee.** L(TI)(50)1.
	:2	**Future work of the Committee.** L(TI)(50)2. Paper endorsed.

Memoranda

5 Jan	L(TI)(49)1	**Progress made by the regional committee for the woollen and worsted industries – S.E.V. Luke and H.W. Morris,** 1+4+7p.
	2	**West Riding publicity campaign – S.E.V. Luke and H.W. Morris,** 1+7p.
17 Jan	3	**Allocations of European volunteer workers between the cotton and wool industries – Board of Trade,** 1p.
20 Jan	4	**Shortage of card clothing for the cotton industry – Edwards, N. covering the Federation of Master Cotton Spinners' Association Ltd.,** 1+5p appendixes.
24 Jan	5	**Public opinion in the Lancashire cotton towns – S.E.V. Luke and H.W. Morris covering the Social Survey,** 1+1+3p.
3 Feb	6	**Progress made by the regional committee for the woollen and worsted industries – S.E.V. Luke and H.W. Morris,** 1+3+7p appendixes.
10 Feb	7	**The Cotton Board trade letter – S.E.V. Luke and H.W. Morris,** 1+8p.
23 Feb	8	**Redeployment in the wool industry – Edwards, J.,** 4p. Assessment of the scope and the means for increasing efficiency.
23 Feb	9	**Progress made by the south-western region working party for the woollen and worsted industry – S.E.V. Luke and H.W. Morris,** 1+2p.
14 Mar	10	**The Cotton Board trade letter – S.E.V. Luke and H.W. Morris,** 1+8p.
19 Mar	11	**The long-term prospects of the wool industry – Edwards, J.,** 4+2p annex. Estimate of demand and labour requirements to 1952.
25 Mar	12	**West Riding publicity campaign – S.E.V. Luke and H.W. Morris,** 1+12p.
25 Mar	13	**Progress made by the regional committee for the cotton industry – S.E.V. Luke and H.W. Morris,** 1+7+23p.

26 Mar	14	Progress made by the regional committee for the woollen and worsted industries – S.E.V. Luke and H.W. Morris, 1+5+7p.
21 Apr	15	The Cotton Board trade letter – S.E.V. Luke and H.W. Morris, 1+8p.
26 Apr	16	Production and manpower targets for 1949 – Edwards, N. covering the Board of Trade and Ministry of Labour, 1+5p annex +2p addendum. Targets based on assumption of sufficient raw materials.
28 Apr	17	Imports of Pirn winding machinery – S.E.V. Luke and H.W. Morris, 1+2p. Extract of a meeting of the official working party on textile machinery supplies, 15 Mar 1949.
2 May	18	Publicity for the textile industries – Edwards, N. covering the public relations officers of the Board of Trade and Ministry of Labour, 1+2p annex.
11 May	19	Progress made by the regional committee for the woollen and worsted industries – S.E.V. Luke and H.W. Morris, 1+5+9p.
26 May	20	The Cotton Board trade letter – S.E.V. Luke and H.W. Morris, 1+8p.
1 June	21	West Riding publicity campaign – S.E.V. Luke and H.W. Morris, 1+9p.
8 June	22	Note by the parliamentary secretary of the Ministry of Health – Blenkinsop, 2+3+6p appendixes +1p addendum.
21 June	23	Training within industry in the wool industry – Edwards, N., 2p.
27 July	24	The Cotton Board trade letter – S.E.V. Luke and H.W. Morris, 1+28p.
27 July	25	Progress made by the regional committee for the woollen and worsted industries – S.E.V. Luke and H.W. Morris, 1+4+16p appendix.
15 Aug	26	Progress made by the regional committee for the cotton industry – S.E.V. Luke and H.W. Morris, 1+7+32p.
16 Aug	27	The Cotton Board trade letter – S.E.V. Luke and H.W. Morris, 1+8p.
12 Sept	28	West Riding publicity campaign – S.E.V. Luke and H.W. Morris, 1+12p.
8 Oct	29	Progress made by the regional committee for the woollen and worsted industries – S.E.V. Luke and H.W. Morris, 1+3+7p.
19 Oct	30	The Cotton Board trade letter – S.E.V. Luke and H.W. Morris, 1+36p.
11 Nov	31	The Cotton Board trade letter – S.E.V. Luke and H.W. Morris, 1+8p.
25 Nov	32	Implications on production and employment of revised dollar import programme – Edwards, J.,

			2p. The new programme significantly revised raw cotton imports.
5 Dec		33	**Progress in 1949 in labour supply to cotton and wool industries – Edwards, N. covering H.N. Grundy,** 1+4p.
5 Dec		34	**Publicity in the wool textile industry – Edwards, J.,** 2p.
6 Dec		35	**Publicity for the textile industries – Edwards, N. covering the director of public relations of the Ministry of Labour,** 1+2p annex.
20 Jan	L(TI)(50)1		**Draft report of the Labour (Textile Industries) Committee to the Production Committee – S.E.V. Luke and H.W. Morris,** 1+5p. Draft of L(TI)(50)3.
20 Jan		2	**Future work of the committee – Edwards, N.,** 1p. The Committee and regional committees would not be formally wound up but should not be reconvened unless really necessary.
24 Feb		3	**Review of the Committee's work – S.E.V. Luke and H.W. Morris covering Edwards, N.,** 1+5p. See PC(50)27.
18 Apr		4	**Termination of the Committee – N. Brook,** 1p.

PC(48)53 and 94 and PC(50)27 are attached.

15.26 Materials Committee (renamed Materials (Allocation) Committee, November 1950)

For the wartime papers of this official committee under the Ministry of Supply (1939–1941), Production Executive (1941–1942) and Ministry of Production (1942–1945), see BT 131 and BT 28. After 1945 it continued to be responsible for the allocation of materials in short supply, in particular steel and timber which were temporarily covered by separate subcommittees (see CAB 134/487). Unresolved issues were adjudicated by the Lord President's Committee and, after October 1947, by the Production Committee.

There was no fixed membership of the committee, representatives of interested departments attending when necessary. The wartime chairman had been a junior minister but in 1945 the wartime secretary, Professor A. Plant, was appointed chairman. After he returned to academic life in June 1946, and in the expectation that shortages would decrease, the chairmanship was divided between several officials on the understanding that N. Brook would chair particularly controversial meetings. Shortages increased, so in December 1946 Attlee decided to revert to the wartime precedent of a junior minister as chairman. These ministers (Gaitskell, Marquand, Jay and Callaghan) were given considerable strategic power by the committee's allocation functions over all economic programmes, especially as they were also *de facto* chairman of the Fuel Allocations Committee (CAB 134/270). For comments on the business-like efficiency of this committee by Gaitskell, who particularly used this power to challenge even Cabinet decisions, see P.M. Williams (ed) *The Diary of Hugh Gaitskell,* pp 38–9.

In September 1947 the secretariat was changed from the Cabinet Office to the C.E.P.S. to increase the general co-ordination of policy. In November 1950 the committee was renamed the Materials (Allocation) Committee to avoid confusion with the Raw Materials Committee. For its papers after 1951 see CAB 134/1006–1009.

Terms (Nov 1945) Subject to the authority of the Lord President, to determine the allocation of raw materials in short supply and to determine any other questions submitted to it regarding the provision and use of raw materials. (Jan 1948) On behalf of the Production Committee, to determine . . .

Members (Nov 1945) A. Plant (Cab. O., ch.). (June 1946) A. Plant (ch. for timber) G. Archer (Supply, ch. for steel, cast iron and non-ferrous metals) R.D. Fennelly (B.T., ch. for all other materials). (Sept 1946) F.G. Lee (Supply) replaced Archer as ch. for iron and steel.
(Jan 1947) Parl. Sec., Min. of Fuel & Power (ch.). (Oct 1947) Paymaster-Gen. (ch.).
(Dec 1947) Ec. Sec. (Try, ch.). (March 1950) Parl. & Fin. Sec., Admiralty (ch.). (Nov 1950) Ec. Sec. (Try, ch.).

Secs. D.N. Lowe (Cab. O.). (June 1946) R.F. Allen (Cab. O.) replaced Lowe. (Dec 1946) F.E. Budd (Cab. O., later C.E.P.S.) replaced Allen. (June 1950) C.D. Smith (C.E.P.S.) replaced Budd. (Oct 1951) K.W.S. Mackenzie replaced Smith.

CAB 134/475   Meetings and Memoranda   2 Nov–22 Dec 1945   M(45)154th–159th and M(45)1068–1081.

Meetings

20 Nov	**M(45)154th:1**	**Flax: review of supply and requirements 1945 and 1946.** M(45)1071. Once minimum government and utility requirements had been met maximum encouragement should be given to exports, particularly to dollar markets.
	:2	**Reorganization of the Committee.** M.(45)1068).
26 Nov	**155th**	Untitled. M(45)1072. Consideration of allocations of paper and board with revised allocations appended.
6 Dec	**156th**	Untitled. M(45)1074. Allocation of jute and jute goods with revised allocations appended.
13 Dec	**157th:2**	**Cotton: supply and requirements for Period I 1946.** M(45)1075. As large as possible an increase to exports should be made without maintaining undue austerity at home. Allocations appended.
19 Dec	**158th:1**	**Rubber: supply and requirements for Period I 1946.** M(45)1079.
	:2	**Steel: supply and requirements for Period I 1946.** M(45)1078.
20 Dec	**159th:1**	**Timber: supply and requirements for the first quarter of 1946.** M(45)1077.
	:2	**Timber: proposal to combine certificate to purchase and licence to acquire.** M(45)1076.

Memoranda

2 Nov	M(45)1068	Reorganization – E.E. Bridges, 1p.
3 Nov	1069	Sisal allocation for export – secretariat, 1p.
7 Nov	1070	Paper and board – secretariat, 1p.
12 Nov	1071	Flax – secretariat covering the Raw Materials Department, 1+9+4p appendixes.
24 Nov	1072	Paper and board – secretariat, 1+2p.
21 Nov	1073	Cotton allocations and planning. Proposed revised arrangements – Raw Materials Department, 1+3p. Recommendation of some relaxation of detailed control.
30 Nov	1074	Jute and jute goods – Raw Materials Department, 4+3p appendixes.
8 Dec	1075	Cotton yarn for Period I 1946 – Raw Materials Department, 2+1p appendix.
10 Dec	1076	Timber: proposal to combine certificates to purchase and licence to acquire – secretariat covering the Raw Materials Department 1+2p. Proposals to simplify procedure and ease work of the Timber Control.
15 Dec	1077	Timber: review of supply and requirements for the first quarter 1946 – Raw Materials Department, 4+1p appendix.
15 Dec	1078	Steel: estimated requirements for Period I 1946 – secretariat covering the Iron and Steel Control, 1+4p.
17 Dec	1079	Rubber: supply and requirements for first quarter 1946 – Raw Materials Department, 8+5p appendixes +3p corrigenda.
21 Dec	1080	Cotton yarn: buying limits – secretary, 2p.
22 Dec	1081	Iron castings: allocations for Period I 1946 – secretariat, 2p.

CAB 134/476   Meetings   11 Jan–18 Dec 1946   M(46)160th–182nd plus three other meetings.

11 Jan	M(46)160th:1	Paper and board. M(46)1084.
	:2	Review of supply position. Paper and board.
	:3	Allocations for twenty-first licensing period. Paper and board.
	:4	Final revision of allocations for twentieth licensing period. M(46)1082. Paper and board.
1 Mar	161st:1	Iron and steel: proposed revision of distribution scheme. M(46)1088
	:2	Allocation of lead. M(46)1089.
8 Mar	162nd	Untitled. M(46)1090. Allocations of linseed oil.
13 Mar	163rd	Steel: supply and requirements for Period II 1946. M(46)1093. Agreed allocations appended.
14 Mar	164th:1	Jute: review of supply and requirements. M(46)1091.

	:2	**Cotton: supply and requirements for the second quarter 1946.** M(46)1092. Agreed allocations appended.
4 Apr	165th:1	**Rubber: supply and requirements for second quarter 1946.** M(46)1098.
	:2	**Timber: supply and requirements for second quarter 1946.** M(46)1097. Agreed allocations appended.
	:3	**Timber: revised licensing procedure.** M(46)1096.
	:4	**Changes in membership.**
10 May	166th	**Paper and board.** M(46)1101. Agreed allocations appended.
14 June	167th:1	**Jute: review of supply and requirements.** M(46)1102. Agreed allocations appended.
	:2	**Cotton: supply and requirements for the third quarter 1946.** M(46)1103. Agreed allocations appended.
	:3	**Birthday Honours List; changes in membership of committee.**
19 June	168th:1	**Steel: supply and requirements for Period III 1946.** M(46)1104. J.C. Carr felt that it was time to review the wartime distribution scheme. A. Plant felt the scheme had been successful but there were two new problems. Some authorizations bore little relation to allocations and the practicability of directing production of those with overloaded order books was very difficult.
	:2	**Lead: review of allocations.** M(46)1105.
	:3	**Changes in membership.**
18 June	169th:1	**Linseed oil: allocations for paint, etc.** M(46)1107.
	:2	**Rape oil: proposed allocations.** M(46)1106. Approved.
28 June	170th:1	**Timber: supply and requirements for third quarter 1946.** M(46)1109. Concern over critical position of softwood. Agreed allocations appended.
	:2	**Change in secretariat.**
21 Aug	171st:1	**Reorganization of the Committee.** M(46)1110.
	:2	**Linseed oil allocations for September 1946.** M(46)1116. Agreed allocations appended.
11 Sept	172nd:1	**Steel: supply and requirements for Period IV 1946; re-authorization of orders for steel sheets.** M(46)1126 and 1128. Agreed allocations appended.
	:2	**Steel Control Board.** F. Lee outlined the new board's relationship with the Committee.
13 Sept	173rd:1	**Linseed oil: supply and requirements fourth quarter 1946.** M(46)1130 and 1132. Agreement on allocations for October only. Consideration

		of whether the division of the allocation imposed cuts of equal severity.
	:2	**Castor oil: supplies and allocations.** M(46)1131. Agreed allocations appended.
	:3	**Rape oil: supplies and allocations.** M(46)1129.
	174th	No record.
24 Sept	**175th**	**Timber: supplies and requirements for the fourth quarter 1946.** M(46)1109 and 1137. The supply situation was deteriorating and the Timber Economy Subcommittee had been reconstituted. Agreed allocations as appended.
1 Oct	**176th**	**Cotton yarn: supply and requirements for the fourth quarter 1946.** M(46)1135. Agreed allocations appended.
24 Oct	**177th**	**Allocation of steel sheets for first quarter 1947.** M(46)1146 and 1141. F. Lee proposed revival of the wartime Steel Economy Subcommittee to consider further economies. He recognized restrictions would raise general issues of policy and suggested that the Lord President act as umpire between competing departmental claims. Agreed allocations appended.
6 Dec	**178th:1**	**Linseed oil: allocations for first quarter 1947.** M(46)1153. Agreed allocations appended.
	:2	**Castor oil: supplies and requirements: first quarter 1947.** M(46)1154. Agreed allocations appended.
	:3	**Rape oil: supplies and allocations first quarter 1947.** M(46)1152. Agreed allocations appended.
6 Dec	**179th**	**Cotton yarn: supply and requirements for first quarter 1947.** M(46)1157. Agreed allocations appended.
10 Dec	**180th**	**Steel: supplies and requirements for the first quarter 1947.** M(46)1156. The coal position could lead to some difficulties although ministers had decided not to cut allocations to steel works. Agreed allocations appended.
13 Dec	**181st:1**	**Timber: second and final reports by Economy Subcommittee.** M(46)1161 and 1162.
	:2	**Timber: supply and requirements for the first quarter 1947.** M(46)1160. Need for further reduction in softwood allocations. Agreed allocations appended.
	:3	**Reorganization of the Committee.**
18 Dec	**182nd:1**	**Lead: allocations for first quarter 1947.** M(46)1159. Agreed allocations appended.
	:2	**Change of secretary.**
18 Jan	*ad hoc*	**Tyre fabric.**
14 Nov	*ad hoc*	**Steel for Ministry of Agriculture.**
19 Dec	*ad hoc*	**Hop wire and baling wire.**

CAB 134/477   Memoranda   9 Jan–30 Dec 1946   M(46)1082–1164.

9 Jan	M(46)1082	**Final revision of allocations for twentieth licensing period** – secretariat, 1+2p appendixes.
8 Jan	1083	**Timber: proposal to combine certificate to purchase and licence to acquire** – secretary, 1p.
10 Jan	1084	**Paper and board: allocations for the twenty-first licensing period** – Raw Materials Department, 1+3p appendix.
14 Jan	1085	**Sisal and manilla** – secretary covering the Raw Materials Department, 1+2+2p appendixes.
24 Jan	1086	**Timber: revised licensing procedure** – secretariat, 1+5p annexes.
8 Feb	1087	**Paper for books** – secretariat, 1p.
19 Feb	1088	**Proposed revision of iron and steel distribution scheme** – secretary, 1+3+3p appendixes. Draft outline of scheme. While the present scheme worked vertically the new system was to be horizontal and provide for the classification of consumers into groups broadly similar to those in the census of production.
25 Feb	1089	**Allocation of lead** – secretary covering the Raw Materials Department, 1+5p. Possible basis of allocation.
6 Mar	1090	**Linseed oil** – secretary covering the Ministry of Food, 1+3p. Request for revised allocation.
11 Mar	1091	**Jute: review of supply requirements** – Raw Materials Department, 3+3p appendixes.
11 Mar	1092	**Cotton yarn: Period II 1946** – Raw Materials Department, 2+1p appendix.
11 Mar	1093	**Steel: estimated requirements for Period II 1946** – secretariat covering the Iron and Steel Control, 1+4p.
18 Mar	1094	**Cotton yarn: buying limits** – secretary, 2p.
19 Mar	1095	**Linseed oil** – secretariat, 1p.
21 Mar	1096	**Timber: revised licensing scheme** – secretariat, 1p.
27 Mar	1097	**Timber: review of supply and requirements for the second quarter 1946** – Raw Materials Department, 4+1p appendix. The size of the gap still depended on the level of supplies from Germany and Russia.
25 Mar	1098	**Rubber: review of supply and requirements for second quarter 1946** – secretary covering the Raw Materials Department, 1+9+4p appendixes.
25 Mar	1099	**Timber and rubber: allocations for Period II 1946** – secretary, 1p.
1 Apr	1100	**Iron castings: allocations for Period II 1946** – secretary, 2p.

8 May	**1101**	**Paper and board: allocations for the twenty-second licensing period – Raw Materials Department,** 1+5p.
6 June	**1102**	**Jute: review of supply and requirements – Raw Materials Department,** 4+2 appendixes.
6 June	**1103**	**Cotton yarn for Period III 1946 – Raw Materials Department,** 1+1p appendix.
17 June	**1104**	**Steel: estimated requirements for Period III 1946 – secretariat covering the Iron and Steel Control,** 1+5p.
14 June	**1105**	**Lead: allocations for Period III 1946 – director of non-ferrous metals of the Ministry of Supply,** 2p.
17 June	**1106**	**Rape oil – Ministry of Food,** 1+1p appendix.
17 June	**1107**	**Paints, varnishes, etc., containing linseed oil – Raw Materials Department,** 5p.
20 June	**1108**	**Paper: reduction in the export allocation for the twenty-second licensing period – secretariat,** 1p.
24 June	**1109**	**Timber: review of supply and requirements for the third quarter 1946 – Raw Materials Department,** 4+1p appendix. Import possibilities were becoming less favourable.
29 June	**1110**	**Reorganization – E.E. Bridges,** 1p.
2 July	**1111**	**Iron castings: allocations for Period III 1946 – secretary,** 1+1p appendix.
6 July	**1112**	**Paints, varnishes, etc., containing linseed oil – secretary covering the Raw Materials Department,** 1+4p.
31 July	**1113**	**Paper and board – secretary,** 1p.
2 Aug	**1114**	**Linseed oil and paints: requirements, fourth quarter 1946 – secretary,** 1p.
16 Aug	**1115**	**Sisal and manilla – secretary covering the Raw Materials Department,** 1+2+2p appendixes. Review of supply position for the second half of 1946, recommending revised allocations.
20 Aug	**1116**	**Linseed oil allocations for September – Ministry of Food,** 2p.
16 Aug	**1117**	**Cast iron pipes – secretariat,** 1p.
23 Aug	**1118**	**Timber: reconstitution of Economy Subcommittee – secretariat,** 1p.
24 Aug	**1119**	Untitled – R.F. Allen, 1p. Administrative arrangements following reorganization.
24 Aug	**1120**	**Raw materials requirements – secretariat,** 1p.
26 Aug	**1121**	**Paint distribution scheme – secretariat,** 2+6p.
29 Aug	**1122**	**Steel sheets – secretariat,** 1p. Increased allocation for housing.
29 Aug	**1123**	**Over-authorization of acquisition of heavy rails, etc. – secretariat,** 2p.
3 Sept	**1124**	**Building board – secretariat,** 1p.
5 Sept	**1125**	**Timber: revised licensing procedure – secretariat,** 1p. List of departments authorized to issue licences.

6 Sept	**1126**	**Steel sheets – secretariat covering the Ministry of Supply,** 1+2+6p. There was a need to confine new authorizations to reduce the overload of orders.
7 Sept	**1127**	**Steel: supplementary allocations sanctioned by the chairman for Period III 1946 – secretariat,** 1p.
9 Sept	**1128**	**Steel: supply and requirements for Period IV 1946 – secretary covering the Iron and Steel Control,** 1+5p.
10 Sept	**1129**	**Rape oil: supplies and allocations – R.F. Allen covering the Ministry of Food,** 1+1p. There were considerable supply difficulties. It had to be decided if allocations were to be further reduced.
11 Sept	**1130**	**Linseed oil: supplies and allocations – secretariat covering the Ministry of Food,** 1+2+2p appendixes.
11 Sept	**1131**	**Castor oil: supplies and allocations – secretariat covering the Ministry of Food,** 1+2p.
11 Sept	**1132**	**Linseed oil for paint for transport purposes – secretariat covering the Ministry of Transport,** 1+4p.
20 Sept	**1133**	**Paper and board: allocations for the twenty-third licensing period – secretariat covering the Paper Control,** 1+5p.
19 Sept	**1134**	**Timber: review of supply and requirements for the fourth quarter 1946 – Raw Materials Department,** 4p. The supply position continued to deteriorate and no improvement was likely until summer 1947. Allocations should take a longer-term view of supply than previously.
19 Sept	**1135**	**Cotton yarn for Period IV 1946 – secretariat,** 1+1p appendix. A meeting was needed to close the existing gap between supply and requirements.
20 Sept	**1136**	**Lead: allocations for Period IV 1946 – secretariat covering the director of non-ferrous metals,** 1+2p.
23 Sept	**1137**	**Timber: report by Economy Subcommittee – R.F. Allen covering the Subcommittee,** 1+10p. Interim report.
25 Sept	**1138**	**Jute: fourth quarter 1946 – secretariat covering the Raw Materials Department,** 1+4+3p appendixes.
26 Sept	**1139**	**Reorganization – N. Brook,** 1p.
2 Oct	**1140**	**Jute: allocations for fourth quarter 1946 – unsigned,** 1+1p appendix.
9 Oct	**1141**	**Iron and steel sheet allocation – secretariat,** 1p.
12 Oct	**1142**	**Iron castings: allocations for Period IV 1946 – secretary,** 1+1p appendix.

18 Oct	1143	Iron and steel distribution scheme. Sheets – secretary, 1p.
21 Oct	1144	Steel and cast iron: supplementary allocations for fourth quarter 1946 – secretary, 1p.
21 Oct	1145	Timber economy: progress report – secretary covering the Raw Materials Department, 1+1+1p appendix.
22 Oct	1146	Steel sheets: re-authorization of orders for fourth quarter 1946 and allocations for first quarter 1947 – R.F. Allen, 1+1p appendix.
23 Oct	1147	Raw materials requirements – secretariat, 4p. Departmental estimates.
31 Oct	1148	Allocations of linseed oil and paints: fourth quarter 1946 – R.F. Allen, 2+1 appendix.
5 Nov	1149	Economy of timber – secretariat covering the Ministry of Health, 1+1p. Proposal to use certain sizes and qualities of softwood only for building.
9 Nov	1150	Linseed oil and paints: requirements first quarter 1947 – secretariat, 1p.
15 Nov	1151	Aluminium – secretariat, 1+4p. Note of a meeting, 7 Nov 1946, to consider tonnage to be made available for housing over the next two years.
2 Dec	1152	Rape oil – secretariat covering the Ministry of Food, 1+1+1p appendix.
4 Dec	1153	Allocations of linseed oil and paints: first quarter 1947 – secretariat covering the Ministry of Food, 1+5p.
3 Dec	1154	Castor oil – secretariat covering the Ministry of Food, 1+1+1p appendix.
3 Dec	1155	Allocations of linseed oil for paints, Dec 1946 – R.F. Allen, 1+3p. Note of a meeting, 18 Nov 1946.
4 Dec	1156	Steel: supply and requirements for first quarter 1947 – R.F. Allen covering the Iron and Steel Board, 1+5p.
5 Dec	1157	Cotton yarn: Period I 1947 – Raw Materials Department, 1+1 appendix.
6 Dec	1158	Iron and steel distribution scheme. Steel sheets – secretariat covering the British Iron and Steel Federation, 1+1p.
12 Dec	1159	Lead allocations for Period I 1947 – secretariat covering the director of non-ferrous metals at the Ministry of Supply, 1+1p.
10 Dec	1160	Timber: review of supply and requirements for the first quarter of 1947 – secretariat covering the Raw Materials Department, 1+4+1p appendix.
11 Dec	1161	Second report by the Economy Subcommittee – secretariat covering the Subcommittee, 1+9p.

11 Dec	**1162**	**Final report by Economy Subcommittee –**
		secretariat covering the Subcommittee, 1+6p.
		Review of departmental programmes and
		possible measures to reduce consumption.
20 Dec	**1163**	**Jute – secretariat covering the Raw Materials**
		Department, 1+1p.
30 Dec	**1164**	**Reorganization – N. Brook,** 1p.

CAB 134/478 Meetings 16 Jan–22 Dec 1947 M(47)1st–29th.

16 Jan	**M(47)1st**	Untitled. M(47)3. Paper and board.
21 Feb	**2nd**	Untitled. M(47)10. Aluminium.
10 Mar	**3rd:1**	**Linseed oil: supplies and allocations for Period**
		II 1947. M(47)19. Agreed allocations
		appended.
	:2	**Castor oil: supply and allocations for Period II**
		1947. M(47)18. Agreed allocations appended.
	:3	**Rape oil: supplies and allocations for Period II**
		1947. M(47)17. Agreed allocations appended.
14 Mar	**4th:1**	**Steel: supplies, requirements and allocations for**
		Period II 1947. Requirements and allocations
		of sheet steel for Period III 1947. M(47)21.
		Gaitskell said that deliveries fell substantially
		short of allocations and that it was impossible
		to estimate production in Period II. It was clear
		from the Fuel Committee that priorities would
		have to be established. For the present,
		departmental allocations should be restricted
		to 70% of Period I. Agreed allocations
		appended.
	:2	**Recommendations regarding proposals in**
		Committee paper M(47)9. M(47)9 and 16. Steel
		allocations.
	:3	**First interim report by the Steel Economy**
		Subcommittee. M(47)14.
17 Mar	**5th**	**Timber: supplies, requirements and allocations**
		for Period II 1947. M(47)22. Agreed allocations
		appended.
21 Mar	**6th**	**Lead: supplies and allocations for Period II**
		1947. M(47)25.
21 Apr	**7th:1**	**Supplies and requirements of steel plates for**
		Period II 1947. M(47)26.
	:2	**Steel problems Period III 1947.** M(47)9.
		Discussion of the problems facing departments
		with regard to supply prospects and the
		backlog. Cancellation of some orders
		considered.
	:3	**First interim report of the Steel Economy**
		Subcommittee. M(47)14. Endorsed with
		amendments. Ministry of Works to investigate
		the impact of the withdrawal of sheet steel
		allocations for the manufacture of certain

equipment on employment in the development areas.

14 May	**8th**	**Allocation of paper and board for the twenty-fifth licensing period.** M(47)39. Agreed allocations appended.
16 May	**9th:1**	**Reduction of backlog of undelivered orders.** M(47)9. Gaitskell felt there was a clear need to reduce demand radically. He proposed to reintroduce from 1 Oct 1947 the provision whereby, after an agreed time, unfulfilled orders were cancelled unless specifically re-authorized.
	:2	**Supplies, requirements and allocations of steel for Period III 1947. Requirements and allocations of sheet steel for Period IV 1947.** M(47)40. Gaitskell proposed general restrictions to concentrate supplies in areas which would directly help exports.
22 May	**10th:2**	**Second interm report by the Steel Economy Subcommittee.** M(47)34.
2 June	**11th:1**	**Rape oil: supplies and allocations for Period III 1947.** M(47)42. Agreed allocations appended.
	:2	**Castor oil: supplies and allocations for Period III 1947.** M(47)43. Agreed allocations appended.
	:3	**Linseed oil: supplies, requirements and allocations Period III 1947.** M(47)44. Agreed allocations appended.
18 June	**12th**	**Cotton yarn: supply, requirements and allocations for Period III 1947.** M(47)46.
20 June	**13th**	**Timber: supplies, requirements and allocations for Period III 1947.** M(47)45. Gaitskell said that in view of the currency problem the allocations proposed would be maximums. Agreed allocations appended.
26 June	**14th**	**Jute: supplies, requirements and allocations for Period III 1947.** M(47)48. Agreed allocations appended.
1 July	**15th**	**Lead: supplies and allocations for Period III 1947.** M(47)49. Agreed allocations appended.
8 July	**16th**	**Sisal and manilla: supplies, requirements and allocations for July–December 1947.** M(47)52. Agreed allocations appended.
25 & 27 Aug	**17th:1**	**Backlog and duplication of orders.** M(47)65. Given the backlog, allocations made by the Materials Committee were ineffective and the pattern of delivery was determined by the steel makers. Gaitskell said that the present scheme had been proved unsatisfactory. Agreement to authorize 75% only of departmental allocations for non-priority building and general steel in Period IV.

	:2	**Supplies, requirements and allocations of steel for Period IV 1947; requirements and allocations of sheet steel for Period I 1948.** Gaitskell felt it was necessary to reduce the allocation for factory building in development areas to allow urgent repairs and extensions elsewhere. Gaitskell emphasized that the only justification for any allocations for non-priority uses was a quick return of foreign currency. It might be necessary to increase direct exports to increase imports of essentials. Agreed allocations appended.
26 Aug	18th	**Rape, castor and linseed oils: supplies and allocations for Period IV 1947.** M(47)59, 60, 61. Agreed allocations appended.
7 Sept	19th	**Cotton yarn: supplies, requirements and allocations for Period IV 1949.** M(47)68. Agreed allocations appended.
19 Sept	20th:1	**Revision of allocations of general and building steel for Period IV 1947.** CP(47)250. Consideration of means to bridge the gap between allocations agreed in M(47)17th and the additional requirements of the new export programmes.
	:2	**Revision of allocations of sheet steel for Period IV 1947 and Period I 1948.**
22 Sept	21st	**Allocations of papers and board for the twenty-sixth licensing period.** M(47)73. Agreed allocations appended.
25 Sept	22nd	**Lead: supplies and allocations for Period IV 1947.** M(47)74. Agreed allocations appended.
26 Sept	23rd:1	**Overdrafts and unhonoured licences.** M(47)58.
	:2	**Timber: supplies, requirements and allocations for Period IV 1947.** M(47)71. Agreed allocations appended.
13 Nov	24th	**Supply, requirements and allocations of steel for Periods I and II 1948.** M(47)86. Gaitskell said that it had proved extremely difficult to devise an acceptable scheme which would ensure the elimination of the backlog and deflation of the steel currency. The cheque system had been made impracticable by objections from industry. It was likely that a modified M form would continue and its use must be more accurate and scrupulous. Ministers were amending priorities. Agreed allocations appended.
1 Dec	25th:1	**Linseed oil: supplies and allocations for Period I 1948.** M(47)90. Agreed allocations appended.
	:2	**Castor oil: supplies and allocations for Period I 1948.** M(47)89. Agreed allocations appended.

	:3	**Rape oil: supplies and allocations for Period I 1948.** M(47)88. Agreed allocations appended.
11 Dec	26th	**Timber: supplies, requirements and allocations for Period I 1948.** M(47)94. Agreed allocations appended.
16 Dec	27th	**Lead: supplies and allocations for Period I 1948.** M(47)98. Agreed allocations appended.
18 Dec	28th	**Cotton yarn: supplies, requirements and allocations for Period I 1948.** M(47)99. Agreed allocations appended.
22 Dec	29th	**Iron and steel distribution scheme: departmental symbols.** M(47)104. List of symbols appended.

CAB 134/479 Memoranda 6 Jan–18 July 1947   M(47)1–55.

6 Jan	**M(47)1**	**Building board – secretariat,** 1p.
7 Jan	2	**Iron castings: allocations for Period I 1947 –** secretary, 1+1p appendix.
14 Jan	3	**Paper and board: allocations for the twenty-fourth licensing period –** secretariat, 1+6p appendix.
10 Jan	4	**Correspondence –** secretary, 1p.
17 Jan	5	**Raw materials requirements –** secretariat, 4+1p appendix. Estimates of requirements.
18 Jan	6	**Economy of timber –** secretariat, 1+1p appendix.
23 Jan	7	**Linseed oil and paints: requirements for second quarter 1947 –** secretariat, 1p.
4 Feb	8	**Departmental estimates of requirements of linseed oil, for paints, varnishes and distempers. Second quarter 1947 –** secretariat, 1+1p appendix.
6 Feb	9	**Steel –** secretariat, 3p. Re-emphasis of the need to sort out past orders if current allocations were to have any meaning. Review of remedial steps being considered.
12 Feb	10	**Aluminium supplies for housing –** secretariat covering the metals division of the Ministry of Supply, 1+3p.
21 Feb	11	**Building board. Allocations for twenty-fourth licensing period –** secretariat, 1+1p appendix.
21 Feb	12	**Tin plate, terne plate and black plate allocations for Period II 1947,** 1+1p appendix.
6 Mar	13	**Economy of timber –** secretariat, 1+1p.
26 Feb	14	**Economy of steel. First interim report by the Steel Economy Subcommittee –** secretariat covering the Subcommittee, 1+17+20p appendixes. Confined to a review of sheet steel, reviewing progress in removing backlog of orders.
26 Feb	15	**Conduit tubing –** secretariat covering the Iron and Steel Board, 1+1p.

28 Feb	16	**Steel – secretariat covering the British Iron and Steel Federation,** 1+2p. Letter to all steel producers on re-authorization.
5 Mar	17	**Rape oil – secretariat covering the Ministry of Food,** 1+1p.
5 Mar	18	**Castor oil – secretariat covering the Ministry of Food,** 1+1+1p appendix.
5 Mar	19	**Linseed oil: allocations for Period II 1947 – secretariat covering the Ministry of Food,** 1+2+2p appendix.
12 Mar	20	**Economy of timber – secretariat,** 1+35p. Reports from departments on action taken to implement the recommendations in M(46)1161 and 1162.
12 Mar	21	**Steel: supply and requirements for Period II 1947 – F.E. Budd covering the Iron and Steel Board,** 1+4p.
13 Mar	22	**Timber: review of supplies and requirements for Period II 1947 – secretariat covering the Raw Materials Department,** 1+3+2p appendixes.
14 Mar	23	**Timber – secretariat covering the Board of Trade,** 1+2p.
14 Mar	24	**Cotton yarn: Period II 1947 – secretariat covering the Raw Materials Department,** 1+2p.
14 Mar	25	**Lead: allocations for Period II 1947 – secretariat covering director of non-ferrous metals,** 1+1p.
17 Mar	26	**Steel plates: requirements – F.E. Budd,** 1p.
17 Mar	27	**Cotton yarn: Period II 1947 – secretariat covering the Raw Materials Department,** 1+1p.
27 Mar	28	**Sisal and manilla – secretariat covering the Raw Materials Department,** 1+3+1p appendix.
27 Mar	29	**Jute – secretariat covering the Raw Materials Department,** 1+3+1p appendix.
9 Apr	30	**Iron castings: allocations for period II 1947 – F.E. Budd,** 1+1p.
17 Apr	31	**Paper and board – secretariat,** 1p.
22 Apr	32	**Departmental estimates of requirements of linseed oil for paints, varnishes, distempers and putty. Period III 1947 – secretariat,** 1+1p appendix.
22 Apr	33	**Raw materials requirements. Cast iron, steel, timber and cotton – secretariat,** 4+1p appendix.
23 Apr	34	**Economy of steel: second interim report by the Steel Economy Subcommittee – secretariat covering the Subcommittee,** 1+4p. Report on economies in building and civil engineering.
25 Apr	35	**Cotton yarn: Period II 1947 – secretariat,** 2+1p appendix.
29 Apr	36	**Iron and steel authorizations – secretariat covering British Iron and Steel Federation,** 2+1p.
6 May	37	**Building board – secretariat,** 1p.

7 May	**38**	**Tin plate, terne plate and black plate allocations for Period III 1947** – unsigned, 1+1p appendix.
9 May	**39**	**Paper and board: supplies and requirements for the twenty-fifth licensing period** – secretariat, 1+5p.
12 May	**40**	**Steel: requirements for Period III 1947, and of sheet steel for Period IV 1947** – secretariat covering the Iron and Steel Board, 1+4p.
27 May	**41**	**Veneers: target allocations for Period II 1947** – secretariat, 1+1p appendix.
28 May	**42**	**Rape oil: supplies and allocations for Period III 1947** – secretariat covering the Ministry of Food, 1+1p.
28 May	**43**	**Castor oil: supplies and allocations for Period III 1947** – secretariat covering the Ministry of Food, 1+1+1p appendix.
28 May	**44**	**Linseed oil: supplies and allocations for Period III 1947** – secretariat covering the Ministry of Food, 1+1+2p appendix.
11 June	**45**	**Timber: review of supplies and requirements for period III 1947** – secretariat covering the Raw Materials Department, 1+4+4p appendix.
13 June	**46**	**Cotton yarn: Period III 1947** – Raw Materials Department, 1+1p appendix.
14 June	**47**	**Iron castings: allocations for Period III 1947** – F.E. Budd, 1+2 appendix.
17 June	**48**	**Jute: Period III 1947** – secretariat covering the Raw Materials Department, 1+3+2p appendixes.
17 June	**49**	**Lead: allocations for Period III 1947** – director of non-ferrous metals of the Ministry of Supply, 1p.
20 June	**50**	**Steel allocations: Period III 1947** – secretary, 1+1p appendix.
27 June	**51**	**Building board** – secretariat, 1+1p appendix.
30 June	**52**	**Sisal and manilla, July–Dec 1947** – secretariat covering the Raw Materials Department, 1+3+3p appendix.
9 June	**53**	**Raw materials requirements. Cast iron, steel, timber and cotton** – secretariat, 4+1 appendix.
14 July	**54**	**Departmental estimates of requirements of linseed oil for paints, varnishes, distempers and putty. Period IV 1947** – secretariat, 2+1p appendix.
18 July	**55**	**Constructional veneers. Target allocations for Period III 1947** – secretariat, 1+1p.

CAB 134/480   Memoranda   21 July–30 Dec 1947   M(47)56–110.

21 July	**M(47)56**	**Cotton yarn: forward buying limits** – secretariat, 1+1p appendix.

24 July	**57**	**Iron and steel: backlog and duplication of orders. First interim report of working party –** secretariat covering the working party, 1+12p appendixes. Recommendation of ways to cancel late orders and to avoid duplication of authorization.
14 Aug	**58**	**Timber: overdrafts and unhonoured licences. Report of working party – secretariat covering the working party,** 1+2+3p appendixes.
15 Aug	**59**	**Rape oil: supplies and allocations for Period IV 1947 – secretariat covering the Ministry of Food,** 1+1p.
15 Aug	**60**	**Castor oil: supplies and allocations for Period IV 1947 – secretariat covering the Ministry of Food,** 1+1+1p appendix.
15 Aug	**61**	**Linseed oil: supplies and allocations for Period IV 1947 – secretariat covering the Ministry of Food,** 1+2+2p appendix.
21 Aug	**62**	**Steel: requirements for Period IV 1947 and of sheet steel for Period I 1948 – secretariat covering the Iron and Steel Board,** 1+4p.
21 Aug	**63**	**Paper and board – secretariat,** 1p.
22 Aug	**64**	**Tin plate, terne plate and black plate allocations for Period IV 1947 – secretariat,** 1+1p appendix.
22 Aug	**65**	**Iron and steel: backlog and duplication of orders. Second interim report of working party –** secretariat covering the working party, 1+6p. Proposals for the basis of a new allocation scheme.
29 Aug	**66**	**Reservation of certain timber for specified purposes – secretariat,** 1+1p appendix.
5 Sept	**67**	**Building board – secretariat,** 1p.
11 Sept	**68**	**Cotton yarn: Period IV 1947 – Raw Materials Department,** 2+1p appendix.
15 Sept	**69**	**Linseed oil allocations for Period IV 1947 –** secretariat, 1p. Substantial reductions in allocations for November and December might be necessary.
16 Sept	**70**	**Iron and steel – secretariat,** 2p.
16 Sept	**71**	**Timber: review of supplies and requirements for Period IV 1947 – secretariat covering the Raw Materials Department,** 1+3+4p appendixes. A tentative import programme for the second half of 1948 had been drafted with the aim of maintaining allocations at present levels.
17 Sept	**72**	**Steel – secretariat,** 1+1p appendix.
18 Sept	**73**	**Paper and board: supplies and requirements for the twenty-sixth licensing period – secretariat,** 1+1p appendix.

19 Sept	74	**Lead: allocations for Period IV 1947 – director of non-ferrous metals of the Ministry of Supply,** 3+4p appendixes.
25 Sept	75	**Linseed oil allocations for Period IV 1947 –** secretariat, 1p.
26 Sept	76	**Iron castings: allocations for Period IV 1947 – F.E. Budd,** 1+1p appendix.
7 Oct	77	**High speed steel – secretariat,** 1p.
9 Oct	78	**Note by secretary of the Cabinet – N. Brook,** 1p.
14 Oct	79	**Jute: Period IV 1947 – secretariat covering the Raw Materials Department,** 1+3+1p appendix.
16 Oct	80	**Building board: allocations for the twenty-sixth licensing period – secretariat,** 1+1p appendix.
16 Oct	81	**Paper and board: fireboard cases: sub-allocations for the twenty-sixth licensing period – secretariat,** 1+1p appendix.
24 Oct	82	**Constructional veneers – secretariat,** 1+1p appendix.
24 Oct	83	**Timber and cotton requirements – secretariat,** 3+1p appendix. Departments were to prepare estimates for 1948.
24 Oct	84	**Departmental estimates of requirements of linseed oil for paints, varnishes, distempers and putty. Period I 1948 – secretariat,** 2+1p appendix.
3 Nov	85	**Iron and steel: small quantity exemptions –** secretariat, 1+1p appendix.
4 Nov	86	**Steel: requirements for Periods I and II 1948 – secretariat covering the Iron and Steel Board,** 1+4p.
11 Nov	87	**Iron and steel distribution scheme – secretariat covering the Ministry of Supply,** 1+3+2p annex. Criticism by industry of the working party's cheque scheme. The Paymaster General's committee had decided not to proceed with it but to tighten up the present scheme instead.
24 Nov	88	**Rape oil: supplies and allocations for Period I 1948 – secretariat covering the Ministry of Food,** 1+1p.
24 Nov	89	**Castor oil: supplies and allocations for Period I – secretariat covering the Ministry of Food,** 1+1+1p appendix.
24 Nov	90	**Linseed oil: supplies and allocations for Period I 1948 – secretariat covering the Ministry of Food,** 1+2+2p appendix.
29 Nov	91	**Tin plate, terne plate and black plate allocations for Period I 1948 – secretariat,** 1+1p appendix.
2 Dec	92	**Revision of the steel priority system – secretariat,** 4p. Sets out revised scheme. Its purpose was that a measure of 'first aid' in obtaining steel should be accorded to

programmes which contribute to the expansion of fuel and power, exports and the saving of imports.

2 Dec	93	**Allocations of building steel, periods I and II 1948** – secretariat, 1+1p annex.
2 Dec	94	**Timber: review of supplies and requirements for Period I 1948** – secretariat covering the Raw Materials Department, 1+3+2p appendixes.
3 Dec	95	**Iron and steel distribution scheme** – secretariat, 1+3p appendix
6 Dec	96	**Iron and steel distribution scheme** – secretary covering the Ministry of Supply, 1+4p. Detailed arrangements for scheme's revision.
6 Dec	97	**Iron and steel: departmental authorizations** – Marquand, 1p. Cripps wished departments to be reminded that authorizations were to be used more accurately and scrupulously and over-authorization stopped.
12 Dec	98	**Lead: allocations for Period I 1948** – director of non-ferrous metals of the Ministry of Supply, 2+5p appendixes.
12 Dec	99	**Cotton yarn: Period I 1948** – Raw Materials Department, 2+1p appendix. Cotton control might be wound up.
12 Dec	100	**Timber: overdrafts and unhonoured licences** – secretariat, 1+1p appendix.
18 Dec	101	**Iron castings: allocations for Periods I and II 1948** – F.E. Budd, 1+3p appendixes.
17 Dec	102	**Paper and board** – secretariat, 1p.
17 Dec	103	**Iron and steel** – secretariat, 1p.
17 Dec	104	**Iron and steel distribution scheme** – secretary, 2+1p appendix. Reallocation of departmental symbols.
19 Dec	105	**Iron and steel distribution scheme** – secretary covering the Ministry of Supply, 1+3+6p annex.
20 Dec	106	**Revision of the iron and steel distribution scheme. Bulk authorization** – Ministry of Supply, 4p. The bulk authorization system was to be extended as far and as fast as practicable. The iron and steel authorization form was to replace the M form.
23 Dec	107	**Sisal and manilla, January–June 1948** – secretariat covering the Raw Materials Department, 1+4+2p appendix.
30 Dec	108	**Jute: Period I 1948** – secretariat covering the Raw Materials Department, 5+2p appendixes.
30 Dec	109	**Building board: requirements for the twenty-seventh licensing period** – secretariat, 1p.
30 Dec	110	**Note by the secretary of the Cabinet** – N. Brook, 1p.

CAB 134/481   Meetings   13 Jan–21 Dec 1948   M(48)1st–22nd + two unnumbered meetings.

13 Jan	**M(48)1st**	**Jute: supplies, requirements and allocations of yarn and rove for Period I 1948: supplies and requirements of cloth and bags for January/ June 1948.** M(47)108. Agreed allocations appended.
19 Jan	**2nd**	**Allocations of paper and board for the twenty-seventh licensing period.** M(48)2. Agreed allocations appended.
3 Feb	**3rd:1**	**Priorities.**
	:2	**Revised iron and steel distribution scheme: transitional arrangements.** M(48)6. Departments were to have special overdraft facilities for the transition.
	:3	**Supplementary allocations of building and general steel for Period II 1948.** Agreed allocations appended.
	:4	**Supplementary allocations of sheet steel for Period II 1948.**
24 Feb	**4th:1**	**Linseed oil: supplies, requirements and allocations for Period II 1948.** M(48)15. Agreed allocations appended.
	:2	**Castor oil: supplies and allocations for Period II 1948.** M(48)14. Agreed allocations appended.
	:3	**Rape oil: supplies and allocations for Period II 1948.** M(48)13. Agreed allocations appended.
1 Mar	**5th**	**Supplies, requirements and allocations of steel for Period III 1948.** M(48)12. Jay set out the principles governing allocations for Period III. E.F. Muir pointed out that, while industrial building was on a rising curve, allocations of steel had been cut to below the level visualized by the Investments Programmes Committee. There was a real danger of holding back industrial production. Agreed allocations appended.
10 Mar	**6th**	**Lead: supplies and allocations for Period II 1948.** M(48)17.
17 Mar	**7th**	**Timber: supplies, requirements and allocations, Period II 1948.** M(48)18.
23 Mar	**8th**	**Cotton yarn: supplies, requirements and allocations for Period II 1948.** M(48)19. Agreed allocations appended.
13 May	**9th**	**Allocations of paper and board for the twenty-eighth licensing period.** M(48)32. Agreed allocations appended.
31 May	**10th:1**	**Linseed oil: paint distribution scheme.** M(48)34.

	:2	**Linseed oil: supplies, requirements and allocations for Period III 1948.** M(48)35. Agreed allocations appended.
	:3	**Castor oil: supplies and allocations for Period III 1948.** M(48)36. Agreed allocations appended.
	:4	**Rape oil: supplies and allocations for Period III 1948.** M(48)37.
9 June	11th	**Lead: supplies and allocations for Period III 1948.** M(48)43. Agreed allocations appended.
14 June	12th:1	**Report on the census of consumers' stocks, receipts and usage of steel.** M(48)38.
	:2	**Steel and iron castings: direct authorizations to small consumers.** M(48)39.
	:3	**Supplies, requirements and allocations of steel for Period IV 1948.** M(48)40. Sets out the principles for allocations in Period IV, as agreed at the Production Committee. Jay said that unless steel supplies were substantially increased in 1949, allocation would be extremely difficult. Certain increases already approved by the Production Committee in principle could only be achieved at the expense of other departmental allocations. Agreed allocations appended.
17 June	13th	**Review of supplies and requirements: allocations for Period III 1948.** M(48)47. On timber. Jay said future allocations were uncertain because future import programmes could not be reliably estimated.
24 June	14th	**Cotton yarn: supplies, requirements and allocations for Period III 1948.** M(48)48. Agreed allocations appended.
16 Sept	15th	**Linseed oil: supplies, requirements and allocations for Period IV 1948.** M(48)68. Agreed allocations appended.
21 Sept	16th	**Timber: supplies, requirements and allocations for Period IV 1948.** M(48)67. Agreed allocations appended.
24 Sept	17th	**Allocations of paper and board for the twenty-ninth licensing period.** M(48)69. Agreed allocations appended.
24 Sept	18th	**Lead: supplies and allocations for Period IV 1948.** M(48)73. Agreed allocations appended.
13 Oct	19th:1	**Removal of iron castings from allocation by the Materials Committee.** M(48)71. Proposal agreed.
	:2	**Direct authorizations to small consumers.** M(48)77.
	:3	**Supplies, requirements and allocations of steel for Period I 1949.** M(48)76. Jay set out the principles behind the allocations proposed.

The Ministry of Supply could not accept its allocations as recommended by the Investment Programmes Committee because it was less than that for Period IV 1948. Jay pointed out that the Investment Programmes Committee, endorsed by the Production Committee, had to be taken into account when making allocations. Agreed allocations appended.

24 Nov	20th	**Linseed oil: supplies, requirements and allocations, Period I 1949.** M(48)85. Agreed allocations appended.
15 Dec	21st	**Timber: supplies, requirements and allocations, Period I 1949.** M(48)87. Jay said that the balance of payments prevented any advantage being taken of the improved supply position. Agreed allocations appended.
21 Dec	22nd	**Lead: supplies and allocations for Period I 1949.** M(48)89.
31 Mar	*ad hoc*	**Steel for the overseas food corporation.**
11 Nov	*ad hoc*	**Tin plate.**

CAB 134/482   Memoranda   12 Jan–23 June 1948   M(48)1–50 and two unnumbered memoranda.

12 Jan	**M(48)1**	**Sheet steel – secretary,** 1+5p. Note of meeting to discuss an alteration in the allocation for Period II.
15 Jan	2	**Paper and board. Supplies and requirements for the twenty-seventh licensing period – secretariat,** 1+7p.
16 Jan	3	**Timber and cotton requirements – secretariat,** 3+1p appendix.
16 Jan	4	**Departmental estimates of requirements of linseed oil for paints, varnishes, distempers and putty. Period II 1948 – secretariat,** 2+1p appendix.
17 Jan	5	**Constructional veneers. Target allocations for Period I 1948 – secretariat,** 1+1p appendix.
31 Jan	6	**Revised iron and steel distribution scheme. Transitional arrangements for firms dependent on many sub-authorizations – secretary,** 3p.
13 Feb	7	**Building board. Allocations for the twenty-seventh licensing period – secretariat,** 1+1p appendix.
16 Feb	8	**Revision of the priority system for components and materials other than steel – secretariat,** 2p.
16 Feb	9	**Revised list of priority programmes – secretary,** 2p. New list attached, excluding coal/oil conversion.
16 Feb	10	**Iron and steel: small quantities exemptions – secretariat,** 1+1p appendix.

18 Feb	11	**Tin plate, terne plate and black plate allocations for Period II 1948** – secretariat, 1+1p.
18 Feb	12	**Steel: requirements for Period III 1948** – secretariat, 1+4p appendix.
18 Feb	13	**Rape oil: supplies and allocations for Period II 1948** – secretariat covering the Ministry of Food, 1+1p.
18 Feb	14	**Castor oil: supplies and allocations for Period II 1948** – secretariat covering the Ministry of Food, 1+1+1p appendix.
18 Feb	15	**Linseed oil: supplies and allocations for Period II 1948** – secretariat covering the Ministry of Food, 1+2+2p appendix.
23 Feb	16	**Paper and board: fireboard cases: sub-allocations for the twenty-seventh licensing period** – secretariat, 1+2p appendix.
5 Mar	17	**Lead: allocations for Period II 1948** – director of non-ferrous metals of the Ministry of Supply, 2+5p appendixes.
10 Mar	18	**Timber: review of supplies and requirements for Period II 1948** – secretariat covering the Raw Materials Department, 1+3+2p appendixes. Import programme to mid-1949 had been prepared providing for allocations of softwoods and plywood at present levels.
18 Mar	19	**Cotton yarn: Period II 1948** – Raw Materials Department, 3+1p appendix.
19 Mar	20	**Allocations of building steel for Period III 1948** – secretary, 1+1p appendix. Recommendations of the Headquarters Building Committee.
24 Mar	21	**Proposed allocations of building timber for Period II 1948** – secretary, 1+1p appendix.
8 Apr	22	**Jute: period II 1948** – secretariat covering the Raw Materials Department, 1+3+1p appendix.
8 Apr	23	**Iron castings: allocations for Period III 1948** – secretary, 1+2p appendixes.
8 Apr	24	**Iron and steel** – secretariat, 3p.
9 Apr	25	**Paper and board** – secretariat, 1p.
9 Apr	26	**Building board: requirements for twenty-eighth licensing period** – secretariat, 1p.
19 Apr	27	**Timber requirements** – secretariat, 2+1p appendix.
17 Apr	28	**Departmental estimates of requirements of linseed oil for paints, varnishes, distempers and putty. Period III 1948** – secretariat, 2+1p appendix.
19 Apr	29	**Cotton requirements: Period III 1948** – secretariat, 1p.
19 Apr	30	**Iron and steel distribution scheme. Bulk authorization. Steel requirements of electrical contractors** – secretariat, 1p.

24 Apr	31	**Veneers: allocations for Period II 1948 –** secretariat, 1+1p appendix.
10 May	32	**Paper and board. Supplies and requirements for the twenty-eighth licensing period – secretariat,** 1+7p appendixes.
12 May	33	**Tin plate, terne plate and black plate allocations for Period III 1948 – secretariat, 1+1p** appendix.
26 May	34	**Linseed oil: paint distribution scheme – Raw Materials Department,** 3p.
26 May	35	**Linseed oil: supplies and allocations for Period III 1948 – secretariat covering the Ministry of Food,** 1+2+2p appendix.
26 May	36	**Castor oil: supplies and allocations for Period III 1948 – secretariat covering the Ministry of Food,** 1+1+1p appendix.
26 May	37	**Rape oil: supplies and allocations for Period III 1948 – secretariat covering the Ministry of Food,** 1+1p.
3 June	38	**Steel: report on the census of consumers' stocks, receipts and usage of steel – F.E. Budd covering the Iron and Steel Board,** 1+5+19p appendixes.
3 June	39	**Steel and iron castings – F.E. Budd covering the Ministry of Supply,** 1+5p. Proposal to remove the smaller consumer from the normal machinery of allocation.
3 June	40	**Steel: requirements for Period IV 1948 – secretariat covering the Iron and Steel Board,** 1+4p.
3 June	41	**Steel and iron castings: decontrol of certain forms of iron and steel – F.E. Budd,** 1p.
3 June	42	**Additions to the revised list of priority programmes – F.E. Budd,** 1p. Additions to list in M(48)9.
4 June	43	**Lead: allocations for Period III 1948 – director of non-ferrous metals of the Ministry of Supply,** 2+5p appendixes.
4 June	44	**Building board: allocations for the twenty-eighth licensing period – secretariat,** 1+2p appendixes.
9 June	45	**Paper and board: fireboard cases: sub-allocations for the twenty-eighth licensing period – secretariat,** 1+2p appendix.
9 June	46	**Linseed oil: paint distribution scheme –** unsigned, 1p.
9 June	47	**Timber: review of supplies and requirements for Period III 1948 – secretariat covering the Raw Materials Department,** 1+3+2p appendixes. Little change since M(48)18.
18 June	48	**Cotton yarn: Period III 1948 – Board of Trade,** 1+1p appendix.

23 June	49	**Proposed allocations of building timber for Period III 1948 – F.E. Budd,** 1+1p appendix.
23 June	50	**Departmental estimates of requirements of linseed oil for paints, varnishes, distempers and putty. Period IV 1948 – secretariat,** 2+1p.
2 Apr		**Circular on the iron and steel distribution scheme – F.E. Budd,** 1p.
1 Jan		**List of principal priority officers for the Materials Committee.**

CAB 134/483   Memoranda   23 June–30 Dec 1948   M(48)51–97.

23 June	**M(48)51**	**Timber requirements – secretariat,** 2+1p appendix.
28 June	52	**Iron and steel – secretariat,** 3p.
28 June	53	**Iron and steel authorization form – F.E. Budd,** 1p.
30 June	54	**Cotton yarn requirements. Period IV 1948 – secretariat,** 1p.
6 July	55	**Building board: withdrawal of insulation board by allocation – F.E. Budd,** 1p.
7 July	56	**Removal of certain materials from allocation by the Materials Committee – F.E. Budd,** 2p. The chairman had reviewed the list of materials subject to allocation by the committee, proposing the abandonment of allocation for those where the supply was in reasonable balance with requirements or where a material was still in short supply but one department had a preponderant interest in it, in which case responsibility for allocation could be transferred to that department.
8 July	57	**Allocations of building steel for Period IV 1948 – F.E. Budd,** 1+1p. Recommended allocations of the Headquarters Building Committee.
8 July	58	**Steel: adjustment of Period IV allocations of general steel to offset inclusion of steel castings among exempt products – F.E. Budd,** 2+1p appendix.
9 July	59	**Jute: Period III 1948 – secretariat covering the Raw Materials Department,** 1+5+2p appendixes.
9 July	60	**Sisal and manilla July-Dec 1948 – secretariat covering Raw Materials Department,** 1+2+2p appendixes.
15 July	61	**Iron castings: allocations for Period IV 1948 – F.E. Budd,** 1+2p appendixes.
15 July	62	**Veneers: allocations for Period III 1948 – F.E. Budd,** 1+1p appendix.

28 July	63	**Removal of certain materials from allocation by the Materials Committee** – F.E. Budd, 2p.
30 July	64	**Tin plate, terne plate and black plate allocations for Period IV 1948** – F.E. Budd, 1+1p appendix.
3 Aug	65	**Paper and board: requirements for twenty-ninth licensing period** – secretariat, 1p.
3 Aug	66	**Building board: requirements for twenty-ninth licensing period** – secretariat, 1p.
9 Sept	67	**Timber: review of supplies and requirements for Period IV 1948** – secretariat covering the Raw Materials Department, 1+3+1p appendix. Framed on the basis of the import programme for July 1948 – June 1949 submitted to Paris.
10 Sept	68	**Linseed oil: supplies and allocations for Period IV 1948** – secretariat covering the Ministry of Food, 1+2+2p appendixes.
16 Sept	69	**Paper and board: supplies and requirements for the twenty-ninth licensing period** – secretariat, 1+9p appendixes.
17 Sept	70	**Departmental estimates of requirements of linseed oil for paints, varnishes, distempers and putty for Period I 1949** – secretariat, 2+1p.
20 Sept	71	**Removal of iron castings from allocation by the Materials Committee** – F.E. Budd covering the Joint Committee on the Working of the Iron and Steel Distribution Scheme, 1+1+1p annex.
22 Sept	72	**Timber requirements** – secretariat, 2+1p appendix.
24 Sept	73	**Lead: allocations for Period IV 1948** – director of non-ferrous metals at the Ministry of Supply, 2+4p appendixes.
30 Sept	74	**Proposed allocations of building timber for Period IV 1948** – F.E. Budd, 1+1p appendix.
30 Sept	75	**Building board: allocations for the twenty-ninth licensing period** – F.E. Budd, 1+2p appendixes.
2 Oct	76	**Steel: requirements for Period I 1949** – secretariat, 1+4p.
2 Oct	77	**Steel** – F.E. Budd covering the Ministry of Supply, 1+4+14p appendixes. Consideration of direct authorizations to small consumers.
13 Oct	78	**Paper and board: fireboard cases. Sub-allocations for the twenty-ninth licensing period** – F.E. Budd, 1+2p appendix.
18 Oct	79	**Veneers: allocations for Period IV 1948** – F.E. Budd, 1+1p appendix.
20 Oct	80	**Steel** – F.E. Budd, 2p.
25 Oct	81	**Allocations of building steel for Period I 1949** – F.E. Budd, 1+1p appendix.
4 Nov	82	**Steel distribution scheme** – F.E. Budd, 3p. Summary of the report of the Joint Committee on the Working of the Steel Distribution Scheme.

4 Nov	83	**Steel economy – F.E. Budd covering the Steel Economy Subcommittee and N. Brook,** 1+14+12p appendixes +1p. Misfiled between M(48)72 and 73. Third interim report of the Steel Economy Subcommittee attached. See PC(48)128. Also M(SE Sub)(48)28. SE(48)1 also attached.
12 Nov	84	**Tin plate, terne plate and black plate allocations for Period I 1949 – F.E. Budd,** 1+1p appendix.
19 Nov	85	**Linseed oil: supplies and allocations for Period I 1949 – F.E. Budd covering the Ministry of Food,** 1+2+2p appendixes.
2 Dec	86	**Steel: decontrol of railway tyres, wheels and axles – F.E. Budd,** 1p.
3 Dec	87	**Timber: review of supplies and requirements for Period I 1949 – F.E. Budd covering the Raw Materials Department,** 1+3+2p appendixes.
19 Dec	88	**Timber: softwood. Discrepancy between recorded consumption and allocations – F.E. Budd,** 1+2p. Record of a meeting on 8 Dec 1948 with representatives of the major timber-consuming departments.
15 Dec	89	**Lead: allocations for Period I 1949 – director of non-ferrous metals at the Ministry of Supply,** 2+4p appendixes.
15 Dec	90	**Steel: report on the census of consumers' stocks, receipts and usage of steel – F.E. Budd covering the Iron and Steel Board,** 1+7+2p appendixes.
17 Dec	91	**Paper and board: requirements for the thirtieth licensing period – F.E. Budd,** 1p.
17 Dec	92	**Building board: requirements for the thirtieth licensing period – F.E. Budd,** 1p.
20 Dec	93	**Proposed allocations of building timber for Period I 1949 – F.E. Budd,** 1+1p appendix.
21 Dec	94	**Timber requirements – F.E. Budd,** 2+1p appendix.
20 Dec	95	**Departmental estimates of requirements of linseed oil for paints, varnishes, distempers and putty – F.E. Budd,** 2+1p appendix.
21 Dec	96	**Steel – F.E. Budd,** 1p.
30 Dec	97	**Steel: requirements for Period II 1949 – F.E. Budd,** 1+4p appendixes.

CAB 134/484 Meetings and Memoranda 12 Jan–21 Dec 1949 M(49)1st–16th, three unnumbered meetings, M(49)1–53 and two unnumbered memoranda.

Meetings

12 Jan	**M(49)1st:1**	**Report on the census of consumers' stocks, receipts and usage of steel. M(48)90.**
	:2	**Supplies, requirements and allocations of steel for Period II 1949. M(48)97.** Jay set out the

general considerations behind the recommendations. Allocations appended.

24 Feb	2nd	**Linseed oil: supplies, requirements and allocations for Period II 1949.** M(49)7. Allocations appended.
14 Mar	3rd	**Timber: supplies, requirements and allocations for Period II 1949.** M(49)8. The Production Committee had agreed to the removal of control on hardwood. Allocations appended.
24 Mar	4th	**Lead: supplies and allocations for Period II 1949.** M(49)10. Allocations appended.
31 Mar	5th	**Supplies, requirements and allocations of steel for Period III 1949.** M(49)11. General considerations behind the allocations explained. Allocations appended.
30 May	6th	**Linseed oil: supplies, requirements and allocations for Period III 1949.** M(49)23. Allocations appended.
15 June	7th	**Timber: supplies, requirements and allocations for Period III 1949.** M(49)25. Allocations appended.
20 June	8th	**Lead: supplies and allocations for Period III 1949.** Allocations appended.
7 July	9th:1	**Report on the census of consumers' stocks, receipts and usage of steel for Period IV 1948.** M(49)24.
	:2	**The future of the steel distribution scheme.**
	:3	**Supplies, requirements and allocations of steel for Period IV 1949.** M(49)29. Allocations appended.
13 Sept	10th	**Linseed oil: supplies, requirements and allocations for Period IV 1949.** M(49)34. Allocations appended.
26 Sept	11th	**Timber: supplies, requirements and allocations for Period IV 1949.** M(49)35. Allocations appended.
27 Sept	12th	**Lead: supplies and allocations for Period IV 1949.** M(49)38. Allocations appended.
4 Oct	13th	**Supplies, requirements and allocations of steel for Period I 1950.** M(49)37 and 39. General consideration behind the allocations explained. Allocations appended.
7 Dec	14th:1	**Economy in government expenditure.**
	:2	**Linseed oil: supplies, requirements and allocations for Period I 1950.** M(49)48. Allocations appended.
15 Dec	15th	**Timber: supplies, requirements and allocations for Period I 1950.** M(49)49. Allocations appended.
21 Dec	16th	**Lead: supplies and allocations for Period I 1950.** M(49)50. Allocations appended.

19 Jan	*ad hoc*	Tin plate for fabricated products.
23 Feb	*ad hoc*	Pre-emption of supplies by the U.K.
22 Mar	*ad hoc*	Steel for British Railways.

Memoranda

18 Jan	M(49)1	**Removal of paper and board from allocation by the Materials Committee** – F.E. Budd, 2p. Responsibility to pass to the Board of Trade.
19 Jan	2	**Steel** – F.E. Budd, 2p.
26 Jan	3	**Allocations of building steel for Period II 1949** – F.E. Budd, 1+1p appendix.
26 Jan	4	**Veneers: allocations for Period I 1949** – F.E. Budd, 1+1p appendix.
4 Feb	5	**Tin plate, terne plate and black plate allocations for Period II 1949** – F.E. Budd, 1+1p appendix.
15 Feb	6	**Removal of building board from allocation** – F.E. Budd, 1p.
17 Feb	7	**Linseed oil: supplies and allocations for Period II 1949** – F.E. Budd covering the Ministry of Food, 1+2+2p appendix.
3 Mar	8	**Timber: review of supplies and requirements for Period II 1949** – F.E. Budd covering the Raw Materials Department, 1+3+2p appendixes.
10 Mar	9	**Timber for export packing** – F.E. Budd covering the Board of Trade, 1+1p.
16 Mar	10	**Lead: allocations for Period II 1949** – director of non-ferrous metals at the Ministry of Supply, 2+3p appendixes.
16 Mar	11	**Steel: supplies and requirements for Period III 1949** – F.E. Budd, 1+4p appendixes.
21 Mar	12	**Timber requirements** – F.E. Budd, 2+1p appendix.
22 Mar	13	**Proposed allocations of building timber for Period II 1949** – F.E. Budd, 1+2p.
21 Mar	14	**Departmental estimates of requirements of linseed oil for paints, varnishes, distempers and putty for Period III 1949** – F.E. Budd, 2+1p appendix.
29 Mar	15	**Steel distribution scheme: over-ordering** – F.E. Budd, 5p.
7 Apr	16	**Expansion of exports to North America** – Jay, 1p.
7 Apr	17	**Steel** – F.E. Budd, 2p.
11 Apr	18	**Allocations of building steel for Period III 1949** – F.E. Budd, 1+1p appendix.
12 Apr	19	**Veneers: allocations for Period II 1949** – F.E. Budd, 1+1p appendix.
14 Apr	20	**Linseed oil** – F.E. Budd, 1p.
5 May	21	**Tin plate, terne plate and black plate allocations for Period III 1949** – F.E. Budd, 1+1p appendix.
13 May	22	**Linseed oil** – F.E. Budd, 1p.

24 May	23	**Linseed oil: supplies and allocations for Period III 1949 – F.E. Budd covering the Ministry of Food,** 1+2+2p appendix.
7 June	24	**Report on the census of consumers' stocks, receipts and usage of steel, fourth quarter 1948 – F.E. Budd covering the Ministry of Supply,** 1+9+2p appendixes.
8 June	25	**Timber: review of supplies and requirements for Period III 1949 – F.E. Budd covering the Raw Materials Department,** 1+3+2p appendixes.
13 June	26	**Lead: allocations for Period III 1949 – director of non-ferrous metals at the Ministry of Supply,** 2+4p appendixes.
21 June	27	**Timber requirements – F.E. Budd,** 2+1p appendix.
21 June	28	**Proposed allocations of building timber for Period III 1949 – F.E. Budd,** 1+1p appendix.
22 June	29	**Steel: supplies and requirements for Period IV 1949 – F.E. Budd,** 1+4p appendixes.
8 July	30	**Steel – F.E. Budd,** 2p.
12 July	31	**Allocations of building steel for Period IV 1949 – F.E. Budd,** 1+1p.
14 July	32	**Veneers: allocations for Period III 1949 – F.E. Budd,** 1+1p appendix.
27 July	33	**Tin plate, terne plate and black plate allocations for Period IV 1949 – F.E. Budd,** 1+1p appendix.
8 Sept	34	**Linseed oil: supplies and allocations for Period IV 1949 – F.E. Budd covering the Ministry of Food,** 1+2+2p appendixes.
13 Sept	35	**Timber: review of supplies and requirements for Period IV 1949 – F.E. Budd covering the Raw Materials Department,** 1+4+2p appendixes.
19 Sept	36	**Timber: allocations for Period IV 1949 – F.E. Budd,** 1p. Sets out the interim procedure for departments for softwood whilst ministers considered the possible need for heavy reductions in allocations.
21 Sept	37	**Steel: supplies and requirements for Period I 1950 – F.E. Budd,** 1+4p appendixes.
21 Sept	38	**Lead: allocations for Period IV 1949 – director of non-ferrous metals at Ministry of Supply,** 2+3p appendix.
26 Sept	39	**Steel: effect of reduced imports on supplies of bottle-neck varieties of steel – F.E. Budd,** 2p.
3 Oct	40	**Proposed allocations of building timber for Period IV 1949 – F.E. Budd,** 1+1p appendix.
7 Oct	41	**Timber requirements – F.E. Budd,** 2+1p appendix.
10 Oct	42	**Steel – F.E. Budd,** 2p.
17 Oct	43	**Allocations of building steel for Period I 1950 – F.E. Budd,** 1+1p appendix.

17 Oct	44	**Veneers: allocations for Period IV 1949 – F.E. Budd,** 1+1p appendix.
3 Nov	45	**Tin plate, terne plate and black plate allocations for Period I 1950 – F.E. Budd,** 1+1p appendix.
11 Nov	46	**Steel: statistics of allocations and deliveries for Period III 1949 – F.E. Budd,** 1+4p appendixes.
15 Nov	47	**Steel: report on the census of consumers' stocks, receipts and usage of steel, second quarter 1949 – F.E. Budd covering the Ministry of Supply,** 1+8+2p appendixes.
29 Nov	48	**Linseed oil: supplies and allocations for Period I 1950 – F.E. Budd covering the Ministry of Food,** 1+1+2p appendixes.
5 Dec	49	**Timber: review of supplies and requirements for Period I 1950 – F.E. Budd covering the Raw Materials Department,** 1+3+1p appendix.
15 Dec	50	**Lead: allocations for Period I 1950 – director of non-ferrous metals at the Ministry of Supply,** 2+4p appendixes.
15 Dec	51	**Steel: supplies and requirements for Period II 1950 – F.E. Budd,** 2+4p appendixes.
20 Dec	52	**Proposed allocations of building timber for Period I 1950 – F.E. Budd,** 1+1p appendix.
20 Dec	53	**Timber requirements – F.E. Budd,** 2+1p appendix.
12 July		**List of principal priority officers – secretariat,** 1+5p.
8 July		**Departmental estimates of requirements of linseed oil for paints, varnishes and distempers for Period IV 1949 – F.E. Budd,** 1+1p appendixes.

CAB 134/485 Meetings and Memoranda 2 Jan–20 Dec 1950   M(50)1st–12th, M(50)1–47 and two unnumbered memoranda.

Meetings

5 Jan	**M(50)1st:1**	**Report on the census of consumers' stocks, receipts and usage of steel, second quarter 1949.** M(49)47.
	:2	**Distribution statistics.** M(49)46 and M(50)1.
	:3	**Supplies, requirements and allocations of steel for Period II 1950.** M(49)51.
16 Mar	2nd:1	**Timber: supplies, requirements and allocations for Period II 1950.** M(50)8. Allocations appended.
	:3	**Change of chairman.**
30 May	3rd	**Supplies, requirements and allocations of sheet and general steel for Period III 1950 and of sheet steel for Period IV 1950.** M(50)10 and 14. The allocations set were to be strictly observed. Allocations appended.

20 June	**4th**	**Review of supplies of steel and of allocations of sheet steel for Period IV 1950.** M(50)24. Allocations appended.
20 June	**5th**	**Allocations of tin plate for Period IV 1950.** M(50)25.
23 June	**6th:1**	**Softwood: supplies, requirements and allocations, Period III 1950.** M(50)23. Allocations appended.
	:2	**Plywood.** M(50)26.
	:3	**Change of secretary.**
14 Sept	**7th**	**Supply, requirements and allocations of steel for Period I 1951.** M(50)32 and 33. There was little shortage of general steel. Consideration of paper by the chairman of the Exports Committee on steel exports. Allocations of sheet steel and tin plate appended.
26 Sept	**8th:1**	**Softwood supplies, requirements and allocations for Period IV 1950.** M(50)34. Allocations appended.
	:2	**Plywood.** M(50)34.
	:3	**Further substitution of hardwood for softwood.** M(50)35.
	:4	**Change in Committee.**
16 Dec	**9th**	**Zinc supplies for Period I 1951.** M(50)46.
18 Dec	**10th:1**	**Softwood supplies, requirements and allocations for Period I 1951.** M(50)43 and 45. Allocations appended.
	:2	**Progress report by the forest products research laboratory on co-operation between departments and the laboratory on the further substitution of hardwood for softwood.** M(50)44.
19 Dec	**11th**	**Supplies, requirements and allocations of steel for Period II 1951.** M(50)41 and 42. Tin plate allocation appended. A working party was to review the sheet steel allocation system.
20 Dec	**12th**	**Zinc.** M(50)47.

Memoranda

2 Jan	**M(50)1**	**Steel: distribution statistics – F.E. Budd covering the Ministry of Supply,** 1+2p.
11 Jan	**2**	**Steel – F.E. Budd,** 2p.
11 Jan	**3**	**Allocations of building steel for Period II 1950 – F.E. Budd,** 1+1p appendix.
31 Jan	**4**	**Tin plate, terne plate and black plate allocations for Period II 1950 – F.E. Budd,** 1+1p appendix.
1 Feb	**5**	**Economy in the use of aluminium for building – Jay,** 2p. Freedom from control had led to aluminium being substituted for steel and timber. Demand had to be reduced to cut dollar expenditure.

2 Feb	6	**Linseed oil – F.E. Budd,** 1+2+2p appendix. Note of a meeting on 1 Feb 1950 considering the ending of allocations.
15 Feb	7	**Economy in the use of aluminium – Jay,** 1p.
7 Mar	8	**Timber: review of supplies and requirements for Period II 1950 – F.E. Budd,** 3+3+1p appendix.
9 Mar	9	**Linseed oil: allocations for Period II 1950 – F.E. Budd,** 1+1p appendix.
17 Mar	10	**Steel: supplies and requirements for Period III 1950 – F.E. Budd,** 1+1p appendix +3p.
20 Mar	11	**Proposed allocations of building timber for Period II 1950 – F.E. Budd,** 1+1p appendix.
23 Mar	12	**Lead: suspension of allocations – F.E. Budd,** 1p. Proposed suspension although the control machinery would be kept in reserve.
24 Mar	13	**Chairmanship of the Committee – N. Brook,** 1p.
27 Mar	14	**Steel: supplies and requirements of sheet steel for Period IV 1950 – F.E. Budd,** 1+1p appendix.
3 Apr	15	**Allocations of building steel for Period III 1950 – F.E. Budd,** 1+1p appendix.
11 Apr	16	**Timber requirements – F.E. Budd,** 2+1p appendix.
11 Apr	17	**Steel – F.E. Budd,** 2p.
	18	**Steel: report on the census of consumers' stocks, receipts and usage of steel, fourth quarter 1947 – F.E. Budd covering the Ministry of Supply,** 1+9+2p appendixes.
3 May	19	**Tin plate, terne plate and black plate allocations for Period III 1950 – F.E. Budd,** 1+1p appendix.
23 May	20	**Steel: discontinuance of allocation of general steel – F.E. Budd,** 1p. Distribution scheme ended except sheet and tin plate steel.
23 May	21	**Linseed oil: discontinuance of allocations – F.E. Budd,** 1p. Ministerial approval for discontinuance.
30 May	22	**Steel: notes for consumers on changes arising from the relaxation of control of general steel – F.E. Budd covering the Ministry of Supply,** 1+4p.
13 June	23	**Timber: review of supplies and requirements for Period III 1950 – Board of Trade,** 2+1p appendix.
13 June	24	**Steel: supplies for Period IV 1950 – F.E. Budd,** 2+1p appendix.
13 June	25	**Tin plate: supplies and requirements for Period IV 1950 – F.E. Budd,** 1+1p appendix.
21 June	26	**Timber: discontinuance of allocation of plywood – F.E. Budd covering the Board of Trade,** 1+3p appendix.
27 June	27	**Change in secretariat – C.D. Smith,** 1p.
29 June	28	**Steel – C.D. Smith,** 1p.
29 June	29	**Timber requirements – C.D. Smith,** 1p.

29 June	30	**Proposed allocations of softwood and allotments of plywood for building purposes – C.D. Smith,** 1+1p appendix.
18 June		**List of principal priority officers – C.D. Smith,** 1+5p.
18 Aug	31	**Steel: 'Notes for consumers, May 1948' – C.D. Smith,** 1p.
2 Sept	32	**Tin plate: supplies and requirements for Period I 1951 – C.D. Smith,** 1+1p appendix.
1 Sept	33	**Steel: supplies for Period I 1951 – C.D. Smith,** 2+1p appendix.
7 Sept	34	**Timber: review of supplies and requirements for Period IV 1950 – Board of Trade,** 3+1p appendix. The value of a reserve had been shown in June and July when there was minimum disruption to essential work although supplies had been scarce.
22 Sept	35	**Timber: possible further substitution of softwood by hardwood – C.D. Smith covering the forestry products research laboratory.** 1+2p annex.
27 Sept		**Timber – C.D. Smith,** 1p.
28 Sept	36	**Timber requirements – C.D. Smith,** 2p.
28 Sept	37	**Steel – C.D. Smith,** 1+2p appendix.
3 Nov	38	**Renaming of Committee – C.D. Smith,** 1p.
10 Nov	39	**Report on the census of consumers' stocks, receipts and usage of steel, second quarter 1950 – C.D. Smith covering the Ministry of Supply,** 1+7+2p appendixes.
22 Nov	40	**Chairmanship of the Committee – N. Brook,** 1p.
1 Dec	41	**Steel: supplies for Period II 1951 – C.D. Smith,** 2+1p appendix. Proposed method of allaying fears of a shortage as a result of companies' stockbuilding following the announcement of the rearmament programme.
1 Dec	42	**Tin plate: supplies and requirements for Period II 1951 – C.D. Smith,** 1+1p appendix.
5 Dec	43	**Review of supplies and timber requirements for Period I 1951 – Board of Trade,** 2+1p appendix.
6 Dec	44	**Timber: progress report by the forest products research laboratory on co-operation between departments and the laboratory on the further substitution of hardwood for softwood – C.D. Smith covering the laboratory,** 1+2p.
11 Dec	45	**Timber – Board of Trade,** 2p.
14 Dec	46	**Zinc: supplies for 1951 for Period I – Ministry of Supply,** 4+13p appendixes.
20 Dec	47	**Zinc – Ministry of Supply,** 1+4p.

CAB 134/486   Meetings and Memoranda   1 Jan–30 Nov 1951   M(51)1st–22nd, M(51)1–73 and three unnumbered memoranda.

Meetings

3 Jan	**M(51)1st**	**Differential deliveries of coal to industry.** M(51)1 and 2. Agreement to the early adoption of a scheme in M(51)1.
8 Jan	**2nd**	**Differential deliveries of coal to industry.** M(51)1 and 2.
18 Jan	**3rd**	**Softwood supplies and allocations for Period I 1951.** M(51)5. Allocations appended.
22 Jan	**4th:1**	**Sheet steel: report by the chairman of the Working Group.** M(51)6.
	:2	**Sheet steel: allocations for Period II 1951.** Allocations appended.
	:3	**Steel: report by the Overseas Negotiations Committee on the effect of a cut in steel exports in 1951.**
	:4	**Supplies of general steel.**
25 Jan	**5th**	**Supplies of sulphur and sulphuric acid.** M(51)9. Allocation schemes based on M(51)9 to be submitted to the Production Committee.
20 Feb	**7th**	**Review of supplies of softwood for Period I 1951.** M(51)11. Allocations appended.
1 Mar	**8th**	**Untitled.** M(51)7(revise) and 12. Consideration of general steel in 1951. Meeting called at short notice and of restricted size in order to obtain a rapid appraisal of departmental views for an early submission to ministers. F.F. Turnbull, summing up, felt there were differences between those concerned with the export and home markets, and, in the home market, between those who would or would not accept 5% reduction on deliveries.
21 Mar	**9th:1**	**Softwood supplies, requirements and allocations for Period II 1951.** M(51)14. Agreement that departments should phase their licensing evenly over Period II. Allocations appended.
	:2	**Plywood.** M(51)14.
	:3	**Substitution of hardwood for softwood.** M(51)13.
4 Apr	**10th**	**Sulphur and sulphuric acid.** M(51)16. Increasingly clear need for allocation. The scheme in M(51)16 was recommended for ministerial approval.
6 Apr	**11th**	**Sheet steel and tin plate allocations for Period III 1951.** M(51)15. Allocations appended.
3 & 4 May	**12th:1**	**Steel allocation and priority schemes.** M(51)21. Broad outlines of the allocation scheme agreed except by the Ministry of Fuel and Power. Approval, with some reservations, of the priority scheme.
	:2	**Procedure for identifying defence contracts.** M(51)22.
	:3	**Supplies of steel in 1951/52.** M(51)23.

15 June	**13th:1**	**Softwood supplies, requirements and allocations for Period III 1951.** M(51)26. Allocations appended.
	:2	**Plywood.** M(51)26.
19 June	**14th:1**	**Priority scheme for general steel.** M(51)21 and 22. Agreement reached.
	:2	**Proposals for rationing alloy steel.** M(51)28.
21 June	**15th**	**Steel position.** M(51)29, 30, 31. Discussion of possible allocation schemes.
31 July	**16th**	**Effect of possible cuts in allocations of softwood.** M(51)38. Views of departments.
16 Aug	**17th:1**	**Sheet steel and tin plate allocations for Period IV 1951.** M(51)32. To go to the Economic Secretary for decision.
	:2	**The working of the sheet steel distributive scheme.** M(51)27. Agreement that the only way to restore order was to cancel orders and then re-validate the most important.
	:3	**Press announcement about the general steel allocation scheme.** M(51)41.
14 Sept	**18th**	**Softwood supplies, requirements and allocations for Period IV 1951.** M(51)49. Edwards, J. emphasized the seriousness of the balance of payments position. Allocations appended.
17 & 19 Oct	**19th:1**	**Availability of steel and general approach to allocation.** M(51)50, 51, 56, 60, 61. F.F. Turnbull suggested how the Committee should approach the subject.
	:2	**Allocation of general steel.** M(51)60.
	:3	**Allocation of general steel: revised proposals.** Second day of the meeting. Agreement on some departmental allocations. The allocation for building was to be by ministers' decision.
	:4	**Allocation of sheet steel.**
	:5	**Level of tin plate production.**
24 Oct	**20th**	**Sulphur and sulphuric acid.** M(51)54. Allocation agreed.
9 Nov	**21st:1**	**Allocation of steel.** M(51)64 and 66. Swinton said that a severe cut in future steel supplies for domestic use was unavoidable and that it should be implemented now whilst industry was sympathetic. Allocations of alloy steel appended.
	:2	**Continuance of the D.O. and P.T. schemes.**
30 Nov	**22nd**	**Softwood supplies, requirements and allocations for Period I 1952.** M(51)68. Allocations appended.

Memoranda

1 Jan	**M(51)1**	**Coal – C.E.P.S.,** 2+5p appendix. The Committee had been directed by the Economic Policy Committee to prepare urgently a scheme

		for the differential allocation of coal to industry. Proposed allocation scheme appended.
1 Jan	2	**Differential deliveries of coal to industry – Ministry of Fuel and Power,** 3p. Sets out the main requirements of a practicable scheme.
4 Jan		**List of principal priority officers – C.D. Smith,** 1+5p.
12 Jan	3	**Timber requirements – C.D. Smith,** 2p.
12 Jan	4	**Steel – C.D. Smith,** 1p.
18 Jan	5	**Timber: review of supplies of softwood for Period I 1951 – C.D. Smith covering the Board of Trade,** 1+2p.
19 Jan	6	**Sheet steel – C.D. Smith covering F.F. Turnbull,** 1+2+2p appendixes. Report of a working party on the existing distribution scheme and how it could be improved.
20 Feb	7	**Steel – C.D. Smith and M.G. Harris,** 1+5p. Revised version. Also ON(51)15(revise). Analysis of the consequences of limiting steel exports to 1.7m tons, 1.5m tons, and even less.
20 Jan	8	**Supplies of sulphur and sulphuric acid – Board of Trade,** 4+5p appendixes.
1 Feb	9	**Sulphur and sulphuric acid – C.D. Smith covering Edwards, J.,** 1+4p appendixes.
6 Feb	10	**Tin plate allocations for Period II 1951 – C.D. Smith,** 1p.
16 Feb	11	**Timber: review of supplies of softwood for Period I 1951 – Board of Trade,** 1p.
19 Feb	12	**Steel supplies in 1951 – Ministry of Supply,** 4+4p appendixes. Also RM(51)51. It could not be assumed that output in 1951 would be greater than 16.25m tons. A reduction in both home and export demand was therefore necessary. Given the problems with the distribution schemes before their abandonment, the best way to restrict home consumption was an all-round reduction in supplies.
15 Mar	13	**Timber: second progress report by the forest products research laboratory on co-operation between departments and the laboratory on the further substitution of hardwood for softwood –** unsigned, 1p. Developments since M(50)44.
15 Mar		**Note by the secretary – C.D. Smith,** 1p.
19 Mar	14	**Review of supplies and timber requirements for Period II 1951 – C.D. Smith,** 2+1p appendix.
31 Mar	15	**Sheet steel and tin plate. Supplies and requirements for Period III 1951 – C.D. Smith,** 2+2p appendixes.
27 Mar	16	**Supplies of sulphur and sulphuric acid – Board of Trade,** 3+4p appendixes.

10 Apr	17	Steel – C.D. Smith, 1+2p appendix.
10 Apr	18	Timber requirements – C.D. Smith, 2+2p appendix.
25 Apr	19	Sulphur and sulphuric acid – C.D. Smith, 1+4p appendixes. Revised allocation schemes attached.
26 Apr	20	Timber – C.D. Smith, 1p. Revised version.
26 Apr	21	Report of the working party on steel allocation – working party, 6+6p appendixes. Also EPB(51)7. Consideration of three alternatives: (a) the old allocation scheme, (b) the cheque scheme, previously examined in 1947, (c) the scheme whereby allocations were made by departments to firms individually to avoid sub-authorizations. Appendixes A and B set out the proposed allocation scheme for general steel and the priority scheme for steel respectively. The dissenting views of the Ministry of Fuel and Power were included separately.
27 Apr	22	Procedure for identifying defence contracts – C.D. Smith, 1+6+2p. Correspondence between Gaitskell, Strauss and Shawcross.
27 Apr	23	Steel – C.D. Smith covering the Ministry of Supply, 1+2p. Sets out the steel supply situation for July 1951–June 1952.
30 Apr	24	Sulphur and sulphuric acid – C.D. Smith, 1+4p appendixes.
5 May	25	Steel – C.D. Smith, 1p.
9 June	26	Timber: review of supplies and requirements of softwood, excluding sleepers, for Period III 1951 – Board of Trade, 2+1p appendix.
11 June	27	Steel – C.D. Smith covering the Ministry of Supply, 1+1p. There was an increasing backlog owing to problems with the sheet steel distribution scheme.
12 June	28	Proposals for rationing alloy steel – Ministry of Supply, 3p.
14 June	29	Steel – C.D. Smith, 1+1p appendix.
14 June	30	Steel position: 1950–53 – Ministry of Supply, 4+1p appendix.
14 June	31	Steel supplies in the second half of 1951 – Ministry of Supply covering E.W. Senior, director of the British Iron and Steel Federation, 1+3p.
28 June	32	Sheet steel and tin plate – C.D. Smith, 1+2p appendixes.
5 July	33	Steel: report on the census of consumers' stocks, receipts and usage of steel, fourth quarter 1950 – C.D. Smith covering the Ministry of Supply, 1+7+2p appendixes.

6 July		**List of principal priority officers – C.D. Smith,** 1+5p.
9 July	34	**Timber requirements – C.D. Smith,** 2p.
11 July	35	**Steel preference scheme – C.D. Smith,** 1p. Recommendations on the level of quotas.
16 July	36	**Civil preference scheme for non-ferrous metals – Ministry of Supply,** 1p.
19 July	37	**Steel – C.D. Smith,** 1p.
30 July	38	**The likely effects of a reduction of softwood allocations – C.D. Smith,** 1p.
28 July	39	**Steel allocation – Edwards, J.,** 2p. The F.B.I. had shown a preference for the old distribution scheme as opposed to that in M(51)21. Strauss and Edwards, J. agreed that the old scheme was preferable and was therefore to be introduced.
14 Aug	40	**Effect on industry of cuts in supplies of sulphur and sulphuric acid – Ministry of Materials,** 2+12p appendixes.
13 Aug	41	**Allocation scheme for general steel – C.D. Smith,** 1+5p annexes. Draft announcement and draft letter to steel-using firms.
15 Aug	42	**Sulphur and sulphuric acid – C.D. Smith,** 2p.
17 Aug	43	**Civil preference scheme for non-ferrous metals – C.D. Smith,** 1p. To be introduced on the lines of M(51)36.
17 Aug	44	**Steel – C.D. Smith,** 1+1p addendum.
23 Aug	45	**Timber – C.D. Smith covering F.F. Turnbull,** 1+4p. Sets out the impact of a reduction of 25,000 softwood standards on the quarterly allocation as requested in M(51)38.
3 Sept	46	**Alloy steel control – K.W.S. MacKenzie,** 1+2p. Proposals for control.
28 Aug	47	**Sheet steel – C.D. Smith,** 2p. Revised allocations.
7 Sept	48	**Alloy steel – K.W.S. MacKenzie,** 1p. Proposals in M(51)46 to be introduced on 1 Jan 1952.
10 Sept	49	**Timber: review of supplies and requirements for Period IV 1951 – Ministry of Materials,** 3+1p appendix.
21 Sept	50	**General steel allocation – Edwards, N.,** 2p. Sets out some general principles on which the first allocation should be approached, including those industries to be given preference.
25 Sept	51	**Steel supplies and requirements for Period I 1952 – Ministry of Supply,** 1+4p appendixes.
24 Sept	52	**Distribution of copper and zinc – Edwards, J. covering the Ministry of Supply,** 1+3+1p appendix.
26 Sept	53	**Allocations of building softwood for Period IV 1951 – K.W.S. MacKenzie,** 1+1p appendix.

12 Oct	54	Sulphur and sulphuric acid – Ministry of Materials, 3+6p appendixes.
29 Sept	55	Softwood – Edwards, J., 1p.
9 Oct	56	General and sheet steel allocations – F.F. Turnbull, 1p.
12 Oct	57	Tin plate – K.W.S. MacKenzie, 1+1p appendix.
13 Oct	58	General and sheet steel allocations. Tin plate requirements for the food industries 1952 – Ministry of Food, 2p.
12 Oct	59	Timber requirements – K.W.S. MacKenzie, 2p.
15 Oct	60	Proposals for general steel allocations for Period I 1952 – F.F. Turnbull, 1+1p appendix.
13 Oct	61	Estimates of general steel consumption – C.E.P.S., 3+3p annexes. See ES(51)67.
15 Oct	62	General and sheet steel allocations. Tin plate requirements for export 1952 – Board of Trade, 3p.
17 Oct	63	Supplies of tin plate for fruit and vegetable canning 1951 – Ministry of Agriculture and Fisheries, 2p.
24 Oct	64	Allocation of steel – K.W.S. MacKenzie covering F.F. Turnbull, 1+7+7p annexes. See ES(51)66.
25 Oct	65	Change in secretariat – F.F. Turnbull, 1p.
7 Nov	66	Allocation of alloy steel – K.W.S. MacKenzie, 1+1p appendix.
21 Nov	67	Steel allocation – K.W.S. MacKenzie covering Swinton, 2+8+3p annexes. Sets out the main policy objectives and the resulting distribution of available steel given the change of government.
27 Nov	68	Timber: review of supplies and requirements of softwood, excluding sleepers and wagon timbers, for Period I 1952 – Ministry of Materials, 1+1p appendix.
7 Dec	69	Steel allocation – F.F. Turnbull, 3+3p annexes. Allocations as agreed by ministers.
17 Dec	70	Allocation of building steel – K.W.S. MacKenzie, 1+1p appendix.
18 Dec	71	Allocations of building softwood for the first half of 1952 – K.W.S. MacKenzie, 1p.
19 Dec	72	Appointment of chairman and amendment of terms of reference – N. Brook, 1p.
22 Oct	73	Tin plate allocation for Periods I and II 1952 – K.W.S. MacKenzie, 1p.

15.27   Materials Committee:

Steel Economy Subcommittee

Set up in October 1946 (see CAB 132/1, LP(46)35th:1) although it did not meet until December 1946. It met once in 1946, fourteen times in 1947 and twelve times in

1948 and dealt mainly with detailed technical proposals for economies. Before being superseded by the Steel Economy Committee (CAB 134/676) it made three reports, the final one being discussed by the Production Committee in October 1948, see CAB 134/639, PC(48)128.

Terms   To examine the main uses to which steel is currently being put (beginning with the uses of sheet steel and then proceeding to other types of steel in particularly difficult supply) with a view to recommending economies in consumption by such means as the use of substitute materials, the alteration of specifications, and the like.

Members   H.A.R. Binney (B.T., ch.); W. Strath (Supply); V.A.G. Lambert (Supply); F. Webster (Works); C.G. Kavanagh (Iron & Steel Fed.).   (Dec 1947) A.S. Le Maitre (B.T., ch.), T. Staves replaced Strath.   (July 1948) E.F. Muir (Works, ch.).

Sec.   H. Barkley (B.T.).   (June 1948) R.E. France (Supply).

CAB 134/487   Meetings and Memoranda   13 Dec 1946–14 Oct 1948   M(SE SUB)(46)1st–M(SE SUB)(48)12th and M(SE SUB)(46)1–M(SE SUB)(48)3.

Timber Economy Subcommittee

Set up in September 1946, it made its final report to the Materials Committee in November 1946, see CAB 134/477, M(46)1137 and CAB 134/476, M(46)175th.

Terms   To examine the present and projected programmes of departments and to recommend such steps as may reasonably be taken to reduce consumption of timber in relation to anticipated supplies.

Members   G.B. Crow (Health, ch.); A.W. McKenzie (B.T.); J. Ross (B.T.); S.R. Walton (Transport); A.J. Filer (Works); J.A. Callen (Timber Control) and others as appropriate.

Sec.   R.F. Allen (B.T.).

CAB 134/487   Meetings and Memoranda   2 Sept–14 Nov 1946   M(TE SUB)(46)1st–10th and M(TE SUB)(46)1–4.

15.28   Ministerial Committee on Economic Planning

Set up in January 1946 to formalize the *ad hoc* committee of ministers responsible for economic planning (GEN 115) and in practice replacing the Industrial Subcommittee of the Lord President's Committee (CAB 71/27) with the same membership but with more specific responsibility for economic planning. It discussed such matters of principle as the period to be covered by the Economic Survey and wages policy. In particular it was concerned with the surveys of 1946, 1946/7 and 1947, which were submitted to it via the Official Steering Committee on Economic Development (CAB 134/186–193). One of its more important tasks was to make suggestions, later endorsed by the Cabinet, on the presentation of the published version of the 1947 survey (CAB 129/16, CP(47)25 and CAB 128/9, CM(47)7, 8 and 9). It continued to function in theory until the establishment of the Economic Policy and Production Committees (CAB 134/215–230 and CAB 134/635–652) but in practice it did not meet after Morrison's illness in January 1947.

Terms   The ministers who exercise, on the Cabinet's behalf, a general oversight over the work of economic planning and supervise the work of the Official Steering Committee on Economic Development will henceforth be known as the Ministerial Committee on Economic Planning.

Members   Ld President (ch.); Ch. of Exchequer; Pres. Bd Trade; Min. of Lab. & N.S. (Mar 1947) Paymaster–Gen. added.   (Aug 1947) Ld Privy Seal added.

Sec.   M.T. Flett (Ld Pres. O.).

CAB 134/503   Meetings and Memoranda   21 Jan 1946–28 Apr 1947
MEP(46)1st–MEP(47)2nd and MEP(46)1–MEP(47)6.

Meetings

21 Jan	**MEP(46)1st**	**Economic survey for 1946.** LP(I)(46)1. Originally GEN 115/1st. Bridges introduced a survey to the committee. His proposals for the future work of breaking down the survey into quarters and also initiating a preliminary survey of the position in 1950 were approved. Morrison stressed the importance of securing the co-operation of industry and of the general public by keeping them well-informed. Dalton was concerned not to tie the work of economic planning too closely to the budget. Agreement that as there was no long-term plan yet prepared there could be no question of publication of an economic plan in the immediate future. Dalton and Cripps both set out what they thought to be the most urgent problems illustrated by the survey. J.E. Meade suggested that the gap could be bridged in the current year by restricting individual investment by use of physical controls.
16 Apr	**2nd:1**	**Control of investment.** ED(46)5. Originally GEN 115/2nd. The steering committee proposed to use existing machinery of control over the national building programme as its main weapon in controlling investment although this meant there would be no detailed control of plant and machinery. The report was approved but Bridges was to satisfy himself that the headquarters building committee had the ability to take on the large responsibility which would devolve to it.
	:2	**Statistics for employment policy.** ED(45)4 and ED(46)6. Agreement that an approach to industry in the first place should be made at

		the official level. Consideration of whether the necessary legislation should be included in the 1946–47 legislative programme.
17 June	3rd	**Publicity for the work of economic planning.** MEP(46)3 & 4. The steering committee recommended that while the information in the economic survey should be made available to the national industrial conference no White Paper should be published in the current year but that the aim should be to publish a White Paper for 1947 on the lines of MEP(46)3. F. Williams pressed for the publication of a leaflet to inform the public and to assist the Prosperity Campaign. Consideration of whether the survey should be on a calendar year or financial year. Agreement that a White Paper on the lines of MEP(46)3 but also containing a brief description of the planning machinery should be prepared with a publication date yet to be determined but probably in the early months of 1947. The steering committee would consider the period to be covered. The steering committee was to prepare a paper on the means by which the U.K. might maintain its balance of trade in a world slump and the instruments at the government's disposal for maintaining demand in the face of a threatened slump.
12 July	4th	Untitled. MEP(46)6. Consideration of the import programme. No discussion recorded and only conclusions listed which were to go to the Cabinet on 15 July 1946.
28 Oct	5th:1	**The import programme 1947.** MEP(46)10. General discussion of the import programme and export targets and more specifically of petrol rationing. Morrison was to do a covering note to the paper for the Cabinet.
	:2	**Metropolitan Water Board schemes.** MEP(46)11.
	:3	**Information for the National Joint Advisory Council.** MEP(46)9.
28 Nov	6th:1	**Planning White Paper.** MEP(46)12. Cripps stressed the lack of information available for the preparation of forecasts and that it was therefore important not to overplay the extent to which planning could as yet be introduced. Continued discussion between Dalton and Morrison over the relationship between the budget and the survey. The steering committee's recommendations were approved.
	:2	**Draft White Paper for the N.J.A.C.** MEP(46)14.

7 Jan	**MEP(47)1st:1**		**Economic Survey for 1947.** MEP(46)15, 16, 18. Morrison set out a number of issues on which ministerial decision was required along with his view of the contents of the White Paper. Morrison was to write a draft report to the Cabinet to be considered by the committee at its next meeting.
	:2		**Wages and price policy and means of carrying out planning decisions.** MEP(46)17 and 19. Isaacs stressed the importance of the N.J.A.C. as a major instrument of wages policy. Cripps felt it was important to decide the objectives of wage policy in a planned economy and that traditional wage differentials should not be allowed to hamper economic planning. Similarly Dalton believed that in a planned economy wages should be determined by social importance of labour. Morrison was concerned that commitments were drawing too heavily on the future and questioned whether the government could stand aside while this happened. Morrison was to prepare a revised statement of the objectives of wages policy.
9 Jan	**2nd**		**Economic Survey for 1947.** MEP(47)2. Consideration of certain detailed aspects and Morrison was to arrange for an amended report to go to the Cabinet.

Memoranda

23 Apr	**MEP(46)1**		**Composition and terms of reference – E.E. Bridges,** 1p.
26 Apr		2	**Note by the secretary – M.T. Flett,** 1p.
26 Apr		3	**Draft White Paper on the Economic Survey for 1946–47 – Official Steering Committee on Economic Development,** 3+6+4p appendixes. Also ED(46)11. Skeleton White Paper attached. Recommendation that no paper be published that year. Distinction from the ministerial version in that supplies and demands had to show a balance. An increase in unemployment was shown and while this could cause public concern this had to be faced. Recommendation that officials considered the period to be covered and no objection to the information going to the national industrial conference. A draft White Paper centred around three tables: (a) supply and distribution of manpower in Great Britain, (b) balance of payments of the U.K., (c) national income and expenditure of the U.K.
3 June		4	**Publicity for economic planning – Morrison covering E.E. Bridges, E.M. Nicholson and F.**

Williams, 1+1+4p. Exchange of minutes on the extent and form of publicity on government's economic plans on the assumption that early publication was inadvisable, in particular with regard to the Prosperity Campaign.

11 July   5   **Economic Survey for 1946/47 – Economic Survey Working Party,** 15+13p appendixes. Also ED(46)20 and EC(S)(46)24(second revise). Report showing developments since the Economic Survey for 1946 consequent on the measures taken since then. The size of the gap had been reduced accordingly and no further action was recommended. However the gap was likely to increase after March 1947 and no solution was readily available. Problems were also likely to be caused in some industries due to a shortage of raw materials including possible coal shortages. Since the prospect of a recurrent shortage of coal for a number of years was likely the use of foreign labour should be considered although there were obvious problems involved.

11 July   6   **U.S. dollar expenditure – Dalton,** 2+1p annex. The committee was to review departmental import programmes once the U.S. loan had been obtained. He felt some small easements could be made.

11 July   7   **Economic Survey for 1946/47 – E.E. Bridges,** 4p. Also ED(46)19. Covering note to the survey. Sets out the reasons why the gap should not be closed although the balance achieved was only temporary and artificial. Concern with over-concentration of employment in group I industries: there had to be some transfer to group III industries. This was perhaps the biggest single issue for economic planning in the next few years. The threatened shortage of coal overshadowed the whole industrial position and it illustrated the important limitation on possibilities of economic planning as an instrument of government because of the difficulty of making quick adjustments to remedy deep-seated industrial problems even when they had long been foreseen. Such difficulties pointed to the need for caution in the claims made for what could be achieved by planning, at least in regard to short-term problems.

15.29 Manpower Committee (1946–47)

For the earlier papers of this committee, see CAB 92/104. It concentrated on immediate manpower issues and its main work was completed in May 1946 with the drafting of a White Paper on future recruitment to the armed services (see CAB 129/10, CP(46)206 and CAB 128/5, CM 52(46)3 and Cmd. 6831). It was served by the Manpower Working Party (CAB 134/510). It was dissolved in October 1947 with responsibility for manpower being assumed by the Labour Committee (CAB 134/469) and the Production Committee (CAB 134/635–652).

Terms (Aug 1945) To submit to the Cabinet periodical reviews of the manpower position and proposals for the redistribution of manpower, and to keep under review the progress of the demobilization scheme.

Members For. Sec. (ch.); Min. of Labour & N.S.; Pres. Bd Trade. (Jan 1947) Min. of Labour & N.S. (ch.) and Home Sec. added.

Sec. W.S. Murrie (Cab. O.).

CAB 134/509 Meetings and Memoranda 2 Jan 1946–17 Sept 1947
MP(46)1st–MP(47)1st and MP(46)1–MP(47)7.

Meetings

2 Jan	**MP(46)1st:1**	**Manpower position up to 30 June 1946.** MP(45)55 and 67.
	:2	**Provision of emergency training centres for building operatives.** MP(45)64.
22 Jan	**2nd:1**	**Manpower employed on supplies and equipment for the forces.** MP(46)2 and 6.
	:2	**Means of reducing the manpower deficit of 30 June 1946.** MP(46)3. Agreement on an appeal to industry to increase output.
	:3	**Recruitment of labour to unattractive industries.** MP(46)4.
31 Jan	**3rd:1**	**Service manpower engaged on storage and on quasi-civilian activities.** MP(46)7.
	:2	**Report to the Cabinet on the manpower position during 1946.** MP(46)9.
	:3	**Manpower employed on the manufacture of supplies and equipment for the forces.** MP(46)8.
14 Feb	**4th:1**	**Release from the army of officers in class B.** MP(46)11.
	:2	**Future manpower needs of the forces.** MP(46)12, 13, 14.
15 Mar	**5th:1**	**Future manpower needs of the forces.** MP(46)18, 19, 23. Agreement to recommend scheme A in MP(46)18 to the Cabinet.
	:2	**Release of bricklayers for the forces.** MP(46)21 and 22.
	:3	**Underemployment in industry.** MP(46)20.
18 Apr	**6th:1**	**Volunteers for underground coal-mining.** MP(46)25 and 28.

	:2	**Future manpower needs of the forces.** MP(46)29.
23 May	7th	**Future manpower needs of the forces.** MP(46)34 and 35. Amended version of the draft White Paper was to go to the Cabinet.
26 Nov	8th:1 (revise)	**Termination of block releases under class B.** MP(46)51.
	:2	**Deferment of call-up of sheet steel workers.** MP(46)52.
17 Sept	MP(47)1st:1	**Direction into productive work of unoccupied persons and persons engaged in unproductive occupations.** MP(47)5. Agreement to recommend to the Cabinet certain powers of direction.
	:2	**Release leave of men released from the forces under class A.** MP(47)6 and 7.

Memoranda

3 Jan	MP(46)1	**Releases from the forces – W.S. Murrie,** 1+6p annex.
13 Jan	2	**Manpower employed on supplies and equipment for the forces at the end of 1945 – Isaacs,** 3p.
	3	**Means of reducing the manpower deficit at 30 June 1948 – Manpower Working Party,** 4p. Report suggesting a solution mainly in terms of increased output.
17 Jan	4	**Problems of recruiting labour in unattractive industries – Isaacs,** 3+5p. Low wages were not the sole problem.
18 Jan	5	**Releases from the forces – W.S. Murrie,** 1+8p annex.
21 Jan	6	**Manpower employed on supplies and equipment for the forces at the end of 1945 – Wilmot,** 4p. Criticism of MP(46)2.
28 Jan	7	**Service manpower engaged in storage and quasi-civilian activities – Manpower Working Party,** 5p.
30 Jan	8	**Manpower employed on the manufacture of supplies and equipment for the forces – Ministry of Labour,** 3p.
28 Jan	9	**Manpower position during 1946 – W.S. Murrie covering the Manpower Working Party,** 1+6+3p annex. Draft report.
5 Feb	10	**Releases from the forces – W.S. Murrie,** 1+6p annex.
11 Feb	11	**Release from the army of class B officers – Lawson,** 2p.
12 Feb	12	**Regular intake and its effect on conscript service – W.S. Murrie covering the service representatives of the Manpower Working Party,** 1+3p annex.

13 Feb	13	**Call-up for the forces after 30 June 1946 – Isaacs covering the Ministry of Labour,** 1+3p annex.
12 Feb	14	**Recruiting for the post-war fighting services – W.S. Murrie covering L.C. Hollis covering Alexander,** 1+3p. Also DO(46)11.
18 Feb	15	**Manpower employed on production for the services – Isaacs,** 2p.
21 Feb	16	**Releases from the forces – W.S. Murrie,** 1+8p annex.
7 Mar	17	**Releases from the forces – W.S. Murrie,** 1+8p annex.
12 Mar	18	**Call-up to the forces in the transitional period – Manpower Working Party,** 3+1p annex. Sets out three alternative schemes.
13 Mar	19	**Arrangements for the call-up of students and apprentices – Isaacs covering the Ministry of Labour,** 1+4p.
12 Mar	20	**Underemployment in industry – W.S. Murrie covering the Ministry of Labour,** 1+2p. Result of an enquiry at selected factories in each region.
14 Mar	21	**Release of experienced brick makers from the forces – Lawson,** 3p.
14 Mar	22	**Release of experienced brick makers from the forces – Isaacs,** 1p.
14 Mar	23	**Call-up to the forces in the transitional period – W.S. Murrie,** 1p. Effect of the proposals in MP(46)19 as against those in MP(46)18 annex.
22 Mar	24	**Releases from the forces – W.S. Murrie,** 1+6p annex.
2 Apr	25	**Releases from the forces of men volunteering for underground coal-mining – Isaacs,** 2p. Proposed scheme.
8 Apr	26	**Releases from the forces – W.S. Murrie,** 1+8p annex.
9 Apr	27	**Releases from the forces of men volunteering for underground coal-mining – Bevin,** 1p.
16 Apr	28	**Releases from the forces of men volunteering for underground coal-mining – Lawson,** 2p. Criticism of MP(46)25.
17 Apr	29	**Call-up to the forces in the transitional period – Manpower Working Party,** 2+2p annexes. Review of schemes suggested in MP(46)18.
27 Apr	30	**Releases from the forces – W.S. Murrie,** 1+8p annex.
1 May	31	**Call-up to the forces in the transitional period – Manpower Working Party,** 2+4+2p annexes.
6 May	32	**Releases from the forces – W.S. Murrie,** 1+8p annex.

17 May	33	**Training of apprentices during their military service – Lawson,** 1+2+2p appendix. Interim report.
21 May	34	**Call-up to the forces during the transitional period – H.H. Wiles,** 3+4p. Draft White Paper attached.
22 May	35	**Call-up to the forces during the transitional period – W.S. Murrie,** 1+4+1p appendix. Revised draft White Paper.
25 May	36	**Releases from the forces – W.S. Murrie,** 1+8p annex.
4 June	37	**Training of apprentices during their military service – De Freitas,** 1+2p annex +1p appendix.
4 June	38	**The training of apprentices called up to the Royal Navy – Dugdale,** 1+1p appendix.
5 June	39	**Distribution of doctors and nurses between the armed forces and the civilian community – H.H. Wiles,** 2+7p appendixes.
6 June	40	**Releases from the forces – W.S. Murrie,** 1+6p annex.
15 June	41	**Distribution of doctors and nurses between the armed forces and the civilian community – Bevin,** 1p.
25 June–23 Aug	42–46	**Releases from the forces – W.S. Murrie.**
20 Sept	47	**Releases from the forces – J.D. Peeke,** 1+6p annex.
13 Sept	48	**Calling up of doctors and dentists – W.S. Murrie** covering Bevan and Westwood, 1+2p.
30 Oct	49	**Manpower for the services and for the manufacture of equipment and supplies, second half 1946 – Isaacs,** 4p. Targets unlikely to be met.
1 Nov	50	**Releases from the forces – J.A. Drew,** 1+6p annex.
12 Nov	51	**Releases from the forces: the class B release scheme – Isaacs,** 3+2p. Schemes to be restricted to key individuals.
14 Nov	52	**Deferment of the call-up of men engaged in the sheet steel industry – Wilmot,** 3p.
23 Nov	53	**Releases from the forces – J.A. Drew,** 1+6p annex.
26 Nov	54	**Strength of the armed forces on 31 March 1946 – W.S. Murrie,** 1p.
29 Nov	55	**Strength of the armed forces – Manpower Working Party,** 4p. The effect on the release programme of manpower targets for the forces in DO(46)135.
23 Nov	56	**Releases from the forces – W.S. Murrie,** 1+6p annex.
28 Jan	**MP(47)1**	**Releases from the forces – W.S. Murrie,** 1+6p annex.

29 Jan	2	**Composition of Committee – N. Brook,** 1p.
14 Apr	3	**Deferment of call-up: claim for special treatment by the iron-founding industry – Isaacs,** 2p.
19 Apr	4	**Deferment of call-up: claim for special treatment by the iron-founding industry – Isaacs,** 1p.
12 Sept	5	**Unproductive employments – W.S. Murrie,** 1+9p annexes. Official report on the directing of productive work to the unoccupied and unproductive.
13 Sept	6	**Period of release leave for men released from the forces in class A – Isaacs,** 2p.
16 Sept	7	**Period of release leave for men released from the forces in class A – Bevin,** 1p.

Manpower Working Party

Set up in November 1945 to provide reports on immediate manpower issues for the ministerial Manpower Committee (CAB 134/509) and long-term forecasts for the Official Steering Committee on Economic Development (CAB 134/186–193). It was dissolved at the same time as the Manpower Committee.

Members   G. Ince (Lab. & N.S., ch. for forecasts) and H.C. Emmerson (Lab. & N.S., ch. for immediate issues).

Secs.   J.D. Peek (Cab. O.).   (Feb 1946) J.A. Drew (Cab. O.).

CAB 134/510   Meetings and Memoranda   5 Dec 1945–29 June 1947
MP(O)(45)1st–MP(O)(46)11th, MP(O)(45)1–MP(O)(47)1 and one
unnumbered memorandum.

Meetings

28 Nov	MP(O)(45)1st:1	**Future procedure.**
	:2	**Survey of manpower in 1946.**
	:3	**Manpower position up to 30 June 1946.**
8 Jan	MP(O)(46)1st	**The manpower deficit at 30 June 1946.** MP(O)(46)1. Supply departments to obtain reports from regional controllers on underemployment in contracted firms and on possible manpower economies. The Ministry of Labour would also carry out enquiries.
24 Jan	2nd:1	**Revised strengths of the services and of supply industries at 31 December 1946.**
	:2	**Means of reducing the manpower deficit at 30 June 1946.** MP(O)(46)4.
	:3	**Underemployment of industrial labour.**
	:4	**Service manpower engaged on storage and on quasi-civilian activities.** MP(O)(46)3, 5, 6.
	:5	**Releases from the forces: fortnightly target figures in the first half of 1946.**

28 Jan	**3rd:1**	**The manpower position during 1946.** MP(O)(46)7.
	:2	**Service manpower engaged on storage and on quasi-civilian activities.** MP(O)(46)8.
23 Feb	**4th**	**Call-up to the forces.** MP(O)(46)10 and 11.
8 Mar	**5th:1**	**Call-up to the forces in the transitional period.** MP(O)(46)12, 13, 14.
	:2	**Permanent peace-time conscription scheme.** MP(O)(46)14.
16 Apr	**6th**	Untitled. Consideration of call-up to the forces.
3 July	**7th:1**	**Recruitment of Poles into the armed forces.** MP(O)(46)19.
	:2	**Release programme for the second half of 1946.**
23 Sept	**8th:1**	**Introduction of a scheme for permanent compulsory national service.** MP(O)(46)22. Consideration of its impact on civil economy.
	:2	**Imposition of a liability for reserve service on men called up on and after 1 January 1948.** MP(O)(46)23.
	:3	**Voluntary recruitment in the fighting services.** MP(O)(46)21. Note on the number of conscripts required for the army attached.
23 Nov	**9th:1**	**Statement by the Prime Minister on the rate of release from the forces.**
	:2	**National Service Bill.**
	:3	**Provision of employment for regulars on discharge from the forces.**
29 Nov	**10th:1**	**Strength of the armed forces on 31 March 1948.** MP(O)(46)34 and 35. Some consideration of the effect on civil economy.
	:2	**Possible lines of criticism of the National Service Bill.** MP(O)(46)33.
9 Dec	**11th:1**	**Industrial restrictions on recruitment.** MP(O)(46)24 and 27.
	:2	**National Service Bill: instructions to parliamentary counsel.**

Memoranda

5 Dec	**MP(O)(45)1**	**Review of manpower during calendar year 1946 – J.D. Peek covering the Ministry of Labour,** 1+5+5p appendixes. Revise version. See ED(45)3.
5 Jan	**MP(O)(46)1**	**The manpower deficit at 30 June 1946 – J.D. Peek,** 1+2p annexes. Extracts from MP(46)1st.
10 Jan	**2**	**The manpower deficit at 30 June 1946 – J.D. Peek covering the Working Party.** 1+4p. Draft report.
11 Jan	**3**	**The manpower deficit at 30 June 1946 – J.D. Peek covering the War Office,** 1+2p.

17 Jan	4	**Manpower deficit at 30 June 1946 – J.D. Peek covering the Working Party,** 1+4p. See MP(46)3. Revised report.
18 Jan	5	**Service manpower engaged on storage and on quasi-civilian activities – J.D. Peek covering the Air Ministry,** 1+2p annex.
18 Jan	6	**Service manpower engaged on storage and on quasi-civilian activities – J.D. Peek covering the Admiralty,** 1+2p annex.
27 Jan	7	**The manpower position during 1946 – J.D. Peek covering the Working Party,** 1+6+3p annex. See MP(46)9.
27 Jan	8	**Service manpower engaged on storage and on quasi-civilian activities – J.D. Peek covering the Working Party,** 1+5p. Draft report of MP(46)7.
11 Feb	9	**Future manpower needs of the services – J.A. Drew covering the Working Party,** 1+9p annexes.
19 Feb	10	**Call-up to the forces – Ministry of Labour,** 3p.
20 Feb	11	**Call-up to the forces – Major-Gen. Jacob,** 2p.
27 Feb	12	**Call-up to the forces, men only. Effect on total strength of variations in period of conscript service – Ministry of Labour,** 2+2p.
4 Mar	13	**Call-up to the forces: chart showing effect of variations in the period of conscript service – J.A. Drew covering the C.S.O.,** 1+2p.
7 Mar	14	**Call-up to the forces: men only. Effect on total strength and variations in period of conscript service – service representatives,** 3+2p.
23 Apr	15	**Call-up in the transitional period – H.C. Emmerson,** 3p.
26 Apr	16	**Call-up to the forces in the transitional period – J.A. Drew covering the Working Party,** 1+2+1+3+3p.
20 May	17	**Call-up to the forces in the transitional period – J.A. Drew,** 1+3p.
21 May	18	**Call-up in the transitional period: deferment of apprentices and learners – J.A. Drew,** 1+2p.
27 June	19	**Recruitment of Poles into the armed forces – J.A. Drew,** 2p.
21 Aug	20	**Relaxation of the schedule of reserved occupations in respect of men who volunteered for regular engagements in the armed forces – Air Ministry,** 2p.
9 Sept	21	**Voluntary recruitment in the fighting services – A.T. Cornwall-Jones covering the Services Working Party,** 1+8+1p annex. Draft report.
6 Sept	22	**The introduction of a scheme for permanent compulsory national service – A.T. Cornwall-Jones covering the Services Working Party,** 1+6+11p appendixes. Draft report for the

		Manpower Committee to submit to the Defence Committee.
4 Oct	23	**Imposition of a liability for reserve service on men called up on and after 1 Jan 1948 – J.A. Drew,** 1+3p. Revise version. Draft report.
30 Sept	24	**Restrictions on voluntary enlistment – J.A. Drew,** 1p.
5 Oct	25	**Scheme for continuing compulsory military service – J.A. Drew,** 1+8p. Amendments to MP(O)(46)22.
18 Oct	26	**Retardation of releases – J.A. Drew,** 1p.
18 Oct	27	**Industrial restrictions on voluntary enlistment – Ministry of Labour,** 2p. Sets out the history and present scope of restrictions.
18 Oct	28	**Retardation of releases from the army in the first quarter of 1947 – J.A. Drew,** 1+1p.
3 Nov	29	**Liability for refresher training under the scheme for compulsory national service – J.A. Drew covering the Services Working Party,** 1+2p. Draft report.
2 Nov	30	**Statement on compulsory military service – J.A. Drew,** 1+5p annex. Revise version. Draft of Prime Minister's speech.
7 Nov	31	**Prime Minister's statement on compulsory military service – J.A. Drew,** 1+7p. Revised draft.
22 Nov	32	**Statement by the Prime Minister on the rate of demobilization – J.A. Drew,** 1+1p.
27 Nov	33	**National Service Bill: possible lines of opposition – J.A. Drew covering Stanley and** *The Economist*, 23 Nov 1946, 1+5p annexes.
27 Nov	34	**Strength of the armed forces on 31 March 1946 – J.A. Drew covering the Economic Section,** 1+3p. Effects on the civil economy of the proposals by Chiefs of Staffs.
28 Nov	35	**Strength of the armed forces at 31 March 1948 – J.A. Drew covering the Services Working Party,** 1+4p.
11 Dec	36	**Strength of the armed forces at 31 March 1948 – J.A. Drew covering the Economic Section,** 1+3p. Revision of MP(O)(46)34.
14 Dec	37	**Speed-up of demobilization: representations by defence and service groups of the Parliamentary Labour Party – J.A. Drew,** 1p.
17 Dec	38	**Industrial restrictions on voluntary recruitment – J.A. Drew covering the Working Party,** 1+3p.
22 Nov	39	**Resolution on demobilization by defence and services group of the Parliamentary Labour Party – J.A. Drew covering the Services Working Party,** 1+4p.

28 Apr   **MP(O)(47)1**   **Revision of arrangements for release of national service entrants consequent on the reduction in period of national service from eighteen months to twelve months – J.A. Drew covering the Working Party,** 1p.

29 Sept   **Intake of national service entrants into the services – Working Party,** 7p. Report.

15.30   Manpower Committee (1949–51)

An official committee set up during the general reorganization of manpower committees in March 1949 (see CAB 139/33 part I, CP(49)54), although it did not meet until January 1950. It was designed to provide a central focus for the reviewing of manpower, working under the aegis of the C.E.P.S. and servicing a wide range of ministerial committees. It became particularly concerned with the manpower requirements of a future war (on which it reported to the Economic Steering Committee in November 1951, see CAB 134/266, ES(51)68) and particular problems arising from the Korean War.

Its terms of reference were deliberately restricted by the C.E.P.S. and the service departments, see CAB 21/2501. The ministerial Labour (Textile Industries) Committee (CAB 134/471–474) and the Joint War Production Staff (DEFE 10/222–228, responsible for the manpower required for the equipment of the armed forces) continued to deal with certain manpower issues. The Ministries of Defence and Labour also retained prime responsibility for the distribution of manpower between the forces and the administration of the National Service Acts respectively, although problems might be referred to the Committee. In February 1950, however, the Committee did acquire responsibility for the schedule of reserved occupations when the Working Party on the Reservation and Withdrawal of Labour replaced the Manpower Subcommittee of the Defence (Transition) Committee. It was served by several other working parties including two on long-term planning (CAB 134/515–516).

Under the Conservative government it merged with the Committee on Productive Capacity (CAB 134/114–116) to form the Manpower and Production Committee and its papers are in CAB 134/1054 (at present retained in the department).

Terms   (a) to consider, in the light of approved policies, questions arising on the allocation and distribution of manpower and on the manpower implications of proposed new policies or proposed modifications of existing policies, and to report to the appropriate ministerial committee as required   (b) to consider, in particular, such questions as may be referred to them connected with the use of foreign labour and the expansion of the labour force in undermanned industries   (c) to supervise preliminary planning for the redistribution of manpower in the early stages of a major war.

Members   E.A. Hitchman (C.E.P.S., ch.); M. Smieton (Lab. & N.S.); D.M. Lloyd (B.T.); R.F. Bretterton (Ec. Sect.); A.J. Newling (M.O.D.); H.R. Camp (Supply, representing the Jt. War Prod. Staff); C.N. Ryan (H.O.). (Jan 1950) W. Strath (C.E.P.S., ch.). (March 1951) E.A. Shillito (C.E.P.S., ch.). Representatives of other ministries might attend when required.

Secs. J.R. Lloyd-Davies (Lab. & N.S.) and R.P. Fraser (Cab O.). (May 1949) J.D. Peek (Cab. O.) replaced Fraser. (Feb 1950) P.J. Moorhouse (Cab. O.) replaced Peek. (May 1951) D. Pointon (Lab. & N.S.) replaced Lloyd-Davies.

CAB 134/511   Meetings and Memoranda   7 Mar 1949–19 Dec 1950   MP(50)1st–5th and MP(49)1–MP(50)13 and one unnumbered memorandum.

Meetings

20 Jan	**MP(50)1st**	**Manpower allocation during the first year of a major war.** MP(50)1.
12 July	**2nd**	**Manpower allocation in the first year of a major war.** MP(50)6.
15 Nov	**3rd:1**	**Manpower distribution at the peak of industrial mobilization in a future war.** MP(50)8.
	:2	**Future work of the Committee.** Sets out a number of points requiring consideration. More frequent meetings were necessary.
6 Dec	**4th:1**	**Defence programme. Labour requirements for Royal Ordnance factory, Swynnerton.** MP(50)10.
	:2	**Manpower distribution at the peak of industrial mobilization in a future war.**
19 Dec	**5th**	**Requirements of the service departments for works staff.** MP(50)11 and 13.

Memoranda

7 Mar	**MP(49)1**	**Composition and terms of reference** – N. Brook, 2p.
16 May		**Change in secretariat** – unsigned, 1p.
16 Jan	**MP(50)1**	**Manpower allocation during the first year of a major war** – Ministry of Labour and C.E.P.S., 2p.
21 Jan	**2**	**Change of chairmanship** – J.R. Lloyd-Davies and J.D. Peek, 1p.
13 Feb	**3**	**Change of secretary** – J.R. Lloyd-Davies and P.J. Moorhouse, 1p.
22 Feb	**4**	**Change in subcommittee organization** – N. Brook, 1p. Also DTC(50)8 and MP(RL)(50)1.
12 May	**5**	**Note by the chairman** – W. Strath, 1p. Also MP(LT)(50)1.
7 July	**6**	**Report by Working Group,** 6+3p appendix. Report on manpower in the first year of a major war.
17 July	**7**	**Manpower in the first year of a major war** – J.R. Lloyd-Davies and R.B. Marshall, 1+8+3p appendix. Also GEN 317/5.
2 Aug	**8**	**Manpower distribution at the peak of industrial mobilization in a future war** – Working Party on Long-term Planning, 4+3p appendixes. Also MP(LT)(50)7.
1 Dec	**9**	**Control of medical manpower in war** – *J.R. Lloyd-Davies and P.J. Moorhouse covering the*

Working Party on the Control of Medical Manpower in War, 1+1+4p. Also DTC(50)21.

2 Dec	10	Defence programme: labour requirements for Royal Ordnance factory, Swynnerton – J.R. Lloyd-Davies and P.J. Moorhouse covering the Ministry of Labour, 1+2p.
11 Dec	11	Requirements of the service departments for works staff – J.R. Lloyd-Davies and P.J. Moorhouse covering the Ministry of Labour, 4p.
12 Dec	12	Manpower distribution at the peak of industrial mobilization in a future war – J.R. Lloyd-Davies and P.J. Moorhouse, 1+3+4p annex +3p appendixes. Also NEW(50)8.
18 Dec	13	Admiralty requirements for works staff – Admiralty, 1p.

CAB 134/512   Meetings and Memoranda   5 Jan–27 Dec 1951   MP(51)1st–5th and MP(51)1–21.

Meetings

18 Jan	MP(51)1st	Requirements of the service departments for works staff. MP(51)1.
1 May	2nd:1	Scientific and technical manpower in wartime. MP(51)3.
	:2	Manpower in a future war. MP(51)4.
13 Sept	3rd	Restriction of production of goods for home consumption. MP(51)8 and 9. Also CPC(51)19th.
30 Oct	4th	Manpower requirements in a future war. MP(51)10.
19 Dec	5th:1	Terms of reference. MP(51)13.
	:2	Manpower requirements in a future war.
	:3	Reservation and withdrawal of labour. MP(51)14.
	:4	Scientific and technical manpower in wartime.
	:5	Working party on nylon.
	:6	Regional working parties. MP(51)17 and 18.
	:7	Transfer of labour within firms for defence work.
	:8	Labour requirements for the Royal Ordnance factory, Swynnerton. MP(51)15.
	:9	Machine tools for defence. CPC(51)82.

Memoranda

5 Jan	MP(51)1	Requirements of the service departments for works staff – Ministry of Labour, 2p. Interim report.
27 Mar	2	Change of chairmanship – W. Strath, 1p.
23 Apr	3	Scientific and technical manpower in wartime – Ministry of Labour, 3+1p annex.
27 Apr	4	Manpower in a future war – E.A. Shillito, 1p.
23 May	5	Change of secretary – unsigned, 1p.

10 Aug	**6**	**Restriction of production of goods for home consumption – E.A. Shillito**, 1+3p. Also CPC(51)49. Note of an *ad hoc* meeting.
13 Aug	**7**	**Dates for war planning – E.A. Shillito**, 1p.
7 Sept	**8**	**The manpower position and measures to deal with labour supply – Minister of Labour**, 1+10+2p appendix. Also CPC(51)56. Recommends the reintroduction of the Control of Engagement Order.
10 Sept	**9**	**Restriction of production of goods for home consumption – P.J. Moorhouse and D. Pointon**, 1+8+40p annexes. Also CPC(51)58.
15 Oct	**10**	**Interim report of the Working Party on Long-term Planning**, 3+8p annex +9p appendixes.
16 Oct	**11**	**Restriction of production of goods for home consumption – D. Pointon and P.J. Moorhouse**, 1+11+2p appendix +9p annex. See GEN 380/8. Also CPC(51)71.
13 Nov	**12**	**Manpower in a future war – Manpower Committee**, 5p. See ES(51)68. Final version of interim report.
11 Dec	**13**	**Terms of reference and composition – N. Brook**, 2p.
13 Dec	**14**	**Reservation and withdrawal of labour – G.J. Nash covering the Working Party**, 1+7+49p. Progress report.
11 Dec	**15**	**Labour requirements for the Royal Ordnance factory, Swynnerton – P.J. Moorhouse and A. Savage covering the Working Party on the Recruitment of Labour to the Royal Ordnance Factory, Swynnerton**, 1+23+18p appendixes +10+1+33p. Interim report, final report and addenda.
18 Dec	**16**	**Labour situation in the Bridgwater area – P.J. Moorhouse and A. Savage covering the Working Party on the Labour Position in Bridgwater**, 1+36+37p appendixes.
19 Dec	**17**	**Labour situation in the Coventry area in relation to the defence programme – P.J. Moorhouse and A. Savage**, 1+2p annex. Amendment to CPC(51)81(revise) made at the Economic Steering Committee.
19 Dec	**18**	**Labour situation in the Preston-Chorley-Blackburn area – P.J. Moorhouse and A. Savage**, 1+1p annex. Amendment to CPC(51)83(revise) made at the Economic Steering Committee.
20 Dec	**19**	**Labour situation in the Bristol area – P.J. Moorhouse and A. Savage covering the Working Party on the Labour Position in Bristol and Weston-super-Mare**, 1+51+51p appendixes.

21 Dec	**20**	**Labour situation in the Gloucester-Cheltenham area – P.J. Moorhouse and A. Savage covering the Working Party on the Labour Position in Gloucester-Cheltenham,** 1+53+40p appendixes.
27 Dec	**21**	**Labour situation in the Redditch area in relation to the defence programme – P.J. Moorhouse and A. Savage,** 1p. A survey was unnecessary at present.

Working Party on Long-term Planning (1950)

Set up by the Manpower Committee in May 1950 (see CAB 134/511, MP(50)5) as an informal group from members of the committee's existing working party. After its report in August 1950 (CAB 134/511, MP(50)8), it was reconstituted under the same name but with different terms of reference, see CAB 134/515.

Terms To consider whether a statistical estimate could be made of the probable distribution of national manpower at the peak of the country's individual effort in a future war.

Members W.A.B. Hopkin (C.S.O.); J.R. Lloyd-Davies (Lab. & N.S.); D.A.V. Allen (C.E.P.S.); P.D. Martyn (M.O.D.).

Secs. M.P. Beazley (C.S.O.).

CAB 134/516 Meetings and Memoranda 12 May–2 Aug 1950 MP(LT)(50)1st–2nd and MP(LT)(50)1–7.

Meetings

12 May	**MP(LT)(50)1st**	**Manpower distribution at the peak of a future war.** GEN 317/2.
18 July	**2nd**	**Manpower distribution at the peak of a future war.** MP(LT)(50)5.

Memoranda

12 May	**MP(LT)(50)1**	**Membership and terms of reference – W. Strath,** 1p. Also MP(50)5.
25 May	**2**	**Manpower estimates 1943 and 1960 – J.R. Lloyd-Davies,** 2+1p. Estimate of the labour force with its distribution by age and sex in 1960.
5 July	**3**	**Appointment of secretary –** unsigned, 1p.
5 July	**4**	**Number of producers required to keep one fighting man supplied in 1960 – P.D. Martyn,** 3p.
14 July	**5**	**Estimated distribution of manpower at the peak of a future war – W.A.B. Hopkin,** 1+2p.
27 July	**6**	**Manpower distribution at the peak of a future war – W.A.B. Hopkin covering the Working**

		Party, 4+3p appendixes. Draft report to the Manpower Committee.
2 Aug	7	**Manpower distribution at the peak of industrial mobilization in a future war – the Working Party,** 4+3p appendixes. See MP(50)8. Report to the Manpower Committee.

Working Party on Long-term Planning (1951)

Set up in April 1951 by the Manpower Committee (see CAB 134/512, MP(51)4) to combine the work of the existing working party of the Manpower Committee and the Working Party on Long-term Planning (CAB 134/516). It produced an interim report for the Committee in October 1951 (CAB 134/511, MP(51)10) and a further submission on manpower in a future war for Conservative ministers in November.

Terms On the basis of information collected from departments, to make an estimate of manpower requirements in the first year of a major war and of the principal distribution of national manpower at the peak of the country's industrial effort in a future war, and to report to the Manpower Committee.

Members A.M. Jenkins (C.E.P.S., ch.); representatives of H.O., M.O.D., Lab. & N.S., B.T., Adm., Supply, Works, Ec. Sect.

Secs. P.J. Moorhouse (Cab. O.) and D.R.F. Turner (Lab. & N.S.).

CAB 134/515   Meetings and Memoranda   22 May–14 Dec 1951   MP(L)(51)1st–7th and MP(L)(51)1–34.

Meetings

26 May	MP(L)(51)1st	**Manpower in a future war: new assumptions.** MP(L)(51)2.
19 July	2nd	**Manpower requirements September 1952 to mid-1954.** MP(L)(51)16.
26 July	3rd:1	**Committee procedure.**
	:2	**Preparation of the Working Party's report.**
	:3	**Manpower requirements September 1952 to mid-1954.** MP(L)(51)16.
6 Sept	4th:1	**Interim report to the Manpower Committee.** MP(L)(51)18, 19, 20. Agreement that the report should be based on the shorter version of MP(L)(51)19.
	:2	**Revised assumptions.** MP(51)7.
20 Sept	5th:1	**Draft interim report to the Manpower Committee.** MP(L)(51)21. Detailed consideration.
	:2	**Revised assumptions.**
26 Oct	6th	**Manpower requirements 1954–1956.** MP(L)(51)30.
30 Nov	7th	**Manpower in a future war: submission to ministers.** MP(L)(51)31 and 32.

Memoranda

22 May	MP(L)(51)1	Composition and terms of reference – P.J. Moorhouse and D.R.F. Turner, 1p.
22 May	2	Manpower in a future war: new assumptions – P.J. Moorhouse and D.R.F. Turner, 2p.
2 June	3	Manpower distribution at March 1951 – Ministry of Labour, 1+2p.
11 June	5	Estimates of the strength of the armed forces – P.J. Moorhouse, 2p.
19 June	6	Estimated requirements of manpower for the building and civil engineering industry and the building materials industries – P.J. Moorhouse, 1p.
19 June	7	Manpower distribution in certain industry groups at September 1952, September 1953 and mid-1954 – Ministry of Labour, 2+1p.
19 June	8	Admiralty manpower requirements – P.J. Moorhouse, 3p.
22 June	9	Note by Ministry of Supply, 2+1p. Estimates of manpower distribution in the industries for which it was responsible.
20 June	10	Colliery manpower in the event of a war starting in 1952 – Ministry of Fuel and Power, 2p.
20 June	11	Board of Trade manpower requirements – Board of Trade, 1+3p annex.
29 June	12	Civil defence manpower requirements – P.J. Moorhouse, 3p.
9 July	13	Estimates of total working population at mid-1952, mid-1953 and mid-1954 – Ministry of Labour, 1+1p.
13 July	14	Building and civil engineering personnel in whole-time civil defence forces – P.J. Moorhouse and D.R.F. Turner, 1p.
14 July	15	Ministry of Supply manpower requirements – P.J. Moorhouse and D.R.F. Turner, 1+1p. Revision of MP(L)(51)9.
16 July	16	Manpower requirements September 1952 to mid-1954 – P.J. Moorhouse and D.R.F. Turner covering C.E.P.S. and Ministry of Labour, 1+3+6p. There was a gap between requirements and supply in all three years.
27 Aug	17	Armed forces at peak of service mobilization – P.J. Moorhouse and D.R.F. Turner, 1p.
1 Sept	18	Manpower for the building and civil engineering and building materials industries – Ministry of Works, 3+1p appendix.
3 Sept	19	Draft interim report – A.M. Jenkins, 1+7+5p appendixes +2p. Long and short versions.
5 Sept	20	Ministry of Supply: manpower requirements for war – Ministry of Supply, 2+1p.
15 Oct	21	Interim report – the Working Party, 3+8p annex +9p appendixes. Final version. See MP(51)10.

3 Oct	22	**Admiralty manpower requirements for a war starting in September 1954** – P.J. Moorhouse and D.R.F. Turner, 2p.
5 Oct	23	**Ministry of Supply manpower requirements for a war starting in September 1954** – Ministry of Supply, 2+1p.
8 Oct	24	**Estimates of the strength of the armed forces** – P.J. Moorhouse and D.R.F. Turner, 3p.
10 Oct	25	**Manpower requirements of the building and civil engineering industry** – P.J. Moorhouse and D.R.F. Turner, 1p.
18 Oct	26	**Civil defence manpower requirements** – P.J. Moorhouse and D.R.F. Turner, 2+1p annex.
19 Oct	27	**Manpower requirements in sectors of industry for which the Ministry of Materials is responsible** – P.J. Moorhouse and D.R.F. Turner, 1p.
19 Oct	28	**Manpower requirements of the coal-mining industry** – P.J. Moorhouse and D.R.F. Turner, 1p.
22 Oct	29	**Manpower requirements: Board of Trade industries** – P.J. Moorhouse and D.R.F. Turner, 2+3p. Revised estimates.
23 Oct	30	**Manpower requirements: 1954–1956** – C.E.P.S. and Ministry of Labour, 4+4p addendum.
26 Nov	31	**Manpower in a future war: report to ministers** – A.M. Jenkins, 1p.
28 Nov	32	**Manpower in a future war** – A.M. Jenkins, 1+11p. Draft submission to ministers.
12 Dec	33	**Manpower requirements at September 1956 compared with estimated manpower distribution at mid-1943** – Ministry of Labour, 3+1p.
14 Dec	34	**Manpower in a future war** – A.M. Jenkins, 1+4+2p appendixes. Revised draft submission.

15.31 Working Party on National Income Forecasts

Set up in January 1950 as a subcommittee of the Economic Survey Working Party. Its main contributions were to the U.K. reports to the O.E.E.C., forecasts of national income and the formulation of national income statistics, and estimates of the impact of defence expenditure on the economy. Its papers after November 1951 are in CAB 134/1058–1061.

Terms   To be responsible under the Economic Survey Working Party for supervising the preparation of forecasts of national income and expenditure.

Members   C.T. Saunders (C.S.O., ch.); E.F. Jackson (C.S.O.); D.A.V. Allen (C.E.P.S.); M.F.W. Hemming, J.C.R. Dow and J. Downie (all Ec. Sect.).

Secs. R.L. Marris (C.E.P.S.) and M. Barbour (C.S.O.).   (March 1950) J. Grieve Smith (Ec. Sect.) replaced Marris.

CAB 134/520   Meetings   25 Jan–4 Dec 1950   NIF(WP)(50)1st–27th.

Meetings

25 Jan	**NIF(WP)(50)1st**	Untitled. NIF(WP)(50)2 and 4. Consideration of work to be done.
30 Jan	**2nd:1**	**Paper by productivity sub-group.** NIF(WP)(50)6.
	:2	**Balance of payments.**
	:3	**Future programme.**
2 Feb	**3rd:1**	**Report for the Investment Programmes Committee.**
	:2	**Outline of draft report for the Investment Programmes Committee.** NIF(WP)(50)7.
	:3	**Forecast of domestic savings.** NIF(WP)(50)9.
	:4	**Future arrangements.**
6 Feb	**4th**	**Revised outline of draft report for Investment Programmes Committee.** NIF(WP)(50)7(revise).
10 Feb	**5th**	**Revised outline of draft report.** NIF(WP)(50)7(second revise).
11 Feb	**6th**	**Revised outline of draft report.** NIF(WP)(50)7(second revise).
3 Mar	**7th**	Untitled. Consideration of investment in 1949.
18 Mar	**8th**	**Revised forecast of national income.** NIF(WP)(50)19.
24 Mar	**9th**	**Revised forecast of gross national product.** NIF(WP)(50)21.
31 Mar	**10th:1**	**Public authorities' accounts.**
	:2	**Capital account.**
	:3	**Consumption.**
17 Apr	**11th:1**	**Supplies of plant and equipment.**
	:2	**Revision of NIF(WP)(50)22.**
25 Apr	**12th**	Untitled. Consideration of public authorities' accounts and capital account.
6 June	**13th**	**Questionnaire for the O.E.E.C. third report.** NIF(WP)(50)29 and 30.
12 June	**14th:1**	**Note by the secretary-general on the preparation of the third report of the O.E.E.C.** CE(50)58.
	:2	**Draft proposals to the O.E.E.C. for questionnaire on third report.** NIF(WP)(50)31(revise).
28 June	**15th**	**The internal balance.** NIF(WP)(50)33 and 34. It was impracticable to produce in the near future more frequent estimates of national income because of the limited data available.
30 June	**16th**	**Preliminary national income estimates for 1954.**
21 July	**17th**	**Production estimates for 1954 in Ministry of Supply industries.**

24 July	18th	Production estimates for 1954 in Board of Trade industries.
30 July	19th:1	NIF(WP)(50)18th meeting: rayon industry.
	:2	Tables on national income and expenditure in 1954. NIF(WP)(50)37.
	:3	The O.E.E.C. third report: draft chapters II and III and general tables. NIF(WP)(50)36.
11 Aug	20th	The impact of defence expenditure on the U.K. economy. NIF(WP)(50)38. Agreement on arrangements for future consideration.
29 Aug	21st	The economic impact of rearmament. NIF(WP)(50)41 and 41 addendum I.
30 Aug	22nd	The economic impact of rearmament. Increase in the gross national product (appendix). NIF(WP)(50)41 addendum II. Appendix attached.
12 Sept	23rd	Review of national food policy. NIF(WP)(50)48 and 50.
27 Oct	24th	National income and expenditure forecasts for 1951 and thereafter. NIF(WP)(50)51.
8 Nov	25th:1	Possible effects of raw material shortages upon the expansion of output. NIF(WP)(50)54.
	:2	Estimates of national income and expenditure in the years 1950 and 1951. NIF(WP)(50)53.
27 Nov	26th	National income estimates for 1951. NIF(WP)(50)55.
4 Dec	27th:1	National income estimates for 1951. NIF(WP)(50)55(first revise) and addendum.
	:2	Notes on consumption trends.

CAB 134/521   Memoranda   23 Jan–2 Dec 1950   NIF(WP)(50)1–55.

23 Jan	NIF(WP)(50)1	Note by the joint secretaries – R.L. Marris and M. Barbour, 1+1p. Also ESWP(50)2.
23 Jan	2	A possible outline of work – R.L. Marris and M. Barbour covering R.L. Marris, 1+2p.
23 Jan	3	Productivity of manufacturing industry – R.L. Marris, 1+7p. Information for background.
23 Jan	4	Projection of national product – R.L. Marris covering J.C.R. Dow, 1+3p.
2 Feb	5	Departmental investment programmes 1948–52 – R.L. Marris and M. Barbour, 1+1+2p. See IPC(WP)(50)44.
27 Jan	6	Productivity sub-group – R.L. Marris, 1+3p.
9 Feb	7	Revised outline of draft report – Working Party, 13p. Second revise version.
7 Feb	8	Estimates of the income of companies, changes in tax reserves and personal incomes – R.L. Marris and M. Barbour covering J.C.R. Dow, 1+3p.
14 Feb	9	Note by the joint secretaries – R.L. Marris and M. Barbour, 1+3p. Revise version.

10 Feb	10	**Consumers' expenditure and the yield of indirect taxation – R.L. Marris and M. Barbour covering R.L. Marris,** 1+13p.
10 Feb	11	**Note by the joint secretaries – R.L. Marris and M. Barbour covering J.C.R. Dow,** 1p. Inland Revenue estimates of tax payments and liabilities.
13 Feb	12	**National income and expenditure during 1951 and 1952 – the Working Party,** 13+2p annexes +2p addendum.
14 Feb	13	**Inventory profits – R.L. Marris and M. Barbour covering J.C.R. Dow,** 1+2+2p annex.
23 Feb	14	**New estimates of fixed investment – C.T. Saunders,** 2+2p.
24 Feb	15	**The supply of equipment and vehicles – C.T. Saunders,** 4+1p. Explanation of the differences between NIF(WP)(50)12 and IPC(WP)(50)46.
6 Mar	16	**Note by the joint secretaries – J. Grieve Smith and M. Barbour covering C.T. Saunders,** 1p. Letter to F.F. Turnbull on the forecast of finance available for investment.
6 Mar	17	**Note by the joint secretaries – J. Grieve Smith and M. Barbour covering C.T. Saunders,** 1+6+1p annex. Letter to F.F. Turnbull on the estimated supplies of plant and equipment 1948–52.
7 Mar	18	**Change in the secretariat – M. Barbour and J. Grieve Smith,** 1p.
17 Mar	19	**Revised forecast of national income – C.T. Saunders,** 3p.
21 Mar	20	**Various notes on investment – C.T. Saunders,** 1+15p annexes. Four papers attached covering the economic balance in 1951 and 1952; the effect of the investment programme on inflation in the consumption field; the effects on tax receipts and financing of investment of more optimistic forecasts of production increases; and the amount of specific investment in the controllable sector.
23 Mar	21	**Revised forecasts of the gross national product – C.T. Saunders,** 1+1p.
3 Apr	22	**Forecasts of national income and expenditure 1950–52 – M. Barbour and J. Grieve Smith covering the Working Party,** 1+7p.
3 Apr	23	**Revision of financial estimates for the Investment Programmes Committee – M. Barbour and J. Grieve Smith covering C.T. Saunders,** 1+3p. Letter to F.F. Turnbull.
5 May	24	**Financing of investment in 1951 and 1952 – M. Barbour and J. Grieve Smith,** 1+9p.
8 May	25	**Financing of investment in 1951 and 1952 – M. Barbour and J. Grieve Smith,** 1+7+6p appendix.

		Report of the Working Party submitted to Gaitskell.
9 May	26	**Financing of investment in 1951 and 1952. 4% productivity assumption – M. Barbour and J. Grieve Smith,** 1+9p. Estimates of national income on that assumption.
8 May	27	**Financing investment in 1951 and 1952 (2½% and 4% productivity assumption) – M. Barbour and J. Grieve Smith,** 1+9p. Draft for Gaitskell covering both assumptions.
11 May	28	**Note by the joint secretaries – M. Barbour and J. Grieve Smith,** 1+7+1p annex. See the appendix to EPC(50)46.
2 June	29	**The next O.E.E.C. report – C.T. Saunders covering R.L. Hall,** 1+2p. Sets out the likely form of the report.
5 June	30	**Note by the chairman – C.T. Saunders,** 1+7p. First draft of questionnaire for the next O.E.E.C. long-term report.
10 June	31	**Third report of the O.E.E.C. Draft proposals to the O.E.E.C. for long-term programme questionnaire – C.T. Saunders,** 4p. Revise version.
14 June	32	**Future supplies of plant and equipment – C.T. Saunders covering the Ministry of Supply and Board of Trade,** 1+6p annexes.
23 June	33	**The internal balance – M. Barbour and J. Grieve Smith covering J. Grieve Smith,** 1+5p. Estimates needed for less than one year ahead.
26 June	34	**Appraising the internal economic situation – M. Barbour and J. Grieve Smith covering J. Downie,** 1+3p. Identifies the minimum information required.
17 July	35	**Movement of industrial production, 1949–1954, by industrial groups – D.A.V. Allen,** 1+1p.
28 July	36	**The O.E.E.C. third report – M. Barbour and J. Grieve Smith,** 1+2p. First draft of chapter II on national income and use of resources.
27 July	37	**The O.E.E.C. third report: national income and expenditure in 1954 – unsigned,** 7p.
10 Aug	38	**Notes on the impact of defence expenditure on the U.K. economy – unsigned,** 13+8p appendixes. Preliminary conclusions.
11 Aug	39	**The impact of the rearmament programme – C.T. Saunders,** 2p. Sets out the possible division of work.
15 Aug	39	**Economic effects of the defence programme – C.T. Saunders,** 1p. Sets out terms of reference for the survey.
25 Aug	40	**Note by the joint secretaries – M. Barbour and J. Grieve Smith,** 1+3p appendixes +5p

			addenda. Further analysis of the additional defence programme.
28 Aug	41		**The economic impact of defence expenditure – M. Barbour and J. Grieve Smith,** 1+9+16p addenda. Drafts of parts I, II, IV, VI and the balance of payments section.
31 Aug	42		**Report on the economic impact of defence expenditure – M. Barbour and J. Grieve Smith,** 1+33p. First draft.
1 Sept	43		**The economic impact of defence expenditure – M. Barbour and J. Grieve Smith,** 1+1p. Outline of internal balance section.
4 Sept	44		**Report on the economic impact of defence expenditure – M. Barbour and J. Grieve Smith,** 1+37+5p appendixes. Revised draft report.
4 Sept	45		**Note by the joint secretaries – M. Barbour and J. Grieve Smith covering the Treasury,** 1+4+1p annex. Effect of the rearmament programme on the sterling area and outline brief for Gaitskell.
6 Sept	46		**Estimates of public authorities' current expenditure on goods and services – E.F. Jackson,** 1+7p.
6 Sept	47		**Estimates of national income and expenditure in the years 1950 to 1953 – E.F. Jackson,** 1+5+3p appendixes.
6 Sept	48		**Review of national food policy – M. Barbour and J. Grieve Smith covering the Ministry of Food,** 1+3+3p appendixes.
6 Sept	49		**Draft report on the economic impact of defence expenditure – M. Barbour,** 1p.
12 Sept	50		**Consumer expenditure on food – M.F.W. Hemming,** 2p.
24 Oct	51		**National income and expenditure forecasts for 1951 and thereafter – C.T. Saunders,** 1p. Sets out two bases for forecasting.
30 Oct	52		**Increase in wage earnings 1950–1951 – J.R.C. Dow,** 1p.
8 Nov	53		**Estimates of national income and expenditure in the years 1950 and 1951–2–3 – M. Barbour and J. Grieve Smith,** 1+5+2p appendix.
7 Nov	54		**Possible effects of raw materials shortage upon the expansion of output – D.A.V. Allen,** 6+1p.
2 Dec	55		**Estimates of national income in 1951 on various assumptions – M. Barbour and J. Grieve Smith,** 1+12+6p addendum. First revise version.

CAB 134/522   Meetings and Memoranda   6 Jan–12 Nov 1951
            NIF(WP)(51)1st–10th and NIF(WP)(51)1–19.

Meetings

10 Jan	**NIF(WP)(51)1st**	**National income and expenditure in 1951 and 1952.** NIF(WP)(51)2.

23 Feb	**2nd:1**	**Economic Survey and Budget Committee.** NIF(WP)(51)2(second revise), 3, 4. Programmes Committee was to reconsider balance of payments situation in 1951.
	:2	**1953 assumptions for Investment Programmes Committee.** NIF(WP)(51)2(second revise).
	:3	**N.A.T.O. and O.E.E.C. questionnaire.**
	3rd	No minutes issued.
7 May	**4th**	**National income forecasting in the U.K.** NIF(WP)(51)10.
14 June	**5th:1**	**The Nitze exercise: other countries' submissions.**
	:2	**The implications of the balance of payments forecast for 1951/52.**
21 June	**6th:1**	**The implications of the latest balance of payments forecasts.** NIF(WP)(51)13.
	:2	**Model for national economy in war.** NIF(WP)(51)12.
29 June	**7th:1**	**General economic prospects.** NIF(WP)(51)13(first revise).
	:2	**Model for national economy in war.** NIF(WP)(51)11 and 12.
3 Oct	**8th:1**	**Timetable.** NIF(WP)(51)15.
	:2	**National income estimates for 1951.** NIF(WP)(51)14.
	:3	**National income forecasts for 1952.** NIF(WP)(51)16.
9 Oct	**9th**	**National income forecasts for 1951 and 1952.** NIF(WP)(51)17.
17 Oct	**10th:1**	**Revised forecasts for 1951 and 1952.** NIF(WP)(51)18.
	:2	**The growth of profits since 1946.** NIF(WP)(51)18 appendix III.

Memoranda

6 Jan	**NIF(WP)(51)1**	**New review of economic prospects for 1951 and 1952 – C.T. Saunders,** 2p.
12 Feb	**2**	**National income and expenditure estimates for 1951, 1952 and 1953 – M. Barbour and J. Grieve Smith,** 2+18+2p appendix. Second revise version. Formulated for the I.P.C.
21 Feb	**3**	**Note by the chairman – C.T. Saunders,** 1p. Sets out future work.
22 Feb	**4**	**National income forecasts in the Economic Survey – J. Grieve Smith and M. Barbour covering J.C.R. Dow,** 1+2p. Problem of forecasting as it was no longer possible to equate changes in real and money national incomes.
8 May	**5**	**National income estimates for the Economic Survey – M. Barbour and J. Grieve Smith,** 1+11p.

8 May	6	**Stock changes – M.F.W. Hemming and J.C.R. Dow**, 3p. Attempt to estimate inventory profits by a global method consistent with the new balance of payments estimates for 1950 and 1951.
5 Apr	7	**National income and expenditure in the Economic Survey for 1951 – M. Barbour and J. Grieve Smith**, 1+9p. Final estimates for the survey.
20 Apr	8	**Revision of survey tables – M. Barbour and J. Grieve Smith**, 1+6+3p addendum. Assesses the effect of budget changes.
30 Apr	9	**Note by the joint secretaries – M. Barbour and J. Grieve Smith covering P. Redfern**, 1+2p. The extent to which defence expenditure should be classified as fixed capital formation.
23 May	10	**National income forecasting in the U.K. – M. Barbour and J. Grieve Smith**, 1+5p. Final version. Description for the O.E.E.C. of its development and role.
8 June	11	**Model for the national economy in war – J.C.R. Dow**, 1+21p.
14 June	12	**Model for the national economy in war – J.C.R. Dow**, 2p. Sets out questions for discussion arising from NIF(WP)(51)11.
4 July	13	**General economic prospects. Revision of survey national income forecasts – M. Barbour and J. Grieve Smith**, 1+12p. Second revise version.
1 Oct	14	**Summary tables of national income and expenditure 1950–51 – C.S.O.**, 2+3p.
2 Oct	15	**Programme of work – C.T. Saunders**, 1p.
2 Oct	16	**Production prospects in 1952 – J. Grieve Smith and J. Bound covering the C.E.P.S.**, 1+4+2p appendix.
8 Oct	17	**National income forecasts for 1951 and 1952 –J. Grieve Smith and J. Bound**, 5p.
16 Oct	18	**Revised forecasts for 1951 and 1952 – C.S.O.**, 2+3+7p appendixes.
12 Nov	19	**National income and expenditure in 1951 and 1952 – J. Grieve Smith and J. Bound**, 1+6+1p appendix. Prepared for the report on economic prospects for 1952. See CAB 130/71, GEN 380.

15.32 Official Coal Committee (1950–51)

Set up in November 1950, as a result of forebodings in the Ministry of Fuel and Power about an impending fuel crisis, to act as a steering committee for a number of new working parties. It was disbanded at its own suggestion in April 1951 with any residual responsibilities being assumed by other inter-departmental committees.

Terms To assist the Ministry of Fuel and Power in carrying through measures for securing an increased output of coal which required co-operation by other departments, and to keep under review the impact of prospective coal supplies on the government's economic plans.

Members E.N. Plowden (C.E.P.S., ch.); D.B. Pitblado (Try); J.A.R. Pimlott (Ld Pres. O.); G. Ince (Lab. & N.S.); L. Watkinson (Fuel & P.).

Secs. R. Gedling (Cab. O.) and D.O. Henley (Try).

CAB 134/523 Meetings and Memoranda 7 Nov–28 Dec 1950 OCC(50)1st–10th and OCC(50)1–33.

Meetings

7 Nov	**OCC(50)1st:1**	**Procedure.** Agreement to act as a steering committee and to appoint working parties.
	:2	**Manpower in the mines.**
	:3	**Incentives to greater production.** Working parties to be established to consider this, supplementary pensions and additional housing for miners.
	:4	**Other methods of increasing coal stocks.** To be a working party on imports.
	:5	**The possibility of reducing consumption of coal.** To be another working party.
13 Nov	**2nd**	**Import of coal.** The committee agreed to report that the gap between needs and supplies could only be filled by imports.
17 Nov	**3rd**	**Draft statement from the Minister of Fuel and Power.**
20 Nov	**4th:1**	**Import of coal.**
	:2	**Progress made by working parties.**
	:3	**First report by Working Party on Fuel Consumption.** OCC(50)4.
	:4	**First report by the Working Party on Manpower Recruitment and Wastage.** OCC(50)5.
23 Nov	**5th:1**	**Manpower recruitment and wastage.** OCC(50)9.
	:2	**Open-cast coal production.** OCC(50)7.
	:3	**Supplementary pensions for miners.**
	:4	**Import of coal.**
	:5	**Exports.**
	:6	**Allocation of coke.** OCC(50)6.
	:7	**Economy drive.** OCC(50)6.
	:8	**Restrictions on use of fuel oil.**
	:9	**The Samson stripper.**
	:10	**Suggested ban on mid-week sport.** Working party to be established.
28 Nov	**6th:1**	**Houses for miners.** OCC(50)10 and 11.
	:2	**Supplementary pensions for miners.**
	:3	**Manpower recruitment and wastage.**
	:4	**Further measures to reduce wastage and increase production in the short term.**

	:5	**Export of coal.** To discuss with the Treasury the effect of further reductions.
	:6	**Import of coal.**
	:7	**Ban on mid-week sport.**
30 Nov	7th:1	**Coal exports.** Recommendation of a 1m ton reduction unless additional supplies became available.
	:2	**Possibility of reducing consumption of coal.**
	:3	**Priority for power stations.**
	:4	**Recruitment of miners.**
	:5	**Personnel management in the mines.**
9 Dec	8th:1	**Houses for miners.**
	:2	**Statement by the Minister of Fuel and Power.**
15 Dec	9th:1	**European voluntary workers.**
	:2	**Winter coal prospects.** OCC(50)21. Acceptance of paper's forecasts.
	:3	**Mid-week sport.** OCC(50)19.
	:4	**Open-cast coal production.** OCC(50)20.
18 Dec	10th:1	**Release of volunteers from the forces.** OCC(50)29.
	:2	**Second report by the Working Party on Fuel Consumption.** Chairman of the Materials (Allocation) Committee was to work out a scheme for the differential allocation of industrial coal.
	:3	**Personnel management in the mines.** OCC(50)26.
	:4	**Up-grading of miners.**
	:5	**Cost of training unskilled workers.**
	:6	**Samson strippers.** OCC(50)22.
	:7	**Shipping for coal imports.** OCC(50)25. Agreement to drop absolute priority for coal but that the Ministry of Transport should continue to co-ordinate government chartering.

Memoranda

7 Nov	OCC(50)1	**Terms of reference – N. Brook,** 1p.
13 Nov	2	**Additional housing for miners – R. Gedling and D.O. Henley,** 1+4p. Note of a meeting of the working party, 10 Nov 1950.
14 Nov	3	**First report to the Minister of Fuel and Power – R. Gedling and D.O. Henley covering the committee.** 1+4+8p annexes. Interim report submitted because emergency action appeared necessary to forestall serious coal shortages that winter.
18 Nov	4	**First report – Working Party on Fuel Consumption,** 5p.
18 Nov	5	**First report – Working Party on Manpower Recruitment and Wastage in the Coal-mining Industry,** 4p.

21 Nov	6	**Second report to the Minister of Fuel and Power – R. Gedling and D.O. Henley covering the Committee**, 1+1p.
22 Nov	7	**First report – Working Party on Open-cast Coal Production**, 2p.
22 Nov	8	**Report – Working Party on Supplementary Pensions for Miners**, 5+3p annexes.
23 Nov	9	**Second report – Working Party on Manpower Recruitment and Wastage in the Coal-mining Industry**, 2+1p appendix.
25 Nov	10	**Houses for miners – Ministry of Health**, 3p.
27 Nov	11	**Houses for miners – R. Gedling and D.O. Henley covering the N.C.B.**, 1+2+3p.
29 Nov	12	**Supplementary pensions for miners: third report to the Minister of Fuel and Power – R. Gedling and D.O. Henley covering the committee**, 1+2p. The majority considered this would not increase manpower.
29 Nov	13	**First report – Working Party on Imports**, 2p. Consideration of the maximum quantity that would be imported Jan–Mar 1951.
1 Dec	14	**Manpower recruitment and wastage: fourth report to the Minister of Fuel and Power – R. Gedling and D.O. Henley covering the committee**, 1+5+1p.
30 Nov	15	**Open-cast coal: fifth report to the Minister of Fuel and Power – R. Gedling and D.O. Henley covering the committee**, 1+1p.
2 Dec	16	**Sixth report to the Minister of Fuel and Power – R. Gedling and D.O. Henley covering the committee**, 1+2p. Further recommendations to counteract the anticipated shortage which now looked even more serious.
4 Dec	17	**Shipping for coal imports – R. Gedling and D.O. Henley covering the committee**, 1+2+2p. Note of an *ad hoc* inter-departmental meeting and memoranda by E.N. Plowden to ministers.
4 Dec	18	**Present manpower position and outlook for 1951 in the coal-mining industry – Inter-departmental Standing Committee on the Increase of Manpower in the Coal-mining Industry**, 4p.
11 Dec	19	**Report – Working Party on Mid-week Sport**, 5p.
11 Dec	20	**Second report – Working Party on Open-cast Coal Production**, 3+8p annexes.
14 Dec	21	**The winter coal prospects – Ministry of Fuel and Power**, 6p. The unexpected deterioration in stocks since mid-November now meant that there was a 3m ton gap.
15 Dec	22	**Samson strippers – C.E.P.S.**, 2p.
15 Dec	23	**Second report – Working Party on Fuel Consumption**, 10p.

14 Dec	**24**	**Coal: export-import prospects for 1951 –** **Ministry of Fuel and Power,** 4+1p annex. Review of the outlook for the 1951 calendar year to determine quantity available for export.
16 Dec	**25**	**Report to the Official Coal Committee –** **Working Group on Coal Shipments,** 3p.
16 Dec	**26**	**Personnel management in the mines – R.** **Gedling and D.O. Henley covering G. Ince,** 1+1p.
15 Dec	**27**	**First report to the Official Coal Committee –** **Working Party on Fuel Efficiency,** 4p.
16 Dec	**28**	**Report of the Manpower Committee of the** **National Consultative Council for the Coal** **Industry – R. Gedling and D.O. Henley covering** **the Manpower Committee,** 1+5+1p annex.
19 Dec	**29**	**Release of volunteers from the forces – Ministry** **of Labour,** 3p.
19 Dec	**30**	**Coal shipments: seventh report to the Minister** **of Fuel and Power – R. Gedling and D.O. Henley** **covering the committee,** 1+1p.
20 Dec	**31**	**Report of the Publicity Subcommittee of the** **Manpower Committee of the National** **Consultative Council for the Coal Industry – R.** **Gedling and D.O. Henley covering the Publicity** **Subcommittee,** 1+5p.
28 Dec	**32**	**Coal for the power stations and for industry –** **L. Watkinson,** 4p. Impact on industry and power stations of the shortage if temperatures were normal and 2% below normal.
28 Nov	**33**	**Report of the Electricity Subcommittee of the** **N.J.A.C. – R. Gedling and D.O. Henley** **covering the Electricity Subcommittee,** 1+5p.

CAB 134/524   Meetings and Memoranda   1 Jan–7 May 1951   OCC(51)1st–4th
and OCC(51)1–17.

Meetings

3 Jan	**OCC(51)1st:1**	**Export of coal.** OCC(51)1. Further fuel shortages were likely but exports could be cut no further unless the situation deteriorated seriously.
	:2	**Coal for power stations.** OCC(50)32. Priority for power stations should continue until the end of winter.
	:3	**Measures to economize in the use of fuel.**
	:4	**Fuel efficiency.** OCC(50)27.
	:5	**Future work of the committee.**
	:6	**Personnel management in the mines.**
	:7	**Recruitment of miners.**
23 Jan	**2nd:1**	**Houses for miners.** OCC(51)6.

	:2	**Possible reduction in the consumption of fuel.** OCC(51)9. The working party was to examine tariffs.
	:3	**Manpower recruitment.**
	:4	**Personnel management in the mines.**
23 Jan	*ad hoc*	**House coal.** Minute of meeting chaired by Edwards, J. to gain a more precise assessment of the problems.
14 Feb	3rd	**Possible restriction of the consumption of electricity.** OCC(51)11. The working party was to examine this.
16 Apr	4th:1	**The load-limiter electricity tariff.** OCC(51)14 and 15.
	:2	**Manpower recruitment.**
	:3	**Employment of Italian miners.**
	:4	**Personnel management in the mines.**
	:5	**Future of the committee.**

Memoranda

1 Jan	OCC(51)1	**Further reduction of coal exports – Ministry of Fuel and Power,** 2+1p annex. Sets out possible effects.
4 Jan	2	**Third report – Working Party on Open-cast Coal Production,** 2+6p annex.
5 Jan	3	**Further reduction of coal exports. Eighth report to the Minister of Fuel and Power – R. Gedley and D.O. Henley covering the committee,** 1+2p. Recommendation against further cuts.
5 Jan	4	**Street lighting – D.B. Pitblado,** 1p.
13 Jan	5	**House coal – Ministry of Fuel and Power,** 6p. The prospects of obtaining additional supplies from other large coal users.
13 Jan	6	**Houses for miners – working party,** 1+1p.
16 Jan	7	**House coal – Ministry of Transport,** 2p. Criticism of OCC(51)5.
19 Jan	8	**House coal – R. Gedling and D.O. Henley,** 1+3p. Note of an *ad hoc* meeting chaired by Edwards, J. which considered OCC(51)5 and 7.
20 Jan	9	**The problem of restricting domestic consumption of electricity and gas – Ministry of Fuel and Power,** 5+14p annexes. The only effective method was a price increase.
29 Jan	10	**The manpower changes in 1950 and revised estimates for 1951 – Inter-departmental Standing Committee on the Increase of Manpower in the Coal-mining Industry,** 2p.
9 Feb	11	**Maintenance of power station stocks. Restriction on consumption of electricity – Ministry of Fuel and Power,** 2+5p annex. Possible restrictions.
15 Feb	12	**Possible restriction of the consumption of electricity – R. Gedling,** 1+5p. Note of an *ad*

hoc meeting of officials, 14 Feb 1951, which considered OCC(51)11.

22 Feb	13	**Emergency plan to conserve electricity supplies: eighth report to the Minister of Fuel and Power** – the committee, 4p.
31 Mar	14	**The load-limiter electricity tariff: report by the Working Party on Fuel Efficiency and Electricity Tariffs** – R. Gedling, 1+5+15p annex. Also OCC(FE)(WP)(51)3.
14 Apr	15	**The load-limiter electricity tariff. Suggested amendments to the draft report to ministers** – Ministry of Fuel and Power, 2p.
5 May	16	**The load-limiter electricity tariff: report to the Minister of Fuel and Power** – the committee, 8p.
7 May	17	**Report to the Minister of Fuel and Power** – the committee, 2p. Covering note to OCC(51)16.

15.33   Productivity (Official) Committee

Set up in August 1948 by E.E. Bridges, with the approval of the Lord President and Chancellor of the Exchequer after the Economic Policy Committee (CAB 134/216, EPC(48)27th:3) had asked the Government Organization Committee (CAB 134/307, GOC(48)4th:1 and GOC(48)23) to make necessary preparations for the Cabinet's campaign to increase productivity. Its purpose was to work under the Production Committee (CAB 134/635–652) to co-ordinate the production departments' drive to ensure the application to specific industries of the most up to date knowledge, thereby allowing the Committee on Industrial Productivity (CAB 132/28–30) to concentrate on scientific problems. After the submission of its report to the Production Committee in September 1949 (CAB 134/642, PC(49)96) it largely lay dormant, see CAB 21/2500.

Terms   To advise on measures to secure higher industrial productivity; and to co-ordinate the activities of government departments in this field.

Members   E.A. Hitchman (C.E.P.S., ch); E.M. Nicholson (Ld Pres. O.); S.C. Leslie (Ec. Info. Unit); L.H. Robinson (Supply); C.H.S. de Peyer (Fuel & P.); G.B. Blaker (Try); M.D. Tennant (Lab. & N.S.); S.A.ff. Dakin (B.T.); O.F. Brown (D.S.I.R.);   (Sept 1948) A.F. Ewing (Works) added.   (Oct 1948) J.A. Diack (Lab. & N.S.) replaced Tennant.   (Dec 1948) E. Whitehead (Ec. Info. Unit) replaced Leslie.   (Mar 1949) T. Brockie (Works) replaced Ewing.

Secs.   J.G. Stewart (Cab. O.), S. Day (Try), J. Frost (B.T.).   (Jan 1949) E.L. Sykes (Cab. O.) replaced Stewart.   (Dec 1949) P.J. Moorhouse (Cab. O.) replaced Sykes.   (Mar 1950) D.R. Williams (Try) replaced Day.

CAB 134/591   Meetings and Memoranda   26 Aug–18 Dec 1948   OP(48)1st–8th and OP(48)1–22.

Meetings

2 Sept	**OP(48)1st:1**	**Composition and terms of reference.** OP(48)1.

	:2	**Changes in productivity in British industry.** OP(48)2.
	:3	**Organization of the committee's work.** Definition of factors concerned in increasing productivity and discussion of productivity in nationalized industries.
	:4	**Publicity about higher productivity.** OP(48)3. Consideration of the section of the report dealing with individual industries particularly coal and cotton.
14 Oct	2nd:1	**C.I.P. (Panel on Technology and Operational Research).** OP(48)8. No decision on its future.
	:2	**Departmental functions in relation to productivity.** E.A. Hitchman summarized departments' different reactions to the suggestion that they should accept responsibility to disseminate knowledge of best techniques.
	:3	**Division of functions between the Ministry of Labour and Production Departments in the field of labour relations.**
3 Nov	3rd:1	**The business of the committee.** OP(48)10.
	:2	**Productivity in the socialized industries.**
	:3	**Activities of the Board of Trade.** OP(48)10 annex 14. Consideration in detail, in particular of the production efficiency service.
	:4	**Activities of the Ministry of Fuel and Power.** OP(48)10 annex 7.
11 Nov	4th:1	**Development councils.**
	:2	**Statistics on productivity.** L. Rostas described progress on the compilation of productivity figures and discussion of their publication.
	:3	**Government organization for industrial productivity. Activities of the Department of Scientific and Industrial Research.** OP(48)10 annex 10a. Consideration also of the information services of the Research Association.
	:4	**Further meetings.** OP(48)10.
17 Nov	5th:2	**Government organization for industrial productivity. Activities of the Admiralty.** OP(48)10 annex 2.
	:3	**Government organization for industrial productivity – activities of the Ministry of Supply.** OP(48)10 annex 13. Consideration of the engineering and iron and steel industries. Agreement that the steel industry's efficiency was high.
19 Nov	6th:1	**Government organization for industrial productivity: activities of the Ministry of Labour.** OP(48)10 annex 9. Consideration by section.

	:2	**Government organization for industrial productivity: activities of the Ministry of Works.** OP(48)10 annex 16.
24 Nov	7th:1	**Government organization for industrial productivity: activities of the Ministry of Agriculture and Scottish Department of Agriculture.** OP(48)10 annexes 3 and 12.
	:2	**Government organization for industrial productivity: activities of the Ministry of Food.** OP(48)10 annex 6.
26 Nov	8th:1	**Future work of the committee: outstanding action by departments.** OP(48)12.
	:2	**Government organization for industrial productivity: activities of the General Post Office.** OP(48)10 annex 11.
	:3	**Government organization for industrial productivity: activities of the Ministry of Education and the Scottish Education Department.** OP(48)10 annex 5.
	:4	**Government organization for industrial productivity: activities of the Treasury.** OP(48)10 annex 1. L. Rostas felt that comparison of British and U.S.A. depreciation allowances might not support the suggestion that productivity was so closely related to fiscal policy.

Memoranda

26 Aug	**OP(48)1**	**Composition and terms of reference – W.S. Murrie,** 1p.
27 Aug	2	**Changes in productivity in British industry – E.A. Hitchman covering L. Rostas,** 1+7p annexes. Draft article for *The Times*.
31 Aug	3	**Publicity about higher productivity – Economic Information Unit,** 5+11p annex. Sections on the general public, industry in general and particular industries. Draft brief to assist the planning of ministerial speeches annexed.
31 Aug	4	**Organization of the committee's work – E.A. Hitchman,** 1+7p annex. GOC(48)22 had identified three main factors concerned in increasing productivity: technical, managerial and labour efficiency. The committee should review and update the activities of government departments on this basis.
21 Sept	5	**Factors concerned in increasing productivity – J.G. Stewart, S. Day and J. Frost,** 1p. Revised statement, adding the provision of conditions for efficient working.
21 Sept	6	**Industrial productivity – J.G. Stewart, S. Day and J. Frost,** 1+1p. Extract from PC(48)18th.

28 Sept	**7**	**Membership of the committee – J.G. Stewart, S. Day and J. Frost**, 1p.
12 Oct	**8**	**Panel on technology and operational research of the Committee on Industrial Productivity. Future of the work done by this panel – J.G. Stewart covering H. Tizard**, 1+4+2p appendix.
19 Oct	**9**	**Membership of the committee – J.G. Stewart**, 1p.
30 Oct	**10**	**Existing departmental activities and organization for the promotion of industrial productivity – E.A. Hitchman**, 1+80p annexes. Annex I – Treasury. Annex II – Admiralty. Annex III – Ministry of Agriculture and Fisheries. Annexes IV, VIII, XI, XII – Ministries of Civil Aviation and Health, the General Post Office and the Scottish Office. Annex V – Ministry of Education and Scottish Education Department. Annex VI – Ministry of Food. Annex VII – Ministry of Fuel and Power. Responsibility for coal lay with the N.C.B. Annex IX – Ministry of Labour. Annex X (A) – Department of Scientific and Industrial Research. Annex XIII – Ministry of Supply, covering the engineering and iron and steel industries. Annex XIV – Board of Trade. Annex XV – Ministry of Transport, including reports from port authorities on improvements in output and shipping performance to the Working Party on the Turnround of Shipping. Annex XVI – Ministry of Works.
25 Nov	**11**	**Human factors involved in industrial productivity – S. Day**, 2p. List as drawn up by the Committee on Industrial Productivity Working Party for the panel on human factors.
25 Nov	**12**	**Future work of the committee: outstanding action by departments – J.G. Stewart**, 1+2p. **List of principal conclusions requiring action.**
10 Dec	**13**	**Dissemination of results of D.S.I.R. work – D.S.I.R.** 10p.
4 Dec	**14**	**Productivity in the socialized industries – J.G. Stewart covering the Ministry of Civil Aviation**, 1+2p. Suggestions for the air transport industry.
4 Dec	**15**	**Membership of the committee – J.G. Stewart**, 1p.
8 Dec	**16**	**Productivity in the socialized industries – J.G. Stewart covering First Lord of the Admiralty**, 1+10p. Productivity in Admiralty industrial establishments.
14 Dec	**17**	**Measures, taken or planned, to promote productivity in the Royal Ordnance factories – Ministry of Supply**, 1+2+2p.

9 Sept	18	**Productivity in the socialized industries – J.G. Stewart covering the Postmaster General,** 1+5+51p. Productivity in the Post Office.
10 Dec	19	**Productivity in the socialized industries – J.G. Stewart covering the Minister of Works,** 1+2p. Industrial productivity in the mobile labour force.
15 Dec	20	**Action being taken by the Ministry of Food to promote operational research into distribution – J.G. Stewart covering the Ministry of Food,** 1+1p.
16 Dec	21	**Productivity in the socialized industries – J.G. Stewart covering the British Transport Commission,** 1+3p.
18 Dec	22	**Getting knowledge to the farmer – Ministry of Agriculture and Fisheries,** 4p.

CAB 134/592   Meetings and Memoranda   4 Jan–30 Dec 1949   OP(49)1st–11th and OP(49)1–50.

Meetings

17 Mar	**OP(49)1st:1**	**Draft first report of the committee.** OP(49)7.
	:2	**Date of further meetings.**
24 Mar	**2nd:1**	**Draft first report of the committee.** OP(49)7.
	:2	**Next meeting.**
26 Apr	**3rd:1**	**Draft first report.** OP(49)7, 10, 11, 13, 14, 15, 16. Detailed consideration of proposed amendments. Departments differed considerably in their assessment of the value of scientific and technical officers.
	:2	**Aspects of motion study.** OP(49)5.
	:3	**Information and publicity services of the research associations.** OP(49)6.
28 Apr	**4th:1**	**Draft first report.** OP(49)7, 8, 10, 11, 13, 14, 15, 16. Continued consideration.
	:2	**Next meeting.**
18 May	**5th**	**Draft first report.** OP(49)8, 17, 20, 21, 22. Detailed consideration of OP(49)17.
2 June	**6th:1**	**Draft first report.** OP(49)17. Continued consideration.
	:2	**Future programme of work.**
8 June	**7th**	**Draft first report.** OP(49)8, 17, 20.
20 June	**8th:1**	**Minutes of previous meeting.**
	:2	**Draft first report.** OP(49)26 and 27.
26 Aug	**9th**	**Productivity publicity.** OP(49)30.
30 Sept	**10th:2**	**U.S. technical assistance and U.K. industrial productivity.** OP(49)33. Consideration of the proposals by item.
	:3	**Relationship between the U.K. government and the Anglo-American Council.** Agreement that the existing policy of non-intervention be

		maintained, but closer liaison and consultation were desirable.
9 Nov	**11th:1**	**Technical journalism in the U.K. – need for a journal of management and productivity.** OP(49)36.
	:2	**U.S. technical assistance and U.K. industrial productivity.** OP(49)35, 37, 40.
	:3	**Self-help in U.K. industry.** OP(49)38.
	:4	**Measures taken to stimulate productivity in the U.K.** OP(49)39.

Memoranda

4 Jan	**OP(49)1**	**Types of liaison arrangements between D.S.I.R. stations and research associations, and government departments – D.S.I.R.,** 8+5p appendixes.
10 Jan	**2**	**Change in secretariat – E.L. Sykes, S. Day and J. Frost,** 1p.
12 Jan	**3**	**Personnel management advisory service. Relations with production efficiency service – Ministry of Labour and the Board of Trade,** 2p. Possibility of closer contact.
25 Jan	**4**	**Action to improve productivity in the coal industry – National Coal Board,** 8+48p. Sets out measures taken. 'Guide to Consultation' attached.
28 Jan	**5**	**Aspects of method study – E.A. Hitchman** covering the Board of Trade, 1+2p.
9 Feb	**6**	**Information and publicity services of the research associations – E.L. Sykes, S. Day and J. Frost,** 1+2p. Note of a meeting, 10 Dec 1948.
11 Mar	**7**	**First report of the committee – E.L. Sykes, S. Day and J. Frost covering the committee,** 1+24p. Draft of OP(49)17. Recommended measures to galvanize government departments, both generally and individually.
14 Mar	**8**	**Publicity about productivity – E.L. Sykes, S. Day and J. Frost covering the Economic Information Unit,** 1+6p. Review of existing measures and prospects.
22 Mar	**9**	**Change in membership – E.L. Sykes, S. Day and J. Frost,** 1p.
22 Mar	**10**	**Amendment to the draft first report – E.L. Sykes, S. Day and J. Frost,** 1+4p.
28 Mar	**11**	**Amendments to the draft first report (2nd series) – E.L. Sykes, S. Day and J. Frost,** 1+7p annexes.
30 Mar	**12**	**Action outstanding on OP(49)7 – E.L. Sykes, S. Day and J. Frost,** 2p.
4–25 Apr	**13–16**	**Amendments to the draft first report – E.L. Sykes, S. Day and J. Frost.**

9 May	**17**	**Draft first report (revised text) – E.L. Sykes, S. Day and J. Frost covering the committee,** 1+28p. Draft of OP(49)26.
10 May	**18**	**Government organization for industrial productivity: General Post Office – E.L. Sykes, S. Day and J. Frost covering the G.P.O.,** 1+16p.
12 May	**19**	**Circulation of statistical papers on productivity trends and of occasional research papers relating to productivity problems – Board of Trade,** 1+2p annexes.
12 May	**20**	**Draft first report – E.A. Hitchman,** 1+4p annex. Conclusions and recommendations to be added to OP(49)17.
13 May	**21**	**Note by the joint secretaries – E.L. Sykes, S. Day and J. Frost,** 1+19p. First annual report of the Advisory Council on Scientific Policy (1947–1948), Cmd. 7465.
16 May	**22**	**Draft first report – E.L. Sykes, S. Day and J. Frost,** 1+2p annexes. Two revised sections.
31 May	**23**	**Draft first report – E.L. Sykes, S. Day and J. Frost,** 1+8p. Redraft of the section dealing with production departments which sponsored privately-owned industries.
31 May	**24**	**Draft first report (2nd revision) – E.L. Sykes, S. Day and J. Frost,** 1+8p. Revised text of introduction and section on departments with general responsibility for nationalized industries.
7 June	**25**	**Management for Production – E.L. Sykes, S. Day and J. Frost covering the British Institute of Management,** 1+47p. Institute handbook.
16 June	**26**	**Draft first report – E.L. Sykes, S. Day and J. Frost covering the committee,** 1+35+13p annexes. Draft of OP(49)31.
18 June	**27**	**Proposed amendments to OP(49)26 – unsigned,** 1p.
5 Aug	**28**	**Note by the chairman – E.A. Hitchman,** 1+2p. Note of a discussion between Wilson, K.M. Nowell, Mr. Balfour and S.C. Leslie, 28 July 1949, to consider a plan for intensified productivity publicity in the autumn.
25 Aug	**29**	**Note by the joint secretaries – E.L Sykes, S. Day and J. Frost covering the Board of Trade,** 1+1+7+12p. Also BTS(G)(49)2(revise). Changes in productivity in 1948 and the first quarter of 1949.
30 Aug	**30**	**Productivity publicity – E.L. Sykes, S. Day and J. Frost covering the committee,** 1+4p. Revise version. Report to Wilson on autumn campaign.

3 Sept	31	**First report – E.L. Sykes, S. Day and J. Frost covering the committee, 1+28+8p** annexes. See PC(49)96.
8 Sept	32	**Future work of the Committee on Industrial Productivity – E.L. Sykes, S. Day and J. Frost covering G.B. Blaker, 1+5p.** Virtually a proposal for abolition.
27 Sept	33	**U.S. technical assistance and U.K. industrial productivity – E.L. Sykes, S. Day and J. Frost, 1+6+3+1p.** Letter from Sir Sydney Caine enclosing U.S. proposals, and note of a meeting, 22 Sept 1949, to consider it and extract from ER(L)(49)64th.
3 Oct	34	**Note by the joint secretaries – E.L. Sykes, S. Day and J. Frost covering the E.C.A. mission, London, 1+1p.** On the work of the Anglo-American Council on Productivity.
6 Oct	35	**Note by the Treasury – Treasury, 2p.** List of additional sectors of industry which might benefit by the despatch of a productivity team to the U.S.A.
31 Oct	36	**Technical journalism in the U.K. – E.L. Sykes, S. Day and J. Frost covering the Economic Information Unit and the Office of the Lord President, 1+3+3p** appendixes. Financial assistance recommended for the British Institute of Management to provide a management production journal.
1 Nov	37	**U.S. technical assistance and U.K. industrial productivity – E.L. Sykes, S. Day and J. Frost, 1+6p.** Note of the meeting of officials with representatives of the U.K. section of the Anglo-American Council, 5 Oct 1949, to consider U.S. proposals.
3 Nov	38	**Self-help in U.K. industry – E.L. Sykes, S. Day and J. Frost covering the Treasury, 1+6p.**
4 Nov	39	**Measures taken to stimulate productivity in the U.K. – E.L. Sykes, S. Day and J. Frost covering the Board of Trade, 1+6p.** Description of the administrative bodies and organization set up to promote productivity.
8 Nov	40	**U.S. technical assistance and U.K. industrial productivity – Treasury, 2p.**
10 Nov	41	**U.S. technical assistance – E.L. Sykes, S. Day and J. Frost covering A.L. Moffat, 1+1p.**
17 Nov	42	**Note by the joint secretaries – E.L. Sykes, S. Day and J. Frost covering the Board of Trade, 1+1+1+3p.** Also BTS(G)(49)3. Changes in productivity in British industry in the first half of 1949.

22 Nov	43	**U.S. technical assistance – E.L. Sykes, S. Day and J. Frost covering the E.C.A. mission, London,** 1+1p.
25 Nov	44	**U.S. technical assistance and U.K. industrial productivity – E.L. Sykes, S. Day and J. Frost covering A. King.** 1p.
23 Nov	45	**U.S. technical assistance: sterling counterpart requirements – E.L. Sykes, S. Day and J. Frost covering the Treasury,** 1+3p.
3 Dec	46	**Note by the joint secretaries – E.L. Sykes, S. Day and J. Frost,** 1+12p appendixes. Note of a meeting of an *ad hoc* working party of the Productivity (Official) Committee, 23 Nov 1949, to prepare a paper for the London Committee on visits of combined European productivity teams to the U.S.A. and of European teams to the U.K. The paper, as approved by the London Committee, is included.
8 Dec	47	**Technical assistance – E.L. Sykes, S. Day and J. Frost covering the Treasury,** 1+5p. Provision of American technical services to assist reductions in cost in British industry.
19 Dec	48	**Visits of European productivity teams to the U.K. – E.L. Sykes, S. Day and J. Frost covering the Treasury and the Foreign Office,** 1+3+3p annex.
28 Dec	49	**Technical assistance – E.L. Sykes, S. Day and J. Frost,** 1+4p. Note of a meeting, 21 Dec 1949, to consider OP(49)47.
28 Dec	50	**Technical assistance – E.L. Sykes, S. Day and J. Frost,** 1+2+1p annex. Note of a meeting of an *ad hoc* working party of the Productivity (Official) Committee, 12 Dec 1949.
30 Dec		**Change in secretariat – E.L. Sykes, S. Day and J. Frost,** 1p.

CAB 134/593   Meetings and Memoranda   3 Jan 1950–16 Mar 1951   OP(51)1st and OP(50)1–OP(51)1.

Meeting

| 16 Mar | **OP(51)1st** | **Mutual aid in industry.** OP(51)1. Agreement that a government initiative to extend industrial mutual aid groups would be untimely if increased productivity were to be presented as one of the main purposes of the groups. |

Memoranda

| 3 Jan | **OP(50)1** | **Productivity teams – Treasury,** 2p. List of teams from U.K. industry which had visited or were about to visit the U.S.A. |

4 Jan		2	**Combined European technical assistance projects – P.J. Moorhouse, S. Day and J. Frost covering the E.C.A. mission, London,** 1+1+2p.
19 Jan		3	**General considerations on the planning of technical assistance projects – P.J. Moorhouse, S. Day and J. Frost covering the Secretary General to the Council of the O.E.E.C.,** 1+12+2p annexes.
25 Jan		4	**Subjects proposed for technical assistance – P.J. Moorhouse, S. Day and J. Frost covering a working party of the Council of the O.E.E.C.,** 1+1+32p appendixes.
8 Feb		5	**Composition and terms of reference of the Subcommittee on Technical Assistance– E.A. Hitchman,** 2p. Also TA(L)(50)1.
23 Feb		6	**Note by the joint secretaries – P.J. Moorhouse, S. Day and J. Frost covering the Board of Trade,** 1+1+1+3p. Also BTS(G)(50)1. Changes in productivity of British industry in the third quarter of 1949.
3 Mar		7	**Change in secretariat – P.J. Moorhouse, D.R. Williams and J. Frost,** 1p.
8 June		8	**Note by the joint secretaries – P.J. Moorhouse, D.R. Williams and J. Frost covering the Board of Trade,** 1+1+3p. Also BTS(G)(50)2. Changes in productivity in British industry in 1949.
11 Nov		9	**Note by the Board of Trade – Board of Trade,** 1+1+16+7p. Also BTS(G)(50)3(revise). Changes in productivity in British industry in 1949 and 1950. Discusses the meaning and significance of overall productivity measurements and updates the estimated changes in output, employment and output per head in selected British industries in 1949 and the first six months of 1950.
13 Mar	OP(51)1		**Mutual aid in industry – P.J Moorhouse and D.R. Williams covering the Information Division of the Treasury,** 1+2p. Proposals for improvement and extension of mutual aid.

15.34 Programmes Committee

Set up in June 1948 during the reorganization of inter-departmental committees concerned with the European Recovery Programme following the establishment of the O.E.E.C., see CAB 129/27, CP(48)137. It absorbed the European Economic Co-operation (London) Committee Programmes Subcommittee and the Exchange Requirements Committee (CAB 134/258–261), and the Accounting Working Party of the European Economic Co-operation (London) Committee became its subcommittee. It met regularly, especially in 1948–49, to take many detailed decisions but membership was kept fluid owing to the frequent absence of key members from Whitehall. Its later papers are in CAB 134/1123–1133.

It received a Monthly Report on Import Commodities Price Movements (later renamed Monthly Report on World Market Prices of Import Commodities) prepared by the C.S.O. and Economic Section and abbreviated below to Monthly Report. It also received many memoranda on other countries' long-term programmes, not cited below.

Terms (i) to collate all programmes of production, consumption, imports, exports, balance of payments, etc., which are to be submitted to the Organization for European Economic Co-operation (ii) where the collation of these programmes shows a need for new decisions of policy affecting more than one department, to arrange for these decisions to be taken (subject to ministerial authority where necessary) either by the committee itself or where appropriate by other inter-departmental committees (e.g. the Investment Programmes Committee or Exports Committee) (iii) to advise the Treasury on authorization to departments for expenditure of foreign exchange (iv) to carry out the existing functions of the Exchange Requirements Committee in relation to bilateral negotiations conducted by the Overseas Negotiations Committee (v) to record progress against the programmes submitted, and to arrange for corrective action and modification accordingly.

Members R.W.B. Clarke (Try, ch.); E. Roll (C.E.P.S. v–ch. for programmes to O.E.C.C.) and M.T. Flett (Try, v–ch. for exchange requirements); representatives of F.O., Ec. Sect., B.T., Food, Ag. & Fish, Supply, Fuel & P., Transport, and others where appropriate. (Jan 1949) J.R. Willis (C.E.P.S.) and A.C. Sparks (Try), new v–ch. (Jan 1950) Pitblado replaced Willis. (Sept 1951) J.A.C. Robertson (C.E.P.S) and E. Jones (Try), new v–ch.

Secs. T.G. Charlton (Cab. O.), P.J. Moorhouse (Cab. O.), G.H. van Loo (Try), A.K. Ogilvy Webb (C.E.P.S.). (Mar 1949) Charlton left. (Apr 1950) R.B. Marshall (Cab. O.) replaced Collyer. (July 1950) J.A. Atkinson (Cab. O.) replaced Marshall.

CAB 134/608 Meetings 8 June–17 Dec 1948 P(48)1st–49th.

8 June	**P(48)1st:1**	**Organization.** R.W.B. Clarke set out the functions of the Committee as outlined in CP(48)137.
	:2	**Preparation for the annual programme from 1 July 1948 to 30 June 1949.** PR(48)20(revise). R.W.B. Clarke set out the proposed timetable.
15 June	**2nd:1**	**The 1948/49 programme for submission to the O.E.E.C.**
	:2	**Cotton purchases from the U.S.A.**
	:3	**Amendments to April/June quarter programme.**
	:4	**Temporary waiver of documentation.**
22 June	**3rd:1**	**Completion of forms for the annual programme.** P(48)4. Agreement that departments should adhere to figures contained in current bilateral agreements even if they were now deemed to be unrealistic.
	:2	**Organization of the Committee.** R.W.B. Clarke set out the work of three subcommittees to take

		over the detailed work of the Exchange Requirements Committee.
	:3	**Timetable for the annual programme.** P(48)2.
	:4	**Report to ministers on the annual programme.** P(48)3. Approval of P(48)3 as a suitable framework for the submission to the Economic Policy Committee on the annual programme.
29 June	4th:1	**Organization of the Committee.**
	:2	**Issues emerging from the completed O.E.E.C. forms and requiring decisions by ministers.**
	:3	**Organization for writing memoranda.** Discussion on whether the export of capital goods should be increased to ensure that necessary supplies of food and raw materials were obtained, or decreased in order that U.K. industry could be re-equipped more rapidly and thereby leading to an increase in exports.
	:4	**Future programme of work.**
1 July	5th:1	**Preparation of the annual programme 1948/49.** Agreement that the Committee should concentrate on the budget programme in order to arrive at a total programme of $1270m. This programme would then have to be re-examined with a view to reducing the total to $1160m, which was the amount of aid which the U.K. would receive on a realistic basis and which would form the basis of the interim import programme as recommended to ministers. Consideration of the problems in compiling a budget programme and the requirements programme, and the need to demonstrate the extent to which the difference between the two contributed to our long-term recovery. Agreement on the criteria for the requirements programme and then consideration of the additional items to be included in the dollar requirements import programme.
	:2	**Future programme of work.**
2 July	6th:1	**Dollar balance of payments.**
	:2	**Table III commodities.** Consideration item by item.
	:3	**Non-dollar balance of payments.** Consideration of the overall U.K. balance of payments estimates on the budget basis and the U.K. position with each geographical area. Agreement that it should be recommended to ministers that present policy *vis-à-vis* the rest of the sterling area should be re-examined.
	:5	**Future programme of work.**
5 July	7th:1	**Draft report on the dollar programme.** P(48)8. Consideration by paragraphs and approval subject to agreed amendments.

	:2	**Draft report on commodity programmes.** P(48)10. Consideration by paragraphs.
	:3	**Draft covering memoranda.** P(48)9. Concern that the paper gave a too optimistic view of the U.K. economic position resulting from the import programme on a budget basis.
6 July	8th:1	**Progress preparation of documents.** R.W.B. Clarke set out the progress in amendment of P(48)8, 9, 10.
	:2	**Non-dollar balance of payments.** P(48)11. R.W.B. Clarke felt that ministers should be warned of the general trends of the policy of bilateral agreements supplemented by increasing purchases from non-dollar sources. Consideration by paragraphs.
	:3	**Date of next meeting.**
9 July	9th:1	**Submission to ministers on the annual programme.** CP(48)177 and 178.
	:2	**Consideration of outstanding points on annual programme for submission to Paris.** R.W.B. Clarke set out the outstanding questions with regard to both policy and mechanics.
13 July	10th:1	**Submission to ministers on the annual programme.**
	:2	**Balance of payments with other participating countries.** P(48)13.
	:3	**Completion of table IV.**
	:4	**Additional break-down of food imports from the third quarter programme.**
	:5	**Future programme of work.**
15 July	11th:1	**Long-term programme.** P(48)15. Detailed consideration of the preparation of the programme.
	:2	**Programme for 1949/50.**
19 July	12th:1	**Non-dollar import policy.** P(48)16.
	:2	**Tobacco purchases.**
	:3	**Long-term programme.** P(48)15(revise) and 18.
	:4	**Programme for 1949/50.** P(48)19. C.E.P.S. would consider the possibility of arranging for major planning to be done on the basis of the July to June year. R.W.B. Clarke said that the programme had to be on a requirements basis but that the definition of requirements presented some difficulty: from the 1952/1953 picture the level of food consumption would be below that of 1946/1947 and it seemed difficult to justify a higher level for 1949/1950.
	:5	**Balance of payments with participating countries.** P(48)14.
	:6	**Items to be included in the loan programme.**
23 July	13th:1	**Third quarter programme.** P(48)25.
	:2	**Fourth quarter programme.** P(48)26.

29 July	**14th:1**	**Third quarter 1948 programme.**
	:2	**Programme for 1949/1950.** M.T. Flett reported the criticisms of the European Economic Co-operation Committee of ER(L)(48)49, which was a revised version of P(48)19. It had been agreed that the 1949/50 programme had to be comparable with the 1952/53 picture, as the E.C.A. was anxious that it should appear as the first step in a four-year plan.
	:3	**Long-term programme.**
	:4	**Annual programme.** R.W.B. Clarke reported that it had been agreed at Paris that the programming procedure should be simplified and that quarterly programming through the O.E.E.C. was to be abandoned except in regard to the commodities in short supply, which would be allocated by the vertical committees, and a simple statement of the intra-European balance of payments.
6 Aug	**15th:1**	**Long-term programme.** R.W.B. Clarke set out the basis, as agreed by the Council of the O.E.E.C., on which the programme was to be drawn up. In particular, there had been lengthy discussion of the price assumptions of the programme. The submission date would also cause problems as only provisional figures would be available for some commodities, in particular steel.
	:2	**Procurements from Canada.** P(48)28.
	:3	**The 1949–50 programme.**
	:4	**Third quarter 1948 programme.**
16 Aug	**16th:1**	**Activity in August and September.** P(48)22. CE(48)52. Consideration of the revised annual programme 1948/49 and the basis on which it should be drawn up. Consideration then of the 1949/50 programme and of the fourth quarter programme.
	:2	**Export of bananas to Belgium.**
	:3	**U.S. surplus agricultural products.**
	:4	**Microfilm copies of other participating countries' returns on the 1948/49 programme.**
24 Aug	**17th:1**	**Microfilm copies of other participating countries' returns on the 1948/49 programme.**
	:2	**Second interim report of the Subcommittee on Accounting Procedure.** P(48)30.
	:3	**Activities in Aug and Sept: timetable.** P(48)32. Agreement on the timetable for the long-term programme, the 1949/50 programme, the 1948/49 programme and the fourth quarter 1948 programme.
	:4	**Revised programme for 1948/49.**

	:5	**Third quarter programme.** The Treasury was to revise the programme.
26 Aug	18th:1	**The 1948/49 annual programme.**
	:2	**Long-term programme.** P(48)33. Conclusion that the estimated net income of the balance of payments was $8.4b, so that an import programme of $7.9b could be afforded, although there was a need to switch purchases to the sterling area. Detailed consideration of the import programmes in P(48)33 on this basis. Agreement to amend the programmes for food, dollar raw materials and manufactured goods from other participating countries.
30 Aug	19th	**Long-term programme 1952/3.** P(48)36. Agreement to cut import programme to allow an increase in net overseas investment. Consideration by paragraphs.
31 Aug	20th	**1948/49 programme.** P(48)38. Subject to Foreign Office reservation, it was agreed to prepare the programme on a basis somewhat higher than the allocation of aid, the difference being shown as 'provision for over-programming'. Agreement on the items to be included on E.R.P. financing.
1 Sept	21st	**Long-term programme.** P(48)36. Consideration of departmental amendments item by item, although R.W.B. Clarke pointed out that it would be difficult to implement the proposed alterations as the paper had already gone forward and policy decisions were being taken. Also the alterations would result in net overseas investment below both what was previously envisaged and what the Treasury felt was desirable.
3 Sept	22nd:1	**Fourth quarter 1948 programme.**
	:2	**U.S. surpluses.**
	:3	**The 1948 loan programme.** P(48)32. Agreement on the loan programme for the second quarter.
	:4	**Third quarter programme.** P(48)41. Agreement on the grant and loan programmes for the third quarter.
	:5	**The 1949/50 programme.** Consideration of the balance of payments tables in relation to the 1948/49 programme.
	:6	**Long-term programme.**
	:7	**Present position on meetings of vertical committees in Paris.**
6 Sept	23rd:1	**The 1949/50 import programme.** Continued consideration of departmental programmes in order to determine a programme which could

be defended in relation to the 1949/50 appropriations being mentioned by the E.C.A.

:2 **Fourth quarter programme.** Agreement on the constituents of the loan programme.

:3 **Treatment of U.S. surpluses in relation to annual programme.**

7 Sept   24th:1   **The 1949/50 programme. Consideration of the balance of payments estimate in relation to each geographical area.**

:2 **Revised programming procedure.**

8 Sept   25th:1   **The 1949/50 programme.** P(48)46. Agreement of cuts in the food and raw materials programmes, and of other amendments.

:2 **Revised programming procedure.** ER(W)(48)22.

:3 **Tobacco.**

:4 **Balance of payments with Canada.**

:5 **Future timetable for the committee.**

9 Sept   26th   **Canada.** P(48)47. Agreement on several amendments to the draft report prior to its submission to the London Committee.

13 Sept   27th:1   **Progress report on the production of the programmes.** Statement by R.W.B. Clarke on the position with regard to the 1949/50 annual programme and the revised 1948/49 programme.

:2 **The 1948/49 balance of payments table.** P(48)48. Agreement to recommend additions to the import programme totalling $24.5m. Agreement on the items to be earmarked for E.R.P. financing.

:3 **Revised prices of U.S. commodities.** P(48)49.

14 Sept   28th   **Revised annual programme 1948/49.** P(48)50 and 51. Approval to some amendments.

17 Sept   29th:1   **Individual country programmes.**

:2 **Rice supplies: South East Asia.** SEAF(48)36.

:3 **Revised 1948/49 programme: procedure at the O.E.E.C.** ER(L)(48)103.

:4 **The O.I.T. questionnaire for the first quarter of 1949.**

21 Sept   30th:1   **Revised 1948/49 programme: procedure at the O.E.E.C.**

:2 **Completion of forms for the 1949/50 programme and the long-term programme.**

:3 **Fourth quarter programme.** Agreement on the additional items to make up the import programme of $591m.

4: **Long-term import programme from Australia.** Detailed consideration of U.K. import programme from Australia for 1948/49, 1949/50 and 1952/53.

	:5	**New Zealand.** Detailed consideration of U.K. import programme from New Zealand for 1948/49, 1949/50 and 1952/53.
	:6	**Revised 1948/49 programme.**
23 Sept	31st:1	**Fourth quarter programme.**
	:2	**Colonial imports for inclusion in the E.R.P. programme for the first and second quarters of 1949.**
	:3	**Tables for 1952/53 programme.** Examination of long-term programme to ensure that no information of commercial importance would be discussed.
	:4	**Tables for 1949/50 programme.**
	:5	**The 1949/50 programme procedure in the O.E.E.C.** There were three issues to consider: the method of handling the forms on arrival in Paris; what the U.K. hoped would result from the O.E.E.C. deliberations; and the way in which the O.E.E.C. was to treat the sum total of bids.
	:6	**Long-term import programme for France.** P(48)57 annex 3. Detailed consideration.
27 Sept	32nd:1	**The 1949/50 and long-term programmes: procedure in the O.E.E.C.** P(48)59. Consideration of paragraphs.
28 Sept	33rd:1	**Tobacco purchases for the period July/Sept 1948.** R.W.B. Clarke cited this as another example of U.S. interests attempting to force the U.K. to spend E.R.P. dollars on unwanted commodities.
	:2	**The 1949/50 programme.** P(48)60. Awareness that the returns under O.E.E.C. table III, detailing import programmes by commodities and country groups, disclosed some commercial secrets. Agreement on remedy.
	:3	**Brief for the ministerial meeting of the O.E.E.C. Council.**
	:4	**Estimated 1952/53 balance of payments of individual countries.** Agreement that examination on the lines of the one with Australia and New Zealand should not yet be carried out with other Commonwealth countries.
	:5	**Summary programmes for the Commonwealth countries.** P(48)62.
	:6	**Revised 1948/49 programme: imports from non-dollar sources.**
5 Oct	34th:1	**Brief for ministerial meeting of the O.E.E.C. Council.**
	:2	**Disclosure of contents of the 1948/49 programmes of the other participating countries.**

	:3	**Estimated 1952/53 balance of payments with the Netherlands and Netherlands Indies.** P(48)66 and 68.
7 Oct	**35th:1**	**The 1948/9 import programme from the rest of the sterling area.** P(48)67. R.W.B. Clarke said that it would be necessary to prepare a realistic balance of payments forecast for 1948/49 for both the O.E.E.C. and the Economic Survey for 1949. Consideration of the import programmes by country.
	:2	**The 1948/49 balance of payments with Eastern Europe.**
12 Oct	**36th:1**	**The 1948/49 import programmes for Middle East and Far East.** P(48)70. Detailed consideration by country.
	:2	**Balance of payments with the non-dollar western hemisphere.** P(48)71.
	:3	**Fourth quarter programme.**
14 Oct	**37th:1**	**Proposed oil sales to participating countries for 1948/49.**
	:2	**The 1948/49 non-dollar balance of payments with the participating countries and Spain.**
	:3	**Future programme of work.**
19 Oct	**38th:1**	**Belgium.**
	:2	**Revised 1948/49 balance of payments.**
	:3	**E.R.P. eligibility.** P(48)58 and 75. Agreement on possible additions to the E.R.P. programme.
28 Oct	**39th:1**	**E.R.P. eligibility.**
	:2	**Belgian 1949 programme.** P(48)85.
	:3	**Belgian long-term programme.** P(48)84.
	:4	**Long-term programme with Switzerland.** P(48)86.
9 Nov	**40th:1**	**Revised balance of payments 1948/49.** P(48)95. Agreement that the figures had changed materially since their submission to Paris.
	:2	**The long-term programme: trade with Argentina.**
	:3	**E.R.P. programme for the first quarter 1949.** P(48)89 and 96.
15 Nov	**41st:1**	**Revised balance of payments for 1948/49.**
	:2	**Survey of first six months of the E.R.P.**
	:3	**Bolivian tin.**
	:4	**U.S. surplus products.** P(48)76 and 79. Only commodities the U.K. might wish to buy were dried eggs and turpentine.
16 Nov	**42nd:1**	**Western Germany.**
	:2	**E.R.P. programme for the first quarter 1949.** P(48)100. Detailed consideration and agreement that the programme should be considered in relation to the revised dollar balance of payments as it might be desirable

		to recommend an increase in the dollar import programme.
22 Nov	**43rd:1**	**E.R.P. financed programme in relation to the revised dollar balance of payments for 1948/49.** P(48)100, 106, 110.
	:2	**Letter of commitment procedure.** P(48)107.
	:3	**Use of private channels of trade (section 112(H) of the Economic Co-operation Act).**
	:4	**The French long-term programme: implications for the U.K. economy.** P(48)108. Detailed consideration.
	:5	**Commodity classification.**
23 Nov	**44th:1**	**E.R.P. programme in relation to 1948/49 dollar balance of payments.**
	:2	**The 1949/50 programme: plan for action.** P(48)111. Detailed examination of proposed submission to the O.E.E.C.
25 Nov	**45th:1 (revise)**	**The 1948/49 programme for bread grains and coarse grains.** P(48)112.
	:2	**The 1948/49 linseed import programme.**
	:3	**Import programme for Western Germany for 1949.** P(48)116.
30 Nov	**46th:1**	**Draft foreword to the White Paper on the U.K. long-term and 1949/50 programmes.** ER(L)(48)199. Detailed consideration and suggestions for revision.
	:2	**Softwood.** P(48)115. M.T. Flett to warn the Materials Committee of the dangers of increasing current allocations.
	:3	**Argentina.**
	:4	**Projects and capital goods.**
9 Dec	**47th:1**	**Matters arising from previous minutes.** Reaction of the Materials Committee to M.T. Flett's warning.
	:2	**Belgium.**
	:3	**Draft foreword to the White Paper on the U.K. long-term and 1949/50 programmes.** Ministry of Food opposed publication of both programmes.
	:4	**E.R.P. programme for first quarter of 1949.**
	:5	**Agricultural surpluses.**
	:6	**Publication of figures relating to deliveries against Marshall Aid.**
	:7	**Use of private channels of trade (section 112(H) of the Economic Co-operation Act).** P(48)125.
	:8	**U.K. long-term programme from Argentina.** P(48)127.
14 Dec	**48th:1**	**Belgium.**
	:2	**Argentina.**
	:3	**Agricultural surpluses.**
	:4	**First quarter 1949: E.R.P. programme.**
	:5	**Coarse grains.** P(48)126 and 129.

	:6	**Economic Survey: 1948/49 imports.** P(48)126 and 131.
17 Dec	49th:1	**First quarter 1949: E.R.P. programme.**
	:2	**Home-grown linseed.** P(48)121.
	:3	**The 1948/49 balance of payments.** P(48)118. Agreement to set up a working party under R. Nowell on the relaxation of import restrictions.
	:4	**U.S. Department of Commerce: export quotas from the U.S.A.**

CAB 134/609   Memoranda   10 June – 5 Oct 1948   P(48)1–68.

10 June	P(48)1	**The 1948–49 programme – T.A.G. Charlton and P.J. Moorhouse,** 1+2p. Note of a meeting of a statistical group held on 9 June 1948.
16 June	2	**The timetable – R.W.B. Clarke,** 2p.
18 June	3	**Skeleton paper for ministers – R.W.B. Clarke,** 3p.
21 June	4	**Distribution of forms for the annual programme – T.A.G. Charlton and P.J. Moorhouse,** 1p.
28 June	5	**Composition and terms of reference – T.A.G. Charlton and P.J. Moorhouse,** 2p.
28 June	6	**Annual programme 1948–1949; Chile and Peru – T.A.G. Charlton and P.J. Moorhouse,** 1p.
28 June	7	**Implications of Article II of the draft bilateral agreement on the preparation of programmes – T.A.G. Charlton and P.J. Moorhouse covering T.L. Rowan,** 1+1p.
5 July	8	**Draft report to Economic Policy Committee on the dollar programme for 1 July 1948–30 June 1949 – T.A.G. Charlton and P.J. Moorhouse,** 1+6+2p annexes. Revise version. Sets out (i) a budget programme in which each country was to use the amount of aid initially allotted to it, i.e. about 10% more than was to be actually available and (ii) a requirements programme in which each country stated what it would like, having regard to availability of commodities.
6 July	9	**Draft covering memorandum – the committee,** 9p. Revise version. Concluded that the budget programme was just sufficient to permit the continuance of existing production and consumption, whilst the requirement programme was seriously limited by shortages, particularly of steel. A level of aid below that in the budget programme would involve cuts in consumption, in raw materials supplied to

industry or delays in the recovery of other countries.

6 July	10	**Draft report on commodity programmes – the committee**, 2+3p. Revise version.
7 July	11	**Report on non-dollar balance of payments – the committee**, 6+1p annex. Revise version. Analysis of the prospective situation by groups of countries and resulting recommendations.
9 July	12	**Report on the annual programme 1948/1949 – T.A.G. Charlton and P.J. Moorhouse**, 1+5p. Record of a meeting of permanent secretaries, 8 July 1948, to consider P(48)8(revise), 9(revise), 10(revise), 11(revise).
13 July	13	**Sterling area balance of payments with participating countries and their overseas territories – T.A.G. Charlton and P.J. Moorhouse**, 1+1p.
20 July	14	**Balance of payments with participating countries – P.J. Moorhouse**, 1+2+1p. Revise version.
16 July	15	**Long-term programme of the O.E.E.C. – C.E.P.S.**, 2+13p appendixes. Revise version. Suggested timetable and guidance to departments on the preparation of the programme.
17 July	16	**Control of import programmes from non-dollar sources – T.A.G. Charlton and P.J. Moorhouse covering the Treasury**, 1+2p.
15 July	17	**Covering memorandum to the annual programme for 1948/1949 – T.A.G. Charlton and P.J. Moorhouse**, 1+6p. See CP(48)178. Revise of P(48)9(revise).
16 July	18	**The 1952–53 programme – T.A.G. Charlton and P.J. Moorhouse covering R.L. Hall**, 1+3p. Proposed form of questionnaire.
19 July	19	**The 1949–50 programme – the committee**, 2p.
19 July	20	**Summary of 1948–49 import programme – C.S.O.**, 1+4p.
20 July	21	**U.K. current account with the rest of the world – P.J. Moorhouse**, 1+1p.
12 Aug	22	**Activity in August and September – T.A.G. Charlton and P.J. Moorhouse covering R.W.B. Clarke**, 1+1p.
20 July	23	**U.K. programme for the year 1948–49: supplementary note on manpower – Ministry of Labour**, 2+1p annex.
21 July	24	**The 1948–49 budget programme – P.J. Moorhouse**, 1+2p.
22 July	25	**July/September programme – E. Roll**, 2p.
21 July	26	**Fourth quarter programme – P.J. Moorhouse**, 1+2p. O.E.E.C. instructions on how to complete the E.C.A. questionnaires.

26 July	27	**U.K. balance of payments with the rest of the world – P.J. Moorhouse, 1+1p.**
28 July	28	**Procurements from Canada – P.J. Moorhouse covering A.E. Bryan, 1+1p.**
14 Aug	29	**U.S. surplus agricultural products – T.A.G. Charlton and P.J. Moorhouse covering T.K. Finletter, 1+2p.** Letter to T.L. Rowan containing a list of the quantities and unit costs of commodities available for assistance to E.C.A. participating countries.
16 Aug	30	**Second interim report for the Subcommittee on Accounting Procedure – T.A.G. Charlton and P.J. Moorhouse covering the subcommittee, 1+6+1p appendix.**
20 Aug	31	**U.S. prices for the year ending June 1949 – P.J. Moorhouse covering T.K. Finletter, 1+2p.** Letter to T.L. Rowan.
23 Aug	32	**Activity in August and September: timetable – P.J. Moorhouse, 1+7p annexes.**
25 Aug	33	**Statistical tables for the O.E.E.C. long-term programme – Statistical Working Group, 1+5p.**
25 Aug	34	**August-September timetable – P.J. Moorhouse, 1p.**
25 Aug	35	**The O.E.E.C. long-term programme – T.A.G. Charlton and P.J. Moorhouse covering the Ministry of Food, 1+4+2p.** Consideration of the import programmes for food and feedingstuffs 1952/53.
31 Aug	36	**The long-term programme – P.J. Moorhouse, 1+9+1p.** Revise version. Chapters 9 and 10.
27 Aug	37	**The O.E.E.C. long-term programme – T.A.G. Charlton and P.J. Moorhouse, 1+1p.** Table attached showing annual export targets by volume for selected Colonial commodities.
30 Aug	38	**Statistical tables of 1948/9 import programme (revised) – Statistical Working Group, 1+4p.**
30 Aug	39	**Work of the O.E.E.C. on the annual programme – P.J. Moorhouse covering C.T. Crowe, 1+5p.** Letter to J.P.C. Henniker.
31 Aug	40	**E.R.P. finance for timber – P.J. Moorhouse covering the Board of Trade, 1+2+2p appendix.**
1 Sept	41	**Third quarter programmes – G.H. van Loo, 1+2p.**
2 Sept	42	**E.R.P. loan programme – P.J. Moorhouse, 1+1p.**
	43	Not issued.
4 Sept	44	**Revised 1948/49 balance of payments table – P.J. Moorhouse, 1+1p.**
6 Sept	45	**The long-term programme – P.J. Moorhouse covering A. Harriman, 1+3p.** Also ER(L)(48)90. Telegram on the preparation of national submissions.

8 Sept	46	**The 1949/59 programme – the committee,** 15+2p. Revise version. See ED(48)9.
9 Sept	47	**Draft report on Canada – P.J. Moorhouse** **covering the committee,** 1+4+1p.
11 Sept	48	**Revised 1948/49 balance of payments table –** **P.J. Moorhouse,** 1+1p.
11 Sept	49	**Note by the Foreign Office,** 1+5p. Letters received by the U.K. delegation to Paris.
13 Sept	50	**Memorandum to the O.E.E.C. and the E.C.A.** **covering revised U.K. programme 1 July 1948** **to 30 June 1949 – R.W.B. Clarke,** 10p. Explanation of U.K. objectives on the assumption of receiving $1263m of E.R.P. aid.
13 Sept	51	**The 1948–49 programme – T.A.G. Charlton and** **P.J. Moorhouse,** 1+2+4p annex. Draft memorandum to be submitted to the Economic Policy Committee, with the Programmes Committee report annexed.
14 Sept	52	**Note by the joint secretaries – T.A.G. Charlton** **and P.J. Moorhouse,** 1+1p. Two letters on U.S. surplus agricultural commodities and grains, fats and oils.
14 Sept	53	**Completion of revised O.E.E.C. forms for** **1948/9 programme – Statistical Working** **Group,** 2+3p appendixes.
16 Sept	54	**E.R.P. quarterly programmes 1948 – G.H. van** **Loo,** 1+1p.
15 Sept	55	**Revised annual programme 1948/49 – T.A.G.** **Charlton and P.J. Moorhouse,** 1+3p. Record of a meeting under E.E. Bridges, 14 September 1948, to consider the submission of the programme to the Economic Policy Committee.
21 Sept	56	**U.K. covering memorandum for the revised** **1948/49 programme – T.A.G. Charlton and P.J.** **Moorhouse,**1+12p. Revision of P(48)50, as amended by the Economic Policy Committee and submitted to the O.E.E.C.
21 Sept	57	**Note by the Statistical Working Group,** 1+4p annexes. Programmes of trade with Australia, New Zealand and France during 1948/9, 1949/50 and 1952/3.
18 Oct	58	**Colonial imports for inclusion in the E.R.P.** **programme – T.A.G. Charlton and P.J.** **Moorhouse,** 1+5p annexes.
27 Sept	59	**The O.E.E.C.: Oct/Nov exercises – R.W.B.** **Clarke,** 1+7p annexes.
27 Sept	60	**The 1949/50 programme – Statistical Working** **Group,** 1+3p.
28 Sept	61	**Long-term programme – Statistical Working** **Group,** 1+5p.

29 Sept	62	The 1948/9 import programme (revised) – Statistical Working Group, 1+3p.
11 Oct	63	1948/9 non-dollar balance of payments: Eastern Europe – Statistical Working Group, 1+1p. Final revise version.
1 Oct	64	The 1949/50 import programme – Statistical Working Group, 1+6p.
1 Oct	65	Digest of programme statistics 1948–49, 1949–50 and 1952–53 – Statistical Working Group, 1+8p.
4 Oct	66	Summary of import-export programmes (Netherlands) – Statistical Working Group,1+2p.
6 Oct	67	The 1948/9 non-dollar balance of payments: sterling area – Statistical Working Group, 1+2p.
5 Oct	68	Balance of payments with the Netherlands monetary area – T.A.G. Charlton, 1+1p.

CAB 134/610   Memoranda   7 Oct–29 Dec 1948   P(48)69–135.

7 Oct	P(48)69	Balance of payments with the Netherlands monetary area – Statistical Working Group, 1+3p.
11 Oct	70	Balance of payments with the Middle East and Far East 1948/9 – Statistical Working Group, 1+2p.
11 Oct	71	Balance of payments with the non-dollar western hemisphere – Statistical Working Group, 1+4p.
14 Oct	73	Balance of payments with Denmark – Statistical Working Group, 1+3p.
16 Oct	75	The 1948/49 E.R.P. programme – G.H. van Loo, 1p.
18 Oct	76	U.S. surplus products – T.A.G. Charlton and P.J. Moorhouse, 1p.
21 Oct	77	Balance of payments with Japan 1948/49 – Overseas Negotiations Committee Working Party, 2p.
23 Oct	79	U.S. surplus products – P.J. Moorhouse, 1+1p. List of products.
25 Oct	83	Belgian Congo long-term balance of payments – P.J. Moorhouse, 1+1p.
27 Oct	84	Long-term balance of payments with Belgium – unsigned, 1+2p.
27 Oct	85	The 1949 import programme from Belgium – P.J. Moorhouse, 1+3p.
30 Oct	87	Balance of payments with Italy – Statistical Working Group, 1+2p.
	88	Not issued.
27 Oct	89	E.R.P. programme first quarter 1949 – M.T. Flett, 2p.

1 Nov	90	**Balance of payments with Sweden – Statistical Working Group,** 1+2p.
1 Nov	91	**Balance of payments with Norway – Statistical Working Group,** 1+2p.
9 Nov	94	**Trade with Western Germany** – unsigned, 1+2p.
6 Nov	95	**Revised 1948–49 programme – Statistical Working Group,** 1+3p.
8 Nov	96	**E.R.P. programme for first quarter 1949 – Treasury,** 2+2p.
10 Nov	97	**Raw materials budget 1948/9 – P.J. Moorhouse,** 1+19+25+3p. Programme by items and country groups, and a summary by countries.
16 Nov	100	**E.R.P. programme for the first quarter 1949 – Treasury,** 1+2p.
15 Nov	102	**Eire: balance of payments forecast 1952/53 – Statistical Working Group,** 1+1p.
18 Nov	105	**The 1948/9 import programme – Statistical Working Group,** 1+1p.
20 Nov	106	**E.C.A. financing programme 1948–49 – R.W.B. Clarke,** 1+2p.
22 Nov	107	**Letter of commitment method – T.A.G. Charlton and P.J. Moorhouse,** 1+4p annexes.
23 Nov	108	**Effect upon the U.K. of the French 1952–53 programme – T.A.G. Charlton and P.J. Moorhouse covering the Committee,** 1+3p. Revise version. The French long-term programme was broadly compatible with the U.K.'s.
19 Nov	109	**The 1952/3 Benelux balance of payments – Statistical Working Group,** 1+2p.
25 Nov	110	**Revised gold and dollar balance of payments for 1948/49 – T.A.G. Charlton and P.J. Moorhouse,** 1+2p. Revise version.
22 Nov	111	**The 1949/50 programme: plan for action – R.W.B. Clarke,** 2+5p annexes.
24 Nov	112	**The 1948/9 import programmes for bread grains and coarse grains – M.T. Flett,** 3p.
4 Dec	113	**Imports of 'other foods' (1934/38, 1949/50, 1952/53) – Statistical Working Group,** 1p. Revise version.
29 Nov	114	**Balance of payments with Argentina (1948/49, 1949/50, 1952/53) – Statistical Working Group,** 1p.
24 Nov	115	**Softwood – Raw Materials Department,** 2+1p appendix. Concern that some considered that the softwood supply position was easy. Increased allocations for 1949/50 depended upon a satisfactory June 1949 stock and current allocations could not be increased yet.
7 Dec	116	**Note by the Statistical Working Group,** 1+2p. Revise version. Bizone imports.

27 Nov	117	**The 1948/49 import programme by countries by half years – Statistical Working Group,** 1+3p.
29 Nov	118	**The 1948–49 balance of payments – R.W.B. Clarke,** 2p. Suggested response to the request by Sir Henry Wilson-Smith's working party to consider modifications to import policy.
29 Nov	119	**U.S. agricultural surpluses – T.A.G. Charlton and P.J. Moorhouse covering M. Thibodeaux,** 1+2p.
1 Dec	120	**Trade with Portugal and dependent overseas territories (1948/49, 1949/50, 1952/53) – Statistical Working Group,** 1p.
2 Dec	121	**Home-grown linseed – T.A.G. Charlton and P.J. Moorhouse covering the Ministry of Agriculture and Fisheries,** 1+1p.
17 Dec	122	**Trade with Poland (1948/49, 1949/50, 1952/53) – Statistical Working Group,** 2p. Revise version.
6 Dec	123	**Trade with South Africa ⟨1948/49, 1949/50, 1952/53) – Statistical Working Group,** 1+2p.
6 Dec	124	**Purchases of U.S. tobacco – T.A.G. Charlton and P.J. Moorhouse covering H.D. Andrews,** 1+1p.
7 Dec	125	**Use of private channels of trade (section 112(H) of the Economic Co-operation Act) – Treasury,** 1+5p annexes.
13 Dec	126	**The 1948/49 imports of coarse grains – T.A.G. Charlton and P.J. Moorhouse covering the Ministry of Agriculture and Fisheries,** 1+5p.
8 Dec	127	**Argentine long-term programme – T.A.G. Charlton and P.J. Moorhouse covering M.T. Flett,** 1+3p.
10 Dec	128	**U.K. imports 1948/49 – T.A.G. Charlton and P.J. Moorhouse,** 1+2p. Comparison of half-yearly programmes with draft economic survey estimates.
11 Dec	129	**Requirements of coarse grains for animal feeding – Ministry of Agriculture,** 2p.
13 Dec	130	**E.R.P. programme for the first quarter 1947 – Treasury,** 1+1p.
13 Dec	131	**Imports compared with departmental programmes – T.A.G. Charlton and P.J. Moorhouse covering the Board of Trade,** 1+3p.
23 Dec	132	**Argentine long-term programme – T.A.G. Charlton and P.J. Moorhouse covering the committee,** 1+4p. Final version.
24 Dec	134	**E.R.P. imports of machinery on private account – T.A.G. Charlton and P.J. Moorhouse covering the Subcommittee on Accounting Procedure,** 1+1+9p annexes. Also P(A)(48)29(revise) and 32.

29 Dec	**135**	**First quarter 1949 programme – T.A.G.** **Charlton and P.J. Moorhouse,** 1p.

CAB134/611   Meetings   4 Jan–17 May 1949   P(49)1st–34th.

4 Jan	**P(49)1st:1**	**Home-grown linseed.**
	:2	**E.R.P. imports of machinery.** P(48)134, P(49)2, 3. Agreement on programme for first quarter of 1949.
	:3	**E.R.P. programme for the first quarter of 1949.**
	:4	**O.I.T. questionnaire.**
	:5	**List of Canadian E.R.P. availabilities.**
6 Jan	**2nd:1**	**Argentina.**
	:2	**Future work on the long-term programme.** P(49)1.
	:3	**Provision of statistical information on non-** **ferrous metals.**
20 Jan	**3rd**	**U.K. revised long-term programme: balance of** **payments.** P(49)5. Examination of the estimates item by item.
25 Jan	**4th:1**	**Resignation of the vice-chairmen.**
	:2	**Timetable.** P(49)9.
	:3	**Revision of the 1952/53 programme of the U.K.** P(49)8. Detailed consideration and discussion of the size of the overall surplus. Consensus that an increase of total exports to over 150% of the 1938 volume should be assumed.
27 Jan	**5th:1**	**U.K. balance of payments for 1952/53.** P(49)8(revise). Detailed consideration.
	:2	**The sterling area 1952/53.** P(49)10.
1 Feb	**6th:1**	**Argentina: long-term contract for meat.** P(49)7. Recommendation to open negotiations.
	:2	**Revised U.K. balance of payments for 1952/53.** P(48)8(second revise). R.W.B. Clarke set out the comments of Sub-group C on P(48)8(second revise). Discussion of the level of imports of food and feedingstuffs.
8 Feb	**7th:1**	**Long-term programme: submission of revised** **figures to Paris.**
	:2	**U.K. long-term balance of payments with** **individual countries.**
	:3	**Revised 1949/50 balance of payments.**
	:4	**E.R.P. programme: first and second quarters** **1949.**
	:5	**Sterling area 1952/53.** P(49)10 and 14. Detailed consideration.
14 Feb	**8th**	**E.R.P. programme: second quarter of 1949 and** **1949/50.** P(49)15. Consideration of the effect of Canadian wheat becoming ineligible for E.R.P. financing. Draft telegram annexed.

17 Feb	*ad hoc*	**The sterling area in 1952/53.** P(49)14, 16, 17. Discussion of the area as a whole and then of individual countries.
15 Feb	9th:1	**Directives for preparation of revised 1949/50 programme.** Agreement over the basis on which the programme should be drawn up.
	:2	**Sterling area 1952/53.** P(49)14, 16, 17. Agreed lay-out for the memorandum to ministers.
21 Feb	10th:1	**Directives for preparation of revised 1949/50 programme.**
	:2	**Proposed long-term agreement with Yugoslavia.** P(49)13.
	:3	**The 1949/50 programme: effect of reduction in U.S. commodity prices.** P(49)19.
	:4	**E.R.P. programme: first and second quarters of 1949.**
	:5	**Preparation of revised 1949/50 programme.**
	:6	**U.K. balance of payments in 1952/53 with each participating country.** P(49)18. Recommendation that a special working party on Benelux should be set up.
24 Feb	11th:1	**Proposed long-term agreement with Yugoslavia.**
	:2	**The 1949/50 programme: the effect of reduction in U.S. commodity prices.**
	:3	**Procedure for second quarter 1949 programme.** P(49)22.
	:4	**U.K. balance of payments in 1952/53 with each participating country.** P(49)18. Continuation of the country by country examination.
26 Feb	12th	**U.K. balance of payments in 1952/53 with each participating country.** P(49)18. Continuation of examination and discussion of the resulting overall position.
1 Mar		**Working party on the sterling area: sterling area in 1952/53.** Consideration of the appendixes to the report.
10 Mar	13th:1	**Change of joint secretary.**
	:2	**E.R.P. programme: first and second quarters of 1949.** P(49)29. Consideration of commodities for inclusion in the programmes.
	:3	**Intra-European situation 1952/53.** P(49)25. Examination of a draft report.
11 Mar		**Working Party on the Sterling Area: draft report on the long-term programme and the Commonwealth.** Detailed consideration.
14 Mar	14th:1	**E.R.P. programme: first and second quarters.** P(49)29 and 30. Consideration of the carry-over and additional dollar purchases.
	:2	**Future timetable.**
15 Mar	15th:1	**E.R.P. programme: first and second quarters.**
	:2	**The 1949/50 programme.**

	:3	**U.K. deficit with Denmark and its bearing on U.K. agricultural policy.** P(49)27.
	:4	**Long-term programme: balance of payments with the three non-participating countries.** P(49)21. Examination country by country.
17 Mar		**Working Party on the Sterling Area.** Consideration of the final draft of the report on the impact of the long-term programme on the Commonwealth, a draft of ER(L)(49)93.
17 Mar	16th:1	**E.R.P. Programme: first and second quarters 1949.**
	:2	**Future timetable.**
	:3	**The 1949/50 programme: questionnaires for 1949/50.** P(49)31 and 32. Consideration in detail of the proposals in P(49)31.
22 Mar	17th:2	**The long-term programme in the light of the resolutions of the O.E.E.C. Consultative Group.** P(49)33, 34, 35, 37.
	:3	**Survey of price changes.** Consideration of the requirements for regular surveys.
	:4	**The 1949/50 programme.**
29 Mar	18th:1	**The 1949/50 programme.**
	:2	**Second quarter 1949 E.R.P. programme.** Agreement on further purchases to reduce the carry-over.
	:3	**Timetable of work on the 1949/50 programme.** P(49)40. Detailed consideration and approval.
	:4	**Long-term programme.** P(49)39. Consideration in detail.
31 Mar	19th	**U.K. 1949/50 programme: food.** P(49)38, 41, 45. Consideration of each commodity.
1 Apr	20th:1	**The Argentine programme.**
	:2	**Raw materials: the 1949/50 programme.** P(49)38. Examination item by item.
	:3	**Iron and steel.**
	:4	**Non-ferrous metals.** Examination item by item.
4 Apr	21st:1	**The 1949/50 programme: agricultural items.** P(49)38. Examination item by item.
	:2	**The 1949/50 programme: oil.** P(49)38. Consideration of stock levels and consumption.
	:3	**Unmanufactured tobacco.** P(49)38.
5 Apr	22nd:1	**Timetable of future work.**
	:2	**The 1949/50 import programme for machinery.** P(49)3. Consideration of programme item by item.
	:3	**The 1949/50 import programme: manufactured goods.** P(49)38. Examination item by item.
8 Apr	23rd:1	**The 1949/50 programme: food.**
	:2	**Second quarter E.R.P. programme.**
	:3	**Sterling area balance of payments with the participants: 1949/50.** P(49)38 and 42.

Examination to agree deficits and supporting data for future negotiations. Examination of the balance of payments with each participant. The Board of Trade reserved its position on export estimates and was to re-examine the overall export position.

12 Apr	24th:1	**The 1949/50 programme.** R.W.B. Clarke questioned the balance of payments forecast based on departmental import programmes. This showed a deficit of £275m. He felt that budgeting for anything less than an overall balance would be very difficult to justify because a surplus was already being run and a £100m surplus was being aimed at in 1952/53.
	:2	**Oil balance of payments.** P(49)48.
20 Apr	25th:1	**Timetable for 1949/50 programme.**
	:2	**Price movements.** P(49)36.
	:3	**Sterling area balance of payments with the French franc area 1949/50.** P(49)51. Examination of the balance item by item.
	:4	**Reports of the subcommittee: 1949/50 programme (commodities).** P(49)49, 50, 52, 53, 54, 55. Consideration of each memorandum individually.
	:5	**The International Monetary Fund.**
21 Apr	26th:1	**The 1949/50 export programme.** P(49)56. Examination by groups of commodities and of countries.
	:2	**The 1949/50 balance of payments.** Consideration of the impact of cutting import programmes of raw materials by £80m and of food by £125m.
	:3	**Maize for starch.**
26 Apr	27th:1	**Timetable for 1949/50 programme.**
	:2	**Food exports.**
	:3	**Third quarter 1949 E.R.P. programme.**
	:4	**O.E.E.C. directions for the preparation of programmes for the year 1949/50.** C(49)46(final).
	:5	**Dollar balance of payments 1949/50.** P(49)58.
28 Apr	28th:1	**Gold and dollar payments 1949/50.** P(49)61. Consideration of the estimates of the 1948/49 E.R.P. and non-E.R.P. balance of payments, the non-E.R.P. dollar import programme (with a view to reducing it to $512m) and the cuts in the E.R.P. programme necessary to bring it into line with likely allocations of aid.
	:2	**Maize for starch.**
29 Apr	29th:1	**The 1949/50 gold and dollar balance of payments.**
	:2	**Timetable.**
	:3	**The 1949/50 balance of payments.** P(49)62.

2 May	30th:1	**U.K. stocks and consumption of petroleum products.** P(49)63.
	:2	**Oil equipment.**
	:3	**The 1949/50 dollar situation.** Agreement on level of the free dollar programme and consideration of alterations to the dollar import programme.
3 May	31st	**Draft report to ministers on the 1949/50 programme. Detailed consideration.** Agreement that all possible instances where dollar savings might be effected without curtailing the import programme should be examined.
5 May	32nd	**Draft report on the 1949/50 programme.** P(49)66. Detailed consideration.
9 May	33rd:1	**Monthly report on import commodity prices.** P(49)67.
	:2	**Balance of payments 1949/50: drafting of covering memoranda.** C(49)46(final).
17 May	34th:1	**Circulation of papers.**
	:2	**The 1949/50 programme.**
	:3	**Third quarter 1949 E.R.P. programme.** P(49)69.

CAB 134/612   Meetings   19 May–28 Nov 1949   P(49)35th–68th.

19 May	P(49)35th:1	**The 1949/50 programme: report to ministers.**
	:2	**Information on the colonies to be submitted to the O.E.E.C. for the 1949/50 programme.** P(49)71.
	:3	**Draft of general memorandum for the O.E.E.C. U.K. 1949/50 programme.** P(49)70. Detailed consideration.
23 May	36th	**Covering memorandum for the 1949/50 programme.** P(49)70(revise).
31 May	37th:1	**Programme of work on the 1949/50 programme.**
	:2	**Revised E.C.A. regulation I and dollar permissions.** P(49)72.
	:3	**Revised 1949/50 programme: report to ministers on expenditure other than imports.** P(49)76.
	:4	**Fourth quarter E.R.P. programme.**
9 June	38th:1	**Programme of work in the 1949/50 programme.**
	:2	**Government overseas expenditure 1949/50.** P(49)73. Examination of the dollar element.
	:3	**Oil: dollar expenditure in 1949/50.** P(49)77.
14 June	39th:1	**Participation of U.S. small business in the E.R.P.**
	:2	**Import commodity price movements.** P(49)79.
	:3	**Changes in E.C.A. procurement procedure.** P(49)80.
	:4	**Agricultural machinery.**
	:5	**Examination of the 1949/50 programme.**
	:6	**Oil equipment: dollar expenditure.** P(49)77.

16 June	**40th:1**	**Participation of U.S. small business in the E.R.P.**
	:2	**Brief for the examination of the revised 1949/50 programme.**
	:3	**Dollar balance of payments.** Concern at the situation.
	:4	**The 1949/50 programme: amended figures.**
30 June	**41st:1**	**Examination of U.K. programmes for 1949/50 in the O.E.E.C.**
	:2	**1949/50 programmes: action arising out of E.P.C. decisions.** Discussion arising from the cuts involved in the standstill policy.
7 July	**42nd:2**	**Imports from the dollar area in the third quarter 1949.** P(49)99(revise).
	:3	**Effects on consumption levels of cuts in dollar import programme of raw materials.** Consideration by item to determine distribution of cuts.
	:4	**Imports of manufactured goods on private account.**
12 July	**43rd:2**	**Monthly report on import commodity price movements No. 3.** P(49)104.
	:3	**Imports of machinery in relation to cuts in the dollar programme.** P(49)101, 102, 103. The Import Licensing Committee was to consider the consequences of applying different criteria for importing machinery from dollar and non-dollar areas; and whether to extend the ban on new licences for machinery from the former to six months. Agreement that there should be only two sets of criteria for granting licences.
	:4	**Import licensing of essential commodities in relation to cuts in the dollar programme.** The Import Licensing Committee was to consider the making of exceptions to the ban on licensing as suggested by R.W.B. Clarke.
16 July	**44th**	**Draft supplementary memorandum on the 1949/50 programme.** Consideration in detail of memoranda, and showing the revised balance of payments for 1949/50.
22 July	**45th**	**Programming and procedural difficulties under E.R.P. finance.** ER(L)(49)209. Consideration of the various items of the import programme which would be ineligible for E.R.P. financing.
4 Aug	**46th**	**U.K. supplementary memorandum to the O.E.E.C. developments in Paris.** Also ER(L)(49)53rd. Part I – agreement that the proposed cuts were unacceptable and involved major policy decisions. Part II – detailed consideration of cuts.
11 Aug	**47th:2**	**Reduction of essential imports from Belgium.**

	:3	**Quarterly report on world price movements.** P(49)108.
	:4	**Proposed switches of imports by other participants to sterling sources.**
16 Aug	48th:1	**Dollar import programme: 1949/50.**
	:2	**Reduction of essential imports from Belgium.** P(49)111, 112, 113.
	:3	**Proposed switches of imports by other participants to sterling sources.**
8 Sept	49th:1	**The balance of payments programme.** P(49)115. Agreement that the programme should be extended to the whole of 1950, and that the dollar and general programmes should be prepared separately. Consideration of the criteria for drafting programme.
	:2	**Report of Working Party on Imports of Dollar Cotton.** P(49)114.
20 Sept	50th:1	**Problems arising from changes in exchange rates.** Consideration of immediate difficulties, the revision of programmes and future procedure relating particularly to price changes.
	:2	**The monthly report on commodity price movements No. 5.** P(49)117.
27 Sept	51st:1	**Problems arising from changes in exchange rates.** Continued consideration.
	:2	**Reprogramming for 1949/50.**
	:3	**Future work of the committee.**
3 Oct	52nd:1	**The 1950 dollar import programme.** P(49)120 and 121. Detailed consideration of P(49)121.
	:2	**Dollar export forecast 1950.** P(49)123.
6 Oct	53rd:1	**Dollar balance of payments 1950.** P(49)125, 126, 127. Agreement on advice to ministers.
	:2	**Submission of 1949/50 import programme to the E.C.A.** SGD(49)90.
10 Oct	54th	**Dollar balance of payments for 1950.** P(49)132. Examination of possible import cuts totalling $55m.
11 Oct	55th	**The 1950 dollar balance of payments.** P(49)131 and addendum. Detailed consideration.
12 Oct	56th	**The 1950 dollar balance of payments.** P(49)135. Detailed consideration.
13 Oct	57th:1	**The dollar programme.** P(49)125(revise), 131(revise), 135(revise), 136.
	:2	**Programming for 1950/51.**
18 Oct	58th:1	**The dollar programme for the period July 1949 to Dec 1950.**
	:2	**The 1949/51 general balance of payments.** Agreement that the general import programme should be based on a commodity analysis.
	:3	**Non-dollar price problems arising from devaluation.** P(49)128, 129, 134, 140.

	:4	**Monthly report on import commodity prices.** P(49)138.
	:5	**Changes in E.C.A. procurement procedure.** P(49)137.
20 Oct	59th:1	**Imports of machinery from dollar sources.** P(49)133. Consideration of the need to import machinery which would increase productivity.
	:2	**The E.C.A. instructions for 1949/50 (final) programme for the U.K. and dependent overseas territories.** P(49)141. Detailed consideration.
25 Oct	60th:1	**Imports of machinery from dollar sources.**
	:2	**E.C.A. instructions for the 1949/50 (final) programme for the U.K. and dependent overseas territories.**
	:3	**The 1950/51, 1951/52 and 1952/53 programmes.**
	:4	**Dollar programme July 1949–Dec 1950.**
	:5	**Progressing of the general import programme.**
	:6	**E.C.A. – finance import programme 1949/50.** Consideration by item, resulting in an agreed programme of $988m.
3 Nov	61st:1	**Submission of the 1949/50 programme to E.C.A.**
	:2	**E.C.A. financed import programme 1949–50.**
	:3	**Imports of machinery from dollar sources.** P(49)144. Agreement that given the balance of payments position, other dollar imports might need to be weighed against the requirements of machinery. Consideration in detail.
	:4	**The 1950/51 programmes.** PR(49)54(1st revise), 55, 56.
	:5	**Draft report on price policy.** P(49)145 and 148.
15 Nov	62nd:1	**Competitive buying in the dollar area.** P(49)151.
	:2	**Machinery imports from dollar sources.**
	:3	**The general balance of payments.** P(49)152, 153, 154. Detailed consideration of P(49)152.
16 Nov	63rd	**The general balance of payments 1949–1951.** P(49)152, 153, 156. The dollar problem's solution lay in increased export earning. The U.K. had to obtain a larger share of world export trade, although this might involve severe price competition with the U.S.A. The Treasury considered that the minimum U.K. surplus required with the non-dollar world was £250m. This should be attainable in 1950 with little drastic action. Detailed consideration of P(49)152.
17 Nov	64th	**General balance of payments mid-1949 to mid-1950.** P(49)152, 153, 156. General agreement that: the position was uncertain and the crucial elements were import prices and export earnings; the U.K., would soon have to depend on indirect controls; the avoidance of general

inflation in the U.K., sterling area and non-dollar world was essential to the success of the present policies in the U.K. internal economy; the U.K. must reduce purchases in the non-dollar world to reduce consumption and thereby keep prices down; more elbow room was required in industries for exports; loans and sterling releases were a loss to consumption and might lose dollars indirectly and upset controls; there should be no major change in import policy but the position should be kept under continuous review.

21 Nov	65th:1	**Regional analysis of the U.K. non-dollar import programme 1950. P(49)159.**
	:2	**General balance of payments mid-1949 to mid-1951.**
	:3	**1950/51 and 1951/52 submissions to the O.E.E.C. P(49)158.** Consideration of the outline of the dollar accounts and then of the general balance of payments for 1950/51 and 1951/52.
24 Nov	66th	**The 1950–51 and 1951–52 submission to the O.E.E.C./E.C.A.: statistics and draft chapter I.** P(49)162 and 164. Agreement on the balance of payments basis for the submissions. Detailed consideration of P(49)162.
25 Nov	67th:1	**Competitive purchasing in the dollar world.**
	:2	**Draft report to ministers on the 1950 balance of payments.** P(49)161 and 163.
	:3	**Submission to the O.E.E.C./E.C.A. on 1950/51 and 1951/52.**
	:4	**Open general licences and purchases of essential items.**
28 Nov	68th:1	**Purchases from Canada.**
	:2	**Submission to the O.E.E.C./E.C.A.: 1950/51, 1951/52.** P(49)166.
	:3	**Submission to the O.E.E.C./E.C.A.: draft covering note for ministers.** P(49)165.

CAB 134/613   Memoranda   1 Jan–8 Apr 1949   T(49)1–37.

5 Jan	**P(49)1**	**Next work on the long-term programme – R.W.B. Clarke,** 3p. Sets out the functions of the committee on this subject.
1 Jan	2	**First quarter 1949 machinery E.C.A. import programme – T.A.G. Charlton and P.J. Moorhouse covering the Ministry of Supply,** 1+1p.
4 Jan	3	**Draft replies to Washington telegrams 5,914 and 5,919 – T.A.G. Charlton and P.J. Moorhouse covering the Ministry of Supply,** 1+3p.

7 Jan	4	**Lists of Canadian E.R.P. availabilities – T.A.G. Charlton and P.J. Moorhouse covering the office of the High Commissioner for Canada.** 1+2p.
19 Jan	5	**U.K. revived long-term programme: balance of payments – statistical working group,** 2+10p.
24 Jan	6	**Change of membership – T.A.G. Charlton and P.J. Moorhouse,** 1p.
24 Jan	7	**Argentine negotiations: long-term contract for meat,** 1p.
27 Jan	8	**Revision of 1952–53 balance of payments – the committee,** 9+5p annexes. 2nd revised version. Request for decisions on certain aspects.
24 Jan	9	**Work on the long-term programme: programme for the period 24 Jan to 4 Feb – T.A.G. Charlton and P.J. Moorhouse,** 2p. Also ER(L)(49)23.
24 Jan	10	**Disturbing area, 1952–53 – T.A.G. Charlton and P.J. Moorhouse covering the Treasury,** 1+11+7p annexes. Substantially revised version of GEN 258/SG/4 setting out estimates of a possible pattern of trade between the sterling area and the rest of the world in 1952/53.
26 Jan	11	**Surplus agricultural commodities in the U.S. – T.A.G. Charlton and P.J. Moorhouse covering E.C.A. Washington,** 1+2p.
25 Jan	12	**Change of membership – T.A.G. Charlton and P.J. Moorhouse,** 1p.
21 Feb	13	**Proposed long-term agreement with Yugoslavia – Ministry of Food,** 2+1p.
7 Feb	14	**Note by Joint Secretaries – T.A.G. Charlton and P.J. Moorhouse covering the Treasury.** 1+12+5p annexes. Examination of the implications for the sterling area as a whole of the present U.K. longterm programme and the combined plans of the European countries.
12 Feb	15	**E.R.P. programmes – A.C. Sparks,** 2p.
14 Feb	16	**The sterling area 1952/53: the impact of the U.K. programme and of European plans – T.A.G. Charlton and P.J. Moorhouse covering the Treasury,** 1+6p. Redraft of P(49)14.
14 Feb	17	**Note by the Chairman – R.W.B. Clarke,** 1+2p. Now to do a paper on the impact of the U.K. long-term programme on the Commonwealth.
17 Feb	18	**Revision of longterm programme: U.K. balance of payments in 1952/53 with each participant – statistical working group,** 1+1+4p.
19 Feb	19	**1949/50 programme: effective reduction in the U.S. commodity prices – T.A.G. Charlton and P.J. Moorhouse covering the E.C.A. mission,** 1+1p annexes.

19 Feb	**20**	**U.K. operating programme for 1949/50 –** **statistical working group,** 3+4p annexes.
21 Feb	**21**	**Revision of long-term programme: balance of** **payments with the three non-participating** **countries – statistical working group,** 1+2p.
22 Feb		**South Africa – T.A.G. Charlton covering W.** **Peters, senior U.K. trade commissioner in South** **Africa,** 1+2+7p.
23 Feb		**Australia and South Africa – T.A.G. Charlton,** 1+12p.
23 Feb	**22**	**Procedure for 2nd quarter E.R.P. programme –** **T.A.G. Charlton and P.J. Moorhouse covering** **U.K. treasury and supply delegation and E.C.A.,** 1+1+4p.
24 Feb		**India and Pakistan – T.A.G. Charlton,** 1+4p.
28 Feb		**Note by the secretary – P.J. Moorhouse,** 1+6p appendix. Commodity appendix to the report on the sterling area in 1952/3.
25 Feb	**23**	**E.C.A. new procedure – T.A.G. Charlton and** **P.J. Moorhouse,** 1p.
1 Mar	**24**	**Programme of E.R.P. deliveries 1st and 2nd** **quarters 1949 – Treasury,** 1+1p.
2 Mar		**Statistical appendix – P.J. Moorhouse,** 1+5p. Statistical appendix to the report on the sterling area in 1952/3.
3 Mar	**25**	**Intra-European situation in 1952/53 – R.W.B.** **Clarke,** 1+3+5p appendixes. Draft report.
4 Mar		**Note by the Chairman – R.W.B. Clarke,** 1+12p. Draft report on the long-term programme and the Commonwealth.
16 Mar	**26**	**Change in secretariat – P.J. Moorhouse and** **P.V. Collyer,** 1p.
7 Mar	**27**	**The U.K. deficit with Denmark and its bearing** **on U.K. agriculture policy – Ministry of** **Agriculture,** 3p. Concern with P(49)25.
9 Mar	**28**	**Linseed production in the U.K. – T.A.G.** **Charlton and P.J. Moorhouse covering** **C.E.P.S.,** 1+1p.
9 Mar	**29**	**E.R.P. programme: 1st and 2nd quarter 1949 –** **A.C. Sparks,** 3p.
10 Mar		**Note by the Chairman – R.W.B. Clarke,** 1+2p appendix. Appendix on Canada of the draft report.
12 Mar	**30**	**E.R.P. programmes, 1st and 2nd quarters 1949** **– A.C. Sparks,** 2+1p.
15 Mar		**The long-term programme and the** **Commonwealth – P.J. Moorhouse covering the** **committee,** 1+11+34p appendixes. Report focusing on Canada, the sterling Commonwealth, and the sterling area and O.E.E.C.

16 Mar	31	**O.E.E.C. programme for 1949/50 – statistical working group**, 1+9p. Proposals for U.K. delegation to put to O.E.E.C. programmes committee.
17 Mar	32	**1949/50 programme: commodity list for import programmes – statistical working group**, 2+3p annex.
21 Mar	33	**Intra-European situation in 1952/53 – P.J. Moorhouse covering the committee**, 1+3+6p appendixes. Report as submitted to the London committee.
21 Mar	34	**Balance of payments with the 'three-nons': forecast for 1952–53 – P.J. Moorhouse and P.V. Collyer**, 1+1p.
21 Mar	35	**U.K. balance of payments: forecast for 1952–53 – P.J. Moorhouse and P.V. Collyer**, 1+1p.
8 Apr	36	**Interim report on price movements and the balance of payments – economic section**, 5+2p annex. Interim report of an *ad hoc* working group on the proposed methods by which price movements might be kept under review with particular reference to their effect on the balance of payments.
21 Mar	37	**Sterling area gold and dollar position 1952/53 – P.J. Moorhouse and P.V. Collyer covering the Treasury**, 1+2p.

CAB 134/614   Memoranda   30 Mar–6 Apr 1949   P(49)38–47.

30 Mar	**P(49)38**	**U.K. 1949/50 programme (revise). Departmental import and export estimates – Statistical Working Group**, 1+2+201p annexes. Annexes I–IV: departmental commodity import programmes; V: general export table, departmental and total import summaries; VI: country import programmes.
25 Mar	39	**U.K. long-term programme – P.J. Moorhouse and P.V. Collyer covering the committee**, 1+4+1p addendum. Re-examination of the long-term balance of payments prior to reconsideration by the O.E.E.C.
26 Mar	40	**Timetable of work on the 1949/50 programme – R.W.B. Clarke**, 3p.
28 Mar	41	**Observations by the Ministry of Agriculture upon the feedingstuffs items included in the Ministry of Food's 1949/50 import programme**, 3p.
7 Apr	42	**Sterling area balance of payments with participants – Treasury**, 1+17p appendixes.
30 Mar	43	**Sterling area gold and dollar position 1952/53 – P.J. Moorhouse and P.V. Collyer**, 1+2p. Revised version of P(49)37.

30 Mar	**44**	**Timetable of work on the 1949/50 programme – P.J. Moorhouse and P.V. Collyer,** 1p.
31 Mar	**45**	**Import programme 1949/50. Food and feedingstuffs – P.J. Moorhouse and P.V. Collyer covering the Ministry of Food,** 1+6p appendixes.
4 Apr	**46**	**Handling of procurement authorizations for projects – P.J. Moorhouse and P. Davenport covering the U.K. Treasury Supply Delegation,** 1+2p.
6 Apr	**47**	**Surplus agricultural commodities in the U.S.A. – P.J. Moorhouse and P.V. Collyer covering H. Siegbert,** 1+2p.

CAB 134/615   Memoranda   11 Apr–22 June 1949   P(49)48–90.

11 Apr	**P(49)48**	**Oil balance of payments, 1949/50 – Ministry of Fuel and Power,** 5+3p.
12 Apr	**49**	**Consumption imports and stocks of American-type cotton in 1949/50 – Board of Trade,** 4p.
13 Apr	**50**	**The 1949/50 food import programme – P.J. Moorhouse and P.V. Collyer covering the Ministry of Food,** 1+1p appendix.
19 Apr	**51**	**Sterling area balance of payments with French monetary area – P.J. Moorhouse and P.V. Collyer covering the Treasury,** 1+1p appendix.
19 Apr	**52**	**Programme of concentrated feedingstuffs – chairman of Working Party on Commodities,** 4p.
14 Apr	**53**	**Raw materials programme, 1949/50 – chairman of the Raw Materials Subcommittee,** 3p. Report on timber and paper pulp and paper board.
19 Apr	**54**	**Food programme 1949/50 – A.C. Sparks,** 5p.
14 Apr	**55**	**The 1949/50 food import programme – P.J. Moorhouse and P.V. Collyer covering the Ministry of Food,** 1+2p.
19 Apr	**56**	**The 1949/50 export programme – Board of Trade,** 6+2p. The programme's object was to provide the best possible estimate of U.K. export earnings during 1949/50. Exports were estimated at 150% of the 1938 volume as against 145% in the original 1949/50 programme for the O.E.E.C.
20 Apr	**57**	**Sterling area balance of payments with non-sterling participants – P.J. Moorhouse and P.V. Collyer covering the Treasury,** 1+4p.
23 Apr	**58**	**Revised gold and dollar balance of payments 1949/50 – P.J. Moorhouse and P.V. Collyer,** 1+10p.
25 Apr	**59**	**U.K. imports (1949) from the dollar area for period ended 2 April 1949 – P.J. Moorhouse and P.V. Collyer,** 1+1p. Actual outturn.

19 May	**60**	**U.K. 1949/50 programme: balance of payments with other participants – C.T. Saunders and others** 3+1p. Consideration of presentation to the O.E.E.C.
28 Apr	**61**	**Gold and dollar balance of payments 1948/49 – P.J. Moorhouse and P.V. Collyer,** 1+2p.
29 Apr	**62**	**Note by the joint secretaries – P.J. Moorhouse and P.V. Collyer,** 1+1p. Revised U.K. general balance of payments for 1949/50.
29 Apr	**63**	**U.K. consumption of motor spirit, gas, diesel and fuel oil in 1949/50 – Treasury and Ministry of Fuel and Power,** 6p.
29 Apr	**64**	**Prices of leading U.K. dollar imports and sterling area dollar exports – P.J. Moorhouse and P.V. Collyer covering the C.S.O.,** 1+2p.
2 May	**65**	**U.K. dollar import programme 1949/50 with possible allocation between the E.R.P., finance and earned dollars – unsigned,** 3p.
4 May	**66**	**The 1949–50 programme – P.J. Moorhouse and P.V. Collyer covering R.W.B. Clarke,** 1+25+13p annexes. Revised draft report covering the 1949–50 dollar situation, the 1949/50 general balance of payments and the problem of presentation to the O.E.E.C. and E.C.A. Draft of ED(49)8 and ER(L)(49)146.
5 May	**67**	**Monthly report on import commodity price movements No. 1 – C.S.O. and Economic Section,** 1+13p. Includes table of price movements and notes on the quotations, relationship between quoted prices and U.K. purchase prices, and on recent trend of prices. Hereafter referred to as monthly report.
7 May	**68**	**Note by the joint secretaries – P.J. Moorhouse and P.V. Collyer,** 1p.
14 May	**69**	**Third quarter E.R.P. programme – Treasury,** 1+3p annexes.
24 May	**70**	**Draft of general memorandum for the O.E.E.C. U.K. 1949/50 programme – the committee,** 45+15p annexes +2p addendum. Second revise version.
18 May	**71**	**Information on the colonies to be submitted to O.E.E.C. for the 1949–50 programme – P.J. Moorhouse and P.V. Collyer covering a working group of the Committee on Colonial Development,** 1+1+2+2p appendixes +1p. Also CD(49)18 and extract from CD(49)6.
20 May	**72**	**Revised E.C.A. regulation 1 and dollar commissions – Treasury,** 3p.
nd	**73**	**Government overseas expenditure 1949/50 – Treasury,** 1+2p.
27 May	**74**	**The 1949/50 programme – P.J. Moorhouse and P.V. Collyer,** 1p.

27 May	75	**General memorandum to the 1949–50 programme – P.J. Moorhouse and P.V. Collyer,** 1+28+19p annexes. U.K. revised 1949–50 programme as submitted to the O.E.E.C.
27 May	76	**The revised U.K. programme for 1949/50 – R.W.B. Clarke covering E.E. Bridges,** 1+2+16+15p annexes. Covering note to the Programmes Committee's report to ministers on the revised U.K. programme by the Official Committee on Economic Development. See EPC(49)52.
7 June	77	**Sundry elements in the oil balance of payments 1949/50 – Ministry of Fuel and Power,** 7+1p.
8 June	78	**U.K. 1949/50 programme revised and submitted to O.E.E.C. on 24 May 1949 – Statistical Working Group,** 1+4p.
10 May	79	**Monthly report No. 2,** 1+12p.
13 June	80	**Changes in E.C.A. procurement procedure – Treasury,** 2p.
15 June	84	**The 1948 balance of payments reported by the O.E.E.C. participating countries – Statistical Working Group,** 1+17p annexes.
22 June	90	**Relative costs and efficiency of bacon and egg production in the U.K. and Denmark – P.J. Moorhouse and P.V. Collyer covering the Working Party on Future Egg Policy,** 1+2p.

CAB 134/616   Memoranda   28 June–12 Sept 1949   P(49)91–117.

25 June	P(49)96	**Dollar expenditure in Persia and the Netherlands Antilles – P.J. Moorhouse and P.V. Collyer covering the Overseas Negotiations Committee,** 1+2p.
7 July	99	**Imports from the dollar area, third quarter 1949 – P.J. Moorhouse and P.V. Collyer,** 1+1p. Revise version.
8 July	101	**Proposed cut in the 1949/50 machinery import programme – Ministry of Supply,** 4p. Possible methods of making cuts.
9 July	102	**Proposed cut in the 1949/50 machinery import programme – D. Carter,** 2+3p. Also ILC 229. Board of Trade views.
9 July	103	**Agricultural machinery import programme 1950 – Ministry of Agriculture and Fisheries,** 2p.
9 July	104	**Monthly report No. 3,** 1+13p.
9 July	105	**Dollar imports on private account – D. Carter,** 2+3p.
22 July	106	**The 1949/50 programme supplementary memorandum for submission to the O.E.E.C. – P.V. Collyer and P.J. Moorhouse,** 1+6+3p appendixes +5p addendum. Second revise

		version. Also ER(L)(49)216. Copy as approved by ministers.
29 July	107	**Surplus agricultural commodities in the U.S.A. – P.V. Collyer covering H. Siegbert,** 1+1p.
8 Aug	108	**Quarterly report on world price movements – P.V. Collyer covering the Economic Section,** 1+6p. First report on recent and future price trends, with particular reference to the U.K. terms of trade and the rest of the sterling area's terms of trade with the U.S.A.
8 Aug	109	**Surplus agricultural commodities in the U.S.A. – P.V. Collyer covering H. Siegbert,** 1+2p.
10 Aug	110	**Monthly report No. 4,** 1+10+9p annex. Review of cereal prices by the Ministry of Food annexed.
15 Aug	111	**Imports of steel from Belgium – Ministry of Supply,** 2p.
15 Aug	112	**Imports of non-ferrous metals from Belgium – Ministry of Supply,** 3p.
15 Aug	113	**Imports of basic slag and superphosphate from Belgium – Ministry of Agriculture and Fisheries,** 1p.
27 Aug	114	**Report of Working Party on Imports of Dollar Cotton – P.J. Moorhouse covering the working party,** 1+4+4p appendix.
6 Sept	115	**The balance of payments programme – R.W.B. Clarke,** 3+4p appendix.
10 Sept	116	**E.R.P. programming – Treasury,** 2+2p annex.
12 Sept	117	**Monthly report No. 5,** 1+8+8p annex. Review of meat and livestock prices by the Ministry of Food annexed.

CAB 134/617   Memoranda   26 Sept–5 Nov 1949   P(49)118–150.

26 Sept	P(49)118	**E.C.A. eligibility – P.J. Moorhouse and P.V. Collyer covering the Working Group on E.C.A. Eligibility,** 1+2p.
22 Sept	119	**Examination of 1950 dollar programme – R.W.B. Clarke,** 1p.
1 Oct	120	**U.K. 1949/50 dollar import programme – Statistical Working Group,** 1+64p annexes. Commodity import programmes of all the importing departments annexed. Annex 1 – food, agriculture and tobacco; Annex 2 – raw materials; Annex 3 – machinery, manufactures and petroleum.
30 Sept	121	**Report on the 1950 dollar import programme – Committee of Three,** 38p. Consideration of the programme's general economic consequences and reports on individual departmental programmes. These totalled over $1,200m and should not be taken as reliable estimates of

future developments given insufficient dollar resources, grave doubts about the overall balance and possible inflation.

1 Oct	122	**Gold and dollar payments to non-dollar countries – P.J. Moorhouse and P.V. Collyer covering the Overseas Negotiations Committee,** 1+7p. Also ON(49)322(revise).
1 Oct	123	**Dollar export forecast 1950 – Board of Trade,** 3p. On optimistic assumptions, exports to the dollar area in 1950 could reach $7,000m.
3 Oct	124	**Food consumption in 1950/51 – P.J. Moorhouse and P.V. Collyer covering the Ministry of Food,** 1+1p.
13 Oct	125	**Dollar programme: appendix I. Sterling area gold and dollar imports – unsigned,** 5p.
5 Oct	126	**Committee of Three revised report on 1950 dollar import programme – C.S.O.,** 1+34p.
5 Oct	127	**Dollar import programme – R.W.B. Clarke,** 3p. Suggested approach.
5 Oct	128	**Price problems arising from devaluation – Ministry of Food,** 7p.
5 Oct	129	**Imports from non-dollar world – Ministry of Supply,** 2p.
7 Oct	130	**Bacon and cheese subsidies – Ministry of Food,** 1p.
12 Oct	131	**Dollar programme: draft report – unsigned,** 8p. Revise version. Deals with the dollar import programme for 1949–50.
10 Oct	132	**Possible reductions in the dollar import programme for 1949/50 – Committee of Three,** 10p. Report on the programme for July 1949–June 1950 as set out in P(49)126, and consideration of possible reductions.
11 Oct	133	**Imports of machinery from dollar sources – Import Licensing Committee,** 3+1p appendix. Also ILC 343. Concern about the consequences of drastic cuts.
11 Oct	134	**The effect of devaluation on prices in the non-dollar world – Raw Materials Department,** 4p.
12 Oct	135	**Dollar programme – P.J. Moorhouse and P.V. Collyer,** 1+8p. Revise version. Redraft of Appendix III of the report to ministers on cuts in the 1949/50 import programme.
13 Oct	136	**The 1950 dollar balance of payments: Appendix II of report – Committee of Three,** 1+18p. Sets out the proposed dollar import programme.
13 Oct	137	**Report on the changes in E.C.A. procurement procedure – P.J. Moorhouse and P.V. Collyer covering the Subcommittee on Accounting Procedure,** 1+5p.
14 Oct	138	**Monthly report No. 6,** 1+9p.

14 Oct	139	**The 1950 dollar programme – P.J. Moorhouse and P.V. Collyer covering the committee,** 1+11+30p appendixes. See EPB(49)19. Also ED(49)16.
14 Oct	140	**Imports of non-ferrous metals from the non-dollar world – Ministry of Supply,** 2p.
18 Oct	141	**E.C.A. instructions for 1949/50 (final) programme – C.S.O.,** 4p.
20 Oct	142	**The dollar programme July 1949–Dec 1950 – P.J. Moorhouse and P.V. Collyer covering E.E. Bridges and the committee,** 1+2+8+22p appendixes. See ED(49)19.
24 Oct	143	**E.C.A. financed import programme 1949/50 – Treasury,** 2+5p.
25 Oct	144	**Imports of machinery from dollar sources: draft report – the committee,** 4+2p appendix. Draft of P(49)150.
26 Oct	145	**Draft report on price policy – the committee,** 3p. Reduced consumption was the main means of avoiding a general price increase for essential goods and raw materials from the non-dollar world.
26 Oct	146	**The second allotment of E.R.P. aid for 1949/50 – Treasury covering P. Hoffman,** 1+3p.
26 Oct	147	**Rates of exchange – Treasury,** 1+7p.
1 Nov	148	**Draft report on price policy – Ministry of Food,** 3p. Criticism of P(49)145.
1 Nov	149	**Change in membership – P.J. Moorhouse and P.V. Collyer,** 1p.
5 Nov	150	**Imports of machinery from dollar sources – P.J. Moorhouse and P.V. Collyer covering the committee,** 1+4+1p appendix. See ED(W)(49)12.

CAB 134/618   Memoranda   9 Nov–30 Dec 1949   P(49)151–174.

9 Nov	**P(49)151**	**Competitive buying in the dollar area – R.W.B. Clarke,** 1+1p appendix.
10 Nov	152	**The general balance of payments: mid-1949 to mid-1951 – Committee of Four,** 37+8p annexes. Introduction – general assumptions; Part I – the general balance of payments; Part II – imports of food, feedingstuffs and tobacco; Part III – imports of raw materials, oil and machinery; total production; Part IV – total supply and demand; Part V – supply and demand for certain groups of commodities; imports of manufactures; Part VI – conclusions. With the weakening of import controls it was useless to build up an import programme from non-dollar sources. A new approach, in which balance of payments

estimates were considered against the probable trend of supply and demand in the whole economy, was necessary. No serious internal difficulty was foreseen to prevent a satisfactory overall balance in the period 1949/51 but the dollar situation remained grave.

14 Nov	153	**General balance of payments; U.K. export prospects 1949/51 – Board of Trade,** 4+8p appendixes. Consideration of the consequences of devaluation on export prospects on each important market.
14 Nov	154	**General balance of payments, 1950/51; 1951/52 – R.W.B. Clarke,** 1p. Suggested approach to dealing with P(49)152 and 153.
14 Nov	155	**Monthly report No. 7,** 1+9p.
15 Nov	156	**The rest of sterling area balance of payments 1949/50 and 1950/51 – P.J. Moorhouse and P.V. Collyer covering S. Goldman,** 1+6+30p appendixes. Examination of the balance of payments of the whole area and individual countries, with implications for the U.K.'s balance of payments.
16 Nov	157	**Invisible items in the general balance of payments: mid-1949 to mid-1951 – Treasury,** 2+1p.
18 Nov	158	**The 1950–51 and 1951–52 models – R.W.B. Clarke,** 3p. Suggested basis for the O.E.E.C. and E.C.A. submissions.
19 Nov	159	**Regional analysis of U.K. non-dollar import programme 1950 – C.S.O.,** 2+1p.
21 Nov	160	**Dollar import programme 1949–50 – C.S.O.,** 1+2p. As submitted to E.C.A.
22 Nov	161	**The balance of payments in 1950: draft report – R.W.B. Clarke,** 5p. Increasing reliance had to be placed on indirect controls.
22 Nov	162	**Memorandum of the O.E.E.C./E.C.A. Draft chapter I: the approach to viability – R.W.B. Clarke,** 8p. Sets out the way in which the U.K. intended to reduce its dependence on economic assistance over the next two years.
23 Nov	163	**Draft report to ministers on balance of payments in 1950 – P.J. Moorhouse and P.V. Collyer covering the Committee of Four,** 1+38p. Appendix to P(49)161.
23 Nov	164	**Import programmes for the O.E.E.C. 1950/51 and 1951/52 – C.S.O.,** 1+2p.
25 Nov	165	**Submission to the O.E.E.C./E.C.A.: draft covering note for ministers – R.W.B. Clarke,** 3p.
26 Nov	166	**Submission to the O.E.E.C. on 1950/51 and 1951/52 programmes – P.J. Moorhouse and**

		P.V. Collyer covering the committee, 1+56p. Draft of P(49)169.
6 Dec	167	**Balance of payments in 1950 – P.J. Moorhouse and P.V. Collyer covering the committee,** 1+5+37p appendix. Revise version. See EPC(49)157.
26 Nov	168	**Preparation of 1950/51 programme – P.J. Moorhouse and P.V. Collyer covering R.S. McCaffrey,** 1+2p.
30 Nov	169	**Submission to the O.E.E.C. on the U.K. position in 1950/51 – P.J. Moorhouse and P.V. Collyer,** 1+4+55p. See ED(49)23. Also ER(L)(49)325.
7 Dec	170	**Monthly report No. 8,** 1+8+10p annex. Review of oils and fats prices by the Ministry of Food annexed.
8 Dec	171	**U.K. current and R.S.A. general balance of payments in gold and dollars 1949–50 – Treasury,** 1+4p appendix.
16 Dec	172	**U.K. programme for 1950/51 – Statistical Working Group,** 2+8+5p addendum + 1p corrigendum.
20 Dec	173	**General memorandum for the O.E.E.C.: U.K. position in 1950/51 – P.J. Moorhouse and P.V. Collyer,** 1+35+7p appendixes. As submitted to the O.E.E.C.
30 Dec	174	**Publication of general memorandum for the O.E.E.C. on the U.K.'s position in 1950–51 – P.J. Moorhouse and P.V. Collyer,** 1+1p.

CAB 134/619   Meetings   5 Jan–8 Dec 1950   P(50)1st–15th.

5 Jan	P(50)1st:1	**Publication of the 1950/51 programme.**
	:2	**Price assumptions in the Economic Survey.** P(50)1. The Official Committee on Economic Development to be informed that prices of imported raw materials and food were higher than forecast. It was too early to estimate their final cost.
	:3	**Central register of returns supplied to the E.C.A.**
	:4	**Changes in membership.**
21 Mar	2nd:1	**Programme for 1950/51.** P(50)6 and 7. Agreement on general procedure to be followed in drawing up the 1950/51 programme and consideration of the more detailed proposals in P(50)7.
	:2	**Monthly report on import commodity price movements.** P(50)5.
	:3	**Progressing of the import programme.** P(50)8.
	:4	**Future work of the committee.**
8 June	3rd:1	**Monthly progress report No. 1, first quarter 1950.** P(50)15.

	:2	**Balance of payments and dollar import programme in 1950/51.** P(50)16. Agreement on how to prepare and consider the broader issues in departmental import programmes.
13 June	**4th**	**The balance of payments and the dollar import programme in 1950/51.** P(50)16. Consideration of the chapters on the total import programme, export prospects in 1950/51, invisibles and the overall balance of payments. Agreement on criteria for the report to ministers on the overall balance.
15 June	**5th**	**The balance of payments and the dollar import programme in 1950/51.** P(50)16 and 19. Consideration of the chapters in P(50)16 on dollar import policy.
27 June	**6th**	**Balance of payments for 1950/51.** P(50)20. Approval with amendment.
29 June	**7th:1**	**Balance of payments for 1950/51.** P(50)21, 22, 23. Approval with amendments.
	:2	**The O.E.E.C. third report.**
11 July	**8th**	**The O.E.E.C. third report.** P(50)26 and 27.
10 Oct	**9th:1**	**Balance of payments programme for 1951.** P(50)37.
	:2	**Monthly progress report No. 4, Jan–June 1950.** P(50)35.
24 Nov	**10th:1**	**Dollar balance in 1951.** P(50)39. Agreement that a conservative estimate of U.K. expenditure on dollar imports in 1951 should be submitted to ministers. Consideration by commodities of the U.K. import programme.
	:2	**General balance of payments for 1950/51.**
27 Nov	**11th**	**The dollar balance in 1951.** P(50)39. Continued consideration by sectors of the dollar accounts.
1 Dec	**12th**	**Overall balance of payments in 1951.** P(50)41. Agreement that an estimate of the import programme should assume reasonable U.S. co-operation on raw material supplies. P(50)41 was discussed on the assumption that the programme for 1951 would be about £2,800m.
4 Dec	**13th:1**	**Dollar programme for 1951.** P(50)42.
	:2	**Future business.**
5 Dec	**14th**	**Overall balance of payments in 1951.** P(50)41. Consideration of certain amendments to the figures in the report and then of closing the gap either by reducing imports or by increasing exports. The former was rejected as impossible. Agreed that it should be recommended to ministers that planning should aim at securing earnings from exports in the second half of 1951 10% higher than the figure forecast. Consideration then turned to certain regional

		problems involved in the overall balance of payments.
8 Dec	15th:1	**Dollar programme for 1951.** P(50)43. R.W.B. Clarke described the comments of the Economic Steering Committee and the Economic Policy Committee on the paper.
	:2	**Overall balance of payments in 1951.** P(50)44.

CAB 134/620   Memoranda   4 Jan–3 July 1950   P(50)1–25.

4 Jan	P(50)1	**Monthly report No. 9,** 1+8p.
12 Jan	2	**U.K. submission on 1950–51–52 position: White Paper – P.J. Moorhouse and M.M. du Merton,** 1+45p. See Cmd. 7862.
17 Feb	3	**Monthly report No. 10,** 1+12p.
18 Feb	4	**U.K. programme for 1950–51 – Colonial Office,** 1+2+3p. Tables covering trade and balance of payments of U.K. dependent overseas territories, 1948–51, as submitted to the O.E.E.C.
8 Mar	5	**Monthly report No. 11,** 1+12p.
9 Mar	6	**New programmes for 1950–51 – R.W.B. Clarke,** 1p.
18 Mar	7	**The programme for 1950–51 – C.S.O.,** 2+6p annexes. Suggested procedure for revising the programme generally, following P(50)6.
20 Mar	8	**Progressing of the import programme – Balance of Payments (Statistics) Subcommittee,** 2+6p appendixes. Report proposing monthly statements on imports of main commodities and more detailed quarterly statements.
24 Mar	9	**The programme for 1950–51 – C.S.O.,** 2+7p annexes. Procedure for drawing up the revised programme.
1 Apr	10	**Change of secretary – P.J. Moorhouse,** 1p.
15 Apr	11	**Monthly report No. 12,** 1+12p.
15 Apr	12	**Programme for 1950/51 – P.J. Moorhouse and R.B. Marshall,** 1p. Revise version.
4 May	13	**Final allotment on E.R.P. aid for 1949/50 – Treasury covering R.M. Bissell,** 1+1+1p.
13 May	14	**Monthly report No. 13,** 1+11p.
26 May	15	**Monthly progress report No. 1, first quarter 1950 – P.J. Moorhouse and R.B. Marshall,** 1+4+5p. First report on imports, balance of payments, consumption and stocks.
1 June	16	**The balance of payments and dollar import programme in 1950/51 – Committee of Four,** 71+9p annexes. Part I – the overall balance of payments, including departmental import programmes, the total import programme, export prospects 1950/51, invisibles and the overall balance. Part II – the dollar import

programme, covering dollar import policy and longer-term aspects. The report forecast at best a balance in the U.K. overall current account, not the desired surplus; and concluded that there was insufficient margin between the proposed dollar programme and the $1,200m ceiling.

2 June	**17**	**Programme for 1950/51 – P.J. Moorhouse**, 1p.
9 June	**18**	**Monthly report No. 14**, 1+11p.
9 June	**19**	**The gold and dollar accounts 1950/51 – Treasury**, 11+4p appendixes.
24 June	**20**	**Balance of payments for 1950–51: draft report for ministers – the committee**, 7p. Draft of P(50)25.
26 June	**21**	**Report of the Programmes Committee on the balance of payments and dollar import programme 1950/51. Annex I: the U.K. import programmes and the overall balance of payments – Committee of Four**, 78+9p appendixes. Redraft of P(50)16 and draft of Annex I of P(50)25.
24 June	**22**	**Report of the Programmes Committee on the balance of payments and dollar import programme in 1950/51. Annex II: the dollar balance of the sterling area 1950/51 – R.B. Marshall and M.M. du Merton covering the Treasury**, 1+12+4p appendixes. Redraft of P(50)19 and draft of Annex II of P(50)25.
26 June	**23**	**Report on the balance of payments in 1950/51. Annex III: the U.K.'s balance of payments in early 1950 – Committee of Four**, 3p. Draft of Annex III of P(50)25.
29 June	**24**	**Monthly progress report No. 2, Jan–April 1950 – R.B. Marshall and M.M. du Merton covering the Treasury, the Board of Trade and the C.S.O.**, 1+3+5p.
30 June	**25**	**Balance of payments for 1950–51 R.B. Marshall covering the committee**, 1+6+78p annexes. See EPC(50)73. Also EPB(50) 15 and ED (50)5.

CAB 134/621   Memoranda   7 July–19 Dec 1950   P(50)26–48.

7 July	**P(50)26**	**The O.E.E.C. third report. Preliminary notes on the general balance of payments 1954 – Third Report Working Group.** 7p. Consideration of the possible effect on import requirements of some preliminary calculations of national output and expenditure.
7 July	**27**	**The O.E.E.C. third report. Preliminary questionnaire for departments – Third Report Working Group**, 2+1p appendix.
14 July	**28**	**Monthly report No. 15**, 1+11p.

18 July	29	The U.K. submission to the O.E.E.C.: third report – Board of Trade, 1+2p. Assessment of the realism of a £2,500m export figure for 1954/55.
18 July	30	Quarterly progress report No. 1, Jan–Mar 1950 – R.B. Marshall and M.M. du Merton covering the Board of Trade, 1+4p.
25 July	31	Change of secretary – P.J. Moorhouse, 1p.
8 Aug	32	Monthly progress report No. 3, Jan–May 1950 – M.M. du Merton and J.A. Atkinson covering the Treasury, the Board of Trade and the C.S.O., 1+1+4p.
10 Aug	33	Monthly report No. 16, 2+12p.
9 Sept	34	Monthly report No. 17, 2+12p.
9 Oct	35	Monthly progress report No. 4, Jan–June 1950 – P.J. Moorhouse and J.A. Atkinson covering the Treasury, the Board of Trade and the C.S.O., 1+6+7p.
17 Oct	36	Monthly report No. 18, 2+11p.
7 Oct	37	Balance of payments programme for 1951 – R.W.B. Clarke, 2p. Proposed procedure.
13 Nov	38	Monthly report No. 19, 2+12p.
22 Nov	39	The dollar balance in 1951: interim report – Committee of Four, 17+10p appendix. Proposed dollar import programme of £547m, with commodity analysis appended.
28 Nov	40	Sterling area gold and dollar accounts 1951 by half years – P.J. Moorhouse and J.A. Atkinson, 1+1p.
30 Nov	41	The overall balance of payments in 1951 – P.J. Moorhouse and J.A. Atkinson covering the Committee of Four, 1+16+10p appendixes +7p addendum +7p appendix. Draft of the appendix to P(50)48.
30 Nov.	42	The dollar programme for 1951 – R.W.B. Clarke, 1+13p. Draft of P(50)43.
5 Dec	43	The dollar programme for 1951 – P.J. Moorhouse and J.A. Atkinson covering the committee, 1+10+16p appendixes. See ES(50)25.
7 Dec	44	Draft report on the U.K. general balance of payments for 1951 – unsigned, 10p. Draft of P(50)45.
9 Dec	45	U.K. general balance of payments for 1951 – P.J. Moorhouse and J.A. Atkinson covering the committee, 1+6+30p appendix. See ES(50)28.
14 Dec	46	Monthly report No. 20, 2+12p.
15 Dec	47	The dollar programme for 1951 – P.J. Moorhouse and J.A. Atkinson covering the committee, 1+7+13p appendixes. See EPC(50)127.

19 Dec	**48**	**Report on the U.K. general balance of payments for 1951 – P.J. Moorhouse and J.A. Atkinson covering the committee,** 1+5+23p appendix. See ES(50)28.

CAB 134/622   Meetings and Memoranda   15 Jan–17 Oct 1951   P(51)1st–19th and P(51)1–28.

Meetings

15 Feb	**P(51)1st**	**Balance of payments work for report to N.A.T.O.** Arrangements agreed.
13 Apr	**2nd:1**	**Balance of payments estimates 1951/52.** P(51)4 and 5. Detailed consideration of P(51)5.
	:2	**Future meetings.**
29 May	**3rd**	**The 1951/1952 import programme.** P(51)12. Consideration of the volume of imports in 1951/52 in detail and of the future trend of prices.
31 May	**4th**	**The 1951/52 balance of payments.** P(51)12, 13, 14, 15. The U.K. overall balance of payments appeared likely to be less unfavourable than the dollar balance.
5 June	**5th**	**The 1951/52 balance of payments.** P(51)16, 17, 18.
8 June	**6th**	**The 1951/52 balance of payments.** P(51)19. Agreement that the report should emphasize the prospective deterioration whilst admitting that forecasts might be unreliable. It should not make firm recommendations but provide ministers with all necessary information. Consideration of how to reduce imports. A reduction in consumption by indirect means, i.e. fiscal measures, offered the best hope.
12 June	**7th**	**Draft report on the balance of payments in 1951/ 52.** P(51)21.
6 July	**8th**	**Action on the 1951/52 balance of payments.** P(51)24. Consideration of import cuts which the Programmes Committee was to draw up at the request of the Economic Policy Committee.
9 July	**9th**	**Action on the 1951/52 balance of payments.** P(51)26 and 27. Further consideration.
11 July	**10th**	**Draft report on import cuts.** P(51)27(revise).
24 July	**11th**	**Import cuts.** P(51)27(2nd revise).
29 Aug	**12th:1**	**Balance of payments since June 1951.** P(51)24. Given the deterioration was greater than expected, a review of the situation for ministers might be desirable.
	:2	**Sterling area balance of payments with Finland.** Consideration of cuts in timber and pulp imports.
	:3	**Import cuts.** P(51)32. Consideration of progress.

	:4	**World market prices of import commodities.** P(51)30.
	:5	**Preparation of next Programme Committee report.**
6 Sept	13th	**The 1952 import programme.** P(51)33. Detailed consideration of proposed procedure.
20 Sept	14th:1	**Authorizations for dollar and near-dollar imports for 1951/52.** P(51)37. Consideration of the import programme to determine in which of the categories in P(51)37 each commodity should be placed.
	:2	**Balance of payments situation.** P(51)36. The Bank of England strongly agreed with the paper but wished to stress further the significance of the U.S. balance of payments.
	:3	**Monthly report on world market prices of import commodities.** P(51)35.
9 Oct	15th:1	**Procedure for considering the 1952 programme.** P(51)41.
	:2	**Export prospects for 1952.** P(51)40.
	:3	**The import programme for 1952.** P(51)39. Examination of the estimated stock levels and whether the price assumptions were satisfactory.
10 Oct	16th:1	**Invisible transactions.** P(51)42.
	:2	**The import programme for 1952.** P(51)39. Consideration of the movement and volume of imports implied by the programme, and of proposals concerning particular commodities.
11 Oct	17th:1	**The import programme for 1952.** P(51)39, 44, 45. Consideration of various commodity import programmes particularly softwoods, pulp and paper.
	:2	**Rest of sterling area balance of payments.** P(51)43. Consideration of paper's assumption and of how the balance of payments of the rest of the sterling area might be improved.
	:3	**Procedure of the committee.**
15 Oct	18th	**Draft report on the 1952 programmes.** P(51)46. Agreement that the urgent need to take decisions required greater emphasis. Consideration in detail.
17 Oct	19th	**Draft report on 1952 programmes.** P(51)46(revise).

Memoranda

15 Jan	P(51)1	**Monthly report No. 21, 2+11p.**
12 Feb	2	**Monthly report No. 22, 2+10p.**
13 Mar	3	**Monthly report No. 23, 2+9p.**
10 Apr	4	**The 1951/52 import programme – P.J. Moorhouse and J.A. Atkinson covering the C.S.O., 1+3p annexes. Proposed schedules.**

7 Apr	5	**The 1951/52 import programme – D.B. Pitblado,** 3p. Proposed procedure.
11 Apr	6	**U.K. submission to N.A.T.O. – C.S.O.,** 1+2p.
11 Apr	7	**Statistical group – E.A. Hitchman, R.W.B. Clarke and F.F. Turnbull,** 2p. See RM(51)98. Also MAC(51)54. Recommendation of a new working group to serve *inter alia* the Mutual Aid, Programmes and Raw Materials Committees.
13 Apr	8	**Monthly report No. 24,** 2+9p.
17 Apr	9	**Progress report No. 5, July–Dec 1950 – P.J. Moorhouse and J.A. Atkinson covering the Treasury, Board of Trade, Economic Section and C.S.O.,** 5+5p.
16 May	10	**Progress report No. 6, Jan–Mar 1951 – P.J. Moorhouse and J.A. Atkinson covering the Treasury, the Board of Trade, the Economic Section and the C.S.O.,** 1+7+4p.
22 May	11	**Monthly report No. 25,** 1+10p.
28 May	12	**The import programme for 1951/52 – Statistical Group,** 64p. Part I – general report, setting out its assumptions and the total programme of £669m. Part II – programmes for individual commodities. Part III – commodity tables.
28 May	13	**U.K. balance of payments: 1951/52. U.K. invisibles – P.J. Moorhouse and J.A. Atkinson covering the Treasury,** 1+6+3p appendix.
31 May	14	**Import programme 1951/52: supplementary notes – Statistical Group,** 6p. Notes on the effect on the programme of a general resumption of price increases, the stockpiling programme, the extent of attrition on the programme as a whole, imports from eastern Europe, and the implications of the programme for industrial production.
31 May	15	**The food programme: supplementary note – Statistical Group,** 2p. Effects of bad weather on cost of imports.
2 June	16	**Balance of payments: 1951/52. Sterling area gold and dollar accounts – P.J. Moorhouse and J.A. Atkinson covering the Treasury,** 1+12p. Conclusion that a sharp deterioration could be expected that year and still more in 1951/52.
2 June	17	**The import programme for 1951/52: shipping availability for imports during 1951/52 – Ministry of Transport,** 2p.
4 June	18	**Estimated U.K. exports in 1951–52 – Board of Trade,** 5+5p appendixes. Estimates volume for 1951–52 158% of 1947.
7 June	19	**The 1951–52 programme – R.W.B. Clarke,** 2p. Basic estimates for 1951–52.

9 June	20	**The 1951/52 import programme: scope for switching food purchases from non-dollar/non-participating countries – Ministry of Food,** 2p.
9 June	21	**Draft report on 1951–52** – unsigned, 17p. Draft of P(51)24.
12 June	22	**Monthly report No. 26,** 1+12p.
13 June	23	**The 1951/52 import programme: supplementary dollar food imports – Ministry of Food,** 3p.
19 June	24	**Balance of payments for 1951–52 – P.J. Moorhouse and J.A. Atkinson covering the committee,** 1+8+41p annex. See EPB(51)13. Also ES(51)40.
28 June	25	**Non-sterling, non-dollar countries – R.W.B. Clarke,** 1p.
29 June	26	**Argentina – P.J. Moorhouse and J.A. Atkinson covering K. Anderson,** 4+2p annex. Also ON(51)89(revise). Examination of prospective sterling area balance of payments with Argentina.
12 July	27	**Import cuts – P.J. Moorhouse and R. Gedling covering the committee,** 1+6+1p annex. See EPC(51)79.
20 July	28	**Monthly report No. 27,** 2+10p.

CAB 134/623   Memoranda   11 Aug–20 Dec 1951   P(51)29–55.

11 Aug	**P(51)29**	**The 1951/52 oils and fats programme – Ministry of Food,** 2+1p annex.
16 Aug	30	**Monthly report No. 28,** 3+10p.
27 Aug	31	**Sterling area balance of payments with Finland – P.J. Moorhouse covering K. Anderson,** 1+2+2p. Also ON(51)122.
28 Aug	32	**The effect of reducing the softwood allocation – P.J. Moorhouse covering F.F. Turnbull,** 1+4p. See M(51)45.
4 Sept	33	**The 1952 import programme – R.W.B. Clarke,** 3+3p annexes. Proposed procedure.
6 Sept	34	**Sterling area balance of payments with Russia and minor satellites 1951/52 – P.J. Moorhouse covering K. Anderson,** 1+3+4p annexes. Also ON(51)123(revise).
12 Sept	35	**Monthly report No. 29,** 2+10p.
11 Sept		**Change of vice-chairmen – P.J. Moorhouse,** 1p.
17 Sept	36	**The balance of payments situation – R.W.B. Clarke,** 12+2p. Sets out the basic considerations for the committee's 1952 report. The problem was no longer solely the dollar area but the weakness of sterling with the rest of the world. The only solution was for the sterling area to import less and export more.
19 Sept	37	**Authorizations for dollar expenditure – P.J. Moorhouse and R. Gedling,** 1+2p. Sets out three

		categories of priority in which to place commodities in preparation for ministerial cuts.
4 Oct	**38**	**Progress report No. 7, Jan/June 1951 – P.J. Moorhouse and R. Gedling covering the Treasury, the Board of Trade, the Economic Section and the C.S.O.,** 1+11+6p.
5 Oct	**39**	**The import programme for 1952 – Statistical Group,** 1+39+16p addenda. Part I – the import programme as a whole (in addenda). Sets out the basis of departmental programmes including stockpiling and the impact of price changes. Part II – commodity analysis, reviewing each commodity. Statistical appendixes in addenda.
8 Oct	**40**	**Export prospects for 1952 – Board of Trade,** 3+2p appendix. Summary of GEN 380/6.
8 Oct	**41**	**Procedure for 1952 report – R.W.B. Clarke,** 4p.
9 Oct	**42**	**Invisible transactions – Treasury,** 8p.
10 Oct	**43**	**Rest of sterling area balance of payments – Treasury,** 10p.
8 Oct	**44**	**Possible reductions in imports of pulp and paper (other than newsprint) – Ministry of Materials,** 4p.
9 Oct	**45**	**Possible reductions in softwood imports – Ministry of Materials,** 4p.
16 Oct	**46**	**Draft report on 1952 programme** – unsigned, 28p. Revise version. Draft of P(51)49.
15 Oct	**47**	**Import content of personal expenditure – C.S.O.,** 3p.
15 Oct	**48**	**The U.K. 1952 import programme: value of consumption at 1952 prices – C.S.O.,** 2p.
18 Oct	**49**	**Note by the secretary – R. Gedling covering the committee,** 1+30p. Draft of P(51)50. Report on the 1952 balance of payments.
22 Oct	**50**	**Balance of payments for 1952 – R. Gedling covering the committee,** 1+12+18p appendix. See ES(51)59.
22 Oct	**51**	**Report on the 1952 balance of payments: statistical appendix – C.S.O.,** 1+17p. Draft of the appendix to P(51)50.
29 Oct	**52**	**The balance of payments in 1952: background material – Statistical Group,** 37p. Material not incorporated in the final report or its statistical appendix (P(51)50).
9 Nov	**53**	**Monthly report Nos. 30 and 31,** 2+10p.
13 Dec	**54**	**Monthly report No. 32,** 2+8p.
20 Dec	**55**	**Progress report No. 8, July/Sept 1951 – P.J. Moorhouse and R. Gedling covering the Treasury, the Board of Trade, the Economic Section and the C.S.O.,** 1+5+6p.

Subcommittee on Country Import Programmes

Set up in July 1948 (CAB 134/608, P(48)3rd) as part of the Programmes Committee organization.

Terms To carry out the detailed examination of the import programmes from each country and to cover the former functions of the Exchange Requirements Committee in relation to bilateral negotiations conducted by the Overseas Negotiations Committee.

Members M.T. Flett (Try, ch.); the members of the Programmes Committee. (Jan 1949) A.C. Sparks (Try, ch.).

Secs. H.A.C. Gill (Try) and P.J. Moorhouse (Cab. O.). (June 1949) J.E. Lucas (Try) replaced Gill. (Dec 1949) L. Bielinky (Try) replaced Moorhouse. (Feb 1950) M.I. Reid (Try) replaced Bielinky.

CAB 134/627   Meetings and Memoranda   1 July–31 Dec 1948
P(CIP)(48)1st–9th and P(CIP)(48)1–44.

628   Meetings and Memoranda   4 Jan–30 Dec 1949
P(CIP)(49)1st–22nd and P(CIP)(49)1–36.

629   Meetings and Memoranda   5 Jan–17 Oct 1950
P(CIP)(50)1st–7th and P(CIP)(50)1–23.

Subcommittee on Food

Set up in July 1948 (CAB 134/608, P(48)3rd) as part of the Programmes Committee organization.

Terms To consider any question that may be referred to them involving the balance of payments aspect of our food policy.

Members M.T. Flett (Try, ch.); W.H. Fisher (Try); C.H. Blagburn (Food); A.C. Sparks (M.A.F.). (Feb 1949) A.C. Sparks (Try, ch.).

Secs. H.A.C. Gill (Try) and P.V. Collyer (Cab. O.). (June 1949) J.E. Lucas (Try) replaced Gill. (Dec 1949) L. Bielinky (Try) replaced Collyer. (Feb 1950) M.I. Reid (Try).

CAB 134/630   Meetings and Memoranda   1 July 1948–23 Feb 1950
P(F)(48)1st–3rd, P(F)(49)1st–5th and P(F)(48)1–2, P(F)(49)1–4,
P(F)(50)1.

631   Meeting   20 June 1951   P(F)(51)1st.

Subcommittee on Raw Materials

Set up in July 1948 (CAB 134/608, P(48)3rd) as part of the Programmes Committee organization it took over the functions of the Exchange Requirements Committee

Subcommittee on Raw Materials (CAB 134/262). Membership varied according to the subject under consideration.

Terms To scrutinize and approve programmes involving expenditure from public funds on raw materials imported on public account, and to examine programmes of imports on private account in cases where it is agreed with the chairman of the Import Licensing Committee that the subcommittee is the appropriate body to do so, for example where the programmes in question are closely related to the purchases on public account and raise similar questions.

Chairman M.T. Flett (Try). (Jan 1949) A.C. Sparks (Try).

Secs. H.A.C. Gill (Try) and P.J. Moorhouse (Cab. O.). (June 1949) J.E. Lucas (Try) replaced Gill. (Dec 1949) L. Bielinky replaced Moorhouse. (Feb 1950) M.I. Reid replaced Bielinky.

CAB 134/632   Meetings and Memoranda   2 July–20 Dec 1948
P(RM)(48)1st–5th and P(RM)(48)1–18.

633   Meetings and Memoranda   25 Jan–29 Dec 1949
P(RM)(49)1st–11th and P(RM)(49)1–38.

634   Meetings and Memoranda   2 Jan 1950–12 Sept 1951
P(RM)(50)1st–3rd, P(RM)(51)1st and P(RM)(50)1–17 and
P(RM)(51)1–9.

15.35   Production Committee

Set up in the major reorganization of October 1947, this committee under the chairmanship of Cripps (1947–50) and Gaitskell (1950–51) became second in importance only to the Economic Policy Committee (CAB 134/215–230). Whilst it did debate issues of major importance, it was also heavily involved in detailed administration, in part because it was a court of appeal for a wide range of committees and especially those involved in the allocation of materials and investment. Its terms of reference overlapped with those of the Economic Policy Committee but in practice it concentrated on the day-to-day internal issues of normal peace-time government rather than issues which had international implications or were thrown up by exceptional circumstances such as the Korean War. It was, according to Douglas Jay, 'where the main work was done', *Change and Fortune* (1980), p 174.

It received a series of monthly reports, itemized here, on the food situation; stocks of food and animal feedingstuffs, raw materials and petroleum products; the movement of wages, hours of work etc. (from July 1948); and changes in the employment position (from June 1951). It established several committees to which it could devolve its responsibilities including the Labour (Textile Industries) Committee (CAB 134/471–474), the Defence (Transition) Committee, which was the reconstituted Headquarters Building Committee, and the Subcommittee on Manufacture in Government-controlled Establishments of Goods for Civilian Use.

Because of the importance to economic planning of the committee, its records up to December 1951 have been listed in full.

Terms   To supervise the production programmes (both for export and for the home market) required to give effect to the general economic plan; and to consider questions of internal economic policy.

Members   Min. of Ec. Aff. (ch.); Ch. of Exchequer (or Fin. Sec.); S./S. Scotland; Mins. of Labour & N.S., Health, Agriculture & Fish, Transport, Food, Supply, Fuel & Power, Works; Pres. Bd Trade; 1st Ld Admiralty; Ch. D. Lancaster; Paymaster-Gen.   (Dec 1947) Ec. Sec. replaced Fin. Sec.   (Mar 1950) Min. State for Ec. Aff. replaced Ec. Sec., Min. of Civil Aviation added.   (Nov 1950) Ec. Sec. (Try) added.   (Jan 1951) Min. of Town & Country Planning replaced Min. of Health.   (May 1951) Ld Privy Seal added.

Secs.   S.E.V. Luke (Cab. O.).   (June 1950) O.C. Morland (Cab. O.) replaced Luke.

CAB 134/635   Meetings and Memoranda   8 Oct–31 Dec 1947
            PC(47)1st–5th and PC(47)1–29.

Meetings

13 Oct	**PC(47)1st:1**	**Work of the committee.**
	:2	**Gas and electricity charges.** PC(47)2.
	:3	**Investment programme.** PC(47)3. Agreement on the reduction of £200m and the continuation of preferential treatment for development areas. Reductions in the housing and other programmes, on which agreement had been impossible, were to go to Cabinet.
4 Nov	**2nd:1**	**Investment programme: draft White Paper.** PC(47)4 and 7. Consideration of its form.
	:2	**Transport of freight and coal.** PC(47)5.
	:3	**Food situation in the U.K.** PC(47)6.
	:4	**Agriculture (Scotland) Bill: housing of crofters and agricultural workers.** PC(47)8.
	:5	**Raw materials: disclosure of allocations.** PC(47)9.
	:6	**Wages policy: claim of Post Office manipulative grades.**
18 Nov	**3rd:1**	**Investment programme: draft White Paper.** PC(47)13. Consideration in detail.
	:2	**Steel: allocations for engineering and shipbuilding exports.** PC(47)15. Allocations proposed by the Materials Committee for the first and second quarters of 1948 were insufficient for the achievement of export targets. Cripps to submit a revised export programme.
	:3	**Essential workers: provision of accommodation.** PC(47)12. A committee of parliamentary secretaries to prepare detailed plans.
	:4	**Statistical review.** PC(47)10.
	:5	**Food situation in the U.K.** PC(47)14.
5 Dec	**4th:1**	**Framework of economic planning.** PC(47)11. General discussion of the basis of economic

planning and the measures necessary to
implement any plan.

:2   **Employment of prison labour.** PC(47)16.

:3   **Building programme: priority for labour.**
PC(47)18. Agreement that W.B.A. priority for
building labour should be strictly limited.

:4   **Production and allocation of alkalis.** PC(47)19.

12 Dec   5th:1   **Mid-week sport in 1948.** PC(47)21.

:2   **Coal: proposed modification of the winter
budget.** PC(47)23. Approval.

:3   **Coal prices.** PC(47)27.

:4   **Bunker coal prices.**

:5   **Oil.** PC(47)24 and 26.

:6   **Winter Transport Executive Committee.**
PC(47)22.

:7   **Stocks of foods and animal feedingstuffs, raw
materials and petroleum products.** PC(47)20.

Memoranda

21 Oct   **PC(47)1**   **Composition and terms of reference – N. Brook,**
1p. Revise version.

8 Oct   2   **Gas and electricity charges – Gaitskell,** 3p.

9 Oct   3   **Report of the I.P.C. – N. Brook** covering the
I.P.C. 1+14+32p appendixes +2p. See
CP(47)284. Also IPC(47)9.

21 Oct   4   **Report of the I.P.C. – Key,** 4p. Sets out the
effect of the proposals on the building industry
and stresses the importance of avoiding an
overlap between the I.P.C. and the
Headquarters Building Committee.

27 Oct   5   **Winter transport prospects – Cripps,** 2p.
Arrangements for a Winter Transport Policy
Committee.

27 Oct   6   **Food situation in the U.K. Report for September
1947 – Strachey,** 9+1p annex.

31 Oct   7   **White Paper on the investment programme –
Cripps,** 1+8+21p appendixes. Draft for
publication setting out the main objectives for
capital investment in 1948 and the criteria on
which cuts had been made.

31 Oct   8   **Agriculture (Scotland) Bill: housing of crofters
and agricultural workers – Woodburn,** 1p.

31 Oct   9   **Disclosure of Materials Committee allocations
– Marquand,** 3p.

4 Nov   10   **Stocks of food and animal feedingstuffs, raw
materials and petroleum products – C.S.O.,**
3+12p appendixes. Also CS(S)(47)37.

11 Nov   11   **The framework of economic planning – Cripps,**
5p. Sets out his views on economic planning.
It should be based on the planning of imports,
investment and consumption. Given the
dependence on foreign trade it should also be

flexible. Three broad considerations should guide detailed planning: (1) in a free society planning should simultaneously seek the satisfaction of consumer wants and the most economical use of resources; (2) since the condition of the economy in the next four years would be far from normal, it would be impossible to give complete freedom to the consumer; (3) it was quite impossible and far from desirable to set production targets over the whole field of industry for every final product. However, in the short term it was necessary both to set general targets for the basic industries and to estimate general levels of production for the main manufacturing industries.

13 Nov	12	**Provision of camp and hostel accommodation for miners, farm workers and European Volunteer Workers** – Isaacs, 1+3p annex.
14 Nov	13	**Capital investment in 1948** – Cripps, 2+5+17p appendixes. Revised draft White Paper. The only major change was a £20m reduction in cuts proposed for the housing programme.
14 Nov	14	**Food situation in the U.K. Report for October 1947** – Strachey, 11+1p annex.
14 Nov	15	**Steel allocations for engineering and shipbuilding exports** – Wilson, H., 2p. On allocations given, export targets could not be met.
26 Nov	16	**Employment of prison labour** – Chuter Ede and Woodburn, 5p.
26 Nov	17	**Emergency Accommodation Committee** – N. Brook, 1p.
29 Nov	18	**The building programme: priority for labour** – Key, 3p. The awarding of W.B.A. priority had become virtually automatic in some cases and its value had depreciated. Recommendation for a more restrictive policy.
2 Dec	19	**Alkalis** – Wilson, H., 4+4p annexes.
3 Dec	20	**Stocks of food and animal feedingstuffs, raw materials and petroleum products** – C.S.O., 3+12p appendixes. Also CS(S)(47)47.
6 Dec	21	**Mid-week sport in 1948** – Chuter Ede, 2p.
9 Dec	22	**Winter Transport Executive Committee** – Cripps, 1p. The committee had been reconstituted, with executive responsibility, to meet the growing crisis.
10 Dec	23	**Coal. Proposed modification of the winter budget** – Gaitskell, 2p. Certain proposed increases.
10 Dec	24	**Oil** – Gaitskell, 5p. Proposals to meet the increasing difficulties.

16 Dec	**25**	**Food situation in the U.K. Report for November 1947 – Strachey,** 9+1p.
11 Dec	**26**	**Tankers – Noel-Baker,** 3p. Gives reasons for the tanker shortage and proposed action.
11 Dec	**27**	**Coal prices – Gaitskell,** 2+4p annex. Recommended increases.
30 Dec	**28**	**Change in membership – S.E.V. Luke,** 1p.
31 Dec	**29**	**Production and allocation of alkalis – Cripps covering Wilson, H.,** 1+2p. Proposed revised allocation.

CAB 134/636   Meetings   12 Jan–17 Dec 1948   PC(48)1st–25th.

12 Jan	**PC(48)1st:1**	**Defence research and development works services.** PC(48)4.
	:2	**Emergency hostel accommodation.** PC(48)5.
	:3	**Effect of cuts in capital investment on employment in development areas and on Merseyside.** PC(48)6. Wilson, H. was seriously concerned. In development areas and Merseyside emphasis had been on production for the home market to avoid the fluctuations of overseas trade, but preference was now being given to the export trade. Agreement that Merseyside should be treated as a development area in the application of both the revised policy for capital investment and any preferential allocation of resources. The Distribution of Industry Committee was to review the revised capital investment programme.
	:4	**Production and allocation of alkalis.** PC(47)29 and PC(48)3.
	:5	**Iron and steel prices.** PC(48)2.
	:6	**Food situation in the U.K.** PC(47)25.
	:7	**Stocks of food and animal feedingstuffs, raw materials and petroleum products.** PC(48)1.
16 Jan	**2nd:1**	**Railway summer passenger services.** PC(48)10.
	:2	**Durex Abrasives factory at Gorseinon, Swansea.** PC(48)7 and 12. Such individual cases were to go to the Chancellor of the Exchequer although the Economic Secretary would normally deal with them.
	:3	**Iron and steel prices.** PC(48)2. Approved.
	:4	**Increase of textile exports: expansion of output.** PC(48)9 and 13. Agreement to establish the Labour (Textile Industries) Committee.
	:5	**Revised export programme.** PC(48)8. Agreement to make every effort to increase textile exports and minimize unrequited exports.

	:6	**The textile exports and the clothing ration.** PC(48)11. Proposals endorsed and to go to Cabinet.
11 Feb	3rd:1	**Staggering of hours.** To continue to 29 Mar 1948.
	:2	**Mid-week sport in 1948.**
	:3	**Passenger transport restrictions.** PC(48)20.
	:4	**First interim report of the Official Working Party on Textile Machinery Supplies.** PC(48)22.
	:5	**Transport during the winter months.** PC(48)14.
	:6	**The effect of electricity shedding on production.** PC(48)19.
	:7	**Food situation in the U.K.** PC(48)16.
	:8	**Statistical review.** PC(48)21.
	:9	**Emergency hostels: committee machinery.** PC(48)17.
27 Feb	4th:1	**Factories Bill.** PC(48)27.
	:2	**Export packing.** PC(48)26.
	:3	**Provision of miners' hostels in the North Midlands region.** PC(48)28.
	:4	**Provision of sheets for hostels.** PC(48)25.
	:5	**Food situation in the U.K.** PC(48)23.
	:6	**Licensing of building maintenance.** PC(48)24. Proposals approved.
12 Mar	5th:1	**Wage claims.** PC(48)30.
	:2	**Commercial work in the royal dockyards.** PC(48)31.
	:3	**Agricultural prices.** PC(48)33. No reaffirmation of prices until the difference between the actual and estimated number of livestock had been calculated.
	:4	**Steel for shipbulding.** PC(48)35. Proposals approved although Barnes wanted a higher allocation in 1949.
	:5	**Medical inspection of day nurseries.**
	:6	**Production and allocation of alkalis.** The Board of Trade had been unable to satisfy oil companies' full requirements and suggested obtaining the balance from Japan.
	:7	**Statistical review.** PC(48)29.
22 Mar	6th:1	**Agricultural prices.** PC(48)38. Agreement to confirm August 1947 prices.
	:2	**Mid-week sport in 1948.** Some greyhound racing was to be allowed.
	:3	**Steel allocation.** PC(48)32, 34, 37. Both PC(48)32 and 37 were appeals against the Materials Committee allocation. Cripps felt it was important to clarify the relationship between the two committees. The Production Committee should give broad guidance to the Chairman of the Materials Committee on

matters of policy and indicate the general priorities and preferences which his committee should keep in mind in making detailed allocations. This guidance should be given before allocations were made and the Production Committee should not thereafter attempt to make or review detailed allocations.

	:4	**Transport during the winter months.** PC(48)36.
9 Apr	7th:1	**The building programme.** PC(48)44. Agreement to an additional allocation of steel for building purposes in Periods II and III.
	:2	**Provision of employment for disabled persons.** PC(48)42.
	:2	**Consumption of dollar-costing metals.** PC(48)45.
	:4	**Development councils.** PC(48)41. Proposed policy approved.
	:5	**Staggering of hours.**
	:6	**Food situation in the U.K.** PC(48)40.
	:7	**Statistical review.** PC(48)43.
23 Apr	8th:1	**Communist activities in factories.** PC(48)51.
	:2	**Indoor allocation of steel.** PC(48)52. General lines endorsed.
	:3	**Oil companies. The expansion programme.** PC(48)47.
	:4	**Housing – Scotland: use of steel in non-traditional houses.** PC(48)48.
	:5	**Steel economy.** PC(48)49.
	:6	**Steel production.** PC(48)56.
	:7	**Interim report by the Labour (Textile Industries) Committee.** PC(48)53.
	:8	**Wage claims.** PC(48)50. Referred to the Economic Policy Committee as there was not enough time to discuss the important issues raised.
	:9	**Food situation in the U.K.** PC(48)46.
3 May	9th:1	**Expansion of alkali production.** PC(48)55.
	:2	**Allocation of caustic soda.** PC(48)54. Agreed that the additional cost of Japanese soda to oil companies should be borne by a general increase in price.
	:3	**Building licensing.** PC(48)57. Approval of an increase in the limit after 1 August 1948.
	:4	**Coal/oil conversion.** PC(48)58 and 59. Proposals endorsed and to go to Cabinet.
	:5	**The clothing ration.** Explanation of impending changes.
14 May	10th:1	**The clothing ration.** Wilson, H., made a statement on the effect of the recent changes.
	:2	**The N.C.B.: resignation of Sir Charles Reid.**
	:3	**Coal prospect for 1948.** PC(48)61.

	:4	**Building licensing.** PC(48)62. Agreement to introduce the new limit from 1 July 1948.
	:5	**Expansion of virgin aluminium production in the U.K.** PC(48)63.
	:6	**Statistical review.** PC(48)60.
28 May	11th:1	**Emergency hostels: Oldham/Rochdale and Burnley/Nelson districts.** PC(48)64.
	:2	**Wage claims.** PC(48)65 and 67. Isaacs said that the White Paper was having a moderating influence. Agreement that disputes in the public sector reported to the Minister of Labour under the Conditions of Employment and National Arbitration Order, 1940 should be referred to the National Arbitration Tribunal at an early stage. The minister should not refrain from pressing the parties concerned to renew their efforts to reach a settlement by agreement.
	:3	**Programme for the 1949 harvest.** PC(48)68. Discussion centred on the proposal to make an early announcement regarding the retention of millable wheat and barley for livestock feeding.
	:4	**Provision of sheets for the armed forces and emergency hostels.** PC(48)66. Alexander could not accept PC(48)66.
	:5	**Price of motor spirit.**
4 June	12th:1	**Consumption of dollar-costing metals.** PC(48)75.
	:2	**Steel for shipbuilding.** PC(48)69. Further consideration of future allocations was deferred until the 1949 I.P.C. Report.
	:3	**Steel prices and subsidies.** PC(48)72. Proposals approved except that for maintenance of subsidy on imported steel for the rest of the financial year.
	:4	**Speed limit for heavy goods vehicles.** PC(48)73.
	:5	**Turn-round of shipping in U.K. ports.** PC(48)74.
	:6	**Food situation in the U.K.** PC(48)70.
	:7	**Statistical review.** PC(48)71.
2 July	13th:1	**Coal: quality problems.** PC(48)80, 81, 82. Bevan acting as chairman. Approval of proposals for the reduction of large coal for home consumption.
	:2	**Arrangements for spreading the industrial electricity load in the winter of 1948–9.** PC(48)85.
	:3	**Report of the Clow Committee on the electricity peak flow problem.** PC(48)88.
	:4	**Development councils.** PC(48)83.
	:5	**Steel economy.** PC(48)78.
	:6	**Food situation in the U.K.** PC(48)79.

16 July	**14th:1**	**Production of aluminium in North Borneo.** PC(48)76 and 87. Isaacs acting chairman and a very small meeting.
	:2	**Second interim report of Official Working Party on Textile Machinery Supplies.** PC(48)90.
	:3	**Wage claims.** PC(48)91. Isaacs thought greater stability had been attained.
	:4	**Statistical review.** PC(48)86.
23 July	**15th:1**	**Capital investment in 1949.** PC(48)93 and 98. Cripps stressed the report's object was not to impose savings but to indicate to departments the way in which resources were likely to be allocated. Wilson, H. agreed in general with the report's principles but felt the figure for 1949 exports of 145% above the 1938 volume should be much higher. Other ministers felt that excessive resources were being devoted to exports at the expense of vital new equipment for basic industries. Then consideration of probable steel supplies in 1949.
	:2	**Building controls.** PC(48)92.
23 July	**16th:1**	**Payment during sickness.** PC(48)96 and 97.
	:2	**Labour for the textile industries.** PC(48)94.
	:3	**Distribution of manpower at end-April 1948.** PC(48)84.
	:4	**Disposal of plant ordered for open-cast coal.** PC(48)95.
	:5	**Capital investment in 1949.** Consideration renewed with a detailed examination of the I.P.C. report. Summing up Cripps said there was general agreement except on coal, electricity and transport industries. The I.P.C. was to reconsider those recommendations.
30 July	**17th:1**	**Coal/oil conversion.** PC(48)101. Bevan acted as chairman.
	:2	**Cement output and demand.** PC(48)102.
	:3	**Steel prices.** PC(48)103.
	:4	**The repair of the Russian ice-breaker 'Kaganovitch'** PC(48)104.
	:5	**Turn-round of shipping in U.K. ports.** PC(48)100.
	:6	**Wage claims.** PC(48)99. Isaacs reported stability but that the recent increase in the cost of living might set off a further wage cycle.
	:7	**Payment during sickness.**
	:8	**Electricity generating station programme.**
	:9	**Eire: trade negotiations.**
6 Sept	**18th:1**	**Capital investment in 1949.** PC(48)108. Approval of proposals for the distribution of additional steel likely to be available in 1949, including provision of the necessary steel for

		defence purposes, although some ministers disliked the consequences.
	:2	**Long-term demand for steels.** PC(48)111. Agreement on the level of demand in the 1950s as a basis for the planning of future steel supplies.
	:3	**Industrial productivity.** Although unwilling to take part in a joint compaign the T.U.C. and the F.B.I. would support such action. General approval of the campaign's arrangements but doubts expressed about effectiveness of propaganda in certain industries where capital equipment and materials limited output.
	:4	**Statistical review.** PC(48)105 and 110.
	:5	**Food situation in the U.K.** PC(48)106.
	:6	**Wage claims.** PC(48)107.
	:7	**Mr. Evan Durbin.**
15 Sept	**19th:1**	**Distribution of industry policy.** PC(48)112. General agreement to publish the White paper but concern that its form might be criticized. Agreement to schedule Merseyside and the Highlands and Islands of Scotland as development areas.
	:2	**Cement distribution.** PC(48)109.
	:3	**Selling prices of non-ferrous metals.** PC(48)114.
	:4	**Standardization of engineering products.** PC(48)113.
	:5	**Surrender of food coupons in hotels.** PC(48)115.
4 Oct	**20th:1**	**Manufacture of crawler tractors in the U.K.** PC(48)117 Isaacs acting chairman.
	:2	**Priority for defence research and development work.** PC(48)119. Priority was not to be granted but everything possible done to expedite production of prototypes.
	:3	**Forth Road Bridge.** PC(48)116 and 118.
	:4	**Wage claim by the N.U.R.** PC(48)123. Serious concern.
	:5	**Movement of wages, hours of work etc. during 1948.** PC(48)120.
	:6	**Food situation in the U.K.** PC(48)122.
29 Oct	**21st:1**	**Wages of Post Office rank and file engineering and allied staff.** PC(48)125.
	:2	**Steel economy.** PC(48)127 and 128. General agreement against the substitution of timber for steel in building construction. Approval of PC(48)128.
	:3	**Ford Motor Co.'s proposals for expansion.** PC(48)130. Extension of the foundry at Dagenham agreed but in future the company should supply a full statement on the effect of transferring part of production to a development area.

	:4	**Food situation in the U.K.** PC(48)126.
	:5	**Statistical review.** PC(48)124.
	:6	**Use of oil facilities installed under the railway coal-oil conversion schemes.** PC(48)121.
	:7	**Movements of wages, hours of work, etc. during September 1948.** PC(48)129. Records the first downward movement in the sliding scales of wages tied to the cost of living index.
9 Nov	**22nd:1**	**Admiralty industrial wage claims.** PC(48)134.
	:2	**Export credit guarantees.** PC(48)135.
	:3	**Coal production and manpower in 1949.** PC(48)133. Isaacs felt the summary of manpower problems was the most realistic yet, but Cripps felt it unduly cautious.
	:4	**Statistical review.** PC(48)131.
23 Nov	**23rd:1**	**U.K. rice stocks.** PC(48)132.
	:2	**Coal prospects in 1948, 1949 and 1950.** PC(48)138 and 142. Isaacs felt manpower could not be increased to the level proposed in PC(48)133 by end-1949. Cripps felt that published manpower figures should in the future be presented as requirements not targets. Agreement not to reduce the estimate for exports and bunkering already given to the O.E.E.C.
	:3	**Provision of employment for disabled persons.** PC(48)137.
	:4	**Relaxation of controls on shipping.** PC(48)136.
	:5	**Claims for improved wages and conditions of employment in agriculture.** PC(48)140. The claim could not be justified under the principles of the White Paper.
	:6	**Cement imports from Germany.** PC(48)139.
2 Dec	**24th:1**	**Electricity generating station programmes.** PC(48)146.
	:2	**Cotton industry conference at Harrogate.** PC(48)143.
	:3	**Movements of wages, hours of work etc. during October 1948.** PC(48)144.
	:4	**Food situation in the U.K.** PC(48)145.
17 Dec	**25th:1**	**Ford Motor Co.'s proposals for expansion.** PC(48)153. Strauss and Wilson, H. approved Ford's proposals since refusal could adversely affect exports but the predominant view was against approval.
	:2	**Census of distribution.** PC(48)151 and 154.
	:3	**Home timber production.** PC(48)141.
	:4	**Feedingstuffs subsidies.** PC(48)149.
	:5	**Survey of agricultural expansion programme.** PC(48)150. Endorsement of the Economic Planning Board conclusions.
	:6	**Statistical review.** PC(48)147.

CAB 134/637   Memoranda   5 Jan–21 April 1948   PC(48)1–52.

5 Jan	**PC(48)1**	**Stocks of food and animal feedingstuffs, raw materials and petroleum products** – C.S.O., 1+3+12p appendixes. Also CS(S)(48)1.
8 Jan	**2**	**Iron and steel prices** – Strauss, 2+3p annex.
6 Jan	**3**	**Production and allocation of alkalis** – Gaitskell, 1p. Recommends a review in order that oil companies could get all their requirements.
6 Jan	**4**	Retained.
9 Jan	**5**	**The emergency hostel programme** – Key, 3+1p appendix. Appointment of an official committee was proposed to focus policy.
8 Jan	**6**	**Employment on Merseyside and in development areas as a result of the cuts in the investment programme** – Wilson, H., 3p.
9 Jan	**7**	**Durex Abrasives Limited factory at Gorseinon, Swansea** – Wilson, H., 2p.
10 Jan	**8**	**Revised export programme** – Wilson, H., covering J.R.C. Helmore, 1+5+5p annex. By end-1948 exports were expected to be 146% above the 1938 volume. No further significant increase was possible without increases in steel supplies.
12 Jan	**9**	**Report by the Working Party on the Increase of Textile Exports** – Wilson, H., 3+24+2p appendixes. Increased labour was needed to realise the full export potential.
12 Jan	**10**	**Railway summer passenger services** – Barnes, 2p. Request for the restrictions to be lifted.
14 Jan	**11**	**Textile exports and the clothing ration** – Wilson, H., 3p.
15 Jan	**12**	**Appeals from decisions of the Headquarters Building Committee** – Key, 2p. Administrative arrangements.
16 Jan	**13**	**Report by the Working Party on the Increase of Textile Exports** – Edwards, N., 1p. Supplementary information.
16 Jan	**14**	**Transport during the winter months** – Barnes, 1+3p annexes.
24 Jan	**15**	**Composition and terms of reference of the Labour (Textile Industries) Committee** – S.E.V. Luke, 1p.
26 Jan	**16**	**Food situation in the U.K.: report for December 1947** – Strachey, 9+1p annex.
29 Jan	**17**	**Emergency hostels** – Cripps, 2p. Sets out changes in the Emergency Accommodation Committee.
3 Feb	**18**	**Electricity policy** – Gaitskell, 4p. Proposals to deal with the need for economy to save coal, for high enough tariffs to cover costs and for spreading of peak demand.

2 Feb	19	**The effect of electricity load shedding on production this winter – Cripps,** 1+2p.
3 Feb	20	**Passenger transport restrictions – Barnes,** 3p.
4 Feb	21	**Stocks of food, animal feedingstuffs, raw materials and petroleum products – C.S.O.,** 1+2+12p appendixes. Also CS(S)(48)2.
9 Feb	22	**First interim report of the Official Working Party on Textile Machinery Supplies – Wilson, H., and Strauss covering the working party,** 1+4p.
16 Jan	23	**Food situation in the U.K. – Strachey,** 8+1p appendix.
17 Feb	24	**Licensing of building maintenance – Key,** 2+2p annex.
18 Feb	25	**Provision of sheets – Shinwell,** 1p.
24 Feb	26	**Export packing – Jay,** 1p. Exports should not be held up for lack of packing materials.
25 Feb	27	**Factories Bill – Isaacs,** 2p.
26 Feb	28	**Provision of miners' hostels in the North Midlands regions – S.E.V. Luke covering the chairman of the Emergency Accommodation Committee,** 1+1p.
3 Mar	29	**Stocks of food, animal feedingstuffs, raw materials and petroleum products – C.S.O.,** 1+3+12p appendixes. Also CS(S)(48)3.
10 Mar	30	**Wage claims – Isaacs,** 1+2+6p appendixes.
9 Mar	31	**The royal dockyards – Viscount Hall,** 10+1p appendix.
10 Mar	32	**Steel for the fuel and power industries – Gaitskell** 4+4p appendixes. Allocations for Period III 1948 were totally inadequate apart from coal.
10 Mar	33	**Agricultural prices – Chuter Ede, Woodburn and Williams,** 1+2p annex. Report on the financial and economic position, recommending the reaffirmation of existing price schedules.
10 Mar	34	**The oil companies' expansion programme – Jay,** 3p. Sets out the criteria for steel allocations on which the programme should be planned.
11 Mar	35	**Steel for shipbuilding – Cripps,** 2p. Basis of steel allocations on which development should be based.
15 Mar	36	**Transport during the winter months: final report – Barnes,** 1+3p. Final report of the Winter Transport Executive Committee. Agreement to terminate the committee.
18 Mar	37	**Steel for industrial building – Wilson, H.,** 4+2p appendix. Concern at the level of allocations.
19 Mar	38	**Agricultural prices – Chuter Ede, Woodburn and Williams,** 3+1p appendix.

19 Mar	39	Livestock expansion programme – Williams, 2p.
10 Mar	40	Food situation in the U.K.: report for February 1948 – Strachey, 8+1p annex.
19 Mar	41	Development councils under the Industrial Organization and Development Act 1947 – Wilson, H., 2+2p appendix. Progress report and proposal to force councils on some industries where employers would not voluntarily establish them.
1 Apr	42	The provision of employment for disabled persons – Isaacs, 2+8p annex.
31 Mar	43	Stocks of food, animal feedingstuffs, raw materials and petroleum products – C.S.O., 1+3+12p appendixes. CS(S)(48)6.
6 Apr	44	The building programme – Key, 1+7+2p appendixes. Report by the Headquarters Building Committee attached. It was essential that allocations of steel were consistent with the approved investment programmes.
6 Apr	45	Consumption of dollar-costing metals – Strauss, 4+1p appendix. With particular regard to aluminium.
15 Apr	46	Food situation in the U.K.: report for March 1948 – Strachey, 8+1p appendix.
16 Apr	47	The oil companies expansion programme – Jay, 1p. He and Gaitskell were unable to agree on steel supplies, so the matter was returned to the committee.
19 Apr	48	Housing: Scotland. Use of steel in non-traditional houses – Woodburn, 2p.
20 Apr	49	Steel economy – Key, 1+3p. Action taken with regard to CIP(IS)(48)14.
19 Apr	50	Wages claims – Isaacs, 1+2+9p appendixes. Appreciation for March.
20 Apr	51	Communist activities in factories to impede production – Cripps, 5p.
21 Apr	52	Steel allocation policy in Period IV 1948 – Jay, 3p. Sets out the principles behind the continuing policy of over-allocation to ensure full use of capacity. In order to retain control over distribution and priorities this policy should not be carried too far.

CAB 134/638   Memoranda   20 April–30 July 1948   PC(48)53–105.

| 20 Apr | PC(48)53 | Labour for the textile industries – Labour (Textile Industries) Committee, 7+2p appendixes. Also L(TI)(48)31. Interim report. Concentration on cotton. |
| 21 Apr | 54 | Caustic soda – Wilson, H., 3p. In relation to oil company requirements. |

21 Apr	55	**The expansion of alkali production – Wilson, H.,** 4p. Proposed measures.
21 Apr	56	**Steel production during the first quarter of 1948 – Strauss covering A.F. Forbes,** 1+6p. Review of the situation and of matters likely to influence output during the rest of the year.
29 Apr	57	**Building licensing – Key,** 2p. Proposal to increase the limit below which no licence was required.
29 Apr	58	**Conversion of locomotives to oil fuel – Barnes,** 3p. Proposal to abandon the policy.
29 Apr	59	**Coal/oil conversion – Gaitskell,** 3p. Broad agreement with PC(48)58.
30 Apr	60	**Stocks of food and animal feedingstuffs, raw materials and petroleum products – C.S.O.,** 1+2+12p appendixes. Also CS(S)(48)7.
8 May	61	**Coal prospects for 1948 – Gaitskell,** 3+1p appendix. The general position was much easier so problems of special importance, in particular the achievement of the export target, were analysed.
10 May	62	**Building licensing: draft of a public announcement – Key,** 1+1p. Recommends introduction of the new ceiling without delay.
12 May	63	**Expansion of virgin aluminium production in the U.K. – Strauss,** 3p. Recommends developments in the Empire, not in the U.K.
12 May	64	**Emergency hostels: Oldham/Rochdale and Burnley/Nelson districts – S.E.V. Luke,** 1+1p annex. Letter from the chairman of the Emergency Accommodation Committee.
13 May	65	**Wage claims in the engineering and shipbuilding industries – Isaacs,** 1+3p. Report on the Inter-departmental Committee on Wages and Conditions of Employment.
21 May	66	**Sheets for the services and industrial hostels – Wilson, H.,** 2+2p. The most pressing need was for increased production in the vital undermanned industries, and so industrial hostels must be made a success. Since the Ministry of Works and the National Service Hostels Corporation were emphatic that experience showed sheets were crucial to that success, they should be supplied regardless of the effect on other consumers.
24 May	67	**Movement of wages, hours of work, etc. during April 1948 – Isaacs,** 1+2+7p appendixes.
25 May	68	**Cropping arrangements for the 1948 harvest – Williams,** 2p.
29 May	69	**Implications for the shipbuilding industry of contemplated steel allocations for 1948–50 – Barnes and Viscount Hall,** 5+3p annex. Grave

		concern. The Shipbuilding Advisory Committee had protested.
28 May	70	**Food situation in the U.K.: report for April 1948** – Summerskill, 9+1p appendix.
29 May	71	**Stocks of food, animal feedingstuffs, raw materials and petroleum products** – C.S.O., 1+3+12p appendixes. Also CS(S)(48)9.
29 May	72	**Steel prices and subsidies** – Strauss, 5p. Request for guidance on future policy.
31 May	73	**Speed limit for heavy goods vehicles** – Barnes, 3p.
1 June	74	**Turn-round of shipping in the U.K. ports** – Barnes, 3+25+17p annex.
2 June	75	**Consumption of dollar-costing metals** – Strauss, 2+4p annexes. Proposals to reduce consumption.
21 June	76	**Production of aluminium in North Borneo** – Strauss, 3p.
21 June	77	**Progress report from the Committee on Industrial Productivity** – Morrison and Cripps, 1+5p annexes. See EPC(48)42.
24 June	78	**Steel economy in building** – Key, 3p.
24 June	79	**Food situation in the U.K.: report for May 1948** – Strachey, 7+1p appendix.
25 June	80	**Coal: quality problems** – Gaitskell, 3+1p appendix. Proposals to deal with the deficit of large and surplus of small coal.
28 June	81	**Railway coal** – Barnes, 3p. Concern at impact on newly nationalized railways of proposals in PC(48)80.
26 June	82	**Coal export prospects** – S.E.V. Luke covering the Overseas Negotiations Committee, 1+4+1p appendix.
28 June	83	**Development councils** – Wilson, H., 2+2p appendix.
29 June	84	**The distribution of manpower at end-April 1948** – Edwards, N., 8p. Labour was not moving fast enough either into undermanned or out of other industries to meet manpower targets of the Economic Survey. Stronger use of direction would be resented and fail. Movement of workers must be by personal choice. Persuasion would have some effect but other controls should be used to restrict less essential jobs.
29 June	85	**Proposals for spreading the industrial electricity load next winter** – Edwards, N., covering the Electricity Subcommittee of the N.J.A.C. Joint Consultative Committee, 1+12p appendix.
30 June	86	**Stocks of food and animal feedingstuffs, raw materials and petroleum products** – C.S.O., 1+3+12p appendixes. Also CS(S)(48)10.

30 June	**87**	**Production of aluminium in North Borneo –** **Woodburn,** 2p. Location in Scotland should be considered first.
29 June	**88**	**The report of the Clow Committee on the** **electricity peak load problem – Gaitskell,** 3+3p appendix. Disappointment at committee's recommendations. The British Electricity Authority should be asked to introduce a seasonal variation in tariffs. Summary of report appended.
14 July	**89**	**Changes in productivity in British industry** **1946–47 – E.E. Bridges covering the Board of** **Trade,** 2+3+3p annex. The Official Committee on Economic Development felt it was no longer possible to expect increased production by an increased labour force. They recommended that the Board of Trade memorandum should be published but under the name of the statistician responsible in order to avoid controversy.
8 July	**90**	**Second interim report of the Official Working** **Party on Textile Machinery Supplies – Wilson,** **H. and Strauss covering the official working** **party,** 1+5p. Progress since PC(48)22.
12 July	**91**	**Movement of wages, hours of work, etc. during** **May 1948 – Isaacs,** 1+2+7p appendixes.
14 July	**92**	**Building controls – Cripps,** 1+12+10p appendixes. Also GOC(48)16(revise) and BCC(48)7(revise). Review of inter-departmental machinery, particularly in relation to Ministry of Works licensing, to reduce delays.
17 July	**93**	**Report on capital investment in 1949 – S.E.V.** **Luke covering the I.P.C.,** 1+87+9p appendixes. Also EPB(48)23, ED(48)6 and IPC(48)8. Sets out general programme and programmes of individual sectors.
19 July	**94**	**Labour for the textile industries – Labour** **(Textile Industries) Committee,** 5+4p appendixes. Second interim report.
20 July	**95**	**Disposal of plant ordered for open-cast coal –** **key covering the working party,** 1+2p.
20 July	**96**	**Sick pay for agricultural workers – Williams,** 4+1p appendix.
21 July	**97**	**Payment during sickness – Isaacs,** 2+2p appendixes.
22 July	**98**	**Report on capital investment in 1949 – Cripps,** 2+2p appendixes. Agreement with PC(48)93 that total investment was determined primarily by steel supplies; national independence required resources to be concentrated on industrial investment; and that therefore social

services investment could be no greater than in 1948. Within industry preference would be given to sectors making a direct and early contribution to the balance of payments. Any additional resources in 1949 and 1950 should be devoted to industrial investment. Views of the Official Committee on Economic Development and the Economic Planning Board appended.

26 July	99	**Movement of wages, hours of work, etc. during June 1948 – Isaacs,** 1+2+9p appendixes.
26 July	100	**Turn-round of shipping in the U.K. ports – Barnes,** 1p.
27 July	101	**Coal-oil conversion (railways) – Barnes,** 2p.
27 July	102	**Cement (supply and demand in 1948 and 1949) – Key,** 3p. Need for economy.
27 July	103	**Steel prices – Strauss,** 2p.
28 July	104	**Repair of the Russian icebreaker 'Kaganovitch' – Viscount Hall,** 3p.
30 July	105	**Stocks of food and animal feedingstuffs, raw materials and petroleum products – C.S.O.,** 1+2+12p appendixes. Also CS(S)(48)13.

CAB 134/639   Memoranda   9 Aug–29 Dec 1948   PC(48)106–156.

9 Aug	**PC(48)106**	**Food situation in the U.K.: report for June 1948 – Strachey,** 7+1p appendix.
30 Aug	107	**Movements of wages, hours of work, etc. during July 1948 – Isaacs,** 1+2+7p appendixes.
1 Sept	108	**Capital investment in 1949: supplementary report – I.P.C.,** 6+10p annex. The programme involved only a suggested distribution of steel, not an allocation. Acceptance of the claim for additional steel for the coal industry and comments on other claims.
7 Sept	109	**Cement distribution in the home market – Key,** 2p. Outline of existing scheme.
31 Aug	110	**Stocks of food and animal feedingstuffs, raw materials and petroleum products – C.S.O.,** 1+3+12p appendixes. Also CS(S)(48)16.
3 Sept	111	**Long-term demand for steel – Cripps and Strauss,** 2+4p annex. Report of a working party estimating demand into the 1950s annexed. It was to provide a basis for the steel industry's investment plans.
6 Sept	112	**Distribution of industry policy – Wilson, H.,** 2+4p annex +51p. Revised version of draft White Paper attached. Merseyside and part of the Scottish highlands to be additional development areas.
8 Sept	113	**Standardizing and simplifying engineering products – Strauss,** 3p.

8 Sept	114	**Selling prices of non-ferrous metals – Strauss,** 2p. Recommends increased prices in line with rising world prices, although contrary to government policy.
13 Sept	115	**Surrender of food coupons in hotels: reversion to former practice – Strachey,** 1p.
15 Sept	116	**Forth Road Bridge – Barnes,** 2p.
14 Sept	117	**Manufacture of crawler tractors in the U.K. – Strauss,** 2p.
17 Sept	118	**Forth Road Bridge – Woodburn,** 1p.
20 Sept	119	**Priority for defence research and development work – Alexander,** 2+3p annexes.
25 Sept	120	**Movement of wages, hours of work, etc. during 1948 – Isaacs,** 1+2+5p appendixes.
5 Oct	121	**Utilization of oil facilities installed under the railways' coal/oil conversion scheme – Official Oil Committee,** 2p. Also OOC(48)14(final).
28 Sept	122	**Food situation in the U.K.: report for July and August 1948 – Strachey,** 8+1p appendix.
29 Sept	123	**Wage claim by the National Union of Railwaymen – Isaacs,** 1+2+2p appendixes.
30 Sept	124	**Stocks of food and animal feedingstuffs, raw materials and petroleum products – C.S.O.,** 1+3+12p appendixes. Also CS(S)(48)19.
19 Oct	125	**Wages of Post Office rank and file engineering and allied staff – Paling,** 1+3+4p appendix.
18 Oct	126	**Food situation in the U.K.: report for September 1948 – Strachey,** 7+1p annex.
18 Oct	127	**Steel economy – Key,** 2p.
22 Oct	128	**Steel economy – Jay,** 1+16+12p appendixes. Also M(SE)(48)3 and M(SE SUB)(48)28. Cuts recommended by the Steel Economy Subcommittee of the Materials Committee.
26 Oct	129	**Movements of wages, hours of work, etc. during September 1948 – Isaacs,** 1+2+7p appendixes.
28 Oct	130	**The Ford Motor Co.'s proposals for expansion – Strauss,** 3p. The Board of Trade wanted part of any expansion to go to a development area. The company felt this would be uneconomic and Strauss agreed.
1 Nov	131	**Stocks of food and animal feedingstuffs, raw materials and petroleum products – C.S.O.,** 1+3+12p appendixes. Also CS(S)(48)25.
9 Nov	132	**U.K. rice stocks – Strachey,** 2p.
2 Nov	133	**Coal production and manpower in 1949 – Gaitskell,** 1+6+10p annexes. Report of the Joint Committee on Production attached.
2 Nov	134	**Admiralty industrial wage claims – Alexander,** 9p.
2 Nov	135	**Export credit guarantees – Wilson, H.,** 2p.
4 Nov	136	**Proposals for further decontrol of British shipping – Barnes,** 5p.

11 Nov	**137**	**The provision of employment for disabled persons – Isaacs,** 3+2p.
15 Nov	**138**	**Coal prospects in 1948, 1949 and 1950 – Gaitskell,** 5+2p annex. Proposal of a 1949 production target of 220m tons. Suggested measures to achieve it and reduce demand to that level.
17 Nov	**139**	**Progress report on cement imports from Germany – Key,** 2p.
18 Nov	**140**	**Claim for increased minimum wages, reduction of the normal working week, and increased annual holidays in agriculture – Isaacs covering the Inter-departmental Committee on Wages and Conditions of Employment,** 2+3p.
18 Nov	**141**	**Home timber production – Wilson, H.,** 2+23p. Report of inter-departmental working party attached.
22 Nov	**142**	**Railway coal – Barnes,** 2p. The B.T.C. felt that proposals in PC(48)138 were risky – but acceptable to Barnes provided railways got regular weekly deliveries.
18 Nov	**143**	**Cotton industry conference at Harrogate – Wilson, H.,** 4p. Also L(TI)(48)85.
26 Nov	**144**	**Movements of wages, hours of work, etc. during October 1948 – Isaacs,** 1+2+6p appendixes.
30 Nov	**145**	**Food situation in the U.K.: report for October 1948 – Strachey,** 8+1 appendix.
30 Nov	**146**	**Electricity generating station programme – Gaitskell,** 4+1p appendix. Estimate of available capacity 1949–51. Little improvement possible before end–1951, so load-spreading must continue. Sets out a programme for construction of power stations and asks for adequate steel supplies.
3 Dec	**147**	**Stocks of food and animal feedingstuffs, raw materials and petroleum products – C.S.O.,** 1+3+12p appendixes. Also CS(S)(48)28.
10 Dec	**148**	**Coal exports – Cripps covering the Overseas Negotiations Committee,** 5+6+5p appendixes.
13 Dec	**149**	**Feedingstuffs subsidies – Cripps and Williams,** 1+9+1p appendix. Also EPB(48)29 and AD(48)25.
13 Dec	**150**	**Survey of agricultural expansion programme – Cripps and Williams,** 1+12+12p appendixes. Also EPB(48)28 and 30 and AD(48)17 and 24.
14 Dec	**151**	**Census of distribution – Wilson, H.,** 2+3p annex. Considerations affecting the choice of first year of the census.
14 Dec	**152**	**The salvage of lead – Wilson, H.,** 1+1p annex.
15 Dec	**153**	**The Ford Motor Co.'s proposals for expansion – Jay,** 1+3p annex.
15 Dec	**154**	**Census of distribution – Marquand,** 1p.

17 Dec	**155**	**Provision of emergency accommodation –** **Emergency Accommodation Committee,** 4+1p annex. Also EAC(48)55.
29 Dec	**156**	**Movements of wages, hours of work, etc. during** **November 1948 – Isaacs,** 1+2+7p appendixes.

CAB 134/640 Meetings 14 Jan–16 Dec 1949 PC(49)1st–27th.

14 Jan	**PC(49)1st:1**	**Coal prospects in 1948, 1949 and 1950.** PC(48)148 and PC(49)7.
	:2	**Vacancies in miners' hostels.** PC(49)6.
	:3	**Prestressed concrete production.** PC(49)2 and 5.
	:4	**Plant and equipment for defence research and development.** PC(49)3.
	:5	**Salvage of lead.** PC(48)152.
	:6	**Provision of emergency accommodation.** PC(48)155. Abolition of the Emergency Accommodation Committee approved.
	:7	**Movements of wages, hours of work, etc. during November 1948.** PC(48)156.
	:8	**Statistical review.** PC(49)1.
	:9	**Food situation in the U.K.** PC(49)4.
26 Jan	**2nd**	**Economic Survey for 1949.** PC(49)8. Agreement that PC(49)8 provided an admirable basis. Whilst it brought out the government's achievements in 1948, it also revealed the government's limited powers; so it was necessary to emphasize the inevitable limits to democratic planning, particularly in relation to manpower policy. Detailed consideration of the survey and targets for production of various commodities.
31 Jan	**3rd:1**	**Prestressed concrete production.**
	:2	**Wage scales of government engineers.**
	:3	**Steel prices and subsidies.** PC(49)10. Approved.
	:4	**Movement of wages, hours of work, etc. during December 1948.** PC(49)9.
	:5	**Turn-round of shipping in U.K. ports.** PC(49)11.
14 Feb	**4th:1**	**Agricultural price reviews.** PC(49)14.
	:2	**Food situation in the U.K.** PC(49)12.
	:3	**Statistical review.** PC(49)13.
	:4	**Restrictions on shop and street lighting.** Agreement to lift restrictions on shops outside periods of peak consumption and that Barnes and Gaitskell should have discretion to relax restrictions on street lighting.
22 Feb	**5th**	**Economic Survey for 1949.** CP(49)29. Consideration of proposed amendments.
2 Mar	**6th:1**	**Charges at industrial hostels.** LP(49)15.
	:2	**The tourist trade.** PC(49)17 and 25.

	:3	**Mid-week sport.** PC(49)19 and 24. Agreement that restrictions on mid-week greyhound racing could be relaxed.
11 Mar	7th:1	**Standardization.** PC(49)18 and 20.
	:2	**Development of alternative sources of supply for jute.** PC(49)29.
	:3	**Steel economy.** PC(49)30.
	:4	**Building work in the newspaper industry.** PC(49)27.
	:5	**Agricultural price reviews.** PC(49)26, 32 and 33.
	:6	**Monopolies and Restrictive Practices (Inquiry and Control) Act 1948.** PC(49)15.
	:7	**Movement of wages, hours of work, etc. during January 1949.** PC(49)21. Concern at the threat of a new wage cycle endangering stabilization policy. It was suggested that a new approach was required, perhaps by a voluntary freeze on wages but with automatic readjustments in line with the cost of living index.
	:8	**Wages of Post Office rank and file engineering and allied staff.** PC(49)22.
	:9	**Statistical review.** PC(49)28.
	:10	**Food situation in the U.K.** PC(49)31.
8 Apr	8th:1	**Supply of sheets to emergency hostels and the services.** PC(49)38.
	:2	**Cost of building.** PC(49)37. Concern at the reduction in productivity from pre-war.
	:3	**Coal/oil conversion: railways.** PC(49)41.
12 Apr	9th:1	**Review of the coal situation.** PC(49)43 and 44. Agreement that an official working party should consider PC(49)43 in detail.
	:2	**The expansion of boilermaking capacity.** PC(49)39.
	:3	**Wage claims in the cotton industry.** PC(49)36.
29 Apr	10th:1	**Ford Motor Co.'s proposals for expansion.** PC(49)48.
	:2	**Future of the General Aircraft Factory at Feltham.** PC(49)49.
	:3	**Responsibility for progressing orders for mining and power station equipment.** PC(49)50.
5 May	11th	**Animal feedingstuffs.** PC(49)46 and 54.
6 May	12th:1	**Coal for export in 1949/50.** PC(49)52. Agreement to allocate 23m tons.
	:2	**Allocation of large coal in 1949–50.** PC(49)43 and 51. Consideration of an additional allocation to the railways above that in PC(49)43.
	:3	**Payment during sickness.** PC(49)34.
	:4	**Movement of wages, hours of work, etc. during February 1949.** PC(49)40.
	:5	**Food situation in the U.K.** PC(49)45.

	:6	**Statistical review.** PC(49)42.
	:7	**Open-cast coal production.**
20 May	13th:1	**Charges at industrial hostels.** PC(49)47.
	:2	**Recruitment of foreign workers for coal-mining.** PC(49)55.
	:3	**Allocation of large coal in 1949/50.** Agreement to reduce the allocation to exports and house coal and to increase that for railways.
	:4	**Location of new industrial projects.** PC(49)57. Approval of PC(49)57 but the Distribution of Industry Committee was to consider further measures to ensure that the geographical distribution of approvals for new projects and extensions was more favourable to development areas.
	:5	**Food situation in the U.K.** PC(49)56.
	:6	**Statistical review.** PC(49)53.
31 May	14th	**Capital investment in 1950–52.** PC(49)59, 60, 61. Some ministers criticized the I.P.C. assumption that physical controls should be relaxed or abandoned when raw material shortages no longer existed. In their view such controls were necessary to regulate investment, as financial controls alone were insufficient to ensure full and beneficial employment of resources. Undue reliance on financial controls might mean less effective control over capital investment outside the public sector. The broad issues of Part I of the report were then considered with some concern expressed at the level of restriction.
21 June	15th:1	**Rotary Hoes Ltd., East Horndon, Essex: proposals for expansion.** PC(49)64.
	:2	**Maximum price for meals.** PC(49)65.
	:3	**Large power-using industries for the Highlands.** PC(49)66.
	:4	**Orders for boilers and components.** PC(49)69.
	:5	**Jute: development of alternative sources of supply.** PC(49)63.
	:6	**Movement of wages, hours of work, etc. during March and April 1949.** PC(49)58. Anxiety that the government seemed powerless to prevent wage increases even when these involved increased public expenditure. Special machinery for considering wage claims within the public sector was suggested. Wilson, H. said that recent wage concessions had greatly increased the difficulties of price control. Industry had found that it could evade prices and incomes policy by permitting claims to go to arbitration, since such awards had to be

		taken into account when the government considered proposed price increases.
	:7	**Food situation in the U.K.** PC(49)62.
	:8	**Statistical review.** PC(49)67.
5 July	16th:1	**London Metal Exchange.**
	:2	**Seasonal variation in electricity tariffs.** PC(49)73. Agreement to discontinue.
	:3	**Future of the steel distribution scheme.** PC(49)75 and 81.
	:4	**Sheet steel for the motor industry.** PC(49)82.
	:5	**Agricultural labour requirements.** PC(49)70.
	:6	**Emergency hostel programme.** PC(49)71.
	:7	**Admiralty industrial wage claims: merit rates for craftsmen.** PC(49)74.
	:8	**Movement of wages, hours of work, etc. during May 1949.** PC(49)79.
11 July	17th:1	**Future of the General Aircraft Factory at Feltham.** PC(49)80.
	:2	**Capital investment in 1950–52.** PC(49)59, 60, 61 and 84. Since 13 May the situation had deteriorated and there was no point in discussing the 1952 programme. It was difficult to settle even the 1950 programme and no commitments should be made which precluded a downward revision of programmes.
19 July	18th:1	**Rehabilitation of private woodlands.** PC(49)87.
	:2	**Maintenance of employment in development areas.** PC(49)72 and 76.
	:3	**Cost of building.** PC(49)68 and 78.
	:4	**Development of aluminium production within the Commonwealth.** PC(49)77 and 83. To go to the Economic Policy Committee.
	:5	**Allocation of public service vehicles for the home market.**
	:6	**Food situation in the U.K.** PC(49)86.
	:7	**Statistical review.** PC(49)85.
23 Sept	19th:1	**The future of the shipbuilding and ship repairing industries.** PC(49)90. Problems arose because pockets of unemployment were appearing outside development areas where Board of Trade powers were limited.
	:2	**Softwood timber supplies.** PC(49)98.
	:3	**Movement of wages, hours of work, etc. during June and July 1949.** PC(49)92 and 93.
	:4	**Food situation in the U.K.** PC(49)89.
	:5	**Statistical review.** PC(49)91 and 94.
30 Sept	20th:1	**Standardization.** PC(49)99. Export needs were to be considered in the determining of standards.
	:2	**Supply of commercial vehicles for the home market.** PC(49)100.

4 Oct	**21st:1**	**Publicity on the economic situation.** PC(49)103. Since there was a divergence of views the issue should go to Cabinet.
	:2	**Report of the Productivity (Official) Committee.** PC(49)96.
	:3	**Maintenance of employment in the development areas.** PC(49)105. Discussion of whether the proposed bill should enable the Board of Trade to acquire buildings for industrial use in development areas.
	:4	**Women's Land Army.** PC(49)102 and 106. Approval of winding up.
7 Oct	**22nd:1**	**Control of labour.** PC(49)107. Agreement that the Control of Engagement Order should be renewed for twelve months and powers of direction retained.
	:2	**Movement of wages and hours of work for August 1949.** PC(49)101.
13 Oct	**23rd**	**Cinematograph Film Production (Special Loans) Act 1949.** PC(49)111.
28 Oct	**24th:1**	**Animal feedingstuffs.** PC(49)115 and 120. An inter-departmental working party was to consider the discontinuation of rationing of feedingstuffs on the withdrawal of the Exchequer's subsidy.
	:2	**Standardization.** PC(49)117.
	:3	**Eradication of wild rabbits.** PC(49)108 and 112.
	:4	**Size of newspapers.**
	:5	**Food situation in the U.K.** PC(49)104.
	:6	**Statistical review.** PC(49)109.
4 Nov	**25th:1**	**Tourist industry: release of requisitioned hotels.** PC(49)114, 118, 119.
	:2	**Special restrictions on workers in coal-mining and agricultural industries.** PC(49)126 and 127. Agreement to lift the ring fence on both industries on 1 Jan 1950.
	:3	**Catering Wages Act 1943.** PC(49)121.
	:4	**Ship repairs abroad.** PC(49)125.
	:5	**Statutory price control of non-ferrous metals.** Agreement to end, in relation to copper, lead and zinc.
2 Dec	**26th:1**	**Economy in government expenditure.** Consideration of a letter from Attlee to chairmen of Cabinet committees.
	:2	**Future of the shipbuilding industry.** PC(49)131.
	:3	**Ship repairs abroad.** PC(49)125.
	:4	**Arbitrary reductions in controlled prices.** PC(49)110, 116, 124 and 129.
	:5	**Food situation in the U.K.** PC(49)123.
	:6	**Movement of wages, hours of work for September and October 1949.** PC(49)122 and 130.

	:7	Statistical review. PC(49)128.
16 Dec	27th:1	Supply of commercial vehicles to the home market. PC(49)135.
	:2	Flat rate transport scheme for fish. PC(49)132.
	:3	Statistical review. PC(49)133.

CAB 134/641   Memoranda   3 Jan–5 May 1949   PC(49)1–55.

3 Jan	PC(49)1	Stocks of food and animal feedingstuffs, raw materials and petroleum products – C.S.O., 1+3+12p appendixes. CS(S)(48)37.
5 Jan	2	Prestressed concrete production: supply of high tensile wire – Strauss, 1p.
7 Jan	3	Plant and equipment for defence research and development – Strauss, 1p.
11 Jan	4	Food situation in the U.K. – Strachey, 9+1p appendix.
10 Jan	5	Prestressed concrete production – Key, 4p.
11 Jan	6	Vacancies in miners' hostels – Gaitskell, 2p.
12 Jan	7	Coal requirements for industry – Jay, 3p. The Fuel Allocations Committee comments on PC(48)138.
19 Jan	8	Economic Survey for 1949 – Cripps, 2+48p. The passages in italics were for colleagues but not for publication. Attention was drawn to the question of publishing targets, the emphasis to be given to coal and electricity, the presentation of manpower issues and the uncertainty of many balance of payments figures. The Survey concluded that, if the forecasts were correct, 1949 would be the first post-war year in which there were no dramatic economic changes and so the object of policy should be increased efficiency. There were, however, some particular problems which should no longer be seen as transitional but requiring permanent solutions.
24 Jan	9	Movement of wages, hours of work, etc. during December 1948 – Isaacs, 1+2+8p appendixes.
26 Jan	10	Iron and steel subsidies and prices – Cripps and Strauss, 5+3p annex. Recommendation to remove subsidies.
27 Jan	11	Turn-round of shipping in the U.K. ports – Barnes, 2p. Report on improvements.
4 Feb	12	Food situation in the U.K.: report for December 1948 – Strachey, 8+1p annex.
7 Feb	13	Stocks of food and animal feedingstuffs, raw materials and petroleum products – C.S.O., 1+3+12p appendixes. Also CS(S)(49)5.
10 Feb	14	Agricultural price reviews – Chuter Ede, Woodburn and Williams, 11+3p appendix.

10 Feb	**15**	**The Monopolies and Restrictive Practices (Enquiry and Control) Act 1948** – Wilson, H., 2p.
11 Feb	**16**	**Agricultural Wages Board recommendations** – Isaacs, 2+1p annex. Concern at proposed increases.
18 Feb	**17**	**Prospects of the tourist trade** – Wilson, H., 3+6p appendixes.
18 Feb	**18**	**Standardization** – Wilson, H., 5+7p annex.
24 Feb	**19**	**Mid-week sport** – Chuter Ede, 3p. Recommends end of ban.
25 Feb	**20**	**Standardization** – Strauss, 1+3p appendix. Extract of the first report of the Lemon Committee on Standardization in the Engineering Industry attached.
25 Feb	**21**	**Movement of wages, hours of work, etc. during January 1949** – Isaacs, 1+2+10p appendixes.
2 Mar	**22**	**Wages of Post Office rank and file engineering and allied staff** – Paling, 1+3p annex.
1 Mar	**23**	**Control of hardwood** – S.E.V. Luke, 1p.
28 Feb	**23**	**Control of hardwood** – Wilson, H., 3p. Proposes removal of control on distribution and use.
28 Feb	**24**	**Mid-week sport** – Woodburn, 2p.
1 Mar	**25**	**Petrol for overseas visitors** – Gaitskell, 1+2p appendix. Criticism of PC(49)17.
1 Mar	**26**	**Agricultural price reviews** – S.E.V. Luke, 1+3p.
2 Mar	**27**	**Building work in the newspaper industry** – Wilson, H., 2+1p annex.
3 Mar	**28**	**Stocks of food and animal feedingstuffs, raw materials and petroleum products** – C.S.O., 1+3+13p appendixes. Also CS(S)(49)7.
4 Mar	**29**	**Development of alternative sources of supply for jute** – Wilson, H., 3+3p annex.
7 Mar	**30**	**Steel economy** – Key, 4p. Progress since PC(48)21st.
8 Mar	**31**	**Food situation in the U.K.: report for January 1949** – Strachey, 7+1p appendix.
8 Mar	**32**	**Agricultural price review for 1949** – Chuter Ede, Woodburn and Williams, 1+7p appendixes. Attached official report reviewing the economic condition and prospects of the industry.
10 Mar	**33**	**Agricultural price review: egg prices** – Strachey, 4p.
21 Mar	**34**	**Payment during sickness** – Isaacs, 1+1p annex.
21 Mar	**35**	**Iron and steel prices** – Strauss, 1+3p appendix.
23 Mar	**36**	**Wage claims in the cotton industry** – Isaacs, 1+3+1p appendix.
29 Mar	**37**	**The cost of building** – Key, 6+3p appendixes.
29 Mar	**38**	**Supply of sheets to emergency hostels and the services** – Wilson, H., 2p.

31 Mar	**39**	**Expansion of boiler making capacity – Strauss,** 3p.
1 Apr	**40**	**Movement of wages, hours of work, etc. during February 1949 – Isaacs,** 1+2+11p appendixes.
5 Apr	**41**	**Coal-oil conversion (railways) – Barnes,** 1p.
6 Apr	**42**	**Stocks of food and animal feedingstuffs, raw materials and petroleum products – C.S.O.,** 1+3+13p appendixes. Also CS(S)(49)12.
8 Apr	**43**	**Review of coal situation – Gaitskell,** 4+2p appendix. Proposed reductions in demand for large coal.
11 Apr	**44**	**Supplies of coal for the railways – Barnes,** 2p. Criticism of cuts in PC(49)43.
13 Apr	**45**	**Food situation in the U.K.: report for February 1949 – Strachey,** 7+1p appendix.
29 Apr	**46**	**Animal feedingstuffs – Williams,** 3p.
25 Apr	**47**	**Charges at industrial hostels – Isaacs,** 3p.
26 Apr	**48**	**Ford Motor Co.'s proposals for expansion – Wilson, H.,** 2p. Events since PC(48)28th.
26 Apr	**49**	**Future of the General Aircraft Factory at Feltham – Wilson, H.,** 1+4p annexes.
27 Apr	**50**	**Responsibility for progressing orders for mining equipment and power station equipment – Strauss,** 2p.
29 Apr	**51**	**Allocation of large coal – Jay,** 1+6p. Report by an official working party on the allocation for July 1949 – June 1950.
3 May	**52**	**Coal exports 1949/50 – Jay,** 4p. Recommends minimum figure for 1949/50 of 23m tons.
4 May	**53**	**Stocks of food and animal feedingstuffs, raw materials and petroleum products – C.S.O.,** 1+3+13p appendixes. Also CS(S)(49)17.
4 May	**54**	**Animal feedingstuffs – Strachey,** 4+6p appendix.
5 May	**55**	**Recruitment of foreign workers for coal-mining – Isaacs,** 2p. The increase in manpower envisaged in the Economic Survey would not be possible but this should not affect production adversely.

CAB 134/642   Memoranda   7 May–7 Oct 1949   PC(49)56–109.

7 May	**PC(49)56**	**Food situation in the U.K.: report for March 1949 – Strachey,** 7+1p appendix.
17 May	**57**	**Location of new industrial projects – Jay,** 3p. The simplified procedure for granting industrial building licences and industrial location certificates, introduced in 1948, had unintentionally changed the geographical distribution of approvals of new industrial projects and extensions. To counter this he proposed a less rigid test of dollar-earning for

new projects and extensions in development areas than in thc rest of the country.

17 May	58	**Movement of wages, hours of work, etc. during March and April 1949 – Isaacs,** 1+2+15p appendixes.
24 May	59	**Report on capital investment in 1950–52 – S.E.V. Luke covering the I.P.C.,** 1+88+10p appendix. Also EPB(49)13, ED(49)10 and IPC(49)3. Conclusion that an increase of £200m in gross fixed investment by 1952 was as much as the country could afford. The powers and machinery required in the long term to control investment should be reviewed since direct physical controls would become less effective as supplies of scarce materials increased. Sets out the general investment programme and individual programmes.
27 May	60	**Capital investment in 1950/52 – Cripps,** 3p. Sets out the recommendations of the Economic Planning Board and the Official Committee on Economic Development. Cripps himself generally endorsed PC(49)59 and believed that any adjustments should be made within the total rather than in addition to it, particularly in the social services field.
27 May	61	**Educational building programme 1950–52 – Tomlinson,** 2p. Criticism of PC(49)59.
30 May	62	**Food situation in the U.K.: report for April 1949 – Strachey,** 7+1p appendix.
3 June	63	**Jute: development of alternative sources of supply – Strachey,** 1p. Progress report.
15 June	64	**Rotary Hoes Ltd., East Horndon, Essex. Proposals for expansion – Jay,** 1+5p annexes. DI(49)13 and DI(49)4th:1 annexed. Referred to the committee because the Distribution of Industry Committee could not agree.
13 June	65	**Maximum prices for meals – Strachey,** 3p.
15 June	66	**Large power-using industries for the Highlands – Woodburn,** 2+5p annex.
15 June	67	**Stocks of food and animal feedingstuffs, raw materials and petroleum products – C.S.O.,** 1+3+14p appendixes. Also CS(S)(49)23.
16 June	68	**House building costs – Bevan,** 2+1p appendix.
16 June	69	**Orders for boilers and components – Strauss,** 3p.
22 June	70	**Agricultural labour requirements – Williams,** 3p.
24 June	71	**The emergency hostel programme – Key,** 3p.
24 June	72	**Maintenance of employment in the development areas – Jay,** 4p. Considerable progress had been made but further measures recommended to deal with (a) vacant Advance and Grenfall

factories in South Wales, (b) anticipated release of labour from shipbuilding and ship repairing, and (c) continued pressure for industrial development and consequent congestion in Greater London.

25 June	73	**Seasonal variation in electricity tariffs** – Gaitskell, 2+2p appendix.
29 June	74	**Merit rates for craftsmen** – Viscount Hall, 2p.
28 June	75	**The future of the steel distribution scheme** – Jay, 5p. Gives details of two alternative policies.
28 June	76	**Maintenance of employment in the development areas** – Strauss, 2p. Need for further official investigation of the problems involved in implementing the proposals in PC(49)72.
29 June	77	**Development of aluminium production within the Commonwealth** – Strauss, 7+12p annexes.
28 June	78	**Softwood prices** – Wilson, H., 3+2p appendixes.
30 June	79	**Movement of wages, hours of work, etc. during May 1949** – Isaacs, 1+2+13p appendixes.
30 June	80	**Royal Ordnance factory, Hayes, and the Electrical Musical Industries Ltd.** – Wilson, H., 2p.
1 July	81	**Future of the steel distribution scheme** – Strauss, 2p. Prepared to accept the second alternative in PC(49)75.
1 July	82	**Sheet steel and the motor industry** – Strauss, 4+1p annex.
6 July	83	**Development of aluminium production within the Commonwealth** – Creech Jones, 3p.
6 July	84	**The investment programme** – Cripps, 2p. Decisions on PC(49)59 could no longer be deferred. Recommends acceptance of the level of investment proposed for 1950 and that for 1952 only exceptional increases should be authorized.
7 July	85	**Stocks of food and animal feedingstuffs, raw materials and petroleum products** – C.S.O., 1+3+14p appendixes. Also CS(S)(49)26.
13 July	86	**Food situation in the U.K.: report for May 1949** – Strachey, 7+1p appendix.
13 July	87	**Rehabilitation of private woodlands** – Woodburn and Williams, 2+8p appendix.
15 July	88	**Headquarters Building Committee: change in terms of reference** – Cripps, 1p.
29 July	89	**Food situation in the U.K.: report for June 1949** – Strachey, 7+1p appendix.
27 July	90	**The future of the shipbuilding and ship repairing industries** – Viscount Hall and Barnes, 6+4p annexes. Permanent reductions in employment expected.

8 Aug	91	**Stocks of food and animal feedingstuffs, raw materials and petroleum products – C.S.O.,** 1+3+14p appendixes. Also CS(S)(49)29.
11 Aug	92	**Movement of wages, hours of work, etc. during June 1949 – Isaacs,** 1+2+12p appendixes.
25 Aug	93	**Movement of wages, hours of work, etc. during July 1949 – Isaacs,** 1+2+12p appendixes.
5 Sept	94	**Stocks of food and animal feedingstuffs, raw materials and petroleum products – C.S.O.,** 1+3+14p appendixes. Also CS(S)(49)32.
19 Sept	95	**Control of investment – the Official Committee on the Control of Investment,** 12p. Also CCI(49)11. Increased reliance would have to be placed on general financial policy rather than physical controls. Each type of control on closer inspection appeared less effective than anticipated and it was hard to devise any practical means to ensure the harmonization of individual investment programmes with general government targets. This was true both for increasing and decreasing investment.
20 Sept	96	**Report of the Productivity (Official) Committee – Jay covering the Productivity (Official) Committee,** 1+28+8p annexes. Also OP(49)31. Preview of the activities of government departments in fostering productivity.
15 Sept	97	**Restoration of Repairs to Ships Order – Viscount Hall,** 1p.
21 Sept	98	**Softwood timber supplies and allocations – Wilson, H.,** 4p. Examines effects of proposed allocation on the housing programme.
21 Sept	99	**Standardization – Wilson and Strauss,** 1+7+14p annexes. Also SI(M)(49)43.
23 Sept	100	**Supply of commercial vehicles to the home market – Strauss,** 2p.
28 Sept	101	**Movement of wages, hours of work, etc. during August 1949 – Isaacs,** 1+2+15p appendixes.
29 Sept	102	**Women's Land Army – Williams,** 2p. Recommends winding up at end-Nov 1950.
29 Sept	103	**Publicity on the economic situation – Cripps,** 3p. Proposed approach to series of conferences and private meetings with industry.
30 Sept	104	**Food situation in the U.K.: report for July and August 1949 – Strachey,** 8+2p appendix.
30 Sept	105	**Proposed Distribution of Industry Amending Bill – Wilson, H.,** 3p. Sets out new powers.
3 Oct	106	**Women's Land Army: Scotland – Woodburn,** 2p.
5 Oct	107	**Control of labour – Isaacs,** 3p. Subject to N.J.A.C. approval, the Control of Engagement Order and use of the power of direction should be withdrawn mid-Nov.

| 6 Oct | 108 | **Eradication of wild rabbits – Woodburn and Williams,** 2+9p appendix. |
| 7 Oct | 109 | **Stocks of food and animal feedingstuffs, raw materials and petroleum products – C.S.O.,** 1+3+14p appendixes. Also CS(S)(49)37. |

CAB 134/643   Memoranda   12 Oct–29 Dec 1949   PC(49)110–139.

12 Oct	PC(49)110	**Proposed arbitrary price reductions – Strachey,** 2p. Repeat of arguments in EPC(49)90 that such reductions were impossible in his areas of responsibility.
10 Oct	111	**Cinematograph Film Production (Special Loans) Act Amendment Bill – Wilson, H.,** 4p.
13 Oct	112	**Eradication of wild rabbits – Strachey,** 2p.
15 Oct	113	**Interim report of the Inter-departmental Committee on Fish Quality – Strachey, Williams and Woodburn,** 2+13+2p appendixes.
18 Oct	114	**Accommodation for overseas visitors. Requisitioned hotels – Wilson, H.,** 3p.
24 Oct	115	**Animal feedingstuffs – Woodburn, Williams and Strachey,** 2+2p appendixes.
24 Oct	116	**Prices of building materials – Key,** 2p.
25 Oct	117	**Standardization – Strauss covering the Official Committee for Standardization of Engineering Products,** 4+35p.
26 Oct	118	**Accommodation for overseas visitors. Requisitioned hotels – Creech Jones,** 3p.
31 Oct	119	**Accommodation for overseas visitors. Requisitioned hotels – Key,** 3p.
27 Oct	120	**Animal feedingstuffs – Strachey,** 4p.
28 Oct	121	**Catering Wages Act 1943 – Isaacs,** 9p.
29 Oct	122	**Movement of wages, hours of work, etc. during September 1949 – Isaacs,** 1+3+13p appendixes.
31 Oct	123	**Food situation in the U.K.: report for September 1949 – Strachey,** 8+1p appendix.
2 Nov	124	**Arbitrary cuts in controlled prices – Strauss,** 1p.
1 Nov	125	**Ship repairs abroad – Jay covering the Overseas Negotiations Committee,** 1+3p.
3 Nov	126	**The coal industry ring fence – Gaitskell,** 1p. Recommends removal as proposed in PC(49)107.
2 Nov	127	**Workers in agriculture and coal-mining: deferment and the ring fence – Isaacs,** 1p.
4 Nov	128	**Stocks of food and animal feedingstuffs, raw materials and petroleum products – C.S.O.,** 1+3+14p appendixes. Also CS(S)(49)43.
17 Nov	129	**Arbitrary reductions in controlled prices – Wilson, H.,** 2p. Effect of 5% reduction in price of certain utility goods.
21 Nov	130	**Movement of wages, hours of work, etc. during October 1949 – Isaacs,** 1+2+10p appendixes.

25 Nov	**131**	**Replacement of obsolescent tonnage – Barnes,** 4+2p annexes.
2 Dec	**132**	**Flat rate transport scheme for fish – Woodburn, Williams and Strachey,** 2p.
7 Dec	**133**	**Stocks of food and animal feedingstuffs, raw materials and petroleum products – C.S.O.,** 1+3+14p appendixes. Also CS(S)(49)46.
10 Dec	**134**	**Release of requisitioned hotels – Key,** 3+1p annex.
13 Dec	**135**	**Supply of commercial vehicles to the home market – Strauss,** 4+2p appendix. Industry was trying to increase exports, but if effective control were wanted it should be on demand.
14 Dec	**136**	**The open-cast coal programme – Gaitskell,** 3p. Target production for next four years.
20 Dec	**137**	**The Grenfall and Advance factories in South Wales – Strauss covering a working party,** 1+9+2p appendix. Proposals for their use, including possibility of government operation.
21 Dec	**138**	**Food situation in the U.K.: report for October 1949 – Strachey,** 9+1p appendix.
29 Dec	**139**	**Movement of wages, hours of work, etc. during November 1949 – Isaacs,** 1+3+8p appendixes.

CAB 134/644   Meetings   4 Jan–8 Dec 1950   PC(50)1st–21st.

4 Jan	**PC(50)1st:1**	**Open-cast coal production.** PC(49)136. Gaitskell revised recommendations.
	:2	**Movement of wages, hours of work during November 1949.** PC(49)139.
	:3	**Food situation in the U.K.** PC(49)138.
16 Jan	**2nd:1**	**Grenfall and Advance factories in South Wales.** PC(49)137.
	:2	**Tourist industry: release of requisitioned hotels.** PC(49)134.
23 Jan	**3rd:1**	**Economic Survey for 1950.** PC(50)3. The Official Committee on Economic Development and the Economic Planning Board had both felt the paper too optimistic but Cripps disagreed. It was argued that the existing policy of publishing annual surveys was open to the criticism that they did not provide an adequate framework for effective economic planning related to the rhythm of production. There were certain fields in which decisions could not be fully effective within a year, e.g. housing. Against this, it was pointed out that the main purpose of the surveys was to provide not a basis for economic planning but an opportunity for reviewing past progress and laying down broad objectives for the current year. Economic planning was achieved

by other means, such as the annual review of the investment programme, which inevitably covered a longer period.

:2 **Length of public service vehicles.** PC(50)5.

:3 **Maintenance of employment in the development areas.** PC(50)5. Wilson, H. felt a more positive policy was required such as preferential treatment in the awarding of contracts. Despite some disagreement, PC(50)6 was approved in principle.

10 Mar   4th:1   **Supply of commercial vehicles to the home market.** PC(50)12. Whilst it was agreed that investment in this sector was too high none of the remedies in PC(50)12 was thought satisfactory.

:2 **Grenfall factories in South Wales.** PC(50)7, 13, 15.

:3 **Economic Survey for 1950.** CP(50)28 and PC(50)17. Bevan did not wish to be committed to the paragraphs on housing.

31 Mar   5th:1   **Working party report on the building industry.** PC(50)25. Agreement that the government should not publish any reply to the criticisms in the report, but should publish the report 24 hours before the Anglo-American Council on Productivity report which was critical of the industry. Proposals on future policy towards the building industry would be prepared by a group of ministers under Bevan.

:2 **Steel economy.** PC(50)14.

:3 **Progress of Remploy factories.** PC(50)20.

:4 **Maintenance of employment in the development areas.** PC(50)24. Agreement that ministers should continue to exert pressure on socialized industries to give proper consideration to development and unemployment areas in the placing of contracts.

:5 **Tourist industry: release of requisitioned hotels.** PC(50)23.

:6 **Discussions with the engineering industry.** PC(50)9.

:7 **Movement of wages and hours of work during December, January and February.** PC(50)8 and 26.

:8 **Food situation in the U.K.** PC(50)22.

27 Apr   6th:1   **Working party on the building industry.** It was not possible to publish the Anglo-American Council on Productivity report just after the working party report.

:2 **House coal.** PC(50)35 and 36. Agreement that a new scheme was necessary to reduce the summer price of coal in the south to encourage stocking.

:3 **Tourist industry: release of requisitioned hotels.** PC(50)38.

:4 **Future of the steel distribution scheme.** PC(50)37 and 39.

:5 **Food situation in the U.K.** PC(50)34.

:6 **Statistical review.** PC(50)31.

:7 **Report of the work of the Labour (Textile Industries) Committee.** PC(50)27.

:8 **The fishing industry at Aberdeen.** PC(50)32.

10 May   7th:1 **Working party report on the building industry.** PC(50)43.

:2 **Milk supplies 1950.** PC(50)40.

:3 **House coal: summer and winter prices.** PC(50)44. The N.C.B. should consider a subsidy to coal merchants for stocking.

25 May   8th:1 **Capital investment in 1951 and 1952.** PC(50)41, 42, 47, 48, 53, 54. Despite concern about cuts in new building and machinery for manufacturing industry, the programmes were approved with slight increases in those for education, the Post Office, and fuel and power.

:2 **Coal.** PC(50)49 and 51. Approval of an additional 1.1m tons of house coal for domestic consumers in summer 1950, leaving 20m tons for export.

:3 **White fish industry.**

13 June   9th:1 **Plan for the Highlands.** PC(50)48.

:2 **House coal: merchants' margins.** PC(50)50.

:3 **Royal Ordnance factories.** PC(50)56.

:4 **Food situation in the U.K.** PC(50)45.

23 June   10th:1 **Report of the Electricity Subcommittee of the Joint Consultative Committee.** PC(50)55.

:2 **White fish industry.** PC(50)64 and 65.

:3 **Future level of the shipbuilding and ship repairing industries.** PC(50)52, 61 and 66.

:4 **Movement of wages and hours of work during March 1950.** PC(50)46.

30 June   11th:1 **Work to places of recreation.** PC(50)58.

:2 **Future level of the shipbuilding and ship repairing industries.** PC(50)52, 61 and 66.

:3 **Food situation in the U.K.** PC(50)59.

5 July   12th:1 **Maintenance of employment in the development areas.** PC(50)41, 47 and 57.

:2 **Manufacture of telephone equipment.** PC(50)62.

:3 **Movement of wages, hours of work, etc. during April and May 1950.** PC(50)77.

12 July   13th:1 **Distributors' margins for price-controlled goods.** PC(50)21.

	:2	**Bulk purchase and Ministry of Food controls.** PC(50)63 and 67.
	:3	**Development councils under the Industrial Organization and Development Act 1947.** PC(50)72.
21 July	14th:1	**Supplies of cement.**
	:2	**Decontrols.** Agreement that for the time being no further relaxation of controls would occur.
	:3	**Interim report by the Working Party on Electric Power-using Industries and the Highlands.** PC(50)75.
	:4	**Acquisition and farming of land.** PC(50)68 and 69.
	:5	**Animal feedingstuffs supplies July 1950–June 1951.** PC(50)77.
	:6	**Capital investment programme: sewerage and sewage disposal works.** PC(50)78.
	:7	**Canned pilchards.** PC(50)73.
	:8	**Food situation in the U.K.** PC(50)76.
28 July	15th:1	**Textile machinery industry: working party report on research and development.** PC(50)82.
	:2	**Standardization and exports.** PC(50)80.
	:3	**Extended use of rayon.** PC(50)83.
	:4	**Subsidy on coal freights.** PC(50)85.
	:5	**Coal exports.** PC(50)84.
	:6	**Powers of the White Fish Industry Board.** PC(50)86.
	:7	**Repair of British ships in Germany.** PC(50)79.
	:8	**Licensing of miscellaneous new building works.** PC(50)81.
	:9	**Supplies of cement.** PC(50)87.
13 Oct	16th:1	**Progress of Remploy factories.** PC(50)90.
	:2	**Tin plate.** PC(50)92. Approval of proposals for the short term only.
	:3	**Supplies of animal feedingstuffs.**
	:4	**Food situation in the U.K.** PC(50)88, 91, 95.
	:5	**Movement of wages, hours of work, etc. during June, July and August 1950.** PC(50)89 and 96. Considerable apprehension at the increase in cost of living.
20 Oct	17th:1	**Proposed increase in the price and meat content of sausages.** PC(50)101.
	:2	**Interim report by the Working Party on Electric Power-using Industries and the Highlands.** PC(50)93.
	:3	**Coal supplies for the winter 1950–51.** PC(50)102. Noel-Baker said that, largely owing to full employment, the outlook was bleak. Agreement to reduce exports in Nov and Dec.
24 Oct	18th:1	**Coal supplies for the winter 1950–51.** Unsuccessful attempt to defer the reduction of exports.

	:2	**Clean coal.** PC(50)97.
	:3	**Coal freight subsidy.** PC(50)98.
	:4	**The N.C.B. national plan.** Pointed out that this did not have government approval.
	:5	**Outlook for coal supplies and particularly for coal exports during the five years 1951–55.** PC(50)100.
1 Nov	19th:1	**Increased productivity in building in relation to the housing programme.** PC(50)94. Submitted to the Subcommittee on the Future Policy towards the Building Industry under Bevan for detailed examination.
	:2	**Export credit guarantees.** PC(50)103.
	:3	**Coal supplies in winter 1950–51.** PC(50)104. Agreement, with the Foreign Office reserving its position, that there was no alternative to PC(50)104 as the situation had deteriorated. Paper to go to Cabinet.
	:4	**Outlook for coal supplies and particularly for coal exports during the five years 1951/55.** PC(50)99 and 100. To be a review of how to increase manpower.
29 Nov	20th:1	**British Electricity Authority investment.** PC(50)108 and 113.
	:2	**Bulk purchases and Ministry of Food controls.** PC(50)110.
	:3	**Alleged opposition by trade unions to the employment of Italian workers in the tin plate industry.** PC(50)112.
	:4	**Raw materials shortages.**
	:5	**Food situation in the U.K.** PC(50)105.
	:6	**Movement of wages, hours of work, etc. during September 1950.** PC(50)106.
	:7	**Statistical review.** PC(50)107.
	:8	**First annual report of the National Research Development Corporation.** PC(50)109.
8 Dec	21st:1	**Future policy towards the building industry.** PC(50)115. Part I was approved but Part II required further examination.
	:2	**Zinc supplies 1951.** PC(50)114.
	:3	**Railway freight rebates fund.** PC(50)117.
	:4	**Grenfall and Advance factories in South Wales.** PC(50)118.
	:5	**Further reference to the Monopolies Commission.** PC(50)116.

CAB 134/645   Memoranda   3 Jan–5 Apr 1950   PC(50)1–29.

3 Jan	**PC(50)1**	**Unemployment in the ship repairing industry – Isaacs,** 3p.
6 Jan	2	**Statistical review – S.E.V. Luke,** 1p.

13 Jan	**3**	**Economic Survey for 1950 – Cripps,** 2+38+4p annex. Draft had been amended in the light of the Economic Planning Board's and the Official Committee on Economic Development's comments. Many statistics were more uncertain than usual because of the unknown level of E.R.P. assistance and devaluation.
17 Jan	**4**	**Food situation in the U.K.: report for November 1949 – Strachey,** 9+1p appendix.
19 Jan	**5**	**Length of public service vehicles – Barnes,** 2+5p appendixes.
19 Jan	**6**	**Placing of government contracts with firms in development and unemployment areas – Wilson, H.,** 2p. Proposals to increase progress.
31 Jan	**7**	**Grenfall factories in South Wales – Isaacs,** 1+1p annex.
2 Feb	**8**	**Movement of wages, hours of work, etc. during December 1949 – Isaacs,** 1+3+7p appendixes.
3 Feb	**9**	**Discussions with the engineering industry on the dollar drive and productivity – Strauss,** 3+2p annexes. Report of the meetings. The industry was trying to overcome its problems but no immediate and dramatic increase in exports could be expected.
17 Feb	**10**	**Manufacture of telephone equipment. Discharge of contractor's work-people on Merseyside – Paling,** 5p.
9 Feb	**11**	**Food situation in the U.K.: report for December 1949 – Strachey,** 10+1p annex.
15 Feb	**12**	**Supply of commercial vehicles to the home market – Strauss,** 6+9p annexes. Rejects the use of steel allocations, licensing manufacture and supply to the home market and licensing the acquisition of commercial vehicles.
15 Feb	**13**	**Grenfall factories in South Wales – Strauss,** 1+2+3p appendixes. Second report of the working party attached.
20 Feb	**14**	**Steel economy – Jay covering the Steel Economy Committee,** 1+13+13p appendix. Also SE(50)1. Fourth report of the Committee setting out recommendations for the major steel-using departments.
2 Mar	**15**	**Grenfall factories in South Wales – Wilson,** 2p.
3 Mar	**16**	**Composition of the committee – S.E.V. Luke,** 1p.
8 Mar	**17**	**The Economic Survey for 1950 – Cripps,** 1+3p annexes. CP(50)28 was much shorter than usual and largely factual.
9 Mar	**18**	**Composition of the committee – S.E.V. Luke,** 1p.

11 Mar	**19**	**Progress report on the long-term programme of the U.K. – Cripps,** 1+23p. Progress in production had exceeded expectations, but its continuation in the second half of the E.R.P. period was uncertain. Investment had been maintained at roughly the level forecast and inflationary pressure had been reduced. Experience had made more apparent the problem of how to achieve a balance in the gold and dollar accounts of the sterling area without an undesirable reduction in trade.
10 Mar	**20**	**Progress of Remploy factories – Isaacs,** 3p.
20 Mar	**21**	**Distributors' margins of price controlled goods – Wilson, H.,** 1+7+9p annexes. Report on the various departmental policies.
21 Mar	**22**	**Food situation in the U.K. – Webb,** 11+1p annex.
24 Mar	**23**	**Tourist industry and release of requisitioned hotels – Stokes,** 3+3p annexes.
24 Mar	**24**	**Placing of government contracts with firms in development and unemployment areas – Cripps,** 1+2p. Sets out the new procedure to be introduced from 1 April 1950.
28 Mar	**25**	**Working party on the building industry – Stokes,** 3p. Sets out responses should the report be used for criticism of government policy.
27 Mar	**26**	**Movement of wages, hours of work, etc. during January and February 1950 – Isaacs,** 1+3+12p appendixes.
31 Mar	**27**	**Report on the work of the Labour (Textile Industries) Committee – S.E.V. Luke covering Edwards, N.,** 1+5p. Also L(TI)(50)3.
4 Apr	**28**	**Gas industry wage claim – Noel-Baker,** 5p.
5 Apr	**29**	**Gas industry wage claim – Isaacs,** 3+3p appendixes.

CAB 134/646   Memoranda   6 Apr–5 June 1950   PC(50)30–57.

6 Apr	**PC(50)30**	**Report on the extent of restrictive trade union practices in the shipbuilding and ship repairing industries – Cripps covering Isaacs,** 1+1p.
19 Apr	**31**	**Stocks of food and animal feedingstuffs, raw materials and petroleum products – C.S.O.,** 1+5+14p appendixes. Also CS(S)(50)6.
18 Apr	**32**	**The fishing industry at Aberdeen – Williams, McNeil and Webb,** 2+17p appendixes.
18 Apr	**33**	**Building industry: working party report – N. Brook,** 1p. Sets out the composition and terms of reference of the Working Party on Future Policy towards the Building Industry under Bevan.

21 Apr	34	**Food situation in the U.K.: report for February 1950** – Webb, 10+1p annex.
21 Apr	35	**House coal** – Noel-Baker, 8p. Recommends increased allocation to the domestic consumer on political grounds.
2 Apr	36	**House coal: summer and winter prices** – Noel-Baker, 8p.
25 Apr	37	**Future of the steel distribution scheme** – Strauss, 4+1p annex. Recommends the abolition of the general steel allocation at home and of formal control of exports whilst retaining statutory power to reintroduce if necessary.
24 Apr	38	**Tourist industry and release of requisitioned hotels** – Stokes, 2+1p appendix.
25 Apr	39	**Steel distribution scheme: views of the Economic Planning Board** – Cripps, 1p. Recommends abolition of allocation of general steel in the home market provided exports did not rise too rapidly. There was no advantage in retaining allocation as a planning instrument in order to assist other objectives. Allocation of sheet steel and tin plate should be retained.
3 May	40	**Milk supplies 1950** – Webb, 6p.
3 May	41	**Factory building in the unemployment areas** – Wilson, H., 3p. Concern that the growth of employment by new industries in development areas scarcely matched the rate of displacement from existing industries. The post-war boom in factory construction was nearly over and capital investment restrictions were likely to increase unemployment. Proposals to remedy the situation.
18 May	42	**Building licensing** – Stokes, 3p. Recommends easing of licensing restrictions.
8 May	43	**Working party report on the building industry** – Bevan, 1p.
8 May	44	**House coal, summer and winter prices** – Noel-Baker, 6p.
12 May	45	**Food situation in the U.K.: report for March 1950** – Webb, 7+1p annex.
16 May	46	**Movement of wages, hours of work, etc. during March 1950** – Isaacs, 1+2+10p appendixes.
23 May	47	**Distribution of industry** – Isaacs, 2p. Need for a comprehensive policy review.
23 May	48	**A plan for the Highlands** – McNeil, 3+1p appendix +18+12p appendixes.
23 May	49	**Review of the coal situation** – Noel-Baker, 5p. Re-emphasizes his concern about improving house coal position.
23 May	50	**Domestic coal problems. Coal merchants' margins** – Noel-Baker, 7+1p appendix.

23 May	**51**	**The consequences of reductions of coal exports in 1950 – Gaitskell covering the Overseas Negotiations Committee,** 1+8+7p annexes.
22 May	**52**	**The future level of the shipbuilding and ship repairing industries – Viscount Hall and Barnes,** 1+17+22p appendixes.
23 May	**53**	**Investment in 1951 and 1952 – Gaitskell,** 3+2p annex. Sets out the Economic Policy Committee's decisions on the level of investment to be used as a basis for the Production Committee's discussions on the programme's detailed composition.
24 May	**54**	**Building licensing – Cripps,** 2p. Criticism of PC(50)42 because it was inconsistent with the recent decision of the Economic Policy Committee on investment.
30 May	**55**	**Report of the Electricity Subcommittee of the Joint Consultative Committee – Isaacs,** 1+4p. Proposals for spreading the industrial electricity load in the winter 1950–51.
6 June	**56**	**Royal Ordnance factories – Strauss,** 1+3p.
5 June	**57**	**Grenfall factories in South Wales – Wilson, H.,** 1p.

CAB 134/647   Memoranda   13 June–12 Sept 1950   PC(50)58–92.

13 June	**PC(50)58**	**Work to places of recreation – Stokes,** 4p. Amplification of PC(50)42.
19 June	**59**	**Food situation in the U.K.: report for April 1950 – Webb,** 6+1p annex.
19 June	**60**	**Secretarial arrangements – N. Brook,** 1p.
19 June	**61**	**Future level of the shipbuilding and ship repairing industries – Viscount Hall and Barnes,** 2p.
20 June	**62**	**Manufacture of telephone equipment. Report by committee officials – Edwards, N.,** 2+6+3p appendixes.
20 June	**63**	**Ministry of Food controls – Webb,** 6+1p appendix. Proposes the removal of obsolete controls so they could concentrate on developing those controls which could play a constructive part in a managed economy.
20 June	**64**	**White fish industry: short-term remedies – Williams covering an official committee,** 1+6+4p annexes.
20 June	**65**	**White fish industry – Williams, McNeil and Webb,** 6+6p appendix.
22 June	**66**	**Future level of the shipbuilding and ship repairing industries – Wilson, H.,** 4p. Concern about the limited scope of remedies in PC(50)52.
22 June	**67**	**Bulk purchase – Wilson, H. and Strauss,** 4p.

30 June	68	Acquisition and management of land in Scotland – McNeil covering the Department of Agriculture for Scotland, 2+7p.
30 June	69	Acquisition, management and farming of land in England and Wales – Williams, 2+6p appendix.
30 June	70	Movement of wages, hours of work, etc. during April and May 1950 – Isaacs, 1+2+12p appendixes.
30 June	71	Subcommittee on Manufacture in Government-controlled Establishments of Goods for Civilian Use – N. Brook, 1p.
5 July	72	Development councils under the Industrial Organization and Development Act, 1947 – Wilson, H., 3+2p appendix.
10 July	73	Canned pilchards – Webb, 1p.
10 July	74	Subcommittee on Manufacture in Government-controlled Establishments of Goods for Civilian Use – O.C. Morland, 1p.
11 July	75	An interim report by the Working Party on Electric Power-using Industries and the Highlands – Wilson, H. and McNeil, 3+6+52p appendixes.
13 July	76	Food situation in the U.K.: report for May 1950 – Webb, 5+1p appendix.
15 July	77	Animal feedingstuffs supplies July 1950 to June 1951 – Webb, 3+1p appendix.
18 July	78	Capital investment programme: sewerage and sewage disposal works – Bevan, 2p.
20 July	79	The repair of British ships in Germany – Viscount Hall and Barnes, 3p.
24 July	80	Standardization and exports – Wilson, H., 4p.
25 July	81	Licensing of miscellaneous new building work – Stokes, 2+1p appendix.
25 July	82	Working party report on research and development in the textile machinery industry – Wilson, H. and Strauss, 5+27p.
25 July	83	Extended use of rayon and other man-made fibres in substitution for imported textile fibres – Wilson, H., 3p.
26 July	84	The summer coal position – Noel-Baker, 3p. Sets out problems and proposed remedies.
26 July	85	Coal freight subsidy – Noel-Baker, 5+2p annex. Recommends its gradual withdrawal.
26 July	86	Powers of White Fish Industry Board – Williams, 1+7p appendix.
26 July	87	Supplies of cement – Stokes, 2p. Review of both immediate and long-term position.
27 July	88	Food situation in the U.K.: report for June 1950 – Webb, 5+1p annex.

1 Aug	89	**Movement of wages, hours of work, etc. during June 1950 – Isaacs,** 1+2+9p appendixes.
25 July	90	**Progress of Remploy factories – Isaacs,** 2p.
11 Sept	91	**Food situation in the U.K.: report for July – Webb,** 6+1p annex.
12 Sept	92	**Tin plate – Strauss,** 5p.

CAB 134/648   Memoranda   15 Sept–28 Dec 1950   PC(50)93–124.

15 Sept	PC(50)93	**Interim report by the Working Party on Electric Power-using Industries and the Highlands – McNeil,** 1+1p appendix.
2 Oct	94	**Increased productivity in building in relation to the housing programme – Stokes,** 3p.
4 Oct	95	**Food situation in the U.K.: report for August – Webb,** 6+1p annex.
5 Oct	96	**Movement of wages, hours of work, etc. during July and August 1950 – Isaacs,** 1+3+12p appendixes.
18 Oct	97	**Clean coal – Noel-Baker,** 11p. Report on the success of remedies introduced after PC(50)35.
17 Oct	98	**Coal freight subsidy – Noel-Baker,** 4+3p appendixes. Recommends gradual withdrawal.
27 Oct	99	**Coal supplies: methods of increasing production and reducing consumption – Noel-Baker,** 28+1p annex. Output had consistently been less than expected in the summer budget. Proposed measures to deal with serious shortage in winter stocks although there was no easy solution.
17 Oct	100	**Outlook for coal supplies and particularly for coal exports during the five years 1951–1955 – Noel-Baker,** 9+1p appendix. Unfavourable since it could not be assumed that consumer demand had peaked.
17 Oct	101	**Proposed increases in the price and meat content of sausages – Webb,** 1p.
18 Oct	102	**Coal supplies in the winter 1950/51 – Noel-Baker,** 5p. The only way to avoid a prolonged fuel crisis was to re-phase exports to give a larger share to the home market in Nov and Dec.
23 Oct	103	**Export credit guarantees – Wilson, H.,** 1p.
30 Oct	104	**Coal supplies in the winter 1950/51 – Noel-Baker,** 2+1p annex. Proposed reduction in exports to reduce prospective domestic shortages.
2 Nov	105	**Food situation in the U.K.: report for September – Webb,** 7+1p annex.
3 Nov	106	**Movement of wages, hours of work, etc. during September 1950 – Isaacs,** 1+3+10p appendixes.
7 Nov	107	**Stocks of food and animal feedingstuffs, raw materials and petroleum products – C.S.O.,** 1+5+14p appendixes. Also CS(S)(50)17.

8 Nov	**108**	**British Electricity Authority investment in 1951** – Noel-Baker, 6p. Proposed £21m increase in 1951 in order to improve productivity and to expedite the defence programme.
8 Nov	**109**	**First annual report of the National Research Development Corporation** – Wilson, H., covering the National Research Development Corporation, 1+22+9p appendixes.
10 Nov	**110**	**Bulk purchase and Ministry of Food controls** – Gaitskell, 2+2p annex. Sets out the lines on which the Official Committee on Government Purchases and Controls should proceed.
13 Nov	**111**	**Additional member of the Committee** – O.C. Morland, 1p.
21 Nov	**112**	**Alleged opposition by trade unions to the employment of Italian workers in the tin plate industry** – Isaacs, 1p.
23 Nov	**113**	**British Electricity Authority investment** – Gaitskell, 5p. Recommends rejection of the proposed increase except where it would expedite completion of generating stations already under construction.
28 Nov	**114**	**Zinc supplies in 1951** – Strauss, 3p.
27 Nov	**115**	**Future policy towards the building industry** – Bevan, 5p. Recommends a review of the building industry investment programme to enable the government to give assurances that the programme would be increased in line with productivity.
27 Nov	**116**	**Further references to the Monopolies Commission** – Wilson, H., 2p.
5 Dec	**117**	**Railway freight rebate scheme. Railway freight rebates fund** – Barnes, 4p. Recommends termination of both.
5 Dec	**118**	**Grenfall and Advance factories in South Wales** – Wilson, H., 2+1p annex.
7 Dec	**119**	**Food situation in the U.K.: report for October 1950** – Webb, 7+1p annex.
12 Dec	**120**	**Movement of wages, hours of work, etc. during October 1950** – Isaacs, 1+3+15p appendixes.
14 Dec	**121**	**A review of progress in the cotton industry** – Wilson, H., 1+13p. His address to the Cotton Board conference.
18 Dec	**122**	**Siting of new factories required to meet the needs of the rearmament programme** – Wilson, H., 2p. New factories would be required and all efforts should be made for them to be built in development areas.
22 Dec	**123**	**Movement of wages, hours of work, etc. during November 1950** – Isaacs, 1+3+12p appendixes.

28 Dec	**124**	**Report of the Electricity Subcommittee, December 1950 – Isaacs covering the subcommittee of the N.J.A.C.,** 1+7p. On load shedding and spreading.

CAB 134/649   Meetings   11 Jan–1 Aug 1951   PC(51)1st–19th.

11 Jan	**PC(51)1st:1**	**Differential allocation of coal to industry.** PC(51)4 and 5. Decision on its introduction to be deferred but preparations were to continue.
	:2	**Railway wagons for the transport of coal.** PC(51)1. Barnes was to ensure that the movement of coal was carried out with minimum delay.
	:3	**Cream.** PC(51)2.
	:4	**Siting of new factories required to meet the needs of the rearmament programme.** PC(50)122. Pointed out that there were many other criteria as well as distribution of industry, in particular strategic considerations and availability of fuel and power supplies.
	:5	**White fish subsidy.** PC(51)3.
	:6	**Report of the Electricity Subcommittee December 1950.** PC(50)124.
	:7	**Food situation in the U.K.** PC(50)119.
	:8	**Movement of wages and hours of work during October and November 1950.** PC(50)120 and 123.
19 Jan	**2nd**	**House coal.** PC(51)5 and 6. Endorsement of PC(51)6.
24 Jan	**3rd:1**	**Cream.** PC(51)2.
	:2	**Tin plate allocation for Period II 1951.** PC(51)9.
	:3	**Price control over white fish and rabbits.** PC(51)7.
	:4	**Dispersal of nationalized boards.** PC(51)8.
	:5	**Allocation of coal to industry.** PC(51)10 and 11. Deferred.
	:6	**Raw materials.**
	:7	**Price control.**
31 Jan	**4th:1**	**Houses for miners.** PC(51)15.
	:2	**Allocation of coal to industry.** PC(51)16 and 17. It was within Noel-Baker's discretion to change the supply to the iron and steel industry to keep essential industries in production.
	:3	**Increase in the price of coal.** PC(51)19.
	:4	**Food situation in the U.K.** PC(51)12.
	:5	**Movement of wages, hours of work, etc. during December 1950.** PC(51)13.
6 Feb	**5th:1**	**Investment in 1951 and subsequent years.** PC(51)18. Some ministers were concerned that the postponement of departmental programmes due to start in 1951 would involve

greater expenditure in 1952 than that approved. Agreement that no revision of the investment programme was possible before a review on the lines suggested in PC(51)18.

	:2	**Raw materials for the building industry.** PC(51)20.
	:3	**Supplies of coal to power stations.** PC(51)21.
	:4	**Supplies of coal to industry.** PC(51)22.
16 Feb	6th	**Allocation scheme for sulphur and sulphuric acid.** PC(51)23.
7 Mar	7th:1	**Raw materials.** PC(51)18, 29, 30, 31. Ministers were to determine minimum and normal stock levels upon which to base departmental purchasing and consumption programmes.
	:2	**Supply of principal materials for the building programme.** PC(51)26. Stokes was concerned that raw material shortages were delaying the programme.
	:3	**Exploitation of home woodlands in emergency.** PC(51)27.
	:4	**Statistical review.** PC(51)24.
15 Mar	8th:1	**General steel supplies in 1951.** PC(51)32. Agreement to reduce direct exports during the first half year to an annual rate of 1.4m tons although some flexibility was permissible where exports could be bartered for urgently-needed raw materials.
	:2	**Distribution of papers.**
	:3	**Coal budget for summer 1951.** PC(51)33 and 36. Approval of PC(51)36.
	:4	**Sulphur.**
	:5	**Movement of wages, hours of work, etc. during January 1951.** PC(51)28.
19 Mar	9th:1	**Economic Survey for 1951.** CP(51)77. Some ministers felt the survey too optimistic, particularly on increased exports and productivity. The investment programme was not included because it was still under review owing to the new defence programme.
	:2	**Import of poultry from countries where fowl-pest is endemic.** PC(51)34.
	:3	**Softwood: allocation for April–June 1951.** PC(51)38 and 39.
	:4	**Provision of houses for skilled workers needed by Hawksley Construction.** PC(51)37.
	:5	**Further reference to the Monopolies Commission.** PC(51)35.
13 Apr	10th:1	**Purchase of bricks from Belgium.**
	:2	**Coal supplies for the copper mines in Northern Rhodesia.** PC(51)41.
	:3	**Allocation schemes for sulphur and sulphuric acid.** PC(51)44.

		:4	**Liberalization of shipbuilding.** PC(51)42.
		:5	**Food situation in the U.K.** PC(51)25 and 40.
		:6	**Movement of wages, hours of work, etc. during February 1951.** PC(51)43.
2 May	11th		**Capital investment in 1951, 1952 and 1953.** PC(51)47, 49, 50. Approval of the report's assumptions and the ban on new office building. Departments were to keep within money limits of programmes, increased costs notwithstanding. Then consideration of individual programmes. Noel-Baker could not accept the programme for coal, electricity and gas.
29 May	12th:1		**Technical manpower for the defence programme.** PC(51)52, 53, 55.
		:2	**The raw materials situation: progress report No. 2 – April 1951.** PC(51)58.
		:3	**Future policy towards the building industry.** PC(51)43.
		:4	**Provision of additional shipping for exports.** PC(51)60.
		:5	**Brick supply and demand: 1951.** PC(51)57.
		:6	**Result of measures to avert a coal crisis.** PC(51)51.
		:7	**Labour supply for the tin plate industry.** PC(51)48.
		:8	**Food situation in the U.K.** PC(51)46.
		:9	**Movement of wages, hours of work, etc. during March and April 1951.** PC(51)56 and 61.
15 June	13th:1		**Investment programme 1951–1953.** PC(51)67. Consideration of the individual programmes remaining.
		:2	**John Deere Plow Co.** PC(51)63.
		:3	**British Standards Institute.** PC(51)68.
		:4	**Food situation in the U.K.** PC(51)62 and 65.
		:5	**Changes in the employment position during April 1951.** PC(51)66.
22 June	14th:1		**Employment of technical manpower on shelter planning.** PC(51)75.
		:2	**Ban on office building.** PC(51)74.
		:3	**Sale of merchant ships for scrap.** PC(51)69 and 71.
		:4	**Iron and steel scrap.** PC(51)64.
		:5	**Removal of train rails for steel scrap.** PC(51)73.
		:6	**Shipping for imported iron ore.** PC(51)72.
29 June	15th:1		**Coal for the Northern Rhodesian copper mines.** PC(51)77.
		:2	**Future raw materials policy.** PC(51)78.
		:3	**Summer coal budget.** PC(51)76. Disagreement between Gaitskell and Noel-Baker over the end-summer stock figure. Noel-Baker was to

		consider ways of reducing consumption and conserving supplies.
4 July	**16th**	**White fish subsidy.** PC(51)81.
20 July	**17th:1**	**Dispersal of nationalized boards: British Electricity Authority.** PC(51)80.
	:2	**Brick supply and demand.** PC(51)82.
	:3	**Steel.** PC(51)87 and 88. Headquarters Building Committee was to examine immediate difficulties in the building industry owing to the shortage of reinforcing steel and the effect of diverting supplies to essential projects. Some ministers were concerned at the treatment of exports as a residual once domestic allocations had been settled.
	:4	**National plan for coal.** PC(51)86.
	:5	**Coal supplies.** PC(51)89 and 90. Noel-Baker recommended increased imports, but officials were first to re-examine coal requirements for winter 1951/52.
	:6	**Movement of wages, hours of work, etc. during May 1951.** PC(51)79.
	:7	**Changes in the employment position during May 1951.** PC(51)84.
	:8	**Food situation in the U.K.** PC(51)85.
27 July	**18th:1**	**Impact of the defence programme on civilian building projects.** PC(51)92.
	:2	**Proposal to build a new hotel in London.** PC(51)91.
	:3	**Fish price control.** PC(51)93.
	:4	**Coke distribution.** Noel-Baker recommended the reimposition of the statutory restriction on supply due to impending shortage.
	:5	**The raw materials situation: progress report for June 1951.** PC(51)95.
1 Aug	**19th:1**	**Land improvement and cattle rearing in the Highlands.** PC(51)94.
	:2	**Coal: measures to increase production and reduce consumption.** PC(51)99. Agreement on some of the proposals in PC(51)99.
	:3	**Steel exports in the second half of 1951.** PC(51)98.
	:4	**Allocation scheme for general steel.** Statements by Edwards, J. and Strauss.
	:5	**Production of sheet steel and tin plate.** PC(51)97.
	:6	**Iron ore.** PC(51)100.

CAB 134/650   Memoranda   8 Jan–29 Mar 1951   PC(51)1–42.

8 Jan	**PC(51)1**	**Railway wagons for the transport of coal –** Noel-Baker, 3p. Recommends priority of movement for coal for the next three months.

9 Jan	2	**Cream – Webb covering the Committee on Future Milk Surpluses,** 5+10+8p appendixes.
9 Jan	3	**White fish subsidy – Williams, McNeil and Webb,** 2+8p appendixes.
10 Jan	4	**Scheme for differential allocation of coal to industry – chairman of the Materials (Allocation) Committee,** 3+4p appendix. See CAB 130/65, GEN 353.
9 Jan	5	**Coal for the power stations, industry, railways and the domestic consumer – Noel-Baker,** 7+1p annex. Power stations must have enough coal and plans provided for the most adverse conditions. A differential scheme for allocations as opposed to a proportionate cut in deliveries should be considered. A more rigorous scheme based on a heavier cut for iron and steel and coke ovens should be ready from mid-Feb (from which less unemployment would ensue than elsewhere). The house coal situation was also serious.
18 Jan	6	**House coal – Edwards, J.,** 3+1p annex. If house coal stocks fell to a dangerous level railways should make further savings.
19 Jan	7	**Price control over white fish and rabbits – Webb,** 3+1p appendix.
19 Jan	8	**Dispersal of nationalized boards – Edwards, J. covering the Official Committee on Dispersal from London of Headquarters Government Offices,** 1+6p.
22 Jan	9	**Tin plate allocation, Period II 1951 – chairman of the Materials (Allocation) Committee,** 2+7p appendixes.
22 Jan	10	**Probable level of unemployment arising from the proposed differential allocation scheme for coal – Edwards, J. covering C.E.P.S.,** 1+5+1p annex. Tentative forecast of unemployment peaking at a maximum of 500,000 to one million. Ministries of Labour and Fuel and Power thought this too optimistic. Edwards, J. believed that unless the coal shortage in industry were greater than 200,000 tons per week unemployment would not be greater than 500,000.
23 Jan	11	**Coal for industry – Noel-Baker,** 4p. Thought PC(51)4 underestimated the possibility of large-scale unemployment. Sets out the machinery to keep stock position under review.
24 Jan	12	**Food situation in the U.K.: report for November 1950 – Webb,** 6+1p annex.
26 Jan	13	**Movement of wages, hours of work, etc. during December 1950 – Isaacs,** 1+2+12p appendixes.

25 Jan	14	**Composition of the committee – O.C. Morland,** 1p.
29 Jan	15	**Houses for miners – Noel-Baker,** 1+2p. Also OCC(51)6.
29 Jan	16	**Allocation of coal to industry: alternative scheme – Edwards, J. covering C.E.P.S.,** 2+4+5p. Recommends maximum overall cut of 50,000 tons per week for the iron and steel industry.
30 Jan	17	**Coal for industry – Noel-Baker,** 4+1p annex.
30 Jan	18	**Investment in 1951 and subsequent years – Gaitskell,** 6+2p appendix. The I.P.C. should review the civil programme for 1951 to see whether reductions were needed to complete defence work without overloading the building industry. Meanwhile, no additions should be made to the programme except shipbuilding. All departments should be warned that the 1952 civil programme would have to be reduced below the officially-approved figure. No 1951 starts should be permitted which would result in the approved cash limit for 1952 being exceeded.
30 Jan	19	**Increase in price of coal – Noel-Baker,** 7p.
2 Feb	20	**Productivity in the building industry. Prospects with regard to raw materials – Edwards, J.,** 3+1p appendix. There would be insufficient bricks to enable productivity to increase by 6% over 1950. Other materials could be in shortage. This made achievement of the approved building programme difficult.
3 Feb	21	**The power stations – Noel-Baker,** 2+1p annex.
5 Feb	22	**Coal for industry – Noel-Baker,** 2p. Situation report.
7 Feb	23	**Allocation scheme for sulphur and sulphuric acid – chairman of the Materials (Allocation) Committee,** 8+4p apendixes.
16 Feb	24	**Stocks of food and animal feedingstuffs, raw materials and petroleum products – C.S.O.,** 1+4+14p appendixes. Also CS(S)(51)7.
28 Feb	25	**Food situation in the U.K. – Webb,** 7+1p annex.
27 Feb	26	**Supply of principal materials for the building programme – Stokes,** 2p. Sets out the supply position and consequences of any shortage.
2 Mar	27	**Exploitation of home woodlands in an emergency – Williams and McNeil,** 2p.
5 Mar	28	**Movement of wages, hours of work, etc. during January 1951 – Isaacs,** 1+3+12p appendixes.
5 Mar	29	**The raw materials situation: progress report No. 1: Feb 1951 – Raw Materials Committee,** 2+23p annex. Also ES(51)19 and RM(51)52(final). First of a series of bimonthly reports assessing

		the implications of any shortages for industrial production and reviewing each major commodity.
5 Mar	30	**Government-held strategic stocks: progress report No. 1 February 1951 – Raw Materials Committee,** 2+1p annex.
6 Mar	31	**Future raw materials policy – Gaitskell covering the Economic Steering Committee,** 1+6p. Also RM(51)75. Moderation of U.S. demand must be the short-term objective but in the long term production must be encouraged since present supplies were insufficient to support full employment worldwide.
13 Mar	32	**General steel supplies in 1951 – Gaitskell,** 3+12p annex. Sets out proposals to remedy anticipated shortfall of 1m tons.
13 Mar	33	**Coal budget for the summer 1951 – Noel-Baker,** 4+1p annex. The outlook was brighter.
13 Mar	34	**Import of poultry from countries where fowl-pest is endemic – Williams,** 4p.
14 Mar	35	**A further reference to the Monopolies Commission – Wilson, H.,** 1p.
14 Mar	36	**Coal exports in 1951 – Wilson, H.,** 2+2p annex. Need for more exports than was recommended in PC(51)33.
14 Mar	37	**Provision of houses for skilled workers needed by Hawksley Constructions – Strauss,** 3p.
15 Mar	38	**Softwood: allocations for April–June 1951 – Wilson, H.,** 2p.
17 Mar	39	**Softwood allocations Period II 1951 – Pakenham,** 3p.
27 Mar	40	**Food situation in the U.K.: report for January 1951 – Webb,** 6+1p annex.
29 Mar	41	**Coal supplies for the copper mines in Northern Rhodesia – Gordon Walker,** 4+2p appendix.
29 Mar	42	**Liberalization of shipbuilding – Viscount Hall,** 2p.

CAB 134/651   Memoranda   3 Apr–12 July 1951   PC(51)43–86.

3 Apr	**PC(51)43**	**Movement of wages, hours of work, etc. during February 1951 – Isaacs,** 1+3+13p appendixes.
10 Apr	44	**Allocation schemes for sulphur and sulphuric acid – Pakenham,** 4+4p appendixes.
13 Apr	45	**Future policy towards the building industry – Isaacs,** 2p.
14 Apr	46	**Food situation in the U.K.: report for February 1951 – Webb,** 7+1p annex.
14 Apr	47	**Capital investment in 1951, 1952 and 1953: nationalized fuel and power industrial programmes – Noel-Baker,** 6p. Criticism of proposed cuts.

18 Apr	48	**Labour supply for the tin plate industry – Isaacs,** 1p.
20 Apr	49	**Capital investment in 1951, 1952 and 1953 – Gaitskell covering E.N. Plowden covering the I.P.C.,** 1+2+2+73+1p. Also ES(51)24, EPB(51)6 and IPC(51)1. Comments of the Economic Planning Board and the Economic Steering Committee including their agreement with the I.P.C. to assume a 5% p.a. increase over three years in building and civil engineering. Some departments reserved their positions. The report's main theme was the modification to the previously approved 1951 and 1952 civil investment programmes occasioned by increased defence investment.
23 Apr	50	**Educational investment in 1953 – Tomlinson,** 2p.
24 Apr	51	**Result of measures taken to avert a coal crisis –** Noel-Baker, 3+1p appendix. A fuel crisis had been averted only by emergency measures. To avoid further crisis everything must be done to build up end-summer stocks.
24 Apr	52	**Technical manpower for the defence programme – Gaitskell covering the Headquarters Building Committee,** 1+8p. Also ES(51)27.
24 Apr	53	**Technical manpower for the defence building programme – Shinwell,** 5p.
26 Apr	54	**Export allocation of steel – Gaitskell,** 1p.
28 Apr	55	**Technical manpower for the defence building programme – Tomlinson,** 3p.
30 Apr	56	**Movement of wages, hours of work, etc. during March 1951 – Isaacs,** 1+3+14p appendixes.
2 May	57	**Brick supply and demand: 1951 – Brown,** 2p.
7 May	58	**The raw materials situation: progress report No. 2 April 1951 – Gaitskell covering the Raw Materials Committee,** 1+2+27p annex. Also RM(51)103(final). Raw materials shortages had not played a considerable part in the decline in the rate of increase of manufacturing output in early 1951.
9 May	59	**Composition of the committee – O.C. Morland,** 1p.
11 May	60	**Provision of additional shipping for exports –** Barnes, 1+3p.
23 May	61	**Movement of wages, hours of work, etc. during April 1951 – Isaacs,** 1+3+13p appendixes.
28 May	62	**Food situation in the U.K.: monthly report for March 1951 – Webb,** 8+1p annex.
30 May	63	**John Deere Plow Co. of U.S.A.: manufacturers of agricultural implements and tractors –** Shawcross, 5+3p annexes.

5 June	64	**Iron and steel scrap – Strauss,** 1+7p appendix.
6 June	65	**Food situation in the U.K.: monthly report for April 1951 – Webb,** 6+1p annex.
7 June	66	**Changes in the employment position during April 1951 – Isaacs,** 1+8p.
12 June	67	**Investment programme 1951–53 – Gaitskell,** 5p. Outcome of discussions on individual departmental programmes. The resulting increases in the annual totals might have to be cut later.
12 June	68	**British Standards Institute – Shawcross covering the Committee on the Organization and Constitution of the B.S.I.,** 2+3p annex +44p.
13 June	69	**Supply of surplus ships for breaking for scrap – Strauss,** 3p.
14 June	70	**Statement on investment – Gaitskell,** 1+3p. Draft statement for the Commons.
14 June	71	**Sale of merchant ships for scrap – Barnes,** 2p.
18 June	72	**Shipping for imported iron ore – Strauss,** 3p.
16 June	73	**Removal of tram-rails for steel scrap – Barnes,** 1p.
19 June	74	**Ban on office building – Brown covering the Headquarters Building Committee,** 1+4p. Detail of proposed ban.
19 June	75	**The employment of technical manpower on shelter planning – Chuter Ede,** 1+1p.
20 June	76	**Summer coal budget – Noel-Baker,** 6+2p appendix. If output could not be increased some coal would have to be imported.
21 June	77	**Coal supplies for the copper mines in Northern Rhodesia – Griffiths,** 2p.
25 June	78	**Future raw materials policy – Gaitskell covering the Raw Materials Committee,** 1+4+5p appendix. Also ES(51)41 and RM(51)127(final).
26 June	79	**Movement of wages, hours of work, etc. during May 1951 – Isaacs,** 1+2+12p appendixes.
27 June	80	**Dispersal of nationalized boards: British Electricity Authority – Noel-Baker,** 3p.
29 June	81	**White fish subsidy – Williams and McNeil,** 4+3p appendixes.
30 June	82	**Brick supply and demand 1951 – Brown,** 1p.
3 July	83	**Revision of iron and steel prices – Strauss,** 6+2p annexes. Recirculated with minor amendments as EPC(51)70.
6 July	84	**Changes in the employment position during May 1951 – Isaacs,** 1+8p.
9 July	85	**Food situation in the U.K.: monthly report for May 1951 – Webb,** 6+1p annex.
12 July	86	**National plan for coal – Noel-Baker,** 4p. Brief summary of the N.C.B.'s plan of investment

up to 1965, concentrating on the principles of investment policy.

CAB 134/652   Memoranda   17 July–17 Oct 1951   PC(51)87–112.

17 July	PC(51)87	**Steel: the level of direct exports in the second half of 1951 – Strauss and Edwards, J. covering the Overseas Negotiations Committee,** 5+4p.
18 July	88	**Shortage of steel for building and civil engineering – Brown,** 2p. Need for a reduction in exports to fulfil the 1951 programme.
18 July	89	**Implications of importing coal – Gaitskell covering a working party,** 1+6+1p annex.
18 July	90	**Coal supplies – Noel-Baker,** 13p. Unless new measures were taken there would be a permanent and increasing deficiency. Output must be increased and consumption cut.
24 July	91	**Proposal to erect a new hotel in London – Shawcross,** 4+2p annex.
24 July	92	**Impact of the defence programme on civilian building projects – Brown,** 1+1+2p appendix. Follow-up to EPC(51)43, based primarily on labour resources.
25 July	93	**Fish price control – Webb,** 3p.
28 July	94	**Land improvement and cattle rearing in the Highlands – McNeil,** 4+1p appendix.
25 July	95	**The raw materials situation: progress report No. 3 June 1951 – Stokes covering the Raw Materials Committee,** 1+24+3p annexes. Also RM(51)154(final). The general prospect was not very different from PC(51)58.
28 July	96	**The import of coal from Poland – Gaitskell covering an official working party,** 1+4p.
31 July	97	**Production of sheet steel and tin plate – Strauss,** 2p.
30 July	98	**Steel exports in the second half of 1951 – Edwards, J.,** 2+3p annex.
30 July	99	**Coal: measures to increase production and reduce consumption – Noel-Baker,** 12+6p annex. Three principles must be accepted: the N.C.B. must be told that increased output was more important than reduced costs; there had to be more miners; and consumption had to be cut by improving the efficiency of use of coal.
31 July	100	**Interim report by the Official Committee on Iron Ore – Gaitskell and Strauss covering the Official Committee,** 1+3+1p appendix.
1 Aug	101	**Movement of wages, hours of work, etc during June 1951 – Isaacs,** 1+2+13p appendixes.
7 Aug	102	**Changes in the employment position during June 1951 – Isaacs,** 1+8p.

21 Aug	**103**	**Food situation in the U.K.: monthly report for June 1951 – Webb,** 6+1p annex.
31 Aug	**104**	**Food situation in the U.K.: monthly report for July 1951 – Webb,** 6+1p annex.
31 Aug	**105**	**Changes in the employment position during July 1951 – Isaacs,** 1+9p.
31 Aug	**106**	**Movement of wages, hours of work, etc. during July 1951 – Isaacs,** 1+2+13p appendixes.
5 Sept	**107**	**Dispersal of nationalized boards – Barnes,** 1+1p annex.
10 Sept	**108**	**Steel supplies – Edwards, J.,** 5+1p annex.
26 Sept	**109**	**Movement of wages, hours of work, etc. during August 1951 – Isaacs,** 1+2+11p appendixes.
4 Oct	**110**	**Changes in the employment position during August 1951 – Isaacs,** 1+8p. Still no signs of large redundancies due to raw material shortages.
11 Oct	**111**	**Food situation in the U.K.: monthly report for August 1951 – Webb,** 6+1p annex.
17 Oct	**112**	**Stocks of food and animal feedingstuffs, raw materials and petroleum products – C.S.O.,** 1+7+11p appendixes. Also CS(S)(51)25.

Subcommittee on Manufacture in Government-controlled Establishments of Goods for Civilian Use

Set up in June 1950 (CAB 134/644, PC(50)9th:3 and CAB 134/647, PC(50)71). Its terms of reference were extended in July to include (b) and (c) (CAB 134/644, PC(50)11th:2 and CAB 134/647, PC(50)74).

Terms To consider and report to the Production Committee (a) on the implications of adopting a more positive policy for manufacturing in government-controlled establishments articles of civil use for supply to government departments or socialized industries or for sale to the public in competition with private industry, and on the practical steps which might be taken to give effect to such a policy; (b) on measures to provide employment in the development areas for male workers in heavy industries, including those who became unemployed in consequence of a reduction in the size of the shipbuilding and ship repairing industries; (c) on the policy for the ordering by the government of commercial tonnage in times of depression in the shipbuilding industry.

Members Min. of Health (ch.); Pres. Bd Trade; S./S. Scot; 1st Ld Admiralty; Mins. of Labour & N.S., Transport, Supply; Fin. Sec. (Try). (July 1950) Min. of Fuel & Power added.

Sec. O.C. Morland (Cab. O.).
CAB 134/653 Meetings and Memoranda 12 July–1 Nov 1950 PC(GE)(50)1st–2nd and PC(GE)(50)1–13.

15.36 Raw Materials Committee

Set up in October 1950 as part of the reorganization of the committee structure occasioned by the Korean War and the ensuing shortages of raw materials, see CAB 134/263, ES(50)1st:3. It acted in close collaboration with the Materials Allocation Committee (CAB 134/475–486) and the Committee on Productive Capacity (CAB 134/114–116). Its main responsibility was to ensure adequate supplies, preparing reports and despatching telegrams to U.K. representatives at the International Materials Conference in Washington, the O.E.E.C., N.A.T.O. and the Commonwealth Liaison Committee. In practice it left food to the Ministry of Food and the stockpiling of strategic materials to a subcommittee of the Joint War Production Committee. A series of bimonthly reports to the Production Committee was started in March 1951 (CAB 134/650, PC(51)29).

Most of the preparatory work for the committee was initially carried out by C.E.P.S., although it provided no secretary between December 1950 and April 1951 owing to pressure of work on the investment programme review. In anticipation of the creation of the Ministry of Materials, ministerial responsibility for the committee was transferred to the Lord Privy Seal in April and one of its officials assumed the chairmanship in June. The committee was discontinued once the new ministry was fully operational, see CAB 21/2512.

Terms (a) to advise the Economic Steering Committee on the measures required to ensure adequate supplies of imported food and raw materials, both for current needs and for stockpiling (b) to direct and co-ordinate the instruction of U.K. representatives in current international discussions on this subject.

Members F.F. Turnbull (C.E.P.S., ch.); E.A. Berthoud (F.O.); M. Stevenson (Try); J.A.C. Robertson (Try); R.F. Bretherton (Ec. Sect.); H.J. Gray (B.T.); G. Clauson (Col. O.); G.T. Field (Supply); F. Hollins (Food). (Jan 1951) E.A. Shillito (C.E.P.S., ch.), A.C. Spark (Try) replaced Stevenson, and L.P. Thompson-McCausland (Bank of Eng.), C.D. Campbell (B.T.), G.M. Wilson (C.E.P.S.) added. (Mar 1951) F.F. Turnbull (C.E.P.S., ch.). (June 1951) E.F. Muir (Privy S.O., ch.).
(Aug 1951) E.F. Muir (Materials, ch.); E.A. Berthoud (F.O.); E. Jones and J.A.C. Robertson (Try); R.L. Hall (Ec. Sect.); H.J. Gray (B.T.); G. Clauson (Col. O.); R.F. Bretherton (Materials); J.M. Franks (Supply); F. Hollins (Food); H. Gresswell (M.O.D.); E.D.T. Jourdain (Ld Pres. O.); L.P. Thompson-McCausland (Bank of Eng.); G.E.B. Shannon (Com. Rel. O.); G.B. Blaker (C.E.P.S.). (Sept 1951) F.E. Figgures (Try) replaced Robertson.

Secs. R.S. Buer (Cab. O.) and E. Jones (C.E.P.S.). (Dec. 1950) Jones left. (Apr. 1951) K.W.S. MacKenzie (C.E.P.S.) added. (Aug 1951) M.P. Lam (Materials) replaced MacKenzie.

CAB 134/658 Meetings and Memoranda 28 Oct–30 Dec 1950 RM(50)1st–18th and RM(50)1–43.

Meetings
31 Oct RM(50)1st:1 Cotton: representations to the U.S.A.

	:2	**N.A.T.O. action on commodities in short supply.**
	:3	**Future business of the committee.**
2 Nov	2nd:1	**Raw materials studies in the O.E.E.C.**
	:2	**Review of scarce raw materials. RM(50)5.**
3 Nov	3rd:1	**Review of scarce raw materials. RM(50)6.**
	:2	**Australian discussions on raw materials. RM(50)7.**
	:3	**N.A.T.O. action on raw materials.**
7 Nov	4th	**Draft report on the raw materials outlook. RM(50)9.**
8 Nov	5th	**Raw materials discussions in N.A.T.O. RM(50)13.**
9 Nov	6th:1	**Report on the raw materials outlook. RM(50)9(revise).**
	:2	**Future business of the committee.**
13 Nov	7th	**Raw materials discussions in N.A.T.O. and the O.E.E.C.**
16 Nov	8th:1	**Stockpiling of oils and fats. RM(50)16.**
	:2	**Co-ordination of Commonwealth stockpiling. RM(50)17.**
	:3	**Raw materials studies in the O.E.E.C.**
	:4	**Proposals to deal with the raw materials shortage. RM(50)15.**
17 Nov	9th:1	**Proposals to deal with the raw materials shortage. RM(50)15 and 18.**
	:2	**Sulphur.**
21 Nov	10th:1	**Danish proposals on raw materials. RM(50)22.**
	:2	**Draft report on measures for dealing with raw material shortages. RM(50)20 and 21.**
29 Nov	11th:1	**Meeting of the Council of the O.E.E.C.: report on raw materials by the Economic Committee. RM(50)25, 26, 27.**
	:2	**Proposed O.E.E.C. delegation to Washington. RM(50)28.**
7 Dec	12th:1	**Zinc.**
	:2	**Rubber.**
8 Dec	13th:1	**Discussions in Washington on raw materials.**
	:2	**Allocations of U.S. exports of sulphur, cotton and cotton linters. EC(50)21.**
	:3	**Pulp, timber and sisal.**
	:4	**Information to colonial governors.**
13 Dec	14th:1	**Rubber.**
	:2	**Raw materials group in N.A.T.O.**
14 Dec	15th	**Central Raw Materials Group.**
15 Dec	16th	**Central Raw Materials Group.**
19 Dec	17th:1	**Anglo-American talks on rubber.**
	:2	**The new raw materials organization and the O.E.E.C.**
	:3	**Central Raw Materials Group.**
21 Dec	18th:1	**Anglo-American talks on rubber.**
	:2	**International Wool Conference.**
	:3	**Central Raw Materials Group.**

		:4	Raw Materials Group in N.A.T.O.

Memoranda

30 Oct	**RM(50)1**		Terms of reference and composition – N. Brook, 2p.
28 Oct	2		Materials in short supply – R.S. Buer and E. Jones covering E.N. Plowden and R.L. Hall, 1+2p. See ES(50)4.
26 Oct	3		Note of an *ad hoc* meeting, 26 Oct 1950, 3p. Consideration of instructions to the U.K. delegation to the O.E.E.C. on timber and cotton.
30 Oct	4		Note of a meeting, 28 Oct 1950, 2p. On cotton.
1 Nov	5		Review of scarce raw materials – R.S. Buer and E. Jones covering the Board of Trade, 1+7p. Review of the Board of Trade materials which were becoming scarce and the industries likely to be affected.
2 Nov	6		Note – Ministry of Supply, 3+2p annex. Review similar to RM(50)5.
1 Nov	7		Note – Board of Trade, 1p. On the recent international discussions.
1 Nov	8		Raw materials policy in the O.E.E.C. – R.S. Buer and E. Jones covering E. Hall-Patch and the Secretary-General of the O.E.E.C., 1+6p.
20 Nov	9		Report on the raw materials outlook – the committee, 6+5p annex. Final version. See ES(50)8.
7 Nov	10		Relationship between the O.E.E.C. and the *ad hoc* N.A.T.O. group – R.S. Buer and E. Jones, 1+3p.
7 Nov	11		The O.E.E.C. raw materials studies: note of a talk on 1 Nov 1950 by the Secretary for Commonwealth Relations with the Commonwealth High Commissioners in London, 1+4p.
7 Nov	12		The inter-relationship of the various N.A.T.O. bodies – R.S. Buer and E. Jones covering the Foreign Office, 1+6+4p appendixes. Also AOC(50)66 and MAC(50)33.
8 Nov	13		Joint meeting of production and economic experts – W. Strath, 2+2p. Also MAC(50)36.
14 Nov	14		Sulphur: the O.E.E.C. Council decision – R.S. Buer and E. Jones covering the Deputy Secretary-General of the O.E.E.C., 1p.
15 Nov	15		Proposals to deal with shortages of raw materials – Board of Trade, 3p.
15 Nov	16		Stockpiling of oils and fats – R.S. Buer and E. Jones covering the Ministry of Food, 1+4+6p appendixes.
15 Nov	17		Co-ordination of Commonwealth stockpiling – R.S. Buer and E. Jones covering the Permanent

		Secretary of the Department of Supply of the Australian government, 1+1p.
15 Nov	18	**Non-ferrous metals: internal control measures – Ministry of Supply**, 4+2p.
20 Nov	19	**U.S. allocations of cotton – R.S. Buer and E. Jones**, 1+4p. Note of meeting between T.L. Rowan and the U.S. Secretary for Agriculture, 7 Nov 1950.
23 Nov	20	**Report on measures for dealing with raw material shortages – the committee**, 7p. Final version. See ES(50)17.
20 Nov	21	**Draft report on measures for dealing with the raw material shortages – F.S. Turnbull**, 2p.
23 Nov	22	**Danish proposals on raw materials – R.S. Buer and E. Jones covering the Danish delegation to the O.E.E.C.**, 1+2p.
22 Nov	23	**Draft brief for the Chancellor's interviews with M. Petsche and M. Buron – R.S. Buer and E. Jones**, 1+10p. See ES(50)14(revise).
23 Nov	24	**Brief for the Chancellor's interviews with M. Petsche and M. Buron – R.S. Buer and E. Jones**, 1+10+2p annex. See ES(50)18.
27 Nov	25	**Minutes of a meeting between the U.K. and the French governments held on 25 Nov 1950 – F.F. Turnbull**, 1+10p.
27 Nov	26	**Information to the O.E.E.C. Coal Committee about purchases of coal – R.S. Buer and E. Jones covering the Ministry of Fuel and Power**, 1+2p.
28 Nov	27	**Ferrous scrap and steel – Ministry of Supply**, 4p.
28 Nov	28	**Draft terms of reference for the O.E.E.C. raw materials mission – E. Jones and R.S. Buer**, 1+1p.
2 Dec	29	**Sulphur – E. Jones and R.S. Buer covering the Board of Trade**, 1+6+2p appendixes.
30 Nov	30	**Briefs for the O.E.E.C. Council meeting – R.S. Buer and E. Jones**, 1+9p. Also ER(L)(50)280.
2 Dec	31	Note of meeting between representatives of the Treasury and the Foreign Office and the E.C.A. London, 29 Nov 1950, 3p.
2 Dec	32	**Rubber: U.S. *aide memoire* – R.S. Buer and E. Jones covering the U.S. Embassy**, 1p.
6 Dec	33	**Measures taken in the U.S.A. to limit civilian use of scarce resources – R.S. Buer and E. Jones**, 1+2p.
6 Dec	34	**Meetings between the Chancellor of the Exchequer and Mr. Foster, the Economic Co-operation Administrator – R.S. Buer and E. Jones**, 1+3p.
7 Dec	35	**Rubber – Board of Trade**, 2p.

8 Dec	**36**	**Statement of principles for economic co-operation between Canada and the U.S.A. – R.S. Buer and E. Jones,** 1+2p.
13 Dec	**37**	**Raw materials organization – R.S. Buer,** 2p. On the tripartite organization.
21 Dec	**38**	**Note of a meeting 20 Feb 1950,** 4p. On the Central Raw Materials Group and cotton.
	39	Retained.
29 Dec	**40**	**Raw materials: the remit from Brussels – R.S. Buer covering F.R. Hoyer Miller,** 1+1p. Also AOC(50)87.
29 Dec	**41**	**Rubber – Board of Trade,** 1+22p. Notes of informal discussions with representatives of the U.S.A. and the Colonial Office.
30 Dec	**42**	**Distribution of European solid fuel – Ministry of Fuel and Power,** 4p.
30 Dec	**43**	**Commodity groups in Washington – R.S. Buer covering the Board of Trade,** 1+3p.

CAB 134/659   Meetings   2 Jan–28 Nov 1951   RM(51)1st–61st.

2 Jan	**RM(51)1st:1**	**Brief for ministerial council meeting of the O.E.E.C.**
	:2	**Report of the N.A.T.O. Advisory Group on Raw Materials.** RM(50)39.
	:3	**Distribution of European solid fuel.** RM(50)42.
	:4	**Composition of the commodity groups in Washington.** RM(50)43 and RM(51)3.
	:5	**International rubber meetings.** RM(50)41 and RM(51)1.
8 Jan	**2nd:1**	**Raw materials adviser to N.A.T.O.**
	:2	**International rubber meeting.**
	:3	**Briefs for the ministerial council meeting of the O.E.E.C.** RM(51)5 and 6.
9 Jan	**3rd:1**	**Proposed rubber conference.**
	:2	**Non-essential uses of zinc.** RM(51)7.
	:3	**Briefs for the Ministerial O.E.E.C. Council.**
12 Jan	**4th:1**	**Proposed rubber conference.**
	:2	**Tin.** RM(51)8.
	:3	**Commodity groups in Washington.** RM(51)9.
	:4	**Secretariat for the Washington organization.** RM(51)10.
16 Jan	**5th:1**	**Import restrictions.** Action was being taken already.
	:2	**Commodity groups in Washington.**
	:3	**Tin.** RM(51)13.
22 Jan	**6th:1**	**Message from the Washington Raw Materials Committee.**
	:2	**Rubber conference.**
	:3	**Measures to implement the O.E.E.C. Council decision on raw materials.**

	:4	Functions and membership of the Raw Materials Central Group.
	:5	Strategic stockpiling: discussions with the U.S.A.
	:6	Supplementary French views on the Washington Raw Materials Organization.
	:7	Stockpiling and military requirements: method of handling in commodity groups. RM(51)14.
	:8	Secretariat for the Washington organization.
	:9	Commodity groups and existing study groups. RM(51)15 and 20.
	:10	Economic Co-operation Administration as a claimant agency. RM(51)17.
25 Jan	7th:1	Functions and membership of the Raw Materials Central Group.
	:2	Progress report on raw materials.
	:3	Restrictions on the consumption of copper.
	:4	Relations between the Washington raw materials organization and the Soviet Bloc. RM(51)16.
	:5	Measures to implement the O.E.E.C. Council decision of 2 Dec 1951 on raw materials. RM(51)21, 22, 23.
30 Jan	8th:1	The Washington organization.
	:2	Harmonization of controls in the O.E.E.C. RM(51)24, 28, 29, 31.
	:3	Rubber. RM(51)27.
31 Jan	9th	Rubber conference. RM(51)27.
2 Feb	10th:1	Parliamentary question on east/west trade.
	:2	Rubber conference. RM(51)27(revise).
	:3	Membership of raw materials organization.
	:4	Clearance of briefs.
	:5	Tin discussions in Washington. RM(51)33.
	:6	Harmonization of raw materials controls in the O.E.E.C. RM(51)28, 29, 31, 32.
8 Feb	11th:1	Sulphur: meeting of the O.E.E.C. Chemical Products Committee. RM(51)39.
	:2	E.C.O.S.O.C.: brief for the twelfth session. RM(51)30.
	:3	Sulphur: representations in Washington. RM(51)35.
	:4	Sulphur: report of the Natural Resources (Technical) Committee. RM(51)38.
	:5	Rubber conference. RM(51)27(revise).
	:6	Harmonization of raw materials controls in the O.E.E.C.
13 Feb	12th:1	Raw materials discussions in the Commonwealth Liaison Committee.
	:2	Harmonization of raw materials controls in the O.E.E.C. RM(51)32(revise).

15 Feb	13th:1	**Raw materials discussions in Washington.** T.L. Rowan's views on the discussions and raw materials shortages.
	:2	**Raw materials discussions in the Commonwealth Liaison Committee.**
	:3	**International rubber conference.** Account of the discussions.
14 Feb	14th:1	**Representation of India on the Copper, Zinc and Lead Supply Committee of the I.M.C.**
	:2	**Briefs for the meetings of the Non-ferrous Metals and Ferro-alloys Supply Committees of the International Materials Committee. RM(51)40.**
16 Feb	15th	**Brief for the Non-ferrous Metals Supply Committee meeting. RM(51)40.**
17 Feb	16th:1	**International rubber conference.**
	:2	**Briefs for the meetings of the Non-ferrous Metals and Ferro-alloys Committees of the I.M.C. RM(51)40.**
19 Feb	17th:1	**Trade negotiations with Portugal.**
	:2	**Defence and stockpiling requirements: discussions in Washington.**
	:3	**Allocation of coal by the O.E.E.C.: bilateral commitment.**
	:4	**Harmonization of controls: discussions in the vertical committees of the O.E.E.C.**
20 Feb	18th	**Brief on cotton for the meeting of the Cotton and Cotton Linters Committee of the I.M.C. RM(51)47.**
20 Feb	19th:1	**Brief on cotton for the meeting of the Cotton and Cotton Linters Committee of the I.M.C. RM(51)47.**
	:2	**Brief on cotton linters for meeting of the Cotton and Cotton Linters Committee of the I.M.C. RM(51)48.**
21 Feb	20th:1	**The I.M.C.: procedure for the commodity committees.**
	:2	**Times of meetings.**
	:3	**Meetings of the O.E.E.C. vertical committees.**
	:4	**International rubber conference.**
	:5	**Harmonization of controls.**
23 Feb	21st:1	**Brief on sulphur for the meeting of the Sulphur Committee of the I.M.C. RM(51)53.**
	:2	**Submission of the requirements of the colonies to the I.M.C.**
	:3	**Raw materials discussions in the Commonwealth Liaison Committee.**
	:4	**Progress report to Production Committee.**
26 Feb	22nd:1	**Report on raw materials to Production Committee. RM(51)52.**

	:2	**Brief for the Cotton and Cotton Linters Committee of the I.M.C. RM(51)47(revise) and 48(revise).**
	:3	**Proposal for Wood Pulp Committee of the I.M.C.: Swedish representations with the Foreign Office.**
28 Feb	23rd:1	**Report on raw materials to the Production Committee.**
	:2	**Tin.**
	:3	**International rubber conference.**
	:4	**Brief for the meetings of the Ferro-alloys Committees of the I.M.C. RM(51)40(final).**
	:5	**Representations to the commodity committees of the I.M.C. by the Iron Curtain countries. RM(51)56.**
	:6	**Briefs for the ministerial council meeting of the O.E.E.C.**
1 Mar	24th	**Report on raw materials to the Production Committee. RM(51)59.**
2 Mar	25th:1	**Report on raw materials to the Production Committee. RM(51)60 and 62.**
	:2	**Second report on raw materials by the O.E.E.C.**
	:3	**Harmonization of controls.**
5 Mar	26th:1	**U.K. strategic stockpiling: discussions with the U.S.A. RM(51)55.**
	:2	**Briefs for the O.E.E.C. Council meeting at ministerial level.**
	:3	**Tin: forthcoming discussions in Washington. RM(51)61.**
7 Mar	27th:1	**International rubber conference: invitation of Germany.**
	:2	**Export policy: proposal to circulate a memorandum to the Commonwealth Liaison Committee.**
	:3	**Briefs for the O.E.E.C. Council meeting at ministerial level. RM(51)64, 65, 66, 67 and EC(51)8 and CES/26.**
12 Mar	28th:1	**Sulphur: decision by the Council of the O.E.E.C. RM(51)70.**
	:2	**Defence and stockpiling requirements: discussions in Washington.**
	:3	**Increased production of raw materials. RM(51)73.**
	:4	**Future raw materials policy. RM(51)75.**
14 Mar	29th:1	**Hides and skins. RM(51)77.**
	:2	**International rubber conference. RM(51)76.**
	:3	**Representation of the O.E.E.C. on the central group of the I.M.C.**
19 Mar	30th:1	**Proposals on raw materials in the O.E.E.C. CE(51)21 and 29.**
	:2	**Secretaries for the commodity committees of the I.M.C.**

	:3	**Tin: discussions in Washington.**
	:4	**Long-term studies of production and conservation. RM(51)80.**
2 Apr	31st:1	**Raw materials discussions in Washington.** Report by Lord Knollys.
	:2	**Sulphur Committee of the I.M.C. RM(51)85 and 86.**
	:3	**Second report on raw materials to the Production Committee.**
	:4	**High level approach in Washington about raw materials shortages. RM(51)87.**
6 Apr	32nd:1	**High level approach in Washington about raw materials shortages.**
	:2	**Raw materials discussions in the Commonwealth Liaison Committee.**
	:3	**Tin: discussions in Washington. RM(51)90.**
	:4	**Disposal of the rubber stockpiles. RM(51)89.**
11 Apr	33rd:1	**Raw materials discussions in the O.E.E.C. RM(51)94. Consideration of hides and skins, sulphur, pulp and paper and liaison between the O.E.E.C. and the supply committees of the I.M.C.**
	:2	**Copper-Lead-Zinc Committee of the I.M.C.: proposed bases of allocation.**
18 Apr	34th:1	**Brief for the meeting of the Pulp-Paper Committee of the I.M.C. RM(51)99.**
	:2	**Future business of the committee. RM(51)100.**
	:3	**International rubber conference.**
20 Apr	35th:1	**Statistical group. RM(51)98.**
	:2	**High level approach to the U.S. authorities. RM(51)101 and 105.**
23 Apr	36th:1	**Sulphur: supplies from Russia.**
	:2	**International rubber conference.**
	:3	**Sulphur Committee of the I.M.C.: proposed basis of allocation.**
	:4	**Central group of the I.M.C.: South African application for membership.**
	:5	**Second progress report to Production Committee. RM(51)103.**
	:6	**Copper-Zinc-Lead Committee of the I.M.C.: proposed bases of allocation.**
25 Apr	37th:1	**Sulphur: U.S. technical mission.**
	:2	**Sulphur: first report of the Sulphur Committee of the I.M.C. RM(51)106.**
	:3	**High level approach to the U.S. authorities. RM(51)101(revise) and 107.**
	:4	**Cotton and Cotton Linters Committee of the I.M.C.: representation of Japan.**
	:5	**Harmonization of controls.**
	:6	**Swedish proposals in the O.E.E.C. for regulating pulp prices.**
27 Apr	38th:1	**Brief for the Lord Privy Seal.**

	:2	**Coal: principles of international allocation.** RM(51)110.
	:3	**Rubber: report on the international rubber conference.** RM(51)109.
30 Apr	39th:1	**Second report to the Production Committee.** RM(51)103(revise).
	:2	**Harmonization of controls.**
	:3	**Tungsten-Molybdenum Committee of the I.M.C.: bases of allocation.**
4 May	40th	**Raw materials studies for the Production Committee.** RM(51)75, 96, 97, 112, 114, 116.
9 May	41st:1	**Food and Agriculture Organization: relationship with the I.M.C. committees.** RM(51)117.
	:2	**Defence and stockpiling requirements.**
	:3	**Coal: principles of international allocation.**
	:4	**Copper: supplies from Northern Rhodesia.**
18 May	42nd:1	**Raw materials studies for the Production Committee: wool.** RM(51)122.
	:2	**Increased production and conservation of raw materials.** RM(51)88, 108, 115, 121, 122, 125.
	:3	**Coal: principles of international allocation.** RM(51)123.
	:4	**Molybdenum: allocation for second quarter 1951.**
23 May	43rd:1	**International Materials Conference: minutes of commodity committee meetings.**
	:2	**Increased production and conservation of raw materials.** RM(51)125. Further studies were to be completed as soon as possible with the forthcoming establishment of a Raw Materials Department.
25 May	44th:1	**Increased production and conservation of raw materials: sulphur and pyrites.** RM(51)120.
	:2	**Raw materials telegrams: submission to the Lord Privy Seal.**
	:3	**New copper mines in Northern Rhodesia.** RM(51)126.
	:4	**International allocations: requirements of Southern Rhodesia.**
28 May	45th:1	**Visit of the Lord Privy Seal to Washington.** E.F. Muir explained that the main purpose had been to make contacts and press the U.K.'s general case, not to negotiate.
	:2	**I.M.C. Sulphur Committee: further report by U.K. representative.** RM(51)128.
	:3	**Future raw materials policy.** RM(51)127.
	:4	**Increased production and conservation of raw materials: sulphur and pyrites.**
4 June	46th:1	**Raw materials discussions in Washington.** Report by H.O. Hooper.

		:2	Cotton and Cotton Linters Committee of the I.M.C.
		:3	Brief for the debate on the Ministry of Materials Bill.
		:2	Increased production and conservation of raw materials: long-term raw materials prospects. RM(51)88(revise).
		:5	Molybdenum: allocation for the third quarter of 1951.
6 June	47th:1	The O.E.E.C.: harmonization of control. RM(51)132.
		:2	Implementing international allocations. RM(51)131. Agreement to consider the matter further in relation to individual commodities.
		:3	E.C.A. development loan for Malaya.
13 June	48th:1	Pulp and Paper Committee of the International Materials Conference. RM(51)139.
		:2	Increased production and conservation: woodpulp. RM(51)138.
		:3	Future raw materials policy. RM(51)127(revise).
		:4	Relations between the O.E.E.C. and the I.M.C.
22 June	49th:1	Tungsten and molybdenum: allocation for third quarter 1951. RM(51)143.
		:2	Development of cotton production in the colonies. RM(51)129.
		:3	Interim allocation by the U.S.A.
		:4	Increased production and conservation: artificial fibres.
		:5	Visit of Lord Knollys to London.
27 June	50th	Price policy: consultations with the U.S. administration. RM(51)144, 146, 147, 148, 151, 153.
29 June	51st:1	Price policy: consultations with the U.S. administration. RM(51)146(revise), 147(revise), 148(revise), 149(revise), 151(revise), 152, 153.
		:2	Raw materials discussions in Washington. Report by Lord Knollys.
6 July	52nd:1	Third progress report to the Production Committee. RM(51)154.
		:2	O.E.E.C. report on raw materials. RM(51)156.
23 July	53rd:1	Raw materials requirements for artificial fibres other than rayon. RM(51)159.
		:2	O.E.E.C. third report on raw materials. RM(51)160.
31 July	54th:1	Price policy: discussions in Washington.
		:2	Sulphur Committee of the I.M.C.: membership of Spain. RM(51)162.
		:3	Tin: price policy. RM(51)161 and 164.
8 Aug	55th:1	Argentina: membership of I.M.C. committees.
		:2	Tin: price policy. RM(51)161(revise).

	:3	**Tin: U.S. contract with Bolivia.**
	:4	**Rubber: price policy.** RM(51)165.
	:5	**Times of meetings.** Agreement to meet weekly in future. Annex attached.
18 Sept	**56th:1**	**Tin: patino concentrates.**
	:2	**Tin: discussions with the U.S.A. and Malaya.** RM(51)170.
3 Oct	**57th**	**Central group of the I.M.C.: proposal to extend membership.** RM(51)172.
17 Oct	**58th:1**	**Principle of coal allocation.** RM(51)173. General view that the procedure accepted by the U.K. in the E.C.E. and the O.E.E.C. was not inconsistent with that asked of raw materials producers in the I.M.C. by the U.K. Nevertheless U.K. exports were not allocated on the principles of equity advanced by the U.K. in the I.M.C. U.K. coal exports must reasonably satisfy other countries' needs as well as meeting existing bilateral commitments. Otherwise the international allocation of scarce raw materials might break down, forcing the U.K. to widen its bilateral arrangements to secure essential needs.
	:2	**Central group of the I.M.C.: proposal to extend membership.**
7 Nov	**59th**	**Exports of non-ferrous semi-manufactures.** RM(51)174. Agreement that it was in the interests of the U.K. and the colonies to retain the allocation scheme.
23 Nov	**60th:1**	**Economy and substitution of scarce materials.** RM(51)175.
	:2	**The International Materials Conference.** Statement by Lord Knollys.
28 Nov	**61st:1**	**Central group of the I.M.C.: representation of Benelux.**
	:2	**Copper prices.**

CAB 134/660   Memoranda   1 Jan–28 Mar 1951   RM(51)1–85.

1 Jan	**RM(51)1**	**Rubber – Board of Trade,** 1+1p.
1 Jan	**2**	**Change of membership –** unsigned, 1p.
1 Jan	**3**	**Commodity groups under the Washington Plan – Ministry of Supply,** 1p.
3 Jan	**4**	**Change of chairmanship –** unsigned, 1p.
5 Jan	**5**	**Brief for the Ministerial Council Meeting of the O.E.E.C. – Board of Trade,** 2p.
5 Jan	**6**	**Brief for the Ministerial Council Meeting of the O.E.E.C. – Ministry of Supply,** 3p.
6 Jan	**7**	**Non-essential uses of zinc – Board of Trade,** 1p.
10 Jan	**8**	**The question of tin allocation – Colonial Office,** 6p.

15 Jan	9	**Commodity groups in Washington – Board of Trade,** 3p. Revise version.
11 Jan	10	**Secretariat for the Washington organization – Board of Trade,** 3p.
11 Jan	11	**Brief for the O.E.E.C. Ministerial Council meeting on 12 Jan 1951: report of the O.E.E.C. mission to Washington – R.S. Buer,** 1+4p. Also ER(L)(51)3.
11 Jan	12	**Brief for the O.E.E.C. Ministerial Council meeting on 12 Jan 1951: raw materials – R.S. Buer,** 1+6+18p annexes.
17 Jan	13	**The question of a commodity group for tin – R.S. Buer,** 1+4p. Revise version.
18 Jan	14	**Stockpiling and military requirements: question of handling in the commodity groups in Washington – R.S. Buer covering the Board of Trade,** 1+3p.
19 Jan	15	**The relationship between commodity groups and study groups – Board of Trade,** 4+2p appendix.
22 Jan	16	**Relations between the Washington raw materials organization and the Soviet Bloc – Foreign Office,** 3p.
20 Jan	17	**The E.C.A. as a claimant agency – R.S. Buer covering E.A. Hitchman,** 1+3p.
22 Jan	18	**Criteria on the size of the commodity groups in Washington – R.S. Buer,** 1+4p.
20 Jan	19	**Vertical committee questionnaires – R.S. Buer,** 1p.
20 Jan	20	**The relationship between commodity groups and study groups – G. Clauson,** 2p.
23 Jan	21	**Report on conservation measures taken in accordance with the decisions of the O.E.E.C. on 2 Dec 1950 – Board of Trade,** 4p.
25 Jan	22	**Reports on measures to implement the O.E.E.C. recommendations of 2 Dec 1950: the fuel industries – Ministry of Fuel and Power,** 2p. Revise version.
25 Jan	23	**Non-ferrous metals and ferrous scrap. The increase of supplies and restriction of demand – Ministry of Supply,** 4p. Revise version.
25 Jan	24	**The O.E.E.C.: harmonization of raw materials controls – Board of Trade,** 1+3p. Also ER(L)(51)8.
24 Jan	25	**The E.C.A. as a claimant agency: reply to letter from the chairman of the Mutual Aid Committee – R.S. Buer covering E.A. Shillito,** 1+1p.
24 Jan	26	**Non-ferrous metals: Washington commodity groups – Ministry of Supply,** 1+2p.
1 Feb	27	**Rubber – Board of Trade,** 6+1p appendix. Revise version.
27 Jan	28	**Harmonization of raw materials controls in the O.E.E.C. – J.A. Atkinson,** 1+2p. Also

		ER(L)(51)9. Conclusions of an *ad hoc* meeting, 26 Jan 1951, to consider RM(51)24.
29 Jan	29	**The O.E.E.C.: harmonization of raw materials controls – Ministry of Supply**, 2p.
30 Jan	30	**Economic and Social Council: twelfth session. Draft brief on commodity questions for the U.K. delegation – R.S. Buer and N.K. Fisher covering the Board of Trade**, 1+9p. Also TN(C)(51)2.
30 Jan	31	**The O.E.E.C.: harmonization of raw materials controls – Ministry of Supply**, 2p.
14 Feb	32	**The O.E.E.C.: harmonization of raw materials controls – Board of Trade**, 4p. Final version.
30 Jan	33	**Tin discussions in Washington – Colonial Office**, 1+10p. Record of discussions.
2 Feb	34	**U.K. strategic stockpiling – R.S. Buer covering the Treasury**, 1+2+10p annexes. Information on progress, authorizations granted and commitments.
31 Jan	35	**Note of a meeting held by the Economic Secretary**, 4p. Consideration of the general raw materials position and of sulphur in particular.
2 Feb	36	**Question of tin allocation – Colonial Office**, 2p.
3 Feb	37	**Briefing for the U.K. representative on Washington commodity groups – E.A. Shillito**, 1p.
5 Feb	38	**Sulphur – R.S. Buer covering the Natural Resources (Technical) Committee**, 1+4p. Interim report.
6 Feb	39	**The O.E.E.C. vertical committee on sulphur – Board of Trade**, 2p.
22 Feb	40	**Brief for Non-ferrous Metals Committee of the I.M.C. – E.A. Shillito covering the Ministry of Supply**, 1+7+53p annexes. Final version.
9 Feb	41	**Washington commodity groups: factual brief on wool – R.S. Buer**, 1+5+7p appendixes.
9 Feb	42	**Washington commodity groups: factual brief on sulphur – R.S. Buer covering the Board of Trade**, 1+4p.
9 Feb	43	**Economic and Social Council: twelfth session. Brief on commodity questions for the U.K. delegation – Trade Negotiations Committee Subcommittee on International Commodity Policy**, 2p. Also TN(C)(51)3.
12 Feb	44	**Non-ferrous metals and the Commonwealth – Ministry of Supply**, 2p.
13 Feb	45	**Supplies of sulphur and sulphuric acid – Board of Trade**, 1+4p.
13 Feb	46	**Rubber conference – Board of Trade**, 2p.
21 Feb	47	**Draft brief for the first meeting of cotton and cotton linters group: cotton – Board of Trade**, 9+2p appendixes. Final version.

23 Feb	48	**Draft brief of first meeting of the cotton and cotton linters commodity group: cotton linters – Board of Trade**, 3+1p annex. Final version.
17 Feb	49	**Place of bilateral agreements involving coal in a multilateral system for the equitable distribution of European solid fuel – Ministry of Fuel and Power**, 3p.
17 Feb	50	**Draft memorandum on cotton for submission to the Commonwealth Liaison Committee – Board of Trade**, 1+3+2p appendixes.
20 Feb	51	**Steel supplies in 1951 – R.S. Buer covering the Ministry of Supply**, 1+4+1p appendix +3p addendum. See M(51)12.
3 Mar	52	**The raw materials situation. Progress report No. 1, Feb 1951 – R.S. Buer**, 1+2+26p annexes. Final version. See PC(51)29. Also ES(51)19.
23 Feb	53	**Brief for the Sulphur Committee of the I.M.C. – Board of Trade**, 1+4p. Final version.
23 Feb	54	**Export policy in relation to negotiations on raw materials with the U.S.A. – R.S. Buer**, 1+1+4+2p. See ES(51)9 and 14.
24 Feb	55	**U.K. strategic stockpiling discussions with the U.S.A. – Treasury**, 3+3p appendix.
24 Feb	56	**Relations between the I.M.C. and the Soviet Bloc – Foreign Office**, 3p.
26 Feb	57	**Report by the Strategic Materials Committee on further requirements of imported strategic materials – chairman of the Strategic Materials Committee**, 1+2+6p appendixes.
27 Feb	58	**Report on the international rubber conference – Board of Trade**, 3p.
28 Feb	59	**Commentary by the Board of Trade on progress report No. 1, Feb 1951 – Board of Trade**, 4+1p annex.
1 Mar	60	**Steel-making raw materials – Ministry of Supply**, 1+1+4p.
1 Mar	61	**The forthcoming tin discussions in Washington – Colonial Office**, 5p.
1 Mar	62	**Commentary on progress report No. 1, Feb 1951 – Ministry of Supply**, 3p.
2 Mar	63	**Report by the Strategic Materials Committee on further requirements of imported strategic materials – R.S. Buer**, 1p.
5 Mar	64	**Briefs for the O.E.E.C. Council meeting of 9 Mar 1951. Coal – Ministry of Fuel and Power**, 5p.
6 Mar	65	**Dr. Stikker's report and the O.E.E.C. representation at the I.M.C. – unsigned**, 2p.
8 Mar	66	**Ministerial brief for the O.E.E.C. Council meeting of 9 Mar 1951. Harmonization of international controls – Board of Trade**, 2p. Revise version.

6 Mar	67	**Second report by the Economic Committee – R.S. Buer covering C.E.P.S.,** 1+7p.
6 Mar	68	**Tin: business talks in Washington – R.S. Buer covering** *Financial Times*, **6 Mar 1951,** 1+3p.
7 Mar	69	**Note of an** *ad hoc* **meeting on the forthcoming discussions in Washington on tin,** 3p. See ES(51)21.
8 Mar	70	**Sulphur: decision by the Council of the O.E.E.C. – R.S. Buer,** 1+1p.
16 Mar	71	**U.K. export policy – Commonwealth Relations Office,** 1+1+3p. Revise version. Also CEA(51)7(revise).
9 Mar	72	**Tin: discussions in Washington – R.S. Buer,** 1+3p.
9 Mar	73	**Increased production of raw materials – R.S. Buer,** 1+1p.
10 Mar	74	**Note of an** *ad hoc* **meeting, 8 Mar 1951,** 4p. On the possibility of securing control of Malayan output of rubber.
10 Mar	75	**Future raw materials policy – R.S. Buer,** 1+6p. See PC(51)31. Also ES(51)18.
10 Mar		**Rubber: possibility of securing control of the Malayan output – D. Pointon,** 1+2p. Draft report.
14 Mar	76	**Rubber – Board of Trade,** 5+3p appendixes. Final version.
13 Mar	77	**Hides and skin: draft reply to Washington telegram No. 717 PRIME – Board of Trade,** 4p.
13 Mar	78	**Allocation of rubber to the Soviet Bloc – R.S. Buer covering the Ministry of Defence,** 1+2p.
15 Mar	79	**Rubber: possibility of securing control of the Malayan output – R.S. Buer covering E.A. Shillito,** 1+3p.
22 Mar	80	**Increased production and conservation of scarce raw materials – E.A. Shillito,** 5p. Final version. It was unclear whether shortages would still have occurred without rearmament given the post-war increase in industrial production. It was necessary to estimate supply and demand over the next five years.
17 Mar	81	**Commodity committees of the I.M.C.: distribution of papers – R.S. Buer,** 1p.
22 Mar	82	**Wool: policy brief – Board of Trade,** 9p. Revise version.
22 Mar	83	**Note of an** *ad hoc* **meeting, 21 Mar 1951,** 3p. Consideration of RM(51)82.
22 Mar	84	**Change of chairman – R.S. Buer,** 1p.
28 Mar	85	**Sulphur: report by the U.K. representative on the Sulphur Committee of the I.M.C., dated 19 Mar 1951 – U.K. representative,** 4+6p annex.

CAB 134/661   Memoranda   29 Mar–1 Dec 1951   RM(51)86–176.

29 Mar	RM(51)86	**Sulphur: U.S. statement to the Sulphur Committee of the I.M.C. on requirements and production for 1951 and 1952 – Board of Trade,** 4p.
31 Mar	87	**High-level approach in Washington about raw material shortages – E.A. Shillito,** 2p.
28 May	88	**Long-term raw materials prospects – Economic Section,** 6+2p. Final version. Even without rearmament it was likely that there would have been considerable raw materials shortages. Given full employment, world demand appeared greater than the supply of raw materials. Assuming the continuation of full employment, therefore, special action was needed. Recent relative price changes between industrial and primary products were also likely to continue.
3 Apr	89	**Disposal of rubber stockpile – Board of Trade,** 1p.
4 Apr	90	**Tin discussions in Washington – Colonial Office,** 1+5p. Summary of discussions.
4 Apr	91	**Coal exports and international allocations – Ministry of Fuel and Power and the Board of Trade,** 3p. Also ON(51)51.
6 Apr	92	**Exports of rubber to the Soviet Bloc – Foreign Office,** 1+4p.
6 Apr	93	**Change of secretary –** unsigned, 1p.
10 Apr	94	**Co-ordinated buying of hides and skins – Board of Trade,** 4p.
9 Apr	95	**Coal exports and international allocations – R.S. Buer and K.W.S. MacKenzie,** 1p.
11 Apr	96	**Possibility of increasing production of pyrites in Cyprus, and of sulphur in the New Hebrides – Board of Trade and Colonial Office,** 3+2p.
11 Apr	97	**Future raw materials policy (RM(51)75). Sisal – Board of Trade,** 3p.
11 Apr	98	**Statistical group – E.A. Hitchman, D.B. Pitblado and F.F. Turnbull,** 2p. Also MAC(51)54 and P(51)7. Proposal for a working group to serve the Raw Materials, Mutual Aid and Programmes Committees and any others dealing with related forecasts.
16 Apr	99	**Pulp and paper – Board of Trade,** 5+11p appendixes +8p addendum.
17 Apr	100	**Future business of the committee – R.S. Buer and K.W.S. MacKenzie,** 1p. List of studies in progress.
28 Apr	101	**High-level approach on raw materials to the U.S. authorities – R.S. Buer and K.W.S.**

		MacKenzie, 1+2+17+5p appendix +5p addendum. Final version. See ES(51)32.
19 Apr	102	**Analysis of E.C.A. estimates of the U.K. import programme – R.S. Buer and K.W.S. MacKenzie,** 1+2+3p. There were large differences between E.C.A. and U.K. estimates.
7 May	103	**Second report to the Production Committee – R.S. Buer and K.W.S. MacKenzie,** 1+2+27p annexes. Final version. See PC(51)58.
20 Apr	104	**Implications of the U.S. economic programme – R.S. Buer and K.W.S. MacKenzie covering R.W.B. Clarke,** 1+3p. Also MAC(51)59.
20 Apr	105	**High-level approach to the U.S. authorities: scope of the U.K.'s defence effort – R.S. Buer and K.W.S. MacKenzie covering Shinwell,** 1+2p. For inclusion in RM(51)101.
21 Apr	106	**Sulphur Committee of the I.M.C. First report of the committee – Board of Trade,** 2p.
23 Apr	107	**High-level approach – F.F. Turnbull,** 1+2p. Draft covering note to RM(51)101.
26 Apr	108	**Increased production and conservation of scarce raw materials – Board of Trade,** 2p.
26 Apr	109	**Inter-governmental rubber conference: second session Rome, April 1951 – Board of Trade representative,** 4p.
26 Apr	110	**International coal allocation: principles of distribution – Ministry of Fuel and Power,** 5+1p annex.
27 Apr	111	**Manganese, Nickel and Cobalt Committee of the I.M.C.: report by the U.K. representative – R.S. Buer and K.W.S. MacKenzie,** 1+4p.
28 Apr	112	**Manganese – Ministry of Supply,** 4+3p.
2 May	113	**Tungsten, Molybdenum Committee of the I.M.C.: report by the U.K. representative – R.S. Buer and K.W.S. MacKenzie covering the U.K. representative,** 1+7p.
3 May	114	**Tin: the U.K. bargaining position – Ministry of Supply,** 5+1p appendix.
4 May	115	**Scarce raw materials – Ministry of Supply,** 2p. Long-term prospects for iron and steel and manganese.
3 May	116	**Supplies of niobium (columbium) – Ministry of Supply,** 2p.
16 May	117	**The relationship between the F.A.O. and the I.M.C. – Board of Trade,** 3p. Final version.
7 May	118	**The O.E.E.C. Steel Committee – Ministry of Supply,** 5+3p annexes. Also ER(L)(51)39.
8 May	119	**Discussions on raw materials for the U.S. authorities – R.S. Buer and K.W.S. MacKenzie,** 1+18+5p appendix +6p annexes. See ES(51)35.
10 May	120	**Raw materials: increased production and conservation: RM(51)80(final). Sulphur and**

		pyrites – Board of Trade, 14p. Long-term prospects.
10 May	121	**Raw materials: increased production and conservation: RM(51)80. Synthetic and artificial fibres – Board of Trade,** 2p. Long-term prospects.
10 May	122	**Future raw materials policy: wool – Board of Trade,** 4p.
15 May	123	**Principles of international coal allocation – R.S. Buer and K.W.S. MacKenzie,** 1+2p.
	124	Not used.
18 May	125	**Long-term raw materials prospects. Increased production: non-ferrous metals – Ministry of Supply,** 1+2p annex.
18 May	126	**New copper mine in Northern Rhodesia – Colonial Office and Ministry of Supply,** 3+7p annexes.
18 June	127	**Future raw materials policy report to the Steering Committee,** 5+5p appendix. Final version. See PC(51)78. Also ES(51)41.
24 May	128	**Sulphur: further report of the U.K. representative of the Sulphur Committee of the I.M.C. – U.K. representative,** 6+4p appendix.
29 May	129	**Development of cotton production in the colonies – R.S. Buer and K.W.S. MacKenzie,** 2p.
31 May	130	**Draft telegrams to Washington on raw materials – F.F. Turnbull,** 1p.
2 June	131	**Problems of implementing international allocations of raw materials – Economic Section,** 6p.
4 June	132	**Harmonization of controls: prohibition on use of copper, copper alloys, etc. – Board of Trade,** 4p.
5 June	133	**Report of the proceedings of the Wool Committee 2 April to 29 May 1951 – Board of Trade,** 6p.
8 June	134	**Change of chairman – unsigned,** 1p.
9 June	135	**Tungsten, Molybdenum Committee of the I.M.C. Second report by the U.K. representative – R.S. Buer and K.W.S. MacKenzie covering the U.K. representative,** 1+9p.
11 June	136	**Sulphur and sulphur-bearing materials: world position and U.K. position 1951–1956 – F.F. Turnbull,** 6p.
9 June	137	**Requests for economic information by U.S. agencies – W. Strath,** 1+2p. Also MAC(51)82, CPC(51)28 and JWPC(51)71. Sets out procedure for satisfying requests.
11 June	138	**Increased production and conservation of raw materials: wood pulp – Board of Trade,** 2+1p.

10 June	**139**	**The I.M.C. Pulp and Paper Committee. Washington 30 April to 24 May 1951 – Board of Trade**, 2p.
11 June	**140**	**The Portway Lead Mine, near Matlock, Derbyshire. Loan by the E.C.A. to H.J. Enthoven and Sons Ltd. – Ministry of Supply,** 1p.
13 June	**141**	**Baluba copper – Ministry of Supply**, 3p.
19 June	**142**	**Baluba copper – R.S. Buer and K.W.S. MacKenzie,** 1+2p. Note of meeting, 15 June 1951, to discuss RM(51)141.
21 June	**143**	**Allocation of tungsten and molybdenum –** unsigned, 2p.
22 June	**144**	**Consultations with the U.S. government on raw material prices – R.S. Buer and K.W.S. MacKenzie,** 1p.
25 June	**145**	**Note of a meeting, 22 June 1951,** 3p. Consideration of briefs on prices for the Washington discussion and on wool.
28 June	**146**	**Rubber – Board of Trade,** 8p. Revise version.
28 June	**147**	**Consultations with the U.S. government on raw material prices – Board of Trade,** 4+3p appendix. Revise version. On cotton and cotton linters.
28 June	**148**	**Consultations with the U.S. government on raw material prices – Board of Trade,** 3p. Revise version. On industrial diamonds.
28 June	**149**	**Consultations with the U.S. government on raw material prices – Board of Trade,** 3+2p appendixes. Revise version. On wood pulp.
28 June	**150**	**Consultations with the U.S. government on raw material prices – Board of Trade,** 1p. Amendment to RM(51)138.
28 June	**151**	**Consultations with the U.S. government on raw material prices: copper, lead and zinc prices – Ministry of Supply,** 5+6p appendixes. Revise version.
26 June	**152**	**Consultations with the U.S. government on raw material prices: tin – Colonial Office and Ministry of Supply,** 6p.
26 June	**153**	**Prices of tungsten ores and concentrates – Ministry of Supply,** 4+2p addendum.
25 July	**154**	**Third report to the Production Committee – R.S. Buer and K.W.S. MacKenzie,** 1+24+3p annexes. Final version. See PC(51)95.
2 July	**155**	**Control of sulphur supplies in the U.S.A. – Board of Trade,** 2p.
5 July	**156**	**Third O.E.E.C. report on raw materials – R.S. Buer and K.W.S. MacKenzie,** 1+2p.
6 July	**157**	**U.K. reply to questionnaire NF(51)6 –** unsigned, 1+4+2p. Questionnaire by the Non-ferrous Metals Committee of the O.E.E.C.

9 July	158	Index to minutes and memoranda, Jan–June 1951 – R.S. Buer and K.W.S. MacKenzie, 1+12p.
17 July	159	Raw materials for synthetic fibres other than rayon – R.S. Buer and K.W.S. MacKenzie covering the Natural Resources (Technical) Committee, 1+5p.
20 July	160	O.E.E.C. third report on raw material situation – R.S. Buer and K.W.S. MacKenzie, 1p.
4 Aug	161	Tin: policy on tin prices – Ministry of Materials, 3p. Revise version.
30 July	162	Sulphur – Ministry of Materials, 1p.
31 July	163	Raw materials requirements for artificial fibres other than rayon – R.S. Buer and K.W.S. MacKenzie covering the secretary of the Natural Resources (Technical) Committee, 1+2p.
31 July	164	Tin: policy on tin prices – Colonial Office, 3p.
3 Aug	165	Rubber: policy on rubber prices – Ministry of Materials, 3p.
9 Aug	166	Report on discussions in Washington, July 1951 – R.S. Buer and K.W.S. MacKenzie covering R.L. Hall and E.F. Muir, 1+5p.
3 Aug	167	Change of secretary – unsigned, 1p.
16 Aug	168	Membership of the committee – R.S. Buer and M.P. Lam, 1p.
17 Sept	169	Raw materials price policy – J.A. Atkinson and M.P. Lam covering the Ministry of Materials, 1+13+8p.
28 Sept	170	Tin: possible long-term arrangements – Ministry of Materials, 2p. Revise version.
24 Sept	171	Change of membership – unsigned, 1p.
1 Oct	172	Proposal to extend central group of the I.M.C. – Ministry of Materials, 2p.
15 Oct	173	Principles of allocating coal and raw materials – Ministry of Materials, 2p.
6 Nov	174	Exports of non-ferrous semi-manufactures – Commonwealth Relations Office and Colonial Office, 2p.
20 Nov	175	Economy and substitution of scarce materials. Exchange of information between the U.K. and the U.S.A. – Ministry of Materials, 2p.
1 Dec	176	Winding up of the committee – N. Brook, 1p.

15.37 Other Committees relevant to Economic Planning

These committees relate mainly to European economic co-operation, the balance of payments and individual industries. The degree of detail provided on their role and membership is determined by the relative importance of the committee.

CAB 134/34–35   Committee on Involuntary Absenteeism in the Coal-mining Industry

Set up in August 1949 (see CAB 128/15, CM(49)40th:3) and wound up in June 1950 once it had reported (AM(50)11, see also CAB 129/41, CP(50)161). Assessors from the N.C.B. and the N.U.M. attended.

Terms   To investigate the causes of the recent increase in involuntary absenteeism in the coal-mining industry and to submit recommendations for remedying it.

Chairman   D. Lidbury.

Sec.   R.F. Fowler (C.S.O.).

34   Meetings and Memoranda   31 Aug–17 Dec 1949   AM(49)1st–4th and AM(49)1–20.
35   Meetings and Memoranda   3 Feb–16 June 1950   AM(50)1st–7th and AM(50)1–12.

CAB 134/45   Exchange Requirements Committee

Prior to October 1947, the secretarial work of the committee was performed by the Treasury, see T 236/1075, 1086–1087 and 1089–1095. As a result of the reorganization of the inter-departmental machinery for handling the balance of payments in September 1949 (CAB 129/21, CP(47)255), it was given wider responsibilities and worked with the Overseas Negotiations Committee (CAB 134/46–48, 555–575) and the Exports Committee (CAB 134/44, 166–169) under the general supervision of the Official Steering Committee on Economic Development (CAB 134/186–193). With the appointment of Cripps as Minister of Economic Affairs on 29 September 1947, there were further readjustments (CAB 129/21, CP(47)287).

   The function of the committee was to collect the data for the production of a six-monthly balance of payments programme. The actual programme, drafted by a working party drawn from its members and the Overseas Negotiations Committee, was submitted to the Chancellor of the Exchequer and the Minister of Economic Affairs. Once accepted, its implementation was the responsibility of the Exchange Requirements Committee. The Import Licensing Committee and the Foreign Exchange Control Committee (T 231/160–163) reported to it as necessary. In practice, its papers relate largely to imports from particular countries or of particular commodities. For later papers see CAB/258–261.

Terms   (Oct 1947)   (a) to scrutinize requirements for imports and other overseas expenditure, and to prepare at regular intervals a table showing the prospective balance of payments as a whole   (b) to ensure that overseas expenditure does not exceed the amounts provided in the balance of payments programme approved by ministers.

Members   (Oct 1947) R.W.B. Clarke (Try, ch.); representatives of Try, B.T., Food, Transport, Fuel & P., M.A.F., Supply, Ec. Sect., C.E.P.S., Com. Rel. O., Col. O., M.O.D.

Secs.   G. van Loo (Try) and P.J. Deacon (Cab. O.).

45 Meetings and Memoranda 8 Oct–30 Dec 1947 BP(ERC)(47)24th–39th and BP(ERC)(47)2–60.

CAB 134/46–48 Overseas Negotiations Committee

Set up in September 1947 as part of the reorganization of the inter-departmental machinery for handling the balance of payments, its main function was to conduct negotiations with important countries to secure supplies (CAB 129/21, CP(47)255 and 287). It took over some of the functions of the Working Party on the Guidance of Exports (CAB 134/303). Its chairman was full-time and departmental representatives had to give it first call on their time. It worked with the Exchange Requirements Committee (CAB 134/45, 258–261) and the Exports Committee (CAB 134/44, 166–169), under the general supervision of the Official Steering Committee on Economic Development (CAB 134/186–193). Its papers relate mainly to negotiations with individual countries but also include 'Methods of Improving the Balance of Payments', the third report of a group of economists, consisting of D.H.F. Robertson (ch.), H.J. Habakkuk, G.D.A. MacDougall and E.A.G. Robinson, set up to consider the situation if I.T.O. plans broke down (CAB 134/47, BP(ON)(47)40). For papers after 1947 see CAB 134/555–575. For its working papers see T 238.

Terms (Oct 1947) To advise on the general principles on which to base trade and financial negotiations with overseas countries; and to supervise the conduct of such negotiations with particular countries.

Members (Oct 1947) T.L. Rowan (Ec. Aff. then Try, ch.); E.W. Playfair (Try); H.C.B. Mynors (B.E.); H.J.B. Lintott (B.T.); R. Makins (F.O.); C.G.L. Syers (Com. Rel. O.); G.H. Baxter (Com. Rel. O.); A.E. Feavearyear (Food); J.M. Fleming (Ec. Sect.); E.A.G. Robinson (C.E.P.S.).

Secs. G.M. Wilson (Cab. O.), J.D. Peck (Cab. O.) and J. G. Marsh (B.T.).

46 Meetings 18 Sept–31 Dec 1947 BP(ON)(47)1st–69th.
47 Memoranda 20 Sept–6 Nov 1947 BP(ON)(47)1–80.
48 Memoranda 6 Nov–31 Dec 1947 BP(ON)(47)81–174.

CAB 134/49–51 Balance of Payments Statistics Subcommittee

Set up as part of the reorganization of the September 1947 inter-departmental machinery for dealing with the balance of payments (CAB 129/21, CP(47)255), the subcommittee was to serve the Overseas Negotiations Committee (CAB 134/46–48, 555–575), the Exchange Requirements Committee (CAB 134/45, 258–261) and the Exports Committee (CAB 134/44, 166–169), see CAB 134/49, BP(STAT)(47)1st. It considered the annual *Economic Surveys*, the annual balance of payments White Papers and the progressing of import programmes. Changes in the overall position since 1946, tourist income and the 1948 dollar import programme were also discussed. Its other major task was to produce a monthly bulletin for use mainly by the Overseas Negotiations Committee. For later papers see CAB 134/781.

Chairman R.G.D. Allen (Try). (May 1948) S. Goldman (Try).

Sec. P.J. Deacon (Cab. O.). (Nov 1947) P.J. Moorhouse. (Feb 1950) C.H. Tylden-Pattenson (Try). (1951) D.M. Hawke (Try).

49 Meetings and Memoranda 5 Nov 1947–1 Nov 1949 BP(STAT)(47)1st–5th, BP(STAT)(48)1st–11th, BP(STAT)(49)1st–4th and BP(STAT)(47)1–2, BP(STAT)(48)1–12(revise), BP(STAT)(49)1–2.
50 Meetings and Memoranda 10 Feb 1950–20 Sept 1951 BP(STAT)(50)1st–2nd and BP(STAT)(50)1–6(revise), BP(STAT)(51)1–2.
51 Monthly Bulletins 13 Jan 1948–15 July 1949 BP(STAT)(MB)(48)1–8 and BP(STAT)(MB)(49)1–3.

CAB 134/68–76 Committee on Colonial Development: Subcommittee on Import Programmes

Set up in 1949 to consider, for the Committee on Colonial Development (CAB 134/64–67), what the colonies could import, in particular with regard to dollar goods, and the formulation of colonial import programmes.

Chairman J.L. Croome (C.E.P.S.). (Aug 1951) A.M. Jenkins (C.E.P.S.).

Secs. P.V. Collyer (Cab. O.) and I.P.M. Cargill. (Aug 51) representatives, Try and Col. O.

68 Meetings 13 Jan–20 Dec 1949 CD(BP)(49)1st–43rd.
69 Memoranda 11 Jan–30 Nov 1949 CD(BP)(49)1–49.
70 Meetings and Memoranda 10 Jan–19 Dec 1950 CD(BP)(50)1st–22nd and CD(BP)(50)1–8.
71 Meetings and Memoranda 4 Jan–30 Nov 1951 CD(BP)(51)1st–20th and CD(BP)(51)1–4.
72–76 Working Papers of the subcommittee (1949–51).

CAB 134/125–128 UK Study Group on Customs Unions

Set up in October 1947 (see CAB 128/10, CM(47)77th:2), it made an interim report in November 1947 (CAB 134/215, EPC(47)11) and a final report in May 1948 (CAB 134/217, EPC(48)37). In June 1948, as a result of the review of machinery following the establishment of the O.E.E.C., it became a subcommittee of the European Economic Co-operation Committee (CAB 134/232–254). To avoid confusion with the International Customs Union Study Group (CAB 133/36–39) it was retitled the European Economic Co-operation Committee Customs Union Working Party. Its papers include some relating to the Havana discussions and the third report by the group of economists on the position if the I.T.O. negotiations failed (CAB 134/125, CU(47)13; see also, the description for the Overseas Negotiations Committee, CAB 134/46–48). Annex E of the report is the group's second report on the U.K.'s attitude to a customs union of which the U.K. was not a member. Papers after June 1948 concentrate on discussions of a European customs union.

Terms To examine and report, as soon as possible, upon possible customs unions or analogous though less far reaching arrangements, between respectively – (a) the U.K. and the colonies; or (b) all the countries of the Commonwealth; and/or (c) some or all of the countries of Europe (with or without their overseas territories) and to examine the relationship of a possible customs union of the U.K. and the colonies or of the whole Commonwealth, to possible customs unions in Europe, particularly as regards the possibility of U.K. participation in a European union if some or all of the countries of the Commonwealth did or did not participate. . . . The study group should also, as a matter of urgency, make recommendations as to the time and methods of consultations with other Commonwealth countries, particularly on the question of which of them would wish to receive invitations to the international study group to be established in connection with the Marshall Plan.

Members R.J. Shackle (B.T., ch.); representatives of the F.O., Try, Col. O., Com. Rel. O., Ec. Sect., Customs & E. (June 1950) S. Holmes (B.T., ch.).

Secs. B. Forbes Adams (B.T.) and J.M. Forsyth (Ec. Sect.). (June 1948) M.F. Hardie (B.T.) and D.J. Robey (Cab. O.).

125 Meetings and Memoranda 17 Oct–31 Dec 1947 CU(47)1st–14th and CU(47)1–48.
126 Meetings 7 Jan–10 Nov 1948 CU(48)1st–22nd.
127 Memoranda 6 Jan–13 Dec 1948 CU(48)1–88.
128 Meetings and Memoranda 6 Jan 1949–9 Aug 1951 CU(49)1st, CU(50)1st–3rd and CU(49)1–14, CU(50)1–11 and CU(51)1.

CAB 134/133–134 Committee on Distribution and Marketing

Set up by Attlee in April 1950. Among the subjects it covered were resale price maintenance, the control of prices, hire purchase, the census of distribution and distributors' margins. Its papers include a memorandum by Wilson, H., and Webb, 'Long-term Arrangements for Control of Prices' (CAB 134/133, DM(50)17), considering whether the new legislation should be included in the Economic Powers Bill, and an interim report to Attlee (CAB 134/133, DM(50)22).

Terms To consider what steps might be taken, by legislation or otherwise, to simplify marketing and distribution, and thus to reduce the general level of retail prices of food and essential consumer goods.

Members Min. of Town and Country Planning (ch.); Mins. of Agriculture and Fish, Nat. Insurance; Min. State Economic Affs.; Parl. Sec. Bd. Trade; Parl. U.-Sec. Scotland. (April 1950) Pres. Bd Trade replaced Parl. Sec. Bd Trade.

Sec. A. Johnston (Cab. O.).

133 Meetings and Memoranda 1 April–13 Dec 1950 DM(50)1st–15th and DM(50)1–32.
134 Meetings and Memoranda 23 June–10 July 1951 DM(51)1st–2nd and DM(51)1–4.

CAB 134/165 Committee on External Economic Policy and Overseas Trade

Set up in December 1945 (see CAB 128/2, (M(45)52nd:3), to be a junior ministerial committee to keep the export position under review and thus relieve the Lord President's Industrial Subcommittee (CAB 71/27) of that function. The Overseas Economic Policy Committee was thereby abolished. Among its papers are memoranda on the prospects of individual industries and monthly reviews of British exports. It was wound up in November 1946 (CAB 129/13, CP(46)389) and replaced by the Overseas Economic Policy Committee (CAB 134/541) made up of senior ministers.

Terms To keep under regular review the development of the export trade, and to consider such general questions of external economic policy as arise from this review, or may be referred to it, reporting as may be necessary to the Cabinet or the appropriate ministerial committee through the President of the Board of Trade.

Chairman Sec. Overseas Trade.

Secs. G.E. Preston (B.T.) and A.N. Coleridge (Ld Pres. O.).

165 Meetings and Memoranda   17 Dec 1945–12 Nov 1946   E(45)1st–4th, E(45)1–2 and E(46)1–50.

CAB 134/180–181 Economic Committee (Washington)

Set up by T.L. Rowan on his appointment as Economic Minister to Washington in 1949, it met regularly to consider U.K. discussions with the U.S.A. and Canada and visits by U.K. ministers or senior officials, who often addressed the committee. After Rowan's return to the U.K. in July 1951, the committee was chaired by either D.H.F. Rickett or S. Caine. For later papers see CAB 134/862–865.

Members T.L. Rowan (ch.) and members of his staff.

180 Meetings and Memoranda   14 Nov 1949–28 Dec 1950   EC(W)(4a)1st–6th, EC(W)(50)1st–39th and EC(W)(49)1–2, EC(W)(50)1–15.
181 Meetings and Memoranda   8 Jan–11 Dec 1951   EC(W)(51)1st–46th and EC(W)(51)1–10.

CAB 134/206–208 Emergency Legislation Committee

For earlier papers and terms of reference see CAB 71/29–30. The committee continued to consider the future of emergency regulations and related legislation. Includes papers on the Supplies and Services (Transitional Powers) Bill, the Emergency Laws (Transitional Provisions) Bill and the Economic Powers Bill. There was a general discussion of emergency powers in July 1948. CAB 134/206 is identical to CAB 71/30. For later papers see CAB 134/870–873.

Chairman Ld Schuster.   (Aug 1945) A. Maxwell (H.O.).   (Sept 1949) T. Sheepshanks (T. & C.P.).

Secs. A. Johnston (Ld Pres. O.) and H.S. Kent (Parl. Counsel).

206 Meetings and Memoranda 6 Mar 1945–24 Sept 1948 EL(45)1st–5th, EL(47)1st, EL(48)1st–2nd and EL(45)1–24, EL(46)1–2, EL(47)1–2, EL(48)1–6.

207 Meetings and Memoranda 17 Jan 1949–20 Dec 1950 EL(49)1st and EL(49)1–5, EL(50)1–15.

208 Meetings and Memoranda 25 Jan–11 Dec 1951 EL(51)1st and EL(51)1–12.

CAB 134/232–254 European Economic Co-operation Committee

For earlier papers see CAB 130/21–26, GEN 188. The committee was changed from an *ad hoc* to a standing committee status in June 1948 with the establishment of machinery for handling the E.R.P. (CAB 129/27, CP(48)137) but was still referred to as the London Committee. It was primarily to be a policy committee on the formulation of submissions to the O.E.E.C., with detailed work carried out by the Programmes Committee (CAB 134/608–623). At the same time, the London Executive Committee (CAB 130/29–30, GEN 209), the Programmes Subcommittee (CAB 130/31–33, GEN 212) and the Supplies Subcommittee (CAB 130/34, GEN 213) were all disbanded, along with other subsidiary committees with the exception of the E.C.E. Working Party (CAB 130/28, GEN 204 and CAB 134/182–185). The Accounting Working Party (CAB 130/35, GEN 217 and CAB 134/624–626) became part of the Programmes Committee machinery. However, the Customs Union Study Group (CAB 134/125–128) became a subcommittee of the London Committee and a new Strategic Materials and Stockpiling Subcommittee (CAB 134/255–257) was established. The chairmen of the London Committee, the Programmes Committee, the Exports Committee (CAB 134/166–169) and the Overseas Negotiations Committee (CAB 134/555–587) were meant to meet regularly to ensure co-ordination of work and there were common elements in the committees' secretariats. Among the subjects considered by the committee were the U.K.–U.S. bilateral agreement, the various reports and programmes for the O.E.E.C., the European Customs Union, the Anglo-American Council on Productivity, U.K.–Canadian relations, the European Payments Union and relations between the O.E.E.C. and N.A.T.O. The committee was abolished in November 1951 with its functions passing to the Mutual Aid Committee (CAB 134/488–496, 1010–1052). A number of membership changes were made without being formalized.

Terms To advise the Economic Policy Committee on matters affecting the European Recovery Programme (except on the programmes to be submitted), including the work of the O.E.E.C. and the Economic Commission for Europe. To instruct H.M. Ambassador in Washington and the U.K. delegations to the O.E.E.C., the Economic Commission for Europe and the negotiations with Canada.

Members T.L. Rowan (Try, ch.); E.A. Berthoud (F.O.); R.W.B. Clarke (Try); M.T. Flett (Try); E.A. Hitchman (C.E.P.S.); E. Roll (C.E.P.S.); W.L. Gorell-Barnes (Col. O.); J.J.S. Garner (Com. Rel. O.); F. Grant (M.A.F.); E.A. Cohen (B.T.); A.F. Rouse (Lab & N.S.); H.A. Hardman (Food); E. Ackroyd (Supply); E.G. Penman (Supply); V.S. Butler (Fuel & P.); A.P. Grafftey-Smith (B.E.); R.L. Hall (Ec. Sect.); E.H.W. Atkinson (E.I.U.). (Oct 1949) E.A. Hitchman (ch.) and Rowan left, and H.G. Lindsell (Supply) replaced Ackroyd. (Sept 1950) H.F. Rossetti (Lab. & N.S.) replaced H.M. Phillips.

Secs. T.A.G. Charlton (Cab. O.) and D.J.B. Robey (Cab. O.). (Mar 1949) M.M. du Merton (Cab. O.) replaced Charlton. (Jan 1950) P.V. Collyer (Cab. O.) replaced Robey. (Mar 1950) P.J. Moorhouse replaced Collyer.

232   Meetings   9 June–22 Dec 1948   ER(L)(48)1st–56th.

233–236   Memoranda   7 June–31 Dec 1948   ER(L)(48)1–65, 66–111, 112–187, 188–236.

237–239   Meetings   5 Jan–30 Dec 1949   ER(L)(49)1st–29th, 30th–62nd, 63rd–87th.

240–245   Memoranda   1 Jan 1949–4 Jan 1950   (ER(L)(49)1–54, 55–129, 130–198, 199–255, 256–306, 307–362.

246–247   Meetings   4 Jan–8 Dec 1950   ER(L)(50)1st–39th, 40th–71st.

248–252   Memoranda   31 Dec 1949–30 Dec 1950   ER(L)(50)1–40, 41–94, 95–153, 155–224, 225–291.

253   Meetings and Memoranda   3 Jan–30 Nov 1951   ER(L)(51)1st–22nd and ER(L)(51) 1–22.

254   Memoranda   12 Mar–30 Nov 1951   ER(L)(51)23–87.

CAB 134/258–262   Exchange Requirements Committee

For earlier papers, terms of reference, membership and role, see CAB 134/45. In March 1948 a Subcommittee on Raw Materials (CAB 134/262) under M.T. Flett (Try) was established to relieve the main committee of detailed consideration of individual programmes of specific raw materials and imports on private account. Both the committee and the subcommittee were wound up in June 1948 with the reorganization of machinery for handling E.R.P. questions. Their functions passed to the Programmes Committee (CAB 134/608–623) and its Subcommittee on Raw Materials (CAB 134/632–634).

Secs.   (Jan 1948) H.A.C. Gill (Try) replaced van Loo.

258   Meetings   2 Jan–20 Apr 1948   ERC(48)1st–19th.

259–261   Memoranda   2 Jan–12 June 1948   ERC(48)1–25, 26–30, 31–58.

262   Subcommittee on Raw Materials   Meetings and Memoranda   3 Mar–29 June 1948   ERC(RM)(48)1st–4th and ERC(RM)(48)1–7.

CAB 134/276   Food Distribution Committee

Set up in May 1948 by the Food Policy Committee (CAB 130/37, GEN 232/1st), its work included consideration of the permanent powers of the Ministry of Food. It no longer functioned after its interim report (CAB 134/276, FD(48)19). The only non-ministerial members were R.L. Hall (Ec. Sect.) and F.W. Smith (C.E.P.S.).

Chairman   Ec. Sec. (Try).

Secs.   R.J.E. Taylor (Cab. O.) and H.L. Jenkyns (Try).

276   Meetings and Memoranda   24 May–16 Aug 1948   FD(48)1st–9th and FD(48)1–19.

CAB 134/293   Committee on Proposed Franco-German Coal and Steel Authority

Attlee appointed this committee of senior officials in May 1950 to report to ministers on the proposed scheme, distinguishing between a scheme with the U.K. included and excluded, the effect on the U.K. economy, the sterling area and the Commonwealth, and the defence aspects of the French proposals. It established a working party (CAB 134/294–297), and its report in June covered that of the working party (CAB 129/40, CP(50)128). It was then wound up.

Terms To collect all available information in relation to the proposed Franco-German coal and steel authority and to advise ministers on the possible effects of the scheme on the U.K.

Members E.E. Bridges (Try, ch.); E.N. Plowden (C.E.P.S.); R. Makins (F.O.); D. Fergusson (Fuel & P.); A. Rowlands (Supply); M. Dean (M.O.D.); S. Holmes (B.T.).

Secs. F.R.P. Vinter (C.E.P.S.) and M.M. du Merton (Cab. O.).

293 Meetings and Memoranda 15 May–21 June 1950 FG(SO)1st–6th and FG(50)1–5.

CAB 134/294–297 Working Party on Proposed Franco-German Coal and Steel Authority

For its establishment in May 1950, see above. After its initial report in June (CAB 129/40, CP(50)128) it was reconstituted to continue consideration of the proposals and if necessary to form the nucleus of a U.K. delegation. In April 1951 an interim report went to the Economic Steering Committee (CAB 134/265, ES(51)29) and then to the Economic Policy Committee (CAB 134/229, EPC(51)44). A further report went to the same committees in July (CAB 134/266, ES(51)45 and CAB 134/230, EPC(51)85). For later papers see CAB 134/899.

Terms To consider practical measures for implementing the French proposals on the assumption that the coal and steel industries of the U.K. would eventually be brought within the projected scheme.
  (June 1950) To consider practical measures for implementing the French proposals for the pooling of the coal and steel industries of Western European countries, on the assumption that the coal and steel industries of the U.K. would eventually be brought within the projected scheme.

Chairman W. Strath (C.E.P.S.). (Sept 1950) D.B. Pitblado (C.E.P.S.). (Sept 1951) J.A.C. Robertson (C.E.P.S.).

Secs. F.R.P. Vinter (C.E.P.S.). (May 1950) E.N.G. Haynes (Supply).

294 Meetings 25 May–9 Nov 1950 FG(WP)(50)1st–31st.
295 Memoranda 26 May–21 Dec 1950 FG(WP)(50)1–82.
296 Meetings and Memoranda 25 Jan –18 Dec 1951 FG(WP)(51)1st–20th and FG(WP)(51)1–15.
297 Memoranda 20 Apr–31 Dec 1951 FG(WP)(51)16–43.

CAB 134/298–300 Committee on Future Legislation

Appointed by Attlee in January 1946 to prepare an annual submission to Cabinet. For later papers see CAB 134/900–901.

Terms To draw up for approval of Cabinet a provisional list of the major bills to be included in the government programme of legislation for the next session.

Members Ld President (ch.); Ld Privy Seal; S./S. Dominions; Chief Whip.   (Oct 1947) Ld President (ch.); Ld Privy Seal; Chief Whip. (1951) Home Sec. (ch.).

Secs. N. Brook (Cab. O.) and W.S. Murrie (Cab. O.).

298 Meetings and Memoranda   30 Jan 1946–9 Oct 1947   FL(46)1st–7th, FL(47)1st–7th and FL(46)1–8 and FL(47)1–12.
299 Meetings and Memoranda   4 Feb–13 Oct 1948   FL(48)1st–8th and FL(48)1–10.
300 Meetings and Memoranda   24 Mar 1949–17 July 1951   FL(49)1st–2nd, FL(50)1st–3rd, FL(51)1st–2nd and FL(49)1–3, FL(50)1–3, FL(51)1–2.

CAB 134/303 Working Party on Guidance of Exports

The working party was established with the approval of Dalton and Cripps in January 1947. Among the subjects considered was the use of the iron and steel distribution scheme to influence the direction of exports. It was dissolved in October 1947 as part of the reorganization of the inter-departmental machinery for handling the balance of payments (CAB 129/21, CP(47)255), with its functions being split between the Exports Committee (CAB 134/44, 166–169) and the Overseas Negotiations Committee (CAB 134/46–48, 555–575).

Terms To consider all questions arising in relation to the implementation of the policy of expanding U.K. exports to certain hard currency markets.

Members H.J.B. Lintott (B.T., ch.); E. Rowe-Dutton (Try); R.W.B. Clarke (Try); G.S. Owen (B.T.); A.E. Welch (B.T.).   (April 1947) Rowe-Dutton left.

Secs G. Parker (B.T.) and R. Marrison (Cab. O.).   (March 1947) E.J. Beaven (B.T.) and T.A.G. Charlton (Cab. O.).

303 Meetings and Memoranda   17 Jan–24 Oct 1947   GE(47)1st–11th and GE(47)1–30.

CAB 134/307–310 Government Organization Committee

The committee was set up in October 1947 under E.E. Bridges as a body of permanent secretaries or their equivalents. It had informal links with the ministerial Committee on the Machinery of Government (CAB 134/504–506) which became more formal after October 1948. In December 1949 it established the Steering Committee for Economic Organization Enquiry (CAB 134/314) and the Economic Organization Working Group (T 222/324–329) and a month later the Subcommittee on Regional Organization (CAB 134/311–313).

Among the subjects taken by the committee were government relations with industry, government organization for encouraging industrial productivity and reviews of controls. More specifically, it considered the report of the Building Controls Committee (CAB 134/307, GOC(47)16(revise)) and progress reports from the Co-ordinating Committee on Controls which co-ordinated departmental reviews of controls and acted as a channel through which the Economic Section passed general information on economic matters to departments. E.E. Bridges changed the membership of the committee regularly after October 1948 in order to keep all permanent secretaries involved. For later papers see CAB 134/903.

Terms   To examine and pass judgment upon proposals for changes in organization and method which are of interest to the Service as a whole, and to recommend to departments for action proposals which they approve.

(Oct 1948) To be responsible, under the supervision of ministers, for laying down the programme of investigations to be undertaken into questions concerning the machinery of government, for directing such investigations and for seeing that any necessary changes are carried into effect.

Chairman   E.E. Bridges (Try).

Secs.   W. Armstrong (Try).   (Feb 1948) W.E. Phillips (Try) added.   (Oct 1948) W. Armstrong and R.P. Fraser (Cab. O.).

307   Meetings and Memoranda   25 Oct 1947–7 Dec 1948   GOC(47)1st–2nd, GOC(48)1st–5th and GOC(47)1–10, GOC(48)1–32.
308   Meetings and Memoranda   18 Jan–14 Dec 1949   GOC(49)1st–4th and GOC(49)1–28.
309   Meetings and Memoranda   12 Jan–29 Dec 1950   GOC(50)1st–5th and GOC(50)1–24.
310   Meeting and Memoranda   2 Jan–17 Dec 1951   GOC(51)1st and GOC(51)1–19.

CAB 134/320   Housing Committee

The committee superseded the earlier Housing Committee under Lord Woolton (CAB 87/36–37). It held meetings irregularly to review progress and to consider major questions of policy. Among such subjects were brick production, the monthly housing returns, the labour situation and the 1947 housing programme. It was abolished in October 1947.

Members   Attlee (ch.).

Secs.   W.S. Murrie (Cab. O.) and J.D. Peek (Cab. O.).

320   Meetings and Memoranda   11 Dec 1945–13 Oct 1947   HG(45)1st, HG(46)1st–5th, HG(47)1st and HG(46)1–9, HG(47)1–3.

CAB 134/321   Committee on the Hotel Industry

321   Meetings and Memoranda   2 Dec 1950–3 July 1951   HI(50)1st, HI(51)1st–2nd and HI(50)1–5, HI(51)1–4.

CAB 134/322   Home Information Services (Ministerial) Committee

322   Meeting and Memoranda   29 May–25 Sept 1951   HIS(51)1st and HIS(51)1–4.

CAB 134/323–340   Legislation Committee

For earlier papers, see CAB 75/15–23. Includes consideration of the Exchange Control Bill but nothing on the Economic Powers Bill or its successors. For later papers see CAB 134/994.

Terms   See CAB 75.

Members   See CAB 75.   (Oct 1947) Ld President (ch.); Ld Privy Seal; Home Sec.; S./S. Scotland; A.–G.; Ld Advocate; Fin. Sec. (Try); Chief Whip.

Secs.   See CAB 75.   (Jan 1947) D.H.F. Rickett.   (July 1947) J.G. Stewart.   (Nov 1947) W.S. Murrie.

323	Meetings 8 Jan–17 Dec 1946 HPC(46)1st–34th.	
324–326	Memoranda 1 Jan–31 Dec 1946 HPC(46)1–50, 51–81, 82–110.	
327	Meetings 2 Jan–16 Dec 1947 HPC(47)1st–28th.	
328–329	Memoranda 2 Jan–22 Dec 1947 HPC(47)1–61, 62–106.	
330	Meetings 13 Jan–14 Dec 1948 HPC(48)1st–28th.	
331–333	Memoranda 1 Jan 1948–10 Jan 1949 HPC(48)1–27, 28–81, 82–108.	
334	Meetings 14 Jan–15 Nov 1949 HPC(49)1st–26th.	
335	Memoranda 11 Jan–12 Dec 1949 HPC(49)1–89.	
336	Meetings 10 Jan–19 Dec 1950 HPC(50)1st–19th.	
337–338	Memoranda 3 Jan–15 Dec 1950 HPC(50)1–44, 45–78.	
339	Meetings 16 Jan–31 July 1951 HPC(51)1st–20th.	
340	Memoranda 13 Jan–19 Sept 1951 HPC(51)1–50.	

CAB 134/349–352   Import Diversion Committee

Set up in July 1948 to meet the requirement in the long-term plan (CAB 134/191, ED(48)5) that £100m of imports had to be switched from Western Hemisphere to soft currency countries or home production in order to achieve viability in 1952. Diversion plans were obtained, as far as possible, from existing committees, working parties and the main importing departments. The committee submitted two reports to E.N. Plowden, the latter of which was considered by the Economic Planning Board (CAB 134/349, ID(48)10 and CAB 134/212, EPB(49)4 and taken by EPB(49)2nd:2). In August 1949 the committee also produced a progress report covering the year July 1948–June 1949 (CAB 134/350, ID(49)13). At the only 1950 meeting it was agreed that little further could be done until the revision of the long-term programme was completed and the committee never met again. A Working Group on Cotton was established in

March 1949 to report to the committee on the possibility of diverting purchases to non-dollar sources given the proposed increased purchases from the Western Hemisphere in 1952–53, which it did in October 1949.

Terms To prepare the necessary programmes of action to secure these switches and to take account of the work of other committees dealing with special aspects of this problem.

Members E.A. Hitchman (C.E.P.S., ch.); S. Caine (Try); A.E. Feavearyear (Food); V.S. Butler (Fuel & P.); R.H. Franklin (M.A.F.); L.B. Hutchinson (Supply); J.R.C. Helmore (B.T.); L. Thompson-McCausland (B.E.); R.L. Hall (Ec. Sect.); E. Roll (C.E.P.S.). (Jan 1949) V.P. Harries (Supply) replaced Hutchinson. (Nov 1949) W. Strath (C.E.P.S., ch.) replaced Hitchman.

Secs. J.K. Ogilvy-Webb (C.E.P.S.) and E.J. Beaven (Cab. O.). (Jan 1949) D. Pointon (C.E.P.S.) replaced Ogilvy-Webb.

349 Meetings and Memoranda 24 July–14 Dec 1948 ID(48)1st–5th and ID(48)1–23.
350 Meetings and Memoranda 1 Jan–7 Dec 1949 ID(49)1st–6th and ID(49)1–22.
351 Meeting and Memoranda 11 Jan 1950–14 Mar 1951 ID(50)1st, ID(50)1–2 and ID(51)1–4.
352 Working Group on Cotton. Meetings and Memoranda 5 Apr–3 Oct 1949 ID(WGC)(49)1st–6th and ID(WGC)(49)1–11.

CAB 154/354 Ministerial Committee on Home Information Services

Superseded in March 1948 by the Information Services Committee (CAB 134/458–460).

354 Meetings and Memoranda 1 April 1946–26 Feb 1948 IH(46)1st–2nd, IH(47)1st–2nd, IH(48)1st and IH(46)1–11, IH(47)1–15, IH(48)1–5.

CAB 134/355–360 Home Information Services (Official) Committee

355 Meetings and Memoranda 11 April–13 Dec 1946 IH(O)(46)1st–6th and IH(O)(46)1–37.
356 Meetings and Memoranda 17 Jan–30 Dec 1947 IH(O)(47)1st–8th and IH(O)(47)1–53.
357 Meetings and Memoranda 5 Jan–2 Dec 1948 IH(O)(48)1st–10th and IH(O)(48)1–65.
358 Meetings and Memoranda 11 Jan–14 Dec 1949 IH(O)(49)1st–8th and IH(O)(49)1–65.
359 Meetings and Memoranda 3 Jan–22 Dec 1950 IH(O)(50)1st–7th and IH(O)(50)1–38.
360 Meetings and Memoranda 19 Jan–30 Nov 1951 IH(O)(51)1st–5th and IH(O)(51)1–36.

CAB 134/361–373   Home Information Services (Official) Committee: Economic Information (Official) Committee

Set up in June 1947 at the same time as the Economic Information Unit in accordance with CAB 134/356, IH(O)(47)7th:4, it was to play a part in the government's greater efforts to increase public awareness of the economic situation. It was to think out problems and to formulate a common background of policy (CAB 134/361, IH(O)(E)(47)1st:1). In November 1949 it was agreed that Clem Leslie could call smaller meetings of departmental information officers instead of full meetings and that there would be a smaller nucleus of members. Among the subjects considered were the Prosperity Campaign Committee, production conferences, joint production committees, the White Paper on *Personal Incomes, Costs and Prices*, productivity and a survey of the machinery for consultation and co-operation between government and industry. Regular surveys of public opinion were also taken, including the survey of knowledge and opinion about the economic situation.

Terms   As a subcommittee of the Home Information Services (Official) Committee, to review and co-ordinate where necessary inter-departmental action on problems of government economic information and the working of the government economic information services within the U.K.

Chairman   S.C. Leslie (E.I.U.).

Secs.   P.H. Boon (Ld Pres. O.) and I.M. Schapiro (C.O.I.).

361   Meetings   12 June–19 Dec 1947   IH(O)(E)(47)1st–16th.
362–363   Memoranda   13 June–23 Dec 1947   IH(O)(E)(47)1–35, 36–86.
364   Meetings   23 Jan–5 Nov 1948   IH(O)(E)(48)1st–14th.
365–367   Memoranda   1 Jan–29 Dec 1948   IH(O)(E)(48)1–71, 72–121, 122–179.
368   Meetings   14 Jan–20 Dec 1949   IH(O)(E)(49)1st–16th.
369–370   Memoranda   8 Jan–30 Dec 1949   IH(O)(E)(49)1–49, 50–103.
371   Meetings and Memoranda   5 Jan–24 Nov 1950   IH(O)(E)(50)1st–16th and IH(O)(E)(50)1–33.
372   Memoranda   1 June–22 Dec 1950   IH(O)(E)(50)34–71.
373   Meetings and Memoranda   1 Jan–15 Nov 1951   IH(O)(E)(51)1st–8th and IH(O)(E)(51)1–44.

CAB 134/458–460   Information Services Committee

Replaced the Ministerial Committee on Home Information Services in March 1948.

458   Meetings and Memoranda   4 Mar–5 Nov 1948   IS(48)1st–6th and IS(48)1–28.
459   Meetings and Memoranda   1 Jan–22 Nov 1948   IS(49)1st–2nd and IS(49)1–14.
460   Meetings and Memoranda   11 Jan 1950–12 Feb 1951   IS(50)1st–2nd, IS(51)1st and IS(50)1–11, IS(51)1–4.

CAB 134/467–468   Committee on the King's Speeches

For earlier files see CAB 98/3 and CAB 78/35, GEN 74. For later papers see CAB 134/ 993 onwards.

467   Meetings and Memoranda   7 July 1948–16 Dec 1949   KS(48)1st–4th, KS(49)1st–3rd and KS(48)1–11 and KS(49)1–6.

468   Meetings and Memoranda   25 Feb 1950–20 Sept 1951   KS(50)1st–3rd, KS(51)1st and KS(50)1–8, KS(51)1–4.

CAB 134/488–496   Mutual Aid Committee

Set up in October 1950 as part of the reorganization of official committees dealing with defence and economic policy (CAB 134/263, ES(50)1). It could report direct to the Economic Policy Committee (CAB 134/215–230) or through the newly established Economic Steering Committee (CAB 134/263–266). Among the subjects considered was the Nitze exercise. The committee had an Accounting and Procedure Subcommittee and Working Parties on Germany, the Nitze Exercise and N.A.T.O. Supply Controls. For later files see CAB 134/1010.

Terms   To consider all inter-departmental questions relating to U.S. financial aid, whether for economic recovery or for defence; and to handle inter-departmental business relating to all forms of military aid from North America, whether in cash or in kind, or arising from the transfer of military supplies or equipment between this country and other powers in N.A.T.O.

Chairman   E.A. Hitchman (Try).

Secs.   G.M. Wilson (Cab. O.) and R.S. Buer (Cab. O.).

488   Meetings and Memoranda   24 Oct–22 Dec 1950   MAC(50)1st–20th and MAC(50)1–65.

489   Meetings   9 Jan–27 Dec 1951   MAC(51)1st–66th.

490–492 Memoranda   8 Jan–31 Dec 1951   MAC(51)1–68, 69–132, 133–200.

493   Accounting and Procedure Subcommittee: Meetings and Memoranda   31 Jan–25 May 1951   MAC(A)(51)1st–7th and MAC(A)(51)1–15.

494   Working Party on Germany: Meetings and Memoranda   17 Aug–27 Dec 1951   MAC(GD)(51)1st–18th and MAC(GD)(51)1–47.

495   Working Party on the Nitze Exercise: Meetings and Memoranda   9 May–2 Aug 1951   MAC(NE)(51)1st–11th and MAC(NE)(51)1–55.

496   Working Party on N.A.T.O. Supply Controls: Meeting and Memorandum   17 Nov–20 Nov 1951   MAC(S)(51)1st and MAC(S)(51)1.

CAB 134/504–506   Committee on Machinery of Government

For earlier files, composition and terms of reference see CAB 87/73–75. The committee was reconstituted in November 1946. It had links with the official Government Organization Committee (CAB 134/307–310) and a Subcommittee on Parliamentary Procedure (CAB 134/507–508).

Terms   (Nov 1946) To keep under review the executive machinery of government and to deal with such machinery of government questions as require consideration by ministers.

Members (Nov 1946) Ld President (ch.); Ch. of Exchequer; Pres. Bd Trade; S./S. Dominions; Home Sec.; Min. Without Portfolio.

(Oct 1947) Ld President (ch.); Ch. of Exchequer; Ld Privy Seal; Home Sec.; Mins. of Defence, Education.

Secs. (April 1946) G.P. Humphreys-Davies (Try) and W. Armstrong (Cab. O.) replaced Fraser. (Nov 1946) Humphreys-Davies left.

504	Meetings and Memoranda 28 Jan 1946–2 Dec 1947 MG(46)1st–2nd, MG(47)1st–2nd and MG(46)1–17 and MG(47)1–3.	
505	Meeting and Memoranda 6 Jan–23 Sept 1948 MG(45)1st and MG(48)1–5.	
506	Meeting and Memoranda 3 Mar 1949–6 Feb 1950 MG(49)1st and MG(49)1–5, MG(50)1–3.	

CAB 134/541   Overseas Economic Policy Committee

Set up in October 1946 as agreed by the Cabinet (CAB 128/6, CM(46)84th:3), it replaced the more junior Committee on External Economic Policy and Overseas Trade (CAB 134/165). Among the subjects considered was the Overseas Economic Survey. The committee was abolished in October 1947 on the reorganization of ministerial standing committees, (CAB 129/2, CP(47)280), its general functions passing to the Economic Policy Committee (CAB 134/215–230).

Terms (a) to watch, on the Cabinet's behalf, the progress of the discussions at the International Conference on Trade and Employment (b) to consider general questions of external economic policy.

Members Prime Minister (ch.); Ld President; Ch. of Exchequer; Pres. Bd Trade; Ss./ S. Dominions, Colonies, India; Mins. of Fuel & Power, Agriculture & Fish, Food; Min. State (F.O.). (March 1947) Paymaster-Gen. added.

Secs. C.G. Eastwood (Col. O.) and R. Marrison (Cab. O.).

541	Meetings and Memoranda 23 Oct 1946–13 Oct 1947 OEP(47)1st–10th and OEP(46)1–10, OEP(47)1–33.

CAB 134/555–587   Overseas Negotiations Committee

For earlier papers, terms of reference, membership and role see CAB 134/46–48. In February 1951, on the abolition of the Exports Committee (CAB 134/166–169), it took over that committee's functions in relation to bilateral negotiations and, when appropriate, country distribution of exports in short supply. As well as the committee's minutes and memoranda, these pieces include a record of agreed minutes of negotiations with other countries (CAB 134/576–579), a series of notes and instructions to production departments on the implementation of bilateral negotiations arising from the abolition of the Exports Committee (CAB 134/581) and the committee's monthly report on external finance (CAB 134/582–585). Files of the committee's working parties on individual countries or commodities can be found in CAB 134/586–587 except for the

Working Party on Egypt (CAB 134/580). For later papers see CAB 134/1087 onwards. For the committee's working papers see T 238.

Members (March 1948) P.S. Beale (B.E.) or L. Thompson-McCausland (B.E.) replaced Mynors. (April 1948) K. McGregor (B.T.) replaced Lintott. (June 1948) D.H.F. Rickett (Try) replaced Hitchman; H. Hardman (Food) replaced Feavearyear; A.E. Welch (B.T.) replaced McGregor; J.J.S. Garner (Com. Rel. O.) replaced Syers. (Nov 1948) G.M. Watson (B.E.) replaced Beale. (Jan 1949) M.T. Flett (Try) replaced Playfair. (April 1949) W.J. Garnett (Com. Rel. O.) replaced Garner and Baxter. (Oct 1949) E.A. Hitchman (C.E.P.S., ch.) replaced Rowan. (March 1950) K. Anderson (Try, dep. ch.).

Secs. (May 1949) E.L. Sykes (Cab. O.) replaced Peek. (Aug 1949) M.M. du Merton (Cab. O.) replaced Sykes. (Dec 1949) E.L. Sykes (Cab. O.) replaced du Merton.

555–556 Meetings 1 Jan–23 Dec 1948 ON(48)1st–54th, 55th, 105th.
557–561 Memoranda 1 Jan–31 Dec 1948 ON(48)1–68, 69–138, 139–209, 210–312, 313–399.
562–563 Meetings 4 Jan–28 Dec 1949 ON(49)1st–54th, 55th–98th.
564–567 Memoranda 4 Jan–31 Dec 1949 ON(49)1–100, 101–228, 229–323, 324–421.
568–569 Meetings 3 Jan–28 Dec 1950 ON(50)1st–56th, 57th–91st.
570–572 Memoranda 31 Dec 1949–29 Dec 1950 ON(50)1–82, 83–169, 170–258.
573 Meetings 1 Jan–28 Dec 1951 ON(51)1st–60th.
574–575 Memoranda 1 Jan–29 Dec 1951 ON(51)1–99, 100–199.
576–579 Agreed Minutes 10 Feb 1948–22 Dec 1951 ON(AG)(48)1st–58th, (49)1st–52nd, (50)1st–55th, (51)1st–34th.
580 Working Party on Egypt: Meetings and Memoranda 25 Oct–25 Nov 1950 ON(E)(50)1st–5th and ON(E)(50)1–3.
581 Exports: Memoranda 19 Feb–24 Dec 1951 ON(EX)(51)1–16.
582–585 Monthly Reports on External Finance 10 Dec 1947–4 Dec 1951 ON(MR)(47)1, (48)1–12, (49)1–12, (50)1–12, (51)1–12.
586–587 Working Parties: 24 June 1948–29 Dec 1949 ON(WP)(48)1–104, (49)1–124.

CAB 134/488–590   Official Oil Committee

Set up in January 1947 on the direction of Attlee (CAB 134/588, OOC(47)1(revise)). The committee produced two reports, the first an interim one on the British oil position (CAB 134/588, OOC(47)12(final)) and the second on the British oil expansion programme (CAB 134/588, OOC(48)1). A Subcommittee on Oil Storage (CAB 134/590) was established in April 1947 to report on alternative methods of storage. Some memoranda in CAB 134/588 and all of CAB 134/589 are closed for fifty years.

Terms To consider questions of oil policy referred to it, and make recommendations; as its first task, to prepare, as a matter of urgency, recommendations for the planning of oil resources, taking into account strategic, political and economic factors.

Chairman D. Fergusson (Fuel & P.).

Secs.   K.L.O. Stock (Fuel & P.) and D. Heber-Percy (Cab. O.).

588   Meetings and Memoranda   29 Jan 1947–23 Nov 1949   OOC(47)1st–5th,
(48)1st–3rd, (49)1st–3rd and OOC(47)1–19, (48)1–15, (49)1–19.

589   Meetings and Memoranda   5 May–1 Nov 1950   OOC(50)1st–3rd and
OOC(50)1–6. Closed for 50 years.

590   Subcommittee on Oil Storage: Meetings and Memoranda   14 April–Sept
1947   OOC(OS)(47)1st–4th and OOC(OS)(47)1–13.

CAB 134/687–692   Committee on the Socialization of Industries

Set up in January 1946 as the ministerial committee to consider rationalization issues
(CAB 129/6, CP(46)1). An official committee had been established a month earlier
(CAB 134/693–696). In October 1947 the committee was reconstituted. Among the
subjects considered were a series of memoranda in July 1947 on taking stock and
reports by official committees on socialized industries and national investment policy
(CAB 134/691, SI(M)(50)25), relations with workers in socialized industries (CAB 134/
692, SI(M)51)25) and the control of prices and charges (CAB 134/692, SI(M)(51)70).

Terms   To consider questions of policy which arise in the working out of schemes to
give effect to approved projects for socializing industries and to ensure a desirable
measure of consistency in the preparation of those schemes.

Members   Ld President (ch.); Ch. of Exchequer; Pres. Bd Trade; Mins. of Fuel & Power,
Supply & Aircraft Production, War Transport, Civil Aviation.   (April 1947) Ld Privy
Seal added.
   (Oct 1947) Ld President (ch.); Ch. of Exchequer; S./S. War; A.-G.; Mins. of Labour,
Transport, Supply, Fuel & Power, Civil Aviation. (Feb 1948) Pres. Bd Trade
added.   (May 1951) Ch. D. Lancaster added.

Secs.   A. Johnston (Ld Pres. O.) and M.T. Flett (Ld Pres. O.).   (Oct 1946) T.M. Wilson
(Ld Pres. O.) replaced Flett.

687   Meetings and Memoranda   1 Jan–13 Dec 1946   SI(M)(46)1st–16th and
SI(M)(46)1–39.

688   Meetings and Memoranda   6 Jan–16 Dec 1947   SI(M)(47)1st–14th and
SI(M)(47)1–50.

689   Meetings and Memoranda   1 Jan–22 Dec 1948   SI(M)(48)1st–14th and
SI(M)(48)1–67.

690   Meetings and Memoranda   4 Jan–19 Dec 1949   SI(M((49)1st–11th and
SI(M)(49)1–52.

691   Meetings and Memoranda   13 Jan–21 Dec 1950   SI(M)(50)1st–10th and
SI(M)(50)1–47.

692   Meetings and Memoranda   5 Jan–2 Oct 1951   SI(M)(51)1st–9th and
SI(M)(51)1–43.

CAB 134/693–696   Official Committee on the Socialization of Industries

Set up in November 1945 as a result of an *ad hoc* meeting on the socialization of
industries (CAB 78/39, GEN 98/1st). Once the ministerial committee was established

in January 1946 the official committee served it although there was no formal change of terms of reference. It made a number of reports to ministers.

Terms To examine in greater detail questions of compensation, finance and organization which were discussed at the meeting in the light of the general conclusions reached, and to submit a report to ministers.

Chairman B.W. Gilbert (Try).

Secs. M.T. Flett (Ld Pres. O.) and P.S. Milner-Barry (Try). (Oct 1946) T.M. Wilson (Ld Pres. O.) and M. Stevenson (Try). (Jan 1948) A.R.W. Bavin (Cab. O.) replaced Wilson. (Feb 1948) J.J.S. Shaw (Try) replaced Stevenson. (April 1948) Shaw left. (May 1949) J.D. Peek (Cab. O.).

693 Meetings and Memoranda   27 Nov 1945–31 Dec 1946   SI(O)(45)1st–3rd, SI(O)(46)1st–11th and SI(O)(45)1–5, SI(O)(46)1–43.
694 Meetings and Memoranda   5 Jan–31 Dec 1947   SI(O)(47)1st–6th and SI(O)(47)1–27.
695 Meetings and Memoranda   7 Jan 1948–8 July 1949   SI(O)(48)1st–4th, SI(O)(49)1st and SI(O)(48)1–17, SI(O)(49)1–3.
696 Meetings and Memoranda   9 Feb 1950–16 Nov 1951   SI(O)(50)1st–2nd, SI(O)(51)1st–3rd and SI(O)(50)1–4, SI(O)(51)1–6.

CAB 134/710   Tourist Accommodation Committee

Set up in December 1945 to consider whether this could prove a source of dollar-earning (CAB 128/2, CM(45)54th:5) and wound up having reported (CAB 129/7, CP(46)66).

Terms To advise and report to the Cabinet on the practicability of using government hostels, universities and public schools for the accommodation of tourists, particularly from the U.S.A., during 1946.

Chairman Overseas Trade Sec.

Secs. R.P.S. Edwards (Dept. Overseas Trade) and J.D. Peek (Cab. O.).

710 Meetings and Memoranda   5 Dec 1945–14 Feb 1946   TAC(45)1st, TAC(46)1st and TAC(45)1–2, TAC(46)1–3, and CP(46)66.

CAB 134/711–716   Trade Negotiations Committee

Set up in February 1946. At the same time Working Parties on Non-tariff Questions (CAB 134/715) and on Tariffs (CAB 134/716) were established. In March 1947 a Subcommittee on International Commodity Policy was set up to ensure that the work of individual departments was consistent with the general principles of U.K. policy and to assist the Board of Trade (CAB 134/714, TN(C)(47)1). Among the subjects covered by the committee were I.T.O., G.A.T.T. and the Havana conference.

Terms   To deal with preliminary work necessary in connection with forthcoming trade negotiations.

Chairman   P. Liesching (B.T.).   (July 1946) J.R.C. Helmore (B.T.).

Secs.   R. Marrison (Cab. O.); P.S. Young (B.T.) and M.F. Hardie (B.T.).   (March 1947) T.A.G. Charlton (Cab. O.) replaced Marrison.

711   Meetings and Memoranda   19 Feb–31 Dec 1946   TN(46)1st–10th and TN(46)1–30.
712   Memoranda   15 Aug–23 Dec 1946   TN(46)31–71.
713   Meetings and Memoranda   1 Jan–26 Nov 1947   TN(47)1st–3rd and TN(47)1–45.
714   Subcommittee on International Commodity Policy: Meetings and Memoranda   3 March–19 Nov 1947   TN(C)(47)1st–2nd and TN(C)(47)1–21.
715   Working Party on Non-tariff Questions: Meetings and Memoranda   20 Feb–30 Aug 1946   TN(N)(46)1st–3rd and TN(N)(46)1–4.
716   Working Party on Tariffs: Meetings and Memoranda   22 Feb 1946–28 April 1947   TN(T)(46)1st–3rd, TN(T)(47)1st and TN(T)(46)1–150, TN(T)(47)1–48.

CAB 134/717–721   European Economic Co-operation Committee: Subcommittee on Intra-European Trade and Payments

Chairman D.H.F. Rickett (Try).   (Jan 1950) E.W. Playfair (Try).

717   Meetings and Memoranda   6 June–17 Dec 1948   TP(L)(48)1st–20th and TP(L)(48)1–48.
718   Meetings   27 Jan–20 Dec 1949   TP(L)(49)1st–47th.
719   Memoranda   19 Jan–30 Dec 1949   TP(L)(49)1–114.
720   Meetings   4 Jan–11 May 1950   TP(L)(50)1st–17th.
721   Memoranda   25 Jan–28 Sept 1950   TP(L)(50)1–73.

CAB 134/729–731   Committee on Food Supplies

Set up in February 1946 it covered world supplies and requirements and the impact of this on U.K. supplies and consumption. There was some consideration of U.K. cereal production and bread rationing.

Chairman   Prime Minister.

Sec.   N. Brook (Cab. O.).

729   Meetings   4 Feb–12 July 1946   WFS(46)1st–14th.
730–731   Memoranda   2 Feb–25 Nov 1946   WFS(46)1–69, 70–131.

CAB 134/733   *Ad hoc* Legislation Meetings

These considered the annual legislative programmes from 1945–46 to 1948–49 and were made up of a mixture of ministers and officials.

733   Meetings 9 Jan 1946–1 Dec 1948.

CAB 134/795   Committee on Iron Ore

Set up in July 1951 in accordance with the wishes of the Production Committee (CAB 134/649, PC(51)14th:6). Among the subjects considered were supplies in 1951–52 and the coke shortage.

Terms   (a) to keep the iron ore position under continuous review and to ensure that any necessary action is taken without delay, report to the ministers concerned whenever necessary and to the Production Committee from time to time   (b) to arrange for the provision of regular statistical returns on the availability and shipping position in respect of iron ore.

Members   E.N. Plowden (C.E.P.S., ch.); F.F. Turnbull (C.E.P.S.); G. Jenkins (Transport); A. Rowlands (Supply).

Secs.   P.J. Moorhouse (Cab. O.) and D.O. Henley (C.E.P.S.).

795   Meetings and Memoranda   3 July 1951–14 Jan 1952   CIO(51)1st–8th and CIO(51)1–16, CIO(52)1.

Chapter 16 Commonwealth and International Conferences

16.1 War Cabinet: Commonwealth and International Conferences

CAB 99 includes the papers of discussions on Article VII (33–35). For conferences from 1945 see CAB 133.

16.2 Commonwealth and International Conferences from 1945

Continuation of CAB 99. CAB 133 includes the papers of the informal meetings of the continuing consultative talks in Washington 1949–50 (1), the Commonwealth Consultative Committee (CCL) (7–12), Commonwealth meetings on general economic and trade questions (CET) (13–14), the Commonwealth Liaison Committee (CLC) and its subcommittees (18–27), the Commonwealth meeting on oil (29), the Committee on Preparations for the Meeting of Commonwealth Prime Ministers (CPM) (30–31), the meeting of Commonwealth ministers concerned with supply and production (CSP) (32–34), the International Study Group on Customs Unions (CU) (36–39), the meeting of Commonwealth finance ministers (EMM) (41), the U.K. delegation to the O.E.E.C. and related papers (42–71), the E.R.P. Washington Committee (73–76), official discussions on economic affairs with regard to the Colombo meeting (79), the meeting of Dominion Prime Ministers (PMM) (86–91), the European Economic Co-operation Committee U.K. delegation (93) and the E.R.P. U.K. Treasury and Supply Delegation, Washington (UKTSD) (94–95).

Chapter 17 Prime Minister's Private Office

British prime ministers have traditionally had a very small private office, headed by a principal private secretary who is a career civil servant. The office dealt with private and party political matters, but files on such issues were removed on the prime minister's resignation. What remains are largely briefs on important or sensitive political issues provided by the secretaries, ministers, civil servants or political advisers; correspondence with ministers; and drafts of speeches etc.

Papers preserved from Churchill's premiership are in PREM 4, those from Attlee's in PREM 8. Files dealing with wartime administration have not been listed and, in PREM 8, the file descriptions have frequently been abbreviated. Churchill's 'operations' files are in PREM 3, whilst the papers of the Defence Secretariat which served him, in his wartime capacity as Minister of Defence, are preserved separately in CAB 120.

For the diary of one of Churchill's private secretaries, see J. Colville, *The Fringes of Power, 1939–55* (1985). For further details of three particularly influential political advisers on economic issues, see R. Harrod, *The Prof: A personal memoir of Lord Cherwell* (1959), A.J.P. Taylor, *Beaverbrook* (1972), and D. Jay, *Change and Fortune* (1980).

17.1 Churchill's Papers

PREM 4

1/3	**Post-war agriculture.** Sept 1942–Oct 1943. Includes some papers by Cherwell.
1/5	**Article VII and the Wheat Act.** Feb–Mar 1944.
1/6	**Agricultural reconstruction.** Mar–Apr 1944. Includes first interim report of the Conservative Subcommittee on Agriculture with comments.
2/18	**Agriculture – various.** Dec 1942–June 1945. Includes papers on rations and on home food production.
6/5	**Consideration by War Cabinet of controversial bills.** Feb–Apr 1945.
6/9	**Cabinet committees – various.** Feb 1940–July 1945. Includes papers on proposed changes and the Machinery of Government Committee report on the Cabinet committee system.
8/6	**The role of the Treasury.** Aug 1943. Includes only MGO 24.
9/5	**Coal and manpower situations.** Nov 1940–May 1945. Includes papers on the recruitment of young boys and on the release of miners from the forces.
9/6	**Conservative Party coal policy.** Apr–June 1945.
9/7	**Coal – various.** Oct 1941–June 1945.
16/4	**Post-war budget.** Apr–May 1944. Cherwell on the post-war budget and the cost of commitments. Figures of expenditure incurred since 1 Mar 1943 for prospective and new legislation as requested by Churchill, with comments.
16/5	**Post-war finance for industry.** July–Nov 1944.

16/6	**Wage regulation. Trade Boards to become Wages Councils.** Nov 1944–Jan 1945.
16/7	**Anglo-French financial agreement.** Mar 1945. Papers leading up to Cmd. 6613.
16/12	**Control of expenditure.** Apr–June 1945. Papers on control after the end of European hostilities.
16/13	**Finance – various.** Sept 1940–May 1945. Includes papers on post-war national income, Cmd. 6520, financial statements, motor taxation and the postponement of the national savings campaign.
17/4	**International Clearing Union.** May 1942–Oct 1943. Papers leading up to Cmd. 6437.
17/6	**Interest-free loan from the U.S.A.** Apr–May 1944. Papers by Laws to Churchill with comments.
17/7	**U.N. bank for reconstruction and development. International investment bank.** June 1944.
17/8	**The I.M.F.** Apr–June 1944. Papers leading to Cmd. 6519 and resulting correspondence.
17/10	**Lord Beaverbrook's opposition to monetary policy.** Feb–Apr 1944. Includes comments on WP(44)95 and 148.
17/11	**Post-war economic co-operation.** Feb–Apr 1944. Various papers and telegrams on co-operation with the U.S.A.
17/12	**Secretary of State for India's memo covering monetary fund scheme and commercial union.** Apr–May 1944. Comments on various memoranda by Amery.
17/13	**Attempt at supersession of White Paper of 10 Sept 1941 on use of materials received under Lend-Lease Act.** May 1943–July 1944.
17/14	**The I.M.F.** Nov 1944–Jan 1945. Includes interim report of the F.B.I. and correspondence relating to Beaverbrook's description of it as a gold standard.
17/15	**Correspondence with President Truman on Lend-Lease arrangements.** May–July 1945. Papers relating to Lend-Lease in Stages II and III.
17/16	**Finance – various.** Dec 1943–July 1945. Largely on international aspects.
18/1	**Anglo-American discussions under Article VII of Mutual Aid Agreement.** July 1943–Mar 1944. Relevant Cabinet minutes and memoranda with some comments and correspondence.
18/2	**Discussions on Article VII of Mutual Aid Agreement with Dominions and India.** Dec 1943–Apr 1944.
18/3	**Mr. Stettinius's mission – Mar–Apr 1944.**
18/4	**Commercial policy – discussions under Article VII of Mutual Aid Agreement and imperial preference.** Jan 1943–Mar 1945. Includes relevant Cabinet minutes and memoranda with some comments and correspondence.
18/6	**Discussions on Lend-Lease Stage II (after the defeat of Germany).** Aug 1944–July 1945. Discussions between Roosevelt and Churchill, papers on British requirements and the resulting White Papers.
18/7	**Budget.** July 1940–Mar 1945. Little after 1942.
34/7	**Cabinet secretariat functions and division of duties.** Apr 1944–Feb 1945. Historical memoranda with commentary.
35/2A	**Future of wartime departments.** Aug 1944–Feb 1945. Some ministerial correspondence and relevant papers of the Machinery of Government Committee.

54/1   **Manpower situation – main file.**
Part 1   Mar 1941–Nov 1943. Mainly on military requirements.
Part 2   Mar 1941–Dec 1942. Mainly on military requirements.

54/2   **Manpower situation – main file.** Sept 1943–Dec 1944. Various papers on requirements during and after the war and on the release from the forces. Includes relevant Cabinet, Reconstruction Committee, Joint War Production Staff and Manpower Committee memoranda and minutes.

55/1   **Manpower situation – main file.** Nov 1943–July 1945. Papers on manpower one year after the defeat of Germany and on demobilization. Includes relevant Cabinet minutes and memoranda.

56/1   **Building programme and manpower.** July 1941–Apr 1945. Papers on demobilization and labour for building and on training for the industry. Includes relevant Cabinet minutes and memoranda.

56/2   **Demobilization.** Jan 1943–July 1945. Various papers on the reallocation of manpower, including consultation with industry and the T.U.C.

56/4   **Statistical Digest series D (Munitions Production and Manpower).** June 1941–July 1945.

56/5   **Manpower – various.** Aug 1940–May 1945.

57/6   **Ministers' speeches submitted for approval.** Jan–Dec 1943.

57/7   **Ministers' speeches and writings and general rulings.**
Part 1   June 1944–Jan 1945.
Part 2   Jan 1941–May 1944.

59/4   **Oil supplies and petrol rationing.** Jan 1940–Apr 1945.

62/4   **Legislative programme.** May 1945.

62/5   **Parliament – various.** Sept 1940–July 1945. Miscellanea.

63/2   **Machinery of government.** Apr 1942–Mar 1945.

69/2   **Prime Minister – various.** Apr 1941–Aug 1945. Miscellanea.

70/2   **Prime Minister's speeches.** Oct 1939–June 1945.

82/2   **The T.U.C. – consultations with.** June 1940–July 1945. Includes demobilization.

85/3   **Minister of Production – appointment and functions of Captain Lyttelton,** Mar 1942–Oct 1944. Includes consideration of the ministry's role during the transition and the relationship with the Board of Trade.

87/7   **Production – various.** Mar 1943–July 1945.

87/8   **Need for decisions on reconstruction.** Jan–Oct 1943. WP(43)255 and resulting comments by Churchill, Wood, Cherwell and E.E. Bridges.

87/9   **Departmental plans for transition period.** Oct–Nov 1943. Replies to WP(43)476.

87/10   **Office of Minister of Reconstruction.** Nov 1943. Papers on its establishment and representation on committees.

87/11   **Reconstruction in transition period – main file.** Sept 1943–Mar 1944. Includes discussions on machinery with Beaverbrook and Cherwell. Various papers on priorities and departmental schedules of schemes prior to R(44)45.

87/12   **Reconstruction booklet.** Nov 1944–July 1945.

87/13   **Reconstruction – various.** Oct 1942–Oct 1943.

88/1   **Reconstruction Problems Committee.** Dec 1940–Dec 1944. List of committees concerned with reconstruction problems, Sept 1942. Various papers on reconstruction and the establishment of a single Reconstruction Committee. Churchill on Labour domination of the Reconstruction Committee.

88/2   **Relaxation and retention of controls.** Aug 1944–May 1945. Includes papers by Beaverbrook on controls with comments. Gap to May 1945 and then on renewal of emergency powers.

88/4   **Reconstruction – various.** Dec 1940–Apr 1945. Includes Ministry of Information 'Public feeling on post-war reconstruction', Nov 1942 and various papers on the presentation of reconstruction and the supply of goods for civilian consumption.

89/1   **Financial aspects of social security plan.** Jan 1943. Papers leading to RP(43)5.

89/2   **Beveridge Report on Social Insurance and Allied Services. Part 1.** Nov 1942. Cmd. 6404.

89/2   **Beveridge Report on Social Insurance and Allied Services. Part 2.** Nov 1942–Apr 1943. Cmd. 6405 and various papers on the White Paper.

90/3   **U.K. stock levels and import programme.** Nov 1944–Mar 1945. Papers mainly on the import programme and the shipping situation.

90/8   **Status of U.K. import programme as Combined Chiefs of Staff's basic objective.** July 1945.

90/9   **Coal in Europe.** Apr–July 1945.

90/10 **Stocks and supplies – various.** May–June 1945.

93/1   **Reconstruction Committee – various papers.** Aug–Sept 1944. On housing.

93/2   **Lord Beaverbrook's committee on prefabricated houses.** Sept 1944.

93/3   **Emergency housing in the transitional period.** Feb–Oct 1944.

93/4   **Machinery for co-ordination and control of housing.** Sept–Nov 1944. Includes papers on standardization and bulk purchase of fitments.

93/5   **Simplified brick construction.** Oct–Nov 1944.

93/6   **Prefabricated houses from the U.S.A.** Oct 1944–Jan 1945.

93/7   **Prefabricated houses from Sweden.** Dec 1944–Mar 1945.

93/8   **Housing squad (ministerial committee).** Nov 1944–July 1945.

93/9   **Housing – various.** Jan 1942–July 1945. Includes papers on division of ministerial responsibility and progress.

94/8   **Committee on Distribution of Industry.** Nov 1944. Papers on its composition and terms of reference arising out of Cmd. 6527.

94/10 **Trade – various.** Sept 1941–June 1945.

95/1   **International regulation of primary products.** Feb–May 1943.

95/2   **Anglo-American discussions under Article VII of Mutual Aid Agreement.** Dec 1943.

95/3   **Overseas resources and liabilities – Ministerial Subcommittee on Industrial Problems (Export Questions).** July–Nov 1944. Includes some minutes and memoranda.

95/4   **Economic co-ordination and exports – various.** Dec 1939–July 1945. Includes Cherwell on increased U.K. export targets depending on the decision about the future of Japanese and German industry.

95/9   **Clothing policy.** May 1943–July 1945.

96/5   **Location of industry.** Jan–Apr 1944.

96/6   **White Paper on employment policy.** Nov 1943–June 1944. Drafts of the White Paper leading to Cmd. 6527. Includes Woolton on the need for speed and Cherwell's comments on the drafts.

96/7   **Distribution of Industry Bill.** Nov 1944–June 1945. Includes papers by Dalton with comments by Beaverbrook and Cherwell.

96/8   **Employment policy – various.** Nov 1943–Jan 1945. Includes various publications.

17.2 Attlee's Papers

PREM 8

12	**Committee on Oil.** Aug–Sept 1945.
13	**Housing Committee.** Aug–Sept 1945.
14	**Prime Minister's note about the standing ministerial committees.** Nov–Dec 1945. Drafts leading to CP(45)333.
17	**Civil Service and Treasury control.** Dec 1942–Nov 1945. Includes some Machinery of Government Committee memoranda and correspondence between Morrison and Attlee.
18	**Appreciation on coal situation. Effect on street lighting.** Aug 1945. Papers arising out of request from Attlee and leading to LP(45)132.
19	**Effect of shortage of railway wagons on the coal situation.** Sept–Nov 1945. Includes relevant Lord President's Committee memoranda and papers by Jay.
20	**Supplies and Services (Transitional Powers) Bill.** Oct 1944–Oct 1945. Drafts with relevant Cabinet minutes and memoranda. In 1944 Churchill felt that given the importance of economic controls in the transition he should answer parliamentary questions on the Bill.
25	**Hydro-electric development in Scotland.** Aug 1945.
35	**Correspondence and discussions with President Truman at Terminal on the subject of Lend-Lease munitions in Stage II. Negotiations with government of Canada following end of Mutual Aid. Lord Keynes's proposal to the U.S.A. for financial assistance. Exchange of telegrams with Prime Minister of New Zealand.** Aug–Nov 1945. Includes relevant Cabinet minutes and memoranda, some memoranda of GEN 89 and various notes on commercial policy, including some by Jay and J.E. Meade.
36	**International wheat supplies.** Oct–Nov 1945.
37	**Food policy and future of the Ministry of Food.** Oct 1945.
38	**Labour for the flour milling industry.** Aug–Sept 1945.
53	**Ministerial responsibility for housing: Parliamentary Counsel's opinion.** Aug–Oct 1945. Demarcation between the Ministries of Works and Health.
72	**Legislative programme for 1946/47 session.** Dec 1945. Includes correspondence between Morrison and Attlee.
73	**Reduction of redundant personnel in the services.** Aug 1945.
74	**Release from the munitions industries.** Aug–Oct 1945.
75	**Publication of information about the demobilization scheme.** Sept 1945.
76	**Report on release from forces June–Nov.** Oct–Dec 1945.
77	**Returns for demobilization.** Sept–Dec 1945. Lack of key local authority technical staff was delaying housing.
78	**Representations from Labour M.P.s for increase in releases.** Aug–Oct 1945.
79	**Review of manpower situation.** Aug–Oct 1945. Papers relating to the end of the Japanese war and demobilization.
80	**Reduction of civilian building labour employed by service departments.** Aug–Oct 1945.

81   **Future of labour controls.** Sept–Dec 1945. Includes relevant Cabinet minutes and memoranda with notes by the Ministry of Labour, pressing for relaxation, and Jay.

92   **Stocks of petroleum spirit.** Dec 1945.

100   **Post-war organization of government publicity abroad.** Aug–Sept 1945.

125   **Agriculture Bill.** Nov 1945–Dec 1946. Relevant Cabinet and Lord President's Committee minutes and memoranda, drafts, and briefs to Attlee.

126   **Agricultural wage increase.** Jan–July 1946. Includes relevant Cabinet and Lord President's Committee minutes and memoranda, notes on agricultural minimum wage and a meeting with the Agriculture and Food Group of the Labour Party.

127   **Transfer of Short Bros. from Rochester to Northern Ireland.** May–June 1946. Papers relating to consideration by the Distribution of Industry Subcommittee of the Lord President's Committee.

152   **Ministerial Coal Committee.** Sept–Dec 1946. Includes ministerial correspondence on the duplication of work by the Lord President's Committee and the Ministerial Committee on Coal for the Coming Winter leading to the establishment of the Coal Committee.

153   **Functions of the Legislation Committee.** May–June 1946.

156   **Future of the steel industry: leakage of information.** Apr–May 1946.

159   **Possibility of easing clothes rationing.** Aug–Sept 1946. Correspondence between Attlee and Cripps following a request by Bevin.

161   **Supply of consumer goods for coal-miners: incentives to production.** Nov 1945–July 1946. Includes relevant Lord President's Committee minutes and memoranda, GEN 105/5, a critical note by Jay and a draft Board of Trade paper on shortages, needs and wishes of miners.

163   **Bulk purchase of cotton.** Mar–Nov 1946. Includes relevant Cabinet and Lord President's Committee minutes and memoranda, 'The government and the control of raw cotton purchases' by the Manchester Cotton Association and drafts, with notes, of the Cotton (Centralized Buying) Bill.

195   **Balance of payments 1946: import programme international commodity policy.** Dec 1945–Nov 1946. Includes relevant Cabinet minutes and memoranda, some with briefs, and various notes by Jay.

196   **Negotiations with Canada for a new loan.** Feb–Mar 1946.

197   **Mr. Churchill talks with the U.S.A. about American loan to Britain.** Feb–Mar 1946.

198   **Composition of U.K. delegation to food and agriculture conference: instructions to Dr. Summerskill, head of delegation.** Mar–June 1946.

199   **Negotiations of long-term wheat contract with Canada.** Mar–July 1946.

200   **Ministry of Food to take over responsibility for publicity on food matters.** Feb–July 1946.

202   **World food supplies. Lord President's mission to the U.S.A. and Canada: wheat supplies for Germany and India.** Apr–June 1946. Includes some papers on bread rationing and the extraction rate.

203   **Oils and fats position.** Feb–June 1946.

205   **Possible measures to economize on use of wheat in the U.K.: bread rationing.** Mar–May 1946. Includes relevant Cabinet and World Food Shortage Committee minutes and memoranda and views of Jay.

207   **Change in standard loaf: effect on cost of living index.** Mar–Apr 1946.

209   **Possibility of obtaining more food from the Argentine if transport difficulties can be eased.** Feb–Mar 1946.

214   **Co-ordination of the German economy with the U.K.** 1946.

226   **Timber for housing: export of timber from Germany and from Austria to the U.K.** Jan–Nov 1946.

228   **Proposed statement of policy by Minister of Health. Draft White Paper on temporary housing plan. Programme of permanent houses to be built by local authorities. Proposals to set up a National Building Corporation.** Oct 1945–Aug 1946.

229   **Shortage of bricks: release of brick makers from the forces.** Mar–July 1946.

230   **Report on slate industry in North Wales by Mr. Ness Edwards.** Mar–May 1946.

231   **Housing return for Feb and Mar 1946.** Mar–May 1946. Includes various progress and statistical reports.

232   **Proposal to set up a housing executive for the co-ordination and control of housing materials, components and labour.** Apr 1946.

233   **Measure to improve the low output of bricklayers in Glasgow.** Mar–Apr 1946.

234   **Minister of Labour, Minister of Works and Minister of Health met the Federation of Building Trades Operatives with a view to removing demarcation difficulties during the period of labour shortage.** Jan–Mar 1946.

235   **Outstanding difficulties to be discussed between the Ministers of Health and Works resulting in the outlining of departmental responsibilities for housing.** Jan–Feb 1946.

267   **Carrying over of uncompleted public bills to next session.** Mar 1946.

269   **Reduction of staff in Civil Service.** Sept 1945–July 1946.

271   **Releases from the forces and from munitions.** Sept 1945–Jan 1946.

272   **Unemployment in Wales and Monmouthshire: deputation to the Prime Minister by M.P.s from Welsh constituencies.** July–Sept 1946. Includes transcript.

273   **Release of R.A.F. camp at Carluke for use by Minister of Labour as industrial training centre.** Sept 1946.

274   **Distribution of doctors and nurses between the armed forces and the civilian community.** Aug 1945–June 1946.

275   **Use of foreign manpower in armed forces and essential services.** Jan–May 1946.

276   **Allocation of raw materials to industries in development areas. Also Greater London plans.** Jan 1945–Feb 1946. Includes notes by Jay on the employment situation and correspondence between Morrison and Attlee on allocation preference for development areas.

277   **Failure to reduce manpower employed on supplies and equipment to the forces.** Jan 1945–Feb 1946.

278   **Distribution of industry: maximum pressure on industry to move to development areas.** Dec 1945–Jan 1946. Includes comments by Attlee, Jay, Dalton and Cripps on LP(I)(45)11.

293   **Committee on the Socialization of Industries.** Dec 1945–Mar 1946.

294   **Boards of government-controlled enterprises and the holding of directorships by their members.** Jan 1946.

421   Chairmanship of Manpower Committee which Foreign Secretary would like to give up. Recommendations for additional members. July 1945–Jan 1947.

422   Changes in Cabinet committees as a result of Sir Stafford Cripps's appointment as Minister of Economic Affairs. Sept–Dec 1947. Also includes changes Dec 1947 on Cripps's appointment as Chancellor of the Exchequer.

423   Investment Programmes Committee. Aug–Dec 1947. Papers on its establishment and reconstitution as a standing committee, including concern of Bevan.

424   Fuel Allocations Committee. June–Oct 1947.

425   Setting up of Fuel (Official) Committee. July–Sept 1947.

426   Setting up of Fuel Committee and membership of Fuel Committee. Feb–May 1947. Includes papers on the committee's procedure once the coal crisis was over and longer-term problems could be considered.

427   Prime Minister's directive re President of the Board of Trade taking over chairmanship of information service committees and in charge of publicity in Lord President's absence. Jan–Mar 1947.

428   Mr. A. Bevan, Minister of Health, expressed dissatisfaction at the present method of taking minutes of Cabinet meetings. July–Oct 1947.

437   Prime Minister considered it was not appropriate for him to correct misleading press statements concerning confidential advice given by economists to the government during the war. Apr–May 1947.

438   Proposed extension of working hours to increase production in the coal-mining industry. Aug–Sept 1947.

439   Discussion on regional reform of the N.C.B. and departmental responsibility for placing orders for mining machinery. July–Aug 1947.

440   Proposal to give food rations to miners. Recruitment for the mines. Substitution of fuel oil for coal. Effect of five-day week on production. Feb 1946–Mar 1947. Includes some minutes and memoranda of the Cabinet, GEN 94 and GEN 126. Various papers by Jay and the Economic Section.

441   Prime Minister wished to know reason for delay in importing 28 austerity locomotives from Europe to help in moving coal. Feb 1947.

442   Prime Minister asked about the progress being made in the reduction of stocks of open-cast coal. Ministry of Fuel and Power sent a report. Jan 1947.

443   Coal crisis (main file).
Part 1 Feb 1947. Setting up of the Fuel Committee and daily reports on the fuel situation.
Part 2 Feb–Mar 1947. Further Fuel Committee memoranda, related papers, including some on rationing, and reports.
Part 3 Mar–June 1947.
Part 4 June–Oct 1947. Papers concerning winter 1947–48.

444   Delays in supply of mining machinery and equipment. Feb–Nov 1947. Papers arising out of N.U.M. complaints.

445   Imports of coal from South Africa. Delivery of coal wagons to South Africa. Mar–Oct 1947.

446   Coal allocations for industry. Mar–Oct 1947. Includes relevant Cabinet and Fuel Committee minutes and memoranda, some with briefs.

447   **Transport of coal.** Feb–Oct 1947. Includes reports on the transport situation and correspondence between Attlee and Barnes on the effects of the five-day week on the transport situation.

448   **Staggering the hours of work in order to ease the industrial electricity load.** Feb–Oct 1947. Includes relevant Fuel Committee minutes and memoranda, some with briefs. Also the report of the Electricity Subcommittee of the Joint Consultative Committee and correspondence between Attlee and Isaacs.

449   **Offer from the U.S.A. to divert coal to this country on route to Europe. Possibility of imports of coal from the U.S.A. and Poland.** Feb–Sept 1947.

450   **Restriction on street lighting.** Apr–June 1947.

451   **Auxiliary generating sets for use in factories.** Apr–June 1947.

452   **Restoration of B.B.C. services.** Feb–Apr 1947. Includes papers on the initial restriction of hours.

453   **Export of U.K. coal and coke to Eire.** Feb–Apr 1947.

454   **Telegrams between the King and Prime Minister re fuel crisis. Press message issued at the King's request.** Feb–Mar 1947.

455   **Coal (N.U.M.).**
Part 1 Feb–May 1947. Agreement of Attlee to the N.U.M.'s request to attend the Fuel Committee and T.L. Rowan's views on the importance of the meeting with regard to the future of planning. Also papers on the five-day week.
Part 2 July–Aug 1947. Further papers on the five-day week and note of N.U.M. and N.C.B. meeting, 30 July 1947.
Part 3 Aug–Oct 1947. Papers on the failure to agree on extra working time and notes of meetings with the N.U.M. and the N.C.B., 21 Aug 1947.

456   **Overlapping of functions between the Colonial Development Corporation and Overseas Food Corporation to develop Colonial resources.** Oct 1947.

457   **Project for a Colonial Development Corporation and Overseas Food Corporation to develop Colonial resources.** Mar–Aug 1947. Includes papers on the ground-nuts scheme.

491   **Report of the Investment Programmes Committee.** Aug–Nov 1947. Includes relevant Cabinet and Production Committee minutes and memoranda, briefs and departmental criticisms of individual programmes leading to Cmd. 7268.

492   **Supplies and Services (Transitional Powers) Bill to extend the Supplies and Services (Transitional Powers) Act 1945. The King raised question re scope of Bill.** Aug–Oct 1947. Includes drafts of Attlee's reply.

493   **Inter-departmental organization for handling balance of payments questions.** Aug–Oct 1947. Papers leading to CP(47)255 and 287, including Bevin's comments.

495   **Discussions on economic recovery of Europe. Talks with Mr. Clayton. The Marshall Plan for U.S. aid.** June–Oct 1947. Includes minutes and memoranda of GEN 179 and briefs and telegrams from various discussions on Marshall Aid.

496   **Establishment of a working party to handle the U.K. case in the discussions arising from the Marshall offer.** July 1947. Proposal by Bevin leading to GEN 188.

501   **Guidance to the U.K. delegates to the Preparatory Commission of the F.A.O. and the final report.** Oct 1946–Feb 1947.

502   Introduction of scheme for rationing bread and other cereals. Supplies
        of wheat and flour for the U.K. May 1946–Apr 1947. Includes relevant
        Cabinet minutes and memoranda, some briefs, including some
        criticism by Jay and papers on when rationing should be rescinded.

503   A request by the Prime Minister that other sources of bacon supplies
        apart from Denmark, Canada and home production in the U.K. should
        be considered. Nov 1947.

505   Consideration of the purchase of a percentage of food and raw materials
        through commercial buying rather than government bulk purchase.
        Aug–Oct 1947. Includes notes on the views of Cripps and Strachey.

506   Food prospects for 1947 and need for new approach to the U.S.A. for
        further supplies. Minister of Food's visit to America and Canada. Oct
        1946–Aug 1947. Includes relevant Cabinet minutes and memoranda,
        some briefs and correspondence between Attlee and Williams.

507   Prime Minister asked Minister of Food to give fuller explanations of
        delays and failure of shipments in the food situation reports. May 1947.

509   Heavy run-down of stocks of food by April 1947. Chancellor of Exchequer
        to bring before Lord President's Committee. Mar 1947.

510   Farmers in the U.K. to be encouraged to increase their production of
        livestock, eggs, etc. despite difficulties over feedingstuffs and labour.
        Jan–Mar 1947.

516   Suggestion by M. Bidault that commercial and financial negotiations
        should be opened in Paris between British and French delegations. Letter
        from M. Blum to Prime Minister re coal export. 1946–47.

530   The Ministry of Works to take over the responsibility for production
        and distribution of building materials and components. May–Sept 1947.
        Papers leading to CP(47)276.

531   Priority for housing to be given to miners, agricultural workers and key
        workers in development areas. Feb–Sept 1947. Includes correspondence
        between Attlee and Bevan on the need for accommodation.

532   *The Times* published three articles on the housing programme which the
        Prime Minister referred to the ministers concerned for comment.
        Apr–May 1947.

533   Meeting of ministers to be held to review progress in housing. Nov
        1946–Feb 1947.

534   Housing campaign in Scotland. Dec 1946–Jan 1947.

589   Amendments to Industrial Organization Bill. Feb–Apr 1947.

590   Proposal to set up emergency power station at Woolwich using German
        plant and Admiralty boilers. Alternative site at Croydon. Project dropped.
        June–Sept 1947.

591   Proposal to construct a power station at Bankside. Rotherhithe suggested
        as alternative site. Prime Minister saw deputation of Labour M.P.s. Nov
        1946–July 1947. Includes correspondence between Attlee and Shinwell.

599   Prime Minister received a deputation from the Agricultural and Food
        Group of the Parliamentary Labour Party on 9 Dec 1947. Notes and
        detailed brief.

605   Employment of prison labour. Nov 1947. Attlee proposed discussion of
        PC(47)16 with the T.U.C.

606   Direction of manpower and the Control of Engagement Order. Aug–Oct
        1947. Includes relevant Cabinet minutes and memoranda and some
        briefs.

607   Double day-shift working in factories. Oct 1944–June 1947. Gap from 1944 to Mar 1947 then papers, including ones by Cripps and Isaacs, leading to Cmd. 7147.

608   Reduction in the Navy and dispositions of the Fleet. Oct–Dec 1947.

609   Proposals for call-up during the transitional period. Manpower requirements of the three services. Mar 1946–Nov 1947.

610   Introduction of a permanent scheme for compulsory national service. Prime Minister's name to appear as supporter of bill. Sept 1946–May 1947. Includes papers on the cost.

615   Functions of Mr. H.A. Marquand in his appointment as Paymaster General. Feb–Aug 1947. From Feb 1947 the functions were to assist the Lord President and, from Mar, to look after finance, fiscal policy and the machinery of planning and to liaise with the party.

619   Nationalization. Prime Minister received a deputation from the Association of Municipal Corporations about compensation for nationalization of electricity, gas and transport undertakings. Feb–July 1947.

620   T.U.C. objection to part-time appointments to Boards of Socialized industries. Mar–Apr 1947.

621   Proposal for the nationalization of transport. Transport Bill. Oct 1945–July 1947.

636   The F.B.I. represented that the time at present allowed between publication of bills and the date of the second reading was insufficient. Feb–Mar 1947.

638   Relations between the Public Relations Adviser at No. 10 and Chief of the Economic Information Unit. Oct–Dec 1947. Papers leading to EPC(47)14.

639   Minister of Agriculture's request that priority be given to production of agricultural machinery to aid food production. Aug–Oct 1947. Includes correspondence between Attlee and Williams and papers leading to CP(47)273.

640   Investigation into the working of the existing machinery for controlling issue of steel and iron to manufacturers. Aug–Oct 1947. Includes relevant Cabinet minutes and memoranda with some briefs and Wilmot on the distribution scheme.

641   Memorandum by the F.B.I., 'Industry and the Way to Recovery'. Aug–Sept 1947. Includes note of a meeting with the F.B.I., 5 Sept 1947.

642   Functions of C.E.P.S. under Sir Edwin Plowden and decision whether it is to be part of Cabinet Office or Lord President's Office. Mar–July 1947. Includes disagreement between E.E. Bridges and E.M. Nicholson. T.L. Rowan felt that it should retain an inter-departmental nature.

643   Reports from the F.B.I. and the T.U.C. on the economic situation. The T.U.C. had discussions with the Prime Minister and other ministers. Mar–June 1947. Includes F.B.I. 'Interim Statement on the Economic Outlook', T.U.C. 'Report of the Special Committee on the Fuel Crisis and the Economic Situation' and verbatim report of the meeting with the T.U.C., 7 May 1947.

644   Purchase of civil engineering plant (mainly excavators) for open-cast coal production from the U.S.A. Purchase of U.S. surplus stocks of excavators, etc. in Germany. Mar–May 1947.

646   White Paper on economic planning. Cabinet decision on raising the school-leaving age. Employment of women. Debate on Economic Survey

	for **1947.** Dec 1946–Apr 1947. Includes some Cabinet and GEN 169 minutes and memoranda, papers on whether the survey would be published, drafts of its foreword. Also notes for the economic debate and on the strengthening of the economic planning staff.
647	**Service requirements of clothing and other equipment in short civilian supply. Prime Minister revised procedure for dealing with the matter.** Mar–Apr 1947.
649	**Ministerial Committee on Home Information Services. Answer to statements in the press.** 1947.
659	**Functions of Chiefs of Staff in regard to financial ceiling for defence estimates and strength of the armed forces. Prime Minister's discussion with Secretary of State for War and Minister of Defence.** 1947.
664	**Shipping prospects for 1946. Priority to be given in first three months to food imports. Prime Minister commented on large tonnage allocated for military purposes and asked the services to propose reductions.** Jan 1946–Jan 1947.
668	**Anglo–Soviet trade.** 1947.
670	**Foreign Secretary saw M. Stalin on 24 Mar 1947 about Anglo-Soviet trade.** 1947.
672	**Road transport strikes.** Jan 1947.
677	**Prime Minister to see T.U.C. deputation to discuss general question of closer consultation between the government and the T.U.C.** Oct 1946–Jan 1947. Notes of meetings 14 Oct and 29 Nov 1946 on the procedure of consultation on increasing miners' rations. Papers leading to CP(47)46 and T.U.C. reaction.
712B	**Deputation from National Farmers' Union headed by Mr. James Turner, President, saw the Prime Minister for discussion on agricultural wages policy and agricultural machinery.** 1947–48.
722	**Question of which committees the new Chancellor of the Duchy of Lancaster, Mr. Hugh Dalton, should become a member.** June 1948.
723	**Alteration in membership of ministerial Committees on Home Information Services and Overseas Information Services. Proposed amalgamation of the two committees.** Oct 1947–Mar 1948.
727	**N.C.B. proposal to introduce differential prices for various grades and qualities of coal. Effect on railways and other socialized industries. etc.** May–July 1948.
728	**Working of open-cast coal in Wentworth Woodhouse Park. Prime Minister saw Lord Fitzwilliam. Protest letters from the N.U.M., etc.** Jan 1946–May 1948.
729	**Coal prospects for winter of 1946/47. Consideration by ministerial committee of means to obtain further economies in civilian and industrial consumption of coal.** Oct 1946–Feb 1948. Includes some minutes and memoranda of the Cabinet and GEN 94. Also Cripps on the need for a compulsory scheme and Shinwell on coal prospects. Gap from Feb 1947 to Feb 1948.
730	**The Prime Minister decided to see representatives of the main firms manufacturing electric generating plant.** Feb 1947–Mar 1948. Papers leading to and resulting from GEN 172/1st.
737	**Prime Minister invited representatives of the cotton industry for discussions at No. 10.** Mar–Apr 1948. Includes the report of the Study Group on Cotton Productivity on manpower utilization in the cotton spinning industry, notes for and transcript of meeting, 22 Mar 1948.

738 **Discussions on wages for cotton industry following the publication of the Evershed Commission report.** Feb 1946–Feb 1948. Papers arising out of the report and on reconversion and expansion of civilian production.

752 **Size and shape of peace-time armed forces and future defence policy for basis of 1948 White Paper.** 1947–48.

759 **Future policy for the royal dockyards. Statement on the future of Rosyth as a naval dockyard in peace-time.** 1945–48.

763 **Electricity peak-load problem and increase in prices. Proposed statement on the report of the Clow Committee.** Aug 1947–July 1948. Papers leading to statement by the Minister of Fuel and Power.

767 **Consultation with the Commonwealth on matters arising on long-term planning and E.R.P.** July–Oct 1948. Includes a report on sterling area planning and papers on arrangements for consultation, including the meeting of Commonwealth prime ministers.

768 **Draft Economic Co-operation Agreement between the U.K. and the U.S.A. in connection with E.R.P. June–July 1948.** Includes relevant Economic Policy Committee minutes and memoranda, some briefs, telegrams with Washington and other papers leading up to Cmd. 7446 and Cmd. 7447.

769 **Revised inter-departmental committee organization following passing of Economic Co-operation Act.** May–June 1948. Papers leading to CP(48)137.

770 **U.K. organization for E.R.P. in Washington, Paris, Brussels and London.** Mar–Apr 1948.

771 **Proposed South African loan following on economic crisis 1947 over balance of payments.** Aug 1947–Feb 1948.

772 **Question of increasing food prices to limit expenditure on food subsidies.** Aug 1947–Feb 1948. Includes relevant Cabinet minutes and memoranda, with briefs on increasing prices and their reconsideration after the *Statement on Personal Incomes and Prices.*

773 **Balance of payments – the dollar programme and food imports in 1948.** Oct 1947–Feb 1948.

774 **Revised export programme after economic crisis. Collection of scrap of iron and steel industry. Textiles exports.** Sept 1947–Jan 1948. Includes Wilmot's report on scrap.

775 **F.A.O. annual conference at Washington Nov 1948. Minister of Agriculture to attend.** Sept–Oct 1948.

776 **Sir John Barlow M.P. wrote to Mr. Moyle about the ground-nut scheme in view of his recent visit to Africa. Minister of Food to visit Tanganyika.** Mar–July 1948.

777 **Legislation to confer permanent powers on Ministry of Food to set up Commodity Commissions as proposed by Lucas Committee to amend Agriculture Marketing Acts.** Apr–May 1948.

778 **Proposals for regulating the distribution of potatoes. 'Grow more food' campaign by National Allotments and Gardens Society – with particular reference to potatoes.** Oct 1947–Apr 1948.

779 **Proposed reduction in the scale of rations for services. Prime Minister minuted service ministers about the prevention of food wastage. Revised overseas ration scales.** Sept 1945–Mar 1948.

780   Prime Minister asked for particulars about the failure of the maize crop in the U.S.A. and its probable effect on the availability of feedingstuffs for the livestock programme. Sept 1947–Mar 1948.

782   Nutritional aspects of food policy. Suggestion of appointment of a scientific advisory committee on food problems (not proceeded with). Official machinery for expansion of world supplies. Oct 1947–Feb 1948.

789   Proposals of the French government for devaluation of the franc. Jan 1948.

793   Supplies of timber from Germany to the U.K. Closing down of North German Timber Control in Sept 1948. Export agreement to be made with Americans for German timber. June 1946–Apr 1948.

796   Accommodation for Minister of State for Economic Affairs and his staff. Sept 1947–Feb 1948.

824   Discussions in London with Mr. De Valera and Ministers for Industry and Commerce, Finance and Agriculture on economic and financial questions. Trade agreement between the two governments. 1947–48.

830   Alleged lack of Co-operative representation on the National Planning Board and on government committees and commissions generally. Prime Minister received deputation from Liaison Committee of the National Council of Labour. Aug 1947–Mar 1948. Papers leading to Attlee's rejection of Co-operative Movement representation.

831   Regional staffs of some ministries considered excessive. Investigation by Civil Service Manpower Committee. Report by Sir Horace Hamilton. Apr 1947–May 1948. Various papers on regional organization of departments.

832   Polish Resettlement Corps. Placing of Polish forces in civil employment. Foreign Labour Committee discussions – manpower. Feb 1946–Jan 1948.

833   Reduction of armed forces overseas and in the U.K. Part I July–Sept 1947. Part II Sept 1947–May 1948.

834   Minister of Defence's paper on plan of manpower requirements in the services in the first three months of possible emergency. Chiefs of Staff discussions on the state of the forces. July–Sept 1948.

836   Prime Minister appealed to demobilized forces to get back into productive employment as soon as possible. Sept 1947–Jan 1948.

846   Prime Minister suggested closer co-operation between management and workers in socialized industries deserved attention of Socialization of Industry Committee. Nov–Dec 1948.

847   Parliamentary enquiries about socialized industries. May–Nov 1947.

848   Prime Minister invited Socialization of Industry Committee to consider future functions and composition of ministries responsible for such industries. Jan–Feb 1948.

849   Proposed measures for nationalization of electricity and gas industries. Electricity Bill – vesting date 1 Apr 1948. Oct 1945–Feb 1948.

854   Negotiations on bulk purchase of food supplies from New Zealand. May–June 1948.

855   Norway – proposals for closer economic co-operation with the U.K. July–Nov 1948.

856   Liaison with oil companies for distribution and dissolution of Petroleum Board. July 1947–Apr 1948.

857   Review of Anglo-American Oil Agreement. Sept 1945–Jan 1948. Gap from Nov 1945 to Jan 1948.

876   Extension of stay of German prisoners of war (due for repatriation) who are working in agriculture in England. Mar 1948. Includes correspondence from Williams.

877   Progress report on industrial productivity. Joint Anglo-American Council on Productivity. June–Oct 1948. Includes papers on the establishment of the Council, Government Organization Committee report on co-ordination of government activities for the promotion of industrial productivity and correspondence between Morrison and Attlee.

878   Possibility of increasing the output of scrap from ship-breaking and question of securing adequate supplies of scrap and pig iron for the U.K. iron and steel industry, in particular from Germany. Dec 1947–July 1948. Includes correspondence between Attlee, Cripps and Strauss and papers leading to and resulting from CP(48)99.

879   Supply of heavy electrical generating plant with particular reference to the effect of export orders on supply of plant to home stations. Feb 1947–Apr 1948. Includes papers on coal/oil conversion.

880   Economic Survey for 1948. Dec 1947–Apr 1948. Includes various drafts and briefs leading to Cmd. 7344.

881   Prohibition of the use of fuel for the purposes of dog racing during coal crisis. Discussions regarding suspension of mid-week sports in 1947 and 1948. Relaxation of restrictions on passenger train services. Jan 1947–Feb 1948.

882   Prime Minister issued directive giving priority for labour and raw materials to projects aimed at expansion of fuel and power resources. Allocation of resources, including steel priority system. Mar 1947–Jan1948. Papers arising out of CP(47)92(revise).

883   Release of civil engineering equipment by the three service departments, primarily for house building, factory construction and open-cast coal working. Sept 1946–Jan 1948. Includes some minutes and memoranda of GEN 152, and Morrison on plant shortage.

895   Surpluses of government stores and disposal to public. Report on progress by General Lindsell and Major-General Geake. Sept 1945–July 1948.

900   Memorandum on the establishment of new towns in two areas of South Wales. Sept 1948.

903   T.U.C. complaint about the Prime Minister's statement on wages policy being issued without prior consultation with them. Feb–Apr 1948. Correspondence between Attlee and Tewson and notes of meetings with the Special Committee of the T.U.C., 11 Feb 1948, and with the General Council, 23 Mar 1948.

925   Prime Minister queries the Minister of Agriculture's amendments to the Agriculture Marketing Bill. Provision for interests of the consumer to be adequately represented on the Boards. Mar–Apr 1949.

949   Size of the clothing ration. Reduction in exports of cotton. Feb 1946–Oct 1949. Includes relevant Cabinet minutes and memoranda, some with briefs, a report on exports and drafts of statements on extent of rationing.

951   Commonwealth consultation on foreign and economic affairs, defence and other matters. 1948–49.

961   Price of coal exported to Denmark increased by the N.C.B. because of the devaluation of the pound. Oct–Nov 1949.

971   Consideration of possibility of relaxing import controls. Apr–Dec 1949. Includes relevant Cabinet and Economic Policy Committee minutes

and memoranda, some with briefs, and drafts of statement by the President of the Board of Trade.

972   **Notification to Commonwealth, Southern Rhodesia and Ireland of devaluation of the pound.** Sept–Oct 1949.

973   **Devaluation of the pound (main file).** Sept–Oct 1949. Includes the reports of the Working Party on Wages Policy and Devaluation and of the Official Working Party on Price Structure after Devaluation. Also various telegrams and notes on the Washington talks, arrangements for informing various bodies and draft of Cripps's broadcast.

974   **Increase in price of bread due to devaluation of the pound. Proposals concerning a reduction in the extraction rate of wheat and an increase in family allowance rejected.** Sept 1949.

975   **Meeting of Commonwealth finance ministers to discuss deterioration in the U.K. dollar situation in July 1949.** June–Aug 1949. Papers on the arrangements and briefs for the meeting. Minutes and memoranda of the meetings (EMM(49)1st–17th and EMM(49)1–28) attached.

976   **Bank of England view of the success of alteration of sterling/dollar exchange rate.** Aug 1949.

978   **Trade negotiations with Canada. Exports during 1948. Discussions in London by Continuing Committee Jan 1949.** Nov 1947–May 1949.

979   **Economic bulletin to be issued by Economic Information Unit. Covering note by Prime Minister to first issue.** Nov 1947–Mar 1949. Includes an enquiry into Ministers' use of bulletin.

980   **Memorandum on the E.R.P. prepared by the London Committee based on the Marshall Plan. Instructions to U.K. delegation in setting up a continuing organization of the E.R.P.** Dec 1947–Jan 1949.

981   **Proposed reduction in cheese ration in summer. Announcement of increased cheese ration on 9 May 1949.** Apr 1946–May 1949. Gap between April 1946 and May 1949.

1019   **Recruitment of foreign labour from among displaced persons in Europe.** Jan 1947–Jan 1949. Includes correspondence between Attlee and Isaacs.

1021   **Size of the armed forces in the next three years. Extension of national service. Financial provision for defence in 1949/50.** Aug 1948–Jan 1949.

1027   **Letter from the Chancellor of the Exchequer about the question of an early election.** July 1949.

1039   **Suggested action to counter current criticisms of nationalized industries.** June–Nov 1941.

1040   **Gas Bill parts 1 and 2.** Apr 1947–Nov 1949.

1048   **Oil and the balance of payments plan for 1948.** Nov 1947–Feb 1949.

1057   **Recall of parliament to debate the economic situation Sept 1949.** Sept 1949.

1060   **Abolition and restoration of basic petrol rationing. Report of the Russell Vick Committee on the black market in petrol.** Aug 1947–Mar 1949. Includes note of a meeting 1 April 1948 on legislation for black market offences.

1062   **Removal of iron and steel subsidies. Statement in the House.** Jan–Mar 1949.

1064   **Concern at cost of government home and overseas information services. Report of the (French) Committee (Cmd. 7836).** Aug 1948–Nov 1949.

1065   **Wage claim by the National Union of Railwaymen.** Sept 1948–May 1949.

1075	**Resumption of Anglo-Soviet trade negotiations. Further negotiations with the U.S.S.R. June 1948.** 1947–49.
1082	**Strikes which threaten the supply of electricity. Question of enforced contracts of service in essential industries.** Feb–Oct 1949.
1110	**Wages policy, prices and profits on devaluation of the pound.** Sept 1949. Includes meeting between Cripps and the employers, 18 Sept 1949, on Cripp's broadcast on a price standstill.
1116	**Proposed improvement of marginal land.** Mar–July 1950.
1146	**European Customs Union Study Group.**1947–50.
1147	**Invitation to Commonwealth ministers to meetings on general economic and trade questions in London.** July–Oct 1950.
1168	**Export of machine tools to Soviet Union: question of orders with Craven Brothers from Soviet Union: question of orders with Craven Brothers from Soviet Union and Poland.** 1950.
1177	**Retail prices for clothing and food: proposals for statutory minimum rates in retail trades: increase in price of clothing and household textiles (blankets).** July 1949–Nov 1950. Includes papers on an arbitrary price reduction of 5% and on grocers' margins.
1178	**Canada and Washington: economic situation and dollar crisis: possible measures by the U.S.A. and Canada: Canada's future trade relations with sterling area.** Part 1 July–Oct 1949. Includes Cabinet and Economic Policy Committee minutes and memoranda, with some briefs. Also Morrison and E.E. Bridges on the economic situation, correspondence between Attlee and Cripps on the dollar situation, Economic Section on the balance of payments and government expenditure, correspondence between Attlee and Bevan on that and CP(49)185. Summary by N. Brook of ministerial discussions 12 July–17 Aug 1949. Part 2 Oct 1949–Nov 1950. Includes relevant Cabinet and Economic Policy Committee minutes and memoranda. Increasingly on the relations with Canada.
1180	**Proposed New Zealand loan following economic crisis 1947 over balance of payments.** Aug 1947–Sept 1950.
1181	**Government trading losses 1948–1949.** June–July 1950.
1182	**Appointment of Royal Commission to enquire into taxation of income.** July 1950.
1183	**Memorandum by the President of the Board of Trade on relations between government and private industry.** Oct 1948–July 1950. Papers arising out of 'State and Private Industry' by Wilson, H., including note of a meeting, 17 May 1950.
1184	**Oil and dollars.** June 1949–July 1950. Proposed cut in oil imports programme for 1949–50. U.S. companies in the U.K. to buy from sterling sources; Australian proposal to deration petrol; abolition of petrol rationing in the U.K. in May 1950. Includes relevant Cabinet and Economic Policy Committee minutes and memoranda, papers on the Washington oil negotiations and drafts of the White Paper on petrol rationing.
1185	**Expansion of exports in North America.** Mar 1949–June 1950. Includes relevant Economic Policy Committee minutes and memoranda, some briefs and papers on the dollar retention incentive scheme.
1186	**Dual price policy.** Dec 1949–June 1950.
1187	**Report on sterling balances.** Nov 1949–May 1950.

1188   Report of financial and economic situation by the Chancellor of the Exchequer after the General Election and his budget proposals. Feb–Mar 1950.

1189   Reports on national and international measures to achieve full employment. Jan–Mar 1950.

1190   Closer economic association between Scandinavia and the sterling area. Nov 1949–Jan 1950.

1191   Governor of Bank of England's request to the Prime Minister to receive a deputation to discuss finance. Jan 1950.

1192   Reorganization of the white fish industry. Parts 1 and 2 Dec 1946–Dec 1950.

1193   Prime Minister to receive Edward Evans M.P.'s deputation on question of a white fish industry board. May–June 1950.

1194   Purchase of coarse grains from the Soviet Union. Oct–Nov 1950.

1195   Agreement with New Zealand government for purchase of butter, cheese and meat over next seven years. July 1948–Sept 1950.

1196   Food prospects for next twelve months: imports of food for 1949–1950; tea ration and the restoration of the London tea market. May 1949–July 1950.

1197   Supplies of wheat and cereals for the U.K.; abolition of bread rationing; discussions on flour extraction rate July 1950. Oct 1947–July 1950.

1198   Modification of points rationing schemes. Apr–May 1950.

1199   Memorandum by the Minister of Food on merchandize marks. Apr 1950.

1212   Request by Minister of Health for adjustment of investment priorities in 1951 and 1952 to allow some increase in the current rate of house-building. Mar–Dec 1950.

1222   Size of civil staffs in government departments. Parts 1 and 2 Sept 1946–June 1950.

1238   Report by Minister of Labour on effect of increase in rates of sickness benefit from July 1948 on absenteeism in industry; report of the Committee on Involuntary Absenteeism in the Coal-mining Industry. Dec 1948–July 1950.

1246   Newspaper circulation: debate in House of Lords on newsprint supply. 1950.

1248   Coal freight subsidy and possible effect of its removal on employment. Apr–Oct 1950.

1249   Economic depression and rate of unemployment in Northern Ireland. Parts 1 and 2 Dec 1949–Aug 1950.

1291   Expansion of traffic and shipping space for tourists from North America; appointment of a committee to deal with accommodation, catering and other facilities for visitors to the Festival of Britain. Feb 1949–Dec 1950. Includes papers on the Festival and dollar-earning.

1302   Wage claim by manual workers in gas industry: boards of socialized industries to keep in touch with minister to whom they are responsible. Apr–Sept 1950.

1311   Reviews of agricultural prices: suggestion of increased prices following increased wages.
Parts 1 and 2 Mar 1946–Oct 1951. Includes relevant Cabinet, Lord President's Committee and Economic Policy Committee minutes and memoranda, with some briefs, correspondence between Attlee and Williams on economic aspects of agricultural policy.

1327   **Ministerial responsibility for supply of oil in a future war: appointment of Committee on Oil Supplies in War.** Dec 1950–Mar 1951.

1337   **Coal production and imports.**
Part 1 June 1950–Feb 1951. Includes relevant Cabinet minutes and memoranda, some briefs, and correspondence between Attlee and Morrison on the need for action and Attlee and Noel-Baker on possible measures, and notes of a meeting of ministers 3 Jan 1951, and with the N.U.M., 3 Jan 1951.
Part 2 July–Oct 1951. Includes relevant Production Committee minutes and memoranda and correspondence between Morrison and Noel-Baker on imports.

1338   **Manpower in the mines: measures to stimulate recruitment.** June 1950–Oct 1951. Includes correspondence between Morrison, Isaacs, Attlee and Noel-Baker. Also note of meeting with the N.U.M., 3 Jan 1951.

1339   **Suggestions for economies in the use of electricity, coal and gas including proposal that the B.B.C. should close down its programmes at 11 p.m.** Aug 1946–June 1951. Includes comments of Shinwell and Dalton and papers on the North of Scotland Hydro-electric Board constructional schemes.

1393   **Hydro-electric development.**

1395   **Future of the emergency powers and question of an economic controls bill.** Oct 1945–June 1951. Includes relevant minutes and memoranda of the Cabinet, Lord President's Committee and Economic Policy Committee, with some briefs. Consideration of whether the bill should include positive powers.

1401   **Proposed cut in licences for export of newsprint to Australia by the Bowater Co.** Apr–May 1951.

1402   **Shortage of coal affecting export contracts.** July 1950–Jan 1951. Includes correspondence between Bevin and Attlee on the possibility of breaking contracts on coal exports.

1403   **Construction of factory in Kilbride by John Deere Plow Co.** May–June 1951.

1412   **Balance of payments.**
Part 1 July 1948–June 1949. Includes relevant Cabinet and Economic Policy Committee minutes and memoranda, with some briefs. Papers on the O.E.E.C. and the long-term balance of payments and also correspondence between Cripps and Attlee on EPC(49)66.
Part 2 June 1949–July 1950. Papers relating to EPC(49)66, the dollar situation and proposed remedies. Includes correspondence from Jay and Wilson to Attlee. Many briefs by R.L. Hall.
Part 3 Oct 1950–Oct 1951. Further papers including relevant Cabinet and Economic Policy Committee minutes and memoranda, with some briefs and correspondence from Edwards, J. and Gaitskell to Attlee.

1413   **Retail grocers' margins.** July–Aug 1951. Alexander's protest against the minutes of the seventeenth meeting of the E.P.C.

1414   **Exports of strategic goods to Eastern Europe.**
Part 1 Nov 1948–Dec 1950.
Part 2 Jan–July 1951.

1415   **Government expenditure.**
Part 1 July–Sept 1949. Papers leading to CP(49)170 and some replies.

Part 2 Oct–Dec 1949. Includes Cabinet and Economic Policy
Committee minutes and memoranda, with some briefs, and some
ministerial correspondence on administrative economies.
Part 3 Nov 1949–Feb 1951. Includes further Cabinet and Economic
Policy Committee minutes and memoranda, with some briefs.
Part 4 June–July 1951. Mainly papers arising from EPC(51)65.

1416 **Conference on international trade and employment at Havana: non-discrimination obligations; control of quantitative restrictions; Torquay negotiations.** Dec 1947–Apr 1951.

1417 **Proposed Australian loan following economic crisis 1947.** Aug 1947–Apr 1951.

1418 **Price control on fish.** Apr 1950–July 1951.

1419 **Meat rations and supplies.** Jan 1949–Oct 1951.

1420 **Simplification of marketing and distribution to reduce level of retail food prices and essential consumer goods: marketing of fruit and vegetables.** July 1950–Aug 1951.

1421 **Proposed increase in animal feedingstuffs ration: withdrawal of subsidies; Cabinet decision in Mar 1950 to continue rationing of feedingstuffs; effect on meat supplies.** Apr 1949–July 1951.

1422 **International Wheat Conferences and negotiations.** Mar 1947–June 1951.

1423 **Sugar.** Nov 1949–May 1951.

1424 **Increase in retail food prices: increase in price of butter and bacon.** Mar 1950–May 1951. Includes correspondence from Webb to Attlee on the problems of showing the economic as well as the actual price of food.

1426 **Scheme for the production of ground-nuts in East Africa.**
Part 1 Oct 1946–Jan 1950.
Part 2 Sept 1950–Jan 1951.

1428 **Schuman Plan.**
Part 1 May 1950–June 1951. Includes relevant Cabinet and GEN 322 minutes and memoranda.
Part 2 July–Sept 1951.

1434 **Economic unification of Europe and relation of the O.E.E.C. to the Council of Europe.** 1949–51.

1442 **Bill for setting up of Ministry of Materials.** May–Aug 1951.

1443 **Review of machinery of government: possible reduction in departments and ministries and reallocations of functions; transfer of functions from Ministry of Health to Ministry of Town and Country Planning.** Nov 1949–May 1951.

1462 **Proposed financial cuts in overseas information expenditure.** Feb–Apr 1951.

1474 **Resettlement of Polish soldiers in British industries.** Dec 1949–Oct 1951.

1480 **Records of Cabinet discussions leading to the resignations of Aneurin Bevan and Harold Wilson.** Apr–May 1951.

1483 **Redistribution of ministerial responsibilities.** Directives by the Prime Minister on duties of the Lord Privy Seal and Lord President of the Council; Cabinet Committee duties of Foreign and Home Secretaries. Mar–May 1951.

1484 **Question of holding of the office of Lord Privy Seal by a peer and consequential rearrangement of Cabinet committee work.** 1951.

1489 **Nationalization. Iron and steel.**

Part 1 Nov 1945–Aug 1947.

Part 2 May 1948–Feb 1951.

1490   **Nationalization. Water.** Mar 1950–Feb 1951.

1497   **Prime Minister to be one of the sponsors of the bill setting up the new materials department.** May–June 1951. Papers leading to Cmd. 8278.

1504   **Reintroduction of double summer time.** Feb 1947–Jan 1951.

1507   **Increased railway charges; financial prospects of the British Transport Commission, including road passenger services.** May 1947–Sept 1951.

1508   **Serious shortage of sulphur: price policy on raw materials imports.** Feb–July 1951.

1509   **Supply position of raw materials.** Includes production of raw materials in the Colonial empire; statement by Minister of Supply on 30 Apr 1951 on stocks of raw materials for steel making; issue of White Paper. Dec 1950–May 1951.

1510   **Sir Hartley Shawcross's opposition to a new government department to deal with raw materials.** Apr–May 1951.

1534   **Reorganization of National Dock Labour Board: proposal to appoint a working party to review dock labour schemes; investigation into labour conditions in the docks; report of committee of enquiry.** May 1949–May 1951.

1538   **Unofficial strike of meat drivers at Smithfield market; possibility of criminal proceedings in unofficial and illegal strikes; memorandum by the Attorney General on communist incitement to strike: communist influence among workers.** June 1950–Jan 1951.

1542   **Idea of creating some form of consumer advisory service; suggestion for legislation to amend the Hire Purchase Act.** Sept 1950–June 1951.

1543   **International Tin Agreement.** Feb 1949–Jan 1951.

1568   **Wages policy (main file).**

Part 1 Jan 1946–July 1947. Includes relevant Cabinet and Lord President's Committee minutes and memoranda, papers by Jay, Isaacs and Bevin.

Part 2 Sept 1947–Feb 1948. Papers, including correspondence from the T.U.C. and its *Interim Report on the Economic Situation,* notes of meetings with the T.U.C., leading to Cmd. 7321.

Part 3 Feb 1948–July 1950. Includes relevant Cabinet and Economic Policy Committee minutes and memoranda, with some briefs on policy after Cmd. 7321 and the September 1949 wages standstill.

Part 4 Oct 1950–May 1951. Includes papers on the possibility of a new approach on wages, including ones by Gaitskell and Isaacs.

1576   **Cabinet consideration of the memorandum by the Lord President on the efficiency and public accountability of nationalized industries.** Mar 1950–May 1951.

Chapter 18   Central Economic Planning Staff

The need for a central planning body had been common to much Labour Party thinking on economic planning during the 1930s and was seriously discussed by the Official Committee on the Machinery of Government (CAB 87/71–72) during its consideration of post-war administrative requirements. After the 1945 election, however, the Labour government's only administrative innovation was the Official Steering Committee on Economic Development (CAB 134/186–193). Morrison, the minister responsible for economic planning, did refer to this committee, the Economic Section (T 230) and C.S.O. (CAB 108 and CAB 139) as an 'Economic General Staff' as did Cripps in his introduction to the *Economic Survey for 1947* (Cmd. 7046); but it did not constitute the planning body that had been envisaged.

Early in March 1947 Marquand was appointed Paymaster General to assist Morrison (who was then ill) with economic planning. Simultaneously Max Nicholson, Norman Brook and Edward Bridges were discussing the need to strengthen the staff for economic planning, given the amount of work relating to fuel, power and material allocations consequent upon the fuel crisis (CAB 124/1079; PREM 8/615). Bridges drafted a note which proposed two steps. First, there was to be a full-time planning staff under a 'departmental planning officer' in each of the departments concerned with economic affairs, trade and industry. Secondly, an inter-departmental planning staff was to be set up, consisting of the departmental planning officers (or their assistants) under a full-time chairman. The latter was to be assisted by a small staff with wartime programming experience and a secretariat. This inter-departmental planning staff, which was to be housed in the Cabinet Office, was normally to report via the Official Steering Committee on Economic Development to the Ministerial Committee on Economic Planning (CAB 134/503) and was to work closely with the Economic Section, C.S.O. and the Materials Committee (CAB 134/475–486). The Economic Section was to retain primary responsibility for longer-term plans while the planning staff concentrated on programmes for the following year. This memorandum was approved at a Cabinet committee under Attlee on 7 March (CAB 130/17, GEN 169/2nd), with the proviso that both sides of industry should be acquainted with the work of economic planning. To this end, the Economic Planning Board (T 229/24–42 and CAB 134/210–214) was proposed.

On 18 March 1947 Bridges's proposals were announced in the House of Commons by Cripps. Sir Robert Sinclair (the wartime Chief Executive of the Ministry of Production) was the first person asked to be Chief Planning Officer, then Ronald Weeks (who had been Vice-Chief of the Imperial General Staff) and finally Edwin Plowden (who had been Chief Executive at the Ministry of Aircraft Production). He accepted at the second time of asking, and his appointment was announced on 27 March although, because of illness, he did not start work until May. All three candidates, it should be noted, were industrialists as this was felt to be an essential requirement for the post.

During the summer of 1947, Bridges's idea of departmental planning officers was dropped and the role of the planning staff discussed – including, within the Treasury, heated discussion on the relationship between financial policy and economic planning. Plowden also started to assemble his staff, which was never to exceed forty and which consisted mainly of administrators on short-term secondment from other departments. Exceptions to this rule were Douglas Allen, who stayed in C.E.P.S. until 1953, and

Austin Robinson (together with Kenneth Berrill and Robin Marris, his protégés from Cambridge) who were trained economists.

Whilst defining its role within Whitehall, C.E.P.S. was involved in crisis-management and the implementation of policy decisions relating in particular to allocations. Then Robinson took over work on the Long-term Economic Survey from the Economic Section and, after the convertibility crisis of August 1947, Plowden was given his first main task of undertaking an investment review in order to effect cuts (CAB 134/437).

In September 1947 C.E.P.S. came to serve Stafford Cripps on his appointment as Minister for Economic Affairs and in November followed him into the Treasury. This greatly strengthened its position. Plowden and Cripps knew each other from their days at the Ministry of Aircraft Production, and so C.E.P.S. (and the Economic Section) now had a direct route to the sympathetic ear of the Chancellor of the Exchequer. Moreover, the Treasury could no longer be so obstructive now that financial policy was clearly to be integrated with economic policy.

The close relationship between Cripps and Plowden was crucial to the improved status of C.E.P.S., but it did not solely advise the Chancellor. Plowden and others of its members played an important part in the co-ordination of various Cabinet committees dealing with economic policy. Plowden was chairman of the Economic Planning Board, a member of the Official Steering Committee on Economic Development and chairman of its Working Group (CAB 134/202). C.E.P.S. also supplied, amongst others, the chairman and secretariat of the Investment Programmes Committee (CAB 134/437–442), the chairmen of the Committee on Productive Capacity (CAB 134/114–116) and the Import Diversion Committee (CAB 134/349–352), the vice-chairman of the Programmes Committee (CAB 134/608–623), and part of the secretariat for the Materials Committee (CAB 134/475–486). On many other committees C.E.P.S. maintained an active representation. It also drafted the annual Economic Survey in conjunction with the Economic Section, was heavily involved in the production of programmes for the O.E.E.C., and both devised and oversaw the implementation of various allocation schemes.

Plowden had taken the position of Chief Planning Officer on a temporary basis and by 1949–50 was under pressure to return to industry. With the strong possibility of a Conservative government in the near future, he approached Bridges to find out the intentions of the Conservatives in relation to C.E.P.S. but Bridges failed to obtain any guarantees from Conservative Central Office (T 273/139). Partly as a result of this, Plowden decided to return to industry and, in 1951, it was announced that Norman Brook, the Secretary to the Cabinet, was to replace him. However, after the 1951 election, the new Chancellor of the Exchequer was R.A. Butler who was a neighbour of Plowden, and he persuaded Plowden to continue. Consequently, he stayed until 1953 when he was replaced by Sir Bernard Gilbert, Joint Second Secretary to the Treasury. His departure marked the beginning of the absorption of C.E.P.S. into the ordinary Treasury machinery and in 1954 it was amalgamated with part of the Overseas Finance Division to form the new Home and Overseas Planning Staff (T 234).

For further information see Lord Plowden, *An Industrialist in the Treasury: the Post-war Years* (Andre Deutsch, 1989).

T 229

1   **Accommodation: chart room.** (CP52/02)   Oct–Nov 1947. Question of an operations room for Cripps.

2   **Agricultural expansion programme. Balance of payments.** (CP269/02) July–Oct 1947. Briefs, mainly for the Lord President, on the programme and its contribution to import savings.

3 **Committee on Agricultural Output. Study Group on U.K. Agricultural Development.** (CP269/03) Jan–Nov 1948. Some minutes and memoranda of the group (SGAD), with comments, leading to its report (AD(48)10).

4 **The agricultural programme. Agricultural priorities for steel etc.** (CP269/12/01) Aug–Dec 1947. Consideration of agricultural requirements as part of the more general discussion on priorities. Includes Morrison's speech at the Agricultural Conference, August 1947.

5 **Agricultural labour.** (CP269/15/01) July–Oct 1947. Labour requirements of the Agriculture Production Programme 1948–51, the progress of recruitment and the need for more houses for agricultural workers.

6 **Agricultural machinery for root crops.** (CP269/25/03) Summer 1947–Apr 1948. Papers relating to the Agricultural Machinery Development Board and the introduction of labour-saving machinery.

7 **Agricultural programme – plant and machinery. Gordon Smith enquiry.** (CP269/25/01) Aug 1947–May 1948. Papers and report on the agricultural machinery manufacturing industry.

8 **Discussions on secondary industrial development in Australia.** (CP138/01) June–Aug 1948. Mainly minutes of meetings.

9 **Export target 1947.** (CP71/23/01) May–Nov 1947. Correspondence and papers relating to the Export Targets Committee (ET).

10 **Balance of payments. Committee on Exports.** (CP71/23/02) Aug–Oct 1947. On C.E.P.S. representation on the Export Committee and the Overseas Negotiations Committee.

11 **Import programme 1947 – balance of payments.** (CP71/47/01) Apr 1947–Apr 1948. Marquand's thoughts on planning. Papers on aspects of the 1947 and 1948 import programme, particularly the dollar programme and Marshall Aid. Questions raised by members of the P.L.P. R.W.B. Clarke on the balance of payments 1948–51.

12 **Balance of Payments Working Party – general.** (CP71/44/01) July–Nov 1947. R.J. Shackle on the balance of payments crisis. Notes on GEN 179 and other papers.

13 **Balance of Payments Working Party. Export Programme.** (CP71/44/02) Aug–Nov 1947. Report of the Export Targets Committee. Papers on unrequited exports and the direction of exports.

14 **Balance of Payments Working Party. Financial measures.** (CP71/44/03) Aug 1947. Notes on GEN 179/14 and GEN 188/52. J.M. Fleming on a 10% devaluation.

15 **Allocation of barley for brewing beer.** (CP141/01) Apr–May 1948.

16 **Earth-moving equipment from services for civilian use.** (CP25/011) Jan–June 1948.

17 **Relaxing of controls of building materials.** (CP62/51/01) Oct 1948. Correspondence resulting from Cripps's refusal to allow the removal of the statutory control over the distribution of certain building materials without further information.

18 **Shortage of railway wagons affecting movement of bricks.** (CP62/30/01) Aug 1947. Papers arising from correspondence from the Midland Federation of Brick and Tile Manufacturers.

19 **Export sales organization in Canada – U.S.A. – Argentina. Information for Chancellor's visit to America.** (CP186/23/01) Apr–Sept 1948. Notes

on the direction of exports to hard currency markets and of the export sales organization.

20 **C.E.P.S. relations with Materials Committee.** (CP11/03) May–June 1947. Correspondence on the lines on which the two bodies could usefully co-operate over raw material allocation.

21 **C.E.P.S. morning staff meetings.** (CP1/02) May 1947–May 1948. Incomplete series of conclusions of the daily meetings of senior staff to discuss informally the action to be taken on various issues.

22 **Miners: compensation for closing of pits.** (CP7/15/03) Feb–Apr 1948.

23 **Rice.** (CP3/01) Oct 1947–Oct 1949.

24 **Planning Board – preliminary discussion. Draft outline of statement to be made at first meeting.** (CP18/03) Apr–July 1947. Drafts of the statement for the first meeting and the terms of reference for the Economic Planning Board.

25 **Planning Board – preliminary discussion – paper on revision of Economic Survey for 1947.** (CP18/04) May–July 1947. Drafts and comments on paper No. 2 'Economic Survey for 1947. Progress and prospects.'

26 **Planning Board – preliminary discussion – paper on coal.** (CP18/7/01) June–July 1947. Drafts and comments on paper No. 3 'Coal' for the first meeting of the board.

27 **Planning Board – preliminary discussions – paper on steel.** (CP18/12/01) June–July 1947. Draft paper No. 4 'Steel' for the first meeting of the board.

28–39 **Economic Planning Board.** (CP18/67/01–011) July–Dec 1947 EPB(47)1st–14th, EPB(47)1–9, 11–26, 28–31.

28 21 July **EPB(47)1st:1 Opening statement by the Lord President and by the Chief Planning Officer.**
:2 **Suggestions of future work of the Board.**
:3 **Economic Survey for 1947: progress and prospects (I) general (II) coal.** EPB(47)2 and 3.
:4 **Future meetings.** To be fortnightly.
10 July **EPB(47)1 Economic planning** – E.N. Plowden, 1p.
16 July **2 Economic Survey for 1947: progress and prospects (I) general** – C.E.P.S., 11p.
16 July **3 Economic Survey for 1947: progress and prospects (II) coal** – C.E.P.S., 5p. Correspondence and drafts of the papers, the Lord President's statement and the minutes of the first meeting also included.

29 5 Aug **EPB(47)2nd Balance of payments crisis.** Sets out Board's views on the necessary corrective action.
7 Aug **EPB(47)3rd:1 Railway wagon position: winter 1947/48.** EPB(47)5.
:2 **Economic Survey for 1948/51.** EPB(47)6. General agreement that integration of fiscal and physical planning was essential and that control over investment was not the sole key to planning.
:3 **Publicity.** EPB(47)4.

	31 July	EPB(47)4	**Publicity** – S.C. Leslie, 4p. Proposed functions of the Economic Information Unit.
	1 Aug	5	**Railway wagon position** – C.E.P.S., 4p.
	1 Aug	6	**Economic Survey for 1948–51** – C.E.P.S., 4p.

Drafts also included.

30	21 Aug	EPB(47)4th:1	**Expansion of agricultural production.** EPB(47)7.
		:2	**Publicity.**
		:3	**Temporary suspension of convertibility of sterling.** R.W.B. Clarke explained the steps taken.
		:4	**Progress of Marshall discussions in Paris.** H.T. Weeks statement of progress.
		:5	**The investment programme.** EPB(47)8.
		:6	**Short-term plan.**
		:7	**Date of meeting.**
	14 Aug	EPB(47)7	**Expansion of agricultural production – Report of Officials placed before Lord President's Committee** – C.E.P.S., 1p. Covering note to the report.
	16 Aug	8	**The investment programme** – C.E.P.S., 4+5p annexes. Outline of the approach to making reductions in the programme.
	19 Aug	9	**Temporary increase in working hours** – C.E.P.S., 1+2+1p annex. Also JCC 207. Outline of short-term crisis measures to achieve an immediate increase in output.

Draft papers and correspondence resulting from the meetings also included.

31	4 Sept	EPB(47)5th:1	**Machinery for control of investment in industry.** EPB(47)11.
		:2	**Memorandum on the economic situation by the F.B.I.**
		:3	**Next meeting.**
	2 Sept	EPB(47)11	**Control of investment by trade associations** – S. Bodington and J.G. Stewart covering Sir Graham Cunningham, 1+3p.

Drafts also included.

32	18 Sept	EPB(47)6th:1	**Review of the present position.** EPB(47)10.
		:2	**Industry and the way to recovery.** EPB(47)12.
		:3	**Dissolution of the Petroleum Board.**
		:4	**Other business.**

	12 Sept	**EPB(47)12**	**Industry and the way to recovery – S. Bodington and J.G. Stewart covering the F.B.I. and C.E.P.S.,** 1+8+5p. F.B.I. proposals to improve the balance of payments and reduce domestic inflation with C.E.P.S. comments.
	25 Sept	**14**	**Termination of the Petroleum Board – S. Bodington and J.G. Stewart covering E.N. Plowden,** 1+2p.

Drafts also included. No copy of EPB(47)10 although there is a paper on suggested amendments.

33	25 Sept	**EPB(47)7th:1**	**Recommendations to ministers on the dollar crisis.** EPB(47)13.
		:2	**Publicity.**
		:3	**Next meeting: Investment Programmes Committee's report.**
		:4	**Co-operation with the F.B.I. on control of investment.**
	13 Oct	**EPB(47)8th**	**Report of the Investment Programmes Committee.** EPB(47)17. General agreement with the proposed cuts.
	26 Sept	**EPB(47)13**	**Recommendations to ministers by the Economic Planning Board to meet the balance of payments problem,** 1+2p.
	26 Sept	**15**	**Economic Planning Board – S. Bodington and J.G. Stewart,** 1p. A Treasury member to be added.
	1 Oct	**16**	**The temporary limitation of industrial capital expenditure – S. Bodington and J.G. Stewart covering the F.B.I.,** 1+5+2p appendix.
	9 Oct	**17**	**Report of the Investment Programmes Committee – S. Bodington and J.G. Stewart covering the Economic Section, C.E.P.S. and the Investment Programmes Committee,** 1+2+14+32p appendixes. See CP(47)284 (CAB 129/21). Also ED(47)48 and IPC(47)9 (CAB 134/190 and 437).
34	16 Oct	**EPB(47)9th:1**	**Statement by the Minister of State for Economic Affairs.** Aimed to soothe complaints that the Board was merely a rubber stamp.
		:2	**Production plans for agricultural machinery.** EPB(47)18.
		:3	**Housing for miners and agricultural workers.** EPB(47)19.
		:4	**Additional capacity for railway wagon repairs.**

		:5	**Dissolution of the Petroleum Board.** EPB(47)14.
		:6	**Next meeting.**
	13 Oct	**EPB(47)18**	**Production plans for agricultural machinery – Ministry of Agriculture and Fisheries,** 5+10p appendixes.
	7 Oct	**19**	**Housing for miners and agricultural workers – C.E.P.S.,** 2p.

Drafts also included.

35	30 Oct	**EPB(47)10th:1**	**Electricity consumption.** EPB(47)22 and 23.
		:2	**Publicity and information on the present crisis.** EPB(47)21.
		:3	**The manning-up of the export- and import-saving industries.** EPB(47)20.
		:4	**White Paper on investment.**
		:5	**Margins.**
		:6	**Dissolution of the Petroleum Board.**
		:7	**Next meeting.**
	28 Oct	**EPB(47)20**	**The manning-up of the export- and import-saving industries – Ministry of Labour,** 5+12p appendixes. Review of existing measures and their impact.
	27 Oct	**21**	**Crisis publicity – Economic Information Unit,** 3p.
	23 Oct	**22**	**Electricity consumption. The relation between the shortages of electricity generating plant, the domestic consumption of electricity and the staggering of hours – S. Bodington and J.G. Stewart covering Sir William Coates,** 1+8+6p appendixes. Need to reduce domestic consumption.
	28 Oct	**23**	**Electricity consumption. Comments on memorandum circulated as paper EPB(47)22 – Ministry of Fuel and Power,** 3p. Most of the proposals were already being carried out.

Drafts also included.

36	13 Oct	**EPB(47)11th:1**	**Change in membership of the Board.**
		:2	**Approval of the minutes of the previous meeting.**
		:3	**Unrequited exports and the direction of exports.** EPB(47)24.
		:4	**Allocation and distribution of raw materials.** EPB(47)26.
		:5	**Publicity.**
		:6	**Review of the investment programmes: housing.**

		:7	**Plans for meeting a deterioration in the economic situation.**
		:8	**Review of Colonial development programme.**
		:9	**Next meeting.**
	8 Nov	EPB(47)24	**Unrequited exports and direction of exports – J.G. Stewart and D.A.V. Allen covering C.E.P.S.,** 1+10+2p appendix.
	7 Nov	26	**Allocation and distribution of scarce raw materials – C.E.P.S.,** 1+10p annex. Review of the general process of allocation and particular commodities.
37	27 Nov	EPB(47)12th:1	**Approval of the minutes of the previous meeting.**
		:2	**Simplification of controls.**
		:3	**Price and profit margins.** EPB(47)25 and 28.
		:4	**Employment in the cotton industry in Lancashire in relation to other local industries.** EPB(47)29.
		:5	**The 1948 non-dollar balance of payments plan.** EPB(47)27.
		:6	**Further meetings.**
	20 Nov	EPB(47)25	**Price and profit margins – J.G. Stewart and D.A.V. Allen covering the Committee on Profit Margins,** 1+11+2p appendix. On the reduction of margins on food distributors.
		27	No copy included.
	24 Nov	28	**Price and profit margins: price control of consumer goods – Board of Trade,** 5p.
	21 Nov	29	**Changes in the distribution of industry between 1939 and 1946 in Lancashire with special reference to their impact on the cotton industry – Board of Trade,** 4+2p appendixes.
38	11 Dec	EPB(47)13th	**Statement by Sir Oliver Franks on the Marshall Plan.** Sets out developments at Washington.
	18 Dec	EPB(47)14th:1	**Minutes of the last meeting.**
		:2	**Economic Survey for 1948.** EPB(47)30. Consideration chapter by chapter.
	12 Dec	EPB(47)30	**Economic Survey for 1948 – J.G. Stewart and D.A.V. Allen,** 1+51+3p appendix. See prefix to EPC(48)1 (CAB 134/217).
39	30 Dec	EPB(47)31	**Distribution of iron and steel – C.E.P.S.,** 2+1p. Explanation of the new distribution scheme. Drafts and final copies of EPB(48)1st and EPB(48)1, 2, 4 also included. See CAB 134/210–211.

40   **Economic Planning Board: second meeting.** (CP18/67/012)   Jan 1948. Drafts and final copies of EP(48)2nd and EP(48)3 with related correspondence. See CAB 134/210–211.

41   **Economic Planning Board: third meeting.** (CP18/67/013)   Jan–Feb 1948. Drafts and final copies of EPB(48)3rd and EPB(48)5 with related correspondence. See CAB 134/210–211.

42   **Economic Planning Board: fourth meeting.** (CP18/67/014)   Feb–Mar 1948. EPB(48)6 and 7 with related correspondence. See CAB 134/ 210–211.

43   **Planning Board – preliminary discussion. Paper on timber.** (CP18/58/ 01)   May–June 1947.

44   **Economic review 1948/51.** (CP201/93/04)   Mar–July 1947. 'Suggestions regarding the planning of the review and the form of the report' – preview paper No. 27 – R.C. Tress. Correspondence on drafts of review and comments by E.A.G. Robinson.

45   **Monthly progress record on Economic Survey. Comments by C.E.P.S.** (CP201/93/02)   May–Oct 1947. Draft progress records and C.E.P.S. comments prior to submission to the Official Steering Committee on Economic Development. Correspondence on the decision to discontinue the series Oct 1947. Social Survey report on meter reading and the fuel target, Sept 1947.

46   **Economic Survey for 1948 general papers.** (CP201/93/03)   July 1947–Aug 1948. Drafts and comments leading to published version (Cmd. 7046) and covering note (EPC(48)1). Papers on the trade and payments agreement with Japan and on inflation and price reductions, including notes of meeting with secretary of the F.B.I. with Cripps's comments.

47   **Comments on Economic Section's Survey for 1948–1951.** (CP201/93/ 0011)   June–Aug 1947. Draft paper for the Economic Planning Board covering the draft economic plan and E.A.G. Robinson's comments as in T 229/44.

48   **Electricity load. Effect of staggering working loads.** (CP14/02)   June 1947–July 1948. Circulars to regional boards, correspondence relating to the Electricity Subcommittee of the N.J.A.C. and reports on developments during 1947–48 winter.

49   **Report of the E.C.A. Mission on U.K. public social services etc.** (CP223/ 02)   Dec 1948.

50   **Food import cuts.** (CP11/47/01)   Oct 1947. Drafts of LP(47)289 (CAB 129/21) and comments on hard currency savings.

51   **Ministry of Food. Committee on Profit Margins report.** (CP102/331/ 01)   July–Nov 1947. Report of committee and its three subcommittees. Also EPB(47)25.

52   **Working Party on Cereal Feedingstuffs 1947/8.** (CP135/44/01)   Nov 1947–Sept 1948. Draft and final versions of relevant papers and minutes of the Committee on Agricultural Output, Economic Policy Committee, Production Committee and Cabinet.

53–54   **The dollar drain 1948.** (CP55/01A and B)   5 Nov 1947–31 Dec 1948. Complete set of minutes and memoranda of the Dollar Drain Committee (DD), some of the Sterling Area Statistical Committee (SASC) and the Balance of Payments Statistics Subcommittee (BP(STAT)). Also weekly statements of the dollars received from the

E.C.A. and the position of procurement authorizations. See also T 229/ 229–231 and 284.

55 **Fuel Committee progress reports. Action arising.** (CP19/02) Apr–June 1947. Briefs on various Fuel Committee papers for Morrison.

56 **Expansion of fuel and power resources. Prime Minister's memorandum dated 20 March 1947.** (CP19/01) May 1947–May 1948. Plowden's job was to check implementation of CP(47)92(revise) (CAB 129/17).

57 **Dissolution of Petroleum Board.** (CP39/01) Aug–Nov 1947. Correspondence and drafts of statement on termination and EPB(47)14 and EPB(47)10th:6.

58 **Fuel/oil: oil programme.** (CP39/01) Jan 1947–Sept 1948. Memoranda, minutes, briefs and correspondence relating to oil stocks, steel requirements of the oil industry and the oil expansion programme and relevant Cabinet, Economic Policy Committee, Production Committee and Exchange Requirement Committee papers.

59 **Production of rail tank wagons for carrying oil fuel.** (CP39/40/01) June–Nov 1947. Railway coal/oil conversion.

60 **Motor spirit: consumption by goods vehicles.** (CP39/10/01) Jan–Mar 1948. Possible means of reducing consumption.

61 **Fuel: motor coaches for private parties, restriction in the use of.** (CP39/ 10/02) Feb 1948.

62 **Import programme 1947.** (CP47/07) May–July 1947. Briefs and comments about CP(47)167 and notes for Morrison's speech on import policy for 8 July 1947.

63 **Federation of British Industries. Meeting to discuss 'Industry and the Way to Recovery'.** (CP17/04) Aug–Sept 1947. Brief and arrangements for meeting, copy of EP(47)12 and correspondence relating to GEN 179/28.

64 **Replacement of imports by home production.** (CP17/81/03) Sept–Dec 1947. Correspondence relating to EP(O)(47)7, 9, 11. See T 229/106.

65 **European economic co-operation: four-year programme for Paris.** (CP129/02) June–Nov 1948. Draft and comments on parts of the programme including French comments.

66 **Investment Programme Committee. White Paper on investment programmes 1948.** (CP45/012) Aug–Dec 1947. Copy of the Investment Review circular. Note of meeting, 6 Oct 1947, to consider further action on the report and comments including the Chancellor's on PC(47)3. Departmental redrafts of individual programmes and notes for the Commons debate.

67 **Temporary limitation of industrial capital expenditure.** (CP72/03) Sept–Oct 1947. F.B.I. note on this (EPB(47)16) and related papers.

68 **Steel economy. Steel Economy Subcommittee and related committees.** (CP12/010) Apr 1947–Nov 1948. Minutes and memoranda of the Committee on Industrial Productivity and its Import Substitution Subcommittee. Cripps's letters to ministers on the steel shortage and their replies with relevant minutes and memoranda of the Production Committee, the Materials Committee and its Steel Economy Subcommittee.

69 **Steel production: short-term and long-term. Memorandum by Sir A. Forbes.** (CP12/08) Jan–Feb 1948. Memorandum stressing the shortage of coke and other limiting factors with resulting correspondence.

70   **Joint Committee on the Working of the Steel Distribution Scheme. Terms of reference and papers and minutes.** (CP12/64/016)   Aug 1948. Revised terms of reference (SDS/28) and SDS 12th, 13th and SDS/29.

71–72   **Materials Committee. Steel Economy Subcommittee.** Dec 1946–Oct 1948.

71   Correspondence. (CP125/013). M(47)14 and 34 and departmental comments on these interim reports. Report by the Panel on Import Substitution of the Committee on Industrial Productivity on steel economy.

72   Memoranda and minutes. (CP125/012) 1948. See CAB 134/487.

73   **Ministry of Agriculture. Steel allocation and flood prevention.** (CP12/70/03)   May–July 1947. Papers related to CP(47)157.

74   **Salzgitter Steelworks.** (CP12/22/02)   Sept 1947.

75   **Steel: pitprops.** (CP12/96/01)   Nov–Dec 1947. Possibility of saving steel.

76   **Steel production.** (CP12/81/01)   Dec 1947–July 1948. Monthly reports from the Iron and Steel Federation to enable C.E.P.S. to monitor production progress. Correspondence on whether the steel target should be altered.

77   **Steel supplies and allocations periods I and II 1948. General.** (CP12/90/02)   June–Oct 1947. F. Lee on the problems of steel allocations in the two periods and their relation to the Investment Programmes Committee. Papers leading to consideration of allocations by the Materials Committee.

78   **Steel supplies and allocations periods III and IV 1948.** (CP12/90/03) Oct 1947–May 1948. Notes of meetings and papers on allocations considered by Materials and Production Committees.

79   **Steel distribution.** (CP12/90/06)   Sept 1947–Nov 1948. Relevant Materials Committee and Steel Distribution Scheme Working Party papers. Notes of discussions with industry and papers on the new distribution scheme.

80   **Steel supplies and allocations periods I and II 1949.** (CP12/90/010) June–Oct 1948. Relevant minutes and memoranda of Materials Committee.

81   **Steel: proposed modification of the priority system.** (CP12/90/013) June 1947–July 1948. Discussions, papers and various committees' memoranda considering the P.M.L. system of priorities and alternative priority schemes.

82   **Steel: exempt products. Proposals to free small consumers of steel from allocations.** (CP12/90/04)   Feb–Oct 1948. Papers leading up to discussion by Materials Committee.

83   **Proposals for increasing employment in the Scottish Development Area.** (CP15/03)   July–Nov 1947. Notes relating to LP(DI)(47)65 and PC(47)8.

84   **Underemployment and short-time in industry.** (CP15/34/01)   May 1947. Evidence of the effect of the fuel crisis on the level of employment and short-time working.

85   **National wages policy. Official Working Party on the Stabilization of Wages.** (CP15/38/02)   Aug 1947–Jan 1948. Various papers on wages policy including E.N. Plowden to Cripps Jan 1948 on need for a standstill for at least a year.

86–87 **Working Party on Statistics for Employment. Post-war statistics.** (CP15/
44/03A and B)   Aug 1943–May 1945.

86   Correspondence and notes on departmental replies originally arising
out of EL(43)4.

87   Memoranda arising out of EL(43)4, mainly by the C.S.O. Includes a
Royal Statistical Society paper on official statistics.

88–89 **Official Committee on Distribution of Industry. Panel A briefs to
ministers and other officers.** (CP29/02A and B).

88   May 1945–Nov 1946. Briefs mainly on papers for the Lord President's
Committee, its Industrial Subcommittee and Distribution of Industry
Committee. See CAB 71/19–25, CAB 132/1–5, CAB 71/26–27 and
CAB 132/21–22.

89   Jan–Dec 1947. Briefs on papers mainly for the Distribution of Industry
Subcommittee and the Distribution of Industry Committee. See CAB
132/21–24 and CAB 134/130–132.

90 **Official Committee on Distribution of Industry. Panel B – general
correspondence.** (CP29/03)   July 1946–May 1948. Various cases but,
in particular, Chrysler Aircraft Ltd. and the Royal Naval Engineering
College of Plymouth.

91 **Visit of the Paymaster General to the regions – suggested topics for
enquiry.** (CP26/01)   May–June 1947.

92 **Talks with Commonwealth countries about their development plans in
the light of the four-year programme.** (CP26/131/03)   Apr–Nov 1948.
Notes of meetings, in particular with Australia and New Zealand. Some
papers of the Sterling Area Development Working Party.

93 **Northern Ireland. Help in export drive and economic difficulties.** (CP80/
04)   Aug–Oct 1947.

94 **Long-term programme. Sir Edwin Plowden's speech in Paris.** (CP129/
01)   Oct–Nov 1948. Notes and briefs for speech.

95 **Publication of long-term programme. Memorandum by Chancellor of
the Exchequer.** (CP129/03)   Nov–Dec 1948. EPC(48)99, drafts of the
foreword and notes on publication. See CAB 134/219.

96–98 **Long-term programme.** (Sept–Nov 1948).

96   Coal. (CP129/7/01). E.A. Hitchman on European coal viability and
resulting comments.

97   Housing. (CP129/20/1)   Notes on key workers' accommodation.
Second report of the Manpower Committee to the Council of the
O.E.E.C.

98   Surplus or deficit between sterling area and other participants. (CP129/
82/01). Future activities of the Sterling Area Development Working
Party and the relationship between the sterling area and the other
O.E.E.C. participating countries.

99–100 **Long-term programme working group** (Nov–Dec 1948) GEN 258 series
I supporting documents. (CP129/44/04).

99   ER(P)(48)118 and correspondence between the Foreign Office and the
U.K. delegation to the O.E.E.C. (Paris).

100   GEN 258 series minutes (CP129/44/06). Incomplete set of minutes.
See CAB 130/42.

101 **Planning for expansion. Lord President's memorandum.** (CP66/06)
May–June 1947. Draft, with comments, and final version of CP(47)169
(CAB 129/19).

102   **Parliamentary debate on 6 Aug 1947.** (CP66/08)   Aug 1947. Notes for Attlee for state of the nation debate in which he proposed remedies for the economic crisis.

103   **Economic situation July–Aug 1947.** (CP66/09)   July–Aug 1947. Drafts of an N.J.A.C. paper on the economic situation in 1947 in response to the T.U.C.'s request.

104   **Contribution of science to long-term economic planning.** (CP66/011) June–Sept 1947. A few papers of the Advisory Committee on Scientific Policy in relation to increased productivity.

105   **Economic Planning (Official) Committee. Adjustments in industry.** (CP21/02)   Aug–Sept 1947. Drafts, with comments, and final version of EP(O)(47)8. See T 229/106.

106   **Economic Planning (Official) Committee. Minutes of meetings etc.** (CP21/67/01)   May–Nov 1947.

20 May	*ad hoc*:1	**Nature of new planning machinery.** E.N. Plowden said the C.E.P.S. was to co-ordinate economic planning and that an Economic Planning Board and an Economic Planning (Official) Committee were to be set up, the latter consisting of planning officers of principal departments and members of C.E.P.S. Its work would be in two parts: long-term planning and devising special remedies for immediate needs.	
	:2	**Steel problems.**	
16 July	EP(O)(47)1st	**Transport problems.** EP(O)(47)5.	
30 July	2nd:1	**Programmes and materials available to meet them.** EP(O)(47)3.	
	:2	**Possible shortages in the near future.** EP(O)(47)4.	
21 Aug	3rd:1	**Temporary increase in working hours.** EP(O)(47)6.	
23 Oct	4th	Untitled. EP(O)(47)10. Agreement on proposals.	
5 June	EP(O)(47)1	**Economic Planning (Official) Committee – A.S. Le Maitre.** Terms of reference and composition.	
14 June	2	**Papers for the Economic Planning Board – H.T. Weeks.** Papers No. 2, 3, 4 for the preliminary discussion of the Planning Board. See T 229/25–27.	
	3	See T 229/107.	
19 July	4	**Possible shortages in the near future – C.E.P.S.** Arrangements for their consideration.	
14 July	5	**Transport problems: winter 1947/8 – C.E.P.S.**	
19 Aug	6	**Temporary increase in working hours – S. Bodington covering the Joint Consultative Committee of the N.J.A.C.** Also JCC 2079(revise).	

16 Sept	7	**Replacement of imports by home production – C.E.P.S.**	
20 Sept	8	**Adjustments in industry – C.E.P.S.** Role of the planning staff in adjusting output of certain industries.	
6 Oct	9	**Replacement of imports by home production – S. Bodington and J.G. Stewart covering the Board of Trade.** Comments on EP(O)(47)7.	
20 Oct	10	**Priorities – S. Bodington.** Proposed modification of steel priority system.	
6 Nov	11	**Replacement of imports by home production – J.G. Stewart and J.L. Croome.** Minutes of an informal meeting, 28 Aug 1947, to consider EP(O)(47)7 and 9 with a draft note for submission to Morrison and Cripps proposing the establishment of an Import Substitutes Committee annexed.	

107   **Economic Planning (Official) Committee first and second meetings.** (CP21/67/02) May–Oct 1947. Drafts, with comments and correspondence, of papers discussed.
    11 July   EP(O)(47)3   **Programmes and materials available to meet them – A.S. Le Maitre.**

108   **Economic Planning (Official) Committee third meeting (temporary increase in working hours).** (CP21/6703) Aug–Sept 1947. Papers and correspondence.

109   **Economic Planning (Official) Committee fourth meeting.** (CP21/67/04) Sept–Oct 1947.

110   **The floods of Mar/Apr 1947. Request for priorities.** (CP50/04) May–June 1947. Brief and correspondence relating to CP(47)157 (CAB 129/19).

111   **Allocations of raw materials.** (CP33/03) Apr 1947–Jan 1948. Notes on the allocation, distribution, control for various industries. Review of the priority system.

112   **Materials Committee. Allocation of scarce raw materials – policy.** (CP124/07) Sept 1939–Apr 1948. Papers on the wartime priority system including J.K. Horsefield's history of raw material allocations.

113   **Steel – priority screening.** (CP124/12/010) Sept 1947. Notes of steel priority allocation for period IV 1947 and period I 1948.

114   **Steel for priority: wagon requirements.** (CP124/12/012) July–Oct 1947. Notes of meetings and correspondence between F.W. Smith and F. Lee.

115   **Materials Committee. Timber Economy Subcommittee – correspondence.** (CP124/58/010) July 1946–Oct 1947. Correspondence on its establishment and running and drafts, with comments, of its reports to the Materials Committee. See CAB 134/ 487.

116   **Economy of containers. Papers and minutes.** (CP124/76/01) Dec 1940–Dec 1945. Papers, minutes and correspondence of the

Subcommittee on Economy of Containers, of the Materials Committee and of the Central Priority Department of the Ministry of Supply, Joint Production and Materials Priority Subcommittees.

117   **Supply of packing materials – correspondence.** (CP124/76/06)   June – Dec 1947. Packaging requirements for expanding the export programme.

118   **Lead – distribution scheme for building materials.** (CP33/60/03) July–Aug 1947. Papers explaining the revised scheme.

119–121   **Sterling Area Development Working Party.**

119   General. (CP82/01)   Feb–Sept 1948. Papers on the development of various goods, commodities and areas. Drafts of reports.

120   Draft working papers. (CP82/03)   Feb–June 1948.

121   Set of papers and minutes. (CP82/90)   Mar–Nov 1948. Almost complete set.

122   **Survey of Welsh slate industry.** (CP130/01)   June 1948. Report by Professor G. Hibberd.

123   **Utilization of slurry.** (CP49/01)   Apr–Nov 1947. Correspondence on its use for fuel.

124–128   **Slurry.** (CP49/03, CP49/05, CP49/07–09)   Apr–Dec 1947.

129   **Prime Minister's correspondence re South African Aid to Britain Fund.** (CP197/196/01)   Mar 1948.

130   **Timber. General supply and allocations.** (CP58/91)   Nov 1947–Nov 1948. Correspondence on supply and requirements and allocations period IV 1947 to period III 1948. Report on the U.K.'s requirements and supplies of timber and plywood 1949–53.

131   **Terms of trade – publicity.** (CP226/28/02)   Oct–Dec 1947.

132   **Memorandum re priority of movement of traffic during winter 1947/48.** (CP30/01)   July 1947–Feb 1948. Some papers of the Central Transport Committee Subcommittee on Transport Requirements. Revised instructions to the Railway Transport Executive on transport priorities and restrictions. Establishment of a Winter Transport Policy Committee.

133   **Winter Transport Executive Committee.** (CP30/64/02)   Nov 1947–Mar 1948. Notes on its establishment and working.

134   **Investigation and wagon repair problems.** (CP8/40/012)   Oct 1947–Jan 1948. Papers leading up to EPC(48)5 (CAB 134/217).

135   **Road Transport Executive.** (CP10/02)   Oct–Nov 1947. Choice of chairman.

136   **Marshall proposals. Alternative action in event of breakdown.** (CP41/02)   July 1947. Drafts of a paper by R.W.B. Clarke and notes of a meeting, 16 July 1947.

137   **Long-term industrial planning. Industries – wool manufacturers.** (CP74/01)   Aug–Sept 1947.

138   **Tractors. Export by Harry Ferguson Ltd. to the U.S.A. and France.** (CP269/25/07)   Oct 1947–Mar 1949.

139   **Crop drying project (M. Samuel and Co. Ltd.)** (CP269/04)   Feb–Apr 1949.

140   **Australian export of lead and zinc.** (CP138/60/01)   Dec 1948–Aug 1949.

141   **Balance of payments. Expansion of exports to North America.** (CP71/41/02)   Dec 1948–June 1949. Papers related to the Export Plans

Subcommittee (E(P)), note of a meeting, Mar 1949, on the export of capital goods in the long term and draft questionnaire on prospects and policy.

158   **The long-term demand for British exports of manufactures.** (CP23/01 annex 1) 1949. Report on the estimated demand in 1951 with detailed analysis of individual industries appended.

159   **Outlook for cereals and feedingstuffs 1947.** (CP135/06) Sept 1949–Apr 1949. Correspondence on the outlook in relation to both the agricultural expansion programme and to dollars.

160–161   **Study Group on Grass Production and Conservation (Zuckerman Report).** (CP135/01A and B) May 1947–Oct 1949. Papers of the Group, the Committee on Agricultural Output and the Panel on Import Substitution of the Committee on Industrial Productivity on feedingstuffs supplies.

162   **Additional animal feedingstuffs required as a result of increases in rations in 1948.** (CP135/02) Oct 1948–Jan 1949.

163   **Anglo-French Economic Committee.** (CP154/64/01) Jan–Feb 1949. Note of meeting, 11 Feb 1949, and Treasury comments on the future development of the European long-term programme.

164–165   **India and Pakistan Working Party on Capital Goods – sterling balances negotiations July 1948.** (CP119/01A and B) Apr 1948–Dec 1949. Various papers of the U.K. delegation and the negotiations. D.H.F. Robertson on the negotiations. Very little after summer 1948.

166   **Long-term industrial planning. General methodology.** (CP17/02) July 1947–July 1949. Correspondence on the methodology including experimental plans for textile industries. More generally on long-term economic planning and the purpose of the long-term survey, disagreements with the Economic Section and the work of C.E.P.S. R.L. Marris's file.

167   **Ford's expansion programme.** (CP45/11/09) Oct 1946–Apr 1949. Correspondence on distribution of industry policy and whether to allow development at Dagenham.

168   **Colonial investment projects submitted to the Investment Programmes Committee.** (CP45/013) Dec 1948–Dec 1949. Report of the Colonial Development Working Party and resulting correspondence on investment.

169   **Committee on Control of Investment – minutes of meetings.** (CP45/51/02) June–Sept 1949. See CAB 134/63.

170–172   **Joint Committee on the Working of the Steel Distribution Scheme.** (CP12/64/015A-C).

170   July 1947–July 1948. Papers of the Joint Committee (SDS) and relevant ones of the Materials Committee and the N.P.A.C.I. reviewing the scheme.

171   July–Sept 1948. Papers of the Joint Committee arising out of SDS/28 in which Cripps asked the Committee to consider alternative schemes, leading to the final report to the Materials Committee (M(48)82). See CAB 134/483.

172   Dec 1948–Apr 1949. Further papers.

173–174   **Working Party on Long-term Demands for Steel (1948). Correspondence and working papers.** (CP12/44/04A and B).

173   Feb 1947–May 1948. C.E.P.S. estimates of Britain's long-term demand leading to concern that the investment programme might be

inadequate. The Working Party (LDS(WP)) was set up to consider this. Early papers.

174   May–Sept 1948. Drafts of report and revised estimates of total home and world demand with papers leading up to the final report (EPB(48)22). See CAB 134/211.

175   Retained.

176–178   **Official Committee on Distribution of Industry. Panel A general correspondence. (CP29/01A-C).**

176   Apr–Dec 1946. Mainly on the location of government industrial establishments.

177   Jan–Dec 1947. Distribution and supply of labour in Huddersfield 1934–46. Progress of building in development areas and correspondence on a number of individual cases.

178   Jan–Dec 1948. Distribution of labour in Bolton 1939, 1946 and 1947. Correspondence arising out of Ian Mikardo's inquiry on the increased participation of managers and technicians in implementing planning. Bruce on the problems of Portsmouth. Jay on Wilson's draft White Paper on the distribution of industry. Correspondence on individual cases.

179   **Meeting between the Chancellor of the Exchequer and Dr. Ludwig Erhard. (CP26/03)** Nov 1948–Mar 1949. Notes and briefs, including the main brief by E.N. Plowden. Note of the meeting, 26 Nov 1948. Notes for the visit of G. Dahrendorf in 1949.

180   **Commonwealth conference. Preparation of brief on the development of the economic resources of the Commonwealth. (CP26/131/02)** Aug 1948–May 1949. Note on the general economic situation and E.R.P. Draft briefs on various Commonwealth countries and the development of Commonwealth economic resources. Some papers of GEN 248.

181   **Talks with South Africa on the four-year programme and related topics. (CP26/131/04)** Sept 1948–Mar 1949. Notes of meetings Nov 1948 on the financial aspects of South Africa's relations with the U.K.

182   **Meeting of Commonwealth finance ministers July 1949. Paper and minutes of meetings etc. (CP26/131/06).** Incomplete set. See CAB 133/41.

183   **Commonwealth finance ministers conference 1949. Working Party papers. (CP26/131/07)** June–July 1949. Incomplete set of papers of GEN 297. See CAB 130/53.

184–185   **Washington discussions with the U.S.A. and Canada 1949. WD(49) series of papers. (CP26/41/01A and B)** July–Aug 1949. WD and TT papers. See T 230/153–154. For T 229/184–189 also see T 232/89–100.

186   **Washington discussions 1949. Tripartite talks in the U.S.A. and Canada. TT(49) series of papers. (CP26/41/05)** Aug 1949. TT(49)1–32. Many are also WD papers.

187   **Tripartite economic discussions 1949. (CP26/41/02)** Aug–Sept 1949. Papers of the Combined Official Committee (COM/OFFICIAL D) and the Combined Top Committee (COM/TOP D).

188   **Washington discussions 1949. Tripartite talks in the U.S.A. and Canada. Sir Edwin Plowden's miscellaneous papers. (CP26/41/06)** June–Sept 1949. Various papers on the dollar position, including one by O. Franks. One paper and one meeting of the Working Party on Wages Policy and Devaluation (WP(C)). J.M. Fleming on the currency unions.

189   **Tripartite discussions held in Washington 1949 between the U.K., Canada and the U.S.A. Continuing organization to follow up discussions.** (CP26/41/07)   Sept–Dec 1949. Arrangements for the continuing organization.

190   **Working Party on the Oil Expansion Programme. Subcommittee on U.K. Consumption (Road and Rail) Subgroup B papers. GEN 295/B series.** (CP27/44/05)   July–Sept 1949. GEN 295/B/1–33. See CAB 130/52.

191   **London Committee – suggestions as to actions which would assist the economic recovery of Europe.** (CP129/64/01)   June–Nov 1948. Departmental suggestions for specific development projects, correspondence with the U.K. delegation to the O.E.E.C. and progress reports on projects.

192   **Liberalization of investments in the O.E.E.C. soft currency countries.** (CP129/72/02)   Aug–Dec 1949.

193–196   **Long-term Programme Sub-group A (Europe).** (CP129/193/01–03).

193   Supporting documents. (CP129/193/03)   Dec 1948–May 1949. Correspondence on proposals for integration and European viability. Comments on GEN 258/A/29.

194–   Papers. (CP129/193/01)   Jan–July 1949. GEN 258/A papers. See
195   CAB 130/43.

196   Minutes. (CP129/193/02)   Jan–June 1949. GEN 258/A minutes. See CAB 130/43.

197   **U.K. long-term programme. General.** (CP129/190/03)   Aug 1948–June 1949. Study of the points raised by the O.E.E.C. secretariat. The programme of 30 Sept 1948. R.L. Hall on the prospects for 1950. E. Roll on the completion of the O.E.E.C.'s consideration of the U.K. programme.

198   **1949/50 and long-term programmes. E.C.A. Mission's report. Departmental comments.** (CP129/010)   Nov 1948–Jan 1949.

199   **Long-term programme. Working Group (GEN 258 series) papers.** (CP129/44/05)   Nov 1948–Jan 1949. Incomplete set. See CAB 130/42.

200   **Country Long-term Programme Studies Subcommittee of the Working Party on Bilateral Discussions.** (CP129/44/03)   Oct 1948–Aug 1949.

201   **European economic co-operation. Joint buying and marketing in South America.** (CP129/64/02)   June 1948–Feb 1949.

202–205   **Long-term programme.**

202   Economic problems arising from study of long-term programmes. (CP129/04)   Nov–Dec 1948. Correspondence between R.W.B. Clarke and E.A.G. Robinson on the problems of Western Europe and correspondence on Western European viability arising out of the O.E.E.C. long-term programme.

203   Chancellor's speech on American aid and European Payments (Financial Provisions) Bill and Economic Secretary's speech on second reading of Bill. (CP129/194/01)   Jan 1949. Drafts, with comments, and final versions of the speeches.

204   O.E.E.C. ministerial meetings. (CP129/08)   Jan–May 1949. ER(L)(49)3 and resulting comments on the future structure of the O.E.E.C.

205 Working Group – Sub-group C (U.K.) (CP129/44/07) Dec 1948–May 1949. Papers on modification of U.K. programme to secure agreement on a European plan.

206 **Butter and egg contract.** (CP129/151/03) May 1949. Overseas Negotiations Committee papers on contracts with Denmark.

207 **Long-term programme (France). Anglo-French talks.** (CP129/154/03) Feb–Apr 1949. Note of meeting with M. Monnet, 17 Feb 1949, and papers on the revision of the French long-term programme.

208 **Problems and methods of planning.** (CP66/013) July 1947–Dec 1949. Correspondence between E.E. Bridges and E.N. Plowden on the role of fiscal measures in planning. C.E.P.S. covering note to the Economic Survey for 1948–51. Note of a meeting with the Czech planning department, Sept 1947. Unsigned draft paper on the progress of economic planning. Gap to 1949 then draft of D.A.V. Allen's 'Note on economic planning' and an unsigned and undated note 'Economic planning'.

209–211 **Talks with Australia and New Zealand on planning and development.**

209 Development in New Zealand. (CP82/138/03) Oct 1948–Dec 1949. Relevant Sterling Area Development Working Party minutes and memoranda with resulting correspondence.

210 U.K. purchase of inessentials from Australia. (CP82/138/012) Oct 1948–April 1949.

211 Diversion of exports from U.K., Australia and New Zealand to dollar areas. (CP82/138/011) Sept 1948–Feb 1949.

212 **Devaluation of sterling.** (CP263/01) Aug–Sept 1949. Draft brief for ministerial talks in Washington. J.M. Fleming on credit policy and currency union. Report by a working party on changes to the price structure after devaluation. Arrangements for informing other countries.

213 **Wages policy following devaluation.** (CP263/02) Aug–Sept 1949. Minutes and memoranda of the Working Party on Wages Policy and Devaluation (WP(C)).

214 **Timber. Requirements for housing.** (CP58/20/01) Oct 1947–Aug 1949. Various papers including some on the Investment Programmes Committee's proposals for the housing programme.

215 **Tourist industry. Short-term plans.** (CP148/01) Nov 1947–Feb 1949. Correspondence relating to the Working Group on Tourism.

216 Retained.

217 **Restrictions on post-war German shipbuilding.** (CP13/157/01) Mar 1949.

218 **Campion Working Party on Statistics for Review of Agricultural Prices – Feb 1950.** (CP269/2/02) Jan–Dec 1950. Some minutes and memoranda for the Working Party on Farm Incomes and Prices (CSO(FP)).

219 **Working Party on the Building Industry. Report (PC(50)43).** (CP5/44/01) Mar–July 1950. Copy of the report and resulting comments. Question of simultaneous publication of the Anglo-American Council of Productivity Report to reduce possible criticism of government. See CAB 134/646.

220 **Colonial Development Working Party – general.** (CP145/01) Nov 1947–Apr 1949. Papers on its establishment and general correspondence. Notes and correspondence on its report.

221   **Cotton industry. Re-equipment, redeployment and productivity.** (CP73/ 81/01)   Aug 1948–May 1950. Notes on the relevant papers of the Labour (Textile Industries) Committee. See CAB 134/471–474.

222   **Economic and social development in South and South-east Asia and the Far East. The Sydney Conference.** (CP35/239/02)   Mar–Nov 1950. Briefs and report.

223–224   **Economic Survey for 1950.** (CP201/93/08B and 08 annex II).

    223   Feb–July 1950. Drafts and proposed amendments following consideration by the Official Committee on Economic Development, the Economic Planning Board, the Production Committee and Cabinet.

    224   Feb–Mar 1950. Proof copies and amendments.

225   **Peak load problem.** (CP14/012)   Oct 1948–Oct 1950. British Electricity Authority on tariffs and the electricity supply industry. The estimated trend of peak load until 1965 and proposed remedies. Economic Section on tariffs with comments. Clow Report (Cmd. 7464). Increasing urgency of the problem with rearmament.

226   **The dollar retention incentive scheme.** (CP23/41/01)   Mar–June 1950. Correspondence arising out of ED(W)(50)21, with which Cripps disagreed, leading to EPC(50)64. See CAB 134/203 and 226.

227–228   **Working Party on Feedingstuffs Subsidies.** (CP135/220/01A and B).

    227   June 1948–Jan 1949. Papers of the Working Party of the Agricultural Output Committee considering removal of subsidies as recommended in EPB(48)17. See CAB 134/211.

    228   Oct 1949–Dec 1950. Minutes, memoranda and correspondence of the Working Party on Feedingstuffs Prices and Derationing (FS P & D).

229–231   **Foreign exchange – the dollar drain (1949).** (CP55/02A-C)   Jan 1949–Jan 1950. Minutes and memoranda of the Sterling Area Statistical Committee (SASC) and the Dollar Drain Committee (DD). Weekly statements of dollars received from E.C.A. and of procurement authorizations issued. See also T 229/53–54 and 284.

232   **Proposed rationing of petrol and other dollar imports.** (CP39/90/01) Oct 1947–June 1950.

233   **Programmes and progress of work. Housing.** (CP20/07)   June 1947–Jan 1950. Various forecasts and reports.

234   **Aluminium houses: production.** (CP20/09)   Feb 1948–Nov 1950.

235   **Imports Diversion Committee – minutes of meetings.** (CP47/64/01) July 1948–Jan 1950. Minutes of the committee (ID).

236   **1949 Colonial import programmes. General.** (CP47/79/047)   Mar 1949–May 1950. Papers on the Colonial dollar import standstill and on its removal.

237   **Committee on Control of Investment – working papers.** (CP45/51/03) June 1949–Feb 1950. Papers of the Committee (see CAB 134/63). Report of the Committee on Economic Controls (CEC(50)2) and note of a meeting, 23 Feb 1950, to consider it. See CAB 134/95.

238   **Investment Programmes Committee. Ministry of Transport purchase tax on commercial vehicles.** (CP45/114/014)   Apr–Nov 1950. Correspondence with motor manufacturing industry on imposition of purchase tax to increase exports. Correspondence between Gaitskell and Stokes, and Gaitskell on the need for fiscal controls if there were not to be physical ones.

239   **Review of steel distribution scheme.** (CP12/64/017)   Dec 1947–Apr 1950. Various papers of the Joint Committee on Working of the Steel

Distribution Scheme (SDS). Jay proposal for review of alternative
schemes and the resulting SDS papers in 1949 on the relaxation of
steel allocation leading to 1950 consideration of the decontrol of general
steel.

240–241   **Substitution of steel and other materials for timber.** (CP12/58/01A and
01 annex I).

240   May 1947–Nov 1949. Papers leading to the establishment of the
Working Party on Timber Substitution (TS) and its correspondence.

241   Working Party – papers and minutes. Apr–Sept 1949. TS(49) minutes
and memoranda leading to its final report (TS(49)20).

242   **Local Government Manpower Committee – Subcommittee on Building
Control Policy.** (CP227/15/01)   July 1949–June 1950. Some minutes,
memoranda, correspondence and its report (LGM(BR)(50)5).

243   **Bilateral discussions in London with U.S. representatives on the defence
programme (Aug–Sept 1950).** (CP253/41/01)   Aug–Sept 1950.

244   **Substitution of sterling for dollar oil. Talks with the U.S.A. 1949/50.**
(CP27/02)   Jan 1949–July 1950. Various papers, including some by
the Oil Working Party (OWP) on substitution and, in particular, of
discussions and correspondence with the Standard Oil Co.

245–247   **Co-ordination of investments.** (CP129/72/01A–C)   Nov 1948–May
1950. Various papers of the European Economic Co-operation
Committee (ER(L)); its Working Group C on the U.K. long-term
programme; and the U.K. delegation to the O.E.E.C. on the integration
of European investment programmes on the basis of long-term plans
submitted to the O.E.E.C.

248–252   **Dual price policy.** (CP2/01A–E)   Oct 1949–Oct 1950. Papers of the
European Economic Co-operation Committee (ER(L)), its Working
Group on Dual Price Policy (GEN 301) and its delegation to the
O.E.E.C. (ER(P)). Also papers of the Overseas Negotiations Committee
(ON) and of the Economic Policy Committee on dual pricing, for
example of coal, with O.E.E.C. attitudes.

253   **Prime Minister's visit to Washington (Dec 1950). Raw materials aspect.**
(CP33/26/01)   Nov 1950–June 1951. General brief and supplement
on raw materials. Notes on the economic effects of the Korean War
and on planning defence expenditure of the North Atlantic Treaty
countries on a comparable basis.

254   **Agriculture – special price review 1951. Increased cost of fertilizers and
wages.** (CP269/2/07)   Aug–Nov 1951. Correspondence on the
restoration of fertilizer subsidy and whether a special review of
agricultural wages and prices was justified.

255–256   **Review of agricultural subsidies (progress of agricultural expansion
programme).** (CP269/220/01A and B)   Mar 1949–May 1951. Review
of agricultural policy leading to a report on the expansion programme
and its economic implications. Some Agricultural Output Committee
(AD) minutes and memoranda included.

257   **Direct agricultural subsidies.** (CP269/220/02)   Dec 1950–Nov 1951.
Papers and meetings on individual subsidies and agricultural subsidies
in general.

258   **Balance of payments. Four-year plan.** (CP71/03B)   June 1948–June
1951. Arrangements for preparation, EPC(48)66 (CAB 134/218) and
resulting correspondence between Cripps and Strachey on the assumed

food consumption levels. Notes on the establishment of the Imports Diversion Committee.

259   **Export target.** (CP71/23/07)   Sept 1948–July 1951. Correspondence on the export target for end-1949 and incompatibility of the balance of payments export target with investment in plant and machinery in the 1949 I.P.C. report.

260   **Coal allocations to industry.** (CP7/90/01)   May 1947–May 1952. Papers on rationing, with preparation of allocations winter 1947–48 and summer 1948. Then little to late 1950. Renewed consideration of an industrial allocation scheme.

261–262   **Coal. Allocations to home and export market.** (CP7/90/04A and B).
261   Nov 1948–Feb 1950. Memoranda of various committees on the supply position and resulting allocations, in particular of large coal. Disagreement between Gaitskell and C.E.P.S. on the role of C.E.P.S. in the coal budget.
262   March 1950–Jan 1951. Increasing consideration, including by the Overseas Negotiations Committee, of whether to reduce export allocations.

263   **Use of Colonial industrial and manpower capacity in the U.K. rearmament programme (Working Party and general papers).** (CP79/136/01)   Nov 1950–Sept 1951. Papers on the establishment of the working party with some of its minutes, memoranda and correspondence.

264   **Possibilities of increasing the supply of Colonial foodstuffs and raw materials to the U.K.** (CP199/04)   Oct–Nov 1951.

265   **Correspondence arising out of the Colonial import programme.** (CP199/47/02)   Oct 1948–Dec 1951. Correspondence on the programme and some papers on the Subcommittee on Import Programmes of the Colonial Development Committee (CD(BP)).

266–267   **Controls and economic powers (Economic Planning and Full Employment Bill).** (CP51/01A and B).
266   May 1947–Dec 1950. Various papers on controls and the delegation of responsibility for their administration to industry. Comments, including Jay's, on the Board of Trade's Operation Bonfire. Then gap to 1950 and papers on the draft Economic Powers Bill. Issue of whether the Bill should include positive as well as negative powers for the maintenance of full employment. Some minutes and memoranda of GEN 324 and GEN 343. See CAB 130/60 and 65.
267   Jan–Nov 1951. Further minutes and memoranda of GEN 324 and GEN 343, including drafts of the Bill (renamed the Full Employment Bill), and monthly reports on developments of economic controls.

268–269   **Expansion of aluminium production within the Commonwealth. Location of new projects.** (CP131/84/01A and B) June 1948–Nov 1952. Some minutes and memoranda on the Working Party on the Production of Primary Aluminium in the Commonwealth sterling area. Possible location in Scotland, North Borneo or the Gold Coast.

270–271   **Economic Survey for 1951.** (CP201/93/09A and B).
270   Sept 1950–Mar 1951. J. Downie pointed out that Ministers were unaware of how favourable the situation was. Work on the economic situation after the increase in defence expenditure. Arrangements for publication, suggested outline and drafts of the survey, including some Economic Survey Working Party (ESWP) papers.

271 Mar–July 1951. Proofs of the White Paper with amendments, summary for the press and economists' opinion published in the *Bulletin of the London and Cambridge Economic Service* (May 1951), with the Economic Section's comments.

272–276 Economic Organization Working Group – memoranda and correspondence. (CP201/44/02A-E).

272 Jan–June 1950. Papers on the Group's establishment by the Steering Committee for Economic Organization Enquiry (GOC(SC)). See CAB 134/314. Memoranda of the Working Group (EOWG) (see T 222/324–326). Comments on D.A.V. Allen's paper on the essential functions of the planning staff. Notes on the terminology of inflation.

273 June–Oct 1950. Further papers, with some drafts and resulting comments, particularly on the paper concerning the Treasury's major responsibilities.

274 Nov 1950–Jan 1951. Further papers. Drafts of report on contacts between government departments and private industry and business.

275 Jan–June 1951. Further papers, including draft of GOC(SC)(51)5. See CAB 134/314.

276 June–Oct 1951. Further papers. Drafts of sections on major economic activities of departments.

277 Economic Organisation Working Group – minutes of meetings. (CP201/44/03) Mar 1950–Aug 1951. See T 222/327.

278 Capital goods – exports for development. (CP23/02) Mar 1951–July 1952. Emphasis on Colombo Plan countries.

279 White fish subsidy. (CP246/01) June 1950–Aug 1951. Briefs on relevant Production Committee papers and draft briefs on quotas for the U.K. delegation to the O.E.E.C.

280–281 National food policy review. (CP11/01A and B) May 1950–Mar 1951. Review of trends in consumer expenditure on food and food supplies with related problems. Problem of co-operation with the Ministry of Food. Later papers on subsidy policy.

282 The possible need for international action in the field of food supplies. (CP11/03) Mar–June 1951. Notes of *ad hoc* meetings and resulting action.

283 Cereal feedingstuffs – policy. (CP135/07) Feb 1948–Nov 1951.

284 Dollar drain. Sterling Area Statistical Committee. (CP55/05) Jan 1950–Jan 1951. Minutes and memoranda of the Statistical Committee (SASC). Bank of England pamphlet on U.K. overseas investment 1938–48. See also T 229/53–54 and 229–231.

285 Electricity publicity. (CP45/104/013) June–Oct 1951. Correspondence concerning the response to British Electricity Authority publicity on the impact of investment cuts.

286–288 Investment Programmes Committee: plant and machinery. (CP45/25/01A-C).

286 Aug 1947–Dec 1948. Various Investment Programmes Committee Working Party papers (IPC(WP)). Concern that decisions on allocations of steel and the division between exports and the domestic market were taken by four bodies and were not always consistent: manufacturers needed guidance on priorities. Need for greater information on investment in the unprogrammed sector.

287 Feb–Nov 1949. Various IPC(WP) papers. Some excerpts from *Engineering.*

288   Jan 1950–Dec 1951. Various IPC(WP) papers. Estimates of the supplies for capital equipment 1949–52 and 1950–53.

289   **Investment prospects, and economic situation 1952 – part of general survey – circular letter 13 Sept 1951, 15 Nov 1951.** (CP45/027) Sept–Dec 1951. Arrangements for a review, the resulting circular and departmental replies. Resulting report showed an overload in the building industry and proposed consideration of controlling investment via starting dates and steel allocations.

290   **Chancellor's visit to Washington – Sept 1951. Talks on general economic problems.** (CP26/201/01)   June–Oct 1951. Correspondence on arrangements, briefs, in particular on coal, defence burden sharing and primary product prices. Note of discussions.

291–292   **The U.K. memorandum to the O.E.E.C. The O.E.E.C. third report – general.** (CP129/018A and B)   May 1950–May 1951. Administrative arrangements, suggested outline of the O.E.E.C. questionnaire, drafts of sections of report and suggested amendments. The report should not be another bid for aid but should assess possibilities and needs of the European economy in the next four/five years. The U.K. report was to say as little as possible on convertibility and non-discrimination.

293   **Railway manpower and winter coal supplies.** (CP8/7/02)   July–Oct 1951. Correspondence on deferring national service call-up for some railwaymen.

294–295   **Raw materials: general.** (CP33/04A and C – part B is missing).
294   Oct–Dec 1950. Correspondence on the Raw Materials Committee, the relationship between the O.E.E.C. Economic Committee and the *ad hoc* group in N.A.T.O. Some papers of the Treasury Stockpiling Committee. The O.E.E.C. draft report on scarcity of raw materials with comments.
295   Mar 1951–July 1954. Papers on Washington discussions with note by O. Franks. Ministerial opposition to a White Paper on the recent history of the raw materials situation. Establishment of the Ministry of Materials and the International Materials Conference.

296–297   **Revised functions of the Commonwealth Liaison Committee (raw materials).** (CP33/07A and B)   Dec 1950–June 1951. Various minutes and memoranda of the Committee on Commonwealth Economic Affairs and of the Commonwealth Liaison Committee concerning the latter's functions.

298   **Long-term measures for increasing production and conserving supplies of raw materials.** (CP33/011)   Feb–June 1951. Minutes and memoranda of various committees, in particular the Raw Materials Committee, after decision to consider the long term.

299–301   **Materials (Allocation) Committee. Steel: 1. Allocation 2. Controls.** (CP124/12/017A-C). See CAB 134/486.
299   Feb–June 1951. Papers on steel allocation and export licensing.
300   July–Sept 1951. Papers on allocation of different types of steel.
301   Sept–Nov 1951. Continued consideration of both allocation schemes, including the decision to delay the introduction of control until after the election.

302   **Raw materials shortages and their effect on U.K. export policy. General policy.** (CP33/23/01)   Jan–Sept 1951. Papers, including one by T.L. Rowan, on the U.K. line in negotiations with the U.S.A. and leading to ES(51)9. See CAB 134/264.

303   **Raw materials: French discussions.** (CP33/154/01)   Nov 1950–June
      1951. Briefs and notes of meetings on whether collective action should
      be international or O.E.E.C. centred.

304   **Lord Privy Seal's visit to Washington (May 1951).** (CP33/26/02)   May
      1951. General and detailed briefs with notes on relationship between
      the International Materials Conference and the O.E.E.C.

305   **Ministerial O.E.E.C. Council. Meetings on raw materials.** (CP33/129/
      02)   Nov 1950–Apr 1951. Briefs for meetings, including the
      relationship between the Washington Organization for Raw Materials
      and the O.E.E.C.

306   **Raw materials: skins and hides.** (CP33/255/01)   Feb–July 1951.
      Includes disagreement of Gaitskell with the official approach.

307   **Timber imports programme.** (CP58/47/01)   Feb 1948–Nov 1951. Very
      little after 1948.

308   **Anti-depression measures.** (CP133/01)   Feb 1948–Aug 1951. Little
      before April 1949, then series of meetings on the impact of a recession
      on various industries. Agreement that the most likely cause was a
      reduction in demand for exports. Consideration of possible remedies.
      July 1949 correspondence between the Ministry of Works and C.E.P.S.
      on preparing a reserve of works. Gap Nov 1949 to May/July 1950
      when Stokes raised with Cripps the state of anti-slump preparations.
      Reply proposing a comprehensive review in Oct. Agreement Sept 1950
      to postpone indefinitely owing to Korean War. See T 229/337.

309   **1. Allocation of shipping for urgent government requirements. 2. Shipping
      for imported iron ore.** (CP13/013)   Feb 1948–Oct 1951. Some minutes
      and memoranda of the Shipping Requirements Committee (SR)
      considering problems arising out of the export and import programmes.
      Renewed activity in 1951 on papers and third report of the Official
      Committee on Shipping for Urgent Government Programmes
      (EPC(51)67). See CAB 134/230.

310   **Working Party on Future Egg Policy.** (CP3/44/01)   Dec 1948–Nov
      1952. Consideration in relation to imports, domestic production and
      prices.

311   **Coal. Long-term plans (investment).** (CP7/66/01)   Nov 1950–May
      1952. Copy of the N.C.B.'s *Plan for Coal* and departmental comments.

312   **House coal.** (CP7/90/05)   May 1950–Feb 1953. Papers on meeting the
      deficiency of house coal. Review of domestic consumption of fuels
      1938–50.

313–314   **Steel: trends in production, consumption and stocks.** (CP12/017A and
      B).

    313   Dec 1947–June 1948. Various statistical papers and some Materials
          Committee and Production Committee memoranda.

    314   Oct 1949–June 1952. Some minutes and memoranda of the Working
          Party on Steel Consumption and later papers.

316   **Conversion value of exports. Reduction of exports of steel-using goods
      of low conversion value.** (CP12/23/04)   Feb 1948–Dec 1952. Little
      before Sept 1951.

317   **1. Exports of fabricated steel. 2. Exports of constructional steel.** (CP12/
      23/06)   Apr 1948–Oct 1952. Meetings and correspondence on exports
      of structural and constructional steel and implications of any cuts.

319   **Steel for oil companies.** (CP12/27/01)   May 1948–May 1952. Papers
      on steel for U.S. oil companies.

320   **Steel: imports (other than from the colonies and the U.S.A.). (CP12/47/
02)** Feb 1948–Dec 1953. In particular from Belgium and Luxembourg.

321   **Transport difficulties. Turn-round of shipping in U.K. ports. (CP13/08)**
Nov 1947–Mar 1952. Papers arising from Glenvil Hall's concern and
the Ministry of Transport Working Party on Shipping Turn-round in
British Ports' interim report on the Port of London. Little after start
of 1949.

322   **Electricity load shedding. Load Limiter electricity tariffs. (CP14/011)**
Jan 1951–Mar 1952. Papers arising from the Working Party on Fuel
Efficiency and Electricity Tariffs of the Official Coal Committee
(OCC(FE)WP)). Little after May 1951.

323   **Policy for full employment. (CP15/09)** July 1949–Apr 1952. Little
before Oct 1950. Papers on the full employment target, the Full
Employment Bill and the White Paper on Full Employment and Wages
Policy. Includes Gaitskell's views on the White Paper, A.T.K. Grant
on full employment and positive financial powers, and the Economic
Section on the lessons of the last five years (EC(S)(51)17 and 20). See
T 230/340.

324   **Houses for miners. (CP20/286/01)** May 1950–Mar 1952. N.C.B.
survey of housing needs and the special drive for houses for miners.
Mainly after Jan 1952.

325   **Oil supplies in wartime. (CP27/64/01A)** 1948–52. Retained.

326–327   **Raw materials – iron and steel. (CP33/12/02A and B)** Nov 1950–Jan
1952. Various papers including some minutes and memoranda of the
Materials Committee.

328   **Raw materials shortages and their effect on U.K. exports. Individual
cases. (CP33/23/02)** Aug 1951–Jan 1952. Shawcross was concerned
that the Economic Policy Committee had no time to consider the
defence programme's impact on present and prospective exports.
Papers leading to official consideration of individual cases.
Correspondence with Sir William Rootes, Chairman of the Dollar
Exports Advisory Council.

329–331   **Economic development of underdeveloped countries. (CP35/02A-C)** Feb
1949–Mar 1954. Papers arising out of President Truman's fourth point
in his inaugural speech.

332   **I.P.C.: composition, terms of reference and procedure. (CP45/03)** Aug
1949–Nov 1952. Papers on its establishment and its later replacement
of the Investment Working Party. Papers on changed membership and
functions. See CAB 134/437–456.

333   **Civil Investment Programme: annual review. (CP45/06A)** 1951–52.
Retained.

336   **Progress of industrial building in development areas. (CP45/5/08)** Aug
1947–Dec 1952. Papers on progress, the impact of investment cuts,
and various papers by Jay.

337   **I.P.C.: reserve of works. (CP45/5/016)** Oct 1947–Feb 1952. Various
papers including E.A.G. Robinson on the protection of steel for public
works; the U.K. reply to the U.N. questionnaire on employment policy;
the state of public works in other countries; and C.E.P.S. comments
on enquiries after late 1950 by Stokes on preparations. See T 229/308.

338   **I.P.C.: industrial building: John Deere Plow Co. (CP45/5/017)** June
1951–Apr 1952. Papers concerning a factory in East Kilbride and
breakdown of communications between committees on the issue.

339 **Control of investment: socialized industries.** (CP45/51/01)   Apr 1949–Nov 1952. Papers relating to the 1949 review of the control of investment and on the relationship between the investment programme and the sanctioning of particular capital projects by supply divisions of the Treasury. See CAB 134/69.

340 **Indirect methods of controlling investment (taxation and credit control).** (CP45/51/04)   Aug 1949–Nov 1952. Papers on schemes abroad.

342–343 **I.P.C.: Ministry of Civil Aviation – correspondence.** (CP45/99/01A and B)   Sept 1947–June 1953. Papers on Ministry's annual investment programme.

344 **I.P.C.: Department of Health for Scotland – housing correspondence.** (CP45/110/01)   Sept 1947–Aug 1953.

345 **I.P.C.: Ministry of Supply direct and assisted schemes excluding housing.** (CP45/112/01)   Aug 1947–June 1952. Papers on the general situation and individual cases.

346 **The motor industry.** (CP45/112/09)   Jan 1949–Oct 1952. Various papers on investment and supplies to the home market and exports.

347–348 **I.P.C.: Ministry of Transport – ports, harbours and canals.** (CP45/114/07A and B).

 347 Correspondence. Dec 1947–Nov 1949. Mainly on the impact of investment cuts 1947 and 1949.

 348 Dock amenities. Mar 1949–July 1950. Papers arising from the National Dock Labour Board report.

349–350 **I.P.C.: Ministry of Transport road vehicles – correspondence.** (CP45/114/010A and B)   Sept 1947–Jan 1953. Papers on investment in public service and commercial vehicles and the division of supplies of the latter between exports and home market.

351 **D.S.I.R. – general and own establishments on building programme.** (CP45/143/01)   Feb 1948–Feb 1952. Includes relevant I.P.C. Working Party and Committee papers.

352 **I.P.C.: Ministry of Materials – general – manufacturing industry.** (CP45/256/01)   Oct 1951–Dec 1952.

354 **Sterling balances.** (CP82/71/01A)   Mar 1950–Dec 1951. Includes long paper by the Sterling Area Working Party on future arrangements with holders of the balances (SA(50)4), and Treasury's Overseas Finance and Treasury Division on the fundamentals of external financial policy. Also papers concerning discussions with the U.S.A. and, after 1951, Commonwealth Supply Ministers' meeting.

355 **Steel: D.O. scheme.** (CP124/12/018)   Apr 1951–Sept 1952. Papers including some by Noel-Baker and Gaitskell on the priority scheme for defence contracts, and some papers of GEN 391.

356 **Steel: P.T. scheme.** (CP124/12/019)   Apr 1951–Jan 1952. Papers on the civil preferential treatment scheme for steel.

357 **Priorities for steel for building (D.O. and P.T. schemes).** (CP124/12/020)   June 1951–Feb 1952. Papers relating to a possible over-application of D.O. and P.T. orders.

358 **General steel allocation – imports on private account.** (CP124/12/022) Nov 1951–May 1952.

361 **Non-ferrous metals.** (CP124/118/01)   1951–52. Retained.

362 **Defence: priority systems in relation to material allocation.** (CP124/136/01A)   Dec 1950–Jan 1952. Proposal by Strauss on the need for priority

defence orders, Dec 1950. Renewed discussions in May 1951 with further papers leading to the introduction of D.O. symbol.

363   **Materials (Allocation) Committee: zinc.** (CP124/252/01)   Dec 1950–Aug 1952.

371   **Wheat and coarse grains import policy.** (CP135/05)   Nov 1949–Nov 1952. Includes papers on possible reduction of feedingstuffs rations.

372–374   **Labour problems arising from expanded defence production – including problems of location of new production capacity.** (CP136/15/02A-C).

372   Aug 1950–Aug 1951. Minutes of various meetings to determine labour needs and minimize new programme's impact.

373   Aug–Dec 1951. Papers on the reintroduction of labour supply inspection, local labour shortages, survey of areas with excess labour demands. Particular attention to proposed Marconi factory in Basildon.

374   Dec 1951–Mar 1953.

375   **Labour requirements for the defence programme at Swynnerton and Radway Green.** (CP136/15/06)   Dec 1950–June 1951. Papers on requirements for two Royal Ordnance factories, including possible conflict with export industries.

376   **The export programme in relation to the accelerated defence programme – proposed increase in volume of export and consumption goods.** (CP135/23/01)   Feb 1951–Feb 1952. Papers on the prospects of achieving the export target and on those targets to be used by production departments in discussion with industry.

377–379   **N.A.T.O. Temporary Council Committee: general papers.** (CP136/64/01A-C)   1951–52. Retained.

380–381   **N.A.T.O. Lisbon meeting: papers leading up to the report.** (CP136/64/02A and B)   1951–52. Retained.

383–385   **Limitation of the production of goods for home consumption to facilitate defence production.** (CP136/81/04A-C).

383   Feb–June 1951. Drafts of CPC(51)4 and 10(final) and other relevant papers of the Committee on Productive Capacity, particularly concerning allocation of raw materials. See CAB 134/115.

384   July–Nov 1951. Papers leading up to EPC(51)97, CPC(51)49 and 58 with resulting correspondence on the possible restriction of production. See CAB 134/115 and 230.

385   Nov 1951–Nov 1952. Further papers reflecting departmental differences on nature of cuts.

386   **Defence share of production and productive capacity.** (CP136/85/01) 1951–52. Retained.

388   **Storage requirements: control of factory and storage space.** (CP136/244/01)   1951–52. Retained.

389–391   **Australian wartime production of food and raw materials.** (CP138/44/01A-C)   1951–52. Retained.

392   **Australian import cuts. Effect upon steel allocation.** (CP138/47/01) Dec 1951–Mar 1952.

393   **Working Group on Tourism.** (CP148/44/01)   Jan 1948–July 1952. Some minutes and memoranda of the group (WGT) to encourage dollar-earning tourism.

394–395   **Nigerian ground-nuts. Transport.** (CP199/30/02A and B)   Nov 1947–Apr 1952. Various papers on Nigerian railways.

396–398   **E.C.A. loan for the development of the Rhodesian railways.** (CP199/30/06A-C)   Mar 1950–Nov 1952.

399-401 **Economic outlook for 1952.** (CP201/01A-C).
399 June–Oct 1951. Includes minutes and memoranda of GEN 380 and minutes of the Second Secretaries' meeting to consider, in accordance with ES(51)53(CAB 134/266), the drafting of a general report on economic prospects (GEN 380/7). See CAB 130/71.
400 Oct 1951–Jan 1952. Further drafts of GEN 380/7 and ES(51)57 with comments.
401 Nov 1951–Dec 1952. Papers on the steps towards solvency after the stop-gap measures recommended in ES(51)57(final). See CAB 134/266.

402 **Urgent economic problems in 1952 and 1953.** (CP201/01) Nov 1951–Jan 1952. Papers and drafts relating to the ministerial Subcommittee on the Economic Situation and drafts of Chancellor's speech.

404-405 **Economic discussions with the T.U.C.** (CP201/08A and B).
404 May 1947–Feb 1949. Various papers, briefs and minutes of meetings on the fuel crisis, equal pay, the statement on personal incomes and the economic situation June 1948, Nov 1948 and Feb 1949.
405 Apr 1949–June 1952. Papers, briefs and minutes of meetings on the 1949 budget, wage restraint and price reductions, the general economic situation, rearmament and long-term fuel policy.

406-408 **Economic Survey for 1952.** (CP201/93/010A-C) Dec 1951–Oct 1952.
406 Dec 1951–Feb 1952. Papers and correspondence on publication arrangements and the role and history of the survey with suggested outline and drafts of various sections.

409 **National income – inflation.** (CP230/02) Sept 1949–Dec 1951. Estimates of the degree of inflation post-devaluation, notes on Economic Section reports on inflationary or deflationary pressure and the change of government, Nov 1951.

410 **Sugar policy – general.** (CP243/01A) May–Nov 1949. Papers relating to the Ministry of Food's Sugar Policy Working Party with its report.

411 **N.A.T.O.: Temporary Council Committee: U.K. submission and comments on report.** (CP253/190/02) 1951–52. Retained.

415 **Review of development areas. General economic problems and policies.** (CP276/01) Dec 1951–Nov 1952.

416 **Chancellor's statement to the N.P.A.C.I. on defence and the economic situation.** (CP288/136/01) Oct 1950–July 1952. Briefs and notes for Butler's speech. Butler had added 'We must beware of the *corporate state*'.

417 **C.E.P.S. General Policy.** (CP1/09) Apr 1947–Dec 1953. Background to the establishment of C.E.P.S. and initial considerations of its role, initially to concentrate on the short term. Various papers and minutes of work during summer 1947 covering the relationship between economic planning and financial and fiscal policy, the planning machinery and the economic situation. Diagram of the planning machinery Dec 1947. Thereafter little until May 1951 review of C.E.P.S. and economic planning review and Mar 1952 consideration of the organization for economic policy.

418-420 **Coal exports and bunkers.** (CP7/23/01A-C) Aug 1947–July 1953.
418 Aug 1947–May 1951. Papers on prospects of increasing exports. Some related minutes and memoranda of the Production Committee, the

Economic Policy Committee and the Overseas Negotiations
Committee.

419   June 1951–Feb 1952. Increasing emphasis on exports and bilateral
agreements.

421   **Coal-mining machinery and equipment.** (CP7/25/01A)   June 1947–Dec
1953. Early papers on N.C.B. requirements and steel supplies. Gap
April 1949–Nov 1950 with correspondence of the Working Party on
Samson Strippers continuing until Mar 1951.

424–425   **Iron ore supplies.** (CP12/021A and B)   June 1951–Mar 1953. Papers
and some minutes and memoranda of the Committee on Iron Ore
(CIO).

427   **Steel exports: 1. Finished steel. 2. Total steel supplies.** (CP12/23/01)
Nov 1947–May 1953. Papers on allocation of steel to exports.

428–429   **Level of exports of steel and tin plate.** (CP12/23/05A and B)   Mar
1949–June 1953. Relevant papers of the Overseas Negotiations
Committee and its Working Party including reports on steel exports
in 1951 and resulting correspondence.

432–433   **International policy for full employment.** (CP15/07A and B)   June
1950–Dec 1953. Papers of the Working Party on the U.N. Report on
National and International Measures to Achieve Full Employment
(NIFE). U.K. reply to the U.N. questionnaire on employment policy
and related papers of the Committee on National and International
Measures for Full Employment (NIFE/UN).

434–441   **Economic Planning Board papers.** (CP18/05A-H).

434   July–Oct 1947. EPB(47)1–22. See T 229/28–35.

435   Oct 1947–June 1948. EPB(47)23–31 and EPB(48)1–20. See T 229/
35–38 and CAB 134/211.

436   July 1948–Feb 1949. See CAB 134/211–212.

437   Apr 1949–Mar 1950. See CAB 134/212–213.

438   Apr 1950–Sept 1951. See CAB 134/213–214.

439   1951–53. Retained. See CAB 134/214 and 877–878.

442–443   **Economic Planning Board minutes.** (CP18/06A and B).

442   July 1947–Dec 1948. See T 229/28–38 and CAB 134/210.

443   Jan 1949–Dec 1951. See CAB 134/212–214.

444   **National fuel policy including the Ridley Report.** (CP19/04)   Jan
1951–Oct 1953. Papers on the committee's establishment with views
of the T.U.C., the F.B.I., ministers and officials. Copy of a report
included.

448–452   **Central Group of Raw Materials Conference and Commodity Groups.**
(CP33/06A-E)   Jan 1950–Dec 1953.

448   Jan 1950–Feb 1951. Papers and telegrams on the establishment of, and
U.K. membership of, the Central Raw Materials Group in Washington
and on relations between the Washington secretariat and the O.E.E.C.
Some minutes and memoranda of the Raw Materials Committee and
its representatives in Washington.

449   Feb 1951. Further papers on the group with telegrams and papers
leading up to the International Materials Conference.

450   Feb–May 1951. Further papers on the group's possible expansion, and
the International Materials Conference. Some papers of the Raw
Materials Committee and its Washington counterpart and of the
Economic Committee (Washington).

451   June 1951–Mar 1953. Further material on the International Materials
       Conference and Ministry of Materials' views on raw material price
       policy.

**454   Economic and social development in South and South-East Asia and the
       Far East.** (CP35/239/01A)   Apr 1949–Aug 1950.

455–459   I.P.C.: policy and reports. (CP45/01A-E).

455   July 1946–Aug 1949. Mainly on drawing up of departmental
       programmes and the committee's annual reports. Also includes
       investment in 1952 and pre-war.

456   Oct 1949–May 1950. Papers on cuts following devaluation and a 1950
       review of the shortfall in investment cuts. A.K. Ogilvy-Webb on the
       degree of success of economic planning. Drafts of various annual
       programmes up to 1952 and papers on the need to control investment.

457   May–Dec 1950. Stokes on capital investment policy and inflation.
       Note of a meeting, May 1950, on credit policy and note, July 1950, on
       the course of investment programmes 1947–52. Other papers on the
       formulation of programmes, particularly the choice between the higher
       and lower programmes for 1950. Some papers on the consequences of
       the additional defence programme.

458   Jan–May 1951. Progress report on post-devaluation cuts. Papers and
       drafts of report on capital investment in 1951, 1952 and 1953 including
       possible ban on office building.

459   June 1951–Oct 1953. Further drafts of 1951–53 programme report.

463   The finance of investment and inflationary pressure. (CP45/023)   Aug
       1949–Mar 1954. Post-devaluation papers on the need for and ways to
       achieve reduced investment. Little thereafter until April 1952.

464–466   Industrial investment: manufacturing industries. (CP45/5/02A-C).

464   Sept 1947–Dec 1949. Various papers, including sponsoring
       departments' views, on the progress of industrial building. Excerpts
       from I.P.C. reports. The F.B.I. on taxation and the shortage of industrial
       capital.

465   Sept 1949–Mar 1953. Disagreement, June 1950, between the Board of
       Trade and Ministry of Supply on the level of new factory building for
       1951 and 1952. Extracts from relevant I.P.C. reports and consideration
       of the criteria for judging manufacturing industry projects. Draft paper
       on post-war investment in manufacturing industry.

466   Mar–Nov 1953. Further drafts of paper on post-war investment leading
       to GEN 422/8.

467–469   Defence programme: building and construction work. (CP45/5/011A-C).

467   Oct 1947–Dec 1950. Odd papers until 1950, then the implications for
       the investment programme of increased defence expenditure, with
       related I.P.C. Working Party and other committee's memoranda.

468   1951. Retained.

469   Apr 1951–Feb 1953. Various papers including extracts from I.P.C.
       meetings and memoranda. Some papers of the Inter-departmental
       Works Services Committee (IWS).

470   Capital investment programme. Ban on office building. (CP45/5/013)
       April 1951–Oct 1953. Draft and final report of the Headquarters
       Building Committee with papers on implementation of the ban after
       1951.

471–472   I.P.C.: building output and productivity. (CP45/5/015A and B).

471   Nov 1948–Feb 1951. Various papers including the Anglo-U.S. Productivity Team's report on building, correspondence between Gaitskell and Stokes and memoranda of the Working Party on Productivity in the Building Industry (PB).

472   Feb 1951–Sept 1953. Ministry of Works note on the measurement of changes in cost and productivity and resulting correspondence including estimates of building capacity in 1952.

473–477   I.P.C.: Ministry of Housing and Local Government (investment programme): housing. (CP45/20/01A-E)   Aug 1947–Nov 1953.

473   Aug 1947–Dec 1949. On the annual and long-term reviews. Includes relevant I.P.C. and I.P.C. Working Party papers and minutes.

474   Dec 1949–Dec 1950. Reviews including correspondence between Cripps and Bevan on economies and the shortfall in investment cuts. Further correspondence on restoring the cut of £30m and proposal to increase the housing programme by increasing productivity.

475   Dec 1950–July 1952. Little before Nov 1951.

479   I.P.C.: machinery and plant. Control of investment. (CP45/25/02)   Dec 1951–Jan 1953. Papers on the establishment of a study group to consider the means of control.

480   I.P.C.: Control of Building Operations Order (Defence Regulations 56A and emergency legislation). Licensing of industrial and agricultural building – raising of licence-free limit. (CP45/51/07A)   Nov 1947–July 1953. Papers on the £100 limit in 1947 and 1948, then gap to Oct 1951.

483   Control of investment – alternative systems (Sir Bernard Gilbert's committee). (CP45/51/09A)   Feb 1949–June 1953. Some minutes and memoranda of the Treasury Organization Committee (TOC) and views of members of C.E.P.S. and R.L. Hall with other papers leading to the review by Gilbert's committee in 1953.

485–487   Investment Committee. Building materials. (CP45/62/01A-C)   Nov 1947–July 1954.

485   Nov 1947–Feb 1951. Papers, including memoranda of the I.P.C. Working Party on various materials including cement, bricks and timber and their likely supply in relation to investment programme, particularly housing.

486   Mar 1951–Apr 1953. Review of brick supply and demand in 1951 and of increased demand.

488   Board of Trade manufacturing industries and miscellaneous investments. (CP45/6901C)   Feb 1951–June 1953. Papers on the approval of individual investments and more general papers on changes in productivity in British industry, including L. Rostas on the inter-relationship of motive power, production and productivity.

489   Board of Trade miscellaneous investment. Hotels. (CP45/69/012)   May 1950–July 1953.

490–491   I.P.C.: Northern Ireland – correspondence. (CP45/80/01B and C)   Apr 1949–Sept 1953.

490   Apr 1949–Dec 1951. Correspondence showing Ulster's concern that it was being treated unfairly.

492–494   I.P.C.: Ministry of Education. (CP45/101/01A-C)   Aug 1947–Aug 1953.

492   Aug 1947–Dec 1949. Papers on the investment reviews 1947 and 1949, particularly correspondence between Attlee and Tomlinson on the proposed cut of 30% in 1949 and the eventual compromise at 15%.

495   **I.P.C.: Ministry of Fuel and Power – general correspondence.** (CP45/104/01)   Aug 1947–Oct 1953. Papers relating particularly to 1947, 1949 and 1950–52 reviews.

496–502   **I.P.C.: electricity – correspondence.** (CP45/104/02B-H)   Jan 1948–Nov 1953.

     496   Jan 1948–June 1949. Papers on the generating station and heavy electrical plant programmes.

     497   Jan–Dec 1949. Papers on the British Electricity Authority generating station programme up to 1952, seasonal variation of tariffs and importation of boilers. Ministerial correspondence on investment cuts late 1949.

     498   Jan–Dec 1950. Continued ministerial correspondence on cuts and importation of boilers. Report to E.C.A. mission to the U.K. on electric power to G.B. and papers on tariffs and the peak load problem. Some minutes and memoranda of the Heavy Electrical Plant Committee (HEP).

     499   Nov 1950–June 1951. Papers covering tariffs, capital investment 1950–54, U.S. assistance for generating plant with regard to rearmament. Also the trend in demand for electricity in the U.K. 1951–65 and the possibility of meeting it.

     500   July–Oct 1951. Various papers and correspondence including some between Edwards, J., Gaitskell and Noel-Baker on the electricity investment programme.

     501   Sept 1951–July 1952. Papers on the impact of certain variables on domestic consumer demand and co-ordination of fuel and power and transport policy. Comparison of the supply of electricity to industry and industrial production from 1924.

503   **I.P.C.: Ministry of Fuel and Power – coal-mining – correspondence.** (CP45/104/04)   Nov 1947–Sept 1953. Includes paper for E.C.A. report on British investment programmes and balance of payments prospects and one by the Minister of Fuel and Power on projected cuts in fuel and power industries for 1950.

504   **I.P.C.: Ministry of Fuel and Power – gas.** (CP45/104/07)   Sept 1947–Oct 1953. Various I.P.C. minutes and memoranda and memoranda of the Working Party with comments, with some correspondence between Noel-Baker and Gaitskell on the impact of steel shortages in 1951.

505–506   **I.P.C.: petroleum – correspondence.** (CP45/104/010A and B)   Sept 1947–Nov 1953. Various papers on the oil refinery investment programme in general and particular companies' proposals.

510–512   **I.P.C.: Post Office – correspondence.** (CP45/107/01A-C)   Sept 1947–Oct 1953.

513–516   **I.P.C.: B.B.C. – correspondence.** (CP45/107/03A-D)   Oct 1947–Nov 1953.

518–519   **Investment Programmes. Scottish Home Department.** (CP45/111/01B and C)   Jan 1950–June 1953. Papers mainly on the Highlands Development Programme and the Department's annual programme.

520–521   **Ministry of Housing and Local Government: 1. Construction of blitzed cities. 2. Miscellaneous investment.** (CP45/113/02A and B)   Dec 1947–Oct 1953.

     520   Dec 1947–Sept 1951. Includes consideration of local unemployment.

522   **I.P.C.: Ministry of Housing and Local Government – water and sewerage.**
            (CP45/113/04A) Feb 1949–May 1953. Includes correspondence
            between Bevan and Cripps on rural sewerage.

523–524   **I.P.C.: Ministry of Transport.** (CP45/114/01A and B) Aug 1947–Oct
            1953.

    523   Aug 1947–Sept 1952. Papers relating to the annual reviews and 1947
            and 1949 reductions. Some papers on the Channel tunnel early 1950.

525–529   **I.P.C.: Ministry of Transport – roads.** (CP45/114/04A-E) Sept
            1947–Nov 1953.

    525   Sept–Dec 1947. Correspondence, including some by ministers and the
            British Road Federation on 1947 cuts.

    526   Jan 1948–Apr 1950. Correspondence on particular cases, including the
            Merthyr Tydfil road scheme and the Runcorn-Widnes bridge, as well
            as on the annual road programme and 1949 investment review.

    527   May 1950–Mar 1952. Correspondence on road maintenance
            expenditure including negotiations with local authorities on
            distribution of total expenditure.

530   **I.P.C.: Public Works Loan Board (local authorities' borrowing).**
            (CP45/227/01) Mar 1950–May 1954. Jay on the place of local
            authorities in the investment programme in 1949 and comparison of
            loan sanctions with investment programmes. Gap from June 1950 to
            1952.

531   **I.P.C.: industrial development in new towns – manufacturing industry.**
            (CP45/261/01) Aug 1948–Sept 1953. Papers mainly on individual
            cases.

532   **I.P.C.: new towns – England and Wales.** (CP45/261/03) Sept
            1947–Oct 1953.

533   **I.P.C.: ban on (a) work on places of recreation and (b) entertainment
            buildings.** (CP45/264/01) Mar 1948–Jan 1953. Papers mainly on
            individual cases.

534   **I.P.C.: Admiralty 1. Works and building.   2. Manufacturing industries.**
            (CP45/285/01) Aug 1947–Jan 1953. Papers on annual investment
            programmes of the Admiralty and its sponsored industries.

537–542   **Dollar drain.** (CP55/03A–F) Jan 1950–Sept 1955. Incomplete set of
            minutes and memoranda of the Dollar Drain Committee (DD) and
            weekly figures of the reserve position.

545   **Talks with Australia and New Zealand on planning and development:
            general discussions of the balance of payments and long-term
            programmes.** (CP82/138/01) Sept 1948–June 1953. Briefs and notes
            for meetings and some minutes and memoranda of the Sterling Area
            Development Working Party (SADWP). One note on long-term
            planning and the Commonwealth. Little between 1948 and 1952.

546–548   **Materials Committee: steel. General supply position. Control procedure.**
            (CP124/12/01F–H).

    546   Feb 1950–May 1951. Papers on supplies and future of the fuel
            distribution scheme, in particular whether allocation of types of steel
            should be ended. Includes some ministerial correspondence.

    547   June–Nov 1951. Papers on steel exports in relation to domestic
            requirements and estimated supplies.

    548   Nov 1951–Dec 1953. Includes notes for consumers on the iron and
            steel distribution scheme.

552–553   **Steel and timber correspondence with Northern Ireland.**

(CP124/12/015A) May 1946–Sept 1956.

552   May 1946–Jan 1952. Papers mainly on allocations of raw materials to Northern Ireland.

554–558   **Materials (Allocation) Committee: allocation of steel.** (CP124/12/05A–E) Oct 1951–Mar 1953.

554   Oct–Nov 1951. Preparation of the paper on the scheme for general steel for the first post-election Cabinet. Includes departmental requirements and proposed allocations. Some minutes and memoranda of GEN 391. See CAB 130/72.

555   Dec 1951–Jan 1952. Drafts and comments on M(51)69. See CAB 134/486.

559   **Materials (Allocation) Committee: steel – working party.** (CP124/12/027) Mar 1951–Nov 1953. Minutes and memoranda of GEN 361 and related papers on a distribution scheme. Note on the steel allocation scheme 1940–53. See CAB 130/66.

562–565   **Materials (Allocation) Committee: timber – general supply position. Control procedure.** (CP124/58/01D–G) Feb 1950–Nov 1955.

562   Feb–Dec 1950. Papers on requirements for various periods and softwood supplies.

563   Dec 1950–Sept 1951. Further papers on requirements and softwood and on the impact of the shipping shortage.

567   **Parliamentary questions and answers – general.** (CP124/274/01) Oct 1947–Dec 1952. Those relating to the Materials Committee, in particular on allocations.

568   **House of Lords: economic debates.** (CP126/201/01) Mar 1949–Nov 1953. Brief for the debate on the economic situation May 1949. Then gap to April 1953.

579   **1. Procedure for carrying out proposals of Commonwealth Economic Conference 1952. International interest.   2. Collective approach to freer trade and currencies.** (CP131/365/04A) Jan–Dec 1953. Includes a note on the finance of investment 1948–52.

581   **Manpower requirements of the defence forces including civil defence organizations.** (CP136/15/01) Oct 1948–Feb 1955. Early papers on the effect of the extension of national service. Then gap to Aug 1950 and consideration of the services manpower requirements.

582–584   **Labour requirements for the defence programme at Coventry.** (CP136/15/03A–C) July 1951–Apr 1953.

582   July–Nov 1951. Relevant minutes and memoranda of the Committee on Productive Capacity (CPC) and its working party.

586   **Information on defence for Commonwealth ministers.** (CP136/78/01) 1951–1954. Retained.

593   **Notes on economic planning.** (CP201/66/01) July 1953–Feb 1955. Notes by D.O. Henley for E.N. Plowden's private use on the meaning of economic planning and Feb 1955 lecture notes on economic planning.

598   **Southern Rhodesia: production of iron steel alloys.** (CP203/12/01) Nov 1948–Mar 1953.

599   **Restrictions on street lighting – shop lighting – electric signs.** (CP218/01) Feb 1949–Oct 1953. Papers on the removal or relaxation of restrictions.

604   **Purchase tax.** (CP262/01) Jan 1951–Mar 1953. Papers on possibility of purchase tax on a wider range of durables and on cars. Inland Revenue on the initial allowances.

605–606   **The agricultural expansion programme.** (CP269/01A and B) June
1947–July 1953.
   605   June 1947–Oct 1949. Papers on the progress of the programme and
particularly its labour requirements. Part B dates from June 1953.

608   **Manpower and Production Committee: papers.** (CP273/01) 1947–53.
Retained.

609   **Manpower and Production Committee (formerly Manpower Committee):
minutes of meetings.** (CP273/64/02) Nov 1950–Oct 1953. See CAB
134/511–512.

613   **Select Committee on Estimates. Sir E. Plowden's evidence before the
subcommittee (20 June 1951).** (CP275/01) June 1951–Nov 1953. Notes
for the meeting and minutes of his evidence on the machinery for
implementation of rearmament policy. C.E.P.S./E.N. Plowden acted
as a clearing-house.

617   **Treasury Delegation Committee. Functions of C.E.P.S. and supply
divisions arising out of the report.** (CP277/01) Oct 1950–Nov 1953.
Final report of the Treasury Organization Committee and papers on
the need to avoid inconsistencies between the investment programme
and supply expenditure approvals. Report of the Treasury Delegation
Committee (TDC) on increased delegation of financial authority to
departments and Dec 1951 training paper on the Treasury's functions.

620   **Retail prices – movements affecting cost of living index. Reports on
import and export price movements.** (CP2/235/01A) Nov 1949–June
1954. Post-devaluation papers on price changes and relevant papers of
the Programmes Committee on import prices with discussion of
revision of interim index and a new family budget enquiry.

621–622   **Open-cast coal.** (CP7/04A and B).
   621   Oct 1947–Jan 1950. Papers on the costs, production and investment.
   622   Nov 1950–Apr 1954. Estimates of production and draft reports for the
Official Coal Committee. Reviews of the excavating plant situation.
Some correspondence on the priority between open-cast coal and
agriculture.

623–624   **Coal – manpower, recruitment and wastage.** (CP7/15/01A and B).
   623   May 1947–Dec 1950. Papers on increasing manpower particularly
European Volunteer Workers and other foreign labour, and on
supplementary pensions. Disagreement between the Ministries of
Labour and Fuel & Power over cause of Nov 1950 shortage. Papers of
the Working Party on Manpower Recruitment and Wastage in the Coal
Industry. Note of a conference, Nov 1950, between Noel-Baker, the
N.C.B. and the N.U.M. and paper by the N.C.B. on wastage.
   624   Jan 1951–Jan 1954. Briefs and note of meeting between ministers and
the N.U.M. Jan 1951 on coal supply. Papers on negotiations with the
N.U.M. on wages, holidays and supplementary pensions. Some Official
Coal Committee papers and Gaitskell's speech to Nottinghamshire
miners June 1951.

628–630   **Coal imports.** (CP7/47/01A–C) Nov 1950–Sept 1954.
   628   Nov 1950–Mar 1951. Papers on need for imports for winter 1950–51.
Drafts of the Working Party on Imports' report to the Official Coal
Committee (OCC(50)13). Consideration of shipping problems and
tables of import programme.

629   Mar 1951–July 1953. Papers on implications of imports and need for them for 1951–52 winter leading to papers on economic prospects for 1952 and transportation of coal.

631   **Steel prices.** (CP12/2/01A) Jan 1948–Dec 1954. Papers on the iron and steel industry subsidy.

632–634   **Iron and steel – coke supplies.** (CP12/31/01A–C) Nov 1947–Apr 1954.

632   Nov 1947–Mar 1952. Mainly after Jan 1951. Some minutes and memoranda of the Committee on Iron Ore (CIO).

635–637   **Steel imports from the U.S.A. in 1952 – under the controlled materials plan.** (CP12/47/01A–C) July 1951–July 1954.

635   July–Sept 1951. Papers leading to U.K. memo requesting imports in 1952.

636   Sept–Dec 1951. E.C.A. discussions on U.K. memorandum on imports of steel, draft note on the consequences of U.K. steel shortage and draft brief for the Prime Minister's visit to Washington.

638–640   **Iron and steel scrap (including steel scrap from ship-breaking).** (CP12/59/01A–C) May 1947–July 1954. Includes paper on German imports and reports of the Scrap Investigation Committee. Little after 1951.

641   **National wages and prices policy.** (CP15/38/01) July 1947–Sept 1954. Discussions and C.E.P.S. views on wages policy in summer 1947. Some papers of the Inter-departmental Committee on Wages (WIB) and of the Official Working Party on the Stabilization of Wages (WS). Papers for debate on the White Paper on Personal Incomes. Gap June 1948–April 1950. Oct 1950 first draft outline of papers on full employment, incomes and prices.

644–645   **Economic Planning Board membership.** (CP18/01A and B) May 1947–Oct 1954.

644   May 1947–Sept 1951. Original soundings to the T.U.C., the F.B.I. and the B.E.C. and minutes from meeting, April 1947, to consider outside membership. Decision to increase industrial representation to three and addition summer 1947 of B.W. Gilbert as as Treasury representative. Consideration of representatives from other groups such as co-operatives, socialized industries and the N.F.U. Papers on the threatened resignation of employers' members Jan 1950. Part B dates from Oct 1952.

646–647   **Economic Planning Board general papers.** (CP18/02A and B).

646   Apr 1947–Dec 1948. Papers on its formation and membership including T.U.C. doubts about joining and officials' doubts on departmental representation. Meeting of officials, June 1947, to consider role of the Planning Board and proposed terms of reference. Correspondence on the relationship of board and ministers over short-term remedial action. Concern 1948 over irregularity of meetings and certain members' absences.

647   Jan 1950–Jan 1955. Further papers on absences. Suggestion by Sir Graham Cunningham to float the pound and the Board's feeling on the internal financial situation and change in exchange rates as expressed by E.N. Plowden to Cripps. A. Rowland's complaint about bias in the Board's minutes and doubts about the Board's value. Paper on Board's future after Oct 1951.

650   **Fuel Economy Working Party papers. Report.** (CP119/231/01) Aug 1951–Oct 1954. Papers of the Working Party considering *inter alia* financial incentives for the installation of fuel-saving equipment, leading to its report (GEN 378/15(final)). See CAB 130/71.

656–657 **Fuel economy and efficiency. Measures to increase production and reduce consumption of coal.** (CP19/231/010A and B). Feb 1949–Oct 1954.

657   May 1951–Oct 1954. Includes some papers of the Fuel Efficiency Advisory Committee and the Working Party on Fuel Economy.

658   **Working Party on Export Trends. General papers.** (CP23/44/03A) July–Aug 1953. Includes papers on post-war investment in manufacturing industry and British Engineers' Association memorandum on foreign competition in export market 1949–52.

662–663 **Strategic stockpiling.** (CP33/08A and B) 1949–1951. Retained.

664   **Raw Materials Strategic Materials Committee and papers on raw materials stockpiling.** (CP33/08C) Apr 1951–Apr 1954.

665   **Treasury Stockpiling Committee memoranda.** (CP33/022B) May 1951–Dec 1952. Includes draft report on revision of stockpiling programme.

670–671 **Miscellaneous investment. Miscellaneous licensed building (Ministry of Works).** (CP45/09A and B) Aug 1947–Feb 1954.

670   Aug 1947–Dec 1951. Papers include various I.P.C. Working Party papers and others on the building labour ceiling and correspondence between Cripps and Stokes on control through licensing.

674–675 **I.P.C.: government building.** (CP45/5/01A and B) Mar 1947–Mar 1954.

674   Mar 1947–Dec 1951. Includes relevant I.P.C. Working Party memoranda and others in particular on office building.

676–678 **Measures to alleviate unemployment in the building industry in London. The London building programme.** (CP45/5/018A–C) May 1951–Aug 1954.

676   May 1951–Jan 1953. Papers on licensing policy and individual cases.

691   **Capital Issues Committee – general correspondence.** (CP63/01A) Aug 1947–July 1954. Papers including Cmd. 6645 setting out committee's procedure in dealing with applications to raise capital. Some individual cases. Notes on C.E.P.S.'s relationship with the committee regarding investment planning and impact of change in monetary policy in Nov 1951 on the committee.

694   **Productive Capacity Committee. Constitution, functions and terms of reference (exercise on location of defence projects).** (CP81/64/02) Dec 1950–Jan 1954. Papers leading to the committee's establishment. See CAB 134/114–116.

696–697 **Materials Committee. Terms of reference and constitution. Procedure and returns of requirements.** (CP124/01A and B) Oct 1945–May 1954. See CAB 134/475–486.

696   Oct 1945–Dec 1953. Papers on the change-over from war to post-war form and functions. Contains papers on its personnel and its role in central planning, including its relationship with C.E.P.S.

702   **Functions of C.E.P.S. in relation to defence and civil defence. Organization and machinery.** (CP136/01) Aug 1948–Dec 1954. Includes papers on Ministry of Production in the next war and on discussions with U.S.A. on Western Union defence and supply questions.

704–705 **The impact on the economy of the defence production programme.** (CP136/201/04A and B).

704   July 1948–June 1951. Little before 1950. Then papers on the expanded defence programme and its impact on civil economy.

705   June–Dec 1951. Papers on the 1951 defence proposals and estimates of the defence effort 1950–53 and of the defence budget 1952–55. Second draft of the memorandum 'Urgent economic problems' to be handed to new government following the election.

710   **O.E.E.C. Stikker–Marjolin Plan: 1. Declaration. 2. 25% expansion programme.** (CP193/81/01A) Feb–Nov 1951. Notes and meetings to discuss the plan with drafts of the declaration and the expansion programme.

711–712   **Colonial development. General.** (CP199/01A and B).

711   Aug 1948–Dec 1949. Papers on economic planning in the colonies and the establishment of the Committee on Colonial Development (CD). Reports of the Working Party on Production of Primary Aluminium in the Commonwealth Sterling Area and of the Colonial Development Working Party.

712   Jan 1950–Mar 1954. Memorandum on colonial borrowing in London 1948–52 and notes and memoranda of the Committee on Colonial Development, including its winding up.

726   **Commonwealth sugar agreement – modifications by the U.K.** (CP243/374/01) Dec 1951–Oct 1954.

734   **Parliamentary questions – C.E.P.S. procedure.** (CP274/01) Nov 1951–Feb 1954. Question of responsibility for steel allocations.

737–738   **N.P.A.C.I. revised procedure and meeting arrangements.** (CP288/02A and B) Feb 1948–Oct 1954.

737   Feb 1948–Oct 1952. Little before Nov 1951. Then correspondence between permanent secretaries on N.P.A.C.I.'s future.

740–743   **Civil defence policy.** (CP298/01A–D) 1948–1954. Retained.

744   **Civil defence shelter policy.** (CP298/312/01) 1948–1954. Retained.

749–764   **European Coal and Steel Community (Schuman Plan).** (CP378/01A–R) May 1950–1954.

749   May–June 1950. Text of French proposals and papers of an inter-departmental Working Party on the Schuman Proposals. Includes views of some ministers and the official line for the House of Commons debate.

750   June–Aug 1950. Continued detailed papers, including comments on the working party report and on the relationship between the Schuman Plan and the O.E.E.C. Papers on U.K. proposals.

751   Aug 1950–Jan 1951. Report on meetings of delegations of six countries June–Aug 1950, report of the Commercial and Tariff Policy Working Party and continued correspondence on developments. U.K. views on E.C.S.C. as a supra-national body.

752   1951. Retained.

753   June–Oct 1951. Notes of meetings of Uniscan, report by the Working Party and correspondence with Commonwealth countries.

754   Nov 1951–Feb 1952. Papers mainly on U.K. relations with E.C.S.C.

778–779   **Work of the C.E.P.S.** (CP1/05A and B) Mar 1947–1956.

778   Mar 1947–Sept 1952. Drafts of a note setting out the role of C.E.P.S. and work to be done in 1949. Draft report of the Working Party on Treasury Administration and Modifications of Economic Surveys and Long-term Plans. Proposal Jan 1949 for weekly meetings of C.E.P.S. representatives on inter-departmental bodies in order to ensure co-ordination. Circular to departmental heads requesting information on changes in home consumption or production not raised at

inter-departmental meetings. Papers on whether to revise 1948–52 survey. Notes on planning for New Zealand High Commissioner. Correspondence on articles on planning machinery by R.S. Milne and G. Walker. Various notes on staff changes. Paper on economic planning for a staff course 1951 and 1952. General description of C.E.P.S. work and objectives.

780–785 **Coal budgets. Trends in production and manpower.** (CP7/01A–F) Feb 1947–Mar 1954.

780 Feb 1947–Mar 1951. Number of preview papers. Concern of H. Tizard about national fuel policy and in particular increasing technical efficiency. Briefs and notes of meeting between ministers and the N.U.M., July 1947. Discussion of 1948 coal target and prospects 1948–50. Statement by Gaitskell to mining unions, Oct 1949. Papers on individual winter and summer coal budgets and prospects to 1955. Jay on winter 1950–51 situation and consideration of possible emergency measures.

781 Mar–Nov 1951. Papers and memoranda on summer 1951 budget and end-summer stocking. Report of *ad hoc* official working party on implications of importing coal. Considerations of coal requirements winter 1951–52. Coal supply outlook 1952 and 1952 coal budget. Coal imports and exports under Conservative government.

782 Dec 1951–July 1952. Further papers on 1952 coal prospects and the budget.

786–787 **Coal prices.** (CP7/2/01A and B) Jan 1947–Jan 1955.

786 Jan 1947–June 1954. Some papers on bunker and coal export prices and F.B.I. pamphlet on the coal price structure. Mainly 1952 onwards.

792–794 **Shipbuilding and ship repairing programme.** (CP13/09A–C) Aug 1947–Sept 1955.

792 Aug 1947–July 1950. Papers relating to the Working Party Report on the Future Level of Shipbuilding and Ship Repairing Industries and of steel supplies. Part B starts Feb 1952.

794 Sept 1954–Sept 1955. Tables of merchant and other shipping statistics 1939 and 1948–54.

801–803 **New export drive including bilateral trade agreements.** (CP23/03A–C) 1950–Nov 1955.

801 1950–52. Closed for 50 years.

807–811 **Oil Working Party – correspondence.** (CP27/44/01A–E).

807 May–Nov 1949. Papers on the establishment and running of the Working Party on Oil Expansion Programme.

808 Nov–Dec 1949. Papers on working party's relations with Ministry of Fuel & Power and on the substitution of sterling oil for dollar oil.

809 Dec 1949–Feb 1950. Further papers on substitution and related tripartite talks.

810 Feb–May 1950. Further papers on Washington tripartite talks and with Commonwealth. Papers on negotiations with individual companies concerning petrol rationing.

811 1950–51. Retained.

812–813 **Raw materials: rubber.** (CP33/250/01A and B) Nov 1950–1951.

812 Nov 1950–Feb 1951. Papers relating to international allocations and negotiations.

813 1951. Retained.

821–822   **I.P.C.: building programme for universities.** (CP45/268/01A and B) Nov 1947–May 1955.

    821   Nov 1947–Dec 1951. Papers on the annual investment programme and particular buildings.

824–825   **Import programming: 1. Procedure. 2. Matters arising.** (CP47/06A and B) Mar 1951–Feb 1955.

    824   Mar 1951–Nov 1953. Papers mainly on procedure.

827–829   **Productivity in British industry.** (CP81/02A–C) June 1947–May 1954.

    827   June 1947–July 1949. Papers relating to the production efficiency campaigns, departmental arrangements for promoting productivity, and the work of the Anglo-American Council on Productivity.

    828   July 1949–Apr 1952. Papers on productivity drive and work of the Official Committee on Productivity. S.C. Leslie on government industrial policy and reaction of C.E.P.S.

830–838   **Materials (Allocation) Committee: tin plate production and allocation.** (CP124/57/01D–N) Apr 1951–Nov 1955.

    830   Apr 1951–Feb 1952. Includes paper by Metal Box Co. on world production of and demand for tin plate.

846–848   **Defence priorities (including conflicts between dollar exports and defence orders).** (CP136/09A–C) Aug 1950–1956.

    846   Aug 1950–Dec 1951. Notes of meeting Aug 1950 on priority guidance to be given to firms with views of the F.B.I. Papers on individual cases.

849   **U.S. assistance. Aid for end-item bids.** (CP136/019) Mar 1951–May 1955. Drafts of briefs for Prime Minister's visit to Washington in relation to U.S. assistance through mutual aid and the Nitze exercise.

850–851   **Defence – production of tanks.** (CP136/81/02A and B) Oct 1950–Apr 1954.

852–853   **Defence production programme.** (CP136/81/010A and B) 1949–Dec 1951.

    852   1949–51. Retained.

    853   Nov–Dec 1951. Papers and progress reports.

854–856   **U.S. assistance.** (CP136/194/01A–C) 1949–1950. Retained.

858   **Defence White Papers 1951, 1952.** (CP136/198/01A) Feb 1949–Feb 1952. Drafts with comments.

863–864   **Council of Europe (Strasbourg Plan) proposals for Europe/ Commonwealth Association (Boothby-ism).** (CP193/131/01A) Dec 1951–July 1955.

872   **Natural Resources (Technical) Committee – correspondence.** (CP266/01A) Nov 1950–Mar 1955. Papers on role of committee and its liaison with the Raw Materials Committee.

875–876   **Manpower and Production Committee: Working Party on Long-term Planning: manpower in a future war.** (CP273/44/02A and B) 1951–53. Retained. See CAB 134/515.

878   **Post Office civil defence measures.** (CP298/107/01) 1949–54.

881   **Report of the Hamilton Committee on Regional Boards for Industry.** (CP333/338/01) Jan–May 1954. Papers and a copy of report reviewing boards' post-war functions.

891   **Tariffs policy in relation to the General Agreement on Trade and Tariffs (G.A.T.T.).** (CP388/01) Oct 1950–May 1955.

Chapter 19 Economic Section

In January 1941, the government's Central Economic Information Service was divided into the Economic Section of the War Cabinet Offices and the Central Statistical Office (CAB 108 and CAB 139). The Section consisted of a small group of professional economists, normally numbering between ten and twenty, to provide general advice on economic policy. Its first four directors were John Jewkes (Jan–Sept 1941), Lionel Robbins (Sept 1941–autumn 1945), James Meade (autumn 1945–April 1947) and Robert Hall (Sept 1947–1961).

During the war, the Section acted as the staff of the Lord President of the Council, Anderson (1940–Sept 1943) and Attlee (Sept 1943–May 1945) and so many of its briefs can be found in CAB 123 and CAB 124. Given the Lord President's role as the focus of decision-making on domestic issues, the Section was involved in most reconstruction issues. For example, Norman Chester was the secretary to the Beveridge Committee on Social Insurance and Allied Services (CAB 87/76–82) and James Meade, in particular, was involved in employment policy. In 1941 he had written 'The Prevention of General Unemployment' (see T 230/13) which had placed demand management at the centre of employment policy. During 1943 a similar line was taken in his 'Maintenance of Full Employment' for the Reconstruction Priorities Committee (CAB 87/12–13). Thereafter, members of the Section continued to play an active role in the discussion of employment policy, pressing for the use of demand management techniques at the Steering Committee on Post-war Employment (CAB 87/63 and CAB 87/70) and in the drafting of the White Paper on *Employment Policy* (Cmd. 6527). Related to this was work on estimating the post-war national income. The Section was also involved in discussions on international reconstruction, including Bretton Woods, commodity policy and the U.K. balance of payments.

During the war there had been consideration of a peace-time central economic staff by the Machinery of Government Committee (CAB 87/73-75) and its official counterpart (CAB 87/72), but nothing new materialized. At the end of the war, Lionel Robbins and some other members of the Section returned to academic life, leaving James Meade to become the director and to spend most of the time serving the new Lord President, Morrison, who had assumed responsibility for (among other things) domestic economic planning. The full range of the Section's responsibilities can be discerned from the files listed below; but its most important role was the preparation from 1946 and publication from 1947 of an annual Economic Survey reviewing the existing situation and forecasting the expected development of the British economy in the coming year. These were then considered by the Official Steering Committee on Economic Development (CAB 134/186-193) and the Lord President's Industrial Subcommittee (CAB 71/27), and its successor, the Ministerial Committee on Economic Planning (CAB 134/503). Between 1945 and 1947 an Overseas Economic Survey was prepared as well (see T 230/19-24) and the Section was further involved in the initial work on the long-term plan.

During Meade's directorship, the importance of the Section declined for three major reasons. First, Morrison did not dominate domestic economic policy as had Anderson before him; he was also not fully at ease with economics and had an alternative source of economic advice in his private secretary, Max Nicholson. Secondly, Dalton as

Chancellor of the Exchequer was himself a trained economist and felt little need for advice from other professional economists. Finally, Meade himself limited his influence both by taking too theoretical an approach with Morrison and by advocating financial policy, as opposed to direct controls, in his advice to Dalton and the Budget Committee.

Meade left in April 1947, disillusioned and ill, and was replaced as director by Robert Hall. Hall was a more pragmatic figure, with considerable experience of Whitehall, and he was able to restore the status of the Section with the assistance of two major organizational changes in 1947: the appointment after March of C.E.P.S. (T 229) under Edwin Plowden, and Cripps's supersession first, in September, of Morrison as minister in charge of economic planning and second, in November, of Dalton as Chancellor. The relationship between the Section and C.E.P.S. was not without its difficulties but, once the professional economists had left C.E.P.S., a good working relationship – especially between Hall and Plowden – was established. The Section provided C.E.P.S. with economic analysis, whilst C.E.P.S. ensured the discussion of this analysis within the Treasury. Plowden's close relationship with Cripps also gave Hall and the Section direct access to the Chancellor and forced the Treasury to be more helpful (see A.K. Cairncross (ed.), *The Robert Hall Diaries, 1947–1953* (Unwin Hyman, 1989.)

Beneath Hall, a continual turnover of staff meant that other members of the Section were mainly young and inexperienced; and it was not until 1949 that Hall was supported by two experienced economists, Russell Bretherton and Marcus Fleming, as deputy directors. These junior staff continued to work as the Section's representatives on various committees, drafting the annual Economic Survey with C.E.P.S. and keeping the economic situation under review. However, the influence of the Section (for example over devaluation) can largely be attributed to Hall, although he did gain increasing support from colleagues who were later to become distinguished economists in their own right: Christopher Dow, Fred Atkinson, Jack Downie and Bryan Hopkin.

Given the importance of T 230, each file which covers some part of this period has been listed. The Section also circulated internal discussion papers and these have also been listed in full for the relevant years. For papers on the development of the Section see T 230/283. For further information see A.K. Cairncross and N. Watts, *The Economic Section 1939–1961* (Routledge, 1989), which includes a full list of the Section's staff; A.K. Cairncross (ed.), *The Robert Hall Diaries 1947–1953* (Unwin Hyman, 1989) and S. Howson (ed.), *The Collected Papers of James Meade vols. I and IV* (Unwin Hyman, 1988 and 1989.)

T 230

1	**Proposed post-war agricultural policy** (EAS14/01) Mar 1941–Mar 1945. Correspondence between Ministry of Agriculture & Fisheries and Board of Trade on protection and stabilization of home agricultural production and the impact of this on trade negotiations. 1943 briefs for the Lord President, then gap to Jan 1945. Draft White Paper on post-war food policy.
2	**Consideration and negotiation of agricultural prices.** (EAS14/34/01) June 1940–Mar 1945. Drafts and amendments of LP(44)192 and LP(45)55 and 56. See CAB 71/18 and 20.
3	**British post-war civil aviation policy.** (EAS172/01) Jan 1945–May 1948. Includes various briefs.
4–6	**U.K. post-war balance of payments. Wartime forecasts.** (EAS29/01A–C) Oct 1940–June 1945.
5	Jan 1942–Feb 1944. Papers dating mainly from 1942. Later papers include estimates for 1950 and Catto on post-war international settlement and U.K. balance of payments.

6   Mar 1944–June 1945. Drafts and amendments of EC(S)(44)11 and 12.
         Estimates for 1945 and survey of the general economic position.
         Includes papers from Bank of England.

7   **Balance of payments. Form of presentation of accounts.** (EAS29/85/01)
         June 1946–Oct 1948. Keynes on the form of forecasts. Papers of the
         Balance of Payments Working Party Sub-Working Party on Form of
         Estimates. Concern of R.L. Hall, summer 1947, over efficiency of
         planning if future balance of payments situation could not be foreseen.
         Resulting papers on the work of the Exchange Requirements
         Committee.

8   **Balance of payments. U.K. exports. Policy and programmes.**
         (EAS29/28/01) Mar 1946–July 1948. Papers forecasting exports in
         1950, reviewing unrequited exports and the possibility of directing
         exports.

9   **Import restrictions on balance of payments grounds.** (EAS29/35/02) Dec
         1942–Nov 1946. General policy file with comments, including J.M.
         Keynes's, on Catto's paper in T 230/5. Papers on quantitative import
         restriction.

10   **Balance of payments. U.K. imports–policy and programmes.**
         (EAS29/35/01) Nov 1945–July 1948. Papers on import control and
         administrative arrangements for import programming. Monthly
         progress analysis of imports in 1946, forecast of raw material imports
         1947–51 and estimate of the import programme July 1947–Dec 1948.

11   **Balance of Payments Working Party. Memoranda.** (EAS29/72/02) Dec
         1945–Apr 1947. BPWP/1/46–BPWP(47)1.

12–21   **Economic Section of the Cabinet War Secretariat: discussion papers.**
         (EAS354/351/01–09B) June 1940–Dec 1948.

13   Jan–Dec 1941. First consideration of reconstruction issues. Includes
         J.E. Meade's 'The Prevention of General Unemployment'.

15   **EC(S)(43) series** (EAS354/351/04) Feb–Dec 1943.

    15 Feb   **1**   **Prevention of mass unemployment – J.E. Meade.**

    17 Feb   **1**   **Prevention of post-war unemployment – J.E.
                          Meade.** Revise version. Outline of paper
                          requested by Anderson.

    17 Feb   **2**   **Prevention of mass unemployment – P. Chantler.**

    19 Feb   **3**   **Creation of employment – J.M. Fleming.** Need
                          to emphasize the reduction of unemployment
                          was dependent on what sacrifices the community
                          was prepared to make. Proposals on that basis.

    22 Feb   **4**   **Methods of preventing mass unemployment –
                          L.C. Robbins.** Written without having read other
                          suggestions.

    10 Mar   **5**   **Maintenance of full employment – J.E. Meade.**
                          Revise version, 12 April. Second revise version,
                          22 April.

    30 Apr   **5**   **Maintenance of full employment – L.C. Robbins.**
                          Third revise version. Somewhat drastic redraft
                          to curtail and rearrange the paper for discussion
                          at the Reconstruction Priorities Committee.
                          Part I – a short statement of the general nature
                          of the problem. Part II – analyses of the various
                          principles and methods of solution. Part III –

		discussion of the application of the principles outlined to the conditions likely to obtain immediately after the war. Concluding section identified the subjects of further enquiry.
5 Apr	6	**Surplus capacity in the immediate post-war period – D.N. Chester.** Primarily concerned with contraction of war industries, e.g. disposal of factories and other assets financed by government.
23 Apr	7	**The budget and the White Paper of 1943 – R.C. Tress.** Revise version 30 April.
27 May	8	**Exports – N. Watts.** Review of wartime export policy and comparison of existing exports with 1938 volume.
28 June	9	**Influences affecting the level of national income. Some reflections on PR(43)35 and on Lord Keynes's note of dissent – J.M. Fleming,** 5p. Need to clarify assumptions involved in national income estimates if ministers were to understand their real meaning, in particular the assumption on the level of increased prices above the 1938 level.
30 June	10	**Influences affecting the level of national income – R.C. Tress.**
5 July	11	**Wages, cost of living and the national income – J.M. Fleming.** Revision of EC(S)(43)9 correcting some errors.
8 July	12	**Bulk purchase (IEP(43)26) – D.N. Chester.** See CAB 87/57.
15 July	13	**Estimates of post-war national income – R.C. Tress.** Tables by R.C. Tress and R. Stone to help comparisons with 1938 and war years.
11 Dec	14	**The post-war international settlement and the U.K. balance of payments – L.C. Robbins covering J.E. Meade.** The strategy for economic settlement discussed informally among U.K. and U.S. officials in Washington fully allowed for, and would assist, the solution of the U.K. post-war balance of payments problem. Covered the transition and long term. Annex on the effect of a change in foreign exchange rate on the balance of current payments.

16	**EC(S)(44) series.** (EAS354/351/05) Jan–Dec 1944.		
	4 Jan	1	**Note on the Economic Section's scheme for varying social security contributions – J.E. Meade covering D. MacDougall.** The scheme was insufficiently responsive.
	4 Jan	2	**Pricing of state products – J.E. Meade.**
	8 Jan	3	**Criteria of operation of state enterprises – J.M. Fleming.**

unemployment. National expenditure should be presented, as in the National Income White Paper, on an income, and not a product basis.

30 Nov	18	**Post-war coal exports – L.C. Robbins covering P. Chantler.** Comments on R(IE)(44)5. See CAB 87/14.
30 Nov	19	**British coal exports under bilateral trading – P. Chantler.**
2 Dec	20	**Employment policy – L.C. Robbins covering J.E. Meade.** Contrasts the White Paper on *Employment Policy* and Beveridge, *Full Employment in a Free Society.*
8 Dec	21	**Employment policy – L.C. Robbins covering R.C. Tress.** Comments on the White Paper on *Employment Policy*, Beveridge and EC(S)(44)20.
16 Dec	22	**Public utility corporations (R(44)199) – L.C. Robbins covering P. Chantler and D.N. Chester.** Consideration of the corporations' general principles and the future financial structure of the electricity supply industry.

17 **EC(S)(45) series.** (EAS354/351/06A) Jan–May 1945.

17 Jan	1	**The balance of gain and loss to U.K. trade from the proposed international multilateral commercial policy convention – J.E. Meade.**
29 Jan	2	**British motor car taxation and the export problem – P. Chantler.** Revise version.
26 Feb	3	**Wages – J. Wood.**
24 Mar	4	**Post-war arithmetic – R.C. Tress.** Comments on N. Kaldor's national income figures and *The Economist*'s criticisms.
21 Apr	5	**Economic forecasting and employment policy – Economic Section.** Second version.
16 Apr	6	**The iron and steel industry. Some reflections on R(45)36 – S.R. Dennison.** See CAB 87/10.
26 Apr	7	**Report on the iron and steel industry (R(45)36) – Economic Section.** Revise version.
24 Apr	8	**The iron and steel industry. Minutes of a staff meeting held on 17 April to discuss the report on the iron and steel industry (R(45)36).**
27 Apr	9	**Report on the iron and steel industry. Minutes of a staff meeting held on 23 April to consider a draft memo by R.C. Tress (EC(S)(45)7).**
2 May	10	**Industrial problems in the transition – S.R. Dennison and J. Wood.** Impressions from visits to eight regions Nov–Dec 1944.
2 May	11	**Notes for Economic Survey – P. Chantler.** Preliminaries of the sections on food, raw materials, shipping and industrial capital equipment.
5 May	12	**Economic Survey. Wages in the first four months of 1945 – J. Wood.**

5 May	13	**Economic Survey: manpower – S.R. Dennison.**
12 May	14	**Economic Survey. Note on 1945/46 coal situation – D.N. Chester.** A shortage predicted that winter.
16 May	15	**Economic Survey. Overseas liabilities and the balance of payments – N. Watts.**
17 May	16	**Economic Survey. Note on post-war housing building situation – D.N. Chester.**
23 May	17	**Economic Survey. Minutes of staff meetings held on 15 and 16 May to discuss the next survey.**
22 May	18	**Copy of a letter sent by Sir E. Bridges to heads of departments concerned with employment policy.** Sets out administrative arrangements including meeting of officials to consider statistics for employment policy and forecasting national income and expenditure.
24 May	19	**Economic Survey. Minutes of a staff meeting held on 17 May to continue the discussion of the next survey.**

18   **EC(S)(45) series.** (EAS354/351/06B)   29 May–30 Oct 1945.

29 May	20	**Economic Survey – minutes of a staff meeting 22 May 1945.** Mainly on the danger of inflation.
31 May	21	**Economic Survey. Note on building labour – D.N. Chester.**
6 June	22	**Capital expenditure by public authorities – D.N. Chester.** Preliminary note on the problems of a questionnaire to local authorities to find out their investment programmes.
25 July	23	**Survey of the general economic position – L.C. Robbins.** Final revise version. See LP(45)127 (CAB 71/21).
25 June	24	**Capital investment by public utility undertakings – P. Chantler.** Problem of the diversity of the organization of public utilities for use in employment policy.
27 June	25	**Capital expenditure by public authorities – D.N. Chester.** On the proposed questionnaire for local authorities.
20 Aug	26	**Survey of the general economic situation – L.C. Robbins.** See LP(45)138 and 139 (CAB 71/21).
30 Aug	27	**Correspondence between E.E. Bridges and J.E. Meade – J.E. Meade.** The future organization of work on certain economic problems and the role of the C.S.O. and Economic Section.
10 Oct	28	**Economic planning – J.E. Meade.** Second revise version. See ED(45)1 (CAB 134/186).
11 Sept	29	**Summary of general ideas on nationalization in** *Socialization and transport* **by H. Morrison – J.E. Meade covering K. Howells.**
12 Sept	30	**Employment and income prospects in the U.S.A. – J.E. Meade covering A.J. Brown.** Background to the Overseas Economic Survey.

20 Sept	**31**	**Compensation – T. Wilson.**
29 Sept	**32**	**The net national income in 1946, 1947 and 1948 – Economic Section and C.S.O.** Also CS(S)(45)77.
2 Oct	**33**	**Nationalization of the coal-mining industry. Memorandum by the Minister of Fuel and Power (LP(45)179) – J.E. Meade covering the Economic Section.** Brief to Morrison.
9 Oct	**34**	**The export drive – J.E. Meade covering T. Wilson.** How to expand export industries immediately without increasing manpower and how to ensure that labour was diverted to them.
24 Oct	**35**	**The distribution of industry policy – Wood.** Concern that long-term policy was different from short-term expedient of filling up development areas with employment. Recommends a ban on development in London and Birmingham with no restrictions elsewhere.
25 Oct	**36**	**Problems and principles of socialization – D.N. Chester.**
31 Oct	**37**	**Draft answers to questions 3, 4 and 6 in Economic Section paper to the Lord President on problems of socialization.**
30 Oct	**38**	**Problems and principles of socialization – J.E. Meade.** Draft introduction.

19	**EC(S)(45) series.**	(EAS354/351/060)	Nov–Dec 1945.
	6 Nov	**39**	**The socialization of industries – Economic Section.** Revise version.
	20 Nov	**40**	**Note by Mr. Fleming – J.M. Fleming.** Revise version. On the pricing policy in socialized industries.
	23 Nov	**41**	**Draft of first part of Overseas Economic Survey – J.E Meade covering A.J. Brown.** Covering introduction, food, coal, materials, manufacturing goods and the level of demand.
	3 Dec	**42**	**Redraft of answers to questions 5–8 of the Lord President's questionnaire on socialization.** Revise version.
	27 Nov	**43**	**Future work of the Section – J.E. Meade.** Highlights four areas: methods of controlling total national expenditure as a means of implementing the proposed economic plan, the socialization of various industries, wage incentives and restrictive practices.
	29 Nov	**44**	**Some random notes on the reparations discussions in Berlin Sept–Nov 1945 – G.D.A. MacDougall.**
	1 Dec	**45**	**Proposed film on 'full employment' – P. Chantler.**
	3 Dec	**46**	**Economic Survey for 1946 (rough draft) – J.E. Meade covering R.C. Tress.**

| 6 Dec | 46 | **Economic Survey for 1946 – J.E. Meade covering R.C. Tress.** See ED(45)5. (CAB 134/186). |
| 15 Dec | 47 | **Further instalment of Overseas Economic Survey – J.E. Meade covering A.J. Brown.** Covering merchandised trade, relief, reparations, international credits and balance of payments and foreign exchange. |

20 **EC(S)(46) series.** (EAS354/351/07A)   Jan–Feb 1946.

2 Jan	1	**Future work on economic planning – J.E. Meade.** Draft minute to E.E. Bridges suggesting revision of the survey, the formulation of a long-term survey, reviews of controls and fiscal weapons, and the preparation of a reserve of works.
4 Jan	2	**Empire Telecommunication Service – J.E. Meade covering N. Watts.**
4 Jan	3	**A buffer-stock-cum-quota commodity regulation scheme – J.E. Meade covering J.M. Fleming.**
26 Jan	3	**A buffer-stock-cum-quota commodity regulation scheme – J.M. Fleming.** Revise version.
9 Jan	4	**Comments on stablization policy and the control of prices – J.E. Meade covering R.S. Sayers.**
18 Jan	5	**Overseas Economic Survey – J.E. Meade covering A.J. Brown.** Conclusion of first draft.
23 Jan	6	**General considerations of centralized importation – Economic Section.** Paper for the Bulk Purchase Committee.
23 Jan	7	**The iron and steel modernization plan – J.E Meade covering R.S. Sayers.**
28 Jan	8	**A summary of previous discussions of commodity policy – J.E. Meade covering J.C.R. Dow.** Paper for the Buffer-stocks Working Party of the Commodity Policy Committee.
20 Jan	9	**Notes on the problems involved in an Economic Survey for 1950 – J.E. Meade covering R.C. Tress, E.A.G Robinson, J. Stafford and C.T. Saunders.**
13 Feb	10	**Draft of Overseas Economic Survey – A.J. Brown.** Complete draft except for sections on petroleum and transport.
14 Feb	11	**The means and possibilities of investment policy – J.E. Meade covering G.L.S. Shackle.** With particular reference to employment policy.
15 Feb	12	**Variations of income tax as a short-term instrument for national income stabilization – J.E. Meade covering J.C.R. Dow.** Consideration as an alternative to varying national insurance contributions.
22 Feb	13	**Postscript to EC(S)(46)11 – J.E. Meade covering G.L.S. Shackle.** Breakdown of total planned domestic capital formation for 1946 into

components sponsored by different government departments.

26 Feb   **14**   **Wages policy – J.E. Meade covering R.S Sayers.** See W(46)3 (CAB 132/88).

21   **EC(S)(46) series.**   (EAS354/351/07B)   Mar–July 1946.

4 Mar   **15**   **Overseas Economic Survey – J.E. Meade covering A.J. Brown.** Revise edition.

13 Mar   **16**   **Capital development and future organization of the iron and steel industry – J.E. Meade covering R.S Sayers.** Revise version.

23 May   **17**   **An economic policy for the socialized coal industry – J.E. Meade covering P. Chantler.** Revise version.

3 May   **18**   **Some fundamental elasticities in British external trade: a preliminary note – J.E. Meade covering A.J. Brown.** Second revise version.

15 Mar   **19**   **Poison! Observations on Mr. Brown's paper (EC(S)(46)18) – J.E. Meade covering J.M. Fleming.** Strong criticism of EC(S)(46)18.

5 Apr   **20**   **Economic Survey for 1946/7. Interim report – J.E. Meade covering the Economic Survey Working Party.** Revise version. Also ESWP(46)3(final).

2 May   **21**   **Variations of national insurance contributions – J.E. Meade covering J.C.R. Dow.** Review of its possibilities as a short-term stabilizer.

7 May   **22**   **Regional differences in wage rates – R.S. Sayers.** Consideration with regard to whether to encourage national wage rates.

13 May   **23**   **Reconversion in the regions – J.E. Meade covering S.R. Dennison and J. Wood.**

18 July   **24**   **Economic Survey for 1946/7 – J.E. Meade covering the Economic Survey Working Party.** Second revise version. See MEP(46)5 (CAB 134/503). Also ED(46)20 (CAB134/189).

20 May   **25**   **Note on international full employment policy – J.E. Meade covering J.M. Fleming.**

22   **EC(S)(46) series.** (EAS354/351/07C) June–Nov 1946.

22 Aug   **26**   **International employment policy – J.M. Fleming.** Revise version. Review of measures in preparation for a draft international convention on employment policy.

3 June   **27**   **Domestic gross capital formation in the financial year 1946/47 – J.E. Meade covering G.L.S. Shackle.**

11 June   **28**   **Housing and investment policy – G.L.S. Shackle.** Possible use of housing investment for employment policy purposes.

18 June   **29**   **Survey of the overseas economic situation as it affects the U.K. – J.E. Meade covering the**

Economic Section. Review encouraged hopes of a current balance in the first half of 1947.

18 June   30   **Supervisory boards and restrictive practices – P. Chantler, R.S. Sayers and J. Wood.**

16 Aug   31   **The cost of living index – J.E. Meade covering N. Watts.** The consequences of basing the index on the 1937–8 household budgets.

15 July   32   **Some thoughts on long-term contracts and commercial policy – J.E. Meade covering J.M. Fleming.**

8 Aug   33   **Regional differences in wage rates – J.E. Meade covering G.P. Jeffries.**

11 Sept   34   **The marketing of home-produced foodstuffs. The economic background – J.E. Meade covering P. Chantler, A.J. Brown and G.L.S. Shackle.** Revise version. Annex by R.C. Tress and J. Stafford on the impact of a fully-developed nutritional policy on the demand for U.K. agricultural produce.

15 Oct   35   **Headings for a survey of the overseas economic situation as it affects the U.K.: Dec 1946 – J.E. Meade covering A.J. Brown.** Notes on the volume and composition of world trading manufactures, of U.K. exports and British price competitiveness.

6 Nov   36   **The possible magnitude of a future depression – J.E. Meade covering J.C.R. Dow.** Revise version. Estimate of the impact of a depression on national income and employment and the extent of counteracting measures.

24 Oct   37   **Wages policy and the undermanned industries – R.S. Sayers covering G.P. Jeffries.**

29 Oct   38   **The present situation in the U.S.A. – J.E. Meade covering A.J. Brown.**

11 Nov   39   **The implementation of planning decisions and the balance between total demand and total supply – J.E. Meade.** Memoranda for a working party on the implementation of planning, illustrating the benefits from a reduction in inflationary pressure.

11 Nov   40   **Industrial production – J.E. Meade covering A.J Brown.** In relation to the Overseas Economic Survey.

23   **EC(S)(46) series.** (EAS354/351/07D) Nov 1946–Jan 1947.

14 Jan   41   **Observations on the reports from the Board of Trade's Industrial Working Parties – J.E. Meade covering P. Chantler.** Second revise version.

15 Nov   42   **The flow of commodities – J.E. Meade covering A.J. Brown.** In relation to the Overseas Economic Survey.

21 Nov	43	**Economic Survey for 1947. Draft of introduction and sections I–III and subject matters of section IV (conclusion) – R.C. Tress.** Also ESWP(46)19.
22 Nov	44	**The financing of international trade – J.E. Meade covering A.J. Brown.** In relation to the Overseas Economic Survey.
25 Nov	45	**The future of retail price stabilization policy – J.E. Meade covering N. Watts.** Response to a Ministry of Food paper recommending its continuation.
17 Dec	46	**The control of consumer expenditure in the interests of employment policy – J.E. Meade covering J.C.R. Dow.** Revise version. Analysis of tools available.
25 Nov	47	**The effect of changes in indirect taxation – J.E Meade covering J.C.R. Dow.** Written in relation to EC(S)(46)46(revise).
25 Nov	48	**Control of depression. Letter from J.E. Meade to B.W. Gilbert – J.E Meade.** Recommendations for conduct of future work as anti-depression measures.
26 Nov	49	**The level of demand – J.E. Meade covering A.J. Brown.** In relation to the Overseas Economic Survey.
2 Dec	50	**Industrial materials – J.E. Meade covering A.J Brown.** In relation to the Overseas Economic Survey.
2 Dec	51	**Coal, shipping and inland transport – J.E. Meade covering A.J Brown.** In relation to the Overseas Economic Survey.
5 Dec	52	**Food, Petroleum – J.E. Meade covering A.J. Brown.** In relation to the Overseas Economic Survey.
1 Jan	53	**Economic Survey for 1947 – Economic Survey Working Party.** Revise version. See MEP(46)15. Also ED(46)51 and ESWP(46)22.
7 Dec	54	**Survey of the overseas economic situation as it affects the U.K. – J.E. Meade covering A.J. Brown.** In relation to the Overseas Economic Survey.
9 Dec	55	**The outlook for world trade in manufactures – J.E. Meade covering A.J. Brown.** In relation to the Overseas Economic Survey.
9 Dec	56	**The settlement of the sterling balances – J.E. Meade covering N. Watts.**

24   **EC(S)(47) series.**   (EAS354/351/08A)   Jan–May 1947.

11 Jan	1	**The Monnet Plan – J.E. Meade covering D. Butt.** Revise version. Summary of the plan and general comments.

22 Jan	2	**Control of next depression – J.E. Meade.** Statement agreed with B.W. Gilbert on method of approach.
25 Jan	3	**Survey of the overseas economic situation as it affects the U.K. – J.E. Meade covering the Economic Section.** As sent to Overseas Economic Policy Committee.
1 Feb	4	**A note on the theory of the integration of the investment programmes of France and Britain – J.E. Meade covering D. Butt.**
4 Feb	5	**Preliminary notes for discussion on implementation of planning decisions – J.E. Meade.** Covering price control, fiscal policy and wages policy.
11 Feb	6	**The C.S.O. price index of consumer goods and the revised cost of living index – J.E. Meade covering G.P. Jeffries.**
19 Feb	7	**Nationalization of the iron and steel industries – J.E. Meade covering R.S. Sayers.**
28 Feb	8	**Planning and coal – J.E. Meade covering R.C. Tress.** Consideration of the nature of a coal budget and how to make coal an efficient instrument of current economic planning.
12 Mar	9	**The control of private investment – J.E. Meade covering R.C. Tress.** Review of possible controls with annexes by G.L.S. Shackle and J.E. Meade.
18 Mar	10	**Transport charges – J.E. Meade covering R.S. Sayers.**
2 May	11	**The extent and effects of recession and depression in the U.S.A. – J.E. Meade covering A.J. Brown.** Revise version. Consideration of the impact of a hypothetical recession.
27 Mar	12	**A note on rationalization in Germany during the war – J.E. Meade covering A.J. Brown.**
2 Apr	13	**The consultant's approach to industrial productivity – J.E. Meade.**
5 May	14	**Note by the Economic Section on paper RC68 by the Royal Commission on Population – R.S. Sayers covering R.S. Sayers, A.J. Brown and G.L.S. Shackle.** Revise version.
20 May	15	**Fuel and power shortages: possible policies – R.S. Sayers covering P. Chantler.**

25		**EC(S)(47) series.**	(EAS354/351/08B) April–July 1947.
	22 Apr	16	**Present conditions in the U.S.A. – J.M. Fleming covering A.J. Brown.** Preliminary draft for the June Overseas Economic Survey.
	24 Apr	17	**Transport charges – J.M. Fleming covering G.P. Jeffries.**
	27 May	18	**Controls – D. Butt.** Factual account for C.E.P.S. of existing economic controls and their purposes.

3 June	**19**	**Financing the deficit and the course of industrial production – A.J. Brown.** Drafts for the June Overseas Economic Survey.
10 June	**20**	**Estimation du Revenu National Français – J.E. Meade covering G.L.S. Shackle.** Summary of the French counterpart of the National Income White Paper.
10 June	**21**	**Coal and the level of demand – J.E. Meade covering A.J. Brown.** Drafts of two parts of the June Overseas Economic Survey.
17 June	**22**	**Survey of the overseas economic situation as it affects the U.K. – A.J. Brown.** The June Overseas Economic Survey.
21 June	**23**	**The available supplies – A.J. Brown.** For the June Overseas Economic Survey.
23 June	**24**	**The philosophy of planning – R.C. Tress.** Correspondence between A.K. Cairncross and R.C. Tress.
25 June	**25**	**Trade and payments – A.J. Brown.** For the June Overseas Economic Survey.
2 July	**26**	**Survey of the Overseas Economic Situation as it affects the U.K. – J.M. Fleming covering N. Watts.**

26   **EC(S)(47) series.**   (EAS354/351/08C)   July–Dec 1947.

17 July	**27**	**Hyper-demand – J.C.R. Dow.** Possibility that price increases were being avoided too much.
17 July	**28**	**Benelux – R.S. Sayers covering G.L.S. Shackle.**
12 Aug	**29**	**The control of consumption expenditure in the interests of employment policy – R.S. Shackle covering J.C.R. Dow.** Redraft of EC(S)(46)46 as agreed by the Inland Revenue and Customs and Excise.
8 Sept	**30**	**Some aspects of the balance of payments crisis – J.M. Fleming.** Attempt to explain the dollar drain in terms of the U.K. deficit on current account and various types of flows.
12 Sept	**31**	**U.K. balance of payments mid–1947 to end–1948 – R.L. Hall covering N. Watts and J.M. Fleming.**
8 Oct	**32**	**Replacement of imports by home production – R.L. Hall covering T. Swan.** Consideration of the issues raised in EP(0)(47)7.
14 Oct	**33**	**Devaluation plus export taxes question – R.L. Hall covering J.M. Fleming and E. Rowe-Dutton.**
16 Oct	**34**	**Under-requited and frustrated exports – R.L. Hall covering J.M. Fleming.**
19 Nov	**35**	**Soft exports from hard materials? – R.L. Hall covering J.M. Forsyth.**
9 Dec	**36**	**The theory of disinflation – R.L. Hall covering J.C.R. Dow.**
13 Dec	**37**	**Economic Survey for 1948 – R.L. Hall covering the Economic Survey Working Party.**

16 Dec	38	**Some thoughts on inflation – R.L. Hall covering J.M. Fleming.** Comments on EC(S)(47)37.
22 Dec	39	**The theory of suppressed inflation – R.L. Hall covering T. Swan.**

27   **EC(S)(48) series.** (EAS354/351/09A)   Jan–June 1948.

7 Jan	1	**Progressing the Economic Survey – R.L. Hall.** Outline arrangements.
7 Jan	2	**A customs union between all the countries of the Commonwealth or the U.K. and the colonies – J.M. Forsyth.** Draft report by the U.K. Study Group on Customs Unions for the Economic Policy Committee.
22 Jan	3	**Not included. Only appendixes A–D.**
23 Jan	4	**Statistics of advertising – J.C.R. Dow.**
23 Jan	5	**Draft outline re incentives to productivity – R.L. Hall covering Mrs. Hemming.**
17 Mar	6	**Fiscal policy and economic planning in 1948 – R.L. Hall covering T. Swan.** Sets out what the Chancellor could do in the budget to meet the objectives of the Economic Survey.
23 Mar	7	**The next Economic Survey – R.L. Hall covering D. Butt.**
2 Apr	8	**Notes on external economic affairs – R.L Hall.**
5 Apr	9	**Money, interest and expenditure – R.L. Hall covering G.L.S. Shackle.** Consideration of a reduction of the quantity of money, without increased interest rates, in order to control inflation.
16 Apr	10	**Budget accounts 1948–49 – R.L. Hall covering J.C.R. Dow.**
21 Apr	11	**Minutes from G.L.S. Shackle to R.L. Hall.** With regard to international trade and consultation.
23 Apr	12	**Reconsideration of the interest rate policy – R.L. Hall covering J.C.R. Dow.** Comments on EC(S)(48)9.
11 May	13	**National income in 1952 and its bearing on long-term investment plans – R.L. Hall covering J.C.R. Dow.** Revise version. Provisional forecast of national income as background for long-term decisions.
5 May	14	**Economic problems of common action – R.L. Hall.** Also GEN 188/199. Sets out the desirable activities of the O.E.E.C.
12 May	15	**Signs of deflation – R.L. Hall covering J.M. Fearn.**
27 May	16	**Report on third session of the Economic Commission for Europe – R.L. Hall covering T. Swan.**
3 June	17	**Signs of deflation – R.L. Hall covering J.M. Fearn.**

28   **EC(S)(48) series.** (EAS354/351/09B) June–Dec 1948.

4 June	**18**	**Economic corollaries of a customs union – R.L. Hall covering J.M. Fleming.** In relation to the work of the Customs Union Study Group.
10 June	**19**	**The problems of socialization – R.L. Hall.**
14 July	**20**	**Numerology – R.L. Hall covering D. Butt.** Concern at the increasing reliance placed on forecasts and estimates.
16 June	**21**	**Price policy in the coal industry – R.L. Hall covering Mrs. Hemming and J.C.R. Dow.**
22 June	**22**	**Pricing and costing in socialized industries – R.L. Hall covering J.C.R. Dow.**
24 June	**23**	**Signs of deflation – R.L. Hall covering K. Howell.**
3 July	**24**	**Price and output policy in socialized industries – R.L. Hall covering J.M. Fleming.**
6 July	**25**	**The impact of deflation – R.L. Hall covering J.C.R. Dow and Miss Hill.** See CE(48)7 (CAB 134/89).
9 July	**26**	**The pricing policy of the nationalized industries – R.L. Hall covering G.P. Jeffries.**
20 July	**27**	**Policy on controls – J.M. Fleming covering J.C.R. Dow and Miss Hill.** Draft ouline of CE(48)13. See CAB 134/89.
29 July	**28**	**Signs of deflation May/June summary – R.L. Hall covering K. Howell.**
12 Aug	**29**	**The pricing policy of the coal industry – J.M. Fleming.** Revised part on coal of EC(S)(48)26.
30 Aug	**30**	**Signs of deflation June/July summary – R.L. Hall covering K. Howell.**
	31	**Ministry of Fuel and Power's memorandum on price policy for the N.C.B. – R.L. Hall covering Mrs. Hemming.** Economic Section comments.
29 Sept	**32**	**Price and output policy in socialized industry – R.L. Hall covering J.M. Fleming.**
2 Nov	**33**	**The alternatives to materials allocations – R.L. Hall covering J.C.R. Dow.** Revise version. See CE(48)19 (CAB 134/89).
4 Oct	**34**	**Signs of deflation July/Aug summary – R.L. Hall covering J.C.R. Dow.**
14 Oct	**35**	**Money and interest in 1948 – R.L. Hall covering G.L.S. Shackle.**
19 Oct	**36**	**Steel in 1948 – R.L. Hall covering W.A.B. Hopkin.**
1 Nov	**37**	**The balance of payments problem of Western Europe – R.L. Hall covering T. Swan.** Considers whether Europe could be viable by 1952–53.
29 Oct	**38**	**Signs of deflation Aug/Sept summary – R.L. Hall covering K. Howell.**
8 Dec	**39**	**European viability 1952/3 – R.L. Hall covering J.M. Fleming and N. Watts.** Revise version.

Survey Working Party (ESWP(47)3)(final)) and consideration of the response by the Economic Section and C.S.O. to the former.

60   Dec 1947–May 1948. Further draft sections with consideration of targets and whether the planning year should be the Marshall Aid year. Correspondence resulting from publication, largely with ex-members of the Section. D. Butt on the functions of the Section as against C.E.P.S.

61–65   **Long-term Economic Survey 1948–51.** (EAS1/05A–C and annex IA and B).

61   Jan 1946–Apr 1947. Relevant minutes and memoranda of the Economic Survey Working Party. Includes some preview papers (see T 230/64–65). Papers on a programme for producing the survey and on likely problems, in particular regarding balance of payments and investment in plant and machinery.

62   June–July 1947. Relevant Economic Survey Working Party minutes and memoranda. Draft sections with departmental views, especially on shipping.

63   July–Nov 1947. Papers on differences with and between departments. Provisional rearrangement of the survey. Concentration in particular on the balance of payments programme and on underlying assumptions, especially on Marshall Aid. Disagreement between the Economic Section and C.E.P.S. on responsibility for the annual and long-term surveys. Final revisions of the latter.

64   Preview papers. Jan–Mar 1947.

nd	1	**Economic review 1948–51.** Meetings of Economic Survey Working Party, 15 and 23 Jan 1947. Consideration of the organization of work for the Economic Review.
nd	2	**Note of meeting 27 Sept 1946 to discuss the contribution which can be made by agriculture to the full employment policy.**
25 Sept	3	**Investment Working Party joint panels on public and private investment.** Capital expenditure on telephone exchange equipment – G.P.O. Also INV(Panels)(46)14.
29 Jan	4	Untitled – **G.P.O.** Review of B.B.C. capital expenditure programme in the next five years.
nd	5	**Ports and inland waterways – Ministry of Transport.**
nd	6	**Gas industry: capital requirements** – unsigned.
13 Feb	7	**1951 balance of payments: note of a meeting 4 Feb 1947.**
nd	8	**Building programme 1948–51** – unsigned.
nd	9	**Building materials 1948–51** – unsigned.
16 Feb	10	**The future demand for clothing – A.K. Cairncross.**
15 Feb	11	**Iron and steel – E. Ackroyd.**
19 Feb	12	**Economic Survey for 1951 – Ministry of Labour.** Probable occupational trends.
19 Feb	13	**Coal – M.F.W. Hemming.**
25 Feb	14	**Electricity programme 1946/7–1950/1 – M.F.W. Hemming.**

25 Feb	15	**Prospects for U.K. shipping and shipbuilding for 1948–51 – P. Chantler.** Revised version, 7 Mar.
25 Feb	16	**Raw material imports – R.W.B. Clarke covering the Raw Materials Department.**
28 Feb	17	**Economic Survey for 1951. Railway transport – G.P. Jeffries.** Revised version, 28 Feb.
28 Feb	18	**Highways – G.P. Jeffries.** Revised version, 18 April.
28 Feb	19	**Road haulage and public passenger vehicles – P. Chantler.**
4 Mar	20	**Economic review 1948–1951.** Note of a meeting 20 Feb to consider preview papers 8–12.
14 Mar	21	**Economic review 1948–1951.** Note of a meeting 5 Mar to consider papers 13–14.
14 Mar	22	**Investment programmes in 1951 – C.T. Saunders.**
18 Mar	23	**Food and agriculture in a post-transition year – G.L.S. Shackle.**
17 Mar	24	**Economic review 1948–51.** Note of a meeting 12 Mar to consider papers 15(revise), 17–19.
	25	Missing.
21 Mar	26	**Economic review 1948–51.** Note of a meeting 20 Mar to consider papers 15(revise), 22, 23.
26 Mar	27	**Suggestions regarding the planning of the review and the form of the report – R.C. Tress.**
28 Mar	28	**First estimate of a total investment programme for 1951 gross fixed investment – C.T. Saunders.**
28 Mar	29	**Manpower for the armed forces and auxiliary services** – A. Reeder.

65	**Apr–June 1947.**		
29 Apr	30	**Review papers. Economic review 1948–51. First draft – R.C. Tress.** Circulated as a basis of discussion.
13 June	30	**Draft economic plan 1948–51 – R.C. Tress.** Revise version. Incomplete survey, based on consistent but optimistic targets, to serve as a basis for debate. The purpose of planning discussed.
28 Apr	31	**Planning estimates of the national income 1948 and 1951 – C.T. Saunders.** Describes the methods used.
9 May	32	**Manpower developments by the end of 1948 – A.** Reeder.
13 May	33	**Economic Survey for 1948–51. Background for a minimum investment programme – C.T. Saunders.**
20 May	34	**Construction programme 1951 – D. Butt.**

66–70   **Employment policy in the U.K. General.** (EAS16/01A–E).

66   July 1941–Aug 1943. Starts with J.E. Meade, 'Internal measures for the prevention of general unemployment' and various other pre-1943 papers on full employment. Comments on Meade, 'Maintenance of full employment' by the Economic Section, J.M. Keynes and others. Correspondence between Meade and Keynes on dividing the current and capital budget, long-term problems and issues for immediate ministerial decision. Correspondence between Meade and H.D. Henderson. J.M. Fleming on the internal buffer-stocks. Meade's concern about the possible division of national income forecasting from post-war employment policy.

67   Aug 1943–Feb 1944. R.C. Tress paper on national income planning and full employment with comments. Treasury note on the maintenance of employment with Economic Section's comments. Various papers of the Steering Committee on Post-war Employment. Notes of two informal talks on employment policy between the Board of Trade, Treasury and Economic Section, including the draft White Paper on employment policy. Revised draft of the White Paper included.

68   Feb–July 1944. Comments by J.M. Keynes on the Steering Committee report and by J.M. Fleming on E.A.G. Robinson's draft of the White Paper. Nuffield College Wartime Research Committee and Social Reconstructions Survey conferences on the international implications of a full employment policy and on full employment in a free society. Comments by Economic Section on the draft White Paper. E.F.M. Durbin on the relative merits of varying taxation and insurance contributions. Correspondence with the Ministry of War Transport on the White Paper. J. Jewkes on the next steps for implementing long-term policy.

69   Aug 1944–Feb 1945. J.E. Meade comments on Jewkes's paper. D.H. Robertson on the role of exchange rate alteration for the restoration of equilibrium. R.H. Coase on statistics of capital expenditure and employment policy with comments. Note of meeting Sept 1944 to discuss Jewkes's paper on the organization required for long-term employment policy leading to the recommendation of a new Treasury division. Comparison by Meade of *Full Employment in a Free Society* and the White Paper with comments. Notes for a conference at Nuffield on full employment, Dec 1944. J.P.R. Maud on moral issues arising from full employment, e.g. over wage restraint.

70   Mar–Dec 1945. J.E. Meade on the Economic Section's functions in relation to employment policy. Note of meeting, Mar 1945, again recommending a new Treasury Division. Correspondence with the Bank of England on cheap money. Circular by E.E. Bridges on administrative arrangements for employment policy, departmental replies and meeting June 1945 to finalize arrangements, with resulting correspondence.

71–73 **Committee on Post-war Employment.** (EAS16/86/01–03). July–Dec 1943.

71   Minutes of meetings. EC(43)1st–28th. See CAB 87/63.

72   Memoranda. EC(43)1–31. See CAB 87/63.

73   Memoranda. EC(O)(43)1–16. See CAB 87/70. Also includes some amendments.

90   **Functions of Cabinet secretariat. Historical memorandum.** (EAS42/02)
             June 1944. First revise of paper on functions since 1904.

91   **Allocation of civilian manpower for industry and armed forces. Group II
             and III.** (EAS128/01) Sept 1943–Aug 194-. Estimates of wartime
             manpower requirements and correspondence on allocations for group
             II and III industries. Some minutes and memoranda of the Manpower
             Committee.

92   **Washington talks on Article VII Mutual Aid Agreement.** (EAS232/01)
             Feb 1942–July 1944. Report by J.E. Meade and telegrams from
             Washington. Other papers on commercial commodity policy and
             various briefs for ministers.

93   **Mutual aid. Anglo-U.S. post-war economic co-operation.** (EAS232/03)
             Dec 1940–Jan 1945. Various papers and speeches. Little after 1942.

94–95   **National debt. Economic proposals.** (EAS12/01A and B).
  94   Apr 1941–Apr 1945. Request by Attlee for paper on a capital levy and
             its impact on the national debt, with J.E. Meade's and J.M. Keynes's
             views. Papers on the formation of the National Debt Enquiry with
             some of its minutes and memoranda.
  95   Apr–July 1945. Further minutes and memoranda with related
             correspondence, including J.M. Keynes, on capital levy and capital
             budget.

96–98   **1. National income and expenditure during wartime. 2. Post-war
             prospects.** (EAS50/01A–C) July 1939–Dec 1943.
  96   July 1939–June 1942. J.E. Meade's papers and correspondence,
             including with J.M Keynes, on national income estimates and wartime
             finances. Papers after 1942 on post-war national income.
  97   May 1942–July 1943. Papers increasingly concentrating on estimates
             of post-war national income and expenditure by the Economic Section,
             W. Eady, J.M. Keynes and H.D. Henderson leading to papers for the
             Reconstruction Priorities Committee.
  98   July–Dec 1943. Further papers on national income and expenditure in
             1948, in particular with regard to commitments for expenditure and
             employment policy.

99   **National Income and Expenditure White Paper 1945.** (EAS50/179/01)
             Jan 1944–Mar 1945. Copy of J.E. Meade's and R. Stone's *National
             Income and Expenditure.* Drafts of sections of the White Paper, in
             particular with regard to statistics and later drafts of White Paper.

100–103 **Proposed reform and developments of social insurance and allied services.**
             (EAS142/01A–D) Sept 1940–Dec 1943.
  102   Sept 1942–Nov 1943. Papers arising out of the Beveridge Report,
             particularly on J.E. Meade's proposal to vary insurance contributions.
  103   Nov–Dec 1943. Further papers leading to the White Paper on the
             government's proposals.

105   **National Insurance. Variations of contributions.** (EAS142/143/01) Dec
             1945–May 1946. Papers by J.E. Meade, J.M. Keynes and others for
             draft of the National Insurance Bill.

106–107 **Preparation of plans for transferring certain industries to public
             ownership.** (EAS144/01A and B) Sept 1945–Apr 1947.

108   **Anglo-U.S. memorandum of understanding on oil and petroleum during
             wartime.** (EAS25/01) Feb–Aug 1944.

109   **O.E.E.C. long-term planning.** (EAS58/02) Jan–Dec 1948. Little before
             Aug. Mainly administrative papers on progress and amendments to

the O.E.E.C. long-term programme. Views on possible Western European co-operation and conflict between the U.K. and other countries, e.g. on liberalization.

110–113   **National wages policy.** (EAS17/01A–D).

110   Feb 1941–May 1942. A few papers, including J.M. Keynes and the Section, on wages and inflation and post-war policy.

111   May 1945–Nov 1946. Note by Jay with Economic Section comments. Papers relating to the Wages Policy Working Party with Economic Section views, in particular, on undermanned industries and relative wages. Conflict between Ministry of Labour and E.M. Nicholson on the state's role.

112   Nov 1946–Feb 1947. Further conflict between the Ministry of Labour and E.M. Nicholson. Some papers of the Board of Trade Committee on Improvements in Undermanned Industries. Drafts of E.E. Bridges's paper on wages and price policy.

113   Apr 1947–June 1948. Papers increasingly concentrating on wages and inflation and not just the undermanned industries, leading to *Statement on Personal Incomes, Costs and Prices* (Cmd. 7321), the reaction to it and matters arising.

114–116   **Price stabilization policy.** (EAS34/01A, B and annex I).

114   Feb 1940–June 1944. Papers on policy's establishment and from 1944 on its continuation. Includes symposium by J.E. Meade and J.M. Fleming on price and output policy of state enterprise (see *Economic Journal*).

115   June 1944–Dec 1945. Correspondence between J.M. Keynes and J.E. Meade on the symposium, with comments. Ministry of Food on employment policy and post-war price control. G.L.S. Shackle, Dec 1945, on an increase in the price level.

116   Graphs and statistics of world wholesale prices. Undated. Tables and graphs of average monthly or annual prices of various commodities for the inter-war period.

121–124   **Inter-departmental Committee on Reparations and Economic Security. Correspondence and RES papers.** (EAS57/86/02A–D) Dec 1941–Aug 1943.

125   **Commercial policy. Proposals for a commercial clearing union.** (EAS4/04) Aug 1942–May 1944. Draft paper by J.E. Meade on an international commercial union with comments by R.F. Harrod, Cherwell and others.

126   **Inter-departmental Committee on Post-war Commercial Policy. PCP papers.** (EAS4/86/01 annex I) 1942. Papers of the Post-war Commercial Policy Committee (PCP/42).

127   **Commercial policy. Committee of officials to examine: (a) levy subsidies (b) bulk purchase (c) programming of supplies.** (EAS4/86/02) Aug–Nov 1944. Minutes and memoranda and related papers of the Committee on Commercial Policy (CCP). See CAB 87/97.

128   **Ministerial Committee on Post-war Commercial Policy GEN 5.** (EAS4/86/03) Apr–July 1943. Minutes and memoranda of GEN 5. See CAB 78/5.

129   **Post-war commercial policy discussions. Committee of Dominion Officials. Sir A. Overton – chairman.** (EAS4/86/04) June 1943. Minutes and memoranda of the Committee (PCP(43)).

148 Jan 1949. Various departmental comments and drafting amendments, including those of Jay and the Economic Planning Board. Consideration of whether there should be output targets, particularly for coal.

149 Jan–Feb 1949. Includes some departmental observations and amendments, including Gaitskell's, although once circulated as PC(49)8 responsibility had passed to C.E.P.S.

150 Feb 1949–Feb 1950. Drafts of the survey for publication and press arrangements.

151 Forward planning of government expenditure. (EAS50/02) Feb–Nov 1949. Papers on J.C.R. Dow's memorandum on government commitments up to 1955 or 1960 covering government expenditure, changes in the national economy and the implications for the budget. E.N. Plowden on the possibility of six-monthly forecasts of budget expenditure for two years ahead.

152 Proposals for increasing and subsequently removing the clothing ration. (EAS141/109/01) Feb 1946–Mar 1949. Includes correspondence between R.L. Hall and the Board of Trade following the 1948 increase in the ration without consultation with those responsible for overall planning.

153–154 Washington discussions with the U.S.A. and Canada. Preparatory discussions to be undertaken – memoranda. (EAS27/86/01A and B).

153 July–Aug 1949. WD(49)2nd and WD(49)1–45. Briefs, notes of previous discussions with other countries and papers setting out the background to the sterling-dollar problem and possible remedies.

154 Aug 1949. WD(49)46–85.

155–160 Intra-European trade and payments. European Payments Union general papers. (EAS81/01A–F) Mar 1949–Sept 1950.

155 Mar–Dec 1949. Various papers relating to discussions at the O.E.E.C. on a payments union and liberalization of trade.

158 Mar–May 1950. Includes E.C.A. comments on the payments union.

159 May–June 1950. Includes papers by the U.K. delegation on reaction to the U.K. proposals.

160 June–Sept 1950. Includes a Foreign Office paper on economic co-operation between free and planned economies in Western Europe. O.E.E.C. draft agreement and published documents relating to the European Payments Union.

161–162 Quarterly surveys of the general economic position. (EAS1/011A and B).

161 Apr 1941–Oct 1944. Papers relating mainly to 1941, apart from J. Jewkes on economic policy in the transition.

162 Oct 1944–Sept 1945. Draft and final versions of the surveys.

163–166 Economic Survey for 1950. (EAS1/08A–D).

163 Jan 1946–Nov 1949. 1946 consideration of a survey of 1950. Then gap to June 1949 and papers on the annual survey for 1950. J.M. Fleming on banking policy in the crisis. Discussion of the survey's nature and some concern about relations with C.E.P.S. Concern about the progress of investment cuts. Draft outlines and sections. Some ESWP memoranda.

164 Nov–Dec 1949. Information from departments, drafts of sections of the survey with comments. J. Downie on new procedure for dealing with the survey. Further ESWP memoranda.

165   Jan–Feb 1950. Drafts of the complete survey for publication, deliberately non-political because of the election.

166   Feb–Mar 1950. Drafts of the popular version and papers relating to publication.

167   Appraisal of the future expectations of the business and commercial world. (EAS70/04) Mar 1949–Mar 1950. Papers on the establishment of periodic departmental reports on industrial prospects before and after devaluation.

168   I.M.F. interpretation of Bretton Woods conference. (EAS39/01) Oct 1944–June 1945. Includes some correspondence by D.H. Robertson and J.M. Keynes on their differing interpretations of Articles IV and VIII. Consideration of proposals of, among others, the American Bankers' Association.

169   Working Party on Price Structure after Devaluation. (EAS34/72/04) Mar 1949–Jan 1950. Drafts and final version of working party report.

170   The internal financial policies of the U.N.I.S.C.A.N. countries. (EAS245/01) Mar – Sept 1950. Papers relating to the question of U.N.I.S.C.A.N. disequilibria and the reports of the U.K., Denmark, Sweden and Norway on their internal financial positions.

171   Inter-departmental Committee on Post-war Commercial Policy (Overton Committee 1942–43). (EAS4/86/01) Nov 1942–May 1943. Minutes, memoranda, papers and report, including H.D. Henderson's note of dissent.

172–175   Article VII: Mutual Aid Agreement. Commercial policy negotiations with the U.S.A. (EAS4/87/02A–D).

172   Sept 1942–Jan 1944. Papers relating to the negotiations, including correspondence on a multilateral tariff reduction and its impact on the U.K.

173   Jan 1944–Jan 1945. Drafts of section of Law's report on commercial policy. Correspondence on imperial preference, tariffs and the negotiations, including the views of J.M. Keynes and J.E. Meade. Concern about the Washington proposals' impact on agriculture.

174   Jan–July 1945. Notes of discussions with U.S. and Canadian officials and resulting papers.

175   Aug 1945–Jan 1947. Includes U.S. views on U.K. agricultural proposals. Notes for discussions with U.S.A on commercial policy and imperial preference and proposals for consideration by an international conference on trade and employment.

176   Commercial policy. Anglo-U.S. discussions leading to the implementation of Article VII of the Mutual Aid Agreement. State trading. (EAS4/87/01) Dec 1942–July 1946. Papers on state trading and drafts of the report by the Working Party on Non-tariff Questions.

177   Dollar Drain Committee papers. (EAS29/86/02) Oct 1947–June 1952. Papers concentrating on 1948–1949 by the Economic Section, including R.L. Hall on fixed and floating exchange rates, Aug 1948. Other committee correspondence.

178   British Transport Commission. Passenger charges scheme 1951. (EAS190/01) May 1951. Papers arising out of a B.T.C. proposal for a scheme for the London area.

179   Draft survey of the U.K. economy 1945–1951. (EAS31/77/01) Nov 1951. Drafts of sections of the factual account of economic developments and first draft of the completed survey (EC(S)(51)37).

area system and convertibility on non-sterling area sterling earnings 1946–51. F.R.P. Vinter on sterling area balance of payments 1946–52.

256   **General post-war housing policy.** (EAS30/01) Oct 1941–Nov 1954. Wartime papers on the post-war building industry and the long-term housing programme. Gap from 1944 to 1952.

257–259   **National economy in the event of war.** (EAS31/111/03A–C) 1950–54. Retained.

262   **Finance of the national insurance scheme. Working papers 1949–54.** (EAS142/03) Aug 1949–Oct 1954. Includes relevant White Papers and notes on the variation of insurance contributions and the effect of subsidy reductions.

266   **Economic planning in foreign countries including discussions with foreign government planners.** (EAS214/02) Feb 1949–Dec 1954. Includes conversations with U.S. and Czech planners. Papers on the economic policy of India, Pakistan, Australia and Denmark. J.C.R. Dow on economic research and organization in government following a visit to the Netherlands and Scandinavia in 1954.

267   **Long-term economic policy.** (EAS214/04) Jan 1953–June 1954. Includes EC(S)(53)12 – the draft Economic Survey for 1948–1952 in retrospect.

276–280   **Balance of payments general policy.** (EAS29/02A–E).

276   Aug 1945–July 1947. Papers relating to 1946 estimates of balance of payments in 1950 and 1947 estimates for 1951. Papers on the balance of payments and Anglo-U.S. relations. Marquand on proposals for C.E.P.S. work by June 1947. R.C. Tress on the financial implications of the draft economic plan for 1948–51.

277   July 1947–Feb 1948. Discussions with U.S. officials and 1947 estimates of the 1948 balance of payments. Papers on the 1948 dollar and non-dollar programmes. Briefs for the Lord President on relevant Cabinet memoranda.

278   Feb 1948–Oct 1950. Papers on the balance of payments and U.S. aid, estimates of the U.K. annual balance of payments to 1950/51. Draft report of an *ad hoc* working party on the effect of price changes on the long-term balance. Briefs for the Lord President on relevant Cabinet and Economic Policy Committee memoranda.

279   Oct 1950–June 1951. Programmes Committee papers on the balance of payments 1951–1952/3, papers on the impact of devaluation and estimates of the balance of payments in 1951. R.L. Hall on the relationship between the cost of living, wages and the balance of payments, Nov 1950. Some minutes and memoranda of GEN 299 (see CAB 130/54).

280   July 1951–Jan 1955. Review of progress in 1951 and on the deterioration of the situation in the second half of that year, leading to papers for the new government. Memorandum on the sterling area balance of payments 1946–52.

281   **Economic Section discussion papers 1955.** (EAS31/351/01) Jan–Oct 1955. Also T 230/345. Includes a memorandum on farm incomes 1947–53.

282   **Profits and dividends policy Dec 1947–Jan 1955.** (EAS34/296/01) Dec 1947–Nov 1955. Brief for the Lord President and comments on EPC(47)27. Discussion of ministers' meeting with the T.U.C. General Council, Nov 1947, and various papers relating to profits up to 1949. Then gap to 1954.

283   1. The role of economists in public administration. 2. Historical notes
             of the Economic Section. (EAS42/01) Jan 1943–Aug 1953.
             Correspondence between L.C. Robbins and·J.M. Keynes on the future
             role of economists in government in relation to the wartime Machinery
             of Government Committee (see CAB 87/73–75). Notes on the
             Economic Section's post-war position. Then gap to 1953. J.C.R. Dow's
             notes for a talk on the situation during and after the war. Paper by the
             Training and Education Division of the Treasury on the functions of
             the Treasury. D. Butt in 1953 on the history of the Economic Section
             and a list of positions of ex-members of the Economic Section in 1959.
             Correspondence between R.L. Hall, L.C. Robbins and J.E. Meade on
             whether the Section should join the Treasury in 1953.

293–301   1. National wages policy. 2. Full employment policy. (EAS17/68/01A–J)
             June 1948–1957.

293   June 1948–July 1950. Reviews of the progress of wage restraint and
             the problems of its possible continuation. W. Eady on wages and the
             cost of living post-war as compared with 1920–21, with resulting
             comments. The T.U.C. on devaluation and wages Nov 1949. Papers,
             spring 1950, on wages policy, the possibility of easing wage restraint,
             and full employment and cost inflation. Discussions with the T.U.C.,
             summer 1950, and consideration of N. Kaldor's proposals for a long-
             term wages policy. Notes on various relevant memoranda for
             committees and Cabinet.

294   July–Nov 1950. Note of a meeting, July 1950, on the relationship
             between wages policy and full employment policy. Economic Section
             on the reasons for a wages policy and first outline draft of a paper on
             the post-war experience and the lessons learned. Draft outline of a
             White Paper on employment policy and wages policy, with comments,
             including those of Gaitskell and Jay.

295   Nov 1950–July 1951. Papers relating to full employment and U.N.
             initiatives, the Full Employment Bill and its suspension with the
             resulting suggestion of a White Paper. Papers on the link between
             wages and the cost of living with discussions between Bevan and
             Gaitskell.

296   July 1951–Jan 1952. Outline of a speech for Gaitskell on the price
             problem. Revised answers to E.C.O.S.O.C. full employment
             questionnaire. Drafts of a White Paper on the problems of employment
             policy leading on to drafts of a White Paper on inflation.

319–322   Development of economic control. (EAS52/31/02A–D) May 1947–1956.

319   May 1947–Dec 1950. Final report to the President of the Board of
             Trade on the examination of controls; note of a meeting, May 1949,
             on the powers for operating economic controls, which led to the
             establishment of Committees on the Control of Investment and on
             Economic Controls (see CAB 134/63 and 95). Review of instructions
             to the Capital Issues Committee. Gaitskell to Cripps, Jan 1950, on
             controls and economic policy, with comments. Various comments on
             EPC(50)9. Review of changes in controls by the Ministries of Food
             and of Supply. Papers on the impact on the cost of living of the removal
             of quantitative restrictions on imports. Memorandum on U.K. controls
             Nov 1950.

320   Jan–Sept 1951. E.N. Plowden and R.L. Hall on the development of
             controls and raw materials statistics. Monthly, then quarterly, reports

on controls. Ministry of Food regular reports and other departmental papers on changes in controls.

321   Sept 1951–May 1952. Further departmental papers.

323   **Economic planning and fiscal policy.** (EAS214/05) 1945–57.

324   **Discussions on problems of sterling balances.** (EAS231/01) 1949–55. Retained.

326–327   **Rent restriction and housing policy.** (EAS30/206/02A and B) May 1951–1958.

328   **Economic policy.** (EAS31/02A) Nov 1950–May 1955. Notes on economic policy in general and the presentation of policy.

332   **Control of expenditure in the interests of employment policy: taxes and benefits.** (EAS168/16/01) 1946–58.

334   **1. Defence burden sharing. 2. Defence expenditure to be borne by N.A.T.O. forces. 3. Economic impact of defence expenditure.** (EAS237/43/01C) Feb 1951–July 1952. Papers relating to the Nitze exercise and the prospects and effect of U.S. aid.

338–339   **Economic Section of the Cabinet secretariat: discussion papers 1950.** (EAS354/351/011A and B) Jan 1950–Jan 1951.

338   **EC(S)(50) series.** (EAS354/351/011A) Jan–July 1950.

4 Jan	1	**Inflationary/disinflationary symptoms Dec 1949 – R.L. Hall covering K. Howell, J. Grieve Smith and J.C.R. Dow.**
4 Jan	2	**A criterion of full employment (a rejoinder) – R.L. Hall covering J. Grieve Smith.** Rejoinder to EC(S)(49)41 on a definition of full employment.
11 Jan	3	**The control of commercial bank credit – R.L. Hall covering S. Abramson.** Review of the need for and possible methods of control.
10 Jan	4	**Summary of U.N. report on national and international measures to achieve full employment – R.L. Hall covering J. Licence.**
11 Jan	5	**One world – some comments – R.L. Hall covering F.J. Atkinson.** Comments on EC(S)(49)30 and 34.
13 Jan	6	**Economic Survey for 1950 – Economic Section.**
28 Jan	7	**The sterling balance problem – R.L. Hall covering J. Jukes.**
27 Jan	8	**Inflationary/disinflationary symptoms. Jan 1950 report – R.L. Hall covering K. Howell, J. Grieve Smith and J.C.R. Dow.** See EPC(50)25.
8 Feb	9	**The future of British agriculture – R.F. Bretherton.** Review of the expansion programme.
13 Feb	10	**European Payments Union: compromise scheme – R.L. Hall covering J.M. Fleming.** Proposed compromise between the experts' and the original U.K. proposals.
14 Feb	11	**Report on the fifth session of the Economic and Employment Commission (New York, Jan 1950) and on a subsequent visit to Washington – R.L. Hall covering J.M. Fleming.** Also NIFE(50)5.

4 Mar	12	**Trade unions and employers' organizations in Great Britain – J. Kelley.** Summary of their structure and activities.
4 Mar	13	**Inflationary/disinflationary symptoms. Feb 1950 report – R.L. Hall covering K. Howell, J. Grieve Smith and J.C.R. Dow.** Draft of EPC(50)37.
8 Mar	14	**Full employment and cost inflation – R.L. Hall covering J. Downie.** If inflation was to be an abiding problem of a fully employed economy then permanent, long-term solutions had to be found. Trade unions and employers were likely to continue to operate sectionally, so the task of policy was to modify or operate the present system of wage determination in order to gain price stability. No suggestion so far was acceptable and more continuous, systematic thought was needed.
9 Mar	15	**U.N. report on national and international measures to achieve full employment – R.L. Hall covering an inter-departmental working party.** See EPC(50)27. Also NIFE(50)2.
17 Mar	16	**European Payments Union – R.L. Hall covering J.E. Meade.**
18 Mar	17	**Western Germany – R.L. Hall covering J. Grieve Smith.**
18 Mar	18	**On mopping up sterling – R.L. Hall covering J.M. Fleming.**
28 Mar	19	**Report by O.E.E.C. countries on internal financial stability – R.L. Hall covering S. Abramson.** Also ER(L)(50)88. Mainly with regard to Belgium.
5 Apr	20	**Internal financial situation. Mar 1950 report – R.L. Hall covering K. Howell and J. Grieve Smith.**
20 Apr	21	**A plan for stabilizing the flow of international trade – R.L. Hall covering J.M. Fleming.**
2 May	22	**The wages problem – R.L. Hall covering F.J. Atkinson.**
9 May	23	**Internal financial situation. April 1950 report – R.L. Hall covering K. Howell and J. Grieve Smith.**
9 May	24	**The problem of wage pressure – R.L. Hall covering J. Downie.** Concentrates on the formulation of, not solutions to, the problem.
9 May	25	**Wage policy and full employment: foreign experience – R.L. Hall covering J. Kelley.**
10 May	26	**The terminology of inflation – R.L. Hall covering J. Downie.** Sets out previous definitions and his own.
18 May	27	**Stable international investment for economic development – R.L. Hall covering J.M. Fleming.**

2 June	28	**Internal financial situation. May 1950 report – R.F. Bretherton covering K. Howell and J. Grieve Smith.** See EPC(50)61.
6 June	29	**Proposed international tin agreement – R.F. Bretherton covering N. Watts.**
19 June	30	**Action against wage pressure – J. Downie.** Continuation of EC(S)(50)24, setting out proposals.
21 June	31	**Visit of the Director to the U.S.A. – R.L. Hall.**
27 June	32	**Wages policy – R.L. Hall covering J.C.R. Dow.** Comments on EC(S)(50)30.
6 July	33	**Working Party on Internal Financial Stability Mar–June 1950 – R.L. Hall covering J.C.R. Dow.**
7 July	34	**Internal financial situation. June 1950 report – R.L. Hall covering J. Grieve Smith.** Revise version, 13 July. See EPC(50)84.
13 July	35	**The present position and future prospects of the development areas – R.L. Hall covering J. Kelley.** The time was ripe for a reappraisal of policy.
14 July	36	**Internal financial position of the U.K. in relation to other countries of Western Europe – R.L. Hall covering J.C.R. Dow.** Summary of O.E.E.C. report on internal financial stability.
18 July	37	**Measures for the reorganization of the white fish industry – R.L. Hall covering J. Kelley.**

339		**EC(S)(50) series.** Aug 1950–Jan 1951.
3 Aug	38	**Internal financial situation. July 1950 report – R.L. Hall covering K. Howell.** See EPC(50)85.
10 Aug	39	**Colonial development: some elementary queries – D. Butt.**
14 Aug	40	**Australian development problems – D. Butt.**
15 Aug	41	**U.K. policy towards Europe – R.L. Hall covering J.C.R. Dow.**
28 Aug	42	**Full employment resolution: E.C.O.S.O.C. July 1950 – R.L. Hall covering J.M. Fleming.**
8 Sept	43	**Internal financial situation. Aug 1950 report – R.L. Hall covering K. Howell.** See EPC(50)93.
20 Sept	44	**Liberalization of trade with the O.E.E.C. – N. Watts.** Departments should be persuaded to reconsider the U.K.'s approach.
4 Oct	45	**The marketing of British agricultural products – R.F. Bretherton.**
5 Oct	46	**Internal financial situation. Sept 1950 report – R.F. Bretherton covering K. Howell and J. Grieve Smith.** See EPC(50)101.
6 Oct	47	**The full employment target – J.M. Fleming covering the Ministry of Labour.** Also NIFE(UN)(50)1. Estimate of the level of unemployment caused by factors other than demand deficiency and the appropriate extent

to which it should be allowed for in a target rate of unemployment.

13 Oct	**48**	**The full employment standard – J.M. Fleming.** Also NIFE(UN)(50)2. Unemployment greater than 2% would necessitate action, but the standard recommended was 3½%.
18 Oct	**49**	**U.K. export prospects – R.L. Hall covering P. Le Cheminant.** Review of the immediate future by an examination of the existing situation in the light of past trends.
26 Oct	**50**	**Cost of living – R.L. Hall covering R.F. Bretherton.** Assessment of the effect of an increase in world prices.
26 Oct	**51**	**Sharing the burden of defence: general considerations – R.L. Hall.**
3 Nov	**52**	**Investment criteria for manufacturing industry – R.L. Hall covering R.F. Bretherton and F.J. Atkinson.** Suggestion of new criteria.
8 Nov	**53**	**Liberalization of trade with the O.E.E.C. – R.L. Hall covering N. Watts.**
10 Nov	**54**	**Internal financial situation. Oct 1950 report – R.L. Hall covering K. Howell and J. Grieve Smith.** See EPC(50)119.
20 Nov	**55**	**Report to the President on foreign economic policies – R.L. Hall covering J. Licence.** See ES(50)13.
27 Nov	**56**	**The presentation of economic policies – R.L. Hall covering R.L. Hall and D. Butt.** Correspondence between the two on the neglect of long-term progressive policies.
13 Dec	**57**	**The cost of living – R.F. Bretherton covering E. Jones.** Attempt to assess the impact of import and excise duties and subsidies on the index.
8 Dec	**58**	**Formulae for determining equitable defence burdens – R.F. Bretherton covering J. Licence.**
15 Dec	**59**	**Monthly reports on the internal financial situation – R.L. Hall.** The series was to be incorporated in the C.S.O. monthly economic report.
15 Dec	**60**	**Economic prospects for 1951 – R.L. Hall covering J. Downie.** See ES(50)29 and EPB(50)20.
1 Jan	**61**	**The cost of living – R.F. Bretherton covering E. Jones.** Supplement to EC(S)(50)57 on the relation of indirect taxes and food subsidies to the total of consumers' expenditure in 1949.
29 Oct	**62**	**The possibility of reducing the cost of living by abolishing quantitative restrictions on imports – R.F. Bretherton covering J. Kelley.**

340   **Economic Section of the Cabinet secretariat: discussion papers 1951. EC(S)(51) series.** (EAS354/351/012) Jan–Nov 1951.

12 Jan	**1**	**The coal situation – R.L. Hall covering F.J.**

		Atkinson. Note on the situation and the prospects for the rest of the winter.
17 Jan	2	**Controls in the U.K.: Dec 1950 – R.L. Hall covering D. Butt.** Review of existing powers to control the economy concluding that they were very powerful and that there were no obstacles to increase them, should that be necessary.
5 Feb	3	**Draft reply to E.C.O.S.O.C. full employment questionnaire – R.L. Hall.** Draft reply.
23 Feb	4	**Proportion of consumers' expenditure on price-controlled goods and services – R.L. Hall covering J. Kelley.**
31 Mar	5	**Overseas development and rearmament – R.L. Hall covering D. Butt.** Examination of the problems arising from the commitment to develop the Commonwealth and South East Asia at the same time as rearmament.
4 Apr	6	**Price policy of the N.C.B. – R.L. Hall covering Mrs. Hemming.**
3 Apr	7	**Price stability – R.F. Bretherton covering F.J. Atkinson.** Concern at a possible long-term upward drift of prices mainly due to wages.
9 Apr	8	**The U.K.'s sterling liabilities – R.F. Bretherton covering N. Watts.**
14 Apr	9	**The Schuman Plan – D. Butt.**
19 Apr	10	**Stock appreciation and bank advances – R.L. Hall covering J. Grieve-Smith.**
20 Apr	11	**Development of economic controls – R.L. Hall.** See ES(51)23.
28 Apr	12	**International effects of U.S. inflation – R.L. Hall covering J. Jewkes.** Summary of likely prospects and possible effects.
3 May	13	**Inter-allied finance in war and reconstruction – D. Butt.**
7 May	14	**The internal distribution of scarce materials – R.L. Hall covering R.F. Bretherton.**
7 May	15	**Proposed paper on lessons of the last five years – D. Butt.** Proposed titles of sections, authors and conclusions with a concentration on the normal peace-time conduct of employment policy rather than an economic history of 1945–50.
28 May	16	**Employment and fluctuations in national expenditure – R.L. Hall covering J. Downie.**
1 June	17	**Full employment and the level of demand – R.L. Hall covering F.J. Atkinson.** Contribution to the paper proposed in EC(S)(51)15.
13 June	18	**Full employment and monetary policy – R.L. Hall covering E. Jones.** Further contribution.
13 June	19	**Full employment and the stability of money incomes – R.L. Hall covering J. Grieve Smith.** Further contribution.

13 June	20	**Full employment and the control of investment –** R.L. Hall covering F.J. Atkinson. Further contribution.
15 June	21	**The N.C.B.'s report for 1950 – R.F. Bretherton covering F.J. Atkinson.**
26 June	22	**O.E.E.C. Working Party on Internal Financial Stability – R.L. Hall covering J.C.R. Dow.**
26 June	23	**Coal and steel – R.L. Hall covering F.J. Atkinson.**
27 June	24	**Full employment and the distribution of industry – R.L. Hall covering P. Le Cheminant.** Further contribution to paper proposed in EC(S)(51)15.
30 June	25	**Raw materials and full employment – R.L. Hall covering P. Le Cheminant.** Further contribution.
2 July	26	**Economists' opinions upon the Economic Survey – R.L. Hall.** Opinions as expressed in the *Bulletin of the London and Cambridge Economic Service*, May 1951.
3 July	27	**The future of the European Payments Union – R.L. Hall covering N. Watts.**
5 July	28	**Industrial relations under full employment – R.L. Hall covering J. Kelley.** Contribution to the paper proposed in EC(S)(51)15.
5 July	29	**The administration of employment policy 1945–50 – R.L. Hall covering D. Butt.** Further contribution.
26 July	30	**Economic controls and full employment – R.L. Hall covering J. Kelley.** Further such paper.
20 Aug	31	**British transport – R.L. Hall covering J. Grieve Smith.** First draft of a general paper on the transport position.
14 Sept	32	**Belgium and the European Payments Union – D. Butt covering N. Watts.**
4 Oct	33	**Government relations with socialized industries – R.L. Hall covering J. Grieve Smith.**
8 Oct	34	**Investment control over the nationalized industries – R.L. Hall covering F.J. Atkinson.**
11 Oct	35	**The state of the U.S. economy – R.L. Hall covering P. Le Cheminant.**
8 Nov	36	**The findings of the report on internal financial stability and its bearing on politico-economic capabilities – R.L. Hall covering J.C.R. Dow.**
13 Nov	37	**Draft survey of U.K economy 1945–51 – R.L. Hall covering J. Grieve Smith.** Factual account of events.
21 Nov	38	**The new-old monetary policy – R.L. Hall covering D.C. Jones.** Review of the post-war capabilities of monetary policy.

341–344 **Economic Section of the Cabinet secretariat: discussion papers 1954. EC(S)(54) series.** (EAS354/351/015A–D) Jan–Dec 1954.

341 Jan–Mar 1954. Includes papers on the supply of U.S. dollars, Jan

Chapter 20   Treasury

The Treasury was the central department of government responsible for financial policy, public expenditure and the management of the Civil Service. The first covered international and bilateral negotiations, the balance of payments, monetary policy and controls over investment. Public expenditure included the co-ordination and supervision of all government expenditure, whilst management of the Civil Service included control over the staffing and organization of all other departments. This combination of advisory and executive responsibilities gave the Treasury an unparalleled influence, both directly and indirectly, over the nature of economic planning.

During the Second World War the Treasury was temporarily in eclipse, with the Chancellor of the Exchequer (Wood) excluded from the War Cabinet from May to October 1940 and from February 1942 to September 1943. This was in part the consequence of the suspicion with which the Treasury was viewed by Churchill and the Labour ministers, a suspicion stemming from the nature of Treasury advice on rearmament and on unemployment during the 1930s. In part it also reflected the fact that manpower had supplanted finance as the major constraint on government policy. The Treasury's influence started to revive when Anderson, who had dominated the Home Front as Lord President, was appointed Chancellor (Sept–July 1945). However, owing to continuing ministerial suspicion, political rivalry and official wariness, its economic role was still restricted largely to financial policy under Dalton's chancellorship (July 1945–Nov 1947) with formal responsibility for economic co-ordination and planning being vested in the Lord President.

The establishment of C.E.P.S. and the appointment of Cripps as Minister of Economic Affairs in September 1947 threatened to make permanent this division between financial aid and economic policy; but following Dalton's resignation, Cripps became Chancellor and his staff, including C.E.P.S., were transferred to the Treasury. Economic and financial policy were thereby reintegrated, with a new ministerial post created to provide assistance for the Chancellor. This post was held by Jay (Economic Secretary, Dec 1947–Feb 1950), Gaitskell (Minister of State for Economic Affairs, Feb–Oct 1950) and Edwards, J. (Economic Secretary, Oct 1950–Oct 1951).

The Treasury's wartime view on reconstruction was well expressed in the memorandum (CAB 87/3, RP(43)5) which led to the creation of the Reconstruction Priorities Committee (CAB 87/12–13); on economic policy, in its submissions to the Committee on Post-war Employment, in particular CAB 87/63, EC(43)6; and on its peace-time role, in its evidence to the Official Committee on the Machinery of Government, particularly CAB 87/72, MGO 24. Between 1945 and 1947 its most direct influence over economic planning was exerted by its permanent secretary, E.E. Bridges, to whom Attlee devolved the task of developing the planning machinery and who consequently chaired the Official Steering Committee on Economic Development (CAB 134/ 186–193). Bridges's instinct was to equate economic planning with full employment policy, as expressed in the 1944 *Employment Policy* White Paper (see T 161/1368/ S.53261/01/4). Moreover, Treasury officials were reluctant either to share any of their transitional responsibilities or to assume new ones. Hence the unseemly dispute over the Economic Survey being based on the calendar year and the budget on the financial year (see, for 1946, CAB 134/503 and T 230/58), and the initial reluctance both to place a Treasury representative on the Economic Planning Board (CAB 134/210–214) and to incorporate C.E.P.S. Nevertheless, after the 1947 crisis and with the continuing crisis over the balance of payments, shortages and potential inflation, officials' attitudes changed. Under the chancellorship of Cripps (Nov 1947–Oct 1950) and Gaitskell (Oct 1950–Oct 1951), they became more amenable to both physical planning and the use of the budget to regulate aggregate demand – if only to achieve their traditional objectives of controlling public expenditure and containing inflation. For a detailed description of how, through a combination of direct responsibility and the chairmanship of inter-departmental committees, the Treasury had become by 1951 the 'central focus of economic co-ordination', see the 'Factual Report on Major Responsibilities' submitted to the Steering Committee for Economic Organization Enquiry, CAB 134/314, GOC(SC)(51)5.

The Treasury has traditionally had three main departments, each containing a number of divisions. The records for each department before 1948 are largely preserved in three discrete classes: Finance (T 160), Supply (T 161), Establishment (T 162). There is also a class of General Files (T 163). In 1948 the registries of each department were decentralized and so records after that date are largely classified by division. There is, however, no hard and fast distinction e.g. files started before 1948 but in use after that date will normally be preserved in the later classes. The smaller size of the post-1948 classes makes documents the more easy to locate. For the pre-1948 classes there are annual subject lists of files closed during the previous year, but the subjects are broad and are not always used consistently e.g. a committee can be classified under a different subject in different years. There is a general index to the divisional classes after 1948 on the open shelves at the P.R.O.; it covers the initial transfers of files but not subsequent ones.

For further details of the organization and functions of the Treasury, See T 165/425 (its Blue Note), T 199/702–704 (organization files), CAB 87/72, MGO 24 (submission to the Machinery of Government Committee, Aug 1943), and more generally T 199. Standard histories are H. Roseveare, *The Treasury* (Allen Lane, 1969), and Lord Bridges, *Treasury Control* (Athlone Press, 1950) and *The Treasury* (Allen and Unwin, 1966). See also the biographies, diaries and memoirs of ministers: B. Pimlott, *Hugh Dalton* (Cape, 1985) and (edited) *The Political Diary of Hugh Dalton* (Cape, 2 vols.) (1986); P. Williams, *Hugh Gaitskell* (Cape, 1979) and (edited) *The Diary of Hugh Gaitskell* (Cape, 1983); D. Jay, *Change and Fortune* (Hutchinson, 1980). A bibliography of work analysing Treasury policy is provided in G.C. Peden, *Keynes, The Treasury and British Economic Policy* (Macmillan, 1988).

Two Treasury classes have been listed separately because of their central importance to economic planning. The records of the C.E.P.S. (T 229) are listed in Chapter 18 and of the Economic Section (T 230), which was transferred to the Treasury in 1953, in Chapter 19. For the papers of the Minister for Economic Affairs in 1947, see BT 195 in Chapter 21.

20.1 Budget Papers

T 171 contains the historical record of the working papers of the official Treasury committee responsible for drafting annual and emergency budgets. The budget was the traditional 'expression of the government's economic policy', determining the means by which government would match its expenditure and revenue over the forthcoming financial year. It was thus the key to much of the Treasury's influence. After the 1941 budget, Keynesian techniques were employed regularly to forecast and adjust the balance between aggregate demand and supply within the economy; and, from the autumn budget of 1947, the Treasury used these techniques to counter inflation. The records include memoranda generated both within and outside the committee, the conclusions reached by the committee and the comments of ministers. The papers for each budget are organized into three broad categories (policy memoranda, submissions by the Customs and Excise and the Inland Revenue, and drafts of the budget speech, broadcast etc.). The material is arranged by subject. There are two lacunae. First, the views recorded are the final, formalized views of the participants; for their development, reference must be made to other Treasury and departmental classes. Secondly, the 1951 budget was the first for which a complete set of the minutes and memoranda of the Budget Committee are preserved. However, there are preserved in this class the summaries of the budget for the King and Cabinet which were never recorded in Cabinet documents. More detailed memoranda on public expenditure and revenue can be found in T 233.

The regular members of the Budget Committee were officials from the Treasury and the revenue departments, with ministers attending when necessary. Representatives of the Economic Section attended after 1945, as did E.N. Plowden after 1947. A detailed description of the drafting process is provided by Sir H. Brittain, *The British Budgetary System* (Allen and Unwin, 1959).

T 171

363-366 **Budget 1943.**

363 General discussions. Includes papers on family allowances, Keynes's proposal for a capital budget, with comments, as well as the usual budget estimates and prospects. Also drafts of the speech, of the budget broadcast and notes on procedure.

364 Customs and Excise proposals.

365 Inland Revenue proposals, including those relating to Excess Profits Tax, the general taxation of profits and the related submissions from industrial organizations.

366 Pay As You Earn: Income Tax (Employments) Bill 1943. Various papers including comments of Keynes and Treasury officials, consultation with industrial representatives and the preparation of the White Paper.

367-368 **Budget 1944.**

367 Indexed papers leading up to the budget, including discussions of the Budget Committee, Treasury notes, the National Income White Paper, Customs and Excise proposals and Inland Revenue proposals. Other papers cover budgetary outturn and prospects, and discussions of various taxation proposals, including excess profits tax, and the Beveridge Report in relation to income tax.

368 Includes drafts and notes of the budget speech, its summary for Cabinet and the King, the budget broadcast and newsreel scripts.

369-370 **Budget 1945.**

369 This volume covers discussions of the Budget Committee, notes by the Treasury, and Customs and Excise and Inland Revenue proposals. There are papers by H. Brittain on the 1945 budget, Keynes on excess profit tax, a paper on purchase tax policy and a report by the Budget Committee and papers on possible income tax relief.

370 Includes drafts and final copy of the budget speech, a summary of it for the King and Cabinet, the budget broadcast, and summaries for the B.B.C. and newsreels.

371-372   **Budget (No. 2) 1945.**

371   This volume covers vote of credit and post-war budget, the post-war budget of 1918, the cost of living and subsidies, the supplementary Financial Statement, summaries for Cabinet and the King, the budget speech and the B.B.C. broadcast. In particular there are papers by the Economic Section on income and expenditure in 1946 and discussions with the T.U.C. on wages. Problems of expenditure and commitments, with estimates of the 1948 position also covered.

372   Covers Inland Revenue and Customs and Excise proposals. Includes papers on post-war credits, income tax and excess profits tax, and purchase tax.

375-376   **Finance Bill 1943.**

375   Includes Financial Statement 1943–44, Cmd. 6438, the bill and its Parliamentary passage.

376   Parliamentary debates.

377-378   **Finance Bill 1944.**

377   Includes Financial Statement, Cmd. 6520, the bill and its Parliamentary passage.

378   Parliamentary debates.

379-380   **Finance Bill 1945.**

379   Includes Financial Statement, Cmd. 6622–6625 and 6615, the bill and the Finance (No.2) Bill and their Parliamentary passage.

380   Parliamentary debates.

381-382   **Finance (No. 3) Bill 1945.**

381   Includes supplementary Financial Statement and the bill's Parliamentary passage.

382   Parliamentary debates.

383-385   **Finance Bill 1946.**

383   Includes Financial Statement, Cmd. 6784, and the bill's initial Parliamentary passage.

384   Further papers on its Parliamentary passage.

385   Parliamentary debates.

386-388   **Budget 1946.**

386   This volume covers balancing the budget and the reduction of defence estimates, the problem of future growth in expenditure on reconstruction and social services, the cost of living and subsidy policy, summaries for discussion with the Prime Minister, for the King and Cabinet, and the B.B.C., the financial outturn 1945–46, drafts of the White Paper on national income, and the Financial Statement, the budget speech. In particular there are Dalton's initial thoughts and comments on 1946 budget estimates; Keynes's views on stabilization policies and subsidies; and consideration of defence expenditure and of the scope of the budget.

387   Customs and Excise proposals, including purchase tax.

388   Inland Revenue proposals, including income tax, the release of post-war credits and excess profits tax.

389-391   **Budget 1947.**

389   Covering general policy, the outturn 1946–47, estimates for 1947–48 and main decisions on the structure of the budget, including income tax. Submissions from the Association of British Chambers of Commerce, the F.B.I., the National Union of Manufacturers, the XYZ Club, Durbin and the Finance Group of the P.L.P. In particular there

are papers by J.M. Keynes on reflections after the 1946 budget; J.E. Meade on points to consider for the 1947 budget, the control of inflation, and the Economic Survey for 1947 and the budget for 1947/48, with Treasury comments on the latter; the Economic Section on the control of consumption expenditure in the interests of the employment policy; and papers on the budgetary outlook 1950 and on the reduction of subsidies. Other subjects covered are subsidies and the new cost of living index, budget estimates of interest on the National Debt and sinking funds, possible changes in income tax, sketch budget and note of a discussion between members of the Budget Committee and the Chancellor, February 1947.

390 Covers the timetable and drafts of statements for Parliament, including the White Paper on national income and expenditure and the Financial Statement of the budget speech and broadcast, and summaries for the King, Cabinet, the B.B.C., newsreels etc. Includes a note on responsibility for various parts of the draft speech, a paper on cheap money, comments on the speech and W. Eady on cheap money and nationalization.

391 Customs and Excise and Inland Revenue proposals. There are papers by J.E. Meade on differential taxation of undistributed profits and on the stabilization and taxation of company profits. Other subjects covered are payment of post-war credits to pensioners, income tax concessions to certain industries in the light of the Board of Trade Working Parties' reports, purchase tax. A number of issues not proceeded with included capital gains tax, gift tax, inheritance levy and the extension of the scope of the National Land Fund.

392-393 Budget (No. 2) 1947.
392 This volume covers general policy and main decisions, subsidies, timetable, procedure, summaries for Cabinet, the King and the B.B.C., drafts of statements for Parliament, including the Financial Statement, and of the budget speech and broadcast. In particular there are papers by Dalton, August 1947, on the possibility of an autumn budget; E.E. Bridges covering R.L. Hall on inflationary pressure, further papers by E.E. Bridges on the need to reduce inflationary pressure and food subsidies, with Dalton's comments; Jay on the budget; and notes of meetings between the Budget Committee and Dalton. Other subjects covered are food subsidies and the differing impact of various reductions, purchase tax and profits tax.

393 Customs and Excise and Inland Revenue proposals. Includes purchase tax, gas and electricity taxation, income tax, profits tax and dividend limitations.

394-396 Budget 1948.
394 This volume covers timetable and procedure, estimates of expenditure, capital-revenue budget, main discussions of policy, briefs for discussion of proposals with the Prime Minister, summary for Cabinet and the King, and draft financial statement. Submissions from the F.B.I., the Association of British Chambers of Commerce, the Finance Group of the P.L.P., and the National Union of Manufacturers. In particular there are papers by the Economic Section on inflation with Treasury comments; Cripps on subsidies and prices; the Treasury on special measures to counter inflationary pressure; R.L. Hall on why tax increases were necessary; Jay on bank deposits, the credit structure

and inflation; and notes of meetings of the Budget Committee with the Chancellor and other economic ministers. Other specific subjects covered are supply estimates and defence expenditure, explanation of a capital budget, the budget forecast on a national income basis, the target surplus and the capital levy.

395   Customs and Excise and Inland Revenue proposals. Includes note of a meeting between Attlee and the T.U.C., 17 Nov 1947, covering income tax, profits, P.A.Y.E. and incentives, and various papers, including R.L. Hall, E.N. Plowden and the Treasury, on the capital levy.

396   Covers timetable, drafts and final versions of the budget speech and broadcast.

397-399   **Budget 1949.**

397   This volume covers notes on general budget policy, Roffey Park discussions, briefs for discussions at Chequers, final decisions, summary for the King and Cabinet, drafts of the White Paper on national income and expenditure and statements for Parliament, including Financial Statement. Submissions from the Engineering Industries Association on initial allowances, the Association of British Chambers of Commerce, the F.B.I., the National Union of Manufacturers, the Finance Group of the P.L.P. and the National Chamber of Trade, and deputations concerning duties on petrol, beer, tobacco and motor car taxation. In particular there are papers by R.L. Hall and E.N. Plowden on the Budget Committee and how it could be improved, R.L. Hall on progress of disinflation and E.N. Plowden on budgetary problems and disinflation; W. Eady on deflation and the supply of money; B.W. Gilbert on the Economic Survey and the 1949/50 budget, and on the reduction of subsidies and indirect taxation; the Economic Section on the problem of inflation in 1949 and on the rationale of the alternative classification; Cripps and Lord Catto on co-operation from bankers; E.G. Compton on the form of the budget statement and the Crick Committee on the form of the Financial Statement; Jay on budgetary inflation and currency inflation (for Roffey Park), and on progress against inflation; the Working Party on Bank Deposits and Advances; and H. Campion on a first look at 1955. Other specific subjects covered are budgetary prospects and policies 1948-52, N.H.S. expenditure, cost of living subsidies, the 1949 budget figures, post-war credits, and supplementary estimates. There are also notes of, and briefs for, the Budget Committee, the Roffey Park discussions, and Chequers.

398   Customs and Excise and Inland Revenue proposals. Includes correspondence between Wilson, H. and Cripps on purchase tax, J.H. Woods on depreciation and the replacement of plant and the Chamber of Shipping and Liverpool Steam Ship Owners' Association on the shipping industry and taxation.

399   Covers drafts and final versions of the budget speech and of the budget forecast, and the newsreel script.

400-402   **Budget 1950.**

400   This volume covers general policy papers of the Budget Committee, its submission to the Chancellor, discussion in Cabinet and the Treasury, the Prime Minister's meetings and final decisions, eve of budget meetings, exchequer accounts, resolutions, administrative

arrangements, a budget timetable, the Finance Bill, restriction of the debate on purchase tax, procedure in the case of government defeat, security and publicity arrangements. In particular there are papers by Jay on motor taxation and his comments on borrowing for local authorities; Addison questioning the need for a budget surplus; submissions from Isaacs, Gordon Walker, Gaitskell, Marquand, Tomlinson and Alexander; and the Economic Section on the problem of inflation in 1950. Other specific subjects covered are capital gains tax, taxation of the middle classes, purchase tax, the feasibility of increasing taxation, investment cuts and prospects, the budgetary position and prospects, N.H.S. expenditure, counterpart funds, wages and prices in 1948 and 1949. There are also notes of, and briefs for, the Budget Committee and Roffey Park discussions, and a summary of the budget speech and proposals.

401   Covering minor proposals and the passage of the Finance Bill through Parliament. Covering drafts of the speech, including the draft outline and allocation of work, the material for various parts, special passages submitted to Cabinet, final comments and the final version of the speech, and drafts and final version of the budget broadcast.

403-407   **Budget 1951.**

403   This volume covers the timetable, preliminary papers, general budgetary problem, dividend limitations and profit tax. Includes the chronological table of the principal events in the run up to the budget. There are papers by the Economic Section on the internal financial situation and on the economic outlook for the 1951 budget; and Gaitskell's notes on economic policy. Other subjects covered are budgetary prospects and taxation of the middle classes. Hereafter the papers are arranged chronologically by meetings of the Budget Committee and of the Chancellor with officials. In particular there are meetings to consider papers by the Economic Section on the general budgetary problem in 1951, and redrafts of it; E.E. Bridges on the general budgetary problem; the Budget Committee on the 1951 budgetary problem, and on the general problem and the size of the gap; W. Eady on dividend limitation; and N. Kaldor's 'A Positive Policy for Wages and Dividends', with comments by Jay, the Treasury and the Inland Revenue. Other specific subjects covered are civil expenditure estimates, sketch budgets, and the general economic situation, all leading to consideration of N.H.S. expenditure and the question of charges, including meetings and related papers with Attlee, Cabinet and other ministers.

404   This volume covers purchase tax and utility, income tax, some other taxes and duties, suspension of initial allowances, and expenditure. In particular there are papers by R.L. Hall on taxation and the control of investment; C.E.P.S. on initial allowances; the Treasury on food subsidies; E.E. Bridges on economics in civil expenditure; and correspondence between Gaitskell and Attlee on cuts in N.H.S. expenditure; and a note on the fiscal and economic effects of suspension of initial allowances. On expenditure, there are general analyses and papers on various increases, especially education, papers on potential economies, including the Treasury on food subsidies. Other specific subjects covered are the fiscal and economic effects of suspension of initial allowances, general and specific analyses of increased

expenditure, especially on education, potential economies, and national insurance.

405   Covers Inland Revenue and Customs and Excise minor proposals, classification of exchequer accounts, resolutions for Parliament, the Financial Statement, Financial Bill and administrative arrangements. Submissions from the National Union of Manufacturers, the Association of British Chambers of Commerce, the T.U.C. and the F.B.I. Also papers on the redrafting of the alternative classification.

406   Covers material for and drafts of the speech, including that by the Economic Section.

407   Includes further drafts of the budget speech and drafts of the broadcast.

417   **Budget Committee minutes 1951.** June 1950–Mar 1951 BC(50)4th–BC(51)10th.

The subjects of the specific minutes include: BC(50)4th taxation of income; 5th dividend limitation; 6th general budgetary policy 1951/52; 7th–8th purchase tax; 9th general economic outlook, purchase tax, middle classes, tax yields; 10th special economy proposals, wages policy, general economic situation; BC(51)1st post-war credits, taxation and control of investment, dividend limitation, timetable; 2nd dividend limitation, initial allowances, food subsidies; 3rd estimate and sketch budget, National Union of Manufacturers, timetable, purchase tax and utility, agricultural land; 4th general budgetary problem in 1951, purchase tax and utility, agricultural land, initial allowances; 5th revenue duties on foodstuffs, profits tax, initial allowances, budgetary problem, Economic Survey; 6th budget outline, profits tax, initial allowances, capital gains tax, purchase tax, post-war credits; 7th (Roffey Park) general discussion, indirect and direct taxation, general taxation proposals, presentation, closing the gap, appendix A – government expenditure, especially N.H.S. and subsidies, appendix B – national insurance; 8th general position, Roffey Park decisions, purchase tax, capital gains, Inland Revenue post-war credits; 9th general budgetary position, timetable, speech; 10th general budgetary position, income tax changes.

418-419   **Budget miscellaneous papers 1951.**

418   2 Mar 1950–19 Jan 1951. There are papers by the National Income Forecasts Working Party on the economic impact of defence expenditure, Wilson, H. on the cost of clothing and household textiles; R.L. Hall on the relation between wages, cost of living and the balance of payments; and note of a meeting, 18 Sept 1950, on wages policy. Other subjects covered are the internal financial situation, full costs estimates, the budgetary outturn, taxation and the control of investment, finance of national insurance, the cost of living index, initial allowances and various economy proposals.

419   23 Jan–31 Mar 1951. Includes the submission of the Association of British Chambers of Commerce, and papers on the alternative classification, national insurance, the budgetary outturn and prospects, decisions at Roffey Park, cost of living subsidies, various taxation proposals, the inflationary gap in 1951, and the draft report of the Budget Committee.

420   **Budget 1951. 1. Dividend limitation 2. Simplification of income tax 3. Purchase tax and utility.** July 1950–June 1951. Includes papers on fiscal policy and the control of investment, whether to introduce a temporary dividend freeze or dividend limitation, the technical aspects of such a measure, and GEN 358/1st.

422   **Budget miscellaneous papers 1952.** 20 Aug 1951–4 Feb 1952. Includes a few papers prior to the election, including Jay on capital gains tax and other measures, an outline of discussion for the Budget Committee and financial estimates.

424   **Budget 1952. 1. Simplification of income tax on small incomes. 2. Dividend limitation 3. D scheme 4. Investment in plant and machinery 5. State of the Nation's Finances - White Paper.** 13 July 1951–7 Mar 1952. Includes further papers prior to the election on dividend limitation with papers by E.N. Plowden and E.E. Bridges, note of a meeting, 13 July 1951, of a deputation from the F.B.I., 20 July 1951, and drafts of the White Paper.

425   **Budget 1952. Budget Committee Working Party BC(WP) papers.** 22 June 1951–5 Feb 1952 BC(WP)(51)1–BC(WP)(52)6. Papers of the working party set up under R.L. Hall to prepare appreciations of the general economic situation for the guidance of the Budget Committee. Papers include methods of estimating the inflationary gap by the National Income Forecasts Working Party; the central government's accounts on a national income basis, and on quarterly estimates of government expenditure; H.A. Copeman on the budget accounts and R.L. Hall on the alternative classification.

426   **Budget 1952. Budget Committee Working Party BC(WP) minutes.** 2 July 1951–17 Jan 1952 BC(WP)(51)1st–BC(WP)(52)2nd. Includes minutes of the working party considering the nature of government accounts.

20.2   Bridges Papers

T 273 contains the working papers of Sir Edward (later Lord) Bridges, including a few inherited from Sir Richard Hopkins, his predecessor, which have not been integrated into other Treasury classes. They fall into two main categories: major economic policy issues, and ministerial and official appointments (with personal assessments). Bridges was Secretary to the Cabinet (1938–47), Permanent Secretary to the Treasury and head of the Civil Service (1945–56). He was one of Attlee's most senior advisers and the administrative responsibility for the co-ordination of economic planning was devolved upon him as chairman of the Official Steering Committee on Economic Development (CAB 134/186–193). His most recent biography is R. Chapman, *Ethics in the British Civil Service* (Routledge, 1988). See also T 269.

T 273

5-8   **Transitional period following 1939-1945 war: plans for Civil Service under Prime Minister's directive of 27 October 1943.** (174 parts 1–4).

5   Oct 1943–June 1944. Papers arising from WP(43)476.

6   Jan–Mar 1944. Papers on problems facing the Reconstruction Committee leading to R(44)45.

7   Nov 1943–Nov 1944. Papers on the drafting of the Cease-Fire Book.

8   Aug 1944–Aug 1945. Further papers on the drafting of the Cease-Fire Book.

20 **Mr. Samuel Clement Leslie.** (284) May 1940–May 1955. Papers on the appointment of the director of the Economic Information Unit and on the Unit itself.

38 **International Bank for Reconstruction Development: appointments.** (29) May 1946–July 1949.

40 **Monopolies Commission: correspondence concerning appointment of Sir A. Carter as Chairman.** (257) May 1948–Jan 1949.

50 **Argentina: trade and financial negotiations with President Peron** (216) Mar–Oct 1946.

57 **Beveridge Report on Social Insurance: Treasury consideration of proposals.** (25) July 1942–Oct 1943. Includes papers by Treasury officials, J.M. Keynes and H.D. Henderson on its cost and post-war expenditure.

63 **Committees and commissions of the Economic and Social Council: U.K. representation and co-ordination among U.K. departments of relations between H.M.G. and international bodies.** (202) Jan–July 1946.

66 **Civil Service manpower: ministerial committee.** (240) Feb–May 1947. Includes briefs by E.E. Bridges for ministers.

67 **Civil Service manpower: official committee.** (239) Jan–Mar 1947. Includes note of the meeting of ministers, 27 January 1947.

74 **Cabinet Office: appointment of Mr. E.E. Bridges as Permanent Secretary and transfer of Sir Norman Brook to H.M. Treasury.** (40 part 3) May 1938–May 1952. Papers on E.E. Bridges giving up the position of Secretary to the Cabinet and on the abortive move of N. Brook to C.E.P.S. to replace E.N. Plowden.

97 **Ministry of Fuel and Power: senior appointments.** (57 part 1) Feb 1942–Nov 1943.

103 **Ministry of Labour and National Service: senior appointments.** (66 part 2) Mar 1945–July 1956.

107 **Lord President's Office: senior appointments.** (70) May 1947–July 1956.

119 **Ministry of Production: creation of and senior staff.** (77) Feb 1942–Aug 1948.

126-127 **Ministry of Supply: changes in appointment and loan of Sir A. Rowlands to Pakistan.** (85 parts 2 and 3) May 1939–Apr 1956.

128 **Ministry of Supply: creation of second Permanent Secretary post and future of ministry.** (85 part 3) May 1951–May 1955.

131 **Board of Trade: senior appointments.** (87 part 3) Nov 1940–Feb 1955.

133 **Board of Trade: Permanent Secretary post.** (87 part 2) Apr 1951–Dec 1956. Includes papers on the replacement for J.H. Woods.

138 **Treasury: senior appointments.** (280) Jan 1942–July 1956. Papers concerning replacements for T.L. Rowan and E.N. Plowden.

139 **Appointment of Sir Edwin Plowden as Chief Planning Officer.** (275) Dec 1947–Feb 1951. Papers on C.E.P.S. amalgamation with the Treasury in 1947 and on E.N. Plowden's concern for his and C.E.P.S.'s future under a Conservative government.

140 **Treasury: ministerial arrangements and appointments.** (279) Sept 1947–Dec 1952. Papers on the administrative arrangements following the appointment of Cripps as Minister for Economic Affairs with T.L. Rowan as his Permanent Secretary, the arrangements during Cripps's illnesses and the appointment of Gaitskell as Minister of State for Economic Affairs.

202   May–Oct 1950. General correspondence. Includes J.H. Woods, with comments, on the higher organization of the Treasury and the Committee's report on the Supply Division.

203   Feb–July 1950. Minutes of meetings. TOC(50)1st–10th and 13th–15th.

205   **Ministry of Works: function and organization.** (108) June 1945–July 1955.

206   **Ministry of Works and Ministry of Health: arrangements for developing non-traditional housing.** (196) Jan–Feb 1946.

209   **Ministerial responsibilities and papers on salaries of supervising ministers.** (23) July 1936–July 1954.

214   **Sir Stafford Cripps: Memorial Fund and inclusion of an article by Sir Edward Bridges and Sir George Schuster's biographical note.** (266) July 1946–Aug 1955.

222   **Broadcasts and speech at Mansion House dinner by Sir Edward Bridges.** (131) July 1952–June 1954.

223-224   **Miscellaneous correspondence.** (parts 1 and 2) June 1940–Apr 1955.

232   **Article attacking civil servants in *Tribune*: request for ministerial intervention.** (222) Nov 1946–Oct 1949. Concerning attacks against the Economic Section and the Treasury.

233   **Professor Hancock's book on British war economy, comments on.** (199) Mar–Dec 1948.

234   **Article for *Cambridge Journal*.** Oct 1950–Jan 1951. 'The Civil Service in 1950', Volume 4 (1950) and correspondence requesting a right of reply.

235   *Keeping Left* **pamphlet 1950: protest to authors by Chancellor of the Exchequer at attack on officials.** (107) Jan 1950.

240   **The recovery of Europe: the Marshall offer.** (51) June–July 1947.

245   **Balance of Payments Working Party on Import Programmes: report 1946.** (52) Jan 1946–June 1947.

246   **Balance of payments 1947: alternative action to U.S. aid.** July–Aug 1947. Includes meetings between the Treasury and the Bank of England and drafts of the Interim Report of the Committee on Alternative Action and consideration of the subject by ministers. Also papers on the convertibility crisis.

247   **Balance of Payments: general.** (20) Sept 1949–July 1953. Papers on balance of payments forecasts.

251   **Coal production since nationalization of industry: correspondence with Mr. Clayton of the U.S. State Department.** (41) Sept 1947. Criticism of nationalization by Clayton and E.E. Bridges's defence of coal.

252   **Coal: measures to increase U.K. supplies (to include for export).** (47) Nov 1950–Sept 1955.

253–254   **Franco-German steel and coal: Schuman Plan.** (84 parts 1 and 2) May 1950–Apr 1954.

258   **Budget Committee 1943 working papers.** (134) May 1942–June 1943. The notes on the first four post-war budgets after 1918, R.V.N. Hopkins on the post-war role of the budget and S.D. Waley, H. Brittain and J.M. Keynes on the nature of the post-war budget. Also H.D. Henderson on net national income in 1948.

259   **Budget Committee 1944 working papers.** (135) Jan–Mar 1944. Further notes on the budget including some by J.M. Keynes.

260   **Budget Committee 1945.** (136) Dec 1944–Jan 1946. Includes papers on purchase tax and excess profits tax, post-war credits, the Bank of

England Bill, investment and the Exchange Control Bill and interest rates.

261   **Manufactured goods for building and export.** (261) June–July 1947. Papers arising from H. Emmerson's request for the appointment of someone to determine priorities.

262   **Building Controls Committee.** (48) Aug 1948–Dec 1949. Consideration of building controls and their complexity.

288–290   **Defence: general papers.** (59A-C) June 1950–Dec 1951.

       288   June–Aug 1950. Includes papers on defence requirements, budget prospects and estimates of expenditure in future years.

       289   Sept–Dec 1950. Includes papers on the economic impact of increased defence expenditure, possible U.S. assistance and Washington meetings, October 1950.

       290   Jan–Dec 1951. Further papers on the defence production programme, the cost of the U.K. defence effort and draft report on economic implications of defence.

291   **Defence and economic policy: new Cabinet committee structure.** (78) Sept–Oct 1950. Papers on the proposed changes, with comments.

298   **Economic planning: creation of steering committee to deal with central economic planning.** (14) May–Dec 1945. Papers on E.E. Bridges's circulars to Permanent Secretaries on proposed machinery and the resulting circulation of 'Planning of Economic Developments' to ministers. J.E. Meade on 'Economic Planning' and papers on membership of the steering committee and its working parties.

299   **Economic planning: general papers March 1947–49.** (102) Dec 1946–Aug 1948. Includes Attlee's draft foreword to the Economic Survey for 1947 with amendments and Mass Observation's report, 'The Language of Leadership' on public understanding of the 1947 Economic Survey. Also includes ministerial correspondence on agricultural production, correspondence on investment and D. Fergusson's criticism of the undermining of departmental responsibility by central planning.

300   **Programming of coal supplies, 1947.** Feb–Mar 1947. Includes correspondence between E.E. Bridges and D. Fergusson, and between N. Brook and Attlee on strengthening the existing organization for programming coal supplies.

301   **Imports of coal from the U.S.A.** Mar–Apr 1947.

302   **Co-ordination and development of fuel resources.** Mar–May 1947. Includes papers on a national fuel policy.

303   **Supply of mining machinery and equipment for conversion programme for coal to oil.** Mar–May 1947.

304   **Economic planning: use of fiscal measures: co-operation between Treasury and Cabinet Office planning staff.** July 1947. Includes P.D. Proctor on the function of the Treasury in the 1948–51 plan and correspondence between E.N. Plowden and E.E. Bridges following a meeting between the Treasury and C.E.P.S. on the role of financial policy in economic planning.

305   **Taxation of fuel, rationing, etc. 1947 papers.** Feb–Mar 1947. Papers on proposals for domestic fuel rationing, the restriction of non-industrial gas and electricity consumption with J.E. Meade on the possible taxation of domestic use of electricity and gas.

306   **1) Memorandum by the F.B.I. on economic outlook.**

2) Report by the T.U.C. (Special Committee) on same and meeting with ministers including Prime Minister.
3) Memorandum by the Association of British Chambers of Commerce.
4) Commentary by the London Chamber of Commerce. March–July 1947. Includes the F.B.I.'s 'An interim statement on the economic outlook', resulting papers and papers relating to the Economic Survey for 1947.

307–308 Economic development: general papers. Dec 1946–Nov 1949.

307 Jan–Mar 1947. Miscellaneous correspondence on economic development and the draft economic White Paper, mid-week sport, the National Savings Movement, R.C. Tress on planning, coal and the coal budget and R.W.B. Clarke on reaction to the *Economic Survey for 1947*.

308 Dec 1946–Nov 1949. Papers on suggested layout of the planning White Paper, the production drive, long-term planning, productivity, reports on production in 1946 and food production in 1948 and drafts by R.W.B. Clarke of parts of the White Paper.

309 ED(W)(49) general: setting up of a working group on economic development 1949. (102) Feb–Nov 1949. Papers arising from TOC(49)3 leading to the establishment of the working group.

310 Economic planning: economic development miscellaneous papers 1949–50 etc. (103) November 1948–May 1950. Includes papers on the annual economic survey, the long-term survey, conferences with industry, arrangements for ministers to meet civil servants concerned at changed economic circumstances, the dollar programme, continuation of the Economic Planning Board and the European Payments Union.

311 Powers for operating economic controls 1949/53 and investment programme. (104) May 1949–Oct 1954. Papers leading to meeting, 25 May 1949, and later papers reviewing economic controls in relation to investments.

315–316 Economic miscellanea. (111–112) Oct 1951–Nov 1954.

315 Oct 1951–Dec 1952. Includes papers and notes of meetings on economic prospects in 1952 and E.E. Bridges's memorandum, 'The Economic Position: analysis of current position and outlook for 1952'.

318 Full employment: central staff to consider 1944–45. July–Oct 1944. Includes papers by J. Jewkes and meetings after Sept 1944 recommending the establishment of a new Treasury division to oversee employment policies.

319 Full employment: arrangements for giving effect to policy 1945. (31) May–Sept 1945. Papers on the Treasury's administrative arrangements and on the C.S.O.'s collection of relevant statistics.

321 Committee on the Economic Planning and Full Employment Bill. (13) Oct 1950–Mar 1951. Papers on the title and contents of the Bill, the full employment standard and the White Paper on full employment.

322–323 Economy and civil expenditure. (9(I–II)) May 1938–Apr 1954.

322 May 1938–Dec 1950. Paper on possible economies in departmental estimates, including social services, 1951/2.

323 Jan 1951–Apr 1954. Progress report on the economy campaign and its renewal with the change of government.

324 Estimates (a) miscellaneous papers 1949–56 (b) questions raised by Estimates Committee. (76) Feb 1949–Oct 1956. Paper on supplementary estimates and note of a meeting, 21 Sept 1950, on methods of handling full cost estimates.

325–327   **Control of expenditure after V.E. Day.** (33 Parts 1–3).

     325   May–Aug 1945. Main policy file. Includes draft circulars on Treasury control.

     326   Apr–May 1945. Preparation of Treasury circular to departments, 14 May 1945.

     327   Jan–June 1945 (1) Functions of Exchange Control Committee. (2) Expenditure overseas and E.E. Bridges's circular letter of 27 April 1945 and service department replies. Papers, including some by Keynes, on the cost of defence in relation to the budget and overseas expenditure.

328   **Overseas publicity and overseas information services expenditure.** (99) Dec 1949.

329   **N.H.S.: miscellaneous expenditure etc.** (110) Mar 1950–Nov 1952. Papers including Cripps on supplementary estimates.

332   **Devaluation of the French franc.** (82) Jan 1948.

336   **I.M.F.** Feb–Mar 1944. Papers on the proposed I.M.F. and J.M. Keynes's misgivings. Also his comments on the proposed International Bank of Reconstruction and Development.

337   **I.M.F./I.B.R.D.: administrative matters of U.K. representatives in appointments.** June 1946–June 1951. Includes note of talk with C.F. Cobbold on a variety of subjects including cheap money and appointments.

338   **Import programme 1947–1948.** (101) Apr–May 1947. Papers relating to the Balance of Payments Working Party report and on proposed import cuts.

339   **Import programme 1941–52 and import cuts 1956: import controls.** (114) Nov 1951–July 1956.

342–344   **Chancellor's and Prime Minister's Washington visits.** (81 Parts 1–3) Mar 1948–Nov 1951.

     342   Aug–Oct 1948. Chancellor's Washington visit September 1948. Includes report of the trip.

     343   Mar 1948–May 1949. (a) Chancellor's visit to the U.S.A. (b) sterling area notes by Sir W. Eady (c) Prime Minister's visit to Washington 1952.

     344   Nov 1951. Prime Minister's visit to Washington Jan 1952.

351   **Paris E.R.P. organization March–September 1948.** (70) Feb 1948–July 1949. Includes papers on the British supply organization in Washington and views, including Cripps's, on U.K. organization for handling E.R.P.

352   **E.R.P. miscellaneous (Programmes, T.I.C.) 1948–50.** (69) Feb 1948–July 1950. Mostly papers on negotiations with U.S.A., administrative arrangements for dealing with E.R.P., and the long-term programme and related policy issues.

353–354   **Oil policies.** (215 Parts 1 and 2) Aug 1942–Feb 1947.

     353   Aug 1942–June 1945. Ministerial and departmental responsibility for oil: liaison with Minister of Fuel and Power and Chairman of Oil Board.

     354   Jan–Feb 1947. Correspondence between Bevin and Attlee on oil storage.

355   **Petrol restriction 1946–49 correspondence.** (66) June 1946–Feb 1949.

359   **Anglo-Persian Oil Co. General 1944–46.** Apr 1944–Dec 1946. Includes papers on Anglo-American oil agreements.

360	**Anglo-Iranian Oil Co. Discussions with government direction 1949–51.** Feb 1949–Feb 1951.
362	**Anglo-Persian Oil Co.** Nov 1950–June 1951. On Iranian nationalization.
363–364	**Anglo-Iranian Oil Co. U.K. sanctions against Persian government for actions against the company.** (Parts 1 and 2) Apr–Dec 1951.
365	**Economic bulletin: publication arrangements.** (52) Oct 1947–Nov 1951. Proposal by S.C. Leslie for fortnightly and, later, monthly bulletins.
368	**Sterling area negotiations 1946.** (62) Jan–Oct 1946. Proposed arrangements.
369	**Gold and dollar reserves: notes to the Chancellor of the Exchequer.** (21) Oct 1947–Aug 1951.
371	**Dollar drain: monitoring of and possible remedial measures Part II.** (24) June–Dec 1949. Various reports and meetings on the dollar situation and some papers of the Dollar Drain Committee.
372	**Dollar drain: monitoring of U.S. gold.** (5) Jan 1950–Dec 1951.
373	**Reports to the Chancellor of the Exchequer on dollar and sterling expenditure in the world.** (22) Mar 1948–Mar 1949.
374	**Cheap sterling: measures to counter, 1950.** (96) Dec 1949–July 1950.
375	**Sterling devaluation: general papers.** (97) June–Oct 1949. Various papers including R.L. Hall recommending devaluation, June 1949, B.W. Gilbert on devaluation and the budget, H. Wilson-Smith on 'Caliban', the Bank of England on alternative measures in the monetary field, O. Franks on the dollar crisis of summer 1949, the Economic Section on the choice of the new exchange rate, and drafts of the paper requested by Cripps on the general inflationary situation. Also various meetings of ministers, officials and U.S. officials.
376	**Sterling balances: possible measures to control increases and decreases.** (20) Feb 1950–Jan 1952.
383	**Western Union Defence Atlantic Pact draft economic clause.** Mar 1949–May 1950.
384	**Western Union defence finance 1949.** Jan–Mar 1949.
385	**Council of Europe.** (74) Jan–Oct 1949. Includes Jay on the proposals for economic unification of Europe.
389	**National Debt Enquiry: introduction of a capital levy after the Second World War: capital budgets and interest rate policy.** (24) Apr 1941–July 1945. Various papers including some by J.M. Keynes and J.E. Meade on post-war budgetary policy and correspondence on the subjects in the title.
390	**Liaison with the F.B.I. on relations with the British government.** (64) May 1946–July 1947. Includes copies of Sir C. Baillieu's speech to A.G.M., 'Industry and the Road Ahead', 30 April 1947.
391	**Disinflationary signs in 1948–50.** (77) July 1948–Mar 1950. Includes correspondence leading up to starting the reports, and copies of the Economic Section reports themselves.
392	**Prime ministers' and financial ministers' conference 1952–56: arrangements for continued financial and economic consultation between Commonwealth etc.** (75) July 1948–Dec 1952.
393	**Food policy and papers concerning Operation Albert (purchase of sugar from Cuba).** (85) Apr 1948–Apr 1953.
394	**Productivity drive: publicity arrangements.** (104) July–Sept 1949. Includes correspondence between Cripps and Wilson, H. on plans for

delegate conferences for industries of particular importance to the general economy on the export drive.

395 **Strikes at electricity generating stations: review of policy.** (44) Dec 1949–Jan 1950.

20.3 Other Treasury Classes

As stated above, Treasury records for the period before 1948 are arranged by department (T 160–T 163) and after 1948 by division. In the following entries, the broad range of subjects covered by each class is summarized and then important individual files are identified. These classes contain much material on Cabinet and inter-departmental committees, be it their minutes, memoranda and working papers or Treasury files relating to their work. Those committees relevant to economic planning are listed at the end of each entry. One idiosyncrasy is that the main Treasury files on general wages policy are to be found in the papers of the Agriculture and Food Division (T 223).

T 160   Finance Files

A very large class dealing with all financial aspects of the Treasury's work up to 1948 and including many papers by Keynes. Files, of which the selection given below is a very small sample, are organized into broad subject areas and must be ordered by their class, box and piece number e.g. T 160/1407/F.18876. The main classes for later papers are T 233 (Home Finance) and T 236 (Overseas Finance).

On the domestic side, there are files on public expenditure commitments (1409/ F.19276, 1163/F.18376, 1383/F.18990, 1407/F.19040, 1407/F.19053), financial controls (1408/F.19130) and specific taxes. There are also discussions of post-war budgetary policy (1407/F.18876), of financial problems in the transition by Keynes (1270/F.18373/ Ann I and /01) and by ministers (1380/F.18604), of the National Income White Papers (1381/F.18833/01 and /02) and of the relationship between purchasing power and consumer goods (1260/F.18083). There are further files on monetary policy (1408/ F.19187) and the Bank of England (1408/F.19155/1–3, 1409/F.19221). Finally, there are a large number of files on capital issues, on the finance and location of industry (1381/F.18757, 1383/F.18960/1–2, 1383/F.18978/1–2 and /01, 1407/F.18960/01) and local authority borrowing for site preparation (1335/F.16352/09/04).

On overseas policy, files relate to international negotiations, including those over the Clearing Union, the I.M.F. and mutual aid, and U.K.–U.S. post-war relations (1375/ F.17942/010/1–6). Included are a general file on post-war commercial policy (1258/ F.18003/016) and many others on exports to specific countries.

Committees: Post-war Commercial Policy (1258/F.18003/020 and 1377/F.18003/ 021/1), Post-war Export Trade (1157/F.17942/03–05).

T 161   Supply Files

This is the class of pre-1948 records most relevant to economic planning, as a result of the Supply Department's responsibility for most questions arising out of public expenditure. It is organized alphabetically by subject and documents must be ordered by their class, box and piece number e.g. T 161/1168/S.52099. For later papers see the classes of relevant divisions (T 223 ff).

Major subjects covered are the distribution of industry (1133/S.50252, 1199/S.52397/ 2–4 and /01/1, 1249/S.52591/05/1, 1293/S.52799, 1294/S.53221/1–2, 1366/S.52591/ 02/1–3, 1366/S.53607/1, 1367/S.52591/02/4–8), wages (1197/S.51926/1–2, 1301/ S.54590/1), industrial relations (1446/S.51652), post-war agricultural policy (1165/ S.48830/1–3), housing and building (1136/S.51920, 1168/S.56618, 1367/S.52591/04), price controls in the transition (1446/S.51649), the post-war general support of trade (1412/S.51361) and the production campaign (1409/S.54085). Bills covered included the Employment and Training Bill (1370/S.53607/1), the Cotton Buying Commission Bill (1294/S.53243/03/02/1–2) and the Supplies and Services (Transitional Powers) Bill (1198/S.52376).

Committees: Steering Committee on Post-war Employment leading to the *Employment Policy* White Paper (1137/S.52098/01–03 and /05, 1168/S.52098 and /04, 1168/ S.52099 and /01–06, 1200/S.52842 and /02–03 and /05, 1412/S.51313/01), Social Insurance and Allied Services (Beveridge) (1129/S.48497/02, /06, /08 and /014, 1164/ S.48497/2, 1165/S.48497/3 and /026, 1193/S.48497/017 and /025, 1242/S.48497/010, 1423/S.48497/01/1–3, 1448/S.48497/03–05 and /020), Official Steering Committee on Economic Development (1294/S.53261/1–3, 1295/S.53261/4–9, 126/S.53261/10), Investment Working Party (1251/S.53555/04 and /07, 1296/S.53555/1–2, 1297/ S.53555/3, /01–02, /05–06, /010/1–2 and /012, 1350/S.53555/03, 1370/S.53555/011/ 1–2), the Headquarters Building Committee (1419/S.54955/1–2), the Wage Stabilization Working Party (1371/S.56131), and the Board of Trade Regional Procedure (Industrial) Committee (1298/S.53640/1).

T 163   General Files

A miscellaneous class of pre-1948 files, including ones on the Supply and Services (Transitional Powers) Bill (135/9) and the Expiring Laws Continuance Bill (136/2).

T 165   Blue Notes

Notes, compiled for the administration of estimates, covering the history, function and estimates of certain departments and services, arranged alphabetically. Prepared annually, with a major revision every five years but suspended 1940–46. For specific file references, see entries for individual departments in chapters 21 and 22. Some blue notes can also be found in T 160 and T 233.

T 172   Chancellor of the Exchequer's Office: Miscellaneous Papers

A miscellaneous collection of papers relating mainly to the Chancellor's correspondence, speeches and meetings, which were not incorporated into other classes. There is relatively little material for the period after 1943. Includes some of Wood's papers on reconstruction and post-war finance (1997, 2001, 2007); a file containing Keynes's comments on the Steering Committee on Post-war Employment report (2016); files for 1947 relating to the economic crisis (2023), industrial morale and incentives (2029) and the start of wages policy (2033); and papers on the 1949 crisis (2037–9).

T 177   Private Office Papers and Private Collections: Phillips Papers

Papers of Sir Frederick Phillips, joint second secretary 1942–45 and head of the Treasury Mission in Washington 1940–43.

T 199   Establishment Officer's Branch: Files

Files relating not only to the internal organization of the Treasury but also to the central organization of government including some individual appointments. See also T 244. In addition to the main Treasury organizational files (236, 305–6, 431–3, 702–4), Treasury issues covered include the appointments of Gaitskell as Minister of State for Economic Affairs (208), Paymasters General (467–70), Permanent Secretaries to the Treasury (351–3) and other Treasury staff. There are sets of press notices (168–9, 231–3) and Chancellors of the Exchequer news bulletins (238–42, 267). Individual policy issues covered are reductions in expenditure (223) and the Long-term Programme and Economic Surveys (234). Finally, there is correspondence concerning certain publications relating to the Treasury, such as Keynes in the *Economic Journal* on the U.S. balance of payments (117).

General administrative issues covered are the organization of the Civil Service (116) and the Whitehall organization to deal with European Economic Co-operation 1947–59 (690). Individual departments covered are the Cabinet Office (65, 375–81), Economic Information Unit (156, 236, 290–1), C.E.P.S. (281–4, but closed for fifty years), C.S.O. (383, 656), Prime Minister's Private Office (408). Transfers of responsibility include those of the Economic Section to the Treasury, 1953 (257) and of Regional Boards of Industry (473).

Committees: Treasury Organization (119–23, 213), Development Areas (Treasury Advisory) (141, 696–7), Machinery of Government (Official) (77–8).

T 214   Establishments (Departmental) Division: Files

Files, largely from 1948, dealing with the organization, reorganization and staffing of other departments. Covers raw materials administration (33, 329–31) and appointment of economic advisers to the Board of Trade (263) and the Ministry of Fuel and Power (364) together with N. Blond's posting to the U.S.A. to increase exports (190). Earlier files are in T 162 and T 243. Contemporary files on general establishments policy are in T 215, and circulars in T 242.

T 216   Establishments (Manning) Division: Files

Files, largely from 1948, on recruitment to and manning of the Civil Service. Includes papers on the Civil Service Manpower Committee (10–14, 98–9) and departmental regional organizations (15).

T 217   Establishments (Professional, Scientific, Technical and Industrial Staff) Division: Files

Includes files on the recruitment of statisticians 1949 (101) and the pay and conditions of economists 1945–55 (205–6).

T 219   Government and Allied Services Division: Files

Files of a mixed supply and establishments division, including some on the government's information services and the papers of the Headquarters Building Committee 1946–48 (307–10).

T 222   Organization and Methods Division: Files

Records of the division set up in 1941 to promote and co-ordinate efforts to achieve administrative efficiency in the Civil Service. Contains much correspondence and many working papers relating to the machinery of government enquiries after 1942 which were registered in the division in 1947. There are several files on the organization of economic policy including a history 1919–47 (54), the role of economists in government (55), the role of the Treasury (231) and its relationship with C.E.P.S. (232). Also other files on specific and general departmental functions (9, 39–51, 63, 67–8, 105, 118, 120, 130, 132, 233–5), controls (213) and the British Institute of Management (157).

Committees: Building Controls (8, 158–161), Civil Service Manpower (14), Controls and Efficiency (36–7), Food Policy Working Party (60), the ministerial and official Machinery of Government committees (61–2, 71–83, 135), Ryan Committee (137–43), Working Party on the Building Industry (162–5), Official Steering Committee on Economic Development (193), Co-ordinating Committee on Controls (214–20), Economic controls (221–6).

T 223   Agriculture and Food Division: Files

Records of the division dealing with agriculture and food policy in all its aspects, including forestry, fisheries and the ground-nut scheme. Surprisingly this is, with T 229 and T 230, the main Treasury class on general wages policy.

There is a major, inter-related series of files on wages (21–2, 25–7, 54–6, 90–1), prices (43–5, 92–4, 165–7), the cost of living (297–8) and subsidies (5, 14, 24, 97–8, 110, 111, 132–5, 161–2). There are papers on import programmes (141–4), rationing (37, 113, 236) and controls (212–4). Other files cover the 1947 Agriculture Bill (33), agricultural expansion programme (216–25) and long-term agricultural policy (193).

Committees: Food Distribution (40–1), The Inter-departmental Committees on Wages (52–3) and Food Policy (76), Wages and Prices (57–8, 87–9), Distribution and Marketing (77), Official Committee on Economic Development: subcommittee on prices (103).

T 225   Defence Policy and Materiel Division: Files

Files on defence programmes, expenditure and their economic impact.

T 227   Social Services Division: Files

Records covering current and capital expenditure on the social services. Includes files on the Employment and Training Bill (34, 163), loans to local authorities (209) and a White Paper on wages and prices (261–2).

T 228   Trade and Industry Division: Files

The main class of records dealing with industry, covering nationalization, stockpiling, strategic materials and individual commodities. General topics covered are: central planning 1947 (17–18), distribution of industry (70, 202–3), rationing (88–9), unemployment during reconversion (128), raw material prices (217, 364–6), the Ministry of Materials (253–4), timber import programme (281–4), government purchases and decontrol (303–4), development councils (388, 441), and the British Institute of Management (624–8).

Committees: various Fuel and Coal committees (33–4, 87, 309–10), Official Steering Committee on Economic Development (20), National Investment Council (81–3), Government Purchases and Controls (195, 237–9), Economic Controls (196), Industrial Productivity (210–13, 252), Productivity (Official) (214–16), Economic Powers and Full Employment (241–4), Materials (275), Dollar Export Council (342).

T 231   Exchange Control Division: Files

Division responsible for exchange control, including the monitoring of overseas investment. There are several historical reviews (167, 179, 586), files relating to the balance of payments (91, 157–8) and the I.M.F. (359–79), as well as records of the monthly liaison meetings between the Treasury and the Bank of England (164, 555). Bills covered are the Exchange Control Bill 1947 (349, 404–6, 408–25, 431–4, 697) and the Investment and Exchange (Control) Bill 1945 (380–8).

Committees: Exchange Control (60–3), and the Treasury Committee (64–7), the Treasury – Bank of England Committee on Post-war Exchange Control Problems (155), Exchange Requirements (156), Foreign Exchange Control (160–3, 392–4, 687–8), Subcommittee on the Future of Exchange Control (174), Inter-departmental Committees on U.S. Investment in the Sterling Area (471) and in the U.K. (474–5), Working Party on Financial Incentives to Exporters to Dollar Markets (611–2).

T 232   European Economic Co-operation Committee: Files

Papers of the committee (see CAB 134/232–54), responsible for O.E.E.C. matters from 1948 until its supersession in 1951 by the Mutual Aid Committee (see T 235). Covers meetings and reports of the O.E.E.C., various proposals for European integration and its impact on the Commonwealth, and U.S. aid. There are individual files on the U.K. 1949/50 and long-term programmes (18, 66, 73–6, 78–80) including weekly correspondence between T.L. Rowan and E.A. Hitchman (200), planning in the colonies (67), the 1949 Washington tripartite discussions (89–100), relations between free and planned economies in Europe (153) and U.K. rationing (253–4) and controls (258). See also T 237.

Committees: Working Group on Long-term Programmes (23), Working Party on Non-dollar Balance of Payments (44), Anglo-American Council on Productivity (101–2), Treasury Organization (192–3), Commonwealth Economic Affairs (223–4).

T 233   Home Finance Division: Files

This division included amongst its responsibilities monetary policy, government accounts and most aspects of domestic policy including nationalization, capital issues and investments, savings, taxation and development areas. For most pre-1948 papers, see T 160.

Individual files are on public expenditure estimates (330, 385, 545, 892, 921, 1445–50) and cuts (268, 276–86, 381, 547–8), monetary policy (143, 299, 1400–1), bank advances (481–4, 1396–8) and dividend limitation (584–96). Bills covered are the Borrowing (Control and Guarantees) Bill 1946 (25–9), Coinage Bill 1946 (260–1), and Economic Planning and Full Employment Bill (627, 819–20).

Committees: National Debt Enquiry (157–9), National Investment Council (161–6, 1021), the Working Party on Treasury – C.E.P.S. liaison (342), Purchase Tax/Utility (629–30, 689–91), Royal Commission on Taxation of Profits and Income (not yet open).

T 235   Mutual Aid Division: Files

Set up in 1950 to serve the Mutual Aid Committee (CAB 134/488–92), which superseded the European Economic Co-operation Committee (CAB 134/232–54, T 232). Covers military and economic aid.

T 236   Overseas Finance Division: Files

The division responsible for most aspects of external financial policy, including relations with the U.S.A., Canada and international organizations (such as the I.M.F., G.A.T.T.), Bretton Woods, commercial policy (including individual commodities), overseas investment and government expenditure, and tourism.

There are major series of files on the balance of payments in relation to the U.K. (311–16, 1756–60, 2296–8, 2651–6, 2733–4, 2936–9, 3296, 3508, 3790, 4240), sterling area (3287–90, 3995–7, 4350–2), statistics (309–10, 437–9), White Papers (2668–72, 2932–3, 3787, 3991–4), exports (853–72, 2509, 2769–72, 3257–8, 3291, 3951–4), imports (1075–1110, 2042–82, 2550–1, 2982–5, 3262, 3734–9, 3741, 3747–8, 4204–12). There are other files on wartime U.S.-U.K. financial relations (in particular 378–88 and W. Eady's papers on stage III, 436–74, 1655–73), devaluation and related issues (2308–16, 2393–9, 2695–7, 2725–30, 3458–9, 4310), and European reconstruction (782–852, 1887–1971). Included also are files on the Economic Surveys (1873, 2301–2, 2304, 2673–5), full employment policy (74, 702–6) and a set of Economic Bulletins (1870–1).

Committees: Bulk Purchase (56), Balance of Payments Working Party (308, 1760), Sterling Area Development Working Party (1569, 2320–1), Dollar Drain (1756–8, 3751–5), Overseas Negotiations (2156–8), the Official Committee on Economic Development Working Group (2502–3), the Working Party on Oil Expansion Programme (2884–90), the Working Party on the Sterling Area (2913), Exports (2972), Commonwealth Economic Affairs (2973–81), Sterling Area Statistical Committee (3839–51, 4259).

T 237   Overseas Finance (Marshall Aid) Division: Files

Division responsible for work on the E.R.P. See also T 232.

T 238   Overseas Negotiations Committee Division: Files

Working papers of the committee (CAB 134/46–8, 555–75), including its minutes and memoranda (3–11), and of its subcommittees. Covers international negotiations, imports and exports generally, and individual commodities. Includes files on decontrol of general steel (61) and national wages policy (65).

Committees: Official Committee on Government Purchases and Controls (51), Economic Organization Working Group (62).

T 241   Bank of England: Papers

A small class of papers relating to the 1945 Bank of England Act.

T 245   Information Division: Files

Set up in 1947 as the Economic Information Unit and transferred to the Treasury in 1950. Six files only, including one on the export programme (4).

T 246   Central Priority Department: Allocation of Raw Materials: Files (1939-46)

Wartime department of the Ministry of Supply, then Production. A few files relate to post-war requirements.

T 247   Keynes Papers

Working papers of Keynes as an economic adviser to the Treasury (1940–46) some of which are reproduced in *The Collected Writings of John Maynard Keynes*. Largely on international reconstruction and external constraints on post-war domestic policy. Individual files are also on general post-war economic policy (69), post-war national income (78), maintenance of employment domestically (80) and internationally (84) and reflections on the 1946 budget (95).

T 249   Training and Education Division: Files

Papers on the training of civil servants, including ones on the control of public expenditure (3) and the place of economic studies in civil servants' training (36).

T 266   Capital Issues Committee

Working papers of the committee responsible, between 1939 and 1959, for the financial control of investment under first the Defence Regulations and then the 1947 Control of Borrowing Order. Includes its minutes (1–9), policy files (10–143) including monthly summaries of decisions (19–31), and case files on individual companies (144–90). Individual policy files are on the Chancellor of the Exchequer's guidance to the committee (48–9), operation of the capital market in the post-war period (94) and the setting up of the National Investment Council (109).

T 267 Treasury Historical Memoranda

Few yet open to the public but the file on the 1947 convertibility crisis is available (3).

T 269 Private Office: Permanent Secretary's Papers

Five large volumes of E.E. Bridges's papers on devaluation and consequential measures, including relevant Cabinet and Cabinet committee minutes and memoranda (June–Nov 1949).

T 277 Committee Section Papers

Not yet available, but expected to contain the records of Treasury committees between 1948 and 1962.

T 278 Papers of Various Senior Officials.

Chapter 21   Board of Trade

During the war, the Board of Trade lost many of its traditional functions either to temporary wartime departments (most notably the Ministries of Supply and Production) or to departments that became permanent after the war (such as the Ministry of Fuel and Power). It retained, however, general responsibility for commercial policy, many aspects of the regulation of commerce and industry, and special responsibility for those trades and industries not specifically allocated to other departments. With the formation of the caretaker government in May 1945, the President of the Board (Lyttelton) assumed responsibility for the Ministry of Production and, later that year, the latter was disbanded by the Labour government – despite having been seen by some as potentially 'the major economic co-ordinating department' (D.N. Chester in G.D.N. Worswick and P.H. Ady, *The British Economy 1945–50* (Clarendon Press, 1952), p 340).

Under the wartime presidency of Dalton (1942–45), the Board played an active role in the planning of post-war reconstruction and, in particular, regional policy (see B. Pimlott, *Hugh Dalton* (Cape, 1985), chapter 23 and B. Pimlott (ed) *The Second World War Diary of Hugh Dalton* (Cape, 1986). Its continuing importance in relation to economic planning was ensured by the appointment of Cripps as President in 1945. He was one of the four members of the Ministerial Committee on Economic Planning and, during Morrison's illness in 1947, assumed more responsibility for economic planning before becoming, successively, Minister of Economic Affairs (see BT 195) and Chancellor of the Exchequer. He was determined to change the Board from a traditionally 'regulative' ministry to one through which the Labour government could exercise 'constructive supervision' over industry in the national interest (BT 13/220). Its traditional responsibilities included external trade relations and the regulation of industry (e.g. company law, bankruptcy and restrictive practices). To these were now added the general co-ordination of government policy towards industry (although many individual industries such as coal were sponsored by other ministries); the fostering of good relations with industry, through eleven Regional Boards and the National Production Advisory Council for Industry; and the stimulation of production in individual industries through their newly-created Development Councils. More specifically the Board was responsible for the supply of raw materials (except metals) and their allocation to a miscellaneous collection of industries including textiles, tobacco, pottery and glass; industrial productivity; the setting of export targets and export promotion; the location of industry; and the collection of industrial information needed for economic planning. To implement these policies, as well as price control and rationing for which it was also responsible, it developed an extensive regional organization. By the end of 1947, the Board's total staff had risen from the pre-war figure of 2,400 to just under 15,000. Given this size and the wide range of responsibilities it was hardly surprising that – despite expedients such as daily meetings between the President and his senior staff (see BT 13) – the permanent secretary was fearful of administrative collapse, see Sir J.H. Woods, 'Administrative Problems of the Board of Trade', *Public Administration* 26 (1948), p 85–91. After Cripps's promotion and his replacement by Harold Wilson, this administrative overload, together with their traditional *laissez-faire* attitudes, gave officials added enthusiasm for the 'bonfire of controls'. The promotion of exports and productivity gained in relative importance.

After the war, there was a major overhaul in the administration of two of the Board's major responsibilities. In April 1946 the Department of Overseas Trade, which had previously been jointly responsible to the Foreign Secretary, was replaced by the Export Promotions Department, answerable solely to the President. It dealt with exports at the trader to trader level, whilst the existing Commercial Relations and Treaties Department continued to deal at a governmental level and with the formulation of policy. In January 1949 the two departments were merged into the Commercial Relations and Export Department. Secondly, in 1950 the Raw Materials Department was disbanded with its functions being distributed amongst various branches of the Board. As a consequence of the Korean War, however, they were re-united and transferred to the newly established Ministry of Materials in July 1951, where they remained until that Ministry's closure in 1954.

BT 5   Minutes

Minutes of the Board: 1943–51 (149–157)

BT 11   Commercial Department: Correspondence and Papers

During the war the department exercised powers of licensing and regulating exports and generally performed functions under the Trading with the Enemy Act 1939. In 1946, a new Exports Promotion Department had been formed within the Board (BT 225) and this merged with the Commercial Relations and Treaty Department in January 1949 to become the Commercial Relations and Export Department (BT 241).

The class is divided into two series, both of which are subject coded. In series 1 (files 1–443), the first relevant code is for commodities (code 3) which is sub-coded by letter according to particular commodities, hence apparel and textiles (code 3A), chemicals (3B), consumer goods (3C). Within these sub-codes are files relating to the export of these individual commodities, relevant international conferences and international commodity policy. There is also a file on the functions and organization of the Commodities Division of the department (3040). Other codes cover Commonwealth trade (code 4); customs (code 5); exchange control (code 9), which includes files on the I.M.F., various Washington negotiations, pound-dollar exchange rate, hard and soft currencies, the guidance of exports and the Exchange Control Bill; League of Nations/ U.N. (code 12), which includes papers relating to the report on national and international measures to achieve full employment (2979–2981), tariff negotiations, the I.T.O., G.A.T.T., Austin Robinson on the viability of Western Europe in 1952–53 (4014) and Anglo-French discussions on long-term programmes (4209); most favoured nations (code 15); payments and debts (code 16); quotas (code 17); shipping (code 18); tariffs (code 19); and U.K. internal (departmental and general) (code 20). This last subject code includes files on controls in the transition, export policy and prospects, bulk purchase, international negotiations, industrial reconstruction and post-war economic policy. There are also some files on employment policy (2331, 2355) and the division of responsibility within the Board of Trade (3571).

Series 1 includes the papers of a number of committees and conferences. Amongst these are the Post-war Commercial Policy Committee, the Post-war Export Trade Committee, the Working Party on Guidance of Exports, the Committee on Export Targets, the Export Diversion Committee, the regional export committees, the Working Party on Import Licensing Relaxations, the Consultative Committee for Industry, the Working Group on U.K. Tin Plate Consumption and the Dollar Export Board. Files also relate to the International Conference on Trade and Employment (2828), economic planning in the colonies (3957), meetings of the T.U.C. Economic Committee with the President of the Board and notes by the department for the N.P.A.C.I.

Series 2, which continues beyond 1951, uses different subject codes. Subjects here include commodities (code 2), including the papers of the Bulk Purchase Committee (5135); Commonwealth matters (code 3); customs (code 5), including the papers of the Customs Union Study Group; currency and financial matters (code 6); import and export matters (code 10), including papers on Anglo-Belgian trade and financial discussions, principles governing the export of scarce raw materials, essential U.K. imports, export policy questions in the Economic Survey for 1951 (4626), and defence and exports (4818). The subject code also contains some papers of the Import Licensing Committee's Working Party on Import Licensing Relaxations. Other codes relate to international organizations (code 13), with files on G.A.T.T., the Torquay and Havana conferences, E.C.E., the U.K. attitude to the Schuman Plan (4902), the international trade organization of the U.N., and papers of the Trade Negotiations Committee and subcommittees; most favoured nation (code 15); quotas (code 16); shipping (code 17); tariffs (code 18); treaties, trade agreements, etc. (code 20) and U.K. (departmental and general) (code 21), which includes files on trade negotiations, the impact of raw materials shortages, 1952 export targets, the regional organization for exports, defence and exports (4627-4628) and the Consultative Committee for Industry.

BT 13   Establishments Department: Correspondence and Papers

This class includes files dealing with the organization of and appointments to various divisions and branches within the Board. There are also files on the Raw Materials Department and its transfer to the Board of Trade, the merger with the Ministry of Production, the amalgamation of the Department of Overseas Trade with the Board, and its regional organization.

The class also contains files on the prosperity campaign, monopolies and restrictive practices, the Export Guarantee Advisory Council, the Cotton Board, the Census of Production Advisory Committee and the Working Party on Import Licensing Relaxations. Perhaps the most important file in the class contains the memoranda of the President's morning meetings (220A). These meetings were held by the President with his senior officials and thus the memoranda cover the whole field of the Board's work and give some guide to the importance or difficulties of particular subjects within the Board's responsibility. Although it is known that the meetings continued under Harold Wilson, only the papers during Cripps's time as President (August 1945-September 1947) exist here.

BT 15   Finance Department: Correspondence and Papers

This class is subject coded. Amongst the subjects are accounting (code 1) including files on the Committee on the Form of Government Accounts (271-272); establishment (code 4), including the transfer of the Department of Overseas Trade to the Board; estimates (code 5), with files on grants to the British Intitute of Management and the Anglo-American Council on Productivity; and industrial assistance and reorganization (code 7), with files on the Distribution of Industry Act, 1945, and related policy, and the correspondence and papers of the Dollar Export Board.

BT 28   Ministry of Production: Correspondence and Papers

Includes files on labour requirements, supplies of materials and production during the war. There are also the papers of a number of committees: the Chief Production Executive Committee and its Industrial Capacity Committee, the Commonwealth Supply Council and its Subcommittees, the London Rubber Committee, the Combined Production and Resources Board, the Anglo-American Packaging Committee, the Utilities Working Party, the Lend-Lease Committee, the Working Party on Reconstruction Policy (1086 and 1088–1089) and the Minister of Production's Council (1131–1136). There is also a file on organization in 1943 (1057) and a report on the work of the ministry (1197). See also BT 87 and BT 168.

BT 29   Ministry of Production: Numerical Indexes to Correspondence

Available in the Reference Room at Kew.

BT 30   Ministry of Production: Subject Indexes to Correspondence

Available in the Reference Room at Kew.

BT 60   Department of Overseas Trade: Correspondence and Papers

The department was created in 1918 and was abolished in 1946, with its functions passing to the Board's new Export Promotions Department (BT 225). However, the Parliamentary Secretary of the Board of Trade with special responsibility for the Export Credits Guarantee Department retained the title of Secretary for Overseas Trade until 1953.

The class contains files on post-war export trade, post-war industries, regional export organization, trade missions, disposal of surplus stocks, 1945 Washington discussions on future trade policy and the export of particular goods. Files also relate to the Reconstruction Committee's Official Subcommittee on Industrial Problems (77/5), the Exchange Control Committee, the Platt report on the textile industry and the reports of the Board of Trade working parties on individual industries.

BT 61   Department of Overseas Trade: Establishment Files

Consists of files on appointments, organization and relations with other departments. The class also includes papers of the Committee on Post-war Commercial Policy and the Post-war Export Trade Committee. There is one file on C.S.O. export forecasts.

BT 64   Industries and Manufactures Department: Correspondence and Papers

This is a very large and important class. The duties of the department were greatly expanded during the war to administer many wartime and post-war controls, including clothes rationing and the utility scheme. The department consisted of many divisions and these can be recognized from the original file reference, for example IM4 22214/44 reveals that the file was opened not only in 1944 but also by IM4, the division responsible for consumer goods other than clothing and textiles. There were four basic divisions which were themselves sub-divided (for example IM1A). Industries and

Manufactures I (or IMI) had existed before the war and amongst its duties were price control and the oversight of retail facilities. Industries and Manufactures II (IM2) was established in 1940 to administer the Limitation of Supplies Orders and was later given responsibility for concentration and for clothes rationing. It also included for a time the Consumer Needs Section and the Directorates of Civilian Clothing and Civilian Footwear. Industries and Manufactures III (IM3) was responsible for the gas and electricity industries until the establishment of the Ministry of Fuel and Power in 1942. By 1943 the coding was assumed by a new division responsible for enforcement, some aspects of the rationing scheme and the Consumer Needs Section. It included also the Accountants Division and the Investigation Branch. Industries and Manufactures IV (IM4) was set up in 1942 to operate controls over production and consumption of consumer goods other than clothing and textiles. There were two other important wartime developments. A separate Industrial Supplies Department (BT 96) was set up in November 1939 to take on work previously done by the Industries and Manufactures Department, including the supply of materials for home needs and for exports, industrial priorities and import licensing. It was wound up in January 1945, with its functions divided between the new Priorities and Engineering Divisions of Industries and Manufactures. In January 1943 an Internal Reconstruction Department was also established to co-ordinate the reconstruction planning of these four divisions. It later became Industries and Manufactures General/IMG.

After the war, the department lost and gained several functions. In December 1945, for example, it lost primary responsibility for engineering to the Ministry of Supply and Aircraft Production although it retained responsibility for general policy questions. On the other hand, a separate Tourist, Catering and Holiday Services Division, established in June 1946, was absorbed into the department in December 1947. Similarly, the Raw Materials Department, which had transferred from the Ministry of Supply in April 1946 (with all its functions except in relation to iron and steel, non-ferrous metals and engineering) was absorbed into the department in 1950, with the exception of responsibility for production and supply of timber which passed to the Forestry Commission. In July 1951 the raw materials function was temporarily transferred to the New Ministry of Materials, returning to the department in August 1954 when the Ministry was abolished.

The class is listed in two ways. There is a subject-coded list which gives a brief description of each individual file. There is also a numerical list which gives a fuller description of the file. However, the subject coding only covers files to piece number 4127. After this there is only the numerical list. Thus in setting out the subjects covered within the class, the lists provide exact references for only a few particularly important files with piece numbers before 4127, but more complete referencing is provided thereafter. Piece numbers 1–84 require the box number as well as the piece number, for example BT 64/81/4678. After this only the piece number is required, for example BT 64/145. At the start of the class list there is also a list of Industries and Manufactures divisions, giving the file series of the division, the broad subject of its work, its period of operation and the relevant piece numbers of its files.

Among the main subjects covered by the Department were indirect taxation and hire purchase, economic controls (in particular price, and utility controls and rationing), international negotiations, and imports and exports. Other subjects were more directly related to industry, for example, industrial efficiency, restrictive practices and monopolies, consultation with respective bodies, distribution of industry and post-war reconstruction. There are a large number of files relating to specific industries and goods. See also BT 258. Committees (listed alphabetically): Board of Trade Working Party on the Allocation of Advance Factories (1963), Beveridge (3393), the Joint Advisory Committee of the Board of Trade (1383–1384), the Building Materials Co-ordinating Committee Subcommittee on Price Control (230), Business Members (3390, 3445, 3470, 3493, 3604, 3653), Capital Issues (4186), the Official Committee on Censuses of Production and Distribution (2251), Central Transport (3907), the Official Coal Committee (2913), Controls and Efficiency (2393), the Disposals Co-ordinating Committee (2130), Official Disposals (2128, 2133) Treasury Disposals (1569), the Distribution of Industry Policy Study Group (2999), the Working Party on the Diversion of Exports (2932–2934), the Dollar Export Board (1266, 1352), E.C.E. Committees (1311–1313, 1560), the Economic Planning Board (2938), the Economic Steering Committee Subcommittee on Prices (433–434, 445, 477, 562–563, 706), the Inter-departmental Committee for the Employment of Supplementary Labour (2904), the Steering Committee on Post-war Employment (3344–3346, 3413, 3430, 3473, 3477), Exports (1236, 1318, 1347–1348), the Working Party for the Cabinet Balance of Payments Exports Committee (2959), Post-war Export Trade (3075, 3176, 3384, 3387), British Exports (Official) (3889–3891), the Inter-departmental Committee on External Economic Policy and Overseas Trade (2886–2888, 2908), the Working Party on Government Purchases and Controls (741), Housing (Official) (2881), Import Licensing (233, 654, 1136, 1581, 1989) and its Working Party on Import Licensing Relaxations (648, 1182, 1582, 2428–2429, 2440, 2488, 4013–4017, 4602, 4641–4649), Improvements in Undermanned Industries (2234, 2244), Incentives to Production (2885), the Steering Committee for Industrial Efficiency (3465), Industrial Management (2232), Industrial Productivity (2360, 2427), the Investment Working Party (726, 2228, 2280), the Jute Goods Working Party (1608), Key Industries (590), the Working Party on the Limitation of Supplies (4659, 4693, 4907), the Working Party on the Lucas Report (2371), Materials (1590, 1592, 2958), the National Joint Advisory Council (2221, 2352), the National Production Advisory Council for Industry (2352, 2969, 3001, 3773), the Overseas Negotiations Committee Working Party (3777, 3782), Official Productivity (2982), Programmes (1048), the Inter-departmental Post-war Projects Committee (3056), Purchase Tax/Utility (Douglas) (4669, 4699, 4701–4703, 4706, 4708), the Advisory Committees on Rationing (1033–1034) and the Joint Rationing Advisory Committee (1390–1400), Raw Materials (3797), the Departmental Reconstruction Committee (3091, 3180–3181, 3185, 3341), and the Board's reconstruction papers (922, 1969, 3308) and reconstruction fortnightly summaries (1970, 3167), the Joint Advisory Council on Reconstruction (3087), the Ministry of Works Advisory Committee on Reconstruction (3054), the Reconstruction Committee Official Subcommittee on Industrial Problems (2844), Resale Price Maintenance (449–450), the Board of Trade Research Committee Subcommittee on Competitive Power (2916, 3760), the Inter-departmental Committee on Restrictive Practices by Supervisory Boards (306, 442), the Parliamentary Secretary's Committee on Special Distribution (1966), the C.S.O. Working Party on Statistics for Employment Policy (3416), the Sterling Area Development Working Party (2962, 3789–3790), the Inter-departmental Working Party on Home Timber Production (3988–3989), the Inter-departmental Committee on Unemployment during the Period of Reconversion (2892–2894), the Inter-departmental Committee on U.S. Investment in the Sterling Area (2484), the Working Party on Wages Policy (2340), the Winter Transport Executive Committee (2952).

Legislation: the Supplies and Services (Transitional Powers) Bill (242, 2941), the Prices of Goods Act (452), the Miscellaneous Goods (Maximum Prices) Order 1948 (511), The Investment (Controls and Guarantees) Bill (2184), the Industrial Organization Bill (2249–2250, 2253, 2255, 2258–2261, 2299, 2301, 2471, 4140–4142, 4689), the Economic Planning and Full Employment Bill (4164).

BT 70 Statistical Department, etc.: Correspondence and Papers

The Department (renamed the Statistics Division in 1945) formulated and published various statistics on trade and industry in the U.K. and abroad. The 1947 Statistics of Trade Act empowered the division to take an annual census of production and to make occasional censuses of distribution and other services. The Division also compiled short-term production returns and statistics on such subjects as retail and wholesale trade, wholesale prices, and the movement of tourists and migrants.

Particular subjects covered include statistics for employment policy (100, 194), the annual *Economic Surveys* (136, 244, 299), and the Anglo-American Productivity Council (292), as well as various files on the balance of payments, the annual White Papers on industry and employment in Scotland, investment and international trade. There are also files of the Census of Distribution Retail Trade Committee, the Inter-departmental Committee on Social and Economic Research, and individual files on the establishment of the Programmes Committee (251) and the Balance of Payments Working Party (252). Organization and Methods also made a report on the Division (351). See also BT 263.

BT 87 Ministry of Production: Ministers' and Officials' Papers

Papers of the private office of the minister (Oliver Lyttelton) and the offices of the chief executives of the ministry (Sir Walter Layton and Sir Robert Sinclair), together with a few other files of senior officials. There is a file on the organization of the ministry (20). Amongst Sinclair's papers are files on the Combined Production and Resources Board, reconversion to peace-time production, manpower, disposals, export policy and Lend-Lease. There is virtually nothing after 1945, when the ministry was merged with the Board of Trade. See also BT 28.

BT 88 Post-war Commodity Policy and Relief Department

In March 1942 responsibility for this subject was given to the Board of Trade, but the department was disbanded in November 1943. There are files coding various commodities.

BT 91 Permanent Secretary's Private Office Papers

There are only seven pieces in this class, covering the period 1946–66. They tend to relate to organization and departmental responsibilities. There is one file containing the working papers of the permanent secretary, Sir John Woods, on the Marshall Plan (7).

BT 94 Central Price Regulation Committee

The class consists of the minutes and files of the committee which was set up in 1939 to enforce the Prices of Goods Act 1939, one of the main wartime measures of price control. General policy files relate to wartime and post-war price control, relations of the committee with government departments and the 80% price sanction. Files also cover the control of various individual commodities. The agenda and minutes of one of the local price regulation committees (Leeds) is also included. The class ends in 1953.

BT 96   Industrial Supplies Department

The department was formed in November 1939 to cover questions relating to priority, other than manpower, including representation of the Board on the subcommittees of the Central Priority Committee, and questions relating to the supply of materials for civil requirements at home and for the export trade. In January 1945 it was wound up with its work being divided between the Engineering and Priorities Divisions of the Industries and Manufactures Department (BT 64). Files relate to the regional boards (122, 133), the post-war reconstruction of various industries, iron and steel requirements, export control after the war and economic controls during the transition (212). There are also papers of the Location of Industry Committee (see BT 168), the Production Departments' Subcommittee of the Official Committee on Post-war Internal Economic Problems (204–205) and the Chief Executive's Advisory Committee (220).

BT 104   Commissioners for the Special Areas

Papers, largely from the inter-war period, relating to the four special areas of Durham, West Cumberland, South Wales and South West Scotland.

BT 131   War Histories (1939–45): Files

Files relating to the writing of the two volumes of the Civil History of the Second World War, J. Hurstfield, *The Control of Raw Materials* (1953) and E.L. Hargreaves and M.M. Gowing, *Civil Industry and Trade* (1952). Includes pieces on various industries and controls during the war, as well as the papers of a number of wartime committees, including the Labour Co-ordinating Committee and the Departmental Reconstruction Committee (63).

BT 132   Parliamentary Branch: Correspondence and Papers

Files on legislation relevant to the Board. It includes papers on the Prices of Goods Act 1939 and the cost of living, and the Iron and Steel Act 1949.

BT 133   Jewellery and Silverware Development Council

Eight files including the minutes etc. of the council.

BT 134   Raw Cotton Commission

The commission was set up as a result of the Cotton (Centralized Buying) Act 1947 and was responsible for the buying, importing, holding and distribution of raw cotton. It operated until August 1954 when private buying was resumed. The class includes the minutes of the commission.

BT 135 United Kingdom–Dominions Wool Disposals Limited

Eleven files, including the minutes, of the company incorporated in 1945 to effect the orderly disposal of the large wartime surpluses of wool held in the U.K. and to arrange for the marketing of future clips. The company was wound up in March 1954.

BT 168 Ministry of Production: Regional Boards for Industry

In January 1940 twelve Area Boards of the Ministry of Supply were established. Later that year they were put under the Production Council's Industrial Capacity Committee, and in 1941 they were renamed the Production Executive's Regional Boards. On the appointment of the Minister of Production in February 1942 the boards became his responsibility and the organization was reformed, the boards now being chaired by the Regional Controllers of the new Ministry of Production. At the end of the war they went to the Board of Trade when the Board and the Ministry of Production merged. This class covers the wartime records of the headquarters organization. It includes files on district and joint production committees, the reconversion of industry and the regional transition machinery. There are also the papers of the Regional Controllers Conferences, the Regional Advisory Committees, the Citrine Committee on Regional Boards, the Cotton Industry Working Party, the Regional Organization Committee and the Location of Industry Committee (238). For post-war files of the headquarters organization see BT 171; for the minutes etc. of the boards themselves, BT 170; and for the administrative files of some of the regions, BT 194.

BT 170 Regional Boards for Industry: Minutes and Circulated Papers

In September 1945 the wartime Regional Boards were dissolved and replaced by eleven Regional Boards for Industry. These had an independent chairman and consisted of three representatives from each side of industry and senior representatives of each department concerned with industrial production. By 1947 the boards were expressing dissatisfaction with their limited role and their lack of support from government departments. These grievances were investigated by the Paymaster General, Marquand. While his report was under consideration, responsibility for the boards was transferred to the Minister of Economic Affairs (Cripps) and, when he became Chancellor of the Exchequer in November 1947, to the Treasury. The boards were then strengthened by an increase in their industrial members to five and their authority to treat industry as a whole. Mining, agriculture and transport were also added to the scope of the boards.

Between 1947 and 1950 the boards were essentially advisory but they occasionally acted in an executive capacity. During the 1947 fuel crisis and the 1947–48 winter, their Fuel Allocation Committees tried to ensure that essential firms received supplies, and they also undertook to arrange electricity load spreading. In January 1950 a committee under Sir John Maud enquired into the regional organization and in February 1952 responsibility for the servicing of the boards at headquarters and regionally returned to the Board of Trade, although the Treasury retained ministerial control. This class consists of the agenda, minutes and memoranda of the Area and Regional Boards along with their subcommittees. See also BT 171, BT 190 and BT 194.

BT 171 Distribution of Industry and Regional Division: Regional Boards for Industry: Files

The class consists of the post-war records of the headquarters organization for dealing with Regional Boards. For wartime papers see BT 168. Subjects covered include the transfer of responsibility for the boards in 1947, the history of the boards and district committees (160), joint consultation (206–210), the production drive, mid-week sport, industrial building licences, shortages and electricity load spreading. There are also the papers of the meetings of the chairmen of the Regional Boards, the Secretaries' Conference meetings, the Regional Organization Committee, the Regional Procedure (Industrial) Committee, the Winter Transport Policy Committee and Regional Board circulars. See also BT 208.

BT 173   Regional Controllers' Conferences: Minutes and Papers

Circulars, agenda, minutes and papers of the conferences 1947–68.

BT 174   Regional Offices: Circulated Papers

Includes Board of Trade regional circulars 1945–53 and Board of Trade export memoranda which were circulated to regional offices.

BT 175   Cotton Board and Textile Council: Minutes and Papers

Although it first met in 1939, the board only had statutory powers from March 1940 to assist the cotton industry, especially with regard to exports and to advise on questions referred to it by any government department. The class includes minutes of the board 1939–66 and progress reports 1940–66.

BT 177   Distribution of Industry and Regionalization Division: Correspondence and Papers

Under the provisions of the Distribution of Industry Acts 1945 and 1950, the Board of Trade was responsible for the provision of premises and financial assistance for industrial undertakings; financial assistance to trading or industrial estate companies; financial assistance for the improvement of basic services; acquisition of land and provisions for dealing with derelict land; and payment towards the cost of removal and resettlement of key workers. These functions were originally undertaken by the Industries and Manufactures Department (BT 64) but a separate division was established in 1946.

In the main, the files of the division relate to particular cases and individual companies. There are some general files and these include ones on government factories and contracts, the use of raw material controls and allocations, investment, building and its licensing, manufacture in government-controlled establishments, new towns, the labour position in certain areas and Industrial Development Certificates. As well as files on individual development areas, there are some reviews of policy (597, 607, 1333) and regional organization (361, 541). The class also includes the papers of, and submissions to, Panel A, some of Panel B, the Consultative Committee on Industrial Estates, the Second Secretaries Committee on Building Projects, the Board of Trade Working Party on the Allocation of Advance Factories, the Regional Controllers' Conferences, the Working Party on Electric Power-using Industries in the Highlands, the Regional Distribution of Industry Panels and the Distribution of Industry Policy Study Group.

BT 187 Financial Advisory Committees

This committee was established under the Distribution of Industry Act 1945 to advise relevant departments on applications for financial assistance by way of grants and loans from companies working to expand in or move to development areas. It was originally known as the Development Areas Treasury Advisory Committee. Files include the minutes of the committee and cover both general policy and individual cases.

BT 190 National Production Advisory Council on Industry

In 1942 the report of the Citrine Committee on regional boards recommended the establishment of a National Production Advisory Council under the Minister of Production. It was to act as a national counterpart to the regional boards and dealt mainly with war production. Between 1942 and 1945 it met twenty-two times whilst its Emergency Committee met seven times. After the war it was renamed the National Production Advisory Council for Industry (N.P.A.C.I.) and given wider terms of reference. It was now 'to advise ministers on industrial conditions and general production questions (excluding matters which are normally handled by the joint organizations of the trade unions and employers in connection with wages and conditions of employment) and on such subjects as may arise from the proceedings of the Regional Boards for Industry'. It was composed of the Chancellor of the Exchequer as chairman, nine members representing employers and nine appointed by the T.U.C., with the eleven chairmen of the Regional Boards and two members from the nationalized industries. Two members of the Northern Ireland Production Council attended as observers. Such ministers as might be directly concerned and their senior officials could also attend. The secretariat of the council also served as the headquarters section of the Regional Boards for Industry. The council met roughly every quarter and received a review of the economic situation by the chairman and a regional report summarizing the views of the regional board chairmen as well as papers on particular topics. There was also a smaller Interim Committee which was consulted on urgent matters and questions not convenient to be put before the whole council.

Most of the files cover the period after 1951. Amongst the earlier ones, however, are minutes and memoranda of the council and its Emergency or Interim Committee (1–7), press notices about the N.P.A.C.I., situation reports from the Regional Boards for Industry (94–117), and files on a possible merger with the N.J.A.C. and on the representation of the Association of British Chambers of Commerce.

BT 192 United Kingdom Commercial Corporation and English and Scottish Commercial Corporation: Papers

Set up in 1940 as a specialist trading company to meet the difficulties of developing U.K. trade with certain neutral countries, the U.K.C.C. went into voluntary liquidation in 1946 whereupon the English and Scottish Commercial Corporation was re-formed. Most files relate to trade with Russia, whilst others are concerned with the Middle East.

BT 194 Regional Boards for Industry: Regional Offices: General Files

This class includes files on regional fuel allocation and its organization, regional aspects of the production drive and unemployment.

BT 195   Economic Affairs Office

Files of the staff of the Minister for Economic Affairs between September and November 1947. The staff also acted as the productivity secretariat and served the N.P.A.C.I. Most of the files relate to this work. Subjects covered include the cotton industry, economy in the use of petrol and oil and productivity in other countries. It also includes the papers of the Committee on Industrial Productivity, its panels, and its Coal Study Group, the Advisory Group for Increased Productivity, the Anglo-American Council on Productivity and the Productivity (Official) Committee. There is also a file on the composition and terms of reference of the N.P.A.C.I. (80) and one on the organization of the Cabinet Office (81).

BT 201   Flax Controller: Miscellaneous Papers

Established by the Ministry of Supply in 1939 and transferred to the Board of Trade in 1946, the controller was the sole buyer and seller of flax in the U.K. and also regulated its spinning, weaving and processing. This post was abolished in 1949.

BT 202   Information Division: Files

In 1940 a Press Section was established to deal with the Board's public announcements and publicity. It was renamed the Public Relations Department and in 1945 assumed responsibility for the *Board of Trade Journal*. In 1948 it was renamed as the Information Division. Files cover various aspects of the information services etc.

BT 204   Wool Control Papers

Full control was assumed in 1939 and retained until 1949 with the objective of ensuring an adequate supply for the needs of the forces and essential Commonwealth and Allied civil requirements; to deny supplies to the enemy; to assist the Dominion economies by guaranteeing a market for exportable surpluses of wool; and to regulate consumption and control prices in accordance with any general plan for the whole U.K. economy. The class includes the papers of Sir Harry B. Shackleton, the Wool Controller 1939–49, and files on the wool clip.

BT 205   Tariff Division: Files

Although the division was not established until 1955 some files were inherited from its predecessor. There are files on G.A.T.T., the Torquay conference, agriculture and the N.F.U., and particular duties.

BT 208   Distribution of Industry Panels: Files

Arising from the 1944 White Paper on *Employment Policy* (Cmd. 6527) ministerial and official committees on the distribution of industry were established. The official committee consisted of Panels A, B and C of which the first two were the responsibility of the Board of Trade. These two dealt respectively with general policy questions and individual projects, and the disposal of government factories. In addition the Board invited departmental representatives in each region to form the Regional Inter-departmental Committees on the Distribution of Industry, which were chaired by the Board of Trade Regional Controller. Files in this class deal with the location and distribution of industry in the specified regions and include the minutes of the various Regional Inter-departmental Committees together with projects considered by Panels A and B.

BT 211   German Division: Files

Established in 1945 as a section of the Priorities Division of the Board. Its work included the procurement and dissemination to British Industry of industrial and scientific knowledge obtained from Germany, the procurement of key workers, and the obtaining of certain imports from Germany.

BT 222   Accountant's Division: Files

Between 1942 and 1951 accountancy work was the responsibility of the Industries and Manufactures Department (BT 64). In 1951 a separate division was established and most of the files in this class date from 1951.

BT 225   Exports Promotion Department: Files

With the dissolution of the Department of Overseas Trade (BT 60) in April 1946, a new Exports Promotion Department was established to act as the executive instrument for fostering exports and providing economic intelligence. In January 1949, to provide a single administrative unit for trade policy and promotion, it was merged with the Commercial Relations and Treaties Department (BT 11) and became the Commercial Relations and Exports Department (BT 241). Files cover some trade negotiations, the export drive and the minutes of various Regional Export Committees 1947–48.

BT 227   Tariff Advisory Committee: Papers

The committee was formed in early 1951 with a Board of Trade chairman and secretariat. It dealt solely with the domestic merits of applications for tariffs. Only the more important tariff applications were referred to the committee, and many of the early ones came from the N.F.U. Files include the agenda, minutes and some papers and progress reports of the committee.

BT 230   Import Licensing Branch

A general control of imports was imposed in June 1940 which, with a few exceptions, prohibited the private importation of goods except under licence from the Board of Trade. An Import Licensing Department was established within the Industries and Manufactures Department to deal with this, which became in 1946 the Import Licensing Branch. Among the subjects covered were import restrictions on particular items, procurements from the U.S.A., frustrated exports, reconstruction policy, dollar imports and import licensing policy. There is a 1952 Organization and Methods report on the branch (428).

BT 231   Iron and Steel Nationalization Papers

A history by S.S. Wilson and papers leading to nationalization.

BT 241   Commercial Relations and Export Division: Policy, General and Record (P, G and R) Files

These files were registered in the CRE series after 1949. Earlier files are in BT 11 and BT 225. The majority deal with British trade interests abroad, covering commercial negotiations on quota arrangements, import-export facilities and control, model draft treaties, international commodity policy and general economic policy measures of other countries that affected the U.K. Files also relate to policy in relation to specific commodities.

BT 246   Export Licensing Branch: Policy, General and Record (P, G and R) Files

Contains files registered in the period 1940–60 covering particular goods of value or necessity, for example industrial diamonds and precious metals.

BT 258   Industries and Manufactures Department: Policy, General and Record (P, G and R) Files

The class starts in 1948 but most of the files cover the period after 1951. Subjects covered include rubber, cotton linters and other goods. There are also some papers of the Committee on Economic Controls and the Full Employment Bill (21), the Rubber Consultative Committee, the Leather, Footwear and Allied Industries Export Corporation, and the Machine Tool Advisory Council Exports Subcommittee. Also see BT 64.

BT 263   Statistics Division: Policy, General and Record (P, G and R) Files

Files of the division after 1950 dealing with policy, general issues or records including policy on the publication of statistics, 1952 papers on the government's 1946 economic plan and the *Economic Survey for 1948* (4–5) and the census of production. See also BT 70.

BT 264   Furniture Development Council: Minutes

Set up by the Furniture Development Council Order 1948 under the provisions of the Industrial Organization and Development Act 1947 and operative from January 1949. It consisted of eighteen members. Minutes only of the council.

Chapter 22   Other Departmental Papers

Almost every department of state had some responsibilities relevant to either the formulation or implementation of economic planning. The criteria for selection of departments included in this chapter are those advanced in the report 'The organization for discharging the major economic responsibilities of government' drafted by the Working Group of the Steering Committee for Economic Organization in October 1951 (CAB 134/314, GOC(SC)(51)6). This, in its turn, informed D.N. Chester's analysis of the machinery of government and planning in G.D.N. Worswick and P.H. Ady, *The British Economy 1945–50* (Clarendon Press, 1952), p 351–353. Further information on departmental papers with regard to housing may be found in the P.R.O. handbook *The development of the Welfare State 1939–1951.*

22.1   Admiralty

The Admiralty's responsibility for the Navy established it as the sponsoring department for the shipbuilding and ship repairing industries. It also maintained close links with the Ministry of Transport over shipping policy.

ADM 1   Admiralty and Secretariat Papers

A vast class of files organized into two series of subject codings. There is also a packing list. Relevant codes in series I cover Cabinet, government policy and general, etc. (code 5) and commerce, trade and economic matters (code 10). In the former code there are files relating to demobilization and post-war manpower allocations (12791, 16579, 16592, 17769, 19085, 19129), post-war shipbuilding (16748), and distribution of industry and local unemployment (17000, 17088, 19113). Pieces relating to the work of committees include the Joint Production Consultative and Admiralty Committees (12504), the Post-war Shipbuilding Committee (16744), the Reconstruction Committee (17037), the Distribution of Industry Committee (17039), the Admiralty Board Reconstruction Committee (17190) and the 1945 Manpower Committee (19074).

In series II the relevant codes are Admiralty, general, etc. (code 5) and dockyards and naval establishments (code 22). These codes include various files on estimates and the strength of the forces, the future of the shipbuilding and ship repairing industries (21688, 22736, 23009), the reconversion of shipping and its effect on unemployment (21679) and surplus capacity at dockyards for industrial production (20929). Amongst the committees covered are the Shipbuilding Advisory Committee (19233), the Admiralty Manpower Economy Committee (20965), the Admiralty Industrial Council (21435, 21441), the Shipbuilding Trade Joint Council (21439), the Merseyside Working Party on unemployment in the ship repairing industry (22724) and the Development Council on Shipbuilding (22727). Code 22 includes the papers of the Admiralty Industrial Council and the Shipbuilding Trade Joint Council.

ADM 116   Admiralty and Secretariat: Cases

A large class, the lists of which are divided into two parts. Part 2 covers this period. It is itself divided into two volumes both of which are arranged on a subject index basis. In volume 1 the relevant code is commerce, trade and economic matters (code 19), which includes wartime files. In volume 2, see government policy, general, economy-policy (code 5). Here there are further wartime files, as well as post-war ones. Subjects covered include demobilization, naval estimates, shipbuilding and ship repairs as an aid to the balance of payments (5649), the shipbuilding industry 1946–50 (5581), post-war cuts in manpower and finance in 1947–48 (5724) and naval construction programmes (5727). Amongst the committee papers included are those of the Joint War Production Staff in 1948 (5668), the Arms Working Party (5666–5667) and the Admiralty Manpower Economy Committee (5825).

ADM 167   Admiralty Board Minutes, Memoranda, etc.

Complete set.

ADM 205   First Sea Lord: Papers

Papers of the various First Sea Lords, covering correspondence with the Prime Minister 1943–45 (27, 35, 43), Korean rearmament (74), various wartime subjects and Admiralty Board minutes and memoranda.

ADM 214   Civil Engineer in Chief: Papers

Miscellaneous collection of documents on significant projects of the Civil Engineering Department.

22.2   Ministry of Agriculture and Fisheries

The Ministry's responsibilities for agricultural and fisheries policy, from wages to production, were intensified rather than changed by the war. The Ministry did, however, acquire new powers in relation to price control and labour issues, whilst the establishment of the Ministry of Food in September 1939 deprived it of some functions, particularly in relation to subsidies. After the war, increased production remained its central concern and it continued to operate locally through County Agricultural Executive Committees. In 1945 it assumed responsibility from the Treasury for the reconstituted Forestry Commission. More significantly, in 1947, the Agricultural Act made permanent the powers it had previously held under emergency legislation to ensure guaranteed markets and assured prices for domestic agricultural produce, and to enforce high standards of farming efficiency. In April 1955 the ministry was amalgamated with the Ministry of Food to form the Ministry of Agriculture, Fisheries and Food. For a later analysis of the ministry's functions see Sir John Winnifrith, *The Ministry of Agriculture, Fisheries and Food* (New Whitehall Series No. 11, Allen and Unwin, 1962).

The Ministry's records are particularly voluminous and the following list is very selective. Classes covering the detailed implementation of policy are grouped broadly by subject at the end.

MAF 34   Agricultural Marketing: Correspondence and Papers

A class mainly on the 1930s but some files carry on to the 1950s on marketing legislation. Files relate to specific marketing boards, the Inter-departmental Committee on Marketing of Agricultural Produce (724) and the Bacon Development Board and its Emergency Committee.

MAF 38   Statistics and Economics: Correspondence and Papers

Includes files on specific and general agricultural statistics, agricultural output and prices, subsidies and grants and the calculation of farmers' net income. There are also files on the cost of the proposed post-war agricultural policy (325), the agricultural expansion programme, and the Agriculture Act 1947. Some papers of the Advisory Economists Conferences and subcommittees, the Farm Management Survey, the National Survey of Rural Resources, the Milk Costs Investigation Committee, the Agricultural Statistics Advisory Group, the Agricultural Output Committee and the Official Committee on Government Purchases and Control, can also be found in this class.

MAF 39   Establishment and Finance: Correspondence and Papers

Includes files of papers for the county war agricultural executive committees, their subcommittees and district committees, notes to heads of divisions, office notices, the reconstitution of the county agricultural executive committees and the Agriculture Act 1947.

MAF 40   Trade Relations and International Affairs: Correspondence and Papers

Includes files on G.A.T.T., the European Customs Union, economic discussions with Eire, discussions with the N.F.U. on import control relaxations and different aspects of agriculture and long-term planning (182, 184, 187–188, 192). The class also has some papers of the following committees: the Import Licensing Committee and its Working Party on Import Licensing Relaxations, the O.E.E.C. Food and Agriculture Committee and its subcommittees, the Tariff Advisory Committee, the Commercial Policy Panel; as well as papers on the International Conference on Trade and Employment.

MAF 41   Fisheries Department: Correspondence and Papers

Includes some general post-war files relating to legislation, international conferences and the white fish industry.

MAF 45   Information and Publicity: Correspondence and Papers

Includes files on the preparation, and final copies, of various wartime and post-war publications, such as the Dig for Victory campaign.

MAF 47   Labour and Wages: Correspondence and Papers

Includes files on the recruitment of labour in Eire, the use of Polish forces and prisoners of war in agriculture, labour controls and the Agricultural Wages Board. There are also papers of the Inter-departmental Committee on Arrangements for Release of Agricultural Workers from the Forces on the Cessation of Hostilities and the Working Party on Agricultural Labour Supply.

MAF 52   Livestock and Dairying: Correspondence and Papers

Includes files relating to legislation and its aftermath with regard to the Milk Marketing Board, the livestock control scheme, and pig and bacon production policy.

MAF 53   Secretariat and Parliamentary Branch: Correspondence and Papers

Includes files on post-war agricultural policy, world wheat supplies, the agricultural minimum wage, a review of wartime emergency legislation (56–57), the Lucas Report, the Agriculture Bill 1947, meetings and correspondence with the National Union of Agricultural Workers and the Food and Agricultural Group of the P.L.P. There are also papers of the minister's monthly policy meetings (202), miscellaneous meetings in his room (257), the Agricultural Improvements Council for England and Wales and copies of some of the ministers' speeches.

MAF 55   Subsidies and Grants: Correspondence and Papers

Files generally on measures for increasing food production and securing farmers against any substantial fall in prices and more specifically on acreage payments, cereal subsidies and the marginal production scheme.

MAF 58   Agricultural Machinery: Correspondence and Papers

The class covers the supply and control of manufacture of agricultural machinery. It includes files on export and import policy, specific machinery, prices, investment, related legislation and papers of the Agricultural Machinery Development Board, the County War Agricultural Executive Committee, the Industrial Subcommittee of the Reconstruction Committee and the Agricultural Machinery Advisory Committee.

MAF 59   Women's Land Army

Files relating to the organization during and after the war, on recruitment, demobilization, organization and publicity. The class also includes some papers of county committees and some photographs.

MAF 61   Wheat Commission

Consists of papers of the commission's various committees between 1932 and 1971, including the Executive Committee and local committees.

MAF 62 Agricultural Wages Board: Correspondence and Papers

Includes papers of the General Purposes Committee, the Standing Advisory Committee and the Inexperienced Workers Committee as well as miscellaneous papers relating to the Board.

MAF 63 Agricultural Wages Board: Minutes

Minutes of meetings.

MAF 64 Agricultural Wages Committees

Minutes of the county committees and their subcommittees.

MAF 79 Animal Feedingstuffs: Correspondence and Papers

Deals with the ministry's responsibilities and liaison with the Ministry of Food in respect of supplies and prices of feedingstuffs for livestock, the preparation and administration of schemes for the control of distribution of feedingstuffs to farmers and the general supervision of the Animal Feedingstuffs Rationing Scheme.

MAF 82 Monthly Agricultural Reports

Monthly crop reports from December 1950 and summaries from July 1906.

MAF 89 General Division: Correspondence and Papers

In 1939 an Intelligence Division was established, which expanded into the General and Intelligence Division two years later and from 1947 was known as the General Division. Its files relate to publications, co-ordination of post-war policy and, until 1943, war damage matters.

MAF 105–MAF 112 Regional Offices

Respectively records of the following M.A.F. regions: Eastern, East Midlands, Northern, South Eastern, South Western, West Midlands, Yorkshire and Lancashire, and Welsh Department.

MAF 183 Registered Files: Office Instructions and Memoranda (EE Series)

Opened 1953, but containing some earlier files, for the use of the Establishments Division. Includes office notices, memoranda to County Agricultural Executive Committees, County Agricultural Officers, local authorities and heads of divisions. See also MAF 39.

MAF 184   Registered Files: Personnel (EP Series)

Opened 1949 for the use of the Establishments Division, dealing with personnel and staff records. Includes lists of officers, ranks and salaries, the Ryan Committee (20, 23–36) and an organization chart of the ministry (21). See also MAF 39.

MAF 185   Registered Files: Hill Farming (HF Series)

Opened 1946 for the use of the Livestock Improvement and Dairy Husbandry Division, dealing with hill farming.

MAF 186   Registered Files: Manpower (MPB Series)

Opened 1939 for the use of the Manpower and Wages Division, dealing with the supply of labour to agriculture, employment of aliens, etc. Files include estimates of the agricultural labour force, the employment of foreign nationals, prisoners of war, European Volunteer Workers and the Women's Land Army, deferment of national service, agricultural efficiency and labour productivity, and the proposal to bring one hundred St. Helenians to the U.K. to relieve unemployment on St. Helena. Also includes some papers of the N.J.A.C. subcommittee on Labour in Agriculture. See also MAF 47.

MAF 187   Registered Files: Marginal Production Scheme (MP Series)

Opened 1950 for the use of the Livestock Improvement and Dairy Husbandry Division, dealing with improvement grants and marginal production. See also MAF 55.

MAF 193   Welsh Land Settlement Society's Records

Formed in 1936 to get unemployed industrial workers to settle on the land and financed by the Commissioner of Special Areas. In 1946 responsibility was taken over by the ministry. The original society was dissolved in 1949 but a new one with the same name was incorporated in that year. For related correspondence see MAF 70/133–140, 187–194.

MAF 194   Registered Files: Marketing Organization (MAO Series)

Opened in 1945 for the use of the Economic Advice and Marketing Division and subsequently the General Agricultural Policy and Marketing Policy Divisions, dealing with post-war marketing policy, the administration of Agricultural Marketing Acts, grant schemes for agricultural and horticultural co-operatives and the Market Development Scheme. Includes some papers of the Agricultural Marketing Committee and the Inter-departmental Committee on Restrictive Practices by Supervisory Boards. See also MAF 34.

MAF 196   Registered Files: Grassland Development (GD Series)

Opened 1948 for the use of the Crops and Feedingstuffs Division and subsequently the Grassland and Crop Improvement Division, dealing with grassland development, silage and fodder supplies.

MAF 197   Registered Files: Public Relations (PR Series)

Opened 1948 for the use of the Information Section of the General Division, dealing with public relations, liaison with the C.O.I. etc. Includes a file on publicity and the 1947 economic situation. See also MAF 45.

MAF 200   Agricultural Research Council: Minutes and Papers

Includes minutes of the council and the Joint Committee on Agricultural Improvement Councils.

MAF 207   Registered Files: Horticultural Produce: Supply and Prices (PDB Series)

Opened 1940 for the use of the Horticulture, Poultry and Pests Division and sub-sequently the Crops, Feedingstuffs and Subsidies, and Horticulture Divisions, dealing with horticulture. Includes files on the Horticulture Subcommittees of the County Agricultural Executive Committees. See also MAF 34.

MAF 208   Registered Files: Horticultural Produce Marketing and Distribution (MHP Series)

Opened 1953, but including some earlier files, for the use of the Horticulture Division, dealing with the marketing and distribution of horticultural produce.

MAF 209   Registered Files: Fisheries (FGB Series)

Opened 1940 for the use of the Fisheries Department, dealing with general fisheries matters. Includes files on the importation of fish, fishermen and national service, international conferences and conventions and the Herring Industry Board. See also MAF 41.

MAF 211   Registered Files: Marketing Eggs and Poultry (MEP Series)

Opened 1953, but containing some earlier files, for the use of the Egg and Poultry Division, dealing with the marketing of eggs and poultry.

MAF 217   Information and Publicity: Leaflets, Photographic Prints and Posters

Consists of a representative sample of the ministry's work in the war and post-war period, including Dig for Victory and Grow More. See also MAF 45.

MAF 224   Registered Files: Headquarters Division: Organization, Functions and Complements (ESC Series)

Opened 1949, although there are some earlier files, for the use of the Personnel Division of the Establishments Department, dealing with organization, functions and complements of the divisions and branches of the ministry.

MAF 225   Registered Files: Finance Policy (FIN Series)

Opened 1949 for the use of the Finance Department, dealing with financial policy, appropriation accounts, etc. Includes files on the Agricultural Mortgage Corporation.

MAF 226   Registered Files: Electricity Supplies to Rural Areas (ES Series)

Opened 1946 for the use of the Land Drainage, Water Supplies and Machinery Division, dealing with policy aspects of electricity supply to rural areas.

MAF 227   Registered Files: Establishment General (EG Series)

Opened 1949, although there are some earlier files, for the use of the Establishments Department, dealing with general establishment policy and organization matters. See also MAF 39.

MAF 228   Registered Files: Agricultural Wages, Health and Housing (SLY Series)

Opened in 1940 for the use of the Manpower and Wages Division, dealing with agricultural wages, health and housing.

MAF 230   Registered Files: Forestry Act 1945: Use and Management of Land (FOR Series)

Opened 1945 for the use of the Land Division, and subsequently the Land Use Division, dealing with the ministry's functions under the Forestry Act 1945 in the use and management of land.

MAF 231   Registered Files: General Administration (GG Series)

Opened 1941 and closed 1954 for the use of the General Branch of the General and Intelligence Division, dealing with any matters not coming within the sphere of any other administrative division and having a co-ordinating role in matters affecting more than one division. Includes files on the legislative programme, the Balance of Payments Working Party, the International Federation of Agricultural Producers and the Co-ordinating Committee on Controls.

MAF 232   Registered Files: Liaison with County Agricultural Executive Committees (CIL Series)

Opened 1951, although there are some earlier files, for the use of the General Division, dealing with liaison with County Agricultural Executive Committees.

MAF 234   Registered Files: Agricultural Housing and Buildings (AHB Series)

Opened 1943 for the use of the Building Branch of the Land Drainage, Water Supply and Building Division, dealing with agricultural housing and farm buildings. The series was closed in 1953 and a number of active files were transferred to MAF 228. See also MAF 47 and MAF 48.

MAF 238   Registered Files: Land Improvement Loans (LI Series)

Originally opened in 1921, stopped in 1940 and re-opened 1952. There are a few files on land improvement loans running between 1940 and 1952, others were transferred to MAF 139. See also MAF 48 and MAF 66.

MAF 243   Registered Files: Statistics: Food Supply and Consumption (SID Series)

Opened in 1952, although there are a few earlier files, for the use of the Agricultural Economics and Statistics Division, dealing with statistical work undertaken in the co-ordination of general food supply, consumption and retail prices.

MAF 245   Registered Files: Agricultural Land Commission (ALC Series)

Opened 1947 for the use of the Agricultural Land Commission, created under the Agriculture Act 1947 to manage all farming land vested in the minister and to advise him in all matters relating to the management of agricultural land. The series also contains papers of the Welsh Agricultural Land Sub-commission.

MAF 250   Registered Files: Defence and Emergency Services (DEF, DEF(M), and Z Series)

Opened 1950 for the use of the Emergency Services and Defence Division, dealing with wartime agricultural defence planning. Including minutes of meetings of heads of divisions on the organization of the industry.

MAF 251   Registered Files: Milk and Milk Products: Supply and Distribution (MK Series)

Opened 1956, although there are a few earlier files, for the use of the Milk, Milk Products and Welfare Foods Division, dealing with milk and milk products supply and distribution.

MAF 252   Registered Files: United Nations Food and Agriculture Organization (FAO Series)

Opened 1946 for the use of the External Relations Division, dealing with work for the U.N. Food and Agriculture Organization.

MAF 254   Registered Files: Export of Animals (XA Series)

Opened 1950 for the use of the Animal Health Division, dealing with the export of animals. Includes papers of the Livestock Export Group.

MAF 255   Ministers' Papers

The papers as kept by their private secretaries covering a great variety of subjects including policy, copies of speeches, correspondence, official diaries, meetings with firms, individuals, etc., agricultural schemes, the fishing industry and the general work of the ministry. The date sequence has not always been maintained. Includes files on a comparison of agriculture after the First and Second World Wars, correspondence with the N.F.U., notes to heads of divisions, the minister's official diary 1950–55, his correspondence ledger 1950–52, his correspondence index June 1948–December 1952 and his outgoing letters 1948–55. There are also files on all relevant legislation after 1946.

MAF 258   Registered Files: Agricultural Wages and Working Conditions (WG Series)

Opened in 1948 to deal with the enforcement of the Agricultural Wages Act 1948 and of orders of the Agricultural Wages Board made under that act in relation to agricultural wages and working conditions. For earlier files on wages see MAF 228. For the papers of the Agricultural Wages Board see MAF 62 and MAF 63.

MAF 260   Registered Files: Food Standards Division (FS Series)

Files of the Food Standards Division, including the papers of the Food Standards Committee.

MAF 265   Registered Files: Analysis of Agricultural Statistics (AAS Series)

Opened 1941 for the use of the Output Analysis Branch of the Agricultural Economics Unit, dealing with the preparation and analysis of agricultural statistics. Includes files on the compilation of statistics on output and value of national farm product, and estimates and forecasts of production.

Agricultural Education	:	MAF 114–115
Crop Production	:	MAF 37, 120, 196
Divisional Office (Records)	:	MAF 145–149, 157–182
Emergency Services and Defence	:	MAF 250
Establishments	:	MAF 183, 224, 227

Fertilizers and Seeds	:	MAF 51, 78, 119
Finance	:	MAF 225
Fisheries	:	MAF 209
Horticulture and Poultry	:	MAF 54, 125–126, 132, 207–208, 211
Land	:	MAF 48, 66, 139, 141–144, 226, 230, 234, 238, 245
Livestock and Dairy	:	MAF 121–124, 185, 187, 251, 254
Wales	:	MAF 70, 193

22.3 Ministry of Food

With the outbreak of war in September 1939, a new Ministry of Food was established to replace the Food (Defence Plans) Department of the Board of Trade. It also took some functions from the Ministry of Agriculture and Fisheries. The new ministry acted as a trading organization for the U.K. by buying food imports, and ran the various food rationing and subsidy schemes. A growing awareness that food shortages would continue into the post-war period encouraged the ministry to negotiate increasingly long-term contracts for overseas food purchases, and in 1945 it was duly decided that the ministry should continue as a separate and permanent department 'to ensure that the supplies available were equitably shared by the whole community, and used to maintain the health and vigour of the people to the best advantage': Sir Ben Smith in *Hansard* (Commons) 5th ser., vol. 415, col. 1284, 7 November 1945. Its policy was not just to deal with shortages but to develop a more positive long-term food policy, with the particular object of minimizing the impact of food imports on the balance of payments. With the relaxation of many controls, by April 1955, the ministry was amalgamated with the Ministry of Agriculture and Fisheries. For a later analysis of the ministry's functions see Sir John Winifrith, *The Ministry of Agriculture, Fisheries and Food* (Allen and Unwin, 1962). The classification used in these classes reflects the administrative structure at the beginning of 1947.

MAF 67   Food Control Committees 1939–54: Selected Minutes

Files of the committees established to provide a link between the ministry and local opinion and to report on the interests of the buying public.

MAF 75   Permanent Record of Operations (1939–54)

Reports from each division of the ministry in 1945 on their peak wartime operations, with further additions on the transition and decontrol.

MAF 83   Supply Department: Supply Secretariat

Consists of files originating in the various supply divisions or branches which were part of either the Economics Division, the General Department or the Supply Secretariat. The Supply Secretariat was established in January 1947 as part of a major reorganization of the ministry which involved the abolition of the General Department and the Supply Department's own reconstitution into five commodity groups and a secretariat. The General Department had been set up in 1941 and some of its divisions were regrouped within the Services Department so that certain of its records can be found in MAF 99–103. Among the divisions of the General Department had been a Post-war Plans (later Reconstruction) Division.

The class has a contents index which is arranged by divisions. Files cover various international conferences, negotiations, supplies of various commodities, Lend-Lease, the combined boards, import programmes, post-war policy, prices and subsidies, and the future and organization of the ministry. There are also papers of a large number of committees, including: Milk Distribution, Post-war Supplies, Freight, the London Food Council, the Food Supply Board, Shipping, the International Emergency Food Council, Post-war Plans, the T.U.C. Advisory Committee, the Inter-departmental Conference on the Post-war Loaf, the Working Party on Food Subsidies and the Cost of Living, the Inter-departmental Committee on Agricultural Marketing, Agricultural Supplies, the Inter-departmental Committee on Restrictive Practices, the Special Committee on Imports, Consumer Demand, Import Licensing, Inland Transport and the Commercial Secretary's memoranda 1943–46.

MAF 84   Supply Department: Cereals Group

Consists of files on general policy, contracts and agreements, 1939–55. Among the subjects covered are alcohol and yeast, animal feedingstuffs, bakery, cereal products, edible pulses, home grown cereals, overseas procurements and international agreements, and rice.

MAF 85   Supply Department: Dairy Produce and Fats Group

Files of the divisions responsible for the procurement, distribution and processing of dairy produce and fats.

MAF 86   Supply Department: Fish and Vegetables Group

Files of the divisions responsible for the movement, distribution and processing of fish and vegetables.

MAF 87   Supply Department: Groceries and Sundries Group

Covering chocolate and sugar confectionery, cocoa, coffee, starch, sugar and tea.

MAF 88   Supply Department: Meat and Livestock Group

Files of the divisions responsible for trading activities and a wide range of control over home-killed and imported meat.

MAF 97   Establishment Department: British Food Mission, Washington

The mission was set up as a result of Lend-Lease but continued after the war. It amalgamated with the British Supply Office in 1948 to form a single supply body to deal with E.R.P. questions, then becoming the U.K. Treasury and Supply Delegation in January 1949. Includes files on the supply and purchase of various commodities, co-ordination between the mission and the ministry, weekly summaries, U.K. requirements and the world food situation. There are also some papers of the Combined Food Board and its subcommittees, the International Wheat Conference, the F.A.O. and the International Emergency Food Council.

MAF 99   Services Department: Distribution Group

Established during the ministry's 1947 reorganization as one of the four groups which, with a secretariat, constituted the department. The files, roughly covering the period 1940–55, are arranged chronologically by their originating division or unit. Amongst these are divisions dealing with storage, transport, rationing and other aspects of distribution. The class also includes the papers of the T.U.C. Advisory Committee 1941–46 (1021–1045) and the 1946 bread rationing scheme (1112–1125).

MAF 100   Services Department: Regional Administration Group

Formed as part of the 1947 reorganization and responsible for the ministry's regional organization and enforcement work. There were seventeen regional food officers in charge of the local food offices in each of the regions, whose work was co-ordinated by the Headquarters Division. This division was also responsible for liaison with local Food Control Committees, set up in 1943 to represent the interests of local consumers and to provide a channel of communication between the ministry and the public.

The class is arranged by divisions: enforcement (1–63) and regional organization (administration) (64–198); and then a series of letters, instructions and manuals issued (199–305). There is also a small selection of files from a regional office (North Midlands) (313–354). Files roughly cover the period 1940–55.

MAF 102   Services Department: Public Relations Group

Set up as part of the January 1947 reorganization although files cover the period 1940–55. It was responsible for transmitting to the public information necessary for the day-to-day operation of food control and for giving advice on the best use of available food supplies. The class includes verbatim reports of the minister's press conferences.

MAF 103   Services Department: Services Secretariat

Set up as part of the January 1947 reorganization although files cover the period 1940–55. The secretariat co-ordinated the work of the Services Department and provided secretarial assistance for departmental sponsored committees. It also dealt with matters of general policy outside the scope of one division. There was also an Export Policy Branch (1–108), responsible for ensuring that policy conformed to that laid down by government. Apart from this files relate to points rationing, licensing policy, food subsidies, and development and unemployment areas. There are also some papers of the T.U.C. Advisory Committee, the Winter Transport Committee and the Food Distribution Committee.

MAF 104   Establishment Department: British Food Mission, Ottawa

Files similar to MAF 97 but relating to Canada. The mission was abolished in 1953.

MAF 127   Establishment Department

Files of the department over the period 1936–55. They are arranged by division. The General Division includes files on organization and reorganization of the ministry (86–88). The Organization and Methods Division also has files on its organization, including charts of the ministry (178), an organizational guide (186) and staff charts of various divisions (211–215).

MAF 129   Finance Secretariat

Contains all the surviving unregistered papers of the Financial Secretary and related Treasury correspondence on the financial aspects of the ministry's work. Files are divided into three main sections. The first covers Treasury and miscellaneous correspondence (1–153), including files on central finance (121, 145), and the minister's letters and speeches (147–148). The second consists of publications related to the Overseas Food and Queensland British Food Corporations (154–166) and the final section (167–246) has cables copied to the ministry.

MAF 138   Finance Department

Consists of files over the period 1938–55 covering financial control, estimates and accounts. It includes files on export policy, food prices, subsidies (209–10, 230, 263, 266, 288, 290, 319), the impact of increased food availability on the economy (256), correspondence with the Treasury (234–235), and organization and charts (222). There are also some papers of the Margins Committee.

MAF 150   Legal Department: Registered Files (L Series)

Consists of advice on various legal matters over the period 1939–55. Includes files on various orders, the maximum prices of particular commodities, controls on food, the revocation of traders' licences and the post-war activities of the ministry.

MAF 151   Committees

Unregistered papers of committees set up under regulations, largely during the war but not all under Ministry of Food auspices. The committees are arranged alphabetically and are: Agricultural Supplies 1946–52 (1–3),Building Programming 1948–53 (4–9), Catering Trade Working Party 1948–50 (10–11), Comparative Consumption Levels 1946–47 (12), Combined Food Board 1942–1946 (13–34), Combined Food Board Committees 1942–46 (35–59), London Food (from 1944 the London Food Council) and its subcommittees 1942–46 (60–83), Combined Working Party on European Food Supplies 1944–45 (84–86), Commonwealth Liaison 1950–52 (87–89), Concentration of Food Production 1941 (90), Consumer Demand 1949–50 (91–92), Economic Advisory 1951–53 (93), Economy Committee and its subcommittees 1947 (94–100), Embassy Food 1946–52 (101–103), Finance Director's memoranda 1945–54 (104–105), Food and Agriculture 1946–52 (106–114), Food Developments 1941–44 (115–116), Food Distribution 1947–54 (117–127), Food Exports and its Working Party, and export circulars 1947–55 (128–131), Food Policy Committee Inter-departmental Working Party 1948–50 (132), Food Standards and subcommittee 1947–55 (133–141), Food Supply Board and its committees 1941–46 (142–161), Freight 1941–45 (162), Inter-departmental Committee on Fresh Fruit and Vegetables 1947–49 (163), Fruit and Vegetables (Marketing and Distribution) Organization 1947–49 (164–165), U.N. Conference on Food and Agriculture (Hot Springs) U.S.A. 1943–44 (167–170), Informal Post-war Plans 1943–44 (171), International Emergency Food Council Washington 1946–47 (172–173), International Emergency Food 1948–49 (174), International Emergency Food Council: Commodity Committees 1946–48 (175–186), International Sugar Council 1939–56 (187–201), International Wheat Conference 1947 and its committees (229–246), International Wheat Conference 1949 and London Conference (247–260), International Wheat Council, preparatory committees and subcommittees for various sessions 1942–53 (261–318), Licensing Working Parties (319), Machinery of Distribution of Unrationed Foodstuffs 1941 (320–321), Margins 1940–58 (322–349), Milk Division (350–352), Minister's Standing Committee 1941–46 (353–355), Orders 1940–59 (356–387), Points Food Supply 1942–50 (388–394), Priority Distribution 1941 (395–396), Profit Margins and its subcommittees 1946–47 (397–404), Rationing 1941 (405–406), Reasonable Expenses 1942–45 (407), Secretary's Committee 1939–40 (408), Secretary's Standing Committee 1946–52 (409–417), Special Committee on Imports 1946 (418), Stationery and Printing 1940–45 (419), Sugar Division 1939–47 (420, 422), Supply Programming 1946–54 (423–437).

MAF 154 Orders Committee

Set up in December 1939, and made responsible in December 1941 for the supervision and co-ordination of the legislative work of the ministry, especially the framing, reviewing and revoking of statutory instruments.

MAF 156 Statistics and Intelligence Division

The division was the focal point for the collection, study and dissemination of statistics and information. Most files contain reports and information on particular commodities. There are also more general files on post-war statistical requirements (175), rationing and points rationing and the cost of living (359–362, 586). There are some papers relating to the Agricultural Supplies Committee, the F.A.O., the Supply Programming Committee, the Wartime, Family and National Food Surveys, the September 1950 Income Study and the Consumer Demand Survey.

MAF 223 Publications

Consists of a variety of publications, 1939–56, although the majority are pre-1950. They are arranged under their main headings, for example administration and organization, catering and diet, bread and cereals, instructional handbooks, rationing, stabilization, etc.

MAF 256 Scientific Advisers Division (SA Series)

Opened in 1947 for the use of the newly formed Scientific Adviser's Division, dealing with nutritional needs, diet, meal planning etc. Includes files on bread rationing and dietary surveys.

MAF 263 Registered Files: Miscellaneous and Manufactured Food (MMF Series)

Opened in 1955 but containing some earlier files on the import of particular commodities, home canning, and chocolate and sugar confectionery. See also MAF 83 – MAF 98 and MAF 99.

MAF 268 Registered Files: Sugar and Sugar Beet (SUG Series)

Opened 1939 to deal with all aspects of sugar and sugar beet as commodities. Originally filed in MAF 87, the series was started in 1958 and some re-registered files are preserved here.

22.4 Ministry of Fuel and Power

The ministry was established in June 1942 largely owing to the problems of coal supply and the unsatisfactory relations between the Board of Trade and the Mines Department. It assumed responsibility for coal from the Mines Department and for petroleum and petroleum products from the Petroleum Department (both of which were wound up) and for gas and electricity from the Board of Trade. This allowed fuel and power policy and rationing to be better co-ordinated, although the ministry continued to operate as three major divisions. In April 1945 the ministry was made permanent, and it subsequently played a major role in the 1947 fuel crisis and the Labour government's nationalization programme. For his experiences at the Ministry from 1946 to 1950, see P.M. Williams (ed) *The Diary of Hugh Gaitskell* (Cape, 1983).

POWE 3 Solid Fuel Control and Rationing 1939–58: Representative Papers

Selected files to illustrate the functioning of the control and rationing systems in operation. The files relate to three regions: the Northern, Wales and the London Regional Group (consisting of London, South Eastern and Eastern Regions).

POWE 7 Annual Reports of Inspectors of Mines

POWE 10 Establishments Division: Correspondence and Papers

Pieces 1–297 are arranged under thirteen subject headings and only a broad indication of the contents of individual files can be obtained. From piece 298, there are individual file descriptions. The class includes files on accounts, appointments and organization, regional organization, the mines inspectorate, the N.C.B., the British Electricity Authority, the North of Scotland Hydro-electric Board, the Gas Board and the Directorate of Open-cast Coal Production. There are also papers relating to departmental committees, the Committee on the Socialization of Industry, the Official Committee on the Machinery of Government, the Government Organization Committee and Area Electricity Board Consultative Councils. There is a file on organization charts (388).

POWE 11 Electricity Commission: Minutes
Minutes to July 1948, when the commission was dissolved, with an index.

POWE 12 Electricity Commission: Correspondence and Papers
Set up under the Electricity (Supply) Act 1919 to be responsible for all aspects of electricity supply. The class consists of correspondence and papers dealing with all aspects of functions with regard to supply, transmission and distribution. It is arranged by subject groupings and within them chronologically. The subject groupings cover administration and legislation including papers on the location of new generating plant and the Inter-departmental Committee on Heavy Electrical Plant; electric lighting companies and responsible authorities; electricity distribution and charges, metering, etc.; financial arrangements; legal matters; overhead lines, etc.; power stations and generating plant (case files); and water resources and barrage schemes, including papers of the committee on the Severn Barrage Scheme.

POWE 13 Ministry of Transport, Electricity Correspondence and Papers
Contains very few files after 1941, but does include some for example on the Severn Barrage Scheme.

POWE 14 Electricity Division: Correspondence and Papers
Consists primarily of post-1942 files, although there are some from the Board of Trade's Gas and Electricity Division. Includes files on the functions of the Electricity Commission and the British Electricity Authority, the siting of power stations, hydro-electric developments in Scotland, appointments, charges and price policy, load shedding and spreading, restrictions on use (including those in 1947), purchase tax, the co-ordination of fuel and power industries, and capital investment. There are also papers of the Ministry of Fuel and Power Steering Committee, the Liaison Committee for Fuel and Power, Under-Secretaries' meetings, the Committee on Peak Demand and Tariffs, the Domestic Fuel Economy Campaign, Consultative Councils and the Ridley Committee.

POWE 16 Coal Division: Early Correspondence and Papers
Covers major problems within the industry since 1920. Few files continue after 1943 but under manpower (code 9) there are some files on recruitment 1945–47; and under N.C.B. (prior to nationalization)(code 11) there are some papers of the Coal Production Subcommittee, the Mining Supplies Committee and the Manpower Subcommittee.

There is a subject list which acts as a key to the class. POWE 17–POWE 21 are arranged similarly for cross-referencing.

POWE 17   Coal Division: Emergency Services: Correspondence and Papers

Consists of files on emergency services, price control, supply and demand for anthracite and retail coal distribution. Includes files on pithead prices, coal and the history of coal supply control. There are also papers of the Public Utilities Coal Committee, the Merchants' Consultative Committee and the Fuel Allocations Committee.

POWE 18   Coal Division: Fuel and Lighting: Correspondence and Papers

Covers subjects related to the Fuel and Lighting Registration and Distribution Order 1942. Includes files on local and regional organization, circulars on industrial and domestic supplies, coal distribution orders and the future planning of coal distribution.

POWE 19   Coal Division: House Coal: Correspondence and Papers

Covers house coal emergency schemes. Includes files on coal distribution, prices and the papers of the Domestic Coal Consumers' Council and the Industrial Coal Consumers' Council. See also POWE 3.

POWE 20   Coal Division: Labour and Labour Relations: Correspondence and Papers

Class running from the 1880s. Includes files on absenteeism, additional manpower for mining, prisoners of war, the employment of foreigners, the release from the forces of ex-miners, training, hours of work, holidays, wages, and the Essential Work Order. There are also papers of the Greene Committee (67–70, 74–76), the Committee on the Employment of Poles, and the Miners Charter (123–126).

POWE 21   Coal Division: Mines Department War Book and Associated Matters: Correspondence and Papers

Largely consists of files on prices and price orders but also includes papers of the Coal Prices Branch.

POWE 22   Coal Division: Production: Correspondence and Papers

Covers drainage schemes, mining subsidence, mining rights, mineral royalties and financial assistance. The class is arranged by subjects. Also includes files of the Reid Committee (174–175, 178–180, 186–192, 195) and the National Joint Committee of the National Association of Colliery Managers and the N.U.M.

POWE 25   Chief Scientist's Division: Correspondence and Papers

Formed in 1948, the division was organized into two branches: Scientific and Fuel Efficiency. The former was concerned with research and development, the latter with both industrial and domestic fuel efficiency. The class is arranged initially by subjects (prices 1–61) and then chronologically. Includes files on fuel utilization and *Fuel Efficiency News.* There are also papers of the Domestic Fuel Planning Committee, the Fuel Efficiency Committee, representative files of the Regional Fuel Efficiency and Government Loan Scheme, the Ministry of Fuel and Power Advisory Council and the Fuel Efficiency Advisory Committee.

POWE 26   A Files

Arranged chronologically, the class relates to various functions of the Mines Department of the Board of Trade and its successors. Includes files on emergency arrangements, labour relations, mineral transport, metalliferous mining, mining royalties, retail distribution, controls and their abolition, legislation and departmental committees.

POWE 28   Statistics and General Division: Correspondence and Papers

Consists mainly of files on statistics, planning and material priorities to the coal, gas, electricity and petroleum industries. Includes files on nationalization, domestic fuel policy, coal production 1948–51, and prices. There are papers of the Inter-departmental Committee on Heating in Government Buildings, the Inter-departmental Committee on Domestic Heating Appliances Subcommittee and the Committee on National Fuel Policy.

POWE 29   Gas Division: Registered Files

The division was responsible for all aspects of policy, including liaison with the Area Boards and Gas Council on matters concerning maintenance, supply and development. Includes papers of the Gas Industry Committee, the Heyworth Committee of Enquiry into the Gas Industry and files on nationalization.

POWE 33   Petroleum Division: Correspondence and Papers

The division took over the functions of the Board of Trade Petroleum Division in 1942 and gained further responsibilities from the Ministry of Supply in 1946. Includes files on sources of supply; shipping; rationing, prices and the black market; Anglo-U.S. oil policy; foreign exchange requirements; sterling-dollar oil problems; U.K. oil balance of payments estimates; coal-oil conversion; and correspondence with individual oil companies. There are also papers of the Exchange Requirements Committee, the Petroleum Standing Advisory Committee, the Oil Advisory Panel, the Committee on National Fuel Policy and the Petroleum Board.

POWE 34   Petroleum Division: Oil Control Board Papers

The board was set up in November 1939 under the Secretary for Petroleum. It was largely an adjudicating and supervisory body and so most of its work was delegated to subcommittees. The class consists of the papers of the Executive Committees of the Oil Control Board and of the Timber Tonnage Committee. The papers of the board itself and the Subcommittee on Supplies can be found in CAB 77.

POWE 35   Valuations and Compensation Division: Coal Industry Nationalization Papers

POWE 36   Solicitor's Branch

Includes files on nationalization.

POWE 37   Coal Division: Registered Files (B Series)

Consists of files after coal nationalization. See also POWE 10, POWE 16–POWE 22, POWE 39–POWE 41. Includes files on N.C.B. members, organization and structure, its relations with the ministry, and its *Plan for Coal*; estimates of production and productivity, and incentives; price policy and wage negotiations; manpower, and the employment of Italian miners; the maintenance of employment in development areas; housing for miners; the coke oven programme; and the O.E.E.C. There are also papers of the Joint Committee on Production and Minister's Joint Production Conference, the Committee on Involuntary Absenteeism in the Coal-mining Industry, the Departmental Investment Programmes Committee and the Inter-departmental Standing Committee on the Increase of Manpower in the Coal-mining Industry.

POWE 38   Electricity Division: Nationalization Files

POWE 39   Coal Division: Finance Files

For earlier files see POWE 16–POWE 22. Mainly on nationalization.

POWE 40   Coal Division: Open-cast Coal Files

For earlier files see POWE 16–POWE 22. Includes files on the conflict between open-cast working and agriculture.

POWE 41   Coal Division: International Matters: OB Files

For earlier files see POWE 16–POWE 22. Includes files on the importation of coal, exports, the Marshall proposals, the O.E.E.C., the Schuman Plan and papers of the Trade Negotiations Committee.

POWE 42   Coal Industry Nationalization Act 1946: Central Valuation Board

POWE 43   Accountant General's Division: Correspondence and Papers

Includes files on the accounts of particular nationalized industries.

POWE 44   Gas Nationalization Papers

22.5   Ministry of Labour

The Ministry of Labour had a central role in the wartime planning of reconstruction owing to the presence of Ernest Bevin as minister, the predominance of manpower budgeting, the need for good industrial relations and the ministry's inter-war responsibilities such as regional policy. For a summary of its views on wages, see CAB 87/9, R(44)182; on regional policy, see CAB 87/63, EC(43)1–2; and on its general post-war role, see CAB 87/74, MG(43)7. See also S. Glynn and A. Booth, *The Road to Full Employment*, chapter 11 (Allen and Unwin, 1987).

It was expected to have a major role after the war as an economic ministry but this did not materialize. The appointment of Isaacs as minister, the removal of labour controls, the decreasing importance of manpower budgets, the ministry's own non-interventionist policies in industrial relations and training, and the transfer of regional policies to the Board of Trade increasingly reduced its importance after the transition period. Its major responsibilities were for labour supply, through its collection and analyses of manpower statistics, and wages policy, through its contacts with the trade union movement.

Full details of its organization, functions and expenditure over the whole period are in T 165/264. Unpublished historical studies of the ministry's wartime role are in LAB 76, a full series of its annual reports in LAB 37 and a number of Information Service publications in LAB 44.

LAB 1   Employment Exchanges: Reports on employment and unemployment

Complete set of quarterly reports by each exchange on existing and prospective situation in its locality, with proposed remedies. Covers 1950/51 only, the reports for all other years having been destroyed.

LAB 3   Arbitration Tribunals

Records of the Industrial Court, Civil Service Arbitration Tribunal and the National Arbitration Tribunal 1940–51, including reports etc. on a wide range of industrial disputes.

LAB 6   Military Recruitment

Records relating to the drafting and implementation of the wartime and post-war National Service Acts, including deferment and prosecution. A history of the Acts is included (688–692) as well as minutes of the Manpower Priority Committee and its subcommittee on the schedule of reserved occupations, 1944 (35–81).

LAB 8   Employment

Contains the major records on the formulation and implementation of manpower and full employment policy in war and peace.

For the war, it includes the minutes and papers of the Labour Co-ordinating Committee, 1941–46 (853–858, 994, 996–997, 1006, 1010, 1021A–B) and the Director-General of Manpower: weekly Principal Assistant Secretaries' meetings 1941–45 (1037). There are also papers on labour controls and demobilization including one for the Inter-departmental Committee on Unemployment during the Period of Reconversion (1026). Further annotated minutes of the wartime Manpower Committee are in LAB 76 and LAB 79.

On full employment policy, it contains papers relating to the 1944 White Paper (733, 864, 913, 947) and the ministry's own Committee on Full Employment, 1944–48 (867, 2177). There are also files on manpower estimates and forecasts for the whole country (131–137, 1402, 2084–2086, 2415) and individual industries; the mobility of labour including the minutes of its Committee on Industrial Mobility, 1945–47 (1020, 1278) and a social survey on industrial mobility (1531) as well as memoranda for the Lord President's Committee and the Official Steering Committee (1276–1277); and regional policy including working papers for the Official Committee on the Balanced Distribution of Industry. There are also numerous files on the recruitment and control of foreign labour and the labour supply for particular industries, such as coal, 1941–50 (1473–1479, 1729). Papers relating to the 1948 Employment and Training Act are also included (1507–1511).

During the Korean War there are reviews of the labour supply for defence industries (1740, 1743–1748, 1796, 1819–1820, 1979) as well as the Regional Controllers' Quarterly Reports on Employment and Unemployment, January 1951–December 1952 (2298–2306). There are also manpower estimates and plans for a future war including some for the Cabinet's Manpower Committee (1703–1704).

There are also numerous files on port labour, the technical and scientific register, women's employment (including the National Institute of Houseworkers, whose minutes and memoranda are in Lab 70) and local employment committees. Some of the returns on which unemployment statistics were based at this time are preserved in LAB 85.

LAB 9   Finance

Records of the Finance Department, including details of expenditure on unemployment insurance, training centres, and recruitment of foreign labour.

LAB 10   Industrial Relations: General

The major class of records on industrial relations including files on general policy and individual firms and disputes. It includes a complete set of the minutes and memoranda of the National Joint Advisory Committee, its Joint Consultative Council (651–658, 1488–1494) and the N.J.A.C. subcommittee on wage incentives 1950–52 (938). It also contains a major paper on post-war industrial relations policy (160) and one on the proposed National Industrial Conference 1946 (662).

On wages policy, it contains the minutes and reports of the Treasury's Wages Co-ordinating Committee 1945–46 (556, 564), papers relating to the 1947 Working Party on the Stabilization of Wages (663–664), the Committee on Wage Incentive Schemes 1949–57 (843–846), and the co-ordination of wage claims in the public sector 1949–50 (847). There are also files relating to industrial working parties 1945–46 (566), the impact of reduced hours on production 1946–48 (594, 788), the Joint Production Committee 1947–50 (720–722) and the machinery for joint consultation 1947–53 (723–728).

There is little on productivity but many files on the personnel management advisory service.

The annual record books of trade disputes recording details of all disputes notified to the Ministry are in LAB 34.

LAB 11   Industrial Relations: Trade Boards and Wages Councils

General administrative records. The minutes of individual boards and councils are in LAB 35.

LAB 12   Establishments

A major class of records concerned with the organization and staffing of the ministry and certain committees, bodies etc for which it was responsible.

On full employment policy, it includes papers on preparations for the ministry's more active post-war role (115, 378), the Investment Working Party 1946–47 (432), the minutes of the Headquarters Committee on Statistics 1940–49 (172, 326, 385, 462, 494, 530), and a few statistical analyses of the unemployed (112, 516–517). There are the records of various publicity campaigns to increase production 1947 (484), educate public opinion about foreign workers 1947–52 (513) and to recruit labour for underm-anned industries 1947–48 (421), cotton 1948 (523) and coal-mining 1946 and 1951 (392, 608) including the minutes of the publicity committee of the Committee on the Employment of Poles in Mines 1947–48 (463).

Also included are papers relating to the post-war implementation of the Essential Works Order (554, 572) and the Control of Engagement Order (507, 556). Finally there are surveys of the work of personnel management advisers 1948–54 (724) and of the ministry's Industrial Information Division 1947–51.

LAB 13   Overseas

Records of, and briefs for, international agencies dealing with labour matters, including reports of U.K. labour attachés abroad, and therefore containing much information about manpower, employment, productivity and migration both in the U.K. and overseas.

It includes many items relating to the O.E.E.C., including the records of its Manpower Committee 1949–51 (45–50, 52–57, 60–64, 649–700); the Brussels Treaty Organization; the International Labour Organization and Conferences; and the U.N., including the 1950 discussion on full employment (660). Other files include memoranda on full employment policy in Sweden 1944 (114), the proposed international employment conference 1944 (120) and wage systems abroad 1950 (670); progress reports for the Foreign Labour Committee 1947 (257); and O.E.E.C. memoranda on urgent economic problems 1950 (781) and manpower aspects of productivity 1949–52 (823–827). There are also papers on the World Federation of Trade Unions (596–603) and the International Confederation of Free Trade Unions (632–642).

LAB 14   Safety, Health and Welfare: General

Papers relating to the interpretation and enforcement of the Factory Acts and other similar regulations and orders, including those on hours of employment. Related papers are in LAB 15, LAB 67 and LAB 33. See also LAB 26.

LAB 18   Training

The major class of records on industrial training for the able-bodied and disabled, covering major policy and particular institutions and schemes including Government Training Centres, Industrial Rehabilitation Units, the Training within Industry Scheme (particularly 139, 542–547) and a large number of vocational training schemes. There are many files on reconstruction planning covering general principles, specific industries and particular groups of workers. Included also are the minutes of major wartime training committees and those of the Inter-departmental Committee on Business Training 1948–54 (568–570).

LAB 19   Youth Employment

Files relating to general policy and individual industries, firms and regions. Contains the papers of the Committee on the Recruitment and Training of Juveniles for Industry 1936–44 and the National Juveniles (Youth) Employment Council 1947–50.

LAB 20   Disabled Persons

Files relating to the employment and training of disabled persons, with regard to general policy (especially the Disabled Persons Employment Act), particular schemes and specific industries and firms, including Remploy. It contains the minutes and memoranda of the Ince Rehabilitation and Resettlement Committee, the National Advisory Council on the Employment of the Disabled and the National Joint Pneumoconiosis Committee.

LAB 25   Private Office Papers: Series I: War Emergency Measures

Contains almost exclusively wartime files, but includes some ministerial papers on the juvenile employment service 1945 (176–178) and papers relating to manpower 1946 (150–152) and labour controls in the Mary Smieton collection (187–195).

LAB 26   Welfare Department

Papers of the department responsible for the welfare of particular occupational groups including the provision of hostels for immigrant labour. Contains the papers of the Standing Committee on Staggered Holidays (250–217).

LAB 32   Resettlement after Demobilization

Contains largely wartime files, including the minutes and memoranda of the Inter-departmental Committee on Release from the Forces and Civil Defence Services and the papers of the resettlement advice service.

LAB 43   Private Office Papers: Series II: Selected Case Files

Post 1946 memoranda on a variety of issues, including a few on unemployment, training, migration and wages policy.

22.6   Ministry of Materials

In 1951, in response to the worldwide stockpiling of raw materials occasioned by the Korean War, Richard Stokes (the Lord Privy Seal) was first given responsibility for monitoring the situation and then, in July, made Minister of Materials. The core of the new ministry was the old Raw Materials Department of the Ministry of Supply, which had been split in 1946 but was not reintegrated. Responsibilities were therefore assumed from the Board of Trade and the Ministry of Supply (which nevertheless retained control over iron and steel). The ministry was generally responsible for the supply of materials until they entered manufacturing industry. It was disbanded in 1954.

BT 161   Ministry of Materials: Files

Relatively few files were opened in 1951, but they include ones on the International Materials Conference, the Raw Cotton Commission, the reversion to private trade (180–182), and the decontrol of raw materials 1945–54 (257). There are also papers on organization and functions (241–243) and some wartime history papers of the Raw Materials Department. Other files relate to individual materials and their control. Some papers of the Trade Negotiations Subcommittee on International Commodity Policy and the Economic Steering Committee Subcommittee on Prices (183–184) are also included, along with a file on the committees on which the ministry was represented (253).

BT 172   Ministry of Materials: Private Office Papers

Files dating from 1951–54 covering *inter alia* particular materials, staff and the Lord Privy Seal's visit to Washington in May 1951.

22.7 Ministry of Supply

The ministry was established in August 1939 to deal with military supplies. Its potential importance grew in 1945 as the incoming Labour government intended it to be the ministry responsible for engineering and heavy industry. Thus in August 1945, it assumed responsibility for the engineering industry from the Board of Trade and merged with the Ministry of Aircraft Production to form a Ministry of Supply and Aircraft Production. Its potential, however, was never fully realized. In April 1946, with the dissolution of aircraft production departments, it reverted to being the Ministry of Supply. Simultaneously it lost its monopoly of the controls over raw materials: it continued to operate controls over iron and steel and non-ferrous metals but those for petroleum and petroleum products passed to the Ministry of Fuel and Power and those over all other raw materials to the Board of Trade. In November 1946 it did gain responsibility for atomic energy (which it retained until 1954) but in 1947 it lost control over most housing supplies to the Ministry of Works. The only other major reorganization of the ministry's functions came in July 1951 with the establishment of the Ministry of Materials, which took over that part of the Ministry of Supply's work concerned with the supply of metals, excluding iron and steel. After October 1951 the Conservative government greatly reduced its civil economic functions.

For the papers of the Iron and Steel Control and Iron and Steel Division of the Ministry of Supply, see BT 255 and POWE 5. Both were responsible for the wartime and post-war distribution of iron and steel, its export and import, and for productivity within the industry. The former contains papers on long-term steel production prospects, the Iron and Steel Act 1949 and price control. The latter includes files on the Control of Iron and Steel Order, Iron and Steel Disposals Ltd., etc.

AVIA 9   Ministry of Aircraft Production: Private Office Papers

Contains the papers of the ministers and parliamentary secretaries of the ministry between 1940 and 1946. Files mainly relate to wartime, including some correspondence with companies, but there are some on post-war industrial organization.

AVIA 10   Ministry of Aircraft Production: Unregistered Papers

Papers to 1946, mainly on wartime problems and administration. Includes A.K. Cairncross's papers.

AVIA 11   Ministry of Supply: Private Office Papers

Includes files on various wartime supply questions, the post-war iron and steel industry, labour in Ministry of Supply factories and the disposal of surplus stores.

AVIA 12   Ministry of Supply: Unregistered Papers

Mainly wartime files but including some papers of the Permanent Secretaries 1940–55 (1–14) with files on iron and steel, the control of supply and the future of the ministry. There are also files on Lend-Lease, including the Keynes-Sinclair negotiations, building construction labour controls 1936–45 and statistics of deliveries. There are organization charts of the ministry (24) and of the Ministry of Aircraft Production (25).

AVIA 15   Ministry of Aircraft Production: Files

This class is subject coded, covering *inter alia* aircraft development and production (codes 5–7), committees (code 15), contracts and contractors (code 18), disposals (code 21), factories (code 25), the ministry itself (code 31), oil and fuel (code 33), post-war industries (code 37), production and manufacture (code 38), and raw materials (code 42).

AVIA 22   Ministry of Supply: Registered Files

There is a contents sheet at the front of the class list arranged by series title and giving relevant piece numbers. Amongst relevant series titles are area organization, which includes minutes of the Regional Controllers Conference; buildings; building labour; contracts; electricity supply; essential works; gas and heat supplies; wartime and post-war labour requirments; the control of machine tools; the ministry's headquarters, including files on the Raw Materials Department, iron and steel control, merger with the Ministry of Aircraft Production and government decisions on reconstruction (222); parliamentary legislation; power; priorities; production; raw materials, including files on finance and foreign exchange and payments; release of men from the services; statistics; stores; demands on U.K. production (752); armistice and post-war supplies, including files on the post-war supply industries and regional development; and civil staffs, with files on labour requirements of various industries and of the Labour Preference Committee and the Labour Supply Committee for Building Materials and Components.

AVIA 33   Handbooks and Directories, etc.

The class includes directories of the distribution of duties of the Ministry of Aircraft Production 1943–45 and the Ministry of Supply 1945–59, showing the organization and structure of successive ministries responsible for supply procurement.

AVIA 34   Departmental Notices

Consists of selected office memoranda and general notices, 1940–56.

AVIA 38   North American Supplies

Mainly wartime class, although some post-war files on procurement. Includes files of the British Ministry of Supply Mission, the British Supply Council, the Combined Production and Resources Board and papers of Sir Henry Self and Sir Ben Smith.

AVIA 46   Ministry of Supply Files: Series 1 (Establishment)

Consists of files on the organization of various branches and divisions of the ministry and on the official war histories. There are organization charts of the ministry 1947–53 (514–515).

AVIA 49   Ministry of Supply Files: Series 2 (General)

Consists of the minutes and papers of various committees, files on general policy, forward planning, iron and steel nationalization, etc. Subjects covered include investment cuts, emergency legislation, the supply of particular materials, the Marshall Plan, disposal policy and the ministry's monthly statistical reports. There is particular emphasis on regional boards, regional controllers' monthly reports and regional aspects of various policies. Files also relate to the Distribution of Industry Committee, the Investment Working Party, the Import Licensing Committee and the Imports Diversion Committee.

AVIA 50   Ministry of Supply Files: Series 3 (Labour)

Includes files on requirements, wages, accommodation and related topics. Also papers of the Manpower Committee.

AVIA 51   Ministry of Supply Files: Series 4 (Finance)

Includes files on Lend-Lease, factories, iron and steel and E.R.P.

AVIA 52   Ministry of Supply Files: Series 5 (Accounting)

AVIA 53   Ministry of Supply Files: Series 6 (Contracts)

Includes files relating to individual companies, progress of rearmament and the labour position in Coventry, Preston, Chorley and Blackburn. Also papers of the Contract Co-ordinating Committee.

AVIA 55   Ministry of Supply Files: Series 8 (Production)

Includes files on building (14–27), imports and exports, iron and steel, various committees (28–76), the Materials (Allocation) Committee, the Coal Carbonization Plant Committee and the International Tin Conference.

AVIA 57   Ministry of Supply Files: Series 12 (Disposals)

BT 255   Iron and Steel Division: Registered Files

A section of the British Iron and Steel Federation within the Ministry of Supply formed the nucleus of control of iron and steel, being responsible for its supply and distribution, supervising imports and exports and co-ordinating efforts to raise production. The control was wound up at the end of the war but the ministry continued to be concerned with the industry. The class consists of the registered files of the division in the Ministry of Power from 1957 but also includes some earlier re-registered Ministry of Supply files. These include ones on long-term steel production prospects, chairmanship of the Iron and Steel Board, the Iron and Steel Act 1949 and price control.

POWE 5   Ministry of Supply, Iron and Steel Control: Registered Files

A section of the British Iron and Steel Federation, the industrial organization embracing most branches of the trade formed the nucleus of the control and its personnel were eventually given the status of temporary civil servants. The control was responsible for the supply and distribution of iron and steel, supervision of imports and exports and co-ordination of all efforts to raise the rate of production. The control continued in a modified form after the war but in July 1955 responsibility passed to the Board of Trade and two years later to the Ministry of Power. Files include scrap, iron ore, the Control of Iron and Steel Order, Iron and Steel Disposals Ltd., etc.

SUPP 14   Ministry of Supply Files

Consists of files covering the period 1939–59, dealing with the supply of materials, individual firms, factories, overseas trade and international bodies. Includes files on individual materials, and their control schemes, price control, machinery and machine tools, the 1947 Anglo-Russian Trade Agreement and other bilateral negotiations. There are also papers of the Steel Economy Committee, the Ministry of Fuel and Power Resources Committee, the International Tin Study Group, the International Materials Conference, various O.E.E.C. committees, the E.C.E. Industry and Materials Committee, the Engineering Advisory Council, the Metals Economy Advisory Committee and the Raw Materials Shipping Committee.

22.8   Ministry of Transport

In May 1941 the Ministry of Transport merged with the Ministry of Shipping to form the Ministry of War Transport in order to combine 'the management of our shipping with all the movement of our supplies by rail and road from our harried ports' (W.S. Churchill, *The Second World War Vol. 3: The Grand Alliance* (Cassell, 1965, p 132)). It was also an active participant in the development of employment policy throughout the war. After the war, it retained its dual responsibility for shipping and inland transport although, in April 1946, it duly dropped 'war' from its title. After the election of the Conservative government in October 1951, responsibility for the ministry and the Ministry of Civil Aviation was assigned to the same minister and, in October 1953, the two departments were formally merged. For a review of its function see Sir G. Jenkins, *The Ministry of Transport and Civil Aviation* (Allen and Unwin, 1959).

Owing to later administrative reorganizations, some ministry records have been classified with those of other departments. Hence the first three classes listed here are Board of Trade classes. The ministry's papers on electricity can be found in POWE 13.

BT 193   Commercial Services (Transport)

Mainly the records of the Commercial Services Division prior to the Board of Trade's assumption of responsibility for merchant shipping and shipbuilding in 1965. Subjects covered include exports, freight rates and papers of the Shipping Requirements Committee.

BT 199   Shipbuilding Advisory Committee

The agenda, minutes and papers of the committee (containing representatives of employees, labour and interested government departments) established in March 1946 to advise the government on the efficiency and stability of the industry. Its chairman was Sir Graham Cunningham, a member of the Economic Planning Board.

BT 217   Civil Aviation: R Series Files

Originally opened in the Air Ministry before passing to the Ministry of Civil Aviation in 1945, this class covers a wide range of civil aviation matters. It includes a file on a letter by J.M. Keynes on civil aviation (231).

MT 6   Railways: Correspondence and Papers

This class reflects the ministry's responsibility for railways since 1919. The pieces are listed by subject headings and there is also a committees subject heading which includes papers relating to the Railways Workshops Capacity Committee, the Wagon Production Committee, the Merseyside Dock Access Committee and the Gowers Committee. Individual committees are also given their own subject headings. Included here are the Control Transport Committee, the Charges Consultative Committee, the Committee on European Economic Co-operation, the Committee on Inland Transport, minutes of meetings of the Controller of Railways, the Defence (Transport) Council, the International Railway Congress Association, the Investment Programmes Committee, the London Passenger Transport Board, the Railway Executive Committee, Railways (London Plan) Committee, the Transport Priority Subcommittee, the War Transport Council, the Welsh Reconstruction Advisory Council and the Winks Transport Executive Committee.

MT 9   Marine: Correspondence and Papers

Consists of files of correspondence and papers from around 1850 arranged by chronological list and a subject index for the period 1903–69. Relevant subjects and their codes include agreements (code 2), clothes rationing (code 111), committees (code 78), crew manning (code 30), defence regulations (code 33), fiscal policy (code 42), food rationing (code 45), legislation (code 62), mercantile marine (code 75), merchant shipping (code 154), the Merchant Shipping Advisory Committee (code 83), the ministry (code 159), provisions (code 108), shipbuilding and ship repairs (code 114), statistics (code 153), training (code 142), and the U.S.A. (code 145).

MT 24   Transport Arbitration Tribunal

Set up as a result of the Transport Act 1947 to deal with valuation and compensation.

MT 33   Road Transport: Correspondence and Papers

Consists of files of correspondence and papers from 1919. The class is arranged with a subject key. Relevant ones include appeals (passenger), covering regional traffic areas, employees (passenger); goods transport, which includes the Winter Transport Executive

Committee and the 1947 road haulage strike; legislation, including various proposals for post-war legislation; licensing and certification; London passenger transport, including the impact of nationalization; organization, which includes the Conference of Chairmen of Traffic Commissioners and Regional Transport Commissioners; public service vehicles; services; and the Transport Act 1947.

MT 34   Road Traffic and Safety: Correspondence and Papers

Includes files on motor and agricultural vehicle taxation.

MT 35   Road Haulage Organization

Set up in March 1943 to secure maximum economy in the use of fuel and rubber and to maintain a fleet of long distance vehicles for emergencies. It was replaced in August 1946 by a new scheme for an emergency reserve of vehicles.

MT 39   Highways: Correspondence and Papers

The papers of the departments set up after 1909 to deal with the construction of new roads. There is a subject index to the class. Relevant subjects include commissions and committees, etc., which covers improvements and new construction, legislation, materials, post-war development, alleviation of unemployment and finance, as well as the papers of the Official Committee on Post-war Internal Economic Problems, and the Investment Programmes Committee (288–290); finance, covering grants and with a file on investment and the draft economic plan (656); land acquisition; post-war development, with a file to the Reconstruction Committee; and war measures.

MT 40   Sea Transport: Correspondence and Papers

Previously with the Board of Trade and then the Ministry of Shipping, it became part of the Ministry of War Transport in 1941. There is a subject key, relevant subjects being committees, conferences and reports, which includes the Freight Movement Co-ordinating Committee; organization; and planning, which includes post-war organization and the release of ships.

MT 45   Ministry of Transport Establishment and Organization: Correspondence and Papers

Arranged with a subject key. Relevant subject headings include appointments and staff recruitment; British Transport Commission; committees; conferences; reports, including relations between the minister and the British Transport Commission; departmental and official histories; legislation; organization and staffing, including post-war reconstruction, the need for an economic policy division (33), organization and functions (347), regional organization and a directory of the ministry; parliamentary briefs; the Railway Rates Tribunal and the Transport Tribunal; road haulage organization; training; transfer of functions and powers; the Transport Act 1947; the Transport Arbitration Tribunal; and war emergency arrangements. See also MT 96.

MT 47   Finance: Correspondence and Papers

Includes three series of files relating to government control of transport (particularly railways and shipping) in time of war, the exercise of various peace-time powers over railways and the nationalization of inland transport. There is a subject index to the class. Relevant files include ones on the Anglo-American Financial Settlement (190–196), the Transport Act 1947; government control of railways, employment policy and reconstruction (326–328), the Investment Programmes Committee (366–377) and borrowing (397–399).

MT 50   Defence Planning and Emergency Transport Committees

Mainly before 1943 but there are some relevant committees' papers, including the Railway Workshops Capacity Committee, the Inland Transport War Council, the Central Transport Committee (120–137), Regional Transport Committees (138–151), the Shipping Advisory Council (152–154) and the Official Committee on Inland Transport (155–156).

MT 52   Inland Waterways: Correspondence and Papers

Correspondence and papers from 1919. Includes files on the Central Canal Committee (59–101), post-war planning and reconstruction (104), the control of canals, the Transport Bill 1947 as well as files on individual canals.

MT 55   Emergency Road Transport Organization

Set up in 1939 and operating on a regional basis under Regional Transport Commissioners, the organization implemented wartime controls such as the rationing of fuel for commercial transport, the economic allocation of transport, zoning of essential commodities and allocation of materials. There is a subject key to the class. Files include circulars to Regional Transport Commissioners, their conferences, post-war reorganization, fuel rationing (including its history), reports to Cabinet committees (215–220), the oil expansion programme (229–232), the production of motor vehicles and their importation from the U.S.A., employment in road transport, and rationalization of services.

MT 56   Rates and Charges: Correspondence and Papers

New division established at the start of the war to exercise control over charges for inland transport. Files include applications for increases in charges, general policy, British Transport Commission charging powers, international inland transport policy, and the papers of the Working Party on Transport Charges and of various users' committees.

MT 59   Shipping Control and Operations: Correspondence and Papers

Set up at the start of the war at the Ministry of Shipping, it dealt with all questions relating to the wartime requisitioning, chartering and allocation of shipping as well as with post-war problems. There is a subject key to the class. Files include coal shipments, oil, the U.K. import programme (610–17) and departmental import programmes (739–1042), post-war foreign shipping relations (2371–2541) and papers relating to the Civil Requirements (Shipping) Committee, the Ship Licensing Committee (1043–1062), the British Mission in Washington (2200–2238) and the Combined Shipping Adjustment Board (2239–2248).

MT 62   Private Office Papers

Includes the papers of Lord Leathers (3–95), most of which are before 1943, but which do include files relating to the Reconstruction Committee's Working Party on Controls (94) and the Official Committee on controls (95–96); Arthur Salter (96–124), again mainly pre-1943; and Alfred Barnes (125–129), including files on shipping and ship-building policy (125) and the road haulage organization (127–128).

MT 63   Port and Transit: Correspondence and Papers

Papers concerning the wartime control and handling of merchant shipping and cargoes. A few post-1945 files include the ports' labour force (370–374), free ports (437–438), capital investment (442–444) and the Transport Bill 1947 (431–434). There are also papers of the Central Transport Committee (228–233), the Working Party on the Turn Round of Shipping (390–398) and the Port Efficiency Committee. See also MT 48, MT 81, MT 82.

MT 64   COT (Co-ordination of Transport) Files

Created in wartime to deal with various aspects of post-war planning in relation to transport. Files include the co-ordinated use of inland transport (1); post-war planning (4–7); reports by the F.B.I. and the Association of British Chambers of Commerce (2) and by H.W. Coates (9); and the papers of the Reconstruction Problems Committee (3) and the Official Committee on Post-war Internal Economic Problems Subcommittee on the Planning and Timing of Investment (8).

MT 65   Stats (Statistics) Files

Consists of various statistical returns, analyses and forecasts. Early papers relate to shipping, import programmes and operational requirements, later ones to post-war activities. Files include shipping earnings in relation to the balance of payments (182–183), shipbuilding prospects (210), turn round of shipping (265), the Marshall Plan (284–292), the Mutual Security (Economic) Programme (293–302), the O.E.E.C. (305–309), the Investment Programmes Committee (310) and the economic organization enquiry (317).

MT 67   Railway Rates Tribunal

Established in 1921 and renamed the Transport Tribunal as a result of the Transport Act 1947. Records of the proceedings of the tribunal, annual reports, etc. See also RAIL 1101 and MT 80.

MT 69   Road Haulage Appeals

Consists of the papers of the Road and Rail Traffic Act 1933 Appeal Tribunal and the Road Haulage Appeals Division of the Transport Tribunal. In 1951 its jurisdiction passed to the Transport Tribunal. Files relate to individual appeals.

MT 72   European Recovery Programme: Shipping Arrangements

In September 1947 the Committee on European Economic Co-operation produced its report on maritime transport which reviewed the state of merchant fleets of participating countries at mid-1947, planned their development to 1951 and examined the availability of shipping services to meet requirements up to 1951. By the summer of 1951 interest had turned from economic considerations to military ones, reflected by the formation of a Mutual Security Programme. Files cover British aspects of these subjects including various aspects of Marshall Aid, applications to E.C.A., counterpart funds, marine insurance and the U.K. export drive to the dollar area. There are also papers relating to the Mutual Defence Agreement (61–67), the Mutual Security Acts (68–77) and the Maritime Transport Committee (37–52).

MT 73   General Shipping Policy: Files (GSP Series)

Includes files on ship repairs abroad (115–119), ship repairing and employment (149), shipbuilding and unemployment (167, 177), nationalization (148), long-term prospects (178, 189), and the papers of the Shipbuilding Advisory Committee (5–13, 274), the Overseas Negotiations Committee (92–103), the Admiralty Working Party on Ship Repairs (155–156), the Investment Programmes Committee (187), the Economic Organization Working Group (197) and the Economic Planning and Full Employment Bill (204).

MT 74   Transport Act 1947, Bill Files and Papers

Papers on nationalization preceding the Act, including discussions with various bodies, draft memoranda, correspondence and minutes of the Cabinet committees on the socialization of industry.

MT 77   Transport Charges Consultative Committees

Consists of proceedings of enquiries by various consultative committees, which were made up of permanent members of the Railway Rates Tribunal (later Transport Tribunal) to advise the minister at his request on applications from transport undertakings for increased charges. See MT 67.

MT 80   Transport Tribunal: Proceedings

Set up as a result of the Transport Act 1947 to replace the Railway Rates Tribunal on applications for increased charges. See also AN 80.

MT 81   Ports: Registered Files: P Series

Created in 1953, although there are some earlier files, dealing with the day-to-day operation of ports. For earlier files see MT 48 and MT 63.

MT 82   Ports: Registered Files: PEP Series

Created in 1952, although there are some earlier files, dealing with port emergency planning. For earlier files see MT 48 and MT 63.

MT 89   International Inland Transport (IIT and IT Files)

Selected ministry files on U.K. participation in the formulation of international inland transport policy. Includes papers relating to the E.C.E. Transport Committee and the Working Party on Road Transport Short-term Problems.

MT 93   Personal Files

Selection of files, particularly on special appointments. Closed for 75 years.

MT 95   Highways Engineering: Registered Files (HE Series)

MT 96   General Division: Registered Files (G and GD Series)

Formed in 1950 to deal with establishment matters other than staffing, general work concerning more than one division and with a parliamentary section. Includes files relating to the Emergency Legislative Commission, the Transport Users Consultative Committee, the Transport Act, and Railway Executive and British Transport Commission appointments. See also MT 45.

MT 97   Road Transport: Registered Files (RT Series)

Consists of files from 1927 dealing with freight transport and public service (passenger) transport. Includes files on freight aspects of the Transport Act 1947, and general administrative work, including the issue of C licences. See also MT 33 and MT 34.

MT 104   Highways Policy: Registered Files (HPA Series)

Series begins in 1965, but contains a number of earlier files.

MT 120   Highways General Planning Division: Registered Files (HGP and GPH Series)

Includes files on the road investment programme (4–11) and new towns.

22.9   Ministry of Works

In October 1940 the responsibilities of the Office of Works were expanded and it was renamed the Ministry of Works and Buildings. Previously it had simply looked after government buildings and accommodation, but Bevin wanted a central authority which would 'plan and execute all building and civil engineering work for the government' (C.M. Kohan, *Works and Buildings* (HMSO, 1952) p 73). In July 1942, on taking over the planning powers of the Ministry of Health, the ministry was renamed the Ministry of Works and Planning; but, in February 1943, it lost these powers to the new Ministry of Town and Country Planning. Its name then stabilized as the Ministry of Works.

During the war, although service departments continued to supervise their own building, the ministry became 'the main governmental building agency and the recognized central authority for dealing with the building and civil engineering industries and industries providing building materials' (F.M.G. Willson, *The Organization of British Central Government 1914-1956* (Allen and Unwin, 1957) p 97-8). A Directorate of Post-war Building was also established with responsibility for the preparation of sites and the manufacture of prefabricated housing. These responsibilities continued after the war with the continued operation of the system of building licensing until 1954. Moreover, in 1945 a regional organization was created and from November 1947 it gained responsibility from the Ministry of Supply for the provision of housing supplies, other than the production of aluminium houses. These responsibilities overlapped seriously with those of the Ministry of Health, and general responsibility for housing remained an issue of contention between the two departments throughout the period.

WORK 22   Administration (General) and Establishment

Consists primarily of matters of general policy affecting executive divisions, dealing with contracts, finance and supplies, and the whole range of the work of organization and establishment. There is a subject index to the class. Files cover individual civil servants and appointments, financial control, organization of divisions, legislation, hostels, preference in awarding contracts to firms in development areas and papers of the Departmental Joint Industrial Council.

WORK 26   Royal Ordnance Factories

WORK 45   Construction Industry and Building Materials

This class covers the ministry's work as the sponsoring department for building, including government consultations with industry during and after the war. It contains files on the control of civil building (29-62), price control, the preparation of a reserve of building (84-86), regional programming circulars (115-117), various statistics and their collection (181-198), building materials production priority, and building priority for development areas. There are also papers of the National Brick Advisory Council (6-9, 11, 13), the Building Programme Joint Committee (21-23), the Building Materials Prices Committee (100, 105-107), and the Headquarters Building Committee Priorities Subcommittee (125).

WORK 46   Official History of the Second World War and Buildings Unpublished Sources

Draft sections and related papers for Kohan's volume.

WORK 49   Regional Building Committees: Minutes

At the end of the war overall responsibility for the national building programme rested with the ministry. As a result building committees in each administrative region were established with a parent committee in London as court of appeal and overall co-ordinator. The committees met infrequently after November 1954. The class contains the surviving files of the regional committees and their subcommittees.

Official War Histories

23.1   CAB 102 Official War Histories (1939–45) (Civil)

Records of the Cabinet Office Historical Section, including the various authors' typescripts, drafts, revisions, and comments as well as unpublished narratives and general correspondence. There is a set of confidential print versions of the histories as published but which contain an additional index to source references (1–26). Other relevant files include the decontrol of raw materials 1945–54 (191); economic policy by W.K. Hancock (266); economic controls during the war (267); a financial history of the war by R. Hawtrey (322); the problems of reconstruction for the gas industry by A. Jenkin (339); wages policy in the war by A.J. Corfield (404); labour, requirements and supply by D. Mack Smith (405); source papers on manpower allocations in 1945 (479, 481); miscellaneous 1945 source papers (483–484); N. Brook's correspondence files on manpower and industry 1942–44 (485, 491, 493–495); W.S. Murrie's files on the manpower position 1943 and 1944 (496–499); organization and administration of the Ministry of Supply 1939–45 (500); Ministry of Supply regional organization (502–503); the War Savings Campaign 1939–46 (523); Anglo-American oil negotiations 1939–45 by P. Rutley (570); the stock crisis 1944–45 by M.A. Ogilvy-Webb (575); the Petroleum Board (578); prices and price policy by R.C. Tress (611); a history of the Ministry of Production by W. Piercy (612–614); reconstruction 1941–43 by A. Baster (619); economy in public expenditure (787); problems with fulfilment of the 1944 and 1945 import programmes (840–841); Ministry of Production departmental meetings (843); and *A People at War* by S.J.L. Taylor on the home front (848).

23.2   CAB 103 Cabinet Office Historical Section Registered Files

Consists of correspondence and comments on both the civil and military histories, including prices and price policy (220), economic controls (246) and a financial history (405–406, but 406 closed).

Abbreviations

1.	**General**

B.B.C.	British Broadcasting Corporation
B.E.	Bank of England
B.E.C.	British Employers' Confederation
B.S.I.	British Standards Institute
B.T.C.	British Transport Commission
C.C.L.	Commonwealth Consultative Committee
C.E.B.	Central Electricity Board
C.E.P.S.	Central Economic Planning Staff
C.L.C.	Commonwealth Liaison Committee
C.O.I.	Central Office of Information
C.P.M.	Committee on Preparations for Meeting of Commonwealth Prime Ministers
C.S.O.	Central Statistical Office
C.W.S.	Co-operative Wholesale Society
D.O. & P.T.	Defence Order Priority Scheme
D.O.T.	Department of Overseas Trade
D.S.I.R.	Department of Scientific and Industrial Research
E.C.A.	European Co-operation Administration
E.C.E.	Economic Commission for Europe
E.C.G.D.	Export Credits Guarantee Department
E.C.O.S.O.C.	Economic and Social Council (of UN)
E.C.S.C.	European Coal and Steel Community
E.I.U	Economic Information Unit
E.P.C.	Economic Policy Committee
E.R.P.	European Recovery Programme
E.S.W.P.	Economic Survey Working Party
F.A.O.	Food and Agriculture Organization
F.B.I.	Federation of British Industries
G.A.T.T.	General Agreement on Tariffs and Trade
G.E.C.	General Electric Company
G.N.P.	Gross National Product
G.P.O.	General Post Office
I.C.I.	Imperial Chemical Industries
I.M.C.	International Materials Conference
I.M.F.	International Monetary Fund
I.P.C.	Investments Programme Committee

I.T.O.	International Trading Organization
J.C.C.	Joint Consultative Committee
J.W.P.C.	Joint War Production Committee
M.E.P.	Ministry (Minister) of Economic Planning
M.F.N.	Most Favoured Nation
N.A.T.O.	North Atlantic Treaty Organization
N.C.B.	National Coal Board
N.F.U.	National Farmers Union
N.I.C.	National Industrial Council
N.J.A.C.	National Joint Advisory Council
N.P.A.C.I.	National Production Advisory Council for Industry
N.U.M.	National Union of Manufacturers; National Union of Miners
N.U.R.	National Union of Railwaymen
O.E.E.C.	Organization for European Economic Co-operation
O.I.T.	See I.T.O.
P.E.P.	Political and Economic Planning
P.L.P.	Parliamentary Labour Party
P.M.L.	Priority Material Licence
P.T.	Preferential Treatment Priority Scheme
R.A.F.	Royal Air Force
R.I.I.A.	Royal Institute of International Affairs
R.J.A.S.	Reconstruction Joint Advisory Council
R.O.F.	Royal Ordnance Factories
R.P.M.	Resale Price Maintenance
S.H.A.E.F.	Supreme Headquarters of Allied Expeditionary Force
T.G.W.U.	Transport and General Workers Union
T.I.C.	Treasury Investment Committee
T.U.C.	Trades Union Congress
U.K.	United Kingdom
U.K.C.C.	United Kingdom Commercial Corporation
U.N.	United Nations
U.N.I.S.C.A.N.	United Kingdom and Scandinavian trading bloc
U.N.R.R.A.	United Nations Relief and Rehabilitation Administration
U.S.	United States

2. Ministers

A.–G.	Attorney-General
Ch. D. Lancaster	Chancellor of the Duchy of Lancaster
Ch. of Exchequer	Chancellor of the Exchequer

Ec. Sec. (Try)	Economic Secretary of the Treasury
Fin. Scc. (Try)	Financial Secretary of the Treasury
1st Ld Admiralty	First Lord of the Admiralty
Foreign Sec.	Secretary of State for Foreign Affairs
Home Sec.	Minister of Home Security
Ld Chancellor	Lord Chancellor
Ld President	Lord President of the Council
Ld Privy Seal	Lord Privy Seal
Min. of:	Minister of:
Agriculture & Fish	Agriculture and Fisheries
Air Prod.	Aircraft Production
Labour & N.S.	Labour and National Service
Soc.(Nat.) Insurance	Social (National) Insurance
M. State Economic Affs	Minister of State for Economic Affairs
M. State (F.O.)	Minister of State for Foreign Affairs
Paymaster-Gen.	Paymaster-General
Prime Min.	Prime Minister
Postmaster-Gen.	Postmaster-General
S./S. Commonwealth Relations	Secretary of State for Commonwealth Relations
Solicitor-Gen.	Solicitor-General

All other ministers have not been abbreviated.

3.   **Departments**

Adm.	Admiralty
Air P.	Ministry of Air Production
B.T.	Board of Trade
Cab. O.	Cabinet Office
Civ. A.	Ministry of Civil Aviation
Col. O.	Colonial Office
Com. Rel. O.	Commonwealth Relations Office
C.S.O.	Central Statistical Office
Dom.	Dominions Office
E. Aff.	Ministry of Economic Affairs
Ec. Sect.	Economic Section of the War Cabinet
Ed.	Board (Ministry) of Education
F.O.	Foreign Office
Fuel & P.	Ministry of Fuel and Power

H.O. & H.S.	Home Office and Ministry of Home Security
Info.	Ministry of Information
Lab. & N.S.	Ministry of Labour and National Service
Ld Chanc. O.	Lord Chancellor's Office
Ld Pres. O.	Lord President's Office
M.A.F.	Ministry of Agriculture and Fisheries
M.O.D.	Ministry of Defence
Nat. Ins.	Ministry of National Insurance
Parl. C.	Parliamentary Counsel
Pen.	Ministry of Pensions
P.M.O.	Prime Minister's Office
Privy S.O.	Privy Seal's Office
Prod.	Ministry of Production
Recon.	Ministry of Reconstruction
Scot.	Scottish Office
Ship.	Ministry of Shipping
T. & C. Plan.	Ministry of Town and Country Planning
Try	Treasury
War Transport	Ministry of War Transport
War	War Office

All other ministries have not been abbreviated.

INDEX

alcohol, *cont.*
    hops, 14.1
    whisky,
        distilling investment programme for,
          15.23
        exports, 15.1, 15.9
Alexander, (Lord), 2.2, 4.1, 7.2, 7.10, 14.1, 15.29,
  15.35, 17.2, 20.1
aliens *see* employment
alkali *see* chemicals
Allen, D.A.V, 13.11, 15.12, 15.30, 15.31, 18,
  20.2
    'Note on economic planning', 18
Allen, P, 6.1
Allen, R.F, 15.26, 15.27
Allen, R.G.D, 15.37
allied,
    control of heavy industry in Germany, 2.1
    economic mobilization, 15.14
    finance in reconstruction, 19
    finance in war, 19
allies, wool supply to, 21
allocation and allocations,
    differential, 15.26, 15.32
        of industrial coal, 15.32
    of/ *see* individual commodities
    removal from, 15.26
    schemes, 18
    to Southern Rhodesia, 15.36
    see also reallocation
Allotments and Garden Society, National, 17.2
alloys *see* steel
aluminium, 14.1, 15.21, 18
    economy in use of, 15.26
    houses, 15.9, 18, 22.9
    for housing, 15.9, 15.26
    industry, 14.1, 15.23
    see also metals
Aluminium in the Commonwealth, Working
  Party on Production of Primary, 18
aluminium production, 15.35
    Commonwealth, 15.13, 15.35, 18
    Commonwealth Sterling Area, 15.13, 15.23
    development of, 15.35
    expansion of, 15.35
    Gold Coast, 15.13, 18
    North Borneo, 15.23, 15.35, 18
    Scotland, 15.35, 18
America,
    Central, exports to, 15.9
    see also North America, South America,
      United States of America
Amery, L, 2.2, 7.1, 7.5, 11, 17.1
ammonia *see* chemicals
Amphlett, E.M, 14.3
Anderson, Sir John, 2.1, 2.2, 3, 4.1, 7.2, 7.4, 7.5,
  7.9, 7.10, 7.12, 10, 11, 19, 20
    Romanes Lecture, 11
    Stamp Memorial Lecture, 3

Anderson, K, 15.13, 15.34, 15.37
Andrew, G.H, 14.8, 15.21
Andrews, H.D, 15.34
Anglo-American etc. *see* individual countries
animal,
    export, 22.2
    see also dogs, farms and farming,
      feedingstuffs, health, livestock, sport
Annecy, France, tariff negotiations at, 15.13
anthracite *see* coal and coalmining
Antilles, Netherlands *see* Netherlands
apples *see* fruit
Appleton, E, 14.3
apprentices *see* employment
arbitration,
    machinery, 2.2, 14.1
    transport, 22.8
    see also strike and strikes
Arbitration Order, Conditions of Employment
  and National, 2.2, 15.35
Arbitration Order, Conditions of Service and
  National, 2.2
Arbitration Tribunal
    Central, 14.1
    Civil Service, 22.5
    National, 15.34, 15.35, 22.5
    Transport, 22.8
Archer, G, 15.26
area and areas,
    coalmining, new towns, 14.2
    congested, 14.2
    depressed, 7.4, 7.8
      industry in, 7.2, 19
    franc, 15.34
    mining, new towns, 14.2
    monetary, Netherlands, 15.34
    regional traffic, 22.8
    restricted, 7.8
    rural, 2.1
      electricity to, 22.2
    textile, 15.25
    see also development areas, dollar areas,
      sterling areas, unemployment areas
Area Board, gas, 22.4
Area Electricity Board Consultative Councils,
  22.4
Areas, Commissioner for the Special, 21, 22.2
Argentina, 2.1
    agreement, 15.9
    balance of payments with, 15.34
    coal for, 15.13
    exports from, 18
    exports to, 15.9
    financial negotiations with, 20.2
    food from, 17.2
    import of coal from Southern Rhodesia, 15.1
    meat shipments from, 2.1, 15.34

Balance of Payments Working Party on Import
Programmes, 20.2
Balance of Payments, Interdepartmental
Committee on Estimates of, 8
Balance of Payments, OEEC programme, 18
Balance of Payments, Working Party on Non-
Dollar, 13.11, 20.3
Balfour, L.G, 15.33
ball and roller bearing industry, 15.21, 15.23
bananas *see* fruit
bank and banks, 2.2
    advances, 19, 20.3
    banking policy, 19
    Coinage Bill, 20.3
    credit, commercial, 19
    deposits, 20.1
    investment, international, 17.1
    UN, 17.1
    see also currency and currencies
Bank of Canada, 15.13
Bank Deposits and Advances, Working Party on,
20.1
Bank of England, 1, 2.2, 5.1, 15.34, 17.2, 18, 19,
20.2, 20.3
    Governor of, 7.2
    meetings with Treasury, 20.3
    Treasury-Bank of England Committee on
      Postwar Exchange Control Problems, 20.3
Bank of England Act, 1945, 20.3
Bank of England Bill, 2.1, 2.2, 20.2
Bank Fund, 15.14
Bank Notes Bill, Currency and, 11
Bank for Reconstruction Development,
International, 20.2
Bankers' Association, American, 19
Bank, International, 2.1, 15.13
bankruptcy, 1, 21
Bankside, London *see* power stations, London
Bannister, M, 15.9
Barbour, M, 15.31
Barkley, H, 15.27
barley *see* alcohol, cereal and cereals, farms and
  farming
Barlow, Sir Alan, 7.8, 7.9, 17.2
Barnes, A, 2.2, 4.1, 6.5, 11, 14.1, 14.2, 15.2,
15.10, 15.13, 15.17, 15.35, 17.2, 22.8
Barnes, J.H, 15.23
barrage balloons *see* defence programme
Barrage Scheme, Severn, 22.4
Barrhead, Scotland, 14.2
Barry Moor Works, Cardiff, Wales, 14.2
Basildon, Essex, Marconi, 18
Baster, A, 7.7, 23.1
Battersea, London, colour-light signalling, 15.23
Bavin, A.R.W, 15.8, 15.21, 15.23, 15.37
Baxter, G.H, 15.1, 15.37
Baxter, T, 7.9
BBC, 2.2, 18, 19

broadcasting, restriction of, 2.1
budget broadcast scripts, 20.1
building programme, 15.21, 15.23
capital investment programme, 15.21
investment programme, 15.23
restoration of services, 15.17, 17.2
see also entertainment, radio, television
Beachley, Gloucestershire, Army Training
  School, 14.2
Beale, P.S, 15.37
Beard, W.B, 14.3
Beaven, E.J, 13.4, 13.5, 15.5, 15.9, 15.10, 15.37
Beaverbrook, (Lord), 1, 2.2, 12, 17.1
Beazley, M.P, 15.30
Beckenham, Kent, Gas Research Board, 14.2,
  15.8
Bedford, Rochester and, Short Bros, 14.2
beer *see* alcohol
Beer, H, 15.5
Belcher, J, 4.3, 14.1, 14.2, 15.8, 15.18, 15.25
Belfast, Northern Ireland, 14.2
Belgian Congo,
    balance of payments with, 15.34
    exports to, 15.9
Belgium, 15.34
    Anglo-Belgian trade discussions, 21
    bananas to, 15.34
    basic slag from, 15.34
    bricks from, 15.35
    exports to, 15.9
    financial stability, internal, 19
    imports from, 15.34
    non-ferrous metals from, 15.34
    steel from, 15.34, 18
    super-phosphate from, 15.34
Bell, G.K, 15.9
Bellenger, F.J, 2.2, 14.1, 14.2
benefits *see* social benefits
Benelux, 19
    balance of payments with, 15.34
    representation to International Materials
      Conference, 15.36
Bennitt, M.W, 15.21
benzole *see* chemicals, refineries, cleaning agents
Berlin, Germany, reparations discussions in, 19
Bermuda, export of coal to, 15.17
Berrill, K, 18
Berthoud, E.A, 15.36, 15.37
Bevan, A, 1, 2.1, 4.1, 11, 14.1, 14.2, 15.13, 15.17,
15.29, 15.35, 17.2, 18, 19
(Beveridge) Committee, Social Insurance and
  Allied Services, 19, 20.3, 21
Beveridge Plan, 2.1, 2.2, 7.2, 7.4
Beveridge Report, 1, 2.1, 2.2, 7.1, 7.4, 10, 11,
20.1
    on Social Insurance and Allied Services,
      17.1, 20.2
Beveridge, Sir William, 7.1, 7.9, 11, 14.2

Ceylon *see* Colombo
Chadwell Heath, Essex,
    factories in, 14.2
    Lewis Burger and Sons Ltd, 14.2
Chamberlain, N, 10
Champion Spark Plugs, Feltham, Middlesex,
    15.9
Chancellor of the Exchequer *see* Exchequer
Channel, tunnel, 18
Chantler, P, 15.23, 19
charges,
    canal, 3
    development, regulations on, 14.1
    docks, 3
    gas, 11, 15.35
    orders, 13.7
    water, 11
    see also transport, health
Charges Consultative Committee, 22.8
Charges, Committee on Development, 3
Charlton, T.A.G, 13.4, 13.5, 15.34, 15.37
Chatham House, Joint Committee of, 9
Chautier, P, 15.5
cheese *see* dairy products
Chelmsford, Essex, labour situation, 15.7
Cheltenham, Roy Feddon Ltd, Gloucestershire,
    factory proposal, 14.2
Cheltenham, Gloucestershire, Gloucester-
    Cheltenham, Working Party on Labour
    Situation in, 15.30
Chemical Industries, Imperial (ICI), 15.21, 15.23
Chemical Products Committee, 15.36
chemicals, 21
    alkali, 15.21, 15.35
        allocation of, 15.35
        production, 15.21, 15.23, 15.35
    ammonia, 15.21, 15.23
    benzole, refineries, 15.23
    British Petroleum Chemicals Ltd,
        Grangemouth, Scotland, 15.21, 15.23
    calcium carbide, 15.17
    carbon black, 14.3
        supplies of, 2.1
    carbonizing industries, 15.23, *see also* coal
        and coalmining
    caustic soda, 15.21
        allocation of, 15.35
        production of, 15.23
    chlorine, 15.21, 15.23
    Cobalt Committee, International Materials
        Committee, Manganese, Nickel and,
        15.36
    industry, 15.21
    manganese, 15.36
    Manganese, Nickel and Cobalt Committee,
        International Materials Committee, 15.36
    Monsanto Chemicals Ltd, Newport
        Monmouthshire, 15.21, 15.23

niobium (columbium), 15.36
nitric acid, 15.21, 15.23
    production, 15.23
nitrogenous fertilizers, 14.3
salt, 15.21, 15.23
soda ash, 15.16
soda, from Japan, 15.35
super-phosphate, import of, 15.34
see also sulphur, sulphuric acid
Cherwell, (Lord), 2.2, 7.2, 7.5, 11, 12, 17.1, 19
Cheshire,
    new towns, 14.1
    North, light industry, 14.2
Chester, D.N, 7.3, 7.8, 7.11, 7.12, 11, 19, 22
Chester, G, 7.14
Chiefs of Staff, function of, 7.11, 17.2
Chile, 15.34
    see also South America
China,
    exports to, 2.1, 2.2
    see also Far East
Chipping Ongar, Essex, new town, 14.2
chlorine *see* chemicals
chocolate *see* foodstuffs
Chorley-Blackburn-Preston, Lancashire, labour
    position, 15.14, 15.30
Chorley, Lancashire,
    defence programme and labour for defence
        in, 15.7
    labour position in, 22.7
chrome *see* metals
Chrysler Aircraft Ltd, 18
Churchill, Sir Winston, 2.1, 2.2, 3, 7.2, 7.5, 7.10,
    7.13, 10, 11, 17.2, 20
    papers, 17.1
cinematograph *see* film amd films
CIP *see* Industrial Productivity, Committee on
Citrine Committee, 21
Citrine, W, 7.14
civil aviation *see* aircraft
civil defence, 2.1, 11
    ARP building, 15.23
    building personnel in, 15.30
    capital investment, 15.21
    civil engineering personnel in, 15.30
    home,
        front, 5.1, 23.1
        guard, 11
    investment programme, 15.23
    London, 4.1
    manpower requirements, 15.30
    measures, Post Office, 18
    organizations, 18
    services, 11
    shelter policy, 18
    see also defence
Civil Defence Corps, 2.2

prices, US, 15.34
programme, 15.34
regulation scheme, 19
in short supply, 15.36
statistics of, 8
supply of, 13.5
see also goods
Commodity Groups, Central Group of Raw
  Materials and, 18
Commodity Policy,
  Subcommittee on Internal, 15.37
  Subcommittee on International, Trade
    Negotiations Committee, 15.36, 15.37,
    22.6
Commodity Policy Committee, 19
Commodity Policy Subcommittee, Trade
  Negotiations Committee, 15.13
Commodity and Relief Department, Postwar,
  Board of Trade, 21
Commonwealth, 15.34, 15.37, 20.3, 21
  aluminium production, 15.13, 15.35, 18
  conference, 3
  consultations, 2.2, 3
    on defence, 17.2
  customs union, 19
  development in, 19
  development plans, 18
  dispersal,
    of industry in, 11
    of population in, 11
  Dominion Officials, Committee of, 19
  Dominions, 7.14, 21
    and the European Recovery
      Programme, 15.13
    governments, exchange of information
      with, 9
    Mutual Aid Agreement, 17.1
    Prime Ministers, 2.1, 2.2, 16.2
    UK-Dominions Wool Disposals Ltd, 21
  economic resources, development of, 18
  emigration to, 15.12
  finance ministers, 2.1, 2.2, 17.2, 18
    meeting, 16.2, 19
  financial co-operation in a total war, 15.14
  Financial and Economic Relations with the
    US and other (sic) Commonwealth
    Countries, Working Party on, 13.11
  goods, duty on, 15.13
  High Commissioners, 15.36
  imports, duties on, 15.13
  meetings,
    on economy, 16.2
    on oil, 16.2
    on production, 16.2
    on supplies, 16.2
    on trade, 16.2
  minister, information on defence, 18
  ministers, meeting of, 15.13

and NATO, 15.14
  negotiations with, commercial policy, 7.14
  and non-ferrous metals, 15.36
  Prime Ministers, 17.2
  relations, 19
  Relations, secretary for, 15.36
  Sterling Area, aluminium production in,
    15.13, 15.23
  Sterling, UK exports to, 15.14
  stockpiling, co-ordination of, 15.36
  sugar policy, 15.13
  Supply Ministers' meeting, 18
  trade customs, 21
  trade, meetings on, 16.2
  UK exports to sterling, 15.14
  wool conference, 15.13
  wool for, 21
  see also colonial, colonies
Commonwealth Association, Europe, 18
Commonwealth Conference Development
  Working Party, 19
Commonwealth Consultative Committee, 16.2
Commonwealth Economic Affairs Committee,
  3, 15.9, 15.14, 18, 20.3
Working Group of, 15.10
Commonwealth Economic Conference, 19
Commonwealth Economic Development, 15.10
Commonwealth Finance Ministers, 15.12
Commonwealth Finance Ministers' Conference,
  3, 15.9, 15.13
  Working Party, 13.11
Commonwealth Finance Ministers' Meeting,
  15.10, 16.2, 19
Commonwealth and International Conferences,
  16.1, 16.2
Commonwealth Liaison Committee, 11, 15.36,
  16.2, 18, 22.3
Commonwealth Meeting on General Economic
  and Trade Questions, Working Group on
  Briefs for, 13.11
Commonwealth Officials on Economic Affairs in
  Colombo January 1950 Committee,
  Preparations for Meetings of, 13.11
Commonwealth Prime Ministers Committee,
  Preparation for Meeting of, 13.11, 16.2
Commonwealth Prime Ministers' Conference, 3
Commonwealth Prime Ministers' and Financial
  Ministers' Conferences, 20.2
Commonwealth Prime Ministers' Meeting,
  Working Party to Prepare Briefs on the
  General Economic Situation, 13.11
Commonwealth Relations Office, 13.5, 15.12,
  15.14, 15.36
Commonwealth Sterling Area, aluminium
  production in, 15.13, 15.23
Commonwealth Supply Council, 21
Commonwealth Supply Ministers' meeting, 18

1065

dollar, 2.1, 2.2, 18
economic, 20.3
management, 18
publicity, 18
see also fuel
Crookshank, (Lord), 7.2, 7.10
Croome, J.L, 15.21, 15.23, 15.37, 18
crops *see* farms and farming
Crow, G.B, 15.27
Crow, H, 15.5
Crowe, C.T, 15.34
Crowther, G, 7.9
Croydon, Surrey, power station at, 17.2
CSO *see* Statistical Office, Central
Cuba,
purchase of sugar from, 20.2
trade talks with, 15.13
see also Havana
Cumberland, West, 7.13, 21
development area, 14.2
roads, 14.2
Cunningham, Sir Graham, 15.21, 18, 22.8
Currency and Bank Notes Bill, 11
currency and currencies,
crisis, 12
hard, 13.2, 21
countries, 2.1
markets, 15.13, 15.37
hard and soft, 15.1, 15.9
scarce, 13.2
soft, 2.1, 18, 21
countries, 15.37
union, 18
see also bank and banks
Curtis, Miss M, 7.9
customs,
Commonwealth trade, 21
procedure, in USA, 15.9, 15.10
union, 2.1, 2.2, 3, 15.13, 19
between Commonwealth, 19
see also European Economic
Cooperation Committee
Customs and Excise, 19
proposals, 20.1
Customs Union Committee, 13.11
Customs Union Study Group, 15.10, 15.13,
15.37, 19, 21
European, 17.2
Interdepartmental, 15.13
Customs Union Working Party, European
Economic Community, European, 15.37
Customs Union, European, 15.13, 15.37, 22.2
Customs Unions, International Study Group on,
16.2
cutlery *see* household goods
cuts, 15.22, 20.3
post-devaluation, 18
cuts in,

building, distribution of, 15.21
coal exports, 2.1
docks capital investment, 15.21
electricity, 2.1, 2.2, 11
expenditure,
overseas, 13.2
overseas information, 17.2
public, 2.1, 15.13
finance, postwar, 22.1
food, 13.2
consumption, 2.2
import, 18
fuel and power industries, 18
imports, 13.2, 15.13, 15.34
by Australia, 18
investment, 19, 20.1, 22.7
investment, capital, 15.8, 15.13
on docks, 15.21
manpower, postwar, 22.1
programme, dock, 15.23
dollar, 15.13
investment, 2.1, 15.21
road, 15.21, 15.23
rationing, 13.2
raw materials, 15.34
Cyprus, pyrites in, 15.36
Czechoslovakia,
economic planning in, 19
exports to, 15.9
planning department, 18

Dagenham, Essex, Ford Motor Company, 14.2,
15.8, 15.35, 18
Dahrendorf, G, 18
Daily Express Newspapers Ltd, factory proposal,
14.2
Daily Graphic, 2.2
Daily News Ltd, factory proposal, 14.2
Daimler Co., 11
Dairy Husbandry Division, Livestock
Improvements and, Ministry of Agriculture
and Fisheries, 22.2
dairy produce,
butter, 2.1, 17.2, 18
from New Zealand, 17.2
butter, contract with Denmark, 18
cheese, 2.1, 15.34, 17.2
from New Zealand, 17.2
rationing, 2.1, 17.2
cream, 15.35
see also milk, foodstuff
Dairy Produce and Fats Group, Supply
Department, Ministry of Food, 22.3
dairying, 22.2
Dakin, S.A, 15.33
Dale, H, 12

Economic White Paper, Draft, 13.1
Economics and Statistics Division, Agricultural,
  Ministry of Agriculture and Fisheries, 22.2
economists, 1, 7.7, 18, 19
    advice to government, 17.2
    in government, 19, 20.3
    opinions on Economic Survey, 19
    pay and conditions of, 20.3
    in public administration, 19
    role of, 7.9, 7.10
    transfer between Britain and Australia, 3
Economists Conferences, Advisory, 22.2
Economist, The, 15.29
economy,
    drive, 15.32
    expansionist, 2.2
    external, 15.13
    internal, 15.13, 15.31
    national, 13.2, 15.10
    wartime, Germany, 19
    see also country and subject
Economy Committee, 22.3
    Admiralty Manpower, 22.1
    Steel, 15.27, 22.7
Economy Committee, Place of Agriculture in the
  National, 13.11
Economy Steering Committee, 15.12
Economy Subcommittee, 15.26
    Steel, 15.26, 15.27, 18
Economy in War Committee, National, 13.11,
  15.14
Economy, British War, 20.2
Economy, Defence and National, Meetings of
  Ministers, 13.11
Ede, J.Chuter, 2.2, 4.1, 14.1, 15.13, 15.17, 15.24,
  15.35
Eden, Sir Anthony, 7.2, 7.10
education,
    in agriculture, 22.2
    arithmetic, postwar, 19
    building, 15.21, 15.23
        programme, 15.35
        in Scotland and Wales, 15.21
    investment in, 15.35
    investment programme, 15.21, 15.23
    raising of the school leaving age, 2.2, 14.1,
      17.2
    school,
        building in Northern Ireland, 15.21,
          15.23
        buildings, 7.2, 14.2, 15.10
        material requirements, 15.23
        meals, 7.2
        public, 15.37
    see also Ministry of Education, training,
      universities
Education Department,
    building programme, 2.2, 4.1

    Scottish, 15.23, 15.33
Education Division, Training and, Treasury, 19,
  20.3
Edwards, F.L, 15.3
Edwards, J, 2.2, 14.1, 15.25, 15.26, 15.32, 15.35,
  17.2, 18, 20
Edwards, N, 2.2, 14.2, 15.8, 15.18, 15.25, 15.35,
  17.2
Edwards, R.P.S, 15.37
EEC *see* European Economic Community
Efficiency, *see also* individual subjects
Efficiency Committee, Controls and, 15.41, 20.3,
  21
egg and eggs, 2.1, 2.2, 13.5, 15.34, 18
    contract with Denmark, 18
    dried, from USA, 15.34
    export of, 15.13
    marketing, 22.2
    prices, 13.5, 15.35
    production, 2.2, 15.34. 2.1
    see also foodstuffs
Egg Policy, Working Party on Future, 18
Egg and Poultry Division, Ministry of
  Agriculture and Fisheries, 22.2
Egg Production, Working Party on Future, 15.34
Egypt,
    exports to, 15.9
    see also Middle East
Egypt, Working Party on, 15.37
Eire,
    balance of payments with, 15.34
    cattle, live, export to UK, 15.13
    coal export to, 15.17, 17.2
    coarse grain for, 13.5
    economical discussions with, 22.2
    exports to, 15.17
    Ministers, discussions with, 13.11
    recruitment of labour in, 22.2
    restriction of men from, 15.17
    trade,
        agreement with, 17.2
        negotiations with, 15.13, 15.35
        statistics, 13.5
    see also Northern Ireland, Ulster
Eire Committee, Economic Relations with, 13.11
El Alamein, 1
elderly persons *see* employment of
electric and electrical,
    contractors, steel for, 15.26
    cookers, 15.4
    energy consumption, 14.3
    fires, 15.4
    lighting companies, 22.4
    plant, 7.5
        heavy, 15.17, 18
    signs, restrictions on, 18
    street lighting, 15.32, 15.35, 18
    see also General Electric Co., hydro-electric

Food Distribution Committee, 3, 14.1, 15.37, 20.3, 22.3

Food Division, Agriculture and, Treasury, 20.3

Food Division, Milk, Milk Products and Welfare, Ministry of Agriculture and Fisheries, 22.2

Food Exports Committee, 22.3

Food Group of Labour Party, Agricultural and, 17.2, 22.2

Food Group, Agricultural, 17.2

Food Mission, British,
    Ottawa, 22.3
    Washington, 22.3

Food Policy Committee, 13.11, 15.37, 20.3
    Government Controls and, 6.4
    Interdepartmental Working Party of, 22.3

Food Policy Working Party, 3, 20.3

Food Problems, Scientific Advisory Committee on, 17.2

Food Production Committee, Concentration of, 22.3

Food Shortage Committee, World, 17.2

Food Standards Committee, 22.2, 22.3

Food Standards Division, Ministry of Agriculture and Fisheries, 22.2

Food Subcommittee, Programmes Committee, 15.34

Food Subsidies and the Cost of Living, Working Party on, 22.3

Food Supplies,
    Combined Working Party on European, 22.3
    Committee on, 11, 15.37

Food Supplies from SE Asia and Certain Other Countries, Official Committee on, 3, 15.13

Food Supplies from SE Asia, Official Committee on, 15.13

Food Supply Board, 22.3

Food Supply Committee, Points, 22.3

Food Survey,
    Family, 22.3
    National, 22.3
    Wartime, 22.3

Food, Department of, 7.9, 15.33

foodstuffs, 19
    castor oil, allocation, 15.26
    chocolate, 15.4, 22.3
    cocoa, 22.3
    coffee, 22.3
    confectionery, 15.4, 22.3
    preserves, 15.4
    pulses, 22.3
    salt,
        industry, 15.23
        Murgatroyd's Saltworks Ltd, Sandbach, Cheshire, 15.21, 15.23
    see also alcohol, bread, cereal and cereals, dairy produce, egg and eggs, fats, fish, flour, fruit, groundnuts, meat, milk, rice, sugar, tea, vegetables

Foodstuffs Committee, Machinery of Distribution of Unrationed, 22.3

Foot, D, 7.9, 7.10

Foot, R, 11

Footscray, Kent, Standard Telephones and Cables Ltd, 14.2

footwear,
    boot and shoe industry, 4.1
    industry, 4.1, 15.4
    see also clothes and clothing, leather

Footwear and Allied Industries Corporation, Leather, 21

Footwear, Directorate of Civilian, 21

Forbes, Sir A, 15.35, 18

Forbes Adams, B, 15.37

Forbes Watson, J, 7.14

Ford Motor Company, Dagenham, Essex, 14.2, 15.8, 15.35
    expansion, 15.35
    expansion programme, 18

forecasts, 15.31
    balance of payments, 15.12, 15.15, 20.2
    budget, 20.1
    economic, 19
    export, 19, 21
    manpower, 22.5
    national expenditure, 8, 15.31
    savings, domestic, 15.31
    wartime, 19

Forecasts, Working Party on National Income, 8, 15.31, 19, 20.1

Foreign Office, 3, 7.9, 13.5, 15.12, 15.13, 15.14, 15.33, 15.34, 15.35, 15.36, 18, 19
    planning staff, 3
    Swedish representations to, 15.36

Foreign Secretary, 21

foreign see individual subjects

forest and forestry, 14.1, 14.2, 20.3
    afforestation in South Wales, 15.8
    employment in, 14.2
    labour supply for, 15.8
    products research laboratory, 15.26
    roads, 14.2, 15.8, 15.21, 15.23

Forestry Act, 1945, 22.2

Forestry Commission, 14.2, 15.23, 21, 22.2
    capital investment, 15.21
    investment programme, 15.23

Forsyth, J.M, 15.37, 19

Forth Road Bridge, Scotland, 7.2, 14.1, 15.35

Foster, E.S, 15.5

Foster, M.B. and Sons, Brentford, Middlesex, 15.8

Foster, S, 7.9

Fowler, R.F, 6.2, 15.37

franc see French franc

France, 1, 15.14, 15.34
    balance of payments, 2.1
    deficit, 2.2

negotiations with, sterling balance, 15.13
Secretary of State for, 17.1
trade questions, 3
wheat supplies for, 17.2
see also Asia, Pakistan
India and Pakistan Working Party on Capital
Goods, 18
India, Secretary of State for, 17.1
Indies, Netherlands *see* Netherlands
Indonesia,
exports to, 15.9
see also Far East
Industrial Building Subcommittee, 15.22
Industrial Capacity Committee, Production
Council, 21
Industrial Classification, Interdepartmental
Committee on, 8
Working Party, 8
Industrial Coal Consumers' Council, 22.4
Industrial Commission, 7.2, 7.8
(Industrial) Committee,
Board of Trade Regional Procedure, 20.3,
21
Regional Committee, 11
Industrial Conference, National, 2.2, 11, 14.1,
14.5, 15.28, 22.5
Industrial Council,
Admiralty, 22.1
Departmental Joint, 22.9
Industrial Court, 22.5
Industrial Departments, Regional Organization
of Trade and, 11
Industrial Development Board, 7.2
Industrial Development Certificates, 21
Industrial Efficiency, Steering Committee for, 21
Industrial Electronics Panel, 14.3
Industrial Estates, Consultative Committee on,
21
Industrial Group, Northern, 11
Industrial Information about the UK
Committee, Working Party on Security of
Economic and, 13.11
Industrial Information Division, Ministry of
Labour, 22.5
Industrial Management Committee, 21
Industrial Mobility, Committee on, 22.5
Industrial Organization Bill, 2.1, 2.2, 14.1, 17.2,
21
Industrial Organization and Development Act,
21, 1947, 2.1, 15.35
Industrial Problems,
Ministerial Committee on, 19
Ministerial and Official Subcommittees on,
Reconstruction Committee, 11
Ministerial Subcommittee on,
Reconstruction Committee, 7.5, 7.6, 7.13
Official Committee on, Home Affairs
Committee, 11, 15.20

Official Subcommittee on, Reconstruction
Committee, 7.6, 11, 15.20, 21
Subcommittee on, 7.5
Industrial Problems Export Questions,
Ministerial Subcommittee on, 7.5, 17.1
Subcommittee, 4.2, 11, 19
Industrial Productivity, Committee on, 11, 14.3,
15.12, 15.33, 15.35, 18, 20.3, 21
Panel on Import Substitution, 18
Panel on Technology and Operational
Research, 15.33
Working Party for the Panel on Human
Factors, 15.33
Industrial Rehabilitation Units, 22.5
Industrial Research Associations, 14.3
Industrial Research, Department of Scientific
and, 14.3, 15.8, 15.10, 15.21, 15.23, 15.33,
15.35, 18
Industrial Staff) Division, Establishments
(Professional, Scientific, Technical and,
Treasury, 20.3
Industrial Subcommittee,
Home Affairs, 4.2, 15.20
Lord President's Committee, 2.2, 4.3, 6.3,
7.5, 14.5, 15.10, 15.28, 15.37, 18, 19
Official, Reconstruction Committee, 11
Industrial Subcommittee on Export Questions,
Reconstruction Committee, 11
Industrial Subcommittee of the Reconstruction
Committee, 22.2
Industrial Supplies Department, Board of Trade,
21
Industrial Working Parties of Board of Trade,
19, 21
industrialists, 18
refugee, 7.5, 11
industrialization, Japanese and overseas, 7.5
Industries Committee,
Improvements in Undermanned, 21
Key, 21
Productivity in the Socialized, 13.11
Socialization of, 2.2, 15.37, 17.2, 22.4
Subcommittee on Relations with
Workers in Socialized Industries,
13.11
Industries Fair, British, 15.12
Industries and Manufacturers, 1, 2, 3, 4, 21
Industries and Manufacturers Department,
Board of Trade,
Engineering Division, 21
Priorities Division, 21
Industries in Overseas Markets, Working Party
on Competitive Ability of UK, 19
Industries, Board of Trade Committee on
Improvements in Undermanned, 15.10, 19
Industries, Boards of Socialized, 17.2
Industries, Committee on Improvement in
Undermanned, 15.10, 19

labour, *cont.*

to industries, unattractive, 15.29
international agencies, 22.5
mobile force, 7.2, 7.4, 7.8, 14.2
mobility of, 19, 22.5
occupational trends, 19
problems and defence production, 18
redeployment of, 11, 15.24
regional policy, 22.5
relations, 15.33
requirements, 21
    wartime, 22.7
    see also individual industries
    reservation of, 15.30
    in *see* individual places and industries
shortages, 11, 17.2
    gas industry, 2.1
supply, 3, 14.5, 15.7, 15.30, 22.5, 23.1
supply to *see* individual industries
targets, 15.21
transfer of, 15.7
volunteer, 2.1
withdrawal of, 15.30 *see also* Communist,
    employment, manpower, recruitment *and*
    individual industries and towns
Labour Committee, 11, 15.18, 15.24, 15.29
Labour Committee, Foreign, 2.2, 11, 15.18,
    15.24, 17.2, 22.5
Labour Conference, International, Paris, 2.2, 3
Labour Controls, Official Committee on, 2.2, 6.3
Labour Co-ordinating Committee, 21, 22.5
    Official, 14.1
Labour Government, 1, 2, 5.2, 15.10
Labour and Labour Relations, Coal Division,
    Ministry of Fuel and Power, 22.4
Labour Organization, International, 22.5
Labour Party, 2.1, 11, 15.13, 15.29, 18
    Agricultural and Food Group, 17.2, 22.2
    Finance Group, 20.1
    Independent, 1
    Keeping Left pamphlet, 20.2
    London, 11
    pamphlets, 11
Labour Position in Bridgwater, Working Party
    on, 15.30
Labour Preference Committee, 22.7
Labour Situation in Bristol and Weston-super-
    Mare, Working Party on, 15.30
Labour Situation in Gloucester-Cheltenham,
    Working Party on, 15.30
Labour Supply Committee for Building Materials
    and Components, 22.7
Labour Supply, Working Party on Agricultural,
    22.2
Labour (Textile Industries) Committee, 15.25,
    15.30, 15.35
Labour, Interdepartmental Committee for
    Employment of Supplementary, 21

Labour, National Council of, Liaison
    Committee, 17.2
Labour, South Wales Regional Council of, 11
Labour, Working Party on Reservation and
    Withdrawal of, 15.30
Laithwaite, G, 5.2
Lam, M.P, 15.36
Lambert, V.A.G, 15.27
Lanarkshire, 11, 14.2, 15.8
    Coltness Foundry, Newmains, 15.8
Lancashire,
    cotton industry, 18
    distribution of industry in, 18
    light industry, 2.1, 14.2
    textile industry, 15.25
land,
    acquisition, 2.2, 7.2, 7.7, 14.1, 15.35, 21
        City of London, 14.1
        for essential civilian needs, 14.1
        highways, 22.8
        for roads, 14.2
        for roadworks, 11
    agricultural, 14.1, 20.1
        loss of, 14.1
        marginal, 14.1
    compulsory purchase of, 7.13, 14.1
    derelict, 14.2, 15.8, 21
    encroachment in Scotland, 14.1
    grassland, development, 22.2
    Grassland and Crop Improvement Division,
        Ministry of Agriculture and Fisheries, 22.2
    improvement in Highlands, 15.35
    improvement loans, 22.2
    management of, 22.2
    marginal, 2.1, 2.2, 17.2
    requisition for defence, 14.1
    restoration after floods, 2.2
    use, economic control of, 4.1
    War Office requirements of, 2.2 *see also*
        farms and farming, woodland
Land Army, Women's *see* Women's Land Army
Land Board, Central, 14.1
Land Commission, Agricultural, 22.2
Land Drainage, Water Supplies and Building
    Division, Ministry of Agriculture and
    Fisheries, 22.2
Land Drainage, Water Supplies and Machinery
    Division, Ministry of Agriculture and
    Fisheries, 22.2
Land Fund, National, 20.1
Land Settlement Society, Welsh, 22.2
Land Subcommission, Welsh Agricultural, 22.2
Land Use Division, Ministry of Agriculture and
    Fisheries, 22.2
Laski, H, 7.9
Latin America *see* South America
law,
    company, 21

negotiations, *cont.*
 sterling balances, 15.13, 18
 tariff, 21
  at Annecy, 15.13
  in Geneva, 2.1, 2.2
  multi-lateral, 15.13
 Torquay, 17.2
 see also trade negotiations
Negotiations Committee Division, Overseas,
 Treasury, 20.3
Negotiations Committee, Overseas, 3, 11, 13.11,
 15.1, 15.9, 15.13, 15.14, 15.26, 15.35, 15.37,
 18, 20.3, 22.8
 Working Party, 3, 15.34, 21
 Working Party on Exports of Finished Steel,
  13.11
Neill, J, 14.3
Nelson, G, 7.14
Nelson, Lancashire,
 /Burnley, district hostels, 15.35
 textile workers' hostels, 15.25
Netherlands, 15.34
 bacon agreement with, 15.13
 balance of payments with, 13.4
 economic policy in, 19
 export to, 15.9
 monetary area, 15.34
Netherlands Antilles, dollar expenditure in,
 15.34
Netherlands East Indies, 15.34
 balance of payments with, 13.4
New Hebrides, sulphur in, 15.36
New Jersey, USA, Standard Oil Company, 15.10,
 15.13
new towns, 14.1, 14.2, 15.21, 21, 22.8
 capital cost to public funds, 14.2
 Cheshire, 14.1
 Development Corporations, 14.1
 development finance, 14.1
 industrial development in, 18
 licenced premises, 14.1
 manufacturing industry in, 15.21
 in mining areas, 14.2
 programme, 14.1
 Scotland, 14.1, 14.2, 15.23
 South Wales, 14.1, 17.2
 transport services in, 14.2
 Wales, 18
 see also town and country planning
new towns: towns,
 Aycliffe, Durham, 14.2
 Bracknell, Berkshire, 14.1
 Chipping Ongar, Essex, 14.2
 Congleton, Cheshire, 14.1
 Corby, Northants, 14.1
 Durham, 14.2
 Harlow, Essex, 14.2
 Hemel Hempstead, Hertfordshire, 14.2
 Houston, Scotland, 14.1

 Mobberley, Cheshire, 14.1, 14.2
 Peterlee, Durham, 14.1
 Pitsea-Laindon, Essex, 14.1
New Towns Bill, 14.1
New Year Honours List, 15.12
New York, Economic Employment Commission,
 19
New Zealand, 17.2
 bulk purchase of food from, 17.2
 butter from, 17.2
 cheese from, 17.2
 development in, 18
 development talks with, 15.13
 economic planning visit to, 15.12
 economic policy, 15.13
 High Commissioner, 18
 meat from, 17.2
 planning talks with, 15.13
 social policy, 15.13
 UK import programme from, 15.34
Newcastle, Salop, 15.21
Newcastle, Wallsend, 11
Newling, A.J, 15.30
Newport, Monmouthshire, 15.23
 Monsanto Chemicals Ltd, 15.21, 15.23
Newsome, N.F, 11
news bulletins, Chancellor of the Exchequer, 20.3
newspapers,
 circulation of, 15.13, 17.2
 Daily Graphic, 2.2
 distribution of, 15.35
 Financial Times, 15.36
 industry,
  building applications for, 11
  building in, 15.21, 15.23, 15.35
  building work in, 15.35
 Kemsley Newspapers (London), 2.2
 Kemsley Newspapers Ltd., factory proposal,
  2.2
 newsprint, 11
  export of, 15.9
  licensing, 17.2
  supply of, 2.2, 17.2
  to Australia, 17.2
 size of, 2.2, 15.13, 15.35
 The Economist, 15.29
 Tribune, attack on Civil Servants, 20.2
 see also journalism
NFU *see* Farmers' Union, National
Nicholson, E.M, 1, 3, 6.6, 11, 14.1, 14.3, 14.4,
 14.5, 15.10, 15.12, 15.14, 15.23, 15.33, 17.2,
 18, 19
nickel *see* metals
Nigeria,
 groundnuts in, 18
 railways in, 18
 see also Africa
niobium *see* metals

Oil Conversion and Mining Supplies
Subcommittee, Coal, 15.2
Oil Expansion Programme, Working Party on,
13.11, 18, 20.3
Oil Working Party, 13.11, 18
Subcommittee on UK Consumption
(General), 13.11
Subcommittee on UK Consumption (Road
and Rail), 13.11
oil refineries,
Caltex Ltd, 15.8
capacity, expansion of, 13.11
investment programme, 18
new, 15.8
Stanlow, Cheshire, 15.23
United Kingdom, 14.2
Vacuum Oil Co. Ltd, 15.8
Oil Requirements, Working Parties on Purchases
of Rice and Services, Exchange Requirements
Committee, 13.11
Oil Storage, Subcommittee on, 15.37
Oil Supplies in War, Committee on, 17.2
Oil, Committee on, 17.2
oils and fats *see* fats
Oldham, Lancashire,
Shaw, General Electric Company, 15.8
textile workers' hostels, 15.25
Oldham/Rochdale, Lancashire, district hostels,
15.35
Operation Albert, 20.2
Operation Bonfire, Board of Trade, 18
Operation Diogenes, 19
Orders Committee, Ministry of Food, 22.3
Orders *see* individual subjects
organization, of *see* individual subjects
Organization Committee,
Regional, 11, 21
Treasury, 18, 20.2, 20.3
Organization for European Economic Co-
operation (OEEC), 1, 2.1-2, 3, 11, 13.5, 15.9,
15.10, 15.12, 15.21, 15.23, 15.31, 15.33-4,
15.36-7, 17.2, 18, 22.4-5, 22.7
activity in field of agriculture, 13.4
activity in field of food, 13.4
allocation of coal, 15.36
Coal Committee, 15.36
commitments, 13.5
Consultative Group, 15.34
controls in, 15.36
Council meeting, 15.36
Council of, 18
Council, Ministerial OEEC, 15.36
deficit, 18
delegation to Washington, 15.36
Food and Agriculture Committee, 22.2
French delegation to, 13.5
import programmes, 15.34
investments in, 18

Italian delegation to, 13.5
long-term programme, 13.5
member countries, financial stability of, 19
NATO relationship with, 19
policy on raw materials, 15.36
programme, Balance of Payments, 18
Programmes Committee, 18
raw materials studies in, 15.36
statistics on, 8
and sterling area, 13.5
Stikker-Marjolin Plan, 18
Submissions of Other Participants, Working
Party on 1950-1951 OEEC, 13.11
surplus, 18
Third report, 15.14
Working Group on OEEC, 13.11
UK delegation to, 16.2
Organization and Methods, 21
Organization and Methods Division,
Establishment Department, Ministry of
Food, 22.3
Treasury, 20.3
Organization for Raw Materials,
Washington, 18
Washington and Soviet Bloc, 15.36
Organization Subcommittee, Regional, 15.37
Organization, Brussels Treaty *see* Brussels
Orr, J.G, 7.3
Ottawa, Canada,
British Food Mission, 22.3
discussions in, 15.13
meetings, 2.1, 2.2
output,
agricultural, 22.2
expansion of, 15.31
per head, 15.33
and prices policy, 19
regulation of, 19
targets for coal, 19
The Battle for Output 1947, COI, 11
see also production, productivity
Output Analysis Branch, Agricultural Economic
Unit, 22.2
Output Committee, Agricultural, 2.2, 11, 15.12,
15.13, 15.14, 18, 22.2
Working Party, 18
Overseas Committees etc. *see* individual subjects
overseas *see* home and overseas *and* individual
subjects
Overton, Sir Arnold, 7.7, 7.8, 7.9, 19
Owen, A.D.K, 7.9
Owen, G.S, 14.4, 15.1, 15.2, 15.37
Oxford University Club, 11

packaging,
for export, 15.1, 15.35
materials, supply of, 18

capital investment, 15.21
deep water quays, Leith, Scotland, 15.21
emergency planning, 22.8
facilities for monster tankers, 15.23
free, 14.2, 22.8
harbours, 18
    capital investment, 15.21
    Shoreham scheme, Sussex, 15.23
and inland waterways, 19
    programme, 15.23
labour force in, 22.5, 22.8
South Wales, 14.2
turn-round of shipping in, 15.35
warehousing, 15.21, 15.23
see also docks, ships and shipping *and*
    individual ports
Ports, Working Party on Shipping Turn-round
  in British, Ministry of Transport, 18
Portsmouth, 18
    Easter Road maintenance scheme, 15.8
    unemployment in, 15.8
Portugal,
    bilateral negotiations with, 15.13
    engineering goods to, 15.9
    exports to, 15.9
    trade negotiations with, 15.36
    trade with, 15.34
Portway Lead Mine, Matlock, Derbyshire, 15.36
Post Office, 15.23, 15.33, 18
    capital investment programme, 15.23
    civil defence measures, 18
    engineering and allied staff wages, 15.35
    investment programme, 15.21
    manipulative grades, wages, 15.35
    tariffs, 2.2
    telephone,
        exchange equipment, 19
        services, 15.21
    wages, 15.35
Postmaster-General, 15.33
postwar,
    policy, 7.1, 10, 22.3 *see also* individual
        subjects
potato(es), 15.13
    distribution, 2.1, 17.2
    production, private, 2.2
    supplies, 2.2
    targets, 2.1
    see also vegetables
Potter-Hyndley mission, 2.2
pottery,
    for export, 15.9, 15.13
    industry, 4.1, 21
        domestic, 15.23
    see also household goods
pottery-making machinery, 15.1
poultry,
    fowl pest, 15.35

import, 15.35
marketing, 22.2
see also livestock, meat
Poultry Division, Egg and, Ministry of
  Agriculture and Fisheries, 22.2
Poultry and Pests Division, Horticulture,
  Ministry of Agriculture and Fisheries, 22.2
pound,
    -dollar exchange rate, 21
    devaluation of, 17.2
    see also sterling
power, water, 15.17
Power) Bill, Ministers (Transfer of, 7.10, 11
Power Station at Bankside Committee, Proposed
  Erection of, 13.11
power stations, 15.2
    Bankside, London, 2.1, 2.2, 11, 17.2
    coal for, 15.32
    Croyden, Surrey, 17.2
    equipment, 15.35
    fuel stockbuilding, 15.17
    Fulham, London, 18
    location of, 2.2, 11
    Poplar, London, 2.2
    priority for, 15.32
    Rotherhithe, London, 17.2
    sabotage at, 2.1
    siting of, 22.4
    stocks and supplies, 15.17
    supplies to, 15.17
    Woolwich, London, 11, 17.2
        proposed, 15.17
    see also electricity
Power, Research Committee Subcommittee on
  Competitive, Board of Trade, 21
powers,
    economic, permanent, 14.1
    emergency, 2.1, 2.2, 3, 4.4, 5.1, 7.2, 11, 13.8,
        14.1, 15.5, 17.1, 17.2
    of licensing, 21
    negative, 13.8
    positive, 13.8, 17.2
        to manufacture, 13.7
        to purchase, 13.7
        to sell, 13.7
    purchasing, 15.23, 20.3
    to control,
        consumption, 13.7
        distribution, 13.7
        production, 13.7
    to expand demand, 13.8
    to requisition, 14.1
    to restrict demand, 13.8
    in transition, 11
Powers Act, Emergency, 13.2
Powers) Act, Supplies and Services (Transitional,
  1, 2.1, 11, 17.2
Powers Bill,

Roy Feddon Ltd, Cheltenham, Gloucestershire,
factory proposal, 14.2
Royal Air Force,
camp at Carluke, 17.2
manpower in, 2.2
rehabilitation centre, Leatherhead, Surrey,
15.21 *see also* armed forces
Royal Commissions, Institutes etc. *see* individual
subjects
Royal Naval Engineering College, Plymouth,
Devon, 18
Royal Navy,
apprentices in, 15.29
release of doctors from, 2.2
see also armed forces, navy and naval
Royal Ordnance Factories, 4.1, 15.1, 15.7, 15.33,
22.9
Hayes, Middlesex, 15.35
labour requirements, 15.13
manpower requirements, 15.7
Radway Green, Cheshire, 15.13, 18
Swynnerton, Working Party on the
Recruitment of Labour to, 15.30
Swynnerton and Radway Green, 15.7
Swynnerton, Staffordshire, 15.13, 18
RSA *see* Sterling Area, Rest of
rubber, 14.1, 15.36, 21
allocation to Soviet Bloc, 15.36
allocations, international, 18
Anglo-American talks on, 15.36
conference, 15.36
economy in road haulage, 22.8
industry, 14.1, 15.23
international meetings, 15.36
negotiations, international, 18
output in Malaya, 15.36
stockpiles, 15.36
supply, 15.26
tyres, 2.1, 15.26
Rubber Committee, London, 21
Rubber Conference,
Inter-governmental, Rome, 1951, 15.36
International, invitation of Germany to,
15.36
Rubber Consultative Committee, 21
Rumney, Wales, 14.2
Runcorn-Widnes bridge, Cheshire, 18
rural,
areas, 2.1
electricity supply to, 22.2
electrification, 7.2
housing, 11, 14.1
sewerage, 18
Rural Resources, National Survey of, 22.2
Russell, L.O, 14.3
Russell Vick Committee, 2.2, 17.2
Russia, 7.5
balance of payments with, 15.34

five year plan, 8
full employment in, 2.2
government of, 1
Iron Curtain countries, representations to
IMC, 15.36
'Kaganovitch' ice breaker, 15.35
machine tools from UK, 17.2
negotiations with, 15.13
orders with Craven Brothers, 17.2
purchase of coarse grains from, 15.13, 17.2
Soviet Bloc, allocation of rubber to, 15.36
Soviet Bloc and Washington Raw Materials
Organization, 15.36
sulphur supplies from, 15.36
timber,
contract with, 15.13
from, 15.26
trade,
Anglo-Soviet, 17.2
negotiations with, 15.13
relations, Anglo-Russian, 3
talks, Anglo-Soviet, 13.2, 17.2
with, 21
unemployment in, 19
see also Communist
Russia and Eastern European Countries
Committee, Export of Strategic Materials to,
EEC, 13.11
Russian Trade Agreement, Anglo-, 22.7
Rutherglen, Scotland, 14.2
Rutley, P, 23.1
Ryan, C.N, 15.30
Ryan Committee, 20.3, 22.2

safety,
in employment, 7.9, 22.5
in industry, 7.9
road traffic, 22.8
see also employment, health, welfare
St. Helena, unemployment on, 22.2
St. Helens, Lancashire, factories, 14.2
salaries *see* wage and wages
salt *see* foodstuff
Salter, Sir Arthur, 22.8
Salzgitter Steelworks, 18
Samson Stripper, 18
Samson Strippers, Working Party on, 18
sanction and sanctions,
economic, against Persia, 3
price, 15.13, 15.14, 21
Sandbach, Cheshire, Murgatroyd's Salt Works
Ltd, 15.21, 15.23
Sandys, D (Lord), 2.2, 7.2
Saunders, C.T, 5.3, 13.11, 15.31, 15.34, 19
sausages *see* meat
Savage, A, 15.7, 15.12, 15.30
saving and savings, 20.3

Russian ice-breaker, 'Kaganovitch', 15.35
seamen, 2.1
shipments,
    of coal, 22.8
    of food, 17.2
shortage, 18
space for North Atlantic tourists, 15.13
statistics, 18, 22.8
Steamship Owners' Association, Liverpool,
    11, 20.1
supplies to ships' shops, 15.9
surplus for scrap, 15.35
survey of postwar, 11
tankers,
    monster, 15.23
    oil, 15.35
tonnage, dry cargo, 2.2
training, 22.8
trawlers, release of, 2.2
turnround, 18
    in UK ports, 15.35
US, 22.8
    dry cargo, 2.2
    see also Admiralty, docks, harbours,
        merchant shipping, naval and navy, ports,
        scrap
shoe industry *see* footwear
shop and shops,
    lighting, 15.35, 18
    supplies to ships', 15.9
    see also retail
shopping trends, 15.4
Shoreham harbour scheme, Sussex, 15.23
Short Bros, (Rochester and Bedford) Ltd., 14.2
Short Bros, Rochester, Kent, 17.2
Short and Harland Ltd., 14.2
shortages, 1, 21
    and defence, 15.14
    investment in period of, 15.3
    of/ *see* individual commodities
Siam,
    rice supplies from, 2.1
    see also Far East
sickness benefit *see* social benefits
Siegbert, H, 15.34
silage *see* farms and farming
silica bricks *see* bricks
silk,
    exports, 15.9
    see also fibres
Silkin, L (later Lord), 4.1, 14.1, 14.2, 15.13
silver *see* metals
Simon, Viscount, 7.10
Simpson, J.R, 15.19
Sinclair, Sir Robert, 2.2, 3, 5.4, 7.10, 18, 21
Singer sewing machines, 15.9
    export of, 15.1, 15.9
sisal, 15.36

allocation for export, 15.26
exports, 15.1, 15.26
see also fibres
slate,
    industry in N.Wales, 17.2
    industry, survey of Welsh, 18
    see also mines and mining
slump, 13.8, 15.28
    anti-slump preparations, 18
    in USA, 11
    world, 19
smallholdings, *see also* agriculture and
    agricultural
Smallholdings Advisory Council, 14.1
Smieton, M, 6.3, 7.11, 15.7, 15.30, 22.5
Smith, Sir Ben, 2.2, 4.1, 4.3, 11, 14.1, 14.2, 22.3,
    22.7
Smith, C.D, 13.9, 15.3, 15.21, 15.22, 15.23, 15.26
Smith, F.W, 15.23, 15.37, 18
Smithfield, London,
    market, 17.2
        drivers' strike, 2.1
        strike, 2.2
soap *see* cleaning agents
social,
    benefits,
        family allowances, 2.1, 7.2, 17.2, 19,
            20.1
        injury, in industry, 2.2
        sickness, 2.1, 2.2, 17.2
        training, 7.4
        unemployment, 2.1, 2.2, 7.4, 14.1, 22.5
        see also employment, health, insurance,
            pensions, welfare
    insurance *see* insurance, pensions,
        unemployment
    policy,
        Australian, 15.13
        New Zealand, 15.13
    security, 1, 2.2, 7.1, 7.2, 7.4, 7.8, 10
        contributions, 19
        plan, 17.1
    services, 2.1, 5.1, 7.4
        capital expenditure on, 20.3
        expenditure on, 2.1, 13.11, 20.1
        public, 18
    welfare *see* welfare
Social Council, Economic and, 2.2, 15.36, 19,
    20.2
Social and Economic Research,
    Interdepartmental Committee on, 21
Social Reconstruction Survey, 11, 19
    Nuffield College, 9
Social Service Division, Treasury, 20.3
Social Survey, 2.2, 11, 15.10, 15.25, 18
    Wartime, 11
socialization, 3
    of aviation, 3

socialization, *cont.*
> of coal, 19
> of electricity, 3
> of gas, 3
> of industries, 3, 19
> of iron and steel, 3
> problems of, 19
> of transport, 3
> *see also* nationalization

Socialization of Industries,
> Ministerial Committee on, 3
> Official Committee on, 11, 15.37

Socialization of Industries Committee, 2.2, 15.37, 17.2, 22.4
> Subcommittee on Relations with Workers in Socialized Industries, 13.11

Socialization of Industry, Cabinet Committees on, 22.8

socialized,
> boards, 11
> industries, 11, 13.8, 15.23, 15.33, 18
> > efficiency in, 2.2
> > public accountability of, 2.2
> > wages in, 4.2, 14.2

Socialized Industries,
> Boards of, 17.2
> Working Party on Price Policy in, 13.7

Socialized Industries Committee, Productivity in, 13.11

soda ash *see* chemicals

soda *see* chemicals

soft currency *see* currency and currencies

softwood *see* wood

Solbury, (Lord), 7.9

Solicitor's Branch, Ministry of Fuel and Power, 22.4

solvency, 18

Soskice, Sir F, 2.2

Sound City Film Studios, Shepperton, Middx, 14.2

South Africa,
> 'Aid to Britain' Fund, 18
> coal from, 2.1, 17.2
> export of coal wagons to, 17.2
> financial relations with, 18
> import controls in, 19
> information received from, 9
> International Materials Committee, membership of, 15.36
> loan from, 17.2
> trade with, 15.34

South America,
> exports to, 15.9
> Latin America,
> > arms for, 15.13
> > trade policies in, 9
> > US trade policies in, 9
> marketing in, 18
> *see also* individual countries

South Wales *see* Wales, South

Southern Rhodesia, 17.2
> allocations to, 15.36
> export of coal to Argentina, 15.1
> iron steel alloys, 18
> locomotives and wagons to, 15.1
> *see also* Rhodesia, Northern Rhodesia

Southwood, (Lord), 9

Soviet *see* Russia

Spaak, P.H, 15.13

Spain, 15.34
> Anglo-Spanish trade and payments negotiations, 15.13
> exports to, 15.9
> membership of Sulphur Committee of IMC, 15.36
> trade negotiations with, 15.13

Sparks, A.C, 13.11, 15.34, 15.36

spectacles *see* health

Spivs and Drones Working Party, 2.2

sport,
> dog racing,
> > during coal crisis, 17.2
> > midweek, 11
> football, midweek, 11
> greyhound racing, 15.17, 15.35
> > regulation of, 14.1
> midweek, 2.2, 3, 11, 15.32, 15.35, 17.2, 20.2, 21
> > limitation of, 15.17
> > regulation of, 15.10
> playing fields, use of, 14.1
> race meetings, regulation of, 14.1
> regulation of, 14.1
> weekday, 2.1
> weekly events, limitation of, 15.10
> *see also* entertainment

Sport, Working Party on Mid-week, 15.32

Squires Gate, Lancashire, Hawker Aircraft Ltd, 15.8

Sri Lanka *see* Colombo

Stability, Working Party on Internal Financial, 19

stabilization, 7.7, 7.8
> of company profits, 20.1
> fund, 9, 19
> of international trade, 19
> of national income, 19
> policy, 7.1, 7.4, 7.7, 14.5, 19
> price, 11
> price, Grondona plan for, 19
> retail price, 19

Stabilization of Wages,
> Official Working Party on, 18
> Working Party on, 2.2, 22.5

Stabilization Working Party, Wage, 20.3

Stacy, R.J.W, 14.2

Stafford, J, 15.9, 15.21, 19

1164

discussions, 15.12

talks, 15.10

Economic Committee (Washington), 15.37, 18

Economic Minister to, 15.37

European Recovery Programme
organization in, 17.2, 20.2

European Recovery Programme UK
Treasury and Supply delegation,
Washington, 16.2

financial talks, 2.2

Food Council, International Emergency,
Washington, 22.3

information sent to Harold Butler, 9

Lord Privy Seal's visit to, 15.36, 18, 22.6

Materials Conference, International, 15.36

meetings, 20.2

mission to, 13.2

Mutual Aid Agreement, Washington talks,
2.2, 19

negotiations, 21

OEEC delegation to, 15.36

oil,

discussions, 5.2

negotiations in, 15.13

talks, 15.10

Raw Materials Organization and Soviet
Bloc, 15.36

talks, 2.2, 13.2

publicity for, 2.2

tin discussions, 15.36

Treasury Mission to, 20.3

visit to,

by Chancellor of the Exchequer, 18, 19,
20.2

by Lord Privy Seal, 15.36

by Prime Minister, 2.1, 18, 20.2

see also United States of America

water, 2.1

charges, 11

main supply,

Cricklewood, London, 15.21, 15.23

Kempton, Salop, 15.23

nationalization of, 17.2

power, 15.17

reservoir, Liverpool, Merseyside, 15.23

resources, 22.4

supply, 11, 14.2, 15.21

in development areas, 14.2

in Scotland, 15.23

to hospitals, 15.21

tanks, controls on, 15.4

works, reservoir, 15.23

Water Board, Fylde (District of Lancashire),
15.23

trunk main, 15.21

Water Board, Metropolitan, 15.23, 15.28

supply main, 15.21

Water Supplies and Building Division, Land
Drainage, Ministry of Agriculture and
Fisheries, 22.2

Water Supplies and Machinery Division, Land
Drainage, Ministry of Agriculture and
Fisheries, 22.2

waterways,

Canal Committee, Central, 22.8

canals, 2.2, 15.23, 18

charges, 3

control of, 22.8

improvements to, 11

inland, 15.23, 19, 22.8

capital investment, 15.21

programme, 15.23

see also transport

Watford, Hertfordshire, Shell Refining and
Marketing Co., 14.2

Watkin, G, 7.9

Watkinson, L, 15.32

Watson and Sons (Electro-medical) Ltd, 14.2

Watson, G.N, 15.37

Watts-Hilger-Swift Group, Grange Hill Estate,
Essex, 14.2

Watts, N, 19

WBA *see* Building Priority 'A', Ministry of
Works

weapons *see* munitions

weaving *see* textile and textiles

Webb, 'Long-term Arrangements for Control of
Prices', 15.37

Webb, M, 2.2, 14.1, 15.13, 15.35, 17.2

Webster, F, 15.27

Weeks, H.T, 13.11, 14.3, 15.1, 15.21, 15.23, 18

Weeks, R, 5, 5.4, 18

Weir, C, 15.10

Welch, A.E, 15.37

welfare,

in employment, 22.5

see also employment

Welfare Department, Ministry of Labour, 22.5

Welfare Food Division, Milk, Milk Products and,
Ministry of Agriculture and Fisheries, 22.2

Welfare State, 22

Welsh, *see also* Wales

Welsh Agricultural Land Subcommission, 22.2

Welsh Land Settlement Society, 22.2

Welsh local authorities, 9

Welsh Parliament, Members of, 9

Welsh Reconstruction Advisory Council, 9, 11,
22.8

Welsh Reconstruction Problems, Advisory
Council on, 9

Committee on Agriculture, 9

Committee on Industry, 9

Welsh Reconstruction Programmes, Advisory
Council on, 9

Welwyn Garden City, Hertfordshire, 14.2

Printed in the United Kingdom for HMSO
Dd 294204   C7   12/91